Introducing
Philosophy
for Canadians

Robert C. Solomon
& Douglas McDermid

OXFORD
UNIVERSITY PRESS

OXFORD
UNIVERSITY PRESS

8 Sampson Mews, Suite 204, Don Mills, Ontario M3C 0H5
www.oupcanada.com

Oxford University Press is a department of the University of Oxford.
It furthers the University's objective of excellence in research, scholarship,
and education by publishing worldwide in

Oxford   New York
Auckland   Cape Town   Dar es Salaam   Hong Kong   Karachi
Kuala Lumpur   Madrid   Melbourne   Mexico City   Nairobi
New Delhi   Shanghai   Taipei   Toronto

With offices in
Argentina   Austria   Brazil   Chile   Czech Republic   France   Greece
Guatemala   Hungary   Italy   Japan   Poland   Portugal   Singapore
South Korea   Switzerland   Thailand   Turkey   Ukraine   Vietnam

Oxford is a trade mark of Oxford University Press
in the UK and in certain other countries

Published in Canada
by Oxford University Press

Library and Archives Canada Cataloguing in Publication
Solomon, Robert C.
Introduction philosophy to Canadians: a text with integrative readings/Robert C. Solomon &
Douglas McDermid.—1st Canadian ed.

Includes bibliographical references and index.
ISBN 978-0-19-543096-7
1. Philosophy—Introductions—Textbooks.
I. McDermid, Douglas   II. Title.
BD21.S642011   100   C2011-900194-2

Cover image: Paul Taylor/Gettyimages

Oxford University Press is committed to our environment. This book
is printed on permanent (acid-free) paper ∞.
Printed and bound in Canada

1 2 3 4 — 14 13 12 11

BRIEF CONTENTS

CONTENTS

Chapter 2: Religion   110

Chapter 3: Knowledge   188

PART III   KNOW THYSELF
Chapter 4: Mind and Body   286

Chapter 5: Self and Freedom   331

PART IV THE GOOD AND THE RIGHT
Chapter 6: Ethics   390

Chapter 7: Justice   477

PREFACE

Introducing Philosophy for Canadians: A Text with Integrated Readings presupposes no background in the subject and no special abilities. Intended primarily as a textbook for a one- or two-semester introductory course, the book provides the course materials from which instructors and students can focus on a variety of problems and perspectives. The point of this textbook is to present students with alternatives on the issues and let them arrive at their own conclusions. These conclusions should be based on arguments in class and with friends or classmates as well as on the discussions in this book. The purpose of philosophy is to encourage each person to think for himself or herself; no single source of arguments or information can take the place of personal dialogues and discussions. A textbook is ultimately a sourcebook; everything in it is to be taken as a cause for further argument, not as a final statement of results. The book does not attempt to sway students toward any particular philosophical positions but rather presents basic philosophical problems and powerful philosophical arguments to encourage students to think for themselves.

Introducing Philosophy for Canadians derives from more than thirty years of teaching in very different schools in various cities, regions, and cultures. The text is based on the belief that philosophy is a genuinely exciting subject, accessible not only to specialists and a few gifted undergraduate majors but to everyone. Everyone is a philosopher, whether enrolled in a philosophy course or not. Most of us are concerned with the same basic problems and use the same essential arguments. The difference is that someone who has studied philosophy has the advantage of having encountered stronger and more varied arguments than might have been available otherwise. In this book, the major philosophers of the past twenty-five hundred years give students these various arguments from their sources.

Introducing Philosophy for Canadians is thus a text that combines the history of philosophy with current thinking about the problems of philosophy, two approaches to the study of philosophy that are too often opposed to each other. But the history of philosophy is the history of thinking about the problems of philosophy, and the problems of philosophy are those problems that have been shaped and motivated by the history of philosophy. There cannot be one without the other. Accordingly, the early chapters of the book follow a rough chronology, from the ancient Greeks and earlier cultures through the medieval and modern periods and the great philosophers who have defined those periods and philosophy as a whole. But the same chapters introduce and present alternative answers to the central problems of philosophy, questions about the nature of reality, the existence and nature of God, the possibility of human knowledge, the nature of truth, and self and personal identity.

This dual approach offers introductory students direct contact with substantial readings from significant works in the history of philosophy but removes the unreasonable demand that they confront these often difficult works in full and without commentary or editing, as they would in the originals or in most anthologies. This book is not, however, a historical introduction but rather an introduction to the problems of philosophy and the various ways in which they have been answered. The history of philosophy thus serves to illuminate these problems and replies, not the other way around.

Although the language of philosophy is often specialized and sometimes difficult, this book is as free of jargon and special terminology as possible. Where necessary, the most important and widely used philosophical terms are carefully introduced within the text and also summarized in a glossary at the end of the book. Brief biographies of the philosophers discussed are also provided at the end of the book to help students understand the place of these philosophers and their ideas within history.

For the Instructor: How to Use This Book

Introducing Philosophy for Canadians is written for a complete course, and the chapters build on one another in logical sequence. Nevertheless, each chapter has been written as an independent unit so that it is possible to use the book in a variety of ways and for a variety of courses. Within each chapter, various sections can be selected for shorter discussion. For example, some instructors may want to use only the first sections of Chapter 2 (Religion) or only a few key sections from Chapter 4 (Mind and Body) and Chapter 5 (Self and Freedom).

A full course might include the Introduction and all seven chapters, but this may be a rather heavy load for an average one-term course. The following outlines are suggestions for a variety of uses of the book adapted to different lengths and kinds of classes:

> **Maximum course** (one very full term)
> Introduction; Chapters 1–7
> **Minimum course** (summer, part-time)
> Introduction; Chapters 2, 3, 6
> **Two-term course**
> First term: Introduction; Chapters 1–3
> Second term: Introduction; Chapters 4–7
> **Ethics and religion/values course**
> Introduction; Chapters 2, 5, 6, 7
> **Metaphysics and epistemology course**
> Introduction; Chapters 1, 3, 4, 5

Some classes may prefer to begin with either Chapter 2 (Religion) or Chapter 6 (Ethics) and reorder the sequence of chapters.

In this edition, we have used alphabetic letters and numbers to designate sections and subsections within the chapters. Because some of the most important chapters (for example, Knowledge, Ethics, and Religion) are longer and more involved, many instructors prefer to assign a few sections rather than an entire chapter. For instance, in Chapter 3 some instructors may prefer to deal only with the standard three theories of truth and dispense with the material on European philosophy (Kant and after). Others may prefer to delete the theories of truth and launch right into Kant following the discussion of Hume. So too, some instructors may prefer to deal with the arguments concerning God's existence but dispense with the problem of evil; some may want to talk only about the basic problem of freedom versus determinism without subjecting students to the (comparative) subtleties and intrigue of the variations of 'soft determinism'. Other instructors may want to teach a brief history of ethics (Aristotle, Hume, Kant, Mill) without treating such general topics as ethical relativism. Some classes might emphasize the global and cross-cultural nature of philosophy; others might choose to ignore the multicultural material altogether and just focus on the Western history of philosophy. Yet others will prefer to focus only on the ongoing problems of philosophy and more or less ignore the historical development of these problems. We are confident that this edition makes all of this much easier to do.

For the Student: Doing Philosophy

Your attempt to develop your own thoughts—to 'do' philosophy as well as to read what others have done—is central to your study of philosophy. Philosophy, more than any other field, is not so much a subject as it is a way of thinking, one that you can appreciate fully only by joining in. While reading each section, therefore, do not hesitate to put down the book at any time and do your own thinking and writing. When reading about metaphysics, for example, think about how you would develop your own view of reality and how you would answer the questions raised by the first philosophers of ancient Greece or Asia. When confronted by an argument, consider how you might argue for or against a given position. When facing an idea that seems foreign, try to put it in your own terms and understand the vision that lies behind it. And when facing a problem, always offer your own answer as well as the answers offered by earlier thinkers. In philosophy, unlike physics or biology, your own answer may be just as legitimate as those given by the philosophers of the past, and there may be equally interesting answers from different traditions. That is what makes philosophy so difficult to learn at first, but it is also what makes it so personally valuable and enjoyable.

Most of the readings and all of the chapters are followed immediately by questions for you to answer, either out loud with other students in class or in writing, perhaps by way of a class journal or as an addition to your class notes. Most of the questions are intended simply to encourage you to articulate the point of what you have just read, putting what you have read in (more or less) your own words. All too often when we are reading new or difficult material we just allow it to 'pass through' on the way to the next reading. We all have had the experience of reading a long passage, even spending a considerable amount of time on it, and then afterward finding that we are unable to say anything about it. The aim of the questions, therefore, is to force you to say or write something. Some of the questions are thought-provoking, but most are aimed simply at providing immediate feedback for you. We ask, therefore, that you take the questions seriously and consider them an integral part of your reading assignment.

Writing Philosophy

With the foregoing ideas in mind, it should be obvious why talking about philosophy with friends and classmates, raising important questions and objections in class, and writing down ideas are so very important. Articulation reinforces comprehension, and arguing against objections broadens understanding. Writing papers in philosophy is a particularly important part of any philosophy course, and there are certain general guidelines to keep in mind:

1. Begin your essay with a leading question. 'Thinking about' some philosophical issue can be fun, but it can too easily lead you to lose direction and purpose. For instance, thinking about 'freedom' involves far too many different problems and perspectives. Asking such questions as 'Is freedom of action compatible with scientific determinism?' or 'Can there be freedom in a socialist state?' gives your thinking a specific orientation and a way of proceeding.

2. Be clear about the difficulties you face in tackling the question. Are the terms of the question clear? It is not always necessary for you to define terms at the start of your essay. Indeed, defining the key term might be the basic and most difficult conclusion you reach. Also, it is often a poor idea to depend on a dictionary

(even a good one) for clarifying your question. Dictionaries are not written by philosophers and generally reflect popular usage—which may include just such philosophical misunderstandings as you are attempting to correct.

3. Clarify the position you are arguing. Don't force the reader (your instructor) to guess where you are going. When you are clear about the question you ask, it will help you clarify the answer you intend to give, and vice versa. In fact, you may well change your mind—both about the question and the answer—several times while you are writing.

4. Argue your case. Demonstrate why you hold the position you do. The most frequent criticism of student papers is 'You have made an assertion, but you haven't made an *argument*.' When an essay question asks you to discuss an idea or a quotation 'critically', this does not mean that you must attack it or find fault with it, but rather that you need to consider the merits and possible inadequacies, consider the reasons given, and give your own reasons for what you say.

5. Anticipate objections to your position and to your arguments, and take the offensive against rival positions. If you don't know what your position is opposed to, it is doubtful you are clear about what your position is. If you can't imagine how anyone could possibly disagree with you, you probably haven't thought through your position carefully.

6. Don't be afraid to be yourself, to be humorous, or charming, or sincere, or personal. The most powerful philosophical writings, those that have endured for centuries, often reflect the author's deepest concerns and attitudes toward life. However, remember that no philosophical writing can be just humorous, or charming, or sincere, or personal. Make sure everything you write—including a joke—is relevant to the topic at hand. What makes your writing philosophical is that it involves general concerns and careful arguments while attempting to prove an important point and answer one of the age-old questions.

7. Finally—and this is very important—don't let your first draft be your last. Write, write, re-write, then re-write some more. And when you think that you have finished your paper, ask yourself the following questions:

    *   *Grammar, Spelling, Punctuation:* Are there any mistakes in grammar, spelling, or punctuation?
    *   *Knowledge of Readings:* Does the paper show that you have read the assigned material carefully and actually understood it? Does your essay contain a reasonable number of direct and specific references to whatever readings are relevant?
    *   *Originality:* Does this paper show that you have thought hard about the problem you are trying to solve? Does it contain any fresh insights or ideas, or does it say nothing but what is perfectly obvious and dull?
    *   *Style:* Is the paper written in lively, lucid, disciplined language? Does it hold the reader's attention? Is it too repetitive?
    *   *Organization:* Does the paper flow logically, or does it jump around in a confusing manner?

NOTES ON THE CANADIAN EDITION

When I was invited by Oxford University Press to develop a Canadian edition of Robert C. Solomon's *Introducing Philosophy: A Text with Integrated Readings*, I accepted with alacrity. My hope was to create a version of Solomon's classic text that would engage Canadians without being parochial, enrich an already diverse menu of readings, and honour philosophy's past while doing justice to its present.

The book you are now holding is the child of that hope. Here are a few of its most noteworthy features:

- A total of fifty-nine new readings, with interpolated commentary and analysis.
- Thirty-two new readings from Canadian sources. Here, conveniently collected in one volume, are works by Lorraine Code, G.A. Cohen, A.R.C. Duncan, Emil Fackenheim, George Grant, Thomas Hurka, Will Kymlicka, Bernard Lonergan, Cheryl Misak, Susan Sherwin, Barry Stroud, Charles Taylor, and other leading Canadian philosophers. Also included are eight stimulating and accessible pieces written by well-known Canadian politicians and public figures: Tommy Douglas on democratic socialism, Phil Fontaine on racism and justice, Michael Ignatieff on rights, W.L. Morton on conservatism, Margaret Somerville on ethics, Pierre Trudeau on justice and multiculturalism, Jean Vanier on Aristotle's ethics, and George Woodcock on anarchism.
- Seven original essays, commissioned especially for this volume and available nowhere else. These essays are by accomplished Canadian philosophers writing on their respective areas of expertise: Alia Al-Saji on Sartre, Christine Daigle on Nietzsche and Sartre, Mark Migotti on pragmatism, J.L. Schellenberg on the problem of divine hiddenness, William Seager on panpsychism, Phillip Wiebe on religious experience, and James O. Young on the coherence theory of truth.
- Substantial excerpts from the Canadian Charter of Rights and Freedoms (sections 1–3, 7–9, 15, 27, and 28).
- Additional coverage of five major historical periods in Western philosophy:
  Ancient: New readings from Plato and Plotinus.
  Medieval: New readings from St John Damascene and Maimonides.
  Early Modern: New readings from Blaise Pascal, Samuel Clarke, Thomas Reid, and Edmund Burke.
  Nineteenth Century: New readings from William Paley, James Fredrick Ferrier, Søren Kierkegaard, and William James.

Twentieth Century: New readings from G.E. Moore, Karl Popper, Roderick Chisholm, Michael Oakeshott, and Simone Weil, among others.

- Expanded coverage of non-Western philosophy, with three important new readings: a selection from *The Questions of King Milinda*, a seminal Buddhist text; an excerpt from Swami Vivekananda's 'Maya and Illusion'; and a reading from Sarvepalli Radhakrishnan's *An Idealist View of Life*.
- More in-depth coverage in six key areas of philosophy: epistemology (Chapter 3), metaphysics (Chapters 1 and 5), philosophy of mind (Chapters 4 and 5), philosophy of religion (Chapter 2), ethics (Chapter 6), and political philosophy (Chapter 7).
- More fiction (by Robert Louis Stevenson and Isaac Bashevis Singer) and poetry (by Jorge Luis Borges and Francis Sparshott) to illustrate philosophical themes and ideas.
- Updated lists of recommended reading and new chapter-review questions at the end of each chapter.
- An updated glossary and enhanced mini-biographies of featured philosophers at the end of the text.
- A revised history-of-philosophy timeline at the beginning of the text.

It's been a great pleasure working on *Introducing Philosophy for Canadians*. If, after reading this book, you have any comments about its contents, please don't hesitate to contact me (dmcdermi@trentu.ca) via email. I would genuinely like to hear from you.

Acknowledgements

For advice, stimulation, encouragement, and for setting good examples of one sort or another, I am indebted to the following people: Felicia Ackerman, Simon Blackburn, Paul Boghossian, Celia Boué, Michelle Boué, James Buckingham, Justin Broackes, Josiah Carberry, Roderick Chisholm, David Conter, Robert Croken, Kerry Cronin, Robert Dornan, Gordon Graham, Jim Kanaris, Jaegwon Kim, Todd Lee, Keith Lehrer, Myrna McDermid, Danny Monsour, Mark Morelli, Alan Musgrave, Martha Nussbaum, Carlos Pereda, Bernard Reginster, David Rondel, Ernest Sosa, Jean-Pierre Schachter, James Van Cleve, William Wainwright, Oliver Whitehead, and Anthony Willing. Some of these individuals are my teachers, some friends and acquaintances, and some correspondents; but all of them have helped me write this book, whether they know it or not.

I wish also to acknowledge the input of Alan Belk, Brendan Moran, Dimitrios Dentsoras, Kent Peacock, and Michael Stack, as well as those reviewers who wish to remain anonymous; their insightful feedback and their enthusiasm for this project were true boons. Speaking of boons, I should like to thank the crack editorial squad at Oxford University Press—Jodi Lewchuk, Kathryn West, Patricia Simoes, and Phyllis Wilson—for their good deeds and their professionalism. Special thanks goes to Oxford's Janice Evans for her meticulous and insightful work as copyeditor.

My gratitude also goes out to the group of seven Canadian philosophers who agreed to contribute original essays for this volume: Alia Al-Saji (McGill University), Christine Daigle (Brock University), Mark Migotti (University of Calgary), John Schellenberg (Mount Saint Vincent University), William Seager (University of Toronto), Phillip Wiebe (Trinity Western University), and James O. Young (University of Victoria).

Finally, I wish to thank the three people to whom my portion of this book is dedicated with love: Michelle, Julia, and Andrea.

—Douglas McDermid
Trent University

PART I
BEGINNING PHILOSOPHY

STARTING WITH SOCRATES

The unexamined life is not worth living.
Socrates

A. Socrates

Socrates (469–399 BCE) was not the first philosopher, but he was, and is still, the ideal of philosophers. Once assured by the oracle at Delphi that he was the wisest man in Athens, Socrates borrowed his view of life from the inscription at Delphi, 'Know Thyself'. Mixing humility with arrogance, he boasted that his superiority lay in his awareness of his own ignorance, and he spent the rest of his life making fools of the self-proclaimed 'wise men' of Athens.

In the opinion of Socrates and other critics of the time, the government of Athens was corrupt and notoriously bumbling, in marked contrast to the 'Golden Age' of Pericles a few years before. Philosophical arguments had become all cleverness and demagoguery, rhetorical tricks to win arguments and legal cases; political ambition replaced justice and the search for the good life. Socrates believed that the people of Athens held their principles glibly, like banners at a football game, but rarely lived up to them and even more rarely examined them. Against this, he developed a technique of asking seemingly innocent questions, trapping his audience in their own confusions and hypocrisies, exploding the pretensions of his times. And against their easy certainties, he taught that 'the unexamined life is not worth living'. He referred to himself as a 'gadfly' (an obnoxious insect with a painful bite), keeping his fellow citizens from ever becoming as smug and self-righteous as they would like to have been. Accordingly, he made many enemies and was satirized by Aristophanes in his play *The Clouds*.

From *The Clouds*
By Aristophanes

STUDENT OF SOCRATES: Socrates asked Chaerephon how many of its own feet a flea could jump—one had bitten Chaerephon's brow and then jumped to Socrates' head.

STREPSIADES: And how did he measure the jump?

STUDENT: Most ingeniously. He melted wax, caught the flea, dipped its feet, and the hardened wax made Persian slippers. Unfastening these, he found their size.

STREPSIADES: Royal Zeus! What an acute intellect!

STUDENT: But yesterday a high thought was lost through a lizard.
STREPSIADES: How so? Tell me.

STUDENT: As he gaped up at the moon, investigating her paths and turnings, from off the roof a lizard befouled him.

In the play, Aristophanes made Socrates and his students look utterly ridiculous, and the 'clouds' refer to the confusion that we mean when we talk of someone 'having his head in the clouds'. Athenians enjoyed the playwright's sarcasm as a mild form of vengeance for Socrates' constant criticisms. Aristophanes probably expressed the general public opinion when he described Socrates as 'shiftless' and merely a master at verbal trickery.

Socrates' students, however, virtually worshipped him. As recorded in *The Phaedo*, they described him as 'the bravest, most wise, and most upright man of our times' and perceived him as a martyr for the truth in a corrupted society. The price of his criticism was not merely the satire of the playwrights. Because he had been such a continual nuisance, the government arranged to have Socrates brought to trial for 'corrupting the youth of Athens' and 'not believing in the gods of the city' (*The Apology*). And for these trumped-up 'crimes', Socrates was condemned to death. But at his trial, he once again became a gadfly to those who condemned him.

From *The Apology*
By Plato

It is not difficult to avoid death, gentlemen of the jury; it is much more difficult to avoid wickedness, for it runs faster than death.

He assesses the penalty at death. So be it. What counter-assessment should I propose to you, gentlemen of the jury? Clearly it should be a penalty I deserve, and what do I deserve to suffer or to pay because I have deliberately not led a quiet life but have neglected what occupies most people: wealth, household affairs, the position of general or public orator or the other offices, the political clubs and factions that exist in the city? I thought myself too honest to survive if I occupied myself with those things. I did not follow that path that would have made me of no use either to you or to myself, but I went to each of you privately and conferred upon him what I say is the greatest benefit, by persuading him not to care for any of his belongings before caring that he himself should be as good and as wise as possible, not to care for the city's possessions more than for the city itself, and to care for other things in the same way. What do I deserve for being such a man? Some good, gentlemen of the jury, if I must truly make an assessment according to my deserts, and something suitable.

Socrates here suggests that the state should give him a pension, rather than a punishment, for being a public benefactor and urging his students to be virtuous.

It is for the sake of a short time, gentlemen of the jury, that you will acquire the reputation and the guilt, in the eyes of those who want to denigrate the city, of having killed Socrates, a wise man, for they will say that I am wise even if I am not. If you had waited but a little while, this would have happened of its own accord. You see my age, that I am already advanced in years and close to death. I am saying this not to all of you but to those who condemned me to death, and to these same jurors I say: Perhaps you think that I was convicted for lack of such words as might have convinced you, if I thought I

(Continued)

should say or do all I could to avoid my sentence. Far from it. I was convicted because I lacked not words but boldness and shamelessness and the willingness to say to you what you would most gladly have heard from me, lamentations and tears and my saying and doing many things that I say are unworthy of me but that you are accustomed to hear from others. I did not think then that the danger I ran should make me do anything mean, nor do I now regret the nature of my defence. I would much rather die after this kind of defence than live after making the other kind. Neither I nor any other man should, on trial or in war, contrive to avoid death at any cost. Indeed it is often obvious in battle that one could escape death by throwing away one's weapons and by turning to supplicate one's pursuers, and there are many ways to avoid death in every kind of danger if one will venture to do or say anything to avoid it. It is not difficult to avoid death, gentlemen of the jury; it is much more difficult to avoid wickedness, for it runs faster than death. Slow and elderly as I am, I have been caught by the slower pursuer, whereas my accusers, being clever and sharp, have been caught by the quicker, wickedness. I leave you now, condemned to death by you, but they are condemned by truth to wickedness and injustice. So I maintain my assessment, and they maintain theirs. This perhaps had to happen, and I think it is as it should be.

Now I want to prophesy to those who convicted me, for I am at the point when men prophesy most, when they are about to die. I say gentlemen, to those who voted to kill me, that vengeance will come upon you immediately after my death, a vengeance much harder to bear than that which you took in killing me. You did this in the belief that you would avoid giving an account of your life, but I maintain that quite the opposite will happen to you. There will be more people to test you, whom I now held back, but you did not notice it. They will be more difficult to deal with as they will be younger and you will resent them more. You are wrong if you believe that by killing people you will prevent anyone from reproaching you for not living in the right way. To escape such tests is neither possible nor good, but it is best and easiest not to discredit others but to prepare oneself to be as good as possible. With this prophecy to you who convicted me, I part from you.

In prison, Socrates was given the opportunity to escape. He refused it. He had always taught that 'the really important thing is not to live, but to live well' (*The Crito*). And 'to live well' meant, along with the more enjoyable things in life, to live according to your principles. When his friend Crito tried to persuade him otherwise, Socrates countered Crito's pleas and arguments with powerful arguments of his own. Look carefully at the structure of these arguments and judge for yourself their soundness.

From *The Crito*
By Plato

Not only now but at all times I am the kind of man who listens only to the argument that on reflection seems best to me.

SOCRATES: My good Crito, why should we care so much for what the majority think? The most reasonable people, to whom one should pay more attention, will believe that things were done as they were done.

CRITO: You see, Socrates, that one must also pay attention to the opinion of the majority. Your present situation makes clear that the majority can inflict not the least but pretty well the greatest evils if one is slandered among them.

SOCRATES: Would that the majority could inflict the greatest evils, for they would then be capable of the greatest good, and that would be fine, but now they cannot do either. They cannot make a man either wise or foolish, but they inflict things haphazardly.

CRITO: That may be so. But tell me this, Socrates, are you anticipating that I and your other friends would have trouble with the informers if you escape from here, as having stolen you away, and that we should be compelled to lose all our property or pay heavy fines and suffer other punishment besides? If you have any such fear, forget it. We would be justified in running this risk to save you, and worse, if necessary. Do follow my advice, and do not act differently.

SOCRATES: I do have these things in mind, Crito, and also many others.

CRITO: Have no such fear. It is not much money that some people require to save you and get you out of here. . . .

Besides, Socrates, I do not think that what you are doing is right, to give up your life when you can save it, and to hasten your fate as your enemies would hasten it, and indeed have hastened it in their wish to destroy you.

* * *

SOCRATES: My dear Crito, your eagerness is worth much if it should have some right aim; if not, then the greater your keenness the more difficult it is to deal with. We must therefore examine whether we should act in this way or not, as not only now but at all times I am the kind of man who listens only to the argument that on reflection seems best to me. I cannot, now that this fate has come upon me, discard the arguments I used; they seem to me much the same. I value and respect the same principles as before, and if we have no better arguments to bring up at this moment, be sure that I shall not agree with you, not even if the power of the majority were to frighten us with more bogeys, as if we were children, with threats of incarcerations and executions and confiscation of property. How should we examine this matter more reasonably? Would it be by taking up first your argument about the opinions of men, whether it is sound in every case that one should pay attention to some opinions, but not to others? Or was that well-spoken before the necessity to die came upon me, but now it is clear that this was said in vain for the sake of argument, that it was in truth play and nonsense? I am eager to examine together with you, Crito, whether this argument will appear in any way different to me in my present circumstances, or whether it remains the same, whether we are to

abandon it or believe it. It was said on every occasion that one should greatly value some opinions, but not others. Does that seem to you a sound statement? . . . Examine the following statement in turn as to whether it stays the same or not, that the most important thing is not life, but the good life.

CRITO: It stays the same.

SOCRATES: And that the good life, the beautiful life, and the just life are the same; does that still hold, or not?

CRITO: It does hold.

SOCRATES: As we have agreed so far, we must examine next whether it is right for me to try to get out of here when the Athenians have not acquitted me. If it is seen to be right, we will try to do so; if it is not, we will abandon the idea. As for those questions you raise about money, reputation, the upbringing of children, Crito, those considerations in truth belong to those people who easily put men to death and would bring them to life again if they could, without thinking; I mean the majority of men. For us, however, since our argument leads to this, the only valid consideration, as we were saying just now, is whether we should be acting rightly in giving money and gratitude to those who will lead me out of here, and ourselves helping with the escape, or whether in truth we shall do wrong in doing all this. If it appears that we shall be acting unjustly, then we have no need at all to take into account whether we shall have to die, if we stay here and keep quiet, or suffer in another way, rather than do wrong.

CRITO: I think you put that beautifully, Socrates, but see what we should do.

SOCRATES: Let us examine the question together, my dear friend, and if you can make any objection while I am speaking, make it and I will listen to you, but if you have no objection to make, my dear Crito, then stop now from saying the same thing so often, that I must leave here against the will of the Athenians. I think it important to persuade you before I act, and not to act against your wishes.

* * *

SOCRATES: Then . . . I ask you: when one has come to an agreement that is just with someone, should one fulfill it or cheat on it?

CRITO: One should fulfill it.

(Continued)

SOCRATES: See what follows from this: If we leave here without the city's permission, are we injuring people whom we should least injure? And are we sticking to a just agreement, or not?

CRITO: I cannot answer your question, Socrates, I do not know.

SOCRATES: Look at it this way. If, as we were planning to run away from here, or whatever one should call it, the laws and the state came and confronted us and asked: 'Tell me, Socrates, what are you intending to do? Do you not by this action you are attempting intend to destroy us, the laws, and indeed the whole city, as far as you are concerned? Or do you think it possible for a city not to be destroyed if the verdicts of its courts have no force but are nullified and set at naught by private individuals?' What shall we answer to this and other such arguments? For many things could be said, especially by an orator on behalf of this law we are destroying, which orders that the judgments of the courts shall be carried out. Shall we say in answer, 'The city wronged me, and its decision was not right.' Shall we say that, or what?

CRITO: Yes, by Zeus, Socrates, that is our answer.

SOCRATES: Then what if the laws said, 'Was that the agreement between us, Socrates, or was it to respect the judgments that the city came to?' And if we wondered at their words, they would perhaps add: 'Socrates, do not wonder at what we say but answer, since you are accustomed to proceed by question and answer. Come now, what accusation do you bring against us and the city, that you should try to destroy us? Did we not, first, bring you to birth, and was it not through us that your father married your mother and begat you? Tell us, do you find anything to criticize in those of us who are concerned with marriage?' And I would say that I do not criticize them. 'Or in those of us concerned with the nurture of babies and the education that you too received? Were those assigned to that subject not right to instruct your father to educate you in the arts and in physical culture?' And I would say that they were right. 'Very well,' they would continue, 'and after you were born and nurtured and educated, could you, in the first place, deny that you are our offspring and servant, both you and your forefathers? If that is so, do you think that we are on an equal footing as regards the right, and that whatever we do to you it is right for you to do to us? You were not on an equal footing with your father as regards the right, nor with your master if you had one, so as to retaliate for anything they did to you, to revile them if they reviled you, to beat them if they beat you, and so with many other things. Do you think you have this right to retaliation against your country and its laws? That if we undertake to destroy you and think it right to do so, you can undertake to destroy us, as far as you can, in return? And will you say that you are right to do so, you who truly care for virtue? Is your wisdom such as not to realize that your country is to be honoured more than your mother, your father, and all your ancestors, that it is more to be revered and more sacred, and that it counts for more among the gods and sensible men, that you must worship it, yield to it, and placate its anger more than your father's? You must either persuade it or obey its orders, and endure in silence whatever it instructs you to endure, whether blows or bonds, and if it leads you into war to be wounded or killed, you must obey. To do so is right, and one must not give way or retreat or leave one's post, but both in war and in courts and everywhere else, one must obey the commands of one's city and country, or persuade it as to the nature of justice. It is impious to bring violence to bear against your mother or father, it is much more so to use it against your country.' What shall we say in reply, Crito, that the laws speak the truth, or not?

CRITO: I think they do.

SOCRATES: 'Reflect now, Socrates,' the laws might say, 'that if what we say is true, you are not treating us rightly by planning to do what you are planning. . . .

'So decisively did you choose us and agree to be a citizen under us. Also, you have had children in this city, thus showing that it was congenial to you. Then at your trial you could have assessed your penalty at exile if you wished, and you are now attempting to do against the city's wishes what you could then have done with her consent. Then you prided yourself that you did not resent death, but you chose, as you said, death in preference to exile. Now, however, those words do not make you ashamed, and you pay no heed to us, the laws, as you plan to destroy us, and you act like the meanest type of slave by trying to run away, contrary to your undertakings and your agreement to live as a citizen under us. First then, answer us on this very point, whether we speak the truth when we say that you agreed, not only in words but by your deeds, to live in accordance with us.' What are we to say to that, Crito? Must we not agree?

CRITO: We must, Socrates.

SOCRATES: 'Surely,' they might say, 'you are breaking the undertakings and agreements that you made with us without compulsion or deceit, and under no pressure of time for deliberation. You have had seventy years during which you could have gone away if you did not like us, and if you thought our agreements unjust. You did not choose to go to Sparta or to Crete, which you are always saying are well governed, nor to any other city, Greek or foreign. You have been away from Athens less than the lame or the blind or other handicapped people. It is clear that the city has been outstandingly more congenial to you than to other Athenians, and so have we, the laws, for what city can please if its laws do not? Will you then not now stick to our agreements? You will, Socrates, if we can persuade you, and not make yourself a laughingstock by leaving the city. . . .

'Be persuaded by us who have brought you up, Socrates. Do not value either your children or your life or anything else more than goodness, in order that you may have all this as your defence before rulers there. If you do this deed, you will not think it better or more just or more pious, nor will any one of your friends, nor will it be better for you when you arrive yonder. As it is, you depart, if you depart, after being wronged not by us, the laws, but by men; but if you depart after shamefully returning wrong for wrong and injury for injury, after breaking your agreement and contract with us, after injuring those you should injure least—yourself, your friends, your country and us—we shall be angry with you while you are still alive, and our brothers, the laws of the underworld, will not receive [you] kindly, knowing that you tried to destroy us as far as you could. Do not let Crito persuade you, rather than we, to do what he says.'. . .

CRITO: I have nothing to say, Socrates.

SOCRATES: Let it be then, Crito, and let us act in this way, since this is the way the god is leading us.

- By choosing to go on living in the city, Socrates has agreed with Athens to obey its laws. Therefore, even if he is wrongly condemned by those same laws, he has the duty to stay and accept his punishment. Do you agree that he has made such a tacit agreement? Do you agree that he has the duty to stay and accept punishment even if he was wrongly condemned? Have you entered into such an agreement with your community? Your country? What would you do if you were Socrates?

Socrates believed that the good of his 'soul' was far more important than the transient pleasures of life. Accordingly, he preferred to die for his ideas than live as a hypocrite. An idea worth living for may be an idea worth dying for as well.

From *The Phaedo*
By Plato

[Socrates] was holding the cup, and then drained it calmly and easily. Most of us had been able to hold back our tears reasonably well up till then, but when we saw him drinking it and after he drank it, we could hold them back no longer; my own tears came in floods against my will. So I covered my face. I was weeping for myself—not for him, but for my misfortune in being deprived of such a comrade. Even before me, Crito was unable to restrain his tears and got up. Apollodorus had not ceased from weeping before, and at this moment his noisy tears and anger made everybody present break down, except Socrates. 'What is this,' he said, 'you

(*Continued*)

strange fellows. It is mainly for this reason that I sent the women away, to avoid such unseemliness, for I am told one should die in good omened silence. So keep quiet and control yourselves.'

* * *

Such was the end of our comrade, Echecrates, a man who, we would say, was of all those we have known the best, and also the wisest and the most upright.

Is there anything that you believe so passionately—anything that makes your life so worth living—that you would die for it? For most people, now as always, life is rather a matter of 'getting by'. One of the more popular phrases of self-praise these days is 'I'm a survivor'. But, ironically, a person who is not willing to die for anything (for example, his or her own freedom) is thereby more vulnerable to threats and corruption. To be willing to die—as Socrates was—is to have a considerable advantage over someone for whom *life is everything*.

If you look closely at your life, not only at your proclaimed ideals and principles but your desires and ambitions as well, do the facts of your life add up to its best intentions? Or are you, too, just drifting with the times: dissatisfied with ultimately meaningless jobs and mindless, joyless entertainments; concerned with the price of tuition, some recent stupidity on the part of your government, the petty competitions of school and society, the hassles of chores and assignments, car troubles, and occasional social embarrassments; interrupted only by all-too-rare and too-quickly-passing pleasures and distractions?

What we learn from Socrates is how to rise above all of this. Not that we should give up worldly pleasures—good food, fun, sex, sports, entertainment—and put our heads in the 'clouds'; but we should see them in perspective and examine for ourselves that jungle of confused reactions and conditioned responses that we have unthinkingly inherited from our parents and borrowed from our peers. The point is not to give up what we have learned or to turn against our culture. Rather, the lesson we can learn from Socrates is that thinking about our experiences and clarifying our ideals can turn life from a dreary series of tasks and distractions into a self-conscious adventure, one even worth dying for and certainly worth living for. This way of being arises from a special kind of **abstract** thinking, one that rises above petty concerns and transforms our existence into a bold experiment in living. This special kind of thinking is called philosophy.

From *The Republic*
By Plato

SOCRATES: Do you agree, or not, that when we say that a man has a passion for something, we shall say that he desires that whole kind of thing, not just one part of it and not the other?

GLAUCON: Yes, the whole of it.

SOCRATES: The lover of wisdom, we shall say, has a passion for wisdom, not for this kind of wisdom and not that, but for every kind of wisdom?

GLAUCON: True.

SOCRATES: As for one who is choosy about what he learns, especially if he is young and cannot yet give a reasoned account of what is useful and what is not, we shall not call him a lover of learning or a philosopher, just as we shall not say that a man who is difficult about his food is hungry or has an appetite for food. We shall not call him a lover of food but a bad feeder.

GLAUCON: And we should be right.

SOCRATES: But we shall rightly call a philosopher the man who is easily willing to learn every kind of knowledge, gladly turns to learning things, and is insatiable in this respect. Is that not so?

B. Making Sense of Socrates

For well over two thousand years, the life and character of Socrates have been an inexhaustible source of fascination to many kinds of thinkers—from philosophers and scholars to novelists, painters, composers, and politicians. Questions about this enigmatic figure pile up fast and thick: What prompted him to live and to die as he did? Why did he polarize his contemporaries? What was he trying to achieve? What *did* he achieve? How did he understand himself and his role as a philosopher, or lover of wisdom? Was he as wise and virtuous as a human being can be? Was his influence entirely for the good? Was he, as many have said, a kind of heroic, self-sacrificing saint? Or was he guilty of impiety, even if not quite in the sense that his accusers had in mind? Could he have been both saintly and impious, a kind of secular martyr who died for the rights of reason and truth? What, in short, are we to make of Socrates?

These questions are difficult to answer, and the task is made even more challenging by the fact that we do not have any texts written by Socrates himself. Indeed, most accounts of his life and teachings survive in the writings of his students, particularly the dialogues of Plato. Yet one way of understanding the man is to look at the metaphors that Plato records to describe Socrates. In *The Apology*, for example, Socrates compares himself to a stinging gadfly, sent by God to rouse the great city of Athens, which is said to resemble a magnificent but rather sluggish thoroughbred.

From *The Apology*
By Plato

I was attached to this city by the god—though it seems a ridiculous thing to say—as upon a great and noble horse which was somewhat sluggish because of its size and needed to be stirred up by a kind of gadfly. It is to fulfill some such function that I believe the god has placed me in the city. I never cease to rouse each and every one of you, to persuade and reproach you all day long and everywhere I find myself in your company.

Another such man will not easily come to be among you, gentlemen, and if you believe me you will spare me. You might easily be annoyed with me as people are when they are aroused from a doze, and strike out at me; if convinced by Anytus you could easily kill me, and then you could sleep on for the rest of your days, unless the god, in his care for you, sent you someone else.

So, what does this metaphor say about Socrates? Let's consider the relationship between the gadfly and the horse. The horse, we might say, is large, powerful, and beautiful, but also passive, slow, and lazy. The gadfly, on the other hand, is small, weak, unsightly, even ugly, but also active, quick, and constantly on the attack. Neither a threatening predator nor a silent parasite, the gadfly seems little more than a noisy nuisance, an inconvenient pain—literally—in the horse's side. But it isn't quite as simple as that, because the gadfly's stings *benefit* the horse. How? Once stung, the drowsy horse wakes up; stirring and starting, it begins to shift and move. Now awake, the once-lethargic horse is reminded of its true nature, of what it is meant to be—reminded, that is, of the powers that lie dormant within itself. In this way the pesky gadfly's stings, sharp and painful as they are, do the horse some good after all—though the horse, of course, is hardly grateful.

> - How is Socrates is like a gadfly? How is Athens like a horse? How might Socrates 'sting' his fellow Athenians? What weapon(s) does he possess?
> - Why do you think Socrates chooses to describe himself as a gadfly in the context of his trial? How might this metaphor be used in defence of his way of life as a philosopher?

We find another descriptive metaphor in *The Meno*. In this text, Socrates and a rather glib, cocky young man named Meno discuss the nature of virtue. Having claimed to know what virtue is, Meno proceeds to define it; but Socrates soon shows that all of Meno's definitions are flawed. Humiliated, perplexed, and stunned, Meno responds by comparing Socrates to a stingray.

From *The Meno*
By Plato

MENO: Socrates, before I even met you I used to hear that you are always in a state of perplexity and that you bring others to the same state, and now I think you are bewitching and beguiling me, simply putting me under a spell, so that I am quite perplexed. Indeed, if a joke is in order, you seem, in appearance and in every other way, to be like the broad torpedo fish, for it too makes anyone who comes close and touches it feel numb, and you now seem to have had that kind of effect on me, for both my mind and my tongue are numb, and I have no answer to give you. Yet I have made many speeches about virtue before large audiences on a thousand occasions, very good speeches as I thought, but now I cannot even say what it is. I think you are wise not to sail away from Athens to go and stay elsewhere, for if you were to behave like this as a stranger in another city, you would be driven away for practising sorcery.

SOCRATES: You are a rascal, Meno, and you nearly deceived me.

MENO: Why so particularly, Socrates?

SOCRATES: I know why you drew this image of me.

MENO: Why do you think I did?

SOCRATES: So that I should draw an image of you in return. I know that all handsome men rejoice in images of themselves; it is to their advantage, for I think that the images of beautiful people are also beautiful, but I will draw no image of you in turn. Now if the torpedo fish is itself numb and so makes others numb, then I resemble it, but not otherwise, for I myself do not have the answer when I perplex others but I am more perplexed than anyone when I cause perplexity in others.

- How is Meno's stingray metaphor similar to the gadfly metaphor? How do the metaphors differ? Does Socrates' sting have the same effect on his audience in both cases?
- How does Socrates respond to the charge that he is like a stingray?

In *The Theaetetus*, Socrates uses a very different metaphor to describe himself. This time he says that he, like his mother Phaenarete, is a midwife who helps those in labour give birth. Socrates adds, however, that the offspring he helps deliver are not children of the body, but children of the mind—not infants, but ideas.

From *The Theaetetus*
By Plato

SOCRATES: Then do you mean to say you've never heard about my being the son of a good hefty midwife, Phaenarete?

THEAETETUS: Oh, yes, I've heard that before.

SOCRATES: And haven't you ever been told that I practise the same art myself?

THEAETETUS: No, I certainly haven't.

SOCRATES: But I do, believe me. Only don't give me away to the rest of the world, will you? You see, my friend, it is a secret that I have this art. That is not one of the things you hear people saying about me, because they don't know; but they do say that I am a very odd sort of person, always causing people to get into difficulties. You must have heard that, surely?

THEAETETUS: Yes, I have.

SOCRATES: And shall I tell you what is the explanation of that?

THEAETETUS: Yes, please do.

SOCRATES: Well, if you will just think of the general facts about the business of midwifery, you will see more easily what I mean. You know, I suppose, that women never practise as midwives while they are still conceiving and bearing children themselves. It is only those who are past child-bearing who take this up.

THEAETETUS: Oh, yes.

SOCRATES: They say it was Artemis who was responsible for this custom; it was because she, who undertook the patronage of childbirth, was herself childless. She didn't, it's true, entrust the duties of midwifery to barren women, because human nature is too weak to acquire skill where it has no experience. But she assigned the task to those who have become incapable of child-bearing through age—honouring their likeness to herself.

THEAETETUS: Yes, naturally.

SOCRATES: And this too is very natural, isn't it?—or perhaps necessary? I mean that it is the midwives who can tell better than anyone else whether women are pregnant or not.

THEAETETUS: Yes, of course.

SOCRATES: And then it is the midwives who have the power to bring on the pains, and also, if they think fit, to relieve them; they do it by the use of simple drugs, and by singing incantations. In difficult cases, too, they can bring about the birth; or, if they consider it advisable, they can promote a miscarriage.

THEAETETUS: Yes, that is so.

SOCRATES: There's another thing too. Have you noticed this about them, that they are the cleverest of matchmakers, because they are marvellously knowing about the kind of couples whose marriage will produce the best children?

THEAETETUS: No, that is not at all familiar to me.

SOCRATES: But they are far prouder of this, believe me, than of cutting the umbilical cord. Think now. There's an art which is concerned with the cultivation and harvesting of the crops. Now is it the same art which prescribes the best soil for planting or sowing a given crop? Or is it a different one?

THEAETETUS: No, it is all the same art.

SOCRATES: Then applying this to women, will there be one art of the sowing and another of the harvesting?

THEAETETUS: That doesn't seem likely, certainly.

SOCRATES: No, it doesn't. But there is also an unlawful and unscientific practice of bringing men and women together, which we call procuring; and because of that the midwives—a most august body of women—are very reluctant to undertake even lawful matchmaking. They are afraid that if they practise this, they may be suspected of the other. And yet, I suppose, reliable matchmaking is a matter for no one but the true midwife.

THEAETETUS: Apparently.

SOCRATES: So the work of the midwives is a highly important one; but it is not so important as my own performance. And for this reason, that there is not in midwifery the further complication, that the patients are sometimes delivered of phantoms and sometimes of realities, and that the two are hard to distinguish. If there were, then the midwife's greatest and noblest function would be to distinguish the true from the false offspring—don't you agree?

THEAETETUS: Yes, I do.

SOCRATES: Now my art of midwifery is just like theirs in most respects. The difference is that I attend men and not women, and that I watch over the labour of their souls, not of their bodies. And the most important thing about my art is the ability to apply all possible tests to the offspring, to determine whether the young mind is being delivered of a phantom, that is, an error, or a fertile truth. For one thing which I have in common with the ordinary midwives is that I myself am barren of wisdom. The common reproach against me is that I am always asking questions of other people but never express my own views about anything, because there is no wisdom in me; and that is true enough. And the reason of it is this, that God compels me to attend the travail of others, but has forbidden me to procreate. So that I am not in any sense a wise man; I cannot claim as the child of my own soul any discovery worth the name of wisdom. But with those who associate with me it is different. At first some of

(Continued)

them may give the impression of being ignorant and stupid; but as time goes on and our association continues, all whom God permits are seen to make progress—a progress which is amazing both to other people and to themselves. And yet it is clear that this is not due to anything they have learned from me; it is that they discover within themselves a multitude of beautiful things, which they bring forth into the light. But it is I, with God's help, who deliver them of this offspring. And a proof of this may be seen in the many cases where people who did not realize this fact took all the credit to themselves and thought that I was no good. They have then proceeded to leave me sooner than they should, either of their own accord or through the influence of others. And after they have gone away from me they have resorted to harmful company, with the result that what remained within them has miscarried; while they have neglected the children I helped them to bring forth, and lost them, because they set more value upon lies and phantoms than upon the truth; finally they have been set down for ignorant fools, both by themselves and by everybody else. One of these people was Aristides the son of Lysimachus; and there have been very many others. Sometimes they come back, wanting my company again, and ready to move heaven and earth to get it. When that happens, in some cases the divine sign that visits me forbids me to associate with them; in others, it permits me, and then they begin again to make progress.

There is another point also in which those who associate with me are like women in childbirth. They suffer the pains of labour, and are filled day and night with distress; indeed they suffer far more than women. And this pain my art is able to bring on, and also to allay.

Well, that's what happens to them; but at times, Theaetetus, I come across people who do not seem to me somehow to be pregnant. Then I realize that they have no need of me, and with the best will in the world I undertake the business of matchmaking; and I think I am good enough—God willing—at guessing with whom they might profitably keep company. Many of them I have given away to Prodicus; and a great number also to other wise and inspired persons.

Well, my dear lad, this has been a long yarn; but the reason was that I have a suspicion that you (as you think yourself) are pregnant and in labour. So I want you to come to me as to one who is both the son of a midwife and himself skilled in the art; and try to answer the questions I shall ask you as well as you can. And when I examine what you say, I may perhaps think it is a phantom and not truth, and proceed to take it quietly from you and abandon it. Now if this happens, you mustn't get savage with me, like a mother over her first-born child. Do you know, people have often before now got into such a state with me as to be literally ready to bite when I take away some nonsense or other from them. They never believe that I am doing this in all goodwill; they are so far from realizing that no God can wish evil to man, and that even I don't do this kind of thing out of malice but because it is not permitted to me to accept a lie and put away truth.

- In what sense are the people who seek out Socrates 'pregnant'? What is the philosophical equivalent of conceiving and bearing children?
- How does Socrates act as a midwife to such people? What specific services does he claim to perform?
- According to Socrates, those who serve as midwives are not in a position to bear children themselves. What does this suggest that Socrates, as an intellectual midwife, cannot do?
- How does the midwife metaphor account for the hostility Socrates encounters among certain people (such as Meno, whom we met earlier)?

In *The Symposium*, one of Plato's most entertaining dialogues, Alcibiades—a worldly, handsome, gifted, seductive, charming, and treacherous Athenian aristocrat—gives a long and splendid speech in praise of Socrates.

From *The Symposium*
By Plato

Socrates is the only man in the world who has made me feel shame . . .

I'll try to praise Socrates, my friends, but I'll have to use an image. And though he may think I'm trying to make fun of him, I assure you my image is no joke: it aims at the truth. Look at him! Isn't he just like a statue of Silenus? You know the kind of statue I mean; you'll find them in any shop in town. It's a Silenus sitting, his flute or his pipes in his hands, and it's hollow. It's split right down the middle, and inside it's full of tiny statues of the gods. Now look at him again! Isn't he also just like the satyr Marsyas?

Nobody, not even you, Socrates, can deny that you look like them. But the resemblance goes beyond appearance, as you're about to hear.

You are impudent, contemptuous, and vile! No? If you won't admit it, I'll bring witnesses. And you're quite a flute player, aren't you? In fact, you're much more marvellous than Marsyas, who needed instruments to cast his spells on people. And so does anyone who plays his tunes today—for even the tunes Olympus played are Marsyas' work, since Olympus learned everything from him. Whether they are played by the greatest flautist or the meanest flute-girl, his melodies have in themselves the power to possess and so reveal those people who are ready for the god and his mysteries. That's because his melodies are themselves divine. The only difference between you and Marsyas is that you need no instruments; you do exactly what he does, but with words alone. You know, people hardly ever take a speaker seriously, even if he's the greatest orator; but let anyone—man, woman, or child—listen to you or even to a poor account of what you say—and we are all transported, completely possessed.

If I were to describe for you what an extraordinary effect his words have always had on me (I can feel it this moment even as I'm speaking), you might actually suspect that I'm drunk! Still, I swear to you, the moment he starts to speak, I am beside myself: my heart starts leaping in my chest, the tears come streaming down my face, even the frenzied Corybantes seem sane compared to me—and, let me tell you, I am not alone. I have heard Pericles and many other great orators, and I have admired their speeches. But nothing like this ever happened to me: they never upset me so deeply that my very own soul started protesting that

my life—my life! was no better than the most miserable slave's. And yet that is exactly how this Marsyas here at my side makes me feel all the time: he makes it seem that my life isn't worth living! You can't say that isn't true, Socrates. I know very well that you could make me feel that way this very moment if I gave you half a chance. He always traps me, you see, and he makes me admit that my political career is a waste of time, while all that matters is just what I most neglect: my personal shortcomings, which cry out for the closest attention. So I refuse to listen to him; I stop my ears and tear myself away from him, for, like the Sirens, he could make me stay by his side till I die.

Socrates is the only man in the world who has made me feel shame—ah, you didn't think I had it in me, did you? Yes, he makes me feel ashamed: I know perfectly well that I can't prove he's wrong when he tells me what I should do; yet, the moment I leave his side, I go back to my old ways: I cave in to my desire to please the crowd. My whole life has become one constant effort to escape from him and keep away, but when I see him, I feel deeply ashamed, because I'm doing nothing about my way of life, though I have already agreed with him that I should. Sometimes, believe me, I think I would be happier if he were dead. And yet I know that if he dies I'll be even more miserable. I can't live with him, and I can't live without him! What can I do about him?

That's the effect of this satyr's music—on me and many others. But that's the least of it. He's like these creatures in all sorts of other ways; his powers are really extraordinary. Let me tell you about them, because, you can be sure of it, none of you really understands him. But, now I've started, I'm going to show you what he really is.

To begin with, he's crazy about beautiful boys; he constantly follows them around in a perpetual daze. Also, he likes to say he's ignorant and knows nothing. Isn't this just like Silenus? Of course it is! And all this is just on the surface, like the outsides of those statues of Silenus. I wonder, my fellow drinkers, if you have any idea what a sober and temperate man he proves to be once you have looked inside. Believe me, it couldn't matter less to him whether a boy is beautiful. You can't

(Continued)

imagine how little he cares whether a person is beautiful, or rich, or famous in any other way that most people admire. He considers all these possessions beneath contempt, and that's exactly how he considers all of us as well. In public, I tell you, his whole life is one big game—a game of irony. I don't know if any of you have seen him when he's really serious. But I once caught him when he was open like Silenus' statues, and I had a glimpse of the figures he keeps hidden within: they were so godlike—so bright and beautiful, so utterly amazing—that I no longer had a choice—I just had to do whatever he told me.

- In Greek mythology, Silenus was a rather ugly companion of Dionysus, the god of wine. What do you think Alcibiades is getting at when he compares Socrates to a figure of Silenus?
- Marsyas, a gifted musician, challenged the god Apollo to a musical contest. He lost and was flayed. In what way does Socrates resemble Marsyas?
- What features of Socrates' way of speaking does Alcibiades find remarkable?

---

1. Reflections on Socrates

Earlier we observed that many have seen Socrates as a saintly martyr, or at least as a person of unimpeachable integrity who died for the truth. Some have even gone so far as to represent Socrates as a forerunner of the biblical figure of Jesus. Both were charismatic teachers; both wrote nothing, but inspired others to write; both defended and embodied lofty moral ideals; both were critical of the mores and institutions of their time; both were falsely accused and wrongly convicted; both freely submitted to unjust death sentences; and both died in ways that defined their respective identities and helped shape influential traditions of thought and feeling that are still with us.

The relation between Socrates and Jesus is the subject of a recent book by the Canadian philosopher Paul Gooch, who compares and contrasts the two figures in an illuminating way.

From *Reflections on Jesus and Socrates*
By Paul Gooch

[W]hat motivates us to put Jesus and Socrates together is, at one level, simply our curiosity.

Almost anything may be compared to some other thing. That's apples and oranges, we protest, when two measures don't map onto each other: naturally enough, for one can't think that this apple has more segments or pith than that orange. Yet we can inquire about their relative vitamin C content in relation to their respective costs at the market. It all depends on what we're after. Likewise, in spite of all the differences between the Greek-speaking Athenian Socrates and the Aramaic-speaking Jesus of Galilee and Jerusalem, we can compare these two men. But it does depend on what we're after.

If it's primarily to understand them in their own contexts through the clash of contrasts and the heightening of similarities, then we would more profitably look for comparisons within their own cultures, and traditions. The Gospels compare Jesus with John the Baptist, for instance, or with Moses. He comes eating and drinking, the friend of sinners; he promulgates new law and commandments. Plato gives us a Socrates often compared to sophists and rhetoricians—thought to be one of that crowd by the Athenians, but distinguished firmly by Plato from a Protagoras or a Gorgias in his philosophical commitment and dialectical skill. Such comparisons work partly because they offer plausible commentary on the self-understanding of Jesus or Socrates. But to compare them with each other in those terms—to think how they might have regarded each other—that would require powers of imagination you will not discover in this book. I don't try to construct a Socrates teleported to Jerusalem to become a contemporary of Jesus, or Jesus sent back in time to Socrates' circle in Athens.

The place from which comparison is made, therefore, is our own place and neither of theirs. And what motivates us to put Jesus and Socrates together is, at one level, simply our curiosity. For when we have learned something of their stories, we find ourselves intrigued with parallels, as we might be struck by resemblances between two members of widely separated branches of a family tree. Their fathers worked with their hands, the one a sculptor and the other a carpenter. They themselves spent their time among the tradespeople and common folk, but were known more for talk than manual work. Neither had any visible means of income; both seemed to hold money of little importance. Their teaching challenged received wisdom and upset religious authorities. Both argued against doing harm to one's enemies and emphasized the value of the soul above the body. Their manner of teaching, in paradoxes and aphorisms and parables, was similarly memorable. Disciples followed them, but they also made determined enemies who set about to bring them down. Though innocent, they were both convicted and died a death of witness to the truth.

Mere curiosity at parallels must be balanced by a recognition of significant differences between Jesus and Socrates. We have physical descriptions of Socrates from which we garner impressions of an unhandsome, snub-nosed man; but of Jesus' appearance we know not a word. The circumstances of their deaths distinguishes them further. One dies, betrayed for silver and deserted by followers, in his prime; the other, with friends, in old and fulfilled age. But it is especially important to appreciate the contrasts between the beliefs or commitments shaping their lives. Socrates lives and dies for philosophy, a pursuit of wisdom that Jesus could not comprehend outside the context of what we'd call his religious existence. The Hebrew Scriptures, Temple, synagogue,

and preeminently his relationship as Son to the Father—all that must be included in the existence of Jesus, and all that is foreign to Socrates. Socrates read Homer and Hesiod, not Isaiah. Unlike Jesus' relation to Scripture, Socrates' stance toward the texts of Olympian religion was critical. In our studies of Jesus and Socrates we must respect the fact that they inhabit their separate religious and cultural spaces, and we must refrain from assimilating one to the other.

That caution is necessary because the comparison between Jesus and Socrates arose originally not from someplace equally distant from each, but as Christians attempted to interpret Socrates in the light of Jesus. And certainly, in spite of their chronological sequence, the development of the character Socrates has been influenced by Jesus much more than Jesus' reputation has been influenced by Socrates. The tendency to see Socrates' death as martyr-like may have been coloured by the death of Jesus, and he has been appropriated by Christian readers in the language of sainthood. Perhaps the odd tradition that Socrates was silent at his trial was somehow influenced by the Gospel accounts of the Passion, for it doesn't appear until a couple of centuries after Jesus.

* * *

So we must exercise discretion in bringing together Socrates and Jesus from their own places into ours. Nevertheless, we still want to reflect on their likenesses and differences, and not only for intellectual recreation. Although parallels and contrasts in their basic stories are readily stated, it's their *experience* we want to compare in these studies. We want to know how they themselves construct the meaning of their deaths; what are their fundamental commitments and motivations; how they relate to authority, temporal and divine; why they use, or refuse, words in order to defend themselves; what it is that they do when they pray; what or who counts among the objects of their loving. As perennially human issues, these sorts of concerns inhabit our own living. It is out of our philosophical and religious questioning that we continue to find Jesus and Socrates compelling figures.

- Do you think the deaths of Socrates and Jesus differ? Do they face death in the same way?
- Do you think that the lives of Socrates and Jesus differ significantly? If so, how?
- Can you think of any other historical figure whom Socrates meaningfully resembles, or who meaningfully resembles Socrates?

To look at Socrates in the light of Christ is, inevitably, to reflect on the religious or quasi-religious significance of Athens' inspired gadfly. But what if it is a more secular and overtly political interpretation of Socrates that we are after? In that case, we would do well to read what Karl Popper, the eminent twentieth-century philosopher of science and society, has to say about him.

In his controversial two-volume work *The Open Society and Its Enemies*, Popper portrays Socrates as an intrepid defender of the democratic spirit. Why? Because Socrates encouraged us to see ourselves in a new, ennobling light: as men and women who know that they have souls to lose; as free spirits, whom no prison of tradition can hold; as reflective, self-critical individuals who cannot live well unless they reason together; as potential paragons of integrity, unmoved by threats or bribes, committed to doing what is right for its own sake. It is this heroic faith in human beings that animates democracy, says Popper; and it was precisely because Socrates lived out that exacting faith so fully—because, in a word, he was a much better democrat than his accusers—that he was sentenced to death by his fellow Athenians in the aftermath of the Peloponnesian War (431–404 BCE).

From *The Open Society and Its Enemies*
By Karl Popper

Socrates' death is the ultimate proof of his sincerity.

As soon as the restored democracy had re-established normal legal conditions, a case was brought against Socrates. Its meaning was clear enough; he was accused of having had his hand in the education of the most pernicious enemies of the state, Alcibiades, Critias, and Charmides. Certain difficulties for the prosecution were created by an amnesty for all political crimes committed before the re-establishment of the democracy. The charge could not therefore openly refer to these notorious cases. And the prosecutors probably sought not so much to punish Socrates for the unfortunate political events of the past which, as they knew well, had happened against his intentions; their aim was, rather, to prevent him from continuing his teaching, which, in view of its effects, they could hardly regard otherwise than as dangerous to the state. For all these reasons, the charge was given the vague and rather meaningless form that Socrates was corrupting the youth, that he was impious, and that he had attempted to introduce novel religious practices into the state. (The latter two charges undoubtedly expressed, however clumsily, the correct feeling that in the ethico-religious field he was a revolutionary.) Because of the amnesty, the 'corrupted youth' could not be more precisely named, but everybody knew, of course, who was meant. In his defence, Socrates insisted that he had no sympathy with the policy of the Thirty, and that he had actually risked his life by defying their attempt to implicate him in one of their crimes. And he reminded the jury that among his closest associates and most enthusiastic disciples there was at least one ardent democrat, Chaerephon, who fought against the Thirty (and who was, it appears, killed in battle).

It is now usually recognized that Anytus, the democratic leader who backed the prosecution, did not intend to make a martyr of Socrates. The aim was to exile him. But this plan was defeated by Socrates' refusal to compromise his principles. That he wanted to die, or that he enjoyed the role of martyr, I do not believe. He simply fought for what he believed to be right, and for his life's work. He had never intended to undermine democracy. In fact, he had tried to give it the faith it needed. This had been the work of his life. It was, he felt, seriously threatened. The betrayal of his former companions let his work and himself appear in a light which must have disturbed him deeply. He may even have welcomed the trial as an opportunity to prove that his loyalty to his city was unbounded.

Socrates explained this attitude most carefully when he was given an opportunity to escape. Had he seized it, and become an exile, everybody would have thought him an opponent of democracy. So he stayed, and stated his reasons. This explanation, his last will, can be found in Plato's *Crito*. It is simple. If I go, said Socrates, I violate the laws of the state. Such an act would put me in opposition to the laws, and prove my disloyalty. It would do harm to the state. Only if I stay can I put beyond doubt my loyalty to the state, with its democratic laws, and prove that I have never been its enemy. There can be no better proof of my loyalty than my willingness to die for it.

Socrates' death is the ultimate proof of his sincerity. His fearlessness, his simplicity, his modesty, his sense of proportion, his humour never deserted him. 'I am the gadfly that God has attached to this city,' he said in his *Apology*, 'and all day long and in all places I am always fastening upon you, arousing and persuading and reproaching you. You would not readily find another like me, and therefore I should advise you to spare me. . . . If you strike at me, as Anytus advises you, and rashly put me to death, then you will remain asleep for the rest of your lives, unless God in his care sends you another gadfly'. He showed that a man could die, not only for fate and fame and other grand things of this kind, but also for the freedom of critical thought, and for a self-respect which has nothing to do with self-importance or sentimentality.

- What does Popper mean when he says that 'Socrates' death is the ultimate proof of his sincerity'?
- If Socrates was truly a defender of the democratic spirit, why was he seen by some contemporaries as democracy's enemy?

As we have seen, Socrates is a very complex character. More than two thousand years after his death, he continues to charm some and repel others, to inspire love and hatred, to call forth both reverence and resentment. Depending on whom you ask, Socrates is the wisest person who ever lived, or a tedious windbag; a great believer in human reason, or a confirmed mystic; a creature of Christ-like purity, or a proud and worldly soul; a life-denying **ascetic** obsessed with eternity, or a lover of this life's fleeting joys; a loyal son of Athens, or a traitor who corrupted the city's youth; a humble inquirer aware of his intellectual limitations, or a condescending show-off; a philosopher who sought truth, or an intellectual street-fighter who used cheap tricks to beat his opponents. In short, there is almost nothing that Socrates has not been called, almost no label that someone or other has not pinned on this elusive man. Original and unclassifiable, he always manages to swim through the nets of words in which we try to catch him.

The truth is that some of us find Socrates attractive, some of us feel threatened by him—and many of us feel both attracted *and* threatened. The one thing we cannot do, it seems, is ignore him. Why? Could it be that we still need him?

Yes, says Søren Kierkegaard, the nineteenth-century Danish philosopher.

ASCETICISM

A life of self-denial and material simplicity, often for philosophical or religious reasons.

From *The Sickness unto Death*
By Søren Kierkegaard

> [W]hat the world . . . needs is a Socrates.

Socrates, Socrates, Socrates! Yes, we may well call your name three times; it would not be too much to call it ten times, if it would be of any help. Popular opinion maintains that the world needs a republic, needs a new social order and a new religion—but no one considers that what the world, confused simply by too much knowledge, needs is a Socrates. Of course, if anyone thought of it, not to mention if many thought of it, he would be less needed. Invariably, what error needs most is always the last thing it thinks of—quite naturally, for otherwise it would not, after all, be error.

- Why does Kierkegaard think that we need a new Socrates? Do we?

C. What Is Philosophy?

Philosophy is not like any other academic subject; rather it is a critical approach to all subjects, the comprehensive vision within which all other subjects are contained. Philosophy is a style of life—a life of ideas, or of reason—which a person like Socrates lives all of the time, which many of us live only a few hours a week. It is thinking, about everything and anything. But mainly, it is living thoughtfully. Aristotle, the student of Plato, called this 'contemplative' life the ideal life for humankind. He did not mean, however, that we should sit and think all of the time without doing anything. Aristotle, like the other Greek philosophers, was not one to abstain from pleasure or from political and social involvement for the sake of isolated thinking. Philosophy need not, as commonly believed, put our heads in the clouds, out of touch with everyday reality. Quite to the contrary, philosophy takes our heads out of the clouds, enlarging our view of ourselves and our knowledge of the world, allowing us to break out of prejudices and harmful habits that we have held since we were too young or too naive to know better. To say that philosophy is 'critical' is not to say that it is negative or nihilistic; it is only to say that it is *reflective*. It looks at and thinks about ideas carefully, instead of unthinkingly accepting them.

'Philosophy' sounds like a new and mysterious discipline, unlike anything you have ever encountered. But the basic ideas of philosophy are familiar to all of us, even if we have not yet formally confronted the problems. In this sense, we are all philosophers already. Watch how we behave in times of crisis; examine the language we use as we argue with friends. Notice how quickly abstract concepts like 'freedom', 'mankind', 'self-identity', 'nature' and 'natural', 'relative', 'reality', 'illusion', and 'truth' enter our thoughts and our conversations. Notice how certain basic philosophical principles—whether conservative or radical, pragmatic or idealistic, confident or skeptical, pedestrian or heroic—enter into our arguments and our thinking as well as our actions. We all have some opinions about God, about morality, about the nature of man and the nature of the universe. But because we haven't questioned them, they are merely the **assumptions** of our thinking. We believe many things without having thought about them, merely assuming them, sometimes without evidence or good **reasons**. What the study of philosophy does for us is to make our ideas explicit, to give us the means of defending our **presuppositions**, and to make alternative suppositions available to us as well. Where once we merely assumed a point of view, passively and for lack of alternatives, now we can argue for it with confidence, knowing that our acceptance is active and critical, systematic rather than merely a collection of borrowed beliefs (who knows from where). To be **critical** means to examine carefully and cautiously—to be willing, if necessary, to change our own beliefs. It does not need to be nasty or destructive. There is *constructive* criticism as well. And *to argue* does not mean 'to have a fight'; an **argument** is nothing less than an attempt to justify our beliefs, to back them up with good reasons.

So what is philosophy? Literally, from the Greek (*philein, sophia*), it is 'the love of wisdom'.[1] It is an attitude of critical and systematic thoughtfulness rather than a particular subject matter. This makes matters very difficult for the beginner, who would like a definition of philosophy of the same kind received when he or she began biology, as 'the study of living organisms'. But the nature of philosophy is itself among the most bitter disputes in philosophy. Many philosophers say that it is a science, in fact, the 'queen of the sciences', the womb in which physics, chemistry, mathematics, astronomy, biology, and psychology began their development before being born into their own distinguished worlds and separate university departments. Historically, this is certainly true. (Thus, in

ARGUMENT

The process of reasoning from one claim to another. It may, but need not, be directed against an explicit alternative.

almost any scientific field, the highest degree is 'doctor of philosophy' ['PhD'].) Insofar as one says that philosophy is the road to reality and that the goal of philosophy is truth, that would seem to make it the ultimate science as well.

But it has also been argued, as far back as Socrates' time, that the main business of philosophy is a matter of definitions—finding clear meanings for such important ideas as truth, justice, wisdom, knowledge, and happiness. Accordingly, many philosophers have taken advantage of the increasingly sophisticated tools of logic and linguistics in their attempts to find such definitions. Other philosophers, however, would insist that philosophy is rather closer to morality and religion, its purpose to give meaning to our lives and lead us down 'the right path' to 'the good life'. Still others insist that philosophy is an art, the art of criticism and argumentation as well as the art of conceptual **system**-building or, perhaps, the art of creating comprehensive and edifying visions, dazzling metaphors, new ways of thinking. So considered, philosophy may be akin to storytelling or mythology. Some philosophers place strong emphasis upon **proof** and argument; others place their trust in intuition and insight. Some philosophers reduce all philosophizing to the study of experience; other philosophers take it as a matter of principle not to trust experience. Also, some philosophers insist on being practical, in fact, insist that there are no other considerations but practicality; and then there are others who insist on the purity of the life of ideas, divorced from any practical considerations. But philosophy cannot, without distortion, be reduced to any one of these preferences. All enter into that constantly redefined critical and creative life of ideas that Socrates was willing to die for. In fact, Socrates himself insisted that it is the *seeking* of wisdom that is the essence of philosophy and that anyone who is sure that he or she has wisdom already is undoubtedly wrong. In *The Apology*, for example, he makes this well-known disclaimer:

PROOF

A sequence of steps that lead to the conclusion to be proved.

From *The Apology*
By Plato

The effect of these investigations of mine, gentlemen, has been to arouse against me a great deal of hostility, and hostility of a particularly bitter and persistent kind, which has resulted in various malicious suggestions, including the description of me as a professor of wisdom. This is due to the fact that whenever I succeed in disproving another person's claim to wisdom in a given subject, the bystanders assume that I know everything about that subject myself. But the truth of the matter, gentlemen, is pretty certainly this: that real wisdom is the property of God, and this oracle is his way of telling us that human wisdom has little or no value. It seems to me that he is not referring literally to Socrates, but has merely taken my name as an example, as if he would say to us 'The wisest of you men is he who has realized, like Socrates, that in respect of wisdom he is really worthless.'

That is why I still go about seeking and searching in obedience to the divine command, if I think that anyone is wise, whether citizen or stranger; and when I think that any person is not wise, I try to help the cause of God by proving that he is not. This occupation has kept me too busy to do much either in politics or in my own affairs; in fact, my service to God has reduced me to extreme poverty.

In the West (that is, Europe and North America, along with those parts of the world most influenced by them), Socrates remains a pivotal figure. But philosophy did not begin in Greece. It is a three-thousand-year-old conversation, or, rather, many conversations, that began in many different places, all around the globe.

The oldest philosophical texts we know are from South Asia, from an area in what is now India, dating from more than a thousand years before Socrates lived. A remarkable series of texts, the Vedas became a source for many of the great religions of the world, beginning with what came to be called Hinduism (a name that for many centuries referred only to a very loose collection of local religious beliefs and practices) and then providing the philosophical foundations for Buddhism. Before Socrates, too, in China, a modest teacher named Kong Fuzi (Confucius) started a very different philosophical tradition, in parallel with another Chinese philosophy called Daoism (sometimes spelled 'Taoism'). And in the Middle East, of course, there was a great deal of philosophical activity, in ancient Persia as well as in the religious cauldron of Jerusalem. Moreover, there had been philosophers in Greece for several centuries by the time Socrates came on the scene, so that the world was already steeped in philosophy. The twentieth-century philosopher Karl Jaspers describes this as the 'Axial Period' and says that it is the turning point of civilization.

From 'The "Axial Period"'
By Karl Jaspers

It would seem that this axis of history is to be found in the period around 500 BCE, in the spiritual process that occurred between 800 and 200 BCE. It is there that we meet with the most deep-cut dividing line in history. Man, as we know him today, came into being. For short we may style this the 'Axial Period'.

The most extraordinary events are concentrated in this period. Confucius and Lao-Tzu were living in China, all the directions of Chinese philosophy came into being, including those of Mo-ti, Chuang-tse, Lieh-tsu, and a host of others; India produced the Upanishads and Buddha, and, like China, ran the whole gamut of philosophical possibilities down to skepticism, to materialism, sophism, and nihilism; in Iran Zarathustra taught the challenging view of the world as a struggle between good and evil; in Palestine the prophets made their appearance, from Elijah, by way of Isaiah and Jeremiah, to Deutero-Isaiah; Greece witnessed the appearance of Homer, of the philosophers—Parmenides, Heraclitus, and Plato—of the tragedians, of Thucydides, and of Archimedes. Everything that is merely intimated by these names developed during these few centuries almost simultaneously in China, India, and the Occident without any one of these knowing of the others.

What is new about this age, in all three of these worlds, is that man becomes aware of Being as a whole, of himself and his limitations. He experiences the terrible nature of the world and his own impotence. He asks radical questions. Face to face with the void he strives for liberation and redemption. By consciously recognizing his limits he sets himself the highest goals. He experiences unconditionality in the depth of selfhood and in the clarity of transcendence.

Although this book is grounded in the Western tradition since Socrates, it is important to keep in mind the traditions from Asia as well. It would be utterly foolish to try to summarize the differences between 'East' and 'West', as too many commentators try to do, especially since the Western tradition is thought to include both the reason-oriented legacy of the Greeks and the faith-oriented religions of the Hebrews and Christians, and eventually Islam, too. Furthermore, the diversity of ideas in Asia is colossal, between the 'all is One' philosophy of the ancient Vedas to the world- and self-as-illusion philosophy of Buddhism and the **Dao-** ('the Way-') oriented philosophy of the Chinese.

Yet we can make a few rather simplified comments about similarities and differences. First, there are remarkable affinities between the philosophies that arose in Greece and the Middle East ('Asia minor') and the ancient Vedic philosophies, particularly in their mutual fascination with unified explanation. (Think of the 'unity of science', evident even in the earliest Greek philosophies, and monotheism, which pretty much defined the three major 'Western' religions.) Second, there is a dramatic contrast between the Greek notion of *logos*, suggesting logic and eternal truth (it also serves a central function in Christianity, as in 'in the beginning was the *logos*'), and the Chinese conception of the Dao, which is more oriented toward change, movement, and process. Third, closely related to the previous point, is the Western affection for polarities and oppositions (good versus evil, reality versus appearance, the sacred versus the secular) and the Chinese insistence on *yin/yang*, the inter-relatedness of such seeming opposites. Fourth, much of Western thought over the past two thousand years has focussed on coming to grips with the idea of the One God. (Atheists, too, are caught up in the arguments concerning God's nature and existence.) Much of Eastern thought, by contrast, has no such concern, or it is a very different kind of concern, although the notion of spirituality plays a central role in many Asian religions.

While these general characterizations brush over a wealth of interesting comparisons, you should not treat the non-Western voices in the text that follows as exotic spice added to the substance of philosophy, nor should you think of them as mere echoes of Western ideas. Rather, consider these excerpts as windows that open to a number of very different perspectives, sometimes in contrast, sometimes in unexpected agreement. Remember—philosophy has many faces and voices, and as you learn to appreciate the profundity of philosophical inquiries, you should learn to appreciate its diversity as well.

With diversity in mind, we can bring this section to a close with a very different description of philosophy from the ancient Chinese Daoist philosopher Lao-zi in the texts of the *Dao De Jing*.[2]

From *Dao De Jing*
By Lao-zi

14

Look for it, and it can't be seen.
Listen for it, and it can't be heard.
Grasp for it, and it can't be caught.
These three cannot be further described,
so we treat them as The One.

Its highest is not bright.
Its depths are not dark.
Unending, unnameable, it returns to nothingness.
Formless forms, and imageless images,
subtle, beyond all understanding.

Approach it and you will not see a beginning;
follow it and there will be no end.
When we grasp the Dao of the ancient ones,
we can use it to direct our life today.
To know the ancient origin of Dao:
this is the beginning of wisdom.

* * *

17

The best leaders are those the people hardly know exist.
The next best is a leader who is loved and praised.
Next comes the one who is feared.
The worst one is the leader that is despised.

If you don't trust the people,
they will become untrustworthy.

(Continued)

The best leaders value their words, and use them sparingly.
When she has accomplished her task,
the people say, 'Amazing:
we did it, all by ourselves!'

D. A Modern Approach to Philosophy

The orientation to philosophy in this book is, inevitably, essentially a modern Western approach in which criticism plays a predominant role. Historically, modern European philosophy has its origins in the rise of science and technology. (As we shall see, philosophy and science both emerged in ancient Greece and Asia Minor and, about the same time, in South and East Asia.) We should understand science, however, not just as a particular discipline or subject matter, but rather as a state of mind, a way of looking at the world. In the European tradition, science sees worldly events as understandable and explainable. It sees the universe as *rational*—operating according to universal laws. And it sees the human mind as rational too—in the sense that the mind can grasp and formulate these laws for itself. European philosophy and science put enormous emphasis on the mind of the individual and the ability of human beings to learn the truth about reality.

Though science is essentially a team effort, requiring the labour and thinking of thousands of men and women, the great breakthroughs in science have often been the insights of one man or woman alone. The most famous modern example of this individual genius is the British philosopher-scientist Isaac Newton. In the eyes of his contemporaries and followers, he single-mindedly mastered the laws of the universe, while sitting (so the story goes) under an apple tree. The ideal of modern Western philosophy is, in a phrase, *thinking for yourself*. That is, philosophy is thinking for yourself about basic questions—about life, knowledge, religion, and what to do with yourself. It is *using* the rationality built into your brain to comprehend the rationality (or lack of it) in the world around you. In some cultures, however, the emphasis lies on the group or community, and thinking for yourself is not as important as maintaining group harmony and cohesiveness. In India and China, for example, it is the elusiveness of scientific knowledge that defines much of philosophy. In many of these traditions, enlightenment rather than scientific knowledge is the main goal of philosophy. It is important to keep this difference in mind.

In much of the Western tradition, modern philosophy depends on the notion that each of us has the ability to ascertain what is true and what is right, through our own thinking and experience, without just depending upon outside authority: parents, teachers, popes, kings, or a majority of peers. This does not mean that you should not listen to or, where appropriate, obey other people. Nor does it mean that whatever you think *is* true or right, even 'for you'. What it means is that you must make decisions by appealing to your own reason and to arguments that you can formulate and examine by yourself. Whether you accept a scientific theory, the existence of God, a doctor's diagnosis, a television network's version of the news, or the legitimacy of a new law are also matters you must decided on the basis of evidence, your evaluation of the testimony or authority of others, principles that you can accept, and arguments that you acknowledge as valid. Nevertheless, all of this—the evidence, your evaluation, testimony, and principles—must be subject to examination by other people and other standards than just your own. The truth is not whatever you believe, but how you come to understand and justify the truth is nevertheless your responsibility. This stress on *individual* **autonomy** stands at the very foundation of contemporary Western thought. We might say that it is our most basic assumption. (Accordingly, we shall have to examine

AUTONOMY

Intellectual independence and
freedom from authority.

it as well; but the obvious place to begin is to assume that we are—each of us—capable of carrying out the **reflection** and criticism that philosophy demands of us.)

Historically, the position of individual autonomy can be found most famously in Socrates, who went against the popular opinions of his day and, consequently, sacrificed his life for the laws and principles he believed to be right. It also appears in many medieval philosophers, some of whom also faced grave danger in their partial rejection or questioning of the authority of the Church. It can also be found in those philosophers who, like the **Buddha**, struck out from established society to find a new way. The stress on individual autonomy came to dominate Western thinking in that intellectually brilliant period of history called the **Enlightenment** (sometimes called 'the Age of Reason'), which began in the late seventeenth century and continued through the French Revolution (1789–99). It appeared in different countries with varying speed and intensity, but ultimately it influenced the thinking of Europe, from England and France to Spain and Russia, and became the ideology of young America. Those principles were, whatever the variations from one country or party to another, the autonomy of the individual and each person's right to choose and to speak his[3] own religious, political, moral, and philosophical beliefs, to pursue happiness in his own way, and to lead the life that he, as a reasonable person, sees as right.

If these principles have often been abused, creating confusion and sometimes anarchy and encouraging ruthlessness in politics and strife in a mixed society, they are principles that can be challenged only with great difficulty and a sense of imminent danger. Once the individual's right or ability to decide such matters for himself or herself is denied, who shall decide? Society no longer agrees on any single unambiguous set of instructions from the scriptures. Those in power are no longer trusted. We are rightfully suspicious of those who attack the individual, because it is not clear what else they have in mind. Whatever the abuses, and whatever political, social, or economic systems might be required to support them, philosophical autonomy is the starting point. Even in the most authority-minded societies, autonomy and the ability to think beyond prescribed limits remain essential.

The metaphor of enlightenment is common to many cultures. The comparison of clear thinking with illumination is present in ancient, Christian, and Eastern thought as well as in modern philosophy and comic-book symbolism (for example, the cartoon light bulb over a character's head). The seventeenth-century French philosopher René Descartes (1596–1650) was one of the founders of the Enlightenment, and he was particularly fond of the illumination metaphor. He is generally recognized as the father of modern philosophy, particularly in its focus on individual autonomy. Like Socrates two thousand years before him, Descartes believed that each person is capable of ascertaining what beliefs are true and what actions are right. But whereas Socrates searched for the truth through dialogue and discussion, Descartes searched in the solitude of his own thinking. With considerable risk to his safety, he challenged the authority of the French government and the Catholic Church. He insisted that he would accept as true only those ideas that were demonstrably true to him. Against what he considered were obscure teachings of the Church and often opaque commands of his government, Descartes insisted upon 'clear and distinct ideas' and arguments based upon 'the light of reason' (*Meditations on First Philosophy*). Yet he retained much of his medieval teachings: he continued to believe in God and the Church, and he made it his first moral maxim to obey the laws and customs of his country. His challenge to authority was rather his **method**, which signified one of the greatest revolutions in Western thought. From Descartes on, the ultimate authority was to be found in man's own thinking and experience, nowhere else.

None of this is meant to deny authority as such, nor is it to deny the 'objectivity' of truth. We must still make appeals to authority, but we must never take authorities as absolutes. For example, none of us would particularly like to go out and establish on our own the figures of the 2011 census of the Canadian population. But it is up to each of us to accept or reject the official 'authoritative' figures, to question the integrity or motivation of the authorities,

CARTESIAN METHOD

Descartes' deductive method that starts with self-evident axioms from which the rest is deduced.

and to appeal, if necessary, to alternative sources of information. Nevertheless, the true figures do exist, whether we or anyone else ever discovers them. Intellectual autonomy and integrity do not demand that we give up the search for truth but rather that we should be continually critical—of both ourselves and others—in the pursuit of it.

For anyone beginning to study philosophy today, Descartes is a pivotal figure. His method is both easy to follow and very much in accord with our own independent temperaments. He proceeded by means of logical arguments, giving his readers a long monologue of presentations and proofs of his philosophical doubts and beliefs. Like Socrates before him, Descartes used his philosophy to cut through the clouds of prejudice and unreliable opinions, to distinguish truth from falsehood. He questioned the truth of commonly held opinions, no matter how many people already accepted them—or, how few.

Philosophy has always been concerned with truth and mankind's knowledge of reality. Not coincidentally, Descartes' new philosophy developed in the age of Galileo and the rise of modern science. In ancient Greece, the origins of philosophy and the birth of science were one and the same. Philosophers understand that the truth is not always what most people believe at any given time. (Most people once believed that the earth was flat and stationary, for example.) But, at the same time that they simply refuse to accept 'common sense', philosophers try not to say things that common sense finds absurd. For example, a philosopher who—in a public speech—denied that anyone existed besides himself would clearly be absurd. So too, the philosopher who argued that he knew that nobody ever knows anything. Nevertheless, philosophers often take such claims very seriously, if only to refute them and show us *why* they are absurd.

Accordingly, two of the most important challenges in the philosopher's search for truth are (1) skepticism and (2) paradox. In **skepticism**, the philosopher finds himself or herself unable to justify what every sane person knows to be the case; for example, that we are not merely dreaming all of the time. In Eastern as well as Western philosophy, skepticism has provided a valuable probe for our everyday presumptions of knowledge, and it sometimes becomes a philosophy in its own right. In a **paradox**, an absurd conclusion seems to result from perfectly acceptable ways of thinking. For example, there is the familiar paradox of Epimenides the Cretan, who claimed that all Cretans are liars. (That sounds reasonable enough.) But if what he said was true, then he was lying and what he said, accordingly, was false. But how can the same statement be both true and false? What Epimenides said was true only if it was false at the same time. That is a paradox, and whenever a philosophical argument ends in paradox we can be sure that something has gone wrong. Again, in both East and West, philosophers have always been intrigued by paradoxes and have often been prompted by them to strike out in bold new directions in search of a resolution.

Skepticism begins with **doubt**. The philosopher considers the possibility that something that everyone believes is possibly mistaken. Some doubt is a healthy sign of intellectual autonomy, but excessive doubting becomes skepticism, which is no longer healthy. It has its obvious dangers: if you doubt whether you are ever awake or not, you might well do things that wouldn't have serious consequences in a dream but would be fatal in real life (jumping out of a plane, for example). Philosophers who have doubts about the most ordinary and seemingly unquestionable beliefs are called *skeptics*. For example, there was the Chinese philosopher who, when he once dreamed that he was a butterfly, started wondering whether he really were a butterfly—dreaming that he was a philosopher. But however challenging skeptics may be as philosophers, in practice their skepticism is impossible. Accordingly, one of the main drives in philosophy has been to refute the skeptic and return philosophy to common sense (to prove, for example, that we are *not* dreaming all of the time).

Opposed to skepticism is the ancient philosophical ideal of **certainty**, the ability to prove beyond a doubt that what we believe is true. Socrates and Descartes, in their very different ways, tried to provide precisely this certainty for the most important beliefs, and thus refute the skeptics of their own times. For Descartes in particular, certainty is the **criterion**, that is, the test according to which beliefs are to be evaluated.

But do we ever find such certainty? It seems that we do, at least in one discipline Descartes suggested—mathematics. Indeed, the precision of mathematics has long served as an ideal of knowledge in Western philosophy. In mathematics, we believe, we can be *certain*. Who can doubt that two plus two equals four or that the interior angles of a triangle total 180 degrees? Using mathematics as his model, Descartes (and many generations of philosophers following him) attempted to apply a similar method in philosophy. First, he had to find, as in Euclidean geometry, a small set of **first principles**, or **axioms**, that were **self-evident**. They had to be assumed without proof or be so fundamental that they seemed not to allow any proof. These would serve as premises or starting points for the *arguments* that would take a person from the self-evident axioms to other principles that might not be self-evident at all. But if these secondary principles could be deduced from first principles that were already certain, then they, like the theorems of geometry, would share the certainty of the principles from which they had been derived.

Descartes was a scientist and a mathematician as well as a philosopher. With that in mind, we can understand his *Discourse on Method*, in which he set out four basic rules that would define philosophy for many years.

> **SELF-EVIDENT**
>
> Obvious without proof or argument.

From *Discourse on Method*
By René Descartes

The first of [my rules] was to accept . . . nothing more than what was presented to my mind so clearly and distinctly that I could have no occasion to doubt it.

The first of [my rules] was to accept nothing as true which I did not clearly recognize to be so; that is to say, carefully to avoid precipitation and prejudice in judgments, and to accept in them nothing more than what was presented to my mind so clearly and distinctly that I could have no occasion to doubt it.

The second was to divide up each of the difficulties which I examined into as many parts as possible, and as seemed requisite in order that it might be resolved in the best manner possible.

The third was to carry on my reflections in due order, commencing with objects that were the most simple and easy to understand, in order to rise little by little, or by degrees, to knowledge of the most complex, assuming an order, even if a fictitious one, among those which do not follow a natural sequence relatively to one another.

The last was in all cases to make enumerations so complete and reviews so general that I should be certain of having omitted nothing.

One might say that the essence of these rules is to be cautious and to think for oneself. The premises, upon which all else depends, must be utterly beyond doubt, perfectly certain, otherwise all else is futile. According to Descartes, the test or criterion of such a premise is that it be a clear and distinct idea, self-evident, and springing from the light of reason alone.

We shall see much more of Descartes in the following chapters. In Chapter 3, we shall see that Descartes' technique for assuring the certainty of his premises was what he called the **method of doubt** (or *methodological doubt*). In order to make sure that he did not accept any principle too quickly before being convinced of its perfect certainty, he resolved to doubt every belief until he could prove it true beyond question, and to show that the very act of doubting this belief led to an intolerable paradox. The point of this kind of argument is not to become a skeptic, but, quite the contrary, to find those premises that even the skeptic cannot doubt. From those premises, Descartes and many generations of philosophers following him have attempted and will attempt to prove that we do indeed know what we think we know. Like Socrates, Descartes begins by questioning what no one but a philosopher would doubt and ends up changing the way we think about ourselves and our knowledge for several centuries. In other cultures, too, entire societies have been dramatically altered by philosophers who challenged what seemed to be obvious; sometimes they challenged reality itself.

To conclude this section on approaches to modern philosophy, let us examine how two contemporary philosophers sum up their views of philosophy. The first is by the great English philosopher Bertrand Russell. The second one is by Mary Midgley.

From *The Problems of Philosophy*
By Bertrand Russell

But further, if we are not to fail in our endeavour to determine the value of philosophy, we must first free our minds from the prejudices of what are wrongly called 'practical' men. The 'practical' man, as this word is often used, is one who recognizes only material needs, who realizes that men must have food for the body, but is oblivious of the necessity of providing food for the mind. If all men were well off, if poverty and disease had been reduced to their lowest possible point, there would still remain much to be done to produce a valuable society; and even in the existing world the goods of the mind are at least as important as the goods of the body. It is exclusively among the goods of the mind that the value of philosophy is to be found; and only those who are not indifferent to these goods can be persuaded that the study of philosophy is not a waste of time.

From *Utopias, Dolphins, and Computers*
By Mary Midgley

Is philosophy like plumbing? . . .

Plumbing and philosophy are both activities that arise because elaborate cultures like ours have, beneath their surface, a fairly complex system which is usually unnoticed, but which sometimes goes wrong. In both cases, this can have serious consequences. Each system supplies vital needs for those who live above it. Each is hard to repair when it does go wrong, because neither of them was ever consciously planned as a whole. There have been many ambitious attempts to reshape both of them, but existing complications are usually too widespread to allow a completely new start.

Neither system ever had a single designer who knew exactly what needs it would have to meet. Instead, both have grown imperceptibly over the centuries, and are constantly being altered piecemeal to suit changing demands, as the ways of life above them have branched out. Both are therefore now very intricate. When trouble arises, specialized skill is needed if there is to be any hope of locating it and putting it right.

Here, however, we run into the first striking difference between the two cases. About plumbing, everybody accepts this need for specialists with painfully acquired technical knowledge. About philosophy, people . . . not only doubt the need, they are often skeptical about whether the underlying system even exists at all. It is much more deeply hidden. When the concepts we are living by function badly, they do not usually drip audibly through the ceiling or swamp the kitchen floor. They just quietly distort and obstruct our thinking.

* * *

Socrates lived, as we do, in a society that was highly articulate and self-conscious—indeed, strongly hooked on words. It may well be that other cultures, less committed to talking, find different routes to salvation, that they pursue a less word-bound form of wisdom. But wisdom itself matters everywhere, and everybody must start from where they are. I think it might well pay us to be less impressed with what philosophy can do for our dignity, and more aware of the shocking malfunctions for which it is an essential remedy.

E. Becoming a Philosopher

Why do philosophy? One reason is that we cannot help it. Asking big questions—about God, reality, the meaning of life, death, sex, love, war, religion, science, morality, politics, history, and art—is something that we are naturally inclined to do, provided we have enough time and leisure. However, when most of us try and think about these big questions on our own, we get lost just as if we were trapped in a large, elaborate maze. We soon discover that we don't really know where to begin, nor where we are heading, nor which paths we should follow, nor which paths are dead ends. The result is that our thinking often gets us nowhere. But it doesn't have to be that way.

This is where the study of philosophy comes in. The best philosophers are people who know their way around the maze much better than the rest of us, because they live there. Like us, they think about the big questions, only they do it much better than we do. Where we are vague, they are precise. Where we are sloppy, they are rigorous. Where our thoughts tend to jump around, theirs are controlled by the rigour and discipline of logic. Where our thinking is inconsistent, theirs is coherent and systematic; and where we are timid or un-imaginative, they are bold and creative. We can therefore learn a great deal by reading their writings and by thinking about what they have to say about the questions that grip us. They may not give us the answers we seek, but they can help us ask better questions.

But where do all these questions come from? What makes us ask them in the first place? According to Plato, philosophy begins in wonder, or with a sense of amazement at the strangeness of things.[4] The twentieth-century Canadian philosopher George Grant, who greatly admired Plato, took a similar view of philosophy's source or origin.

From 'What Is Philosophy?'
By George Grant

Philosophy is for those who have moved beyond any simple certainty.

I want to try to describe what philosophy is. My job is to teach philosophy to youngsters. Just what is this subject that we try to teach them, and which is taught at all the universities of the world? Why is it that in all the great civilizations there have always been philosophers and that indeed we often judge the greatness of a society by the greatness of its philosophy?

The word philosophy comes from two Greek words, love and wisdom. Philosophy means the love of wisdom. Now most of us have some knowledge of what it is to love. Parents love their children—that is, the children are infinitely precious to them. Some of us at our worst moments love money in the same way. Money is what is infinitely precious to us. That is, to love somebody in the real sense, not the Hollywood sense, is to say that that person is not of relative but of absolute worth to one. People who love themselves think themselves of absolute worth. They are for themselves the centre of the universe.

But if it is fairly easy from our own experience to say what love is, it is far more difficult to know what we mean by the word *wisdom*. It is indeed quite easy to say what wisdom is not. It is not, for instance, knowledge in any specialized sense. We know people who have a great deal of knowledge about mathematics or medicine, of fixing radios or selling insurance, who despite that knowledge we would not call wise. The great atomic scientist in the United States, Dr Oppenheimer, obviously is a man of vast knowledge, but nobody who has followed his career could easily call him a wise man. Just like Einstein, outside his specialized field of physics he talks like a child. On the other hand, most of us have met people who have very little specialized knowledge and who one would yet call wise. For instance, I know a retired minister in Halifax who is no great specialist in any field but is one of the wisest men I have ever met.

Now I think that gives us the clue to what wisdom is. We call people wise if they know how to live—if

(Continued)

they know what is important in living. And when we speak about living we mean something to do with the whole of the person—that which goes to the very roots of an individual's life. And that is what we mean when we say philosophy is the love of wisdom. It is the desire to seek that which will give purpose and meaning and unity to life. That is the difference between philosophic and scientific knowledge. Scientific knowledge is always concerned with some part or aspect of life; philosophic knowledge is always concerned with the whole of human existence.

In other words, philosophy begins when we ask the questions: 'How should I live? What is life for? Why do I exist in the world?' Now of course for many people such questions as these do not arise as real questions. They think they know what life is really for. They think they know what is important. For instance, in North America today more and more people think they are certain what is of prime importance to living. It is to get more money, to buy a more expensive house, to have wider and more varied pleasures, to be a social success—that is what is known as getting on in the world. Once one has got a Chevrolet, get an Oldsmobile; once one has got an Oldsmobile, get a Buick. Among such people—and of course this kind of mood is present in all of us—there is little desire for wisdom, little desire to think what life is about. The practical getting on in the world is their philosophy—so they don't feel the need to think further.

In a nobler and deeper way the same thing is true of people who are held very simply by some clearly defined religion. If they take that religion seriously it tells them directly what is important about living. It gives them such certainty that they feel no need to think deeply about the meaning of life—that is, to ask philosophic questions. They live in tradition. And when I speak about religion I do not mean only as ancient and wise a tradition as Christianity. It is equally true of the great political religions of the twentieth century. In Soviet Russia, for instance, there is practically no philosophy, for the religion of communism provides for many people a simple Sunday school faith which tells them how to live.

Philosophy is for those who have moved beyond any simple certainty. It is for those who have come face to face with the mystery of existence and who have seen how profound a mystery it is. Philosophy is the attempt to fathom that profundity—that is, to find the wisdom which will enable us to live as we ought.

Now the sense of mystery arises for people in two ways; first from just plain wonder at the world around

them, and secondly from the anguish of their own lives. That glorious man Plato—the greatest of all philosophers—said once that philosophy begins in wonder. We look at the immense spaces of the night—the worlds beyond worlds beyond worlds that the astronomers tell us about, and how can we not wonder what it is all for, where it all came from? We look at human history—at all the vast numbers of civilizations and billions of people who have existed, the traces of whom have entirely disappeared from the world—and we ask what human life is for. Has it any meaning at all? I think this wonder exists deep down in everybody. Certainly it exists in all children. When I say to my six-year-old daughter that God made the world, she looks up in wonder to ask who then made God. When we meet a blind person, my four-year-old son asks why did God make some people blind—or why did God make mosquitoes or sharks? Of course, the tragedy is that we kill that wonder in our children. We fill them with complacent conventional opinions and tame them to accept unquestioningly. We make them adjusted little members of the ant community. But still that spontaneous wonder in children is evidence that it is deeply in all of us. It is just our humanity that we desire to know, and that desire to know is the very root of philosophy.

Of course, this sense of mystery comes to us not only in this natural spontaneous way—but also arises in the anguish and suffering which is so near the heart of all our lives. This anguish arises for us when people we love are dead or going to die—when we face the fact that inescapably we too must die. It faces us in all the suffering we undergo when we are disappointed in what we have desperately wanted. It arises for us most deeply in the guilt and shame we rightly feel when we have treated some other person cruelly or let some other person down. That is, when we see our shoddy little selves for what we truly are.

Most of us will try to do anything to avoid that anguish. We will do anything to forget that someday we shall die; we try to push aside the thought that we have treated people unfairly, by dubbing all our guilts 'neurotic'. We try to surround ourselves with pleasant thoughts—the next cigarette, the next dance, the next promotion, the next act of love. But inescapably the fact of our situation is there. At some moment—perhaps when we lie awake at night, perhaps when we are in pain, perhaps when we face the fact that somebody we love has no real care for us, perhaps even at our greatest moments of happiness when we know this happiness is bound to pass—at such moments we admit our situation and experience anguish. The whole mystery of human existence arises for us and we start to philosophize—to fathom that mystery in thought. For instance, these days if any of us really faced what the cobalt bomb may mean—that human existence perhaps will cease to exist on this planet—that is, you and I and our children—we might really begin to face that mystery. Has the human story then been meaningless? Is my life, are my children's lives meaningless? It is in such moments that philosophy in its deepest sense arises.

Of course, the practical man will say, get on with the job—why think about such things—earn your living, bring up your family, do your duty, make the world more comfortable for other people. All one can say in answer to such practical people is that those who feel this anguish, meet this mystery, have no alternative to philosophy. It is what God has called them to do. Perhaps we may say even more. After all, an ape or a bee gets on with the job, earns his living, procreates and cares for his children, accepts his existence, adjusts to his society. Only man is capable of this attempt to understand the mystery of existence. It is only man who can rebel, feel anguish, think. Perhaps then in a very real sense, it is the ability to philosophize which gives man his real dignity, which makes him more valuable than a

clever ape. One of the finest philosophers of all time, a Frenchman named Pascal, once expressed this brilliantly. He said:

> Man is but a reed, the weakest thing in nature; but a thinking reed. It does not need the universe to take up arms to crush him; a vapour, a drop of water is enough to kill him. But, though the universe should crush him, a man would still be nobler than his destroyer, because he knows that he is dying, knows that the universe has got the better of him; the universe knows nothing of this.

This means that philosophy is something inescapable to being a man. It is an activity rooted in the very nature of our humanity—not a pleasant academic exercise reserved for a few professors and students in a university. The farmer must find himself as much as the teacher; the businessman as much as the coal miner. It also means that philosophy is something that a man must do for himself. Nobody can make another man's philosophy for him. Other people can grow our food for us; other people can make our atom bombs for us; somebody else can cure us when we are sick—but nobody else can do our thinking for us. This is the ultimate truth of freedom. A man must do his own believing as he does his own dying.

- What are the two sources of philosophy identified by Grant?
- Why does Grant think that philosophy isn't just for professional philosophers and academic specialists, but for everyone?
- Why does Grant say that philosophy is 'inescapable' and 'rooted in the very nature of our humanity'?

According to George Grant, philosophy isn't just another academic subject or university department; it is a pursuit open to all of us, because its roots lie deep in human nature. By engaging in philosophy, by thinking carefully and hard about what matters most, our minds may move 'out of the shadows and imaginings into the truth' (to use a phrase of St Augustine that Grant was fond of quoting). However, there is no guarantee that we will succeed. Like any other human activity, philosophy can go wrong in many different ways. For example, we may make mistakes in reasoning or logic—and, alas, we often do. We may also allow ourselves to be blinded by our preconceptions and our prejudices. We may take things for granted that really should be questioned; and we may question things that really should be taken for granted. We may fail to ask the right questions; we may also ask the wrong questions. We may mistake a part for the whole, or the whole for a part. These, sadly, are only a few examples of the intellectual vices we need to guard against if we are not to go astray as philosophers.

The dangers inherent in doing philosophy are highlighted by the Canadian philosopher and poet Francis Sparshott, in a splendid short poem entitled 'Philosopher':

'Philosopher'
By Francis Sparshott

Brooding over chaos and the waste places,
He saw that it was bad.
His idle fingers swirled the jigsaw pieces
Till he went mad.

Looking for bits with one straight edge to form
His picture's border, he found none at all:
Only obscene curves quantified disorder.
No green trees, no blue sky, no red-brick wall.

And even the dapple faded, year by year,
To indeterminate greys and browns. But his hand
Still stirs the pieces round, his hooked eyes peer
At the rubbed contours. Can't he understand

That there's no jigsaw? No mind ever fitted
These scraps of card together, no fret cut
A pretty picture up. More to be mocked than pitied,
All nails and pupils, he keeps his bed now. But

How long will nurses bring the pan? How long
Will meals come up from the kitchen? Can he pay
For his private room forever? And isn't it wrong
To tie scarce facilities up this way?

His cracked gaze stirs the bits of his distress.
He knows they won't fit,
But what else can he do? He would be in a worse mess
If he solved it . . . .

Sparshott's philosopher has set himself a simple-sounding task: that of putting together the pieces of a jigsaw puzzle. To perform this task successfully would be to recover a lost unity, to re-create a harmonious whole, to bring order out of chaos. Note, however, that the chaos and the order here are of a rather peculiar sort. The chaos is apparent and undeniable—remember, our philosopher *sees* 'that it was bad'—whereas the order is so hidden as to be invisible. Undeterred, our philosopher works away sedulously, fortified by the firm hope that the appearance of chaos will eventually give way to the reality of order if he can just discover how the puzzle pieces were arranged in the first place, before the 'pretty picture' was 'cut . . . up'. And so he keeps 'stir[ring] the pieces round', obsessed with finding that elusive, saving combination.

It turns out, however, that our neurotic philosopher is the victim of his own false assumptions. The pieces he is obsessed with are not pieces of a jigsaw at all—indeed, 'there's no jigsaw'—but are instead just 'scraps of card', stray odds and ends that 'won't fit' together now *because they never did*. The truth is tragic: there was no order to begin with, no lost unity, no antecedently given whole of which the pieces are parts. Small wonder, then, that the philosopher 'went mad', for he has spent his life looking for something that is nothing but an unacknowledged projection of his own mind. Ironically enough, the philosopher's stubborn insistence that reality must conform to the preconceptions of his reason has led to the loss of reason itself.

- Do you think the figure in the poem is supposed to represent all philosophers, or just certain types of philosophers? Why or why not?
- What do you think the last two lines of the poem mean? Why would the philosopher 'be in a worse mess / If he solved it . . .'?

Sparshott's poem makes it clear that philosophers face certain temptations. One of these temptations is looking for order—a nice, neat, tidy arrangement—where it simply doesn't exist. Another temptation—one Sparshott's poem does not address directly—is *impatience*. Philosophical problems are just that—problems—and it is natural for us to want problems to go away. However, we won't get anywhere in philosophy if it we are in too much of a hurry. We cannot hope to solve philosophical problems if we do not understand them, and we cannot hope to understand them unless we take the time to think hard about them. This means that we need to slow down and make sure we have a firm grasp of the questions before we try and answer them. And since these questions are so deep and broad and abstract, we cannot hope to wrap our minds around them without getting a bit confused. Because philosophy gets us to look at familiar things in a new way, its questions can leave us feeling lost and dizzy and disoriented. This is why philosophy is one subject in which perplexity is very often a sign of progress. Here confusion can be proof of understanding, not its opposite.

In a sense, then, part of the point of this book is *to get you confused*. You will be presented with many philosophical theories, all of which are answers to challenging questions. If you think about these questions with care and attention, you should find yourself perplexed about many things: about the nature of right and wrong, good and evil, justice and liberty, truth, knowledge, science, perception, reason, free will, God, consciousness, and reality (to name only a few). Of course, you should think about how to solve these problems, but always remember to take your time—be patient.

The need for patience in philosophy was succinctly expressed by the twentieth-century French philosopher Simone Weil.

From *First and Last Notebooks*
By Simone Weil

The proper method of philosophy consists in clearly conceiving the insoluble problems in all their insolubility and then in simply contemplating them, fixedly and tirelessly, year and after year, without any hope, patiently waiting.

By this standard, there are few philosophers. And one can hardly even say a few.

There is no entry into the transcendent until the human faculties—intelligence, will, human love—have come up against a limit, and the human being waits at this threshold, which he can make no move to cross, without turning away and without knowing what he wants, in fixed, unwavering attention.

It is a state of extreme humiliation, and it is impossible for anyone who cannot accept humiliation.

Many of us want to forget about problems we cannot solve. Simone Weil encourages us to do something different. If we are truly philosophers, she suggests, we will continue to contemplate the problems we are unable to solve, dwelling on precisely those aspects of them that make them insoluble. This contemplation of the insoluble is a potentially lifelong task: we are to do it 'fixedly and tirelessly, year and after year'. And not only that: we are advised to ponder our problems 'without any hope, patiently waiting'.

- Do you think the philosopher in Sparshott's poem practises what Weil preaches? Can you think of any differences between their methods?
- Why might someone find it worthwhile to think about problems she cannot solve? What might be gained by the sort of contemplation Weil describes?

What Simone Weil recommends is not easy, as she herself admits. Whether we agree with her advice or not, one thing seems fairly clear: unless we approach philosophical questions with a measure of patience and humility, any answers we come up with will likely be empty and superficial. This point was made powerfully by George Grant: If 'we are not willing to wait for answers in philosophy', he warns us, our answers will be 'cheap'. And this tendency toward impatience may have grave consequences for us as philosophers and for our culture as a whole.

From 'What Is Philosophy?'
By George Grant

The life of philosophy is open to all of us.

The way I have described philosophy has been as a very intimate and personal activity—something dealing with the core of the human mind. Of course, in the university it is presented to students in a more formal way. We try to put before the students what has been most illuminating in the great philosophizing of the past. The students study the writings that incorporate the fullest wisdom of the greatest philosophers. This study of the past is necessary, for, after all, each generation does not come into a new world—it comes into a world made rich by the tradition of the ages. Therefore, one of the things a man must do if he is to be wise himself is to partake of all that accumulation of wisdom. This study of the history of philosophy is the raw material out of which men can begin to build a philosophy of their own. After all, any man who has even elementary humility will want to find out what Aristotle and St Paul, Kant and Calvin, said about a problem, and see in the great man's solution of that problem the beginnings of a solution of his own.

For instance, to such a central problem as 'what is truth?' we cannot expect any easy answer, and we need all the help we can get from those in the past who have had clearer minds and greater vision than ourselves. Do you remember Francis Bacon's wonderful description of the meeting between Pilate and Jesus? '"What is truth?" said jesting Pilate and would not wait for an answer.' If we are not willing to wait for answers in philosophy, if we are not willing to learn from the wisdom of the past, how can we expect to get anything but a cheap answer to the problem 'What is truth?' And if we have a cheap answer to such a problem we are liable to have a cheap life.

* * *

Yet we must never despair, for none of us is a slave to our society. The life of philosophy is open to all of us. And its reward is in truth infinite. For as we face the mystery of existence and pass in thought beyond a superficial view of the world, there will come to us, out of the mystery and the anguish, the certainty which is rooted not in foolishness but in truth.

- Why is patience so crucial in philosophy, according to Grant?

If we are going to become philosophers, therefore, it seems that we must seek answers with patience as well as with daring. The road that leads to truth in philosophy is long and crooked and hard and steep; unless we are ready for an arduous journey—unless we are prepared to keep going, no matter how high and rough the road—we won't get too far. However, if we persevere and refuse to give up, we may move in the presence of the truth—of that good for which any free mind yearns by nature. That, at any rate, is what Grant is saying to us; and it is very much in the spirit of Plato, as you shall realize after reading Chapter 1.

At this point, you may find yourself thinking along the following lines: 'The truth we seek as philosophers is said to lie at the end of a road. Very well; but there may be many roads, and each may lead to a different sort of truth. For instance, there may be one road meant for scientists, another meant for artists, another meant for mathematicians, another meant for mystics; and so on. So, which road should philosophers travel?'

This is a very good question. The nineteenth-century Scottish philosopher James Frederick Ferrier gives the following classic answer to this question: The road that philosophers must travel is the high road of reason.

From *Institutes of Metaphysic*
By James Frederick Ferrier

A system of philosophy is bound by two main requisitions,—it ought to be true, and it ought to be reasoned.

2. A system of philosophy is bound by two main requisitions,—it ought to be true, and it ought to be reasoned. If a system of philosophy is not true, it will scarcely be convincing; and if it is not reasoned, a man will be as little satisfied with it as a hungry person would be by having his meat served up to him raw. Truth is the ultimate end of philosophy: hence a system of philosophy ought to be true. The formation of reason (as affected by the discharge of its proper function, which is the ascertainment and concatenation of necessary principles and conclusions) is the proximate end of philosophy; hence a system of philosophy ought to be reasoned. Philosophy, therefore, in its ideal perfection, is a body of reasoned truth.

3. Of these obligations, the latter is the more stringent: it is more proper that philosophy should be reasoned, than that it should be true; because, while truth may perhaps be unattainable by man, to reason is certainly his province, and within his power. In a case where two objects have to be overtaken, it is more incumbent on us to secure the one to which our faculties are certainly competent, than the other, to which they are perhaps inadequate. Besides, no end can be so important for man as the cultivation of his own reason.

4. This consideration determines the value of a system of philosophy. A system is of the highest value only when it embraces both of these requisitions—that is,

when it is both true and reasoned. But a system which is reasoned without being true is always of higher value than a system which is true without being reasoned.

5. The latter kind of system is of no value; because philosophy is 'the attainment of truth by the way of reason'. That is its definition. A system, therefore, which reaches the truth, but not by the way of reason, is not philosophy at all; it has no scientific worth. No man can be called upon to take truth upon trust at the hands of his brother man. But truth not reasoned is truth proposed upon trust. The best that could be said of such a system would be, that it was better than one which was neither true nor reasoned.

6. Again,—an unreasoned philosophy, even though true, carries no guarantee of its truth. It may be true, but it cannot be certain; because all certainty depends on rigorous evidence—on strict demonstrative proof. Therefore no certainty can attach to the conclusions of an unreasoned philosophy.

7. Further,—the truths of science, in so far as science is a means of intellectual culture, are of no importance in themselves, or considered apart from each other. It is only the study and apprehension of their vital and organic connection which is valuable in an educational point of view. But an unreasoned body of philosophy, however true and formal it may be, has no living and essential interdependency of parts on parts;

(Continued)

and is, therefore, useless as a discipline of the mind, and valueless for purposes of tuition.

8. On the other hand, a system which is reasoned, but not true, has always some value. It creates reason by exercising it. It is employing the proper means to reach truth, although it may fail to reach it. Even though its parts may not be true, yet if each of them be a step leading to the final catastrophe—a link in an unbroken chain on which the ultimate disclosure hinges—and if each of the parts be introduced merely because it is such a step or link,—in that case it is conceived that the system is not without its use, as affording an invigorating employment to the reasoning powers, and that general satisfaction to the mind which the successful extrication of a plot, whether in science or in romance, never fails to communicate.

9. Such a system, although it falls short of the definition of philosophy just given, comes nearer to it than the other; because to reach truth, but not by the way of reason, is to violate the definition in its very essence; whereas to miss truth, but by the way of reason, is to comply with the fundamental circumstance which it prescribes. If there are other ways of reaching truth than the road of reason, a system which enters on any of these other paths, whatever else it may be, is not a system of philosophy in the proper sense of the word.

10. But, as has been said, a system of philosophy ought to be both true in all its positions, and also thoroughly reasoned out in a series of strict demonstrations, which, while each is complete and impregnable in itself, shall present, in their combination, only one large demonstration from the beginning to the end of the work. This, indeed, is the only kind of system to which much value can be assigned, or from which any large intellectual profit can be expected. Philosophical books may be read; philosophical lectures may be listened to; but nothing except a strictly-reasoned system can be either taught or learned.

- According to Ferrier, a system of philosophy aims at two things. How would you explain these aims in your own words?
- Which of these two aims is regarded as more important? Why?

Ferrier states that philosophers seek the truth 'by the way of reason'—that is, by means of argument, evidence, and proof, not by means of blind guesses and gut feelings. Does Ferrier mean you should dismiss all of your pre-philosophical convictions once you start studying philosophy? No, not at all. However, reason must become the judge of your beliefs, not vice versa; simply stating your deepest convictions won't make you a philosopher. You must get in the habit of backing up what you say with reasons—and your reasons had better be as good as you can make them. If you are not prepared to submit to reason—if all you are interested in doing is telling people what you happen to think—then you can be sure of one thing: whatever you are doing, you are not playing the exacting and exciting game that we have come to call philosophy. Ever since the days of Socrates, playing that game has meant participating in a *dialogue*, a civilized exchange of ideas in which answers to questions are judged by whether they can be defended with *good arguments*. In this game, the referee whose authority all players acknowledge is reason: not tradition, not custom, not revelation, not power, not force, not wealth, but reason. What counts is how well you can defend your position, not whether your position is brand-new or old-fashioned, shocking or reassuring, popular or unfashionable, innocuous or subversive.

So how can you advance in the game of philosophy? Simply by developing the skill of good reasoning. But what counts as good reasoning? Is there more than one way of arguing well? And just what is an 'argument', anyway? How can we distinguish the sheep from the goats, the good ones from the not-so-good ones? Finally—and this is crucial—how can each of us learn to make our arguments as good as possible?

Asking these questions leads us to that branch of philosophy known as *logic*.

F. A Brief Introduction to Logic

Many great thinkers—from Socrates to Descartes to contemporary philosophers—present their thoughts in the form of arguments. But—to return to a question raised at the end of the last section—what *is* an argument?

An argument is a verbal attempt to get other people to accept a belief or opinion by providing reasons why they should accept it. We usually think of an argument as a confrontation between two people. When they try to convince each other, they usually resort to certain verbal means, and it is with these means that a philosopher is concerned. Of course, there are other ways of getting people to agree with you—tricks, bribes, brainwashing, threats of physical force. But the use of arguments is the most durable and trustworthy, as well as the most respectable, way of getting others to agree. Freedom of speech is the cornerstone of democracy (and the bane of totalitarianism) precisely because of the power of argument to determine the best among competing opinions. On the other hand, we should not think of an argument as a political weapon whose purpose is to shut down conversation or put other people and their opinions on the defensive. It is always reasonable to ask for arguments, but it may not be reasonable to push a person for arguments that he or she cannot provide. To fail to argue for a position is not necessarily to give up on it, and to refute the arguments for a position is not necessarily to reject the position.

You don't have to be arguing with anyone in particular in order to construct an argument. Editorials in newspapers, for example, argue for a position, but not necessarily against anyone. But whether your argument is a letter to a magazine, in which you are trying to convince the entire population of your views, or a personal letter, in which you are trying to convince a friend not to do something foolhardy, the main point of argument is to demonstrate or establish a point of view. A scientist describing an experiment tries to demonstrate to other scientists the truth of his or her theory. A politician tries to demonstrate to his or her constituency the need for higher taxes. A philosopher tries to demonstrate to us the value of a certain view of life, a certain view of reality, a certain view of ourselves. In each case, these people try to give as many reasons as possible why other people should accept their view of things; in short, they use arguments to persuade others.

Argument involves at least two components: logic and rhetoric. **Logic** concerns those reasons that should hold for anyone, anywhere, without appealing to personal feelings, sympathies, or prejudices. **Rhetoric**, on the other hand, does involve such personal appeals. Personal charm may be part of rhetoric, in a writer as well as in a public speaker. Jokes may be part of rhetoric. A personal plea is an effective rhetorical tool; so is trying to be sympathetic to readers or playing off their fears. None of these personal tactics are part of logic, however. Logic is impersonal. For this reason, logic may be less flamboyant and personally exciting, but it has the advantage of being applicable to everyone. A logical argument goes beyond rhetorical appeal.

Yet logic and rhetoric virtually always function together. Although it is possible to be persuasive through pure rhetoric without being at all logical, such efforts often disappear as soon as readers have had a chance to think again about how they have been persuaded. One can also be logical without attention to rhetoric, but such arguments will be dry and unattractive, even if they do convince anyone who would take the time to read them. However, logic and rhetoric in combination can be very persuasive and are rarely separable in any great work of philosophy. In all of the readings of this book, you will notice the combination of impersonal logic and personal appeal, all aimed at getting the reader to agree with the author's point of view.

There are good arguments and there are bad arguments. Good arguments require good logic as well as effective rhetoric to survive the passing moods, reflection, and criticism of readers. To argue well, you must master the basic rules of argument, as well as be aware of the all-too-common pitfalls that lie in wait for those who ignore the rules. Knowing these rules and warnings will not only help you avoid **fallacies**, it will allow you to criticize

FALLACY

An apparently persuasive argument that is really an error in reasoning, a mistake in the deductive form.

effectively other people's arguments as well. Have you ever heard someone say, 'Well, there's something wrong with that argument, but I'm not sure what it is'? Knowing a little logic may help you see clearly what is wrong with an argument.

Standard logic textbooks emphasize two primary forms of logical argument:

1. **Deductive arguments**, which *reason* from one statement to another by means of accepted logical rules; anyone who accepts the premises is bound logically to accept the conclusion.
2. **Inductive arguments**, which *infer* one statement from another. In this type of argument, it is possible for the conclusion to be false even if all of the premises are true. The most familiar example of an inductive argument is a **generalization** from a set of observations to a general statement called a *hypothesis*.

1. Deductive Arguments

VALID

An argument that correctly follows agreed-upon rules of inference.

A deductive argument is **valid** when it correctly conforms to the rules of deduction, when it is impossible for the premise(s) to be true and the conclusion false. In this sense, the premise (or premises) guarantee the truth of the conclusion. The following are some examples of the most familiar rules.

1. It was *either* Phyllis *or* Juan. (It was Phyllis *or* it was Juan.)
   It wasn't Phyllis.
   Therefore it was Juan.
2. *Both* Tom *and* Jerry went to the circus last night. (Tom went to the circus last night *and* Jerry went to the circus last night.)
   Therefore Tom went to the circus last night.
3. *If* Carol did that all by herself, *then* she's courageous.
   Carol did it all by herself.
   Therefore Carol is courageous.

It is important to emphasize that whether or not an argument is valid depends only on the form of the argument. A valid argument—one in the correct form—can still have a conclusion that is false. Consider this:

4. If Carol did that all by herself, then elephants can fly.
   Carol did it all by herself.
   Therefore elephants can fly.

Notice that example 4 is identical in form to example 3. The conclusion is patently false, but the argument is still valid.

But what good is a deductive argument if its conclusion can be false? The answer is that if the initial statements (called **premises**) are true, then the truth of the conclusion is guaranteed. It is important to remember that a deductive argument cannot prove its own premises. To be effective, you must be sure of the premises before beginning the deductive argument. Thus the following argument, although it is valid, is an appallingly bad argument:

5. If someone argues for socialized medicine, then he or she is a communist.
   Communists want to kill people.
   Therefore if someone is for socialized medicine, he or she wants to kill people.

The argument in example 5 has the valid form:

5'. If *p*, then *q*.
    If *q*, then *r*.
    Therefore if *p*, then *r*.

But although the argument is valid, its premises are not true, and therefore they provide no guarantee that the conclusion is true. Remember: a valid argument guarantees the truth of the conclusion only if the premises are true. Therefore, in using or evaluating any deductive argument, you must always ask yourself two things:

    a.   Are the premises true?
    b.   Is the argument valid?

If the answer to both of these is yes, then the argument is said to be **sound**.

An argument in an essay may not appear exactly in the form provided by the rules of deduction. This does not mean that the argument is invalid. In example 5, the second premise, 'communists want to kill people', must be restated in '*if . . . then . . .*' form. In fact, straight-forward copying of the rules of deduction in an essay makes boring reading, so arguments usually must be restated in order to fit these forms exactly. When you are writing an argument, it is necessary to pay attention both to the validity of the argument and to the degree of interest with which it is stated. Sometimes you can leave out one of the premises, if it is so obvious to every reader that actually stating it would seem absurd. For example,

    6.   Men can't give birth.
         Therefore Robert can't give birth.

The missing premise, of course, is

    Robert is a man.

But it would be unnecessary in most contexts to say this. When using deductive arguments effectively, rhetorical considerations are important too.

A common form of deductive reasoning is the **syllogism**. This form contains two premises and a conclusion, usually involving membership in groups and using the terms *all*, *some*, and *none*. The best-known example is

    7.   All men are mortal.
         Socrates is a man.
         Therefore Socrates is mortal.

The first statement, 'all men are mortal', is called the *major premise*; the second statement, 'Socrates is a man', is called the *minor premise*. The final statement, following from the other two, is the *conclusion* and is generally preceded by the word *therefore*. In this example, the words *men* and *man* are called the *middle term*, the word *mortal* is called the **predicate**, and the name *Socrates* is called the *subject*. The middle term serves to link the subject and the predicate, both of which are joined in the conclusion. The form of this syllogism is

    7'.   All *A*'s are *B*'s.
         C is an *A*.
         Therefore *C* is a *B*.

Any nouns can be substituted for the *A*, *B*, and *C* in this deductive form. For example,

    8.   All cows are pigeons.
         Sir John A. Macdonald is a cow.
         Therefore Sir John A. Macdonald is a pigeon.

Argument 8 is valid, although its conclusion is false. The reason, of course, is that the premises are false. Again, a valid argument does not guarantee a true conclusion unless the premises are true, so always be certain that you have adequately defended the premises before beginning your deduction.

Valid arguments sometimes proceed from negative premises as well as positive **assertions**. For example,

ASSERTION

A statement or declaration that takes a position.

9. No Canadian has ever become president of the United States.
    Terry Fox was a Canadian.
    Therefore Terry Fox was not president of the United States.

The form is

9'. No *A*'s are *B*'s.
     C is an *A*.
     Therefore *C* is not a *B*.

Another common argument is

10. Some elephants weigh more than six thousand kilograms.
     Elephants are animals.
     Therefore some animals weigh more than six thousand kilograms.

The form, with a little rephrasing, is

10'. Some *A*'s are *B*'s. (Some elephants are more than six thousand kilograms in weight.)
      All *A*'s are *C*'s. (All elephants are animals. The 'all' is implicit.)
      Therefore, some *C*'s are *B*'s. (Some animals are more than six thousand kilograms in weight.)

Not all deductive arguments are syllogisms in this traditional sense. For example, the following is a valid deductive argument, but not a syllogism:

11. Jones is an idiot, and he (Jones) is also the luckiest man alive.
     Therefore Jones is an idiot.

The form of this argument is

11'. *p* and *q*.
      Therefore *p*.

In the discussion that follows, we will talk about deductive arguments in general and not worry whether they are properly to be called 'syllogisms' or not.

It is impossible in this introduction to list all of the correct forms of deduction. We will, however, describe some of the most dangerous *fallacies*. The following example is one, for it looks dangerously like example 10':

12. Some elephants are domesticated.
     Some camels are domesticated.
     Therefore some elephants are camels.

This form

12'. Some *A*'s are *B*'s.
      Some *C*'s are *B*'s.
      Therefore some *A*'s are *C*'s.

INVALID

An argument that does not follow agreed-upon rules of inference.

is **invalid**, and is thus a fallacy. This fallacy often appears in political arguments. For example,

13. We all know that some billionaires are corrupt.
     We all know that some communists are corrupt.
     Therefore we know that some billionaires are communists.

When stated so simply, the fallacy is obvious. But when spread through a long-winded speech, such fallacies are often accepted as valid arguments. Using the logician's symbolic forms to analyze a complex speech or essay will often make clear the validity or invalidity of an argument.

Another common fallacy closely resembles the deductive form in example 3:

14. If this antidote works, then the patient will live.
    The patient lived.
    Therefore the antidote works.

This looks valid at first glance, but it is not. The patient may have recovered on his or her own, proving nothing about the antidote. The form of this argument is

14'. If p, then q.
    q.
    Therefore p.

The correct deductive form of example 3 was

If p, then q.
p.
Therefore q.

Be particularly careful of the difference between these two.

'*If . . . then . . .*' statements are often used in another pair of arguments, one valid, one invalid. The valid one is

15. If this antidote works, then the patient will live.
    The patient did not live.
    Therefore the antidote did not work.

The form is

15'. If p, then q.
    Not q.
    Therefore not p.

This is valid, although one might insist on adding an explicit qualification to the first premise. The qualification is 'for nothing else whatever can save the patient', since one might argue that something else, perhaps a miracle, might save the patient rather than the antidote. Notice that this qualification doesn't save the invalid argument in example 14, however, nor does it save the invalid argument in the following example:

16. If this antidote doesn't work, then the patient will die.
    The antidote works.
    Therefore the patient won't die.

Again, the patient might very well die of other causes, despite the antidote. The form

16'. If p, then q.
    Not p.
    Therefore not q.

is invalid.

Most valid and invalid deductive argument forms are a matter of common sense. What makes fallacies so common is not ignorance of logic so often as sloppy thinking or writing, or talking faster than one can organize thoughts in valid form. Most important, therefore, are careful thinking and writing. Yet even the greatest philosophers commit fallacies, and you will likely encounter some of them in your studies.

2. Inductive Arguments

In deduction, the conclusion never states more than the premises. (It is often said that the conclusion is already contained in the premises.) In an inductive argument, the conclusion *always* states more than the premises. It is, therefore, a less certain form of argument, but that does not mean that it is any less important. Many of the premises in deductive arguments will come from inductive arguments, and most of our knowledge and almost all of science depend upon induction. Induction takes various forms and defies rigid characterization. For example, while most inductive arguments proceed from evidence to a generalized conclusion, some proceed to a specific conclusion, as in the case of detectives moving from the evidence in a criminal investigation to the indictment of a particular individual. (What Sherlock Holmes refers to as his 'powers of deduction' is in fact his remarkable ability with induction.) A more typical form of an inductive argument that works toward a generalization is

> Every *A* we have observed is a *B*.
> Therefore *A* is a *B*.

The argument, in other words, is from an observed set of things to an entire class of things. For example

> 17. Every crow we have observed in the past twenty years is black.
>   Therefore all crows are black.

But induction, unlike deduction, does not guarantee the truth of the conclusion, even if we know that the observations are all correct. So the conclusion of example 17 should properly read

> It is probable that all crows are black.

This tentative conclusion is called a **hypothesis**. A hypothesis is an educated guess made on the basis of the evidence collected thus far. It is always possible, when we are using induction, that a new piece of evidence will turn up that will refute the hypothesis. This new piece of evidence is called a **counter-example**. Inductive arguments must always be ready for such counter-examples because no inductive argument guarantees certainty. This is not to say, however, that we should not accept such arguments. Human beings have observed millions of rabbits, and never has a rabbit weighed more than six thousand kilograms. This does not mean that it is impossible to find a six-thousand-kilogram rabbit, but neither does it mean that we should therefore hesitate to believe that no rabbits weigh more than six thousand kilograms. Induction is never certain, but, on the basis of the evidence, we can nevertheless agree on the best hypothesis. It is worth noting, however, that some philosophers, following David Hume (see Chapter 2), have claimed that induction is without rational justification, no matter how undeniably useful it may be.

There are good (sound) and bad (unsound) inductive arguments. The most familiar reason why an inductive argument may be called **unsound** is generalization on the basis of too few examples. For instance, the following argument is clearly unsound:

> 18. Every Canadian prime minister from British Columbia has been a Conservative.
>   Therefore we can suppose that every Canadian prime minister from British Columbia will be a Conservative.

There has only been one prime minister from British Columbia (Kim Campbell in 1993) and the intricacies of Canadian politics are clearly such that the next prime minister from British Columbia could as likely be a Liberal or a member of the NDP as a Conservative. Similarly,

19. The driver of every bus we rode in Winnipeg had a beard.
    Therefore all bus drivers in Winnipeg have beards.

is unsound. Although the sampling involves more than one example, this is still not sufficient to make a sound inductive generalization.

How many examples are required? It varies with the case. If a chemist, conducting an experiment, adds chemical g to chemical h and gets j, that in itself will probably warrant the hypothesis that

$$g + h \rightarrow j,$$

although this hypothesis, like all hypotheses, will have to be tested by further experiments and observations. (Deductions, on the contrary, do not have to be tested, assuming the truth of their premises.) A chemist can usually assume that one set of pure chemicals will react like any other set of the same chemicals. But when the hypothesis is about people, generalizations should be made with extreme caution, especially when writing about sensitive subjects such as 'national character'. For example, comments beginning with 'Italians are . . .', 'Russians tend to be . . .', or 'Canadians are too . . .' require extreme care. But caution does not mean that it is impossible to write about such subjects. It has often been done brilliantly, and you might even agree that a person who refuses to see the general differences between different peoples and societies is even more foolish than someone who generalizes too quickly and carelessly. But all generalizations (even this one) must be made with care for the context and the subject matter.

A different kind of inductive unsoundness comes from generalizing to a hypothesis that goes too far beyond what the evidence will support. For example,

20. Every graduate we know of from Melonville Secondary School is an excellent athlete.
    Therefore we can suppose that the physical education teachers there must be very good.

The problem here is not too small a sampling; in fact, we might even look at *every* graduate of Melonville Secondary School. The problem is that this kind of evidence isn't sufficient to prove anything about the teachers. The students might come from athletic homes. Or the food in the school's cafeteria might be loaded with extra vitamins and protein. Or the students may enjoy playing sports outside of school, even though their gym classes are badly taught. It is important to be sure that the hypothesis you defend is supported by the right kind of evidence. In this case, we need evidence about the physical education teachers, not just about the students.

A very different kind of problem arises for induction when the hypothesis is *self-confirming*. A self-confirming hypothesis creates its own confirmation or, alternatively, blocks all possible counter-examples from the start. Consider the following two familiar examples. First, a uniformed policeman who is visible to all passersby tries to evaluate the driving patterns of the cars that pass him, making sure that they all drive at the legal speed. Of course they do! But the same sort of self-confirmation often goes on in subtle ways in science, for example, where the equipment itself is designed to present precisely the evidence it is supposed to be looking for. Second, a paranoid individual advances the hypothesis that 'they're all out to get me'. Given that way of looking at the world, indeed 'they' are. Not only does this individual systematically interpret other people's behaviour in a hostile way, he also behaves in such a way that people really do become wary of him, if not hostile to him. But again, this extreme case has thousands of more everyday instances; persons who feel friendless may easily work on a mild version of the paranoid hypothesis and confirm their own thesis. A person who entertains the hypothesis that 'all people are basically selfish' will have little trouble finding what he or she is looking for, and, within that investigation, some selfish motive can always be found (for example, 'in order not to feel guilty') for even the most generous and unselfish behaviour. (We might note that there are also *self-defeating* hypotheses; for example, the policeman, hypothesizing that everyone breaks the law, may and goes out, in uniform, to catch them, thereby undermining his own hypothesis.)

It is also worth noting that while most philosophers recognize the usefulness of deduction, not every philosopher thinks that induction is important for knowledge. For example, Karl Popper believes that the logic of science (and police investigations) proceeds not by way of induction but by way of the *disconfirmation* of **proposed** hypotheses with counter-examples. In other words, knowledge proceeds from hypothesis to hypothesis, not from evidence to hypothesis by way of induction. But whatever one thinks of the justifiability of induction and its importance, it is essential not to think of induction as occurring in a vacuum. Inductive reasoning always goes on against a background of other hypotheses, theories, and scientific viewpoints as well as an abundance of other evidence that is taken for granted, built into the hypothesis itself or, perhaps, ignored as irrelevant, undependable, or unimportant. Because of its formality, deduction can deal with isolated arguments. But induction, even when subjected to the formal rigours of probability theory, can never be so understood out of context. Background conditions and the state of knowledge at the moment are always in some sense presupposed. Because of this informal (if not chaotic) complexity, induction is just as much a matter of insight as logic.

3. Argument by Analogy

An argument by analogy defends the similarity between some aspect of two things on the basis of their similarity in other respects. Such arguments may employ both deductive and inductive arguments; insofar as *A* is like *B*, deductions appropriate in discussing *A* will be appropriate in discussing *B* as well. And if *A* and *B* are similar in so many ways, then it is inductively plausible that they will be similar in other ways as well. As such, arguments by analogy are a valuable form of reasoning, if not always a reliable form of proof.

Consider the following example of an argument by analogy. A politician defends the need for more efficient government and fewer unnecessary jobs on the basis of an argument by analogy between government and business. A government is like a business, the politician argues. It has a certain product to turn out, namely, services to the people, and receives a certain income from the sale of that product, namely, taxes. It employs a certain number of people, whose job it is to turn out that product and who are paid with that income. Their business is to produce the product as cheaply but as well as possible, to keep the cost down while ensuring quality, and make a profit in order to be able to offer new and better services. Thus, the politician argues, the more efficiently it is run and the fewer unnecessary employees it must support, the better a government will be.

Such an argument is valuable in getting people to see similarities and in clarifying complex and confusing issues, but it must be used with care. The danger, and the reason why many logicians reject arguments by analogy altogether, is that no two things are similar in every respect. (Otherwise, they would be the same.) And just because two things are similar in certain respects, it doesn't follow that they will be similar in others. But this objection is too strong. If two things are similar in several respects, it is at least plausible to suggest that they will be similar in others. For example, running the government *is* like running a business. Both involve managing an organization. Both require skill in handling money. The success of both depends on the quality of the products and services they produce. When using this type of argument, pay careful attention to each particular analogy, to make sure that the two things compared are significantly similar and, most importantly, that the aspect that is argued about is significantly similar in both cases.

In traditional Western philosophy, analogies and metaphors play an enormous but often unappreciated role in the great philosophical classics. The assumption, or at least the expectation, is that these analogies and metaphors can be recast in terms of deductive and inductive arguments. But not all philosophical traditions make this assumption. In Chinese philosophy, for example, analogical reasoning is far more central to philosophical disputation than deductive arguments. What the philosopher does, in certain traditions, is to provide new ways of seeing things—a particular virtue of arguments by analogy. So too, in many folk philosophies around the world, the use of myth and metaphor has not yet been replaced—and probably cannot be replaced—by the standard logics of Western reasoning. The place of logic itself can be an important philosophical problem.

The three kinds of arguments discussed above—deductive, inductive, and argument by analogy—attempt to defend a view or an opinion. But part of almost every argument is an attack on alternative views and opinions. In general, someone else's position can be questioned by asking the following questions:

    a.   What is he or she arguing? Is the position clear?

    b.   What are the arguments? Are they deductive? Inductive? Or by analogy?

          If deductive:

              Are the premises all true?

              Are the deductive arguments valid?

         If the answer to either of these questions is no, a good counter-argument exists to show that the adversary has not given us a reason for accepting his or her view.

          If inductive:

              Is there enough evidence to support the hypothesis?

              Does the evidence support the hypothesis?

              Is the hypothesis sufficiently clear?

              Is this the best hypothesis to explain the evidence?

         If the answer to any of these is no, a good counter-argument exists to show that the adversary has not defended his or her general claim.

          If argument by analogy:

              Are the things compared similar?

              Are the things similar in the relevant respects in question?

         If the answer to either of these is no, a good argument exists to show that the opponent's analogy is not a good one.

    c.   Does the conclusion mean what the opponent says it means?

4. Necessary and Sufficient Conditions, Logical Possibility, and Arguments by Counter-example

As you begin to study the arguments of the great philosophers, you must understand the concepts of *necessary and sufficient conditions* and *logical possibility*. A is a necessary condition for B when B can't happen without A. So B requires A; if A doesn't happen, then B can't happen—necessarily, if B, then A. A is a sufficient condition for B when A is enough to guarantee B, so A implies B—necessarily, if A, then B. Consequently, A is necessary and sufficient for B when A is both required for B and enough to guarantee B ('A if, and only if, B'). When this happens, A and B necessarily go together—you can't have one without the other.

    A definition supposedly supplies necessary and sufficient conditions. Thus, a way of challenging a philosophical definition or theory put forward—for example, a definition or theory of 'justice' or 'freedom'—is to show that it is logically possible to have an A without B, or a B without A. What you have supplied are counter-examples, not to an inductive argument or hypothesis, but to a philosophical claim. Since definitions or philosophical claims or theories give necessary and sufficient conditions, the person who has thus defined A in terms of B has to go back to the drawing board.

One need not actually find a counter-example in order to challenge a philosophical definition. Insofar as definitions claim to provide *logically* necessary and sufficient conditions, it is enough that you can merely *imagine* a possible counter-example. That is to say, since a definition proffers logically necessary and sufficient conditions that cover all *possible* cases, the mere logical possibility of a counter-example suffices to challenge the definition. Whenever a philosopher makes a general or a universal claim, it is possible to challenge it with a counter-example.

In Section 2, we mentioned counter-examples with respect to inductive generalizations. A counter-example that refutes a hypothesis, such as 'here is an *A* that is not *B*', will always give trouble to someone who argues that 'all *A*'s are *B*'s'. For example, if a bigot says, 'all people from Poland are naturally unintelligent', the single counter-example of Copernicus, a Pole, is sufficient to undermine that claim. Counter-examples may also work in the face of deductively defended claims, however. Consider the following common philosophical argument:

21. All events in nature are determined by physical forces (gravity, chemistry, electromagnetic forces, and so on).
     All human actions are events in nature.
     Therefore all human actions are determined by physical forces.

This syllogism is a valid argument, of the form

21'. All *A*'s are *B*'s.
     All *C*'s are *A*'s.
     Therefore all *C*'s are *B*'s.

One way to attack this valid argument, even if you don't see any reasons to reject the premises as such, is to use the method of counter-examples: 'Look. I decided to come to this college of my own free will. I thought about it for a few days, and I remember the exact moment when I made my decision—while eating pizza at Harry's restaurant. I made that decision. It wasn't caused in me by physical forces. Therefore, I reject your conclusion.'

What has happened here is this: On the one hand, if we accept the premises as true and the argument as valid, it would seem that we have to accept the conclusion. But what the counter-example does in this case is force the person who has argued the syllogism to clarify what is meant by 'determined by physical forces' in both the premise and the conclusion. Does this phrase mean only that *some* forces must be present? If so, the argument is not nearly so interesting as we thought, for everyone will admit that when a person makes a decision there is an electrical charge or a chemical change in the brain. Does it mean rather that there are *only* physical causes present, in which case free will is indeed excluded? But what then of the counter-example (your college decision)? The burden of proof is on the person who argued the syllogism; he or she is forced to explain how it seems that you made a decision of your own free will when in fact there is no such thing as free will. You can see how this philosophical argument could become very complicated, but we only want to make a simple point. A single, well-placed counter-example can open up a whole new discussion, even when it might seem as if the matter had already been settled.

Although it might seem to you as if arguments are conclusive, one way or the other, this is almost never the case. An argument can be convincing and persuasive, but there is always room for further argument if someone is stubborn or persistent enough. A good counter-example can always be explained away, and even a large number of counter-examples might be explained away if one is willing to adjust other aspects of the theory, by refining definitions, for example. What ultimately sinks a bad hypothesis or general claim is the weight of the extra explanations it needs. For example, someone argues that there are Martians currently living on earth. You point out that no one on earth has ever seen a Martian. Your opponent explains this away by suggesting that the Martians are invisible to the human eye. You argue that the atmosphere on earth would not support Martian life. Your opponent argues that they are a different form of life, different from any that we can understand. You ask your opponent what these Martians do and how we might come to test his or her view. Your opponent says that the Martians don't want us to know that they are here, so they are careful not to do anything that would let us discover their presence. At this point, you will probably walk away in disgust. You have not silenced your opponent. In fact, he or she might go on inventing new ways out of your arguments forever. But, at a certain point, your opponent's explanations will have become so obviously self-serving and defensive that you and everyone else will be completely justified in ignoring them. The point of argument, remember, is to persuade. Absolute proof is impossible. But this means too that persuading some people is also impossible. There are limits to argument—at least, practical limits.

5. *Reductio ad Absurdum*

One last argument deserves mention. It is usually called by its Latin name, ***reductio ad absurdum***, and is a form of deductive argument. It is, however, an indirect argument. It consists of taking your opponent's view and showing that it has intolerable or **contradictory** consequences. For example, someone argues that one can never know whether minds exist other than one's own. You counter by pointing out that the very act of arguing this with you contradicts his point. He replies, no doubt, that he can't know that you exist. You show that he cannot even know that he exists. What you have done is reduce your opponent's view to absurdity, showing that it leads to consequences that no one could accept—in this case, the idea that he cannot have self-knowledge at all. A *reductio ad absurdum* argument, like a good counter-example, is often an excellent way of forcing other people to clarify their positions and explain more carefully exactly what they mean to argue.

> **CONTRADICTION**
>
> The logical relation of two principles in which the truth of one requires the falsity of the other.

6. The Most Insidious Kinds of Fallacies

No brief survey of logic would be adequate without identifying other fallacies, more general and more tempting than those we discussed previously under deductive arguments. Whatever kinds of arguments you employ, be careful when you are tempted by the following fallacies.

Mere assertion: The fact that you accept a position is not sufficient for anyone else to believe it. Stating your view is not an argument for it, and unless you are just answering a public opinion survey, every opinion always deserves a supporting argument. There are statements, of course, that everyone would accept at face value, and you need not argue those. But that does not mean that they cannot be argued, for even the most obvious facts of common sense must be argued when challenged—this is what much of philosophy is about.

Begging the question: This fallacy occurs when something looks like an argument but simply accepts as a premise what is supposed to be argued for as a conclusion. For example, suppose you are arguing that one ought to be a Christian and your reason is that the Bible tells you so. This may, in fact, be conclusive for you, but if you are trying to convince someone who doesn't believe in Christ, he or she will probably not believe what the Christian Bible says either. As an argument for becoming a Christian, therefore, referring to the Bible begs the question. Question-begging often consists of a reworded conclusion, as in 'this book will improve your grades because it will help you to do better in your courses'.

Vicious circle: Arguing in a vicious circle, like begging the question, is usually a short-cut to nowhere that results from careless thinking. Consider a more elaborate version of the above fallacy. A person claims to know God exists because she has had a religious vision. Asked how she knows that the vision was religious rather than just the effect of something she ate, she replies that such an elaborate and powerful experience could not have been caused by anyone or anything but God. Asked how she knows this, she replies that God himself told her—in the vision. If you argue *A* because of *B*, and *B* because of *C*, but then *C* because of *A*, you have argued in a vicious circle. It is vicious because, as in begging the question, you have assumed just what you want to prove. But remember: ultimately, all positions may come full circle, depending upon certain beliefs that can be defended only if you accept the rest of a great many beliefs. Debates between religious people and atheists are often like this, or arguments between free marketeers and Marxists, where many hours of argument show quite clearly that each person accepts a large system of beliefs, all of which depend on the others. Some logicians refer to such a development of an entire worldview, which requires a great deal of thinking and organizing, as a 'virtuous circle' because it has (arguably) favourable results.

Irrelevancies: You have seen people who argue a point by arguing everything else, throwing up charts of statistics and complaining about the state of the universe and telling jokes—everything but getting to the point. This may be a technique of wearing out your opponent, but it is not a way of persuading him or her to agree with you. No matter how brilliant an argument may be, it is no good to you unless it is relevant to the point you want to defend.

Ad hominem **arguments:** The most distasteful kind of irrelevancy occurs when you attack your opponent personally instead of arguing against his or her position. It may well be that the person you are arguing against is a liar, a sloppy dresser, bald and ugly, too young to vote or too old to work, but the only question is whether what he or she says is to be accepted. Harping on the appearance, reputation, manners, intelligence, friends, or possessions of your opponent may sometimes give your readers insight into why he or she holds a certain position, but it does not prove or disprove the position itself. As insight into an opponent's motives, personal considerations may, in small doses, be appropriate. But more than a very small dose is usually offensive, and it will often weigh more against you than against your opponent. Whenever possible, avoid this kind of argument completely—it usually indicates that you don't have any good arguments yourself.

Unclear or shifting conclusions: One of the most frustrating arguments to read is an argument that has a vague conclusion or that shifts conclusions with every paragraph. If something is worth defending at all, it is worth stating clearly and sticking with. If you argue that drug users should be punished, but aren't clear whether you mean people who traffic in heroin or people who take aspirin, you are not worth listening to. If you say that you mean illegal drug offenders, don't argue that drugs are bad for your body, since this is true for both legal and illegal drugs. If you say that you mean amphetamine users, then don't switch to talking about the illegality of drugs when someone explains to you the several medical uses of amphetamines. Know what you are arguing, or your arguments will have no point.

Changing meanings: It is easy to miss a fallacy when the words seem to form a valid argument. For example, consider the following argument:

> People are free as long as they can think for themselves.
> Prisoners in jail are free to think for themselves.
> Therefore, prisoners in jail are free.

This paradoxical conclusion is due to the ambiguity of the word *free*, first used to refer to a kind of mental freedom, second to refer to physical freedom. An interesting example is the argument often attributed to the well-known British philosopher John Stuart Mill: 'Whatever people desire, that is what is desirable.' But notice that this argument plays with an ambiguity in the English language. Not everything that is in fact desired should be desired (for example, alcohol by alcoholics), so the argument is deductively invalid. (Mill makes the case, however, that the only evidence that x is desirable is that people in fact desire it.) Be careful that the key terms in your argument keep the same meaning throughout.

Distraction: Another familiar form of fallacy is the 'red herring', the sometimes long-winded pursuit of an argument leading away from the point at issue. For example, in the middle of an argument about the relation between the mind and the brain, a neurologist may well enjoy telling you, in impressive detail, any number of odd facts about neurology, about brain operations he or she has performed, about silly theories that neurology-ignorant philosophers have defended in the past. But if these do not bear on the issue at hand, they are only pleasant ways of spending the afternoon, not steps to settling a difference of opinion.

Pseudo-questions: Sometimes fallacious reasoning begins with the very question being asked. For example, some philosophers have argued that asking such questions as 'How is the mind related to the body?' or 'Could God create a mountain so heavy that even he could not move it?' are pseudo-questions; that is, they look like real questions—even profound questions—but are ultimately unanswerable because they are based on some hidden piece of nonsense. (For the first question, it has been suggested that there is no legitimate distinction between mind and body, and therefore any question about how they are 'related' is pointless; the second question presumes that God is omnipotent in the sense that he can do the logically impossible, which is absurd.) Pseudo-questions, like distractions, lead us down a lengthy path going nowhere, except that, with pseudo-questions, we start from nowhere as well.

Dubious authority: We mentioned earlier that modern philosophy is based on the assumption that we have a right—and sometimes a duty—to question authority. Yet, most of our knowledge and opinions are based on appeals to authorities—whether these authorities are particularly wise or not. It would be extremely foolish, if not fatal, not to so appeal to authorities, especially in a world that has grown so technologically and socially complicated. We ask an economist what will happen if interest rates fall. We ask Miss Manners which fork to use for the salad. The fallacy of dubious authority arises when we ask the *wrong* person, when we appeal to an expert who is not in fact an expert in the area of concern. For example, when physicians are asked questions about nuclear policy or physicists are asked questions about high school education, their expertise in one field does not necessarily transfer to the other. Appealing to opinions in books and newspapers depends on the authority of the authors and publications in question. What is in print is not necessarily authoritative.

Slippery slope: As the name suggests, this type of fallacy occurs when we begin an argument by taking the first, often small step on a greased incline that carries the argument from the top (the initial premise) to the bottom (the ultimate conclusion) so quickly that it misses important steps along the way. For example, some have argued that any interference with free speech whatsoever, even forbidding someone to scream 'fire' in a crowded auditorium, will sooner or later lead to the eradication of free speech of every kind, including informed, responsible political discussion. But is it the case that, by attacking an extreme instance, we thereby endanger an entire institution? Sometimes, this may be so. But more often than not, the slippery slope leads us to think that there is such inevitability when in fact there is no such thing.

Attacking a straw man: Real opponents with real arguments and objections are sometimes difficult to refute, and an easy way out is to attack an unreal opponent with easily refutable arguments and objections. This unreal fellow is called a 'straw man', and he provides us with the extra advantage of not fighting back. For example, a writer of religion attacks those who have suggested that Mohammed never existed, when in fact his opponents have only questioned a particular interpretation of his claim to divinity. A writer discussing the mind–body problem lampoons those who believe that there is *no* possible correlation between mental events and some (perhaps unknown) physical events—a position that has been argued by virtually no one.

Pity (and other emotional appeals): Some forms of fallacy appeal to the better parts of us, even as they challenge our fragile logical abilities. The appeal to pity has always been such an argument. Photographs of suffering people may well be an incentive to social action, but the connection between our pity—which is an undeniable virtue—and the social action in question is not yet an argument. The appeal to pity—and all appeals to emotion—have a perfectly legitimate place in philosophical argument, but such appeals are not yet themselves arguments for any particular position. An orator may make us angry, but what we are to do about the problem must be the product of further argument.

Appeal to force: Physical might never makes philosophical right. Sometimes a person can be intimidated, but he or she is not thus refuted. Sometimes one has to back up a philosophical conviction with force, but it is never the force that justifies the conviction.

Inappropriate arguments: The last fallacy we will mention has to do with choice of methods. To insist on deductive arguments when there are powerful inductive arguments against you is a fallacy too—not a fallacious argument, perhaps, but a mistake in logic all the same. For example, if you are arguing deductively that there cannot be any torture going on in a certain country, since Mr Q rules the country and Mr Q is a good man (where the implicit premise is that 'good men don't allow torture in their country'), you had better be willing to give up the argument when dozens of trustworthy eyewitnesses publicly describe the tortures they have seen or experienced. To continue with your deduction in the face of such information is foolish. This may not tell you where your argument has gone wrong: Perhaps Mr Q is not such a good man. Or perhaps he has been overpowered. Or perhaps good men can't prevent torture if they aren't told about it. But in any case, the argument must now be given up.

The same may be true the other way around. Certain abstract questions are answerable only by deduction. When arguing about religious questions, for example, looking for evidence upon which to build an inductive argument may be foolish. What is at stake are your basic concepts of religion and their **implications**. Evidence, in the sense of looking around for pertinent facts, may be irrelevant.

To be caught in one of these fallacies is almost always embarrassing and damaging to your overall argument. If you have a case to make, then make it in the most powerfully persuasive way. An intelligent combination of deductive and inductive arguments, coupled with analogies and proper criticisms of alternative positions, is the most effective persuasion available. If you think your opinions are important, then they deserve nothing less than the best supporting arguments you can put together.

As you proceed with your course, you will have the opportunity to use many of these logical forms, not only as you interpret the ideas of the great philosophers of the past but as you develop your own arguments as well. You will find that philosophical criticism is a powerful tool in the arguments you have with your friends and the debates you carry on, whatever the topic. Most importantly, logic is a valuable aid to getting together your own thoughts about things, about the problems of philosophy that you will encounter in this book, and about life in general.

But then again, why should we assume that the truth is all that **coherent** or logical? As Ralph Waldo Emerson once wrote,

> A foolish consistency is the hobgoblin of little minds, adored by little statesmen and philosophers and divines. With consistency a great soul has simply nothing to do. He may as well concern himself with his shadow on the wall. Speak what you think now in hard words and to-morrow speak what to-morrow thinks in hard words again, though it contradict every thing you said to-day.—'Ah, so you shall be sure to be

IMPLICATION

A statement that logically follows from another.

misunderstood.'—Is it so bad then to be misunderstood? Pythagoras was misunderstood, and Socrates, and Jesus, and Luther, and Copernicus, and Galileo, and Newton, and every pure and wise spirit that ever took flesh. To be great is to be misunderstood.[5]

Nevertheless, it would be prudent to advise you to avoid contradicting yourself. Even if you are 'great', it is unpleasant to be misunderstood, especially by your instructor. A prudent **consistency** is the salvation of most students.

CONSISTENT

Fitting together in an orderly, logical way.

SUMMARY AND CONCLUSION

As you begin your studies in philosophy, you will find that thinking like a philosopher helps you put your life and your beliefs in perspective. How? By enabling you to see afresh the ways in which you view the world, to bring into focus just what you assume, what you infer, and what you know for certain. Philosophy allows you to see the justification (or lack of it) for your most treasured beliefs, and to separate what you will continue to believe with confidence from what you should consider doubtful or reject. Philosophy also gives you the intellectual strength to defend what you do and what you believe to others and to yourself. It forces you to be clear about the limits as well as the warrants for your acts and beliefs. Consequently, it gives you the intellectual strength to understand, tolerate, and even sympathize with or adopt views very different from the ones you currently hold.

REVIEW QUESTIONS

1. Suppose a friend of yours puts forward the following argument (with the steps numbered for easy reference): '(1) If you reject the discipline of philosophy without giving any reasons or arguments, then you are not being reasonable (because you aren't bothering to justify your opinion or back up what think). But (2) if you try to support your rejection of philosophy with reasons and arguments, then you end up doing philosophy after all. So (3) in order to criticize philosophy, you must engage in philosophy. Therefore, (4) philosophy's only reasonable critics—and what other kind of critics are worth paying attention to?—are themselves philosophers.' What are your initial thoughts about this line of reasoning? What parts, if any, do you agree with? What parts, if any, do you disagree with?

2. The philosopher William James once wrote that 'philosophy is at once the most sublime and the most **trivial** of human pursuits'. What do you think he means? In what way is philosophy 'trivial'? In what sense is philosophy 'sublime'?

3. What makes Socrates such a complex, many-sided figure? How is this complexity conveyed by the metaphors used to characterize him? What does his relationship to Athens suggest about the philosopher's place in society?

4. According to George Grant, the price we pay for accepting 'cheap answers' to philosophical questions is a 'cheap life'. What does he mean? What does this say about his understanding of philosophy? If Grant is right, why is patience essential in philosophy?

5. According to Descartes, philosophy begins with radical doubt—that is, with an attempt to wipe the slate clean and start from scratch. Why does Descartes begin in this way? Exactly what is he hoping to achieve? What does his choice of this starting-point take for granted?

6. How do you think philosophy differs from science? From poetry? From religion? From pure logic? Does it have anything in common with any of these fields? If so, what?

KEY TERMS

abstract	Dao	predicate
ad hominem argument	deductive argument	premise
aphorism	dialectic	presupposition
argument	doubt	proof
asceticism	Enlightenment	proposition
assertion	fallacy	reason
assumption	first principles	reasons
autonomy	generalization	*reductio ad absurdum*
axiom	hypothesis	reflection
begging the question	implication	rhetoric
Buddha	inconsistent	self-evident
Cartesianism (Cartesian	inductive argument	skepticism
method)	inference	sound
certainty	invalid	syllogism
coherence	logic	system
consistent	method (sometimes,	trivial
contradiction	methodology)	unsound
counter-example	method of doubt (or	valid
criterion	methodological doubt)	vicious circle
critical	paradox	

FURTHER READING

General Introductions to Philosophy

Robert Audi, ed., *The Cambridge Dictionary of Philosophy* (New York: Cambridge University Press, 1999).

Edward Craig, *Philosophy: A Very Short Introduction* (Oxford: Oxford University Press, 2002).

James Fieser and Bradley Dowden, eds, *The Internet Encyclopedia of Philosophy* (www.iep.utm.edu).

Ted Honderich, ed., *The Oxford Companion to Philosophy*, 2nd edn (Oxford: Oxford University Press, 2005).

Thomas Nagel, *What Does It All Mean?* (New York: Oxford University Press, 1987).

T.L.S. Sprigge, *Theories of Existence: A Sequence of Essays on the Fundamental Questions of Philosophy* (Harmondsworth: Pelican Books, 1984).

Edward N. Zalta, ed., *The Stanford Encyclopedia of Philosophy* (http://plato.stanford.edu/)

On Socrates

Sara Ahbel-Rappe and Rachana Kamtekar, eds, *A Companion to Socrates* (Oxford: Blackwell, 2006).

G.M.A. Grube, trans., *The Trial and Death of Socrates,* 3rd edn, (Indianapolis, IN: Hackett, 2001).

A.E. Taylor, *Socrates* (New York: Doubleday, 1959).

Emily Wilson, *The Death of Socrates* (Cambridge, MA: Harvard University Press, 2007).

On the Enlightenment

Peter Gay, *The Enlightenment* (New York: Norton, 1995).

Isaac Kramnick, *The Portable Enlightenment Reader* (New York: Penguin, 1995).

On Logic

Graham Priest, *Logic: A Very Short Introduction* (New York: Oxford University Press, 2001).

PART II
THE WORLD AND BEYOND

CHAPTER 1

REALITY

It must be that what can be spoken and thought is: for it is possible for it to be, and it is not possible for what is nothing to be.

Parmenides

Well over three thousand years ago, philosophers in India, in the *Rig Veda* (the oldest of those holy books called the Vedas), contemplated the nature and origins of the whole of reality ('Brahman'), concluding, with considerable skepticism, that reality as such was not, or at least not normally, known by us, and perhaps it could not be known at all. Now, at the beginning of the twenty-first century, some philosophers and some of our best-known physicists have come to question that ultimate reality, those evasive particles that seem to multiply as the experiments get more sophisticated and the origin of everything ('the big bang') gets more and more (rather than less and less) mysterious. Some theorists even suggest that we *create* reality through our observation of it and there is no independent reality at all.

Questions about the ultimate nature of reality and the origins of the universe (or, from the Greek *cosmos*, thus, **cosmology**, the nature of the universe, and **cosmogony**, the origins of the universe) have defined much of philosophy from ancient times until today. (And we have no reason to suppose that the questions are getting any easier.) The ways the questions are asked, of course, vary considerably with the growth of science and among various religious and cultural contexts, but they remain among the most fundamental of philosophical questions.

A. The Way the World Really Is

We are all aware that the ultimate reality, the way the world really is, may not correspond to our everyday views of the world, the way it seems to be. For example, we casually talk of 'sunrises' and 'sunsets', and surely it does seem as if the sun goes 'up' and 'down', while we and our earth stay in place. It took several thousand years for people in general to recognize that, despite appearances, our earth actually moves around the sun. We now accept that without question, even if there is little in our everyday experience to support it. Similarly, consider the chair on which you are sitting: Does it seem to you that it is composed mostly of empty space and tiny electrically charged colourless particles whirling about at fantastic speeds? Of course not, but modern science has taught you that 'solid' objects are indeed made up of just such spaces and particles. The world is not as it seems, and the beginnings of both philosophy and science were the first attempts of men and women to see the reality beyond their 'common-sense' views of things.

How do you begin to answer questions about the way the world really is? To begin, you would likely appeal to the authority of modern science, and that is a reasonable beginning. But you know that the 'science' of one generation is seen as the superstitions of another. (Remember, people once people believed that the earth was flat.) You have probably, at least once in your school career, caught one of the 'authorities'—perhaps a teacher, perhaps even a noted scientist—in a mistake. You cannot simply accept what scientists tell you without question, any more than Descartes could accept the teachings of his teachers without question. Have you ever examined the evidence for the theory that the earth goes around the sun? If not, why should you believe it? Or, to take a very different example, scientists are generally agreed that some version of Darwin's theory of evolution is true. Does that mean that you have to believe it? Many people do not, because it seems to contradict the story of creation in the Bible. Even within science there are always disagreements and debates. There are different theories to answer the same questions, and you have to decide. Which are you to believe?

Your view of reality is influenced by modern science, but it is also influenced by twenty-five hundred years of philosophy, even if you've never studied it before. Today we can say, with some confidence, that we know much more about the world than the ancient philosophers knew, but we must not be too confident. Not only are there still many scientific problems unsolved, there are and always will be conflicting views of how we are to see our world in more general terms. How much faith should we have in religion? How much should we see the world as a world of people and how much as a world of physical objects? How much should we accept 'common sense' and how much should we indulge in scientific and philosophical speculation, all of which change all of the time?

As we begin to consider such questions, we can look back from our modern vantage point to many ancient traditions—both Western and Eastern—that were philosophical in the sense that they looked beyond ordinary experience for an understanding of reality. The ancient philosophers did not have the advantage of either our scientific sophistication or a long history of philosophical thinking to give them support, yet they offered many new and profoundly thoughtful opinions about reality.

B. The First Greek Philosophers

Because it was a Greek who coined the term *philosophy* and in Greece where philosophy was first recognized as a formal discipline, Western philosophers today often refer to the first Greek thinkers as the first 'philosophers'. Philosophy in this sense is said to begin with a seemingly odd claim made by the Greek philosopher Thales on the coast of Turkey sometime around 580 BC. He suggested that the source of everything was water. The earth floats upon water, and it and all things on it are made of water. In his essay 'On the Heavens', Aristotle later called this theory 'childish', but he also acknowledged that it was the 'oldest view that has been transmitted to us'. In his *Metaphysics*, Aristotle went on to consider Thales' view in some detail.

From *Metaphysics*
By Aristotle

There must be some nature—either one or more than one—from which the other things come into being.

Most of the first philosophers thought that principles in the form of matter were the only principles of all things. For they say that the element and first principle of the things that exist is that from which they all are and from which they first come into being and into which they are finally destroyed, its substance

(Continued)

remaining and its properties changing. . . . There must be some nature—either one or more than one—from which the other things come into being, it being preserved. But as to the number and form of this sort of principle, they do not all agree. Thales, the founder of this kind of philosophy, says that it is water (that is why he declares that the earth rests on water). He perhaps came to acquire this belief from seeing that the nourishment of everything is moist and that heat itself comes from this and lives by this (for that from which anything comes into being is its first principle)—he came to his belief both for this reason and because the seeds of everything have a moist nature, and water is the natural principle of moist things.

So too, the commentator Simplicius suggested that 'Thales was the first to introduce the study of nature to the Greeks'. Thales' seemingly simple claim, that the world rests on water, was in fact one of the most remarkable claims of the ancient world, not because it was so implausible (which it was, as his own students pointed out to him) but because it was one of the first recorded attempts to describe the way the world really is, beyond all appearances and day-to-day opinions. Accordingly, Thales' theory marks the beginning of Western science as well as philosophy. He was the first Greek thinker to break with common sense and religion and offer a general theory about the ultimate nature of reality. In place of mythological accounts of nature and human behaviour in terms of divine agencies (gods, goddesses, and spirits), he and other thinkers of the period provided explanations in terms of laws and abstract generalizations. Knowledge became an end in itself, one of the noblest pursuits of humanity.

> - Do you consider Thales' theory that the source of everything is water 'childish'? How would you make his theory more plausible?
> - In what ways are contemporary physicists' theories that subatomic particles are the basis of the physical world anticipated by Thales?

1. The Ionian Naturalists

NATURALISM

The belief that ultimate reality is a natural property.

Thales' answer, that ultimate reality is water, should not surprise nearly so much as the fact that he attempted such a theory at all. Indeed, we should be impressed by the fact that he even asked 'what is the world really like?' because as far as we know, no one had attempted to ask such a question in such a way before him. Thales was not willing to accept the opinions and mythologies that had been handed down for generations. He insisted, instead, on observing the world for himself, on thinking out his own answer, and on discussing it with his friends and neighbours, many of whom, no doubt, thought that he was slightly peculiar. (It is also said, however, that his cosmic speculations helped him to make a fortune in the olive oil business. No doubt his neighbours respected that.)

Thales was the first of a group of philosophers—or rather, the first of several groups of pre-Socratic philosophers—scattered around the various Greek islands and the coasts of Asia Minor, or Ionia, who lived in the sixth and fifth centuries BCE, just before the time of Socrates. Accordingly, they are called Ionians. Their opinions varied greatly. Among them they developed a wide range of systematic views of the universe and the ultimate nature of reality. Unlike Socrates and most later philosophers, they were not very concerned with questions of method. They went straight to the heart of the problem, to the nature of the universe itself. As we shall see, some of them came strikingly close to our modern scientific conceptions.

The idea that everything was water did not satisfy Thales' friends and students. They appreciated his attempt to find the 'One Reality', but they thought that it must be something else. Thales' first student, Anaximander, argued against his teacher that some things, for example, the dry, dusty cliffs of Asia Minor, could not possibly be made of water, which was naturally wet and never dry. Anaximander was the first recorded student to talk back to his teacher (which in philosophy, unlike most other subjects, is considered a virtue rather than a discourtesy). Thales had made the first gigantic step, rejecting the 'obvious' answers of common sense and trying to find out the way the world really is. But notice that Thales' answer to that question still appeals to a common ingredient, water, which is so familiar to us. Thales' defence of his thesis also depended on some very commonsensical claims: for example, the idea that if you dig deep enough into the earth, you will eventually hit water.

Once Thales had made the break with common sense and said that the way the world really is need not be at all like the way it seems to us, it was no longer necessary to suppose that reality was anything like our experiences. Anaximander, consequently, argued that ultimate reality could not be composed of any of the then-known elements—earth, air, fire, or water—since these were each so different from the others. They might be mixed together, as when earth and water are mixed to make mud or clay, but it made no sense to suppose that any of them might really be made up of any of the others. So Anaximander suggested that the ultimate nature of reality was something else—let us simply call it 'primordial stuff'—that is not like anything we could ever experience.

The word Anaximander actually used was the **apeiron**, which is sometimes translated as 'the indefinite' or 'the unlimited'. The *apeiron*, or 'primordial stuff', was a chaos or void that yielded the variety of things in the world. This notion of 'stuff' was a second major step in philosophy and science. Today, we feel comfortable with the idea that things are made of 'stuff' (atoms and molecules) that we never experience in everyday life. But in the ancient world, this suggestion must have seemed extremely exciting.

Anaximander's student, Anaximenes, thought his teacher's notion of 'stuff' was too mysterious, but he also rejected Thales' theory and replaced it with the idea that air is the basic 'stuff'. Just as our soul, which is air, integrates us, so breath and air surround the whole cosmos. Air makes up the other elements and the various things of the world by becoming thicker and thinner. (Think of steam condensing to form water and then ice.) Anaximenes thus introduced the idea that changes in the quantity of basic elements can produce changes in quality as well—a key principle of modern science.

- How is Anaximander's theory that 'primordial stuff' is the ultimate reality an improvement on Thales' theory? In what ways is it more problematic?
- To what extent must you reject 'common sense' when trying to explain reality? What are the limitations to such speculation and theorizing?

---

2. Monism, Materialism, and Immaterial 'Stuff'

The attempt to find the ultimate reality by reducing all of the varied things in the world to one kind of thing—as Thales and his students did with water, air, and *apeiron*—is called **monism**. So the scientific and philosophical debate began: Is the world really made of water? Is it made of some other kind of 'stuff'? Today, the debate continues: Is everything made up of matter, or energy, or matter-energy? Are there basic particles that cannot be reduced to anything else? Scientists once thought that atoms were such particles; then they discovered electrons, protons, and neutrons that made up atoms. Since then, they have discovered dozens of other particles, and today much debate surrounds a mysterious particle called a quark, which physicists think may lead to the ultimate answer to Thales' ancient question. But notice that all of these views are strictly physical. That is, they are concerned about basic questions of what we now call physics and chemistry, concerned about the material 'stuff' of which all things are composed. Accordingly, these philosophies can be called **materialism**, the view that reality is ultimately composed of some kind of material 'stuff'. (In this context, *materialism* does not mean 'concern about the material things in life—money, cars, jewellery, getting a new garbage disposal every year, etc.'.)

If you think like a physical scientist, the idea that the universe is made up of some kind of material 'stuff' sounds very plausible. In fact, you might wonder, what else could it be made of? Consider this: There are some things in the universe that could not plausibly be made of material 'stuff'. For example, what about your thoughts and feelings? Are they simply bits of matter, or are they composed of some entirely different kind of 'stuff', perhaps some kind of mental or spiritual 'stuff'? Some early philosophers, particularly in Asia, claimed that reality was not made of just physical elements, but rather that reality was inherently spiritual. Many of these thinkers claimed that the primordial 'stuff' was divine, or godly.

3. Heraclitus

At this same time, another pre-Socratic philosopher, Heraclitus, was groping for a conception of an **immaterial** 'stuff', something that was spiritual or non-physical. (*Immaterial*, in a philosophical context, does not mean, as it does in law, 'irrelevant'.) Quite independent of the monists, he defended the idea that fire was the fundamental 'stuff' of reality. For Heraclitus, however, *fire* seemed to connote both the natural element it was for the Ionians and a spiritual power. Heraclitus' philosophy was cryptically expressed, and his contemporaries and commentators did not understand him very well, calling him such things as 'riddler'. Nonetheless, Heraclitus' profound and provocative claims have been an inspiration to many philosophers since, especially during the nineteenth century.

Although Heraclitus claimed that everything in the world was a manifestation of fire, he did not understand fire as an eternal and unchanging origin. Quite the opposite; he claimed that everything that exists is fleeting and changeable. Fire was the element that best explained, or at least represented, the constant flux that Heraclitus claimed underlay nature. 'It is in changing that things find repose,'[1] he stated, indicating that the only thing in the world that is constant is change. 'You cannot step into the same river, for other waters are continually flowing on,'[2] he claimed. The fact that we refer to 'the' river at all, however, shows that something is constant—the change and flow itself.

'This world that is the same for all', one fragment of his work reads, '. . . ever was and is and shall be ever-living fire that kindles in regular measures and goes out by regular measures.'[3] This fire, like the fluctuating flow of the river, itself seems to have measure, a rhythm, underlying it. Although the world never stops changing, the measure with which it does so can be understood. So, Heraclitus claimed, our ever-changing reality has a *form* that remains the same, which he called the *logos*. The *logos* is the deeper nature behind natural, changing things, but you cannot see it, or hear it, or touch it. Thus, 'nature loves to hide'[4] beneath the constant flux of the ordinary world we perceive.

Heraclitus' doctrines were provocative, confusing, and sometimes maddening, as the following fragments indicate:

1. Man's character is his fate.
2. Wisdom is one thing: to understand the *logos* by which all things are guided through all things.
3. The sun will not overstep his measures; if he does, the Erinyes [furies], the handmaids of justice, will find him out.
4. The sea is the purest and the impurest water. Fish can drink it, and it is good for them; to men it is undrinkable and destructive.
5. Good and ill are one.
6. To God all things are fair and good and right, but men hold some things wrong and some right.
7. We must know that war is common to all and strife is justice, and that all things come into being and pass away.
8. The way up and the way down is one and the same.

- How does Heraclitus' view improve upon the materialism/immaterialism debate? (How does Heraclitus bridge the materialism/immaterialism divide?)
- Why does fire seem to be the appropriate element for Heraclitus?
- How can an ever-changing reality, or 'flux', have form (a *logos*)?
- What does Heraclitus mean when he says that you can't step into the same river twice?

4. Democritus, Atoms, and Pluralism

Not all materialists thought that there was only one ultimate component of reality. A number of philosophers appeared in the ancient world who believed in **pluralism**, that is, that more than one basic type of 'stuff' made up the universe. The best known of the pluralists was Democritus, who suggested that the universe was made up of tiny bits of 'stuff' that he called atoms. These combined together to form the many different things and qualities of the world. (The soul, he suggested, consists of smooth, round, unusually mobile atoms, disposed throughout the body.) Other pluralists stressed the idea that these different bits of 'stuff' were very different in kind as well, so that the bits of 'stuff' that composed water, for example, would be very different from those that composed fire. You can appreciate how these concepts echo in our own time, given our current ideas in chemistry and physics. These ancient Greek issues and answers have not become obsolete; they have changed and become more refined. Some have been more in favour at one time and others at other times. But they are still very much with us.

- What are the merits of Democritus' 'atomic' view in its own terms, beyond its anticipation of modern physics?
- What, if anything, is problematic about the claim that reality is made of individual atoms?

5. Animism

While the theories of 'stuff' were indeed the precursors of modern physics and chemistry, these philosophers were also concerned with what we would call the mental and the spiritual aspects of the world. Even the most materialistic among them—for example, Thales—did not believe that the basic matter of the universe was cold and lifeless 'stuff'. All of these philosophers believed that the universe itself, as well as everything in it, was alive in at least some limited way. That is, they all believed in **animism**, the doctrine that everything, volcanoes and stones as well as elephants and flowers, are living things. Furthermore, animism has not disappeared because of the advances of science, though in certain periods (like our own) it has been treated less favourably than in others. But even in the nineteenth century, when physics and chemistry were making some of their most spectacular advances, animism was an extremely popular doctrine, even among scientists. A great many people today still accept a modified version of it. The place of mind and spirit in a world of matter and energy is still among our basic problems.

- How is animism still alive today?

6. Pythagoras

Another Greek pre-Socratic philosopher, Pythagoras, also attempted to defend a view of the world that did not depend upon the usual kinds of material 'stuff'. He believed, however, that numbers were the real nature of things, and he taught his students to worship the mathematical order of the universe. (His legacy in geometry is still remembered today in the theorem named after him.) He was particularly inspired by new Greek discoveries in music and harmony, and he saw the universe itself as a grand harmony. (The term 'the music of the spheres' was part of his teachings.) Pythagoras was also a **mystic** and the leader of a powerful underground cult that believed in reincarnation and the **immortality** of the soul, which he understood as the part of man that is capable of abstract thought, such as mathematics. In accordance with his religion, he gave the mind and the soul a much more prominent place in his view of the world than did other pre-Socratic philosophers.

Despite the sometimes mysterious views of Pythagoras and his cult, he is still recognized as one of the most important thinkers of the ancient world. With Heraclitus, he was one of the first Greeks to defend a view of reality that depended more on logic and thought than purely material 'stuff'.

> • How is modern science still very much in the spirit of Pythagoras? Why is it necessary, in studying physics or engineering, to know a lot of math?

MYSTICISM

The belief that one can grasp certain fundamental religious truths through a form of direct experience that differs from ordinary understanding.

7. The Appearance/Reality Distinction

All of the thinkers we have considered so far, whatever their differing views and outlooks, have espoused an underlying reality that is different from the way the world appears in one's ordinary experiences. In Greece, the profound discrepancy between the way the world seems and the way it really must be grew wider and wider. The problem has come to be called, not surprisingly, the appearance/reality distinction.

For Thales, water was the eternal and unchanging element, although the forms it took might be very different and change constantly. For Democritus, atoms were unchanging and indestructible, although the things they combined to compose might change and be destroyed. Heraclitus' *logos* and Pythagoras' notion of the immortal 'soul' were right on the edge of an investigation into how the world can be both one and many, both changing and stable. Because he believed that the nature of reality was fire-like, Heraclitus appreciated the importance of change, as in the flickering of a flame. But he insisted that the *logos*, or logic, underlay the constant changes in the world. We shall see that the presupposition that reality cannot change, however much things seem to change, will remain one of the most important beliefs in Western culture. (In Christianity, for example, the eternal and unchanging nature of God and the human soul are built upon the same philosophical foundation.)

None of the early thinkers, however, offered an explanation as to *why* the world should appear so different to people than their philosophical investigations led them to believe it really was. Nor did these thinkers present any convincing argument that this should be so. The conflict finally came to a head, and the argument was finally offered. The philosopher who brought it out most clearly was a pre-Socratic Greek, Parmenides.

8. Parmenides

Parmenides was an accomplished mathematician who thought far more of the eternal certainties of arithmetic than he did the transient things of everyday experience. He, too, was a monist and believed in a single reality, 'the One'. Because he shared the assumption that reality must be eternal and unchanging, he came to an astonishing conclusion: This world, the world of our experience, cannot be real! Our world is constantly changing. Objects are created and destroyed; organisms live and die; people grow old, change their appearance, and move from place to place. So this world, with all its changes, cannot be the real world, nor can we ever know the real world, since we are as inconstant and changing as the other things of our experience. We are, at best, living in a kind of illusion, not in reality at all.

Parmenides gave us what is sometimes postulated to be the first full-scale philosophical argument.

From *Fragments*
By Parmenides

It is right that what is for saying and knowing should be, for it can be; but nothing can not *be.*

(The goddess addresses the young philosopher) Come, I will tell you—and you, take the story when you have heard it—about the only routes there are for seeking to know: One says is and that there is no not being; this is the path of Persuasion (for she goes the way of Truth). The other says is not, and that not being is right. This I point out to you is an utterly ignorant footway. For you could not either get to know that which is not (for it is not attainable) or point to it.

. . . because the same thing is for knowing (or 'thinking about') that is for being.

It is right that what is for saying and knowing should *be*, for it can be; but nothing can *not be*.

. . . what is is unborn and imperishable, a whole of a single kind, unshakable and not incomplete. It neither was nor will be, because it is now, all of it together, one cohesive. For what birth will you seek for it? From what would it have grown? I will not let you say or think that it came from what is not. For 'is not' cannot be said or thought.

The argument is: What really is cannot have come to be, for there is nothing outside of reality (what really is) that could have been its source. It is an argument that is the source of much of Western **metaphysics**. Naturally, no two scholars agree about what it means. But all agree on the main point: that philosophers should be interested only in *what is* in the fullest sense, and not in *what is not*, or in what sometimes is and sometimes is not. This means that philosophers should not be interested in anything that changes. The weather in Saskatoon is cold one day, and not cold the next. Because it sometimes *is not* cold, it is not a proper subject for the pure philosopher. What *is*, according to Parmenides, is *unchanging and eternal*.

A simple way to understand the root of this argument is this: We cannot put non-existent apples in a sack or non-existent dollars in our wallet. By the same token, Parmenides assumes, we cannot put things that do not exist in our mind; we can only truly think about or know things that *are*. Moreover, only one kind of thought really contains knowledge of the thing we are thinking about. Suppose we are thinking about beer. It is no use thinking about all the things beer is not—like wine and orange juice. Really thinking about beer is thinking about what beer really is.

Since thinking about change involves thinking about things that are not always the same, it involves thinking, in a sense, about things that are not (as the weather is not cold today). But this, according to Parmenides' assumption, is impossible: We can only think about what is.

Since Thales proposed his theory of nature, the main achievement of philosophy had been to break away from common sense and ordinary experience in order to find out the way the world really is. But now we can see how far away from common sense and ordinary experience this breaking away can lead us. In Parmenides' philosophy, if the results of his logic are incompatible with common sense and ordinary experience, so much the worse for common sense and ordinary experience. The followers of Parmenides, particularly the mathematician Zeno of Elea, extended these bizarre conclusions to new lengths. Zeno argued, by means of a series of famous paradoxes, that all motion and change is nothing but an illusion.

- How do you understand the claim that what is cannot have come to be?
- Is it helpful when explaining what something is to explain what it is not? Is it necessary?

9. The Sophists

The following generation of philosophers, who called themselves **sophists** (who have ever since given 'sophistry' a bad name because of their rhetorical debating tricks), went even further. They argued that there is no reality, and even if there were, we couldn't know anything about it anyway. (So argued the sophist Gorgias.) The teaching of Protagoras, another sophist, is still well known today; he said that 'Man is the measure of all things', which means that there is no reality except for what we take to be reality. We shall later see that the sophists, despite their bad reputation, anticipated many of the most important philosophical concerns of the twentieth century. In particular, they stressed practical questions rather than abstract questions, and thus anticipated the American pragmatists. In suggesting that truth is relative to people, they anticipated the much-disputed question of relativism, the idea that truth might be different at different times for different people. Wandering around the countryside, giving lessons in debating and rhetoric, the sophists used the accomplishments of the earlier philosophers to ridicule philosophy and make fools of practically everyone. That is, until they met Socrates, whose arguments against them changed the course of philosophy and Western thought in general.

> • How do you understand the claim that 'man is the measure of all things'? What does this mean?

10. Metaphysics

These various theories about the way the world really is are called metaphysical doctrines, and the attempt to develop such doctrines, in which we have been taking part for these past pages, is called metaphysics. The business of metaphysics is to ask and attempt to answer the most basic questions about the universe, its composition and the 'stuff' of which it is composed, the rule of man and mind, and the nature of the immaterial aspects of the universe as well as its physical nature. But now that we are about to discuss metaphysics in its maturity, with Plato and Aristotle, let us also give 'stuff' its proper name. It is called (first by Aristotle) **substance**. Accordingly, metaphysics, the study of 'the way the world really is', begins with the answers to a series of questions about substance and how it is manifested in particular things (such as people and trees):

SUBSTANCE

A unit of existence that stands by itself; the essential reality of a thing or things that underlies the various properties and changes of properties.

1. How many substances are there? (Monism versus pluralism.)
2. What are they? (Water, air, fire, numbers, something unknown, minds, spirit, atoms?)
3. How are individual things composed? (And how do we tell them apart, identify them, reidentify them?)
4. How do different things and (if there is more than one) different substances interact?
5. How did substance come into being? (Was it created by God? Or has it always been there?)
6. Are substances 'in' space and time? Are space and time substances? (If not, what are they?)

The first four questions are central to **ontology**, the study of being. The final two questions are central to cosmology, the study of the universe. (For the pre-Socratics, these were the same.) Cosmological questions are necessarily shared between philosophers, physicists, and astronomers, and it is impossible for us to give them more than a cursory review within a strictly philosophical book. Ontology, on the other hand, is still considered by many philosophers to be the heart of metaphysics. Therefore, the rest of this chapter will be primarily concerned with ontology.

You should note, at this point, that ontology and cosmology are not all there is to metaphysics. One further set of problems explores the existence of God, which is both an ontological problem (God has been identified as the 'substance of the universe') and a cosmological problem (God as creator; God as eternal); this topic will be studied in greater depth in Chapter 2. Another realm of metaphysics questions the existence of the human soul, or, in a more secular and transient context, the relationship between mind and body (see Chapter 4). Finally, there are questions surrounding metaphysical freedom (discussed in Chapter 5), which have serious implications for the more 'practical' questions involving human action, ethics (Chapter 6), and justice (Chapter 7).

- How would a materialist understand thoughts and feelings, which seem immaterial? How would a materialist understand numbers (not numerals)?
- Why have philosophers and scientists tried so hard to find the basic 'stuff' of the universe? Why not just say 'everything is what it is and is not another thing'?

C. Ultimate Reality in the East: India, Persia, and China

1. Reality as Spirit: The Upanishads

While the Ionian naturalists were pursuing their protoscientific inquiries in Greece, sages in India were developing their own doctrines about the nature of reality that were essentially religious. The earliest articulation of the concept of God as reality appears in the ancient Indian Vedic literature, especially in the appendages called **Upanishads**, 'secret doctrines', from which later Eastern religious and spiritual notions emerged. In addition to the innumerable sects and divisions of religious belief and practice traditionally termed Hindu or Buddhist, other Indic religions such as Jainism and Sikhism also owe a conceptual debt to the early Upanishads.

A passage from one of the oldest Upanishads (*c.* 800 BCE) relates to the spiritual aspiration that sets the tone for much Upanishadic teaching (whom or what is invoked in this passage is not clear):

From the *Brhadāranyaka Upanishad* (1.3.28)

From non-being (*asat*) to true being (*sat*) lead me.
From darkness to light lead me.
From death to immortality lead me.

The 'seeking' expressed in the early Upanishads centres on '**Brahman**', considered the ultimate secret both of ourselves and of the universe. The Upanishadic notion of Brahman is a seeking of a 'Unity' underlying all individual selves and things. So too, the 'Emptiness' and absolutist notions of much of Buddhist thought are concerned with 'the One', this underlying unity. Buddhism's view of the supremely real as 'Emptiness' or 'Openness' developed out of similar notions suggested in the early Upanishads. In these texts, the 'Absolute' is considered to have a peculiar 'logic', or 'nature', unlike that of everyday, finite, physical things. It is important *not* to think of the 'Emptiness' suggested in the following passages as merely *nothing*, the *absence* of all things. Paradoxically, it is rather a 'fullness', but unlike anything in our ordinary experience.

From the *Brhadāranyaka Upanishad* (4.3.32)

An ocean, a single seer without duality becomes he whose world [of vision] is *brahman*. This is his supreme attainment. This is his highest fulfillment. This is his best world. This is his supreme bliss. Other creatures subsist on a small bit of this bliss.

From the *Īśā Upanishad* (4–6)

He who experiences all things in the Self and the Self in all things . . . does not fear.

Not moving the One is swifter than the mind. The gods do not reach That running [always] before. . . . That moves; That moves not. It is far, and It is near.

It is within all this; It indeed is outside all this. He who experiences all things in the Self and the Self in all things thereupon does not fear.

From the *Brhadāranyaka Upanishad* (5.1.1)

Om. That is the Full. This is the Full. From the Full, the Full proceeds. Taking away the Full of the Full, it is just the Full that remains.

Indian conceptions of reality often invoke doctrines that are called **pantheism**, an identification of God with the natural world, the universe. Whether the following passage illustrates pantheism or not, it reveals a doctrine of divine immanence, of divine *indwelling* in all things. It also suggests an 'Inner Controller' who is thought to be 'other' than the things, and selves, in which it indwells.

From the *Brhadāranyaka Upanishad* (3.7.3–23)

Who standing in the earth is other than the earth, whom the earth knows not, whose body the earth is, who within controls the earth, that is this, the Self, the Inner Controller, the Immortal. Who standing in the waters is other than the waters, whom the waters know not, whose body the waters are, that is this, the Self, the Inner Controller. . . . Who standing in the wind is other than the wind, whom the wind knows not, whose body the wind is, who within controls the wind, that is this, the Self, the Inner Controller, the Immortal. . . . Who standing in all beings is other than all beings, whom all beings know not, whose body all beings are, that is this, the Self, the Inner Controller, the Immortal. . . . Who standing in the eye is other than the eye, whom the eye knows not, whose body the eye is, who within controls the eye, that is this, the Self, the Inner Controller, the Immortal. Who standing in the ear is other than the ear, whom the ear knows not, whose body the ear is, that is this, the Self, the Inner Controller, the Immortal. . . . Who standing in the understanding is other than the understanding, whom the understanding knows not, whose body the understanding is, who within controls the understanding, that is this, the Self, the Inner Controller, the Immortal. . . . Who standing in the seed of generation is other than the seed of generation, whom the seed of generation knows not, whose body the seed of generation is, that is this, the Self, the Inner Controller, the Immortal. Unseen, the seer, unheard, the hearer, unthought, the thinker, unknown, the knower; there is no other seer than this, no other hearer than this, no other thinker than this, no other knower than this. That is this, the Self, the Inner Controller, the Immortal; valueless is anything other.

The passage above—one that is quoted repeatedly over centuries of commentary and discussion—illustrates a 'spiritually monist' view that has enjoyed substantial prominence in India, a view that finds the 'self' (or *ātmān*) as the key to life and reality. Clearly the 'self' referred to here is not the individual, personal self. It is rather the 'self' of all reality, an all-encompassing spirit that includes us all. Indian spiritualism in the

Upanishads recognizes the small worth of worldly desires and attachments in the light of inevitable death and the possibility of an extraordinary knowledge, or experience, that can carry us beyond this great fear.

From the *Chandogya Upanishad* (6.11)

'Were someone to hack the root of this large tree, dear child, it would bleed but live; were someone to hack its trunk, it would bleed but live; were someone to hack its tops, it would bleed but live. Pervaded by the living self (*ātmān*), it stands continually drinking and exulting. If life were to leave one branch, then that branch would dry up; if a second, then that would dry up; a third, then that would dry up; if the whole, then the whole would dry up. Just in this way indeed, dear child,' he [Ávetaketu's teacher] said, 'understand: this endowed most surely with life dies; life does not die. That which is this, this is the most subtle, everything here has that as its soul (*ātmā*). That is the reality; that is the self (*ātmān*); you are that O Ávetaketu.' 'Please, sir, instruct me even further.' 'Alright, dear one,' he said. . . .

From the *Katha Upanishad* (1.25–27, 2.11–12, and 2.20–23)

[Yama, 'Death':] 'Whatever desires, (even) the most difficult to win in the world of mortals, have them all at your demand. Delightful females with chariots, with music—none like these may be won by mortal men—be entertained by them, O Naciketas, given by me. Do not inquire into dying.' [Naciketas:] Existing only until tomorrow are such desires of a mortal, and, O Bringer-of-the-end, they wear away the splendor and vigour of every sense and power one has. Even all that is alive is of small worth indeed. Yours alone are the chariots; yours the dancing and the singing. A person is not to be satisfied with wealth. Are we to have wealth once we have seen you? But the boon that I wish to choose is this (answer this question): 'Will we continue to exist while you rule?' . . . [Death:] Having seen in your grasp, O Naciketas, the fulfillment of desire and the foundation of the world and an infinity of power, of self-will, and the safe shore of fearlessness, and great fame sung far and wide, you wisely let it all go. A person who is wise and steadfast, discerning the God through spiritual discipline and study—the one that is difficult to experience, who has plunged deep into the hidden and is established in the secret place, standing in the cavern, the ancient—leaves joy and sorrow behind. . . . Subtler than the subtle, grander than the grand, the self is set in the secret heart of the creature. One who is without self-will experiences this (and becomes) free of sorrow; through his clearness and purity towards material things [or, 'through the grace of the Creator'[5]], one experiences the self's greatness and breadth. Seated he travels far; lying down he goes everywhere. Who other than I is fit to know this God, the one that has both maddening pleasure and freedom from maddening pleasure? The wise person, recognizing the bodiless in bodies, the settled in things unsettled, the great and pervasive self (*atma*), does not grieve nor suffer. This the self is not to be won by eloquent instruction, nor by intelligence, nor by much study. Just that person whom this chooses, by such a person is this to be won; to such a person this the self reveals, uncovers its very own form and body.

- How can 'Emptiness', or nothing, be 'Fullness' or 'Oneness'?
- How do you understand the idea of a 'Self' that is different from things, but nonetheless inhabits all things and is unknown?
- Do you think the inevitability of death diminishes or augments the worth of worldly goods?

2. Reality, Good, and Evil: Zarathustra

Greek materialism conceived of a world that was morally neutral (even if, as Thales said, 'all things are filled with gods'). Not all early thinkers conceived of reality that way. In the sixth century BCE, a Persian reformer named Zarathustra broke away from the Indic peoples who were the progenitors of the Upanishads. He preached a **monotheism** over and against the early Indian **polytheism**. Zarathustra claimed that his god—called **Ahura Mazda**—was not just spiritual or divine nature, but a creator, the one origin of all that existed. Ahura Mazda was a personal and all-good god, who created all natural things. Thus, Zarathustra and the religion he began (called **Zoroastrianism**) was extremely influential on the later monotheistic religions of Christianity, Judaism, and Islam.

Zarathustra was the first to recognize and formulate a doctrine regarding the existence and origin of good and evil in the universe. Ahura Mazda, the One Lord, created first among all things two twin spirits, lower sorts of divinities. The character of the first, called **Spenta Mainyush**, drew him and everything that followed him to goodness and good acts. The character of the other, called **Angra Mainyush**, led him and everything in his service to do evil. The twins are described in the following passage from the Gathas (the original portion of the **Zend-Avesta**, the scripture of Zoroastrianism).

From the Zend-Avesta

Thus are the primeval spirits who as a pair (combining their opposite strivings), and (yet each) independent in his action, have been famed (of old). (They are) a better thing, they two, and a worse, as to thought, word, and as to deed. And between these two let the wisely acting choose right. (Yasna XLV:2)

Although Angra Mainyush and Spenta Mainyush are born with natural tendencies toward evil and good, respectively, they choose quite freely to express it in action. Thus, while Ahura Mazda is responsible for the creation of everything, Angra Mainyush is responsible for unleashing evil, whose forms are deceit, destructiveness, and death. The natural world, according to Zoroastrianism, is set against itself like two armies, in an eternal battle between good and evil. Everything that exists freely chooses its alliance in accordance with its tendencies. Human beings, however, are free and conscious decision-makers, and so have more choice about their moral alliances than do other creatures.

It followed that all natural entities were things either to be worshipped or reviled. Fire, which represented the 'Beneficent Immortal' spirit, **Asha** (or 'Righteousness'), was especially to be worshipped, as the best of the 'good creation'. In fact, in their own time, Zoroastrians were referred to as 'fire worshippers'.

In the following passage, also from the Gathas, Ahura Mazda despairs for his creation, should Asha find no good guardian for it.

From the Zend-Avesta

Upon this the creator of the Kine (the holy herds) asked of Righteousness: How (was) thy guardian for the Kine (appointed) by thee when, as having power (over all her fate), ye made her? . . . Whom did ye select as her (life's) master who might hurl back the fury of the wicked? Asha: . . . (Great was our perplexity); a chieftain who was capable of smiting back (their fury), and who was himself without hate (was not to be obtained by us). (Yasna XXIX:2–3)

Zarathustra freely takes initiative on behalf of the herd. Recognizing his worthiness, God names Zarathustra its guardian. Zarathustra, then, takes a profoundly spiritual perspective on the question of the underlying nature of reality.

Although Zoroastrianism originally had no full-blown notion of 'immaterial stuff', or thought, as the essential nature of reality, Zarathustra's Ahura Mazda is an immortal, conscious entity that creates from thought, and it is the human's ability to think, according to Zarathustra, that gives humankind its unique moral capacity. In addition, Zoroastrianism had a notion of eternity—of which our time here on earth is only a part. At the end of our time, so it was claimed, the evil creation would be eternally vanquished.

- How do you think that Zoroastrianism anticipates the monotheistic religions of Christianity, Judaism, and Islam? How is it similar to them? How is it different?

---

3. Confucius

In its earlier form in China, philosophy was not so concerned with the questions we have called protoscientific but rather with human beings, human relationships, and human actions. One Chinese thinker of the sixth century BCE, **Confucius**, insisted that thinking is our fundamental nature. He was concerned essentially for the human good, which he described as 'gentlemanly', and he and his followers set the forms for Chinese society for millennia afterward. Confucian metaphysics, unlike the ontologies of the West, was primarily concerned with people.

Confucius and his followers claimed that human beings were divided within themselves—that the muddle of human passions, ambitions, and confused loyalties distracted people from their moral duty. Through conscious and attentive adherence to propriety, they claimed, human beings could overcome their 'personal selves' and their desires and achieve a goodness that was 'impersonal'. This impersonal life—the life of propriety—however, was a person's more 'real' way of living. Through thinking, a person gained a sense of 'self' as a Good Man. To 'think', in the Confucian sense, was to become a different, better person; and Confucius believed that few if any men were capable of such profound thought, as the following passages from *The Analects* (Confucius' collected sayings) attest.

From *The Analects*
By Confucius

He who learns but does not think is lost.

The Master [Confucius] said, 'He who learns but does not think is lost. He who thinks but does not learn is in grave danger.' (XI:5)

The Master said, 'I have never yet seen anyone whose desire to build up his moral power was as strong as sexual desire.' (IX:17)

The Master said, 'I have never yet seen a man who was truly steadfast.' Someone answered, 'Shen Ch'eng'. The Master said, 'Ch'eng! He is at the mercy of his desires. How can he be called steadfast?' (V:10)

Confucian 'thinking' was a form of attention, in which the Good Man fixed upon his 'inner self'. Thus, the thinking of the 'gentleman' did not so much involve contemplation as unerring attention to duty, where 'duty' was understood essentially as social propriety. The Confucian 'doctrine of the mean' directed that the 'gentleman' always avoid extremity. 'Moderation in all things' was the way of propriety. Thus, Confucius' dicta were often concerned with delineating proper dress, proper diet, proper manner, proper government, and proper respect for the examples set by the 'Good Men' of past ages. This inner truth, attention to which led one always to act with propriety, was called the 'Way' (or Dao) of Goodness.

> Wealth and rank are what every man desires; but if they can only be retained to the detriment of the Way he possesses, he must relinquish them. . . . The gentleman who ever parts company with goodness does not fulfill that name. Never for a moment does a gentleman quit the way of Goodness. (IV:5)

For Confucius, harmony represented not only the unity that could be achieved in music, but also that between the inner person and his exterior self, which was distracted by so many concerns between the self and society and within society as such. For Confucius, propriety and singleness of spirit were practical, not merely contemplative, activities; but they pointed, at least in the realm of human affairs, to a path between oneness and dispersion, inner reality and exterior appearance.

> [B]oth small matters and great depend upon it [harmony]. If things go amiss, he who knows the harmony will be able to attune them. But if harmony itself is not modulated by ritual, things will go amiss. (I:12)

- Do you think our passions and ambitions distract us from our moral duty? Is this always so?
- What is your 'personal self'? How does Confucius think that it can be overcome?
- Why is etiquette, or acting in socially appropriate ways, important?

4. Lao-zi, or the Poets of the *Dao De Jing*

In China during Confucius' own lifetime, or so the story goes, a religious mystic named Lao-zi espoused a doctrine that rebelled against the powerful Chinese dynasty and the ancient heroes whom Confucius revered. This radical doctrine, which developed into the religion Daoism, also rejected the Confucian faith in ritual, or the exterior expression of moral goodness.

More likely, the poems attributed to Lao-zi, called the poems of the *Dao De Jing* (or 'Way of Life'), were composed by several authors who shared Confucius' frustration with unethical behaviour and political corruption but responded in a radically different way. They were mystic recluses who claimed that there was a nature of reality, called the **Dao**, or 'Way', which they understood quite differently from Confucius. They claimed that the Dao could not be taught or understood through discourse or rules, nor mimicked through the constancy of gentlemanly conduct. Rather, they claimed, the Dao could be known only through direct acquaintance with it. The seeker after the Dao could only be prepared for its revelation to him through meditation—not ever through ritual. Thus, although the poets of the *Dao De Jing* shared Confucius' primarily practical and moral focus, including the impersonality of goodness, they believed that 'impersonal goodness' could be neither sought nor expressed in any visible, speakable, observable way. They claimed the Dao was '**ineffable**' and could not be known through words or thought.

INEFFABLE

Indescribable.

From *Dao De Jing*
By Lao-zi

Existence is beyond the power of words
To define:
Terms may be used
But are none of them absolute.
When people lost sight of the way to live
Came codes of love and harmony,
Learning came, charity came,
Hypocrisy took charge; . . .

Thus, these mystics were monists. They believed that the nature of reality is one, and that this One is, in a sense, living or conscious. But they did not go the way of the scientific and animistic doctrines of Greece. The poets of the *Dao De Jing* claimed that the One, living reality, is fully beyond the visible, sensible world of our ordinary experience. It was certainly not one of the physical elements, nor could it be known by way of the rules set down by our ancestors.

What we look for beyond seeing
And call the unseen
Listen for beyond hearing,
And call the unheard,
Grasp for beyond reaching
And call the withheld,
Merge beyond understanding
In a oneness. . . .
Knowledge studies others,
Wisdom is self-known; . . .
A realm is governed by ordinary acts,
A battle is governed by extraordinary acts,
The world is governed by no acts at all.

> • How can one follow or seek the Dao if it is beyond description? How can one act without acting?

5. Buddha

Buddhism's historical founder, Siddhārtha Gautama of the Sakya clan, was born a prince in India (or perhaps what is now southern Nepal) near the year 560 BCE. As a young man, before he became the **Buddha** (from the Sanskrit term *buddha*, 'the awakened one'), he led a life of pleasure and enjoyment. His father, fearing the prophecy that his son would become a religious mendicant, tried to protect him from the sight of anything unpleasant or evil. However, one day the young prince journeyed some distance from the royal enclave and encountered first a diseased person, then a wrinkled and decrepit old man, and then a corpse. Inquiring about each of these and being told that all persons are subject to such infirmities, the prince renounced his life of enjoyments and vowed to search tirelessly for the origin and cause of these evils—and for the power to root them up. The Buddha's experience of enlightenment did not occur immediately, however; he had to try various paths before arriving at the 'Middle Way', a way of life he later proclaimed to his disciples. Eventually, after a long ordeal of meditation under a Bodhi tree, the Buddha achieved the *summum bonum* (the highest good)—'*nirvāna*', an extinction of evil at its roots. The Buddha spent the remainder of his life travelling and preaching—helping others to reach this supreme good and developing a picture of reality to support this conception.

Although the Buddha did not record anything himself, his disciples preserved his teachings and sermons over the years, first through the oral tradition and later in writing. Through the centuries—first in India and then in almost every Asian country east of India—Buddhist doctrines and practices evolved; in each culture and epoch in which Buddhism prospered, local customs and indigenous religious beliefs were assimilated, giving the religion everywhere a unique form and expression.

Among the most important of the Buddha's teachings are the **Four Noble Truths**:

1. All is suffering (and transitory).
2. The root of suffering is desire, attachment, and personal clinging.
3. There is a way to eliminate desire, and thereby eliminate suffering, namely *nirvāna*.
4. The way to this supreme good is the Eightfold Noble Path: right thought, right resolve, right speech, right conduct, right livelihood, right effort, right mindfulness, and right concentration or meditation.

The Buddhist vision of the universe was, in one sense, much like Parmenides', in that the world as we know it must be understood as *illusion*. But, like the Hindus of the Upanishads, the underlying reality was One, except that the Buddhists called this 'Emptiness' or 'Nothingness'. Also like the Hindus, the Buddha proclaimed the 'wheel of becoming', which shows the connectedness between life, craving, rebirth (rebirth seems never to have been doubted by the Buddha), and the causal interdependence of all things, their insubstantiality, and similarly the insubstantiality of the self or soul—there is 'no soul' according to the Buddha.[6] Although each of these doctrines and others received much thought and elaboration in later years, it is the practice-doctrines' emphases on meditation and compassion that underpin the main themes of the Buddha. What follows is one of the most famous of the many hundreds of sermons and discourses attributed to the Buddha.

From 'Fire Sermon'
Attributed to the Buddha

The learned and noble discipline . . . becomes divested of passion, and by the absence of passion he becomes free.

And there The Blessed One addressed the priests:

'All things, O priests, are on fire. And what, O priests, are all these things which are on fire?

'The eye, O priests, is on fire; forms are on fire; eye-consciousness is on fire; impressions received by the eye are on fire; and whatever sensation, pleasant, unpleasant, or indifferent, originates in dependence on impressions received by the eye, that also is on fire.

'And with what are these on fire?

'With the fire of passion, say I, with the fire of hatred, with the fire of infatuation; with birth, old age, death, sorrow, lamentation, misery, grief, and despair are they on fire.

'The ear is on fire; sounds are on fire; . . . the nose is on fire; odours are on fire; . . . the tongue is on fire; tastes are on fire; . . . the body is on fire; things tangible are on fire; . . . the mind is on fire; ideas are on fire; . . . mind-consciousness is on fire; impressions received by the mind are on fire; and whatever sensation, pleasant, unpleasant, or indifferent, originates in dependence on impressions received by the mind, that also is on fire.

'And with what are these on fire?

'With the fire of passion, say I, with the fire of hatred, with the fire of infatuation; with birth, old age, death, sorrow, lamentation, misery, grief, and despair are they on fire.

'Perceiving this, O priests, the learned and noble disciple conceives an aversion for the eye, conceives an aversion for forms, conceives an aversion for eye-consciousness, conceives an aversion for the impressions received by the eye; and whatever sensation, pleasant, unpleasant, or indifferent, originates in dependence on impressions received by the eye, for that also he conceives an aversion. Conceives an aversion for the ear, conceives an aversion for sounds, . . . conceives an aversion for the nose, conceives an aversion for odours, . . . conceives an aversion for the tongue, conceives an aversion for tastes, . . . conceives an aversion for the body, conceives an aversion for things tangible, . . . conceives an aversion for the mind, conceives an aversion for ideas, conceives an aversion for mind-consciousness, conceives an aversion for the impressions received by the mind; and whatever sensation, pleasant, unpleasant, or indifferent, originates in dependence on impressions received by the mind, for this also he conceives an aversion. And in conceiving this aversion, he becomes divested of passion, and by the absence of passion he becomes free, and when he is free he becomes aware that he is free; and he knows that rebirth is exhausted, that he has lived the holy life, that he has done what it behooved him to do, and that he is no more for this world.'

Now while this exposition was being delivered, the minds of the thousand priests became free from attachment and delivered from the depravities.

- The Buddha claimed that attachment or desire is the root of suffering. Is there a difference between attachment and desire? How might either cause us to suffer?
- Does one become free from suffering when one becomes devoid of passion?

D. Two Kinds of Metaphysics: Plato and Aristotle

The term *metaphysics* is relatively new (from about 70 BCE or so), but it is generally agreed that the first great systematic metaphysicians were Plato (427–347 BCE) and Aristotle (384–322 BCE). Plato had been a student of Socrates and his most faithful recorder. (Almost all that we have of Socrates' teachings comes to us through Plato.) Yet Socrates was a moralist, not a metaphysician, and most of the metaphysical doctrines that Plato discusses using Socrates as his mouthpiece are probably Plato's own. Aristotle never tried to be a faithful disciple of Plato, and he became his teacher's harshest and most famous critic.

Metaphysics is what Aristotle called 'first philosophy', the investigation of 'Being as Being', or ultimate reality. What does it mean for something to exist? What is it for something to change? What makes one thing like another? Sometimes these questions, or at least the answers to these questions, are presupposed in our everyday thinking, whether we actually think about them or not. For example, we 'naturally' believe that a tree continues to exist when we aren't looking at it. But why do we believe this? Even when such questions are the creations of philosophers, they outline views of the world that nonphilosophers share with them. The problem is, as we shall see, that people disagree violently about these issues, even from one generation to the next (for example, from Plato to Aristotle). What seems to be clear and obvious to one philosopher will seem obscure, merely metaphorical, or downright paradoxical to another. But as we watch the warring history of metaphysics, we too should be humbled by it, for it cannot be that all of those geniuses got it wrong while we now have it right. We too, whether explicitly or not, have metaphysical views, and we too may have to be ready to give them up as we think more about them and face further arguments.

With Plato and Aristotle, metaphysics becomes a cautious consuming enterprise, producing monumental systems of many volumes that require a lifetime of study to master. All we can do here is present a thumbnail sketch, with some brief selections of Plato's metaphysics and a very brief introduction to Aristotle's philosophy, which seems, at first glance, to be primarily a refutation of Plato. But like so many philosophers who seem to be attacking each other from completely opposed viewpoints, Plato and Aristotle have much in common. Both attempted to resolve the problems they inherited from the pre-Socratics: to find the ultimate substance of the universe, to understand what was eternal and unchanging, to understand change, and to show that the universe as a whole is intelligible to human understanding. Plato, following Parmenides and the other pre-Socratics who trusted their **reason** more than common sense, gave reason a grander position in human life and in the universe in general than it had ever received before. Aristotle, although he too defended reason, insisted that philosophy return to common sense and have a respect for ordinary opinion, which many of the Greek philosophers seemed to have lost. But whatever their differences, it is the shared grandeur of their enterprise that should impress us most about Plato and Aristotle. Between them, they established what we today call 'philosophy'. And between them, they also laid the intellectual foundations for Christian theology. St Augustine, for example, was very much a Platonist, and St Thomas Aquinas was thoroughly indebted to Aristotle.

1. Plato

FORM

An independently existing entity in the world of Being, which determines the nature of the particular things of this world. (For Aristotle, forms have no independent existence.)

The most important single feature of Plato's philosophy is his theory of **Forms**. (The Greek word is *Eidos*.) Plato's Forms are sometimes referred to as **Ideas**, but Plato does not mean ideas in a person's mind, but rather ideal forms or perfect examples—the perfect circle or perfect beauty. To avoid confusion, we shall use not the word *Ideas*, but *Forms*.

Forms are the ultimate reality. Things change, people grow old and die, but Forms are eternal and unchanging. Thus Plato could agree with Heraclitus that the world of our experience is constantly changing; but he could also agree with Parmenides, who insisted that the real world, the eternal and unchanging world, was not the same as the world of our experience. According to Plato, the real world was a *world of Forms*, a world of eternal truths. There were, in other words, two worlds: (1) the world in which we live, the world of constant change or the *world of **Becoming***, and (2) the world of Forms, the unchanging world, the *world of **Being***. We can see here Plato's close connection with Parmenides, holding that ultimate reality (the Forms) must be changeless and eternal. Furthermore, also in accordance with Parmenides, it is only such changeless and eternal things that truly can be known. Our only access to this latter world, the real world, is through our reason, our capacity for intellectual thought. Plato's 'two-worlds' view was to have a direct and obvious influence on Christian theology. It would also affect philosophers, mathematicians, mystics, poets, and romantics of all kinds until the present day. But in his own time it had a more immediate importance; it allowed him to reconcile Heraclitus and Parmenides, to resolve the problems of the pre-Socratics, and to finally give ideas their proper place in human thought.

Plato thought of the Forms as having the special features of *what is* according to Parmenides. The most exciting Form for Plato was the Form of beauty. Plato thought a person could get to know beauty by falling in love in the right way and by realizing that the excitement of love is really aimed not at the personality of the person loved but at the link between that person and eternal beauty.

From *The Symposium*
By Plato

You see, the man who has been thus far guided in matters of Love, who has beheld beautiful things in the right order and correctly, is coming now to the goal of Loving: All of a sudden he will catch sight of something wonderfully beautiful in its nature; that, Socrates, is the reason for all his earlier labours: First, [Beauty] always is, and neither comes to be nor passes away, neither waxes nor wanes. Second, it is not beautiful this way and ugly that way, nor beautiful at one time and ugly at another; nor beautiful in relation to one thing and ugly in relation to another; nor is it beautiful here but ugly there, as it would be if it were beautiful for some people and ugly for others. Nor will the beautiful appear to him in the guise of a face or hands or anything else that belongs to the body. It will not appear to him as one idea or one kind of knowledge. It is not anywhere in another thing, as in an animal, or in earth, or in heaven, or in anything else, but itself by itself with itself, it is always one in form; and all the other beautiful things share in that, in such a way that when those others come to be or pass away, this does not become the least bit smaller or greater nor suffer any change.

For Plato, it is the world of Forms, the world of Being, that is real. But this is not to say (as Parmenides had argued) that the world we live in, the world of becoming, is unreal. It is, however, less than real, not an illusion, but without those qualities of eternity and necessity that are the marks of true reality. This might seem like a verbal trick; it is not. The idea of a hierarchy of realities was already familiar in religions that antedated Plato's philosophy by centuries. We still use such notions in our own thinking, comparing, for example, the world of film and novels to 'the real world', or the dreary humdrum of working-day life to 'really living'. But the best illustration of Plato's two-worlds view is his own, which he offers us in a parable called the Myth of the Cave.

It is a parable about bringing people from the less real to the really real. Indeed, one of the most striking features of Plato's philosophy (and much of Greek philosophy in general) is its emphasis on the *love* of wisdom, the irresistibility of reality; and what is too easily lost in translation is the very erotic imagery Plato uses to describe our passion for the truth. The Myth of the Cave not only illustrates two kinds of knowledge, two kinds of worlds; it is also a parable about human timidity, the difficulties we have in facing the truth, and our resistance to the dazzling light of truth itself.

From *The Republic*
By Plato

One must turn one's whole soul from the world of becoming until it can endure to contemplate reality, and the brightest of realities, which we say is the Good.

SOCRATES: Imagine men to be living in an underground cave-like dwelling place, which has a way up to the light along its whole width, but the entrance is a long way up. The men have been there from childhood, with their neck and legs in fetters, so that they remain in the same place and can only see ahead of them, as their bonds prevent them turning their heads. Light is provided by a fire burning some way behind them, and on a higher ground, there is a path across the cave and along this a low wall has been built, like the screen at a puppet show in front of the performers who show their puppets above it.

(Continued)

GLAUCON: I see it.

SOCRATES: See then also men carrying along that wall, so that they overtop it, all kinds of artifacts, statues of men, reproductions of other animals in stone or wood fashioned in all sorts of ways, and, as is likely, some of the carriers are talking while others are silent.

GLAUCON: This is a strange picture, and strange prisoners.

SOCRATES: They are like us, I said. Do you think, in the first place, that such men could see anything of themselves and each other except the shadows which the fire casts upon the wall of the cave in front of them?

GLAUCON: How could they, if they have to keep their heads still throughout life?

SOCRATES: And is not the same true of the objects carried along the wall?

GLAUCON: Quite.

SOCRATES: If they could converse with one another, do you not think that they would consider these shadows to be the real things?

GLAUCON: Necessarily.

SOCRATES: What if their prison had an echo which reached them from in front of them? Whenever one of the carriers passing behind the wall spoke, would they not think that it was the shadow passing in front of them which was talking? Do you agree?

GLAUCON: By Zeus, I do.

SOCRATES: Altogether then, I said, such men would believe the truth to be nothing else than the shadows of the artifacts?

GLAUCON: They must believe that.

SOCRATES: Consider then what deliverance from their bonds and the curing of their ignorance would be if something like this naturally happened to them. Whenever one of them was freed, had to stand up suddenly, turn his head, walk, and look up toward the light, doing all that would give him pain, the flash of the fire would make it impossible for him to see the objects of which he had earlier seen the shadows. What do you think he would say if he was told that what he saw was foolishness, that he was now somewhat closer to reality and turned to things that existed more fully, that he saw more correctly? If one then pointed to each of the objects passing by, asked him what each was, and forced him to answer, do you not think he would be at a loss and believe

that the things which he saw earlier were truer than the things now pointed out to him?

GLAUCON: Much truer.

SOCRATES: If one then compelled him to look at the fire itself, his eyes would hurt, he would turn round and flee toward those things which he could see, and think that they were in fact clearer than those now shown to him.

GLAUCON: Quite so.

SOCRATES: And if one were to drag him thence by force up the rough and steep path, and did not let him go before he was dragged into the sunlight, would he not be in physical pain and angry as he was dragged along? When he came into the light, with the sunlight filling his eyes, he would not be able to see a single one of the things which are now said to be true.

GLAUCON: Not at once, certainly.

SOCRATES: I think he would need time to get adjusted before he could see things in the world above; at first he would see shadows most easily, then reflections of men and other things in water, then the things themselves. After this he would see objects in the sky and the sky itself more easily at night, the light of the stars and the moon more easily than the sun and the light of the sun during the day.

GLAUCON: Of course.

SOCRATES: Then, at last, he would be able to see the sun, not images of it in water or in some alien place, but the sun itself in its own place, and be able to contemplate it.

GLAUCON: That must be so.

SOCRATES: After this he would reflect that it is the sun which provides the seasons and the years, which governs everything in the visible world, and is also in some way the cause of those other things which he used to see.

GLAUCON: Clearly that would be the next stage.

SOCRATES: What then? As he reminds himself of his first dwelling place, of the wisdom there and of his fellow prisoners, would he not reckon himself happy for the change, and pity them?

GLAUCON: Surely.

SOCRATES: And if the men below had praise and honours from each other, and prizes for the man who saw most clearly the shadows that passed before them, and who could best remember which usually came earlier and which later, and which came together and thus could most ably prophesy the future, do you think our man would desire those rewards and envy those who were honoured and held power among the prisoners, or would he feel, as Homer put it, that he certainly wished to be 'serf to another man without possessions upon the earth'[7] and go through any suffering, rather than share their opinions and live as they do?

GLAUCON: Quite so, I think he would rather suffer anything.

SOCRATES: Reflect on this too. If this man went down into the cave again and sat down in the same seat, would his eyes not be filled with darkness, coming suddenly out of the sunlight?

GLAUCON: They certainly would.

SOCRATES: And if he had to contend again with those who had remained prisoners in recognizing those shadows while his sight was affected and his eyes had not settled down—and the time for this adjustment would not be short—would he not be ridiculed? Would it not be said that he had returned from his upward journey with his eyesight spoiled, and that it was not worthwhile even to attempt to travel upward? As for the man who tried to free them and lead them upward, if they would somehow lay their hands on him and kill him, they would do so.

GLAUCON: They certainly would.

SOCRATES: This whole image, my dear Glaucon, must be related to what we said before. The realm of the visible should be compared to the prison dwelling, and the fire inside it to the power of the sun. If you interpret the upward journey and the contemplation of things above as the upward journey of the soul to the intelligible realm, you will grasp what I surmise since you were keen to hear it. Whether it is true or not only the god knows, but this is how I see it, namely that in the intelligible world the Form of the Good is the last to be seen, and with difficulty; when seen it must be reckoned to be for all the cause of all that is right and beautiful, to have produced in the visible world both the light and the fount of light, while in the intelligible world it is itself that which produces and controls truth and intelligence, and he who is to act intelligently in public or in private must see it.

GLAUCON: I share your thought as far as I am able.

SOCRATES: Come then, share with me this thought also: do not be surprised that those who have reached this point are unwilling to occupy themselves with human affairs, and that their souls are always pressing upward to spend their time there, for this is natural if things are as our parable indicates.

GLAUCON: That is very likely.

SOCRATES: Further, do you think it at all surprising that anyone coming to the evils of human life from the contemplation of the divine behaves awkwardly and appears very ridiculous while his eyes are still dazzled and before he is sufficiently adjusted to the darkness around him, if he is compelled to contend in court or some other place about the shadows of justice or the objects of which they are shadows, and to carry through the contest about these in the way these things are understood by those who have never seen Justice itself?

GLAUCON: That is not surprising at all.

SOCRATES: Anyone with intelligence would remember that the eyes may be confused in two ways and from two causes, coming from light into darkness as well as from darkness into light. Realizing that the same applies to the soul, whenever he sees a soul disturbed and unable to see something, he will not laugh mindlessly but will consider whether it has come from a brighter life and is dimmed because unadjusted, or has come from greater ignorance into greater light and is filled with a brighter dazzlement. The former he would declare happy in its life and experience, the latter he would pity, and if he should wish to laugh at it, his laughter would be less ridiculous than if he laughed at the soul that has come from the light above.

GLAUCON: What you say is very reasonable.

SOCRATES: We must then, if these things are true, think something like this about them, namely that education is not what some declare it to be; they say that knowledge is not present in the soul and that they put it in, like putting sight into blind eyes.

GLAUCON: They surely say that.

SOCRATES: Our present argument shows that the capacity to learn and the organ with which to do so are present in every person's soul. It is as if it were not possible to turn the eye from darkness to light without turning the whole body; so one must turn one's whole soul from the world of becoming until it can endure to contemplate reality, and the brightest of realities, which we say is the Good.

(Continued)

GLAUCON: Yes.

SOCRATES: Education then is the art of doing this very thing, this turning around, the knowledge of how the soul can most easily and most effectively be turned around; it is not the art of putting the capacity of sight into the soul; the soul possesses that already but it is not turned the right way or looking where it should. This is what education has to deal with.

GLAUCON: That seems likely.

Our world is like a set of shadows of the real world; that does not make it an illusion, but it does make it a mere imitation of the bright originals. Notice, too, the saviour-like role of the philosopher that Plato is setting up here. (His famous argument that philosophers should be kings, and kings philosophers, is included in *The Republic* too.) Like Pythagoras, Plato believed that knowledge of pure Forms, knowledge of the world of 'Being', is a person's only hope for salvation and the 'good life'.

- Do you see any similarities between Plato's theory of Forms and the doctrines about the nature of reality found in Eastern philosophy?
- In what sense is ignorance like being imprisoned in a cave? What are the shadows in Socrates' story?

Socrates had taught his students, Plato among them, that the truth, if we can know it at all, must be in us. Plato (using his teacher as his literary spokesman) gives this revelation a new twist. It begins with a puzzle. How is it possible to learn anything? If we don't already know it, how will we recognize it when we find it? And if we already do know it, it makes no sense to say that we 'learn it'. Now, this puzzle sounds like nonsense if we think only of examples such as 'what is the beer consumption rate in Antigonish, Nova Scotia?' To answer such questions, obviously we can't simply 'look into ourselves'; we have to go out into the world and get information. But Plato insists that he is after much bigger game than 'information'; he wants Knowledge (with a capital K), knowledge of reality, to which we have access only through thinking. That world, unlike the world of change and 'information' in which we live, is characterized by the fact that everything in it is eternal and necessary. In this eternal world, reality is not discoverable merely through observation and experience. For example, consider the simple truth, $2 + 2 = 4$; it never changes—no experience is necessary to know it; it is one of those eternal truths that deserves its place in Plato's world of Being.

Perhaps the best way to understand Plato's exciting but somewhat mysterious notion of the Forms is to think of them in terms of *definitions*. The Forms are what different things of the same kind have in common and what make them things of the same kind. For example, two horses have in common the Form horse, and you recognize a horse, Plato would say, because of its Form. Suppose that you've never seen a horse before. Is it possible for you to know what a horse is? The answer is, 'of course'. It is enough that you have learned what a horse is (from pictures or descriptions) even if you've never seen one. But how is such learning possible? According to Plato, it is possible because we know a definition and thus recognize the Form of a horse, like the ideal Form of a triangle, and with it we are able to know what a horse is, even if we have never seen one, and we recognize horses when we do see them. In Plato's terms, we can recognize all horses, no matter what their age, shape, colour, or peculiarities, just because they 'participate' in the Form horse. For Plato, the Form horse has even more reality than particular, flesh-and-blood horses.

The concept of Form allows Plato to explain what it is that one comes to understand when one learns that two or more things are of the same kind. But for Plato the notion of Form serves another purpose as well. In addition to what we know about things from experience, we also know some things independent of experience, and we know these things with certainty (the same certainty Descartes sought, which we discussed in the Introduction). For example, we know that every horse is an animal. We know that not simply because every horse that we have seen has turned out to be an animal, but because we know, apart from any particular experiences with horses, that the very Form horse includes the Form animal. (In our times, we would say that the meaning of the English word 'horse' already includes the concept of 'being an animal'; accordingly, philosophers refer to this kind of truth as **conceptual truth**. But this term was not available to Plato.)

Definitions are essential because without them it is difficult to know exactly what one is talking about. But this quest for definitions should not be confused with the high school debating technique of asking your opponent to 'define his or her terms'. Rather, a definition is the *conclusion* of a philosophical argument—and it is very hard to come by. In his dialogue *The Meno*, Plato has Socrates push for a definition of 'virtue'; his arguments here are a good illustration of the Socratic pursuit of the Forms as definitions.

> **CONCEPTUAL TRUTH**
>
> A statement that is true and that we can see to be true by virtue of the meanings of the words (or the 'concepts') that compose it.

From *The Meno*
By Plato

. . . there is no teaching but recollection, in order to show me up at once as contradicting myself.

MENO: Can you tell me, Socrates, can virtue be taught? Or is it not teachable but the result of practise, or is it neither of these, but men possess it by nature or in some other way?

SOCRATES: Before now, Meno, Thessalians had a high reputation among the Greeks and were admired for their horsemanship and their wealth, but now, it seems to me, they are also admired for their wisdom, not least the fellow citizens of your friend Aristippus of Larissa. The responsibility for this reputation of yours lies with Gorgias, for when he came to your city he found that the leading Aleuadae, your lover Aristippus among them, loved him for his wisdom, and so did the other leading Thessalians. In particular, he accustomed you to give a bold and grand answer to any question you may be asked, as experts are likely to do. Indeed, he himself was ready to answer any Greek who wished to question him, and every question was answered. But here in Athens, my dear Meno, the opposite is the case, as if there were a dearth of wisdom, and wisdom seems to have departed hence to go to you. If then you want to ask one of us that sort of question, everyone will laugh and say: 'Good stranger, you must think me happy indeed if you think I know whether virtue can be taught or how it comes to be; I am so far from knowing whether virtue can be taught or not that I do not even have any knowledge of what virtue itself is.'

I myself, Meno, am as poor as my fellow citizens in this matter, and I blame myself for my complete ignorance about virtue. If I do not know what something is, how could I know what qualities it possesses? Or do you think that someone who does not know at all who Meno is could know whether he is good-looking or rich or well-born, or the opposite of these? Do you think that is possible?

MENO: I do not; but, Socrates, do you really not know what virtue is? Are we to report this to the folk back home about you?

SOCRATES: Not only that, my friend, but also that, as I believe, I have never yet met anyone else who did know.

MENO: How so? Did you not meet Gorgias when he was here?

SOCRATES: I did.

MENO: Did you then not think that he knew?

SOCRATES: I do not altogether remember, Meno, so that I cannot tell you now what I thought then. Perhaps he does know; you know what he used to say, so you remind me of what he said. You tell me yourself, if you are willing, for surely you share his views.

MENO: I do.

SOCRATES: Let us leave Gorgias out of it, since he is not here. But, Meno, by the gods, what do you yourself say that virtue is? Speak and do not begrudge us, so that I may have spoken a most

(Continued)

unfortunate untruth when I said that I had never met anyone who knew, if you and Gorgias are shown to know.

MENO: It is not hard to tell you, Socrates. First, if you want the virtue of a man, it is easy to say that a man's virtue consists of being able to manage public affairs and in so doing to benefit his friends and harm his enemies and to be careful that no harm comes to himself; if you want the virtue of a woman, it is not difficult to describe: she must manage the home well, preserve its possessions, and be submissive to her husband; the virtue of a child, whether male or female, is different again, and so is that of an elderly man, if you want that, or if you want that of a free man or a slave. And there are very many other virtues, so that one is not at a loss to say what virtue is. There is virtue for every action and every age, for every task of ours and every one of us—and Socrates, the same is true for wickedness.

SOCRATES: I seem to be in great luck, Meno; while I am looking for one virtue, I have found you to have a whole swarm of them. But, Meno, to follow up the image of swarms, if I were asking you what is the nature of bees, and you said that they are many and of all kinds, what would you answer if I asked you: 'Do you mean that they are many and varied and different from one another in so far as they are bees? Or are they no different in that regard, but in some other respect, in their beauty, for example, or their size or in some other such way?' Tell me, what would you answer if thus questioned?

MENO: I would say that they do not differ from one another in being bees.

SOCRATES: If I went on to say: 'Tell me, what is this very thing, Meno, in which they are all the same and do not differ from one another?' Would you be able to tell me?

MENO: I would.

Meno continues to try to satisfy Socrates with a definition of virtue, but every time he either contradicts himself or argues in a circle. So how does one know a definition? The answer, according to Plato, is that we recognize the Forms. We know what a horse is because we recognize the Form of a horse. We recognize that 2 + 2 = 4 because we know the Forms. But how do we *know* the Forms? If we do not and cannot learn of them from experience (the changing world of Becoming in everyday life), then how do we know them at all? The answer, according to Plato, is that they already are 'in us'.

> • Are you persuaded that we do not know what something is if we cannot define it? What would a Daoist say?

The second principle of Plato's metaphysics, our bridge between the two worlds, is the immortality and immateriality of the human soul. Our souls contain knowledge of the world of Being that is already in us at birth. Such knowledge and ideas are called **innate**. Experience only triggers them off and allows us to 'remember' them. Here is the answer to Plato's puzzle, 'How is it possible to learn a truth about the world of Being?'—we already 'know' it; it's just a matter of recalling it. Consider his famous illustration, again given in *The Meno*.

MENO: How will you look for it, Socrates, when you do not know at all what it is? How will you aim to search for something you do not know at all? If you should meet with it, how will you know that this is the thing that you did not know?

SOCRATES: I know what you want to say, Meno. Do you realize what a debater's argument you are

bringing up, that a man cannot search either for what he knows or for what he does not know? He cannot search for what he knows—since he knows it, there is no need to search—nor for what he does not know, for he does not know what to look for.

MENO: Does that argument not seem sound to you, Socrates?

SOCRATES: Not to me.

MENO: Can you tell me why?

SOCRATES: I can. I have heard wise men and women talk about divine matters. . . .

MENO: What did they say?

SOCRATES: What was, I thought, both true and beautiful.

MENO: What was it, and who were they?

SOCRATES: The speakers were among the priests and priestesses whose care it is to be able to give an account of their practices. Pindar too says it, and many others of the divine among our poets. What they say is this; see whether you think they speak the truth: They say that the human soul is immortal; at times it comes to an end, which they call dying, at times it is reborn, but it is never destroyed, and one must therefore live one's life as piously as possible:

> Persephone will return to the sun above in the ninth year the souls of those from whom she will exact punishment for old miseries, and from these come noble kings, mighty in strength and greatest in wisdom, and for the rest of time men will call them sacred heroes.

As the soul is immortal, has been born often and has seen all things here and in the underworld, there is nothing which it has not learned; so it is in no way surprising that it can recollect the things it knew before, both about virtue and other things. As the whole of nature is akin, and the soul has learned everything, nothing prevents a man, after recalling one thing only—a process men call learning—discovering everything else for himself, if he is brave and does not tire of the search, for searching and learning are, as a whole, recollection. We must, therefore, not believe that debater's argument, for it would make us idle, and faint-hearted men like to hear it, whereas my argument makes them energetic and keen on the search. I trust that this is true, and I want to inquire along with you into the nature of virtue.

MENO: Yes, Socrates, but how do you mean that we do not learn, but that what we call learning is recollection? Can you teach me that this is so?

SOCRATES: As I said just now, Meno, you are a rascal. You now ask me if I can teach you, when I say there is no teaching but recollection, in order to show me up at once as contradicting myself.

MENO: No, by Zeus, Socrates, that was not my intention when I spoke, but just a habit. If you can somehow show me that things are as you say, please do so.

At this dramatic point in the dialogue, Socrates calls over an illiterate, uneducated slave boy and with minimal instructions leads him to discover an elementary geometrical proof. What is crucial is that Socrates does not tell the boy the answer but 'draws it out of him'. But then the question becomes, where was this answer 'in him', and how did he recognize it? After the demonstration, Socrates draws his conclusions:

SOCRATES: What do you think, Meno? Has he, in his answers, expressed any opinion that was not his own?

MENO: No, they were all his own.

SOCRATES: And yet, as we said, he did not know a short time ago?

MENO: That is true.

SOCRATES: So these opinions were in him, were they not?

MENO: Yes.

SOCRATES: So the man who does not know has within himself true opinions about the things that he does not know?

MENO: So it appears.

SOCRATES: These opinions have now just been stirred up like a dream, but if he were repeatedly asked these same questions in various ways, you know that in the end his knowledge about these things would be as accurate as anyone's.

MENO: It is likely.

SOCRATES: And he will know it without having been taught but only questioned, and find the knowledge within himself?

MENO: Yes.

SOCRATES: And is not finding knowledge within oneself recollection?

MENO: Certainly.

(Continued)

SOCRATES: Must he not either have at some time acquired the knowledge he now possesses, or else have always possessed it?

MENO: Yes.

SOCRATES: If he always had it, he would always have known. If he acquired it, he cannot have done so in his present life. Or has someone taught him geometry? For he will perform in the same way about all geometry, and all other knowledge. Has someone taught him everything? You should know, especially as he has been born and brought up in your house.

MENO: But I know that no one has taught him.

SOCRATES: Yet he has these opinions, or doesn't he?

MENO: That seems indisputable, Socrates.

SOCRATES: If he has not acquired them in his present life, is it not clear that he had them and had learned them at some other time?

MENO: It seems so.

SOCRATES: Then that was the time when he was not a human being?

MENO: Yes.

SOCRATES: If then, during the time he exists and is not a human being he will have true opinions which, when stirred by questioning, become knowledge, will not his soul have learned during all time? For it is clear that during all time he exists either as a man or not.

MENO: So it seems.

SOCRATES: Then if the truth about reality is always in our soul, the soul would be immortal so that you should always confidently try to seek out and recollect what you do not know at present—that is, what you do not recollect?

MENO: Somehow, Socrates, I think that what you say is right.

SOCRATES: I think so too, Meno.

The doctrine of the immortality of the soul did not originate with Plato, of course. The ancient Egyptians believed the soul to be immortal many centuries before the first Greek philosophers existed, and Pythagoras had taught it to his students. But Plato's doctrine had more than religious significance; it was his answer to the skeptics and our bridge to the eternal world of Being. Of course, as a student of Socrates, he also appreciated the advantages of believing in an afterlife. Socrates could face death so calmly, he told his students, just because he believed in life after death. But for Plato it signified something more; it provided us with knowledge in this life as well as continued existence in another.

Plato's doctrines of the world of Being and the immortality of the soul introduce a clearly immaterialist conception of reality, as opposed to all of the more or less materialist conceptions we have encountered so far (the world as 'stuff'). Even Pythagoras' numbers and Heraclitus' *logos* had their materialistic foundations, for neither philosopher was willing to grant these things an existence independent of the material things of our world. The things of Plato's world of Being can exist apart from the things of the world of Becoming.

What is in this 'other world', this world of Being? We have already met one of its inhabitants: the simple truth, $2 + 2 = 4$. Its inhabitants are Forms. Consider the following familiar example: Your geometry teacher asks you to prove that the internal angles of a triangle total 180 degrees. Simple enough. You remember how: You extend the base of the triangle, draw a line parallel to the base through the apex, and then proceed with your proof. But now, how do you know that you have not only shown that the internal angles of *this* triangle total 180 degrees? As a matter of fact, it is pretty obvious that what you have drawn isn't even a triangle; the sides sag, one of the angles is broken, and the lines are fat (after all, a real line has no width at all). But yet you claim to have proved something about all triangles. Well, it is clear that you needn't do the proof even twice, much less an infinite number of times, to make your claim. How come? Because what you have been working with is not this particular poorly drawn triangle in your notebook but an ideal triangle, the form of all and any triangles. And there it is—Plato's Form of a triangle. It is not identical to any particular triangle. (How could it be, for it would have to be acute, isosceles, right, and nonright all at the same time!) It is their ideal Form, which each particular triangle approximates, that has its own existence in the world of Being. Plato says that every triangle that we can draw participates in the ideal Form and that it is only through reason, not through observation of particular triangles, that we come into contact with these ideal Forms.

To know a Platonic Form is not just to *see* something. It is to *fall in love* with it; in fact, it is to fall madly in love. So Socrates, in nearly all of Plato's dialogues, repeats the claim that a philosopher is a kind of lover. Indeed, he says that to know the Forms is to want to reproduce, to propagate, to teach everyone else to see them and to love them too. The Myth of the Cave and the metaphor of the sun and shadows have two sides. The first is that the changing world of our everyday experience is only a shadow, an imitation of reality. But the second side is that the world of our everyday experience is also an image of the divine and ultimate reality, and so in the things of everyday life we get at least a glimpse of perfection.

Among the Forms are those ideals of human perfection that we should not only recognize but try to realize here in the world of Becoming: Wisdom, Justice, Beauty, and Goodness. To these ideals of perfection each of us aspires, and it is the definition of these ideals that is the task of every philosopher. His or her job (Socrates' main task in all of Plato's dialogues) is to sort out the common confusions about such vital matters. The business of the philosopher, in short, is to make others recognize eternal Forms and make it possible to achieve that heroic wisdom to which Plato's teacher, Socrates, devoted his life.

By this point you should be able to appreciate, even from this brief sketch, the power of the metaphysical doctrines Plato developed. You may also be aware of some of their difficulties. Most importantly, the gap between our world and the real world makes us exceedingly uncomfortable; none of us likes to think of ourselves living merely in the shadows. (As Plato himself warns, wouldn't the prisoners who had never been released laugh at and even kill the philosopher who thus instructs them?) The connection between the world of Being and our own world of Becoming is not at all clear. Plato does say that the things of this latter world 'participate' in the Forms of the former, but one thing that we shall have to learn right away in philosophy (and in every other discipline) is that the words that pretend to be explanations are often only cosmetic cover-ups. It looks as if we have a theory when in fact we have only a word. This is particularly true of Plato's word '*participates*' (*methexis*), and he himself raises serious doubts about it in his later dialogues. But the real attack comes, as it should come in philosophy, from his own students, and in particular, from one, perhaps the greatest of them all, Aristotle.

> - How does the slave boy discover the proof without being told? Do you find Socrates' explanation at all plausible?

2. Aristotle

Aristotle claimed that he did not understand Plato's concept of '**participation**'. (When a philosopher claims 'not to understand' something, it means that he is pushing for a better account of it, that he is not at all satisfied so far. Aristotle probably understood Plato as well as anybody ever has.) Aristotle's objection, as he expressed it in his *Metaphysics*, was essentially that Plato had failed to explain the relationship between the Forms and particular things, and that the word 'participation' was no more than 'a mere empty phrase and a poetic metaphor'. Furthermore, Plato's emphasis on the Forms made it impossible to appreciate the full reality of particular things, and the eternal permanence of the Forms made them useless for understanding how particular things could change. Indeed, the question 'How do things change?' becomes the central theme of Aristotle's philosophy.

Aristotle also wanted to determine the nature of reality. But Plato had argued that reality was something other than the world of our experience. Aristotle, a practical man of the earth, a great biologist, physicist, and worldly tutor to Alexander the Great, would have none of this. This world, our world, *is* reality. He agreed with Plato that knowledge must be universal and concerned with what things have in common, but he rejected Plato's idea that these common universal ingredients—the Forms of things—could be separated from

PARTICIPATION

For Plato, the obscure relationship between the things of this world and the Forms of which they are manifestations.

particular things. But this meant that Aristotle also rejected Plato's separation of the human soul from the body, and Aristotle, unlike Plato, saw human beings entirely as creatures of nature—'*rational* animals', but still animals. Metaphysics, for Aristotle, was not the study of another world, recollected in our eternal souls; it was simply the study of nature (*physis*) and, as importantly, the study of ourselves. Accordingly, he brought metaphysics 'back home'. But it must not be thought that he made it any simpler. The beginning student of Aristotle—as well as the trained scholar—will attest to the fact that he is among the most difficult authors in philosophy.

From *Metaphysics*
By Aristotle

There is a branch of knowledge that studies being qua being, and the attributes that belong to it in virtue of its own nature. Now this is not the same as any of the so-called special sciences, since none of these enquires universally about being *qua* being. They cut off some part of it and study the attributes of this part—that is what the mathematical sciences do, for instance. But since we are seeking the first principles, the highest causes, it is of being qua being that we must grasp the first causes.

The study of being *qua* being is metaphysics, which Aristotle was the first to isolate from other branches of philosophy. It is, first of all, the study of the different ways the word *be* can be used. This leads Aristotle to his famous theory of categories:

There are several senses in which a thing may be said to 'be'. In one sense the 'being' meant is 'what a thing is' or a 'this', while in another sense it means a quality or a quantity or one of the other things that are predicated as these are. While 'being' has all these senses, the primary type of being is obviously the 'what', which indicates the substance of the thing. For when we say of what quality something is, we say that it is good or bad, not that it is six feet long or that it is a man; but when we say what it is, we do not say 'white' or 'hot' or 'six feet long', but 'a man' or 'a god'. All other things are said to be because they are quantities of that which is in this primary sense, or qualities of it, or in some other way characteristics of it.

The primary use of *be* is to tell us what something *really is*, what it is in an unqualified sense: We are, in this sense, a certain individual human being. We are also a certain number of inches tall; but that fact is secondary, it is something *about* us, which could change without changing what we *are*, first and foremost, and belongs to the category of *quantity*. We may also be pale or dark; that fact also is secondary and belongs to the category of *quality*. The primary category is that of *substance*. As Aristotle defines it, *substance* is 'that which stands alone'. In other words, *substance* is *independent* being. You would exist, for instance, even if you didn't have hair. But *your* hair could not exist without you, and so it is not a substance. Substances are the basic elements in Aristotle's metaphysics. A horse, a tree, and a butterfly are substances.

Tables and chairs are not primary beings for Aristotle, because he thinks of primary beings as having their own natures. Something made by a human being, such as a table, can only exist *along with* human beings. It cannot move or fulfil its nature—in this case, supporting our food—by itself. Our nature is what we will do if nothing stops us. A human being grows up and leads a human life, if nothing stops him; that's his nature. But a wooden table will inevitably rot if no one stops it, since that is the nature of the wood it is made of. Wood has a nature, tables do not. For that reason, Aristotle treats artifacts (things we make) as having a lower level of being than have human beings.

From *Physics*
By Aristotle

Some people think that the nature and real being of a natural object is the primary material in it (material in itself unformed)—in a bed it would be the wood, in a statue the bronze. It is an indication of this, according to Antiphon, that if you bury a bed, and the rotting wood becomes able to send up a shoot, what comes up will not be a bed, but wood—suggesting that the arrangement in accordance with the rules of the art belongs only incidentally, and that the reality—what the thing really is—is what actually persists through all those changes.

* * *

But there is another way of speaking, according to which the nature of a thing is its shape or form as given in its definition . . . and this rather than its matter is a thing's nature. For (i) each thing is called whatever it is, when it is that thing actually rather than just potentially [the wood or the seed, the matter, is not a table or a lettuce—though it may have the potentiality of being one—until it has actually been put together or has actually germinated and grown]. Further, (ii) men come to be from men, but not beds from beds. That is precisely why people say that the nature of a bed is not the shape but the wood; if it sprouts it is not a bed but wood that comes up. But if this shows that the wood is nature, form too is nature; for men come to be from men.

The doctrines of Aristotle's metaphysics sound as simple as they could be. This world, the world of our experience, is reality; there is no other world. The ultimate things of reality, substances, are individual things—people, horses, trees, and butterflies. Change is real and much of reality is subject to change. Forms are real, but they cannot exist separately from the particular substances whose forms they are. This is not as radical a departure from Plato as it may seem. Aristotle did believe that the highest level of reality was not subject to change. Gods, the heavens, and even the forms of biological species were changeless in his system; Aristotle did not believe in any form of evolution.

For Aristotle, the primary substances are individual things; secondary substances (less real than individuals) are what he called the 'species' and the 'genus' to which a thing belongs. To return to our equestrian example, this particular horse, for Aristotle, is the primary substance. The species, 'horse', and the even broader genus, 'animal', are less real than the horse itself. Aristotle, like Plato, has a hierarchy of reality. But he turns Plato's hierarchy upside down. Plato holds that the more abstract things are the more real; Aristotle argues that the more concrete things, individuals, are the more real. For Aristotle, as in common sense, the most tangible things are considered to be the most real things.

What is a substance? Aristotle spends many pages giving a number of definitions, enough to keep the philosophers of the Middle Ages busy for a thousand years sorting them out. For our purposes, it will be enough to mention three different descriptions of substance, each of which is important for Aristotle and for later philosophy. The first characterization of substance is presented in terms of grammar. In *Categories*, Aristotle says, 'a substance is that which is neither predictable of a subject nor present in a subject; for instance, the individual man or horse'. More simply, a substance is the thing referred to by a noun, which is the subject of a sentence; for example, 'the man is . . .' or 'Socrates is . . .' or 'the horse is. . .'. (This characterization would have been less confusing in Ancient Greek.) A more ontological way of saying this, but unfortunately very confusing too, is to say that a substance is independent of anything else. (We shall see how important this becomes in the modern metaphysics of Spinoza and Leibniz.) Other things might depend upon a substance, but a substance does not depend upon them. This is an awkward way of saying, perhaps, that the colour of a horse could not exist without the horse; indeed, nothing could be true of a horse if it did not exist.

A second way of characterizing substance is to say that substance is what underlies all of the properties and changes in something. In this sense, you can say that you are the same person (that is, the same substance) that you were ten years ago, despite the fact that you are, quite obviously, very different in a great many ways. (Aristotle says, again in *Categories*, 'Substance, while remaining the same, is capable of admitting contrary properties.') Combining this characterization with the first, we can say that a substance is whatever is most basic to reality, like the pre-Socratic philosophers' notion of 'stuff'. It is the concrete individual thing, which remains constant despite the fact that it changes and has different properties at different times. You are the same person before and after you've gotten a haircut, tried on a new suit of clothes, or had your appendix removed.

The third characterization of substance requires the introduction of another new term, which became a central concern of philosophers before the twentieth century. A substance can be defined in terms of what is *essential*. An **essence** (or an essential **property**) is that aspect of an individual that identifies it as a particular individual. For example, it is part of the essence of being Socrates that he is a human being, that he lived in the fourth century BCE, and that he was wise. Anything that does not have these properties could not possibly be Socrates. There are other properties that Socrates has, of course; for example, the fact that he had a wart on his nose. But this is not an essential property. (Aristotle calls it an *accident* or an *accidental property*.) Socrates still would have been Socrates without it. But Socrates could not have been a centipede, for it is part of his essence to be human.

A substance is a combination of form and matter. Aristotle's 'form' is roughly the same as Plato's Form,[8] except that for Aristotle, it does not exist apart from the individual things that have it; it is always *informing* some matter. In this sense, matter is a discovery of Aristotle's. It is, basically, what things are made out of; it is what is given shape and structure by the form. The matter of a boat is wood; its form is the design that the boat builder realized in the wood.

With both concepts available, Aristotle thinks he can explain change by avoiding the mistakes of his predecessors, especially the mistake of Parmenides, which he blames on inexperience:

The first people to philosophize about the nature and truth of things got side-tracked and driven off course by inexperience. They said that nothing comes to be or passes away, because whatever comes to be must do so either from what is, or from what is not—and neither of these is possible. For what is cannot come to be, since it is already; and nothing can come to be from what is *not*, since there must [in all change and coming into being] be something underlying.

While these earlier philosophers believed only in matter that by itself would stay the same (for example, Plato believed only in Forms that are eternally unchanging), Aristotle believes in things that combine matter and form in a variety of ways. It is in this *combination* that Aristotle finds change. Even though the *essence* of a thing cannot change (or it would no longer be the same thing), and it is of little metaphysical importance if *accidents* change, substantial change—the 'coming to be and passing away' of a substance—takes place when matter is given a new form.

Let's examine this conclusion in more detail. Form and matter, Aristotle says, cannot exist separately, but they can be *distinguished* everywhere in nature. The best examples can be found in human craftsmanship. One can take a lump of clay, for example, and make it into a bowl of any number of shapes. Or one can take a piece of silver and make it into a fork, a spoon, a bracelet, or a couple of rings. The clay or the silver is the matter; the shape and the function define the form. Aristotle also says that the matter itself can be analyzed in terms of form and matter. The matter of the clay and the silver would be the basic elements—earth, air, fire, and water. The form would be the shape and proportion these elements assume to make clay or silver. Indeed, Aristotle even holds that the basic elements themselves can be analyzed in terms of more primitive matter—hotness, coldness, dryness, and wetness—which combine to give the form of the elements. It is the form of things that we can know and explain, according to Aristotle, never the matter. Thus, we can *talk* about form and matter separately, and so *understand* change. His predecessor, he thought, mistook the way we talk about reality for the way it is. The form, *by itself*, can never change, nor can the matter, but the way they combine can change. By changing their form, caterpillars turn into butterflies and seeds into fruits and flowers. Thus, Aristotle explains both change and stability.

You may already anticipate certain troubles that will plague later philosophers. How much can we change a person, for example, and still have him or her be the same? Provide a haircut? A college education? A ten-year jail sentence? A sex-change operation? But before we worry about such problems, let us appreciate the importance of this notion of essence in Aristotle's philosophy. With it, he can do everything that Plato wanted to do with his notion of Forms, but without invoking anything otherworldly. According to Aristotle, we can know that Socrates is a man, for instance, just because the essence of Socrates includes the property of being a man. We can know that a horse is an animal because the essence of being a horse includes the property of being an animal. For Plato, a conceptual truth of this kind was a truth about eternal Forms; for Aristotle, it is the form that changes, and a conceptual truth is rather a statement about essences.

In both medieval and modern philosophy, the concepts of substance and essence will take on a particularly important role in debates about God and his relation to his creations as well as in the continuing controversies in ontology that accompanied the rise of modern science. But Aristotle's ontology, much more than the philosophy of his predecessors, was linked up with an exciting prescientific cosmology, an account of the nature and purpose of the universe. In the Middle Ages, these theories profoundly inspired the great Christian theologian St Thomas Aquinas, who would refer to Aristotle as simply 'The Philosopher'.

- What are the three definitions of substance that Aristotle gives? How are they all expressions of the same thing? Give an example of how the form–matter combination explains change.

To understand Aristotle's cosmology, we have to begin with a notion that is extremely foreign to people today; it is that the universe as a whole, and all things in it, have a purpose, a goal. The Greek word for 'purpose' or 'goal' is *telos*, and Aristotle's view is called **teleology**. Teleology can be directly contrasted with our modern scientific view of reality, which is primarily a causal view. Teleology explains something by looking for its purpose, goal, or end; causal explanations seek to understand how something came about, not why it came about. If you were asked why a frog has a heart, for example, the teleological answer would be 'in order to keep it alive, by pumping the blood through its body'. The causal answer, on the other hand, would be an explanation of the genetics, the evolutionary process, the development of the frog. If you were asked why a plant turns its leaves toward the sunlight, the teleological answer would be 'in order to face the sun'. The causal explanation, instead, would refer you to the fact that the cells grow faster on one side of the stem and that certain chemicals present in the leaves react to sunlight,

TELEOLOGY

The belief that all phenomena have a purpose, end, or goal.

and so on. In modern science, a causal answer is always preferable, and if a teleological answer is allowed at all it is always with the qualification that either there is an underlying causal explanation or we do not yet have (but someday will have) an adequate causal explanation. In Aristotle's metaphysics, on the other hand, one does not have an explanation at all unless one knows what purpose a thing or an event serves. 'Nature does nothing in vain' is the motto of the teleologist.[9]

Aristotle believed that every substance, every individual thing whether human, animal, vegetable, or mineral, had its own nature, its own internal principles, certain tendencies that were part of its essence. This was, for example, the basis of his famous theory of falling objects: Every object has its 'place', and if that object is moved, it will return to its rightful place on its own power. That means that any object of sufficient size, whose place is on (or under) the ground, will fall toward the earth immediately if it is lifted into the air. And larger objects, which are not slowed down by the air's resistance, will fall faster than smaller ones. Indeed, this seemed so inherently reasonable to Aristotle and everyone around him that it never occurred to them to test it under experimental conditions. But gravitation, which Newton would not discover for another two millennia, is essentially a causal concept. Aristotle's explanation was a teleological one, which the Greeks found far more convincing. Moreover, even if they had had the equipment for a test, which they did not, the Greeks still might not have believed the answer. Aristotle could not understand how causation could possibly operate at a distance. Thus, Aristotle thought that the cause of an object falling had to be in the object and not in the earth.

A reader who begins Aristotle may be initially confused by his use of the word *cause* (*aition*) to include not only what we have been calling causal explanation but teleological accounts as well. In fact, Aristotle lists four different kinds of **cause**, all of which together explain why a thing is as it is at any given time. The first of these is the matter that makes it up, the *material cause*, the silver in the spoon or the flesh and blood in our bodies. The second is the principle or law by which it is made, the *formal cause*, the architect's blueprint or the craftsman's model. The third is what we would call 'the cause', which Aristotle calls the *efficient cause*, the person or event that actually makes something happen by doing something—pushing a button, causing an explosion, calling the person in charge. Fourth, there is the purpose of the thing, its *final cause*, its *telos*.

You might notice that Aristotle's four causes are better suited for explaining human activities than giving what we would call scientific explanations about things that happen in nature. But this is indeed Aristotle's paradigm, and he even says in *Physics*, 'If purpose is present in art, it must also be present in nature'. For him, it is the final cause that provides us with the most important explanation. We can understand this without any difficulty when we are explaining human activities. We want to know, first of all, what purpose a person has in doing something. But when it comes to nature, we do not generally ask about purpose; we are more likely to ask about (efficient) causes. We might ask of an animal, what purpose is served by a long neck, or certain features in its feet, or some kind of fur, but we are less likely to ask that of a plant and would find such a question unintelligible with reference to rocks, clouds, and stars. Aristotle and his fellow Greeks would not find this unintelligible at all. Indeed, he believed (and thousands of scientists followed him until the seventeenth century) that everything that existed had to be accounted for in terms of its inner purposes and the overall purpose it served in nature. Thus a magnet literally 'attracts' little pieces of metal, and the stars really do have a purpose in their heavenly wanderings. Not only do all the things and creatures of the universe have their purposes, but the universe itself has its purpose too. Indeed, it is this ultimate purpose of the universe that gives all the particular things their significance. Indeed, for Aristotle, the idea that the universe as a whole might *not* have a purpose would have been absurd. One of his most famous arguments is aimed at showing why there must be an ultimate purpose, a 'first (Final) cause', or what he calls, 'the **prime mover**'.

PRIME MOVER

The 'cause-of-itself' which initiates all changes but is not itself affected by anything prior.

From *Metaphysics*
By Aristotle

Moreover, it is obvious that there is some first principle, and that the causes of things are not infinitely many either in a direct sequence or in kind. For the material generation of one thing from another cannot go on in an infinite progression (for example flesh from earth, earth from air, air from fire, and so on without a stop); nor can the source of motion (for example man be moved by air, air by the sun, the sun by Strife, with no limit to the series). In the same way neither can the Final Cause [that is, purposes] recede to infinity—walking having health for its object, and health happiness, and happiness something else: one thing always being done for the sake of another. And it is just the same with the Formal Cause [that is, the essence]. For in the case of all intermediate terms of a series which are contained between a first and last term, the prior term is necessarily the cause of those which follow it; because if we had to say which of the three is the cause, we should say 'the first'. At any rate it is not the last term, because what comes at the end is not the cause of anything. Neither, again, is the intermediate term, which is only the cause of one (and it makes no difference whether there is one intermediate term or several, nor whether they are infinite or limited in number). But of series which are infinite in this way, and in general of the infinite, all the parts are equally intermediate, down to the present moment. Thus if there is no first term, there is no cause at all.

The argument, simply stated, is that teleological explanations cannot go on forever, there can be no **infinite regress**. For Aristotle, if x exists for the purpose of y and y exists for the purpose of z, there must be some ultimate purpose that will explain them all. A similar argument can be made with regard to efficient causes, that if p makes q happen and r makes p happen and so on, there must be an end to the 'and so on', and so too with the material cause and the formal cause. But the most exciting aspect of this infinite regress argument is the idea that the universe itself must have a purpose, a Final cause, a 'prime mover' that Aristotle characterizes as 'pure thought, thinking about itself'. It is an obscure but intriguing idea, which was taken up by Christian theology as an apt characterization of the Christian God (see Chapter 2). But Aristotle's prime mover has few of the characteristics of the Judeo-Christian-Islamic God; he (it) did not create the universe and has no special concern for man. The prime mover is more of a metaphysical necessity than a proper object of worship. But it is not too far-fetched to say that Aristotle, like most of the Greeks, viewed the universe as something like a cosmic organism, with an ultimate purpose, whose ultimate goal was thinking itself.

We can appreciate how this cosmology would become a source of inspiration for a great many philosophers, poets, and religious people. In more recent centuries, for example, it was used as a welcome alternative to the nuts-and-bolts materialism of modern Newtonian science (as we shall see in Leibniz). Aristotle's imaginative cosmology—with its depiction of the universe as purposeful, developing according to its own goals and principles—is a fascinating picture and still an attractive alternative to the lifeless sketch of the physical universe that is so central to our modern scientific outlook.

> • What is teleology? To what extent do we still rely on teleological explanations?

INFINITE REGRESS

A sequence going back endlessly—*A* caused by *B*, *B* by *C*, *C* by *D* . . . and so on to infinity.

E. Modern Metaphysics

Throughout the Middle Ages, philosophers and theologians developed elaborate systems of metaphysics, many of them derived directly or indirectly from the thoughts and theories of Plato and Aristotle. Inherent in all such systems was the confidence that the world is ultimately intelligible, and that the truths that reason can discern about reality are not only true, but necessarily true. Throughout this rich millennium of philosophy (from the later days of the Roman Empire through the Renaissance and Reformation), philosophy and theology in Europe became pretty much a single subject.

All of this changed with the rise of the 'new' science in the sixteenth and seventeenth centuries. At that time, a series of revolutions took place that justify a discussion about the beginning of the 'modern' era of philosophy. What distinguished these revolutions was not a separation from religion and theology (most of these philosophers were pious theists whose God played a central role in their thinking), but rather a new boldness of thought, often in contradiction with Church authority and strikingly original in its form. The father of these revolutions was René Descartes (whom we met earlier in the Introduction), whose philosophy represented a radically new turn in some very old ways of metaphysical thinking. (We should remind ourselves that no thinker, however bold or brilliant, carries off a revolution all alone. Generations paved the way for Descartes' revolution.)

Descartes' metaphysics was derived from ancient concerns, and in particular from the Aristotelian notion of *substance* as it had developed through the intervening centuries of Judeo-Christian and Arabic-Islamic theology during the Middle Ages. It was also a product of modern science, which was rapidly developing under the guidance of such geniuses as Copernicus, Galileo, and Newton. And as with Aristotle, one of Descartes' central concerns was teleology, the purposiveness of the world, but in the new religious climate the question of purposiveness was focussed wholly on the Being through whom all purposes were to be ultimately explained, the Judeo-Christian-Islamic God. But this sense of purpose (or final causality) started to run counter to the notions of efficient and material causality that had already come to rule modern science. With the birth of modern science and the modern world, the clash between the teleological visions of faith and the causal explanations of science became inevitable.

The most dramatic new ingredient in modern metaphysics, however, was a concept that played virtually no role in ancient metaphysics at all, and that was the notion of *mind* or *consciousness*. To be sure, the Greeks talked about their own psychological states. (Aristotle wrote long discussions of such emotions as anger, for example. Homer often described the psychology of his heroes, but almost always in physiological terms.) But the idea of a mind as a self-contained arena—what the contemporary philosopher Daniel Dennett has dubbed 'the Cartesian theatre'—is distinctively new. One can trace its development through the centuries by way of the ever-increasing Christian emphasis on the soul and inner personal experience, but it is only in modern metaphysics that we get the full-blown view that what the world is made of, the ultimate reality of things, is the mind. This view, in general, is called **idealism**. For a few eccentric philosophers, this might be taken to mean that the reality of the world is a function of one's individual mind, but most idealists had something much grander in mind, as we shall see. Deriving their views from medieval Christianity, for example, some philosophers suggested that there is ultimately only one mind, or one supreme mind, and that is the mind of God. Others suggested that mind pervades everything including God. In one sense, idealist views are plausible: we realize that we know about the things of reality only by way of their effects (direct or indirect) on our minds. But whether they exist only because of our minds is a much more radical proposition, and whether our minds are 'free' to conceive of things and determine our actions, in the light of modern science, will become one of the most pressing concerns of philosophy.

Descartes' metaphysical system was an amalgam of the latest theories in science and mathematics (some of which he discovered), established theology, and the new science of psychology. His method itself (discussed briefly in the Introduction) was based on the model of mathematical proof, starting with premises that were self-evident and arguing deductively to conclusions that were therefore equally certain. We consider Descartes' contributions to knowledge—and his famous *cogito* arguments ('I think, therefore I am')—in the Chapter 3. Here we consider Descartes' equally famous metaphysical model of the world, one that has set the stage for much of philosophy ever since. (The basic idea that mind and body are distinct is still referred to as Cartesian dualism.) We also look at Descartes' two most famous and brilliant followers, who developed elaborate metaphysical systems quite different from—and in opposition to—his own. The first is a Jewish philosopher, excommunicated for his heresies, who lived his life in poverty on the outskirts of Amsterdam. He is Benedictus de Spinoza (1632–1677). The second is his slightly younger contemporary, Gottfried Wilhelm von Leibniz (1646–1716), Germany's first great modern philosopher. Together, they present us with the classics in modern Western metaphysics, three very different speculations on the nature of the world.

1. René Descartes

Modern metaphysics begins with Descartes' insistence upon perfect certainty and mathematical deduction as the legitimate methodology. But methodology aside, metaphysics is a continuous enterprise from the Greeks through medieval philosophy, with Descartes its direct heir. We should not be surprised, for example, to find that the central concept of Descartes' metaphysics is substance. Indeed, his definition of the term, which he puts forth in *Principles of Philosophy*, comes straight from Aristotle: 'a thing existing in such a manner that it has need of no other thing in order to exist'. (Both Spinoza and Leibniz follow Descartes in taking substance as their central concept, and they follow him also in their method. The three philosophers are usually grouped together as a single school of thought called Rationalism.)

Descartes' metaphysics can be understood best in terms of a monumental historical conflict between the 'new' science (developed by Galileo and others) and the established authority of the Roman Catholic Church. Descartes, like many of the most important philosophers to follow him, was both an enthusiast of the new science—in fact he was an important contributor to both science and its mathematical foundations—and a religious man. He could not tolerate the idea that science should replace the orderly, meaningful worldview of Christianity with a Godless, amoral universe of mere 'matter in motion'. Neither could Descartes ever agree that science should reduce human existence—in particular, the thinking self—to another mere machine. (It is often noted that Descartes did think that animals were mere machines: What we too generously attribute to them by way of learning and responding to the environment, Descartes interpreted as nothing more than mechanical adjustments.) Accordingly, his metaphysics divides the world into three sorts of 'substances': God; the mind, or the self; and physical, material being. The latter two sorts of substances are, of course, created by and dependent on God. Indeed, Descartes begins all his studies with a proof of the existence of the world (and one's knowledge of it) that rests on the presumption of God's goodness. Because God is rational and good, we can trust (within limits) our own limited knowledge of the world. (We examine some of these proofs and arguments in the following chapter.) But because the world (of minds and matter) depends on God, there is no danger that science should leave us with a Godless, meaningless, mechanical universe. In Aristotelian terms, the ultimate causes in the universe are 'final' (or purposive) causes, not 'efficient' (or mechanical) causes. The physical world is God's creation; and though it must be understood by science according to causal mechanisms, it is, nevertheless, within the domain of God's providence.

Within the domain of nature there are two sorts of substances: mind and body. Because these are substances, they are utterly distinct and independent. One immediate advantage of this 'Cartesian dualism' is that the science of minds and the science of physical bodies (like theology and science) do not and cannot contradict one another. There is a science of the self and a science of physics, and there is no reason to suppose that science will deny the freedom of the self anymore than there is reason to fear that science will ultimately conflict with theology. What is true of physical bodies is not what is true of minds, and vice versa. Bodies may be wholly constrained by the laws of physics, but minds are free.

What *is* substance, according to Descartes? He delineates three different kinds:

On Substance
By René Descartes

Extension in length, breadth, and depth constitutes the nature of corporeal substance; and thought constitutes the nature of thinking substance.

Principle LI

What substance is, and that it is a name which we cannot attribute in the same sense to God and to His creatures.

As regards these matters which we consider as being things or modes of things, it is necessary that we should examine them here one by one. By substance, we can understand nothing else than a thing which so exists that it needs no other thing in order to exist. And in fact only one single substance can be understood which clearly needs nothing else, namely, God. We perceive that all other things can exist only by the help of the concourse of God. That is why the word substance does not pertain *univoce* to God and to other things, as they say in the Schools, that is, no common signification for this appellation which will apply equally to God and to them can be distinctly understood.

Principle LII

That it may be attributed univocally to the soul and to body, and how we know substance.

Created substances, however, whether corporeal or thinking, may be conceived under this common concept; for they are things which need only the concurrence of God in order to exist. But yet substance cannot be first discovered merely from the fact that it is a thing that exists, for that fact alone is not observed by us. We may, however, easily discover it by means of any one of its attributes because it is a common notion that nothing is possessed of no attributes, properties, or qualities. For this reason, when we perceive any attribute, we therefore conclude that some existing thing or substance to which it may be attributed, is necessarily present.

Principle LIII

That each substance has a principal attribute, and that the attribute of the mind is thought, while that of body is extension.

But although any one attribute is sufficient to give us a knowledge of substance, there is always one principal property of substance which constitutes its nature and essence, and on which all the others depend. Thus extension in length, breadth, and depth constitutes the nature of corporeal substance; and thought constitutes the nature of thinking substance. For all else that may be attributed to body presupposes extension, and is but a mode of this extended thing; as everything that we find in mind is but so many diverse forms of thinking. Thus, for example, we cannot conceive figure but as an extended thing, nor movement but as in an extended space; so imagination, feeling, and will only exist in a thinking thing. But, on the other hand, we can conceive extension without figure or action, and thinking without imagination or sensation, and so on with the rest; as is quite clear to anyone who attends to the matter.

This is to say, following Aristotle, everything is either a substance or an attribute of a substance, and a substance (as opposed to an attribute) can be thought of independently and can exist independently. Strictly speaking, this is true only of God. But we can also so define physical and mental substances. What defines physical substance, Descartes tells us, is its *extension in space*. Mind, by contrast, is unextended; that is, a thought does not have (in the sense that a wooden box has) a location in the physical dimensions of space.

Principle LIV

That the nature of body consists . . . in . . . extension alone.

The nature of matter or of body in its universal aspect does not consist in its being hard, or heavy, or coloured, or one that affects our senses in some other way, but solely in the fact that it is a substance extended in length, breadth, and depth. . . . If, whenever we moved our hands in some direction, all the bodies in that part retreated with the same velocity as our hands approached them, we should never feel hardness; and yet we have no reason to believe that the bodies which recede in this way would on this account lose what makes them bodies. It follows from this that the nature of body does not consist in hardness. The same reason shows us that weight, colour, and all the other qualities of the kind that is perceived in corporeal matter may be taken from it, it remaining meanwhile entire: it thus follows that the nature of body depends on none of these.

Principle XIII

What external place is . . .

The words place and space signify nothing different from the body which is said to be in a place, and merely designate its magnitude, figure, and situation as regards other bodies. . . . For example, if we consider a man seated at the stern of a vessel when it is carried out to sea, he may be said to be in one place if we regard the parts of the vessel . . . : and yet he will be found continually to change his position, if regard be paid to the neighbouring shores. . . . But if at length we are persuaded that there are no points in the universe that are really immovable, as will presently be shown to be probable, we shall conclude that there is nothing that has a permanent place except in so far as it is fixed by our thought.

Although physical nature is ruled by mechanical, causal laws, mental substance (the mind, the self) is defined by its freedom.

Principle XXXIX

That freedom of the will is self-evident.

Finally it is so evident that we are possessed of a free will that can give or withhold its assent, that this may be counted as one of the first and most ordinary notions that are found innately in us. We had before a very clear proof of this, for at the same time as we tried to doubt all things and even supposed that He who created us employed His unlimited powers in deceiving us in every way, we perceived in ourselves a liberty such that we were able to abstain from believing what was not perfectly certain and indubitable. But that of which we could not doubt at such a time is as self-evident and clear as anything we can ever know.

But the mind not only 'wills'; it also understands. We perceive the world and come to know its objects. But since the physical world and the mind are two distinct substances, how can there be a link between the two? The answer is that we have *ideas*, which are states of mind but nevertheless represent objects in the world that are their causes. However, this raises a number of ancient and more modern problems. Descartes, like Plato and Aristotle, has far more faith in reason and its favourite methods (for example, mathematics) than he does in perception and the information gleaned from the senses. The senses can fool us, and we tend to rush to judgment prematurely on the basis of sensory experience, as Descartes explains in the following passage from *Meditations on First Philosophy*.

FREEDOM OF THE WILL

Actions undetermined by external causes, including the power of God.

From 'Meditation VI'
By René Descartes

When I feel pain in my foot, my knowledge of physics teaches me that this sensation is communicated by means of nerves dispersed through the foot, which, being extended like cords from there to the brain, when they are contracted in the foot, at the same time contract the inmost portions of the brain which is their extremity and place of origin, and then excite a certain movement which nature has established in order to cause the mind to be affected by a sensation of pain represented as existing in the foot. But because these nerves must pass through the tibia, the thigh, the loins, the back, and the neck, in order to reach from the leg to the brain, it may happen that although their extremities which are in the foot are not affected, but only certain ones of their intervening parts, this action will excite the same movement in the brain that might have been excited there by a hurt received in the foot, in consequence of which the mind will necessarily feel in the foot the same pain as if it had received a hurt. And the same holds good of all the other perceptions of our senses.

* * *

From this it is quite clear that, notwithstanding the supreme goodness of God, the nature of man, inasmuch as it is composed of mind and body, cannot be otherwise than sometimes a source of deception.

But there is another source of ideas in addition to those caused in us by perception. There are also *innate* ideas, those implanted in us by God. Because of innate ideas we can know certain propositions to be true *for certain* (for example, the propositions of geometry, as Plato also had argued). It is because of innate ideas that we are able to *reason* and, in particular, to do philosophy, to know God, to know universal truths. But even here a dramatic difference must be noted between Descartes and his ancient predecessors. Plato and Aristotle would have claimed to know reality itself (whether this consisted of Forms or essences). But Descartes ultimately claims that we know only the ideas. There is always that gap between the mind and the world that the ancients never allowed and never entertained. Thus the doctrine of innate ideas might be said to play an even more essential role in Descartes' philosophy than in Plato's. Nevertheless, in his time Descartes was accused by the Roman Catholic Church of overreaching our claim to knowledge: His claim that the human mind has access to the truth through innate ideas was a challenge to the Church's claim to being the sole authority in all ultimate matters.

The most difficult problem facing Descartes' philosophy, however, was the relationship between the various substances. How could God create a substance if that so-called substance were then dependent on God? For example, how could one substance interact with another as physical objects must do if they are to cause in us a perception? In general, how do the mind and the body interact, as surely they must, on Descartes' account? By definition substances are distinct and independent; interaction would seem to be interdependence and not logically possible. These are the questions that most bothered Spinoza and Leibniz—the questions that would define much of philosophy for years to come.

With the rise of modern science, it became the generally accepted view that the universe was a giant machine, perhaps set up by God, but in any case a well-coordinated and predictable mechanism. Isaac Newton's discovery of the causal laws of motion and gravity only brought to a climax a scientific worldview that had been in the making for centuries. And though ancient animism was still alive and belief in God and spirituality was still virtually universal, the modern mechanical view of reality was an absolutely unavoidable consideration for any metaphysician.

Both Spinoza and Leibniz fully appreciated this modern scientific view, although they interpreted it in very different way. They were both religious men. (Spinoza, ironically, was branded an atheist and his philosophy banned from most of Europe.) They both accepted Descartes' 'rationalist', deductive method and both developed their thinking along the lines of a geometrical system. They both began by considering the concept of substance. Yet

Spinoza emerged as a monist, Leibniz as a pluralist. In viewing their impressive systems of thought, it is important to keep in mind the long history we have quickly reviewed, the powerful influences of Christianity and science, and, most importantly, the various meta-physical problems to which we were introduced earlier in this chapter.

- What are the similarities between Cartesian dualism and Plato's view of reality?
- Do we perceive substances, according to Descartes? If not, what do we perceive?
- Why does Descartes think that the body is a source of deception? Give evidence from your own experience that supports his claim.

---

2. Benedictus de Spinoza

Spinoza was an avid political reformer, particularly on the issue of religious toleration, yet many of his ideas were deemed heretical in his own time. His major work, *Ethics* (which, as you will see, is much more than a study in ethics), was his most forceful contribution to the issue of tolerance. It is also one of the few modern works that is accepted as an unqualified classic by virtually everyone in philosophy. In this work, Spinoza introduced a shockingly radical reinter-pretation of God and His relation to the universe. He also gave an equally shocking theory of our roles in the universe. So, while you are attempting to comprehend the difficult statements and proofs about 'substance' that follow, keep your mind open for the dramatic changes in the way Spinoza teaches us to look at our world and for his radical rethinking of Judaism.

Spinoza begins with a set of definitions:

From *Ethics*
By Benedictus de Spinoza

Everything which exists, exists either in itself or in something else.

Definitions

I. By that which is *self-caused*, I mean that of which the essence involves existence, or that of which the nature is only conceivable as existent.

II. A thing is called *finite after its kind*, when it can be limited by another thing of the same nature; for instance, a body is called finite because we always conceive another greater body. So, also, a thought is limited by another thought, but a body is not limited by thought, nor a thought by body.

III. By *substance*, I mean that which is in itself, and is conceived through itself: in other words, that of which a conception can be formed in-dependently of any other conception.

IV. By *attribute*, I mean that which the intellect perceives as constituting the essence of substance.

V. By *mode*, I mean the modifications of sub-stance, or that which exists in, and is con-ceived through, something other than itself.

VI. By *God*, I mean a being absolutely infinite—that is, a substance consisting in infinite at-tributes, in which each expresses eternal and infinite essentiality.

VII. That thing is called *free*, which exists solely by the necessity of its own nature, and of which the action is determined by itself alone. On the other hand, that thing is necessary, or rather constrained, which is determined by something external to itself to a fixed and def-inite method of existence or action.

VIII. By *eternity*, I mean existence itself, in so far as it is conceived necessarily to follow solely from the definition of that which is eternal.

These definitions sound much more forbidding than they really are. Notice first how many of these terms and definitions are familiar to us from Aristotle: for example, the def-inition of substance as the basic 'stuff' that has various properties but is dependent only on itself and can be thought of without thinking of anything else. **Attributes** and **modes**, on the other hand, are properties: attributes consist of essential characteristics of a substance; modes are modifications of attributes. (For example, having a body is an attribute of substance; being blond and blue-eyed are merely modes.) The self-caused, or the **cause-of-it-self**, is like Aristotle's prime mover, but with some very important differences. Spinoza's 'mover' turns out to be identical to the universe, and Spinoza's 'God' is much more than 'thought thinking itself', as in Aristotle. But the basic starting point of the entire system, as summarized in these definitions and axioms, is the Aristotelian notion of substance. Like the ancient metaphysicians, Spinoza insists that whatever really exists, exists eternally (Definition VIII). But that also means that *there can be no Creation and no Creator*!

As in geometry, the definitions are followed by a set of *axioms*, that is, principles that are so obvious that they need no defence. In plane geometry, such an axiom would be 'the shortest distance between two points is a straight line'. Spinoza's axioms may not seem quite so obvious at first glance, partly because of the unfamiliarity of his metaphysical terminology.

Axioms

I.   Everything which exists, exists either in itself or in something else.

II. That which cannot be conceived through anything else must be conceived through itself.

III. From a given definite cause an effect necessarily follows, and, on the other hand, if no definite cause be granted, it is impossible that an effect can follow.

IV. The knowledge of an effect depends on and involves the knowledge of a cause.

V.   Things which have nothing in common cannot be understood, the one by means of the other; the conception of one does not involve the conception of the other.

VI. A true idea must correspond with its ideate or object.

VII. If a thing can be conceived as non-existing, its essence does not involve existence.

You can see that the axioms follow approximately the same sequence as the definitions, and the axioms in most cases are based on the definitions, although they do not strictly follow from them. For example, Axiom I, like Definition I, concerns the idea that everything has an explanation. Definition I, although stated in terms of 'cause' ('self-caused'), concerns that which must exist if it can just be thought of. Axiom I says that everything must either be explainable through itself (that is, 'self-caused') or through something else.

Similarly, Definition II uses a technical term ('finite after its kind') to talk about things that can be explained only by reference to something greater, while Axiom II says that anything that cannot be so explained must be explained simply in terms of itself ('self-caused' again). Axioms III and IV outline the basic principles of cause and effect; that is, that a cause makes its effect happen necessarily, and without the cause, there would be no effect, and that the knowledge of the effect depends on knowing the cause. (These two principles have had a long and important history in both metaphysics and theories of science and knowledge. They will play a key role in Spinoza's theory of determinism [the idea that everything happens necessarily because of its causes] and in 'deterministic' theories generally, which will be discussed in Chapter 5.) Axioms V–VII return to the central theme of explanation begun in Axioms I and II; Axiom V insists that one thing can be explained in terms of another only if they have something in common. Thus you explain one physical event in terms of another physical event (since they have in common certain physical properties). Axiom VI repeats the important assumption we made explicit at the end of the introduction to this section on modern metaphysics, namely, that our ideas are capable of grasping reality. (This axiom also states a seemingly innocent theory of truth, often called 'the correspondence theory of truth,' which says that 'a true idea corresponds with some actual fact [*ideate* or *object*] in the world'.) Axiom VII returns to the idea of essence involving existence, in other words, that which is self-caused, or substance or God. Axiom VII is stated negatively, however, and says that if we can think of something as not existing (for example, we can imagine what it would be like to live in a world without freeways, or without stars, or even without other people), then 'its essence does not involve existence'. That is, existing is not one of its essential characteristics and it is not 'self-caused'.

The general theme of the axioms is that everything has an explanation for its existence, either by reference to something else or because it is 'self-caused' or self-explanatory, that is, its 'essence involves its existence' or it is entirely 'in itself, and is conceived through itself'. This last phrase is from the definition of 'substance' (Def. III), so you can see how, even in his axioms and definitions, Spinoza is setting up his main thesis—that there can only be one substance.

Starting with these definitions and axioms, which he takes to be unobjectionable, Spinoza begins the 'proofs' of his 'propositions', which follow like the theorems of Euclidean geometry from the definitions of terms such as 'line', 'point', and 'parallel'. Again, these proofs look forbidding, but their philosophical relevance should be clear.

Propositions

PROP. I. *Substance is by nature prior to its modifications.*

Proof.—This is clear from Def. iii. and v.

PROP. II. *Two substances, whose attributes are different, have nothing in common.*

Proof.—Also evident from Def. iii. For each must exist in itself, and be conceived through itself; in other words, the conception of one does not imply the conception of the other.

PROP. III. *Things which have nothing in common cannot be one the cause of the other.*

Proof.—If they have nothing in common, it follows that one cannot be apprehended by means of the other (Ax. v.), and, therefore, one cannot be the cause of the other (Ax. iv.). *Q.E.D.* [Latin, *quod erat demonstrandum*, a phrase used in traditional logic meaning 'thus it is proven'.]

PROP. IV. *Two or more distinct things are distinguished one from the other either by the difference of the attributes of the substances, or by the difference of their modifications.*

Proof.—Everything which exists, exists either in itself or in something else (Ax. i.),—that is (by Def. iii. and v.), nothing is granted in addition to the understanding, except substance and its modifications. Nothing is, therefore, given besides the understanding, by which several things may be distinguished one from the other, except the substances, or, in other words (see Ax. iv.), their attributes and modifications. *Q.E.D.*

PROP. V. *There cannot exist in the universe two or more substances having the same nature or attribute.*

Proof.—If several distinct substances be granted, they must be distinguished one from the other, either by the difference of their attributes, or by the difference of their modifications (Prop. iv.). If only by the difference of their attributes, it will be granted that there cannot be more than one with an identical attribute. If by the difference of their modifications—as substance is naturally prior to its modifications (Prop. i.),—it follows that setting the modifications aside, and considering substance in itself, that is truly (Def. iii. and vi.), there cannot be conceived one substance different from another,—that is (by Prop. iv.), there cannot be granted several substances, but one substance only. *Q.E.D.*

PROP. VI. *One substance cannot be produced by another substance.*

Proof.—It is impossible that there should be in the universe two substances with an identical attribute, *i.e.*, which have anything common to them both (Prop. ii.), and, therefore (Prop. iii.), one cannot be the cause of another, neither can one be produced by the other. *Q.E.D.*

So far, the main point is quite simple: if there is more than one substance, the substances could have no possible relation to each other. Therefore, by a kind of *reductio ad absurdum* argument, there can only be one substance. In the propositions that follow (and especially the note to Prop. VIII) this is demonstrated again:

PROP. VII. *Existence belongs to the nature of substance.*
Proof.—Substance cannot be produced by anything external (Corollary, Prop. vi.), it must, therefore, be its own cause—that is, its essence necessarily involves existence, or existence belongs to its nature.

PROP. VIII. *Every substance is necessarily infinite.*
Proof.—There can only be one substance with an identical attribute, and existence follows from its nature (Prop. vii.); its nature, therefore, involves existence, either as finite or infinite. It does not exist as finite, for (by Def. ii.) it would then be limited by something else of the same kind, which would also necessarily exist (Prop. vii.); and there would be two substances with an identical attribute, which is absurd (Prop. v.). It therefore exists as infinite. *Q.E.D.*

Note.—No doubt it will be difficult for those who think about things loosely, and have not been accustomed to know them by their primary causes, to comprehend the demonstration of Prop. vii.: for such persons make no distinction between the modifications of substances and the substances themselves, and are ignorant of the manner in which things are produced; hence they attribute to substances the beginning which they observe in natural objects. Those who are ignorant of true causes, make complete confusion—think that trees might talk just as well as men—that men might be formed from stones as well as from seed; and imagine that any form might be changed into any other. So, also, those who confuse the two natures, divine and human, readily attribute human passions to the deity, especially so long as they do not know how passions originate in the mind. But, if people would consider the nature of substance, they would have no doubt about the truth of Prop. vii. In fact, this proposition would be a universal axiom, and accounted a truism. For, by substance, would be understood that which is in itself, and is conceived through itself—that is, something of which the conception requires not the conception of anything else; whereas modifications exist in something external to themselves, and a conception of them is formed by means of a conception of the thing in which they exist. Therefore, we may have true ideas of non-existent modifications; for, although they may have no *actual* existence apart from the conceiving intellect, yet their essence is so involved in something external to themselves that they may through it be conceived. Whereas the only truth substances can have, external to the intellect, must consist in their existence, because they are conceived through themselves. Therefore, for a person to say that he has a clear and distinct—that is, a true—idea of a substance, but that he is not sure whether such substance exists, would be the same as if he said that he had a true idea, but was not sure whether or not it was false (a little consideration will make this plain); or if anyone affirmed that substance is created, it would be the same as saying that a false idea was true—in short, the height of absurdity. It must, then, necessarily be admitted that the existence of substance as its essence is an eternal truth. And we can hence conclude by another process of reasoning—that there is but one such substance.

This last phrase summarizes the key doctrine of the entire *Ethics*, that there can be but one substance. The argument in this note, which insists that the essence of substance includes its existence, was a very popular argument throughout the Middle Ages. It means, quite simply, that if you can even imagine something whose essence includes existence, then you know that thing necessarily exists. In a further digression (yet it is the digressions that often contain the most philosophy), Spinoza adopts Aristotle's insistence (see p. 80) that everything (or every event) must have its cause:

There is necessarily for each individual existent thing a cause why it should exist.

This cause of existence must either be contained in the nature and definition of the thing defined, or must be postulated apart from such definition.

Such an assertion gives Aristotle the basis for his 'prime mover' argument. But Spinoza, unlike Aristotle, has no qualms about the idea of an 'infinite regress'; in his view, the universe extends back in time forever, has always existed, and at no time ever came into existence.

What then follows is the working-out of the notion that there is one substance:

PROP. IX. *The more reality or being a thing has, the greater the number of its attributes* (Def. iv.).

PROP. X. *Each particular attribute of the one substance must be conceived through itself.*

Proof.—An attribute is that which the intellect perceives of substance, as constituting its essence (Def. iv.), and, therefore, must be conceived through itself (Def. iii.). *Q.E.D.*

Spinoza goes on to explain that, although we might think of different attributes separately (for example, think of minds and bodies as totally different from each other), we must not conclude that they are different substances. They are rather separate properties of one and the same substance. He then concludes:

Consequently it is abundantly clear, that an absolutely infinite being must necessarily be defined as consisting in infinite attributes, each of which expresses a certain eternal and infinite essence.

If anyone now ask, by what sign shall he be able to distinguish different substances, let him read the following propositions, which show that there is but one substance in the universe, and that it is absolutely infinite, wherefore such a sign would be sought for in vain.

Now this looks complicated, but we can appreciate its straightforward significance by looking at it through our earlier questions in ontology and cosmology (p. 60): first, 'How many substances does Spinoza say that there are (and must be)?' Only one—he is a monist, like the earliest pre-Socratics. Descartes, Spinoza's immediate predecessor, had argued that there are three kinds of substance: bodies, minds, and God. Spinoza, however, argues that the very definition of substance makes it necessary that there be only one substance and that bodies and minds are attributes of this one substance, not substances themselves.

So the answer to our second ontological question, 'What kind of substances?' is 'one infinite substance', the full nature of which we cannot know. But at least we know two of its properties, namely body and mind. Now notice that this gets around a problem that will plague Descartes (see Chapter 4): How can different substances, which by definition are independent, interact with one another (our fourth question)? If mind and body are separate substances, then how can they come together to form a person? For Spinoza, since there is only one substance, this problem does not arise. With regard to our third question, 'How do we distinguish different things (attributes, bodies, and minds)?' Spinoza's answer is fantastic; there is ultimately only one body, namely the physical universe, and one mind, namely all of the thinking in the universe (which in turn are different attributes of the one substance). This means that distinctions between our bodies ('my' body and 'your' body) and between our bodies and the rest of the physical universe are ultimately unwarranted, a humanistic pretension that has no basis in reality. But even more surprising is the idea that there is but a single mind and that our individual minds are somehow only 'part of it' (that is, particular modes) but not individual minds at all! Your pride in your 'individuality', therefore, has no foundation in reality. You are only a part of that one cosmic substance, the universe.

But the universe is also God. Here is where the innocent-looking obscurity of Spinoza's system becomes the heresy that was banned throughout Europe. By Proposition X, Spinoza has proved that God, substance, and the cause-of-itself are all identical. In the next few propositions, he proves that God necessarily exists (we shall see similar proofs in Chapter 2). Then, Proposition XIV: '*Besides God, no substance can be granted or conceived.*' This means that God and the universe are one and the same. This position, called pantheism (literally, 'everything is God'), was considered sacrilege, even in liberal Amsterdam. It means, against all traditional Judeo-Christian teachings, that God has no existence independent of the universe and that He therefore cannot be its Creator. Look again at the explanation to Definition VIII and then at Proposition XV and those that follow:

PROP. XV. *Whatsoever is, is in God, and without God nothing can be, or be conceived.*

PROP. XVI. *From the necessity of the divine nature must follow an infinite number of things in infinite ways—that is, all things which can fall within the sphere of infinite intellect.*

PROP. XVII. *God acts solely by the laws of his own nature, and is not constrained by anyone.*

PROP. XVIII. *God is the indwelling and not the transient cause of all things.*

PROP. XIX. *God, and all the attributes of God, are eternal.*

PROP. XX. *The existence of God and his essence are one and the same.*

PROP. XXI. *All things which follow from the absolute nature of any attribute of God must always exist and be infinite, or, in other words, are eternal and infinite through the said attribute.*

PROP. XXII. *Whatever follows from any attribute of God, in so far as it is modified by a modification, which exists necessarily and as infinite, through the said attribute, must also exist necessarily and as infinite.*

PROP. XXIII. *Every mode which exists both necessarily and as infinite must necessarily follow either from the absolute nature of some attribute of God, or from an attribute modified by a modification which exists necessarily and as infinite.*

PROP. XXIV. *The essence of things produced by God does not involve existence.*

PROP. XXV. *God is the efficient cause not only of the existence of things, but also of their essence.*

Yes, Spinoza believes in God. But God is nothing other than the universe. He has few of the characteristics traditionally attributed to Him and worshipped in Him. For example, Spinoza goes on to argue, on the basis of what he has said already, that God has no will, that He doesn't do anything, and, ultimately, He doesn't care about anything either, including humanity. Here is a scientific worldview that is so unrelenting that even Newton himself would be shocked by it. This does not mean that Spinoza is a materialist; quite to the contrary, the importance of his constant insistence upon 'the infinite attributes of God', of which we are capable of knowing only two (could you imagine what some of the others might be like?), is to say that God has not only physical existence but mental existence as well.

But where the scientific outlook becomes most dramatic is in Spinoza's defence of the doctrine we shall call **determinism**, the thesis that every event in the universe necessarily occurs as the result of its cause. The ultimate cause is God, which is to say, the universe itself. Once again, the terms come from Aristotle, but it is therefore important to remind ourselves that Spinoza does not believe—with either Aristotle or Christendom—that the universe has any purpose whatsoever. Nor does he believe that the universe or God has any beginning or end, thus answering our two sets of cosmological questions with a single necessary truth, once again, derived directly from the definition of substance.

The ultimate meaning of Spinoza's arguments for determinism is that no action, whether of man or God, is ever free. Everything in the universe, according to Spinoza, is exactly as it must be; the universe couldn't be any other way. Nothing is so pointless as struggling against a universe in which everything, including our own natures and actions, is already determined.

PROP. XXVI. *A thing which is conditioned to act in a particular manner has necessarily been thus conditioned by God; and that which has not been conditioned by God cannot condition itself to act.*

PROP. XXVII. *A thing, which has been conditioned by God to act in a particular way, cannot render itself unconditioned.*

PROP. XXVIII. *Every individual thing, or everything which is finite and has a conditioned existence, cannot exist or be conditioned to act, unless it be conditioned for existence and action by a cause other than itself, which also is finite and has a conditioned existence; and likewise this cause cannot in its turn exist or be conditioned to act, unless it be conditioned for existence and action by another cause, which also is finite and has a conditioned existence, and so on to infinity.*

PROP. XXIX. *Nothing in the universe is contingent, but all things are conditioned to exist and operate in a particular manner by the necessity of the divine nature.*[10]

PROP. XXX. *Intellect, in function finite, or in function infinite, must comprehend the attributes of God and the modifications of God, and nothing else.*

PROP. XXXI. *The intellect in function, whether finite or infinite, as will, desire, love, & c., should be referred to passive nature and not to active nature.*

PROP. XXXII. *Will cannot be called a free cause, but only a necessary cause.*

PROP. XXXIII. *Things could not have been brought into being by God in any manner or in any order different from that which has in fact obtained. [God is determined too.]*

PROP. XXXIV. *God's power is identical with his essence.*

PROP. XXXV. *Whatsoever we conceive to be in the power of God, necessarily exists.*

PROP. XXXVI. *There is no cause from whose nature some effect does not follow.*

Part II of the *Ethics* discusses 'the nature and origin of the mind'. It begins with a further set of definitions and axioms, most importantly, the definition of body as '**extended** thing', that is, extended in space (which Spinoza got directly from Descartes and the medieval philosophers) and idea, 'the mental conception which is formed by the mind as a thinking thing'. Mind, unlike body, is defined as **unextended** (that is, it has no spatial dimensions). It is in this part that Spinoza argues those surprising doctrines that we have already summarized: Mind and body are each one of an infinite number of attributes of God, not substance themselves (as they were for Descartes), and our individual minds are really indistinguishable modifications of the one Great Mind of the One Substance. And Spinoza joins with all of his metaphysical colleagues in insisting that the order and connection of ideas is the same as the order and connection of things (Prop. VII). Here again is Spinoza's affirmation of his confidence in thought to grasp reality.

The upshot of Part II, and the subject that dominates the *Ethics* for the remaining three parts, is Spinoza's determinism.

PROP. XLVIII. *In the mind there is no absolute or free will; but the mind is determined to wish this or that by a cause, which has been determined by another cause, and this last by another cause, and so on to infinity.*

Spinoza has none of Aristotle's fears of an 'infinite regress', and if he believes in a 'cause-of-itself', it is not the same as a 'first cause', for there is no such thing in Spinoza's worldview. We shall talk more about this 'free will' and 'determinism' problem in Chapter 5; but it is worth noting, as a way of summing up, Spinoza's drastic answer to the problem. As an unyielding determinist, he rejects every attempt to save some space for freedom of human action. But he assures us that we can, with heroic effort (Prop. XLVII), understand the nature of this determinism, and accept it gracefully. The folly is in the fighting, he tells us. The remainder of the *Ethics* is given over to the attempt to draw out the logical consequences of this stoic conclusion.

Part III is a long argument against emotions and what we would call 'emotional involvement', which he perceives as the needless cause of suffering and vice. Spinoza argues the virtues of human reason, which penetrates the useless involvements of the emotions and allows us to understand the causes of our actions and feelings. To understand an emotion, Spinoza believes, is to change and eliminate it. For example, to understand why we are angry is sufficient to let us get rid of our anger, and to realize that we are unable to change is the only freedom we can really be said to have.

What you have just seen is modern metaphysics at its most brilliant. The geometrical method, however, is no longer fashionable, and much of Spinoza's language is, to us, antiquated and unnatural. But the intricacies of his system—the way he ties so many different ideas together, the answers he gave to ancient philosophical problems, and the boldness with which he sets out a new vision of the universe—have made Spinoza's philosophy widely appreciated despite his difficult style. What you are about to read, though, is no less astonishing, no less brilliant, and its author no less remarkable a genius.

- How does Spinoza 'solve' the problem of interaction among substances?
- What is the essence of God, according to Spinoza?

---

3. Gottfried Wilhelm von Leibniz

Leibniz begins with the same technical notion of substance, but from it he draws an entirely different but equally fantastic picture of the universe. (Leibniz and Spinoza met several times and discussed these issues, but Leibniz found Spinoza's opinions too shocking and acquaintanceship with him too dangerous.) Where Spinoza's universe was mechanical and wholly dependent upon causes, Leibniz's universe is very much alive, and everything happens for a purpose (as in Aristotle's ancient teleology). The guiding principle of Leibniz's philosophy is called the '**Principle of Sufficient Reason**', which says, simply, that there must be a reason for everything. Even God, on this account, cannot act capriciously but must have a reason for whatever He has created. We shall see that this principle is among the most important guidelines to Leibniz's philosophy. From it, he develops a radical alternative to Isaac Newton's physics and a spectacularly optimistic view that, because God acts according to this principle, this world that He created must be 'the **best of all possible worlds**'.

Where Spinoza argues that there can be at most one substance, Leibniz argues that there are many. He calls them **monads**. Every monad is different from every other, and God (who is something of a supermonad and the only 'uncreated monad') has created them all. The excerpts presented here, accordingly, are from a short work (of about ninety paragraphs) called the *Monadology* ('the study of monads'), written in 1714. It is a very condensed summary of Leibniz's metaphysics:

From *Monadology*
By Gottfried Wilhelm von Leibniz

Every present state of a simple substance is a natural consequence of its preceding state, in such a way that its present is pregnant with its future.

1. The Monad, of which we will speak here, is nothing else than a simple substance, which goes to make up composites; by simple, we mean without parts.

2. There must be simple substances because there are composites; for a composite is nothing else than a collection or *aggregatum* of simple substances.

A simple substance is one that cannot be divided. The argument is curious: any 'composite' is obviously divisible. That means that every composite must be 'composed' of some simple substances that make it up. (There is a hidden infinite regress argument here: If there weren't ultimately simple substances, then we could go on dividing things forever.) But if the simple substances were extended in space, then they too would be further divisible, for anything that has length, for example, no matter how small, can be cut in two (at least in theory). Therefore, Leibniz concludes, these basic simple substances, or monads, must be immaterial and have no extension. They can have neither parts, nor extension, nor divisibility:

3. Now, where there are no constituent parts there is possible neither extension, nor form, nor divisibility.

These Monads are the true Atoms of nature, and, in fact, the Elements of things.

Here, in Leibniz's first three propositions, are the answers to our first two ontological questions: 'How many substances are there?' Many. This answer makes Leibniz a pluralist. 'What kind of substances are they?' Simple and immaterial substances, which makes Leibniz an *immaterialist*. (Don't be misled by the term '*atoms*': we are used to thinking of atoms as the smallest material substances, but Leibniz's atoms are *im*material.) Now, in three more propositions, Leibniz answers our cosmological questions: 'Are these substances eternal, or do they come into being at some time? How do they come into being? Are they destructible?'

4. This dissolution, therefore, is not to be feared and there is no way conceivable by which a simple substance can perish through natural means.
5. For the same reason there is no way conceivable by which a simple substance might, through natural means, come into existence, since it cannot be formed by composition.

6. We may say then, that the existence of Monads can begin or end only all at once, that is to say, the Monad can begin only through creation and end only through annihilation. Composites, however, begin or end gradually.

Spinoza had argued that the one substance could neither be created nor destroyed; it had neither beginning nor end. Leibniz's monads can be created or destroyed, but not by any 'natural' means. They can be created or destroyed only 'all at once'. Anticipating later propositions, we can guess that Leibniz will have God create them. But notice that compounds of monads, for example, 'material objects', can be created and destroyed 'naturally'.

Now our third question, 'How do we distinguish different substances or monads?'

8. Still Monads must have some qualities, otherwise they would not even be existences. And if simple substances did not differ at all in their qualities, there would be no means of perceiving any change in things. Whatever is in a composite can come into it only through its simple elements and the Monads, if they were without qualities, since they do not differ at all in quantity, would be indistinguishable one from another. For instance, if we imagine *a plenum* or completely filled space, where each part receives only the equivalent of its own previous motion, one state of things would not be distinguishable from another.

9. Each Monad, indeed, must be different from every other. For there are never in nature two beings which are exactly alike, and in which it is not possible to find a difference either internal or based on an intrinsic property.

Only God could actually know everything about every monad in order to compare and contrast them. But even God can distinguish different monads only because they in fact have differences between them. This leads Leibniz to suggest one of his most controversial principles, the so-called 'Principle of the **Identity of Indiscernibles**': no two monads can have the same properties (Prop. 9). Why is this? According to the 'Principle of Sufficient Reason' (Prop. 32), nothing can be without good reason. Even God, therefore, would have no good reason for duplicating any monad. If two monads were identical, Leibniz argues, God could have no reason for putting one in one place and the other in another place, or for creating them both in the first place. Therefore, no two monads could be exactly alike. A strange kind of argument, but very much at the heart of Leibniz's philosophy, as we shall see.

How does a monad, which is by definition 'simple', alter or combine with other monads to form the changing and familiar universe of our experience? (Here you should be reminded of the similar problems that faced the ancient pre-Socratics and Plato.) Here is our fourth question, and the most difficult Leibniz has to answer: 'How do substances interact?' By definition, monads cannot literally 'interact'. So Leibniz's answer is extremely speculative and imaginative:

7. There is also no way of explaining how a Monad can be altered or changed in its inner being by any other created thing, since there is no possibility of transposition within it, nor can we conceive of any internal movement which can be produced, directed, increased, or diminished there within the substance, such as can take place in the case of composites where a change can occur among the parts. The Monads have no windows through which anything may come in or go out.

The problem is that different substances, by definition, are independent and cannot, therefore, have anything to do with one another. Descartes, as we shall see in Chapter 4, had a terrible time getting together his two substances of mind and body. Spinoza, as a monist, solved the problem in the simplest possible way; since there is only one substance, no question of 'interaction' is applicable. But Leibniz is a pluralist; there are many substances. They cannot interact as such. They cannot even perceive each other in the usual sense. They 'have no windows', in his peculiar but now famous expression; 'nothing can come in or go out'. Unlike the ancient (and modern) materialist atomists, Leibniz cannot have his monads simply combine and recombine to form new compounds in any usual sense. They cannot, in Leibniz's words, 'be altered or changed in [their] inner being by any other created thing'. So, how do monads change? They must have all changes already created (by God) within themselves.

Remember the animism that was so prevalent in the ancient Greek philosophers. For them, the phenomenon of life was the model for metaphysics; the idea of Newtonian mechanics would have been incomprehensible to them. Leibniz, we may now say, was vehemently anti-Newton. He was, we may also say, one of the outstanding modern animists. A monad is as different as can be from a Newtonian material atom; a monad is alive, and its changes come from within, never from without. (Except, that is, for its initial creation.) Think of a monad as a living being, 'programmed' with all of the information and experiences it needs to develop in a certain way, like an acorn developing into an oak tree. Thus the changes in the monad are all internal, programmed by God at the creation. Now keep in mind that a monad is immaterial, and so its 'growth' cannot be thought of as a development in the physical world. The growth too, therefore, must be internal, and the apparent interaction between monads must really be changes in the perceptions of the monads themselves.

10. I assume it as admitted that every created being, and consequently the created Monad, is subject to change, and indeed that this change is continuous in each.

11. It follows from what has just been said, that the natural changes of the Monad come from an internal principle, because an external cause can have no influence upon its inner being.

12. Now besides this principle of change there must also be in the Monad a manifoldness which changes. This manifoldness constitutes, so to speak, the specific nature and the variety of the simple substances.

13. This manifoldness must involve a multiplicity in the unity or in that which is simple. For since every natural change takes place by degrees, there must be something which changes and something which remains unchanged, and consequently there must be in the simple substance a plurality of conditions and relations, even though it has no parts.

14. The passing condition which involves and represents a multiplicity in the unity, or in the simple substance, is nothing else than what is called Perception. This should be carefully distinguished from Consciousness.

Leibniz argues that what we are really describing when, for example, we talk about a squirrel climbing a particular tree at a particular moment in time is ourselves. The perception of the squirrel is a permanent part of one unchanging monad—our perception as a whole. The apparent differences between parts of a monad are really changes in perception. Leibniz is arguing that the sense in which material things seem to exist in space is as different perceptions or experiences of a perceiving monad. What is ultimately real, therefore, is the perceiving monad. Perceptions change, within each monad, to create the appearance of a moving and changing material world. Notice that Leibniz carefully distinguishes 'Perception' from what he calls 'Consciousness'. Perception is experience, in general, and is present, in some degree, in every monad. Consciousness, on the other hand, is a very special kind of experience, reflective and articulate, and is to be found only in a few monads. (With this distinction, Leibniz precociously introduces the concept of 'the unconscious' into German philosophy two hundred years before Freud.)

Here is the attack on Newton's more materialist view of the universe. Such a view, Leibniz complains, cannot account for experience (perception), in other words, the immaterial aspects of the universe.

17. It must be confessed, however, that Perception, and that which depends upon it, are inexplicable by mechanical causes, that is to say, by figures and motions. Supposing that there were a machine whose structure produced thought, sensation, and perception, we could conceive of it as increased in size with the same proportions until one was able to enter into its interior, as he would into a mill. Now, on going into it he would find only pieces working upon one another, but never would he find anything to explain Perception.

   It is accordingly in the simple substance, and not in the composite nor in a machine that the Perception is to be sought. Furthermore, there is nothing besides perceptions and their changes to be found in the simple substance. And it is in these alone that all the internal activities of the simple substance can consist.

18. All simple substances or created Monads may be called Entelechies, because they have in themselves a certain perfection. There is in them a sufficiency which makes them the source of their internal activities, and renders them, so to speak, incorporeal Automatons. [In other words, every monad is alive, to a certain extent.]

19. If we wish to designate as soul everything which has perceptions and desires in the general sense

(Continued)

that I have just explained, all simple substances or created Monads could be called souls. But since feeling is something more than a mere perception I think that the general name of Monad or Entelechy should suffice for simple substances which have only perception, while we may reserve the term Soul for those whose perception is more distinct and is accompanied by memory. [Again, Leibniz insists that 'Perception' is most primitive and is common to all monads.]

20. We experience in ourselves a state where we remember nothing and where we have no distinct perception, as in periods of fainting, or when we are overcome by a profound, dreamless sleep. In such a state the soul does not sensibly differ at all from a simple Monad. As this state, however, is not permanent and the soul can recover from it, the soul is something more.

21. Nevertheless it does not follow at all that the simple substance is in such a state without perception. This is so because of the reasons given above; for it cannot perish, nor on the other hand would it exist without some affection and the affection is nothing else than its perception. When, however, there are a great number of weak perceptions where nothing stands out distinctively, we are stunned; as when one turns around and around in the same direction, a dizziness comes on, which makes him swoon and makes him able to distinguish nothing. Among animals, death can occasion this state for quite a period.

22. Every present state of a simple substance is a natural consequence of its preceding state, in such a way that its present is pregnant with its future. [Here is Leibniz's version of the thesis that one cause necessarily follows another.]

23. Therefore, since on awakening after a period of unconsciousness we become conscious of our perceptions, we must, without having been conscious of them, have had perceptions immediately before; for one perception can come in a natural way only from another perception, just as a motion can come in a natural way only from a motion.

* * *

29. It is the knowledge of eternal and necessary truths that distinguishes us from mere animals and gives us reason and the sciences, thus raising us to a knowledge of ourselves and of God. This is what is called in us the Rational Soul or the Mind.

30. It is also through the knowledge of necessary truths and through abstractions from them that we come to perform Reflective Acts, which cause us to think of what is called the I, and to decide that this or that is within us. It is thus, that in thinking upon ourselves we think of *being*, of *substance*, of the *simple* and *composite*, of a *material* thing and of *God* himself, conceiving that what is limited in us is in him without limits. These Reflective Acts furnish the principal objects of our reasonings.

As we have seen, the answer to our fourth question is, 'Monads don't interact'. Each is locked into itself and contains within itself its own view of the universe as a whole.

56. Now this interconnection, relationship, or this adaptation of all things to each particular one, and of each one to all the rest, brings it about that every simple substance has relations which express all the others and that it is consequently a perpetual living mirror of the universe.

57. And as the same city regarded from different sides appears entirely different, and is, as it were multiplied respectively, so, because of the infinite number of simple substances, there are a similar infinite number of universes which are, nevertheless, only the aspects of a single one as seen from the special point of view of each monad.

But, of course, the perspective of any one monad is extremely one-sided and confused.

60. Besides, in what has just been seen can be seen the *a priori* reasons why things cannot be otherwise than they are. It is because God, in ordering the whole, has had regard to every part and in particular to each monad; and since the Monad is by its very nature *representative*, nothing can limit it to represent merely a part of things. It is nevertheless true that this representation is, as regards the details of the whole universe, only a confused representation, and is distinct only as regards a small part of them, that is to say, as regards those things which are nearest or greatest in relation to each Monad. If the representation were distinct as to the details of the entire universe, each Monad would be a Deity. It is not in the object represented that the Monads are limited, but in the modifications of their knowledge of the object. In a confused way they reach out to infinity or to the whole, but are limited and differentiated in the degree of their distinct perceptions.

Now Leibniz has an alternative to Newton: bodies (composite monads) only seem to interact; in fact, it all happens within each monad, programmed and created by God in '**pre-established harmony**'.

PRE-ESTABLISHED HARMONY

The belief that the order of the universe is prearranged by God.

61. In this respect composites are like simple substances, for all space is filled up; therefore, all matter is connected. And in a plenum or filled space every movement has an effect upon bodies in proportion to this distance, so that not only is every body affected by those which are in contact with it and responds in some way to whatever happens to them, but also by means of them the body responds to those bodies adjoining them, and their intercommunication reaches to any distance whatsoever. Consequently every body responds to all that happens in the universe, so that he who saw all could read in each one what is happening everywhere, and even what has happened and what will happen.

62. Thus although each created Monad represents the whole universe, it represents more distinctly the body which specially pertains to it and of which it constitutes the entelechy. And as this body expresses all the universe through the interconnection of all matter in the plenum, the soul also represents the whole universe in representing this body, which belongs to it in a particular way.

Every monad develops as a reflection of the development of all the other monads in the universe as well. Returning to our example of watching a squirrel climb around a tree, Leibniz's view is that the reality of the squirrel climbing around the tree is actually our perception of this occurrence. But you can see that this alone is not sufficient; we might simply dream or hallucinate this view, and it would then not be 'real' at all. The difference between the dream and the reality is in the changes in the other monads, for instance, the monads that constitute the squirrel and any other observers of the same scene, including God. Reality is composed of the totality of all monads, each perceiving from its own perspective (although God, Leibniz insists, perceives from all perspectives at once). The 'pre-established harmony' guarantees that all of these views from all of these perspectives are in agreement, so that our view of the squirrel, for example, is matched by the squirrel's view of us.

Returning to our fourth question, we can see how this view of the pre-established harmony between monads allows Leibniz to explain how different substances interact. Although substances, by definition, cannot interact as such, they can seem to interact if their perceptions are coordinated. Thus, the collision of two billiard balls is in fact a harmony of perceptions about the collision of two billiard balls. Two people fighting is in fact a harmony of perceptions by each of the two people (and anyone else who is watching) about those two people fighting. This explanation may seem to be extreme, but given Leibniz's conception of the universe as composed of a great number of immaterial substances, it is an explanation that is necessary for his philosophy to be consistent. It is an explanation that is also necessary, however, to enable him to reject Newton's cosmology.

The last of our initial set of questions about substance (and our second cosmological question) is, 'Are space and time themselves substances?' According to Leibniz, the answer to this question is an emphatic 'No'. It is on this question that Leibniz makes his sharpest break with Newton's physics. Are monads 'in' space? Leibniz would have said no. But he also seems to give the surprising answer that not only are monads not 'in' space (since they are immaterial), they are, strictly speaking, not 'in' time either. The monad does not change in time, but rather, time is in the monad. That is, time is a relation between experiences of the monad. It is not something independent. These views of space and time are intimately tied to Leibniz's analysis of the *seeming* 'interaction' between monads. Both are rejections of Newton's theory and an attempt to offer an alternative.

To our way of thinking, Leibniz's views seem bizarre, compared to the almost common-sense character of Newton's theory. Newton had argued that the universe was the motion of (material) atoms in empty space, acting against each other according to the laws of motion, force, and gravity that he had so elegantly formulated. But Newton's theories, which seem almost quaintly obvious to us now, contained what most people of his and Leibniz's time—including Newton himself—considered to be manifest absurdities. One such theory, relating to our fourth ontological question, was the idea of **action-at-a-distance**, the idea that one object could affect another although the two were not even in contact. (For example, the idea that the moon and the earth have gravitational attraction for each other.) Thus Leibniz's conception of windowless monads, each seeming to interact with others but in fact only developing within itself, would have seemed to his contemporaries no more absurd than Newton's view of causality. Leibniz didn't need causality; he had his 'pre-established harmony'. Newton, meanwhile, had a great deal of trouble reconciling his mechanistic theories with the traditional ideas of God and Creation, ideas which he continued to hold for the rest of his life.

The most famous disagreement between Leibniz and Newton concerns the nature of space and time, a topic that is still being debated because of the impact of Einstein's theory of relativity at the beginning of the twentieth century. Newton's mechanical theory seemed to presuppose the existence of some permanent container, namely space, in which the material atoms of his theory could mutually attract and bounce against each other. This container, which could exist independently of its contents, is called **absolute space**. In itself, this sounds entirely reasonable; we talk about things 'moving in space' and 'taking up space'. But then, can we also talk about the entire universe being 'in' space, the way a basketball can be said to be 'in' the basket? This idea has some absurd consequences that led Leibniz and many of his contemporaries to reject it. The idea that space could exist apart from all things in it, perhaps even entirely empty (or what many philosophers called the **void**), would mean that it makes sense to talk about movement or location in space even when there isn't anything in space, not even points and rulers with which to measure distances or dimensions. Bertrand Russell, one of Leibniz's most famous admirers, pointed out the absurdity of this idea by asking, 'If space is absolute, then wouldn't it make sense to suggest that the universe might have doubled in size last night?' But what would it mean to say that the universe has gotten larger? An elephant or a planet or even a galaxy can get larger, but only in comparison to some measuring stick and a frame of reference. It is only by such comparisons that such 'size' talk makes sense. But to say that the universe doubles in size is to say that our measuring stick, and we ourselves, double in size also. So all comparisons remain the same. Similarly, what would it mean to say that the universe in its entirety moved one foot to the left? All of the one-foot measurements are in the universe. There is no way to talk about the universe itself moving. On the basis of such considerations, Leibniz rejected Newton's idea of absolute space as absurd. In its place, he insisted that space is relative, that is, relative to measurements and things that are measured. There is no absolute space; there is only space relative to the various positions of the monads, that is, to observers.

The same is true of time. Newton believed in **absolute time** also, time as existing apart from anything happening 'in' it. But the same consequences follow this initially reasonable idea. If time is absolute, it seems to make sense to ask, 'When did the universe begin?' (In fact, astronomers are again asking this question.) But what could this 'when' refer to? It can't refer to any measurement in the universe (clocks, the age of rocks or stars), for it is the universe itself that is being measured, and there aren't any measures of time outside of the universe. Consequently, Leibniz rejected absolute time along with absolute space. Both are relative to the monads and have no possible existence of their own. This means, among other things, that there could be no void or empty space, nor could there be any sense of time in which literally nothing happened. Space and time, according to Leibniz, are relative to our own perceptions.

Once again we encounter an intersection between the realm of philosophy and that of science. Current physics and astronomy are still very much involved with these questions of space and time, and both alternatives, from Newton and from Leibniz, are still very much alive. Scientists still talk about the beginning of the universe, and with awesome sophistication; of course, they also talk in strictly relativistic terms, like Leibniz, but now à la Einstein. To delve into these issues any further, therefore, we should have to leave eighteenth-century metaphysics and move into twentieth- and twenty-first-century physics. Indeed, the new and sometimes strange experimental findings that continually emerge from the sciences are often relevant to philosophical debates as well. For example, late twentieth-century experiments with the speed of light have brought about startling changes in our views of space and time. One consequence of this changed view is the idea that we cannot talk intelligibly about two events happening 'at the same time' if they are a sufficiently great distance apart, say several billion light years. The discovery of radiation from outer space and the expansion of galaxies has raised old issues about creation in a new way: whether the universe was created all at once and then started to expand and change (the 'big-bang theory') or whether there is continuous creation going on even now (the 'steady-state theory'). Because of recent theories in science, philosophers are now willing to say things that would have seemed like utter nonsense to both Newton and Leibniz—for example, that 'space is curved'.

These are not issues to be settled by scientists alone, however; it is philosophical theories that give structure and meaning to the scientific experiments. But neither can philosophers simply cut themselves off from science and pretend that they can solve these problems 'just in their heads'. At the outer reaches of science, you will find philosophy, just as, at the beginnings of philosophy, you will find the unanswered problems of science.

Earlier in this chapter, we stressed the importance of a basic assumption of all metaphysics, that the universe is intelligible. In Leibniz's philosophy, this assumption is presented as one of the basic presuppositions of all thinking; again, he calls it

32. . . . the Principle of Sufficient Reason, in virtue of which we believe that no fact can be real or existing and no statement true unless it has a sufficient reason why it should be thus and not otherwise. Most frequently, however, these reasons cannot be known by us.

These reasons can, however, be known to God, who knows everything. It is on the basis of this principle, for example, that Leibniz defends the claim he made in Proposition 9, that two monads can never be identical ('the identity of indiscernibles'). The reasoning is this: Since God is the supremely rational Being (monad), He must have a reason for all that He does. But Leibniz also argues (Prop. 58) that God must have created the universe 'with the greatest possible variety together with the greatest order that may be'. Here is the reason why God would not have created any two monads alike. But the Principle of Sufficient Reason has a further implication; it also serves as a principle of divine ethics. Among the various possible worlds (that is, among the infinitely many ways in which the world might have been), God chooses the most perfect, that is, 'the best of all possible worlds'. Leibniz took this concept of 'the best of all possible worlds' very seriously, and in the next century, it was to provide a foundation for much of the optimism of the Enlightenment. And in Leibniz's own metaphysics, it provides the concluding propositions of *Monadology*, a joyous optimism that creates as close to a happy ending as one can expect to find in a serious philosophical treatise.

85. Whence it is easy to conclude that the totality of all spirits must compose the city of God, that is to say, the most perfect state that is possible under the most perfect monarch.

* * *

90. Finally, under this perfect government, there will be no good action unrewarded and no evil action unpunished; everything must turn out for the well-being of the good; that is to say, of those who are not disaffected in this great state, who, after having done their duty, trust in Providence and who love and imitate, as is meet, the Author of all Good, delighting in the contemplation of his perfections according to the nature of that genuine, pure love which finds pleasure in the happiness of those who are loved. It is for this reason that wise and virtuous persons work in behalf of everything which seems conformable to presumptive or antecedent will of God, and are, nevertheless, content with what God actually brings to pass through his secret, consequent, and determining will, recognizing that if we were able to understand sufficiently well the order of the universe, we should find that it surpasses all the desires of the wisest of us, and that it is impossible to render it better than it is, not only for all in general, but also for each one of us in particular, provided that we have the proper attachment for the author of all, not only as the Architect and the efficient cause of our being [our Creator] but also as our Lord and the Final Cause [purpose of our existence] who ought to be the whole goal of our will, and who alone can make us happy.

This theological 'happy ending' is not an afterthought for Leibniz; it is the heart of his philosophy. Like his older contemporary Spinoza, his involvement in metaphysics is ultimately a very personal concern for religion and for his own view of himself and his place in the world. From this perspective, it is revealing to see the vast differences between the two philosophers. Spinoza's view of humanity is extremely anti-individualistic, and each individual is wholly submerged in the concept of the one substance. In Leibniz, however, his pluralism reinforces the view that each individual is a world in himself or herself, and his idealism places an emphasis on mind and thought that is in sharp contrast with Spinoza's balance between thought and body (although many critics have charged Spinoza with emphasizing body to an alarming degree). Spinoza's determinism and his view that ultimately we can do nothing but understand is surely a gloomy view compared to Leibniz's happy confidence that this is the 'best of all possible worlds'. Of course, Spinoza's heretical view of God as the one substance is very different from Leibniz's more traditional and pious view.

But these considerations are far from being merely coincidental or curious implications of Descartes', Spinoza's, and Leibniz's metaphysical views. These religious concerns lie at the heart of their philosophical concerns, and one might well say that their metaphysics is constructed as an ingenious form of support for their religious convictions. Indeed, for most of the past two thousand years, and until very recently, the Judeo-Christian-Islamic religious tradition has provided much of the motivation and the structure of Western philosophy. And this brings us to the subject of our next chapter: the rich and fascinating field of the philosophy of religion.

- What does Leibniz mean by pre-established harmony and how does this notion solve the problem of interaction among substances?
- What is a monad and how do we distinguish among them? What is the 'Principle of the Identity of Indiscernibles'?
- If even God must act for a reason, as Leibniz claims, can God be said to be free? *Is* this the best of all possible worlds?

SUMMARY AND CONCLUSION

Metaphysics is the study of ultimate reality, the attempt to find out the way the world really is. The first recognized metaphysical theory in Western philosophy is Thales' suggestion that everything is ultimately made of water. After Thales, a number of schools of metaphysics suggested alternative theories, all of them depending on the speculative powers of human reason and diverging in various and important ways from 'common sense'. But these thinkers were not only the first significant Western philosophers; they were also the first theoretical scientists, anticipating in many ways some of the most sophisticated theories of contemporary physics, astronomy, and chemistry.

The first turning point in Western metaphysics came with Socrates, although Socrates himself was more interested in moral issues than in metaphysics as such. Socrates' student Plato and Plato's student Aristotle in turn became the first great systematic metaphysicians, and philosophy ever since has been deeply indebted to them. Plato introduced an elaborate theory in which ultimate reality consisted of Forms, in contrast to the particular and changing things of everyday life. To support this 'two-worlds' theory of Forms versus individual things, he offered a theory of learning, a 'theory of recollection', in which he argued that the human soul is immortal and that each of us already knows, in some sense,

what we appear to learn in our lives. Aristotle argued instead that only individual things deserve the ultimate claim to reality, for these individual things are the primary substances. Since Aristotle, metaphysicians have typically used the term *substance* as the name of the basic entities that compose reality.

The second turning point came with the rise of the 'new' science in Europe in the sixteenth and seventeenth centuries. At that time, beginning with Descartes, some of the greatest metaphysical thinkers of modern times took the concept of 'substance' and attempted to use deduction as a method for proving the ultimate nature of reality. Their answers were extremely different. For example, Spinoza argued that there can only be one substance; Leibniz argued that there are many. For Spinoza, God is identical to the universe, to the one substance; for Leibniz, God is distinct from all other substances, which He created. For Spinoza, mind and body are but two of an infinite number of attributes of God, the only two that we can know; for Leibniz, all substances are ultimately immaterial. But beneath these technical concerns is a struggle by both philosophers to answer the most important problems of human existence: the nature of God and religion, the place of human beings in the universe, and the role and foundations of science.

REVIEW QUESTIONS

1. What similarities do you find among modern philosophy (Descartes, Leibniz, Spinoza), the pre-Socratics, and Eastern thought (the Upanishads, Confucianism, Daoism, Buddhism) in their attempts to explain the ultimate reality?

2. What pre-Socratic influences can you identify in Plato? (Be specific: for example, 'Plato, like Parmenides, believes that . . .'.)

3. How do you think about metaphysical issues today? What problems are still very much alive for you?

4. Which modern theories about the nature of reality are materialist? Which are immaterialist?

5. How is Plato responding to the pre-Socratics with the theory of Forms? What is Aristotle's response to Plato's theory of Forms?

6. How would you explain the problem of substances interacting with each other? How do Descartes, Leibniz, and Spinoza solve this problem? Could any of these solutions help Plato solve the problem of participation? Are there any similarities between participation and substance interaction? Why or why not?

7. What is the value of talking about different 'possible worlds' in Leibniz? Are these literally different worlds?

8. How is metaphysics related to science? Are they competitors and rivals? Are they friends and collaborators? Or do they have nothing to do with each other?

KEY TERMS

absolute space
absolute time
action-at-a-distance
Ahura Mazda
Angra Mainyush
animism
apeiron
Asha
attribute
Becoming (in Plato)
Being (in Plato)
best of all possible
    worlds
Brahman
Buddha
cause
cause-of-itself (*causa sui*)
conceptual truth
cosmogony
cosmology
Dao
determinism

essence (or an essential
    property)
extended
extended (substance)
Form (in Plato)
Four Noble Truths
freedom of the will
Idea
idealism
Identity of Indiscernibles
immaterialism
immortality
ineffable
infinite regress
innate ideas
materialism
metaphysics
modes (in Spinoza)
monad (in Leibniz)
monism
monotheism
mysticism

naturalism
ontology
pantheism
participation
pluralism
polytheism
pre-established harmony
prime mover (in Aristotle)
Principle of Sufficient Reason
    (in Leibniz)
property
reason
sophists
Spenta Mainyush
substance
teleology (teleological)
unextended
Upanishads
void
Zend-Avesta
Zoroastrianism

FURTHER READING

On Ancient Greek Philosophy

Julia Annas, *Plato: A Very Short Introduction* (Oxford: Oxford University Press, 2003).

Jonathan Barnes, *Aristotle* (Oxford: Oxford University Press, 1982).

W.K.C. Guthrie, *The Greek Philosophers: From Thales to Aristotle* (New York: Harper & Row, 1960).

G.S. Kirk and J.E. Raven, *The Presocratic Philosophers* (Cambridge: Cambridge University Press, 1957).

A.E. Taylor, *Plato: The Man and His Work* (New York: Dial, 1936).

Nicholas P. White, *Plato on Knowledge and Reality* (Indianapolis, IN: Hackett, 1976).

On Medieval Philosophy

A. Hyman and J. Walsh, *Philosophy in the Middle Ages* (Indianapolis, IN: Hackett, 1973).

On World Philosophy

Daniel Bonevac and Stephen Phillips, eds, *Introduction to World Philosophy: A Multicultural Reader* (New York: Oxford University Press, 2009).

R. Solomon and K. Higgins, *World Philosophy* (New York: McGraw-Hill, 1995).

On Spinoza and Leibniz

Jonathan Bennett, *A Study of Spinoza's Ethics* (Indianapolis, IN: Hackett, 1989).

Stuart Hampshire, *Spinoza* (London: Penguin, 1951).

Hidé Ishiguro, *Leibniz's Philosophy of Logic and Language* (Ithaca, NY: Cornell University Press, 1972).

Robert Merrihew Adams, *Leibniz: Determinist, Theist, Idealist* (New York: Oxford University Press, 1994).

Bertrand Russell, *A Critical Exposition of the Philosophy of Leibniz* (London: George Allen and Unwin, 1937).

Roger Scruton, *Spinoza* (Oxford: Oxford University Press, 1982).

On More Recent Metaphysical Systems

Tim Crane and Katalin Farkas, eds, *Metaphysics: A Guide and an Anthology*. (New York: Oxford University Press, 2004).

Richard Gale, *Blackwell Guide to Metaphysics* (Oxford: Blackwell Press, 2002).

Peter Van Inwagen, *Metaphysics*, 2nd edn (Boulder, CO: Westview Press, 2002).

Jaegwon Kim and Ernest Sosa, eds, *A Companion to Metaphysics* (Oxford: Blackwell, 1999).

Jaegwon Kim and Ernest Sosa, eds, *Metaphysics: An Anthology* (Oxford: Blackwell, 1995).

A.O. Lovejoy, *The Great Chain of Being* (Cambridge, MA: Harvard University Press, 1936).

Ted Sider and Earl Conee, *Riddles of Existence: A Guided Tour of Metaphysics* (Oxford: Oxford University Press, 2007).

CHAPTER 2

RELIGION

As I went through the city and looked carefully at the objects of your worship,
I found among them an altar with the inscription, 'To an unknown god.'

Acts 17:23

The age-old efforts of metaphysicians to know the way the world really is have rarely been motivated by curiosity or the scientific spirit alone. Most often, metaphysics and philosophy in general have been motivated by religious devotion. The search for truth and the concern with what we can know and how we ought to behave have often been tied to concern about the nature of the divine and its relationship to us. For many thoughtful people, there is no more powerful an experience than religious experience, and they have no more important beliefs than their religious beliefs. Religion defines their lives, and their religious views define reality.

Although the issues of religion are philosophically within the domain of metaphysics, epistemology, and ethics, their importance demands special attention. They involve experiences of a kind that are not common to other ontological and cosmological concerns. Religious beliefs involve emotions that are not relevant to the technical concerns with substance and science. It is this emotional involvement in religion that has inspired some of the greatest art, the bloodiest wars, the kindest actions, and the most brilliant philosophy in history.

A. What Is Religion?

Religion has played an important role in the history of philosophy. Indeed, some scholars would claim that philosophy grew out of religion and only occasionally has turned against its religious heritage. Although religion and philosophy are intimately linked, we certainly wouldn't want to identify them. Central to both, however, is the question of religious belief. A person who believes in a single, independent Being, God, who is the Creator of the universe, is a **theist**, a believer. To refuse to believe in God—to deny that God exists—is to be an **atheist**. To suspend judgment—to neither believe in God nor disbelieve in God—is to be an **agnostic**. We will discuss some atheistic and agnostic claims, as well as several different religious traditions, later in this chapter.

Before we investigate specific religious-philosophical debates, however, let us take a look at how some philosophers have answered a preliminary question: What is religion? For the twentieth-century philosopher John Wisdom, a student of Ludwig Wittgenstein, the essential feature of religious belief is a certain 'attitude' that the religious person has toward his or her surroundings; and the gap between the religious 'attitude' and that of the philosopher or scientist interested in explanation is unbridgeable.

From 'Gods'
By John Wisdom

The one says: 'A gardener comes unseen and unheard. He is manifested only in his works with which we are all familiar.' The other says 'There is no gardener.'

Two people return to their long-neglected garden and find among the weeds a few of the old plants surprisingly vigorous. One says to the other 'It must be that a gardener has been coming and doing something about these plants.' Upon inquiry they find that no neighbour has ever seen anyone at work in their garden. The first man says to the other 'He must have worked while people slept.' The other says 'No, someone would have heard him and besides, anybody who cared about the plants would have kept down these weeds.' The first man says 'Look at the way these are arranged. There is purpose and a feeling for beauty here. I believe that someone comes, someone invisible to mortal eyes. I believe that the more carefully we look the more we shall find confirmation of this.' They examine the garden ever so carefully and sometimes they come on new things suggesting the contrary and even that a malicious person has been at work. Besides examining the garden carefully they also study what happens to gardens left without attention. Each learns all the other learns about this and about the garden. Consequently, when after all this, one says 'I still believe a gardener comes' while the other says 'I don't' their different words now reflect no difference as to what they have found in the garden, no difference as to what they would find in the garden if they looked further, and no difference about how fast untended gardens fall into disorder. At this stage, in this context, the gardener hypothesis has ceased to be experimental; the difference between one who accepts and one who rejects it is now not a matter of the one expecting something the other does not expect. What is the difference between them? The one says: 'A gardener comes unseen and unheard. He is manifested only in his works with which we are all familiar.' The other says 'There is no gardener.' And with this difference in what they say about the gardener goes a difference in how they feel toward the garden, in spite of the fact that neither expects anything of it which the other does not expect.

But is this the whole difference between them—that the one calls the garden by one name and feels one way toward it, while the other calls it by another name and feels in another way toward it? And if this is what the difference has become, then is it any longer appropriate to ask 'Which is right?' or 'Which is reasonable?'

- How would you decide whether there is a gardener or not?
- Do you think that belief is necessary for religion? If so, belief in what?
- Is the belief in God's existence the same sort of belief as the belief that it is raining outside? Do you think that there is scientific evidence for God's existence? Does there need to be?

For Wisdom, religious belief is obviously different from the scientific quest for causal explanation. Since the scientific revolution of the sixteenth to eighteenth centuries, many philosophers have tried to define religion and science in contrast to one another, and many have tried to cast their lots with science. But there is plenty of resistance to such a move. Many scientists are deeply religious people, and many religious thinkers accept the authority of science without compromising their religious **faith**. No less a scientist than Albert Einstein, for example, has argued that it is this religious awe and appreciation for the complex regularities of nature that has spawned the great efforts of science to understand it. Indeed, he says, science itself inspires a 'cosmic religious feeling'.

FAITH

The trust that a believer has in God's ultimate grace and fairness.

On the Design of the Universe
By Albert Einstein

I maintain that the cosmic religious feeling is the strongest and noblest motive for scientific research.

It is easy to see why the churches have always fought science and persecuted its devotees. On the other hand, I maintain that the cosmic religious feeling is the strongest and noblest motive for scientific research. Only those who realize the immense efforts and, above all, the devotion without which pioneer work in theoretical science cannot be achieved are able to grasp the strength of the emotion out of which alone such work, remote as it is from the immediate realities of life, can issue. What a deep conviction of the rationality of the universe and what a yearning to understand, were it but a feeble reflection of the mind revealed in this world, Kepler and Newton must have had to enable them to spend years of solitary labour in disentangling

the principles of celestial mechanics! Those whose acquaintance with scientific research is derived chiefly from its practical results easily develop a completely false notion of the mentality of the men who, surrounded by a skeptical world, have shown the way to kindred spirits scattered wide through the world and the centuries. Only one who has devoted his life to similar ends can have a vivid realization of what has inspired these men and given them the strength to remain true to their purpose in spite of countless failures. It is cosmic religious feeling that gives a man such strength. A contemporary has said, not unjustly, that in this materialistic age of ours the serious scientific workers are the only profoundly religious people.

Einstein's statement of scientific faith is particularly important in times such as our own when science and religion seem at each other's throats. Current controversies over 'Creation' versus 'evolution', for example, have made it seem as if science and religion are utterly irreconcilable, with completely opposed visions of the world. But consider the following response from Keiji Nishitani, a Japanese philosopher conversant in both Christianity and Buddhism. Nishitani claims that the distinguishing feature of religion is the 'personal/impersonal', or in other words, the deeply personal recognition that each of us must give to the existence that we share with all other things in the universe. To step outside of ourselves, to consider the world from an impersonal perspective—called 'personal **nihility**' by Nishitani—is an intimate and unique activity. But it is a necessary one. Everyone, whether consciously or unconsciously, must engage in it at some point in his or her life.

NIHILITY

'The Nothing', 'nothingness'.

From 'What Is Religion?'
By Keiji Nishitani

Religion is at all times the individual affair of each individual.

'What is religion?' we ask ourselves, or, looking at it the other way around, 'What is the purpose of religion for us? Why do we need it?' Though the question about the need for religion may be a familiar one, it already contains a problem. In one sense, for the person who poses the question, religion does not seem to be something he needs. The fact that he asks the question at all amounts to an admission that

religion has not yet become a necessity for him. In another sense, however, it is surely in the nature of religion to be necessary for just such a person. Wherever questioning individuals like this are to be found, the need for religion is there as well. In short, the relationship we have to religion is a contradictory one: those for whom religion is *not* a necessity are, for that reason, the very ones for whom religion is a necessity. There is no other thing of which the same can be said.

When asked, 'Why do we need learning and the arts?', we might try to explain in reply that such things are necessary for the advancement of mankind, for human happiness, for the cultivation of the individual, and so forth. Yet even if we can say why we need such things, this does not imply that we cannot get along without them. Somehow life would still go on. Learning and the arts may be indispensable to living well, but they are not indispensable to living. In that sense, they can be considered a kind of luxury.

Food, on the other hand, is essential to life. Nobody would turn to somebody else and ask him why he eats. Well, maybe an angel or some other celestial being who has no need to eat might ask such questions, but men do not. Religion, to judge from current conditions in which many people are in fact getting along without it, is clearly not the kind of necessity that food is. Yet this does not mean that it is merely something we need to live *well*. Religion has to do with life itself. Whether the life we are living will end up in extinction or in the attainment of eternal life is a matter of the utmost importance for life itself. In no sense is religion to be called a luxury. Indeed, this is why religion is an indispensable necessity for those very people who fail to see the need for it. Herein lies the distinctive feature of religion that sets it apart from the mere life of 'nature' and from culture. Therefore, to say that we need religion, for example, for the sake of social order, or human welfare, or public morals is a mistake, or at least a confusion of priorities. Religion must not be considered from the viewpoint of its *utility*, any more than life should. A religion concerned primarily with its own utility bears witness to its own degeneration. One can ask about the utility of things like eating for the natural life, or of things like learning and the arts for culture. In fact, in such matters the question of utility should be of constant concern. Our ordinary mode of being is restricted to these levels of natural or cultural life. But it is in breaking through that ordinary mode of being and overturning it from the ground up, in pressing us back to the elemental source of life where life itself is seen as useless, that religion becomes something we need—a *must* for human life.

Two points should be noted from what has just been said. First, religion is at all times the individual affair of each individual. This sets it apart from things like culture, which, while related to the individual, do not need to concern each individual. Accordingly, we cannot understand what religion is from the outside. The religious quest alone is the key to understanding it; there is no other way. This is the most important point to be made regarding the essence of religion.

Second, from the standpoint of the essence of religion, it is a mistake to ask, 'What is the purpose of religion for us?' and one that clearly betrays an attitude of trying to understand religion apart from the religious quest. It is a question that must be broken through by another question coming from within the person who asks it. There is no other road that can lead to an understanding of what religion is and what purpose it serves. The counterquestion that achieves this breakthrough is one that asks, 'For what purpose do I myself exist?' Of everything else we can ask its purpose for us, but not of religion. With regard to everything else we can make a *telos* of ourselves as individuals, as man, or as mankind, and evaluate those things in relation to our life and existence. We put ourselves as individuals/man/mankind at the centre and weigh the significance of everything as the *contents* of our lives as individuals/man/mankind. But religion upsets the posture from which we think of ourselves as *telos* and centre for all things. Instead, religion poses as a starting point the question: 'For what purpose do I exist?'

We become aware of religion as a need, as a must for life, only at the level of life at which everything else loses its necessity and its utility. Why do we exist at all? Is not our very existence and human life ultimately meaningless? Or, if there is a meaning or significance to it all, where do we find it? When we come to doubt the meaning of our existence in this way, when we have become a question to ourselves, the religious quest awakens within us. These questions and the quest they give rise to show up when the mode of looking at and thinking about everything in terms of how it relates to *us* is broken through, where the mode of living that puts us at the centre of everything is overturned. This is why the question of religion in the form, 'Why do we need religion?' obscures the way to its own answer from the very start. It blocks our becoming a question to ourselves.

The point at which the ordinarily necessary things of life, including learning and the arts, all lose their necessity and utility is found at those

(Continued)

times when death, nihility, or sin—or any of those situations that entail a fundamental negation of our life, existence, and ideals, that undermine the roothold of our existence and bring the meaning of life into question—become pressing personal problems for us. This can occur through an illness that brings one face-to-face with death, or through some turn of events that robs one of what had made life worth living.

* * *

Nihility refers to that which renders meaningless the meaning of life. When we become a question to ourselves and when the problem of why we exist arises, this means that nihility has emerged from the ground of our existence and that our very existence has turned into a question mark. The appearance of this nihility signals nothing less than that one's awareness of self-existence has penetrated to an extraordinary depth.

Normally we proceed through life, on and on, with our eye fixed on something or other, always caught up with something within or without ourselves. It is these engagements that prevent the deepening of awareness. They block off the way to an opening up of that horizon on which nihility appears and self-being becomes a question. This is even the case with learning and the arts and the whole range of other cultural engagements. But when this horizon does open up at the bottom of those engagements that keep life moving continually on and on, something seems to halt and linger before us. This something is the meaninglessness that lies in wait at the bottom of those very engagements that bring meaning to life. This is the point at which that sense of nihility, that sense that 'everything is the same' we find in Nietzsche and Dostoevsky, brings the restless, forward-advancing pace of life to a halt and makes it take a step back. In the Zen phrase, it 'turns the light to what is directly underfoot'.

In the forward progress of everyday life, the ground beneath our feet always falls behind as we move steadily ahead; we overlook it. Taking a step back to shed light on what is underfoot of the self—'stepping back to come to the self', as another ancient Zen phrase has it—marks a conversion in life itself. This fundamental conversion in life is occasioned by the opening up of the horizon of nihility at the ground of life. It is nothing less than a conversion from the self-centred (or man-centred) mode of being, which always asks what *use* things have for us (or for man), to an attitude that asks for what *purpose* we ourselves (or man) exist. Only when we stand at this turning point does the question 'What is religion?' really become our own.

- What does Nishitani mean when he says, '[T]hose for whom religion is *not* a necessity are, for that reason, the very ones for whom religion *is* a necessity'?

For another intriguing non-Western view on religion, we turn to the writings of Swami Vivekananda, an eloquent exponent of Hinduism who travelled widely in North America and Europe after leaving his native India in the 1890s. Well acquainted with many major faiths—Judaism, Christianity, Islam, Buddhism, and, of course, Hinduism—Vivekananda was struck not so much by their obvious differences as by their underlying similarities. Yes, he tells us, different religions have different beliefs, creeds, and dogmas; and yes, they engage in different rituals, practices, and acts. And yet all religions are expressions of the same deep impulse, the same passionate aspiration. For the heart and soul of religion, Vivekananda contends, is nothing less than freedom: freedom from the deceptions and disappointments of life, freedom from the limitations that are part of being in the world, freedom from meaningless suffering, freedom from the tyranny of Nature and her inexorable laws. Religion, in short, presents itself to us as a way out of the everyday world of illusions, flux, and half-truths, the world to which Hinduism has given the name '*maya*'.

From 'Maya and Illusion'
By Swami Vivekananda

All religions are more or less attempts to get beyond nature—the crudest or the most developed, expressed through mythology or symbology, stories of gods, angels or demons, or through stories of saints or seers, great men or prophets, or through the abstractions of philosophy—all have that one object, all are trying to get beyond these limitations. In one word, they are all struggling towards freedom. Man feels, consciously or unconsciously, that he is bound; he is not what he wants to be. It was taught to him at the very moment he began to look around. That very instant he learnt that he was bound, and he also found that there was something in him which wanted to fly beyond, where the body could not follow, but which was as yet chained down by this limitation. Even in the lowest of religious ideas, where departed ancestors and other spirits—mostly violent and cruel, lurking about the houses of their friends, fond of bloodshed and strong drink—are worshipped, even there we find that one common factor, that of freedom. The man who wants to worship the gods sees in them, above all things, greater freedom than in himself. If a door is closed, he thinks the gods can get through it, and that walls have no limitations for them. This idea of freedom increases until it comes to the ideal of a Personal God, of which the central concept is that He is a Being beyond the limitation of nature, of Maya.

- Where do Vivekananda and Nishitani seem to agree? Do you see any differences between their views of religion?

So far we have been chiefly concerned with the question, 'What is *religion*?' But there is a closely related question that we cannot ignore—'What is it *to be religious*?' That is, what is religion like from the inside? How does a deeply religious person think of herself, of what she believes, of what she does, of what she refrains from doing? Does a genuinely religious person think that he has it all more or less figured out—that he is in secure possession of the truth and that he only needs to continue attending worship services, saying prayers, giving to charity, and following the rest of the rules of his religion? In other words, does being deeply religious lead to complacency?

Absolutely not, says the twentieth-century Canadian theologian and philosopher Bernard Lonergan. According to Lonergan, authentic religious life, far from being static or fixed, is all about development. And the kind of development that religious life exhibits isn't linear—as when you walk in a straight line from point A to point B over flat, solid ground. Rather, being genuinely religious is like progressing along an ever-expanding loop. The more a person loves God, the more aware she is of what separates her from God; and the more aware she is of what separates her from God, the more she loves God.

From *Method in Theology*
By Bernard Lonergan

It is the greatest saints that proclaim themselves the greatest sinners . . . .

Religious development is not simply the unfolding in all its consequences of a dynamic state of being in love in an unrestricted manner. For that love is the utmost in self-transcendence, and man's self-transcendence is ever precarious. Of itself, self-transcendence involves tension between the self as

(Continued)

transcending and the self as transcended. So human authenticity is never some pure and serene and secure possession. It is ever a withdrawal from unauthenticity, and every successful withdrawal only brings to light the need for still further withdrawals. Our advance in understanding is also the elimination of oversights and misunderstandings. Our advance in truth is also the correction of mistakes and errors. Our moral development is through repentance for our sins. Genuine religion is discovered and realized by redemption from the many traps of religious aberration. So we are bid to watch and pray, to make our way in fear and trembling. And it is the greatest saints that proclaim themselves the greatest sinners though their sins seems slight indeed to less holy folk that lack their discernment and their love. . . .

I have conceived being in love with God as an ultimate fulfillment of man's capacity for self-transcendence; and this view of religion is sustained when God is conceived as the supreme fulfillment of the transcendental notions, as supreme intelligence, truth, reality, righteousness, goodness. Inversely, when

the love of God is not strictly associated with self-transcendence, then easily indeed it is reinforced by the erotic, the sexual, the orgiastic. On the other hand, the love of God also is penetrated with awe. God's thoughts and God's ways are very different from man's and by that difference God is terrifying. Unless religion is totally directed to what is good, to genuine love of one's neighbour and to a self-denial that is subordinated to a fuller goodness in oneself, then the cult of a God that is terrifying can slip over into the demonic, into an exultant destructiveness of oneself and of others.

Such, then, is what is meant by saying that religious development is dialectical. It is not a struggle between any opposites whatever but the very precise opposition between authenticity and unauthenticity, between the self as transcending and the self as transcended. It is not just an opposition between contrary propositions but an opposition within the human reality of individuals and of groups. It is not to be defined simply by some *a priori* construction of categories but also to be discovered *a posteriori* by a discerning study of history.

- Why does Lonergan think that 'it is the greatest saints that proclaim themselves the greatest sinners'?
- What does Lonergan mean when he says that religious development is 'dialectical'?

While we are on the subject of the religious life, there is one knotty question we need to consider—a question that has long troubled philosophers and non-philosophers alike. It is just this: 'Are some ways of being religious *better* than others?' According to the Jewish philosopher Maimonides, one of the great minds of the Middle Ages, the answer to this question is a firm and definite 'Yes'. In his classic *The Guide for the Perplexed*, Maimonides tells a story—a parable, really—about a king who lives in a magnificent palace. Many of the king's subjects seek him, says Maimonides, but only a few find him. Why is this?

From *The Guide for the Perplexed*
By Maimonides

A king is in his palace, and all his subjects are partly in the country, and partly abroad. . . .

A king is in his palace, and all his subjects are partly in the country, and partly abroad. Of the former, some have their backs turned towards the king's palace, and their faces in another direction; and some are desirous

and zealous to go to the palace, seeking 'to inquire in his temple', and to minister before him, but have not yet seen even the face of the wall of the house. Of those that desire to go to the palace, some reach it, and go round about in search of the entrance gate; others have passed through the gate, and walk about in the antechamber; and others have succeeded in entering into the inner part of the palace, and being in the same room with the king in the royal palace. But even the latter do not immediately on entering the palace see the king, or speak to him; for, after having entered the inner part of the palace, another effort is required before they can stand before the king—at a distance, or close by—hear his words, or speak to him.

What is the point of Maimonides' allegorical tale? We don't need to engage in guesswork, actually, because Maimonides tells us what he has in mind, decoding every last detail for the benefit of his readers:

I will now explain the simile which I have made. The people who are abroad are all those that have no religion, neither one based on speculation nor one received by tradition. . . . I consider these as irrational beings, and not as human beings; they are below mankind, but above monkeys, since they have the form and shape of man, and a mental faculty above that of the monkey.

Those who are in the country, but have their backs turned towards the king's palace, are those who possess religion, belief, and thought, but happen to hold false doctrines, which they either adopted in consequence of great mistakes made in their own speculations, or received from others who misled them. Because of these doctrines they recede more and more from the royal palace the more they seem to proceed. These are worse than the first class, and under certain circumstances it may become necessary to slay them, and to extirpate their doctrines, in order that others should not be misled.

Those who desire to arrive at the palace, and to enter it, but have never yet seen it, are the mass of religious people; the multitude that observe the divine commandments, but are ignorant. Those who arrive at the palace, but go round about it, are those who devote themselves exclusively to the study of the practical law; they believe traditionally in true principles of faith, and learn the practical worship of God, but are not trained in philosophical treatment of the principles of the Law, and do not endeavour to establish the truth of their faith by proof. Those who undertake to investigate the principles of religion have come into the antechamber; and there is no doubt that these can also be divided into different grades. But those who have succeeded in finding a proof for everything that can be proved, who have a true knowledge of God, so far as a true knowledge can be attained, and are near the truth, wherever an approach to the truth is possible, they have reached the goal, and are in the palace in which the king lives.

- According to Maimonides, are all believers equally close to God? Why or why not?
- Does Maimonides see philosophy as threatening the religious life, or as supporting it?

B. The Western Religions

Among the world religions, Judaism, Christianity, and Islam bear a special relationship to each other and to philosophy. They might be called the **'Abrahamic' religions**, because all three trace their roots to Abraham of the Old Testament. Thus, the God worshipped in all three of these religions is the 'God of Abraham'. We might also call these the three 'Western' religions, in that they all originate among peoples living west of the Indus River (one traditional dividing line between East and West).

Judaism, Christianity, and Islam are closely associated together and with the West for another reason, as well. The early religious thinking of all three was heavily influenced by the Greek philosophy of Plato and Aristotle. Although some other religions make use of Greek philosophy, its influence in other faiths does not approach the status it holds in Christian, Jewish, and Muslim thought.

Yet the God who appears in the Old Testament is not readily understood in either Platonic or Aristotelian terms. (You might look back at our discussions of Plato and Aristotle in Chapter 1 and see if you can find anything described there that is akin to the Judeo-Christian God.) Therefore, early thinkers, particularly in the Middle Ages, had their work cut out for them in offering defences of their beliefs, or in arriving at rational religious beliefs, using the Greeks as their model. The medieval philosophers' attempts to do so are among the most monumental of efforts in the history of philosophy, with some of the most provocative and widely influential results.

In many cases, philosophy played a crucial role in the conversions of individuals, and whole countries, to one of these religions. In others, philosophical disputes were the primary cause of sectarian secessions. In all cases, philosophical arguments were a vital ingredient in the development of the doctrines that have come down to us today.

1. The Traditional Conception of God

The principal issues for all three of these great monotheisms, of course, are the existence and character of God. The God of Judaism, Christianity, and Islam has many characteristics that must be identified for our understanding. Most importantly, it is generally believed that God is an independent being, the Creator of the universe, and distinct from the universe He created. It is generally agreed that God is the supremely rational and moral being with concern for human justice and human suffering. It is agreed that He is all-powerful (**omnipotent**), all-knowing (**omniscient**), and that He is everywhere at once (**omnipresent**). In the Old Testament, it is made evident that God has emotions; for example, we read of God as 'a jealous God' and we hear of the 'wrath of God'. The attempt to understand the being who has these characteristics defines Western theology and a great deal of Western metaphysics.

To insist that God is an independent being, the Creator of the universe but distinct from that universe, is of the utmost importance for Western religion. When people try to reinterpret God so that He is nothing other than some universal quality—as in 'God is love', or 'God is ultimate force', or 'God is life', or 'God is the universe'—there is a very real possibility that they are denying God's existence as an independent being. One can say 'God is love' as shorthand for 'God loves us and wants us to love each other' without this danger. But if one believes that God simply is identical to people's loving one another, then it is evident that this belief is no different from that of a person who might not believe in God at all but just believes in love. Similarly, it is one thing to believe that God is a 'force', among other things, who created the universe; but if you believe that God is nothing other than a force that created the universe, without consciousness or concern, then your belief does not differ from that of someone who also believes that some force created the universe but does not believe in God.

In Judaism, Christianity, and Islam, the independence of God from the universe He created is an all-important belief. Philosophers and theologians refer to this independence as the **transcendence** of God. We say that God 'transcends' the universe and humankind. We also say that He 'transcends' all human experience. This notion of transcendence raises an immediate epistemological problem. If God transcends our experience, how can we know that He exists at all? If He is outside of our every possible experience—if we cannot see, hear, or touch Him—what possible evidence can we have for His existence, and how can we have any way of knowing what He must be like?

In some ancient religions, gods and goddesses were very much like human beings, although they were usually stronger and perhaps smarter. The Greek and Roman gods, for example, were like this. Although they were immortal, they often misbehaved and became jealous or furious at one another. Philosophers use the word **anthropomorphism** when they refer to the perception of gods more or less as human. It is quite natural, when people try to envision their deities, that they should endow them with those characteristics they understand best—human characteristics.

The Greek philosopher Xenophanes criticized popular Greek religion around 500 BCE by noting that 'if cows, horses, and lions had hands, or could draw and work like men with their hands, horses would draw gods in the shape of horses, etc.'. He also noted that 'Ethiopians make their gods black and snub-nosed, Thracians give them red hair and gray eyes'—in other words, all humans envision their gods as having physical characteristics similar to their own. There is one God, he concluded, but he is 'in no way like mortals in body and mind'.

The God of Judaism, Christianity, and Islam is much less anthropomorphic than the gods and goddesses of ancient Greece and Rome, yet He is conceived of in certain anthropomorphic ways. The God of the Hebrews frequently took their side in battle in the Old Testament, helping them to fell the walls of Jericho, keeping the sun still for extra hours, and holding apart the waters of the Red Sea. The God of the Old Testament has many human emotions: He becomes jealous or angry when His commands are not carried out, having people swallowed by whales and sometimes destroying whole cities. Even the notion that God is a loving God carries with it anthropomorphism. It is often said that these descriptions are mere approximations, based on the idea that we can never really know or understand what God is like. (For example, it is said that we cannot understand divine love and that we use our all-too-human conception of love as the only example we can find.) But such anthropomorphic projections are in no way an objection to belief in God; it is only to be expected that people will try to understand religion in those terms that they know best.

The scriptural emphasis on God's sense of justice and His concern for humankind also demonstrates anthropomorphic characteristics, even if it is true, as we are so often told, that God's conception of justice may be very different from our own. These characteristics are so important that if a person does not believe that God is a merciful and concerned being with a strong sense of justice, then that person probably does not believe in God at all. (For example, Aristotle's 'prime mover', despite the Western theologians' marvellous adaptation of the concept to their religions, is not on the face of it very much like the Judeo-Christian God.) Prayer is meaningful only on the assumption that God listens to us and understands us; faith is intelligible only on the assumption that God cares about us. Without these characteristics, God would not be a moral force in our lives.

Some sophisticated theists and theologians have tried to purge belief in God of all anthropomorphic characteristics, speaking, for example, only of 'Being Itself' rather than the usual characterization of God as 'Him'. Still, although we might not actually believe that God, like Zeus, resembles some superhuman immortal being, it is clear that our traditional conception of God is far more anthropocentric than some theologians would no doubt prefer.

The Western religions' conception of God has been varied in so many ways that we can't even begin to consider them. There are the often-debated differences between the God of the Old Testament and the God of the New Testament. Then there are the obvious differences in the way God is interpreted by the various sects of Judaism, Christianity, and Islam. And the differences between this God and other gods (for example, Zeus, Krishna, Isis) are so enormous that traditional Christians, Jews, and Muslims would hesitate to call any of these figures 'God' at all.

ANTHROPOMORPHIC

A non-human thing or being to which human attributes have been ascribed.

- If God is transcendent and independent from creation, then how do we know that God has the qualities that we ascribe to him (for example, omniscient, good, omnipotent)?

C. Proving God: The Ontological Argument

It is one thing to be taught that there is a God; it is another to believe in God for good reason, rationally, and to know what one believes. Of course, many people have insisted that belief in God is not a matter of rationality or knowledge at all but only of faith. But the turn to faith logically comes after attempts to know. So before we turn to examine other philosophical questions raised by religious belief, let us ask whether or not we *can* know that God exists.

Let's return to the question we brought up in the previous section: Since God by definition transcends our experience, how can we have evidence for His existence? (This problem is similar to the one we faced with substance in Chapter 1, where you likely noticed that notions of God and substance are highly intertwined in metaphysics, as for example in Spinoza's philosophy). There are people who claim to have been direct witnesses to miracles or to have heard God's own voice. But, assuming that none of us is one of them, our problem remains: Should we believe their reports? Might they have been victims of imagination or hallucination? Is there any evidence in our experience that would allow us to know of God's existence? If not, what reasons can we give for a belief in God?

In the long history of Western theology, three major sets of 'proofs' have emerged as attempts to demonstrate God's existence. Each has received various formulations, and all are still being discussed today. They are called (1) the **ontological argument**, (2) the **cosmological argument**, and (3) the **teleological argument** (the latter two will be discussed in the following sections).

Here, we will begin by discussing the *ontological argument*. This is the most difficult of the three, for it is a purely logical proof—it attempts to argue from the *idea* of God to His *necessary existence*. Descartes used this argument in his *Meditations* to prove God's existence; Spinoza and Leibniz formulated similar arguments. But the man who is generally credited with the invention of the argument is an eleventh-century monk named St Anselm. Because his argument depends wholly on the idea of God's existence, it is called *ontological*.

ONTOLOGICAL ARGUMENT

An argument for God's existence based on the very concept of 'God'.

COSMOLOGICAL ARGUMENT

An argument for God's existence based on the idea that there must have been a first cause or an ultimate reason for the universe.

TELEOLOGICAL ARGUMENT

An argument for God's existence based on the perceived intricacy and 'design' of nature.

On the Ontological Argument
By St Anselm

For God is that than which a greater cannot be thought, and whoever understands this rightly must understand that he exists in such a way that he cannot be non-existent even in thought.

Some time ago, at the urgent request of some of my brethren, I published a brief work, as an example of meditation on the grounds of faith. I wrote it in the role of one who seeks, by silent reasoning with himself, to learn what he does not know. But when I reflected on this little book, and saw that it was put together as a long chain of arguments, I began to ask myself whether *one* argument might possibly be found, resting on no other argument for its proof, but sufficient in itself to prove that God truly exists, and that he is the supreme good, needing nothing outside himself, but needful for the being and well-being of all things. I often turned my earnest attention to this

problem, and at times I believed that I could put my finger on what I was looking for, but at other times it completely escaped my mind's eye, until finally, in despair, I decided to give up searching for something that seemed impossible to find. But when I tried to put the whole question out of my mind, so as to avoid crowding out other matters, with which I might make some progress, by this useless preoccupation, then, despite my unwillingness and resistance, it began to force itself on me more persistently than ever. Then, one day when I was worn out by my vigorous resistance to the obsession, the solution I had ceased to hope for presented itself to me, in the very turmoil of my thoughts, so that I enthusiastically embraced the idea which in my disquiet, I had spurned.

* * *

God Truly Is

And so, O Lord, since thou givest understanding to faith, give me to understanding—as far as thou knowest it to be good for me—that thou dost exist, as we believe, and that thou art what we believe thee to be. Now we believe that thou art a being than which none greater can be thought. Or can it be that there is no such being, since 'the fool hath said in his heart, "There is no God"'? But when this same fool hears what I am saying—'A being than which none greater can be thought'—he understands what he hears, and what he understands is in his understanding, even if he does not understand that it exists. For it is one thing for an object to be in the understanding, and another thing to understand that it exists. When a painter considers beforehand what he is going to paint, he has it in his understanding, but he does not suppose that what he has not yet painted already exists. But when he has painted it, he both has it in his understanding and understands that what he has now produced exists. Even the fool, then, must be convinced that a being than which none greater can be thought exists at least in his understanding, since when he hears this he understands it, and whatever is understood is in the understanding. But clearly that than which a greater cannot be thought cannot exist in the understanding alone. For if it is actually in the understanding alone, it can be thought of as existing also in reality, and this is greater. Therefore, if that than which a greater cannot be thought is in the understanding alone, this same thing than which a greater cannot be thought is that than which a greater can be thought. But obviously this is impossible. Without doubt, therefore, there exists, both in the understanding and in reality, something than which a greater cannot be thought.

God Cannot Be Thought of as Non-existent

And certainly it exists so truly that it cannot be thought of as non-existent. For something can be thought of as existing, which cannot be thought of as not existing, and this is greater than that which *can* be thought of as not existing. Thus, if that than which a greater cannot be thought can be thought of as not existing, this very thing than which a greater cannot

be thought is *not* that than which a greater cannot be thought. But this is contradictory. So, then, there truly is a being than which a greater cannot be thought—so truly that it cannot even be thought of as not existing.

And *thou* art this being, O Lord our God. Thou so truly are, then, O Lord my God, that thou canst not even be thought of as not existing. And this is right. For if some mind could think of something better than thou, the creature would rise above the Creator and judge its Creator; but this is altogether absurd. And indeed, whatever is, except thyself alone, can be thought of as not existing. Thou alone, therefore, of all beings, has being in the truest and highest sense, since no other being so truly exists, and thus every other being has less being. Why, then, has 'the fool said in his heart, "There is no God",' when it is so obvious to the rational mind that, of all beings, thou dost exist supremely? Why indeed, unless it is that he is a stupid fool?

How the Fool Has Said in His Heart What Cannot Be Thought

But how did he manage to say in his heart what he could not think? Or how is it that he was unable to think what he said in his heart? After all, to say in one's heart and to think are the same thing. Now if it is true—or, rather, since it is true—that he thought it, because he said it in his heart, but did not say it in his heart, since he could not think it, it is clear that something can be said in one's heart or thought in more than one way. For we think of a thing, in one sense, when we think of the word that signifies it, and in another sense, when we understand the very thing itself. Thus, in the first sense God can be thought of as non-existent, but in the second sense this is quite impossible. For no one who understands what God is can think that God does not exist, even though he says these words in his heart—perhaps without any meaning, perhaps with some quite extraneous meaning. For God is that than which a greater cannot be thought, and whoever understands this rightly must understand that he exists in such a way that he cannot be non-existent even in thought. He, therefore, who understands that God thus exists cannot think of him as non-existent.

Thanks be to thee, good Lord, thanks be to thee, because I now understand by thy light what I formerly believed by thy gift, so that even if I were to refuse to believe in thy existence, I could not fail to understand its truth.

The logic of the argument is deceptively simple: The concept of 'God' is defined, innocently enough, as 'a being greater than which none can be thought'. Then, Anselm asks, 'which would be greater, a being who is merely thought, or a being who actually exists?' The answer, of course, is a being who actually exists. But since God is, by definition, the greatest being who can be thought, He must therefore exist. 'God cannot be non-existent even in thought'. Anselm goes on to argue that the idea of an eternal being who either does not yet exist or no longer exists is self-contradictory, so that the very idea we have of such a being requires existence. It is worth noting that, while formulating the ontological argument, Anselm was also putting into place some of the final ingredients in the Christian conception of God, as not only a perfect or even the most perfect being but rather as the greatest (most perfect) *conceivable* being.

The argument has had a long, influential history, and logicians are still arguing about it. The argument was not seriously altered until five centuries later, when Descartes took up Anselm's argument and gave it its modern formulation. In the seventeenth century, Descartes (in his *Meditations*) made explicit the presupposition of the argument: existence is a property that, like colour, shape, weight, and charm, a thing may either have or not have. Some properties, however, are essential to a thing: three angles are essential to a triangle, spots are essential to a Dalmatian. So too, Descartes suggests, perfection is essential to the most perfect being, and existence is a perfection. One can no more conceive of a most perfect being without existence than one can conceive of a triangle without three angles or a Dalmatian without spots.

On the Ontological Argument
By René Descartes

From the fact that I cannot conceive God without existence, it follows that existence is inseparable from Him, and hence that He really exists.

But now, if just because I can draw the idea of something from my thought, it follows that all which I know clearly and distinctly as pertaining to this object does really belong to it, may I not derive from this an argument demonstrating the existence of God? It is certain that I no less find the idea of God, that is to say, the idea of a supremely perfect Being, in me, than that of any figure or number whatever it is; and I do not know any less clearly and distinctly that an [actual and] eternal existence pertains to this nature than I know that all that which I am able to demonstrate of some figure or number truly pertains to the nature of this figure or number, and therefore, although all that I concluded in the preceding Meditations were found to be false, the existence of God would pass with me as at least as certain as I have ever held the truths of mathematics (which concern only numbers and figures) to be.

This indeed is not at first manifest, since it would seem to present some appearance of being a sophism. For being accustomed in all other things to make a distinction between existence and essence, I easily persuade myself that the existence can be separated from the essence of God, and that we can thus conceive God as not actually existing. But, nevertheless, when I think of it with more attention, I clearly see that existence can no more be separated from the essence of God than can its having its three angles equal to two right angles be separated from the essence of a [rectilinear] triangle, or the idea of a mountain from the idea of a valley; and so there is not any less repugnance to our conceiving a God (that is, a Being supremely perfect) to whom existence is lacking (that is to say, to whom a certain perfection is lacking), than to conceive of a mountain which has no valley.

But although I cannot really conceive of a God without existence any more than a mountain without a valley, still from the fact that I conceive a mountain with a valley, it does not follow that there is such a mountain in the world; similarly although I conceive of God as possessing existence, it would seem that it does not follow that there is a God which exists; for my thought does not impose any necessity upon things, and just as I may imagine a winged horse, although no horse with wings exists, so I could perhaps attribute existence to God, although no God existed.

But a sophism is concealed in this objection; for from the fact that I cannot conceive a mountain without a valley, it does not follow that there is any mountain or any valley in existence, but only that the mountain and the valley, whether they exist or do not exist, cannot in any way be separated one from the other. While from the fact that I cannot conceive God without existence, it follows that existence is inseparable from Him, and hence that He really exists; not that my thought can bring this to pass, or impose any necessity on things, but, on the contrary, because the necessity which lies in the thing itself, i.e., the necessity of the existence of God determines me to think in this way. For it is not within my power to think of God without existence (that is of a supremely perfect Being devoid of a supreme perfection) though it is in my power to imagine a horse either with wings or without wings.

And we must not here object that it is in truth necessary for me to assert that God exists after having presupposed that He possesses every sort of perfection, since existence is one of these, but that as a matter of fact my original supposition was not necessary, just as it is not necessary to consider that all quadrilateral figures can be inscribed in the circle; for supposing I thought of this, I should be constrained to admit that the rhombus might be inscribed in the circle since it is a quadrilateral figure, which, however, is manifestly false. Although it is not necessary that I should at any time entertain the notion of God, nevertheless whenever it happens that I think of a first and a sovereign Being, and, so to speak, derive the idea of Him from the storehouse of my mind, it is necessary that I should attribute to Him every sort of perfection, although I do not get so far as to enumerate them all, or to apply my mind to each one in particular. And this necessity suffices to make me conclude (after having recognized that existence is a perfection) that this first and sovereign Being really exists; just as though it is not necessary for me ever to imagine any triangle, yet, whenever I wish to consider a rectilinear figure composed only of three angles, it is absolutely essential that I should attribute to it all those properties which serve to bring about the conclusion that its three angles are not greater than two right angles, even although I may not then be considering this point in particular. But when I consider which figures are capable of being inscribed in the circle, it is in no way necessary that I should think that all quadrilateral figures are of this number; on the contrary, I cannot even pretend that this is the case, so long as I do not desire to accept anything which I cannot conceive clearly and distinctly. And in consequence there is a great difference between the false suppositions such as this, and the true ideas born within me, the first and principal of which is that of God. For really I discern in many ways that this idea is not something factitious, and depending solely on my thought, but that it is the image of a true and immutable nature; first of all, because I cannot conceive anything but God himself to whose essence existence [necessarily] pertains; in the second place because it is not possible for me to conceive two or more Gods in this same position; and, granted that there is one such God who now exists, I see clearly that it is necessary that He should have existed from all eternity and that He must exist eternally; and finally, because I know an infinitude of other properties in God, none of which I can either diminish or change.

Descartes' version is

> *I cannot conceive of a God without the property of existence.*
> *(His existence cannot be separated from His essence.)*
> *Therefore, God exists.*

Then he adds

> *My conception of God is such that He has every sort of perfection.*
> *Existence is a perfection.*
> *Therefore, God necessarily exists.*

These arguments are valid as stated, but are they also sound? Consider the following argument, which is structured in the same form as the above arguments. Define a 'grenlin' as 'the greenest imaginable creature'. Now, which is greener, a green creature that does exist or one that does not? Obviously the one that exists. Therefore, at least one grenlin exists.

It is worth noting that this objection had been raised against Anselm too, by Gaunilo of Marmoutier, who suggested the existence of an island more perfect than any other, on the same grounds that it would be contradictory for the most perfect island not to exist. Anselm replied that the argument cannot be applied to islands or anything else whose non-existence is conceivable. The question, then, is what it means for non-existence to be conceivable or for existence to be a necessary property of a thing.

Descartes faced a similar challenge to his formulation when a critic attacked his analogy with triangles and insisted that, while it may be true that *if* a triangle exists, then it must have three angles, it does not follow that triangles must exist, or that any in fact do exist. Descartes' answer is similar to Anselm's response to his critic: The essence of triangle does not include the perfection of existence, as God's surely does.

The ontological argument makes a special case for God, because He is the only 'greatest conceivable' or 'most perfect' being. Nevertheless, the argument has made many believers uneasy and has been dismissed as a clever trick by nonbelievers. But, whatever our unease, the argument is clearly valid.

The argument is a straightforward syllogism of the 'All men are mortal/Socrates is a man/Socrates is mortal' type, the only real (but significant) difference being that, while there can be any number of men, there can be only one God, one 'most perfect' being. But what we have so far taken for granted in the above presentations of the argument is the presupposition that existence is a property, like a colour or shape. One way of attacking the logic of the argument, even while accepting its validity, is to challenge this presupposition, and thus the soundness of the argument. In other words, is 'exists' a predicate, like 'barks' and 'is green'? Or is it rather a quantifier, like 'all' and 'none' and 'some' (which is, essentially, 'there exists at least one . . .')? The objection that 'existence is not a predicate' was formulated against the ontological argument by the great philosopher Immanuel Kant.

Kant suggested that the problem lies in the central idea, shared by the ontological argument and the unacceptable arguments that follow the same form, that existence is one of the essential properties, that is, part of the definition of a thing. But existence, Kant argues, is not a property and cannot be part of a definition. In an often quoted passage of his *Critique of Pure Reason*, he presents this argument:

Against the Ontological Argument
By Immanuel Kant

Being is evidently not a real predicate, or a concept of something that can be added to the concept of a thing.

I answer:—Even in introducing into the concept of a thing, which you wish to think in its possibility only, the concept of its existence, under whatever disguise it may be, you have been guilty of a contradiction. If you were allowed to do this, you would apparently have carried your point; but in reality you have achieved nothing, but have only committed a tautology. I simply ask you, whether the proposition, that *this* or *that thing* (which, whatever it may be, I grant you as possible) *exists*, is an analytical or a synthetical proposition? If the former, then by its existence you add nothing to your thought of the thing; but in that case, either the thought within you would be the thing itself, or you have presupposed existence, as belonging to possibility, and have according to your own showing deducted existence from internal possibility, which is nothing but a miserable tautology. The mere word *reality*, which in the concept of a thing sounds different from existence in the concept of the predicate, can make no difference. For if you call all accepting or positing (without determining what it is) reality, you have placed a thing, with all its predicates, within the concept of the subject, and accepted it as real, and you do nothing but repeat it in the predicate. If, on the contrary, you admit, as every sensible man must do, that every proposition involving existence is synthetical, how can you say that the predicate of existence does not admit of removal without contradiction, a distinguishing property which is peculiar to analytical propositions only, the very character of which depends on it?

I might have hoped to put an end to this subtle argumentation, without many words, and simply by an accurate definition of the concept of existence, if I had not seen that the illusion, in mistaking a logical predicate for a real one (that is the predicate which determines a thing), resists all correction. Everything can become a *logical predicate*, even the subject itself may be predicated of itself, because logic makes no account of any contents of concepts. *Determination*, however, is a predicate, added to the concept of the subject, and enlarging it, and it must not therefore be contained in it.

Being is evidently not a real predicate, or a concept of something that can be added to the concept of a thing. It is merely the admission of a thing, and of certain determinations in it. Logically, it is merely the copula of a judgment. The proposition, *God is almighty*, contains two concepts, each having its object, namely, God and almightiness. The small word *is*, is not an additional predicate, but only serves to put the predicate *in relation* to the subject. If, then, I take the subject (God) with all its predicates (including that of almightiness), and say, *God is*, or there is a God, I do not put a new predicate to the concept of God, but I only put the subject by itself, with all its predicates, in relation to my concept, as its object. Both must contain exactly the same kind of thing, and nothing can have been added to the concept, which expresses possibility only, by my thinking its object as simply given and saying it is. And thus the real does not contain more than the possible. A hundred real dollars do not contain a penny more than a hundred possible dollars. For as the latter signify the concept, the former the object and its position by itself, it is clear that, in case the former contained more than the latter, my concept would not express the whole object, and would not therefore be its adequate concept. In my financial position no doubt there exists more by one hundred real dollars, than by their concept only (that is their possibility), because in reality the object is not only contained analytically in my concept, but is added to my concept (which is a determination of my state), synthetically; but the conceived hundred dollars are not in the least increased through the existence which is outside my concept.

What Kant is arguing is that the existence of a thing can never be merely a matter of logic. (This is what he means when he says that the proposition that a thing exists cannot be analytic.) 'Existence', or 'being', he argues, isn't a 'real predicate' (though it is a grammatical predicate) because it does not tell us anything more about whatever is said to have existence. In other words, there is something odd about the statement, 'this apple is red, round, ripe, and exists'. What is odd is that 'exists' does not give a characteristic of the apple but rather says that there is an apple with these characteristics. The proper characterization of God, therefore, includes the various characteristics we discussed earlier in this chapter, but it should not include, according to Kant, any characteristic that implies God's existence. It is one thing to say that God, if He exists, has such-and-such characteristics; it is something more to say that such a God exists. (This is what Kant means by his example about the one hundred real versus one hundred possible dollars; they both have exactly the same number of cents, but only the one hundred real dollars are worth anything.)

Many contemporary philosophers agree with Kant's argument, but many do not. The ontological argument is by no means put to rest. Charles Hartshorne, for example, has provided us with a twentieth-century version of the argument.

On the Ontological Argument

By Charles Hartshorne

The ontological argument turns logically upon the unique relation between the possibility and the actuality, the 'essence' and the 'existence', of God. With ordinary finite ideas the task of knowledge is to decide among three cases: (1) the type of thing conceived is impossible, and hence non-existent (for example, a moral being totally without 'freedom'); (2) the type of thing is possible, but there is no actual example (a Euclidean space?); (3) the thing is possible, and there is an example (a speaking animal). The ontological argument holds that with the idea of God only two of these three cases need be considered, since one of the three, (2), is meaningless. If, the argument holds, there exists no God, then there also can be no possibility of the existence of a God, and the concept is nonsense, like that of 'round square'. If, further, it can be shown that the idea of God is not nonsensical, that it must have an at least possible object, then it follows that it has an actual object, since a 'merely possible' God is, if the argument is sound, inconceivable. *Where impossibility and mere actualized possibility are both excluded, there nothing remains but actuality, if the idea has any meaning at all.*

The ontological argument itself does not suffice to exclude the impossibility or meaninglessness of God, but only to exclude his mere possibility. Or, as Leibniz said, it must assume that God is not impossible. (We shall consider presently whether the argument can be extended so as to justify this assumption.) The inventor of the argument, Anselm, took it for granted that the man with religious experience, to whom he addressed his discourse, though he may doubt God's existence, will not easily doubt that in hoping that there is a God he is at least hoping for something with a self-consistent meaning. Now, given a meaning, there must be something which is meant. We do not think just our act of thinking. What we think may not be actual, but can it be less than possible—unless it be a self-contradictory combination of factors, singly and separately possible? In short, when we think, can we fail to refer to something beyond our thought which, either as a whole or in its elements, is at least possible? Granting this, the ontological argument says that, with reference to God, 'at least possible' is indistinguishable from 'possible *and* actual' (though, as we shall see, 'possible' here means simply 'not impossible' and has no positive content different from actuality). Let us now present the reasons for the contention that 'at least possible' and 'actual' are indistinguishable in the case of the divine.

According to one theory of possibility, a given type of entity is possible if the most general features, the strictly generic characters, of existence or of the universe are compatible with the production of such an entity. Thus, there is no contradiction of the most general features of reality in the supposition that nature has really produced Mr Micawber. There is contradiction of the details of nature (such as the detail that Micawber is a character in a novel written by a highly imaginative author), but these may be supposed otherwise without destroying the meaning, the generic content, of 'existence'. But the idea of God is the idea of a being everlasting in duration, and independent, in a certain aspect of his being (in his individual 'essence'), from everything else. Such a being could not be produced, since he must then be both derivative and underivative, everlasting and yet not everlasting. To create the omniscient, one must endow him with a perfect memory of the past before he existed; to create the omnipotent, one must endow him with incomparably more power, a metaphysically different order of power, than that which created him. It is hardly necessary to prolong the discussion: no theologian holding either type-one or type-two theism has ever rejected that portion of the ontological argument which consists in the proof that *God could not be a mere possibility*; and (as we are about to show) it is demonstrable that in order to reject this proof one must construct a theory of possibility which would not be required for ordinary purposes, so that the tables may be turned upon those who accuse the argument of making God an exception to all principles of knowledge. The argument does make God an exception, but only in the sense that it *deduces* this exceptional status from a generally applicable theory of possibility together with the definition of God. Nothing else is required. The opposition, on the contrary, sets up a general principle which, but for God and the desire to avoid asserting his existence (as following from his possibility), would be without merit.

* * *

The old objection that if a perfect being must exist then a perfect island or a perfect devil must exist is not perhaps very profound. For it is answered simply by denying that anyone can conceive perfection, in the strict sense employed by the argument, to be possessed by an island or a devil. A perfect devil would have at the same time to be infinitely responsible for all that exists besides itself, and yet infinitely averse to all that exists. It would have to attend with unrivalled care and patience and fullness of realization to the lives of all other beings (which must depend for existence upon this care), and yet it must hate all these things with matchless bitterness. It must savagely torture a cosmos every item of which is integral with its own being, united to it with a vivid intimacy such as we can only dimly imagine. In short, whether a perfect God is sense or nonsense, a perfect devil is unequivocally nonsense, and it is of no import whether the nonsensical does or does not necessarily exist, since in any case it necessarily does not exist, and its existence would be nothing, even though a necessary nothing. Clearly, again, an island is not in essence unproducible and self-sufficient. Of course one can arbitrarily put concepts together and suppose that an island which could never be destroyed and had never been produced would be better than one

capable of production, since some form of eternal life might go on upon it, undisturbed by any possibility of an end to such a world. But it is not apparent what would make such a world an island, if the 'waters' which 'washed' it never wore its shores, and if it were not a part of the surface of a body in space surrounded by other bodies capable of smashing it to pieces, and were not composed of particles capable of ultimately separating, etc. The question is if such a conception would in the end be distinguishable from the idea of the cosmos as the perpetually renewed body of God, that is, not an island in the least, but an aspect of the very idea of God whose self-existence is upheld by the argument.

* * *

Thus to make God's existence exceptional in relation to his conceivability is a result, not a violation, of the general principle of existence. Whatever is merely possible, this possibility as such is real, is other than nothing, only thanks to something which itself is not merely possible but is reality itself as self-identical, or as that which, being the ground of possibility, is more than merely possible. It is an implication of the idea of God that he is that ground.

Whether or not the argument succeeds in anything like its classical form, it can be understood in another way, which clearly distinguishes it from all the absurd arguments that apparently have the same form. If you believe in God, then the argument might be taken in a very different way, not as a 'proof' but as an attempt to articulate your belief. The theologian Karl Barth has argued that this is what Anselm's argument really tries to do, and as you read over his argument a second or third time it becomes clear that he is expressing his faith as much as he is offering a logical proof. In general, the 'proofs' of God's existence have been such articulations and expressions as well as proper logical arguments. Even if they fail as proofs, they often succeed in this other, and perhaps more important, function. Descartes' and Anselm's arguments are, ultimately, that we cannot think about God and at the same time doubt His existence.

It is clear that, considered simply as a logical argument, the ontological argument does not have the power to convert nonbelievers into believers. And if you are a believer, it is clear that an objection to the 'proof' is not going to shake your faith in any way whatsoever. So the significance of the proof is ambiguous; as a logical exercise it is brilliant, as an expression of faith it may be edifying, but as an actual proof that God exists it seems to have no power at all.

- What are some major objections to the ontological argument? How have philosophers countered such objections?
- What does it mean to say that a 'proof' for God's existence is not really a proof at all, but an articulation of belief?

D. Proving God: The Cosmological Argument

The ontological argument is a fascinating exercise in logic and rationality, but critics often object that it does not seem to say anything about the all-important role of God as creator. Other arguments, however, take creation as their central focus, either by arguing the necessity of a creator (as in the cosmological argument), or by paying attention to the detailed design of the world that was created (as in the teleological argument).

The cosmological argument is actually a series of arguments, all of which involve something like Aristotle's premise that there must be a first cause ('a prime mover'), some ultimate explanation for the existence and nature of the universe. If there were no such first cause or ultimate explanation, that would suggest an infinite regress (arguing backward forever), which Aristotle and most Western logicians until modern times considered incomprehensible. In the next selection, St Thomas Aquinas presents several of the best-known formulations of the cosmological argument in the first four of what he calls the 'five ways' of proving God's existence.

On the Cosmological Argument
By St Thomas Aquinas

We cannot but admit the existence of some being having of itself its own necessity, and not receiving it from another, but rather causing in others their necessity.

The first and more manifest way is the argument from motion. It is certain, and evident to our senses, that in the world some things are in motion. Now whatever is moved is moved by another, for nothing can be moved except it is in potentiality to that towards which it is moved whereas a thing moves inasmuch as it is in act. For motion is nothing else than the reduction of something from potentiality to actuality. But nothing can be reduced from potentiality to actuality, except by something in a state of actuality. Thus that which is actually hot, as fire, makes wood, which is potentially hot, to be actually hot, and thereby moves and changes it. Now it is not possible that the same thing should be at once in actuality and potentiality in the same respect, but only in different respects. For what is actually hot cannot simultaneously be potentially hot; but it is simultaneously potentially cold. It is therefore impossible that in the same respect and in the same way a thing should be both mover and moved, i.e., that it should move itself. Therefore, whatever is moved must be moved by another. If that by which it is moved be itself moved, then this also must needs be moved by another, and that by another again. But this cannot go on to infinity, because then there would be no first mover, and consequently, no other mover, seeing that subsequent movers move only inasmuch

as they are moved by the first mover, as the staff moves only because it is moved by the hand. Therefore, it is necessary to arrive at a first mover, moved by no other; and this everyone understands to be God.

The second way is from the nature of efficient cause.[1] In the world of sensible things we find there is an order of efficient causes. There is no case known (neither is it, indeed, possible) in which a thing is found to be the efficient cause of itself; for so it would be prior to itself, which is impossible. Now in efficient causes it is not possible to go on to infinity, because in all efficient causes following in order, the first is the cause of the intermediate cause, and the intermediate is the cause of the ultimate cause, whether the intermediate cause be several, or one only. Now to take away the cause is to take away the effect. Therefore, if there be no first cause among efficient causes, there will be no ultimate, nor any intermediate cause. But if in efficient causes it is possible to go on to infinity, there will be no first efficient cause, neither will there be an ultimate effect, nor any intermediate efficient causes; all of which is plainly false. Therefore it is necessary to admit a first efficient cause, to which everyone gives the name of God.

The third way is taken from possibility and necessity, and runs thus. We find in nature things that are possible to be and not to be, since they are found to be generated, and to be corrupted, and consequently, it is possible for them to be and not to be. But it is impossible for these always to exist, for that which can not-be at some time is not. Therefore, if everything can not-be, then at one time there was nothing in existence. Now if this were true, even now there would be nothing in existence, because that which does not exist begins to exist only through something already existing. Therefore, if at one time nothing was in existence, it would have been impossible for anything to have begun to exist; and thus even now nothing would be in existence—which is absurd. Therefore, not all beings are merely possible, but there must exist something the existence of which is necessary. But every necessary thing either has its necessity caused by another, or not. Now it is impossible to go on to infinity in necessary things which have their necessity caused by another, as has been already proved in regard to efficient causes. Therefore we cannot but admit the existence of some being having of itself its own necessity, and not receiving it from another, but rather causing in others their necessity. This all men speak of as God.

In his 'fourth way', Aquinas combines the form of the cosmological argument with some of the ideas from the ontological argument:

The fourth way is taken from the gradation to be found in things. Among beings there are some more and some less good, true, noble, and the like. But *more* and *less* are predicated of different things according as they resemble in their different ways something which is the maximum, as a thing is said to be hotter according as it more nearly resembles that which is hottest; so that there is something which is truest, something best, something noblest, and, consequently, something which is most being, for those things that are greatest in truth are greatest in being, as it is written in [Aristotle's] *Metaphysics*. . . . Now the maximum in any genus is the cause of all in that genus, as fire, which is the maximum of heat, is the cause of all hot things, as is said in the same book. Therefore, there must also be something which is to all beings the cause of their being, goodness, and every other perfection; and this we call God.

The cosmological argument, in all of these versions, is also both an attempt at 'proof' and an expression of an individual's belief in God. Accordingly, it must be appreciated for its role in articulating the concept of God in traditional Christianity and evaluated as a logical argument. As a logical argument, two modern objections seem to have considerable weight.

First, even if the argument is formally valid, it proves only that there is some 'first mover' or 'first cause' or 'necessary being'. It does not prove that this being has all of the other attributes that allow us to recognize God. (Aquinas' fourth way, however, includes moral attributes of perfection as well.) Taken at face value, Aquinas' first three versions of the cosmological argument are similar to Aristotle's argument for the 'prime mover' (which we explored in Chapter 1) except that Aquinas takes the 'first cause' to be an 'efficient' as well as 'final' cause, that is, as the creator as well as the meaning of the universe. (Furthermore, while Aristotle, in his *Physics*, allows that there might be several prime movers, Aquinas is clear that there can be only one.) Nevertheless, one might accept the argument and believe only in a 'first cause' yet deny the existence of God. From this perspective we might ask, 'Why could the universe itself not be its own cause?' In current physics, scientists would argue that this idea is just as plausible as the idea that there must have been something else that caused our universe to exist.

This leads us to the second modern objection: the cosmological argument is too quick to dismiss the possibility of an infinite regress. While the idea that the universe did not have a beginning but has always existed would have seemed absurd to Aquinas (and to Aristotle), it is generally accepted today. Now, even though scientists and mathematicians talk about the beginning of the universe and the relativity of time, they no longer consider an infinite regress as necessarily impossible. Without the idea that every infinite regress is an absurdity, the cosmological argument loses its main premise.

In fact, Aquinas admits that there is no valid argument against the claim that God and the universe existed for all eternity, but he has another argument to help him here. He says that the beginning of the universe required an *act*, which means that the universe could not have been the cause of itself. Furthermore, even if the universe existed eternally, it would still require a prime mover to keep it in motion. Therefore, he concludes, God must exist even if the infinite regress argument by itself does not prove this.

- Is an infinite regress absurd? Do you find the idea of an uncaused cause any less absurd?

Although Aquinas' formulations of the cosmological argument have been influential, we mustn't suppose that they are the only possible formulations, let alone the best. Many other philosophers have presented their own versions of the cosmological argument—versions that differ significantly from what we find in Aquinas. For instance, Samuel Clarke, a distinguished eighteenth-century British philosopher, presents a sophisticated statement of the cosmological proof in propositions I and II of *A Demonstration of the Being and Attributes of God*.

From *A Demonstration of the Being and Attributes of God*
By Samuel Clarke

Consequently there must, on the contrary, of necessity have existed from eternity some one immutable and independent being.

I

First, then, it is absolutely and undeniably certain that *something has existed from all eternity*. This is so evident and undeniable a proposition, that no atheist in any age has ever presumed to assert the contrary, and therefore there is little need of being particular in the proof of it. For, since something now is, it is evident that something always was, otherwise the things that now are must have been produced out of nothing, absolutely and without a cause, which is a plain contradiction in terms. For, to say a thing is produced and yet that there is no cause at all for that production, is to say that something is effected when it is effected by nothing, that is, at the same time when it is not effected at all. Whatever exists has a cause, a reason, a ground of its existence, a foundation on which its existence relies, a ground or reason why it does exist rather than not exist, either in the necessity of its own nature (and then it must have been of itself eternal), or in the will of some other being (and then that other being must, at least in the order of nature and causality, have existed before it). . . .

II

There has existed from eternity some one unchangeable and independent being. For, since something must needs have been from eternity, as has been already proved and is granted on all hands, either there has always existed some one unchangeable and independent being from which all other beings that are or ever were in the universe have received their original, or else there has been an infinite succession of changeable and dependent beings produced one from another in an endless progression without any original cause at all. Now this latter supposition is so very absurd that, though all atheism must in its accounts of most things (as shall be shown hereafter) terminate in it, yet I think very few atheists ever were so weak as openly and directly to defend it. For it is plainly impossible and contradictory to itself. I shall not argue against it from the supposed impossibility of infinite succession, barely and absolutely considered in itself, for a reason which shall be mentioned hereafter. But, if we consider such an infinite progression as one entire endless series of dependent beings, it is plain this whole series of beings can have no cause from without of its existence because in it are supposed to be included all things that are, or ever were, in the universe. And it is plain it can have no reason within itself for its existence because no one being in this infinite succession is supposed to be self-existent or necessary (which is the only ground or reason of existence of anything that can be imagined within the thing itself, as will presently more fully appear), but everyone dependent on the foregoing. And, where no part is necessary, it is manifest the whole cannot be necessary—absolute necessity of existence not being an extrinsic, relative, and accidental denomination but an inward and essential property of the nature of the thing which so exists.

An infinite succession, therefore, of merely dependent beings without any original independent cause is a series of beings that has neither necessity, nor cause, nor any reason or ground at all of its existence either within itself or from without. That is, it is an express contradiction and impossibility. It is a supposing something to be caused (because it is granted in every one of its stages of succession not to be necessarily and of itself), and yet that, in the whole, it is caused absolutely by nothing, which every man knows is a contradiction to imagine done in time; and because duration in this case makes no difference, it is equally a contradiction to suppose it done from eternity. And consequently there must, on the contrary, of necessity have existed from eternity some one immutable and independent being.

To suppose an infinite succession of changeable and dependent beings produced one from another in an endless progression without any original cause at all is only a driving back from one step to another and, as it were, removing out of sight the question concerning the ground or reason of the existence of things. It is, in reality and in point of argument, the very same supposition as it would be to suppose one continued being of beginning-less and endless duration neither self-existent and necessary in itself, nor having its existence founded in any self-existent cause, which is directly absurd and contradictory.

What, exactly, is Clarke's argument? What are his main premises, what is his conclusion, and how is that conclusion supposed to follow logically from those premises? Here is a simple reconstruction of Clarke's basic line of reasoning:

(1) *Something has existed from eternity.*

Therefore,

(2) *One of the following two things must be true: either (a) 'there has always existed some one unchangeable and independent being from which all other beings that are or ever were in the universe have received their original', or (b) 'there has been an infinite succession of changeable and dependent beings produced one from another in an endless progression without any original cause at all'.*

(3) *But option (b) cannot be true: 'An infinite succession . . . of merely dependent beings without any original independent cause is . . . an express contradiction and impossibility'.*

Therefore,

(C) *Option (a) must be true: 'There has existed from eternity some one unchangeable and independent being'.*

As we can see from this reconstruction, the form of Clarke's argument is that of an *argument from elimination*. That is, he argues that there are only two possibilities worth considering, then rules one of them out. If only (a) *or* (b) can be true, and if (b) is ruled out, then we must conclude that (a) is true. So far, so good. But why is Clarke convinced that (a) and (b) are the only possible options here? And why does he think that option (b) can be ruled out? To address these questions, we need to dig a bit deeper.

Let's begin at the very beginning, then, with premise (1). According to Clarke, there has never been a time when there was absolutely nothing. Why? If, once upon a time, there was absolutely nothing, there would still be nothing now; for nothing comes from nothing. But it is as plain as the print on this page that there isn't nothing now. Because something exists right now, therefore, we can conclude that *something* has existed from all eternity (or 'since time began', as we might put it). Now, simply saying that '*something* has existed from all eternity' isn't very informative; we want to know what *kinds* of things—what kinds of beings—could exist or must exist. And it is at this point, in premise (2), that Clarke introduces a distinction between **dependent beings** (so named because they depend on some other being for their existence) and **independent beings** (so named because they don't depend on any other being for their existence). Ask yourself: Could dependent beings be the only things that have ever existed? If your answer is yes, you have committed yourself to option (b). If your answer is no, then you must hold that not all beings are dependent—that at least one independent being exists. And that conclusion is equivalent to option (a). So you must say one of two things: either (a) there has always existed at least one independent being, or (b) nothing has ever existed but dependent beings.

This brings us to premise (3). Why does Clarke think that the very idea of (b), according to which there has never been anything other than dependent beings, is absurd or impossible? Here Clarke invokes a metaphysical principle very similar in spirit to Leibniz's celebrated '**Principle of Sufficient Reason**' (which we first encountered in Chapter 1). Leibniz insists that there must be a 'sufficient reason' or a satisfactory explanation for everything, whether we can know it or not. Whenever we ask 'Why?'—as in 'Why did that leaf just fall from the tree?', or 'Why did the water in the pond freeze last night?', or 'Why did their canoe capsize?', or 'Why was the professor late for yesterday's class?'—we are assuming the Principle of Sufficient Reason, or something like it. For if we think it makes sense to ask 'Why?'—to demand an explanation—we must think that there *is* an explanation, whether or not any of us will ever know what that explanation is. And since human beings cannot help asking 'Why?' questions, it looks very much as if the Principle of Sufficient Reason must be one of the iron laws of human thought. And Leibniz is convinced that this is the case, for he tells us that the Principle of Sufficient Reason is a rule by which we are bound to reason:

From *Monadology*
By Gottfried Wilhelm von Leibniz

Our reasoning is based upon two great principles: first, that of Contradiction, by means of which we decide that to be false which involves contradiction and that to be true which contradicts or is opposed to the false. And second, the Principle of Sufficient Reason, in virtue of which we believe that no fact can be real or existing and no statement true unless it has a sufficient reason why it should be thus and not otherwise. Most frequently, however, these reasons cannot be known by us.

Although Samuel Clarke agrees with the drift of what Leibniz is saying, he formulates the Principle of Sufficient Reason in his own way. Here is Clarke's formulation, taken from Proposition I of *A Demonstration of the Being and Attributes of God*:

From *A Demonstration of the Being and Attributes of God*
By Samuel Clarke

Whatever exists has a cause, a reason, a ground of its existence, a foundation on which its existence relies, a ground or reason why it does exist rather than not exist, either in the necessity of its own nature (and then it must have been of itself eternal), or in the will of some other being (and then that other being must, at least in the order of nature and causality, have existed before it).

As we have said, this is the principle that Clarke relies upon to defend premise (3), according to which (b) is absurd. Since 'whatever exists has a cause, a reason, a ground of its existence', it follows that *if* an infinite series of dependent beings existed, there would have to be 'a cause, a reason, a ground of its existence'—in other words, a satisfactory explanation of why it exists. Now, ask yourself: If there is such a reason or explanation, what could it be? Where is it to be sought? If (b) is true, the explanation of the series cannot lie *outside* the series of dependent beings. Why? Because (b) says that *everything* that exists, or has ever existed, is part of that series. So if (b) is true, there is *nothing* outside of that series. And so we must conclude that 'this whole series of beings can have no cause from without of its existence because in it are supposed to be included all things that are, or ever were, in the universe'. Very well; let's try again. Could the explanation or 'sufficient reason' of the series lie *within* the series? Again the answer is no, says Clarke. Since nothing can be its own sufficient reason unless it is 'self-existent or necessary', no dependent being can be its own sufficient reason. But every member of the series described by (b) is a dependent being; and 'where no part is necessary, it is manifest that the whole cannot be necessary'. And so we must conclude that the series of dependent beings 'can have no reason within itself for its existence'.

Can you see where all this is leading? If the reason or ground of the series described by (b) doesn't lie beyond the series or within the series—if the existence of that series cannot be explained either by appealing to something outside the series or by appealing to something inside the series—then an infinite series of dependent beings can have *no* reason or ground of its existence. But 'whatever exists has a cause, a reason, a ground of its existence'. Therefore, there cannot exist an infinite series of dependent beings: it would be a 'contradiction', an 'impossibility'. So, option (b) is impossible—and that is precisely what premise (3) asserts. But if (b) isn't true, then (a) must be true, according to premise (2). So (a) must be true—and that is Clarke's conclusion, (C).

Hence if Clarke's cosmological argument succeeds—if his premises are true and his logic impeccable—then there must exist an 'independent and unchangeable being'. Is that the same as proving that God exists? No; and Clarke is well aware of this, though he is untroubled by it. Why? For Clarke, the cosmological argument is the beginning, not the end, of his argument for God's existence; it is the first step of the journey, not the final destination.[2]

- How is Clarke's version of the cosmological argument different from Aquinas' first and second ways? Does Clarke agree with what Aquinas says about the impossibility of an infinite regress?
- How is Clarke's argument similar to Aquinas' third way? How is it different?
- What are some major objections to the cosmological argument? How do such objections compare to those raised against the ontological argument?
- Of all the versions of the cosmological argument we have examined, which strikes you as the most promising? Which strikes you as the least promising? Why?

E. Proving God: The Teleological Argument

The most familiar 'proof' of God's existence is often called the **argument from design**. The question at the centre of the argument is clear enough: How could the world be as complex and intricate and orderly as it is if it were the product of blind chance and not divine design?

Immanuel Kant called the argument from design the 'teleological argument', because it attributes purpose to the creation of the world. William Paley, an Anglican philosopher active in the late eighteenth and early nineteenth centuries, puts forth a classical form of the argument in his analogy of the Watchmaker:

From *Natural Theology*
By William Paley

Suppose I had found a watch upon the ground, and it should be enquired how the watch happened to be in that place. . . .

In crossing a heath, suppose I pitched my foot against a *stone*, and were asked how the stone came to be there, I might possibly answer, that, for any thing I knew to the contrary, it had lain there forever: nor would it perhaps be very easy to shew the absurdity of this answer. But suppose I had found a *watch* upon the ground, and it should be enquired how the watch happened to be in that place, I should hardly think of the answer which I had before given, that, for any thing I knew, the watch might have always been there. Yet why should not this answer serve for the watch, as well as for the stone? Why is it not as admissible in the second case, as in the first? For this reason, and for no other, viz. that, when we come to inspect the watch we perceive (what we could not discover in the stone) that its several parts are framed and put together for a purpose, for example that they are so formed and adjusted as to produce motion, and that motion so regulated as to point out the hour of the day; that, if several parts had been differently shaped from what they are, of a different size from what they are, or placed after any other manner, or in any other order, than that in which they are placed, either no motion at all would have been carried on in the machine, or none which would have answered the use, that is now served by it.

What we have here is an *argument from analogy*—a non-deductive form of argument (as we described in the Introduction). The world, we are told, resembles a giant watch; but watches are plainly the products of intelligent design, not of blind chance; and so it stands to reason that the world, too, is most likely the product of intelligent design. In short, the fact that there is a kind of order in Nature gives us good (but not conclusive) reasons for thinking that there is a Divine Mind behind it all, a Celestial Watchmaker of unparalleled power, wisdom, and skill.

The Watchmaker argument was endorsed by many European philosophers in the eighteenth century, and its prestige lasted well into the nineteenth century. Indeed, even a young Charles Darwin was greatly impressed by Paley's *Natural Theology* when he read it as a theology student at Cambridge University. Later, of course, Darwin took a rather different view of Paley's argument, as we shall discuss later in this section.

Yet the Watchmaker argument, though famous and influential, is not the only version of the teleological argument. Indeed, it would be rather odd if it were, given that (a) the teleological argument has been around at least since Plato's *Timaeus*—almost 2,500 years ago—and (b) philosophers who agree that a certain kind of argument is a good one seldom agree about the best way to formulate it. In a sense, then, there is no such thing as *the* teleological argument, just as there is no such thing as *the* cosmological argument or *the* ontological argument. Though handy, each of these labels simply refers to a basic type or style of argument, which different philosophers have developed in different ways.

So how else has the teleological argument been formulated? Let's begin with a look at two different versions, that of St John Damascene and that of St Thomas Aquinas, neither of which is an argument from analogy. Both are deductive arguments, both come from medieval philosophy, and both give us much philosophical food for thought.

Writing well over a thousand years ago, St John Damascene maintained that the order present in the natural world—what he calls 'the harmony of creation'—proves that God exists. Although Damascene wasn't the first to argue in this way (he acknowledges that the argument, far from being original, had already been around for centuries), his brief and elegant formulation of the teleological argument is worth reading:

From *An Exact Exposition of the Orthodox Faith*
By St John Damascene

The very harmony of creation, its preservation and governing, teach us that there is a God.

What is more, the very harmony of creation, its preservation and governing, teach us that there is a God who has put all this together and keeps it together, ever maintaining it and providing for it. For how could such contrary natures as fire and water, earth and air, combine with one another to form one world and remain undissolved, unless there were some all-powerful force to bring them together and always keep them that way?

What is it that has ordered the things of heaven and those of earth, the things which move through the air and those which move in the water—nay, rather, the things which preceded them: heaven and earth and the natures of fire and water? What is it that combined and arranged them? What is it that set them in motion and put them on their unceasing and unhindered courses? Or is it that they had no architect to set a principle in them all by which the whole universe be moved and controlled? But who is the architect of these things? Or did not he who made them also bring them into being? We shall certainly not attribute such power to spontaneity. Even grant that they came into being spontaneously; then, whence came their arrangement? Let us grant this, also, if you wish. Then, what maintains and keeps the principles by which they subsisted in the first place? It is most certainly some other thing than mere chance. What else is this, if it is not God?

According to Damascene, Nature is made up of things with opposite or contrary natures: fire and water, earth and air, and so forth. Now, things with opposite or contrary natures do not automatically form a stable and harmonious order—an 'indissoluble union'—all on their own. And yet the natural world forms such an order. Hence there must exist a Being who, existing outside of Nature, governs Nature; a Being who 'bound things together and is always preserving them from dissolution'; a Being who ensures that the natural world never devolves into utter chaos, but remains an enduring and unified whole. And if there really is a Being who has what it takes to do all that, asks Damascene, why shouldn't we call that Being 'God'?

Another classic version of the teleological argument from the medieval period is St Thomas Aquinas' 'fifth way':

On the 'Fifth Way'
By St Thomas Aquinas

The fifth way is taken from the governance of the world. We see that things which lack knowledge, such as natural bodies, act for an end, and this is evident from their acting always, or nearly always, in the same way, so as to obtain the best result. Hence it is plain that they achieve their end, not fortuitously, but designedly. Now whatever lacks knowledge cannot move towards an end, unless it be directed by some being endowed with knowledge and intelligence; as the arrow is directed by the archer. Therefore some intelligent being exists by whom all natural things are directed to their end; and this being we call God.

Aquinas states this argument so tersely, so succinctly, and so quickly that it is easy for the reader to miss what is going on. So how, exactly, does the fifth way unfold? Let us take a closer look.

According to Aquinas, things in nature act for an end. Take a humble acorn, for example. If experience teaches us anything about acorns, it is that there is something that an acorn is supposed to *become*—namely, an oak tree. An acorn, we might say, is a *potential* oak tree: if left alone and given what it needs—light, water, oxygen, and so on—it will grow and eventually become a mighty oak. Now, here's what Aquinas wants to know: How is this sort of goal-directed development possible? That is, how can things in nature act for an end? *You* can act for an end, and so can I; but that is because we are *persons* (that is—beings with intelligence and will). For example, I can go to the corner store to buy milk (that's my end, or goal) because I know what milk is and where to get it (intelligence) and because I have decided to buy milk (will). But something lacking intelligence and will cannot act for an end, says Aquinas, unless it is directed to that end by a being with intelligence and will, just 'as the arrow is directed by the archer' to its target. And who is this intelligent and powerful Being 'by whom all natural things are directed to their end'? None other than God, Aquinas answers.

- Is Aquinas' God a watchmaker, like Paley's God? Why or why not?
- How does Aquinas' fifth way differ from Damascene's argument? Do you think that they prove the same type of God? Why or why not?
- Which of these two arguments seems better to you? Why?

Aquinas' argument is psychologically powerful, but it has its problems. For one thing, we may wonder whether Aquinas' idea that natural bodies act for ends is tenable in light of modern advances in the sciences of biology, physics, and chemistry. If we can no longer take that idea seriously, it doesn't follow that Nature isn't orderly—it may or may not be—but it does follow that Aquinas has incorrectly described whatever order there is in Nature. And this matters, because once old-fashioned natural teleology goes—once we jettison the idea that things in nature act for ends or goals—the fifth way will crumble and collapse. After all, if things in nature are not goal-directed, there is no need to wonder *how* they can be goal-directed.

We may also wonder whether there is quite as much order in Nature as Aquinas seems to think. In addition to order, isn't there also a good deal of disorder in the natural world? In addition to things 'acting always, or nearly always, in the same way, so as to obtain the best result', aren't there also things that often turn out very badly indeed? Think about floods and hurricanes, earthquakes and tsunamis, mudslides and droughts, plagues and epidemics. Such natural disasters may seem relatively rare—at any rate, they don't happen *to us* every day—but we know what havoc and harm they can wreak. If Nature were truly the work of a divine designer, we may ask, would she be so capricious or cruel, so indifferent or chaotic? If we look at Nature objectively—warts and all—do we really find the sort of beautiful harmony that we would expect to find if Aquinas' conclusion were true?

Absolutely not, concludes David Hume in his superb *Dialogues Concerning Natural Religion*:

On an Imperfect Universe
By David Hume

This world, for aught he knows, . . . was only the first rude essay of some infant deity who afterwards abandoned it.

In a word, Cleanthes, a man who follows your hypothesis is able, perhaps, to assert or conjecture that the universe sometime arose from something like design; but beyond that position he cannot ascertain one single circumstance and is left afterwards to fix every point of his theology by the utmost licence of fancy and hypothesis. This world, for aught he knows, is very faulty and imperfect compared to a superior standard and was only the first rude essay of some infant deity who afterwards abandoned it, ashamed of his lame performance; it is the work only of some dependent, inferior deity and is the object of derision to his superiors; it is the production of old age and dotage in some superannuated deity and, ever since his death, has run on at adventures from the first impulse and active force which it received from him.

Begun in the 1750s, Hume's *Dialogues Concerning Natural Religion* were finally published in 1779, three years after Hume's death and almost a quarter century before Paley's *Natural Theology* (1802). Because the *Dialogues* contain a hard-hitting critique of the idea that Nature is the creation of a supernatural designer, some readers have concluded that William Paley's case for a Watchmaker was intellectually stillborn. Not so, insists Richard Dawkins, the prominent contemporary evolutionary biologist, popular author, and leading New Atheist. In *The Blind Watchmaker*, Dawkins argues that philosophers have underestimated the merits of Paley's original argument, just as they have overestimated the force of Hume's objections to it. So just who does Dawkins think should get the credit for dealing the death-blow to Paley's Celestial Watchmaker? Hint: it's not a philosopher.

From *The Blind Watchmaker*
By Richard Dawkins

Natural selection is the blind watchmaker, blind because it does not see ahead, does not plan consequences, has no purpose in view.

Paley's argument is made with passionate sincerity and is informed by the best biological scholarship of his day, but it is wrong, gloriously and utterly wrong. The analogy between telescope and eye, between watch and living organism, is false. All appearances to the contrary, the only watchmaker in nature is the

(*Continued*)

blind forces of physics, albeit deployed in a very special way. A true watchmaker has foresight: he designs his cogs and springs, and plans their interconnections, with a future purpose in his mind's eye. Natural selection, the blind, unconscious, automatic process which Darwin discovered, and which we now know is the explanation for the existence and apparently purposeful form of all life, has no purpose in mind. It has no mind and no mind's eye. It does not plan for the future. It has no vision, no foresight, no sight at all. If it can be said to play the role of watchmaker in nature, it is the *blind* watchmaker.

I shall explain all this, and much else besides. But one thing I shall not do is belittle the wonder of the living 'watches' that so inspired Paley. On the contrary, I shall try to illustrate my feeling that here Paley could have gone even further. When it comes to feeling awe over living 'watches' I yield to nobody. I feel more in common with the Reverend William Paley than I do with the distinguished modern philosopher, a well-known atheist, with whom I once discussed the matter at dinner. I said that I could not imagine being an atheist at any time before 1859, when Darwin's *Origin of Species* was published. 'What about Hume?', replied the philosopher. 'How did Hume explain the organized complexity of the living world?', I asked. 'He didn't', said the philosopher. 'Why does it need any special explanation?'

Paley knew that it needed a special explanation; Darwin knew it, and I suspect that in his heart of hearts my philosopher companion knew it too. In any case it will be my business to show it here. As for David Hume himself, it is sometimes said that that great Scottish philosopher disposed of the Argument from Design a century before Darwin. But what Hume did was criticize the logic of using apparent design in nature as *positive* evidence for the existence of a God. He did not offer any *alternative* explanation for apparent design, but left the question open. An atheist before Darwin could have said, following Hume: 'I have no explanation for complex biological design. All I know is that God isn't a good explanation, so we must wait and hope that somebody comes up with a better one.' I can't help feeling that such a position, though logically sound, would have left one feeling pretty unsatisfied, and that although atheism might have been *logically* tenable before Darwin, Darwin made it possible to be an intellectually fulfilled atheist. I like to think that Hume would agree, but some of his writings suggest that he underestimated the complexity and beauty of biological design. The boy naturalist Charles Darwin could have shown him a thing or two about that, but Hume had been dead for 40 years when Darwin enrolled in Hume's university of Edinburgh.

* * *

Natural selection is the blind watchmaker, blind because it does not see ahead, does not plan consequences, has no purpose in view. Yet the living results of natural selection overwhelmingly impress us with the appearance of design as if by a master watchmaker, impress us with the illusion of design and planning.

- What does Dawkins mean when he says that 'Darwin made it possible to be an intellectually fulfilled atheist'? Why doesn't he think that Hume made this possible? In other words, what did *The Origin of Species* do to Paley-esque design arguments that the *Dialogues* didn't?

The prestige of the Watchmaker argument has suffered enormously from the shock of Darwin's theory of evolution. Nevertheless, the argument from design does not lack its defenders and enthusiasts in our time. While current theory does not always invoke God explicitly, it argues more generally that the universe does show design and cannot be the product of pure chance. Such arguments are explored in the following selections from physicist Paul Davies and philosopher Cory Juhl.

From *The Mind of God*
By Paul Davies

All the evidence suggests that this is not just any old universe, but one that is remarkably well adjusted to the existence of certain interesting and significant entities (for example, stable stars).

The situation becomes even more intriguing when we take into account the existence of living organisms. The fact that biological systems have very special requirements, and that these requirements are, happily, met by nature, has been commented upon at least since the seventeenth century. It is only in the twentieth century, however, with the development of biochemistry, genetics, and molecular biology, that the full picture has emerged. Already in 1913 the distinguished Harvard biochemist Lawrence Henderson wrote: 'The properties of matter and the course of cosmic evolution are now seen to be intimately related to the structure of the living being and to its activities; . . . the biologist may now rightly regard the Universe in its very essence as biocentric.' Henderson was led to this surprising view from his work on the regulation of acidity and alkalinity in living organisms, and the way that such regulation depends crucially upon the rather special properties of certain chemical substances. He was also greatly impressed at how water, which has a number of anomalous properties, is incorporated into life at a basic level. Had these various substances not existed, or had the laws of physics been somewhat different so that the substances did not enjoy these special properties, then life (at least as we know it) would be impossible. Henderson regarded the 'fitness of the environment' for life as too great to be accidental, and asked what manner of law is capable of explaining such a match.

In the 1960s the astronomer Fred Hoyle noted that the element carbon, whose peculiar chemical properties make it crucial to terrestrial life, is manufactured from helium inside large stars. . . . Hoyle was struck by the fact that the key reaction proceeds only because of a lucky fluke. Carbon nuclei are made by a rather tricky process involving the simultaneous encounter of three high-speed helium nuclei, which then stick together. Because of the rarity of triple-nucleus encounters, the reaction can proceed at a significant rate only at certain well-defined energies (termed 'resonances'), where the reaction rate is substantially amplified by quantum effects. By good fortune, one of these resonances is positioned just about right to correspond to the sort of energies that helium nuclei have inside large stars. . . . A detailed study also revealed other 'coincidences' without which carbon would not be both produced and preserved inside stars. Hoyle was so impressed by this 'monstrous series of accidents', he was prompted to comment that it was as if 'the laws of nuclear physics have been deliberately designed with regard to the consequences they produce inside the stars'. Later he was to expound the view that the universe looks like a 'put-up job', as though somebody had been 'monkeying' with the laws of physics.

On the 'Fine-Tuning' Argument
By Cory Juhl

As Paul Davies notes in *The Mind of God*, there appear to be a large number of surprising 'coincidences' in the structure of physical laws. For instance, he notes that in 1913 the Harvard biochemist Lawrence Henderson pointed out how remarkable was the 'fit' of the earth's environment to life, and in the 1960s astronomer Fred Hoyle was struck by the fact that the reactions that made life possible were 'a lucky fluke'. It seems that the fundamental constants of physics, such as the gravitational constant and dozens of others, seem 'finely tuned' to allow for life as we know it. According to the fine-tuning argument, the surprising way in which the various constants 'fit together' strongly suggests that an intelligent being was involved in the production of our universe. The reasoning is straightforward. Of all the combinations of values that the constants might have taken, their values are distributed in just the right way to yield a universe that can produce life as we know it. If there is a God who wants life as we know it to arise, this is not surprising. If there is no God, the probability

(*Continued*)

that such a combination would come into being spontaneously, or accidentally, is infinitesimally small. Since these hypotheses exhaust the class of possible explanations, we should infer that God (or at least some extremely powerful intelligent being) 'fine-tuned' the universe and its laws.

A number of responses have been given to this argument. One common response made by a number of physicists is that, granting the prior improbability of any single universe being 'fine-tuned', it may be that there are an enormous number of universes, whose fundamental constant values vary randomly across the collection. Given enough such universes, it is not surprising that some universe should be fine-tuned. Furthermore, intelligent observers will be around asking such questions only in fine-tuned universes, so it should not be surprising that we (intelligent observers) find ourselves in a universe of this sort. Fine-tuning advocates have responded that such a 'many-universes' response seems ad hoc, since, they claim, there is no independent motivation (aside from theism-avoidance) for positing such worlds. Whether the 'many-universes' hypothesis can be independently supported is an interesting open question.

Another response to the fine-tuning argument raises concerns about our assignments of prior probabilities to the various 'universe production' scenarios. Unlike types of events that are produced regularly within our universe, we are only able to observe one universe. For example, it seems possible, for all we know, that there is a 'law of universe production' that guarantees that only fine-tuned universes are ever produced. In the absence of further relevant data, which data seems impossible in principle to gather (that is, data about other universes), we simply have no justification for thinking that universes like ours are probable or improbable.

A common reaction to the proposal of a 'law of universe production' that necessarily yields fine-tuned universes like ours is that 'this just pushes the question back', as to why such an improbable law obtains. However, a *tu quoque* is possible here: why should a God of just the sort theists propose exist? The arguments are reminiscent of those pertaining to the cosmological argument discussed earlier. As to our ability to know prior probabilities, advocates of fine-tuning will insist that on any reasonable assignment of prior probabilities to various possible universes, fine-tuned universes will turn out to have an extremely low probability. Just as we make our best guesses on the basis of what we know in other more familiar cases, we should make our best guess in this case, which is without a doubt the conjecture that there is an Intelligent Designer.

Whether this is our best guess, though, remains questionable. In order to see why, we can consider any hypothesis as to the probability that God would produce a universe of any given type. Given any hypothesis of this sort, there is an atheistic hypothesis (involving, say, a law of universe production) that yields universes of any given type with exactly the same probability. In a nutshell, given any theistic hypothesis about the probabilities of various types of universes, there is an 'equivalent' atheistic hypothesis that assigns exactly the same probabilities to the creation of exactly the same types of universes. So the question becomes, is it obvious that in general we should prefer theistic hypotheses of that sort over atheistic hypotheses of the same sort? Opinions will differ, but it is far from clear that of any such pair of analogous pairs of hypotheses, the theistic hypotheses are intrinsically more plausible.

- How does the new argument from 'fine-tuning' resembles Damascene's version of the teleological argument? How do the two arguments differ?
- Of all the versions of the teleological arguments we have examined, which strikes you as the most promising? The least promising? Why?
- Do you think that one must believe either in God or in evolution? Could you believe in both?
- What are some major objections to the teleological argument? How do such objections compare to those raised against the ontological and cosmological arguments?
- Do you think any of the arguments for God's existence we've examined establish the existence of the traditional God with all of His qualities? Why or why not?
- Are the ontological, cosmological, and teleological arguments the only arguments for God's existence? Can you think of any others?

F. Mystical Experience and God

In the last three sections of this chapter, we have scrutinized versions of three major arguments for God's existence: the ontological proof, the cosmological proof, and the teleological proof. What if, after examining all these arguments with due care, you conclude that none of them succeeds? To begin with, you can rest assured that you are not alone. Skepticism about the traditional theistic proofs has become increasingly common among philosophers since the time of Kant, who offered a rigorous critique of 'rational theology' (that is—the part of philosophy that attempts to demonstrate the existence of God and to deduce his attributes by means of reason alone, without appealing to 'revelation' or 'sacred tradition'). Few post-Kantian philosophers—even those who were by no means ardent disciples of Kant—have approached the arguments in the same spirit as their pre-Kantian counterparts.

Take William James, for example. Writing a little over a century after the publication of Kant's *Critique of Pure Reason*—and less than half a century after the publication of Darwin's *The Origin of Species*—James had this to say about the traditional philosophical proofs of God's existence:

From *The Varieties of Religious Experience*
By William James

The arguments for God's existence have stood for hundreds of years with the waves of unbelieving criticism breaking against them, never totally discrediting them in the ears of the faithful, but on the whole slowly and surely washing out the mortar from between their joints. If you have a God already whom you believe in, these arguments confirm you. If you are atheistic, they fail to set you right. The proofs are various. The 'cosmological' one, so-called, reasons from the contingence of the world to a First Cause which must contain whatever perfections the world itself contains. The 'argument from design' reasons, from the fact that Nature's laws are mathematical, and her parts benevolently adapted to each other, that this cause is both intellectual and benevolent. The 'moral argument' is that the moral law presupposes a lawgiver. The 'argument *ex consensu gentium*' is that the belief in God is so widespread as to be grounded in the rational nature of man, and should therefore carry authority with it.

As I just said, I will not discuss these arguments technically. The bare fact that all idealists since Kant have felt entitled either to scout or to neglect them shows that they are not solid enough to serve as religion's all-sufficient foundation. Absolutely impersonal reasons would be in duty bound to show more general convincingness. Causation is indeed too obscure a principle to bear the weight of the whole structure of theology. As for the argument from design, see how Darwinian ideas have revolutionized it. Conceived as we now conceive them, as so many fortunate escapes from almost limitless processes of destruction, the benevolent adaptations which we find in Nature suggest a deity very different from the one who figured in the earlier versions of the argument. The fact is that these arguments do but follow the combined suggestions of the facts and of our feeling. They prove nothing rigorously. They only corroborate our pre-existent partialities.

Suppose we grant, for the sake of argument, that James is right, and concede that traditional arguments for God's existence 'prove nothing rigorously' but 'only corroborate our pre-existent partialities'. Does it follow from this that you have no reason to believe in God? No. Why? Simple: because there may be other ways for you to defend or justify that belief. For instance, it may be possible for you to justify your belief in God by appealing, not to metaphysical proofs, but to your religious experiences—to your own intuitive awareness of God's presence, say, or to your sense that God is 'there' in a way you find hard to describe but even harder to doubt. As we shall see, James himself holds something like this view about the justification of religious belief; and he is by no means alone in doing so. For example, Sarvepalli Radhakrishnan, the eminent Indian philosopher (and former president of India) takes a very similar view. In *An Idealist View of Life*, Radhakrishnan argues that the world's major religions all grow out of the rich soil of individual experience, not from the rough dust of impersonal argument.

From *An Idealist View of Life*
By Sarvepalli Radhakrishnan

The direct apprehension of God seems to be as real to some men as . . . the perception of the external world is to others.

Philosophy of religion is religion come to an understanding of itself. It attempts a reasoned solution of a problem which exists directly only for the religious man who has the spiritual intuition or experience and indirectly for all those who, while they have no personal share in the experience, yet have sufficient belief that the experience does occur and is not illusory. The direct apprehension of God seems to be as real to some men as the consciousness of personality or the perception of the external world is to others. The sense of communion with the divine, the awe and worship which it evokes, which to us are only moments of vision or insight, seem to be normal and all-pervading with the saints. If philosophy of religion is to become scientific, it must become empirical and found itself on religious experience.

* * *

All the religions owe their inspiration to the personal insights of their prophet founders. The Hindu religion, for example, is characterized by its adherence to fact. In its pure form, at any rate, it never leaned as heavily as other religions do on authority. It is not a 'founded' religion; nor does it centre round any historical events. Its distinctive characteristic has been its insistence on the inward life of spirit. To know, possess, and be the spirit in this physical frame, to convert an obscure plodding mentality into clear spiritual illumination, to build peace and self-existent freedom in the stress of emotional satisfactions and sufferings, to discover and realize the life divine in a body subject to sickness and death has been the constant aim of the Hindu religious endeavour.

According to Radhakrishnan, '[t]he direct apprehension of God seems to be as real to some men as the consciousness of personality or the perception of the external world is to others'. Taken as a historical observation, what Radhakrishnan says seems quite true. If we study different civilizations and cultures, we find that there have always been men and women who have claimed to enjoy a 'direct apprehension of god': men and women, that is, who have had intense experiences in which the divine seemed to them undeniably present. Now, whether we should regard any of these experiences as *veridical*—whether, that is, all such experiences are delusions or whether at least some of them are more or less what they seem—is a hugely important question; and we shall return to it in just a moment. For now, however, all that interests us is the fact—and there is no doubt that it is a fact, according to Radhakrishnan—that such compelling experiences are the true root of the religious life:

The whole scheme of Buddhism centres on Buddha's enlightenment. Moses saw God in the burning bush, and Elijah heard the still small voice. In *Jeremiah* we read: 'This is the covenant which I will make with the house of Israel after those days, saith the Lord. I will put my hand in their inward parts, and in their heart will I write it.' Jesus' experience of God is the basic fact for Christianity: 'As he came up out of the river he saw the heavens parted above him and the spirit descending like a dove towards him: and he heard a voice sounding out of the heavens and saying "Thou art my beloved son. I have chosen thee."' According to St Mark, the baptism in the Jordan by John was to Jesus the occasion of a vivid and intense religious experience, so much so that he felt that he had to go for a time into absolute solitude to think it over. He obviously spoke of the ineffable happening, the sudden revelation, the new peace; and joy in words that have come down to us. He emphasizes the newness of the reborn soul as something which marks him off from all those who are religious only at second hand. 'Verily I say unto you, among men born of women there hath not arisen a greater than John the Baptist; but the least in the Kingdom of God is greater than he.' The vision that came to Saul on the Damascus road and turned the persecutor into an apostle is another illustration. Faith means in St James acceptance of dogma; in St Paul it is the surrender of heart and mind to Christ; but in the Epistle to the Hebrews, faith is defined as that outreaching of the mind by which we become aware of the invisible world. The life of Mohammad is full of mystic experiences. Witnesses to the personal sense of the divine are not confined to the East. Socrates and Plato, Plotinus and Porphyry, Augustine and Dante, Bunyan and Wesley, and numberless others, testify to the felt reality of God. It is as old as humanity and is not confined to any one people. The evidence is too massive to run away from.

Consider also the following argument by the Sufi philosopher Mohammad al-Ghazali, a renowned Islamic **mystic** from the Middle Ages:

From *The Deliverance from Error*
By Mohammad al-Ghazali

What is most distinctive of mysticism is something which cannot be apprehended by study, but only by immediate experience . . . by ecstasy and by a moral change.

When I had finished with [philosophy and theology], I next turned with set purpose to the method of mysticism (or Sufism). I knew that the complete mystic 'way' includes both intellectual belief and practical activity; the latter consists in getting rid of the obstacles in the self and in stripping off its base characteristics and vicious morals, so that the heart may attain to freedom from what is not God and to constant recollection of Him.

The intellectual belief was easier to me than the practical activity. I began to acquaint myself with their belief by reading their books. . . . I thus comprehended their fundamental teachings on the intellectual side, and progressed, as far as is possible by study and oral instruction, in the knowledge of mysticism. It became clear to me, however, that what is most distinctive of mysticism is something which cannot be apprehended by study, but only by immediate experience (*dhawq*—literally 'tasting'), by ecstasy and by a moral change. What a difference there is between *knowing* the definition of health and satiety, together with their causes and presuppositions, and *being* healthy and satisfied! What a difference between being acquainted with the definition of drunkenness—namely, that it designates a state arising from the domination of the seat of the intellect by vapours arising from the stomach—and being drunk! Indeed, the drunken man while in that condition does not know the definition of drunkenness nor the scientific account of it; he has not the very least scientific knowledge of it. The sober man, on the other hand, knows the definition of drunkenness and its basis, yet he is not drunk in the very least. Again the doctor, when he is himself ill, knows the definition and causes of health and the remedies which restore it, and yet is lacking in health. Similarly there is a

(Continued)

difference between knowing the true nature and causes and conditions of the ascetic life and actually leading such a life and forsaking the world.

I apprehended clearly that the mystics were men who had real experiences, not men of words, and that I had already progressed as far as was possible by way of intellectual apprehension. What remained for me was not to be attained by oral instruction and study but only by immediate experience and by walking in the mystic way.

Many of the reports of mystical experience with which we are most familiar come from adherents of widespread religious traditions, such as Hinduism, Buddhism, Judaism, Christianity, and Islam (as in the case of al-Ghazali). However, we mustn't conclude from this that no one else has mystical experiences. The fact is that there have always been purely philosophical mystics: free spirits and independent souls who have sought to experience God without benefit of clergy or creed, unsupported by revelations or rituals. In the West, the philosophical mystic *par excellence* is Plotinus, a renowned Neoplatonist thinker who has often been described as the last great philosopher of the ancient world. In *The Enneads*, a sequence of six lyrical treatises on metaphysics, Plotinus movingly conveys the ecstatic rapture enjoyed by a soul liberated from the brutal prison of the body. Reading his poetic descriptions of the free soul's joyful and elevated state, we immediately realize something: instead of trafficking in pale conjectures or second-hand speculations about these esoteric matters, Plotinus is telling us about his own experiences of vivid mystical bliss:

From *The Enneads*
By Plotinus

Many times it has happened: lifted out of the body into myself . . . .

Many times it has happened: lifted out of the body into myself; becoming external to all other things and self-centred; beholding a marvellous beauty; then, more than ever, assured of community with the loftiest order; enacting the noblest life, acquiring identity with the divine; stationing with It by having attained that activity; poised above whatsoever within the Intellectual is less than the Supreme: yet, there comes the moment of descent from intellection to reasoning, and after that sojourn in the divine, I ask myself how it happens that I can now be descending, and how did the Soul ever enter into my body, the Soul which, even within the body, is the high thing it has shown itself to be.

Do these sorts of mystical experiences have any important philosophical implications? Yes, Plotinus replies: the knowledge that the mystic's soul has of itself when 'lifted out of the body' furnishes us with a convincing proof of the soul's immortality.

That the soul is of the family of the diviner nature, the eternal, is clear from our demonstration that it is not material: besides it has neither shape nor colour nor is it tangible. But there are other proofs.

Assuming that the divine and the authentically existent possesses a life beneficent and wise, we take the next step and begin with working out the nature of our own soul.

Let us consider a soul, not one that has appropriated the unreasoned desires and impulses of the bodily life, or any other such emotion and experience, but one that has cast all this aside, and as far as possible has no commerce with the bodily. Such a soul demonstrates that all evil is accretion, alien, and that in the purged soul the noble things are immanent, wisdom and all else that is good, as its native store.

If this is the soul once it has returned to itself, how deny that it is of the nature we have identified with all the divine and eternal? Wisdom and authentic virtue are divine, and could not be found in the chattel mean and mortal: what possesses these must be divine by its very capacity of the divine, the token of kinship and of identical substance.

Hence, too, any one of us that exhibits these qualities will differ but little as far as soul is concerned from the Supernals; he will be less than they only to the extent in which the soul is, in him, associated with body.

This is so true that, if every human being were at that stage, or if a great number lived by a soul of that degree, no one would be so incredulous as to doubt that the Soul in man is immortal. It is because we see everywhere the spoiled souls of the great mass that it becomes difficult to recognize their divinity and immortality.

To know the nature of a thing we must observe it in its unalloyed state, since any addition obscures the reality. Clear, then look: or, rather, let a man first purify himself and then observe: he will not doubt his immortality when he sees himself thus entered into the pure, the Intellectual. For, what he sees is an Intellectual-Principle looking on nothing of sense, nothing of this mortality, but by its own eternity having intellection of the eternal: he will see all things in this Intellectual substance, himself having become an Intellectual Cosmos and all lightsome, illuminated by the truth streaming from The Good, which radiates truth upon all that stands within that realm of the divine.

Thus he will often feel the beauty of that word, 'Farewell: I am to you an immortal God', for he has ascended to the Supreme, and is all one strain to enter into likeness with it.

If the purification puts the human into knowledge of the highest, then, too, the science latent within becomes manifest, the only authentic knowing. For it is not by running hither and thither outside of itself that the Soul discerns Moral Wisdom and Justice: it learns them of its own nature, in its contact with itself, in its intellectual grasp of itself, seeing deeply impressed upon it the images of its primal state; what was one mass of rust from long neglect it has restored to purity.

Imagine living gold: it files away all that is earthy about it, all that kept it in self-ignorance preventing it from knowing itself as gold; seen now unalloyed it is at once filled with admiration of its worth and knows that it has no need of any other glory than its own, triumphant if only it be allowed to remain purely to itself.

You may not find this lengthy passage easy to follow, partly because of its rich poetic diction, partly because of its unfamiliar jargon, and partly because of Plotinus' exasperating refusal to state his proof in a straightforward, linear fashion. There is no need to be discouraged by these things, however; all they signify is that if we want to understand Plotinus, we need to roll up our sleeves and get down to work. To be more specific, we must seek answers to three questions. First, what is the argument's starting-point? Second, what are its main premises? Third, by what sequence of logical steps does Plotinus approach his startling conclusion?

Here is one way of reconstructing Plotinus' argument that seems to shed some light on our three questions:

(1) *To know the true nature of a thing, we must get to know that thing as it is in itself, apart from other things:* 'To know the nature of a thing we must observe it in its unalloyed state, since any addition obscures the reality.'

Therefore,

(2) *To know the true nature of your own soul, you must become acquainted with your soul as it is in itself, apart from the body:* 'Let us consider a soul, not one that has appropriated the unreasoned desires and impulses of the

bodily life, or any other such emotion and experience, but one that has cast all this aside, and as far as possible has no commerce with the bodily.'

(3) *When your soul is thoroughly purified—that is, when its 'commerce with the bodily' has been suspended—your soul will know itself as wholly and innately good, as invested with perfections that belong to it essentially, or in virtue of its very nature*: 'Such a soul demonstrates that all evil is accretion, alien, and that in the purged soul the noble things are immanent, wisdom and all else that is good, as its native store. . . . [W]hat he sees is an Intellectual-Principle looking on nothing of sense, nothing of this mortality, but by its own eternity having intellection of the eternal. . . . [I]t is not by running hither and thither outside of itself that the Soul discerns Moral Wisdom and Justice: it learns them of its own nature, in its contact with itself, in its intellectual grasp of itself, seeing deeply impressed upon it the images of its primal state; what was one mass of rust from long neglect it has restored to purity.'

(4) *This discovery is strong evidence of the soul's kinship with what is divine and eternal*: 'If this is the soul once it has returned to itself, how deny that it is of the nature we have identified with all the divine and eternal? Wisdom and authentic virtue are divine, and could not be found in the chattel mean and mortal: what possesses these must be divine by its very capacity of the divine, the token of kinship and of identical substance.'

Therefore,

(C) *The purified soul's knowledge of itself gives us reason to believe in the soul's immortality*: '[H]e will not doubt his immortality when he sees himself thus entered into the pure, the Intellectual. . . . [I]f every human being were at that stage, or if a great number lived by a soul of that degree, no one would be so incredulous as to doubt that the Soul in man is immortal. It is because we see everywhere the spoiled souls of the great mass that it becomes difficult to recognize their divinity and immortality.'

- What premises of Plotinus' argument strike you as reasonable? What premises don't? Why?
- In the final paragraph, Plotinus compares the soul to gold. What is the point of this comparison? What do you think Plotinus is getting at?
- In what way(s) is Plotinus' argument for the immortality of the soul reminiscent of Plato's philosophy?

Some people—and you may well be one of them—are firmly convinced that philosophy and mysticism are sworn enemies; that philosophers must despise mystics as self-indulgent dreamers deficient in reason, and that mystics must condemn philosophers as soulless logic-choppers devoid of vision. If Plotinus is right, however, this unnuanced opposition between philosophy and mysticism cannot be sustained. Once you grant that philosophy is not an academic subject but a way of life; once you agree that the philosophical life is an expression of your soul's deepest desire; once you admit that this desire cannot be satisfied as long as your soul is ruled by your body and enslaved by your senses—once you grant all this, why shouldn't you expect philosophers to be mystics, and mystics philosophers? Why shouldn't you hope that philosophy and mysticism will be joined together, with each enriching and fructifying the other when and where it can? For those who share this bold high hope, Plotinus will always be an inspiration.

As we have learned, religious experiences of the sort described by Plotinus and al-Ghazali—ecstatic experiences in which a person directly encounters the ultimate reality behind the veil of sensuous appearances—are typically labelled 'mystical' experiences. But what, exactly, are mystical experiences? What is special or distinctive about them? Once again, we turn to William James, who devised an influential definition of what is *mystical*:

From *The Varieties of Religious Experience*
By William James

Our own more 'rational' beliefs are based on evidence exactly similar in nature to that which mystics quote for theirs.

One may say truly, I think, that personal religious experience has its root and centre in mystical states of consciousness; so for us, who in these lectures are treating personal experience as the exclusive subject of our study, such states of consciousness ought to form the vital chapter, from which the other chapters get their light. Whether my treatment of mystical states will shed more light or darkness, I do not know, for my own constitution shuts me out from their enjoyment almost entirely, and I can speak of them only at second hand. But though forced to look upon the subject so externally, I will be as objective and receptive as I can; and I think I shall at least succeed in convincing you of the reality of the states in question, and of the paramount importance of their function.

First of all, then, I ask, What does the expression 'mystical states of consciousness' mean? How do we part off mystical states from other states?

The words 'mysticism' and 'mystical' are often used as terms of mere reproach, to throw at any opinion which we regard as vague and vast and sentimental, and without a base in either facts or logic. For some writers a 'mystic' is any person who believes in thought-transference, or spirit-return. Employed in this way the word has little value: there are too many less ambiguous synonyms. So, to keep it useful by restricting it, I will do what I did in the case of the word 'religion', and simply propose to you four marks which, when an experience has them, may justify us in calling it mystical for the purpose of the present lectures. In this way we shall save verbal disputation, and the recriminations that generally go therewith.

1. *Ineffability.*—The handiest of the marks by which I classify a state of mind as mystical is negative. The subject of it immediately says that it defies expression, that no adequate report of its contents can be given in words. It follows from this that its quality must be directly experienced; it cannot be imparted or transferred to others. In this peculiarity mystic states are more like states of feeling than like states of intellect. No one can make clear to another who has never had a certain feeling, in what the quality or worth of it consists. One must have musical ears to know the value of a symphony; one must have been in love oneself to understand a lover's state of mind. Lacking the heart or ear, we cannot interpret the musician or the lover justly, and are even likely to consider him weak-minded or absurd. The mystic finds that most of us accord to his experiences an equally incompetent treatment.

2. *Noetic quality.*—Although so similar to states of feeling, mystical states seem to those who experience them to be also states of knowledge. They are states of insight into depths of truth unplumbed by the discursive intellect. They are illuminations, revelations, full of significance and importance, all inarticulate though they remain; and as a rule they carry with them a curious sense of authority for aftertime.

These two characters will entitle any state to be called mystical, in the sense in which I use the word. Two other qualities are less sharply marked, but are usually found. These are:

3. *Transiency.*—Mystical states cannot be sustained for long. Except in rare instances, half an hour, or at most an hour or two, seems to be the limit beyond which they fade into the light of common

(*Continued*)

day. Often, when faded, their quality can but imperfectly be reproduced in memory; but when they recur it is recognized; and from one recurrence to another it is susceptible of continuous development in what is felt as inner richness and importance.

4. *Passivity.*—Although the oncoming of mystical states may be facilitated by preliminary voluntary operations, as by fixing the attention, or going through certain bodily performances, or in other ways which manuals of mysticism prescribe; yet when the characteristic sort of consciousness once has set in, the mystic feels as if his own will were in abeyance, and indeed sometimes as if he were grasped and held by a superior power. This latter peculiarity connects mystical states with certain definite phenomena of secondary or alternative personality, such as prophetic speech,

automatic writing, or the mediumistic trance. When these latter conditions are well pronounced, however, there may be no recollection whatever of the phenomenon, and it may have no significance for the subject's usual inner life, to which, as it were, it makes a mere interruption. Mystical states, strictly so-called, are never merely interruptive. Some memory of their content always remains, and a profound sense of their importance. They modify the inner life of the subject between the times of their recurrence. Sharp divisions in this region are, however, difficult to make, and we find all sorts of gradations and mixtures.

These four characteristics are sufficient to mark out a group of states of consciousness peculiar enough to deserve a special name and to call for careful study. Let it then be called the mystical group.

Although James mentions four marks of mystical states in this passage, he lays particular emphasis upon the first two: ineffability and noetic quality. As he sees it, mystical experiences are essentially '**ineffable**', that is, impossible to describe to anyone else, and he compares this experience with the experience of listening to a symphony or being in love. But he also insists that mystical experiences provide us with knowledge, 'states of insight into depths of truth unplumbed by the discursive intellect'. Indeed, James goes so far as to tell us is that we cannot rule out the possibility that mystical experiences may serve as a source of *justification* for religious beliefs. Why? Here is his argument:

[M]ystical states of a well-pronounced and emphatic sort *are* usually authoritative over those who have them. They have been 'there', and know. It is vain for rationalism to grumble about this. If the mystical truth that comes to a man proves to be a force that he can live by, what mandate have we of the majority to order him to live in another way? We can throw him into a prison or a madhouse, but we cannot change his mind—we commonly attach it only the more stubbornly to its beliefs. It mocks our utmost efforts, as a matter of fact, and in point of logic it absolutely escapes our jurisdiction. Our own more 'rational' beliefs are based on evidence exactly similar in nature to that which mystics quote for theirs. Our senses,

namely, have assured us of certain states of fact; but mystical experiences are as direct perceptions of fact for those who have them as any sensations ever were for us. The records show that even though the five senses be in abeyance in them, they are absolutely sensational in their epistemological quality, if I may be pardoned the barbarous expression—that is, they are face-to-face presentations of what seems immediately to exist.

The mystic is, in short, *invulnerable*, and must be left, whether we relish it or not, in undisturbed enjoyment of his creed. Faith, says Tolstoy, is that by which men live. And faith-state and mystic state are practically convertible terms.

Ask yourself: What justifies your beliefs about the physical world: about trees, tables, chairs, books, and the like? The answer is obvious: your perceptions. If you are asked how you know that there is a book on the table, you will naturally say 'Because I can see it'; if you are asked how you know there is a bird singing outside your window, you will say 'Because I can hear it'; if you are asked how you know that someone is frying bacon downstairs, you will say 'Because I can smell it'; and so on. In each case, your evidence for what you believe—and let us agree that it can be excellent evidence—comes in the form of your perceptual experiences: what you see, hear, smell, taste, and touch. Now, adds James, if you grant that your perceptual experiences can justify some of your beliefs about the physical world, what right have you to deny that mystical experiences may justify some of the mystic's beliefs about God? After all, as Radhakrisnan asserts, 'mystical experiences are as direct perceptions of fact for those who have them as any sensations ever were for us'. And if this is the case—if '[o]ur own more "rational" beliefs are based on evidence exactly similar in nature to that which mystics quote for theirs'—then it looks as if we have no good reason to treat them differently. So if we think that our perceptions may justify some beliefs about physical objects—and we all do think that—shouldn't we concede that mystical experiences *may* justify at least *some* of the mystic's beliefs about the supernatural?

Here you may object that, for all we know, mystical experiences might simply be delusions or hallucinations, and that there may be nothing in reality to which they correspond. The problem with this objection is simple: it seems that the very same thing can be said about our ordinary perceptual experiences. Whether we have good reasons to trust our senses is a large topic—a topic we shall explore more thoroughly in Chapter 3, Section A, where our focus will be on Cartesian skepticism. At this point, however, let us just note that there *is* a distinction between appearance (how things seem to an individual) and reality (how things truly are). For it is a fact of life, familiar to all, that things may not be as they seem. Remember the plight of Shakespeare's Macbeth:

> Is this a dagger which I see before me,
> The handle toward my hand? Come, let me clutch thee.
> I have thee not, and yet I see thee still.
> Art thou not, fatal vision, sensible
> To feeling as to sight? Or art thou but
> A dagger of the mind, a false creation,
> Proceeding from the heat-oppressèd brain?[3]

While some of our perceptions may be mistaken (as in the case of Macbeth and his 'dagger of the mind'), we do not conclude from this that perception is unreliable, let alone that we should *never* trust our perceptions. You can see where this line of reasoning is leading: If we do not conclude that perceptions can never be trusted simply because they may occasionally deceive us, why should we conclude that mystical experiences can *never* be trusted simply because some of them may turn out to be delusions or hallucinations? In short, how can you be a skeptic about mystical experiences in general without also being a skeptic about perceptual experiences in general? What argument can you use to discredit the first class of experiences that doesn't also discredit the second?

Here, then, is James' challenge to skeptical critics of religious experience: if you think that mystical experiences cannot be used to justify a belief in God, just what is it about them that prevents them from playing that role? Canadian philosopher Phillip Wiebe, author of *God and Other Spirits: Intimations of Transcendence in Christian Faith*, finds this

Jamesian challenge compelling and thought-provoking. In the following new piece, written specifically for this text, Wiebe helpfully describes several varieties of religious experience; he also explores what we are—and are not—entitled to conclude from them.

'Religious Experience and Religious Belief'
By Phillip Wiebe

The ancient ideal of proving God's existence by deducing it from indubitable premises, which followed Aristotle's interpretation of science, has given way to searching for evidence that might lend probability to religious claims. In this respect theism is again following the lead of science, but probabilistic arguments are no easy solution to the shortcomings of deduction on the topic of religion.[4] The gods and goddesses of traditional religions have been widely considered unobservable, and the interpretation of probability in such contexts is unclear, since probability is known to us primarily from contexts in which statements derive from and can be tested by observation. A third form of argumentation, identified by C.S. Peirce as 'abduction' or 'retroduction',[5] might be of value, however. This strategy involves the cautious postulation of entities (possibly unobservable) in a theory, with the understanding that the theory is assessed by such criteria as relative simplicity over other conjectures, capacity to predict novel events, capacity to receive confirming or disconfirming evidence, and consistency with well-established theories. The theories central to chemistry, atomic physics, genetics, evolutionary theory, and plate tectonics, in the last two centuries, have all postulated unobserved (possibly unobservable) entities or mechanisms. Their rationality cannot be straightforwardly assessed, inasmuch as complex conceptual structures, rather than isolable claims, are involved.

Let me now bring this abductive methodological background to bear on religious experience. I will begin with an incident told to me by a seminary professor, who got it first-hand:

Tom Arthur (not his real name) of Abbotsford, British Columbia, said he was a nominal theist for most of his life. He occasionally went to church, but did not take 'religion' seriously until he was asked to be a pallbearer at the funeral of a friend, by which time Tom was retired. The service made him think about God, and when it was over he prayed, asking God to reveal himself if he was real. Tom added, 'But please don't scare me.' Nothing happened for a week or so, but when he and his wife returned home from shopping one day they noticed that their bedroom light was on. They were sure they had shut it off before going out, and wondered if someone had been in their house. They did not notice anything missing, and so gave the incident little attention at the time, thinking that maybe they had absentmindedly left the light on. A similar incident occurred a few days later when they again went out, only this time the light and the television set in their bedroom were both on when they returned. They examined the doors and windows, but none of them showed any evidence of an attempted entry. They phoned their son to find out if he had paid them an unexpected call, but he had not. They even phoned the previous owners of the house, just in case they had kept a key to the house and had come over for some reason. The former owners assured them that they had not been to the house. Tom's wife was so spooked by these incidents that she wanted to sell the house, but Tom wasn't ready. Then a third incident occurred a week or so later. They came home to find their bedroom light on and Tom's good suit laid out on the bed, as though he was supposed to go somewhere. It was the same suit he had worn to the funeral. Tom wondered if 'someone' was trying to get him to go to church, and the strange events stopped when he and his wife started going.

Tom, in effect, postulated the existence of God (or some emissary) in order to account for the strange set of events that he witnessed. The sequence of events—the prayer, the disturbances in the home, and their cessation—within a relatively short period of time understandably gave Tom the impression that they were causally related. Naturally, those of us with a modern bent want a large number of comparable cases to justify a causal claim, but religion might not cooperate with this legitimate demand of science, for the knowledge religion offers might be personal, rather than public. Inasmuch as Tom considered the effect of the experience as positive and beneficial in his life, he also construed the source of the events in similar terms. God has been interpreted in many prominent religious traditions as infinite, but nothing of an experiential character would ever warrant postulating an infinite being. Tom was not irrational in conjecturing, however, that *something* was trying to get his attention.

Apparitions and locutions form another important class of religious experiences in which a being is perhaps conjectured to be the cause. The following account was given first-hand to me, as part of a larger study of Christic apparitions:

Helen Bezanson reported two Christic visions at different times of her life, the first of which (in a church service) began with a tactile sensation of someone touching her hand. Her eyes were closed in prayer at the time, so she opened them to see if someone had touched her, but no one was even near enough to do so. She closed them again, and again felt the same touch. When she opened them a second time she saw a figure standing on a pedestal some nine feet away whom she immediately identified as Jesus. He appeared much as tradition has imagined him, that is, with a long robe, long hair, and a beard. He was surrounded by radiance, not simply in a halo around his head but in an oval shape around his entire body. Helen reported that she had the sense that she was looking at God, but she could not explain exactly what gave her that impression. She looked around the room at the other people who were present, to see if any of them gave any indication that they saw the same thing, but none did. Helen was able to look away and back again to the front to see the same figure. It finally disappeared, but not before communicating the sense to Helen that she was accepted and loved. Helen was not interested in religion when this event occurred, and only attended this service to please her mother-in-law.[6]

Helen also conjectured that she had 'encountered' some transcendent being, a postulation that made sense of what she 'touched' and 'saw'. Yet, because she was apparently the only one to see the vision, we must consider the possibility that Helen's experience was hallucinatory.

The *perceptual release theory* attempts to explain a possible mechanism responsible for 'aberrant' sensations, and was advanced by prominent psychiatric pioneers Sigmund Freud, John Hughlings Jackson, and Jean Esquirol in the nineteenth century. This theory claims that bits of memory deriving from perceptions, feelings, and other elements of lived experience are combined and transformed in fairly realistic ways to produce a cluster that is 'dropped' into consciousness, where it is experienced as an apparition or vision, much as similar clusters are released during sleep, where they are experienced as dreams. The visual components that Helen reported—a pedestal that was not actually a part of the building, a man who resembled popular images of Christ, and the glow around a body—could likely be traced to previous events in Helen's life where she saw these as possibly isolated images.

The claim that Helen's experience was hallucinatory needs to be treated with some reserve, however. Helen's complex experience began with tactile sensations for which she could not account, followed by visual sensations that did not follow her eyes. If a single 'cluster' of transformed memories was dropped into her conscious experience, as the *perceptual release theory* implies, why did her experience begin with identical *tactile* impressions and then feature identical *visual* perceptions? One would think that if the *perceptual release theory* is the proper theory to invoke, the sensory perceptions would have been all the same. Moreover, one would think that the visual image would have followed her eyes rather than remaining at the front of the building where the initial vision was seen. The position of her head seems insufficient to account for the consistent occurrence and then disappearance of the identical vision. Helen's conjecture that she encountered a being from a transcendent domain is not devoid of evidence, given the success of the reality-check she conducted, and the difficulties we've encountered in the perceptual release theory.

Even if we admit that *she really saw something*, modern physics has taught us that things do not exist in the way they appear to us, so we need to be circumspect in asserting too much about this experience. The scrutiny of religious experiences requires

(*Continued*)

close attention to their phenomenological character, with openness to the possibility that some concealed form of reality is exhibiting its existence. Whether religious realities will be reduced in some futuristic science is unclear, but such a reduction will never be effected if we are unaware of the detailed nature of religious experience. Neurophysiological advances in the study of mental states are to be welcomed, for they will assist us in differentiating experiences in which the causal source is wholly within a person from those in which it is not.

A final experience I will comment on briefly comes from a study undertaken by Emma Heathcote-James, who has researched more than eight hundred first-hand accounts of 'encounters with angels' in Britain. One of these was subsequently researched by Carol Midgley, a reporter for *The Times* of London, who found that about half the people in a church saw what they considered to be an angel during a baptismal service (the font was at the back, and not everyone looked in the direction of the event). In her report, Midgley quotes the resident priest of the church as saying

> Suddenly there was a man in white standing in front of the [baptismal] font about eighteen inches away [from me]. He was a man but he was totally, utterly different from the rest of us. He was wearing something long, like a robe, but it was so white it was almost transparent. . . . He was just looking at us. It was the most wonderful feeling. Not a word was spoken; various people began to touch their arms because it felt like having warm oil poured over you. The children came forward with their mouths wide open. Then all of a sudden—I suppose it was a few seconds, but time seemed to stop—the

angel was gone. Everyone who was there was quite convinced that the angel came to encourage us.[7]

This report is interesting for the intersubjective observation that it alleges, for such experience places events in the space-time-causal world. This account also pairs the phenomenological sense of having warm oil poured over one's body with the reported intersubjective observation. Many people who attend religious services report that at some point in their lives they experience thoughts, emotions, or impressions that are remarkable (for them), and seem to disclose a largely hidden reality. Very rarely can such experiences be directly associated with some intersubjectively observed event suggesting the reality of a transcendent order. This fact seems to have contributed to the widespread belief that religious experience has no significance for anyone but the experiencer.

Religion can be plausibly interpreted as a descriptive and explanatory domain postulating the existence of intelligent and intentional beings that have causal capacities to act in the world. This conjecture must be cautious and open-ended, for we do not know exactly what we are dealing with—is this *God* who turns on lights and television sets? Was this the *resurrected Christ* who appeared to Helen? Are angels real? Such questions, and innumerable others, including questions about possible malevolent powers, are triggered by accounts of religious experience. The scope of religious experience (in detailed terms) is currently unknown, as is the percentage of reliable accounts. This domain of experience offers intriguing grounds for advancing the existence of transcendent realities, grounds that cannot be easily dismissed as irrational.

- Do you agree with James and Radhakrishnan that experience, not philosophical argument, is the true root of religious belief? Why or why not?
- How are some religious experiences like perceptual experiences? How are they different?
- Can you think of a reason not to trust religious experiences that isn't also a reason not to trust ordinary perceptual experiences?
- According to Wiebe, 'the knowledge religion offers might be personal, rather than public'. What is personal, as opposed to public, knowledge? What is the difference between them, and why might it be important?

G. Religion and Practical Reason

As we have seen, if the three traditional forms of 'proof' of God's existence don't seem to be adequate, it may be partly because what each of them proves is not the existence of *God*, but at most the existence of *something*—something that is defined by its existence, something that is a first cause, or something that is an intelligent 'designer'. But a very different view of God is defended, for example, by Immanuel Kant. In this view, the most important attribute of the traditional Western God—the reason why men and women have worshipped Him, prayed to Him, feared Him, fought wars in His name, and died for Him—is His divine justice. Thus the most important attributes of God in Western religion are His moral qualities. Without them, our notion of God would be very different than it is.

According to this view, the importance of God in Western thought is His role as the source of our moral laws, as the judge of our actions and feelings, and as the sanction that stands behind those laws and judgments. The traditional 'proofs' of God's existence are not wholly convincing, even if they are valid, just because they leave out this all-important moral aspect of belief in God. What distinguishes theists from atheists is not a matter of mere theory or argument ('a mere hypothesis', the French philosopher Pierre-Simon Laplace called it), but a difference in conduct and confidence. The theist believes in a divine source of morality, in a judgment of one's actions that transcends everyday life, and the promise of reward (or threat of punishment) after death. The atheist also believes in morality—but not in divine morality—and believes that all judgments of our actions and all rewards and punishments must take place in this life or not at all. Accordingly, the question of God's existence has a distinctly moral dimension. For believers, the conception of the human good depends on the conception of God.

With this conception of God in mind, Kant offered his own argument for the existence of God. Unlike supporters of the ontological, cosmological, and teleological arguments, he did not try to 'prove' God's existence as such and even said that, strictly speaking, we could have no knowledge of God at all, since God, as transcendent, cannot be the object of any possible experience. So Kant, following a long tradition in Christianity, said that belief in God is a matter of faith. But this does not mean, as people so often take it to mean, that it is an irrational belief. Quite to the contrary, Kant insisted that it is the most rational belief of all. For without it, we would not have the anchor for our morality, nor would we have any reason to suppose that our good deeds would in fact be eventually rewarded or evil deeds punished. It was obvious to Kant, as it has been to every person with his or her eyes open since ancient times, that justice is not always delivered in this life. Innocent children are butchered in wars; evil men live grand lives well into old age. Therefore, according to Kant, it is rational to believe in God, rational to have faith, even if faith is not, strictly speaking, a matter of knowledge. It is, as he says in *The Critique of Practical Reason*, a 'postulate of pure practical reason'.

On God and Morality
By Immanuel Kant

The moral law led, in the foregoing analysis, to a practical problem which is assigned solely by pure reason and without any concurrence of sensuous incentives. It is the problem of the completeness of the first and principal part of the highest good, viz., morality; since this problem can be solved only in eternity, it led to the postulate of immortality. The same law must also lead us to affirm the possibility of the second element of the highest good, i.e., happiness proportional to that morality; it must do so just as disinterestedly as heretofore, by a purely impartial reason. This it can do on the

(*Continued*)

supposition of the existence of a cause adequate to this effect, i.e., it must postulate the existence of God as necessarily belonging to the possibility of the highest good (the object of our will which is necessarily connected with moral legislation of pure reason). We proceed to exhibit this connection in a convincing manner.

Happiness is the condition of a rational being in the world, in whose whole existence everything goes according to wish and will. It thus rests on the harmony of nature with his entire end and with the essential determining ground of his will. But the moral law commands as a law of freedom through motives wholly independent of nature and of its harmony with our faculty of desire (as incentives). Still, the acting rational being in the world is not at the same time the cause of the world and of nature itself. Hence there is not the slightest ground in the moral law for a necessary connection between the morality and proportionate happiness of a being which belongs to the world as one of its parts and as thus dependent on it. Not being nature's cause, his will cannot by its own strength bring nature, as it touches on his happiness, into complete harmony with his practical principles. Nevertheless, in the practical task of pure reason, i.e., in the necessary endeavour after the highest good, such a connection is postulated as necessary: we *should* seek to further the highest good (which therefore must be at least possible). Therefore also the existence is postulated of a cause of the whole of nature, itself distinct from nature, which contains the ground of the exact coincidence of happiness with morality. This supreme cause, however, must contain the ground of the agreement of nature not merely with a law of the will of rational beings but with the idea of this law so far as they make it the supreme ground of determination of the will. Thus it contains the ground of the agreement of nature not merely with actions moral in their form but also with their morality as the motives to such actions, i.e., with their moral intention. Therefore, the highest good is possible in the world only on the supposition of a supreme cause of nature which has a causality corresponding to the moral intention. Now a being which is capable of actions by the idea of laws is an intelligence (a rational being), and the causality of such a being according to this idea of laws is his will. Therefore, the supreme cause of nature, in so far as it must be presupposed for the highest good, is a being which is the cause (and consequently the author) of nature through understanding and will, i.e., God. As a consequence, the postulate of the possibility of a highest derived good (the best world) is at the same time the postulate of the reality of a highest original good, namely, the existence of God. Now it was our duty to promote the highest good; and it is not merely our privilege but a necessity connected with duty as a requisite to presuppose the possibility of this highest good. This presupposition is made only under the condition of the existence of God, and this condition inseparably connects this supposition with duty. Therefore, it is morally necessary to assume the existence of God.

The key to Kant's argument is the obvious fact that good deeds are not always rewarded in this life and evil deeds are often not punished. Why then, he asks, should a person be moral and do what is right? If we are to rationally decide to be moral, we must also believe that happiness and morality will be in harmony (what Kant calls 'the highest good'), that good people will be rewarded with happiness and evil people will be punished. But if this does not happen in this life, then we must believe that it happens in another life ('this problem can be solved only in eternity'). Further, we must believe in some ultimate source of justice, a divine judge who will weigh good against evil and make certain that eternal happiness and punishment are meted out fairly. This argument is at one and the same time a defence of the Christian belief in the immortality of the human soul and a defence of the belief in God. It is necessary to believe in both, according to Kant, in order to sustain our willingness to be moral: 'Therefore, it is morally necessary to assume the existence of God.'

A similar, albeit more pragmatic, position was argued more recently by William James. He argues that believing in God is 'rational' insofar as it doesn't conflict with our other beliefs (for example, our beliefs in science, a matter that Kant stressed also) and if it tends to make us lead better lives.

From 'The Will to Believe'

By William James

The universe is no longer a mere It to us, but a Thou, if we are religious; and any relation that may be possible from person to person might be possible here.

Science says things are; morality says some things are better than other things; and religion says essentially two things.

First, she says that the best things are the more eternal things, the overlapping things, the things in the universe that throw the last stone, so to speak, and say the final word. 'Perfection is eternal'—this phrase of Charles Secrétan seems a good way of putting this first affirmation of religion, an affirmation which obviously cannot yet be verified scientifically at all.

The second affirmation of religion is that we are better off even now if we believe her first affirmation to be true.

Now, let us consider what the logical elements of this situation are *in case the religious hypothesis in both its branches be really true*. (Of course, we must admit that possibility at the onset. If we are to discuss the question at all, it must involve a living option. If for any of you religion be a hypothesis that cannot, by any living possibility, be true, then you need go no farther. I speak to the 'saving remnant' alone.) So proceeding, we see, first, that religion offers itself as a *momentous* option. We are supposed to gain, even now, by our belief, and to lose by our non-belief, a certain vital good. Secondly, religion is a *forced* option, so far as that good goes. We cannot escape the issue by remaining skeptical and waiting for more light, because, although we do avoid error in that way *if religion be untrue*, we lose the good, *if it be true*, just as certainly as if we positively chose to disbelieve. It is as if a man should hesitate indefinitely to ask a certain woman to marry him because he was not perfectly sure that she would prove an angel after he brought her home. Would he not cut himself off from that particular angel-possibility as decisively as if he went and married someone else? Skepticism, then, is not avoidance of option; it is option of a certain particular kind of risk. *Better risk loss of truth than chance of error*—that is your faith-vetoer's exact position. He is actively playing his stake as much as the believer is; he is backing the field against the religious hypothesis, just as the believer is backing the religious hypothesis against the field. To preach skepticism to us as a duty until 'sufficient evidence' for religion be found is tantamount therefore to telling us, when in presence of the religious hypothesis, that to yield to our fear of its being error is wiser and better than to yield to our hope that it may be true. It is not intellect against all passions, then; it is only intellect with one passion laying down its law. And by what, forsooth, is the supreme wisdom of this passion warranted? Dupery for dupery, what proof is there that dupery through hope is so much worse than dupery through fear? I, for one, can see no proof; and I simply refuse obedience to the scientist's command to imitate his kind of option, in a case where my own stake is important enough to give me the right to choose my own form of risk. If religion be true and the evidence for it be still insufficient, I do not wish, by putting your extinguisher upon my nature (which feels to me as if it had after all some business in this matter), to forfeit my sole chance in life of getting upon the winning side—that chance depending, of course, on my willingness to run the risk of acting as if my passional need of taking the world religiously might be prophetic and right.

All this is on the supposition that it really may be prophetic and right, and that, even to us who are discussing the matter, religion is a live hypothesis which may be true. Now, to most of us religion comes in a still further way that makes a veto on our active faith even more illogical. The more perfect and more eternal aspect of the universe is represented in our religions as having personal form. The universe is no longer a mere *It* to us, but a *Thou*, if we are religious; and any relation that may be possible from person to person might be possible here. For instance, although in one sense we are passive portions of the universe, in another we show a curious autonomy, as if we were small active centres on our own account. We feel, too, as if the appeal of religion to us were made to our own active goodwill, as if evidence might be forever withheld from us unless we met the hypothesis half-way. To take a trivial illustration: just as a man who in a company of gentlemen made no advances, asked a warrant for every concession, and

(Continued)

believed no one's word without proof, would cut himself off by such churlishness from all the social rewards that a more trusting spirit would earn—so here, one who should shut himself up in snarling logicality and try to make the gods extort his recognition willy-nilly, or not get it at all, might cut himself off forever from his only opportunity of making the gods' acquaintance. This feeling, forced on us we know not whence, that by obstinately believing that there are gods (although not to do so would be so easy both for our logic and our life) we are doing the universe the deepest service we can, seems part of the living essence of the religious hypothesis. If the hypothesis *were* true in all its parts, including this one, then pure intellectualism, with its veto on our making willing advances, would be an absurdity; and some participation of our sympathetic nature would be logically required. I, therefore, for one, cannot see my way to accepting the agnostic rules of truth-seeking, or willfully agree to keep my willing nature out of the game. I cannot do so for this plain reason, that *a rule of thinking which would absolutely prevent me from acknowledging certain kinds of truth if those kinds of truth were really there, would be an irrational rule.* That for me is the long and short of the formal logic of the situation, no matter what the kinds of truth might materially be.

This 'practical' argument for belief in God ruled philosophy from the time of Kant until the present century. It has its origins in a short but brilliant argument by the seventeenth-century French philosopher, mathematician, scientist, writer, and religious thinker Blaise Pascal. Pascal offered an argument that he called a wager, literally a bet, about God. It isn't a proof of God's existence in any sense; in fact, one of its explicit terms is the fact that we can't know whether God exists or not. But then, he says, if God exists, and we believe in Him, we are entitled to an infinite reward. If He exists and we don't believe in Him, on the other hand, we are really in for it—eternal damnation. Even if he doesn't exist, we are still better off believing in God because of the qualities faith brings to life in us. In support of the decision to believe, Pascal asks,

> Now, what harm will befall you in taking this side? You will be faithful, honest, humble, grateful, generous, a sincere friend, truthful. Certainly you will not have those poisonous pleasures, glory and luxury; but will you not have others? I will tell you that you will thereby gain in this life, and that, at each step you take on this road, you will see so great certainty of gain, so much nothingness in what you risk, that you will at last recognize that you have wagered for something certain and infinite, for which you have given nothing.[8]

So, if we treat this as a betting situation, in which our option is simply to believe or not believe, our betting odds look like this:

'Pascal's Wager'

	AND GOD EXISTS	AND GOD DOESN'T EXIST
If we believe	We will enjoy eternal reward.	We've wasted a little piety but perhaps been better people.
If we don't believe	We will suffer eternal damnation.	No reward, no punishment.

Looking at these odds, it is obvious which option we ought to choose. The risk of eternal damnation overwhelms the promise of a few 'poisonous' pleasures; and the promise of eternal reward is well worth the risk that we may be wrong, considering what is gained even in this life. The conclusion, then, on strictly practical grounds, is that we ought to believe in God.

As you have seen, Kant, James, and Pascal each base their argument on the all-important assumption that 'God is just'. On the basis of this assumption, they then argue that it is rational to believe in God, even if it is not possible to prove (or even know) that He exists. Accordingly, belief in God is a matter of faith, but this faith can be argued and justified as rational belief. Just because it is faith and not knowledge, it does not follow that it is 'blind faith' or irrational, beyond argument or arbitrary. To insist that belief in God is a matter of faith, therefore, is not to say that it is beyond the reach of philosophy or rational consideration.

- What does Pascal's wager fail to capture about religious belief and devotion?

H. God and Evil

These 'moral' arguments for believing in God are sound only as long as we accept the assumption that 'God is just'. There have been few sophisticated theists who have actually denied this, of course, but there have been a great many, particularly in modern times, who have worried about it considerably. These worries have resulted from what is called 'the **problem of evil**'. It can be stated very simply, but its solution, if you believe in God, is not simple at all. The problem is this: If God is all-powerful (omnipotent), all-knowing (omniscient), and just, then how is it possible that there is so much unearned suffering and unpunished wickedness in the world? Or simply, if God exists, how can the world be so full of evil? It cannot be that He does not know of these misfortunes, for He is all-knowing. Nor can it be that He is unable to do anything about them, for He is all-powerful. And if He is just and has concern for human beings, then He must care about protecting the innocent and punishing or preventing evil.

The problem of evil is a significant problem because few believers in any religion are willing to give up their faith in the power of Nature or of its Creator, its innate goodness, or the belief that there is real justice in it. The clearest and most widely known characterization of the problem of evil for the religious belief is probably still the one found in the biblical Book of Job, in which Job, deeply pious yet undeservedly suffering, struggles to keep his faith:

> Then his wife said to him, 'Are you still unshaken in your integrity? Curse God and die!' But he answered, '. . . If we accept good from God, shall we not accept evil?' (2:9–10)

But eventually, Job asks God:

> 'Why should the sufferer be born to see the light? Why is life given to men who find it so bitter?' (3:20)

The most common solution to the problem of evil is offered to Job by his friend Eliphaz:

> 'Mischief does not grow out of the soil, nor trouble spring from the earth; man is born to trouble, as surely as birds fly upwards.' (5:6)

In other words, Eliphaz suggests that man has been created by God with the kind of nature that brings with it its own creation of troubles.

This has often been the solution offered by philosophers and theologians to the problem of evil. There are several versions even of this solution, most centred around the assumption that human beings have 'free will'. The version most influential in Christianity was offered by St Augustine. In his youth, Augustine had come under the influence of a religion called

Manichaeism, which was branded as heresy by all of the great monotheisms (including, at that time, the Persian religion Zoroastrianism, whose founder we studied in Chapter 1) precisely because of the explanation of evil that it espoused. The Manichaeans claimed that there were two equally powerful gods, one of which was good and one evil. The good god ruled the spirit and mind, and the evil god ruled the body. According to the Manichaeans, then, neither god was all-powerful and human beings were not free, but rather at the mercy of one or the other of the gods. Only at death, claimed the Manichaeans, when the soul is separated forever from the body, could human beings achieve real moral goodness.

Augustine abandoned Manichaeism and embraced Christianity. As a Christian, he wrote eloquently about the freedom of the will and the ability of human beings to observe the moral obligations to which God has commanded them.

From *Confessions*
By St Augustine

Whatever is, is good; and evil . . . is not a substance, because if it were a substance, it would be good.

But although I declared and firmly believed that you, our Lord God, the true God who made not only our souls but also our bodies and not only our souls and bodies but all things, living and inanimate, as well, although I believed that you were free from corruption or mutation or any degree of change, I still could not find a clear explanation, without complications, of the cause of evil. Whatever the cause might be, I saw that it was not to be found in any theory that would oblige me to believe that the immutable God was mutable. If I believed this, I should myself become a cause of evil, the very thing which I was trying to discover. So I continued the search with some sense of relief, because I was quite sure that the theories of the Manichees were wrong. I repudiated these people with all my heart, because I could see that while they were inquiring into the origin of evil they were full of evil themselves, since they preferred to think that yours was a substance that could suffer evil rather than that theirs was capable of committing it.

I was told that we do evil because we choose to do so of our own free will, and suffer it because your justice rightly demands that we should. I did my best to understand this, but I could not see it clearly. I tried to raise my mental perceptions out of the abyss which engulfed them, but I sank back into it once more. Again and again I tried, but always I sank back. One thing lifted me up into the light of your day. It was that I knew that I had a will, as surely as I knew that there was life in me. When I chose to do something or not to do it, I was quite certain that it was my own self, and not some other person, who made this act of will, so that I was on the point of understanding that herein lay the cause of my sin. If I did anything against my will, it seemed to me to be something which happened to me rather than something which I did, and I looked upon it not as a fault, but as a punishment. And because I thought of you as a just God, I admitted at once that your punishments were not unjust.

But then I would ask myself once more: 'Who made me? Surely it was my God, who is not only good but Goodness itself. How, then, do I come to possess a will that can choose to do wrong and refuse to do good, thereby providing a just reason why I should be punished? Who put this will into me? Who sowed this seed of bitterness in me, when all that I am was made by my God, who is Sweetness itself? If it was the devil who put it there, who made the devil? If he was a good angel who became a devil because of his own wicked will, how did he come to possess the wicked will which made him a devil, when the Creator, who is entirely good, made him a good angel and nothing else?'

These thoughts swept me back again into the gulf where I was being stifled. But I did not sink as far as that hell of error where no one confesses to you his own guilt, choosing to believe that you suffer evil rather than that man does it.

* * *

'Where then is evil? What is its origin? How did it steal into the world? What is the root or stem from which it grew? Can it be that there simply is no evil? If so, why do we fear and guard against something which is not there? If our fear is unfounded, it is itself an evil, because it stabs and wrings our hearts for nothing. In fact the evil is all the greater if we are afraid when there is nothing to fear. Therefore, either there is evil and we fear it, or the fear itself is evil.

'Where then does evil come from, if God made all things and, because he is good, made them good too? It is true that he is the supreme Good, that he is himself a greater Good than these lesser goods which he created. But the Creator and all his creation are both good. Where then does evil come from?

'Can it be that there was something evil in the matter from which he made the universe? When he shaped this matter and fitted it to his purpose, did he leave in it some part which he did not convert to good? But why should he have done this? Are we to believe that, although he is omnipotent, he had not the power to convert the whole of this matter to good and change it so that no evil remained in it? Why, indeed, did he will to make anything of it at all? Why did he not instead, by this same omnipotence, destroy it utterly and entirely? Could it have existed against his will? If it had existed from eternity, why did he allow it to exist in that state through the infinite ages of the past and then, after so long a time, decide to make something of it? If he suddenly determined to act, would it not be more likely that he would use his almighty power to abolish this evil matter, so that nothing should exist besides himself, the total, true, supreme, and infinite Good? Or, if it was not good that a God who was good should not also create and establish something good, could he not have removed and annihilated the evil matter and replaced it with good, of which he could create all things? For he would not be omnipotent if he could not create something good without the help of matter which he had not created himself.'

These were the thoughts which I turned over and over in my unhappy mind, and my anxiety was all the more galling for the fear that death might come before I had found the truth. But my heart clung firmly to the faith in Christ your Son, our Lord and Saviour, which it had received in the Catholic Church. There were many questions on which my beliefs were still indefinite and wavered from the strict rule of doctrine, yet my mind never relinquished the faith but drank it in more deeply day by day.

* * *

It was made clear to me also that even those things which are subject to decay are good. If they were of the supreme order of goodness, they could not become corrupt; but neither could they become corrupt unless they were in some way good. For if they were supremely good, it would not be possible for them to be corrupted. On the other hand, if they were entirely without good, there would be nothing in them that could become corrupt. For corruption is harmful, but unless it diminished what is good, it could do no harm. The conclusion then must be either that corruption does no harm—which is not possible; or that everything which is corrupted is deprived of good—which is beyond doubt. But if they are deprived of all good, they will not exist at all. For if they still exist but can no longer be corrupted, they will be better than they were before, because they now continue their existence in an incorruptible state. But could anything be more preposterous than to say that things are made better by being deprived of all good?

So we must conclude that if things are deprived of all good, they cease altogether to be; and this means that as long as they are, they are good. Therefore, whatever is, is good; and evil, the origin of which I was trying to find, is not a substance, because if it were a substance, it would be good. For either it would be an incorruptible substance of the supreme order of goodness, or it would be a corruptible substance which would not be corruptible unless it were good. So it became obvious to me that all that you have made is good, and that there are no substances whatsoever that were not made by you. And because you did not make them all equal, each single thing is good and collectively they are very good, for our God made his whole creation *very good*.

* * *

For you evil does not exist, and not only for you but for the whole of your creation as well, because there is nothing outside it which could invade it and break down the order which you have imposed on it. Yet in the separate parts of your creation there are some things which we think of as evil because they are at variance with other things. But there are other things again with which they are in accord, and then they are good. In themselves, too, they are good. And all these things which are at variance with one another are in accord with the lower part

(Continued)

of creation which we call the earth. The sky, which is cloudy and windy, suits the earth to which it belongs. So it would be wrong for me to wish that these earthly things did not exist, for even if I saw nothing but them, I might wish for something better, but still I ought to praise you for them alone. For all things *give praise to the Lord on earth, monsters of the sea and all its depths; fire and hail, snow and mist; and the storm-wind that executes his decree; all you mountains and hills, all you fruit trees and cedars; all you wild beasts and cattle, creeping things and birds that fly in air; all you kings and peoples of the world, all you that are princes and judges on earth; young men and maids, old men and boys together; let them all give praise to the Lord's name*. The heavens, too, ring with your praises, O God, for you are the god of us all. *Give praise to the Lord in heaven; praise him, all that dwells on high. Praise him, all you angels of his, praise him, all his armies. Praise him, sun and moon; praise him, every star that shines. Praise him, you highest heavens, you waters beyond the heavens. Let all these praise the Lord*. And since this is so, I no longer wished for a better world, because I was thinking of the whole creation, and in the light of this clearer discernment I had come to see that though the higher things are better than the lower, the sum of all creation is better than the higher things alone.

The problem arises once again, however, if we ask 'How could God have given people free will, knowing—as He must have—that they would misuse it so badly?' Would everyone be much better off if we had a bit less 'free will', or at least if we had more desires to do good and fewer impulses to cause trouble and suffering?

There are several traditional responses to this question. One is that God has allowed us moral latitude to provide a test of our virtue, for if we were all 'naturally' good, there would be little question of good versus evil or salvation versus damnation. But it is open to question whether these distinctions are themselves desirable; wouldn't it have been better for humanity to have stayed in the Garden of Eden? Why did God have to create temptation, and what would have been lost from the world if Adam and Eve had been created with a bit more fortitude and obedience?

Then there is the familiar defence, 'but doesn't the world need some evil, in order that we recognize the good?' But it isn't at all obvious that we need anything like the amount of evil and suffering we have in the world in order to recognize what is good. Yet even if we were to agree on this 'free will' defence of the traditional conception of God as omnipotent, omniscient, and perfectly just, laying the blame for suffering on people's own choices, that would not solve the problem of evil. This is why we said that this line of 'free will' defence is, at best, a partial solution. For not all human hardships and sufferings seem to be our own doing; much of the evil in the world does not seem to depend on human action in any way.

Even if we accept the claim that we cause evil through free choice, we still need to explain how the effects of our choices can seem so unrelated to the actions that are supposedly their cause. The Western religions' concept of 'original sin' offers one such explanation, and it too finds its first expression in the Book of Job. When Job insists that he has done nothing to warrant his suffering, his friend Bildad suggests: 'Inquire now of older generations and consider the experience of their fathers' (8:8), implying that the 'sins of the fathers', the original sin of the whole human race, justifies Job's punishment. The punishment by God of any individual person, so goes the claim, is just, even though that particular individual did nothing to deserve it. Thus, God remains both just and good.

But this solution, rejected by Job himself, undermines our hopes that right action will be rewarded, and so again it belies the moral force that God is supposed to play in our lives. For if we were destined to suffer anyway for sins committed by others, then God would not appear to be just, and there would be little incentive for us to be faithful and follow God's commandments.

Some philosophers answered the problem of evil in a very different way, by denying one of the main tenets of traditional theistic thinking, namely, the idea that God is good. For example, Spinoza's **pantheism** (discussed in Chapter 1) was one of these many attempts to save belief in God while maintaining a rational picture of nature. More radical versions of pantheism deny that God is just and that He has any moral characteristics at all. In Spinoza's theory, however, which has often been compared to that of the Eastern religions, God is identical to the universe. He is not its creator. He is not a moral agent, so He has neither concern nor ability for the misfortunes and suffering of the world. He has no special concern for people. If one defends an extreme determinism in which no one—not even God—has 'free will', questions of moral responsibility, reward, and punishment become irrelevant, a matter of human vanity, nothing more. It is not surprising, then, that Spinoza, though devout, was long branded an atheist and his books were proscribed.

So too, the German philosophers Johann Fichte and G.W.F. Hegel defended versions of pantheism in which God was immanent (instead of transcendent) and identical to the one universe as 'Spirit' as well as Spinoza's substance. They, too, fought off accusations of atheism in their careers (and Fichte was actually fired in a great scandal over this). In France, the anti-clerical Enlightenment was trying to replace the increasingly dubious authority of the Church with rationality, but this often meant gutting religion (Christianity, in particular) of much of its content, especially most of its rituals and its 'superstitions'. Jean-Jacques Rousseau and his devoted followers in the French Revolution (for example, Maximilien Robespierre) advocated belief in a 'Supreme Being' but jettisoned most of Christianity nevertheless. Foremost in this fight was Voltaire, who also held onto his belief in God but sheared Him of all of His moral attributes, thus avoiding the problem of evil by denying God His attribute of 'justice'. For Voltaire, God was simply a 'hypothesis', the creator who turned on the giant Newtonian machine but then left it to go on its own. This peculiarly truncated version of theism is usually called **deism**. It believes in a God, but not much of one. It is essentially an appeal to the cosmological argument; and it is satisfied with a minimal deity, which stops far short of our traditional conception of God. Voltaire also despised the 'argument from design' with all of its hidden moralizing. The world is full of evil, Voltaire insisted, and there is no denying it. And since there is evil, there cannot be an all-powerful, all-knowing God who is also just, and there can be no appeal to His 'mysterious ways'. He has no 'mysterious ways'; in fact, He has no 'ways' at all. (Voltaire famously made his point against Leibniz and his 'best of all possible worlds' hypothesis in his novel *Candide*, where he lampooned the Leibnizian Dr Pangloss.) Thus by saving rationality of faith the French philosophers lost a great deal of the religion. But the question for many believers would be the following: Is the deist God (or Hegel's 'Spirit' or Spinoza's 'substance') God at all?

PANTHEISM

The belief that God is identical to the universe as a whole, everything is divine, or that God is in everything.

DEISM

The belief that God existed to create the universe but that there is no justification for our belief that God has any special concern for mankind or justice, or any anthropomorphic attributes.

- What attributes of God are necessary for there to be a 'problem' of evil?
- Do you think free will accounts for evil? Does it account for all the evil in the world?
- Do you think that good deeds must be rewarded and bad deeds punished for the universe to be moral?
- Do you think that the deist's conception of God can properly be called 'God'? Does deism solve the problem of evil?
- What does it mean to say that God is a 'hypothesis'?

---

1. Hinduism, Buddhism, Karma, and Compassion

The difficulties stemming from the 'free will' solution to the problem of evil may indicate to some that the Western religions' conceptions of God and of human nature are just not adequate. The Western religions characterize human beings as so limited in our understanding of God's justice that we can never predict the evil or good effects of our actions. But then how can we have any meaningful moral theory at all? Similarly, these religions claim that the wrongdoings we engage in during our short life here on earth are punished eternally by God and our occasional good actions are rewarded eternally. Yet the view that each and every human lifetime belongs to a unique eternal soul would seem to make all of God's rewards and punishments intrinsically unjust—way out of proportion to the insignificant actions that are supposedly their cause.

One interesting alternative to these conceptions of humans and God is offered by the Hindu religion, whose solution to the problem of evil is unique in its use of the notion of **karma**.

Hinduism is not actually a single religion; rather, it is best understood as a family of religious beliefs and practices united, among other things, by a belief in the notion of social caste and a shared lineage from the Indic religions, such as Upanishadism, which we discussed in Chapter 1. There are no identifiable 'core' Hindu *beliefs*—beyond a 'reverence' for the Veda, though it is rarely read, and a participation in a social organization. Nevertheless, one may speak of 'scriptures' and of ideas that over the centuries have been more at the centre of Hindu culture than others. In general, a theistic worldview has dominated Hindu belief and guided religious practices. However, the Hindu conception of God is radically different from that shared by Judaism, Christianity, and Islam. The Hindu notion of human nature also radically differs from the Western notion. For most Hindus, human beings have free will, but the free exercise of that will *changes* the human being. This is the doctrine of karma, which claims that any course of action that one undertakes creates a psychological tendency, or habit, to repeat it. One's free will thus becomes limited by one's own dispositions to action, or habits, dispositions that according to much ancient Indian thought continue even into a new birth. The inveterate smoker, for instance, is drawn to the taste of tobacco at a young age in her next incarnation.

Of all the many, many scriptures and sacred texts that over the centuries have moved the hearts of the faithful in India, the **Bhagavadgītā** (or '**Gītā**'), the 'Song of God' (*c.* 200 BCE), clearly stands out as the most important. The Gītā is a small portion of a long epic poem. The central theme of the passages given below is the unique Hindu response to the 'problem of evil'. The warrior Krishna is the ruler of a neighbouring state. Throughout most of the long poem, Krishna is an ordinary person though an able, just, clever, and politically astute one. The key event of the entire epic is a battle over political succession. The political issues involved are complex, but only one side of the warring family has a just claim. Five brothers are the principal representatives of the just family (although many noble and venerable sages and heroes fight against them). Krishna joins the battle line as charioteer for the third of the five brothers, a champion archer named Arjuna. The Gītā is a dialogue between Krishna and Arjuna that occurs just minutes before the battle begins. In the dialogue, Krishna ceases to be a mere mortal and reveals Himself to Arjuna as God incarnate. So His advice to Arjuna, at least according to Hindu theists, is not simply the encouragement of a friend or the wise teachings of a guru; His words are the voice of God speaking to a human being in a time of personal moral crisis. At the beginning of the Gītā, Arjuna insists that it cannot be the morally right thing to do to fight and kill his kinsmen, teachers, friends, and loved ones who face him in battle.

KARMA

The tendency of any course of action to be repeated; the limitation of one's free will by one's own habits and dispositions.

From the Bhagavadgītā[9]

[Arjuna:] No good do I see in killing my own family in battle. I desire not victory, nor rule, nor pleasures, Krishna; what is power to us, enjoyments, or life, Govinda? Those who make rulership desirable for us, and enjoyments and pleasures, it is they that are arrayed in battle (against us), abandoning life and wealth. Teachers, fathers, sons, grandfathers, uncles, inlaws—these I do not wish to kill even if it means that I must die, Krishna—not even to rule the three worlds, why then for the earth?

Despite the passion and sincerity of moral feeling that Arjuna expresses, Krishna insists that the right thing to do in the circumstances is to fight, to kill the opposing warriors, and to win the battle.

There are several dimensions to Krishna's explanation why fighting is the right course of action for Arjuna, and more commentary has been elicited by His response to Arjuna's plea for guidance than by any other comparably brief text, except perhaps the Torah and the Gospels. In the verses that follow (part of Krishna's reply), Krishna first explains the cosmic foundations of human action. Next He states His own motive as God for assuming mortal birth. Krishna goes on to talk again about human action and closes with a refrain recurring throughout the Gītā—injunctions about the practice of *yoga* (that is, spiritual 'discipline'). Through such self-discipline in general—whether *karmayoga* (the yoga of action), *jnānayoga* (the yoga of knowledge and meditation), or *bhaktiyoga* (the yoga of love and devotion)—Krishna lays out the three 'paths' by which one may live a spiritually transformed life.

[Krishna:] Without personal attachment undertake action, Arjuna, for just one purpose, for the purpose of sacrifice. From work undertaken for purposes other than sacrifice, this world is bound to the law of karma. Having loosed forth creatures along with sacrifice, the Creator said of old, 'With this may you bring forth fruit, let it be your horn-of-plenty.[10] Make the gods flourish with this and may the gods make you flourish. Mutually fostering one another, you will attain the supreme good. For made to flourish by sacrifice, the gods will give you the enjoyments you desire. One who not giving to them enjoys their gifts is nothing but a thief.' . . . Know action to have its origin in the Absolute, Brahman, and Brahman to have its foundation in the Immutable. Therefore is the omnipresent Brahman established through all time in sacrifice. . . . Although I exist as the unborn, the imperishable self (*ātmān*), and although I exist as the Lord of beings, resorting to and controlling my own nature I come into (phenomenal) being by my own magical power of self-delimitation. Whenever there is a crisis of *dharma* [righteousness, the good, the cosmic direction], Arjuna, and a rising up of *adharma*, then I loose myself forth. For the protection of good people and for the destruction of evil-doers, for the establishment of *dharma*, I take birth age after age. . . . Just in the ways in which I am approached, so do I receive to my love. People on all sides follow the path that is mine, Arjuna. . . . Actions do not stain me; nor do I have desire for the fruits of works. The person who recognizes me as this way is himself not bound by dispositions of action. So knowing, very ancient seekers of liberation and enlightenment carried out works. Therefore simply do actions as were done of old by the ancients. What action is (and all its implications), and what inaction, even the seer-sages are confused on this

score. To you I will explain that kind of action which when understood you will be free from the untoward and evil. . . . For action must be understood, and wrong action as well; inaction must be understood—deep, dark, and dense is the nature of action. Were one to see inaction in action and action in inaction, that person among mortals would be the one with wisdom; he, spiritually disciplined, would be the agent of all works. One whose instigations and undertakings are all free from the motive of personal desire, the wise see that person as the truly learned, as one whose personal dispositions have been burned up in the fire of knowledge. . . . Satisfied with whatever gain comes by him, passed beyond oppositions and dualities, untouched by jealousy, equal-minded and balanced in the face of both success and failure, such a person though he acts is not bound (by karmic dispositions). All dispositions dissolve and wash away when a person is free from attachment, 'liberated', and has his mind firmly fixed in knowledge—acting in a spirit of sacrifice. . . . This world does not belong to one who fails to sacrifice, so how could the next, Arjuna? In this way, numerous diverse sacrifices are spread wide in the mouth of Brahman. Know them all as born in action. Thus knowing, you will be 'liberated' and enlightened. The sacrifice that is knowledge, O you who are a great warrior, is superior to any sacrifice involving material things. All work and action in its entirety, Arjuna, culminates and is fulfilled in (spiritual) knowledge. . . . Even if of all sinners you are now the very worst evil-doer, once in the boat of knowledge you will safely cross over the crookedness of evil. As a fire kindled reduces its fuel to ashes, Arjuna, so the fire of knowledge makes ashes all *karma*. . . . In yoga, in 'spiritual discipline', take your stand; son of Bharata, stand up and fight.

Yet another approach to religion and the problem of evil is offered in Buddhism, whose Indian roots and spread throughout Asia was briefly discussed in Chapter 1. In Buddhism, the problem of evil is avoided entirely, since Buddhism abandons any conception of an anthropomorphic God. Yet Buddhism retains a belief in moral obligation and in reason. The highest form of Buddhism confronts evil—or, rather, human suffering—by working to help others in need. The answer to 'the problem of evil', in other words, is *compassion*. This is particularly true of the Northern, or Mahāyāna, doctrines. Against those Buddhists who encourage a course of spiritual discipline toward a solely personal end, the Mahāyāna argue that such an end is not the best and the highest. If we strive for our own personal salvation alone and if we intend to follow no career (*yāna*) helping others to the supreme good of *nirvāna*, we would belong to the 'Hīnayāna', literally 'a being with no career' (a term used by Mahāyānists in deprecation of such a 'path'). Mahāyānists, 'beings with wide and great careers', however, seek not only personal salvation but 'deliverance of all sentient beings from suffering and ignorance'. A follower of this 'wide path' attempts to acquire the six moral, intellectual, and spiritual perfections (*pāramitā*) possessed by Siddhārtha Gautama—liberality or charity, good moral character, patience or peace in the face of anger or desires, energy (energy to strive for the good), ability to maintain deep meditation, and last, the most important, insight or wisdom (*prajnā*). (In this conception, Siddhārtha Gautama is less 'the **Buddha**' than a *Bodhisattva*—one who has one foot in the bliss of *nirvāna*, so to say, but whose being is turned naturally through compassion toward achieving the welfare of all beings.) Thus Mahāyāna is more world-affirming than 'Hīnayāna', in that the development of individual perfections, rather than an extinction of individuality and personality in an otherworldly bliss, is the goal. One does not aim at extinction of individual form; one needs individual form and body as a medium with which to help others.

Thus the Mahāyānists do not view the natural world as an evil place to be abandoned but as—could we only perceive it as such—the 'Body of the Buddha', the *dharmakāya*. But even though nature comes to be viewed in such a positive way, Buddhist philosophy throughout the long history of Mahāyāna tends to be thoroughly 'idealistic', and the answer to evil lies not in the world but in us.

> • What is karma and how does it relate to free will?

I. A Hidden God?

In Section H, we examined the traditional problem of evil: if God exists, why is there evil—and so much evil—in the world? Now we shall consider a related problem: the **problem of divine hiddenness**. Simply put, the problem is this: if God exists, why doesn't He make His existence more obvious? That is, if there really is a God, why is it so hard for people to know Him? If God is all-good, He surely wants us to know Him; and if God is all-powerful, He can certainly make it possible for us to know Him; and if God is all-knowing, then He knows that we exist, and He also knows that our highest good lies in knowing Him. And yet, the argument continues, God is 'a hidden God': remote, silent, and elusive. How, then, can a perfectly good, omnipotent, and omniscient God exist?

These questions provide a hasty sketch of the problem of divine hiddenness, but they by no means get to the heart of the matter. For a more refined and detailed formulation of the problem, we now turn to an essay written especially for this text. Its author is J.L. Schellenberg, a Canadian philosopher of religion known for his work on divine hiddenness—especially his book *Divine Hiddenness and Human Reason*.

'Would a Loving God Hide from Anyone? Assembling and Assessing the Hiddenness Argument for Atheism'

By J.L. Schellenberg

The idea of a person-like God represents one way in which the religious idea of an ultimate reality has been interpreted by human beings. As you might expect, given the word *ultimate*, God is commonly regarded as having all knowledge and all power—or at least as much as it makes sense to suppose a person could have. For the same reason of ultimacy, God is said to be the source of our existence and all-good. But God is also said to be all-loving toward created beings, and this attribute is at least as obviously essential as the others. For love is one of the most impressive features any person can display. How could a candidate for 'greatest possible person' be anything but a fraud if she or he weren't always as loving to all other beings as it is possible for a person to be? Whatever stunning attributes such a candidate displayed, we would still be able to imagine an even greater person who *is* that loving.

This point provides the first premise for our argument:

(1) *If no perfectly loving God exists, then God does not exist.*

Now think about people in your life whom you would regard as being loving, even if not half as loving as what we would expect from the greatest possible person. What does it mean to say they love you? At least this much is clear: people who love you are invariably open to some kind of personal relationship with you, in which the two of you can interact meaningfully with each other. Indeed, since they love you, they want to be close to you, and close in a way you can appreciate, so you can turn to them for advice or draw on their support or just feel their presence when that's what you need. (Of course, if they love you, they'll value being with you for its own sake, too.) Now, it's true that they won't force any of this on you, which is why I used the expression *open to*. But if they aren't at least open to such a relationship, it would be a mistake to say they love you.

To see the implications of this point with full clarity, imagine that you're listening to a friend describe his parents: 'Man, they're great—I wish everyone could have parents like mine, who are so genuinely loving! Granted, they don't want anything to do with me. They're never around. Sometimes I find myself looking for them—once, I have to admit, I even called out for them when I was sick—but no dice. Apparently they're just not open to a relationship with me right now. But it's so good that they love me!' If you heard your friend talking like this, you'd think he was seriously confused. And you'd be right. His parents, if your friend's description of them is correct, could certainly be lots of other things—even impressive things, like the best corporate lawyer in the country or the prime minister—but they are not loving parents.

I expect you'll see how all of this can be applied to God. A careful look at the concept of love should lead us to affirm that God—who, if he exists, is necessarily perfectly loving—is always open to forming a personal relationship with each of us (or at least that God is thus disposed toward anyone capable of forming such a relationship—I will assume this restriction has been noted from here on in). So we have another premise:

(2) *If a perfectly loving God exists, then there is a God who is always open to a personal relationship with each human person.*

Instead of trying immediately to draw some conclusions, let's look a bit more closely at the expression *open to*. Consider the following situation: person A, without resisting a relationship with person B, is at some time not at a conscious level aware of B's existence; person B knows this and has the ability to make A consciously aware of his existence, but chooses not to do so. Clearly, at the given time, B is not open to a personal relationship of the sort I've described with A. Indeed, in this situation, B is preventing such a relationship from existing. Now reconsider this situation, with God standing in for person B. What is the result, in light of what we've already said about God? We can say that if any of us is ever—as I will put it—nonresistantly unaware of God's existence, then there is no God who is always open to a relationship with each of us. Another way of putting that point conveniently turns it around for us as follows:

(3) *If there is a God who is always open to a personal relationship with each human person, then no human person is ever non-resistantly unaware that God exists.*

(*Continued*)

And now we can draw a conclusion! Taking (2) and (3) together, it follows by an elementary logical rule called *hypothetical syllogism*[11] that

(4) *If a perfectly loving God exists, then no human person is ever non-resistantly unaware that God exists.*

But clearly there are lots of human persons who have been, for one reason or another (geographical or temporal location, social influence, personal interpretation of the evidence, and so on), non-resistantly unaware that God exists. Perhaps more people than ever are in that position today. So we can add this premise:

(5) *Some human persons are non-resistantly unaware that God exists.*

And now we are in a position to draw additional conclusions. Taking (4) and (5) together, it follows by a logical rule called *modus tollens*[12] that

(6) *No perfectly loving God exists.*

And from (1) taken together with (6) it follows by a logical rule called *modus ponens*[13] that

(7) *God does not exist.*

In other words, what love and logic combine to show is the truth of atheism.

Points (1) to (7) constitute one way of developing the hiddenness argument. Perhaps surprisingly, this is a relatively new argument, the product of thinking in the last decades of the twentieth century. Why, you may ask, did it lie hidden for so long?

There are various reasons, but here I'll focus on the main two. Across time, many humans have been inclined to think of God in exclusively masculine terms; at the same time, and until very recently, they have also considered a certain relational 'distance' to be a perfectly acceptable feature of masculinity. You may have noticed how father characters in old TV shows and movies tend to be rather aloof and are often absent from their children's lives, often away on important business. Well, it has long seemed natural to think of 'God the Father' in the same way. This, together with the commonness of references in theology to God as hidden, has made it possible for us to forget what is implied by being loving.

A second reason stems from the rising tide of secularity. In modern and postmodern culture, life without religion has become thinkable, but we should remember that this was not always the case.

This complex phenomenon of secularization has brought with it much more uncertainty about the existence of God than once existed, and thus more of a chance for people to start wondering why God should be 'hidden' from them. From such wondering, a hiddenness argument for atheism can grow.

But is the hiddenness argument a sound argument? That is certainly a question worth asking at this point. To assess the hiddenness argument, let's consider how a critic might respond to it, and see whether the critic can be answered. Premises (1) and (3) look very solid—you should check this for yourself—and we have seen how conclusions (4), (6), and (7) all follow from the earlier premises by elementary rules of logic. That leaves premises (2) and (5). Is either of these premises a weak link?

Let's start with (2). Someone might say that the kind of relational closeness (2) expects God to be open to is in fact impossible in this case, since God is not a physical being. God has no body with which to give us a comforting hug, no eyes with which to look kindly on us.

This point is answerable, for the same dispositions we humans express in these physical ways can be communicated by what is sometimes called religious experience. Imagine here a rich, subtly varying, constantly modulating sense of the presence of God. Even if we think it best to avoid the rather 'chummy' talk of, say, some forms of evangelical Christianity, we're just disagreeing with the way the experiential relationship is described. Clearly we can still speak of, for example, prayer and the observation of God's work in one's life, perhaps thinking of the latter as in some way causally related to prayer. All theistic (God-centred) religious traditions speak of such things as Divine guidance, support, or forgiveness, and—on the human side—trust, gratitude, and worship. Even if there is in fact no God, what they describe does seem possible. And what do they describe if not forms of personal interaction?

So the first objection to (2) doesn't get off the ground. But here's another: Maybe God is a bit like a good prime minister, governing the universe carefully and well and in this way ensuring benefits for us all even if not open to us in a relationship. Why shouldn't such a benevolent God count as loving?

The answer is this: Benevolence is indeed part of love, but it's not the whole. We think of benevolence as loving because it's a giving attitude. Such giving certainly belongs to any admirable love. But someone might give a lot 'from afar' while always refusing to give of herself in the closeness of a relationship. Such a person would be benevolent but would lack one of the things that belong to love and make it admirable.

You may notice here that by giving of ourselves in a relationship we become even more benevolent. That's an important observation, and it provides one reason for supposing that a perfectly benevolent God would be open to a relationship in the manner in question. But be sure to notice that, as I suggested earlier, admirably loving people don't open themselves to a relationship just from benevolence! ('Oh well, I guess she needs a relationship with me right now, so I'd better open up.') No, in a loving relationship each participant values the relationship for its own sake and not just for what can be gotten from it, whether for themselves or for others.

A third objection to (2) is perhaps the most common: Maybe some of the good things that God, as benevolent, wants us to have require that some people lack explicit awareness of God, at least for a time. If so, God has a reason to give up openness to a relationship, at least for that time. And if God is otherwise open to a relationship, doesn't God remain perfectly loving?

Here, of course, we first need to know what the 'good things' in question are. The ones most often mentioned are such things as the freedom to choose to live a bad life, cooperation with others in seeking knowledge of God, and a deep awareness of our spiritual deficiencies as opposed to spiritual complacency. We also need to check to see whether such good things might really be impossible for someone without that person at some time being unaware of God.

And that's where this objection runs into trouble, for the benefits that the critic can appeal to, though significant, all seem to be ones that in one way or another can be worked into a relationship with God, or at least made compatible with God's continuing openness to it. For example, we can point out that awareness of God doesn't have to come through the kind of overwhelming, constantly 'in your face' earth-shattering manifestation of Divine presence that would obliterate moral freedom. In this connection, notice how rather many people who are convinced there is a God still lead very bad lives! As for cooperation in spiritual investigation, if God is unsurpassably rich and deep, then there will always be more to learn about God! Finally, spiritual complacency resulting from closeness to God can always be stemmed by a strategic

experiential retreat, just as a parent who thinks you're taking her for granted can step back for a bit and allow you to appreciate how good you've had it without disappearing from view altogether. But if our own limited imaginations are in these ways able to reveal how a perfectly loving God can have the good things in question without giving up openness to a relationship, the objection is answered.

Objections to premise (2) seem therefore to be without force. But what about premise (5)? Might it plausibly be said that no one has ever really been non-resistantly unaware of God—that those who don't believe in God are invariably hiding from God? Might we have managed to get things backward in this way?

I think not. Many people who don't believe in God still have an admirable track record of investigation, and emotionally are, if anything, biased in favour of God. Many people who find that the evidence of argument and experience has taken belief in God away would love to believe in God. And, of course, we don't need to stay focussed on such support for (5). Behind it, in places far distant from any affected by Western culture and also in times long ago, before humans had so much as thought of an all knowing, perfectly good, and perfectly loving creator of the universe, we find individuals and communities who lack belief in God without ever having resisted God in any way. The critic of (5) needs you to look away from all this evidence for non-resistant non-belief. But to do so would be to fall prey to a failing of another kind. Hence this objection to the hiddenness argument, too, is without force, and the argument, all things considered, wins a positive assessment.

Two comments in conclusion. First, the fact that there are all these objections to the hiddenness argument is not in itself a reason to suspect it of weakness. Lots of very plausible views are adamantly opposed. Indeed, by raising many objections to an argument and answering them all we show the strength of that argument.

Second, giving up on the idea of a person-like God, if this is the point to which we are driven by the hiddenness argument, does not mean giving up on religion. The personal-God idea, as I said at the beginning, represents only one way—the way that is most familiar, closest to us—of giving more detail and content to the religious notion of an ultimate Divine reality. This personal picture of the Divine may indeed turn out to be one of humanity's most elementary or primitive, representing an early

(Continued)

attempt to come to grips with ultimate things. What we often fail to notice in this connection is that the human race has really just gotten started in religious investigation. We've been at it for only a few thousand years, and science tells us that the earth may remain habitable for a billion more! If so, human beings, and perhaps other species to follow, may yet have a lot of ground to cover along the road to illumination about things religious.

Now we have an example of an atheistic argument from divine hiddenness, but how have religious believers responded to the problem? Do they deny that God is hidden? If they do, then what arguments do they employ? And if they don't deny God's hiddenness, how do they account for it? How do they explain why a loving and perfect God would hide from his creatures?

Let's see what three figures—Blaise Pascal, Emil Fackenheim, and Isaac Bashevis Singer—have had to say about this tangle of topics.

First we will turn to Blaise Pascal, whose 'wager' we encountered earlier in this chapter, and his most celebrated work, the *Pensées* (or 'Thoughts'), a defence of Christianity. Unlike some of the Christian philosophers we have encountered—St Thomas Aquinas, for instance—Pascal does not think that the way to God is through proof or metaphysical argument. When we look out into the world, writes Pascal, what we see is ambiguous and confusing. On the one hand, we find good; on the other hand, evil; one the one hand, evidence that God exists; on the other hand, evidence that God does not exist. The conclusion we should draw from these facts is that God's existence cannot be inferred from Nature; to that extent, Pascal the theist allows, the atheists are right. If there is a God, Pascal concludes, He must be a **Deus absconditus**—'a hidden God'.

Although Pascal grants that God, if He exists, must be hidden, he denies that this makes belief in the God of Christianity unreasonable. Why? Let us allow Pascal to speak for himself:

From *Pensées*
By Blaise Pascal

If man is not made for God, why is he only happy with God? If man is made for God, why is he so hostile to God?

13

Instead of complaining that God has kept himself hidden, you will give him thanks that he has made himself so visible. And you will give him further thanks that he has not revealed himself to the wise people full of pride, unworthy of knowing so holy a God.

18

If man is not made for God, why is he only happy with God? If man is made for God, why is he so hostile to God?

260

What do the prophets say of Jesus Christ? That he will obviously be God? No. Rather that he is *a truly hidden God*, that he will be unrecognized, that no one will think he is who he is, that he will be a stumbling block for many to fall over, etc.

266

God wants to motivate the will more than the mind. Absolute clarity would be more use to the mind and would not help the will.

Humble their pride.

267

Jesus Christ came to blind those who see clearly and give sight to the blind, to heal the sick and allow the healthy to die, to call sinners to repent and justify them and leave the righteous in their sinfulness, to feed the poor and *send the rich away hungry*.

271

Man is not worthy of God, but he is not incapable of being made worthy of him.

It is unworthy of God to associate himself with man's wretchedness, but not unworthy of him to extricate man from his wretchedness.

274

Wishing to appear openly to those who seek him wholeheartedly, and to remain hidden from those who single-mindedly avoid him, God qualified the way he might be known so that he gave visible signs to those who seek him, and none to those who do not.

There is enough light for those whose only desire is to see, and enough darkness for those of the opposite disposition.

275

That God wanted to be hidden.

If there were only one religion, God would be clearly manifest.

If there were martyrs only in our religion, the same.

God being therefore hidden, any religion which does not say that God is hidden is not true. And any religion which does not give the reason why does not enlighten. Ours does all this. *Vere tu es Deus absconditus*. ['Truly, God is hidden with you' (Isaiah 45:15).]

644

I admire the boldness, with which these people set about speaking of God. In addressing their arguments to unbelievers, their first chapter is about proving the existence of God from the works of nature. I would not be surprised about their venture if they were addressing their arguments to the faithful, for it is clear that those with a keen faith in their hearts can see straightaway that everything which exists is the work of the God they worship. But for those in whom this light has been extinguished and in whom these authors are trying to rekindle it, these people deprived of faith and grace who, scrutinizing with all their intelligence everything they see in nature which can lead them to this knowledge, but finding only obscurity and darkness; to say to them that they only have to look at the least of the things surrounding them and they will see God revealed there, and then to give them as a complete proof of this great and important matter the course of the moon and the planets, and to claim to have achieved a proof with such an argument, is to give them cause to believe that the proofs of our religion are indeed weak. I see by reason and experience that nothing is more likely to arouse their contempt. This is not how Scripture, which understands better the things which are God's, speaks of them. It says on the contrary, that God is a hidden God; and that since the corruption of nature, he has left men in a blind state from which they can emerge only through Jesus Christ, without whom all communication with God is barred: *Nemo novit Patrem, nisi Filius, et cui Filius voluerit revelare*. ['Just as no one knows the Father except the Son and those to whom the Son chooses to reveal him' (Matthew 11:27).]

That is what Scripture points out to us, when it says in so many places that those who seek God will find him. It is not this light we are speaking of, like the midday sun. We do not say that those who seek the sun at midday, or water in the sea, will find it. And so clearly the evidence of God is not of such a kind in nature. It also tells us elsewhere: *Vere tu es Deus absconditus*. ['Truly, God is hidden within you' (Isaiah 45:15).]

681

Let them at least learn the nature of the religion they attack, before attacking it. If this religion boasted that it had a clear vision of God, and to have it plain and unhidden, it would be attacking it to say that nothing can be seen in this world which obviously proves it. But since, on the contrary, it says that humanity is in darkness, estranged from God, that he has hidden himself from its knowledge, that this is the very name that he gives himself in the Scriptures: *Deus absconditus* ['the hidden God' (Isaiah 45:15)]; and if, finally, it strives equally to establish these two facts: that God has established visible signs in the Church by which those who seek him sincerely should know him; and that he has nevertheless

(Continued)

hidden them in such a way that he will only be perceived by those who seek him whole-heartedly, what advantage can they derive when, in their professed unconcern in seeking the truth, they protest that nothing reveals it to them? For the darkness by which they are surrounded, and with which they castigate the Church, establishes simply one of the things the Church upholds, without affecting the other, and, far from destroying its doctrine, confirms it.

In order to attack it, let them protest that they have made every effort to seek it everywhere, even in what the Church offers for their instruction, but without any satisfaction at all. If they spoke like that, they would indeed be attacking one of these claims. But I hope to show here that no reasonable person could speak like that, and I even dare to say that no one has ever done it. We know well enough how people in this state of mind behave. They think they have made great efforts to learn, when they have spent a few hours reading a book of the Bible, and have questioned some ecclesiastic about the truths of the faith. After that, they boast that they have consulted books and men unsuccessfully. But in fact I would tell them what I have often said, that such negligence is intolerable. It is not a question here of the passing interest of some stranger for us to treat it like this. It is a question of ourselves, and our all.

708

As far as I am concerned, I admit that as soon as the Christian religion reveals this principle—that man's nature is corrupt and has fallen away from God—this opens eyes to see the nature of that truth everywhere. For nature is such that it points everywhere to a God who has been lost, both within man and elsewhere.

And a corrupt nature.

709

Greatness. Religion is so great a thing that it is right that those who would not want to take the trouble to seek it, if it is obscure, should be denied it. So what is there to complain about if it can be found simply by looking for it?

> • Why does Pascal think that we should *expect* God to be hidden? Why would God want to hide?

Next we will turn to Emil Fackenheim, a German-born rabbi and thinker who emigrated in 1940 to Canada, where he spent decades as a highly regarded professor of philosophy. In one of Fackenheim's essays, included in his collection *Quest for Past and Future: Essays in Jewish Theology*, he asks how a religious believer should deal with the apparent absence or hiddenness of God when tragedy strikes. Does the sufferer's painful experience of God's absence—his sense that God has withdrawn in the face of tragedy—prove that faith is foolish? Does the fact that God seems terribly distant at such moments mean that belief in God has been refuted? Not at all, says Fackenheim:

From 'On the Eclipse of God'
By Emil Fackenheim

Religious faith can be, and is, empirically verifiable; but nothing empirical can possibly refute it.

In one of his writings, Martin Heidegger quotes with approval, as applying to the present, these words of the early nineteenth-century German poet Hölderlin: 'Alas, our generation walks in night, dwells as in Hades, without the Divine.' When Hölderlin wrote those words, there cannot have been many people who agreed with him, for it was an age which thought of itself as about to reach the very summit of religious enlightenment. In our own age, by contrast—an age which is acquainted with catastrophe and stands in fear of even greater catastrophes to come—hardly anyone can think of himself as walking in anything but night. And while it is not immediately clear whether this means that we must dwell 'without the Divine'—indeed, that is the question to which these reflections are addressed—it is at any rate perfectly clear that we are undergoing an unprecedented crisis of religious faith.

According to a widespread view, it is the very catastrophes of the twentieth century which have brought the crisis about. The ancient belief that the Divine is with us—that God lives and cares—cannot, it is said, be sustained in the face of these catastrophes, for to sustain it requires smugness and blindness to tragedy. Yet the fact is that this view reflects a complete lack of understanding of the nature of religious faith in general and Biblical faith in particular. Biblical faith—and I mean both Jewish and Christian—is never destroyed by tragedy but only tested by it; and in the test it both clarifies its own meaning and conquers tragedy. Here, precisely, lies the secret of its strength.

Consider a few representative examples. The prophet Jeremiah lives to see the destruction of the Temple, of Jerusalem, of the whole national existence of Judah. He does not deny the tragedy or seek to explain it away. But neither does it occur to him that God's existence has now been refuted, or that He can no longer be conceived as just, or as loving His people, Israel. To Jeremiah the destruction of the Temple is a manifestation of divine justice. And it does not mark the end of divine love: 'There is hope for the future.'

The case of Job is still more extreme because Job is struck by tragedies which are explicitly said to be beyond the bounds of any conceivable divine justice. Yet Job never denies the existence of God; nor does he follow his wife's suggestion that he curse God and die. His faith is reduced to utter unintelligibility, yet he persists in it.

Let me give a final example which, at least in one respect, is still more extreme—the example of the Psalmist. Even in the midst of unintelligible tragedy, Job never wholly loses his sense of the presence of God. The Psalmist in extremis, however, does, when he complains that God has 'hidden His face'. God is not—at least not now—present. Unlike Job, the Psalmist does not ask that God's ways be made intelligible to him. He does not ask that the valley of the shadows or the netherworld be made to vanish; he asks only that God be present while he walks through them, as God was present to him before. Yet even in this most extreme of all crisis situations—God having 'hidden His face'—the Psalmist never loses his faith. He never says that God does not, after all, exist; nor that, though existing, He has finally ceased to care. (In practice the two assertions would amount to the same thing.) What he does say is that, unaccountably, God has hidden His face; that He has hidden it for only a while; and that He will turn His face back to man again.

Put radically, this means that there is no experience, either without or within, that can possibly destroy religious faith. Good fortune without reveals the hand of God; bad fortune, if it is not a matter of just punishment, teaches that God's ways are unintelligible, not that there are no ways of God. A full heart within indicates the Divine Presence; an empty heart bespeaks not the non-existence or unconcern of God, but merely His temporary absence. *Religious faith can be, and is, empirically verifiable; but nothing empirical can possibly refute it.*

Philosophers of science rightly assert that such an attitude toward the empirical is in principle illegitimate in the sciences. It is, however, hardly surprising that it should be of the essence of religious faith. Science is forever hypothetical. But what could one make of a religious faith which was forever hypothetical, wavering between belief in good times and unbelief in bad? Since, as we have seen, the characteristic of genuine faith is not only to survive in tragic times but to survive in them most triumphant, it is no accident that adherents of Biblical faith should always have regarded times of external or internal darkness not as evidence against God, but rather—to use Martin Buber's expression—as evidence of an 'eclipse of God'. To follow Buber's metaphor, an eclipse of the sun is something that occurs, not to or in the sun, but between the sun and the eye; moreover, this occurrence is temporary. Hence the catastrophes of our time, however great, cannot by themselves account for the contemporary crisis of religious belief.

- What does Fackenheim mean when he claims that '[b]iblical faith—and I mean both Jewish and Christian—is never destroyed by tragedy but only tested by it'? How does he support this statement?
- What does Fackenheim mean by 'the eclipse of God'? How is 'the eclipse of God' related to the idea of a 'hidden God'?
- According to Fackenheim, '[r]eligious faith can be, and is, empirically verifiable; but nothing empirical can possibly refute it'. What do you think he would say about John Wisdom's parable of the gardener (included above, in Section A)? Where do you think Fackenheim would agree with Wisdom? Where would he disagree?

Finally, we will turn to Isaac Bashevis Singer, winner of the 1978 Nobel Prize for Literature. The protagonist of Singer's short story 'Joy' is a rabbi whose great sufferings—including the death of his children—cause him to lose his faith in God. Forlorn and broken, he withdraws from his friends, neglects his pupils, retreats into his study, even rejects food. Then, one day, something unexpected happens: the rabbi has a vision in which Rebecca, his youngest daughter—one of his dead children—appears to him. His faith restored, the rabbi rejoins his assembled friends, just as Rebecca has instructed him to do. Here is what he tells them:

From 'Joy'
By Isaac Bashevis Singer

If one knew the truth how could there be freedom?

After taking some broth, the rabbi commented on the Torah, a thing he had not done in years. His voice was low, though audible. The rabbi took up the question of why the moon is obscured on Rosh Hashona. The answer is that on Rosh Hashona one prays for life, and life means free choice, and freedom is Mystery. If one knew the truth how could there be freedom? If hell and paradise were in the middle of the marketplace, everyone would be a saint. Of all the blessings bestowed on man, the greatest lies in the fact that God's face is forever hidden from him. Men are the children of the Highest, and the Almighty plays hide-and-seek with them. He hides his face, and the children seek him while they have faith that He exists. But what if, God forbid, one loses faith? The wicked live on denials; denials in themselves are also a faith, faith in evil-doing, and from it one can draw strength for the body. But if the pious man loses his faith, the truth is shown to him, and he is re-called. This is the symbolic meaning of the words, 'When a man dies in a tent': when the pious man falls from his rank, and becomes, like the wicked, without permanent shelter, then a light shines from above, and all doubts cease.

- The rabbi tells his friends: 'If one knew the truth how could there be freedom? If hell and paradise were in the middle of the marketplace, everyone would be a saint.' What do you think this means? Do you think the rabbi has a point? Why or why not?
- Where do you think Pascal and Singer agree about the hiddenness of God?

J. Beyond Reason: Faith and Irrationality

Whenever you can defend your belief rationally, it is obviously desirable to do so. The move from rationality to irrationality in the defence of religion, therefore, is a serious step. Kant, who defended belief in God as a matter of faith, nevertheless defended this belief as rational. But there have always been religious people who have defended faith against reason, emphasizing the impossibility of rational justification and the irrelevance of the usual forms of understanding and knowledge where religion is concerned. In some cases, particularly in modern times, this step away from rationality may be a convenient escape from arguments and doubts that have become too overpowering. But it is not always, or even usually, taken for this reason, as we shall see.

1. The Leap of Faith

Following the Enlightenment, particularly in Germany, religion took a dramatic swing to the subjective. Attempts at rational defence were given up entirely. The German Romantic philosopher Friedrich Schleiermacher insisted that religion was simply a matter of intense feelings of dependence, nothing more. (His contemporary, Hegel, wryly retorted that this would make a dog a better Christian than most of us.)

The best and most famous of all of these 'new' Christians was Søren Kierkegaard, an eccentric Danish philosopher who is often claimed as the father of both the 'new' Christianity and that non-religious philosophy called existentialism. Kierkegaard was born into a society in which almost everyone was a Christian. They all believed the same dogmas, without thinking about them. They all went to the same (Lutheran) churches for Sunday services and Friday afternoon bingo games and enjoyed these social gatherings immensely. They were all entitled to call themselves 'Christians' just by virtue of the fact that they had been born of certain parents, brought as children to certain churches, and continued to mouth certain doctrines that they didn't understand or care to understand in the slightest. What they all lacked was passion. Their religion and they themselves, according to Kierkegaard, were boring through and through. Whatever happened to the phrase 'the fear of God in their hearts'? These people felt no 'fear', just the security of a comfortable and self-righteous society and the warm swill of beer in their bellies, he complained. Kierkegaard, who had been brought up in an unusually devout Lutheran home, was disgusted with them. This isn't Christianity, he insisted, and the sophisticated disputes over doctrine and dogma had nothing more to do with being religious than the calculations of an accountant at tax time.

Accordingly Kierkegaard offered his alternative—a new (in fact, very old) way of seeing oneself as a Christian. Rational argument was irrelevant. The doctrines of Christianity, he admitted, were absolutely absurd. But that didn't matter. In fact, it was the very absurdity of these beliefs that made the passion of Christianity possible. After all, if it were simply a matter of accepting some proposition, why should we feel anything? And 'proofs' of God's existence, needless to say, were as irrelevant—in fact, offensive—as you could imagine. 'Christianity is passion!' he insisted. 'Religion is feeling and commitment.' No talk of 'truth'—unless you mean simply **subjective truth**. No talk of 'proof' and no talk of 'rationality'. There is simply, to use his most famous phrase, *the leap of faith*—the leap across the borders of rationality and thinking to the passion-filled life of old-fashioned Christian fear and awe of God. He summed up his position in an article he wrote shortly before his death: 'My only analogy is Socrates. My task is a Socratic task—to revise the conception of what it means to be a Christian.'

Kierkegaard's move away from rationality is characterized as a rejection of 'objectivity'. Being a Christian, he says, is not a matter of 'objective faith' (consisting of reason, doctrines, and 'proofs') but of subjectivity, passion, and 'inwardness'.

SUBJECTIVE TRUTH

What is true for the individual; the 'truth' of strong feelings and commitment.

On Subjective Truth
By Søren Kierkegaard[14]

If God does not exist, it would be impossible to prove it, but if God does exist, it would be folly to try to prove it.

Objective faith: what does that mean? It means a sum of dogmas. But suppose Christianity is nothing of the kind; suppose, on the contrary, it is inwardness, and therefore also the paradox, so as to push away objectively; and thus to acquire significance for the existing individual in the inwardness of his existence, in order to place him more decisively than any judge can place the accused, between time and eternity in time, between heaven and hell in the time of salvation. Objective faith: it is as if Christianity had also been heralded as a kind of little system, although not quite so good as the Hegelian system; it is as if Christ—yes, no offence intended—it is as if Christ were a professor, and as if the Apostles had formed a little professional society. Truly, if it was once no easy thing to become a Christian, I believe now it becomes more difficult every year, because by now it has become so easy to become one—one finds a little competition only in becoming a speculative philosopher. And yet the speculative philosopher is perhaps most removed from Christianity, and perhaps it is far preferable to be an offended individual who nonetheless continually relates himself to Christianity, than to be a speculative philosopher who supposes he has understood it.

* * *

Suppose, however, that subjectivity is truth, and that subjectivity is the existing subjectivity, then, to put it this way, Christianity is an exact fit. Subjectivity culminates in passion, Christianity is paradox, paradox and passion fit one another exactly, and paradox exactly fits one whose situation is in the extremity of existence. Yes, in the wide world there could not be found two lovers so well fitted for one another as paradox and passion, and their argument is like a lovers' argument, when they argue whether he first aroused her passion, or she his. So it is here: by means of the paradox itself, the existing person has been situated in the extremity of existence. And what is more delightful for lovers than that they are allowed a long time together without any change in the relationship between them, except that it becomes more intensive in inwardness?

Religion is a confrontation with the unknown, not something knowable.

But what is this unknown thing, with which reason in its paradoxical passion is affronted, and which even upsets for man his self-knowledge? It is the Unknown. But it is certainly something human, insofar as we know what it is to be human, nor is it some other thing humans know. Let us call this unknown something: *the God*. That is merely the name we give to it. To want to prove that this unknown something (the God) exists could hardly occur to reason. For of course if God does not exist, it would be impossible to prove it, but if God does exist, it would be folly to try to prove it; for, in the very moment I began my proof, I would have presupposed it, not as dubious but as certain (a presupposition is never dubious, just because it is a presupposition); since otherwise I would never begin, understanding that the whole would be impossible if he did not exist. But if when I speak of proving God's existence I mean that I propose to prove that the Unknown, which exists, is God, then I express myself less fortunately; for then I prove nothing, least of all existence, but merely develop the content of a concept. In general, to try to prove that something exists is a difficult matter, and what is still worse for the bold who would attempt it, the difficulty is of a kind that will not bring fame to those who occupy themselves with it. The whole proof always turns into something entirely different, turns into an additional development of the consequences that come from my having assumed that the object in question exists. Thus I continually deduce not toward existence, but I deduce from existence, whether I exert myself indeed in the world I can grasp with my hands or in thought. So I do not prove that a stone exists, but that something which exists is a stone; a court of justice does not prove that a criminal exists, but that the accused, who certainly exists, is a criminal. Whether one calls existence an *accessorium* [a predicate] or the eternal *prius* [first given], it can never be proven. Let us take our time; for us there is no reason to hurry, as there is for those, who from concern for themselves or for God or for some other thing, must hurry to show they exist. When it is so, there is indeed excellent reason to hurry, especially if the prover sincerely tries to appreciate the danger that he himself or the thing in question may not exist until the proof is complete, and does not secretly entertain the thought that it exists whether he succeeds in proving it or not.

So if from Napoleon's actions one tried to prove Napoleon's existence, would it not be of the greatest peculiarity, since his existence very well explains his actions, but actions cannot prove *his* existence, unless I have already understood the word 'his' such that I assume that he exists. But Napoleon is only an individual, and insofar there is no absolute relationship between him and his actions; after all, another person may have performed the same actions. Perhaps this is why I cannot deduce from actions to existence. If I call these actions the actions of Napoleon, then the proof is superfluous, since I have already named him; if I ignore this, I can never prove from the actions that

they are Napoleon's, but (purely ideally) prove that such actions are the actions of a great general, etc. But between God and his works there is an absolute relationship; God is not a name, but a concept, and perhaps it follows from that, that his *essentia involvit existentiam* [essence entails existence]. God's works can only be done by God; quite right, but where then are the works of God? The works from which I would deduce his existence are not immediately given. Or does the wisdom in nature, the goodness, the wisdom in the governance of the world, reside on the very face of things? Are we not here confronted with the most terrible temptations to doubt, and is it not impossible finally to dispose of those doubts? But from such an order of things I will certainly not prove God's existence, and even if I began I would never finish, and furthermore would live constantly *in suspenso* [in suspense], that something terrible should suddenly happen that would demolish my little proof. So, from what works will I prove it? From the works as apprehended through an ideal interpretation, i.e., such as they do not immediately reveal themselves. But in that case it is not from the works that I prove it, but I develop only the ideality I have presupposed; because of my confidence in *this* I boldly defy all objections, even those that have not yet been made. As soon as I begin I have presupposed the ideal interpretation, and presuppose that I will be successful in carrying it through; but this is just to presuppose that God exists, and that in confidence in him is how I am actually beginning.

You can see how little Kierkegaard thinks of the ingenious 'proofs' of God's existence, as well as all attempts to 'know' Him. The point of religion, he says, is precisely not to know, but rather to feel. It is the absurdity and the irrationality of Christian doctrines, he insists, that makes this rare intensity of feeling possible.

Precisely its objective repulsion, the absurd is the measure of the intensity of faith in inwardness. There is a man who wants to have faith, well, let the comedy begin. He wants to have faith, but he also wants to ensure himself with the help of an objective inquiry and its approximation-process. What happens? With the help of the approximation-process, the absurd becomes something else; it becomes probable, it becomes more probable, it becomes extremely and exceedingly probable. Now he is prepared to believe

it, and he boldly supposes that he does not believe as shoemakers and tailors and simple folk do, but only after long consideration. Now he is prepared to believe it, but lo and behold, now it has become impossible to believe it. The almost probable, the very probable, the extremely and exceedingly probable: that he can almost know, or as good as know, to a greater degree and exceedingly almost *know*—but *believe* it, that is impossible, for the absurd is precisely the object of faith, and only that can be believed.

Christianity, Kierkegaard concludes, is suffering, the suffering that comes with the anticipation of our own death and our feeling of smallness and insignificance when we consider the eternal order of things. For those who try to minimize this suffering through professional 'understanding' and knowledge, Kierkegaard has little but sarcasm, as he suggested in his journals: '*The two ways*. One is to suffer; the other is to become a professor of the fact that another suffered.'

Also in his journals, Kierkegaard expands on his notion of subjective truth:

What I really lack is to be clear in my mind what I am to do, not what I am to know, except insofar as a kind of understanding must precede every action. The thing is to understand myself, to see what God truly wishes me to do; the thing is to find a truth which is true for me, to find the idea I can live and die for. What would be the use of discovering so-called objective truth, of mastering all the systems of philosophy and of being able, if required, to discuss them all and reveal the inconsistencies within each; what good would it do me to be able to develop a theory of the state and synthesize all details into one whole, and so to create a world I did not live in, but only held up for others to see; what good would it do me to be able to explain the meaning of Christianity if it had no deeper significance for me and for my life; what good would it do me if truth herself stood before me, cold and naked, not caring whether I recognized her or not, and producing in me a shudder of terror rather than a trusting devotion? Indeed I do not deny that I yet acknowledge an imperative of understanding and that with it one can control men, but it must be taken up into my life, and that is what I now recognize as the most important thing.[15]

- How does subjectivism differ from mysticism?
- Why does Kierkegaard claim that absurdity or paradox is the essence of faith?

---

2. God as Ultimate Concern

Following Kierkegaard, Christian 'irrationalism' changed the complexion of Western religion and gave faith a meaning that is not vulnerable to rational arguments. Early twentieth-century philosopher Paul Tillich proposed an extremely powerful form of Christianity that also gives up the traditional view of God and moves the focus of the religion to purely personal concerns and commitments. These are our religion, and we don't need anything more.

On the Ultimate Concern
By Paul Tillich

God as the ultimate in man's ultimate concern is more certain than any other certainty, even that of oneself.

We have discussed the meaning of symbols generally because, as we said, man's ultimate concern must be expressed symbolically! One may ask: Why can it not be expressed directly and properly? If money, success, or the nation is someone's ultimate concern, can this not be said in a direct way without symbolic language? Is it not only in those cases in which the content of the ultimate concern is called 'God' that we are in the realm of symbols? The answer is that everything which is a matter of unconditional concern is made into a god. If the nation is someone's ultimate concern, the name of the nation becomes a sacred name and the nation receives divine qualities which far surpass the reality of the being and functioning of the nation. The nation then stands for and symbolizes the true ultimate, but in an idolatrous way. Success as ultimate concern is not the natural desire of actualizing potentialities, but its readiness to sacrifice all other values of life for the sake of a position of power and social predominance. The anxiety about not being a success is an idolatrous form of the anxiety about divine condemnation. Success is grace; lack of success, ultimate judgment. In this way concepts designating ordinary realities become idolatrous symbols of ultimate concern.

The reason for this transformation of concepts into symbols is the character of ultimacy and the nature of faith. That which is the true ultimate transcends the realm of finite reality infinitely. Therefore, no finite reality can express it directly and properly. Religiously speaking, God transcends his own name. This is why the use of his name easily becomes an abuse or a blasphemy. Whatever we say about that which concerns us ultimately, whether or not we call it God, has a symbolic meaning. It points beyond itself while participating in that to which it points. In no other way can faith express itself adequately. The language of faith is the language of symbols. If faith were what we have shown that it is not, such an assertion could not be made. But faith, understood as the state of being ultimately concerned, has no language other than symbols. When saying this I always expect the question: Only a symbol? He who asks this question shows that he has not understood the difference between signs and symbols nor the power of symbolic language, which surpasses in quality and strength the power of any non-symbolic language. One should never say 'only a symbol', but one should say 'not less than a symbol'. With this in mind we can now describe the different kinds of symbols of faith.

The fundamental symbol of our ultimate concern is God. It is always present in any act of faith, even if the act of faith includes the denial of God. Where there is ultimate concern, God can be denied only in the name of God. One God can deny the other one. Ultimate concern cannot deny its own character as ultimate. Therefore, it affirms what is meant by the word *God*. Atheism, consequently, can only mean the attempt to remove any ultimate concern—to remain unconcerned about the meaning of one's existence. Indifference toward the ultimate question is the only imaginable form of atheism. Whether it is possible is a problem which must remain unsolved at this point. In any case, he who denies God as matter of ultimate concern affirms God, because he affirms ultimacy in his concern. God is the fundamental symbol for what concerns us ultimately. Again, it would be completely wrong to ask: So God is nothing but a symbol? Because the next question has to be: A symbol for what? And then the answer would be: For God! God is symbol for God. This means that in the person of God we must distinguish two elements: the element of ultimacy, which is a matter of immediate experience and not symbolic in itself, and the element of concreteness, which is taken from our ordinary experience and symbolically applied to God. The man whose ultimate concern is a sacred tree has both the ultimacy of concern and the concreteness of the tree which symbolizes his relation to the ultimate. The man who adores Apollo is ultimately concerned, but not in an abstract way. His ultimate concern is symbolized in the divine figure of Apollo. The man who glorifies Jahweh, the God of the Old Testament, has both an ultimate concern and a concrete image of what concerns him ultimately. This is the meaning of the seemingly cryptic statement that God is the symbol of God. In this qualified sense God is the fundamental and universal content of faith.

It is obvious that such an understanding of the meaning of God makes the discussions about the existence or non-existence of God meaningless. It is meaningless to question the ultimacy of an ultimate concern. This element in the idea of God is in itself certain. The symbolic expression of this element varies endlessly through the whole history of mankind. Here again it would be meaningless to ask whether one or another of the figures in which an ultimate concern is symbolized does 'exist'. If 'existence' refers to something which can be found within the whole of reality, no divine being exists. The question is not this, but: Which of the innumerable symbols of faith is most adequate to the meaning of faith? In other words, which symbol of ultimacy expresses the ultimate without idolatrous elements? This is the problem, and not the so-called 'existence of God'—which

(Continued)

is in itself an impossible combination of words. God as the ultimate in man's ultimate concern is more certain than any other certainty, even that of oneself. God as symbolized in a divine figure is a matter of daring faith, of courage and risk.

God is the basic symbol of faith, but not the only one. All the qualities we attribute to him, power, love, justice, are taken from finite experiences and applied symbolically to that which is beyond finitude and infinity. If faith calls God 'almighty', it uses the human experience of power in order to symbolize the content of its infinite concern, but it does not describe a highest being who can do as he pleases. So it is with all the other qualities and with all the actions, past, present, and future, which men attribute to God. They are symbols taken from our daily experience, and not information about what God did once upon a time or will do sometime in the future. Faith is not the belief in such stories, but it is the acceptance of symbols that express our ultimate concern in terms of divine actions.

Another group of symbols of faith are manifestations of the divine in things and events, in persons and communities, in words and documents. This whole realm of sacred objects is a treasure of symbols. Holy things are not holy in themselves, but they point beyond themselves to the source of all holiness, that which is of ultimate concern.

Notice how far Tillich has moved from the traditional Judeo-Christian-Islamic conception of God. He is still a theist and a Christian, but it is not clear that 'God' means the same for Tillich as it does in the Old and New Testaments. For Tillich, God is a symbol of the 'ultimate concern', yet he expands the belief in God to represent the fact that one finds his or her life meaningful. Tillich says that this 'makes the discussions about the existence or non-existence of God meaningless'. It also undercuts the Western idea that God is a single kind of being with the characteristics we discussed earlier and brings Tillich's theism very close to the *general* idea of religion, which Nishitani described in the passage we looked at in Section A of this chapter. God is whatever concerns us ultimately, whatever is most important in our lives. This is even true, Tillich says, when one denies the existence of God: 'Where there is ultimate concern, God can be denied only in the name of God'.

- For Tillich, what is an 'ultimate concern'? Why does it make the question of God's existence 'meaningless'?
- How is God a symbol of the 'ultimate concern'? Can you have an ultimate concern and not believe in God?

K. Doubts about Religion

It is often said that religion is a matter of personal belief and faith, suggesting that the objects of religious belief are beyond criticism and no one's business but one's own. But it is a questionable slide from this view—which is amiably suited to promoting tolerance between believers of different faiths—to the idea that true faith is immune to doubt, or, for that matter, to criticisms of a very different kind. On the one hand, religious belief might necessarily involve doubts; indeed, it might be argued that the dogmatic certainty sought by many believers is something less than real faith. Such a view is implied by Kierkegaard, for example, and his insistence on passionate commitment arises precisely in order to confront the 'objective uncertainty' of faith. An even more profound doubt *within* the bonds of faith is expressed by the great Russian author Fyodor Dostoyevsky. He was a devout Christian whose faith was shaken many times, not least by the cruelty he often witnessed (and of which he was sometimes the victim) in feudal Tsarist Russia. In his novel *The Brothers Karamazov*, Alyosha is a devout but still naive religious novice, whereas his brother Ivan is entertaining serious doubts about the justification for belief in a good God. (The author clearly recognized himself in both brothers.) In a conversation between the two of them, Ivan presents us with a vivid and horrible picture of human evil challenging his faith.

From *The Brothers Karamazov*
By Fyodor Dostoyevsky

It's not God that I don't accept, Alyosha, only I most respectfully return Him the ticket.

'One picture, only one more, because it's so curious, so characteristic, and I have only just read it in some collection of Russian antiquities. I've forgotten the name. I must look it up. It was in the darkest days of serfdom at the beginning of the century, and long live the Liberator of the People! There was in those days a general of aristocratic connections, the owner of great estates, one of those men—somewhat exceptional, I believe, even then—who, retiring from the service into a life of leisure, are convinced that they've earned absolute power over the lives of their subjects. There were such men then. So our general, settled on his property of two thousand souls, lives in pomp, and domineers over his poor neighbours as though they were dependants and buffoons. He has kennels of hundreds of hounds and nearly a hundred dog boys—all mounted and in uniform. One day a serf boy, a little child of eight, threw a stone in play and hurt the paw of the general's favourite hound. "Why is my favourite dog lame?" He is told that the boy threw a stone that hurt the dog's paw. "So you did it." The general looked the child up and down. "Take him." He was taken—taken from his mother and kept shut up all night. Early that morning the general comes out on horseback, with the hounds, his dependants, dog boys, and huntsmen, all mounted around him in full hunting parade. The servants are summoned for their edification, and in front of them all stands the mother of the child. The child is brought from the lockup. It's a gloomy, cold, foggy autumn day, a capital day for hunting. The general orders the child to be undressed; the child is stripped naked. He shivers, numb with terror, not daring to cry. . . . "Make him run," commands the general. "Run! run!" shout the dog boys. The boy runs. . . . "At him!" yells the general, and he sets the whole pack of hounds on the child. The hounds catch him, and tear him to pieces before his mother's eyes! . . . I believe the general was afterward declared incapable of administering his estates. Well—what did he deserve? To be shot? To be shot for the satisfaction of our moral feelings? Speak, Alyosha!'

'To be shot,' murmured Alyosha, lifting his eyes to Ivan with a pale, twisted smile.

'Bravo!' cried Ivan delighted. 'If even you say so . . . You're a pretty monk! So there is a little devil sitting in your heart, Alyosha Karamazov!'

'What I said was absurd, but—'

'That's just the point, that "but"!' cried Ivan. 'Let me tell you, novice, that the absurd is only too necessary on earth. The world stands on absurdities, and perhaps nothing would have come to pass in it without them. We know what we know!'

'What do you know?'

'I understand nothing,' Ivan went on, as though in a delirium. 'I don't want to understand anything now. I want to stick to the fact. I made up my mind long ago not to understand. If I try to understand anything, I shall be false to the fact, and I have determined to stick to the fact.'

'Why are you trying me?' Alyosha cried, with sudden distress. 'Will you say what you mean at last?'

'Of course, I will; that's what I've been leading up to. You are dear to me. I don't want to let you go, and I won't give you up to your Zossima.'

Ivan for a minute was silent; his face became all at once very sad.

'Listen! I took the case of children only to make my case clearer. Of the other tears of humanity with which the earth is soaked from its crust to its centre, I will say nothing. I have narrowed my subject on purpose. I am a bug, and I recognize in all humility that I cannot

(Continued)

understand why the world is arranged as it is. Men are themselves to blame, I suppose; they were given paradise, they wanted freedom, and stole fire from heaven, though they knew they would become unhappy, so there is no need to pity them. With my pitiful, earthly, Euclidian understanding, all I know is that there is suffering and that there are none guilty; that effect follows cause, simply and directly; that everything flows and finds it level—but that's only Euclidian nonsense, I know that, and I can't consent to live by it! What comfort is it to me that there are none guilty and that effect follows cause simply and directly, and that I know it—I must have justice, or I will destroy myself. And not justice in some remote infinite time and space, but here on earth, and that I could see myself. I have believed in it. I want to see it, and if I am dead by then, let me rise again, for if it all happens without me, it will be too unfair. Surely I haven't suffered, simply that I, my crimes and my sufferings, may manure the soil of the future harmony for somebody else. I want to see with my own eyes the hind lie down with the lion and the victim rise up and embrace his murderer. I want to be there when everyone suddenly understands what it has all been for. All the religions of the world are built on this longing, and I am a believer. But then there are the children, and what am I to do about them? That's a question I can't answer. For the hundredth time I repeat, there are numbers of questions, but I've only taken the children, because in their case what I mean is so unanswerably clear. Listen! If all must suffer to pay for the eternal harmony, what have children to do with it, tell me, please? It's beyond all comprehension why they should suffer, and why they should pay for the harmony. Why should they, too, furnish material to enrich the soil for the harmony of the future? I understand solidarity in sin among men. I understand solidarity in retribution, too; but there can be no such solidarity with children. And if it is really true that they must share responsibility for all their fathers' crimes, such a truth is not of this world and is beyond my comprehension. Some jester will say, perhaps, that the child would have grown up and have sinned, but you see he didn't grow up, he was torn to pieces by the dogs, at eight years old. Oh, Alyosha, I am not blaspheming! I understand, of course, what an upheaval of the universe it will be, when everything in heaven and earth blends in one hymn of praise and everything that lives and has lived cries aloud: "Thou art just, O Lord, for Thy ways are revealed." When the mother embraces the fiend who threw her child to the dogs, and all three cry aloud with tears, "Thou art just, O Lord!" then, of course, the crown of knowledge will be reached and all will be made clear. But what pulls me up here is that I can't accept that harmony. And while I am on earth, I make haste to take my own measures. You see, Alyosha, perhaps it really may happen that if I live to that moment, or rise again to see it, I, too, perhaps, may cry aloud with the rest, looking at the mother embracing the child's torturer, "Thou art just, O Lord!" But I don't want to cry aloud then. While there is still time, I hasten to protect myself, and so I renounce the higher harmony altogether. It's not worth the tears of that one tortured child who beat itself on the breast with its little fist and prayed in its stinking outhouse, with its unexpiated tears to "dear, kind God"! It's not worth it, because those tears are unatoned for. They must be atoned for, or there can be no harmony. But how? How are you going to atone for them? Is it possible? By their being avenged? But what do I care for avenging them? What do I care for a hell for oppressors? What good can hell do, since those children have already been tortured? And what becomes of harmony, if there is hell? I want to forgive. I want to embrace. I don't want more suffering. And if the sufferings of children go to swell the sum of sufferings which was necessary to pay for truth, then I protest that the truth is not worth such a price. I don't want the mother to embrace the oppressor who threw her son to the dogs! She dare not forgive him! Let her forgive him for herself, if she will, let her forgive the torturer for the immeasurable suffering of her mother's heart. But the sufferings of her tortured child she has no right to forgive; she dare not forgive the torturer, even if the child were to forgive him! And if that is so, if they dare not forgive, what becomes of harmony? Is there in the whole world a being who would have the right to forgive and could forgive? I don't want harmony. From love for humanity I don't want it. I would rather be left with the unavenged suffering. I would rather remain with my unavenged suffering and unsatisfied indignation, *even if I were wrong*. Besides, too high a price is asked for harmony; it's beyond our means to pay so much to enter on it. And so I hasten to give back my entrance ticket, and if I am an honest man I am bound to give it back as soon as possible. And that I am doing. It's not God that I don't accept, Alyosha, only I most respectfully return Him the ticket.'

Doubt, however, is not limited to those who have faith, and the more vicious attacks on the Judeo-Christian tradition challenge not only the theology of religion but its underlying motivation. It could be that religious faith is a perfectly understandable expression of hope for a better world or an appeal for some justice that transcends what we witness here in secular life. But it has been charged that religion is something more problematic than this, an escape from worldly responsibilities, an irresponsible reaction to a world we cannot cope with, or perhaps a childish unwillingness to give up an **illusion** of security we ought to have outgrown in adolescence. Below, we will examine how these critical views of religion have been forcefully argued by three influential thinkers from the eighteenth and early nineteenth centuries—Karl Marx, Friedrich Nietzsche, and Sigmund Freud.

Karl Marx is often quoted for his incisive critique of religion. His point is simple, and he makes it powerfully: Humans invent religion to escape their intolerable social conditions. And once we see this, we should reject religion as an escape and turn instead to the correction of those conditions that make such an escape necessary.

ILLUSION

A false belief motivated by intense wishes.

From *Critique of Hegel's Philosophy of Right*
By Karl Marx

Religion is the sigh of the oppressed creature, the sentiment of a heartless world, and the soul of soulless conditions.

The basis of irreligious criticism is this: *man makes religion*; religion does not make man. Religion is indeed man's self-consciousness and self-awareness so long as he has not found himself or has lost himself again. But *man* is not an abstract being, squatting outside the world. Man is *the human world*, a state, society. This state, this society, produces religion which is an *inverted world consciousness*, because they are an *inverted world*. Religion is the general theory of this world, its encyclopedic compendium, its logic in popular form, its spiritual *point d'honneur*, its enthusiasm, its moral sanction, its solemn complement, its general basis of consolation and justification. It is *the fantastic realization* of the human being inasmuch as the *human being* possesses no true reality. The struggle against religion is, therefore, indirectly a struggle against *that world* whose spiritual *aroma* is religion.

Religious suffering is at the same time an *expression* of real suffering and a *protest* against real suffering. Religion is the sigh of the oppressed creature, the sentiment of a heartless world, and the soul of soulless conditions. It is the *opium* of the people.

The abolition of religion as the *illusory* happiness of men, is a demand for their *real* happiness. The call to abandon their illusions about their condition is a *call to abandon a condition which requires illusions*. The criticism of religion is, therefore, *the embryonic criticism of this vale of tears* of which religion is the *halo*.

Criticism has plucked the imaginary flowers from the chain, not in order that man shall bear the chain without caprice or consolation but so that he shall cast off the chain and pluck the living flower. The criticism of religion disillusions man so that he will think, act, and fashion his reality as a man who has lost his illusions and regained his reason; so that he will revolve about himself as his own true sun. Religion is only the illusory sun about which man revolves so long as he does not revolve about himself.

* * *

It is clear that the arm of criticism cannot replace the criticism of arms. Material force can only be overthrown by material force; but theory itself becomes a material force when it has seized the masses. Theory is capable of seizing the masses when it demonstrates *ad hominem*, and it demonstrates *ad hominem* as soon as it becomes radical. To be radical is to grasp things by the root. But for man the root is man himself. What proves beyond doubt the radicalism of German theory, and thus its practical energy, is that it begins from the resolute *positive* abolition of religion. The criticism of religion ends with the doctrine that *man*

(Continued)

is the supreme being for man. It ends, therefore, with the *categorical imperative to overthrow all those conditions* in which man is an abased, enslaved, abandoned, contemptible being—conditions which can hardly be better described than in the exclamation of the Frenchman on the occasion of a proposed tax upon dogs: 'Wretched dogs! They want to treat you like men!'

Fifty years later, Friedrich Nietzsche opened an even more blistering attack on religion in general, on Christianity in particular. He accused Christianity of being nothing other than rationalizations for impotence, an expression of everything that is most contemptible in human nature.

From *Beyond Good and Evil*
By Friedrich Nietzsche

The Jewish 'Old Testament', the book of divine justice, has people, things, and speeches in such grand style that Greek and Indian literature have nothing to set beside it. One stands in awe and trembling before this monstrous vestige of what humanity once was, and has sorrowful thoughts about old Asia and its protruding little peninsula Europe, which would like to stand out over and against Asia as the 'progress of humanity'. To be sure: there will be nothing in these ruins to astonish or distress anyone who is just a wretched tame house pet himself and understands only house pet needs (like our cultured people of today, including the Christians of 'cultured' Christianity)—the taste for the Old Testament is a touchstone for the 'great' and the 'small'—perhaps he will find the New Testament, the book of mercy, more to his taste (it is full of the true delicate musty odour of devotee and petty soul). To have glued this New Testament, a kind of rococo of taste in every respect, on to the Old Testament to make a single book, a 'Bible', a 'book in itself': this is perhaps the greatest piece of temerity and 'sin against the spirit' that literary Europe has on its conscience.

From *The Antichrist*
By Friedrich Nietzsche

Who alone has good cause to lie his way out of reality? One who suffers from it!

Christianity should not be prettified and ornamented: it has waged deadly war against the higher type of human being; it has raised an edict against all the basic instincts . . . and out of these instincts it has distilled evil and the Evil One: the strong as the characteristically reprehensible, the 'reprobate'. Christianity takes sides with everything weak and base, with every failure; it has made an ideal of what *contradicts* the instinct of strong life to maintain itself; it has corrupted the reason of even the strongest in spirit . . . in its fear of them it has bred the opposite sort:—the house pet, the herd animal, the sick human animal:—the Christian. As long as the priest is considered a *higher* type of human—this *career* refuter, slanderer, and poisoner of life—there is no answer to the question: what is truth? For truth has been stood on her head when the conscious proponent of nothingness and negation is welcomed as the representative of 'truth'. In Christianity, morality and religion do not have even a single point of contact with reality.

* * *

This world of *pure fiction* is greatly inferior to the world of dreams, so far as the latter *mirrors* reality, and the former falsifies, devalues, and negates reality. . . . Who alone has good cause to lie his way out of reality? One who suffers from it!

* * *

The Christian concept of God—God as god of the sick, God as a spider, God as spirit—is among the most corrupt concepts of the divine the world has ever accepted. It may well represent the low-water mark in the descending development of divine kinds.

* * *

This pitiful god of Christian monotono-theism! This hybrid creation of decay, this mix of zero, concept and contradiction, in which every instinct of decadence, every timorousness and exhaustion of the soul, finds its justification!

From *The Gay Science*
By Friedrich Nietzsche

The meaning of our cheerfulness.—The greatest recent event—that 'God is dead', that belief in the Christian god has become unbelievable—is even now beginning to cast its first shadows over Europe. At least for the few, whose eyes—in whose eyes the *suspicion* is strong and fine enough for this spectacle, some sun seems to have set and some ancient deep trust has been transformed into doubt; to them our old world with every day looks more like evening: more mistrustful, stranger, 'older'. But in general one may say: the event itself is much too great, too distant, too removed from the capacity of the many for understanding, for even its harbingers to be supposed as having *arrived* yet. One should suppose all the less that many people yet know *what* this event truly means—and how much must collapse now that this belief has been undermined, because it is built on the foundation of this belief, is supported by it, has developed on it: for example, our entire European morality. This long abundance and succession of collapse, destruction, ruin, and disaster that is now

upon us—who today could guess enough of it to feel the need to play the teacher and first prophet of this monstrous logic of horror, the proclaimer of a darkness and an eclipse of the sun the like of which has probably yet to occur on earth?

* * *

The first consequences, the consequences for *us*, are just the opposite of what one might expect: they are not at all sad and dark but rather like a new barely describable sort of light, happiness, relief, exhilaration, encouragement, daybreak. Indeed, we philosophers and 'free spirits' feel, when we hear the news that 'the old god is dead', as if a new dawn shines on us; our hearts overflow with gratitude, astonishment, presentiments, expectations. At long last the horizon looks free to us once more, even if it is not bright; at long last our ships may venture out once more, venture out to brave any risk; all the daring of the lover of knowledge is allowed once more; the sea, *our* sea, lies open once more; perhaps never yet has there been such an 'open sea'.

Finally, in the early twentieth century, the attack was given a psychoanalytic foundation by Sigmund Freud, who also reduces the grand aspirations of religion to mere illusions, but, even worse, the illusions of an insecure child who has never properly grown up.

From *The Future of an Illusion*
By Sigmund Freud

Illusions need not necessarily be false—that is to say, unrealizable or in contradiction of reality.

. . . the psychical origin of religious ideas. These, which are given out as teachings, are not precipitates of experience or end results of thinking: they

are illusions, fulfillments of the oldest, strongest, and most urgent wishes of mankind. The secret of their strength lies in the strength of those wishes.

(Continued)

As we already know, the terrifying impression of helplessness in childhood aroused the need for protection—for protection through love—which was provided by the father; and the recognition that this helplessness lasts throughout life made it necessary to cling to the existence of a father, but this time a more powerful one. Thus the benevolent rule of a divine Providence allays our fear of the dangers of life; the establishment of a moral world-order ensures the fulfillment of the demands of justice, which have so often remained unfulfilled in human civilization; and the prolongation of earthly existence in a future life provides the local and temporal framework in which these wish-fulfillments shall take place. Answers to the riddles that tempt the curiosity of man, such as how the universe began or what the relation is between body and mind, are developed in conformity with the underlying assumptions of this system. It is an enormous relief to the individual psyche if the conflicts of its childhood arising from the father-complex—conflicts which it has never wholly overcome—are removed from it and brought to a solution which is universally accepted.

When I say that these things are all illusions, I must define the meaning of the word. An illusion is not the same thing as an error; nor is it necessarily an error. Aristotle's belief that vermin are developed out of dung (a belief to which ignorant people still cling) was an error; so was the belief of a former generation of doctors that *tabes dorsalis* is the result of sexual excess. It would be incorrect to call these errors illusions. On the other hand, it was an illusion of Columbus' that he had discovered a new sea route to the Indies. The part played by his wish in this error is very clear. One may describe as an illusion the assertion made by certain nationalists that the Indo-Germanic race is the only one capable of civilization; or the belief, which was only destroyed by psychoanalysis, that children are creatures without sexuality. What is characteristic of illusions is that they are derived from human wishes. In this respect they come near to psychiatric delusions. But they differ from them, too, apart from the more complicated structure of delusions. In the case of delusions, we emphasize as essential their being in contradiction with reality. Illusions need not necessarily be false—that is to say, unrealizable or in contradiction of reality. . . . Thus we call a belief an illusion when a wish-fulfillment is a prominent factor in its motivation, and in doing so we disregard its relations to reality, just as the illusion itself sets no store by verification.

In conclusion, Freud agrees with Marx and Nietzsche that the only proper concern of man is humanity. But is this conclusion necessarily an indictment of religion? Freud was fascinated by Jewish mysticism, and Nietzsche offered extravagant praise of Buddhism. Many Christians, Muslims, and Jews have used their religion as a metaphysical support for concerted social activism and humanism, and for many people religion is an emotional support without which they could not even function as human beings. The balance is precarious. No one can deny that there have been thousands of atrocities—to both spirit and body—in the name of religion. But neither has it been proved that such cruelty is necessary for religion nor that religion is as easily dispensable as some of its critics have suggested.

- What does Dostoyevsky's Ivan mean when he says that he wants to 'respectfully return' to God his 'entrance ticket'? Do you agree with him that 'too high a price is asked for harmony'?
- How would you explain Marx's favourite remark that religion is 'the opium of the people'?
- What are the human characteristics that religion emphasizes that Nietzsche finds so contemptible?
- What does Freud mean when he says that the religious person is like a child?

SUMMARY AND CONCLUSION

Religion is one of the most important, controversial, and sensitive parts of our lives. It is not surprising, then, that it is also one of the most important, controversial, and sensitive areas of philosophy. Initially, religion seems to be part of metaphysics, an examination of the way the world really is, and the answer of religion is that reality is, in a word, divine. But we have seen that religion is much more than a search for knowledge; it is also a search for meaning, for morality, for ultimate justice, and for a type of experience that is like no other. Philosophy of religion begins as a metaphysical discipline, attempting to define a supreme entity of a certain type (God) and to demonstrate His existence through rational arguments and proofs. But many philosophers and religious people deny that such a metaphysical approach is either possible or appropriate. Some philosophers deny that we can *know* God but insist that it is necessary to have faith. But while some philosophers interpret this faith as a form of rationality, others claim that it is strictly an emotional commitment beyond the domain of rational argument and understanding.

These various approaches to the philosophy of religion are all very much alive, and so too are the doubts that accompany each approach. Those who believe that we can know God are at odds with those who deny that we can know Him. Those who insist on faith disagree among themselves whether this faith can be, or ought to be, justified. There are those who want to believe in God but find that certain problems (for example, the problem of evil or the problem of divine hiddenness) make it difficult or impossible for them to do so. There are those who see belief in God as an outmoded belief, left over from the inadequate science and metaphysics of previous centuries. And there are those who attack religion as not only outmoded but as insidious, as a symptom of decadence, weakness, or immaturity. But in the face of these various doubts and attacks, traditional religious beliefs continue to grow and to raise new questions. Religion is humanity's oldest philosophy, and it is still the most controversial area of philosophical concern.

REVIEW QUESTIONS

1. Is there a difference between a philosopher's belief that God exists and a religious person's belief in God? If so, what do you think the difference is? What light, if any, does this difference shed on the concept of faith?

2. Suppose your friend argues as follows: '(1) If you already believe in God, you don't need a proof of His existence. And (2) if you don't believe in God, no proof will persuade you to believe in Him. Therefore, (3) there is no point in offering proofs of God's existence, for such proofs are either unnecessary or insufficient.' Do you agree with your friend's argument? What seems right to you about it? What seems wrong with it?

3. What practical difference does the existence of God make? In what way(s) would a world in which God exists be different from a world in which there is no God? What does a person who believes in God believe in?

4. How would you summarize Anselm's version of the ontological argument for the existence of God, Descartes' revision of the argument, and Kant's attack on the argument? Do you agree with Kant that existence is not a predicate? Can you think of any other apparent predicates that are not actual predicates? If existence is a special case, why?

5. Hume argues that if God built the universe, he wasn't a very good architect. Some theists respond that the universe was built as well as it could be and that any changes would only make it worse. Do you find this response convincing? Can you imagine a better world? What would you change?

6. Of the three metaphysical arguments for theism we have examined, which strikes you as the best? Which one do you think is the worst? Why?

7. What is mystical experience? How does it resemble perceptual experience? How is it different? Can you think of any reasons to doubt mystical experiences that are not also reasons to doubt our ordinary perceptual experiences?

8. How would you characterize the pragmatic argument for God's existence? What are its weaknesses, if any? Do you think that it undermines belief in God?

9. What is the problem of evil and what are some theistic responses to it? What do you think of them?

10. What is the problem of divine hiddenness, according to Schellenberg? Why isn't Pascal threatened by the idea that God, if He exists, is a hidden God—a '*Deus absconditus*'?

11. What does Kierkegaard think about the very idea of proving the existence of God? What do you think about what Kierkegaard thinks?

12. How did the attack on Christianity developed from Marx and Nietzsche into Freud? What does Freud mean by the word 'illusion'? Are illusions always bad? Could Christianity and other forms of religion be good, helpful illusions? How would Nietzsche respond?

KEY TERMS

Abrahamic religions	*Deus absconditus*	omniscient
agnostic	*dharma*	ontological argument
anthropomorphic	faith	pantheism
argument from design	illusion	Principle of Sufficient Reason
atheist	independent being	problem of divine hiddenness
Bhagavadgītā ('Gītā')	ineffable	problem of evil
Brahma ('Brahman')	karma	subjective truth
Buddha	mysticism	Sufism
cosmological argument	nihility	teleological argument
deism	omnipotent	theist
dependent being	omnipresent	transcendence

FURTHER READING

On the Philosophy of Religion in General

Louise Antony, ed., *Philosophers without Gods: Meditations on Atheism and the Secular Life* (New York: Oxford University Press, 2007).

Richard M. Gale, *On the Philosophy of Religion* (Belmont, CA: Thomson Wadsworth, 2007).

Thomas V. Morris, ed., *God and the Philosophers: The Reconciliation of Faith and Reason* (New York: Oxford University Press, 1994).

Graham Oppy and Michael Scott, eds, *Reading Philosophy of Religion: Selected Texts with Interactive Commentary* (Oxford: Blackwell, 2010).

Stephen Phillips, *Philosophy of Religion: A Global Approach* (Belmont, CA: Wadsworth, 1995).

Louis Pojman, *Philosophy of Religion: An Anthology*, 3rd edn (Belmont, CA: Wadsworth Press, 1998).

Philip Quinn and Charles Taliaferro, eds, *Blackwell Companion to the Philosophy of Religion* (Cambridge, MA: Blackwell, 1999).

William Rowe, *Philosophy of Religion: An Introduction*, 4th edn (Belmont, CA: Wadsworth/Thomson, 2007).

Charles Taliaferro, *Evidence and Faith: Philosophy and Religion since the Seventeenth Century* (Cambridge: Cambridge University Press, 2005).

William J. Wainwright, *Philosophy of Religion*, 2nd edn (Belmont, CA: Wadsworth Press, 1999).

Linda Zagzebski, *Philosophy of Religion: An Historical Introduction* (Oxford: Blackwell, 2007).

On the Existence of God

William Lane Craig and Walter Sinnott-Armstrong, *God? A Debate between a Christian and an Atheist* (Oxford: Oxford University Press, 2003).

Hans Küng, *Does God Exist? An Answer for Today* (New York: Crossroads, 1980).

J.L. Mackie, *The Miracle of Theism: Arguments for and against the Existence of God* (New York: Oxford, 1982).

T.J. Mawson, *Belief in God: An Introduction to the Philosophy of Religion* (Oxford: Oxford University Press, 2005).

Graham Oppy, *Arguing about Gods* (New York: Cambridge University Press, 2006).

Alvin Plantinga and Michael Tooley, *Knowledge of God* (Oxford: Blackwell, 2008).

J.J.C. Smart and John Haldane, *Atheism and Theism* (Oxford: Blackwell, 2003).

Jordan Howard Sobel, *Logic and Theism: Arguments for and against Belief in God* (Cambridge: Cambridge University Press, 2004).

Richard Swinburne, *Is There a God?* (Oxford: Oxford University Press, 1996).

Richard Swinburne, *The Existence of God* (Oxford: Clarendon Press, 2004).

On the Problem of Evil

Austin Farrer, *Love Almighty and Ills Unlimited* (London: Collins, 1966).

John Hick, *Evil and the Love of God* (London: MacMillan, 1966).

Alvin Plantinga, *God, Freedom and Evil* (Grand Rapids, MI: William B. Eerdmans, 1974).

J.L. Schellenberg, *Divine Hiddenness and Human Reason* (Ithaca, NY: Cornell University Press, 1993).

On St Thomas Aquinas

Brian Davies, *The Thought of Thomas Aquinas* (Oxford: Clarendon Press, 1992).

Timothy McDermott, ed. and trans., *Aquinas: Selected Philosophical Writings* (Oxford: Oxford University Press, 1993).

On Samuel Clarke

Ezio Vailati, ed., *A Demonstration of the Being and Attributes of God and Other Writings* (Cambridge: Cambridge University Press, 1998).

On David Hume

J.C.A. Gaskin, *Hume's Philosophy of Religion* (London: Macmillan, 1978).

On Mysticism and Religious Experience

William P. Alston, *Perceiving God: The Epistemology of Religious Experience* (Ithaca, NY: Cornell University Press, 1991).

William James, *The Varieties of Religious Experience: A Study in Human Nature* (New York: Modern Library, 2002).

W.T. Stace, *Mysticism and Philosophy* (Philadelphia: Lippincott, 1960).

Evelyn Underhill, *Mysticism, A Study in the Nature and Development of Man's Spiritual Consciousness* (London: Methuen, 1945).

Phillip Wiebe, *God and Other Spirits: Intimations of Transcendence in Christian Faith* (New York: Oxford University Press, 2004).

On the Sufi Mystical Tradition in Islam

James Fadiman and Robert Frager, eds, *The Essential Sufism* (San Francisco: Harper Collins, 1998).

On Plotinus

Stephen MacKenna, trans., *The Enneads* (New York: Penguin, 1991).

On Søren Kierkegaard

J. Collins, *The Mind of Kierkegaard* (Chicago: Regnery, 1953).

C. Stephen Evans, *Kierkegaard: An Introduction* (Cambridge: Cambridge University Press, 2009).

On Medieval Religions

A. Hyman and J. Walsh, *Philosophy in the Middle Ages* (Indianapolis, IN: Hackett, 1973).

On Nishitani

D.T. Suzuki, *Zen Buddhism* (New York: Doubleday, 1956).

CHAPTER 3

KNOWLEDGE

Once upon a time, I, Zhuang-zi, dreamt I was a butterfly, fluttering hither and thither, to all intents and purposes a butterfly. I was conscious only of following my fancies as a butterfly, and was unconscious of my individuality as a man. Suddenly, I waked, and there I lay, myself again. Now I do not know whether I was then a man dreaming I was a butterfly, or whether I am now a butterfly dreaming I am a man.

Zhuang-zi[1]

After an evening of heated but fruitless metaphysical debate with a number of his friends, the British physician John Locke turned to them and asked, 'Shouldn't we first determine whether we are capable of answering such questions?' They agreed. Perhaps, having encountered such debates in the previous chapters, you are thinking much the same thing. These great metaphysical systems are surely monuments to human intelligence, but do they achieve what they are intended to? Do they tell us 'the way the world really is'? Since each of the contending systems claims that it does, how can it be that they disagree? Which is right? And how can we decide?

In 1690 Locke took philosophy around a sharp turn, one that had been suggested by Descartes a half century before. But Descartes had broached the question 'What can we know?' only as a preface to his metaphysics. Locke, on the other hand, decided to put questions about reality on the shelf until he could develop an adequate theory of human knowledge. Accordingly, his greatest work, *An Essay Concerning Human Understanding*, is not primarily an inquiry into substance or reality or God or truth (although all of these enter in), but rather an exploration of *human understanding*. From metaphysics, the study of ultimate reality, we now turn to that area of philosophy known as **epistemology**, a term coined in the nineteenth century by James Frederick Ferrier, the Scottish philosopher whose acquaintance we made in the Introduction. Epistemology is the theory of knowledge: how we get it, what it is, what its limits are, whether we have it, or why we don't.

Even before Plato, Parmenides had seen that between a false belief and knowledge of reality are many opinions and **appearances** of reality, which might be very different from reality itself. Plato's Myth of the Cave is a graphic illustration of this distinction. Descartes, although he distrusted his senses and wasn't certain that they gave accurate representations of reality, at least could be certain of the appearances themselves—he could not be mistaken about them. And here is the problem that has defined epistemology, the seeming abyss between reality and mere appearance: Perhaps we know the appearances of things, but how can we know that we know the reality 'behind' them?

EPISTEMOLOGY

The study of human knowledge, its nature, its sources, and its justification.

Let us return for a moment to the central idea of traditional metaphysics, that of **substance**. Substance is that which underlies all of the various properties of a thing (or things); and it is the properties, never the substance itself, that are experienced by us. Now, presumably, there can be no properties unless they are properties of something. That seems to be a platitude. But yet, we cannot experience the nature of the substance itself. And here begins the embarrassment of metaphysics.

The problem was stated succinctly by the best-known British philosopher of the twentieth century, Bertrand Russell, in a little volume called *The Problems of Philosophy*, in which he says the following:

From *The Problems of Philosophy*
By Bertrand Russell

The real table, if there is one, is not immediately known to us at all, but must be an inference from what is immediately known.

In daily life, we assume as certain many things which, on a closer scrutiny, are found to be so full of apparent contradictions that only a great amount of thought enables us to know what it is that we really may believe. In the search for certainty, it is natural to begin with our present experiences, and in some sense, no doubt, knowledge is to be derived from them. But any statement as to what it is that our immediate experiences make us know is very likely to be wrong. It seems to me that I am now sitting in a chair, at a table of a certain shape, on which I see sheets of paper with writing or print. By turning my head I see out of the window buildings and clouds and the sun. I believe that the sun is about ninety-three million miles from the earth; that it is a hot globe many times bigger than the earth; that, owing to the earth's rotation, it rises every morning, and will continue to do so for an indefinite time in the future. I believe that, if any other normal person comes into my room, he will see the same chairs and tables and books and papers as I see, and that the table which I see is the same as the table which I feel pressing against my arm. All this seems to be so evident as to be hardly worth stating, except in answer to a man who doubts whether I know anything. Yet all this may be reasonably doubted, and all of it requires much careful discussion before we can be sure that we have stated it in a form that is wholly true.

To make our difficulties plain, let us concentrate attention on the table. To the eye it is oblong, brown, and shiny, to the touch it is smooth and cool and hard; when I tap it, it gives out a wooden sound. Anyone else who sees and feels and hears the table will agree with this description, so that it might seem as if no difficulty would arise; but as soon as we try to be more precise our troubles begin. Although I believe that the table is 'really' of the same colour all over, the parts that reflect the light look much brighter than the other parts, and some parts look white because of reflected light. I know that, if I move, the parts that reflect the light will be different, so that the apparent distribution of colours on the table will change. It follows that if several people are looking at the table at the same moment, no two of them will see exactly the same distribution of colours, because no two can see it from exactly the same point of view, and any change in the point of view makes some change in the way the light is reflected.

For most practical purposes the differences are unimportant, but to the painter they are all-important: the painter has to unlearn the habit of thinking that things seem to have the colour which common sense says they 'really' have, and to learn the habit of seeing things as they appear. Here we have already the beginning of one of the distinctions that cause most trouble in philosophy—the distinction between 'appearance' and 'reality', between what things seem to be and what they are. The painter wants to know what things seem to be, the practical man and the philosopher want to know what they are; but the philosopher's wish to know this is stronger than the practical man's, and is more troubled by knowledge as to the difficulties of answering the question.

To return to the table. It is evident from what we have found, that there is no colour which pre-eminently appears to be *the* colour of the table, or even

(Continued)

of any one particular part of the table—it appears to be of different colours from different points of view, and there is no reason for regarding some of these as more really its colour than others. And we know that even from a given point of view the colour will seem different by artificial light, or to a colour-blind man, or to a man wearing blue spectacles, while in the dark there will be no colour at all, though to touch and hearing the table will be unchanged. This colour is not something which is inherent in the table, but something depending upon the table and the spectator and the way the light falls on the table. When, in ordinary life, we speak of *the* colour of the table, we only mean the sort of colour which it will seem to have to a normal spectator from an ordinary point of view under usual conditions of light. But the other colours which appear under other conditions have just as good a right to be considered real; and therefore, to avoid favouritism, we are compelled to deny that, in itself, the table has any one particular colour.

The same thing applies to the texture. With the naked eye one can see the grain, but otherwise the table looks smooth and even. If we looked at it through a microscope, we should see roughnesses and hills and valleys, and all sorts of differences that are imperceptible to the naked eye. Which of these is the 'real' table? We are naturally tempted to say that what we see through the microscope is more real, but that in turn would be changed by a still more powerful microscope. If, then, we cannot trust what we see with the naked eye, why should we trust what we see through a microscope? Thus, again, the confidence in our sense with which we began deserts us.

The *shape* of the table is not better. We are all in the habit of judging as to the 'real' shapes of things, and we do this so unreflectingly that we come to think we actually see the real shapes. But, in fact, as we all have to learn if we try to draw, a given thing looks different in shape from every different point of view. If our table is 'really' rectangular, it will look, from almost all points of view, as if it had two acute angles and two obtuse angles. If opposite sides are parallel, they will look as if they converged to a point away from the spectator; if they are of equal length, they will look as if the nearer side were longer. All these things are not commonly noticed in looking at a table, because experience has taught us to construct the 'real' shape from the apparent shape, and the 'real' shape is what interests us as practical men. But the 'real' shape is not what we see; it is something inferred from what we see. And what we see is constantly changing in shape as we move about the room; so that here again the senses seem not to give us the truth about the table itself, but only about the appearance of the table.

Similar difficulties arise when we consider the sense of touch. It is true that the table always gives us a sensation of hardness, and we feel that it resists pressure. But the sensation we obtain depends upon how hard we press the table and also upon what part of the body we press with; thus the various sensations due to various pressures or various parts of the body cannot be supposed to reveal *directly* any definite property of the table, but at most to be *signs* of some property, which *causes* all the sensations, but is not actually apparent in any of them. And the same applies still more obviously to the sounds which can be elicited by rapping the table.

Thus it becomes evident that the real table, if there is one, is not the same as what we immediately experience by sight or touch or hearing. The real table, if there is one, is not *immediately* known to us at all, but must be an inference from what is immediately known. Hence, two very difficult questions at once arise; namely, (1) Is there a real table at all? (2) If so, what sort of object can it be?

In these few pages, Russell succeeds in summarizing the problems that have dominated British philosophy since Locke's original epistemological studies. But why say 'British philosophy'? Why should this problem have been more serious there than on the continent of Europe, where most of the great metaphysicians were working? Why should it have had more impact on Locke and his followers than on Descartes, Spinoza, Leibniz, and their latter-day followers? Because of a single profound difference, which has always created a general gap in understanding between British (and North American) philosophy and European philosophy. Descartes, Spinoza, and Leibniz retained their faith in human

reason's ability to give us knowledge of reality, despite the fact that reality was beyond our every possible experience. Because of their confidence in the powers of reason, they are usually called **rationalists**. Because it happens that all three were Europeans (Descartes was French; Spinoza, Dutch; and Leibniz, German), they are often called *continental rationalists*. The movement developed by John Locke, on the other hand, is generally called **empiricism**, because of its insistence upon the data of experience (or *empirical* data) as the source of all knowledge. (A **datum** [plural, *data*] is a bit of 'given' information; modern empiricist philosophers sometimes talk of **sense-data**, that is, the information immediately given by the senses.) Also included in this group of empiricists are Bishop George Berkeley[2] and David Hume, whom we shall also meet in this chapter. Because they were all from Great Britain (Berkeley was Irish; Hume, Scottish), they are often called *British empiricists*. (Russell is generally considered a more contemporary member of this same movement.)

> **EMPIRICISM**
>
> The philosophy that demands that all knowledge, except for certain logical and mathematical truths, comes from experience.

- What problem does Russell suggest lies at the heart of epistemology? What problem does the distinction between appearance and reality pose?
- Is there a 'problem of knowledge'? What is it?

Although epistemology received a renewed attention and a new kind of treatment in the era after Descartes, the rift between the claims of rationalists and those of empiricists was not new. The basics of the debate were laid out by Plato, in his dialogue *Theaetetus*:

From *Theaetetus*
By Plato

SOCRATES: But the question you were asked, Theaetetus, was not, what are the objects of knowledge, nor yet how many sorts of knowledge there are. We did not want to count them, but to find out what the thing itself—knowledge—is. . . . Perception, you say, is knowledge?

THEAETETUS: Yes.

SOCRATES: The account you give of the nature of knowledge is not, by any means, to be despised. It is the same that was given by Protagoras, though he stated it in a somewhat different way. He says, you will remember, that 'man is the measure of all things—alike of the being of things that are and of the not-being of things that are not'. No doubt you have read that.

THEAETETUS: Yes, often.

SOCRATES: He puts it in this sort of way, doesn't he, that any given thing 'is to me such as it appears to me and is to you such as it appears to you', you and I being men?

THEAETETUS: Yes, that is how he puts it.

SOCRATES: Well, what a wise man says is not likely to be nonsense. So let us follow his meaning. Sometimes, when the same wind is blowing, one of us feels chilly, the other does not, or one may feel slightly chilly, the other quite cold.

THEAETETUS: Certainly.

SOCRATES: Well, in that case are we to say that the wind in itself is cold or not cold? Or shall we agree with Protagoras that it is cold to the one who feels chilly and not to the other? . . . [I]ndeed the doctrine is a remarkable one. It declares that nothing is *one* thing just by it-self, nor can you rightly call it by one definite name, nor even say it is of any definite sort.

In this way, Socrates claims that the empiricist cannot have any knowledge at all. He defends the rationalist's claim earlier in the dialogue:

SOCRATES: You do not suppose a man can understand the name of a thing when he does not know what the thing is?

THEAETETUS: Certainly not.

SOCRATES: Then, if he has no idea of knowledge, 'knowledge about shoes' conveys nothing to him?

THEAETETUS: No.

SOCRATES: 'Cobblery' in fact, or the name of any other art, has no meaning for anyone who has no conception of knowledge.

Russell, like Theaetetus, associates knowledge with **perceptions**, or 'sense-data'. Thus, he assumed that any notion of 'substance' we might have must be *derived* from our perceptions. Socrates claimed that our varied perceptions can never give us a notion of substance. All we would be able to get out of a bunch of differing perceptions is a bunch of differing perceptions. However, since we *have* a notion of substance (in Russell's example, of a table), we must have gotten it from something other than our perceptions. Knowledge, concludes Socrates, must be something other than an accumulation of perceptions. The continental rationalists, in a sense, agreed with Socrates on this point and claimed that the non-perceptual source of knowledge must be 'reason' itself. The British empiricists went the other way, claiming that there simply wasn't any other source of ideas aside from perceptions. (*Perception* actually can mean 'a sense-datum', 'the mind's ability to interpret sense-data', and 'the ability to understand'. In philosophy, we generally restrict the meaning to the first two senses.)

So, how are we to know reality? By retaining confidence in our own powers of abstract reason? Or by appeal to experience, which carries with it the threat that we may never know reality beyond our experience at all? In the pages that follow, you will be introduced to one of the most vigorous and long-lasting dialogues in philosophy, not only between the rationalists and the empiricists but (as we saw in the juxtaposition of Spinoza and Leibniz in Chapter 1) between various rationalists and empiricists as well.

Is the choice between reason and experience a 'false dilemma' (a kind of pseudo-question)? Among the issues in dispute are not only the emphasis on and faith in reason versus experience but also the nature of reason and the nature of experience. What is an idea that can be known to be true by reasons alone—a '**truth of reason**'? How can we infer from the nature of our private experience what the world 'outside' is like? How do we even know that there *is* an 'external' world? How is it possible to have 'abstract' ideas, that is, ideas that are not simply based on the concrete particulars of experience, such as *this* dog, *this* table, *that* star over there to the left of the Big Dipper? How do we get the idea, for example, of 'dog' in general, not this dog or that dog or big dog or little dog or Chihuahua or German Shepherd but just 'dog', which includes all of them?

The question of *substance* comes up again and again: What is a substance? How do we know of substances? So does the notion of **cause**: Is an idea *caused* by an object of which it is the idea, or do we make the idea up, and so 'cause' it ourselves? We also encounter a more specific set of questions: What aspects of a thing are *in it*? What aspects of a thing are rather *in us*, that is, in the way we perceive it, in the mental apparatus that we use in our knowledge? But beneath the welter of questions and debates, there is a singular shared concern. All of the rationalists and empiricists are men of science who appreciate the advances of modern physics and its kindred disciplines, who think of knowledge as one of the highest human attributes, and who want to understand knowledge and its foundations as a way of justifying their faith in science. At the bottom of all of these disputes is that basic admiration and concern for knowledge as such, and the central question 'How is this knowledge possible?' is itself an extension of that same admiration and concern.

A. The Rationalist's Confidence: René Descartes

Let's return to the philosopher who began the modern emphasis on methodology, René Descartes. We have already mentioned his 'method of doubt', the goal of which is not to defend doubts but, quite to the contrary, to move from doubt to knowledge and certainty. Descartes' doubt is intended only to separate what is doubtful from what is not. He never doubted, nor did his followers, that he would be able to find beliefs about reality. As he describes them in his *Meditations on First Philosophy*, these beliefs would be 'clear and distinct' and 'perfectly certain'. (Spinoza refers to such ideas as 'adequate ideas'; Leibniz calls them 'truths of reason'.) Once Descartes had found even one such belief, he could use it as a premise from which he could deduce all of his other beliefs about reality. And none of this depends upon the data of experience; it is entirely a process of reason, of examining the clarity of his beliefs and the logical connections between them.

Once again, it is important to remind ourselves that these problems and their sometimes radical complications and solutions do not appear in a vacuum. Descartes lived in the time of Galileo, and Galileo's new science is always in the background of Descartes' method of doubt. In undermining the traditional science of Aristotle and the Middle Ages, Galileo raised the doubt that what we think that we see we might not really see at all. Colours, for example, seemed to be more in the minds of men and women than in the objects themselves. But if we could be mistaken about something so seemingly certain as the colour of objects, Descartes reasons, could we not be mistaken about much else besides? Indeed, could we not be mistaken in our perceptions *in general*? For this reason Descartes appeals to reason rather than to experience (although, as we shall see, he dangerously calls reason into question as well). We might also add that, although he was a devout Catholic, Descartes could not help but be affected by Martin Luther's challenge to Church authority the century before. Thus the insistence on resolving these doubts for oneself, instead of appealing to established authority, was very much a part of the radical temperament of the time.

In six famous 'meditations', Descartes begins with the resolve to doubt everything that he believes, that is, until he can find a first premise that is beyond doubt, from which he can then argue for the truth of other beliefs, which he can then use as premises to prove more beliefs, and so on. In the first meditation, he states his method of doubt and begins to eliminate all of those beliefs about which he could possibly be mistaken. He doubts his senses—could they not mislead him, as they do in an optical illusion or a hallucination? He examines his belief in God—could it be that his Jesuit teachers had been fooling him? He even doubts the existence of the world—is it not conceivable that he is merely dreaming? Here is how he begins the first of the meditations.

From 'Meditation I'
By René Descartes

I was convinced that I must . . . build anew from the foundation.

Of the Things Which May Be Brought within the Sphere of the Doubtful

It is now some years since I detected how many were the false beliefs that I had from my earliest youth admitted as true, and how doubtful was everything I had since constructed on this basis; and from that time I was convinced that I must once and for all seriously undertake to rid myself of all the opinions which I had formerly accepted, and commence to build anew from the foundation, if I wanted to establish any firm and permanent structure in the sciences.

In order to 'build anew' his system of beliefs and eliminate his false beliefs, Descartes resolves to doubt everything that he believes. But this does not mean that he has to list every belief he has; that might take forever. Instead, it is necessary only for him to examine those 'first principles' upon which all of his other beliefs are based.

Now for this object it is not necessary that I should show that all of these are false—I shall perhaps never arrive at this end. But inasmuch as reason already persuades me that I ought no less carefully to withhold my assent from matters which are not entirely certain and indubitable than from those which appear to me manifestly to be false, if I am able to find in each one some reason to doubt, this will suffice to justify my rejecting the whole. And for that end it will not be requisite that I should examine each in particular, which would be an endless undertaking; for owing to the fact that the destruction of the foundations of necessity brings with it the downfall of the rest of the edifice, I shall only in the first place attack those principles upon which all my former opinions rested.

The first set of principles to be doubted is that 'common-sense' set of beliefs that relies upon the senses: seeing, hearing, tasting, smelling, and touching. Descartes argues that, despite our common-sense reliance on these, it is nevertheless possible that we could be deceived by our senses.

All that up to the present time I have accepted as most true and certain I have learned either from the senses or through the senses; but it is sometimes proved to me that these senses are deceptive, and it is wiser not to trust entirely to any thing by which we have once been deceived.

But it may be that although the senses sometimes deceive us concerning things which are hardly perceptible, or very far away, there are yet many others to be met with as to which we cannot reasonably have any doubt, although we recognize them by their means. For example, there is the fact that I am here, seated by the fire, attired in a dressing gown, having this paper in my hands and other similar matters. And how could I deny that these hands and this body are mine, were it not perhaps that I compare myself to certain persons, devoid of sense, whose cerebella are so troubled and clouded by the violent vapours of black bile, that they constantly assure us that they think they are kings when they are really quite poor, or that they are clothed in purple when they are really without covering, or who imagine that they have an earthenware head or are nothing but pumpkins or are made of glass. But they are mad, and I should not be any the less insane were I to follow examples so extravagant.

Now Descartes makes one of his most famous philosophical moves: He wonders whether he could possibly be dreaming all of his experience; for in a dream, as we all know, everything can still seem perfectly real, as if we were actually awake:

At the same time I must remember that I am a man, and that consequently I am in the habit of sleeping, and in my dreams representing to myself the same things or sometimes even less probable things, than do those who are insane in their waking moments. How often has it happened to me that in the night I dreamt that I found myself in this particular place, that I was dressed and seated near the fire, whilst in reality I was lying undressed in bed! At this moment it does indeed seem to me that it is with eyes awake that I am looking at this paper; that this head which I move is not asleep, that it is deliberately and of set purpose that I extend my hand and perceive it; what happens in sleep does not appear so clear nor so distinct as does all this. But in thinking over this I remind myself that on many occasions I have in sleep been deceived by similar illusions, and in dwelling carefully on this reflection I see so manifestly that there are no certain indications by which we may clearly distinguish wakefulness from sleep that I am lost in astonishment. And my astonishment is such that it is almost capable of persuading me that I now dream.

Almost four centuries later, Descartes' dream argument for skepticism is still keeping philosophers awake at night. One contemporary analysis of this argument comes from the Canadian philosopher Barry Stroud, who has written insightfully about its intuitive power and pull:

From *The Significance of Philosophical Scepticism*
By Barry Stroud

With this thought, if he is right, Descartes has lost the whole world. He knows what he is experiencing, he knows how things appear to him, but he does not know whether he is in fact sitting by the fire with a piece of paper in his hand. It is, for him, exactly as if he were sitting by the fire with a piece of paper in his hand, but he does not know whether there really is a fire or a piece of paper there or not; he does not know what is really happening in the world around him. He realizes that if everything he can ever learn about what is happening in the world around him comes to him through the senses, but he cannot tell by means of the senses whether or not he is dreaming, then all the sensory experiences he is having are compatible with his merely dreaming of a world around him while in fact that world is very different from the way he takes it to be. That is why he thinks he must find some way to tell that he is not dreaming. Far from its being mad to deny that he knows in this case, he thinks his recognition of the possibility that he might be dreaming gives him 'very powerful and maturely considered'[3] reasons for withholding his judgment about how things are in the world around him. He thinks it is eminently reasonable to insist that if he is to know that he is sitting by the fire he must know that he is not dreaming that he is sitting by the fire. That is seen as a necessary condition of knowing something about the world around him. And he finds that that condition cannot be fulfilled. On careful reflection he discovers that 'there are no certain indications by which we may clearly distinguish wakefulness from sleep'. He concludes that he knows nothing about the world around him because he cannot tell that he is not dreaming; he cannot fulfill one of the conditions necessary for knowing something about the world.

The Cartesian problem of our knowledge of the external world therefore becomes: how can we know anything about the world around us on the basis of the sense if the senses give only what Descartes says they give us? What we gain through the senses is on Descartes' view only information that is compatible with our dreaming things about the world around us and not knowing anything about that world. How then can we know anything about the world by means of the senses? The Cartesian argument presents a challenge to our knowledge, and the problem of our knowledge of the external world is to show how that challenge can be met.

When I speak here of the Cartesian argument or of Descartes' skeptical conclusion or of his negative verdict about his knowledge I refer of course only to the position he finds himself in by the end of his first meditation. Having at that point discovered and stated the problem of the external world, Descartes goes on in the rest of his *Meditations* to try to solve it, and by the end of the sixth meditation he thinks he has explained how he knows almost all those familiar things he began by putting in question. So when I ascribe to

(Continued)

Descartes the view that we can know nothing about the world around us I do not mean to suggest that that is his final and considered view; it is nothing more than a conclusion he feels almost inevitably driven to at the early stages of his reflections. But those are the only stages of his thinking I am interested in here. That is where the philosophical problem of our knowledge of the external world gets posed, and, before we can consider possible solutions we must be sure we understand exactly what the problem is.

I have described it as that of showing or explaining how knowledge of the world around us is possible by means of the senses. It is important to keep in mind that that demand for an explanation arises in the face of a challenge or apparent obstacle to our knowledge of the world. The possibility that he is dreaming is seen as an obstacle to Descartes' knowing that he is sitting by the fire, and it must be explained how that obstacle can either be avoided or overcome. It must be shown or explained how it is possible for us to know things about the world, given that the sense-experiences we get are compatible with our merely dreaming. Explaining how something is nevertheless possible, despite what looks like an obstacle to it, requires more than showing merely that there is no impossibility involved in the thing—that it is consistent with the principles of logic and the laws of nature and so in that sense could exist. The mere possibility of the state of affairs is not enough to settle the question of how our knowledge of the world is possible; we must understand how the apparent obstacle is to be got round.

Descartes' reasoning can be examined and criticized at many different points, and has been closely scrutinized by many philosophers for centuries. It has also been accepted by many, perhaps by more than would admit or even realize that they accept it. There seems to me no doubt about the force and the fascination—I would say the almost overwhelming persuasiveness—of his reflections.

As Stroud notes, Descartes discovered a deep philosophical problem: the problem of understanding how knowledge of the external world is possible if beliefs about that world are ultimately based on nothing but sense-perceptions. Why, you ask, is this a problem? To answer that question, try asking another: What does it mean to say that your beliefs about the external world are ultimately based on sense-perception? Just this: that your beliefs about the world outside your mind are based on *appearances*—based, that is, solely on how things *seem* to you. It was this thought that led to Descartes' subversive discovery, because everybody knows (or at least, they *think* they know!) that it is perfectly possible for things to appear one way to us and yet not be that way in reality. Think of Descartes' dream scenario as a way of making that abstract possibility—that potential gap between appearance and reality, that slippage between seeming and being—dramatic and vivid. It *seems* to Descartes as if he were seated by the fire; and yet it is still theoretically possible that he is not seated by the fire, but is dreaming instead. In the same way, it *seems* to you as if you are reading a philosophy book right now; and yet it is still theoretically possible that you are just having a dream.

You can see where this is leading—back to Descartes' problem of knowledge. If your beliefs about the external world are based on nothing but appearances, and if you can never know that appearances are a reliable guide to the way that the world really is, then how can you ever claim to have knowledge of anything outside your own mind? The answer, it seems clear, is that you are in no position to claim any such thing. And if this is the last word on the subject, then the skeptic has won—and we have lost the everyday world of fire and paper, rocks and trees, books and bodies.

Returning to the first meditation, you can understand how Descartes has brought himself to the point where he doubts the existence of the whole of nature, even the existence of his own body. After all, you may dream that your body has changed grotesquely; you may even dream that you have left your body altogether. So isn't it possible, according to this strict method of doubt, to wonder whether you do indeed have a body, just as it is possible to wonder how you knows of the existence of the 'external world' in general?

Yet there is one sphere of knowledge that would seem to be immune even to Descartes' radical doubting—the principles of arithmetic and geometry:

From 'Meditation I'
By René Descartes

Arithmetic, Geometry, and other sciences of that kind which only treat of things that are very simple and very general, without taking great trouble to ascertain whether they are actually existent or not, contain some measure of certainty and an element of the indubitable. For whether I am awake or asleep, two and three together always form five, and the square can never have more than four sides, and it does not seem possible that truths so clear and apparent can be suspected of any falsity [or uncertainty].

But these can be doubted, too. To do so, Descartes turns his attention to God, his Creator, and asks whether God might be able to deceive him, even about these apparently certain principles:

Nevertheless I have long had fixed in my mind the belief that an all-powerful God existed by whom I have been created such as I am. But how do I know that He has not brought it to pass that there is no earth, no heaven, no extended body, no magnitude, no place, and that nevertheless [I possess the perceptions of all these things and that] they seem to me to exist just exactly as I now see them? And, besides, as I sometimes imagine that others deceive themselves in the things which they think they know best, how do I know that I am not deceived every time that I add two and three, or count the sides of a square, or judge of things yet simpler, if anything simpler can be imagined? But possibly God has not desired that I should be thus deceived, for He is said to be supremely good. If, however, it is contrary to His goodness to have made me such that I constantly deceive myself, it would also appear to be contrary to His goodness to permit me to be sometimes deceived, and nevertheless I cannot doubt that He does permit this.

Descartes' argument, which he will use again later in his *Meditations*, is that God is good and would not deceive him. But suppose, just suppose, that God did not exist?

There may indeed be those who would prefer to deny the existence of a God so powerful, rather than believe that all other things are uncertain. But let us not oppose them for the present, and grant that all that is here said of a God is a fable; nevertheless in whatever way they suppose that I have arrived at the state of being that I have reached—whether they attribute it to fate or to accident, or make out that it is by a continual succession of antecedents, or by some other method—since to err and deceive oneself is a defect, it is clear that the greater will be the probability of my being so imperfect as to deceive myself ever, as is the Author to whom they assign my origin the less powerful. To these reasons I have certainly nothing to reply, but at the end I feel constrained to confess that there is nothing in all that I formerly believed to be true, of which I cannot in some measure doubt, and that not merely through want of thought or through levity, but for reasons which are very powerful and maturely considered; so that henceforth I ought not the less carefully to refrain from giving credence to these opinions than to that which is manifestly false, if I desire to arrive at any certainty [in the sciences].

To bring his method to its extreme conclusion, Descartes now introduces a drastic supposition: that not a good God but an evil genius, a malicious demon, is constantly deceiving him, even about those things of which he seems to be most certain:

I shall then suppose, not that God who is supremely good and the fountain of truth, but some evil genius not less powerful than deceitful, has employed his whole energies in deceiving me; I shall consider that the heavens, the earth, colours, figures, sound, and all other external things are nought but the illusions and dreams of which this genius has availed himself in order to lay traps for my credulity; I shall consider myself as having no hands, no eyes, no flesh, no blood, nor any senses, yet falsely believing myself to possess all these things; I shall remain obstinately attached to this idea, and if by this means it is not in my power to arrive at the knowledge of any truth, I may at least do what is in my power [that is, suspend my judgment], and with firm purpose avoid giving credence to any false thing, or being imposed upon by this arch deceiver, however powerful and deceptive he may be. But this task is a laborious one, and insensibly a certain lassitude leads me into the course of my ordinary life. And just as a captive who in sleep enjoys an imaginary liberty, when he begins to suspect that this liberty is but a dream, fears to awaken, and conspires with these agreeable illusions that the deception may be prolonged, so insensibly of my own accord I fall back into my former opinions, and I dread awakening from this slumber, lest the laborious wakefulness which would follow the tranquility of this repose should have to be spent not in daylight, but in the excessive darkness of the difficulties which have just been discussed.

Descartes has taken his doubt as far as he can possibly go; he now doubts everything, until, that is, he finds the one principle that is beyond all doubt and perfectly certain—the fact of his own existence. That he cannot doubt, for if he doubts it, he still knows that he must exist to doubt. From this first principle, Descartes proceeds, through the meditations that follow, to re-establish his confidence in other things he believes as well—the existence of God, the existence of the 'external world', and the existence of his own body.

- Why does Descartes undertake his enterprise of 'methodological doubt'? What does he hope to get out of it?
- What does Descartes' dream argument demonstrate? Why does he introduce the idea of an evil genius? What does the possibility of the evil genius allow us to doubt?
- What, according to Descartes, is indubitable (beyond doubt)? How can we be certain of anything if we assume that we are being deceived?

Many philosophers have challenged the extremity of Descartes' method and have often objected that once you begin to doubt things so thoroughly, you will never again be able to argue your way back to certainty. One way of making this objection is to ask, how can Descartes possibly get rid of an 'evil genius' who is deceiving him about everything once he has introduced this possibility? Indeed, the supposition of an evil genius was so extreme that even Descartes, in the years that followed the publication and many disputes about his *Meditations*, insisted that no one should take his argument too seriously. But in the meditations themselves he tried to show that we could indeed get rid of the evil genius. Having watched Descartes work his way into the depth of Plato's cave, let us now watch him work his way out again.

From 'Meditation II'

By René Descartes

I am, I exist, is necessarily true each time that I pronounce it, or that I mentally conceive it.

Of the Nature of the Human Mind; and that It Is More Easily Known than the Body

The Meditation of yesterday filled my mind with so many doubts that it is no longer in my power to forget them. And yet I do not see in what manner I can resolve them; and, just as if I had all of a sudden fallen into very deep water, I am so disconcerted that I can neither make certain of setting my feet on the bottom, nor can I swim and so support myself on the surface. I shall nevertheless make an effort and follow anew the same path as that on which I yesterday entered, i.e., I shall proceed by setting aside all that in which the least doubt could be supposed to exist, just as if I had discovered that it was absolutely false; and I shall ever follow in this road until I have met with something which is certain, or at least, if I can do nothing else, until I have learned for certain that there is nothing in the world that is certain. Archimedes, in order that he might draw the terrestrial globe out of its place, and transport it elsewhere, demanded only that one point should be fixed and immovable; in the same way I shall have the right to conceive high hopes if I am happy enough to discover one thing only which is certain and indubitable.

I suppose, then, that all the things that I see are false; I persuade myself that nothing has ever existed of all that my fallacious memory represents to me. I consider that I possess no senses; I imagine that body, figure, extension, movement, and place are but the fictions of my mind. What, then, can be esteemed as true? Perhaps nothing at all, unless that there is nothing in the world that is certain.

But how can I know there is not something different from those things that I have just considered, of which one cannot have the slightest doubt? Is there not some God, or some other being by whatever name we call it, who puts these reflections into my mind? That is not necessary, for is it not possible that I am capable of producing them myself? I myself, am I not at least something? But I have already denied that I had senses and body. Yet I hesitate, for what follows from that? Am I so dependent on body and senses that I cannot exist without these? But I was persuaded that there was nothing in all the world, that there was no heaven, no earth, that there were no minds, nor any bodies; was I not then likewise persuaded that I did not exist? Not at all; of a surety I myself did exist since I persuaded myself of something [or merely because I thought of something]. But there is some deceiver or other, very powerful and very cunning, who ever employs his ingenuity in deceiving me. Then without doubt I exist also if he deceives me, and let him deceive me as much as he will, he can never cause me to be nothing so long as I think that I am something. So that after having reflected well and carefully examined all things, we must come to the definite conclusion that this proposition: I am, I exist, is necessarily true each time that I pronounce it, or that I mentally conceive it.

Here it is, the one, certain truth that Descartes needs to start his argument. His most famous formulation of this truth is *cogito, ergo sum*: 'I think, therefore I am'. (It may be worth pointing out that a similar argument appears in the work of St Augustine, more than one thousand years earlier.)

But now that Descartes knows that he exists, what is he? His answer: 'a thing which thinks'.

But I do not yet know clearly enough what I am, I who am certain that I am; and hence I must be careful to see that I do not imprudently take some other object in place of myself, and thus that I do not go astray in respect of this knowledge that I hold to be the most certain and most evident of all that I have formerly learned. That is why I shall now consider anew what I believed myself to be before I embarked

(Continued)

upon these last reflections; and of my former opinions I shall withdraw all that might even in a small degree be invalidated by the reasons which I have just brought forward, in order that there may be nothing at all left beyond what is absolutely certain and indubitable.

What then did I formerly believe myself to be? Undoubtedly I believed myself to be a man. But what is a man? Shall I say a reasonable animal? Certainly not; for then I should have to inquire what an animal is, and what is reasonable; and thus from a single question I should insensibly fall into an infinitude of others more difficult; and I should not wish to waste the little time and leisure remaining to me in trying to unravel subtleties like these. But I shall rather stop here to consider the thoughts which of themselves spring up in my mind, and which were not inspired by anything beyond my own nature alone when I applied myself to the consideration of my being. In the first place, then, I considered myself as having a face, hands, arms, and all that system of members composed of bones and flesh as seen in a corpse which I designated by the name of body. In addition to this I considered that I was nourished, that I walked, that I felt, and that I thought, and I referred all these actions to the soul: but I did not stop to consider what the soul was, or if I did stop, I imagined that it was something extremely rare and subtle like a wind, a flame, or an ether, which was spread throughout my grosser parts. As to body I had no manner of doubt about its nature, but thought I had a very clear knowledge of it; and if I had desired to explain it according to the notions that I had then formed of it, I should have described it thus: By the body I understand all that which can be defined by a certain figure: something which can be confined in a certain place, and which can fill a given space in such a way that every other body will be excluded from it; which can be perceived either by touch, or by sight, or by hearing, or by taste, or by smell:

which can be moved in many ways not, in truth, by itself, but by something which is foreign to it, by which it is touched [and from which it receives impressions]: for to have the power of self-movement, as also of feeling or of thinking, I did not consider to appertain to the nature of body: on the contrary, I was rather astonished to find that faculties similar to them existed in some bodies.

But what am I, now that I suppose that there is a certain genius which is extremely powerful, and, if I may say so, malicious, who employs all his power in deceiving me? Can I affirm that I possess the least of all those things which I have just said pertain to the nature of body? I pause to consider, I revolve all these things in my mind, and I find none of which I can say that it pertains to me. It would be tedious to stop to enumerate them. Let us pass to the attributes of soul and see if there is any one which is in me? What of nutrition or walking [the first mentioned]? But if it is so that I have no body it is also true that I can neither walk nor take nourishment. Another attribute is sensation. But one cannot feel without body, and besides I have thought I perceived many things during sleep that I recognized in my waking moments as not having been experienced at all. What of thinking? I find here that thought is an attribute that belongs to me; it alone cannot be separated from me. I am, I exist, that is certain. But how often? Just when I think; for it might possibly be the case if I ceased entirely to think, that I should likewise cease altogether to exist. I do not now admit anything which is not necessarily true: to speak accurately I am not more than a thing which thinks, that is to say a mind or a soul, or an understanding, or a reason, which are terms whose significance was formerly unknown to me. I am, however, a real thing and really exist; but what thing? I have answered: a thing which thinks. . . . What is a thing which thinks? It is a thing which doubts, understands, affirms, denies, wills, refuses, which also imagines and feels.

In other words, Descartes cannot know for certain that he has a body, much less a particular kind of body, since the evil genius could fool him about that. The only thing that the evil genius could not possibly fool him about is his own thinking; therefore, the 'I' that he knows to exist can only be a thinking 'I', not a person or a man in the more usual sense. Later on, this discovery will cause Descartes to raise a gigantic problem, namely, how to explain the connection between this thinking self and the body with which it is associated. But for now, we are more interested in the way he will use his discovery of a single, certain truth. (His discussion of the 'mind–body' connection occurs in 'Meditation VI', which we shall discuss in Chapter 4.)

Descartes has his premise, the fact of his own existence as a 'thinking thing'. What must follow, then, is the use of this premise in an argument that will 'prove' the beliefs he began by doubting: the existence of his own body, the existence of the 'external' world, and the existence of God. Finally, he must somehow get rid of his tentative supposition of the evil demon. But first, he raises once again the old metaphysical question of substance. In a famous example from 'Meditation II', he argues:

Let us begin by considering the commonest matters, those which we believe to be the most distinctly comprehended, to wit, the bodies which we touch and see; not indeed bodies in general, for these general ideas are usually a little more confused, but let us consider one body in particular. Let us take, for example, this piece of wax: it has been taken quite freshly from the hive, and it has not yet lost the sweetness of the odour of the honey which it contains; it still retains somewhat of the odour of the flowers from which it has been culled; its colour, its figure, its size are apparent; it is hard, cold, easily handled, and if you strike it with the finger, it will emit a sound. Finally all the things which are requisite to cause us distinctly to recognize a body, are met with in it. But notice that while I speak and approach the fire what remained of the taste is exhaled, the smell evaporates, the colour alters, the figure is destroyed, the size increases, it becomes liquid, it heats, scarcely can one handle it, and when one strikes it, no sound is emitted. Does the same wax remain after this change? We must confess that it remains; none would judge otherwise. What then did I know so distinctly in this piece of wax? It could certainly be nothing of all that the senses brought to my notice, since all these things which fall under taste, smell, sight, touch, and hearing are found to be changed, and yet the same wax remains.

Perhaps it was what I now think, viz. that this wax was not that sweetness of honey, nor that agreeable scent of flowers, nor that particular whiteness, nor that figure, nor that sound, but simply a body which a little while before appeared to me as perceptible under these forms, and which is now perceptible under others. But what, precisely, is it that I imagine when I form such conceptions? Let us attentively consider this, and, abstracting from all that

does not belong to the wax, let us see what remains. Certainly nothing remains excepting a certain extended thing which is flexible and movable. But what is the meaning of flexible and movable? Is it not that I imagine that this piece of wax being round is capable of becoming square and of passing from a square to a triangular figure? No, certainly it is not that, since I imagine it admits of an infinitude of similar changes, and I nevertheless do not know how to compass the infinitude of my imagination, and consequently this conception which I have of the wax is not brought about by the faculty of imagination. What now is this extension? Is it not also unknown? For it becomes greater when the wax is melted, greater when it is boiled, and greater still when the heat increases; and I should not conceive [clearly] according to truth what wax is, if I did not think that even this piece that we are considering is capable of receiving more variations in extension than I have ever imagined. We must then grant that I could not even understand through the imagination what this piece of wax is, and that it is my mind alone which perceives it. I say this piece of wax in particular, for as to wax in general it is yet clearer. But what is this piece of wax which cannot be understood excepting by the [understanding or] mind? It is certainly the same that I see, touch, imagine, and finally it is the same which I have always believed it to be from the beginning. But what must particularly be observed is that its perception is neither an act of vision, nor of touch, nor of imagination, and has never been such although it may have appeared formerly to be so, but only an intuition of the mind, which may be imperfect and confused as it was formerly, or clear and distinct as it is at present, according as my attention is more or less directed to the elements which are found in it, and of which it is composed.

This 'intuition of mind' is the key to all rationalist thinking. **Intuition** is where the rationalist obtains his premises, from which he argues to all other conclusions. The difference between the rationalist and the empiricist, at least in what they say that they are doing, is the rationalist's heavy reliance on non-empirical intuition. Both would agree on the legitimacy of the deductions that follow; it is the source of the premises that is in dispute. And intuition, according to the rationalists, has its source in reason alone. (Notice that 'reason' refers not only to the activity of reasoning but to unreasoned intuitions and insights as well.) As we shall see, it is this reliance on intuition, rather than the actual arguments that Descartes uses to 'prove' his other beliefs, that will be at the centre of the dispute between rationalists and empiricists.

The strategy of Descartes' argument is as follows. First, he establishes his premise, which you have seen:

> I exist (*as a thinking thing*).

Then (in 'Meditation III'), Descartes uses this premise to prove the existence of God. The argument itself is a version of two arguments for God's existence: the cosmological argument and the ontological argument. As you may recall from our discussion in Chapter 2, the basic logic of both arguments is this: If a finite, dependent, and merely **contingent** being like myself can even think of an infinite, independent, and necessary being, then such a being must exist. (We also discussed Descartes' arguments for the existence of God in Chapter 2. The details of these arguments are not so much the concern of epistemology or the theory of knowledge as they are of the special logical considerations necessary when talking about the Supreme Being, so we will not explore Descartes' arguments in full in this chapter. For now, let us simply grant Descartes his second step.) So, with this new development in the argument, we have

> I exist (*as a thinking thing*). (*premise*)
> God exists (*because I could not exist without Him*).

Now we can say that, by His very nature (another intuition), God is good, in fact, perfectly good. So, as Descartes says in 'Meditation VI',

From 'Meditation VI'
By René Descartes

Since He has given me a very strong inclination to believe that these ideas (of trees, houses, etc.) arise from corporeal objects, I do not see how he could be vindicated from the charge of deceit, if in truth they proceeded from any other source, or were produced by other causes than corporeal things? (For example, by the evil demon, or in dreams.)

Therefore,

We *cannot be deceived* [whether by the evil demon or whatever else]. . . . I cannot doubt but that there is in me a certain passive faculty of perception, that is, of receiving and taking knowledge of the ideas of sensible things; but this would be useless to me, if there did not also exist in me, or in some other thing, another active faculty capable of forming and producing those ideas. But this active faculty cannot be in me [in as far as I am but a thinking thing], seeing that it does not presuppose thought, and also that those ideas are frequently produced in my mind without my contributing to it in any way, and even frequently contrary to my will. This faculty must therefore exist in some substance different from me, in which all the objective reality of the ideas that are produced by this faculty is contained formally or eminently, as I before remarked: and this substance is either a body, that is to say, a corporeal nature in which is contained formally [and in effect] all that is objectively [and by representation] in those ideas; or it is God himself, or some other creature, of a rank superior to body, in which the same is contained eminently. But as God is no deceiver, it is manifest that he does not of himself and immediately communicate those ideas to me, nor even by the intervention of any creature in which their objective reality is not formally, but only eminently, contained. For as he has given me no faculty whereby I can discover this to be the case, but, on the contrary, a very strong inclination to believe that those ideas arise from corporeal objects, I do not see how he could be vindicated from the charge of deceit, if in truth they proceeded from any other source, or were produced by other causes than corporeal things: and accordingly it must be concluded, that corporeal objects exist. Nevertheless they are not perhaps exactly such as we perceive by the senses, for their comprehension by the senses is, in many instances, very obscure and confused; but it is at least necessary to admit that all which I clearly and distinctly conceive as in them, that is, generally speaking, all that is comprehended in the object of speculative geometry, really exists external to me.

The argument is not convincing, as Descartes' critics were quick to point out. Where does Descartes get his confidence in reason to begin with, such that he feels confident in his own abilities to prove God's existence? Descartes' answer is that we get that confidence from God Himself. But with this answer he has begged the question; that is, he has presumed the existence of God in order to get the confidence with which he then proves God's existence. (This circularity of argument is often called 'the Cartesian Circle'.) Another way of criticizing the same strategy is to say that, having once introduced the evil demon, Descartes has no way of getting rid of him, since that supposition undermines his confidence in his own reason just as thoroughly as his confidence in God bolsters it.

> - Why is Descartes considered a 'rationalist'? What does this designation mean?
> - What is the 'Cartesian Circle'? Why is it a problem?

Our primary concern in our study of epistemology, however, is with Descartes' rationalist claim that certain beliefs are self-evident, or 'clear and distinct', on the basis of intuition and reason alone. These are beliefs that we don't have to learn—in fact, couldn't learn—from experience. It is not just Descartes' 'I exist' premise that is such a belief; all of the **rules of inference**, which he uses in his arguments, are also beliefs of this kind. Ultimately, his confidence in reason itself is one, too. In particular, John Locke, in his disillusionment with metaphysics, begins his philosophy with an assault on the very idea of knowledge that is independent of experience. Thus he begins with an attack on the heart of the rationalist methodology.

B. Innate Ideas Concerning Human Understanding: John Locke

Regarding metaphysics, John Locke is reported to have commented to a friend, 'you and I have had enough of this kind of fiddling'. Against the sometimes fantastic claims of the metaphysicians, Locke sought a restoration of common sense.[4] Just as Aristotle had acted as a critic of Plato's extravagant two-worlds view, Locke acted as a corrective to the metaphysical enthusiasm of the medieval and modern worlds. He accepted Descartes'

SKEPTICISM

The belief that knowledge is not possible, that no argument can overcome doubt.

tentative **skepticism**, but he questioned his French predecessor's urge to metaphysics as well as his confidence in the insights of pure reason. He rejected the unsupportable 'intuitions' that provided Descartes with his rules and his premises, and he turned instead to the data of experience as the ultimate source of all knowledge. He therefore rejected Descartes' exclusively deductive method and supplanted it with a method appropriate to **generalizations from experience**, or **induction**. In inductive reasoning, unlike in deductive reasoning, the conclusion always goes beyond the premises and therefore it is always less certain than they are. (For example, from the observed fact that all the philosophy professors that you have met have been absent-minded [the premise] you conclude by **inductive generalization** that all philosophy professors are probably absent-minded.) Accordingly, Locke also modified Descartes' demand for 'perfect certainty' and allowed for probability and 'degrees of assent'. Yet Locke did not reject reason as such. He still accepted the certainty of mathematical reasoning and the validity of deductive inferences; but he also expanded the concept of rationality to include inductive reasoning and probability as well as deduction and certainty.

- What is induction? (You can refer back to pp. 40–2 in the Introduction.) Give an example of inductive reasoning. How does induction differ from deduction?

Locke's *An Essay Concerning Human Understanding* (1689) is built on a single premise, namely, that all our knowledge comes from experience. This means, in his view, that there cannot possibly be ideas that are prior to experience, ideas that are 'born into us', as suggested so vividly by Plato. In other words, Locke refuses to accept the notion of **innate ideas**, by which he means not only those ideas that are literally 'born into us' but all ideas that are derived without appeal to experience. This includes, in his opinion, Descartes' 'clear and distinct ideas', Spinoza's 'adequate ideas', and Leibniz's 'truths of reason'.

From *An Essay Concerning Human Understanding*
By John Locke

No proposition can be said to be in the mind which it never yet knew, which it was never yet conscious of.

1. *The way shown how we come by any knowledge, sufficient to prove it not innate.*—It is an established opinion among some men, that there are in the understanding certain innate principles; some primary notions, κοιναί ἔννοιαι, characters, as it were, stamped upon the mind of man which the soul receives in its very first being, and brings into the world with it. It would be sufficient to convince unprejudiced readers of the falseness of this supposition, if I should only show (as I hope I shall in the following parts of this discourse) how men, barely by the use of their natural faculties, may attain to all the knowledge they have, without the help of any innate impressions, and may

arrive at certainty, without any such original notions or principles. . . .

2. *General assent the great argument.*—There is nothing more commonly taken for granted, than that there are certain principles, both speculative and practical (for they speak of both), universally agreed upon by all mankind, which therefore, they argue, must needs be constant impressions which the souls of men receive in their first beings, and which they bring into the world with them, as necessarily and really as they do any of their inherent faculties.

3. *Universal consent proves nothing innate.*—This argument, drawn from universal consent, has

this misfortune in it, that if it were true in matter of fact that there were certain truths wherein all mankind agreed, it would not prove them innate, if there can be any other way shown how men may come to that universal agreement in the things they do consent in, which I presume may be done.

4. *'What is, is', and 'It is impossible for the same thing to be and not to be', not universally assented to.—* But, which is worse, this argument of universal consent, which is made use of to prove innate principles, seems to me a demonstration that there are none such; because there are none to which all mankind give an universal assent. I shall begin with the speculative, and instance in those magnified principles of demonstration, 'Whatsoever is, is' and 'It is impossible for the same thing to be, and not to be'; which, of all others, I think, have the most allowed title to innate. These have so settled a reputation of maxims universally received that it will no doubt be thought strange if anyone should seem to question it. But yet I take liberty to say that these propositions are so far from having an universal assent that there are a great part of mankind to whom they are not so much as known.

5. *Not on the mind naturally imprinted, because not known to children, idiots, &c.—*For, first, it is evident that all children and idiots have not the least apprehension or thought of them; and the want of that is enough to destroy that universal assent which must needs be the necessary concomitant of all innate truths: it seeming to me near a contradiction to say that there are truths imprinted on the soul which it perceives or understands not; imprinting, if it signify anything, being nothing else but the making certain truths to be perceived. For to imprint anything on the mind without the mind's perceiving it, seems to me hardly intelligible. If therefore children and idiots have souls, have minds, with those impressions upon them, they must unavoidably perceive them, and necessarily know and assent to these truths; which since they do not, it is evident that there are no such impressions. For if they are not notions naturally imprinted, how can they be innate, and if they are notions imprinted, how can they be unknown? To say a notion is imprinted on the mind, and yet at the same time to say that the mind is ignorant of it, and never yet took notice of it, is to make this impression nothing. No proposition can be said to be in the mind which it never yet knew, which it was never yet conscious of.

The argument is straightforward: there is no universal agreement regarding supposedly 'innate' principles, and even if there were, that would not prove their 'innateness'. Rather, he argues:

Let us suppose the mind to be, as we say, a blank tablet (tabula rasa) of white paper, void of all characters, without any ideas; how comes it to be furnished? Whence comes it by that vast store, which the busy and boundless fancy of man has painted on it with almost endless variety? Whence has it all the materials of reason and knowledge? To this I answer in one word, from *experience*: in that all our knowledge is founded, and from that it ultimately derives itself.

- What does Locke mean when he says that the mind is like a blank tablet (tabula rasa) of white paper? What is he arguing against?

It is this premise that Locke is concerned to defend and use, and his attack on innate ideas is by way of introduction. But Locke fails to prove that the human mind does not have inborn potentials and limitations, and more importantly, he fails to recognize that inference from experience might itself require principles that are not drawn from experience. In fact, Leibniz, one of the chief targets of Locke's attack, was not long in providing what we might call 'the rationalist's reply'. Turning Locke against himself, Leibniz argued that, by his own principles, he could not attack the concept of innate ideas.

From *New Essays on Human Understanding*
By Gottfried Wilhelm von Leibniz

The question at issue is whether the soul in itself is entirely empty, like the tablet upon which nothing has yet been written (tabula rasa), as is the view of Aristotle and the author of the *Essay* (Locke), and whether all that is traced on it comes solely from the senses and from experience; or whether the soul contains originally the principles of various notions and doctrines which external objects merely awaken from time to time, as I believe, with Plato and even with the Schoolmen, and with all those who take in this sense the passage of St Paul (Romans 2:15) where he remarks that the law of God is written in the heart. . . . From this there arises another question, whether all truths depend on experience, that is to say, on induction and examples, or whether there are some that have some other basis. For if some events can be foreseen before any trial has been made of them, it is clear that we must here contribute something of our own. The senses, although necessary for all our actual knowledge, are not sufficient to give us the whole of it, since the senses never give anything except examples, that is to say, particular or individual truths. All examples which confirm a general truth, however numerous they may be, are not enough to establish the universal necessity of this same truth; for it does not follow that what has happened will happen again in the same way.

* * *

It would seem that necessary truths, such as are found in pure mathematics, and especially in arithmetic and in geometry, must have principles the proof of which does not depend on examples, nor, consequently, on the testimony of the senses, although without the senses it would never have occurred to us to think of them. This ought to be well recognized; Euclid has so well understood it that he often demonstrates by reason what is obvious enough through experience and by sensible images.

Logic also, together with metaphysics and ethics, one of which forms natural theology and the other natural jurisprudence, are full of such truths; and consequently their proof can only come from internal principles, which are called innate. It is true that we must not imagine that these eternal laws of the reason can be read in the soul as in an open book, as the edict of the praetor can be read in his *album* without difficulty or research; but it is enough that they can be discovered in us by dint of attention, for which opportunities are given by the senses. The success of experiments serves also as confirmation of the reason, very much as proofs serve in arithmetic for better avoiding error of reckoning when the reasoning is long.

* * *

It seems that our able author claims that there is nothing potential in us and nothing even of which we are not at any time actually conscious; but he cannot mean this strictly, or his opinion would be too paradoxical; for acquired habits and the contents of our memory are not always consciously perceived and do not even always come to our aid at need, although we often easily bring them back to mind on some slight occasion which makes us remember them, just as we need only the beginning of a song to remember the song. Also he modifies his assertion in other places by saying that there is nothing in us of which we have not been at least formerly conscious. But besides the fact that no one can be sure by reason alone how far our past apperceptions, which we may have forgotten, may have gone, especially in view of the Platonic doctrine of reminiscence, which, mythical as it is, is not, in part at least, incompatible with bare reason; in addition to this, I say, why is it necessary that everything should be acquired by us through the perceptions of external things, and that nothing can be unearthed in ourselves? Is our soul, then, such a blank that, besides the images borrowed from without, it is nothing? . . . [T]here are a thousand indications that lead us to think that there are at every moment numberless perceptions in us, but without apperception and without reflections; that is to say, changes in the soul itself of which we are not conscious, because the impressions are either too slight and too numerous, or too even, so that they have nothing sufficient to distinguish them one from the other; but, joined to others, they do not fail to produce their effect and to make themselves felt at least confusedly in the mass.

- How does Locke refute the notion that 'whatsoever is, is' and 'It is impossible for the same thing to be, and not to be' are innate ideas? What kind of truths does Leibniz cite as innate in rebuttal?

Locke himself did not continue the debate; he was already convinced of his position and had more urgent problems to worry about (the political chaos in London following the 'Glorious Revolution' of 1688). But the debate continued in different forms. The rise of anthropology in the nineteenth century, with the discoveries of societies whose basic ideas were radically different from traditional Western ideas, seemed to support Locke's claim that no one will believe in innate universal principles if they 'ever look beyond the smoke of their own chimneys'. But in the nineteenth century a great many philosophers still argued for the existence of universal principles not learned through experience. (Immanuel Kant did this in a very powerful set of arguments that we will encounter in chapters 5 and 6.) In the early twentieth century, opinion was in general accord with Locke, but recently it has taken another swing back to Leibniz, this time supported by anthropology. A major movement in the social sciences, usually called structuralism (whose main proponent was Claude Lévi-Strauss in France), has argued that underneath the many superficial differences between very different societies there are certain basic 'structures' that are universal and innate. In North America, the notion of innate ideas has appeared once again in the work of the well-known linguist Noam Chomsky. According to Chomsky, certain capacities for language are built into us from birth; this assertion allows him to explain not only the similarities of human thinking (which was the view that Locke attacked) but also the enormous capacity for learning different languages quickly (the average three-year-old learns a language in six months). The Locke–Leibniz debate is still very much alive.

C. The Empiricist Theory of Knowledge

The **tabula rasa** ('blank tablet') view of the mind is Locke's most famous epistemological concept. Leaving aside those special concerns that involve only 'the relations between ideas' (as in mathematics, logic, and trivial **conceptual truths** such as 'a horse is an animal'), all of our ideas are derived from experience. Epistemology (and philosophy in general) now became a kind of psychology (indeed, the two disciplines were not yet distinguished), a study of the history of our common experiences in order to discover where we get our ideas, particularly ideas relating to substance, God, and our various conceptions of reality. In his theory, Locke uses three familiar terms: **sensation** (or what more modern empiricists call sense-data), **ideas** (not in the Platonic sense but simply 'the immediate object of perception, thought, or understanding'), and **quality** (or what we have so far been calling property, for example, being red, being round, being heavy).

From *An Essay Concerning Human Understanding*
By John Locke

The ideas of primary qualities of bodies are resemblances of them, and their patterns do really exist in the bodies themselves, but the ideas produced in us by these secondary qualities have no resemblance of them at all.

1. Concerning the simple ideas of sensation, it is to be considered—that whatsoever is so constituted in nature as to be able, by affecting our senses, to cause any perception in the mind, doth thereby produce in the understanding a simple idea; which, whatever be the external cause of it, when it comes to be taken notice of by our discerning faculty, it is by the mind looked on and considered there to be a real positive idea in the understanding, as much as any other whatsoever; though, perhaps, the cause of it be but a privation of the subject.

2. Thus the ideas of heat and cold, light and darkness, white and black, motion and rest, are equally clear and positive ideas in the mind; though perhaps, some of the causes which produce them are barely privations, in those subjects from whence our senses derive those ideas. These the understanding, in its view of them, considers all as distinct positive ideas, without taking notice of the causes that produce them: which is an inquiry not belonging to the idea, as it is in the understanding, but to the nature of the things existing without us. These are two very different things, and carefully to be distinguished; it being one thing to perceive and know the idea of white or black, and quite another to examine what kind of particles they must be, and how ranged in the superficies, to make any object appear white or black.

* * *

7. To discover the nature of our *ideas* the better, and to discourse of them intelligibly, it will be convenient to distinguish them *as they are ideas or perceptions in our minds*; and *as they are modifications of matter in the bodies that cause such perceptions in us*: that so we may not think (as perhaps usually is done) that they are exactly the images and resemblances of something inherent in the subject; most of those of sensation being in the mind no more the likeness of something existing without us, than the names that stand for them are the likeness of our ideas, which yet upon hearing they are apt to excite in us.

8. Whatsoever the mind perceives *in itself*, or is the immediate object of perception, thought, or understanding, that I call *idea*; and the power to produce any idea in our mind, I call *quality* of the subject wherein that power is. Thus a snowball having the power to produce in us the ideas of white, cold, and round—the power to produce those ideas in us, as they are in the snowball, I call qualities; and as they are sensations or perceptions in our understanding, I call them ideas; which *ideas*, if I speak of sometimes as in the things themselves, I should be understood to mean those qualities in the objects which produce them in us.

Notice that the basis of Locke's theory is the 'common-sense' distinction between physical objects in the world and sensations and ideas in our minds. Accordingly, we may talk of two types of qualities or properties. The first type, which Locke refers to as **primary qualities**, are those that are inherent in the objects in the world (for example, solidity of form and extension in space). The second type, which Locke calls **secondary qualities**, are those that an object merely appears to have, qualities that do not exist independently of the objects' effects on our sense organs (for example, colour and texture).

Primary Qualities

Qualities thus considered in bodies are, *First*, such as are utterly inseparable from the body, in what state soever it be; and such as in all the alterations and changes it suffers, all the force can be used upon it, it constantly keeps; and such as sense constantly finds in every particle of matter which has bulk enough to be perceived; and the mind finds inseparable from every particle of matter, though less than to make itself singly be perceived by our senses: e.g. Take a grain of wheat, divide it into two parts; each part has still solidity, extension, figure, and mobility: divide it again, and it retains still the same qualities; and so divide it on, till the parts become insensible; they must retain still each of them all those qualities. For division (which is all that a mill, or pestle, or any other body, does upon another, in reducing it to insensible parts) can never take away either solidity, extension, figure, or mobility from any body, but only makes two or more distinct separate masses of matter, of that which was but one before; all which distinct masses, reckoned as so many distinct bodies; after division, make a certain number. These I call *original* or *primary qualities* of body, which I think we may observe to produce simple ideas in us, viz. solidity, extension, figure, motion or rest, and number.

* * *

Secondary Qualities

Secondly, such qualities which in truth are nothing in the objects themselves but powers to produce various sensations in us by their primary qualities, i.e., by the bulk, figure, texture, and motion of their insensible parts, as colours, sounds, tastes, &c. These I call *secondary qualities*. To these might be added a *third* sort, which are allowed to be barely powers; though they are as much real qualities in the subject as those which I, to comply with the common way of speaking, call qualities, but for distinction, secondary qualities. For the power in fire to produce a new colour, or consistency, in *wax* or *clay*—by its primary qualities, is as much a quality in fire, as the power it has to produce in *me* a new idea or sensation of warmth or burning, which I felt not before—by the same primary qualities, viz. the bulk, texture, and motion of its insensible parts.

The question, then, is how physical objects cause us to have sensations and ideas. Locke's answer (which, like his theory as a whole, is very strongly influenced by the physical theories of his contemporary Isaac Newton) is, by impulse. This might not seem illuminating until you think of the Newtonian theory of force as a product of particles and masses in motion. It is on this model that Locke develops what is now called his '**causal theory of perception**'. First, for the primary qualities,

CAUSAL THEORY OF PERCEPTION

The view that our sensations and ideas are caused by physical objects acting upon our sense organs.

If then external objects be not united to our minds when they produce ideas therein; and yet we perceive these *original* qualities in such of them as singly fall under our senses, it is evident that some motion must be thence continued by our nerves, or animal spirits, by some parts of our bodies, to the brains or the seat of sensation, there to produce in our minds the particular ideas we have of them. And since the extension, figure, number, and motion of bodies of an observable bigness may be perceived at a distance by the sight, it is evident some singly imperceptible bodies must come from them to the eyes, and thereby convey to the brain some motion; which produces these ideas which we have of them in us.

Then, for secondary qualities,

After the same manner that the ideas of these original qualities are produced in us, we may conceive that the ideas of *secondary* qualities are also produced, viz. by the operation of insensible particles on our senses. For, it being manifest that there are bodies and good store of bodies, each whereof are so small, that we cannot by any of our senses discover either their bulk, figure, or motion—as is evident in those particles of the air and water, and others extremely smaller than those; perhaps as much smaller than the particles of air and water, as the particles of air and water are smaller than peas or hail-stones;—let us suppose at present that the different motions and figures, bulk and number, of such particles, affecting the several organs of our senses, produce in us those different sensations which we have from the colours and smells of bodies; e.g., that a violet, by the impulse of such insensible particles of matter, of peculiar figures and bulks, and in different degrees and modifications of their motions, causes the ideas of the blue colour, and sweet scent of that flower to be produced in our minds. It being no more impossible to conceive that God should annex such ideas to such motions, with which they have no similitude, than that he should annex the idea of pain to the motion of a piece of steel dividing our flesh, with which that idea hath no resemblance.

What I have said concerning colours and smells may be understood also of tastes and sounds, and other the like sensible qualities; which, whatever reality we by mistake attribute to them, are in truth nothing in the objects themselves, but powers to produce various sensations in us; and depend on those primary qualities, viz. bulk, figure, texture, and motion of parts [as I have said].

Therefore,

I think it easy to draw this observation—that the ideas of primary qualities of bodies are resemblances of them, and their patterns do really exist in the bodies themselves, but the ideas produced in us by these secondary qualities have no resemblance of them at all. There is nothing like our ideas, existing in the bodies themselves. They are, in the bodies we denominate from them, only a power to produce those sensations in us: and what is sweet, blue, or warm in idea, is but the certain bulk, figure, and motion of the insensible parts, in the bodies themselves, which we call so.

Flame is denominated hot and light; snow, white and cold; and manna, white and sweet, from the ideas they produce in us. Which qualities are commonly thought to be the same in those bodies that those ideas are in us, the one the perfect resemblance of the other, as they are in a mirror, and it would by most men be judged very extravagant if one should say otherwise. And yet he that will consider that the same fire that, at one distance produces in us the sensation of warmth, does, at a nearer approach, produce in us the far different sensation of pain, ought to bethink himself what reason he has to say—that this idea of warmth, which was produced in him by fire, is *actually in the fire*; and his idea of pain, which the same fire produced in him the same way, is *not* in the fire. Why are whiteness and coldness in snow, and pain not, when it produces the one and the other idea in us; and can do neither, but by the bulk, figure, number, and motion of its solid parts?

The particular bulk, number, figure, and motion of the parts of fire or snow are really in them—whether anyone's senses perceive them or no: and therefore they may be called *real* qualities, because they really exist in those bodies. But light, heat, whiteness, or coldness, are no more really in them than sickness or pain is in manna. Take away the sensation of them; let not the eyes see light or colours, nor the ears hear sounds; let the palate not taste, nor the nose smell, and all colours, tastes, odours, and sounds, *as they are such particular ideas*, vanish and cease, and are reduced to their causes, i.e., bulk, figure, and motion of parts.

- What does Locke mean by 'primary qualities'? Give an example.
- What does Locke mean by 'secondary qualities'? Give an example.

This is the basic empiricist theory as Locke presented it. The logical consequences of empiricism, as we shall see when we study Berkeley and Hume, are not nearly so palatable. But how does the causal theory of perception allow Locke to approach the traditional questions of metaphysics? Significantly, the first two steps in his argument are identical with those we traced in Descartes—one's own existence and the existence of God—and Locke even includes the problematic notion of 'intuition':

1. The knowledge of our own being we have by intuition. The existence of God, reason clearly makes known to us.

   The knowledge of the existence of *any other thing* we can have only by *sensation*: for there being no necessary connection of real existence with any *idea* a man hath in his memory; nor of any other existence but that of God with the existence of any particular man: no particular man can know the existence of any other being, but only when, by actual operating upon him, it makes itself perceived by him. For, the having the idea of anything in our mind, no more proves the existence of that thing, than the picture of a man evidences his being in the world, or the visions of a dream make thereby a true history.

But then, the strict empiricist re-emerges:

2. It is therefore the *actual receiving* of ideas from without that gives us notice of the existence of other things, and makes us know, that something doth exist at that time without us, which causes that idea in us; though perhaps we neither know nor consider how it does it. For it takes not from the certainty of our senses, and the ideas we receive by them, that we know not the manner wherein they are produced: e.g., whilst I write this, I have, by the paper affecting my eyes, that idea produced in my mind, which, whatever object causes, I call *white*; by which I know that that quality or accident (i.e. whose appearance before my eyes always causes that idea) doth really exist, and hath a being without me. And of this, the greatest assurance I can possibly have, and to which my faculties can attain, is the testimony of my eyes, which are the proper and sole judges of this thing; whose testimony I have reason to rely on as so certain, that I can no more doubt, whilst I write this, that I see white and black, and that something really exists that causes that sensation in me, than that I write or move my hand; which is a certainty as great as human nature is capable of, concerning the existence of anything, but a man's self alone, and of God.

Here Locke asserts his alternative to the strict Cartesian limitation of knowledge to matters of certainty and deduction:

3. The notice we have by our senses of the existing of things without us, though it be not altogether so certain as our intuitive knowledge, or the deductions of our reason employed about the clear abstract ideas of our own minds; yet it is an assurance that deserves the name of *knowledge*. If we

(*Continued*)

persuade ourselves that our faculties act and inform us right concerning the existence of those objects that affect them, it cannot pass for an ill-grounded confidence: for I think nobody can, in earnest, be so skeptical as to be uncertain of the existence of those things which he sees and feels. At least, he that can doubt so far, (whatever he may have with his own thoughts,) will never have any controversy with me; since he can never be sure I say anything contrary to his own opinion. As to myself, I think God has given me assurance enough of the existence of things without me: since, by their different application, I can produce in myself both pleasure and pain, which is one great concernment of my present state. This is certain: the confidence that our faculties do not herein deceive us, is the greatest assurance we are capable of concerning the existence of material beings. For we cannot act anything but by our faculties; nor talk of knowledge itself, but by the help of those faculties which are fitted to apprehend even what knowledge is.

Locke then answers Descartes:

8. But yet, if after all this anyone will be so skeptical as to distrust his senses, and to affirm all that we see and hear, feel and taste, think and do, during our whole being, is but the series and deluding appearance of a long dream, whereof there is no reality; and therefore will question the existence of all things, or our knowledge of anything: I must desire him to consider, that, if all be a dream, then he doth but dream that he makes the question, and so it is not much matter that a waking man should answer him. But yet, if he pleases, he may dream that I make him this answer, that the certainty of things existing in *rerum natura* when we have the testimony of our senses for it is not only as great as our frame can attain to, but as our condition needs. For, our faculties being suited not to the full extent of being, nor to a perfect, clear, comprehensive knowledge of things free from all doubt and scruple; but to the preservation of us, in whom they are; and accommodated to the use of life: they serve to our purpose well enough, if they will but give us certain notice of those things, which are convenient or inconvenient to us. For he that sees a candle burning, and hath experimented the force of its flame by putting his finger in it, will little doubt that this is something existing without him, which does him harm, and puts him to great pain: which is assurance enough, when no man requires greater certainty to govern his actions by than what is as certain as his actions themselves. And if our dreamer pleases to try whether the glowing heat of a glass furnace be barely a wandering imagination in a drowsy man's fancy, by putting his hand into it, he may perhaps be wakened into a certainty greater than he could wish, that it is something more than bare imagination. So that this evidence is as great as we can desire, being as certain to us as our pleasure or pain, i.e., happiness or misery; beyond which we have no concernment, either of knowing or being. Such an assurance of the existence of things without us is sufficient to direct us in the attaining the good and avoiding the evil which is caused by them, which is the important concernment we have of being made acquainted with them.

9. In summary, then, when our senses do actually convey into our understanding any idea, we cannot but be satisfied that there doth something *at that time* really exist without us, which doth affect our senses, and by them give notice of itself to our apprehensive faculties, and actually produce that idea which we then perceive.

Locke is now ready to incorporate the traditional metaphysical notion of substance into his theory; for him, substance is that which underlies both the primary and the secondary qualities of a thing.

1. *Ideas of substances, how made.*—The mind being, as I have declared, furnished with a great number of the simple ideas conveyed in by the senses, as they are found in exterior things, or by reflection on its own operations, takes notice, also, that a certain number of these simple ideas go constantly together; which being presumed to belong to one thing, and words being suited to common apprehensions, and made use of for quick dispatch, are called, so united in one subject, by one name; which, by inadvertency, we are apt afterward to talk of and consider as one simple idea, which indeed is a complication of many ideas together: because, as I have said, not imagining how these simple ideas can subsist by themselves, we accustom ourselves to suppose some substratum wherein they do subsist, and from which they do result; which therefore we call 'substance'.

2. *Our ideas of substance in general.*—So that if anyone will examine himself concerning his notion of pure substance in general, he will find he has no other idea of it at all, but only a supposition of he knows not what support of such qualities which are capable of producing simple ideas in us; which qualities are commonly called 'accidents'. If anyone should be asked, 'What is the subject wherein colour or weight inheres?' he would have nothing to say but, 'The solid extended parts.' And if he were demanded, 'What is it that solidity and extension inhere in?' he would not be in a much better case than the Indian . . . who, saying that the world was supported by a great elephant, was asked what the elephant rested on? to which his answer was, 'a great tortoise'; but being again pressed to know what gave support to the broad-backed tortoise, replied—something, he knew not what. And thus here, as in all other cases where we use words without having clear and distinct ideas, we talk like children, who, being questioned what such a thing is which they know not, readily give this satisfactory answer, that it is something, which in truth signifies no more, when so used, either by children or men, but that they know not what; and that the thing they pretend to know and talk of is what they have no distinct idea of at all, and so are perfectly ignorant of it, and in the dark. The idea, then, we have, to which we give the general name 'substance' being nothing but the supposed, but unknown, support of those qualities we find existing, which we imagine cannot subsist *sine re substante*, 'without something to support them', we call that support *substantia*; which, according to the true import of the word, is, in plain English, 'standing under', or 'upholding'.

* * *

Hence, when we talk or think of any particular sort of corporeal substances, as horse, stone, &c., though the idea we have of either of them be but the complication or collection of those several simple ideas of sensible qualities which we used to find united in the thing called 'horse' or 'stone'; yet because we cannot conceive how they should subsist alone, nor one in another, we suppose them existing in, and supported by some common subject; which support we denote by the name 'substance', though it be certain we have no clear or distinct idea of that thing we suppose a support.

- Why does Locke claim that substance is 'we know not what'? Is this conclusion reason to say that we don't know what substance (a thing in itself) is?

For Locke, substance is 'we know not what'. Yet he hesitates to reject all of the pre-existing notions of substance, for he cannot escape the suspicion that talk of 'qualities' makes no sense unless the qualities are the qualities of something. But this suspicion is dispensable according to Locke's own principles. So, it turns out, is his central distinction between primary and secondary qualities, as Berkeley is soon to point out. And, as we shall see, the conclusions that later empiricists develop from Locke's arguments will be shocking, to say the least.

D. Common Sense Undone: Bishop George Berkeley

Beginning from John Locke's 'common-sense' philosophy, Bishop George Berkeley developed the most provocative thesis in all philosophy: **subjective idealism**. It is the doctrine that there are no material substances, no physical objects, only minds and ideas in mind. (His concept of 'idea' comes directly from Locke.) Berkeley developed this surprising position from Locke's thesis by three simple steps. First, he accepted the argument that we have no idea whatsoever what a substance might be, and he agreed that all that we can ever know of a thing are its sensible properties (or 'qualities'). Second, he showed that the distinction between primary and secondary qualities cannot be, as Locke had argued, a distinction between properties inherent in the objects themselves as opposed to properties that the objects simply cause in us. Third, he observed that once one has agreed that all knowledge of the world (except for knowledge of one's own existence and of God) must be based upon experience, the question becomes why we should ever think that there is anything other than our experiences. Locke had argued that our experiences were caused by physical objects, but how could this claim be justified by experience? Since we have no experience of either the objects themselves or their causation, but only of their effects (that is, the ideas they cause in us), a consistent empiricist must give up not only the causal theory of perception but the notion of physical objects as well.

Berkeley developed his theory of subjective idealism in *Treatise Concerning the Principles of Human Knowledge* (1710):

From *Treatise Concerning the Principles of Human Knowledge*
By Bishop George Berkeley

But whatever power I may have over my own thoughts, I find the ideas actually perceiv'd by sense . . . are not creatures of my will. There is therefore some other will or spirit that produces them.

1. It is evident to anyone who takes a survey of the objects of human knowledge, that they are either ideas actually imprinted on the senses, or else such as are perceiv'd by attending to the passions and operations of the mind, or lastly ideas formed by help of memory and imagination; either compounding, dividing, or barely representing those originally perceiv'd in the aforesaid ways. By sight I have the ideas of light and colours with their several degrees and variations. By touch I perceive hard and soft, heat and cold, motion and resistance, and of all these more and less either as to quantity or degree. Smelling furnishes me with odours; the palate with tastes, and hearing conveys sounds to the mind in all their variety of tone and composition. And as several of these are observ'd to accompany each other, they come to be marked by one name, and so to be reputed as one thing. Thus, for example, a certain colour, taste, smell, figure, and consistence having been observ'd to go together, are accounted one distinct thing, signified by the name *apple*. Other collections of ideas constitute a stone, a tree, a book and the like sensible things; which as they are pleasing or disagreeable excite the passions of love, hatred, joy, grief, etc.

2. But besides all that endless variety of ideas or objects of knowledge, there is likewise something which knows or perceives them, and exercises divers operations, as willing, imagining, remembering about them. This perceiving, active being is what I call *mind*, *spirit*, *soul*, or *myself*. By which words I do not denote any one of my ideas, but a thing entirely distinct from them, wherein they exist, or, which is the same thing, whereby they are perceiv'd, for the existence of an idea consists in being perceiv'd.

3. That neither our thoughts, nor passions, nor ideas formed by the imagination, exist without the mind, is what every body will allow. And to me it is no less evident that the various sensations or ideas imprinted on the sense, however blended or

combin'd together (that is whatever objects they compose) cannot exist otherwise than in a mind perceiving them. I think an intuitive knowledge may be obtain'd of this, by anyone that shall attend to what is meant by the term *exist* when apply'd to sensible things. The table I write on, I say, exists, i.e., I see and feel it, and if I were out of my study I should say it existed, meaning thereby that if I was in my study I might perceive it, or that some other spirit actually does perceive it. There was an odour, i.e. it was smelt; there was a sound, i.e. it was heard; a colour or figure and it was perceiv'd by sight or touch. This is all that I can understand by these and the like expressions. For as to what is said of the absolute existence of unthinking things without any relation to their being perceiv'd, that is to me perfectly unintelligible. Their *esse* is *percipi*, (to be is to be perceived) nor is it possible they shou'd have any existence, out of the minds or thinking things which perceive them.

4. It is indeed an opinion strangely prevailing amongst men, that houses, mountains, rivers, and in a word all sensible objects have an existence natural or real, distinct from their being perceiv'd by the understanding. But with how great an assurance and acquiescence soever, this principle may be entertained in the world: yet whoever shall find in his heart to call it in question may, if I mistake not, perceive it to involve a manifest contradiction. For what are the foremention'd objects but the things we perceive by sense, and what do we perceive besides our own ideas or sensations, and is it not plainly repugnant that any one of these or any combination of them shou'd exist unperceiv'd?

So Berkeley has established his central thesis—that 'to be is to be perceived' (*esse est percipi*). In what follows, he argues that there is nothing other than these perceptions, or 'ideas', and it is nonsense to suppose that there are things outside of the mind 'like' our ideas—for 'an idea can be like nothing but an idea'.

6. Some truths there are so near and obvious to the mind that a man need only open his eyes to see 'em. Such I take this important one to be, viz. that all the choir of heaven and furniture of the earth, in a word all those bodies which compose the mighty frame of the world, have not any subsistence without a mind, that their *being* is to be perceiv'd or known; that consequently so long as they are not actually perceiv'd by me, or do not exist in my mind or that of any other created spirit, they must either have no existence at all, or else subsist in the mind of some eternal spirit: it being perfectly unintelligible and involving all the absurdity of abstraction, to attribute to any single part of them an existence independent of a spirit. To make this appear with all the light and evidence of an axiom, it seems sufficient if I can but awaken the reflection of the reader, that he may take an impartial view of his own meaning, and turn his thoughts upon the subject itself, free and disengaged from all embarras of words and prepossession in favour of received mistakes.

7. From what has been said, 'tis evident, there is not any other substance than *spirit* or that which perceives. But for the fuller demonstration of this point, let it be consider'd, the sensible qualities are colour, figure, motion, smell, taste, etc. the ideas perceiv'd by sense. Now for an idea to exist in an unperceiving thing is a manifest contradiction, for to have an idea is all one as to perceive, that therefore wherein colour, figure, etc. exist must perceive them; hence 'tis clear there can be no unthinking substance or *substratum* of those ideas.

8. But say you, though the ideas themselves do not exist without the mind, yet there may be things like them whereof they are copies or resemblances, which things exist without the mind, in an unthinking substance. I answer an idea can be like nothing but an idea, a colour, or figure, can be like nothing but another colour or figure. If we look but never so little into our thoughts, we shall find it impossible for us to conceive a likeness except only between our ideas. Again, I ask whether those suppos'd originals or external things, of which our ideas are the pictures or representations, be themselves perceivable or no? If they are, then they are ideas and we have gain'd our point; but if you say they are not, I appeal to anyone whether it be sense, to assert a colour is like something which is invisible; hard or soft, like something which is intangible, and so of the rest.

At this point Berkeley takes up Locke's distinction between 'primary' and 'secondary' qualities, and maintains that the arguments Locke put forward regarding the latter also can be applied to the former. Primary qualities too can be ideas only, and not properties of matter.

9. Some there are who make a distinction betwixt *primary* and *secondary* qualities: by the former, they mean extension, figure, motion, rest, solidity or impenetrability, and number: by the latter they denote all other sensible qualities as colours, sounds, tastes, etc. The ideas we have of these they acknowledge not to be the resemblances, of any thing existing without the mind or unperceiv'd, but they will have our ideas of the primary qualities to be patterns or images of things which exist without the mind, in an unthinking substance which they call *matter*. By matter, therefore, we are to understand an inert, senseless substance, in which extension, figure, motion, etc. do actually subsist, but it is evident from what we have already shewn, that extension, figure, and motion are only ideas existing in the mind, and that an idea can be like nothing but another idea, and that consequently neither they nor their archetypes can exist in an unperceiving substance. Hence it is plain, that the very notion of what is called *matter* or *corporeal substance*, involves a contradiction in it.

* * *

10. They who assert that figure, motion, and the rest of the primary or original qualities do exist without the mind, in unthinking substances, do at the same time acknowledge that colours, sounds, heat, cold, do not, which they tell us are sensations existing in the mind alone, that depend on and are occasion'd by the different size, texture, motion, of the minute particles of matter. This they take for an undoubted truth, which they can demonstrate beyond all exception. Now if it be certain, that those original qualities are inseparably united with the other sensible qualities, and not, even in thought, capable of being abstracted from them, it plainly follows that they exist only in the mind. But I desire anyone to reflect and try, whether he can by any abstraction of thought, conceive the extension and motion of a body, without all other sensible qualities. For my own part, I see evidently that it is not in my power to frame an idea of a body extended and moving, but I must withal give it some colour or other sensible quality which is acknowleg'd to exist only in the mind. (In short, extension, figure, and motion, abstracted from all other qualities, are inconceivable. Where therefore the other sensible qualities are, there must these be also, i.e. in the mind and no where else.)

* * *

14. I shall further add, that after the same manner, as modern philosophers prove colours, tastes, to have no existence in matter, or without the mind, the same thing may be likewise prov'd of all other sensible qualities whatsoever. Thus, for instance, it is said that heat and cold, are affections only of the mind, and not at all patterns of real beings, existing in the corporeal substances which excite them, for that the same body which appears cold to one hand, seems warm to another. Now why may we not as well argue that figure and extension, are not patterns or resemblances of qualities existing in matter, because to the same eye at different stations, or eyes of a different texture at the same station, they appear various, and cannot therefore be the images of any thing settled and determinate without the mind? Again, 'tis prov'd that sweetness is not really in the sapid thing, because the thing remaining unalter'd the sweetness is changed into bitter, as in case of a fever or otherwise vitiated palate. Is it not as reasonable to say, that motion is not without the mind, since if the succession of ideas in the mind become swifter, the motion, it is acknowledg'd, shall appear slower without any external alteration

15. In short, let anyone consider those arguments, which are thought manifestly to prove that colours, tastes, exist only in the mind, and he shall find they may with equal force, be brought to prove the same thing of extension, figure, and motion. Though it must be confess'd this method of arguing does not so much prove that there is no extension, colour, in an outward object, as that we do not know by sense which is the true extension or colour of the object. But the arguments foregoing plainly shew it to be impossible that any colour or extension at all, or other sensible quality whatsoever, shou'd exist in an unthinking subject without the mind, or in truth, that there shou'd be any such thing as an outward object.

Must there be substances apart from the mind? Berkeley asks. It is true that we are some-how 'affected', but it does not follow that there must be material objects. How would we know of any such objects?

18. But though it were possible that solid, figur'd moveable substances may exist without the mind, corresponding to the ideas we have of bodies, yet how is it possible for us to know this? Either we must know it by sense or by reason. As for our senses, by them we have the knowledge only of our sensations, ideas, or those things that are immediately perceiv'd by sense, call 'em what you will: but they do not inform us that things exist without the mind, or unperceiv'd, like to those which are perceiv'd. This the materialists themselves acknowledge. It remains therefore that if we have any knowledge at all of external things, it must be by reason, inferring their existence from what is immediately perceiv'd by sense. But I do not see what reason can induce us to believe the existence of bodies without the mind, from what we perceive, since the very patrons of matter themselves do not pretend, there is any necessary connection betwixt them and our ideas. I say it is granted on all hands (and what happens in dreams, frenzys and the like puts it beyond dispute) that it is possible we might be affected with all the ideas we have now, though there were no bodies existing without resembling them. Hence it is evident the supposition of external bodies is not necessary for the producing our ideas: since it is granted they are produced sometimes, and might possibly be produced always in the same order, we see them in at present, without their concurrence.

19. But, though we might possibly have all our sensations without them, yet perhaps it may be thought easier to conceive and explain the manner of their production, by supposing external bodies in their likeness rather than otherwise, and so it might be at least probable there are such things as bodies that excite their ideas in our minds. But neither can this be said, for though we give the materialists their external bodies, they by their own confession are never the nearer knowing how our ideas are produced: since they own themselves unable to comprehend in what manner body can act upon spirit, or how it is possible it shou'd imprint any idea in the mind. Hence it is evident the production of ideas or sensations in our minds, can be no reason why we shou'd suppose matter or corporeal substances, since that is acknowledged to remain equally inexplicable with, or without this supposition. If therefore it were possible for bodies to exist without the mind, yet to hold they do so, must needs be a very precarious opinion; since it is to suppose, without any reason at all, that God has created innumerable beings that are entirely useless, and serve to no manner of purpose.

20. In short, though there were external bodies, 'tis impossible we shou'd ever come to know it; and if there were not, we might have the very same reasons to think there were that we have now. Suppose, what no one can deny possible, an intelligence without the help of external bodies to be affected with the same train of sensations or ideas that you are, imprinted in the same order and with like vividness in his mind. I ask whether that intelligence hath not all the reason to believe the existence of corporeal substances, represented by his ideas, and exciting them in his mind, that you can possibly have for believing the same thing? Of this there can be no question, which one consideration were enough to make any reasonable person, suspect the strength of whatever arguments he may think himself to have, for the existence of bodies without the mind.

21. Were it necessary to add any further proof against the existence of matter, after what has been said, I cou'd instance several of those errors and difficulties (not to mention impieties) which have sprung from that tenet. It has occasion'd numberless controversies and disputes in philosophy, and not a few of far greater moment in religion. But I shall not enter into the detail of them in this place, as well because I think, arguments a posteriori are unnecessary for confirming what has been, if I mistake not, sufficiently demonstrated a priori, as because I shall hereafter find occasion to speak somewhat of them.

22. I am afraid I have given cause to think, I am needlessly prolix in handling this subject. For to what purpose is it to dilate on that which may be demonstrated with the utmost evidence in a line or two, to anyone that's capable of the least reflection?

(Continued)

It is but looking into your own thoughts, and so trying whether you can conceive it possible for a sound, or figure, or motion, or colour to exist without the mind, or unperceiv'd. This easy trial may make you see, that what you contend for, is a downright contradiction. Insomuch that I am content to put the whole upon this issue; if you can but conceive it possible for one extended, moveable substance, or in general, for any one idea or any thing like an idea to exist otherwise than in a mind perceiving it, I shall readily give up the cause: and as for all that *compages* of external bodies you contend for, I shall grant you its existence, though you cannot either give me any reason why you believe it exists, or assign any use to it when it is supposed to exist. I say, the bare possibility of your opinions being true, shall pass for an argument that it is so.

23. But say you, surely there's nothing easier than to imagine trees, for instance, in a park, or books existing in a closet, and no body by to perceive them. I answer you may so, there is no difficulty in it: but what is all this, I beseech you, more than framing in your mind certain ideas which you call *books* and *trees*, and at the same time omitting to frame the idea of anyone that may perceive them? But do not you your self perceive or think of them all the while? This therefore is nothing to the purpose: it only shews you have the power of imagining or forming ideas in your mind; but it does not shew that you can conceive it possible, the objects of your thought may exist without the mind; to make out this, it is necessary that you conceive them existing unconceiv'd or unthought of, which is a manifest repugnancy. When we do our utmost to conceive the existence of external bodies, we are all the while only contemplating our own ideas. But the mind taking no notice of itself, is deluded to think it can and does conceive bodies existing unthought of or without the mind; though at the same time they are apprehended by or exist in itself.

- What is subjective idealism? How does Berkeley argue that Locke's view leads to subjective idealism?
- What is Berkeley's argument against the distinction between primary and secondary qualities?
- Do the objects in your bedroom cease to exist when you are not there to perceive them, according to Berkeley? Why is God so important for Berkeley's idealism?

But what, then, can explain the fact that we cannot simply 'think' things into existence by imagining them? And how can we say that a thing exists when no one is there to perceive it? (If a tree falls in the forest, and there's no one there to hear it, does it make a sound?) It is here that God enters the picture as a matter of necessity.

---

29. But whatever power I may have over my own thoughts, I find the ideas actually perceiv'd by sense have not a like dependence on my will. When in broad daylight I open my eyes, 'tis not in my power to chuse whether I shall see or no, or to determine what particular objects shall present themselves to my view; and so likewise as to the hearing and other senses, the ideas imprinted on them are not creatures of my will. There is therefore some other will or spirit that produces them.

30. The ideas of sense are more strong, lively, and distinct than those of the imagination, they have likewise a steddiness, order, and coherence, and are not excited at random, as those which are the effects of human wills often are, but in a regular train or series, the admirable connection whereof sufficiently testifies the wisdom and benevolence of its author. Now the set rules or establish'd methods, wherein the mind we depend on excites in us the ideas of sense, are called the *laws of nature*: and these we learn by experience, which teaches us that such and such ideas are attended with such and such other ideas, in the ordinary course of things.

31. This gives us a sort of foresight, which enables us to regulate our actions for the benefit of life. And without this we shou'd be eternally at a loss, we cou'd not know how to act any thing that might procure us the least pleasure, or remove the least pain of sense. That food nourishes, sleep refreshes, and fire warms us; that to sow in the seed-time is the way to reap in the harvest, and, in general, that to obtain such or such ends, such or such means are conducive, all this we know, not by discovering any necessary connection between our ideas, but only by the observation of the settled laws of nature, without which we shou'd be all in uncertainty and confusion, and a grown man no more know how to manage himself in the affairs of life, than an infant just born.

* * *

33. The ideas imprinted on the senses by the Author of nature are called *real things*, and those excited in the imagination being less regular, vivid, and constant, are more properly termed *ideas*, or *images of things*, which they copy and represent. But then our sensations, be they never so vivid and distinct, are nevertheless *ideas*, i.e. they exist in the mind, or are perceived by it, as truly as the ideas of its own framing. The ideas of sense are allow'd to have more reality in them, i.e. to be more strong, orderly and coherent than the creatures of the mind; but this is no argument that they exist without the mind. They are also less dependent on the spirit, or thinking substance which perceives them, in that they are excited by the will of another and more powerful spirit: yet still they are *ideas*, and certainly no *idea*, whether faint or strong, can exist otherwise than in a mind perceiving it.

This formulation, that the things of the world are nothing other than ideas in the mind of God, is the subject of an intriguing poem by the Argentinian writer Jorge Luis Borges:

'Things'
By Jorge Luis Borges

The fallen volume, hidden by the others
from sight in the recesses of the bookshelves,
and which the days and nights muffle over
with slow and noiseless dust. Also, the anchor
of Sidon, which the seas surrounding England
press down into its blind and soft abyss.
The mirror which shows nobody's reflection
after the house has long been left alone.
Fingernail filings which we leave behind
across the long expanse of time and space.
The indecipherable dust, once Shakespeare.
The changing figurations of a cloud.
The momentary but symmetric rose
which once, by chance, took substance in the shrouded
mirrors of a boy's kaleidoscope.
The oars of Argus, the original ship.
The sandy footprints which the fatal wave
as though asleep erases from the beach.
The colours of a Turner when the lights
are turned out in the narrow gallery
and not a footstep sounds in the deep night.

(Continued)

The other side of the dreary map of the world.
The tenuous spiderweb in the pyramid.
The sightless stone and the inquiring hand.
The dream I had in the approaching dawn
and later lost in the clearing of the day.
The ending and beginning of the epic
of Finsburgh, today a few sparse verses
of iron, unwasted by the centuries.
The mirrored letter on the blotting paper.
The turtle in the bottom of the cistern.
And things that cannot be. The other horn
of the unicorn. The Being, Three in One.
The triangular disc. The imperceptible moment
in which the Eleatic arrow,
motionless in the air, reaches the mark.
The violet pressed between the leaves of Bécquer.
The pendulum which time has stayed in place.
The weapon Odin buried in the tree.
The volume with its pages still unslit.
The echo of the hoofbeats at the charge
Of Junín, which in some enduring mode
never has ceased, is part of the webbed scheme.
The shadow of Sarmiento on the sidewalks.
The voice heard by the shepherd on the mountain.
The skeleton bleaching white in the desert.
The bullet which shot dead Francisco Borges.
The other side of the tapestry. The things
Which no one sees except for Berkeley's God.

- **What do the things listed by Borges have in common? How are they different?**

Returning to Berkeley's *Principles of Human Knowledge*, we find one more argument central to the rationalist–empiricist debate—the Berkeleyan defence against common sense:

38. But after all, say you, it sounds very harsh to say we eat and drink ideas, and are clothed with ideas. I acknowledge it does so; the word 'idea' not being used in common discourse to signify the several combinations of sensible qualities which are called 'things'; and it is certain that any expression which varies from the familiar use of language will seem harsh and ridiculous. But this doth not concern the truth of the proposition, which in other words is no more than to say, we are fed and clothed with those things which we perceive immediately by our senses.

39. If it be demanded why I make use of the word 'idea', and do not rather in compliance with custom call them 'thing'; I answer, I do it for two reasons—first, because the term 'thing' in contradistinction to 'idea', is generally supposed to denote somewhat existing without the mind; secondly, because 'thing' hath a more comprehensive signification than 'idea', including spirit or thinking things as well as ideas. Since therefore the objects of sense exist only in the mind, and are withal thoughtless and inactive, I chose to mark them by the word 'idea', which implies those properties.

Is this where Locke was leading us? If so, it looks as if the 'new' metaphysics is every bit as fantastic as the old ones. But the controversial development of Locke's empiricism has still another step to go.

E. The Congenial Skeptic: David Hume

It isn't very far from Berkeley's subjective idealism to David Hume's outrageous, but seemingly irrefutable, skepticism. Russell, writing about Hume two hundred years later (in 1945), says,

> To refute him has been, ever since he wrote, a favourite pastime among metaphysicians. For my part, I find none of their refutations convincing; nevertheless, I cannot but hope that something less skeptical than Hume's system may be discoverable.

And,

> Hume's skeptical conclusions . . . are equally difficult to refute and to accept. The result was a challenge to philosophers, which, in my opinion, has still not been adequately met.[5]

There have been philosophers who have said—or feared—that Hume's skepticism is the last word in philosophy. In any case, it is one of those positions that no philosophy student can avoid taking seriously.

Hume's *A Treatise of Human Nature* (1739) was written when he was in his early twenties; his ambition was no less than to be the Isaac Newton of philosophy and psychology, following and outdoing John Locke. The book failed to attract much attention (he said 'it fell stillborn from the press'), and Hume turned his attention to other matters, making himself famous as a historian. Later, in 1748, he wrote a more popular version of his earlier *Treatise*, which he called *An Enquiry Concerning Human Understanding*. It was extremely successful, and Hume became widely known as a 'devil's advocate' during his lifetime, a position he generally enjoyed. Both the *Treatise* and the *Enquiry* are firmly committed to Locke's empiricist methodology, but where Locke was generous with doubtful ideas with no clear experiential basis (notably, substance and God), Hume was ruthless. In a famous threatening passage, he bellowed,

> When we run over libraries, persuaded of these [empiricist] principles, what havoc must we make? If we take in our hand any volume of divinity or school metaphysics, for instance, let us ask, Does it contain any abstract reasoning concerning quantity or number? No. Does it contain any experimental reasoning concerning matter of fact and existence? No. Commit it to the flames, for it can contain nothing but sophistry and illusion.[6]

In this unveiled threat to traditional metaphysics we can see in a glance Hume's formidable tactics—the insistence that every justifiable belief must be either a 'relation of ideas'—for example, a statement of mathematics, logic, or a trivial conceptual truth—or a '**matter of fact**', which can be confirmed by appeal to our experience. (This 'either-or' is sometimes called '**Hume's fork**'.) Of course, most of the modern philosophers we have discussed shared this insistence upon justifiability either by reason ('relation of ideas') or by experience. But it is only Hume who realizes the severity of this demand and the embarrassing number of our fundamental beliefs that do not allow **justification** either by reason or experience.

Like his empiricist predecessor, Hume insists that all knowledge begins with basic units of sensory experience. Hume's '**impressions**' (Locke's 'sensations') are these basic units (what we would still call 'sensations' or 'sense-data').

From *A Treatise of Human Nature*
By David Hume

That idea of red, which we form in the dark, and that impression, which strikes our eyes in sun-shine, differ only in degree, not in nature.

All the perceptions of the human mind resolve themselves into two distinct kinds, which I shall call *impressions* and *ideas*. The difference betwixt these consists in the degrees of force and liveliness with which they strike upon the mind, and make their way into our thought or consciousness. Those perceptions, which enter with most force and violence, we may name *impressions*; and under this name I comprehend all our sensations, passions, and emotions, as they make their first appearance in the soul. By *ideas* I mean the faint images of these in thinking and reasoning; such as, for instance, are all the perceptions excited by the present discourse, excepting only, those which arise from the sight and touch, and excepting the immediate pleasure or uneasiness it may occasion. I believe it will not be very necessary to employ many words in explaining this distinction. Everyone of himself will readily perceive the difference betwixt feeling and thinking. The common degrees of these are easily distinguished; tho' it is not impossible but in particular instances they may very nearly approach to each other. Thus in sleep, in a fever, in madness, or in any very violent emotions of soul, our ideas may approach to our impressions: As on the other hand it sometimes happens, that our impressions are so faint and low, that we cannot distinguish them from our ideas. But notwithstanding this near resemblance in a few instances, they are in general so very different, that no one can make a scruple to rank them under distinct heads, and assign to each a peculiar name to mark the difference.

There is another division of our perceptions, which it will be convenient to observe, and which extends itself both to our impressions and ideas. This division is into *simple* and *complex*. Simple perceptions or impressions and ideas are such as admit of no distinction nor separation. The complex are the contrary to these, and may be distinguished into parts. Tho' a particular colour, taste, and smell are qualities all united together in this apple, 'tis easy to perceive they are not the same, but are at least distinguishable from each other.

Having by these divisions given an order and arrangement to our objects, we may now apply ourselves to consider with the more accuracy their qualities and relations. The first circumstance, that strikes my eye, is the great resemblance betwixt our impressions and ideas in every other particular, except their degree of force and vivacity. The one seem to be in a manner the reflection of the other; so that all the perceptions of the mind are double, and appear both as impressions and ideas. When I shut my eyes and think of my chamber, the ideas I form are exact representations of the impressions I felt, nor is there any circumstance of the one, which is not to be found in the other. In running over my other perceptions, I find still the same resemblance and representation. Ideas and impressions appear always to correspond to each other. This circumstance seems to me remarkable, and engages my attention for a moment.

Upon a more accurate survey I find I have been carried away too far by the first appearance, and that I must make use of the distinction of perceptions into *simple and complex*, to limit this general decision, *that all our ideas and impressions are resembling*. I observe, that many of our complex ideas never had impressions, that corresponded to them, and that many of our complex impressions never are exactly copied in ideas. I can imagine to myself such a city as the *New Jerusalem*, whose pavement is gold and walls are rubies, tho' I never saw any such. I have seen *Paris*; but shall I affirm I can form such an idea of that city, as will perfectly represent all its streets and houses in their real and just proportions?

I perceive, therefore, that tho' there is in general a great resemblance betwixt our *complex* impressions and ideas, yet the rule is not universally true, that they are exact copies of each other. We may next consider how the case stands with our *simple* perceptions. After the most accurate examination, of which I am capable, I venture to affirm, that the rule here holds without any exception, and that every simple idea has a simple impression, which resembles it; and every simple impression a correspondent idea. That idea of red, which we form in the dark, and that impression, which strikes our eyes in sunshine, differ only in degree, not in nature. That the case is the same with all our simple impressions and ideas, 'tis impossible to prove by a particular enumeration of them. Everyone may satisfy himself in this point by running over as many as he pleases. But if anyone should deny this universal resemblance, I know of no way of convincing him, but by desiring him to show a simple impression that has not a correspondent idea, or a simple idea, that has not a correspondent impression. If he does not answer this challenge, as 'tis certain he cannot, we may from his silence and our own observation establish our conclusion.

Thus we find, that all simple ideas and impressions resemble each other; and as the complex are formed from them, we may affirm in general, that these two species of perception are exactly correspondent. Having discover'd this relation, which requires no further examination, I am curious to find some other of their qualities. Let us consider how they stand with regard to their existence, and which of the impressions and ideas are causes, and which effects.

The *full* examination of this question is the subject of the present treatise; and therefore we shall here content ourselves with establishing one general proposition. *That all our simple ideas in their first appearance are deriv'd from simple impressions, which are correspondent to them, and which they exactly represent.*

- What is the difference between 'impressions' and 'ideas'?

According to Hume, simple ideas are derived from simple impressions. A simple idea would be something like a red, round image; a simple impression would be seeing a red, round image. More complex ideas, for example, the idea of an apple, are complex arrangements and associations of simple ideas. To justify a belief as knowledge, therefore, we must break up its complex ideas into simple ideas and then find the impressions upon which those ideas are based. If I claim to see an apple, for example, I analyze my experience; my idea that there is an apple out there depends upon my seeing several red, round images from different angles, feeling something smooth, tasting something fruity and tart, and so on. If I claim that there are objects of a certain kind (apples, for example), I must identify the simple ideas and impressions upon which my supposed knowledge is based. And if I make a metaphysical claim about the existence of God or substances, I must either be pre-approved to identify the ideas and impressions upon which such a claim is based, or I must show that it is nothing other than a 'relation of ideas'; otherwise, the claim cannot be justified ('commit it to the flames').

But, to the embarrassment of most metaphysical doctrines, such claims cannot be defended by either of the methods allowed by Hume. They are, by their very nature, about things beyond everyday experience (for example, God, substance) and so are not based upon 'impression'; nor are they '**relations of ideas**' that can be demonstrated by a simple logical or mathematical proof. Therefore, they cannot be justified. The problem, however, is that the same argument extends far beyond the debatable claims of metaphysics and undermines some of the beliefs that are most essential to our everyday experiences as well.

In Hume's philosophy, three such beliefs in particular are singled out for analysis. On the one hand, they are so fundamental to our daily experience and common knowledge that no sane man or woman could possibly doubt them; on the other hand, they are completely without justification.

First, there is our idea of **causation** (or causality), of one event bringing about or causing another event. From this idea, which provides what Hume calls 'the strongest connections' of our experience and 'the cement of the universe', we derive a most important principle, the **principle of universal causation**, which states that every event has its cause (or causes). We invoke such a principle every time we explain anything; for example, the

RELATIONS OF IDEAS

Knowledge that is based solely on the logical and conceptual connections between ideas.

car won't start. We search for the cause, but everything seems to check out—the carburetor, the electrical system, and so on. Now, we might search for hours without finding the cause, but there is one thing that we believe that we know for certain: there must be a cause somewhere—even if it is a very complex cause. What we cannot believe to be possible is that there is no cause. (You may recognize this principle as a version of Leibniz's Principle of Sufficient Reason, which substitutes the more Newtonian notion of 'cause' for the notion of 'reason'.)

Second, because of our presupposed belief in causation and its universal applicability, we are able to think beyond our immediate 'ideas' and predict the future and explain the past. But to do so, we must also believe that our observations of the present will have some relevance in the future, that we can in fact draw valid inductive generalizations from our experience. Of course, we do so all of the time; for example, when I wake up at 6:00 in the morning in the middle of February, I expect the sun to rise within the hour. Why? Because it has always done so. In making every such prediction, we presuppose a **principle of induction,** that is, that the laws of nature that have always held in the past will continue to hold in the future. The principle of induction is sometimes summarized as 'the future will be like the past', which is all right only so long as it is not taken too literally; for of course the future is never just like the past—since you began reading this paragraph, for example, you have aged by fifteen seconds, you have added a whole expression to your knowledge, and (unless you were eating or drinking) you have lost a tiny bit of weight as well. But the laws of nature, at least, do not change from moment to moment.

Third, there is our belief in the 'external world', that is, a physical or material world that exists independently of our impressions and ideas, which it presumably causes in us. Berkeley had already done Hume's work for him here. Hume, following Berkeley, also rejects all notions of substance as unintelligible, including even that minimal 'we know not what' of John Locke. But where Berkeley turned the rejection of matter and substance into a metaphysics (namely, his subjective idealism) and used it to defend the existence of God, Hume rejects this idealist metaphysics as well and remains wholly skeptical, refusing to accept the existence of God. He remains firm in his insistence that our belief in the existence of anything is no different from 'the idea of what we conceive to be existent'.

We can see that these three basic beliefs are intimately tied together; the notion of cause supports the principle of induction,[7] and the causal theory of perception supports our belief in the 'external world'. Accordingly, Hume takes causation to be the central idea of all reasoning,[8] that is, all attempts to connect separate ideas together in a single belief. Hume's arguments are both elegant and simple to follow. He begins with a statement that all human knowledge must be either 'relations of ideas' or 'matters of fact', explains what he means by each of these two terms, shows how it is that 'the relations of cause and effect' are the basis of all reasoning, and then proceeds to show that such reasoning can be neither a relation of ideas nor a simple matter of fact.

From *An Enquiry Concerning Human Understanding*
By David Hume

All inferences from experience . . . are effects of custom, not of reasoning.

All the objects of human reason or enquiry may naturally be divided into two kinds, to wit, *Relations of Ideas*, and *Matters of Fact*. Of the first kind are the sciences of Geometry, Algebra, and Arithmetic; and in short, every affirmation which is either intuitively or demonstratively certain. *That the square of the hypotenuse is equal to the square of the two sides*, is a proposition which expresses a relation between these figures.

That three times five is equal to the half of thirty, expresses a relation between these numbers. Propositions of this kind are discoverable by the mere operation of thought, without dependence on what is anywhere existent in the universe. Though there never were a circle or triangle in nature, the truths demonstrated by Euclid would for ever retain their certainty and evidence.

Matters of fact, which are the second objects of human reason, are not ascertained in the same manner; nor is our evidence of their truth, however great, of a like nature with the foregoing. The contrary of every matter of fact is still possible; because it can never imply a contradiction, and is conceived by the mind with the same facility and distinctness, as if ever so conformable to reality. *That the sun will not rise tomorrow* is no less intelligible a proposition, and implies no more contradiction than the affirmation, *that it will rise*. We should in vain, therefore, attempt to demonstrate its falsehood. Were it demonstratively false, it would imply a contradiction, and could never be distinctly conceived by the mind.

It may, therefore, be a subject worthy of curiosity, to enquire what is the nature of that evidence which assures us of any real existence and matter of fact, beyond the present testimony of our senses, or the records of our memory. This part of philosophy, it is observable, has been little cultivated, either by the ancients or moderns; and therefore our doubts and errors, in the prosecution of so important an enquiry, may be the more excusable; while we march through such difficult paths without any guide or direction. They may even prove useful, by exciting curiosity, and destroying that implicit faith and security, which is the bane of all reasoning and free enquiry. The discovery of defects in the common philosophy, if any such there be, will not, I presume, be a discouragement, but rather an incitement, as is usual, to attempt something more full and satisfactory than has yet been proposed to the public.

All reasonings concerning matter of fact seem to be founded on the relations of *Cause and Effect*. By means of that relation alone we can go beyond the evidence of our memory and senses. If you were to ask a man, why he believes any matter of fact, which is absent; for instance, that his friend is in the country, or in France; he would give you a reason; and this reason would be some other fact; as a letter received from him, or the knowledge of his former resolutions and promises. A man finding a watch or any other machine in a desert island, would conclude that there had once been men in that island. All our reasonings concerning fact are of the same nature. And here it is constantly supposed that there is a connection between the present fact and that which is inferred from it. Were there nothing to bind them together, the inference would be entirely precarious. The hearing of an articulate voice and rational discourse in the dark assures us of the presence of some person. Why? Because these are the effects of the human make and fabric, and closely connected with it. If we anatomize all the other reasonings of this nature, we shall find that they are founded on the relation of cause and effect, and that this relation is either near or remote, direct or collateral. Heat and light are collateral effects of fire, and the one effect may justly be inferred from the other.

Hume's argument, which we shall see again and again, is that we explain our experiences and events by appeal to other experiences and events. If I burn my finger and wonder how, I look down and see that I have just placed my hand too near the stovetop burner. I explain that the heat of the burner is the cause and the burn is the effect of the hot burner. Indeed, we are perplexed whenever we cannot find some causal **explanation**, and the suggestion that there might not be one ('there was no cause; you just burned yourself, that's all') is all but unintelligible to us. But now, Hume asks, where do we get this knowledge of causes and effects?

If we would satisfy ourselves, therefore, concerning the nature of that evidence, which assures us of matters of fact, we must enquire how we arrive at the knowledge of cause and effect.

I shall venture to affirm, as a general proposition, which admits of no exception, that the knowledge of this relation is not, in any instance, attained by reasonings a priori; but arises entirely from experience,

(Continued)

when we find that any particular objects are constantly conjoined with each other. Let an object be presented to a man of ever so strong natural reason and abilities; if that object be entirely new to him, he will not be able, by the most accurate examination of its sensible qualities, to discover any of its causes or effects. Adam, though his rational faculties be supposed, at the very first, entirely perfect, could not have inferred from the fluidity and transparency of water that it would suffocate him, or from the light and warmth of fire that it would consume him. No object ever discovers, by the qualities which appear to the senses, either the causes which produced it, or the effects which will arise from it; nor can our reason, unassisted by experience, ever draw any inference concerning real existence and matter of fact.

This proposition, *that causes and effects are discoverable, not by reason but by experience*, will readily be admitted with regard to such objects, as we remember to have once been altogether unknown to us; since we must be conscious of the utter inability, which we then lay under, of foretelling what would arise from them. Present two smooth pieces of marble to a man who has no tincture of natural philosophy; he will never discover that they will adhere together in such a manner as to require great force to separate them in a direct line, while they make so small a resistance to lateral pressure. Such events, as bear little analogy to the common course of nature, are also readily confessed to be known only by experience; nor does any man imagine that the explosion of gunpowder, or the attraction of a lodestone, could ever be discovered by arguments a priori. In like manner, when an effect is supposed to depend upon an intricate machinery or secret structure of parts, we make no difficulty in attributing all our knowledge of it to experience. Who will assert that he can give the ultimate reason, why milk or bread is proper nourishment for a man, not for a lion or a tiger?

But the same truth may not appear, at first sight, to have the same evidence with regard to events, which have become familiar to us from our first appearance in the world, which bear a close analogy to the whole course of nature, and which are supposed to depend on the simple qualities of objects, without any secret structure of parts. We are apt to imagine that we could discover these effects by the mere operation of our reason, without experience. We fancy, that were we brought on a sudden into this world, we could at first have inferred that one billiard ball would communicate motion to another upon impulse; and that we

needed not to have waited for the event, in order to pronounce with certainty concerning it. Such is the influence of custom, that, where it is strongest, it not only covers our natural ignorance, but even conceals itself, and seems not to take place, merely because it is found in the highest degree.

But to convince us that all the laws of nature, and all the operations of bodies without exception, are known only by experience, the following reflections may, perhaps, suffice. Were any object presented to us, and were we required to pronounce concerning the effect, which will result from it, without consulting past observation; after what manner, I beseech you, must the mind proceed in this operation? It must invent or imagine some event, which it ascribes to the object as its effect; and it is plain that this invention must be entirely arbitrary. The mind can never possibly find the effect in the supposed cause, by the most accurate scrutiny and examination. For the effect is totally different from the cause, and consequently can never be discovered in it. Motion in the second billiard ball is a quite distinct event from motion in the first; nor is there anything in the one to suggest the smallest hint of the other. A stone or piece of metal raised into the air, and left without any support, immediately falls: but to consider the matter a priori, is there anything we discover in this situation which can beget the idea of a downward, rather than an upward, or any other motion in the stone or metal?

And as the first imagination or invention of a particular effect, in all natural operations, is arbitrary, where we consult not experience; so must we also esteem the supposed tie or connection between the cause and effect, which binds them together, and renders it impossible that any other effect could result from the operation of that cause. When I see, for instance, a billiard ball moving in a straight line towards another; even suppose motion in the second ball should by accident be suggested to me, as the result of their contact or impulse; may I not conceive, that a hundred different events might as well follow from that cause? May not both these balls remain at absolute rest? May not the first ball return in a straight line, or leap off from the second in any line or direction? All these suppositions are consistent and conceivable. Why then should we give the preference to one, which is no more consistent or conceivable than the rest? All our reasonings a priori will never be able to show us any foundations for this preference.

Hume's argument so far is that we do not know particular causes and effects through reason, but only through experience. Because you have seen it so many times, you know that a billiard ball moving toward and striking another billiard ball sets the second in motion on a predictable path. But if you had never seen anything like it before—perhaps if you were Adam or Eve (pool tables were not created until the eighth day of creation)—you would not have any idea of what to expect. Both balls might stop dead. Both might explode. The second might start a lawsuit. Prediction of cause and effect, in other words, depends upon prior experience, and no amount of mere reasoning will suffice by itself.

In a word, then, every effect is a distinct event from its cause. It could not, therefore, be discovered in the cause, and the first invention or conception of it, a priori, must be entirely arbitrary. And even after it is suggested, the conjunction of it with the cause must appear equally arbitrary; since there are always many other effects, which, to reason, must seem fully as consistent and natural. In vain, therefore, should we pretend to determine any single event, or infer any cause or effect, without the assistance of observation and experience.

* * *

When we reason a priori, and consider merely any object or cause, as it appears to the mind, independent of all observation, it never could suggest to us the notion of any distinct object, such as its effect; much less, show us the inseparable and inviolable connection between them. A man must be very sagacious who could discover by reasoning that crystal is the effect of heat, and ice of cold, without being previously acquainted with the operations of these qualities.

In this argument, we see Hume applying the first half of his 'fork' to the idea of causation. The idea of cause and effect cannot be a relation of ideas, because, for example, no matter how closely we examine the idea of fire, we will never discover the idea of its causing gunpowder to explode. Reasoning alone cannot reveal the causes or effects of particular events. At the outset of this argument, Hume also suggests that the idea of causation is not discoverable through perception either: Although we perceive many different qualities of fire, we never perceive its power to cause gunpowder to explode. Hume concludes that the idea of cause and effect must be derived from our experience of the constant conjunction of two events. We observe, for example, that every time we set a match to gunpowder it explodes; and because we expect the future to be like the past, we infer that the application of fire is the cause of the gunpowder's exploding. In short, our knowledge of causes is arrived at through induction from past experiences.

Hume's argument against induction, and in particular against the inductive principle that the future will be like the past, takes exactly the same form. Again he begins with his 'fork' between 'relations of ideas' and 'matters of fact', and again he proves that one of the basic assumptions of all our thinking, the principle of induction, cannot be established either way:

But we have not yet attained any tolerable satisfaction with regard to the question first proposed. Each solution still gives rise to a new question as difficult as the foregoing, and leads us on to further enquiries. When it is asked, *What is the nature of all our reasonings concerning matter of fact?* the proper answer seems to be, that they are founded on the relation of cause and effect. When again it is asked, *What is the foundation of all our reasonings and conclusions concerning that relation?* it may be replied in one word, Experience. But if we still carry on our shifting humour, and ask, *What is the foundation of all conclusions from experience?* this implies a new question, which may be of more difficult solution and explication. Philosophers, that give themselves airs of superior wisdom and sufficiency, have a hard task when they encounter

(*Continued*)

persons of inquisitive dispositions, who push them from every corner to which they retreat, and who are sure at last to bring them to some dangerous dilemma. The best expedient to prevent this confusion, is to be modest in our pretensions; and even to discover the difficulty ourselves before it is objected to us. By this means, we may make a kind of merit of our very ignorance.

I shall content myself, in this section, with an easy task, and shall pretend only to give a negative answer to the question here proposed. I say then, that, even after we have experience of the operations of cause and effect, our conclusions from that experience are *not* founded on reasoning, or any process of the understanding. This answer we must endeavour both to explain and to defend.

It must certainly be allowed, that nature has kept us at a great distance from all her secrets, and has afforded us only the knowledge of a few superficial qualities of objects; while she conceals from us those powers and principles on which the influence of those objects entirely depends. Our senses inform us of the colour, weight, and consistence of bread; but neither sense nor reason can ever inform us of those qualities which fit it for the nourishment and support of a human body. Sight or feeling conveys an idea of the actual motion of bodies; but as to that wonderful force or power, which would carry on a moving body forever in a continued change of place, and which bodies never lose but by communicating it to others; of this we cannot form the most distant conception. But notwithstanding this ignorance of natural powers and principles, we always presume, when we see like sensible qualities, that they have like secret powers, and expect that effects, similar to those which we have experienced, will follow from them. If a body of like colour and consistence with that bread, which we have formerly eat, be presented to us, we make no scruple of repeating the experiment, and foresee, with certainty, like nourishment and support. Now this is a process of the mind or thought, of which I would willingly know the foundation. It is allowed on all hands that there is no known connection between the sensible qualities and the secret powers; and consequently, that the mind is not led to form such a conclusion concerning their constant and regular conjunction, by anything which it knows of their nature. As to past *Experience*, it can be allowed to give *direct* and *certain* information of those precise objects only, and that precise period of time, which fell under its cognizance: but why this experience should be extended to future times, and to other objects, which for aught we know, may be only in appearance similar; this is the main question on which I would insist. The bread, which I formerly eat, nourished me; that is, a body of such sensible qualities was, at that time, endued with such secret powers: but does it follow, that other bread must also nourish me at another time, and that like sensible qualities must always be attended with like secret powers? The consequence seems nowise necessary. At least, it must be acknowledged that there is here a consequence drawn by the mind; that there is a certain step taken; a process of thought, and an inference, which wants to be explained. These two propositions are far from being the same, *I have found that such an object has always been attended with such an effect*, and *I foresee, that other objects, which are, in appearance, similar, will be attended with similar effects.*

The argument so far is just like the argument regarding cause and effect, namely, that it is only from experience that we know the properties and effects of things and events, that moving bodies cause others to move, for instance, or that eating bread gives humans nourishment. But now Hume distinguishes two propositions: (1) I have recognized a certain cause-and-effect relationship in my past experience, and (2) I predict that a similar cause-and-effect relationship will hold in the future also. The reference is surely reasonable, Hume says, but again he forces us to say *why* such an inference is reasonable, and he argues that we cannot do so.

I shall allow, if you please, that the one proposition may justly be inferred from the other: I know, in fact, that it always is inferred. But if you insist that the inference is made by a chain of reasoning, I desire you to produce the reasoning. The connection between these propositions is not intuitive. There is required a medium, which may enable the mind to draw such an inference, if indeed it be drawn by reasoning and argument. What that medium is, I must confess, passes my comprehension; and it is incumbent on those to produce it, who assert that it really exists, and is the origin of all our conclusions concerning matter of fact.

This negative argument must certainly, in process of time, become altogether convincing, if many penetrating and able philosophers shall turn their enquiries this way and no one be ever able to discover any connecting proposition or intermediate step, which supports the understanding in this conclusion. But as the question is yet new, every reader may not trust so far to his own penetration, as to conclude, because an argument escapes his enquiry, that therefore it does not really exist. For this reason it may be requisite to venture upon a more difficult task; and enumerating all the branches of human knowledge, endeavour to show that none of them can afford such an argument.

Next, Hume presents his 'fork': the division of all knowledge into reasoning about relations of ideas (which he here calls 'demonstrative') and reasoning about matters of fact (which he here calls 'moral'). He says that it is clear from the above arguments that no demonstrative reasoning is available to justify our predictions of the future. But then he goes on to argue that no reasoning about matters of fact—no appeal to experience— can justify our propensity to make predictions either. For in order to justify our belief that the future will resemble the past on the basis of our experience, we would in effect be arguing that we know that the future will be like the past because in the past the future has always been like the past, and this is 'begging the question' and a 'vicious circle', in which one defends a proposition by referring it back to itself. Therefore our propensity for predicting can't be justified by appealing to experience either, which leaves us without any justification at all.

All reasonings may be divided into two kinds, namely, demonstrative reasoning, or that concerning relations of ideas, and moral reasoning, or that concerning matters of fact and existence. That there are no demonstrative arguments in the case seems evident; since it implies no contradiction that the course of nature may change, and that an object, seemingly like those which we have experienced, may be attended with different or contrary effects. May I not clearly and distinctly conceive that a body, falling from the clouds, and which, in all other respects, resembles snow, has yet the taste of salt or feeling of fire? Is there any more intelligible proposition than to affirm, that all the trees will flourish in December and January, and decay in May and June? Now whatever is intelligible, and can be distinctly conceived, implies no contradiction, and can never be proved false by any demonstrative argument or abstract reasoning a priori.

If we be, therefore, engaged by arguments to put trust in past experience, and make it the standard of our future judgment, these arguments must be probable only, or such as regard matter of fact and real existence, according to the division above mentioned. But that there is no argument of this kind, must appear, if our explication of that species of reasoning be admitted as solid and satisfactory. We have said that all arguments concerning existence are founded on the relation of cause and effect; that our knowledge of that relation is derived entirely from experience; and that all our experimental conclusions proceed upon the supposition that the future will be conformable to the past. To endeavour, therefore, the proof of this last supposition by probable arguments, or arguments regarding existence, must be evidently going in a circle, and taking that for granted, which is the very point in question.

* * *

When a man says, *I have found, in all past instances, such sensible qualities conjoined with such secret powers*; and when he says, *Similar sensible qualities will always be conjoined with similar secret powers*, he is not guilty
(Continued)

of tautology, nor are these propositions in any respect the same. You say that the one proposition is an inference from the other. But you must confess that the inference is not intuitive; neither is it demonstrative: Of what nature is it, then? To say it is experimental, is begging the question. For all inferences from experience suppose, as their foundation, that the future will resemble the past, and that similar powers will be conjoined with similar sensible qualities. If there be any suspicion that the course of nature may change, and that the past may be no rule for the future, all experience becomes useless, and can give rise to no inference or conclusion. It is impossible, therefore, that any arguments from experience can prove this resemblance of the past to the future; since all these arguments are founded on the supposition of that resemblance. Let the source of things be allowed hitherto ever so regular; that alone, without some new argument or inference, proves not that, for the future, it will continue so. In vain do you pretend to have learned the nature of bodies from your past experience. Their secret nature, and consequently all their effects and influence may change, without any change in their sensible qualities. This happens sometimes, and with regard to some objects: Why may it not happen always, and with regard to all objects? What logic, what process of argument secures you against this position? My practice, you say, refutes my doubts. But you mistake the purport of my question. As an agent, I am quite satisfied in the point; but as a philosopher, who has some share of curiosity, I will not say skepticism, I want to learn the foundation of this inference. No reading, no enquiry has yet been able to remove my difficulty, or give me satisfaction in a matter of such importance. Can I do better than propose the difficulty to the public, even though, perhaps, I have small hopes of obtaining a solution? We shall at least, by this means, be sensible of our ignorance, if we do not augment our knowledge.

- What is 'Hume's fork'? Which three beliefs does he claim are unjustified as a result? How does Hume undermine our ability to make predictions?

Hume's arguments against the principle of universal causation and the principle of induction are also arguments against rationalism in general. What he is saying is that reasoning alone, without information from experience, cannot tell us anything whatever about the world. Reasoning **a priori**, that is, thinking without any appeal to experience, is incapable of proving any of those theorems so important to the rationalists, such as the existence of substances, a God, and causes, as well as the conformity of future events to past ones. His arguments are at the same time skeptical ones, since he reasons that even an appeal to experience cannot prove the reality of any of these things.

What is the solution to these skeptical doubts? If we seek a justification or defence, there is none, according to Hume. But in everyday life, such philosophical doubts need have no effect at all, for though there is no justification of our beliefs, we can yet remain confident that at least there is an explanation for them.

Suppose a person, though endowed with the strongest faculties of reason and reflection, to be brought on a sudden into this world; he would, indeed, immediately observe a continual succession of objects and one event following another, but he would not be able to discover anything further. He would not at first, by any reasoning, be able to reach the idea of cause and effect, since the particular powers by which all natural operations are performed never appear to the senses; nor is it reasonable to conclude, merely because one event in one instance precedes another, that therefore the one is the cause, the other the effect. The conjunction may be arbitrary and casual. There may be no reason to infer the existence of one from the appearance of the other: and, in a word, such a person without more experience could never employ his conjecture or reasoning concerning any matter of fact or be assured of anything beyond what was immediately present to his memory or senses.

Suppose again that he has acquired more experience and has lived so long in the world as to have observed similar objects or events to be constantly conjoined together—what is the consequence of this experience? He immediately infers the existence of one object from the appearance of the other, yet he has not, by all his experience, acquired any idea or knowledge of the secret power by which the one object produces the other, nor is it by any process of reasoning he is engaged to draw this inference; but still he finds himself determined to draw it, and though he should be convinced that his understanding has no part in the operation, he would nevertheless continue in the same course of thinking. There is some other principle which determines him to form such a conclusion.

This principle is *custom* or *habit*. For wherever the repetition of any particular act or operation produces a propensity to renew the same act or operation without being impelled by any reasoning or process of the understanding, we always say that this propensity is the effect of *custom*. By employing that word we pretend not to have given the ultimate reason of such a propensity. We only point out a principle of human nature which is universally acknowledged, and which is well known by its effects. Perhaps we can push our inquiries no further or pretend to give the cause of this cause, but must rest contented with it as the ultimate principle, which we can assign, of all our conclusions from experience. It is sufficient satisfaction that we can go so far without repining at the narrowness of our faculties, because they will carry us no further. And it is certain we here advance a very intelligible proposition at least, if not a true one, when we assert that after the constant conjunction of two objects, heat and flame, for instance, weight and solidity, we are determined by custom alone to expect the one from the appearance of the other. This hypothesis seems even the only one which explains the difficulty why we draw from a thousand instances an inference which we are not able to draw from one instance that is in no respect different from them. Reason is incapable of any such variation. The conclusions which it draws from considering one circle are the same which it would form upon surveying all the circles in the universe. But no man, having seen only one body move after being impelled by another, could infer that every other body will move after a like impulse. All inferences from experience, therefore, are effects of custom, not of reasoning.

In other words, there is no 'solution to these skeptical doubts', but, at most, what Hume calls 'a skeptical solution'. It means an end, not only to philosophy, but to all **rational** inquiry and all claims that we can know anything (even that the sun will rise tomorrow, or that you are reading this text). You might think that such conclusions would have driven Hume mad or caused him such confusion that he would have been incapable of coping with the most everyday chores. Yet we know that he was a most jovial and practical sort of fellow. As a philosopher, he has been driven right up against the wall of Plato's cave. But he remains unperturbed. In a famous passage at the end of the *Treatise*, he simply remarks:

Most fortunately it happens, that since reason is incapable of dispelling these clouds, nature herself suffices to that purpose, and cures me of this philosophical melancholy and delirium, either by relaxing this bent of mind, or by some avocation, and lively impression of my senses, which obliterate all these chimeras. I dine, I play a game of backgammon, I converse, and am merry with my friends; and when after three or four hours' amusement, I wou'd return to these speculations, they appear so cold, and strain'd, and ridiculous, that I cannot find in my heart to enter into them any further.[9]

> • Why does Hume think that rationality alone is unable to give us knowledge? Why does he think empiricism alone is unable to give us knowledge? What is Hume's 'solution' to this problem?

Perhaps you too find these speculations cold, strained, and ridiculous. If so, however, this is not the time to run off to dinner and an evening of games and conversation. Something has gone very wrong. The empiricist attempt to restore common sense to philosophy has ended in the least commonsensical philosophy imaginable. A person who really believed that there is no material world or that the future will not resemble the past (and therefore, having been hit by a truck last week, steps into the street convinced that it will not happen again) would be crazy! How can our intellects be so out of joint with our experience or our philosophy so far away from practical life? How serious is Hume's skepticism?

F. Common Sense Defended: Thomas Reid and G.E. Moore

One thinker who emphatically denied that Humean skepticism was the last word in epistemology was Hume's countryman and contemporary, Thomas Reid. According to Reid, philosophy must respect the authority of common-sense beliefs; and when a philosopher's conclusions contradict such beliefs, we should agree with common sense and disagree with the philosopher, no matter how ingenious or cogent her arguments may initially seem:

> If there are certain principles, as I think there are, which the constitution of our nature leads us to believe, and which we are under a necessity to take for granted in the common concerns of life, without being able to give a reason for them—these are what we call *the principles of common sense*; and what is manifestly contrary to them is what we call absurd.[10]

What, exactly, does Reid mean by 'the **principles of common sense**'? He uses this term to refer to certain fundamental beliefs or assumptions that fit the following descriptions: (a) Principles that have been accepted by virtually all human beings at all times, in all places, and in all cultures. In other words, belief in them is practically universal. (b) Principles that we begin to believe so early in our lives that we are unable to remember a time when we did not take them for granted. So such convictions are evidently derived not from experience or education, but from human nature itself. (c) Principles for which we can give no positive arguments as support because there is nothing more evident or obvious from which they could be deduced or derived (hence Reid calls them 'first principles'). (d) Principles that are psychologically irresistible—those that we can't help but believe and cannot doubt or shake off—since they have their root in 'the constitution of our nature' (that is—they are not the product of reasoning or inference). (e) Principles that we find indispensable and take for granted 'in the common concerns of life'. (And it is a very good thing for us that we do. If we could doubt them, the consequences would be dire. For without common sense to guide us through life, we would either meet with a quick and nasty end, or find ourselves locked up for our own protection.) (f) Principles that we cannot sensibly deny or negate. Indeed, the denial or negation of such a principle would strike us not merely as false, but as downright preposterous. If anyone other than a philosopher professed to doubt such principles, we would most likely regard that person as a fool or a madman.

Here are just a few examples of Reidian 'principles of common sense', or 'first principles':

From *Essays on the Intellectual Powers of Man*
By Thomas Reid

1. First, then, I hold, as a first principle, the existence of everything of which I am conscious.
2. Another first principle, I think, is, *That the thoughts of which I am conscious, are the thoughts of a being which I call MYSELF, my MIND, my PERSON.*
3. Another first principle I take to be—*That those things did really happen which I distinctly remember.*
4. Another first principle is, *Our own personal identity and continued existence, as far back as we remember anything distinctly.*
5. Another first principle is, *That those things do really exist which we distinctly perceive by our senses, and are what we perceive them to be.*
6. Another first principle, I think, is, *That we have some degree of power over our actions, and the determinations of our will.*
7. Another first principle is—*That the natural faculties, by which we distinguish truth from error, are not fallacious.*
8. Another first principle relating to existence, is, *That there is life and intelligence in our fellow-men with whom we converse.*
9. Another first principle I take to be, *That certain features of the countenance, sounds of the voice, and gestures of the body indicate certain thoughts and dispositions of mind.*
10. Another first principle appears to me to be— *That there is a certain regard due to human testimony in matters of fact, and even to human authority in matters of opinion.*
11. *There are many events depending upon the will of man, in which there is a self-evident probability, great or less, according to circumstances.*
12. The last principle of contingent truths I mention, is, *That, in the phenomena of nature, what is to be, will probable be like to what has been in similar circumstances.*

I do not at all affirm, that those I have mentioned are all the first principles from which we may reason concerning contingent truths. Such enumerations, even when made after much reflection, are seldom perfect.

To see how Reid's commitment to common sense informs his epistemology, let's look at his reply to external world skepticism (that is—the thesis that no one can know anything about the world outside his or her own mind). Observing that such skepticism contradicts the common-sense belief that our senses can be trusted, Reid answers the skeptic's challenge with a challenge of his own:

From *An Inquiry into the Human Mind on the Principles of Common Sense*
By Thomas Reid

Why, sir, should I believe the faculty of reason more than that of perception?

I am aware that this belief which I have in perception stands exposed to the strongest batteries of skepticism. But they make no great impression upon it. The skeptic asks me, Why do you believe the existence of the external object which you perceive? This belief, sir, is none of my manufacture; it came from the mint of Nature; it bears her image and superscription; and, if it is not right, the fault is not mine: I even took it upon trust, and without suspicion. Reason, says the skeptic, is the only judge of truth, and you ought to throw off every opinion and every belief that is not grounded on reason. Why, sir, should I believe the faculty of reason more than that of perception?—they came both out of the same shop, and were made by the same artist; and

(Continued)

if he puts one piece of false ware into my hands, what should hinder him from putting another?

Perhaps the skeptic will agree to distrust reason, rather than give any credit to perception. For, says he, since, by your own concession, the object which you perceive, and that act of your mind by which you perceive it, are quite different things, the one may exist without the other; and, as the object may exist without being perceived, so the perception may exist without an object. There is nothing so shameful in a philosopher as to be deceived and deluded; and, therefore, you ought to resolve firmly to withhold assent, and to throw off this belief of external objects, which may be all delusion. For my part, I will never attempt to throw it off; and, although the sober part of mankind will not be very anxious to know my reasons, yet, if they can be of use to any skeptic, they are these—

First, because it is not in my power: why, then, should I make a vain attempt? It would be agreeable to fly to the moon, and to make a visit to Jupiter and Saturn; but, when I know that Nature has bound me down by the law of gravitation to this planet which I inhabit, I rest contented, and quietly suffer myself to be carried along in its orbit. My belief is carried along by perception, as irresistibly as my body by the earth. And the greatest skeptic will find himself to be in the same condition. He may struggle hard to disbelieve the informations of his senses, as a man does to swim against a torrent; but, ah! it is in vain. It is in vain that he strains every nerve, and wrestles with nature, and with every object that strikes upon his senses. For, after all, when his strength is spent in the fruitless attempt, he will be carried down the torrent with the common herd of believers.

Secondly, I think it would not be prudent to throw off this belief, if it were in my power. If Nature intended to deceive me, and impose upon me by false appearances, and I, by my great cunning and profound logic, have discovered the imposture, prudence would dictate to me, in this case, even to put up [with] this indignity done me, as quietly as I could, and not to call her an impostor to her face, lest she should be even with me in another way. For what do I gain by resenting this injury? You ought at least not to believe what she says. This indeed seems reasonable, if she intends to impose upon me. But what is the consequence? I resolve not to believe my senses. I break my nose against a post that comes in my way; I step into a dirty kennel; and, after twenty such wise and rational actions, I am taken up and clapped into a mad-house. Now, I confess I would rather make one of the credulous fools whom Nature imposes upon, than of those wise and rational philosophers who resolve to withhold assent at all this expense. If a man pretends to be a skeptic with regard to the informations of sense, and yet prudently keeps out of harm's way as other men do, he must excuse my suspicion, that he either acts the hypocrite, or imposes upon himself. For, if the scale of his belief were so evenly poised as to lean no more to one side than to the contrary, it is impossible that his actions could be directed by any rules of common prudence.

Thirdly, although the two reasons already mentioned are perhaps two more than enough, I shall offer a third. I gave implicit belief to the informations of Nature by my senses, for a considerable part of my life, before I had learned so much logic as to be able to start a doubt concerning them. And now, when I reflect upon what is past, I do not find that I have been imposed upon by this belief. I find that without it I must have perished by a thousand accidents. I find that without it I should have been no wiser now than when I was born. I should not even have been able to acquire that logic which suggests these skeptical doubts with regard to my senses. Therefore, I consider this instinctive belief as one of the best gifts of Nature. I thank the Author of my being, who bestowed it upon me before the eyes of my reason were opened, and still bestows it upon me, to be my guide where reason leaves me in the dark. And now I yield to the direction of my senses, not from instinct only, but from confidence and trust in a faithful and beneficent Monitor, grounded upon the experience of his paternal care and goodness.

Now, what is Reid telling us in this passage? Three things, essentially. First, he is reminding us that his skeptical adversary takes it for granted that reason is trustworthy. (Why? Well, remember that our skeptic relies on reason to argue for the thesis of skepticism; and if she thinks the faculty of reason can be trusted to lead us to the truth, she must surely think that this faculty is basically trustworthy, mustn't she?). Second, Reid is reminding us that the skeptic does not think nearly so highly of perception. (Why? Because our skeptic is convinced that there are good philosophical grounds for doubting the testimony of the senses.). Third, and most importantly, he is accusing the skeptic of gross inconsistency. Reid's challenge is simple: Why favour reason over perception? In other words, what gives the skeptic the right to trust the first faculty but distrust the second? Epistemologically speaking, reason and perception appear to be in the same boat: both are cognitive faculties human beings possess by nature—'natural faculties, by which we distinguish truth from error'. And when you come right down to it, isn't whatever justification you have for believing in reason also a justification for believing in perception? Isn't whatever excuse you have for not believing in perception also an excuse for not believing in reason? After all, both faculties 'came out of the same shop' and have the same origin, be it Nature or be it God; and neither faculty can be used to prove itself trustworthy, because any such 'proof' would assume the very thing to be proven. As Reid remarks elsewhere, trying to use reason to prove reason's reliability, or perception to prove perception's reliability, would be rather like asking a man whom you suspect may be a liar if you can trust him.

The moral? If you are willing to trust reason, you should be willing to trust perception as well; and if you distrust perception, you should also distrust reason. If, however, you choose to distrust reason instead of trusting perception, you have effectively silenced yourself; for without reason, you can no longer argue for skepticism—or, for that matter, anything else. So skepticism, instead of being the flower of philosophy, is its death.

It is important to see that Reid's treatment of external world skepticism is really an instantiation of a more general anti-skeptical strategy—a strategy in which common-sense principles play a central role. Here is the basic idea:

(1) *Suppose that a philosophical skeptic argues against some principle of common sense,* X. (For present purposes, it doesn't matter exactly what *X* is; it could be our belief in the reliability of our cognitive faculties—perception, consciousness, memory, or reason; our belief in the self or in personal identity; our belief in other minds; our belief that Nature is uniform, and that the future will resemble the past; or even our belief that there is a real difference between right and wrong, virtue and vice.)

(2) *If you reject one principle of common sense, you have no right to any of the rest.* (It would be inconsistent to pick and choose among them, since the principles of common sense are all created equal, having the same basic status and the same basic claim on us.)

Therefore,

(3) *Our skeptic has no right to help herself to any principles of common sense; so if she accepts any such principle, she is guilty of an inconsistency.*

(4) *Inevitably, however, the philosophical skeptic will help herself to some principle(s) of common sense.* (We have already seen one example of this: that of the skeptic who questions perception but takes reason's reliability for granted. And here is another example: that of Descartes and Hume, who assume without proof that the faculty of consciousness, through which I know the contents of my own mind, is credible.)

Therefore,

(5) *The philosophical skeptic is inconsistent.*

According to this way of looking at things, there are ultimately two—and only two—options open to a philosopher: either she mustn't accept *any* principles of common sense, or she must accept *all* of them. And this puts the skeptic between a rock and a hard place. If, on the one hand, a skeptic refuses to accept *any* common-sense principles, how will she be able to argue for skepticism? Any would-be defender of a philosophical thesis must set out from *some* premises; but what premises are available to you, once you have turned your back on the republic of common sense? None, it would appear. If, on the other hand, a philosopher accepts *all* of the principles of common sense, then she won't end up being much of a skeptic, will she? For Reid considers all the propositions that skeptics have been most keen to take aim at to be 'first principles': belief in perception; belief in reason; belief in memory; belief in the self; belief in personal identity; belief in other minds; belief in substance; belief that every event has a cause; belief in free will; belief in a real distinction between right and wrong; and belief in nature's uniformity.[11] In the end, then, philosophy and skepticism just don't mix: a consistent skeptic cannot be a philosopher, and a consistent philosopher cannot be a skeptic.

What, then, is Reid's grand conclusion? It is that skeptics such as Descartes and Hume are in the wrong, not because skepticism is demonstrably *false*—Reid doesn't claim to have refuted it—but because skepticism is something we are not in a position to defend given our natural and inescapable commitment to common sense. So skepticism is *indefensible*, if not *irrefutable*.

But there is actually a bit more to it than that. For if Reid is right, then Descartes was wrong not just about external world skepticism, but also about *the very nature of philosophy*. According to Descartes, philosophy begins with *doubt*: we are told to second-guess our senses, to question everything, to admit nothing except what is absolutely certain or infallible. In this way, we are to purge our minds of inherited error, prejudice, common sense, natural beliefs, conventional assumptions, and miscellaneous half-truths. Underlying this project is the thought that our ordinary beliefs are guilty until proven innocent, that they are groundless until we can find a foundation for them, that they are objectionable until we can come up with some positive reason for thinking otherwise. In short, the burden of proof—and it is a crushing burden—is on us. That, at any rate, is what Descartes thinks.

According to Reid, philosophy begins not with doubt, but with *trust*. Instead of questioning all our beliefs and preconceptions, we begin by assuming that our natural faculties of reason, sense-perception, memory, and introspection are all more or less trustworthy—not infallible, to be sure, but fundamentally sound. Now, you can see what this implies: if you have no choice but to trust your cognitive equipment—if you can't help but have a basic confidence in its ability to generate mostly true beliefs under normal conditions—then your ordinary beliefs will appear innocent until proven guilty. That is, your run-of-the-mill beliefs about the world (for example—about the book being on the table, say, or about the sun rising tomorrow) will automatically count as justified unless you are given some good reason to doubt them. (Here it is important to remember that Reid does not think that skeptical arguments applying to whole classes of beliefs—to *all* our perceptual beliefs, for example, or to *all* beliefs arrived at through induction—can constitute good reasons for doubt.)

So the burden of proof is no longer on us: we are not required to justify our ordinary beliefs from the ground up. Because we are no longer obsessed with absolute certainty or haunted by the thought that we might be totally out of touch with reality, there is no need for us to 'build anew from the foundation' *à la* Descartes (assuming it were possible for us to do so). Instead of wiping the slate of the mind perfectly clean or starting over from scratch, we should just begin from where we find ourselves in real life, with the worldview we happen to hold *right now*. While we may occasionally be mistaken about particular matters of fact—remember, Reid doesn't claim that our faculties are *infallible*—we do not need to prove that we exist, or that there is an external world, or that nature is uniform, or that there are other minds, or any other basic proposition that skeptics have put on trial. Our irresistible common-sense convictions are justified by default, produced as they are by faculties philosophers cannot sensibly question.

So what does all this mean? It means that a wise philosopher will acknowledge the authority of common sense and submit humbly to its dictates, just as ordinary folk do every day of their lives:

From *An Inquiry into the Human Mind on the Principles of Common Sense*
By Thomas Reid

Common Sense holds nothing of Philosophy, nor needs her aid.

In this unequal contest betwixt Common Sense and Philosophy, the latter will always come off both with dishonour and loss; not can she ever thrive till this rivalship is dropt, these encroachments given up, and a cordial friendship restored: for, in reality, Common Sense holds nothing of Philosophy, nor needs her aid. But, on the other hand, Philosophy (if I may be permitted to change the metaphor) has no other root but the principles of Common Sense; it grows out of them, and draws its nourishment from them. Severed from this root, its honours wither, its sap is dried up, it dies and rots.

The philosophers of the last age, whom I have mentioned, did not attend to the preserving this union and subordination so carefully as the honour and interest of philosophy required: but those of the present have waged open war with Common Sense, and hope to make a complete conquest of it by the subtleties of Philosophy—an attempt no less audacious and vain than that of the giants to dethrone almighty Jove.

Another thinker famous for opposing skepticism in the name of common sense was G.E. Moore, the distinguished twentieth-century British philosopher. Like Thomas Reid (with whose writings he was familiar), Moore was not favourably impressed by the attempts, made by his predecessors and his contemporaries, to deny the validity of our ordinary judgments about reality. Indeed, Moore found the paradoxical statements of philosophers—statements such as 'Time is unreal' or 'To be is to be perceived'—deeply perplexing, because such statements fly in the face of what all of us are disposed to say and think outside of the philosophy lecture hall. According to Moore, the job of the philosopher is not to question our common-sense beliefs, but to analyze them; not to doubt them, but to unpack their meaning with clarity and precision.

Although Moore can be classified as 'a defender of common sense', he was a much more subtle and critical philosopher than this prosaic label might suggest. (The same, as we have already seen, was true of Thomas Reid.) An example of Moore's patient and meticulous way of undoing the paradoxes of other philosophers can be found his reply to Humean skepticism.

From *Some Main Problems of Philosophy*
By G.E. Moore

I think, therefore, those philosophers who argue, on the ground of Hume's principles, that nobody can ever know of the existence of any material object, are right so far as the first step in their argument is concerned. They are right in saying: *If* Hume's principles are true, nobody can ever *know* of the existence of any material object—nobody can ever know that any such object even probably exists: meaning by a material object, an object which has shape and is situated in space, but which is not similar, except in these respects, to any of the sense-data which we have ever directly apprehended. But are they also right in the second step of their argument? Are they also right, in concluding: *Since* Hume's principles are true, nobody ever *does* know, even probably, of the existence of any material object? In other words: Are Hume's principles true?

You see, the position we have got to is this. If Hume's principles are true, then, I have admitted, I do *not* know *now* that this pencil—the material object—exists. If, therefore, I am to prove that I *do* know that this pencil exists, I must prove, somehow, that Hume's

(Continued)

principles, one or both of them, are *not* true. In what sort of way, by what sort of argument, can I prove this?

It seems to me that, in fact, there really is no stronger and better argument than the following. I *do* know that this pencil exists; but I could not know this, if Hume's principles were true; *therefore*, Hume's principles, one or both of them, are false. I think this argument really is as strong and good a one as any that could be used: and I think it really is conclusive. In other words, I think that the fact that, if Hume's principles were true, I could not know of the existence of this pencil, is a *reductio ad absurdum* of those principles. But, of course, this is an argument which will not seem convincing to those who believe that the principles are true, nor yet to those who believe that I really do not know that this pencil exists. It seems like begging the question. And therefore I will try to shew that it really is a good and conclusive argument.

* * *

But whether the exact proposition which formed my premise, namely: I do know that this pencil exists; or only the proposition: This pencil exists; or only the proposition: The sense-data which I directly apprehend are a sign that it exists; is known by me immediately, one or other of them, I think, certainly is so. And all three of them are much more certain than any premise which could be used to prove that they are false; and also much more certain than any other premise which could be used to prove that they are true. That is why I say that the strongest argument to prove that Hume's principles are false is the argument from a particular case, like this in which we do know of the existence of some material object. And similarly, if the object is to prove *in general* that we do know of the existence of material objects, no argument which is really stronger can, I think, be brought forward to prove this than particular instances in which we do in fact know of the existence of such an object. I admit, however, that other arguments may be more convincing; and perhaps some of you may be able to supply me with one that is. But, however much more *convincing* it may be, it is, I think, sure to depend upon some premise which is, in fact, less certain than the premise that I do know of the existence of this pencil; and so, too, in the case of any arguments which can be brought forward to prove that we do not know of the existence of any material object.

What is Moore's anti-skeptical argument? Let's break it down into five steps. *Step 1*: If Hume's argument for skepticism is logically sound, then both of 'Hume's principles'—call them A and B—must be true. *Step 2*: So if I am to be justified in thinking that Hume's argument for skepticism is sound, then i must know (or at least have very good reason for thinking) that both A and B are true. *Step 3*: But if Hume's argument is sound, then I do not know any concrete and particular matters of fact (for example—that there is a pencil on my desk). *Step 4*: However, it is more evident to me that I know some concrete and particular matter of fact (for example—that there is a pencil on my desk) than that I know that both A and B are true. *Step 5*: Therefore, I am justified in rejecting Hume's argument for skepticism.

For Moore as for Reid, common sense functions not as a substitute for philosophical reflection, but as a constraint on it. In other words, if a philosopher's conclusion cannot be squared with common sense, that becomes a good reason to reject her conclusion and to suspect that something *must* be wrong with the arguments for that conclusion. Of course, common-sense philosophers are free to do more than this—to engage in philosophical analysis or constructive theory-building, for instance—provided that they do not contradict common sense in the process. In fact, Reid and Moore do advance positive theses in many of their writings. In short, they are not nit-picking critics who do nothing but find fault with the work of others.

As our brief discussion of Reid and Moore suggests, philosophical appeals to common sense needn't be crude, dogmatic, careless, or simple-minded. Nevertheless, a few readers may wonder whether there isn't something anti-philosophical about such appeals. After all, isn't philosophy supposed to be free to question everything? Shouldn't philosophers refuse to take things at face value? Doesn't Plato's famous Myth of the Cave suggest that our common-sense view of the world—the view that, according to Plato, the philosophically enlightened person learns to see through—is false and superficial, inadequate and misleading? Indeed, doesn't Plato tell us that the vast majority of people—all firm believers in 'common sense'—are prisoners who don't realize they are prisoners, deluded dwellers in a world of mere shadows and phantasmagoria?

If you agree with Plato about this, then it is unlikely that you will be captivated by the writings of Reid or Moore, let alone converted by their arguments. But the next philosopher we will study—Immanuel Kant—will probably be much more to your liking.

- What is 'common sense'? Should we expect philosophical theories to conform to it? Why or why not?
- What is Reid's argument against skepticism? How is it similar to Moore's reply to the skeptic? How do you think their arguments differ? Which argument strikes you as the better of the two?

G. Immanuel Kant's Revolution

Immanuel Kant is considered by a great many philosophers to be the greatest thinker since Plato and Aristotle. He stands at the beginning of almost every modern movement in Western philosophy, as an inspiration and as a kind of founder. Existentialism would not be possible without him; nor would **phenomenology**, **pragmatism**, or many of the varieties of **linguistic philosophy** that dominated English and North American philosophy for most of the twentieth century. He brings together the often opposed threads of rationalism and empiricism and weaves them into a single monumental philosophical system, which he published primarily in three 'critiques' (*The Critique of Pure Reason*, *The Critique of Practical Reason*, and *The Critique of Judgement*) in the last two decades of the eighteenth century. His writing is notoriously difficult to interpret, but it is possible for even a beginning philosophy student to appreciate the main theme of his self-proclaimed 'revolution' in philosophy. It is, in one sense, a total reorientation of what we mean when we talk about reality and knowledge.

Ever since the ancient Greeks, almost all philosophers had accepted the idea that there is a reality 'out there', whether or not they accepted that we could ever come to know this reality. The idea of an 'external world' seemed innocent enough, until metaphysicians began to find that their contradictory views about this world could not be reconciled. This dilemma prompted Locke to turn away from metaphysics and pay more attention to the way we acquire knowledge. The shift of attention to knowledge led Hume to argue that we couldn't even know that the sun would rise tomorrow, or that one billiard ball in fact causes the movement of another, or that there is indeed a world outside of our own ideas.

This skeptical conclusion seemed utterly absurd to Kant, who admitted, in his *Prolegomena to Any Future Metaphysics*, that he had been awakened from his 'dogmatic slumbers' by Hume's work. Kant had been a metaphysician (a follower of Leibniz), but reading Hume convinced him that there was a serious problem, not only for metaphysics, but for our claims to know the world at all. And Kant, who was also a scientist and an enthusiastic supporter of Isaac Newton and the new physics, saw that he had to refute Hume if he was going to keep claiming that scientists (and everyone else) could know anything at all. But the problem, as he diagnosed it, turned out to be the unquestioned idea that there was a distinction to be made between our beliefs and experience of the world, on the one hand, and the world itself, Reality or Truth, on the other.

What Kant suspected, and what many philosophers believe today, is that our 'ideas' do not just correspond to reality but in some sense shape and set up the world, impose upon the world the structures we experience. We see material objects instead of just patterns of light and colours (as seen perhaps by a newborn baby), and this is our contribution to experience. We experience events in a cause-and-effect relationship instead of as mere sequences of events, and this is not because of experience alone, but because we *make* our experience conform to causal rules. We expect certain events in the future on the basis of what we have experienced in the past, and this too is not mere habit, but a set of rules we impose necessarily on every experience. According to Kant, space and time do not exist 'out there', independent of our experience; we impose the forms of three-dimensional space and one-dimensional time on our experience, and through these forms we come to know the world. So too, Kant argues, all of our knowledge of the world is in part a product of the various forms and rules that we impose upon, or use to set up, our experience. The word Kant uses for 'set up' is '*constitute*' (think of a 'constitution' that sets up a government, provides it with its rules and structures). We constitute our own experience in the sense that we provide the rules and structures according to which we experience objects, as objects in space and time, as governed by the laws of nature and the relations of cause and effect. Kant writes, 'the understanding does not derive its laws from, but prescribes them to, nature'.

According to Kant's philosophy, reality has no existence that we can understand except as we constitute it through our basic concepts. Kant took these concepts—or what he called '**categories**'—to be the basic rules of the human mind as such, common to all peoples in all places at all times.[12] Truth and knowledge are a function of our concepts. Kant's revolution rejects the very idea of an external reality and instead looks to the concepts through which we constitute reality. Thus there is no point to wondering whether our concepts match up to reality, since there would be no reality without our concepts. Our concepts not only cohere with each other; they set up a corresponding reality as well. Of course those concepts 'work'— it is as if someone were to wonder how it is that a ceramic mold exactly fits a piece of jewellery, when the mold gave shape to the jewellery in the first place.

Previous philosophers had asked, 'How can we know that our ideas correspond with the way the world really is?' Kant rejected that question. Instead, he asked, '*How do our ideas constitute the world*? What is the structure and what are the rules (the *concepts* or *categories*) of the human mind according to which we set up our world, the world of our experience?'

- What does Kant mean when he says that we 'constitute' our world?

The project of Kant's *The Critique of Pure Reason* is to analyze and prove the **necessity** of these concepts, which we can know a priori—independently of all experience and with certainty, just because they are the rules within which all of our knowledge is possible. Think of it this way: You take a number of pieces of wood and a checkerboard and set up the game by making up rules about what can be moved where, how, and when. Then, within the game, you are free to make any number of moves, some brilliant, some stupid, but you are always bound by the rules that you yourself have set up. And since you yourself have established these rules, it would be absurd to wonder whether or not they are 'true'.

Kant's revolution changed our conception of reality, our conception of knowledge, and, most importantly, our conception of ourselves. Truth is no longer correspondence between our ideas and reality, but our own system of rules (concepts or categories) by which we constitute our reality. Knowledge, accordingly, is no longer the comprehending of a reality beyond our experience, but knowledge of our experience. But this does not mean knowledge of experience, distinct from knowledge of objects, for the objects of our experience are all there is to reality. Moreover, in making this move, Kant gives the philosophers something that they thought they had lost, a renewed ideal of certainty, for, he argued, we can be certain of the rules of our own experience. Kant defended the necessity of the truths of arithmetic and geometry as those rules that have to do with the a priori forms of our intuitions of space and time. According to Kant's philosophy in general, reality is the world of our experience, as we constitute it through the concepts of our understanding. Therefore, we can know it with certainty, for truth, in general, is our own construction.

You might at first think that there is some trick here, as if Kant is saying, 'Well, if we can't have knowledge in the hard sense, then I'll simply redefine the words *knowledge*, *reality*, and *truth*'. But what he has done is point to the difficulty of the picture that other philosophers had accepted; he has shown that what we normally mean by *truth*, *knowledge*, and *reality* is not an insatiable appeal to a world beyond our experience. Underneath Kant's spectacular pronouncements there is, once again, a return to common sense. This world, the one you stand in, touch, and see, *is* the real world. But what makes it real, according to Kant, is not just that you stand in, touch, and see it, but that you actively constitute it as the way it is, apply your own rules for understanding it, and structure it through your own experience.

Kant gives us a general way of describing of all those truths that metaphysicians have always argued about. Using Kant's terminology, we can say they are forms of **synthetic a priori knowledge**. Such knowledge is, briefly characterized, knowledge of our own rules with which we (necessarily) constitute reality. If a truth is not true because of our experiences, nor is it true because of the grammar or meanings of the sentences of our language, how else could it be defended? This was Hume's dilemma, and with this two-test system of justification, he eliminated many of our most important beliefs as 'unjustifiable', as neither 'truths of reason' nor 'matters of fact'. But now, we have our third way: A belief can be true, necessarily true, if it is one of those rules that we impose to constitute our experience. Thus Kant defended the truths of arithmetic and geometry by showing that they were the '(a priori) forms of intuition', the ways in which we must experience our world. So too did he defend all of those truths that Hume had claimed to be unjustifiable.

Accordingly, the principle of universal causation is neither a generalization from experience nor an **analytic** truth, but rather a *rule* for 'setting up' our world. That rule is, 'Always look for regular (or "law-like") connections between events, so that you can explain an event as an *effect* of previous events, and therefore predict future events as well'. Like a rule in chess, this is not a move within the game but one of those rules that defines the game. So too with the principle of **induction**; it is neither based upon experience nor a trivial truth but a rule with which we govern all of our experience. So too for our belief in the 'external' or material world, which Berkeley and Hume found so problematic. Our experience alone will not tell us whether we are dreaming or not, and the idea of the material ('external') world is not a **tautology** or a conceptual truth. It too is one of the rules that we use to constitute our experience, namely, that we shall *always* interpret our experience of objects in space as external to us and as material or *substantial*. But notice, our metaphysical notion of substance is no longer that which is, by definition, outside of our experience. It is now part of the rules by which we set up our experience.

SYNTHETIC A PRIORI KNOWLEDGE

Knowledge that is necessary and known independently of experience (and thus a priori), but that does not derive its truth from the logic or meaning of sentences (thus synthetic).

ANALYTIC

Demonstrably true by virtue of the logical form or the meanings of the component words.

From *The Critique of Pure Reason*
By Immanuel Kant

The Distinction between Pure (a Priori) and Empirical (a Posteriori) Knowledge

That all our knowledge begins with experience there can be no doubt. For how should the faculty of knowledge be called into activity, if not by objects which affect our senses, and which either produce representations by themselves, or rouse the activity of our understanding to compare, or connect, or to separate them, and thus to convert the raw material of our sensuous impressions into a knowledge of objects, which we call experience? In respect of time, therefore, no knowledge within us is antecedent to experience, but all knowledge begins with it.

(Continued)

But although all our knowledge begins with experience, it does not follow that it arises from experience. For it is quite possible that even our empirical experience is a compound of that which we receive through impressions, and of that which our own faculty of knowledge (incited only by sensuous impressions), supplies from itself, a supplement which we do not distinguish from that raw material, until long practice has roused our attention and rendered us capable of separating one from the other.

It is therefore a question which deserves at least closer investigation, and cannot be disposed of at first sight, whether there exists a knowledge independent of experience, and even of all impressions of the senses? Such *knowledge* is called a priori, and distinguished from *empirical* knowledge, which has its source a posteriori, that is, in experience.

From *Prolegomena to Any Future Metaphysics*
By Immanuel Kant

My purpose is to persuade all those who think metaphysics worth studying that it is absolutely necessary to . . . propose first the preliminary question, 'Whether such a thing as metaphysics can be even possible at all?'

My purpose is to persuade all those who think metaphysics worth studying that it is absolutely necessary to pause a moment and, regarding all that has been done as though undone, to propose first the preliminary question, 'Whether such a thing as metaphysics can be even possible at all?'

If it be science, how is it that it cannot, like other sciences, obtain universal and lasting recognition? If no, how can it maintain its pretensions and keep the human mind in suspense with hopes never ceasing, yet never fulfilled? Whether then we demonstrate our knowledge or our ignorance in this field, we must come one and for all to a definite conclusion respecting the nature of this so-called science, which cannot possibly remain on its present footing. It seems almost ridiculous, while every other science is continually advancing, that in this, which pretends to be wisdom incarnate, for whose oracle everyone inquires, we should constantly move round the same spot, without gaining a single step. And so its votaries having melted away, we do not find men confident of their ability to shine in other sciences venturing their reputation here, where everybody, however ignorant in other matters, presumes to deliver a final verdict, because in this domain there is actually as yet no standard weight and measure to distinguish sound knowledge from shallow talk.

*   *   *

Hume started chiefly from a single but important concept in metaphysics, namely, that of the connection of cause and effect (including its derivatives force and action, and so on). He challenged reason, which pretends to have given birth to this concept of herself, to answer him by what right she thinks anything could be so constituted that if that thing be posited, something else also must necessarily be posited; for this is the meaning of the concept of cause. He demonstrated irrefutably that it was perfectly impossible for reason to think a priori and by means of concepts such a combination, for it implies necessity. We cannot at all see why, in consequence of the existence of one thing, another must necessarily exist or how the concept of such a combination can arise a priori. Hence he inferred that reason was altogether deluded with reference to this concept, which she erroneously considered as one of her own children, whereas in reality it was nothing but a bastard of imagination, impregnated by experience, which subsumed certain representations under the law of association and mistook a subjective necessity (habit) for an objective necessity arising from insight. Hence he inferred that reason had no power to think such combinations, even in general, because her concepts would then be purely fictitious and all her pretended a priori cognitions nothing but common experiences marked with a false stamp. In plain language, this means that there is not and cannot be any such thing as metaphysics at all.

* * *

I openly confess my recollection of David Hume was the very thing which many years ago interrupted my dogmatic slumber and gave my investigations in the field of speculative philosophy a quite new direction. I was far from following him in the conclusions at which he arrived by regarding, not the whole of his problem, but a part, which by itself can give us no information. If we start from a well-founded, but undeveloped, thought which another has bequeathed to us, we may well hope by continued reflection to advance farther than the acute man to whom we owe the first spark of light.

I therefore first tried whether Hume's objection could not be put into a general form, and soon found that the concept of the connection of cause and effect was by no means the only concept by which the understanding thinks the connection of things a priori, but rather that metaphysics consists altogether of such concepts. I sought to ascertain their number; and when I had satisfactorily succeeded in this by starting from a single principle, I proceeded to the deduction of these concepts, which I was now certain were not derived from experience, as Hume had attempted to derive them, but sprang from the pure understanding. This deduction (which seemed impossible to my acute predecessor, which had never even occurred to anyone else, though no one had hesitated to use the concepts without investigating the basis of their objective validity) was the most difficult task which ever could have been undertaken in the service of metaphysics; and the worst was that metaphysics, such as it is, could not assist me in the least because this deduction alone can render metaphysics possible. But as soon as I had succeeded in solving Hume's problem, not merely in a particular case, but with respect to the whole faculty of pure reason, I could proceed safely, though slowly, to determine the whole sphere of pure reason completely and from universal principles, in its boundaries as well as in its contents. This was required for metaphysics in order to construct its system according to a safe plan.

Kant gives us a way of resolving the age-old disputes of metaphysics—questions concerning reality as such. Since the claims of the metaphysicians are all synthetic a priori, Kant provides us with the following policy:

1. Those claims that are rules by which we must interpret our experience are true—necessarily true.
2. Those claims that contradict rules by which we must interpret our experience are false—necessarily false.
3. Those that are not rules by which we must interpret our experience are either analytic, contingently true, or contingently false.
4. Finally, those claims that cannot be decided by appeal to the rules of our experiences and make no difference to our experience one way or the other are to be rejected as possible topics of knowledge.

The logical positivists in the twentieth century took this last part of Kant's policy as a program for a devastating attack on metaphysics in general. Although the logical positivists, as empiricists in the tradition of David Hume, did not accept much of Kant's theory, they wholeheartedly endorsed his rejection of claims that made no difference whatever to our experience. They said that any claim that makes no difference to our experience—that cannot be tested in any way—is meaningless.

Kant also upheld some of the metaphysicians' claims even as he denied others. For example, he saves Newton's (and Spinoza's) determinism in his rule of causality, thus rejecting Leibniz's 'pre-established harmony' view as necessarily false. With some revisions, he accepts a large part of Leibniz's view of space and time as relative, that is, relative to our experience. He saves the notion of substance because he says that one of the most important rules of our experience is that we see objects as substantial (that is, as 'real'). But he does not accept the view that substance is something independent of human experience, for such a view, by definition, means that substance would be irrelevant to our experience. Nor does he accept the central dispute between Spinoza and Leibniz, whether there is but one substance or many, for no rule of our experience is concerned one way or another. It makes no difference to our experience. It is a metaphysician's game and not a possible topic for knowledge.

Again, Kant's revolution is the elimination of 'reality' and 'truth' as external to ourselves. Since Kant, many philosophers no longer view human knowledge as the passive reception of sensations or intuitions. And, needless to say, the problems of philosophy have become radically changed.

CORRESPONDENCE THEORY OF TRUTH

A statement or belief is true if it 'corresponds' with 'the facts'.

In rejecting the **correspondence theory of truth** and the idea of an 'external' reality, Kant destroyed the old problems, resolved the old disputes, and answered Hume's skepticism, at least for a while. But you can probably see a new and even more virulent version of those problems, disputes, and doubts on the horizon. By denying us our anchor in reality, Kant launches philosophy in a bold new direction, and he creates the dilemma that still defines philosophy today: If we supply our own rules for experience, is there any uniquely correct way of describing the way the world is?

The basis of Kant's theory is that we supply the rules according to which we constitute our experience. We can talk about truth only within our experience and according to our own rules. But you can see what happens when we raise the following questions: What about people (or creatures) who are very different from us? Will they use the same rules? Will they have the same experiences? And, if we do differ from them, who is 'right'? Whose rules are 'better'? Whose experience is 'true'? You can see here the problems of the **coherence theory of truth** coming to haunt Kant's philosophy. Suppose there are two (or more) sets of rules, equally coherent? Can they both be 'true'? You can appreciate how easily the German Romantic philosophers who immediately followed Kant replaced his notion of 'constitution' with the more exciting notion of 'creation'. We create our realities, they announced. We are all artists, building our worlds. Notice the words 'reali*ties*' and 'worlds'; there is no longer confidence, much less a guarantee, that there is only one reality or one world.

COHERENCE THEORY OF TRUTH

A statement or a belief is true if it 'coheres' with a system of statements or beliefs.

PRAGMATIC THEORY OF TRUTH

A statement or a belief is true if it 'works', if it allows us to function effectively in everyday life.

Kant's most immediate follower, a German philosopher named Johann Gottlieb Fichte, used the **pragmatic theory of truth** to come to the same conclusion; the truth is, according to him, that which is most practical, most conducive to the good life, and the evaluation of different realities depends wholly on the practical consequences. With Kant's revolution, the one truth that earlier philosophers had sought seems destined to be replaced by many truths, our knowledge with the possibility of different kinds of knowledge.

But before we go on to explore these intriguing complications, let us make it clear that Kant himself never accepted a word of all this. According to him, there was still but one possible set of rules and therefore only one way of constituting our experience, whoever we are, wherever we're from, and no matter what kind of conscious creature we happen to be. This means: one world, one science, one reality, and one truth. Kant tries to prove this in the central section of *The Critique of Pure Reason* in a formidable argument that he calls a '**transcendental deduction**'.

What does Kant mean by this term? You already know that a deduction is an inference from one statement to another according to a set of rules of inference. 'Transcendental' refers to the basic rules of human experience. In this case, Kant attempts to infer from various statements that we believe, the basic rules (concepts, categories) of human experience. But a transcendental deduction is not satisfied with simply deducing some such rules; it also proves that they are the *only* rules that we are able to use to constitute our experience. That is why it is so important to Kant. It allows him his revolution without its anarchist consequences.

The argument itself is enormously complicated and scholars who have studied it for half their lives still do not agree on what it is or whether it is a valid argument. While we won't try to summarize it for you here, we can say that Kant believed that such a transcendental deduction would prove that, although it is we ourselves who supply the rules of our experience and determine what can be true for us, we don't have a choice in the matter. There is still only one truth for all of us.

Philosophers are still arguing whether any such transcendental argument (Kant's or not) might succeed. If one does, then people must, in their basic rules, all agree. (Of course, they will always disagree about particular matters; no two chess players make all the same moves.) But if there is no successful transcendental argument, then there need be no such universal agreement. It then makes sense to talk about different truths for different people. This, we may say, continues to be the dominant battle of twenty-first-century Western philosophy. But obviously, it is not new; it is merely an extension of a debate that began with the earliest philosophers. On the one side have been the **absolutists**—those who believe that there is only one set of rules and one truth. On the other side have been the **relativists**—those who believe that there are different rules for different people and therefore different 'truths'. Plato, and Descartes, for example, were absolutists; Protagoras and the Sophists were relativists. Kant was an absolutist. Most of his followers were relativists. (Don't be confused by their discussions of 'the Absolute'; they were in fact still relativists.)

> • What consequences do you see following from the difference between relativism and absolutism on questions of knowledge?

ABSOLUTISM

The thesis that there is but one correct view of reality, one single truth.

RELATIVISM

The thesis that there is no single correct view of reality, no single truth.

H. The Battle in Europe after Kant: Relativism and Absolutism

The story of philosophy in Europe since Kant is largely the story of a war between relativism and absolutism, in which even the politics and arts of the times play a continuing role. The philosophers immediately following Kant, as we have already mentioned, pursued relativism with relish, developing alternative systems of philosophy as fast as they could find publishers. The German philosopher Friedrich Schelling, for example, produced about one system a year at the turn of the century. He became the best-known Romantic philosopher of a large group of Romantic intellectuals, poets, and critics throughout Europe who turned to the virtual worship of individual 'genius' and competed for the most extravagant and creative view of the world. The virtually undisputed winner of this contest, however, was not Schelling but one of his schoolmates, Georg Wilhelm Friedrich Hegel.

1. Georg Wilhelm Friedrich Hegel

Hegel was in college (Tübingen Lutheran seminary) when the French Revolution was raging just across the border. He was just starting to put together his mature philosophy when Napoleon was attempting to take over all of Europe. This international turmoil helps us understand the global reach of Hegel's philosophy and his bold effort to proclaim an 'absolute' position with reference to knowledge. Like many young German intellectuals in that exciting period, he was trying to get outside his provincial perspective and to understand the world from a larger, even a 'divine', point of view. Accordingly, Hegel's theory of truth is part and parcel of his all-embracing system of thought.

Hegel begins by rejecting many key metaphors that have ruled modern philosophy, especially all the 'correspondence' metaphors in which the world in itself (or 'the Absolute') is on one side and our knowledge (beliefs, sentences, utterances) are on the other, separated by some distorting filter (our senses) or actively altered by the machinery of our understanding. In place of such metaphors (and the skepticism they inevitably engender), Hegel suggests a holistic worldview in which consciousness and the world are not separate but inseparably integrated. In traditional terms, this means that there is no world, no reality-in-itself, apart from consciousness.

It also means that we must give up our view of consciousness and the self as self-enclosed and, in some sense, 'inside' us. Indeed, Hegel also suggests that we give up the view that the self is essentially a feature of the individual: the self—or 'Spirit'—is shared by all of us; or rather, in more Platonic language, we all 'participate' in Spirit. Not surprisingly, Hegel was familiar with some Asian thinkers and incorporated some Eastern views into his notion of truth. However, the truth, according to Hegel, 'is the whole'—that is, the unity of all our consciousnesses and the world. This means that there is no saying (and no point in attempting to say) what the world might be apart from our conceptions of it. But neither is this to invite skepticism, for the world is nothing but the synthesis of all our possible conceptions of it.

Hegel, like Kant, is an idealist. He calls himself an 'absolute idealist' (in contrast to Kant's 'transcendental idealism'), by which he means that he believes that reality is the product of mind—not individual minds, of course, but the cosmic mind, 'Spirit'. This belief opens the way for a radical departure from Kant, who argued at great length that there could be but one possible way of conceiving the world—that is, one a priori set of forms of intuition (space and time) and one set of categories (substance, causality, etc.). Hegel's predecessor (Kant's immediate successor) Fichte had already argued that there are at least two basically different ways of envisioning the world—the scientific, objective ('dogmatic') way and the practical, moral, activist ('idealist') way—and rather than being simply 'right' or 'wrong', Fichte had declared famously that 'The philosophy a man chooses depends upon the kind of man that he is.' Hegel goes a giant step further and provides a long series of possible conceptions of the world—or 'forms of consciousness'—conceptions that are not divided into 'practical' and 'theoretical' but, Hegel tells us, all of which have both their practical and their theoretical aspects. (Once again Hegel rejects an age-old dichotomy.) Such views are not simply alternative options, as if we could each simply chose one or another (as Kierkegaard would argue some years later). The way we view the world is already determined by our place in history, our language, and our society. Nor is the variety of forms of consciousness a demonstration of the now-popular view that there is no 'correct' way of knowing. The various forms of consciousness emerge one from another by way of improvement or by way of opposition (as, for example, scientific theories tend to follow one another), and (again, as in science) there is always the necessary sense that they are all moving toward some final end—the correct view. So, too, Hegel insists that all these different conceptions and ways of viewing the world are leading up to something—to a viewpoint that is not relative to any particular viewpoint or perspective. This is the standpoint he calls 'absolute knowing'.

This idea that the various forms of consciousness emerge one from another and lead us eventually to the absolute is perhaps Hegel's most exciting philosophical contribution to Western thinking. Virtually every other philosopher we have discussed, whether metaphysician or epistemologist, essentially offered us a static view of knowledge, a concept of the understanding that—except for education from childhood and the detailed knowledge gained by the sciences—did not change, did not grow, did not develop. Hegel provides philosophy (and humanity) with a historical perspective. Our knowledge is not, as many philosophers had insisted ever since ancient times, about what is apart from our knowledge of it. Truth develops, as the human mind develops. Truth is not *being* but *becoming*. Knowledge develops through conflict and confrontation, or what Hegel famously calls a **dialectic** (a term he borrowed from Kant but that goes back to the Greeks).

In an important sense, it is Hegel who discovers (or invents) the history of philosophy. Other philosophers had talked about their predecessors, of course. (Aristotle, for instance, provided us with much of what we know about the pre-Socratic philosophers.) But what Hegel suggests is that something more is to be gleaned than a mere sequence of refutations, additions, and improvements to thought; it is reality itself that is being converted. The history of philosophy, accordingly, is but one aspect of an incredible cosmic odyssey, a 'phenomenology of spirit'—the development through time not only of consciousness but of reality too.

The selection that follows is from the Introduction of Hegel's 1807 masterpiece, *The Phenomenology of Spirit*. In this book, Hegel presents a dialectic of various forms of consciousness, from the most primitive sensory perception to the most sophisticated views of the Enlightenment and 'Revealed Religion' (Christianity), culminating in that final stage of 'Absolute Knowing'. In these paragraphs, Hegel rejects the traditional metaphors of epistemology and argues that skepticism should not be taken at all seriously. He then suggests the holistic form of his overall system.

From *The Phenomenology of Spirit*
By G.W.F. Hegel

The Absolute alone is true, or the truth alone is absolute.

It is a natural assumption that in philosophy, before we start to deal with its proper subject-matter, *viz.* the actual cognition of what truly is, one must first of all come to an understanding about cognition, which is regarded either as the instrument to get hold of the Absolute, or as the medium through which one discovers it. A certain uneasiness seems justified, partly because there are different types of cognition, and one of them might be more appropriate than another for the attainment of this goal, so that we could make a bad choice of means; and partly because cognition is a faculty of a definite kind and scope, and thus, without a more precise definition of its nature and limits, we might grasp clouds of error instead of the heaven of truth. This feeling of uneasiness is surely bound to be transformed into the conviction that the whole project of securing for consciousness through cognition what exists in itself is absurd, and that there is a boundary between cognition and the Absolute that completely separates form. For, if cognition is the instrument for getting hold of absolute being, it is obvious that the use of an instrument on a thing certainly does not let it be what it is for itself, but rather sets out to reshape and alter it. If, on the other hand, cognition is not an instrument of our activity but a more or less passive medium through which the light of truth reaches us, then again we do not receive the truth as it is in itself, but only as it exists through and in this medium. Either way we employ a means which immediately brings about the opposite of its own end; or rather, what is really absurd is that we should make use of a means at all.

It would seem, to be sure, that this evil could be remedied through an acquaintance with the way in which the *instrument* works; for this would enable us to eliminate from the representation of the Absolute which we have gained through it whatever is due to the instrument, and thus get the truth in its purity. But this 'improvement' would in fact only bring us back to where we were before. If we remove from a reshaped thing what the instrument has done to it, then the thing—here the Absolute—becomes for us exactly what it was before this (accordingly) superfluous effort. On the other hand, if the Absolute is supposed merely to be brought nearer to us through this instrument, without anything in it being altered, like a bird caught by a lime-twig, it would surely laugh our little ruse to scorn, if it were not with us, in and for itself, all along, and of its own volition. For a ruse is just what cognition would be in such a case, since it would, with its manifold exertions, be giving itself the air of doing something quite different from creating a merely immediate and therefore effortless relationship. Or, if by testing cognition, which we conceive of as a *medium*, we get to know the law of its refraction, it is again useless to subtract this from the end result. For it is not the refraction of the ray, but the ray itself whereby truth reaches us, that is cognition; and if this were removed, all that would be indicated would be a pure direction or a blank space.

Meanwhile, if the fear of falling into error sets up a mistrust of Science, which in the absence of such scruples gets on with the work itself, and actually cognizes something, it is hard to see why we should not turn

(*Continued*)

round and mistrust this very mistrust. Should we not be concerned as to whether this fear of error is not just the error itself? Indeed, this fear takes something—a great deal in fact—for granted as truth, supporting its scruples and inferences on what is itself in need of prior scrutiny to see if it is true. To be specific, it takes for granted certain ideas about cognition as an *instrument* and as a *medium*, and assumes that there is a *difference between ourselves and this cognition*. Above all, it presupposes that the Absolute stands on one side and cognition on the other, independent and separated from it, and yet is something real; or in other words, it presupposes that cognition which, since it is excluded from the Absolute, is surely outside of the truth as well, is nevertheless true, an assumption whereby what calls itself fear of error reveals itself rather as fear of the truth.

This conclusion stems from the fact that the Absolute alone is true, or the truth alone is absolute.

* * *

Now, because it has only phenomenal knowledge for its object, this exposition seems not to be Science, free and self-moving in its own peculiar shape; yet from this standpoint it can be regarded as the path of the natural consciousness which presses forward to true knowledge; or as the way of the Soul which journeys through the series of its own configurations as though they were the stations appointed for it by its own nature, so that it may purify itself for the life of the Spirit, and achieve finally, through a completed experience of life itself, the awareness of what it really is in itself.

Natural consciousness will show itself to be only the Notion of knowledge, or in other words, not to be real knowledge. But since it directly takes itself to be real knowledge, this path has a negative significance for it, and what is in fact the realization of the Notion, counts for it rather as the loss of its own self; for it does lose its truth on this path. The road can therefore be regarded as the pathway of *doubt*, or more precisely as the way of despair. For what happens on it is not what is ordinarily understood when the word 'doubt' is used: shilly-shallying about this or that presumed truth, followed by a return to that truth again, after the doubt has been appropriately dispelled—so that at the end of the process the matter is taken to be what it was in the first place. On the contrary, this path is the conscious insight into the untruth of phenomenal knowledge, for which

the supreme reality is what is in truth only the unrealized Notion. Therefore this thoroughgoing skepticism is also not the skepticism with which an earnest zeal for truth and Science fancies it has prepared and equipped itself in their service: the *resolve*, in Science, not to give oneself over to the thoughts of others, upon mere authority, but to examine everything for oneself and follow only one's conviction, or better still, to produce everything oneself, and accept only one's deed as what is true.

The series of configurations which consciousness goes through along this road is, in reality, the detailed history of the *education* of consciousness itself to the standpoint of Science. That zealous resolve represents this education simplistically as something directly over and done with in the making of the resolution; but the way of the Soul is the actual fulfillment of the resolution, in contrast to the untruth of that view. Now, following one's own conviction is, of course, more than giving oneself over to authority; but changing an opinion accepted on authority into an opinion held out of personal conviction, does not necessarily alter the content of the opinion, or replace error with truth. The only difference between being caught up in a system of opinions and prejudices based on personal conviction, and being caught up in one based on the authority of others, lies in the added conceit that is innate in the former position. The skepticism that is directed against the whole range of phenomenal consciousness, on the other hand, renders the Spirit for the first time competent to examine what truth is. For it brings about a state of despair about all the so-called natural ideas, thoughts, and opinions, regardless of whether they are called one's own or someone else's, ideas with which the consciousness that sets about the examination (of truth) *straight away* is still filled and hampered, so that it is, in fact, incapable of carrying out what it wants to undertake.

The necessary progression and interconnection of the forms of the unreal consciousness will by itself bring to pass the *completion* of the series. To make this more intelligible, it may be remarked, in a preliminary and general way, that the exposition of the untrue consciousness in its untruth is not a merely *negative* procedure. The natural consciousness itself normally takes this one-sided view of it; and a knowledge which makes the one-sidedness its very essence is itself one of the patterns of incomplete consciousness which occurs on the road itself, and will manifest itself in due course. This is just the skepticism which only ever sees pure nothingness in its result and abstracts from the fact that this nothingness is specifically the nothingness of that *from which it results*. For it is only when it is taken as the result of that from which it emerges, that it is, in fact, the true result; in that case it is itself a *determinate* nothingness, one which has a *content*. The skepticism that ends up with the bare abstraction of nothingness or emptiness cannot get any further from there, but must wait to see whether something new comes along and what it is, in order to throw it too into the same empty abyss. But when, on the other hand, the result is conceived as it is in truth, namely, as a *determinate* negation, a new form has thereby immediately arisen, and in the negation the transition is made through which the progress through the complete series of forms comes about of itself.

* * *

This contradiction and its removal will become more definite if we call to mind the abstract determinations of truth and knowledge as they occur in consciousness. Consciousness simultaneously *distinguishes* itself from something, and at the same time *relates* itself to it, or, as it is said, this something exists *for* consciousness; and the determinate aspect of the *relating*, or of the *being* of something for a consciousness, is *knowing*. But we distinguish the being-for-another from *being-in-itself*; whatever is related to knowledge or knowing is also distinguished from it, and posited as existing outside of this relationship; this *being-in-itself* is called *truth*. Just what might be involved in these determinations is of no further concern to us here. Since our object is phenomenal knowledge, its determinations too will at first be taken directly as they present themselves; and they do present themselves very much as we have already apprehended them.

Now, if we inquire into the truth of knowledge, it seems that we are asking what knowledge is *in itself*. Yet in this inquiry knowledge is *our* object, something that exists *for us*; and the *in-itself* that would supposedly result from it would rather be the being of knowledge *for us*. What we asserted to be its essence would be not so much its truth but rather just our knowledge of it. The essence or criterion would lie within ourselves, and that which was to be compared with it and about which a decision would be reached through this comparison would not necessarily have to recognize the validity of such a standard.

Starting from a clearly Kantian perspective, Hegel taught that we have to stop talking about 'true' and 'false' philosophies, religions, political systems, societies, scientific theories, and values. There are only different 'forms of consciousness', some more sophisticated and perspicacious than others, but none wholly true (or false) to the exclusion of others. Hegel wholly endorsed the Kantian thesis that the world is nothing other than the way in which we constitute it.

Hegel's dialectic was essentially a dialectic of ideas, a series of confrontations of various forms of consciousness so that we could see how they all form an interlocking view of reality. But although philosophy and human history improve through time—eventually reaching a form of absolute knowledge and (Hegel hoped) world peace and universal freedom—the movement itself is by no means a smooth progression. It is often violent, both in the intellectual realm and in the flesh-and-blood world of human politics, which Hegel grimly referred to as the 'slaughter-bench' of history.

One of Hegel's most enthusiastic followers, Karl Marx (whose critique of Hegel we encountered in Chapter 2), thought that Hegel had the dialectic of history turned upside down. It is not ideas that determine world history, Marx argued, but rather the details of history—in particular the economic details—that determine the ideas, including the ideas of philosophers. From this notion of dialectic Marx developed his powerful and influential view of history as class conflict, replacing Hegel's abstract 'forms of consciousness' with the day-to-day battles of wages, jobs, exploitation, and profits.[13]

In what follows, Hegel presents an overview of his all-embracing notion of 'Spirit' (also called 'the Idea'). Spirit, in one sense, is God, but the concept embraces all of humanity, all of history, and all of nature as well. The point of the argument is that the world itself *develops* and *changes*, and so the virtues and truths of one generation may well become inadequate to the next generation. Yet this is not relativism in the crude sense, such that a truth, for example, is only true for a particular person or people. First, truth is not, in this sense, subjective; it is to be found in the world and not just in the minds of individuals or groups. Second, and even more important, to say that a truth is inadequate from a later, probably more expansive, point of view is not to say that it 'was true but now is false'; rather, it shows that we are slowly approaching an ever more adequate conception of the truth and knowledge, which Hegel calls 'Freedom'. Freedom is God's purpose developing through history and humanity.

From *Reason in History*
By G.W.F. Hegel

Reason governs the world and has consequently governed its history.

The question of the *means* whereby Freedom develops itself into a world leads us directly to the phenomenon of history. Although Freedom as such is primarily an internal idea, the means it uses are the external phenomena which in history present themselves directly before our eyes. The first glance at history convinces us that the actions of men spring from their needs, their passions, their interests, their characters, and their talents. Indeed, it appears as if in this drama of activities these needs, passions, and interests are the sole springs of action and the main efficient cause. It is true that this drama involves also universal purposes, benevolence, or noble patriotism. But such virtues and aims are insignificant on the broad canvas of history. We may, perhaps, see the ideal of Reason actualized in those who adopt such aims and in the spheres of their influence; but their number is small in proportion to the mass of the human race and their influence accordingly limited. Passions, private aims, and the satisfaction of selfish desires are, on the contrary, tremendous springs of action. Their power lies in the fact that they respect none of the limitations which law and morality would impose on them; and that these natural impulses are closer to the core of human nature than the artificial and troublesome discipline that tends toward order, self-restraint, law, and morality.

When we contemplate this display of passions and the consequences of their violence, the unreason which is associated not only with them, but even—rather we might say *especially*—with *good* designs and righteous aims; when we see arising therefrom the evil, the vice, the ruin that has befallen the most flourishing kingdoms which the mind of man ever created,

we can hardly avoid being filled with sorrow at this universal taint of corruption. And since this decay is not the work of mere nature, but of human will, our reflections may well lead us to a moral sadness, a revolt of the goodwill (spirit)—if indeed it has a place within us. Without rhetorical exaggeration, a simple, truthful account of the miseries that have overwhelmed the noblest of nations and polities and the finest exemplars of private virtue forms a most fearful picture and excites emotions of the profoundest and most hopeless sadness, counter-balanced by no consoling result. We can endure it and strengthen ourselves against it only by thinking that this is the way it had to be—it is fate; nothing can be done. And at last, out of the boredom with which this sorrowful reflection threatens us, we draw back into the vitality of the present, into our aims and interests of the moment; we retreat, in short, into the selfishness that stands on the quiet shore and thence enjoys in safety the distant spectacle of wreckage and confusion.

But in contemplating history as the slaughterbench at which the happiness of peoples, the wisdom of states, and the virtue of individuals have been sacrificed, a question necessarily arises: To what principle, to what final purpose, have these monstrous sacrifices been offered?

From here one usually proceeds to the starting point of our investigation: the events which make up this picture of gloomy emotion and thoughtful reflection are only the means for realizing the essential destiny, the absolute and final purpose, or, what amounts to the same thing, the true result of world history. We have all along purposely eschewed that method of reflection which ascends from this scene of particulars to general principles. Besides, it is not in the interest of such sentimental reflections really to rise above these depressing emotions and to solve the mysteries of Providence presented in such contemplations. It is rather their nature to dwell melancholically on the empty and fruitless sublimities of their negative result. For this reason we return to our original point of view. What we shall have to say about it will also answer the questions put to us by this panorama of history.

The first thing we notice—something which has been stressed more than once before but which cannot be repeated too often, for it belongs to the central point of our inquiry—is the merely general and abstract nature of what we call principle, final purpose, destiny, or the nature and concept of Spirit. A principle, a law is something implicit, which as such, however true in itself, is not completely real (actual). Purposes, principles, and the like, are at first in our thoughts, our inner intention. They are not yet in reality. That which is in itself is a possibility, a faculty. It has not yet emerged out of its implicitness into existence. A second element must be added for it to become reality, namely, activity, actualization. The principle of this is the will, man's activity in general. It is only through this activity that the concept and its implicit ('being-in-themselves') determinations can be realized, actualized; for of themselves they have no immediate efficacy. The activity which puts them in operation and in existence is the need, the instinct, the inclination, and passion of man. When I have an idea I am greatly interested in transforming it into action, into actuality. In its realization through my participation I want to find my own satisfaction. A purpose for which I shall be active must in some way be my purpose; I must thereby satisfy my own desires, even though it may have ever so many aspects which do not concern me. This is the infinite right of the individual to find itself satisfied in its activity and labour. If men are to be interested in anything they must have 'their heart' in it. Their feelings of self-importance must be satisfied. But here a misunderstanding must be avoided. To say that an individual 'has an interest' in something is justly regarded as a reproach or blame; we imply that he seeks only his private advantage. Indeed, the blame implies not only his disregard of the common interest, but his taking advantage of it and even his sacrificing it to his own interest. Yet, he who is active for a cause is not simply 'interested', but 'interested in it'. Language faithfully expresses this distinction. Nothing therefore happens, nothing is accomplished, unless those concerned with an issue find their own satisfaction in it. They are particular individuals; they have their special needs, instincts, and interests. They have their own particular desires and volitions, their own insight and conviction, or at least their own attitude and opinion, once the aspirations to reflect, understand, and reason have been awakened. Therefore people demand that a cause for which they should be active accord with their ideas. And they expect their opinion—concerning its goodness, justice, advantage, profit—to be taken into account. This is of particular importance today when people are moved to support a cause not by faith in other people's authority, but rather on the basis of their own independent judgment and conviction.

We assert then that nothing has been accomplished without an interest on the part of those who brought it about. And if 'interest' be called 'passion'—because the whole individuality is concentrating all its desires and powers, with every fibre of volition, to the neglect of all other actual or possible interests and aims, on one object—we may then affirm without qualification that *nothing great in the world* has been accomplished without passion.

* * *

[O]ne may indeed question whether those manifestations of vitality on the part of individuals and peoples in which they seek and satisfy their own purposes are, at the same time, the means and tools of a higher and broader purpose of which they know nothing, which they realize unconsciously. This purpose has been questioned, and in every variety of form denied, decried, and denounced as mere dreaming and 'philosophy.' On this point, however, I announced my view at the very outset, and asserted our hypothesis—which eventually will appear as the result of our investigation—namely, that Reason governs the world and has consequently governed its history. In relation to this Reason, which is universal and substantial, in and for itself, all else is subordinate, subservient, and the means for its actualization. Moreover, this Reason is immanent in historical existence and reaches its own perfection in and through this existence. The union of the abstract universal, existing in and for itself, with the particular or subjective, and the fact that this union alone constitutes truth are a matter of

(Continued)

speculative philosophy which, in this general form, is treated in logic. But in its historical development (*the subjective side, consciousness, is not yet able to know what is*) the abstract final aim of history, the idea of Spirit, for it is then itself in process and incomplete. The idea of Spirit is not yet its distant object of desire and interest. Thus desire is still unconscious of its purpose; yet it already exists in the particular purposes and realizes itself through them. The problem concerning the union of the general and the subjective may also be raised under the form of the union of freedom and necessity. We consider the immanent development of the Spirit, existing in and for itself, as necessary, while we refer to freedom the interests contained in men's conscious volitions.

- How does Hegel address the problem of skepticism in rejecting the 'correspondence metaphors' of philosophy?
- What is Hegel's dialectic and how does it relate to truth and knowledge as he understands it? How do you think Marx revises this notion?

---

2. Arthur Schopenhauer

Arthur Schopenhauer claimed to be a faithful student of Kant. Indeed, he claimed to be the only faithful interpreter of what he took to be Kant's central idea, the distinction between the constituted world of our experience and an underlying reality, which could be found in the realm of 'the will'. But Schopenhauer, who was one of the great eccentrics in the history of philosophy, gave Kant's philosophy a dramatic twist, encouraged by his readings of Eastern philosophy. In place of Kant's confidence in the truth of the world of our experience, Schopenhauer invokes the Buddhist conception of the 'veil of Maya' and declares our experience of the world to be largely illusion. Meanwhile the will, which Kant takes to be inherently rational, becomes an irrational, impersonal, inner force for Schopenhauer, exerting itself to no particular purpose within us. The most evident manifestation of the will, in us and in all creatures, Schopenhauer suggests, is sexual desire—the often urgent and foolish desire to reproduce ourselves so that our offspring can reproduce themselves, and so on and so on, to no end whatever. Thus Schopenhauer, like the Buddha, stresses the futility of desire, and his whole philosophy is aimed at giving us some relief from the will. But the will is ultimate reality, and within its purposeless striving dwell all of the peoples and all of the creatures of nature. The following selection is from Schopenhauer's greatest book, *The World as Will and Representation*.

From *The World as Will and Representation*
By Arthur Schopenhauer

Now man is nature herself, and indeed nature at the highest grade of her self-consciousness, but nature is only the objectified will-to-live.

The will, considered purely in itself, is devoid of knowledge, and is only a blind, irresistible cure, as we see it appear in inorganic and vegetable nature and in their laws, and also in the vegetative part of our own life. Through the addition of the world as representation, developed for its service, the will obtains knowledge of its own willing and what it wills, namely that this is nothing but this world, life, precisely as it exists.

We have therefore called the phenomenal world the mirror, the objectivity, of the will; and as what the will wills is always life, just because this is nothing but the presentation of that willing for the representation, it is immaterial and a mere pleonasm if, instead of simply saying 'the will', we say 'the will-to-live'.

As the will is the thing-in-itself, the inner content, the essence of the world, but life, the visible world, the phenomenon, is only the mirror of the will, this world will accompany the will as inseparably as a body is accompanied by its shadow; and if will exists, then life, the world, will exist. Therefore life is certain to the will-to-live, and as long as we are filled with the will-to-live we need not be apprehensive for our existence, even at the sight of death. It is true that we see the individual come into being and pass away; but the individual is only phenomenon, exists only for knowledge involved in the principle of sufficient reason, in the *principium individuationis*. Naturally, for this knowledge, the individual receives his life as a gift, rises out of nothing, and then suffers the loss of this gift through death, and returns to nothing. We, however, wish to consider life philosophically, that is to say, according to its Ideas, and then we shall find that neither the will, the thing-in-itself in all phenomena, nor the subject of knowing, the spectator of all phenomena, is in any way affected by birth and death. Birth and death belong only to the phenomenon of the will, and hence to life; and it is essential to this that is manifest itself in individuals that come into being and pass away, as fleeting phenomena, appearing in the form of time, of that which in itself knows no time, but must be manifested precisely in the way aforesaid in order to objectify its real nature. Birth and death belong equally to life, and hold the balance as mutual conditions of each other, or, if the expression be preferred, as poles of the whole phenomenon of life. The wisest of all mythologies, the Indian, expresses this by giving to the very god who symbolizes destruction and death (just as Brahma, the most sinful and lowest god of the Trimurti, symbolizes generation, origination, and Vishnu preservation), by giving, I say, to Shiva as an attribute not only the necklace of skulls, but also the lingam, that symbol of generation which appears as the counterpart of death. In this way it is intimated that generation and death are essential correlatives which reciprocally neutralize and eliminate each other. It was precisely the same sentiment that prompted the Greeks and Romans to adorn the costly sarcophagi, just as we still see them, with feasts, dances, marriages, hunts, fights between wild beasts, bacchanalia, that is with presentations of life's most powerful urge. This they present to us not only through such diversions and merriments, but even in sensual groups, to the point of showing us the sexual intercourse between satyrs and goats. The object was obviously to indicate with the greatest emphasis from the death of the mourned individual the immortal life of nature, and thus to intimate, although without abstract knowledge, that the whole of nature is the phenomenon, and also the fulfillment, of the will-to-live. The form of this phenomenon is time, space, and causality, and through these individuation, which requires that the individual must come into being and pass away. But this no more disturbs the will-to-live—the individual being only a particular example or specimen, so to speak, of the phenomenon of this will—than does the death of an individual injure the whole of nature. For it is not the individual that nature cares for, but only the species; and in all seriousness she urges the preservation of the species, since she provides for this so lavishly through the immense surplus of the seed and the great strength of the fructifying impulse. The individual, on the contrary, has no value for nature, and can have none, for infinite time, infinite space, and the infinite number of possible individuals therein are her kingdom. Therefore nature is always ready to let the individual fall, and the individual is accordingly not only exposed to destruction in a thousand ways from the most insignificant accidents, but is even destined for this and is led towards it by nature herself, from the moment that individual has served the maintenance of the species. In this way, nature quite openly expresses the great truth that only the Ideas, not individuals, have reality proper, in other words are a complete objectivity of the will. Now man is nature herself, and indeed nature at the highest grade of her self-consciousness, but nature is only the objectified will-to-live; the person who has grasped and retained this point of view may certainly and justly console himself for his own death and for that of his friends by looking back on the immortal life of nature, which he himself is.

- What follows from Schopenhauer's celebration of the will as the 'thing-in-itself', the truth behind all reality?

3. Friedrich Nietzsche

After Hegel, relativism became ever more sophisticated. Marx explained differences in philosophical worldviews in terms of different economic and social circumstances; for him, the question was no longer 'Which view of the world is true?' but rather, 'What circumstances would make a person believe that?' Hegel's rival Arthur Schopenhauer defended the radical idea that what we called reality was in fact an illusion; and a few years later, following Schopenhauer, the eccentric but brilliant iconoclast Friedrich Nietzsche defended a similar view. He too attacked the traditional notions of truth and knowledge with a vengeance and argued that there could be as many equally 'true' (or equally 'false'—it doesn't matter) worldviews as there were creative people and societies. He also urged that every person adopt for himself or herself as many different worldviews as possible, at one time or another, as a matter of 'experiment'.

Like Schopenhauer, he considered all such views as dictated by the will and not merely as knowledge as such, and, like Marx, he replaced the old question, 'which view of the world is true?' with a question of circumstances. But Nietzsche was not interested in economic or social circumstances so much as psychological factors. So he asked, 'What kind of personality would need to believe that?' Truth is no longer even an issue. In fact, even rationality is starting to feel the threat of relativism. For, with Nietzsche, not only is truth out the window, but coherence and pragmatism are forced to take second place as well. What comes first? Excitement, adventure, heroism, creativity, and what Nietzsche generally calls 'the will to power'. Of course, one must still act rationally if one is to achieve these things, but thinking, according to Nietzsche, plays at most a secondary role in our lives.

Nietzsche's view of truth was, to put it mildly, startling. His basic claim was a paradox: 'truth is error'. This can be interpreted in many different ways, and Nietzsche himself interprets and reinterprets it from many different perspectives—which is quite in line with his view of truth itself. 'There are no facts,' he tells us, 'only interpretations'. Elsewhere he tells us that there are only 'perspectives', various ways of viewing the world and no ultimately correct (or incorrect) way. The very idea of 'truth', he writes, and the curious obsession with truth enjoyed by the scholars, is a kind of pathology, or at least a real curiosity, that requires examination. Why are we so enamoured with the idea of 'truth'? How and why did philosophers ever get the idea that there is another world, more real and 'better' than this one?

On Truth
By Friedrich Nietzsche[14]

Sense for Truth.—I welcome every skepticism to which I may answer: 'Let us try it out!' But I no longer want to hear anything about things and questions that cannot be tested. This is the limit of my 'sense for truth': for courage has there lost its right.

Life No Argument.—We have organized for ourselves a world to live in—by postulating bodies, lines, surfaces, causes and effects, motion and rest, form and content: without these instances of belief no one could manage to live today! But nevertheless they are yet unproven. Life is no argument; error might be among the conditions of life.

Ultimate Skepticism.—But in the end what are human truths?—They are our *irrefutable* errors.

Truth is the sort of error without which a particular species of life could not live. In the end the value for *life* is what decides the matter.

The criterion of truth is in the enhancement of the feeling of power.

What Is Truth?—Inertia; that supposition that provides ease; the smallest cost in spiritual power; etc.

There are all kinds of eyes. Even the sphinx has eyes:—and thus there are all kinds of 'truths', and thus there is no truth.

For us the falseness of a judgment is not on that account an objection to a judgment. . . . The question is how far is it life-promoting, life-preserving, species-preserving, perhaps even species-propagating; and our fundamental inclination is to insist that the falsest judgments (such as synthetic a priori judgments) are for us the most indispensable, that without admitting as true the fictions of logic, without measuring reality against the entirely invented world of the unconditional and self-identical, without constant falsification of the world through numbers, human beings could not live—that to renounce false judgments would be to renounce life, would be to deny life.

How the 'True World' at Last Became a Fable: The History of an Error

1. The true world:—attainable for the wise, the pious, the virtuous; he lives in it, *he is it*. (The oldest form of the idea, comparably sensible, simple, and compelling. . . .')

2. The true world:—unattainable for now, but promised for the wise, the pious, the virtuous ('for the sinner who repents'). (Progress of the idea: it becomes more subtle, sinister, incomprehensible: it becomes Christian.)

3. The true world:—unattainable, indemonstrable, unpromisable; but the very thought of it—a consolation, a duty, an imperative. (The old sun, really, but viewed through fog and skepticism. The idea has become elusive, pale, Nordic. Kantian.)

4. The true world:—unattainable? At least, unattained. And as unattained, also *unknown*. Thus no consolation, redemption, or obligation: how could something unknown obligate us? (Grey dawn. Reason's first yawn. . . .)

5. The 'true' world:—an idea that is no longer of any use, not even for obligating—an idea that has become worthless and superfluous—*consequently*, a refuted idea: let us abolish it! (Bright day; breakfast, return of *bons sense* and cheerfulness; . . .)

6. The true world:—we have abolished. What world is left? Perhaps the apparent? But no! *With the true world we have abolished the apparent as well*. (Noon; . . . end of the longest error; high point of humanity.)

Although Nietzsche wrote in the last half of the nineteenth century, his works were ignored until the twentieth century, when they made an enormous impact (not all of it positive), first in Germany and then in Europe and in North America. Nietzsche's relativistic view of truth, while very much at home with many current thinkers, was still quite alien to the ideas of the nineteenth century, when thinkers—following Hegel or Kant or natural science—were still trying to develop a unified and 'true' picture of the world.

However, one of Nietzsche's German colleagues, Wilhelm Dilthey, did provoke extensive activity and comment at the end of the nineteenth century with his less extreme relativistic view. The doctrine he promoted, which is still tremendously influential in both Europe and North America, is called **historicism**. Historicism is Hegel's dialectic of forms of consciousness pinned down to precise social and historical periods. It is the thesis, simply, that truth and rationality are relative to particular peoples at particular times in history and that overall comparison of them, with the intention of finding out which is 'true', is totally mistaken. It is, obviously, a very strong relativist doctrine, so strong and so influential that the absolutists in philosophy, who had had much less publicity and success than the relativists in the late nineteenth century, started looking around for a champion. They found him in the 'phenomenologist' Edmund Husserl.

• Is 'historicism' a form of relativism? What is the difference between them?

I. Phenomenology

Phenomenology is the study of the essential structures of the human mind, consciousness itself; and because the structures of the mind are essential, they can be known to be true, universally and necessarily. It is a self-consciously scientific and rigorous discipline, modelled after mathematics (just as the theories of Descartes and the ancient Greeks were based on mathematical principles). Edmund Husserl, widely regarded as the founder of modern phenomenology, was a new kind of rationalist: he believed that the truths of arithmetic and geometry are known—and known with certainty—by appeal to a certain kind of intuition, which he called 'essential' intuition. Finding such intuitions adequate for arithmetic and geometry, Husserl turned his theory elsewhere, to philosophy in general. Husserl was horrified by what he saw as rampant relativism. He saw it, in fact, not only as a crisis in philosophy but as 'a crisis in European civilization'. So he turned his phenomenology to attack it.

From 'Philosophy as Rigorous Science'
By Edmund Husserl

Historicism takes its position in the factual sphere of the empirical life of the spirit. To the extent that it posits this latter absolutely, without exactly naturalizing it (the specific sense of nature in particular lies far from historical thinking and in any event does not influence it by determining it in general), there arises a relativism that has a close affinity to naturalistic psychologism and runs into similar skeptical difficulties.

* * *

In view of this constant change in scientific views we would actually have no right to speak of sciences as objectively valid unities instead of merely as cultural formations. It is easy to see that historicism, if consistently carried through, carries over into extreme skeptical subjectivism. The ideas of truth, theory, and science would then, like all ideas, lose their absolute validity. That an idea has validity would mean that it is a factual construction of spirit which is held as valid and which in its contingent validity determines thought. There would be no unqualified validity, or validity-in-itself, which is what it is even if no one has achieved it and though no historical humanity will ever achieve it. Thus too there would then be no validity to the principle of contradiction nor to any logic, which latter is nevertheless still in full vigour in our time. The result, perhaps, will be that the logical principles of non-contradiction will be transformed into their opposites.

Using both Kant's terminology and his absolutist intentions, Husserl attacked all forms of relativism and attempted to develop a *transcendental phenomenology*—a phenomenology that discovers the basic rules of all experience (just as he had discovered them for arithmetic and geometry before). Because these rules (or 'ideal laws') were discovered to be essential, they were, Husserl concluded, the only rules possible. (In Husserl as in Kant, the word *transcendental* means the basic and the only rules with which we 'constitute' our world. Husserl used the notion of 'constitution' also, with much the same meaning that Kant did.)

Whereas previous philosophers had found such essential rules of experience in a mysterious Platonic 'world of Being' or simply in our language, Husserl, as a phenomenologist, found them in human consciousness. Thus consciousness itself, with the objects of its own constitution, becomes our new anchor. Starting from Descartes, Husserl suggests that we go back to that 'subjective' starting point and look again.

From *The 1929 Paris Lectures*
By Edmund Husserl

The splintering of contemporary philosophy and its aimless activity makes us pause. Must this situation not be traced back to the fact that the motivations from which Descartes' meditations emanate have lost their original vitality? Is it not true that the only fruitful renaissance is one which reawakens these meditations, not in order to accept them, but to reveal the profound truth in the radicalism of a return to the *ego cogito* with the eternal values that reside therein?

* * *

We thus begin, everyone for himself and in himself, with the decision to disregard all our present knowledge. We do not give up Descartes' guiding goal of an absolute foundation for knowledge. At the beginning, however, to presuppose even the possibility of that goal would be prejudice. . . . Science demands proof *by reference to the things and facts themselves, as these given in actual experience and intuition.* Thus guided, we, the beginning philosophers, make it a rule to judge only by the evidence.

* * *

Here, specifically following Descartes, we make the great shift which, when properly carried out, leads to *transcendental subjectivity*. . . . Let us consider: as radically meditating philosophers we now have neither knowledge that is valid for us nor a world that exists for us. . . . However, whatever be the veracity of the claim to being made by phenomena, whether they represent reality or appearance, phenomena in themselves cannot be disregarded as mere 'nothing'. On the contrary, it is precisely the phenomena themselves which, without exception, render possible for me the very existence of both reality and appearance. This epistemological abstention is still what it is: it includes the whole stream of experienced life and all its particulars, the appearances of objects, other people, cultural situations, etc. Nothing changes, except that I no longer accept the world simply as real; I no longer judge regarding the distinction between reality and appearance. . . . This ubiquitous detachment from any point of view regarding the objective world we term the *phenomenological epoché*. It is the methodology through which I come to understand myself as that ego and life of consciousness in which and through which the entire objective world exists for me, and is for me precisely as it is. . . . Through the phenomenological *epoché* the natural human ego, specifically my own, is reduced to the transcendental ego. This is the meaning of the phenomenological reduction.

- Why does Husserl think that the method of phenomenology is a form of rationalism?
- What does Husserl mean by 'transcendental subjectivity'? How is it related to Descartes' project?
- How is phenomenology supposed to defeat relativism? How might it invite relativism?

Husserl's battle, from beginning to end, was a battle against relativism, against all of those philosophies that held that there can be different but equally true or equally rational worldviews. And his phenomenology, for all of its internal struggles, has been immensely influential. But phenomenology was not the solution to relativism. Husserl thought that phenomenology could be transcendental and prove that certain rules were basic and essential to all human thinking. But just as Kant opened the door to relativism with his view that we constitute our world, Husserl opened it wider with his view that a study of consciousness was the way to do philosophy. For were there not, his followers asked, many different forms of consciousness? (Thus returning to Hegel rather than Kant.) And phenomenology as it developed in France, rather than Germany, became the source of a new relativism, which is extremely fashionable today.

Phenomenology continues to attract the attention of many philosophers who are interested in coming to terms with consciousness and its structures. A good example of the phenomenological tradition's ongoing influence can be found in the work of John Russon, a contemporary Canadian philosopher. In his recent, provocative book *Human Experience: Philosophy, Neurosis, and the Elements of Everyday Life*, he examines our understanding of the world as reflected in everyday experience.

When we start thinking about epistemology, we may find it perfectly natural to embrace the Cartesian picture of knowledge as a relation between a subject and an object. According to this familiar picture, the subject that does the knowing (you) is on one side on the divide, the object known (trees, say) is on the other, and each side is to be thought of as absolutely independent of the other. Knowledge becomes a matter of the subject (you) copying or representing objects (trees) as they are apart from the subject, without adding or subtracting anything to them. Implicit in this picture is the idea that your mind—the true locus of knowledge—is akin to an inner mirror in which the outer world is reflected without any distortion.

According to Russon, this Cartesian picture of our relation to the world is anything but natural or self-evident. One of the themes running through his critique of that picture is that human experience is not a matter of duplication, but of interpretation. Instead of the world being given to us as it exists 'in itself', our experience is of things as they are *for us*. In other words, our view of ordinary things—the sense we make of them, the meaning we give them—is inescapably conditioned by our expectations, our interests, our projects, and our preconceptions.

Understanding the structure of our lived experience, appreciating how it is shaped by us, exploring what that shaping reveals about us—this is what interests Russon as a phenomenologist.

From *Human Experience*
By John Russon

[O]ur experience is always interpretive: whatever perception we have of the world is shaped by our efforts to organize and integrate all of the dimensions of our experience into a coherent whole.

Challenging Traditional Prejudices

What could be more obvious than that there is a world outside us and that we must make choices about how to deal with it? When we think about our place in the world, this is almost always what we imagine. Is it so obvious though? Is this the proper way to describe our situation? We can be a bit more precise.

When we reflect on ourselves, we typically start by recognizing ourselves as discrete agents facing a world about which we must make choices. The world is made up, it seems, of things with discrete identities that are present to us, right here, right now. On this familiar view, then, reality is a kind of aggregate, a bunch of distinct, separately existing things, one of which—me—faces those others and must self-consciously orchestrate her dealings with those things. These last few sentences, it seems to me, sum up the

very core of almost all of our thinking experience of ourselves. Though quite simple, they nonetheless express the 'theory' of reality with which we typically operate. The significance of these familiar views for our lives is immense. 'And why not?' one might ask, since, 'after all, those sentences describe how things really are, so they should be the foundation for everything we think'. Indeed, this view seems so compelling as to be indubitable. It is, in fact, a standard way to mock philosophers to claim that they do doubt these ideas, wondering whether chairs exist, or whether they themselves really exist: these claims, in other words, seem so obvious that one would have to be a fool to entertain doubt about them.

Whether or not the philosophers should be mocked, it remains true that this cartoon of philosophical activity does in an important way describe the real work of philosophy. Indeed, it seems to me that the history of philosophy in general, and twentieth-century thought in particular, has taught us to be wary of the vision of the world described in my first sentences. As suggested above, the significance of these views is indeed immense, but not because they are true. Rather, their significance comes from the extent to which our lives are crippled by too readily accepting this 'theory' of things and of ourselves.

In the twentieth century, opposition to these views has come from many quarters. In recent years, ecologists have done a great deal to show us that our identities cannot be easily severed from the natural environments in which we live. Psychologists, for one hundred years at least, have investigated a wide range of experiences in which people do not seem to be free agents with full possession of the power of choice. Sociologists and anthropologists have shown how the way in which we see the world is largely reflective of cultural prejudices, so the identities of the objects we encounter are not clearly separable from our own social identities. All of these insights challenge the easy separation of subject and object upon which our familiar view is based.

Probably the single most important aspect of the critique of this familiar view is found in the recognition that our experience is always interpretive: whatever perception we have of the world is shaped by our efforts to organize and integrate all of the dimensions of our experience into a coherent whole. How we go about this will be dictated by the level of our education, by our expectations, and by our desires, and so the vision we have will always be as much a reflection of ourselves and our prejudices as it is a discovery of 'how things really are'. In other words, the very way that we see things reveals secrets about us: what we see reveals what we are looking for, what we are interested in. This is as true of our vision of things that we take to be outside us as it is of our vision of ourselves.

Focussing on the interpretive dimension to all experience allows us to shift away from the typical perspective we have upon ourselves on one side and the world on the other. We can now turn to our experience of the world and ask, 'What do we reveal about ourselves through the way we experience?' or, 'Who do we reveal ourselves to be by the way in which we see ourselves and our world?' When, for example, one of us experiences America as 'home', this is not because there is some intrinsic property to America that makes it 'homey'. Rather, what we experience as the character of this object is fundamentally a reflection of our own expectations of security and ease of operation, based upon our memories of, and habituation to, this place. To others, of course, this same setting is threatening and oppressive. The homey or threatening character of this site is a reflection of our developed identities, and not of an inherent feature of the independent objects that confront us. Similarly, the experience of a woodland setting as a site for camping or as a site for logging reveals the interpretive perspective with which one engages with the world, rather than revealing the independent essence of the forest. This interpretive dimension, we shall see, is at play at every level of experience, from the most basic to the most developed forms of experience.

Shifting our focus to the interpretive dimension of experience opens up for us a new field of inquiry, a new object of study, namely, the field of our interpretive acts, the field of those acts through which we reveal the forms and limits of our powers of interpretation. Instead of accepting our immediate view of ourselves as obviously being discrete agents facing a world of present things about which we must make choices, we are now led to find our own identities to be a problem, a question. The same holds true for the things of the world. We are led to ask what the principles are behind the interpretive acts that give to us an integrated vision of ourselves and our world, who or what the agency is that enacts those interpretive principles, whether those principles are right, what consequences this structure of interpretation has, and so on. We are left, in short, with a task of discerning and evaluating the acts of interpretation that make our experience appear the way it does. We must, then, get clear on just how our experience does appear to us, with an eye to uncovering its founding acts of interpretation. I now want to give brief descriptions of some familiar experiences in order to show how interpretation is at play in our experience, and thereby to launch us into a new account of who we are and what our world is, that is, a new account of the relation of subject and object that is opposed to our familiar prejudices about ourselves and our world.

* * *

Description, Happening, and Situation

If we free ourselves of the traditional prejudices about the subject and the object as fully present and mutually alien entities between which a relation has

(*Continued*)

to be created, what our description of experience reveals instead is that the relation itself comes first, that is, it is from the primary relation—the act of experiencing—that subject and object come to be established, and not vice versa. What is first is a situation of experience in which all of the participants—subjects and objects—are already shaped and defined by the others. The subject and the object are not indifferent beings that might or might not come into relation: they are already involved, each having a grip on the other. How the object exists is reflective of the interpretive demands of the subject; equally, the subject is already subordinated to the demands of the object. In other words, each taken by itself is an abstraction, something that can only be separated in reflective thought and not in reality. We must, therefore, reorient our thinking and conceive of a subject who is intrinsically situated, or an environment that intrinsically calls for someone to resolve it. What exists is a situation that is meaningful, a situation that is experienced as a range of tensions, a situation that needs certain things to be done. Human reality is this situation, this event of meaning, this happening of a subject-object pair.

In identifying the subject-object pair as the human reality, we have gone beyond any appeal either to a more original choosing agent that goes out to meet an alien object, or to an objective truth that forces itself onto an alien subject for explaining why things are the way that they are. This is because we have seen that the subject and the object so conceived only exist as abstracted aspects of the meaningful situation, the comprehending relation. This entails that there is nothing beyond this meaningful situation to which one could turn to justify, explain, test, or prove the significance of human reality. Consequently, it is what occurs as the situation of human meaning that must be the ground, guide, and measure of all our investigations and self-interpretations. In order to know, then, we will rely on the authority neither of the scientist nor the theologian. Knowledge will ultimately be a matter of describing what happens, and this description of the form experience takes will be the last word.

- What does it mean to say that 'our experience is always interpretive'? What are some of the implications of this view, according to Russon?

J. Hermeneutics and Pragmatism: Relativism Reconsidered

Absolutism seems to deny the obvious fact that people are different and disagree, not only in superficial ways but in terms of their most basic beliefs. Relativism, on the other hand, seems to deny the obvious similarities among people and imply that we will never be able to understand one another—or find the truth—at all. One attempt to bridge the gap between dogmatic absolutism and solipsistic relativism is **hermeneutics**.

Hermeneutics is an old name for 'interpretation', with an eye to getting at the truth. For many centuries, this formidable word was applied exclusively to the interpretation of the Bible, with the aim of understanding the Word of God. Today, however, the term has a much broader meaning. It is often used in literary criticism to talk about the interpretation of texts—not only the Bible, but any text. It is also used in philosophy to refer to the discipline of interpreting and understanding the world, which becomes, in effect, our text, and different cultures' views of the world, which may seem initially to be mutually incommensurable.

The modern father of hermeneutics is the German 'historicist' Wilhelm Dilthey, whom we encountered in Section H, above. Dilthey came to realize that the methods of the physical sciences were not very successful when applied to the 'human sciences', in part because history played such enormous importance in human life. He also realized that there was a very real danger in the Kantian attempt to overcome traditional philosophical distinctions between appearance and reality, subjectivity, and objective truth. While his historicism lent itself to relativism, Dilthey himself was vehemently antirelativist. The problem, he argued, was to develop a method for *understanding* human differences. But he believed that all of these were ultimately superficial and thus not incommensurable at all.

Contemporary hermeneutics attempts to provide a way of understanding viewpoints other than our own. It is simply dogmatic to insist—as Kant and many other philosophers have insisted—that the structures of the human mind are everywhere the same and, consequently, that we all share a common basis of knowledge. But is it simpleminded, on the other hand, to insist that we are all different and have different truths, since there is at least enough overlap for us to understand that we do disagree. For example, how can the modern-day scientist understand the commonly held medieval view of God and the earth as the spiritual and spatial centres of the universe? Well, not by dismissing their views as nonsense, and not by simply saying, 'Well, they have their opinions and we have ours'. Rather, we can turn to hermeneutics and attempt to step into their shoes (but without taking off our own shoes first).

In the twentieth century, hermeneutics was turned into a powerful style of philosophizing by the German metaphysician Martin Heidegger. It was Heidegger, in his monumental book *Being and Time* (1928), who suggested that life is like a text, and the purpose of our lives is to understand that text. Heidegger was a student of Husserl and was thus a phenomenologist. But in his hermeneutical phenomenology he tries to 'uncover' the hidden meanings in our experience. He rejects the scientific tone of Husserl's phenomenology and prefers to talk about the structures of life itself, including our profound sense of history, which he believes defines human life.

The most important proponent of hermeneutics, however, was a student of Heidegger, Hans-Georg Gadamer. In fact, Gadamer was so wary of the fact that method—and not only the scientific method—may distort our understanding that he insisted that hermeneutics must resist the temptation to become another method. Rather, it should attempt to overcome methods, to dispense with the overemphasis on proofs and arguments and the quest for certainty and emphasize instead the shared understandings that we already have with one another. The substance of philosophy then becomes dialogue rather than individual phenomenology or abstract proofs. Interpretation thus becomes not an abstract function of the intellect but a process that permeates our every activity.

Gadamer's hermeneutics does not reject the notion of truth, but it does give up entirely the idea that there is a single truth wholly outside of us that we need a method (rationalism, empiricism, scientific psychology) to discover. Like the coherence theorist and the pragmatist, Gadamer gave up the idea of secure *foundations* for our knowledge—such as the raw experiences or 'sense-data' discussed by some empiricists, or the a priori principles defended by Kant. But where both the coherence theorist and the pragmatist tend to interpret truth as a function of the present—coherence of beliefs and workability, respectively—the hermeneuticist insists that truth must be understood *historically*, in terms of a *tradition*. While the philosophical tradition had tended to ignore the importance of its own tradition and look for strictly eternal truths, Gadamer's hermeneutics hold rather that it is only within this tradition, and by looking at this tradition, that philosophical truth is possible at all. Does this mean that we must accept whatever our tradition may be, even if it is wrong? But what would it mean, Gadamer asked, for a tradition to be wrong? We can criticize ourselves, of course, and that is just the point of hermeneutics. But does it mean that we must also justify ourselves and what we have always believed? 'Do we need to justify,' he asked rhetorically, 'that which has always supported us?'

Does relativism mean that there can be no truth? Does relativism apply only to philosophical views, not to *real* theories? Could there be *really* different views of the world—and different worlds? But does it even make sense to talk about relative truth, that is, a truth that is only 'true' for one person or group and not another?

If it even makes sense to say that something is only true for some but not for others, it must mean that a statement is true for a person or group by virtue of the scheme or conceptual framework they employ; thus it is true for a certain society that the witch doctor embodies the power of the devil, but true for another society that the powers of the so-called witch doctor are nothing but the combination of natural pharmaceuticals plus the power of suggestion. But we must not fall into the radical trap of Protagoras and claim that 'man is the measure of all things'—if we are to continue using the word *truth* at all. A statement or a belief cannot be true just by virtue of its being believed, in other words, if there is no possibility that a person or a group can believe what is false (or, not believe some statement that is nevertheless true). Furthermore, as in hermeneutics, it is essential that we do not close off the possibility that one truth might be understandable—perhaps in different terms—by those who believe another, apparently contradictory truth. This would be to deny the possibility of cross-cultural communication—to cut people of different cultures off from each other completely.

- **What is hermeneutics? What role does history play in hermeneutical understanding of truth?**

Hermeneutics has had a recent resurgence in American philosophy, particularly in discussions of relativism and multiculturalism. In the following essay, the twentieth-century American philosopher Richard Rorty, who claimed a profound debt to hermeneutics, defends a vision of 'solidarity'—which he contrasts with the traditional notion of 'objectivity', which he associates with 'pragmatism'. His claim is that the pragmatic theory of truth (which we outlined previously) is essentially the theory that truth has a moral standard—the solidarity of a community—rather than a metaphysical one—objectivity. In other words, he claims that pragmatism defines *truth* as 'what it is morally best for our community to believe', and using this definition, he can claim that it is morally best for us to believe in pragmatism.

From 'Solidarity or Objectivity?'
By Richard Rorty

[T]he question is not about how to define words like 'truth' or 'rationality' or 'knowledge' or 'philosophy', but about what self-image our society should have of itself.

There are two principal ways in which reflective human beings try, by placing their lives in a larger context, to give sense to those lives. The first is by telling the story of their contribution to a community. This community may be the actual historical one in which they live, or another actual one, distant in time and place, or a quite imaginary one, consisting perhaps of a dozen heroes and heroines selected from history or fiction or both. The second way is to describe themselves as standing in immediate relation to a non-human reality. This relation is immediate in the sense that it does not derive from a relation between such a reality and their tribe, or their nation, or their imagined band of comrades. I shall say that stories of the former kind exemplify the desire for solidarity, and that stories of the latter kind exemplify the desire for objectivity. Insofar as a person is seeking solidarity, he or she does not ask about the relation between the practices of the chosen community and something outside that community. Insofar as he seeks objectivity, he distances himself from the actual persons around him not by thinking of himself as a member of some other real or imaginary group, but rather by attaching himself to something which can be described without reference to any particular human beings.

* * *

Those who wish to ground solidarity in objectivity—call them 'realists'—have to construe truth as correspondence to reality. So they must construct a metaphysics which has room for a special relation between beliefs and objects which will differentiate true from false beliefs. They also must argue that there are procedures of justification of belief which are natural and not merely local. So they must construct an epistemology which has room for a kind of justification which is not merely social but natural, springing from human nature itself, and made possible by a link between that part of nature and the rest of nature. On their view, the various procedures which are thought of as providing rational justification by one or another culture may or may not really *be* rational. For to be truly rational, procedures of justification *must* lead to the truth, to correspondence to reality, to the intrinsic nature of things.

By contrast, those who wish to reduce objectivity to solidarity—call them 'pragmatists'—do not require either a metaphysics or an epistemology. They view truth as, in William James' phrase, what it is good for *us* to believe. So they do not need an account of a relation between beliefs and objects called 'correspondence', nor an account of human cognitive abilities which ensures that our species is capable of entering into that relation. They see the gap between truth and justification not as something to be bridged by isolating a natural and transcultural sort of rationality which can be used to criticize certain cultures and praise others, but simply as the gap between the actual good and the possible better. From a pragmatist point of view, to say that what is rational for us now to believe may not be *true*, is simply to say that somebody may have come up with a better idea. It is to say that there is always room for improved belief, since new evidence, or new hypotheses, or a whole new vocabulary, may come along. For pragmatists, the desire for objectivity is not the desire to escape the limitations of one's community, but simply the desire for as much intersubjective agreement as possible, the desire to extend the reference of 'us' as far as we can. Insofar as pragmatists make a distinction between knowledge and opinion, it is simply the distinction between topics on which such agreement is relatively easy to get and topics on which agreement is relatively hard to get.

'Relativism' is the traditional epithet applied to pragmatism by realists. Three different views are commonly referred to by this name. The first is the view that every belief is as good as every other. The second is the view that 'true' is an equivocal term, having as many meanings as there are procedures of justification. The third is the view that there is nothing to be said about either truth or rationality apart from descriptions of the familiar procedures of justification which a given society—*ours*—uses in one or another area of inquiry. The pragmatist holds the ethnocentric third view. But he does not hold the self-refuting first view, nor the eccentric second view. He thinks that his views are better than the realists, but he does not think that his views correspond to the nature of things. He thinks that the very flexibility of the word 'true'—the fact that it is merely an expression of commendation—insures its univocity. The term 'true', on his account, means the same in all cultures, just as equally flexible terms like 'here', 'there', 'good', 'bad', 'you', and 'me' mean the same in all cultures. But the identity of meaning is, of course, compatible with diversity of reference, and with diversity of procedures for assigning the terms. So he feels free to use the term 'true' as a general term of commendation in the same way as his realist opponent does—and in particular to use it to commend his own view.

However, it is not clear why 'relativist' should be thought an appropriate term for the ethnocentric third view, the one which the pragmatist *does* hold. For the pragmatist is not holding a positive theory which says that something is relative to something else. He is, instead, making the purely *negative* point that we should drop the traditional distinction between knowledge and opinion, construed as the distinction between truth as correspondence to reality and truth as a commendatory term for well-justified beliefs. The reason that the realist calls this negative claim 'relativistic' is that he cannot believe that anybody would seriously deny that truth has an intrinsic nature. So when the pragmatist says that there is nothing to be said about truth save that each of us will commend as true those beliefs which he or she finds good to believe, the realist is inclined to interpret this as one more positive theory about the nature of truth: a theory according to which truth is simply the contemporary opinion of a chosen individual or group. Such a theory would,

(Continued)

of course, be self-refuting. But the pragmatist does not have a theory of truth, much less a relativistic one. As a partisan of solidarity, his account of the value of cooperative human inquiry has only an ethical base, not an epistemological or metaphysical one. Not having *any* epistemology, *a fortiori* he does not have a relativistic one.

* * *

[T]he question is not about how to define words like 'truth' or 'rationality' or 'knowledge' or 'philosophy', but about what self-image our society should have of itself. The ritual invocation of the 'need to avoid relativism' is most comprehensible as an expression of the need to preserve certain habits of contemporary European life. These are the habits nurtured by the Enlightenment, and justified by it in terms of an appeal of Reason, conceived as a transcultural human ability to correspond to reality, a faculty whose possession and use is demonstrated by obedience to explicit criteria. So the real question about relativism is whether these same habits of intellectual, social, and political life can be justified by a conception of rationality as criterionless muddling through, and by a pragmatist conception of truth.

I think that the answer to this question is that the pragmatist cannot justify these habits without circularity, but then neither can the realist. The pragmatists' justification of toleration, free inquiry, and the quest for undistorted communication can only take the form of a comparison between societies which exemplify these habits and those which do not, leading up to the suggestion that nobody who has experienced both would prefer the latter. It is exemplified by Winston Churchill's defence of democracy as the worst form of government imaginable, except for all the others which have been tried so far.

* * *

My suggestion that the desire for objectivity is in part a disguised form of the fear of the death of our community echoes Nietzsche's charge that the philosophical tradition which stems from Plato is an attempt to avoid facing up to contingency, to escape from time and chance. Nietzsche thought that realism was to be condemned not only by arguments from its theoretical incoherence, the sort of argument we find in Putnam and Davidson, but also on practical, pragmatic grounds. Nietzsche thought that the test of human character was the ability to live with the thought that there was no convergence. He wanted us to be able to think of truth as

> *a mobile army of metaphors, metonyms, and anthromorphisms—in short a sum of human relations, which have been enhanced, transposed, and embellished poetically and rhetorically and which after long use seem firm, canonical, and obligatory to a people.*[15]

Nietzsche hoped that eventually there might be human beings who could and did think of truth in this way, but who still liked themselves, who saw themselves as *good* people for whom solidarity was *enough*.

I think that pragmatism's attack on the various structure–content distinctions which buttress the realist's notion of objectivity can best be seen as an attempt to let us think of truth in this Nietzschean way, as entirely a matter of solidarity. That is why I think we need to say, despite Putnam, that 'there is only the dialogue', only *us*, and to throw out the last residues of the notion of 'transcultural rationality'. But this should not lead us to repudiate, as Nietzsche sometimes did, the elements in our movable host which embody the ideas of Socratic conversation, Christian fellowship, and Enlightenment science. Nietzsche ran together his diagnosis of philosophical realism as an expression of fear and resentment with his own resentful idiosyncratic idealizations of silence, solitude, and violence. Post-Nietzschean thinkers like Adorno and Heidegger and Foucault have run together Nietzsche's criticisms of the metaphysical tradition on the one hand with his criticisms of bourgeois civility, of Christian love, and of the nineteenth century's hope that science would make the world a better place to live, on the other. I do not think that there is any interesting connection between these two sets of criticisms. Pragmatism seems to me, as I have said, a philosophy of solidarity rather than of despair. From this point of view, Socrates' turn away from the gods, Christianity's turn from an Omnipotent Creator to the man who suffered on the Cross, and the Baconian turn from science as contemplation of eternal truth to science as instrument of social progress, can be seen as so many preparations for the act of social faith which is suggested by a Nietzschean view of truth.

The best argument we partisans of solidarity have against the realistic partisans of objectivity is Nietzsche's argument that the traditional Western metaphysico-epistemological way of firming up our habits simply isn't working anymore. It isn't doing its job. It has become as transparent a device as the postulation of deities who turn out, by a happy coincidence, to have chosen *us* as their people. So the pragmatist suggestion that we substitute a 'merely' ethical foundation for our sense of community—or, better, that we think of our sense of community as having no foundation except shared hope and the trust created by such sharing—is put forward on practical grounds. It is *not* put forward as a corollary of a metaphysical claim that the objects in the world contain no intrinsically action-guiding properties, nor of an epistemological claim that we lack a faculty of moral sense, nor of a semantic claim that truth is reducible to justification.

Rorty makes the point that our metaphysical theory of 'truth' has political overtones. The belief that there is one single truth can lead to condescension and disrespect toward people who believe differently from oneself. Only, however, if the absolutist believes, in addition to his absolutism, that he or his culture is closer to that one truth than are others.

> • What is the difference between 'objectivity' and 'solidarity' according to Rorty? Why does he favour 'solidarity'?

Rorty's new-fangled pragmatism is rooted in a rejection of two ideas that have been central to Western philosophy ever since Plato: first, the idea that the nature of truth is a deep and weighty philosophical topic; second, the idea that philosophy is a discipline that can judge the practices of our culture by appealing to ahistorical or 'transcultural' standards (for example—Plato's Forms, or the will of God, or Natural Law, or the timeless dictates of pure reason). Because Rorty thinks these old-fashioned ideas are now more trouble than they are worth, he is happy to abandon them; and he encourages us to do likewise. According to Rorty's version of pragmatism, truth is little more than what your cultural peers will let you get away with saying, and philosophy is a way of describing and re-imagining our culture's most fruitful practices from a perspective internal to those practices and their history.

What Rorty is telling us, in effect, is that we can never leave Plato's cave—that we can never get outside of our culture or our history and compare our worldview to an unconditioned reality existing 'in itself'. But if we cannot get out of the cave that is our culture, then there are no absolute or universal standards to which we can appeal. From this, Rorty thinks, two things follow. First, we cannot meaningfully contrast 'truth' with consensus among our fellow cave dwellers, so 'objectivity' is supplanted by 'solidarity'. Second, philosophy cannot judge what the cave dwellers tend to say or do from some higher, God-like perspective external to our shared practices. Once we get rid of the traditional ideas of 'truth' and 'objectivity' and 'knowledge' and 'justification', there is really nothing left for epistemologists to talk about. So enlightened philosophers should abandon epistemology altogether.

Must pragmatists agree with Rorty about all this? Absolutely not. Canadian philosopher Cheryl Misak, another leading pragmatist, defends a very different view of truth and of philosophy in her recent book *Truth, Politics, Morality: Pragmatism and Deliberation*. In the following excerpt, she singles out Rorty's radical views for criticism:

From *Truth, Politics, Morality*
By Cheryl Misak

Without the idea of truth, some core practices of inquiry, belief, and assertion cannot be explained or accounted for.

Rorty and the Abandonment of Justification

Richard Rorty has campaigned over the last two decades to explode an old philosophical picture of truth and objectivity and replace it with his version of pragmatism. In some quarters he has been so successful that the first task for any other kind of pragmatist is to wrest the label from him.

Many of Rorty's negative points are well within what I take to be the real spirit of pragmatism. We must, he urges, cease thinking of the mind as a 'great mirror, containing various representations' of the world.[16] For this thought requires us to attempt the impossible—to try to get outside of our own minds and see the world as it really is. And we must resist the temptation to seek answers to questions such as 'Is reality intrinsically determinate, or is its determinacy a result of our activity?' All the potential answers share presuppositions which we would be better off dropping. We cannot find solutions to insoluble problems—problems which are mischaracterized and which take us down ill-chosen paths.

It is Rorty's positive arguments which, upon scrutiny, break with the pragmatist aim of elucidating the notions of truth and knowledge in human terms. Rorty thinks that the philosopher should happily jettison the notion of truth altogether and speak rather of justification relative to one group of inquirers or another. Truth, right reason, rationality, validity, and the like are myths. Truth is merely what passes for good belief; it 'is not the sort of thing one should expect to have a philosophically interesting theory about'.[17] Indeed, Rorty is generally dismissive of theory. We must simply describe practice as we find it.

Were we to hold on to the term 'truth', against Rorty's advice, we would have to take it to mean that beliefs which are currently approved of are true. The notion of objectivity must be reinterpreted to mean intersubjectivity or 'solidarity'.[18] It is what we have come to take as true.

What, we might well ask, is left of philosophy? Sometimes Rorty suggests that the role left for the philosopher is to become a 'kibitzer'[19]—a kind of informal cultural critic. We must abandon the 'spirit of seriousness' and get down to some 'play'.[20] At other times, he says that philosophy must lower its sights and become a genre of literature or cultural studies.[21] It is a conversation governed not by truth and reasonableness, but by convention, culture, and personal interests. And at yet other times, he says that the philosopher's job is to produce generations of 'nice' liberal students.[22]

Of course, if truth is as Rorty describes, philosophy is not the only area of inquiry which must face up to the fact. Even in science, on his view, we can identify no standards over and beyond the ones we happen to find ourselves with. Rorty thinks that it has been a pernicious mistake for humanists (philosophers, historians, literary critics, etc.) to take the 'objectivity' of science for their model, for there is there no objectivity there either.[23]

And in politics, morals, and political philosophy, we should not expect to find a rational justification of democracy or liberalism, or of this or that conception of the good, for nowhere are rational justifications to be had. What we have is the ongoing conversation in which we must make our decisions, form our policies, and live our lives. Here, as everywhere, we are to 'substitute the idea of "unforced agreement" for that of "objectivity".'[24]

Rorty is a democrat and a liberal. The fact that he has given up the search for foundations does not, of course, lead him to give up his beliefs. But how, we will want to ask, can he assert that democracy, liberalism, and unforced agreement are best, if what is best is simply what is taken by some group to be best? It turns out that the 'we' in his claim that truth is what we take to be true is spelled out as follows: 'us twentieth-century Western social democrats',[25] 'Western liberal intellectuals',[26] 'us postmodernist bourgeois liberals'.[27] What is best to believe is what democrats and liberals take to be best to believe.

* * *

We might say that, as a pragmatist, Rorty is committed to bridging the gap between theory and practice and that the way he does it is by getting rid of theory and leaving only parochial practice. His is exactly the wrong way of looking at the relationship between philosophy and the ways we have of going on. The problem comes out starkly in the following passage, where it is recommended that philosophy be drawn from local custom:

> Given the preferences that we Americans share, given the adventure on which we are embarked, what should we say about truth, knowledge, reason, virtue, human nature, and all the other traditional philosophical topics?[28]

Taking the parochial status quo as a given and then going on to philosophy seems to be a strategy which arises out of despair—out of the realization that philosophy cannot provide us with a rock-solid, entirely universal, foundation for our beliefs. If we cannot be put 'in touch with the way things are', Rorty thinks we are left with no general criteria for justification at all. We are left with nothing but this or that way of doing things.

But surely the appropriate response to Rorty here is that philosophy need not adopt the foundationalist universalist model, nor need it abandon standards altogether. If certainty or an utterly secure grounding is what is being sought by philosophy, philosophy is not going to be of much use. We shall see that this is a point at the heart of pragmatism. But following hard on the heels of that point ought to be the insistence that philosophy need not be so useless. We shall see that there are other kinds of justifications which can go hand in hand with the requirement that philosophy be connected to practice.

We should, I think, cast our lot in with those attempts rather than abandon ship as quickly as Rorty advises. If we take inquiry as seriously as all pragmatists, including Rorty, recommend, the notion of truth cannot simply drop out of our vocabulary. For without the idea of truth, some core practices of inquiry, belief, and assertion cannot be explained or accounted for.

We assume, for instance, that it is appropriate to criticize the beliefs and actions of others and that we can make discoveries, mistakes, and progress. All of these practices need to appeal to something which goes beyond the parochial. We also require the concept of truth to distinguish between a belief which is adequate on the evidence and argument available, and a belief which would be adequate were all the evidence and argument available. Inquirers do not usually think that they have the truth in their hands, no matter how pleased they are with their views. In order to make sense of this thought, we must appeal to something which goes beyond what is reasonable here and now—we must appeal to truth. The pragmatist is well-advised to see what can be made of the notion of truth, before he recommends what the inquirer will find impossible.

- Where does Misak disagree with Rorty? Does she agree with any of his ideas?

K. The Nature of Truth: Three Theories

We have already mentioned the correspondence theory of truth, which has probably been the single most influential theory of truth in the history of Western philosophy. At first, the basic idea behind the correspondence theory may sound criminally simple: true beliefs (propositions, statements, sentences, ideas) are those that 'correspond' to reality. True beliefs, in other words, agree with the way things are. False beliefs don't.

Consider the following example. A man believes that his cat—Emerald, the world's laziest feline—is sitting on the mat in front of him. Ask yourself: What would make his belief true? What would make his belief false? If his belief is true, it is true because it corresponds to the way the world is—that is, it is true *because* Emerald is actually on the mat. If his belief is false, it is false because it fails to correspond to the way the world is—that is, it is false *because* Emerald is not on the mat.

According to the traditional correspondence theory of truth, truth is simply a matter of representing reality accurately: our beliefs, descriptions, and theories all aim to fit, match, picture, or reflect facts 'out there' in a world existing independently of our minds, our concepts, our language, and our culture. In a way, then, our beliefs and statements are like maps: they purport to describe something existing outside themselves, and they either get it right (in which case they are true) or they get it wrong (in which case they are false). Because what decides the truth-value of what we think or utter is nothing but the world, truth in this view is objective, not relative; found, not made; discovered, not constructed.

Although the correspondence theory of truth may seem both simple and plausible—a rare combination in a philosophical theory!—it has been criticized by many philosophers. Here are four common objections to the correspondence theory.

First, the theory itself doesn't define what, exactly, is meant by 'correspondence' or 'agreement'. We know that 'correspondence' is supposed to name the relation that holds between true beliefs and reality; but how are we to understand that relation? Unless we can specify what 'correspondence' means, a theory that appeals to 'correspondence' to explain truth isn't very informative. Until this question is answered, therefore, talk of 'correspondence' seems more of a metaphor than a philosophical theory.

Second, the theory doesn't satisfactorily explain what true beliefs *correspond to*. With what kind of thing or entity are they supposed to 'agree' or 'correspond'? To many philosophers, the answer has seemed obvious: true beliefs correspond to 'the facts'. But what, exactly, are facts? Here we need to be careful. Sometimes when we speak of '*facts*', we are simply using that word as a **synonym** for *truths*, meaning 'true propositions or beliefs'. However, a defender of the correspondence theory had better not be using the word *fact* in this sense; for then all she would be saying is that true beliefs correspond to true beliefs— and that certainly isn't very helpful. Perhaps what is meant by *fact* is something like an actual state of affairs in the world, such as the cat being on the mat in the kitchen. This suggestion sounds more promising; but it, too, faces problems. For what are we to say about beliefs such as 'There is no cat on the mat', or 'There is no milk in the refrigerator', or 'I do not have a brother'? If beliefs of this sort can be true—and they obviously can— doesn't this mean that there must be lots of shadowy 'negative' facts out there in the world, as well as positive ones? And here is another problem: How are we to identify facts? How do we count them or distinguish them? For instance, is the fact that makes the man's belief 'My cat is on the mat' true *the same fact* as the fact that makes his belief 'There is an animal in my house' true? Questions like these have kept the defenders of facts busy.

Third, the correspondence theory rests on a distorted picture of the mind's relation to the world. How so, you ask? For one thing, traditional formulations of the correspondence theory of truth presuppose some form of metaphysical **realism**; that is, the view that the world that our minds are trying to represent is objective and mind-independent. But what if such realism is false? What if the world of ordinary objects—of stones, trees, and streams—is in some sense *shaped* or *constituted* by the mind, as Kant and Schopenhauer maintained? If we get rid of the idea of a mind-independent reality against which our thoughts and theories can be measured, then we must also get rid of the idea of truth as correspondence with such a reality. Moreover, the idealist tradition beginning with Kant has rightly emphasized that the mind is fundamentally active and constructive in knowledge, imposing its forms on the raw and chaotic data of sensation. In contrast, the traditional correspondence theory of truth seems tied to a pre-Kantian picture of the mind as a fixed and passive mirror of the outside world. According to certain versions of the correspondence theory, the mind is not a creative source of order but a kind of glorified copying-machine whose chief function is to make mental duplicates of whatever already exists. And this has seemed flat-out wrong to many philosophers.

Fourth, some philosophers—especially philosophers influenced by Kant's 'revolution'— have alleged that the correspondence theory leads straight to external world skepticism. According to these thinkers, our only access to reality is mediated by our conceptual scheme. Because of this, even our most humdrum perceptions (for example—'There is a cat on yonder mat') are interpretations of sensory data conditioned by our scheme of concepts. And because of this, we can never compare our beliefs to an unconceptualized reality—to the way the world is 'in itself'—and determine that our beliefs correspond to it. Trapped within the iron ring of our representations, we have absolutely no way of telling whether any of those representations accurately reflect external things. The moral is as clear as it is grim: if truth is correspondence, we can never know whether *any* of our beliefs about the world are true. And this is a conclusion few find palatable.

All these objections are serious and important, but it would be premature to conclude that any of them actually *refutes* the correspondence theory of truth. Defenders of the theory have replied to these arguments (as well as to many others) with considerable ingenuity. So the correspondence theory in some form may survive after all.

Suppose, however, that the critics of correspondence are right. Ask yourself: if truth is not a matter of correspondence with reality, what could it possibly be?

Here we find much disagreement among philosophers. Of course, some philosophers respond by rejecting all questions about the nature of truth because they believe that there is no 'deep' philosophical answer to be found. For such philosophers, truth cannot be defined, analyzed, or identified with *any* property (of which correspondence is but one example). But such absolute rejections have become popular only recently, promoted by contemporary philosophers such as Richard Rorty, whom we met earlier in this chapter. Until the late twentieth century, almost all philosophers who thought hard about truth subscribed to the view that truth *does* have a nature that philosophical analysis can uncover and elucidate. If we accept this earlier view of truth, we are left with two common alternatives to the correspondence theory: the coherence theory of truth and the pragmatic theory of truth.

According to the coherence theory, truth is best understood as coherence among one's beliefs, not as correspondence between one's beliefs and a reality lying outside of them. Now, what does this dictum mean? Essentially this: that truth is a property of wholes, not of parts; it is a property that belongs to an entire system of beliefs, as opposed to a component of such a system. Thus we must understand the truth of an individual belief in terms of that belief's membership in a *coherent* set of beliefs, that is, a set that is logically consistent (it contains no contradictions), suitably comprehensive (it leaves nothing out), and systematically integrated (its parts are unified, with no part floating free from the rest).

Where correspondence theorists fall back on mirror metaphors (to capture the idea that true beliefs *represent* reality), coherence theorists are partial to a different metaphor: that of a spider's web. To understand this metaphor, ask yourself: What makes a web a *good* web? The answer is simple: the excellence of a web is essentially a matter of how well its threads *hang together*. In a well-spun web, innumerable fine threads are woven together in such a way that the whole thing becomes broad and strong, with no weak parts, frayed threads, bald patches, or whispy strands. And what, you ask, does this have to do with the coherence theory? Well, explains the coherentist, we are the web-spinning spiders, the threads are individual beliefs, and the web is the worldview constituted by our beliefs. And just as what makes a web good is its cohesiveness, what makes a system of beliefs true is its coherence. What really counts, in other words, is how well our worldview hangs together, not whether it can be said to 'correspond' to a realm of mind-independent fact.

This, at any rate, is the view taken in one form or another by many philosophers, especially those who have followed Kant in thinking that we cannot compare our beliefs to reality as it is 'in itself'. As they see it, the coherence theory of truth saves us from an intolerable skepticism; for if the truth of our beliefs consisted in their correspondence to the way things are in themselves, we could never know whether any of our beliefs about the world were true. But we can know whether our beliefs cohere or hang together, they maintain, because we have direct access to them and immediate knowledge of them. So if truth is correspondence, they conclude, we are prevented from having knowledge of the world; but if truth is coherence, they add, we are not.

However, critics of the coherence theory have frequently pointed out that a system of beliefs can be coherent without being true. A fairy tale might be coherent, they remind us, but that doesn't make it true. Critics also object that there could be two equally coherent system of beliefs that contradict each other, and thus cannot both be true. And if such contradiction is possible, shouldn't we conclude that mere coherence isn't sufficient for truth?

Defenders of a coherence theory of truth have come up with thoughtful replies to these and other objections. In our next reading, the Canadian philosopher James O. Young, author of *Global Anti-realism*, discusses some of the attractions of a coherence theory of truth while calling attention to certain problems that coherentists cannot afford to ignore.

'Could Truth Be Coherence with a System of Beliefs?'
By James O. Young

Most people, when asked what it is for a proposition to be true, will give an answer something like the one Plato gave thousands of years ago: 'a true proposition says that which is, and a false proposition says that which is not.'[29] What Plato believed, and what most people who have thought about truth since his time have believed, is that true propositions represent (or correspond to) objective features of reality. This view of truth, usually called the correspondence theory of truth, can seem like unassailable common sense. A few philosophers have, however, had doubts about the correspondence theory and opted, instead, for a coherence theory of truth (or *coherentism*). These philosophers believe that to say that a proposition is true is to say that it coheres with a system of beliefs. A proposition is true, in this view, not when it stands in a relation (correspondence) to reality, but when it stands in a relation (coherence) to other propositions that are held to be true (or believed). A proposition coheres with beliefs when they justify it. While this theory of truth may seem counterintuitive, it is a consequence of two widely held philosophical premises.

The first premise that leads to coherentism is that truth is an epistemic concept, that is, it is linked to what users of propositions (or speakers) can be justified in believing. The correspondence theory of truth entails that truth is a non-epistemic concept: a proposition can be true even if no one could ever *know* that it is true. Consider, for example, the proposition that

(1) Sir John A. MacDonald wrote ten sentences on 17 November 1877.

There is no way to tell whether (1) is true. Nevertheless, the correspondence theorist holds that either (1) is true or its negation is. Some philosophers believe, however, that if speakers cannot be justified in believing a proposition, then it cannot be true. The coherence theory of truth is such an epistemic theory of truth.

Philosophers are led to adopt an epistemic conception of truth by reflecting on meaning. The concepts of meaning and truth are closely connected, and many philosophers believe that when speakers know the *meaning* of a proposition, they know the conditions under which the proposition is *true* (its *truth-conditions*). Arguably, when speakers know the meaning of a proposition, they also know what would justify the proposition. Several arguments have been advanced for this view. One of these is the *acquisition argument*, which is based on the premise that whenever speakers know the meaning of a proposition, they may be said to understand it. The acquisition argument states that the only understanding that speakers can acquire is knowledge of justification conditions. The only training that speakers can be given teaches them that a proposition is rightly asserted when conditions that justify the proposition obtain. Consequently, the understanding that speakers possess when they understand a proposition consists in knowledge of justification conditions.

If the meaning of a proposition consists in its truth-conditions and when speakers understand a proposition they grasp what would justify it, then the truth-conditions of a proposition consist in what would justify it. This conclusion, in turn, leads to the conclusion that for a sentence to be true is for it to be justifiable. If the conditions that justify a proposition obtain, then the proposition is true. If a proposition cannot be justified, then it cannot be true.

The second premise is the coherence theory of justification. In this theory, any proposition is justified when it coheres with a system of beliefs. Our beliefs are inter-connected in such a way that they lend each other mutual support. We do not believe any propositions that stand alone, not needing justification by other beliefs. For example, the proposition 'This greenish, salt-like compound contains copper' is justified by beliefs such as the belief that copper can form compounds that are greenish and salt-like, the belief that copper is an element that can exist within a compound, the belief that the compound is observed to be greenish and salt-like, and so on. Even reports of observation need to be justified, according to the coherence theory of justification, by our beliefs. The proposition that I am seeing something greenish is justified by the belief that the conditions of observation (lighting, for example) are normal and by the belief that I am not dreaming.

The coherence theory of justification leads to some startling conclusions when it is combined with the Duhem thesis. According to the Duhem thesis, we can adopt any hypothesis we like, so long as we make enough adjustments elsewhere in our system of beliefs. Suppose, to continue with the example of the copper compound, that I combine the contents of two test tubes, one of which I believe to contain copper sulfate, the other of which I believe to contain sodium carbonate; I further believe that, when these substances are combined, the result will be copper carbonate, which is a greenish, salt-like compound. Now, suppose that the mixture fails to turn green. One of my beliefs has to be given up, but we cannot know with certainty which one must be abandoned. I can give up my belief that the first test tube contained copper sulfate, my belief that the second test tube contained sodium carbonate, my belief that the two compounds yield copper carbonate, or my belief that copper carbonate is greenish and salt-like. I can even give up my belief that the mixture failed to turn green. The system of beliefs we adopt must enable us to navigate around the world, but any number of systems of beliefs are equally good for this purpose. The Duhem thesis has another striking consequence: we are never in a position to say *which* propositions correspond to how reality is. We can only determine which hypotheses cohere with a given system of beliefs.

A coherence theory of truth results when an epistemic conception of truth is combined with a coherence theory of justification. Speakers can only know that a given proposition is justified by coherence with a system of beliefs. They can never know how the world is, only how their system of beliefs says the world is. Their understanding of a proposition can only consist in what they can know (and this is the only understanding that they can acquire). Consequently, their understanding of a proposition can only consist in knowledge of the conditions under which the proposition is justified with a system of beliefs. The argument for this coherentism can be summarized as follows:

(P1) *For a proposition to be true is for it to be justifiable.*

(P2) *A proposition can only be justified by coherence with a system of beliefs.*

∴ (C) *For a proposition to be true is for it to be justified by coherence with a system of beliefs.*

A feature of this version of the coherence theory of truth needs to be highlighted. The system is not to be identified with the beliefs of any individual speaker. Rather, the system is the maximal consistent that can be derived from the beliefs of a community of speakers. The system is chosen because it is composed of the beliefs that speakers have available to them as they learn a language. Other versions of the coherence theory maintain that truth is coherence with some ideal set of beliefs: what would be believed once all of the possible evidence is collected. Still other versions of the theory hold that truth is coherence with an even more ideal set: what an omniscient being would believe. As we will see, saying that for a proposition to be true is for it to cohere with an actual system of beliefs can lead to questions about coherentism.

Over the years, many objections to the coherence theory of truth have been advanced. According to one common objection, a proposition could be true even though it does not cohere with any system of beliefs. Advocates of this objection will invite us to consider again a proposition such as (1). This proposition does not cohere with any system of beliefs: no one has, or ever will have, beliefs with which (1) coheres. Nevertheless, someone may argue, it could be true. If so, then truth cannot be identified with coherence with a system of beliefs.

The coherence theory can easily be defended against this objection. Coherentists can reply that, in asserting that (1) may be true even though it does not cohere with a system of beliefs, the objector begs the

(Continued)

question against the coherence theory. As stated, the objection simply assumes that a proposition can be true even if it does not cohere with a system of beliefs. This is what is at issue. The objection gives no *reason* to believe that a proposition can be true even though it fails to cohere with a system of beliefs.

One could hold that classical logic provides us with a reason for believing that (1) could be true even though it does not cohere with a system of beliefs. The opponent of the coherence theory could argue that the negation of (1), namely,

(2) Sir John A. MacDonald did not write ten sentences on 17 November 1877

does not cohere with a system of beliefs either and, so, according to the coherence theory cannot be true. Yet, according to the law of excluded middle, either (1) or its negation must be true. So it seems that truth cannot be coherence with a system of beliefs. Coherentists can defend themselves against this objection, but only at the cost of rejecting the law of excluded middle. Anyone who adopts an epistemic conception of truth will need to reject parts of classical logic. Fortunately for the coherentist, alternative logics, such as intuitionist logic, are available.

Some philosophers have rejected the coherence theory of truth on the grounds that it is committed to an idealist metaphysics: the view that reality is dependent on mind. Certainly some early adherents of the coherence theory were idealists; in fact, some philosophers were moved to adopt coherentism precisely because they were antecedently committed to idealism. According to an idealist, the distinction between reality and our mental representation of reality does not exist. (Think, for example, of Berkeley's dictum that 'to be is to be perceived'.) When this distinction is collapsed, then truth cannot be understood in terms of a relationship between mental representations of reality (such as propositions) and reality. Since many philosophers find idealism implausible, they are moved to reject the coherence theory as well.

A coherentist need not, however, be committed to idealism. As the theory is formulated in this essay, it is purely a theory about truth and has, qua theory of truth, no metaphysical implications. Whether coherentists are idealists or physicalists will depend on which (if either) of these doctrines coheres with their system of beliefs. The proposition that there is a mind-independent world may cohere with a system, in which case coherentists would be physicalists, but they would not be committed to physicalism by their coherentism.

This may seem to be an inadequate response to the charge that coherentism leads to idealism. Consider again (1). According to coherentism, neither this sentence nor its negation is true, because neither is justifiable. An opponent of coherentism could charge that, as a result, there is no fact of the matter about how many sentences MacDonald wrote on the day in question. This seems to make the facts depend on what we can be justified in believing, and so to make reality dependent on our minds, as idealists believe. The coherentist can reply to this objection by saying that from the premise that (1) is neither true nor false, we cannot conclude that there is no fact about how many sentences MacDonald wrote. Correspondence theorists typically believe that what is true and what is real are closely linked. But coherentists have no such view. From the failure of a proposition to be true, one can only conclude that it does not cohere with a system of beliefs. One cannot infer anything about reality. This may be an odd view, but it is not an idealist view.

Another objection to the coherence theory challenges the coherentist to specify the system of beliefs with which propositions cohere. The charge is that coherentists cannot do so without contradicting their position. A simple version of this objection, developed by Bertrand Russell, states that the coherence theory has the consequence that patent falsehoods are true. The proposition that

(3) Sir John A. MacDonald was a teetotaler

coheres with some set of propositions. But MacDonald was known to have drank quite a lot of alcohol in his lifetime, and accounts of his behaviour survive for us in historical records. One could write an alternative universe novel in which MacDonald never drank alcohol, yet (3) is obviously false, when faced with what is recorded in history. More generally, any proposition can be made to cohere with some set of propositions. Russell charged that coherentists cannot respond to this objection by saying that that (3) is false because it coheres with a set of propositions that do not correspond to reality. This would be to contradict their theory of truth, by assuming that some propositions correspond to reality. The coherentist can, however, simply say that Russell's objection misses the mark because it mischaracterizes the coherence theory. Coherentists never said that true propositions cohere with just any set of propositions.

They cohere with a set of beliefs, of propositions held to be true.

Finally the coherentism described can be accused of leading to relativism about truth. A coherence theory that identifies truth with coherence with an ideal set of beliefs does not lead to relativism. There is only one ideal set of beliefs, and so only one set of true propositions. The set of beliefs that a community of speakers actually holds is, however, constantly changing. Consequently, the propositions that cohere with a community's set of beliefs will also be constantly changing. This is just to say that propositions are true relative to the beliefs of a community of speakers.

The coherence theory sketched here appears to have no response to this objection. The coherentist can only grasp the thistle and accept relativism. For some readers this may be too much to accept. Perhaps they were willing to embrace an epistemic conception of truth. Perhaps they were willing to revise classical logic. Perhaps they were even willing to reject the link between truth and reality. Relativism may, however, be the last straw. At any rate, readers should now have some idea about what would lead someone to adopt a coherence theory of truth, and some idea about the consequences of accepting such a theory.

Finally, we turn to the pragmatic theory of truth. Perhaps we should not speak of 'the' pragmatic theory, however, since there are at least two theories of truth to which that vague label has been applied. According to one version—a version first formulated by C.S. Peirce, the founder of pragmatism—truth is explained in terms of the practice or conduct of inquiry. To say, as Peirce does, that truth is what we would accept at 'the end of inquiry' is to say that the true opinion on some matter (for example—the number of stars in our solar system) is that opinion which a community of rational and responsible inquirers would ultimately arrive at, if they were allowed to push their investigations as far as possible. According to a second version of the pragmatic theory—a version associated with William James and John Dewey—true ideas and theories are best thought of not as maps or mirrors meant to represent reality, but as tools or instruments that empower us to remake the world in our own image. Like tools and instruments generally, the intellectual conceptions and categories we use to interpret our experience are human creations that are to be judged by their consequences—that is, by how well they serve our various interests, purposes, and needs. So truth isn't a matter of copying reality, but of coping with it.

Why have pragmatic accounts of truth struck certain philosophers as attractive? What do such accounts seem to get right? What do they seem to get wrong? And how are such theories related to the correspondence and coherence theories? In our next reading, Mark Migotti, a Canadian philosopher with a profound knowledge of the pragmatist tradition, helps us understand what is distinctive about the pragmatist approach—or approaches—to the problem of truth.

'Pragmatist Theories of Truth'
By Mark Migotti

Pragmatism was conceived by its founders, Charles Sanders Peirce and William James, as a fresh, reformist approach to philosophy. Peirce's description of his philosophy as '[growing out of] a contrite fallibilism, combined with a high faith in the reality of knowledge, and an intense desire to find things out'[30] nicely captures an important common feature of pragmatist theories of truth: trying to do justice both to our manifest ability to bring truth within our grasp (hence the 'high faith in the reality of knowledge'), and to the no less manifest impossibility of ever making our human hold on the truth perfectly secure and immune to revision (hence the 'contrite fallibilism').

(Continued)

In the late 1870s, Peirce set forth the basic elements of a pragmatist conception of truth in a seminal article entitled 'How to Make Our Ideas Clear'. Here, he sets the stage for his analysis of truth with a critique of the Cartesian doctrine of clear and distinct ideas. According to Descartes, what is perceived clearly and distinctly cannot be false. According to Peirce, once we recognize that something that *seems* to be clearly and distinctly perceived can turn out to be wrong, we realize that it is not clear what, exactly, 'clear and distinct' means.

Instead of Descartes' dual distinction, Peirce distinguishes three 'grades of clarity' (or levels of understanding) of ideas or concepts. At the first level of clarity, an idea is understood well enough for everyday use, and its object can be easily recognized in most circumstances; at the second level, it can be given a verbal definition. For example, the concept of a triangle is clear at the first grade when slices of pie, doorstops, etc. can be distinguished from other things in respect of shape, and it achieves the second grade when it is defined as 'a three-sided plane figure'.

At the first level, the idea of truth is clear; we are introduced to it in early childhood with the distinction between a true story and a 'made-up' one, a true statement and a lie. As Peirce observes, however, our ability to use the concept of truth in daily life does not guarantee that we understand in general terms what it means for that concept to apply, and it would 'probably puzzle most men' to produce an abstract definition of truth. Undaunted, philosophers have proposed to define truth with such forms of words as '*adequatio intellectus et rei*' (adequacy of mind and thing), or 'correspondence to the facts', or 'agreement with reality'. Pragmatists, however, do not believe that any such 'nominal' definition of truth can deliver real insight into what it is for an idea to be true.

According to what would later become known as 'the Pragmatic Maxim', 'the rule for attaining the third grade of clearness of apprehension is as follows: Consider what effects which might conceivably have practical bearings we conceive the object of our conception to have. Then, our conception of these effects is the whole of our conception of the object.'[31] According to Peirce, the truth of an idea has two chief practical effects. First, if an idea is true, then, when acted on, it 'will carry us to the point we aim at and not astray'; and second, when a subject is inquired into, the truth about that subject will emerge in the indefinitely long run. So truth, pragmatically understood, is 'the *opinion* which is fated to be ultimately agreed to by all who investigate'[32] (emphasis added).

All pragmatists share Peirce's dissatisfaction with philosophical definition by verbal formula alone; and they all agree that the concept of truth is intimately and intricately linked to the concepts of action, inquiry, and belief. Pragmatists are unanimous too in developing their theories of truth not in isolation from the rest of their philosophy but in harness with their larger concerns. But different pragmatists have different larger concerns, and so conceive the details of these conceptual linkages differently.

Like Kant, whom he once described as 'nothing but a somewhat confused pragmatist',[33] Peirce sought to set philosophy on the path of science. But *qua* fallibilist, Peirce would have been disinclined to follow Kant in describing the path of science as especially 'secure',[34] and *qua* pragmatist, he would have been completely opposed to Kant's idea that a scientific philosophy must be a priori. In Peirce's view, a scientific philosophy will not sit in judgment on the rest of science, but will play its part within the ongoing effort to explain things; and a crucial first step in making philosophy scientific is to take to heart the fact that, since philosophy is a branch of inquiry, its goal, like that of inquiry generally, is truth. The first qualification of 'a man of science', Peirce writes, is that 'the dominant passion of his whole soul . . . be to find out the truth in some department, regardless of what the colour of that truth may be'.[35]

That truth is the goal of inquiry is a mere platitude; what is philosophically substantial, and contested, is Peirce's claim that at the third, pragmatic level of understanding, what it is to be true is made clear by reference to what it is to inquire, rather than the other way around. 'Absolutist', 'metaphysical realist' philosophers think this is a big mistake. As they see it, truth simply is what it is, quite independently of anything to do with us. Pragmatists think that this superficially innocuous claim is dangerously ambiguous. On one interpretation, 'truth is independent of us' is a truism; truth *must* be independent of us if it is to be the goal of inquiry. When we inquire we seek to discover how things are, not to alter them or express how we think they should be or would like them to be; and if discovery is to occur, there must be things independent of us and our inclinations to discover.

But the independence of truth from us can also be taken in a philosophically contentious sense that, pragmatists hold, compromises the intelligibility of inquiry 'from the other side', so to speak; for if seeking something is to be a coherent undertaking, the object sought must be not only independent of us but also accessible to us. If what we are seeking in our inquiries, the truth, is something that might forever escape our grasp and could never, even in principle, be established as the genuine article, then how do we begin to search for it? If you were offered a chance to search for the Holy Grail, but told beforehand that you could never be confident that you had actually found the real thing as opposed to a fake, the undertaking would probably strike you as a great waste of time. Truth, understood as something utterly transcendent, wholly divorced from human activity, has no pragmatic meaning at all.

That truth and inquiry are related to each other in the doubly reciprocal fashion outlined above does not entail that there can be truth *only* where there is also inquiry. There are many things that human beings will never know or care to find out; and the pragmatist can be fairly asked how his theory can account for the truth of such 'buried secrets'. In response to this challenge, Peirce pointed out that we can never tell in advance how much it may be possible to find out, and he noted how often unexpected advances in knowledge have allows us to uncover much about the universe and its history long thought to be utterly beyond recovery, and to draw the moral that we can never tell how much it might be possible to find out. Whether or not Peirce can solve the problem of buried secrets without compromising his pragmatism—a question that continues to be discussed among interpreters of his thought—the fact that he takes the problem seriously distinguishes his version of pragmatism from James', Dewey's, and Richard Rorty's; for from their various perspectives, the problem of buried secrets is at best a minor annoyance, at worst a specious distraction.

Like Peirce, James held that the meaning of truth must be given 'in experiential terms';[36] but he was also concerned to put philosophy to practical use in ways often quite foreign to Peirce's scientific, logically oriented philosophy. And where Peirce was inveterately hostile to nominalism, the doctrine that only particulars are real, James was a lifelong nominalist, and his nominalistic emphasis on the concrete and the 'particular go' of things leads him to be more impressed than Peirce—or perhaps better, impressed in a different way—by the variety of vocabularies and schemes of classification in which candidates for truth and falsity are formulated. The night sky, for example, can be divided up into different constellations with different names, no one of which is the uniquely correct grouping of the heavenly bodies. When James avers that 'the trail of the human serpent is over everything',[37] he sounds as if, like his contemporary the English pragmatist F.C.S. Schiller, he takes pragmatism to be closely allied to a quite unPeircean kind of neo-Protagorean humanism.

John Dewey, the last major pragmatist of the 'classical' phase of the movement, was especially concerned to move philosophy beyond such hidebound philosophical dualisms as mind versus body, theory versus practice, fact versus value, sensation versus thought, and so on. So it will be no surprise to learn that he rejects both sides of the debate between coherence and correspondence theorists of truth. Like Peirce and James, and defenders of a coherence account of truth, Dewey denies that an appeal to a mysterious, *sui generis* correspondence relation between something in the mind (e.g. a belief) and reality or facts can do any useful work in the theory of truth. But like defenders of a correspondence account of truth, Dewey (and Peirce and James) deny that a theory of truth which purports to do away with things outside the mind altogether can be satisfactory.

Dewey endorses Peirce's pragmatist definition of truth as the opinion fated to be ultimately agreed to by all who investigate, but embeds it in a radically novel account of investigation. According to Dewey, the seductively uncomplicated fact that *to inquire* is *to seek to discover how things are* should not be taken to license what he called 'the spectator theory of knowledge', the view that to know things is to 'see them in the mind's eye'. According to the spectator theory, knowledge is a matter of accurately registering the contents of a world of 'ready-made', antecedently existing objects; we know best when we interfere least. Dewey holds that this conception of the relationship between mind and world is blind to the manifold ways in which that relationship is *trans*active and mutually transformative. As Dewey conceives it, inquiring is a kind of coping. He argues that theory is not opposed to practice, but is a specific form of practice, having little to do with sheer contemplation of the world, and everything to do with purposeful intervention in the world—in the form of inquisitive experimentation, intelligent manipulation, creative conjecture, rigorous testing, and so on. And the ultimate end of inquiry is not a redundant representation of the world in thought, but a reduction of its ability to frustrate us in our diverse endeavours.

(Continued)

Fundamentally, the Deweyan inquirer is a problem-solver striving to enhance human life by overcoming intellectual obstacles to fruitful, efficient action.

A century after the pragmatist tradition was inaugurated by Peirce, Richard Rorty began to articulate his influential brand of neo-pragmatism, according to which the movement culminates in a sweeping rejection of philosophical ambition. Like Dewey, Rorty is concerned with the place of philosophy in culture and society. But instead of Dewey's goal of reforming philosophy by replacing worse theories with better ones, Rorty urges a frank abandonment of traditional philosophical projects across the board, and of the philosophical theory of truth in particular. Rorty distinguishes efforts to answer technical logico-semantic questions about truth—to which he insists he has no objection—from efforts to achieve the traditional philosophical goal of laying bare the true nature of truth. He is convinced that the latter enterprise is intellectually bankrupt: according to his pragmatist theory, 'truth is not the sort of thing one should expect to have a philosophically interesting theory about'.[38]

Rorty's hostility to philosophical theorizing is fuelled by his conviction that no philosophical theories have thus far been successful, those of the classical pragmatists included. So why does he think of his work as contributing to the pragmatist tradition?

Because, having written Peirce off as a failed revolutionary, he then (mis)reads James and Dewey as anti-theoretical philosophers like himself. In Rorty's version of what has nicely been called 'the higher dismissiveness', James' idea that vocabularies or conceptual schemes should be judged as more or less adequate to different purposes (rather than simply true or false, correct or incorrect) becomes the idea that creative redescription is a more fruitful, achievable ideal than accurate representation; and Dewey's idea of inquiry as coping becomes the idea of inquiry as negotiation, aimed not at truth but at persuasion, or 'unforced agreement'.

Peirce wanted pragmatism to make philosophy scientific; Rorty wants it to make philosophy literary. James hoped that pragmatism would 'unstiffen' our philosophical theories; Rorty hopes it will rid us of them. Dewey viewed pragmatist philosophy as advancing the cause of democratic politics; Rorty views it as highlighting 'the priority of democracy *over* philosophy'. This is a strange state of affairs, one that perhaps proves the French adage that '*les extrêmes se touchent*' (the extremes meet). For if anti-pragmatist metaphysical realists dwell on the independence of truth at the expense of making its accessibility an impenetrable mystery, the revolutionary pragmatist Rorty—in reducing truth to agreement, something he presumes to be readily accessible—denies its independence outright.

- What differences do you see between the correspondence theory and the coherence theory? Which theory strikes you as superior? Why?
- Why is there no such thing as the pragmatist theory of truth? Which pragmatist ideas about truth strike you as most plausible? Why?

L. Feminist Epistemology

In the second half of the twentieth century, feminism grew from a worldwide social protest movement to a profound philosophical challenge to traditional theories of knowledge. Today, it is no longer just a social-political movement striving to attain equal opportunities for women in education and in advancement in the sciences (although that is still a serious issue), but comprises a claim that women's knowledge—and pursuit of knowledge—is actually different from men's. The argument is that epistemology and knowledge, while they are presented as gender-neutral, are in fact largely male defined, that is, 'patriarchal' in the now-established language of feminist discourse. In the following selections, the idea of a feminist epistemology is presented by two eminent feminist philosophers: the Australian Elizabeth Grosz and the Canadian Lorraine Code.

On Feminist Knowledge
By Elizabeth Grosz

No one method, point of view, position for subjects and objects is the norm or model for all philosophy.

There is considerable disagreement among feminists about which approach to take in questioning philosophy's sexist, patriarchal, and phallocentric assumptions. They are divided over whether to accept philosophy on its own terms, to undertake a revision of it in the light of feminist knowledges, to abandon it, or actively to undermine it. Radical feminists challenge philosophy's orientation around *oneness*, unity, or identity—one truth, one method, one reality, one logic, and so on. Many have insisted that there are a plurality of perspectives and a multiplicity of models on which philosophy could base itself.

In their endorsement of plurality and multiplicity, feminists such as Le Doeuff, Irigaray, and Lloyd are not, however, committed to relativism. Relativism is the belief that there are no absolute positions of judgment or knowledge. There are many positions, each of which is *equally valid*. Relativism or pluralism implies the existence of frameworks and positions which each have their own validity and standards; and the belief that none of these positions is comprehensive or all-inclusive.

Pluralism and relativism imply abandoning the right to criticize actively other positions, even those we find offensive and disturbing—phallocentric or racist statements, for example—and to accept them as having equal validity to our own positions. Radical feminists instead aim to expand and multiply the criteria for what is considered true, rational, or valid and to reject or condemn those they perceive to be discriminatory. They insist on retaining the right to judge other positions, to criticize them, and also to supersede them. Radical feminists are not absolutists nor objectivists nor relativists nor subjectivists. They advocate a *perspectivism* which acknowledges other points of view but denies them equal value.

It is at this time impossible to specify what a philosophy compatible with feminism would be like; given that it does not exist as a definite body of texts, any definition or description would be overly prescriptive. Nevertheless, some general tendencies can be briefly outlined.

Among the features a feminist philosophy may develop are the following:

(a) Instead of a commitment to truth and objectivity, it can openly accept its own status (and that of all discourses) as context-specific. It accepts its *perspectivism*, that fact that all discourses represent a point of view, have specific aims and objectives, often not coinciding with those of their authors. Rather than seeing itself as disinterested knowledge, it can openly avow its own political position: all texts speak from or represent particular positions within power relations.

(b) Instead of regarding philosophy as the unfolding of reason, a sure path of progress towards truth, a feminist philosophy can accept itself as the product of a specific socio-economic and textual-discursive history. Neither relativist nor subjectivist, it aims to render these and other binary oppositions problematic. A feminist philosophy defies modes of conventional evaluation. This is not, however, to claim that it cannot be evaluated in any terms; simply that the criteria used must be different. A theory's validity is not judged simply according to its adoption of a fixed or pre-given form, but it may be judged according to its *intersubjective* effects, that is, its capacity to be shared, understood, and communicated by those occupying similar positions; and also by its *intertextual* effects, that is, its capacity to affirm or undermine various prevailing or subordinated discursive systems, and the effects it has on other discourses.

(c) Instead of separating the subject and object of knowledge, a feminist philosophy may instead assert a continuity or contiguity between them. The gulf necessary for objectivity is an attempt to guarantee a knowing subject free of personal, social, political, and moral interests (a Cartesian subject), unimplicated in a social context, and uninfluenced by prior ideas and knowledges. A feminist philosophy would need to reconceptualize their interrelations so that reason and knowledge include history, context, and specificity. A

(*Continued*)

feminist philosophy could accept, as patriarchal discourses cannot, that subjects occupying different positions may develop different types of theory and have different investments in their relation to the object. Above all, it can accept that all knowledge is *sexualized*, that it occupies a sexually coded and structured position. However, the sexual position of the text cannot be readily identified with the sexual identity of its author; a female author, for example, does not in any way guarantee a feminine text.

(d) Instead of the dichotomous, oppositional structure, which separates subject and object, teacher and pupil, truth and falsity, etc., a feminist philosophy may regard these terms as continuities or *differences*. Distinctions or oppositions imply that two binary terms are mutually exclusive and exhaustive of the field; that one term defines the other as its negative; that this other can have a place in the binary structure; however, when terms are conceived as two among many others, they are neither contradictory nor all-inclusive. If anything, the relation of difference is based on contrariety not contradiction.

(e) Instead of aspiring to the status of truth, a feminist philosophy prefers to see itself as a form of *strategy*. Strategies are not abstractions, blueprints, or battle-plans for future action. Rather, they involve a provisional commitment to goals and ideals; a recognition of the prevailing situation, in opposition to which these ideals are erected; and an expedient relation to terms, arguments, and techniques that help transform the prevailing order into the ideal. To deny that a feminist philosophy aspires to truth is not to claim it is content with being regarded as false; rather, the opposition between truth and falsity is largely irrelevant for a strategic model.

(f) Instead of dividing theory from practice—so that practice is located chronologically before and after theory (construed as either a plan or a *post facto* reflection, respectively)—a feminist philosophy may regard theory as a form of practice, a textual, conceptual, and educational practice, one involved in struggles for theoretical ascendancy, where dominant and subordinated discourses battle with each other. Theory is not privileged by its isolation from practice and its relegation to a pure conceptual level. When it is seen as a material process, theory can be seen as a practice like any other, neither more nor less privileged in its ability to survey and assess other practices. As a material labour or practice, theory relies on concepts, words, and discursive 'raw materials', processes of theoretical production (e.g., the form of argument, narrative, or linguistic structure needed to make coherent discourses) and a determined product (a text or theory). It is not hierarchically privileged over other practices, reserving the right of judgment; rather it is itself capable of being assessed by other practices.

(g) Instead of opposing reason to its others, a feminist philosophy expands the concept of reason. It has analyzed how reason as we know it is allied with masculinity and relegates feminine attributes to a repressed or subordinated status. A feminist philosophy would not reverse the relation between reason and its others, but would expand reason so that its expelled others are now included. In beginning with women's lived experiences in the production of knowledge it seeks a reason that is not separated from experience but based upon it, that is not opposed to the body but accepts it, not distinct from everyday life but cognizant of it.

(h) Instead of accepting dominant models of knowledge (with their logic, binary structure, desire for precision and clarity) a feminist philosophy can accept its status as material, textual, and institutional. As such, it can accept the provisional, not eternal, status of its postulates. It aims for the production of new methods of knowing, new forms of analysis, new modes of writing, new kinds of textual objects, new texts. No *one* method, point of view, position for subjects and objects is the norm or model for all philosophy.

You may still be wondering just how the sex or gender of a knower can be epistemologically significant. After all, you might say, knowledge is knowledge, no matter whose it is; so what possible difference does it make whether a knower is male or female? In our next reading, Lorraine Code, a pioneer in the field of feminist epistemology, addresses this very question.

From 'Is the Sex of the Knower Epistemologically Significant?'
By Lorraine Code

The question arises, then, whether there are distinct male and female languages which point to a sexual relativism in knowledge.

Kant's concept of the creative synthesis of the imagination is a revolutionary concept in the history of epistemology in its placing of the epistemological subject at the centre of the cognitive process. It is possible, without losing sight of its original sense, to extend the scope of the Kantian creative synthesis to a full recognition of the knowing subject as person, rather than merely as knower in a more anonymous sense. This points to the further contention that each individual's knowledge has its particular shape as much as a result of what he or she is as because of what the world is. Knowledge comes into existence as a result of a cooperative interaction of the will, feeling, thought, and perception of individual knowing subjects. This is not to deny that the objective nature of reality and of human cognitive structures determine and delimit the ways of knowing which can have validity and stand fast. Nor is it to deny that knowledge must develop according to logical principles, where contradiction and inconsistency can be recognized and eradicated. Nevertheless, within these limits there is a wide spectrum of diversity.

The person with strongly fundamentalist religious convictions, for example, may well see and understand Darwinian theory in a manner quite different from that of the person who is not committed to any form of religious belief. (Edmund Gosse, in his work *Father and Son*, depicts his biologist father's conflict between his scientific and his religious knowledge.) The nature of an individual's contribution to knowledge on a broader level is influenced by such conflicts in knowledge acquisition. Thomas Kuhn makes this point for science in general when he writes:

> Observation and experience can and must drastically restrict the range of admissible scientific belief, else there would be no science. But they cannot alone determine a particular body of such belief. An apparently arbitrary element, compounded of personal and historical accident, is always a formative ingredient of the beliefs espoused by a given scientific community at a given time.[39]

Kuhn acknowledges that science has seemed to provide an illustration of the generalization, so important for epistemology, that truth and falsity are determined by the confrontation of statement with fact. Yet the act of judgment which leads scientists to reject a previously accepted theory, or to accept one which had seemed unacceptable, is always based upon more than a simple comparison of that theory with the world.

These considerations are relevant to the question of epistemological significance of the sex of the knower in the following way. A woman who is strongly aware of her femininity, a member of a feminist organization, for example, and a man who is self-consciously masculine, a so-called 'male chauvinist', will very likely show that their possibilities of structuring experience are constrained by these facts. But a female Christian and a female atheist would be equally far apart in their ways of knowing certain kinds of things, just as would a male Marxist and a female capitalist. In an important sense, one's attitude to one's sexuality is similar to an ideological stance. Just as some people are fervently ideological and others less so, and this is significant in the acquisition of knowledge, so some people are keenly aware of sexuality and others less so, and this is a constraint upon the acquisition of knowledge. At this general level then, it is reasonable to suggest that the sex of the knower is a subjective factor similar to emotional, professional, and religious orientations. It does influence the form and content of knowledge in a manner similar to these factors. But the degree of influence is by no means constant for members of one sex as opposed to members of the other sex.

The historical circumstances of the knower are closely linked with the kind and amount of knowledge which can be acquired. A fifteenth-century man could no more know about the DNA molecule or about nuclear physics than he could know about the Nazi regime in Germany. This is not because certain biological and physical information would not have been true in his time, but because it would constitute novelty of a degree which he could not accommodate within the body of his knowledge. The level of

(Continued)

existing knowledge dictates what kind of knowledge it is possible (i.e. logically and practically possible) to acquire at any time in history.[40]

In periods of history when the academies are closed to women, it is difficult to the point of impossibility for women to acquire knowledge of the 'academic' variety. This is not to suggest that the closed doors of the institutions of learning produce feminine stupidity. But the evidence about the adaptability of the human brain, and the need for certain skills to be acquired at an early developmental stage if they are to be acquired at all, is pertinent here. If one branch of the species is prevented, in practical terms, from developing in certain ways, higher levels of knowledge will simply be inaccessible, at least to most of these people. The rare individual will achieve the desired results by independent efforts: one might argue that any Renaissance woman *could*, by her own efforts and with great difficulty, have achieved the intellectual status of the Renaissance man. Nonetheless, I think one must take seriously Christine Pierce's observation that

> . . . certain abilities of persons can be manifested only in circumstances of cooperativeness. One cannot, for instance, manifest intelligence in an interpersonal situation with someone priorly convinced of one's stupidity.[41]

The word 'cannot' is well chosen. Most women, in eras prior to the rise of feminist movements, *can* know much less than men.

Location within a particular language is a further subjective constraint upon the possibility of complete objectivity for knowledge in general. Because language is so powerful a formative force in determining the structure of knowledge, the recognition of a measure of linguistic relativism, which I urge, is equivalent to a measure of epistemological relativism. This is true not only from one natural language to another, but of various sub-languages within a particular natural language. The language of physics, for example, construes reality in one way; the language of sociology in another. Apart from mathematics and the mathematically formalized branches of the natural sciences, with their precise symbolism, problems of interpretation, understanding, and evaluation attend all human speech situations. Any act of communication between human beings is, at the same time, an act of translation. The creative

synthesis which leads to knowledge is shaped, to some extent, by the language in which it takes place.

The question arises, then, whether there are distinct male and female languages which point to a sexual relativism in knowledge. Differences of pitch and intonation, for example, which linguistic studies detect in men's and women's speech[42] are epistemologically equivocal: one might make a case for their epistemological significance by arguing that the image of self reflected in speech is indicative of the knower's way of approaching the world, and thence of knowing it. This suggestion is supported in Robin Lakoff's study of *Language and Woman's Place*[43] and in Miller and Swift's *Words and Women*.[44] Here there is persuasive evidence for woman's place in the world being linguistically defined and maintained in innumerable subtle ways: ways which determine her approach to the world and hence must have an effect upon her knowledge of it.

Furthermore, the suggestion that 'in general men have been in control of determining what is labelled. . .'[45] points to a crucial epistemological difference related to the sex of the knower. If this suggestion is in any way plausible, it leads to the conclusion that men establish the limits of the conceptual structuring which is central to the growth of knowledge. Women, then, find the limits of their creativity (i.e. the limits of their knowledge) dictated by men. The kinds of knowledge available to the entire species are dictated by half of its members.[46] These conclusions, however, are extremely tentative. They are relevant more to the psychology of individual knowers than to conditions for the growth of knowledge in general. Like poets and scientists, women can make a creative leap beyond the dominant communal language. Galileo and Kepler, for example, were successful in creating new forms of scientific discourse. One can acknowledge that

> there is a problem (for women) both of concept formation within an existing male constructed framework and a problem of language use in developing and articulating an authentic understanding of the world and one's relationship to it.[47]

But one must at the same time recognize that this does not hold equally for all women, and that feminist movements are slowly altering the epistemological significance of woman's place in language.

Finally, the affective side of human nature, the fact that human beings are as much feeling creatures as they are thinking creatures, constitutes a subjective constraint upon objectivity for knowledge in general. Susanne Langer points out that epistemology finds the entire area of feeling unmanageable because it eludes propositional formulation, yet she designates it 'The generic basis of all mental experience—sensation, emotion, recollection, and reasoning, to mention only the main categories.'[48] The interests, inclinations, and enthusiasms of the knower have a central effect upon how and what he or she can know. This is true of the scientist and of the artist, and of the everyday knowledge of human beings in general. It is in this sense that Thomas Kuhn, in the remarks cited above, might amplify the notions of 'personal and historical accident'.

It is in this subjective constraint in particular that male and female knowledge differ. There is an entire range of affective experience bound up specifically with being male or being female: experiences of sexuality and of parenthood, of general self-awareness as a physical and emotional being, and some aspects of interpersonal relations, which must of necessity be different for men and for women. The experience of what it is to be male or what it is to be female (in those aspects not connected with roles imposed by society) must constitute an area where it is logically impossible for one group of human beings to know what another does.

The greater proportion of human knowledge could roughly be designated 'knowledge by description'.[49] But the acceptance of a knowledge claim involves the tacit assumption that what is known could be, or could have been, experienced at first hand. Such a condition does not hold for this kind of experience. In the same way that a blind person cannot really know colour, that a deaf person cannot really know sound, so it is reasonable to argue that a person who is male cannot really know what it is to be female, and vice versa.

Even here, however, the boundaries are not as clear as they may seem to be. This is knowledge which belongs to the realm where the affective side of the knower is most active, just as mathematics belongs to that area which is most purely intellectual. And I think one possible solution to the lack of vocabulary for dealing with the problem of feelings is to be found in the 'vocabulary' of art. Knowledge which has its source in the experience of works of art falls between Russell's acquaintance/description distinction, very broadly used. It can be designated 'knowledge-by-second-hand-acquaintance'. Just as a photograph displays a person's appearance more adequately than any verbal description can evoke it, so an artist's creation shows what a situation is like. The artist provides a means of letting one 'see' for oneself, experience it for oneself in such a way that one is able to enter into an entire and immediate experience of 'what it is like to be x'; either to be in an x kind of situation, or to be an x kind of person. As one enters into the experience in this way it becomes very close to knowledge by acquaintance. It is true that a woman can never know at first hand just what it is like to be a man. But it is possible that the reading of a novel or a poem, or the viewing of a painting or a sculpture will allow her to know some aspect of 'maleness' almost as though she were experiencing it for herself. And the same can be said of a male apprehension of aspects of 'femaleness'. Even in this apparently clear-cut area, then, the logical impossibility is not as absolute as it might seem.

The historical accounts to which I have referred suggest that female knowledge cannot achieve the degree of objectivity male knowledge can achieve. Female knowledge is characterized as more subjective than male knowledge. And the assumption is that it is therefore inferior to male knowledge, the more objective being necessarily the 'better' knowledge. But this assumption must not go unquestioned. Perhaps total objectivity in knowledge is both impossible and undesirable. One might argue that women bring a richness of feeling and a depth of understanding to cognitive activity such that the final known Gestalt is richer, more multifaceted, and better. Perhaps the admission of women to the kingdom of knowers, on an equal footing, will effect a shift in the standard evaluation of knowledge claims, granting greater respectability to the contribution made by the affective side of human nature.

In any case, most of these comments refer to socially acquired characteristics rather than to cognitive capacity. As male and female roles become less rigidly specified by society, so it will become more common for men to acknowledge the affective side of their nature and for women to acknowledge their intellectual side. The differences between male and female knowledge, language, and experience will no longer be equivalent to differences between 'forms of life'. And the epistemological significance of being male or being female will not be so great.

- How does gender supposedly make a difference in our ability to know?
- Do you think that a feminist epistemology diminishes our ability to have universal and objective knowledge?
- Feminist philosophy claims to advocate 'perspectivism', which acknowledges other points of view but denies that they have equal value. Is there anything about this view that you find problematic? How is feminist theory (as outlined by Grosz) supposed to achieve the balance between recognizing that truth is perspectival and denying all perspectives equal value?

SUMMARY AND CONCLUSION

Epistemology is the study of human knowledge—what we can and cannot know. In this sense, epistemology and metaphysics are complementary disciplines. Epistemology becomes the method of approach to the knowledge of the way the world really is. For some philosophers—for example, Descartes—this approach places its primary trust in reason; accordingly, they are called rationalists. For other philosophers—for example, Locke—the preferred approach is to trust the senses and experience; they are called empiricists. The problem for both the rationalists and the empiricists is to get beyond the mere appearance of things to the reality behind them. The rationalist tries to do this by appealing to intuition and certain principles from which he or she can deduce the way the world really is. The empiricist, on the other hand, appeals to his or her experiences, trying to find there evidence for the nature of reality. For both views, however, the danger is that their methods do not always seem to achieve as much as they would like. Rationalists disagree about which principles to start with and which intuitions to trust. Empiricists find that their own method of experience makes it impossible to say anything about what lies beyond experience. Thus Berkeley argues that only our ideas (including God) and the minds that have these ideas exist, and Hume concludes that we can never know anything about reality, but only about our own **associations of ideas**.

Epistemologists are still working on more satisfactory answers to the questions of knowledge, and

they are still trying to defeat or defend once and for all the skeptical conclusions so brilliantly argued by Hume. This sophisticated anti-skeptical tradition begins in a sense with Reid, whose subtle brand of common-sense realism has appealed to many. Since the writings of Kant, however, the questions about knowledge have shifted from the question of how we know what the world is like to questions that presume that reality is not independent of consciousness, that we somehow 'constitute' the world through our concepts. The German idealists Fichte, Hegel, and Schopenhauer developed very different conceptions of knowledge based on the new Kantian philosophy, while other philosophers—most notably Nietzsche—reacted violently against certain aspects of Kant's philosophy. Contemporary phenomenology, hermeneutics, and pragmatism put even more emphasis on culture and practicality, and, finally, attention to the differences between the sexes has further added to the complexity of our questions about knowledge.

Yet the age-old epistemological questions remain. What can we know? How can we know it? What are the limitations of our possible knowledge? How personal is knowledge—how relative to the individual and his or her cultural context, biology, and gender? And what is the nature of truth? Is it objective or relative? If objective, how can we claim to know it? If relative, relative to what? And is the pronouncement that 'truth is relative' itself relative or not?

REVIEW QUESTIONS

1. Can you think of any way for Locke to defend his claim that substances exist, but we do not know what they are? How would Locke respond to Berkeley's conclusion that we can only know ideas?

2. Descartes re-establishes his system of beliefs based on his famous statement 'I am a thing that thinks'. Where is the place of the thing that thinks in Locke's system? What is the difference between inductive and deductive reasoning, and how do these methods of reasoning relate to the systems of Descartes and Locke?

3. How would you characterize skepticism? In what ways have the various thinkers responded to the skeptics' challenge? How might the skeptics reply in each case?

4. What are the difficulties associated with rationalism and empiricism?

5. How does Kant answer Hume's skeptical challenge? Does he succeed?

6. What does Reid mean by 'common sense'? How does Reid answer Hume's skeptical challenge? Does he succeed?

7. Compare and contrast the ways Reid and Kant reply to Humean skepticism. Which way do you favour? Why?

8. What is pragmatism, according to Rorty? Why does Misak think Rorty sets a bad example for pragmatists? Do you agree?

9. What is the difference between 'absolutism' and 'relativism'? What problems are associated with each school of thought? How do you see this debate being played out today in the popular press and in the views of the public toward science, ethics, and religion?

10. What do you see as the role of language in the theories discussed in this chapter? Why would a concern with language be so central to questions about truth?

11. Do you think the correspondence theory of truth is correct? If not, what view of truth do you think is best? Why? If, on the other hand, you think the correspondence theory *is* correct, how would you go about answering some of the standard objections to it?

KEY TERMS

absolutism

analytic (of a sentence
   or truth)

a posteriori (knowledge)

appearance

a priori (knowledge)

association of ideas

categories

causal theory of perception

causation (or causality)

cause

cogito, ergo sum

coherence theory of truth

conceptual truth

constitute

contingent (truth)

correspondence theory
   of truth

criterion

datum

dialectic

empirical (knowledge)

empiricism

epistemology

explanation

generalization from
   experience (or induction)

hermeneutics

historicism

Hume's fork

idea

impression

induction; inductive reasoning;
   inductive generalization

innate ideas

intuition

justification

law of the excluded middle

linguistic philosophy
   (or analytic philosophy)

logical truth

matter of fact (in Hume)

necessary (truth)

necessity

perception

phenomenology

pragmatic theory of truth

pragmatism

primary qualities

principles of common sense

principle of induction

principle of universal
   causation

probable

quality

rational

rationalism

realism

reason

relations of ideas

relativism

rules of inference

secondary qualities

semantics

sensation

sense-data

skepticism

subjective idealism

substance

synonym	synthetic (statement)	transcendental
synthetic a priori knowledge	tabula rasa	transcendental deduction
	tautology	truth of reason

FURTHER READING

On Epistemology in General

Robert Audi, *Epistemology: A Contemporary Introduction* (New York: Routledge, 2003).

Jonathan Dancy and Ernest Sosa, eds, *A Companion to Epistemology* (Oxford: Blackwell, 1992).

Susan Haack, *Evidence and Inquiry: A Pragmatist Reconstruction of Epistemology* (Amherst, NY: Prometheus Books, 2009; expanded edition).

On Skepticism

John Greco, *Putting Skeptics in Their Place* (New York: Cambridge University Press, 2000).

Barry Stroud, *The Significance of Philosophical Skepticism* (Oxford: Oxford University Press, 1984).

Peter Unger, *Ignorance* (London: Oxford University Press, 1975).

Michael Williams, *Unnatural Doubts* (Princeton, NJ: Princeton University Press, 1995).

On Hermeneutics

David Hoy, *The Critical Circle* (Berkeley: University of California Press, 1978).

On Relativism

M. Krausz and J. Meiland, eds, *Relativism* (Notre Dame, IN: University of Notre Dame Press, 1982).

On Truth

Douglas McDermid, *The Varieties of Pragmatism: Truth, Realism, and Knowledge from James to Rorty* (New York and London: Continuum, 2006).

Richard Rorty, *Philosophy and the Mirror of Nature* (Princeton, NJ: Princeton University Press, 1979).

Frederick F. Schmitt, *Truth: A Primer* (Boulder, CO: Westview, 1995).

R.C.S. Walker, *The Coherence Theory of Truth: Realism, Anti-realism, Idealism* (London: Routledge, 1989).

On Feminist Theories of Knowledge

Lorraine Code, *What Can She Know? Feminist Theory and the Construction of Knowledge* (Ithaca, NY: Cornell University Press, 1991).

Ann Garry and Marilyn Pearsall, *Women, Knowledge and Reality* (Boston: Unwin Hyman, 1989).

On German Idealism

R. Solomon, *Introducing the German Idealists* (Indianapolis, IN: Hackett, 1981).

On the British Empiricist Tradition

Jonathan Bennett, *Locke, Berkeley, Hume: Central Themes* (Oxford: Clarendon Press, 1971).

On European (Continental) Philosophy

Robert Solomon and David Sherman, *Blackwell Guide to Continental Philosophy* (Oxford: Blackwell, 2003).

On René Descartes

Willis Doney, ed., *Descartes* (New York: Doubleday, Anchor, 1967).

Bernard Williams, Chapter 2, 'The Project', in *Descartes: The Project of Pure Enquiry* (London: Penguin, 1978).

On Friedrich Nietzsche

Maudemarie Clark, *Nietzsche on Truth and Philosophy* (Cambridge: Cambridge University Press, 1990).

John T. Wilcox, *Truth and Value in Nietzsche: A Study of His Metaethics and Epistemology* (Ann Arbor: University of Michigan Press, 1974).

On Thomas Reid

Philip de Bary, *Thomas Reid and Scepticism: His Reliabilist Response* (London: Routledge, 2002).

Keith Lehrer, *Thomas Reid* (London: Routledge, 1989).

Nicholas Wolterstorff, *Thomas Reid and the Story of Epistemology* (New York: Cambridge University Press, 2001).

On Immanuel Kant

Henry E. Allison, *Kant's Transcendental Idealism: An Interpretation and Defense* (New Haven, CT: Yale University Press, 2004).

Paul Guyer, *Kant* (New York: Routledge, 2006).

Stephan Körner, *Kant* (New Haven: Yale University Press, 1982).

P.F. Strawson, *The Bounds of Sense: An Essay on Kant's Critique of Pure Reason* (London: Methuen, 1966).

James Van Cleve, *Problems from Kant* (New York: Oxford University Press, 1999).

Allen W. Wood, *Kant* (Malden, MA: Blackwell, 2005).

PART III
KNOW THYSELF

CHAPTER 4

MIND AND BODY

It is certain that I (that is, my mind, by which I am what I am) is entirely and truly distinct from my body, and may exist without it.

René Descartes

Whatever our attempts to answer the problems of self-identity, they begin with a single 'fact': our own consciousness. This was the logical beginning for Descartes, who used the fact of his own consciousness as the starting point for his whole philosophy. It was true for Locke, who argued that our identity is to be found in the continuity of our consciousness rather than in the continuity of our bodies. It was even acknowledged by Hume, who used his own consciousness as the basis of his denial that there was any such thing as the self. It was the starting point of Kant's philosophy; his transcendental ego, like Descartes' 'I think', gave him the basis for the rest of his philosophy. Even those philosophers who have not been interested in these logical arguments—Buddhists, Marxists, existentialists—have begun with at least one of a variety of considerations of consciousness: the fact of our own self-consciousness, the facts of consciousness, or just the fact that only people seem capable of or interested in asking the question 'Who am I?' But now what is this 'consciousness'? As soon as we ask the question, we find ourselves once again in the labyrinth of traditional metaphysics.

A. What Is Consciousness?

We can begin to appreciate the problems of consciousness by returning to the attempts of the eighteenth-century rationalist metaphysicians to be clear about their notion of 'substance'. Descartes said that there were two different kinds of substances: mind or mental substance and body or physical substance. Accordingly, he is usually called a *dualist* and the position, in general, that mind and body are different substances is called Cartesian **dualism**.[1] You remember that Descartes insisted that his identity was as a 'thinking thing', in other words, a mental substance. But now, what of his body? We have seen that he believed that he could intelligibly doubt the existence of his body but not of his mind. But what is so special about this body that, unlike other bodies (the chair in front of him, the body of the king), was so intimately connected to his mind? It moved when he willed it to move, it walked when he decided to walk, it wrote what he wanted to write. In the last of his six *Meditations*, he turns to this problem.

From 'Meditation VI'
By René Descartes

Because, on the one hand, I have a clear and distinct idea of myself . . . as . . . only a thinking and unextended thing, and as, on the other hand, I possess a distinct idea of body . . . only an extended and unthinking thing, it is certain that I am entirely and truly distinct from my body, and may exist without it.

Firstly, then, I perceived that I had a head, hands, feet, and other members composing that body which I considered as part, or perhaps even as the whole, of myself. I perceived further, that that body was placed among many others, by which it was capable of being affected in diverse ways, both beneficial and hurtful; and what was beneficial I remarked by a certain sensation of pleasure, and what was hurtful by a sensation of pain. And, besides this pleasure and pain, I was likewise conscious of hunger, thirst, and other appetites, as well as certain corporeal inclinations toward joy, sadness, anger, and similar passions.

* * *

Nor was I altogether wrong in likewise believing that that body which, by a special right, I called my own, pertained to me more properly and strictly than any of the others; for in truth, I could never be separated from it as from other bodies: I felt in it and on account of it all my appetites and affections, and in fine I was affected in its parts by pain and the titillation of pleasure, and not in the parts of the other bodies that were separated from it. But when I inquired into the reason why, from this I know not what sensation of pain, sadness of mind should follow, and why from the sensation of pleasure joy should arise, or why this indescribable twitching of the stomach, which I call hunger, should put me in mind of taking food, and the parchedness of the throat of drink, and so in other cases, I was unable to give any explanation, unless that I was so taught by nature; for there is assuredly no affinity, at least none that I am able to comprehend, between this irritation of the stomach and the desire of food, any more than between the perception of an object that causes pain and the consciousness of sadness which springs from the perception. And in the same way it seems to me that all the other judgments I had formed regarding the objects of sense, were dictates of nature; because I remarked that those judgments were formed in me, before I had leisure to weigh and consider the reasons that might constrain me to form them.

But, afterward, a wide experience by degrees sapped the faith I had reposed in my senses; for I frequently observed that towers, which at a distance seemed round, appeared square when more closely viewed, and that colossal figures, raised on the summits of these towers, looked like small statues, when viewed from the bottom of them; and, in other instances without number, I also discovered error in judgments founded on the external senses; and not only in those founded on the external, but even in those that rested on the internal senses; for is there aught more internal than pain? and yet I have sometimes been informed by parties whose arm or leg had been amputated, that they still occasionally seemed to feel pain in that part of the body which they had lost,—a circumstance that led me to think that I could not be quite certain even that any one of my members were affected when I felt pain in it. And to these grounds of doubt I shortly afterward also added two others of very wide generality: the first of them was that I believed I never perceived anything when awake which I could not occasionally think I also perceived when asleep, and as I do not believe that the ideas I seem to perceive in my sleep proceed from objects external to me, I did not any more observe any ground for believing this of such as I seem to perceive when awake; the second was that since I was as yet ignorant of the author of my being, or at least supposed myself to be so, I saw nothing to prevent my having been so constituted by nature as that I should be deceived even in matters that appeared to me to possess the greatest truth.

* * *

But now that I begin to know myself better, and to discover more clearly the author of my being, I do not, indeed, think that I ought rashly to admit all which the senses seem to teach, nor, on the other hand, is it my conviction that I ought to doubt in general of their teachings.

And, firstly, because I know that all which I clearly and distinctly conceive can be produced by

(Continued)

God exactly as I conceive it, it is sufficient that I am able clearly and distinctly to conceive one thing apart from another, in order to be certain that the one is different from the other, seeing they may at least be made to exist separately, by the omnipotence of God; and it matters not by what power this separation is made, in order to be compelled to judge them different; and, therefore, merely because I know with certitude that I exist, and because, in the meantime, I do not observe that aught necessarily belongs to my nature or essence beyond my being a thinking thing, I rightly conclude that my essence consists only in my being a thinking thing [or a substance whose whole essence or nature is merely thinking]. And although I may, or rather, as I will shortly say, although I certainly do possess a body with which I am very closely conjoined; nevertheless, because, on the one hand, I have a clear and distinct idea of myself, in as far as I am only a thinking and unextended thing, and as, on the other hand, I possess a distinct idea of body, in as far as it is only an extended and unthinking thing, it is certain that I [that is, my mind, by which I am what I am] am entirely and truly distinct from my body, and may exist without it.

Then comes Descartes' proof that, in general, he could not be fooled about the existence of bodies 'outside' of him.

But there is nothing which that nature teaches me more expressly [or more sensibly] than that I have a body which is ill affected when I feel pain, and stands in need of food and drink when I experience the sensations of hunger and thirst, etc. And therefore I ought not to doubt but that there is some truth in these informations.

Nature likewise teaches me by these sensations of pain, hunger, thirst, etc., that I am not only lodged in my body as a pilot in a vessel, but that I am besides so intimately conjoined, and as it were intermixed with it, that my mind and body compose a certain unity. For if this were not the case, I should not feel pain when my body is hurt, seeing I am merely a thinking thing, but should perceive the wound by the understanding alone, just as a pilot perceives by sight when any part of his vessel is damaged; and when my body has need of food or drink, I should have a clear knowledge of this, and not be made aware of it by the confused sensations of hunger and thirst: for, in truth, all these sensations of hunger, thirst, pain, etc., are nothing more than certain confused modes of thinking, arising from the union and apparent fusion of mind and body.

Besides this, nature teaches me that my own body is surrounded by many other bodies . . . some are agreeable, and others disagreeable, there can be no doubt that my body, or rather my entire self, in as far as I am composed of body and mind, may be variously affected, both beneficially and hurtfully, by surrounding bodies.

But how can two different substances, particularly two such different kinds of substances, interact? We know what it is for two bodies to interact, but how can a body make contact with a mind, which seems so intangible and 'ghostly'? Descartes never answers this problem to his own or to his critics' satisfaction. Spinoza, seeing Descartes' troubles, insists that there is only one substance and that body and mind are but different 'attributes' of that one substance. That avoids the metaphysical question, for there is no trouble about interaction within a substance. But it still leaves a sizable problem, namely, how these two attributes are coordinated. That is a question Spinoza never answers; and Leibniz, attacking the same problem, finds it preferable to deny the reality of physical substance altogether. There are only mental substances, monads, each locked into its own experience. The extravagance of these two solutions should give you some idea of the difficulty of the problem.

We can get a more specific clue to the mysterious quality of 'consciousness' if we consider the following. Descartes, Spinoza, and Leibniz, you recall, define mind as 'unextended', that is, unextended in space. (Bodies, on the other hand, *are* extended in space.) In other words, it is essential that minds, unlike bodies, cannot be said to be of a particular size or located in such and such a place. But despite this definition, notice how much of our talk about consciousness consists of metaphors of spatial form. We talk about something being 'in' our minds. We talk about something 'slipping (out of)' our minds. Philosophers often talk about the 'contents' of consciousness, and a popular phrase from William James is the 'stream of consciousness'. Now we might say, 'those are just metaphors'; but why are such metaphors necessary?

In general, we tend to rely on comparisons to express our abstract thoughts. When we try to describe an image, we do so in terms appropriate to physical things (namely, what it is an image *of*). We try to describe a pain and come out with metaphors ('it's as if a vice were closing on my head') or comparisons ('it feels the same as touching a hot stove'). When we try to describe the unseen mind, we resort to using spatial metaphors to explain what we believe to exist but cannot describe on its own terms. So, how would you describe 'what it is to be conscious' without resorting to metaphor? You might say something about 'aware-ness' or 'feelings', but you would only be restating the problem in different words.

There is a further difficulty: If I can talk about my mind only with difficulty, how can I talk about your mind at all? I can experience only what is 'in' my mind, I can't feel your pain. Even if I feel 'sympathy pains' with you, it is my pain I feel. So I can't describe your mind at all, and evidently I have difficulty describing my mind as well. Therefore, how can we talk about 'mind' at all? Not surprisingly, many psychologists and philosophers have rejected the idea of 'mind' altogether, preferring to talk only about what is mutually observable and 'extended' in physical space (for example, neurological processes and overt behaviour).

We shall later consider some of these attempts to reject the idea of 'mind' altogether. But what should seem fairly obvious to you is that this idea can be rejected only with reference to other people, not with reference to yourself. *Why? Because of Descartes' first premise.* The same logic that allows him to assert with certainty 'I am thinking' and 'I exist as a thinking thing' now forces us to admit that 'I am not thinking' and 'I am not a thinking thing' are utterly absurd and unintelligible statements. They are self-refuting in exactly the same sense that 'I am thinking' is self-confirming. (This isn't to say that you are thinking clearly, or well, or enjoying it; only that, in some minimal sense, you are thinking.) Therefore, you must have a mind. The fact that you are conscious is the last thing you could ever deny.

- What does Descartes mean when he says that the mind and body are a unity due to the mind's awareness of bodily sensations and interactions? Can you think of counter-examples to this claim (that is, times when your mind was unaware of something occur-ring within your body or times when something was occurring within your mind with no bodily manifestations)? Do these counter-examples prove Descartes wrong? Or are they impossible in some way? What might be another explanation for the perceived intimacy between physical and mental states?
- Is the existence of your consciousness irrefutable? Can you deny the existence of particu-lar conscious states (moods, ideas, sensations, emotions)? How can you be certain of your knowledge of them?

It is important to appreciate the fact that Descartes did not defend the idea of a radical difference between mind and body only as a metaphysical or scientific thesis. There is much in 'common sense' that supports it, and the separation of mind or soul from physical body obviously serves a long-standing religious concern as well. It makes sense of the thesis that the soul might survive the body after death, and it safely separates the realms of religion and science. It even provides an argument for the necessity of God's existence. As Descartes discusses in 'Meditation III', he believes that his various fleeting thoughts could not be unified into a coherent, enduring self without the intervention of a higher power.

From 'Meditation III'
By René Descartes

But though I assume that perhaps I have always existed just as I am at present, neither can I escape the force of this reasoning, and imagine that the conclusion to be drawn from this is, that I need not seek for any author of my existence. For all the course of my life may be divided into an infinite number of parts, none of which is in any way dependent on the other; and thus from the fact that I was in existence a short time ago it does not follow that I must be in existence now, unless some cause at this instant, so to speak, produces me anew, that is to say, conserves me. It is as a matter of fact perfectly clear and evident to all those who consider with attention the nature of time, that, in order to be conserved in each moment in which it endures, a substance has need of the same power and action as would be necessary to produce and create it anew, supposing it did not yet exist, so that the light of nature shows us clearly that the distinction between creation and conservation is solely a distinction of the reason.

And in the dedication to his *Meditations*, he writes,

And as regards the soul, although many have considered that it is not easy to know its nature, and some have even dared to say that human reasons have convinced us that it would perish with the body, and that faith alone could believe the contrary, nevertheless, inasmuch as the Lateran Council held under Leo X (in the eighth session) condemns these tenets, and as Leo expressly ordains Christian philosophers to refute their arguments and to employ all their powers in making known the truth, I have ventured in this treatise to undertake the same task.

B. The Problem of Dualism

How is consciousness connected to your body? You decide to raise your hand, and your hand goes up. You formulate an answer to your friend's question, and it comes out of your mouth. How does what takes place 'in your mind' determine what happens with your body? A familiar image, borrowed from untold numbers of cartoons, is the little man (or woman) in your head, operating your body as a construction worker operates a giant steam shovel. But this is no answer at all. First, there is no little man. But even if there were, the same problem would then focus on him (or her). How does he or she move a body by making certain mental decisions? The same problem arises in the other direction, from body to mind. A friend steps on your toe—your physiology teacher can explain to you what happens: nerves are pinched and signals are sent through your central nervous system into that huge complex of fat cells called your brain. But then, at some point, there is something else, the feeling, the pain. How does this happen? How does a feeling emerge from that complex and still unknown network of neurological reactions going on in your body?

You can see that this problem of mind–body interaction is no longer just a technical metaphysical problem having to do with the special notion of substance. The problem of 'interaction' is the same for Spinoza and his one substance as it is for Descartes and his dualism. Even if you don't want to talk of substances at all, there is still the problem of explaining how your mind affects your body and how your body affects your mind. For whether or not you accept the special problems of the eighteenth-century metaphysicians, you have to admit that your mind is very different from your body, and that is the source of the trickiest of all modern philosophy problems—the mind–body problem. How are mind and body related?

The human body, like any other physical body, can be described in terms of its size, weight, chemical composition, and movements in space. The workings of the human nervous system, although very complex and not yet adequately understood, can be described just like any other biological reaction, in terms of the changes in cell membranes and chemical reactions, the procession of chemoelectric nerve 'impulses', and the computer-like network of different nerve components that are stimulated at any given time. The human brain can be seen as a complex machine, like a gooey computer. The human mind, however, is not to be characterized in any such spatial or chemical terms. The mind is not the same as the brain. It has no shape or weight, and it has the awkward property of being observable—in any particular case—by one and only one person.

We can understand how a body might interact with another body, even when the 'forces' involved are hard to picture (for example, the gravitational attraction between two distant planets). But how does a body interact with something that has none of the crucial characteristics of a body? You might think of 'energy' here, for energy would seem to have at least some of the intangible and 'unextended' features of mind. It too, in a very limited sense, 'has no size or weight'. But energy is a function of physical bodies, force is a function of mass and acceleration. They are not, like our experiences, 'private': a lightning bolt is observable to anyone who looks. Energy states, unlike our ideas, can be identified and described by science. And while it has often been demonstrated (most notably by Einstein) that energy and mass are interconvertible, any such 'interconvertibility' of mind and matter is still at the highly speculative stage, limited to questionable performances by 'psychics' and such. We may well talk about 'mental energy', but it is far from clear what we mean.

How can something so abstract as ideas and sensations interact with physical nervous systems and brain cells? Philosophers have proposed a number of solutions, all of them controversial and none of them yet satisfactory. But even before we look at some of them, it is important to stress the following point: The mind–body problem is not simply a matter of how little we know about the human nervous system. No matter how our knowledge develops, we will still be faced with that mysterious gap between the last known neurological occurrence and the experience. Right now we can trace our neural impulses only so far, and the 'last known neurological occurrence' is not very far along. But even when we have complete 'brain maps' and can say for every mental occurrence what is going on in the brain at the same time, the problem will still remain: How are the two related?[2]

For a classic attempt to resolve the problem of dualism, let's return to Descartes. The following selection is from his essay 'The Passions of the Soul'.

From 'The Passions of the Soul'
By René Descartes

The soul is really joined to the whole body, and . . . we cannot, properly speaking, say that it exists in any one of its parts to the exclusion of the others.

But in order to understand all these things more perfectly, we must know that the soul is really joined to the whole body, and that we cannot, properly speaking, say that it exists in any one of its parts to the exclusion of the others, because it is one and in some manner indivisible, owing to the disposition of its organs, which are so related to one another that when any one of them is removed, that renders the whole body defective; and because it is of a nature which has no relation to

(*Continued*)

extension, nor dimensions, nor other properties of the matter of which the body is composed, but only to the whole conglomerate of its organs, as appears from the fact that we could not in any way conceive of the half or the third of a soul, nor of the space it occupies, and because it does not become smaller owing to the cutting off of some portion of the body, but separates itself from it entirely when the union of its assembled organs is dissolved.

It is likewise necessary to know that although the soul is joined to the whole body, there is yet in that a certain part in which it exercises its functions more particularly than in all the others; and it is usually believed that this part is the brain, or possibly the heart: the brain, because it is with it that the organs of sense are connected, and the heart because it is apparently in it that we experience the passions. But, in examining the matter with care, it seems as though I had clearly ascertained that the part of the body in which the soul exercises its functions immediately is in nowise the heart, nor the whole of the brain, but merely the most inward of all its parts, to wit, a certain very small gland which is situated in the middle of its substance and so suspended above the duct whereby the animal spirits in its anterior cavities have communication with those in the posterior, that the slightest movements which take place in it may alter very greatly the course of these spirits; and reciprocally that the smallest changes which occur in the course of the spirits may do much to change the movements of this gland.[3]

* * *

Let us then conceive here that the soul has its principal seat in the little gland that exists in the middle of the brain, from whence it radiates forth through all the remainder of the body by means of the animal spirits, nerves, and even the blood, which, participating in the impressions of the spirits, can carry them by the arteries into all the members. Recollecting what has been said above about the machine of our body, that is, that the little filaments of our nerves are so distributed in all its parts, that on the occasion of the diverse movements which are there excited by sensible objects, they open in diverse ways the pores of the brain, which causes the animal spirits contained in these cavities to enter in diverse ways into the muscles, by which means they are capable of being moved; and also that all the other causes which are capable of moving the spirits in diverse ways suffice to conduct them into diverse muscles; let us here add that the small gland which is the main seat of the soul is so suspended between the cavities which contain the spirits that it can be moved by them in as many different ways as there are sensible diversities in the object, but that it may also be moved in diverse ways by the soul, whose nature is such that it receives in itself as many diverse impressions, that is to say, that it possesses as many diverse perceptions as there are diverse moments in this gland. Reciprocally, likewise, the machine of the body is so formed that from the simple fact that this gland is diversely moved by the soul, or by such other cause, whatever it is, it thrusts the spirits which surround it toward the pores of the brain, which conduct them by the nerves into the muscles, by which means it causes them to move the limbs.

CAUSAL INTERACTIONISM

The theory that mind and body causally interact, that mental changes can cause bodily changes and vice versa.

The technical name given to this theory is **causal interactionism**. Unlike his followers, Descartes did not take seriously the problem of separate substances or radically different changes causally affecting one another. He apparently felt satisfied, if not exactly comfortable, with such a causal account. He was vigorously attacked in this by most of his immediate followers, including Spinoza, Leibniz, and many of the empiricists, who insisted that 'different substances cannot interact'. In other words, they argued that physical bodies can causally interact only with other physical bodies and not with anything so different as minds. Yet one thing remains obvious—the familiar coordination of our mental activities and the movements of our bodies must be accounted for. To do so, without bringing in causal interaction, required considerable ingenuity on the part of Descartes' critics.

We have already seen (in Chapter 1) the two metaphysical alternatives that immediately followed Descartes. The first was formulated by Leibniz as part of his overall theory of monads. He insisted that there could be no causal interaction between monads, and specifically, there could be no sense made out of the claim that mental substances interact with anything that we call 'physical bodies'. So what could he suggest as an alternative? His answer to the problem was that God, who had created monads in the first place, had also 'programmed' them in such a way that our mental activities and what we call our bodily activities are exactly coordinated. Leaving aside the rest of Leibniz's theory and looking just at the mind–body problem, we can restate his solution as a form of what is called **parallelism**. His '**pre-established harmony**' between monads can now be viewed as the somewhat strange theory that our mental lives and the movements of our bodies are exactly coordinated (so that I feel pain when you step on my toe and so that my hand goes up just when I 'decide' that it should). Yet there is no causal interaction between them whatsoever. It is like the sound and visual tracks of a film playing in a cinema, moving along exactly parallel but never in fact interacting. (That is, the character who appears to be talking in the movie does not cause the sounds that you hear as if he or she were producing them. The sounds are actually produced separately and would continue even if the projector bulb burned out and the figure on the screen disappeared altogether.) Of course, to accept this theory you must also accept the considerable metaphysical and theological supports that it requires. If you don't believe in a God who could set up this complex system, there is absolutely no way of explaining the remarkable coordination of mind and body. Even if you do believe in God, you may well think that the mind–body problem requires some more plausible and secular solution.

Spinoza's theory need not be kept in the 'one substance' metaphysics that he used to present it. In fact, much the same theory was defended by Bertrand Russell in the twentieth century, without reference to the metaphysical notion of substance at all. Russell said, as Spinoza had said centuries before, that mind and body, mental events and physical changes, were different aspects of one and the same 'something'. For Spinoza, the 'something' was 'the one substance' and the aspects were what he called 'attributes'. Russell claimed only that our experiences and ideas were one aspect of some events or activities of which the various chemical reactions of the brain were another aspect. Accordingly, the theory has often been called the **dual aspect theory**, whether or not it is specifically addressed to the problem of substances and their attributes. Since we are now talking about two 'aspects' of the same thing rather than two different things, the problem of interaction doesn't arise. But again, this only rephrases the problem rather than solves it. What is this mysterious 'something' of which mind and body are merely 'aspects'? It is neither brain nor mind, so what could it be? By the nature of the case, we can't find out, which leaves us with the equally embarrassing question, 'How could one and the same thing have such different aspects?' You might say, 'Well, a hot coal has both "aspects" of being heavy and being hot'. But that we can explain. What are we to say of a 'something' that is neither brain nor mind but both?

- How would you describe and differentiate between the various solutions to the mind–body problem (for example, causal interactionism, parallelism, dual aspect theory)?

C. The Rejection of Dualism

If the problem is dualism, then perhaps the answer is the rejection of dualism. Of course, we still have to account for the obvious facts of the case: that we feel something when certain things happen to our bodies, that we do something when we mentally will it to be done. So philosophers of recent years—and nearly all psychologists—have taken a dim view of dualism in all of the above forms.

1. Epiphenomenalism

A first step toward eliminating dualism consists of minimizing, though not rejecting, the mental side of dualism. This theory is usually called **epiphenomenalism**. Epiphenomenalism

---

PARALLELISM

The thesis that mental events and bodily events parallel each other and occur in perfect coordination but do not interact.

DUAL ASPECT THEORY

The theory that mind and body are simply different aspects of one and the same substance.

EPIPHENOMENALISM

The thesis that mental events are side effects of physical processes in the brain and nervous system but of little importance themselves.

allows for causal interaction, but only in one direction. Bodies and changes in bodies cause mental events. You might think of the body as a boiler system equipped with various gauges to tell us how the machine is functioning at any given time. The machine works on, registering certain results on the attached gauges. But notice that the gauge is relatively unimportant to the working of the machine. In fact, the gauge can break and the machine can function for years. What is the significance of such a theory? It allows philosophers and psychologists who are interested in the continuity of physical and physiological laws to concentrate on the physical side of the matter while ignoring the problematic disruption of the mysterious 'mind'. If an objection is raised, they can always insist: 'Oh, I'm not denying that you feel something too.' But they believe that such feelings—and mental processes in general—are unimportant details, side-products, epiphenomena, that need not be taken all that seriously.

> • Does epiphenomenalism solve the problem of dualism? Why or why not?

2. Radical Behaviourism

Epiphenomenalism is a timid rejection of dualism. It doesn't actually reject dualism, but it minimizes one half the duality. Other forms of attack are much more bold. In psychology, many authors have long accepted that all talk of 'the mental' is a hopeless tangle of confusions that, by the nature of the case, cannot be resolved through any experiment whatsoever. (That is, only one person could observe the results of the experiment in any given case, and the very nature of a scientific experiment is that it must be observable by anyone.) Accordingly, many psychologists have followed the American theorist John Watson in practising what they call **behaviourism**.

Today the best-known behaviourist is the late psychologist B.F. Skinner. Behaviourism, as a form of science, refuses to even consider any events that cannot be publicly witnessed. That immediately and logically excludes, but need not deny the existence of, mental events. Most behaviourists, however, have gone beyond the method—which only says that they will not scientifically study such events—and have done a bit of metaphysics as well; they also deny that there can be any mental events. Watson, for example, goes so far as to suggest that belief in consciousness goes back to the ancient days of superstition and magic. He insists that any good behaviourist can catch the average undergraduate student in a mess of tongue-tied contradictions but concludes from this not that our concept of consciousness is complicated and confused but rather that there could not possibly be any such thing. His argument is self-consciously 'scientific', the alternative to which is being a mere 'savage and still believing in magic'. His test is simply whether the soul (philosophers and psychologists often shift too easily between 'soul' and 'consciousness') can be experienced; 'no one has ever touched a soul, or seen one in a test tube, or has in any other way come into relationship with it as he has with the other objects of his daily experience.'[4] Thus Watson shifts from his view as a scientist, able to write about only what he can measure and observe, to a view as a metaphysician, insisting that there cannot be any such thing as consciousness and that no rational person should believe that there is.

BEHAVIOURISM

The thesis that only what is publicly observable can be used as subject matter or evidence in scientific research regarding human beings.

> • In denying the legitimacy of anything that cannot be 'publicly witnessed', how has behaviourism rejected dualism?
> • Do you think behaviourism is a sensible scientific program?

3. Logical Behaviourism

Philosophers too have turned to behaviourism as a way of escaping the problems of Cartesian dualism. Oxford philosopher Gilbert Ryle, following some suggestions by Ludwig Wittgenstein, established a new form of behaviourism—logical behaviourism—in his book *The Concept of Mind* (1949). Its first chapter is appropriately called 'Descartes' Myth'. First he describes what he calls 'the official doctrine':

From *The Concept of Mind*
By Gilbert Ryle

The phrase 'there occur mental processes' does not mean the same sort of thing as 'there occur physical processes', and, therefore . . . it makes no sense to conjoin or disjoin the two.

There is a doctrine about the nature and place of minds which is so prevalent among theorists and even among laymen that it deserves to be described as the official theory. Most philosophers, psychologists and religious teachers subscribe, with minor reservations, to its main articles and, although they admit certain theoretical difficulties in it, they tend to assume that these can be overcome without serious modifications being made to the architecture of the theory. It will be argued here that the central principles of the doctrine are unsound and conflict with the whole body of what we know about minds when we are not speculating about them.

The official doctrine, which hails chiefly from Descartes, is something like this. With the doubtful exceptions of idiots and infants in arms every human being has both a body and a mind. Some would prefer to say that every human being is both a body and a mind. His body and his mind are ordinarily harnessed together, but after the death of the body his mind may continue to exist and function.

Human bodies are in space and are subject to the mechanical laws which govern all other bodies in space. Bodily processes and states can be inspected by external observers. So a man's bodily life is as much a public affair as are the lives of animals and reptiles and even as the careers of trees, crystals, and plants.

But minds are not in space, nor are their operations subject to mechanical laws. The workings of one mind are not witnessable by other observers; its career is private. Only I can take direct cognizance of the states and processes of my own mind. A person therefore lives through two collateral histories, one consisting of what happens in and to his body, the other consisting of what happens in and to his mind.

The first is public, the second private. The events in the first history are events in the physical world, those in the second are events in the mental world.

It has been disputed whether a person does or can directly monitor all or only some of the episodes of his own private history; but, according to the official doctrine, of at least some of these episodes he has direct and unchallengeable cognizance. In consciousness, self-consciousness, and introspection he is directly and authentically apprised of the present states and operations of his mind. He may have great or small uncertainties about concurrent and adjacent episodes in the physical world, but he can have none about at least part of what is momentarily occupying his mind.

It is customary to express this bifurcation of his two lives and of his two worlds by saying that the things and events which belong to the physical world, including his own body, are external, while the workings of his own mind are internal. This antithesis of outer and inner is of course meant to be construed as a metaphor, since minds, not being in space, could not be described as being spatially inside anything else, or as having things going on spatially inside themselves. But relapses from this good intention are common and theorists are found speculating how stimuli, the physical sources of which are yards or miles outside a person's skin, can generate mental responses inside his skull, or how decisions framed inside his cranium can set going movements of his extremities.

Even when 'inner' and 'outer' are construed as metaphors, the problem of how a person's mind and body influence one another is notoriously charged with theoretical difficulties. What the mind wills, the legs, arms, and the tongue execute; what affects the ear and the eye has something to do with what the mind

(Continued)

perceives; grimaces and smiles betray the mind's moods and bodily castigations lead, it is hoped, to moral improvement. But the actual transactions between the episodes of the private history and those of the public history remain mysterious, since by definition they can belong to neither series. They could not be reported among the happenings described in a person's autobiography of his inner life, but nor could they be reported among those described in someone else's biography of that person's overt career. They can be inspected neither by introspection nor by laboratory experiment. They are theoretical shuttlecocks which are forever being bandied from the physiologist back to the psychologist and from the psychologist back to the physiologist.

Underlying this partly metaphorical representation of the bifurcation of a person's two lives there is a seemingly more profound and philosophical assumption. It is assumed that there are two different kinds of existence or status. What exists or happens may have the status of physical existence, or it may have the status of mental existence. Somewhat as the faces of coins are either heads or tails, or somewhat as living creatures are either male or female, so, it is supposed, some existing is physical existing, other existing is mental existing. It is a necessary feature of what has physical existence that it is in space and time; it is a necessary feature of what has mental existence that it is in time but not in space. What has physical existence is composed of matter, or else is a function of matter; what has mental existence consists of consciousness, or else is a function of consciousness.

* * *

What sort of knowledge can be secured of the workings of a mind? On the one side, according to the official theory, a person has direct knowledge of the best imaginable kind of the workings of his own mind. Mental states and processes are (or are normally) conscious states and processes, and the consciousness which irradiates them can engender no illusions and leaves the door open for no doubts. A person's present thinkings, feelings, and willings, his perceivings, rememberings, and imaginings are intrinsically 'phosphorescent'; their existence and their nature are inevitably betrayed to their owner. The inner life is a stream of consciousness of such a sort that it would be absurd to suggest that the mind whose life is that stream might be unaware of what is passing down it.

* * *

On the other side, one person has no direct access of any sort to the events of the inner life of another. He cannot do better than make problematic inferences from the observed behaviour of the other person's body to the states of mind which, by analogy from his own conduct, he supposes to be signalized by that behaviour. Direct access to the workings of a mind is the privilege of that mind itself; in default of such privileged access, the workings of one mind are inevitably occult to everyone else. For the supposed arguments from bodily movements similar to their own to mental workings similar to their own would lack any possibility of observational corroboration. Not unnaturally, therefore, an adherent of the official theory finds it difficult to resist this consequence of his premises, that he has no good reason to believe that there do exist minds other than his own. Even if he prefers to believe that to other human bodies there are harnessed minds not unlike his own, he cannot claim to be able to discover their individual characteristics, or the particular things that they undergo and do. Absolute solitude is on this showing the ineluctable destiny of the soul. Only our bodies can meet.

Then Ryle argues that the 'official doctrine' is 'absurd' and is based upon what he calls 'a category mistake':

Such in outline is the official theory. I shall often speak of it, with deliberate abusiveness, as 'the dogma of the Ghost in the Machine'. I hope to prove that it is entirely false, and false not in detail but in principle. It is not merely an assemblage of particular mistakes. It is one big mistake and a mistake of a special kind. It is, namely, a category mistake. It represents the facts of mental life as if they belonged to one logical type of category (or range of types or categories), when they actually belong to another. The dogma is therefore a philosopher's myth. In attempting to explode the myth I shall probably be taken to be denying well-known facts about the mental life of human beings, and my plea that I aim to do nothing more than rectify the logic of mental-conduct concepts will probably be disallowed as mere subterfuge.

I must first indicate what is meant by the phrase 'category mistake'. This I do in a series of illustrations.

A foreigner visiting Oxford or Cambridge for the first time is shown a number of colleges, libraries, playing fields, museums, scientific departments, and administrative offices. He then asks 'But where is the university? I have seen where the members of the Colleges live, where the Registrar works, where the scientists experiment, and the rest. But I have not yet seen the University in which reside and work the members of your University.' It has then to be explained to him that the University is not another collateral institution, some ulterior counterpart to the colleges, laboratories and offices which he has seen. The University is just the way in which all that he has already seen is organized. When they are seen and when their coordination is understood, the University has been seen. His mistake lay in his innocent assumption that it was correct to speak of Christ Church, the Bodleian Library, the Ashmolean Museum, *and* the University, to speak, that is, as if 'the University' stood for an extra member of the class of which these other units are members. He was mistakenly allocating the University to the same category as that to which the other institutions belong.

* * *

One more illustration. A foreigner watching his first game of cricket learns what are the functions of the bowlers, the batsmen, the fielders, the umpires, and the scorers. He then says 'But there is no one left on the field to contribute the famous element of team-spirit. I see who does the bowling, the batting, and the wicket-keeping; but I do not see whose role it is to exercise *esprit de corps*.' Once more, it would have to be explained that he was looking for the wrong type of thing. Team-spirit is not another cricketing-operation supplementary to all of the other special tasks. It is, roughly, the keenness with which each of the special tasks is performed, and performing a task keenly is not performing two tasks. Certainly exhibiting team-spirit is not the same thing as bowling or catching, but nor is it a third thing such that we can say that the bowler first bowls *and* then exhibits team-spirit or that a fielder is at a given moment *either* catching *or* displaying *esprit de corps*.

These illustrations of category mistakes have a common feature which must be noticed. The mistakes were made by people who did not know how to wield the concepts *University . . .* and *team-spirit*. Their puzzles arose from inability to use certain items in the English vocabulary.

A category mistake, in general, is mistaking one *type* of thing for another. For example, it would be a category mistake to ask, 'what colour is the number 3?' The philosophically interesting mistakes, of course, are neither so obvious nor so silly as the above examples. They are mistakes we make when we try to think abstractly. Most significant are the category mistakes that philosophers make when they talk about 'the mind':

My destructive purpose is to show that a family of radical category mistakes is the source of the double-life theory. The representation of a person as a ghost mysteriously ensconced in a machine derives from this argument. Because, as is true, a person's thinking, feeling, and purposive doing cannot be described solely in the idioms of physics, chemistry, and physiology, therefore they must be described in counterpart idioms. As the human body is a complex organized unit, so the human mind must be another complex organized unit, though one made of a different sort of stuff and with a different sort of structure. Or, again, as the human body, like any other parcel of matter, is a field of causes and effects, so the mind must be another field of causes and effects, though not (Heaven be praised) mechanical causes and effects.

This disastrous category mistake, which Ryle attributes primarily to Descartes, is thinking that 'the mind' and its events are some strange and mysteriously private sort of *thing* behind our behaviour, when, in fact, mind is the *pattern* of our behaviour and not 'behind' behaviour at all.

When two terms belong to the same category, it is proper to construct conjunctive propositions embodying them. Thus a purchaser may say that he bought a left-hand glove and a right-hand glove, but not that he bought a left-hand glove, a right-hand glove, and a pair of gloves. 'She came home in a flood of tears and a sedan-chair' is a well-known joke based on the absurdity of conjoining terms of different types. It would have been equally ridiculous to construct the disjunction 'She came home either in a flood of tears or else in a sedan-chair'. Now the dogma of the Ghost in the Machine does just this. It maintains that there exist both bodies and minds; that there occur physical processes and mental processes; that there are mechanical causes of corporeal movements and mental causes of corporeal movements. I shall argue that these and other analogous conjunctions are absurd; but, it must be noticed, the argument will not show that either of the illegitimately conjoined propositions is absurd in itself. I am not, for example, denying that there occur mental processes. Doing long division is a mental process and so is making a joke. But I am saying that the phrase 'there occur mental processes' does not mean the same sort of thing as 'there occur physical processes', and, therefore, that it makes no sense to conjoin or disjoin the two.

The key to Ryle's analysis is what he calls 'a disposition', by which he means a tendency for something to happen given certain conditions. For example, we say that 'if the lever is disturbed, then the mousetrap will snap closed'. The key is the *'if . . . then'* (or 'hypothetical') form of the statement. Ryle explains this in the following way:

There are at least two quite different senses in which an occurrence is said to be 'explained'; and there are correspondingly at least two quite different senses in which we ask 'why' it occurred and two quite different senses in which we say that it happened 'because' so and so was the case. The first sense is the causal sense. To ask why the glass broke is to ask what caused it to break, and we explain, in this sense, the fracture of the glass when we report that a stone hit it. The 'because' clause in the explanation reports an event, namely the event which stood to the fracture of the glass as cause to effect.

But very frequently we look for and get explanations of occurrences in another sense of 'explanation'. We ask why the glass shivered when struck by the stone and we get the answer that it was because the glass was brittle. Now 'brittle' is a dispositional adjective; that is to say, to describe the glass as brittle is to assert a general hypothetical proposition about the glass. So when we say that the glass broke when struck because it was brittle, the 'because' clause does not report a happening or a cause; it states a law-like proposition. People commonly say of explanations of this second kind that they give the 'reason' for the glass breaking when struck.

How does the law-like general hypothetical proposition work? It says, roughly, that the glass, *if* sharply struck or twisted, etc. *would* not dissolve or stretch or evaporate but fly into fragments. The matter of fact that the glass did at a particular moment fly into fragments, when struck by a particular stone, is explained, in this sense of 'explain', when the first happening, namely the impact of the stone, satisfies the protasis of the general hypothetical proposition, and when the second happening, namely the fragmentation of the glass, satisfies its apodosis.

He then applies this concept of disposition to his analysis of 'mind'. (This task occupies him for most of his book.) The main idea is this: Everything 'mental' is really a disposition to behave in certain ways. Consider, for example, his brief analysis of acting from vanity:

The statement 'he boasted from vanity' ought, on one view, to be construed as saying that 'he boasted and the cause of his boasting was the occurrence in him of a particular feeling or impulse of vanity'. On the other view, it is to be construed as saying 'he boasted on meeting the stranger and his doing so satisfies the law-like proposition that whenever he finds a chance of securing the admiration and envy of others, he does whatever he thinks will produce this admiration and envy'.

Then the general argument:

To say that a person knows something, or aspires to be something, is not to say that he is at a particular moment in process of doing or undergoing anything, but that he is able to do certain things, when the need arises, or that he is prone to do and feel certain things in situations of certain sorts. . . .

Abandonment of the two-worlds legend involves the abandonment of the idea that there is a locked door and a still to be discovered key. Those human actions and reactions, those spoken and unspoken utterances, those tones of voice, facial expressions, and gestures, which have always been the data of all the other students of men, have, after all, been the right and the only manifestations to study. They and they alone have merited, but fortunately not received, the grandiose title 'mental phenomena'.

Ryle's (and Wittgenstein's) logical behaviourism differs from the radical behaviourism of the psychologists in that it is not a theory about behaviour and its causes so much as it is a theory about the language of mind, about the meaning of 'mentalistic' terms such as 'wants', 'believes', 'hurts', 'loves', 'feels', and 'thinks'. Ryle's basic thesis, stripped of his polemic against 'the ghost in the machine', is that applying a mental term—attributing a mental property—to a person is logically equivalent to saying that the person will act in a certain way. The advantage of this is that it eliminates all mysterious things mental by translating the mental terminology into statements about behaviour, not 'inner events'. Instead of thinking of love as 'a feeling deep inside', for example, the logical behaviourist would say, unromantically perhaps, that 'John loves Mary' means that John will be with Mary every chance he gets, he will buy her flowers if flowers are available, he will take her to the movies if she utters the stimulating words, 'Let's go to the movies!' As you can see from this example, the number of acts and possible acts involved in the translation of a mentalistic term can be indefinitely large, since, in various circumstances and with various opportunities, a person in love might do almost anything. (The case is not so complicated, usually, with such mental predicates as 'is thirsty' and 'has an itch'.) But however complicated the translation from mental language to behavioural disposition, the problem of dualism does not arise. The causal interaction between mind and body has been reformulated as the causal connection between a physical state—a disposition to behave in certain ways—and the actual consequent behaviour. Saying 'he will marry her because he loves her' is therefore no more metaphysically problematic than saying 'the glass will break because it is brittle'.

There is a problem with all forms of behaviourism—both radical and logical. However tempting such a theory might be when we are studying other people at a distance, it seems utterly absurd when we try to think behaviouristically while talking to a friend or listening to someone talk to us. And behaviourism becomes pure nonsense when we are trying to understand and talk about our own mental states. My pain is not the same as my behaviour, and no matter how easy it may be for you to infer from my behaviour that I am in pain, that is certainly not how *I* know that I am in pain, and it is not what I mean by my report, 'I am in pain'. Indeed, when I tell you 'I am in pain', I am not predicting my behaviour. I am telling you what I *feel*, quite apart from anything I might *do*. Whatever the logic of mental language, that undeniable feeling seems to remind us that behaviourism, however therapeutic in psychology and however powerful as an antidote to Cartesianism, cannot be the whole story. Watson's behaviourism helped correct an absurd amount of mentalistic theorizing about the behaviour of animals ('the rat is trying to figure out how to get the door open'). So too, Ryle's behaviourism is a vital challenge to the too-easy supposition that our 'minds' are ghostly containers filled with equally ghostly entities and processes. But as an alternative account of the mind, behaviourism inevitably bangs up against that ultimate mark of the mental, Descartes' 'I think'. There is no way you can think consistently that you never think or think that your thinking is nothing but your tendency to behave. As one of Watson's early critics commented, 'What behaviourism shows is that psychologists do not always think very well, not that they don't think at all'.

The rejection of dualism need not be a rejection of the mental side of the duality, although that is the obvious preference of most scientists. We have seen at least one philosopher, however, who escapes the problems of Cartesian dualism by rejecting the physical side of the problem. That philosopher is Bishop George Berkeley, who quite clearly, in attacking Locke and defending his own 'subjective idealism', provided a radical solution to the mind–body problem. His theory is that there are only minds and their ideas, no physical bodies. Therefore, there is no problem of interaction. Yet he, like Leibniz, needs God to hold his system together. Although we see little of it nowadays, idealism was a common answer to the mind–body problem in previous times. For much of the nineteenth century, in North America as well as in England and Europe, the idealists were so powerful that they virtually ruled philosophy.

- How has dualism committed a 'category mistake', according to Ryle? Do you think our use of the term *mind* is akin to the use of *university* in the example he provides?
- Can the mind be described in dispositional terms? How does doing so avoid making the mind a substance?

---

4. The Identity Theory

The most powerful and most plausible rejection of dualism, however, consists neither of denying consciousness nor of denying physical bodies. To deny dualism by denying mind or body strikes us as a bit simple-minded. There is a better way. Why not say that there are not two things at all, as there appear to be, but only one. In other words, mind and body, or more accurately, mental events and certain bodily events (presumably brain events) are identical. This theory, accordingly, is called the **identity theory**, and it was one of the hottest controversies in philosophy in the second half of the twentieth century. You can see that it was anticipated, in a sense, by Spinoza and Russell with their dual aspect theories. But the identity theory, unlike the others, tries to tie itself as closely as possible with current scientific research, and although it is not a scientific theory itself, it will allow no mysterious 'something' such as we found in Spinoza and Russell. Accordingly, it is usually considered a form of materialism (although it does not deny the existence—only the ontological independence—of mental events).

The identity theory says that there are mental events, but they are identical to—the same thing as—certain physical events, that is, processes in the brain. Unlike behaviourism (radical or logical), the identity theory does not deny that mentalistic terms refer to something. The identity theory rather denies dualism by insisting that what mentalistic terms such as 'wants', 'believes', and 'loves' refer to is not only some further unspecifiable mental state; it is also a neurological process that scientists will someday be able to specify precisely. Dualism is eliminated because there are no longer two things to interact; there is just a single event, a mental-neurological event, which can be described in either of two ways, in either of two quite different languages. One can (truthfully) say, 'I have a headache' or, if one knows an extensive amount of neurology, one could just as well describe the sensation in terms of physical processes in the brain.

The following excerpt contains Australian philosopher J.J.C. Smart's classic statement of the identity theory.

From 'Sensations and Brain Processes'
By J.J.C. Smart

Sensations are nothing over and above brain processes.

It seems to me that science is increasingly giving us a viewpoint whereby organisms are able to be seen as physico-chemical mechanisms: it seems that even the behaviour of man himself will one day be explicable in mechanistic terms. There does seem to be, so far as science is concerned, nothing in the world but increasingly complex arrangements of physical constituents. All except for one place: in consciousness. That is, for a full description of what is going on in a man you would have to mention not only the physical processes in his tissue, glands, nervous system, and so forth, but also his states of consciousness: his visual, auditory, and tactual sensations, his aches and pains. That these should be *correlated* with brain processes does not help, for to say that they are *correlated* is to say that they are something 'over and above'. You cannot correlate something with itself. You correlate footprints with burglars, but not Bill Sikes the burglar with Bill Sikes the burglar. So sensations, states of consciousness, do seem to be the one sort of thing left outside the physicalist picture, and for various reasons I just cannot believe that this can be so. That everything should be explicable in terms of physics (together of course with descriptions of the ways in which the parts are put together—roughly, biology is to physics as radio-engineering is to electromagnetism) except the occurrence of sensations seems to me to be frankly unbelievable. Such sensations would be 'nomological danglers', to use Feigl's expression. It is not often realized how odd would be the laws whereby these nomological danglers would dangle. It is sometimes asked, 'Why can't there be psychophysical laws which are of a novel sort, just as the laws of electricity and magnetism were novelties from the standpoint of Newtonian mechanics?' Certainly we are pretty sure in the future to come across new

ultimate laws of a novel type, but I expect them to relate simple constituents: for example, whatever ultimate particles are then in vogue. I cannot believe that ultimate laws of nature could relate simple constituents to configurations consisting of perhaps billions of neurons (and goodness knows how many billion billions of ultimate particles) all put together for all the world as though their main purpose in life was to be a negative feedback mechanism of a complicated sort. Such ultimate laws would be like nothing so far known in science. They have a queer 'smell' to them. I am just unable to believe in the nomological danglers themselves, or in the laws whereby they would dangle. If any philosophical arguments seemed to compel us to believe in such things, I would suspect a catch in the argument. In any case it is the object of this paper to show that there are no philosophical arguments which compel us to be dualists.

* * *

Why should sensations just be brain processes of a certain sort? There are, of course, well-known (as well as lesser-known) philosophical objections to the view that reports of sensations are reports of brain-processes, but I shall try to argue that these arguments are by no means as cogent as is commonly thought to be the case.

Let me first try to state more accurately the thesis that sensations are brain processes. It is not the thesis that, for example, 'afterimage' or 'ache' means the same as 'brain process of sort X' (where 'X' is replaced by a description of a certain sort of brain process). It is that, in so far as 'afterimage' or 'ache' is a report of a process, it is a report of a process that *happens to be* a brain process. It follows that the thesis does not claim that sensation statements can be *translated* into statements about

(*Continued*)

brain processes. Nor does it claim that the logic of a sensation statement is the same as that of a brain-process statement. All it claims is that in so far as a sensation statement is a report of something, that something is in fact a brain process. Sensations are nothing over and above brain processes. Nations are nothing 'over and above' citizens, but this does not prevent the logic of nation statements being very different from the logic of citizen statements, nor does it ensure the translatability of nation statements into citizen statements. (I do not, however, wish to assert that the relation of sensation statements to brain-process statements is very like that of nation statements to citizen statements. Nations do not just *happen to be* nothing over and above citizens, for example. I bring in the 'nations' example merely to make a negative point: that the fact that the logic of *A*-statements is different from that of *B*-statements does not insure that *A*'s are anything over and above *B*'s.)

Remarks on identity. When I say that a sensation is a brain process or that lightning is an electric discharge, I am using 'is' in the sense of strict identity. (Just as in the—in this case necessary—proposition '7 is identical with the smallest prime number greater than 5'.) When I say that a sensation is a brain process or that lightning is an electric discharge I do not mean just that the sensation is somehow spatially or temporally continuous with the brain process or that the lightning is just spatially or temporally continuous with the discharge. When on the other hand I say that the successful general is the same person as the small boy who stole the apples I mean only that the successful general I see before me is a time slice of the same four-dimensional object of which the small boy stealing apples is an earlier time slice. However, the four-dimensional object which has the general-I-see-before-me for its late time slice is identical in the strict sense with the four-dimensional object which has the small-boy-stealing-apples for an early time slice. I distinguish these two senses of 'is identical with' because I wish to make it clear that the brain-process doctrine asserts identity in the *strict* sense.

As compatible as the identity theory may seem with contemporary science and as plausible as it may seem as a way of rejecting dualism without rejecting the obvious facts about feelings and thinking, the identity theory too runs up against its share of paradoxes. The idea that one thing (a brain event that is the same thing as a mental event) can be referred to and described in two different languages sounds plausible and impressive. But, in this case, the two languages are so very different that there is very good reason to suppose that the thing(s) they refer to is/are very different as well. To pursue this line of criticism, here is a reevaluation of the identity theory by the American philosopher Jerome Shaffer.

Against the Identity Theory
By Jerome Shaffer

What are the advantages of the identity theory?

The sense of 'identity' relevant here is that in which we say, for example, that the morning star is 'identical' with the evening star. It is not that the expression 'morning star' means the same as the expression 'evening star'; on the contrary, these expressions mean something different. But the object referred to by the two expressions is one and the same; there is just one heavenly body, namely, Venus, which when seen in the morning is called the morning star and when seen in the evening is called the evening star.

The morning star is identical with the evening star; they are one and the same object.[5]

Of course, the identity of the mental with the physical is not exactly of this sort, since it is held to be simultaneous identity rather than the identity of a thing at one time with the same thing at a later time. To take a closer example, one can say that lightning is a particularly massive electrical discharge from one cloud to another or to the earth. Not that the word 'lightning' *means* 'a particularly massive electrical discharge . . .';

when Benjamin Franklin discovered that lightning was electrical, he did not make a discovery about the meaning of words. Nor when it was discovered that water was H_2O was a discovery made about the meanings of words; yet water is identical with H_2O.

In a similar fashion, the identity theorist can hold that thoughts, feelings, wishes, and the like are identical with physical states. Not 'identical' in the sense that mentalistic terms are synonymous in meaning with physicalistic terms but 'identical' in the sense that the actual events picked out by mentalistic terms are one and the same events as those picked out by physicalistic terms.

* * *

What are the advantages of the identity theory? As a form of materialism, it does not have to cope with a world which has in it both mental phenomena and physical phenomena, and it does not have to ponder how they might be related. There exist only the physical phenomena, although there do exist two different ways of talking about such phenomena: physicalistic terminology and, in at least some situations, mentalistic terminology. We have here a dualism of language, but not a dualism of entities, events, or properties.

But do we have merely a dualism of languages and no other sort of dualism? In the case of Venus, we do indeed have only one object, but the expression 'morning star' picks out one phase of that object's history, where it is in the mornings, and the expression 'evening star' picks out another phase of the object's history, where it is in the evenings. If that object did not have these two distinct aspects, it would not have been a *discovery* that the morning star and the evening star were indeed one and the same body, and, further, there would be no point to the different ways of referring to it.

Now it would be admitted by identity theorists that physicalistic and mentalistic terms do not refer to different phases in the history of one and the same object. What sort of identity is intended? Let us turn to an allegedly closer analogy, that of the identity of lightning and a particular sort of electrical phenomenon. Yet here again we have two distinguishable aspects, the appearance to the naked eye on the one hand and the physical composition on the other. And this is also not the kind of identity which is plausible for mental and physical events. The appearance *to the naked eye* of a neurological event is utterly different from the experience of having a thought or a pain.

It is sometimes suggested that the physical aspect results from looking at a particular event 'from the outside', whereas the mental results from looking at the same event 'from the inside'. When the brain surgeon observes my brain he is looking at it from the outside, whereas when I experience a mental event I am 'looking' at my brain 'from the inside'.

Such an account gives us only a misleading analogy, rather than an accurate characterization of the relationship between the mental and the physical. The analogy suggests the difference between a man who knows his own house from the inside, in that he is free to move about within, seeing objects from different perspectives, touching them, etc., but can never get outside to see how it looks from there, and a man who cannot get inside and therefore knows only the outside appearance of the house, and perhaps what he can glimpse through the windows. But what does this have to do with the brain? Am I free to roam about inside my brain, observing what the brain surgeon may never see? Is not the 'inner' aspect of my brain far more accessible to the brain surgeon than to me? He has the X-rays, probes, electrodes, scalpels, and scissors for getting at the inside of my brain. If it is replied that this is only an analogy, not to be taken literally, then the question still remains how the mental and the physical are related.

* * *

One of the leading identity theorists, J.J.C. Smart, holds that mentalistic discourse is simply a vaguer, more indefinite way of talking about what could be talked about more precisely by using physiological terms. If I report a red afterimage, I mean (roughly) that something is going on which is like what goes on when I really see a red patch. I do not actually *mean* that a particular sort of brain process is occurring, but when I say something is going on I refer (very vaguely, to be sure) to just that brain process. Thus the thing referred to in my report of an afterimage is a brain process. Hence there is no need to bring in any non-physical features. Thus even the taint of dualism is avoided.

Does this ingenious attempt to evade dualistic implications stand up under philosophical scrutiny? I am inclined to think it will not. Let us return to the man reporting the red afterimage. He was aware of the occurrence of something or other, of some feature or other. Now it seems to me obvious that he

(Continued)

was not necessarily aware of the state of his brain at that time (I doubt that most of us are ever aware of the state of our brain) nor, in general, necessarily aware of any physical features of his body at that time. He might, of course, have been incidentally aware of some physical feature but not insofar as he was aware of the red afterimage as such. Yet he was definitely aware of something, or else how could he have made that report? So he must have been aware of some non-physical feature. That is the only way of explaining how he was aware of anything at all.

Of course, the thing that our reporter of the afterimage was aware of might well have had further features which he was *not* aware of, particularly, in this connection, physical features. I may be aware of certain features of an object without being aware of others. So it is not ruled out that the event our reporter is aware of might be an event with predominantly physical features—he just does not notice those. But he must be aware of some of its features, or else it would not be proper to say he was aware of *that* event. And if he is not aware of any physical features, he must be aware of something else. And that shows that we cannot get rid of those non-physical features in the way that Smart suggests.

* * *

If by X-rays or some other means we were able to see every event which occurred in the brain, we would never get a glimpse of a thought. If, to resort to fantasy, we could so enlarge a brain or so shrink ourselves that we could wander freely through the brain, we would still never observe a thought. All we could ever observe in the brain would be the *physical* events which occur in it. If mental events had location in the brain, there should be some means of detecting them there. But of course there is none. The very idea of it is senseless.

Shaffer disagrees with the identity theory, but both his presentation and his criticism of it continue to be debated. In defending the identity theory, it is most important to stress that the identity of brain processes and thoughts is an empirical identity, that is, an identity that must be discovered through experiment and experience. It is not a logical identity, as if the terms *brain process* and *thought* are synonymous. The latter suggestion is obviously false, and modern defenders of the identity theory emphasize that future neurophysiological research will prove them right. Shaffer's criticism, however, is based on a principle that must be distinguished from the all-too-easy attack on the logical identity suggestion. The principle is that if two things are identical, then they must have all the same properties. But, Shaffer argues, no amount of research could possibly show that brain processes and thought have the same properties. Most importantly, brain processes take place in the brain and can be traced like any other physical processes; thoughts, on the other hand, have no spatial location, and there is nothing that research can 'discover' that will show that they do. Of course, research can and has shown that certain thoughts are correlated with certain brain processes, but correlation is not yet identity.

- Is the identity theory of mind a form of materialism? How does it differ from most forms of materialism? How does it differ from epiphenomenalism?
- How could psycho-physics describe your experience of pain or of seeing red? Do you think that psycho-physics could fully capture what it is like to have these experiences? Does the identity theorist claim to capture your experience of pain when he describes it in terms of physical laws?
- What does Smart mean when he claims, 'sensations are nothing over and above brain processes'? What does he mean by 'strict identity'?
- How are mental properties different from physical properties? Does this show that they cannot be identical?

5. Eliminative Materialism

To most materialists, the identity theory seemed promising, even if its arguments proved inadequate. The real question was whether there might be some other version of the thesis—that mental states were 'nothing but' brain states—that did not claim the kind of one-to-one match required by the identity theory. One suggestion (still popular in many quarters) is the thesis called **eliminative materialism**, which proposes to defend materialism without claiming an identity between what we call 'mental states' and the workings of the brain. Rather, the argument goes, our increasing knowledge of the workings of the brain will make outmoded our 'folk-psychology' talk about the mind and we will all learn to talk the language of neurology instead.

In the following excerpt, Paul Churchland defends the opposition (rather than the complementarity) of neurological explanations of human behaviour and the familiar mentalistic accounts. With increased knowledge of neurology, he argues, our ordinary language will be replaced or, at least, seriously revised.

On Eliminative Materialism
By Paul M. Churchland

The most central things about us remain almost entirely mysterious from within folk psychology.

The identity theory was called into doubt not because the prospects for a materialist account of our mental capacities were thought to be poor, but because it seemed unlikely that the arrival of an adequate materialist theory would bring with it the nice one-to-one match-ups, between the concepts of folk psychology and the concepts of theoretical neuroscience, that intertheoretic reduction requires. The reason for that doubt was the great variety of quite different physical systems that could instantiate the required functional organization. *Eliminative materialism* also doubts that the correct neuroscientific account of human capacities will produce a neat reduction of our common-sense framework, but here the doubts arise from a quite different source.

As the eliminative materialists see it, the one-to-one match-ups will not be found, and our common-sense psychological framework will not enjoy an intertheoretic reduction, *because our common-sense psychological framework is a false and radically misleading conception of the causes of human behaviour and the nature of cognitive activity.* On this view, folk psychology is not just an incomplete representation of our inner natures; it is an outright *mis*representation of our internal states and activities. Consequently, we cannot expect a truly adequate neuroscientific account of our inner lives to provide theoretical categories that match up nicely with the categories of our common-sense framework. Accordingly, we must expect that the older framework will simply be eliminated, rather than be reduced, by a matured neuroscience.

Historical Parallels

As the identity theorist can point to historical cases of successful intertheoretic reduction, so the eliminative materialist can point to historical cases of the outright elimination of the ontology of an older theory in favour of the ontology of a new and superior theory.

* * *

It used to be thought that when a piece of wood burns, or a piece of metal rusts, a spirit-like substance called 'phlogiston' was being released: briskly, in the former case, slowly in the latter. Once gone, that 'noble' substance left only a base pile of ash or rust. It later came to be appreciated that both processes involve, not the loss of something, but the *gaining* of a substance taken from the atmosphere: oxygen. Phlogiston emerged, not as an incomplete description of what was going on, but as a radical misdescription. Phlogiston was therefore not suitable for reduction to or identification with some notion from within the new oxygen chemistry, and it was simply eliminated from science.

* * *

(Continued)

The concepts of folk psychology—belief, desire, fear, sensation, pain, joy, and so on—await a similar fate, according to the view at issue. And when neuroscience has matured to the point where the poverty of our current conceptions is apparent to everyone, the superiority of the new framework is established, we shall then be able to set about *reconceiving* our internal states and activities, within a truly adequate conceptual framework at last. Our explanations of one another's behaviour will appeal to such things as our neuropharmacological states, the neural activity in specialized anatomical areas, and whatever other states are deemed relevant by the new theory. Our private introspection will also be transformed, and may be profoundly enhanced by reason of the more accurate and penetrating framework it will have to work with—just as the astronomer's perception of the night sky is much enhanced by the detailed knowledge of modern astronomical theory that he or she possesses.

The magnitude of the conceptual revolution here suggested should not be minimized: it would be enormous. And the benefits to humanity might be equally great. If each of us possessed an accurate neuroscientific understanding of (what we now conceive dimly as) the varieties and causes of mental illness, the factors involved in learning, the neural basis of emotions, intelligence, and socialization, then the sum total of human misery might be much reduced. The simple increase in mutual understanding that the new framework made possible could contribute substantially toward a more peaceful and humane society. Of course, there would be dangers as well: increased knowledge means increased power, and power can always be misused.

Arguments for Eliminative Materialism

The arguments for eliminative materialism are diffuse and less than decisive, but they are stronger than is widely supposed. The distinguishing feature of this position is its denial that a smooth intertheoretic reduction is to be expected—even a species-specific reduction—of the framework of folk psychology to the framework of a matured neuroscience. The reason for this denial is the eliminative materialist's conviction that folk psychology is a hopelessly primitive and deeply confused conception of our internal activities. But why this low opinion of our commonsense conceptions?

There are at least three reasons. First, the eliminative materialist will point to the widespread explanatory, predictive, and manipulative failures of folk psychology. So much of what is central and familiar to us remains a complete mystery from within folk psychology. We do not know what *sleep* is, or why we have to have it, despite spending a full third of our lives in that condition. (The answer, 'For rest', is mistaken. Even if people are allowed to rest continuously, their need for sleep is undiminished. Apparently, sleep serves some deeper functions, but we do not yet know what they are.) We do not understand how *learning* transforms each of us from a gaping infant to a cunning adult, or how differences in *intelligence* are grounded. We have not the slightest idea how *memory* works, or how we manage to retrieve relevant bits of information instantly from the awesome mass we have stored. We do not know what *mental illness* is, nor how to cure it.

In sum, the most central things about us remain almost entirely mysterious from within folk psychology.

* * *

This argument from explanatory poverty has a further aspect. So long as one sticks to normal brains, the poverty of folk psychology is perhaps not strikingly evident. But as soon as one examines the many perplexing behavioural and cognitive deficits suffered by people with *damaged* brains, one's descriptive and explanatory resources start to claw the air. . . . As with other humble theories asked to operate successfully in unexplored extensions of their old domain (for example, Newtonian mechanics in the domain of velocities close to the velocity of light, and the classical gas law in the domain of high pressures or temperatures), the descriptive and explanatory inadequacies of folk psychology become starkly evident.

The second argument tries to draw an inductive lesson from our conceptual history. Our early folk theories of motion were profoundly confused, and were eventually displaced entirely by more sophisticated theories. Our early folk theories of the structure and activity of the heavens were wildly off the mark, and survive only as historical lessons in how wrong we can be. Our folk theories of the nature of fire, and the nature of life, were similarly cockeyed. And one could go on, since the vast majority of our past folk conceptions have been similarly exploded. All except folk psychology, which survives to this day and has only recently begun to feel pressure. But the phenomenon of conscious intelligence is surely a more complex and difficult phenomenon than any of those just listed. So far as accurate understanding is concerned, it would be a *miracle* if we had got *that* one right the very first time, when we fell down so badly on all the others. Folk psychology has survived for so very long, presumably, not because it is basically correct in its representations, but because the phenomena addressed are so surpassingly difficult that any useful handle on them, no matter how feeble, is unlikely to be displaced in a hurry.

* * *

Arguments against Eliminative Materialism

The initial plausibility of this rather radical view is low for almost everyone, since it denies deeply entrenched assumptions. That is at best a question-begging complaint, of course, since those assumptions are precisely what is at issue. But the following line of thought does attempt to mount a real argument.

Eliminative materialism is false, runs the argument, because one's introspection reveals directly the existence of pains, beliefs, desires, fears, and so forth. Their existence is as obvious as anything could be.

The eliminative materialist will reply that this argument makes the same mistake that an ancient or medieval person would be making if he insisted that he could just see with his own eyes that the heavens form a turning sphere, or that witches exist. The fact is, all observation occurs within some system of concepts, and our observation judgments are only as good as the conceptual framework in which they are expressed. In all three cases—the starry sphere, witches, and the familiar mental states—precisely what is challenged is the integrity of the background conceptual frameworks in which the observation judgments are expressed. To insist on the validity of one's experiences, *traditionally interpreted*, is therefore to beg the very question at issue. For in all three cases, the question is whether we should *reconceive* the nature of some familiar observational domain.

* * *

A final criticism draws a much weaker conclusion, but makes a rather stronger case. Eliminative materialism, it has been said, is making mountains out of molehills. It exaggerates the defects in folk psychology, and underplays its real successes. Perhaps the arrival of a matured neuroscience will require the elimination of the occasional folk-psychological concept, continues the criticism, and a minor adjustment in certain folk-psychological principles may have to be endured. But the large-scale elimination forecast by the eliminative materialist is just an alarmist worry or a romantic enthusiasm.

Perhaps this complaint is correct. And perhaps it is merely complacent. Whichever, it does bring out the important point that we do not confront two simple and mutually exclusive possibilities here: pure reduction versus pure elimination. Rather, these are the end points of a smooth spectrum of possible outcomes, between which there are mixed cases of partial elimination and partial reduction. Only empirical research . . . can tell us where on that spectrum our own case will fall. Perhaps we should speak here, more liberally, of 'revisionary materialism', instead of concentrating on the more radical possibility of an across-the-board elimination.

Churchland's primary aim in this final argument is to present as at least intelligible his position that 'our collective conceptual destiny lies substantially toward the revolutionary end of the spectrum'.

- In what sense do the eliminative materialists (Churchland) agree with those who reject the identity theory (Shaffer)? In what important ways do they differ?
- What is 'folk psychology'? Can you give an example of a folk-psychological explanation for falling in love, being sad, embarrassment followed by anger, hunger dissipating after a few days of fasting, the need for sleep?

6. Functionalism: The Mind and the Computer

Despite the claims of Cartesians that 'minds are non-physical', at least in the obvious sense, Churchland and other materialists based their notion of the 'self' on what they felt to be scientific fact, the physical basis of minds—the brain and the central nervous system. It is the brain that makes minds possible.

On the one hand, this was a rather remarkable discovery in the history of biology. It is by no means obvious, looking at the gooey cauliflower-shaped stuff inside the skull, that in that space is packed billions of tiny neural networks that control our every experience, our every action, including the inner actions of our bodies of which we may not even be aware (control of metabolism and blood flow, for example). But since the introduction of computers, scientific criticisms of dualism have taken another line. Is it so obvious that minds could *only* be the product of brains? Could mental processes be based on physical processes that are not brain processes? Could, for example, mental processes be based upon a network of electronic signals in a properly designed complex of transistors and circuit boards? In other words, could mental processes be the product of a computer? Could the brain be nothing but an organic computer? Could computers—the kind that we make out of metal and minerals—have minds?

It is no coincidence that the past two decades or so of computer breakthroughs has produced a revolution in the way some philosophers think about selves and minds. This new philosophical position is called **functionalism**, and its basic insight is that minds are produced not so much by particular kinds of materials (for example, brains) but rather by the *relations* between parts. In the near future, it may in fact be possible, according to the most optimistic functionalists, to build a fully functioning human mind out of computer parts. But whether or not computer scientists achieve such a (frightening) miracle, functionalists still hold that the mind is, in effect, a *function* of the patterns of neurological activity in the brain.

In computer technology, there is a crucial distinction between 'hardware' and 'software'. Hardware is the actual computer with its circuits. In the case of human minds, the hardware would be the brain and its neurological circuits. Software is the program that gives the computer specific instructions. (Sometimes, specific instructions can be 'hard-wired', as in the case of instinct, but these are not the exciting cases that inspire most functionalists and computer scientists.) The view of the functionalists is that the mind is nothing other than an elaborate program of sorts, which is the product of a spectacularly complicated pattern embodied in the physical workings of the brain.

In the following selection, David Braddon-Mitchell and Frank Jackson give a brief defence of functionalism.

FUNCTIONALISM

The view that the mind is the product of patterns in the brain.

From *Philosophy of Mind and Cognition*
By David Braddon-Mitchell and Frank Jackson

The world is full of states, devices, stations in life, objects, processes, properties, and events that are defined wholly or partly by their functional roles. Thermostats are defined by how they control temperature by switching machines on and off; burglar alarms are defined by how they function to produce loud noises on being disturbed in various ways (only sometimes by burglars, unfortunately); the office of vice-chancellor is defined by its function in a university; filtration is defined as a process that takes as input solids in liquid suspension and delivers as separate outputs the solid and the liquid; a graduation ceremony is an event in part defined by its role of producing graduates; a dangerous corner is the kind that tends to take approaching cars and deliver accidents; and so on and so forth. In all these cases there is a distinction to be drawn between the functional role and what occupies or fills it. Some thermostats are bi-metallic strips; some are more complex electronic devices. Either way, they count as thermostats provided they do the required regulating of temperature. Many different people might be vice-chancellor of the university. Burglar alarms come in many shapes and sizes. There are many ways a corner can be dangerous.

In the same way functionalists about the mind distinguish the functional roles specified by the input, output, and internal role clauses from what occupies them, and insist that what matters for being in one or another mental state are the roles that are occupied, not what occupies them. Provided the right roles are occupied, it does not matter what occupies them. Sometimes it is claimed that as a matter of empirical fact what occupies the relevant roles most likely varies. It is claimed that what plays the belief-that-there-is-food-nearby role in dogs is most likely different from what plays that role in cats; or perhaps the occupant of the role varies from one kind of dog to another; or perhaps it is different in left-handed people as opposed to right-handed people. Sometimes the claim is simply that it is abstractly possible that what plays or realizes the role associated with a given mental state varies. What is agreed though is that what matters for being in a given mental state are the roles occupied, not what occupies them. This is the famous multiple realizability thesis distinctive of functionalist theories of mind. Multiple realizability is appealing for a number of reasons:

1. We ascribe mental states on the basis of behaviour in circumstances and without much regard to what realizes the various functional roles. Indeed, we do not know in any detail what realizes the roles, and until relatively recently we did not know even in broad outline.

2. We have all read science fiction stories about creatures—traditionally called 'Martians' in philosophical discussions—whose chemistry is, say, silicon-based, instead of carbon-based like ours, and who interact with the environment much as we do, plan our defeat, fall in love with some of us, admire characteristics that we abhor, shame us with their compassion and understanding, are vastly more intelligent than we are, or whatever. These stories strike us as perfectly coherent, despite the fact that it is part of the story that the states that realize the relevant functional roles in them are quite different from those that realize the roles in us. As the conclusion from these science fiction considerations is often put, we should not be chauvinists about the mind.

3. There is considerable evidence that our brains start out in a relatively plastic state, and that as we grow and the environment impacts on us, states come to occupy new functional roles, those subserving language, for instance. The usual explanation as to why language cannot be learnt past a certain age appeals to this point. Past a certain age it is too late for the right changes in brain function to occur. This opens up the possibility that the way your brain changed to subserve the functional roles needed for language was different from the way my brain did. But, provided the job gets done, it does not seem to matter.

4. An important part of making a good recovery from a stroke is getting an undamaged part of the brain to do something previously done by the part damaged by the stroke. Stroke victims do not worry about whether the new part of the brain counts as a different realizer of the old role. What they worry about is whether the job will be well done, and that seems exactly the right attitude to take.

5. Prosthetic surgery for the brain seems no more problematic *in principle* than does prosthetic surgery in general. We can imagine that, as they degenerate, parts of someone's brain are progressively replaced by silicon implants. Provided the implants fill the same functional roles, surely the surgery would count as successful. But then it must be the case that mental life is preserved despite the radical change in what realizes the various functional roles.

Multiple realizability, then, in addition to being common ground among functionalists, is a point in favour of their theory. It is widely accepted that any theory of mind should accommodate multiple realizability, and it is very much a point in functionalism's favour that it does this so naturally. What is not common ground is the question of which functional roles are essential to which mental states and the more general question of where functionalism should stand on how we might answer this question.

One response is to leave the question to someone else. Some functionalists hold that the question of which functional roles mental states occupy should be left to empirical psychology and neuroscience. We can distinguish very many functional roles played by mental states, and the study of the mind is the study of these many functional roles. But it is no part of

(Continued)

functionalism, on this view, to argue for one or another answer to conceptual issues concerning how to analyze what it is to be in pain, believe that it will rain soon, or whatever. But if the key to the mind lies in functional roles, it seems fair to ask for some sort of guide as to which functional roles matter. A burglar alarm may play many functional roles. Perhaps it plays the role of being a drain on your bank balance, being a conversation piece at dinner parties, and making a loud noise when burglars are near. We know which role matters for its being a burglar alarm. The last role is the one that matters. That is why if it stops breaking down—and so stops being a drain on your bank balance—and if it stops being unusual in the neighbourhood—and so stops being a conversation piece—it will still be a burglar alarm. Among the various functional roles it has, we discriminate between those that matter for its counting as a burglar alarm and those that do not matter. The same is true for all the examples we gave earlier. Any particular vice-chancellor, thermostat, or dangerous corner will play many roles, but only some will matter for being a vice-chancellor, a thermostat, or a dangerous corner. Why, then, should it be impossible to make the same kind of discrimination in the case of mental states? We know that not all the roles which various mental states fill matter equally for its being the mental state that it is—for instance, pain's playing the role of being the example most often chosen for discussion by philosophers is irrelevant to its being pain; it wouldn't hurt any less if philosophers instead began to discuss itching—so surely it is fair to ask the functionalist for some guide as to which functional roles of a mental state matter for its being the mental state that it is.

The best answer, in our view, to the question of which functional roles matter is the answer given by common-sense functionalism. Common-sense functionalism aims to give an analysis of what it is to be in one or another mental state in broadly functional terms, in the same general way that we can give an analysis of being a burglar alarm in broadly functional terms.

The idea that the computer will someday provide a single model of mental states and information processes has been called into question recently. It is not at all clear that the mind works like a computer, or whether instead it works on different parallel levels in a manner substantially more complicated and considerably faster than any known computer.

Nevertheless, like any bold new hypothesis, the functionalist analogy analysis of the mind as a computer has crashed head-on into some of the most entrenched ideas and experiences of common sense. In defence of common sense, John Searle—one of the leading analysts of ordinary human language and the special features of human communication—attacks the notion that computers are sufficiently intelligent to threaten or to challenge human intelligence anytime soon. He suggests a powerful counter-example to the widespread claim that 'the conclusive proof of the presence of mental states and capacities [in a computer system or elsewhere] is the ability to convince a competent expert, for example, if a machine could converse with a native Chinese speaker in such a way as to convince the speaker that it understood Chinese'.[6]

From 'The Myth of the Computer'
By John R. Searle

Since brains do produce minds, and since programs by themselves can't produce minds, it follows that the way the brain does it can't be by simply instantiating a computer program.

The details of how the brain works are immensely complicated and largely unknown, but some of the general principles of the relations between brain functioning and computer programs can be stated quite simply. First, we know that brain processes cause mental phenomena. Mental states are caused by and realized in the structure of the brain. From this it follows that any system that produced mental states would have to have powers equivalent to those of the brain. Such a system might use a different chemistry, but whatever its chemistry it would have to be able to cause what the brain causes. We know from the [previous] argument digital computer programs by themselves are never sufficient to produce mental states. Now since brains do produce minds, and since programs by themselves can't produce minds, it follows that the way the brain does it can't be by simply instantiating a computer program. (Everything, by the way, instantiates some program or other, and brains are no exception. So in that trivial sense brains, like everything else, are digital computers.)

And it also follows that if you wanted to build a machine to produce mental states, a thinking machine, you couldn't do it solely in virtue of the fact that your machine ran a certain kind of computer program. The thinking machine couldn't work solely in virtue of being a digital computer but would have to duplicate the specific causal powers of the brain.

A lot of the nonsense talked about computers nowadays stems from their relative rarity and hence mystery. As computers and robots become more common, as common as telephones, washing machines, and forklift trucks, it seems likely that this aura will disappear and people will take computers for what they are, namely useful machines.

- How is the mind similar to a computer? In what ways does it differ? How does a functionalist view of mind argue that they are the same?

From *Minds, Brains, and Science*
By John R. Searle

Imagine that a bunch of computer programmers have written a program that will enable a computer to simulate the understanding of Chinese. So, for example, if the computer is given a question in Chinese, it will match the question against its memory, or database, and produce appropriate answers to the questions in Chinese. . . . Does the computer, on the basis of this, understand Chinese, does it literally understand Chinese, in the way that Chinese speakers understand Chinese? Well, imagine that you are locked in a room, and in this room are several baskets full of Chinese symbols. Imagine that you (like me) do not understand a word of Chinese, but that you are given a rule book in English for manipulating these Chinese symbols. The rules specify the manipulations of the symbols purely formally, in terms of their syntax, not their semantics. So the rule might say: 'Take a squiggle-squiggle sign out of basket number one and put it next to a squoggle-squoggle sign from basket number two.' Now suppose that some other Chinese symbols are passed into the room, and that you are given further rules for passing back Chinese symbols out of the room. Suppose that unknown to you the symbols passed into the room are called 'questions' by the people outside the room, and the symbols you pass back out of the room are called 'answers to the questions'. Suppose, furthermore, that the programmers are so good at designing the programs and that you are so good at manipulating the symbols, that very soon your answers are indistinguishable from those of a native Chinese speaker. There you are locked in your room shuffling your Chinese symbols and passing out Chinese symbols in response to incoming Chinese symbols. On the basis of the situation as I have described it, there is no way you could learn any Chinese simply by manipulating these formal symbols.

Now the point of the story is simply this: by virtue of implementing a formal computer program from the point of view of an outside observer, you behave exactly as if you understood Chinese, but all the same you don't understand a word of Chinese. But if going through the appropriate computer program for understanding Chinese is not enough to give *you* an understanding of Chinese, then it is not enough to give *any other digital computer* an understanding of Chinese. . . . All that the computer has, as you have, is a formal program for manipulating uninterpreted Chinese symbols.

- How would you answer Searle and his 'Chinese room' thought experiment? Does it prove what he wants it to prove?

7. Connectionism

Not all criticisms of functionalism are non-materialist. Recently, objections have been brought against functionalism from neurophysiologists who claim that functionalism is just too simplistic in its vision of the brain and of computers. Connectionists complain that functionalism is a 'top-down', 'software' approach, which can never be accurate in its representation of the 'hardware' of either the brain or the computer. In other words, say the connectionists, a functionalist starts with behaviour—either human behaviour or computer behaviour—and claims that understanding human consciousness is just a matter of finding the 'program' for that behaviour. The functionalist claims that to understand the 'program' is to understand the behaviour, regardless of the mechanical and physical interactions that make the program run. The connectionist, on the other hand, claims that the mechanical and physical interactions that occur in the brain determine the kinds of behaviour—which kinds of software—that computers are capable of processing. Connectionists therefore advocate a 'bottom-up' approach to understanding the mind. Connectionists are still materialists, but not in the simple, reductionist, way of their predecessors. They believe that consciousness—in its full colour and quality—is a result of the complicated 'connections' that really do go on in the brain. There is no one-to-one correspondence between neurons and thoughts or perceptions; rather, they claim, the 'hardware' of the brain is an immensely complex mechanism to which the functionalists do not do justice.

- What are the similarities and differences between functionalists and connectionists?

D. The Problem of Consciousness

IMMEDIATE

For certain and without need for argument.

Descartes claimed he knew what was going on in his mind with an **immediate** certainty that he could never have about what was going on in the world 'outside' him. In his first 'Meditation', he talks about his seeming to be sitting in front of the fire and the fact that he might be wrong about his actual position in space (for example, if he were in bed asleep at the time). But what he could not be wrong about is his *seeming* to be sitting in front of the fire. Similarly, imagine that you think you see a friend walking across the street. You are wrong, for your friend is in fact in Alaska this week. But you can still be certain that you thought that you saw him, even if you didn't *actually* see him. Philosophers often refer to this special kind of 'immediate' certainty in the case of our own conscious experiences as **incorrigibility**. You might make a mistake in any factual claim about the world, for you might be hallucinating, or dreaming, or simply fooled by circumstances. But nothing could lead you to suspect you might be mistaken about your own experiences. Given enough evidence against you, you might be willing to change from 'but I know that I saw it' to 'well, I thought I saw it', but nothing could convince you that you were wrong in thinking that you saw whatever it was. That claim, the claim about your experience, is incorrigible. Your claim about what you saw, however, is always open to further questioning.

INCORRIGIBILITY

Impossible to correct; cannot be mistaken.

For many years, this notion of incorrigibility served as part of the definition of *mind* and therefore, as Churchland implies, also defence against materialism. Whatever was mental could be described incorrigibly and this is very different than is the case with physical things. But doubts have begun to creep in recently. Part of the problem was Freud's introduction of the notion of the **unconscious**. According to his famous 'psychoanalytic' theory, not everything mental is knowable, and therefore surely not everything 'in the mind' can be described incorrigibly. In a famous passage from his 'Introductory Lectures', Freud says the following:

On the 'Unconscious'
By Sigmund Freud

There is no need to discuss what is to be called conscious: it is removed from all doubt. The oldest and best meaning of the word *unconscious* is the descriptive one; we call a psychical process unconscious whose existence we are obliged to assume—for some such reason as that we infer it from its effects—, but of which we know nothing. In that case we have the same relation to it as we have to a physical process in another person, except that it is in fact one of our own. If we want to be still more correct, we shall modify our assertion by saying that we call a process unconscious if we are obliged to assume that it is being activated *at the moment* though *at the moment* we know nothing about it.

Notice that Freud starts from a Cartesian position, the idea that conscious is 'removed from all doubt'. But then he suggests what no Cartesian can tolerate—the idea that there are ideas (experiences, intentions) in our minds that we do not and sometimes cannot know, much less know with certainty. And if we accept this notion of 'the unconscious' (or even the weaker notion of 'preconscious'), the traditional notion of the 'incorrigibility' of the mental is seriously challenged.

The argument, however, cuts both ways. Many philosophers have rejected Freud just because his notion of 'the unconscious' goes against the notion of incorrigibility. 'If it isn't knowable incorrigibly,' these philosophers have said, 'then it can't be mental at all.' Even Freud himself was forced to admit that his theory flew in the face of our normal 'manner of speaking'. The debate continues. Can you be wrong about what is going on in your own mind? For a long time, it was generally agreed that you could not be. Now we aren't so sure. You are certain that you are over an old love affair, but, without too much difficulty, a friend or a psychologist convinces you that you have been thinking about it constantly. You are certain that you are angry, but on closer examination, and in retrospect, you decide that you really felt guilty. You thought that you were thinking about your professor, when suddenly you realize that in fact it was the face of your father!

Is there anything about which we could not be mistaken? What of those basic bits of data that the empiricists talked about—sensations or impressions? Could we possibly be wrong in our confidence that 'right now, I am experiencing a cold feeling in my hand'? The empiricists assumed that one could not be wrong about this, for it was on the basis of such certainties that we were able to construct, through inductive reasoning, our theories about the world. Could we be wrong even about our own sensations? Consider this example (it comes from Berkeley): A mischievous friend tells you that he is going to touch your hand with a very hot spoon. When you aren't looking, he touches you with a piece of ice. You scream and claim, with seeming certainty, that he has given you an uncomfortable sensation of heat. But you're wrong. What you felt was cold. What you seemed to feel was heat. But even your 'seeming', in this case, was mistaken.

Philosophers have also pointed out that what is unique to mind as opposed to body is the fact that one and only one person can (and must) experience what is going on. I can (and must) feel only my pains, I can't experience your pains. Philosophers have referred to this as **privileged access**, sometimes as the **privacy** of mental events. The 'privilege' is the fact that, whatever is going on in your mind, you are not only the first but the only one to

PRIVACY

The seeming inaccessibility of mental states and events to anyone other than the person who 'has' them.

know of it directly. The 'privacy' refers to the fact that if you decide not to tell anyone or betray yourself (through your facial expressions or your behaviour), no one else need ever know. If you have a wart on your thigh, you can keep it contingently 'private' by choosing suitable clothing. But if you have a 'dirty little secret' in your mind, you have a logical guarantee of its privacy—it is private necessarily.

Incorrigible means 'beyond correction'; *privileged access* means 'known in a special way'. (These concepts must be kept separate.) Because of privileged access and the 'privacy' of consciousness, our states of mind have the very peculiar status of being always knowable to ourselves (though whether or not we want to say 'knowable with certainty' depends on our views about incorrigibility) and yet possibly unknowable to anyone else. That is why, as you learned in grade school, you could always fake a headache to stay home for the day but you couldn't fake a fever or a sore. As long as it was purely mental, it was also purely private. Your success depended wholly upon how good (or bad) an actor you were. But when it comes to your body, you were in no privileged position. It was the thermometer, not your opinions, that told whether you had a fever or not. And it was the doctor, not you, who decided how serious your sore really was. But when it came to your own consciousness, you were in a truly privileged and irrefutable position.

> • What does it mean to say that your own mental experiences are 'incorrigible'? How does this notion resist materialism? How does Freud undermine the claim to incorrigibility?

This peculiarity of the first-person position, of our relationship to our own consciousness, is one of the things that makes the notion of 'self' so difficult and that makes the problem so seemingly unresolvable. It makes the way that we establish our own identity seem categorically different from how others know it. Against all forms of reductionism and materialism, philosopher Thomas Nagel has argued in an ingenious fashion that it is consciousness, or what he calls 'subjectivity', that makes the problem so 'intractable'. Defining *subjectivity* in terms of 'what it's like' to be something, Nagel introduces his concern about the mind–body problem with an intriguing question: 'What is it like to be a bat?'

From *Mortal Questions*
By Thomas Nagel

Fundamentally an organism has conscious mental states if and only if there is something that it is like to be that organism—something it is like for the organism.

Conscious experience is a widespread phenomenon. It occurs at many levels of animal life, though we cannot be sure of its presence in the simpler organisms, and it is very difficult to say in general what provides evidence of it. (Some extremists have been prepared to deny it even of mammals other than man.) No doubt it occurs in countless forms totally unimaginable to us, on other planets in other solar systems throughout the universe. But no matter how the form may vary, the fact that an organism has conscious experience *at all* means, basically, that there is something it is like to be that organism. There may be further implications about the form of the experience; there may even (though I doubt it) be implications about the behaviour of the organism. But fundamentally an organism has conscious mental states if and only if there is something that it is like to *be* that organism—something it is like *for* the organism.

We may call this the subjective character of experience. It is not captured by any of the familiar, recently devised reductive analyses of the mental, for all of them are logically compatible with its absence.

It is not analyzable in terms of any explanatory system of functional states, or intentional states, since these could be ascribed to robots or automata that behaved like people though they experienced nothing. It is not analyzable in terms of the causal role of experiences in relation to typical human behaviour—for similar reasons. I do not deny that conscious mental states and events cause behaviour, nor that they may be given functional characterizations. I deny only that this kind of thing exhausts their analysis. Any reductionist program has to be based on an analysis of what is to be reduced. If the analysis leaves something out, the problem will be falsely posed. It is useless to base the defence of materialism on any analysis of mental phenomena that fails to deal explicitly with their subjective character.

* * *

I assume we all believe that bats have experience. After all, they are mammals, and there is no more doubt that they have experience than that mice or pigeons or whales have experience. I have chosen bats instead of wasps or flounders because if one travels too far down the phylogenetic tree, people gradually shed their faith that there is experience there at all. Bats, although more closely related to us than those other species, nevertheless present a range of activity and a sensory apparatus so different from ours that the problem I want to pose is exceptionally vivid (though it certainly could be raised with other species). Even without the benefit of philosophical reflection, anyone who has spent some time in an enclosed space with an excited bat knows what it is to encounter a fundamentally *alien* form of life.

I have said that the essence of the belief that bats have experience is that there is something that it is like to be a bat. Now we know that most bats (the microchiroptera, to be precise) perceive the external world primarily by sonar, or echolocation, detecting the reflections, from objects within range, of their own rapid, subtly modulated, high-frequency shrieks. Their brains are designed to correlate the outgoing impulses with the subsequent echoes, and the information thus acquired enables bats to make precise discriminations of distance, size, shape, motion, and texture comparable to those we make by vision. But bat sonar, though clearly a form of perception, is not similar in its operation to any sense that we possess, and there is no reason to suppose that it is subjectively like anything we can experience or imagine. This appears to create difficulties for the notion of what it is like to be a bat. We must consider whether any method will permit us to extrapolate to the inner life of the bat from our own case, and if not, what alternative methods there may be for understanding the notion.

Our own experience provides the basic material for our imagination, whose range is therefore limited. It will not help to try to imagine that one has webbing on one's arms, which enables one to fly around at dusk and dawn catching insects in one's mouth; that one has very poor vision, and perceives the surrounding world by a system of reflected high-frequency sound signals; and that one spends the day hanging upside down by one's feet in an attic. Insofar as I can imagine this (which is not very far), it tells me only what it would be like for *me* to behave as a bat behaves. But that is not the question. I want to know what it is like for a *bat* to be a bat. Yet if I try to imagine this, I am restricted to the resources of my own mind, and those resources are inadequate to the task. I cannot perform it either by imagining additions to my present experience, or by imagining segments gradually subtracted from it, or by imagining some combination of additions, subtractions, and modifications.

To the extent that I could look and behave like a wasp or a bat without changing my fundamental structure, my experiences would not be anything like the experiences of those animals. On the other hand, it is doubtful that any meaning can be attached to the supposition that I should possess the internal neurophysiological constitution of a bat. Even if I could by gradual degrees be transformed into a bat, nothing in my present constitution enables me to imagine what the experiences of such a future stage of myself thus metamorphosed would be like. The best evidence would come from the experiences of bats, if we only knew what they were like.

- How would you explain 'privileged access'? How is it distinct from incorrigibility? How does 'privileged access' lead to the problems involved in trying to know what it is like to be a bat? (What *would* it be like to be a bat?)

Taking this argument one step farther, Colin McGinn insists that consciousness is a 'mystery' that neither philosophy nor science can resolve. He introduces the important notion of **intentionality**, the 'aboutness' of consciousness, its relation to the world. For him, the question is whether a 'naturalistic' (materialistic) theory of the mind can account for this essential feature of mind.

On the 'Mystery of Consciousness'
By Colin McGinn

The mind–body problem is a 'mystery' and not merely a 'problem'.

Naturalism in the philosophy of mind is the thesis that every property of mind can be explained in broadly physical terms. Nothing mental is physically mysterious. There are two main problems confronting a naturalistically inclined philosopher of mind. There is, first, the problem of explaining consciousness in broadly physical terms: in virtue of what does a physical organism come to have conscious states? And, second, there is the problem of explaining representational content—intentionality—in broadly physical terms: in virtue of what does a physical organism come to be intentionally directed toward the world? We want to know how consciousness depends upon the physical world; and we want to know, in natural physical terms, how it is that thoughts and experiences get to be *about* states of affairs. We want a naturalistic account of subjectivity and mental representation. Only then will the naturalist happily accept that there are such things as consciousness and content.

* * *

[I]ntentionality is a property precisely of conscious states, and arguably only of conscious states (at least originally). Moreover, the content of an experience (say) and its subjective features are, on the face of it, inseparable from each other. How then can we pretend that the two problems can be pursued quite independently? In particular, how can we prevent justified pessimism about consciousness spreading to the problem of content? If we cannot say, in physical terms, what makes it the case that an experience is *like* something for its possessor, then how can we hope to say, in such terms, what makes it the case that the experience is *of* something in the world—since what the experience is like and what it is of are not, prima facie, independent properties of the experience? That is the question I shall be addressing.

* * *

This question is especially pressing for me, since I have come to hold that it is literally impossible for us to explain how consciousness depends upon the brain, even though it does so depend. Yet I also believe (or would like to believe) that it is possible for us to give illuminating accounts of content. Let me briefly explain my reasons for holding that consciousness systematically eludes our understanding. Noam Chomsky distinguishes between what he calls 'problems' and 'mysteries' that confront the student of mind. Call that hopeful student *S*, and suppose *S* to be a normal intelligent human being. Chomsky argues that *S*'s cognitive faculties may be apt for the solution of some kinds of problem but radically inadequate when it comes to others. The world need not in all of its aspects be susceptible of understanding by *S*, though another sort of mind might succeed where *S* constitutionally fails. *S* may exhibit, as I like to say, *cognitive closure* with respect to certain kinds of phenomena: her intellectual powers do not extend to comprehending these phenomena, and this as a matter of principle. When that is so Chomsky says that the phenomena in question will be a perpetual mystery for *S*. He suspects that the nature of free choice is just such a mystery for us, given the way our intellects operate. That problem need not, however, be intrinsically harder or more complex than other problems we can solve; it is just that our cognitive faculties are skewed away from solving it. The structure of a knowing mind determines the scope *and limits* of its cognitive powers. Being adept at solving one kind of problem does not guarantee explanatory omniscience. Human beings seem remarkably good (surprisingly so) at understanding the workings of the physical world—matter in motion, causal agents in space—but they do far less well when it comes to fathoming their own minds. And why, in evolutionary terms, should they be intellectually equipped to grasp how their minds ultimately operate?

Now I have come to the view that the nature of the dependence of consciousness on the physical world, specifically on the brain, falls into the category of mysteries for us human beings, and possibly for all minds that form their concepts in ways constrained by perception and introspection. Let me just summarize why I think this; a longer treatment would be needed to make the position plausible. Our concepts of the empirical world are fundamentally controlled by the character of our perceptual experience and by the introspective access we enjoy to our own minds. We can, it is true, extend our concepts some distance beyond these starting-points, but we cannot prescind from them entirely (this is the germ of truth Kant recognized in classical empiricism). Thus our concepts of consciousness are constrained by the specific form of our own consciousness, so that, we cannot form concepts for quite alien forms of consciousness possessed by other actual and possible creatures. Similarly, our concepts of the body, including the brain, are constrained by the way we perceive these physical objects; we have, in particular, to conceive of them as spatial entities essentially similar to other physical objects in space, however inappropriate this manner of conception may be for understanding how consciousness arises from the brain. But now these two forms of conceptual closure operate to prevent us from arriving at concepts for the property or relation that intelligibly links consciousness to the brain. For, first, we cannot grasp other forms of consciousness, and so we cannot grasp the theory that explains these other forms: that theory must be general, but *we* must always be parochial in our conception of consciousness. It is as if we were trying for a general theory of light but could only grasp the visible part of the spectrum. And, second, it is precisely the perceptually controlled conception of the brain that we have which is so hopeless in making consciousness an intelligible result of brain activity. No property we can ascribe to the brain on the basis of how it strikes us perceptually, however inferential the ascription, seems capable of rendering perspicuous how it is that damp grey tissue can be the crucible from which subjective consciousness emerges fully formed. That is why the feeling is so strong in us that there has to be something *magical* about the mind–brain relation. There must *be* some property of the brain that accounts non-magically for consciousness, since nothing in nature happens by magic, but no form of inference from what we perceive of the brain seems capable of leading us to the property in question. We must therefore be getting a partial view of things. It is as if we were trying to extract psychological properties themselves from our awareness of mere physical objects; or again, trying to get normative concepts from descriptive ones. The problem is not that the brain lacks the right explanatory property; the problem is that this property does not lie along any road we can travel in forming our concepts of the brain. Perception takes us in the wrong direction here. We feel the tug of the occult because our methods of empirical concept formation are geared toward properties of kinds that cannot in principle solve the problem of how consciousness depends upon the brain. The situation is analogous to the following possibility: that the ultimate nature of matter is so different from anything we can encounter by observing the material world that we simply cannot ever come to grasp it. Human sense organs are tuned to certain kinds of properties the world may instantiate, but it may be that the theoretically basic properties are not ones that can be reached by starting from perception and working outward; the starting point may point us in exactly the wrong direction. Human reason is not able to travel unaided in just any theoretical direction, irrespective of its basic input. I think that honest reflection strongly suggests that nothing *we* could ever empirically discover about the brain *could* provide a fully satisfying account of consciousness. We shall either find that the properties we encounter are altogether on the wrong track or we shall illicitly project traits of mind into the physical basis. In particular, the essentially spatial conception we have, so suitable for making sense of the non-mental properties of the brain, is inherently incapable of removing the sense of magic we have about the fact that consciousness depends upon the brain. We need something radically different from this but, given the way we form our concepts, we cannot free ourselves of the conceptions that make the problem look insoluble. Not only, then, is it *possible* that the question of how consciousness arises from the physical world cannot be answered by minds constructed as ours are, but there is also strong positive reason for supposing that this is actually the case. The centuries of failure and bafflement have a deep source: the very nature of our concept-forming capacities. The mind–body problem is a 'mystery' and not merely a 'problem'.

1. Changing Our Minds: Holism and Consciousness
When Aristotle wrote about 'the soul', he meant nothing other than 'the form of the body':

From *De Anima*
By Aristotle

One can no more ask if the body and the soul are one than if the wax and the impression it receives are one, or speaking generally the matter of each thing and the form of which it is the matter; for admitting that the terms unity and existence are used in many senses, the paramount sense is that of actuality. We have, then, given a general definition of what the soul is: it is substance expressed as form. It is this which makes a body what it is.

This is not behaviourism. Aristotle is not denying the existence of anything that we normally believe in. Yet it is clearly not a dualism of the Cartesian variety, and this raises the following question: Are there ways of conceiving of ourselves without falling into the Cartesian trap of talking about minds and bodies?

We can only suggest a few possibilities here. One was advanced by Ludwig Wittgenstein in his *Philosophical Investigations*. Although he is usually considered to be an unconfessed behaviourist, a more recent and perhaps more plausible interpretation is that Wittgenstein wanted to deny the very idea that human beings are a curious combination of two very different substances or kinds of entities or events. Rather, there are just people, not minds plus bodies.

A very different kind of answer comes to us from Edmund Husserl's phenomenology. Although Husserl was not particularly concerned with the mind–body problem as such, he was obviously very interested in the nature of consciousness, since consciousness provides the subject matter of his entire life's work. Husserl's argument began with a violent attack on the spatial metaphors we use in talking about consciousness. At the beginning of the chapter, we suggested that such metaphors were 'just metaphors', symptoms of a problem but not a problem themselves. Well, Husserl shows that they are a problem, that philosophers have not used them merely as metaphors, and that it is because of their taking these metaphors literally that our problems about consciousness arise in the first place.

What Husserl attacks is the very idea of consciousness as a mysterious container, 'in' which one finds ideas, thoughts, feelings, desires, and so on. The same objection holds of such metaphors as 'the stream of consciousness', with emotions, thoughts, and feelings floating by like so much flotsam and jetsam. Consciousness must rather be viewed in two parts (though Husserl insists these must not be thought of as a separate 'dualism'): There are the acts of consciousness, and there are the objects of those acts.

Simply stated, a phenomenologist would analyze my seeing a tree into (1) my act of seeing and (2) the tree as seen. So far, this looks simple enough. But its consequences are not so straightforward. First, just in passing, notice what this does to Berkeley's idealism. Berkeley's whole argument rested on his thesis that all we can experience are ideas. But this is a confusion, Husserl insists, of our act of experiencing with the objects experienced. The object experienced (the tree) is not merely my idea. Accordingly, Husserl concludes that Berkeley's idealism is 'absurd'. And in general, Husserl's phenomenological theory insists that philosophers have been neglectful of this crucial distinction. Many attributes of the act of experiencing do not hold of the object; for example, the object, unlike the act, is not 'private'. One and only one person, namely, myself, can perform my act of seeing. But any number of people can see the object of my seeing, the tree. Moreover, there can be no such thing, Husserl argues, as a conscious act without an object. You can see how this might provide a powerful argument against many traditional forms of skepticism.

Our concern here is Husserl's conception of consciousness, which depends (as in McGinn) on intentionality. (Accordingly, the act is often called the 'intentional act', and the object is called the 'intentional object'.) To say that consciousness is intentional means (among other things) that our conscious acts are always directed toward objects and that we should not, therefore, talk about conscious acts as self-contained 'contents' that are mysteriously coordinated with the movements of our bodies. Rather, we can simply say that among our various acts as persons are intentional conscious acts as well as physical actions. We can look at a tree and we can kick a tree. But there is no problem of 'coordination' or interaction.

This theory was never actually developed by Husserl himself, but it was worked out in great detail by one of his 'existential' followers in France, Maurice Merleau-Ponty (a close friend and student of Sartre). Coming from a very different starting point, Merleau-Ponty arrives at a position surprisingly close to that of Wittgenstein. It must not be called 'behaviourist', but like Wittgenstein, Merleau-Ponty does reject the traditional way of dividing up mind and body and thereby suggests a very different conception of persons in which such problematic distinctions are not allowed to arise.

Merleau-Ponty attacks dualism from the side that has so far seemed least controversial—the idea that the human body is just another 'bit of matter'. He introduces the notion of a 'dialectic' between mind and body, by which he means that there is no ultimate distinction between them. From one point of view—for example, that of a physiologist interested in the workings of the brain and the sense organs—it is possible to see the body as 'the cause of the structure of consciousness'. From another point of view—for example, that of a medical student dissecting a body in her anatomy class—it is possible to see the body as a mere 'object of knowledge'. But it is a mistake, Merleau-Ponty argues, to confuse either of these viewpoints with the 'correct' view of the body, either as a cause of consciousness or as something wholly distinct from it. Only the *living* body can count as *my* body, except in a very special and not everyday sense, namely, the sense in which I can talk about what will happen to my body after I die.

'The body is not a self-enclosed mechanism,' he argues, nor does it makes sense to treat 'the soul' or consciousness as a distinct entity with some mysterious relationship with the body. 'There is not a duality of substances,' he writes, but only 'the dialectic of living being in its biological milieu.' Merleau-Ponty sometimes says the consciousness is nothing but 'the meaning of one's body', all of which is to say, in extremely difficult prose, that mind and body are nothing other than a single entity, and the distinctions we make between them are always special cases. As he says, 'I live my body'; there is no enigma of 'my body' to be explained.[7]

In his difficult 'dialectical' language, Merleau-Ponty defends a thesis that is strikingly similar to that defended by Wittgenstein: One cannot treat a person as an uneasy conglomerate of mental parts and body parts but must begin with the whole person. But where Wittgenstein proceeds by attacking the mental side of Cartesian dualism, Merleau-Ponty attacks anyone who would treat the human as 'just another body'. The body itself is not only alive but, in an important sense, conscious. This does not mean, as in Descartes, that it is connected with a consciousness. It is itself aware, as we often notice when we talk of 'bodily awareness' or 'feeling our way'. The difference between the body of a living person and a corpse is not just a difference in physiology, nor is it the difference between an 'inhabited' body and an 'uninhabited' body. My body and myself are essentially one, and to try to separate them, as Descartes had done, is to make the relationship between 'me' and 'my body' into an unnecessary mystery.

A similar view has been defended by analytic philosopher Galen Strawson, following Husserl and Merleau-Ponty but objecting to a standard analysis of consciousness by analytic philosophy. According to that analysis, consciousness consists of two elements: sensations and intentionality (Hume's 'impressions and ideas'). Strawson objects that there is a more holistic concept that is essential, what he calls 'cognitive experience'.

On 'Cognitive Experience'

By Galen Strawson

Consider (experience) the difference, for you, between my saying: 'I'm reading *War and Peace*' and my saying 'barath abalori trafalon'. In both cases you experience sounds, but in the first case you experience something more: you have understanding-experience, cognitive experience.

Why isn't this point universally acknowledged? *Have you had only sensory experience for the last two minutes?* One problem is that there has been a terminological lock-in. When analytic philosophers talk generally about what I call 'EQ content'—when they talk generally of the 'subjective character' of experience, or 'what-it's-likeness', or 'qualitative character', or 'phenomenology' in the current deviant use of the term (it is incorrect first because 'phenomenology' is the study of experience, not experience itself, second because when it is used to mean experience itself it is used too narrowly to mean only sensory content)—they standardly have only *sensory* EQ content, in mind, and the mistake has already been made. For this terminological habit simply forbids expression of the idea that there may be non-sensory or *cognitive* EQ content.

One doesn't have to be Husserl to be astounded by this terminological folly, and the metaphysical folly that it entrains—the denial of the existence of cognitive experience—as one negotiates the unceasing richness of everyday experience. It beggars belief. It amounts to an outright denial of the existence of almost all our actual experience, or rather of fundamental features of almost all (perhaps all) our experience. And yet it is terminological orthodoxy in present-day analytic philosophy of mind.

How did this happen? It was, perhaps, an unfortunate by-blow of the correct but excessively violent rejection, in the twentieth century, of the 'image theory of thinking' or 'picture theory of thinking' seemingly favoured, in various degrees, by the British empiricists and others. But rejecting the picture theory of thinking didn't require denying the existence of cognitive experience. On the contrary. Liberation from the picture-theory idea that cognitive experience centrally and constitutively involves sensory experience, and is indeed (somehow or other) a kind of internal sensory experience, is a necessary first step toward a decent account of what

cognitive experience is. Schopenhauer certainly didn't reject the existence of cognitive experience when he refuted the picture theory of thinking in 1819 in terms that no one has improved on:

> While another person is speaking, do we at once translate his speech into pictures of the imagination that instantaneously flash upon us and are arranged, linked, formed, and coloured according to the words that stream forth, and to their grammatical inflexions? What a tumult there would be in our heads while we listened to a speech or read a book! This is not what happens at all. The meaning of the speech is immediately grasped, accurately and clearly apprehended, without as a rule any conceptions of fancy being mixed up with it.

When it comes to EQ content, then, when it comes to the strictly qualitative character of experience, which is wholly what it is considered entirely independently of its causes, there is cognitive EQ content as well as sensory or non-cognitive EQ content. There is cognitive experience. Its existence is obvious to unprejudiced reflection, but some philosophers have denied it fiercely and, it must be said, rather scornfully.

It can seem difficult to get a decent theoretical grip on it. It is, for one thing, hard to pin down the contribution to the character of your current experience that is being made now by the content of this very sentence in such a way as to be able to take it as the object of reflective thought. (It is far easier to do this in the case of the phenomenological character of an experience of yellow, let the 'transparentists' say what they will.) In fact, when it comes to the attempt to figure to oneself the phenomenological character of understanding a sentence like 'Consider your hearing and understanding of this very sentence and the next' it seems that all one can really do is rethink the sentence as a whole, comprehendingly; and the trouble with doing this is that it seems to leave one with no mental room to stand back in such a way as to be able to take the phenomenological character of one's understanding of the sentence, redelivered to one by this rethinking, as the principal object of one's attention: one's mind is taken up with the sense of the thought in such a way that it is very hard to think about the experience of having the thought.

This is, as it were, a merely practical difficulty. It is I think a further point that there is in any case something fundamentally insubstantial, intangible, unpindownable, about the character of much cognitive experience, and that this is so even though cognitive experience can also and simultaneously have a character of great determinacy. Consider, for example, your experience of understanding this very sentence, uneventful as it is. Or the sentence 'This sentence has five words.' Determinate but insubstantial.

I use quiet sentences to make the point, rather than sentences like 'A thousand bonobos hurtled past on bright green bicycles', simply because it helps to still the imagistic or emotional accompaniments of thought or understanding as far as possible. It is then easier to see that what is left is something completely different, something that is equally real and definite and rich although it can seem troublesomely intangible when one tries to reflect on it: the experience that is standardly involved in the mere comprehending of words, read, thought, or heard—right now—, where this comprehending is (once again) considered quite independently of any imagistic or emotional accompaniments. Cognitive experience, we may say, is a matter of whatever EQ content is involved in such episodes after one has subtracted any non-cognitive EQ content trappings or accompaniments that such episodes may have.

I think we have no choice but to grant that our capacity for cognitive experience is a distinct naturally evolved *experiential modality* that is, whatever its origins, fundamentally different from all the sensory experiential modalities (at least as we currently understand them). This is a radical claim in the current context of discussion of experience or consciousness, especially given all the input from psychology and neuropsychology, which very strongly constrains people to think that all experience *must* be somehow sensory.

We also have to think through very clearly the initially difficult fact that cognitive EQ content is, in itself, purely a matter of experiential qualitative character, wholly what it is considered entirely independently of its causes. We may have to dwell on the point, work on it, especially if we have been trained up as analytic philosophers at any time in the last fifty years. Try now to imagine life without cognitive experience being part of the (experiential) qualitative character of experience. Consider yourself reading this now and try to convince yourself that all that is going on is sensory experience (accompanied by non-experiential changes in your dispositional set).

Next, we turn to William James, who defended a view that is strikingly similar to the phenomenological theory. But instead of giving consciousness the attention it receives in Husserl, he argues that there is no such thing as consciousness as an entity, only different functions of experience:

From 'Does Consciousness Exist?'
By William James

Consciousness . . . is fictitious, while thoughts in the concrete are fully real. But thoughts in the concrete are made of the same stuff as things are.

'Thoughts' and 'things' are names for two sorts of objects, which common sense will always find contrasted and will always practically oppose to each other. Philosophy, reflecting on the contrast, has varied in the past in her explanations of it, and may be expected to vary in the future. At first, 'spirit and matter', 'soul and body', stood for a pair of equipollent substances quite on a par in weight and interest. But one day Kant undermined the soul and brought in the transcendental ego, and ever since then the bipolar relation has been very much off its balance. The transcendental ego seems nowadays in rationalist quarters to stand for

(*Continued*)

everything, in empiricist quarters for almost nothing. In the hands of . . . writers . . . the spiritual principle attenuates itself to a thoroughly ghostly condition, being only a name for the fact that the 'content' of experience *is known*. It loses personal form and activity—these passing over to the content—and becomes a bare [consciousness], of which in its own right absolutely nothing can be said.

I believe that 'consciousness', when once it has evaporated to this estate . . . is on the point of disappearing altogether. It is the name of a nonentity, and has no right to a place among first principles. Those who still cling to it are clinging to a mere echo, the faint rumour left behind by the disappearing 'soul' upon the air of philosophy. During the past year, I have read a number of articles whose authors seemed just on the point of abandoning the notion of consciousness, and substituting for it that of an absolute experience not due to two factors. But they were not quite radical enough, not quite daring enough in their negations. For twenty years past I have mistrusted 'consciousness' as an entity; for seven or eight years past I have suggested its non-existence to my students, and tried to give them its pragmatic-equivalent in realities of experience. It seems to me that the hour is ripe for it to be openly and universally discarded.

To deny plumply that 'consciousness' exists seems so absurd on the face of it—for undeniably 'thoughts' do exist—that I fear some readers will follow me no farther. Let me then immediately explain that I mean only to deny that the word stands for an entity, but to insist most emphatically that it does stand for a function. There is, I mean, no aboriginal stuff or quality of being, contrasted with that of which material objects are made, out of which our thoughts of them are made; but there is a function in experience which thoughts perform, and for the performance of which this quality of being is invoked.

That function is *knowing*. 'Consciousness' is supposed necessary to explain the fact that things not only are, but get reported, are known. Whoever blots out the notion of consciousness from his list of first principles must still provide in some way for that function's being carried on.

* * *

My thesis is that if we start with the supposition that there is only one primal stuff or material in the world, a stuff of which everything is composed, and if we call that stuff 'pure experience', then knowing can easily be explained as a particular sort of relation toward one another into which portions of pure experience may enter. The relation itself is a part of pure experience; one of its 'terms' becomes the subject or bearer of the knowledge, the knower, the other becomes the object known.

* * *

I am as confident as I am of anything that, in myself, the stream of thinking (which I recognize emphatically as a phenomenon) is only a careless name for what, when scrutinized, reveals itself to consist chiefly of the stream of my breathing. The 'I think' which Kant said must be able to accompany all my objects, is the 'I breathe' which actually does accompany them. There are other internal facts besides breathing (intracephalic muscular adjustments, etc. . . .), and these increase the assets of 'consciousness', so far as the latter is subject to immediate perception; but breath, which was ever the original of 'spirit', breath moving outwards, between the glottis and the nostrils, is, I am persuaded, the essence out of which philosophers have constructed the entity known to them as consciousness. *That entity is fictitious, while thoughts in the concrete are fully real. But thoughts in the concrete are made of the same stuff as things are.*

- What does James mean when he claims 'I mean only to deny that the word [consciousness] stands for an entity, but to insist most emphatically that it does stand for a function'? Is James simply a functionalist?

Finally, Friedrich Nietzsche suggests that consciousness, far from being the most immediate, self-evident thing, is ultimately dispensable:

On the 'Genius of the Species'
By Friedrich Nietzsche

The problem of consciousness (more precisely, of becoming conscious of something) confronts us only when we start to understand how we might dispense with it; and now physiology and animal history put us at the beginning of such understanding (it took them two centuries to catch up with Leibniz's suspicion that soared ahead). For we could think, feel, will, and remember, and we could also 'act' in all senses of the word, and yet none of any of it would have to 'enter our consciousness' (as one metaphorically says). The whole of life would be possible without its, so to speak, seeing itself in the mirror. Indeed by far the largest part of our life even now in fact takes place without this mirroring; and that is true even of our thinking, feeling, and willing life, however offensive this may sound to older philosophers. So *what purpose* has any consciousness at all when it is generally *superfluous*?

What if consciousness is neither independent of Nature (as old-school dualists think), nor dependent on Nature (as old-school materialists think), but is instead a basic feature built right into Nature? According to this third view—a view known as **panpsychism**—a skein of mind-stuff is woven into the very fabric of the world. Being shot through with spirit, Nature can no longer be seen as alien or 'other', as 'disenchanted' or 'dead'. All is drenched in sentience, says the panpsychist; and there is nothing without some measure of mentality.

> **PANPSYCHISM**
>
> The view that everything is invested with some degree of mentality or consciousness.

Now, what would induce anyone to adopt this odd-sounding view? Here is one argument. It is a fact that conscious beings exist—you and I, for example. It is also a fact that we evolved from lower forms of life. Add these two facts together, and you've got the makings of a first-class conundrum: At what point did consciousness make its appearance in Nature? Either consciousness was there in some form from the very beginning, or it wasn't. But there is reason to believe that if consciousness wasn't there in some rudimentary form from the very beginning, it couldn't have developed later on in the way that it has. For how could the novelty of consciousness just 'emerge', suddenly bursting or blossoming into being? How could the wild flower of mind bloom in the bone-dry deserts of matter? Unless we can answer these world-riddles—and what wise mortal can claim to do that?—we had better conclude that Nature and everything in it was conscious to *some* degree from the get-go. And that is what panpsychists maintain.

A philosophical theory with a long and rich history, panpsychism could claim numerous well-known adherents as recently as the early twentieth century. By the middle of the twentieth century, however, the view had pretty much faded away into obscurity; and many came to see it more as a curiosity belonging to the past than as a live option with a future. In the last two decades, however, panpsychism has made a modest comeback. Why? In an essay written especially for this text, Canadian philosopher William Seager, author of *Metaphysics of Consciousness* and *Theories of Consciousness*, explains the sources of the view's appeal while identifying several problems that continue to pester panpsychists.

'Panpsychism'
By William Seager

Consciousness Is Special

We categorize the world via a number of ordinary, common-sense distinctions. Among these are the division between natural things and artifacts, the division between things that are alive versus those that are inanimate, and the division between things with minds and those without. It's an interesting feature of the way

(*Continued*)

humans think that we are ready and eager to attribute mental states pretty indiscriminately. Children seem to naturally assume that most things that can move (and some that cannot) can think and act intentionally. Preliterate societies were generally animistic. Even adults in today's society tend to perceive awareness and intention in other-than-human things.[8]

When philosophers try to provide an overarching account of the structure and makeup of the world, they naturally wonder about the status of these common-sense distinctions. Is there anything deeply significant about the difference between artifacts and natural things? Not really. Both are made of the same kind of stuff, put together in more or less complex ways. It doesn't matter to these things whether they were purposefully built by an intelligent agent or were put together by some natural process, such as evolution by natural selection.

Now, it is true that for a long time the divide between the animate and the inanimate was thought to be fraught with metaphysical import. Many thinkers believed that there had to be some immaterial component that generated the spark of life in otherwise dead matter. These *vitalists* allowed that animals were made of material substance but thought that life demanded some infusion beyond matter.[9] Vitalism now seems a quaint relic of chemical ignorance. The discovery of the material basis of heredity in the DNA molecule, the unravelling of the complex details of metabolism, the decipherment of the chemical activity of drugs, and a host of other scientific victories have gone far to show that life is nothing but complex organized chemistry.[10]

Science has obliterated the idea that there are some inexplicable, immaterial differences lying behind the natural divisions of natural versus artifact and living versus dead. What of the divide between things with minds and the rest of the world? Many aspects of the mind have been scientifically linked to material neurological processes in ways not unlike the ways life was linked to chemistry. Modern brain-scanning technology is beginning to provide us a window into the mind and promises much more.

In a remarkable recent study, researcher Adrian Owen compared the brain signatures of subjects with normal brain function to those of patients diagnosed with being in a persistent vegetative state (PVS). First, he had the normal subjects either imagine playing tennis or imagine walking around their home. Using an fMRI scanner, Owen was able to pin down the brain's signature for these two mental activities so that he could, in real time, tell what a subject was imagining. He then tried the experiment with the PVS patients and discovered that when he asked them to imagine playing tennis, in many cases their brains immediately 'lit up' in the pattern of neural activity characteristic of that task (and the same for the home imagination task). These people were not PVS but were suffering from some form of locked-in syndrome (an affliction whose victims remain fully conscious but are so completely paralyzed that they cannot perform any voluntary action and are often mistakenly thought to be in a coma).

It is possible to envisage that some day we will have decoded the mind and that we will possess mind-reading machines and neural lie detectors. This would have vast social implications, but would the distinction between mind and non-mind have then followed our other examples into the oblivion of philosophical insignificance?

I think that one feature of mind—perhaps its most central and essential feature—would at least resist this conclusion: consciousness. Our experiments in brain scanning are helping us to discover the correlations between brain states and states of consciousness, but these correlations do not reveal that consciousness has a merely material nature. Why not? Consciousness has a unique property that is intimately familiar to us all but curiously difficult to describe. This property is sometimes called the subjectivity of consciousness or its phenomenality. Conscious states, such as being in pain from a toothache or tasting strawberries, have a bizarre feature: it is like something to be in them, or, in other words, there is a way these states are to an experiencing subject. This idea can be intuitively explicated by considering that there is nothing it is like to be in many states, such as being an uncle or weighing 75 kilograms. Consider that one can gain or lose such properties without feeling anything at all. Contrast the experience of tasting a ripe strawberry. Presumably, there is something it is like for a squirrel, for example, to taste a nut or feel the rush of fear inspired by the sight of a stalking cat. Presumably, there is nothing at all it is like for a rock to roll down a hill or bump hard into a boulder.

Conscious creatures thus have two aspects. They have their objective properties, but they also have a subjective inner aspect found in what it is like to be in their conscious states. If you've never tasted marmite, then no description will convey the intrinsic nature of this dubious experience, and no amount of knowledge of brain processes will help either. This division of the world into the conscious and the non-conscious seems to be fundamental and resists the kind of scientific breakdown of distinctions discussed above. This is the root of the mind–body problem in philosophy and particularly the source of what David Chalmers has called the 'hard problem' of consciousness, a constellation of basic questions about the conscious mind: why is there any consciousness in the world at all, what difference does consciousness make to the physical world, and how exactly does matter generate or constitute consciousness in all its various but completely specific forms?

Emergence

The natural way to tackle the problem of consciousness is to hark back to the success science has had with features of life. The scientific picture of the world envisages a long cosmological history almost all of which is utterly lifeless but at some point, on earth at least, conditions allowed for the slow development of the complex chemical reactions we call life. Generally speaking, when there is a transition in a system from lacking a certain property to possession of that property, we say that the property emerged or is an emergent phenomenon. Emergence is very commonplace. Hurricanes and tornadoes are emergent phenomena of the atmosphere. From the point of view of the long history of the earth, life is an emergent feature of its chemical evolution.

Is it reasonable to think that consciousness is an emergent feature of the brain, presumably, more specifically, of the activity of the brain's complex network of inter-signalling neurons? It is certainly reasonable to suppose that there are many emergent processes in and properties of the brain and these will include the large-scale neural patterns of activity that correlate with conscious experience. But is this enough to show that consciousness itself is an emergent feature? Many have worried that this is not sufficient and that consciousness presents a special problem for the idea of neural emergence.

Standard cases of emergence are one and all instances of complex interactions of the constituents subsystems, and they seem to share one salient trait: it is possible to understand, at least in principle and in outline, exactly how the emergent phenomenon appears because of the properties of the basic constituents. A typical example is how the liquidity of water is an emergent phenomenon of the oxygen and hydrogen atoms. It is possible to explain how liquidity appears based upon the properties of the constituent elements—their typical bonding strengths and modes of combination, for example. Of course, many emergent features depend on a level of complexity that we cannot actually grasp, but it remains true that such an explanation is possible in principle.

The problem of consciousness is that it is very hard to see how complex interactions of neurons within the brain could produce the subjective aspect of experience, the 'what it is like' of experience. This problem was perhaps first noticed by the seventeenth-century philosopher Gottfried Wilhelm Leibniz, who wrote:

> . . . supposing there were a machine, so constructed as to think, feel, and have perception, it might be conceived as increased in size. . . so that one might go into it as into a mill. That being so, we should, on examining its interior, find only parts which work one upon another, and never anything by which to explain a perception.[11]

Leibniz is worried that nothing about the operation of the machine (or, by extension, the brain) could reveal how something like experience could arise from its mechanical actions. This worry has never been overcome. And it does not arise in other cases of emergence. If we look inside a living organism we can see (given the proper scientific equipment) how the chemical activity can produce processes we call reproduction, metabolism, and, in short, life itself. In the case of consciousness, though we can or will eventually be able to explain how the brain stores information, organizes perception, generates actions, underlies complex cognition, etc., this information will never explain why consciousness, or the subjective aspect of experience, and precisely the kind of subjective experience we have, should be produced. Thomas Huxley put this point like this, back in 1886: 'How it is that anything so remarkable as a state of consciousness comes about as a result of irritating nervous tissue, is just as

(Continued)

unaccountable as the appearance of the djinn when Aladdin rubbed his lamp in the story.'

It seems that if consciousness is an emergent property of brains, it must be of quite a different and more mysterious kind than the forms of emergence we are familiar with. Some philosophers, writing in the early part of the twentieth century, embraced this mystery and accepted a sort of emergence that was utterly inexplicable. They believed that there were laws of nature in addition to the basic laws of physics that linked material processes to entirely novel emergent properties. However, they were of the opinion— reasonable at the time—that chemistry furnished an uncontroversial example of this mysterious and radical kind of emergence. Unfortunately for them, scientific advances soon revealed how chemistry emerges from underlying physical processes and there followed soon after the revolutions in molecular biology that so strongly support the claim that life, too, is a standard emergent. But despite our burgeoning knowledge of the brain, no scientific advance to date has helped us to even begin to understand how consciousness could be a standard emergent.

Universal Mind

If one is moved by the argument that consciousness is a special problem but cannot stomach inexplicable emergence, there is an alternative. This is the doctrine of panpsychism, which asserts that consciousness is fundamental and ubiquitous. Fundamentality means that consciousness does not reduce to anything else, even in the relatively weak sense embodied in standard emergence; ubiquity is the claim that consciousness is, in some sense, universal. A basic form of panpsychism holds that every physically fundamental entity—those things that form the foundation of the physical world (quarks, superstrings, whatever)—possesses some measure of consciousness. To be sure, the kind of consciousness associated with the physical simples is utterly remote from our own rich, varied, and finely articulated system of experience, but it shares the essential feature of inherent subjectivity.

Panpsychism has a very long history, and for most of the history of philosophy it has, in one form or another, perhaps been the generally favoured view. It is only in the last century, with the rise of the scientific account of the world, that philosophical orthodoxy demanded that consciousness must be a standard emergent constituted by complex material processes.

Panpsychism avoids the difficulties of explicating consciousness as an emergent (though a problem lurks here, as we shall see), but apart from this negative virtue, what arguments can be advanced in support of panpsychism? I want to look at two arguments. The first, the genetic argument, stems from the problem of emergence. The second, the intrinsic nature argument, tries to find a crack in the scientific account of the world that opens a passage toward panpsychism.

The genetic argument starts with the premise that nature never suffers discontinuous ontological leaps. We never find completely new things appearing but rather observe nature reworking and remoulding pre-existing features in endlessly novel ways. There are of course many sudden transitions in nature. After many years of quiescence or minor rumblings, a volcano violently erupts. This is no change in the fundamental stuff of nature, but only a swift reconfiguring of the already existing physical conditions within and below the fiery mountain. Nature also exhibits what are called 'phase transitions', as when slowly cooled water suddenly freezes or when molten iron becomes magnetized if cooled in an external magnetic field. But again, phase transitions are just a reordering or restructuring of already present features.

The jump from non-conscious assemblies of insensate matter to a conscious being is a discontinuity of an entirely different order of magnitude. Finding no other examples of such a leap in nature, the panpsychist concludes that consciousness must be a fundamental feature built into reality, so to speak, from the start and on the ground floor.

The intrinsic nature argument begins with an observation about the nature of physical science, which is that science never tells us about the intrinsic nature of things but only about the relations into which they enter. The concept of 'intrinsic nature' is obscure and difficult to define, but roughly speaking the intrinsic properties of something are what it has in and of itself. Although it is natural to think of a physical property such as mass as intrinsic, in fact mass is defined in terms of its relation to force and motion. The same goes for all physical attributes: charge, momentum, spin, etc. This point is sometimes put by saying that matter is inscrutable—its true nature is invisible to a science that only reveals its relational, structural, and mathematical properties.

Presumably, there are some intrinsic properties that must ground the reality of material things and underpin their ability to stand in the relational structures observed and postulated by scientific theory. What are these intrinsic features? In general, we have no access to them, but we do have acquaintance with one purely intrinsic property: consciousness itself. The subjective aspect of experience is seemingly entirely non-relational by nature. This point must not be confused with any claim about the causes of experience or the role that experience plays in generating behaviour. Consciousness does stand in a host of relations to other things. But the point is that consciousness is not defined or constituted by its relational proclivities. Do we have any evidence that this intrinsic feature is associated with matter? Perhaps we do. The evidence we have of the correlations between brain processes and states of consciousness suggests that in consciousness we are experiencing the intrinsic features of a certain chunk of matter, namely our own brains. The argument then goes that we need to assign an intrinsic nature to matter, we know of only one intrinsic nature, consciousness, and we have some evidence that at least some material objects actually do have this intrinsic nature. It therefore seems not unreasonable to assign consciousness as the universal intrinsic nature of matter, that is, to embrace panpsychism.

Problems for Panpsychism

The most obvious difficulty facing panpsychism is simply the intuitive absurdity of the claim that everything is conscious. But an incredulous stare is not much of an argument. A simple argument against panpsychism that leverages its implausibility can, however, be easily constructed. We expect that a creature's consciousness should make some kind of difference to its behaviour, but most of the things in the world and certainly the fundamental entities posited by physics give no sign whatsoever of being conscious. This argument is not really very strong. We might expect that as entities get smaller and simpler they give less sign of their conscious component. Gravity is taken to be a fundamental feature of all matter and energy, but an individual electron gives no observable sign of possessing gravitational powers. We might also argue that the causal powers of matter ultimately stem from their intrinsic nature, which, as argued above, in consciousness itself, so that everything we observe in the physical world is in a way an efflorescence of consciousness. We would not expect

everything to behave in the overtly mentalistic way that hyper-complex creatures such as ourselves and other animals do.

What about other large material objects, such as rocks and planets? While some panpsychists did accept that such beings had minds (the German psychologist Gustav Fechner was one) a more common reply is that only properly organized matter can possess complex unitary minds. Yet Leibniz's distinction between what he called 'organic unities' and 'mere aggregates' can be used to distinguish such things as rocks from creatures with their own consciousnesses. The panpsychist can easily reject the canard that panpsychism entails that rocks and tables have feelings.

But this sort of reply leads to another objection against panpsychism, which was developed by William James in 1890; it is often called the 'combination problem'. James' complaint was that no set of distinct and independent mental states can by themselves constitute a single, new, unified mental state. In James' own words,

> Take a sentence of a dozen words, and take twelve men and tell to each one word. Then stand the men in a row or jam them in a bunch, and let each think of his word as intently as he will; nowhere will there be a consciousness of the whole sentence . . . . Where the elemental units are supposed to be feelings, the case is in no wise altered. Take a hundred of them, shuffle them and pack them as close together as you can (whatever that might mean); still each remains the same feeling it always was, shut in its own skin, windowless, ignorant of what the other feelings are and mean.[12]

It seems the panpsychist can answer this objection only by endorsing a form of emergentism that postulates that certain structures of simpler mental states can give rise to and constitute more complex states of consciousness. James is describing a mere aggregate of feelings that will never rise above the simple collection of its elements. There must be another way the simple conscious states can combine and unify.

But then, will come the objection, if the panpsychist must admit that there are emergent conscious states, why not forgo the extravagant hypothesis of universal mind and simply endorse a materialist emergentism. Although the objection has some force, the obvious reply is that the panpsychist need only accept
(*Continued*)

what we called above standard emergence—the re-arrangement and combination of pre-existing features into novel forms. The opponents of panpsychism must endorse the radical emergence of consciousness as completely inexplicable and metaphysically brute.

Finally, there is a kind of methodological objection to panpsychism that I believe has some force. The sciences have been extraordinarily successful in integrating all aspects of the world into one deeply inter-connected vision. It is natural for philosophers to want to rework this spectacular accomplishment into a complete metaphysical account of the world. This ongoing project is far from complete but it has no room for theories like panpsychism. Such theories have, in the words of Thomas Nagel, the 'faintly sickening odour of something put together in the metaphysical laboratory'.[13] But, given that the science-based metaphysics remains unfinished and given the apparently insurmountable problem of integrating consciousness into it, a more radical metaphysical outlook may be needed and at least provides a new perspective on the ancient problem of discovering a unified, complete picture of the world.

- What are the two arguments for panpsychism that Seager outlines? Which argument seems best to you? Why?
- What problems facing panpsychism does Seager identify? Which seems the most serious to you? Why?

SUMMARY AND CONCLUSION

Since Descartes' discussion of mind and body as two separate and different substances, philosophers have struggled with a number of theories to explain how mind and body work together to constitute a complete human being. Certain properties of mind—its lack of 'extension' and seeming 'privileged access'—and the 'incorrigibility' of mental claims made the connection between mind and body extremely problematic. Therefore, philosophers suggested that mental events and bodily events are different aspects of some other event (dual aspect theory), or that they occur in parallel, like the sound and visual tracks on a film (parallelism or pre-established harmony), or that bodily events cause mental events but not the other way around (epiphenomenalism), or that mental events and bodily events are in fact identical (identity theory). Many philosophers and psychologists embraced behaviourism, arguing that 'mental event' is in fact only shorthand for a complex description of patterns of behaviour. More recently, many philosophers have come to reject the distinction between mind and body altogether, insisting on the primacy and indivisibility of the concept of a person. Other philosophers have come to embrace functionalism, which holds that the brain is in fact an extremely sophisticated computer, and the mind is causally but not logically dependent on the brain. And then there are the panpsychists, for whom consciousness is a built-in feature of the world in which we live. Yet other philosophers dismiss all such theories as essentially hopeless, insisting on the intractability of the mind–body problem.

REVIEW QUESTIONS

1. What is Cartesian dualism? What about it seems right to you? What seems wrong with it? What problems does it solve? What problems does it create?

2. What is the identity theory? What problem is it called on to answer? In what ways is the dual aspect theory a version of the identity theory?

3. Functionalism argues that mental acts occur as a 'function' of elements of the brain. Logical behaviourism claims that mind is only the 'pattern' of our behaviour. What is different about these two accounts? What is similar about them? In what ways are they using the same ideas to provide different accounts of the mind?

4. What is eliminative materialism? What are some arguments for it? What are some arguments against it? Which arguments do you find the most convincing? Why?

5. Recall that Ryle rejects dualism because, according to him, Descartes committed a category mistake. What is a category mistake? Do you think Cartesian dualism really rests on one? In what respect does William James' theory resemble Ryle's? How do they differ?

6. Discuss how Nagel's question 'What is it like to be a bat?' confronts the challenge of the eliminative materialists. Can you think of how an eliminative materialist might respond? How might some of the other theorists who reject dualism respond to the claim that 'subjectivity' is essential to our concept of ourselves?

7. Consider the following claim: 'Panpsychism is the best solution to the mind–body problem.' Why might a thoughtful person think this is true? What reasons could she or he have? Why might an equally thoughtful person think that this is false? What reasons could she or he have?

KEY TERMS

behaviourism
causal interactionism
dual aspect theory
dualism
eliminative materialism
emergence

epiphenomenalism
functionalism
identity theory
immediate
incorrigibility
intentionality

panpsychism
parallelism
pre-established harmony
privacy
privileged access
unconscious

FURTHER READING

On Problems of Consciousness

Donald Davidson, *Essays on Actions and Events* (Oxford: Oxford University Press, 1980).

Fred Dretske, *Naturalizing the Mind* (Cambridge, MA: MIT Press, 1995).

Jerry Fodor, *Representations: Philosophical Essays on the Foundations of Cognitive Science* (Cambridge, MA: MIT Press, 1981).

John Foster, *The Immaterial Self: A Defence of the Cartesian Dualist Conception of Mind* (London: Routledge, 1996).

Jaegwon Kim, *Philosophy of Mind* (Boulder, CO: Westview Press, 2006).

Jaegwon Kim, *Supervenience and Mind* (Cambridge: Cambridge University Press, 1993).

Colin McGinn, *The Character of Mind* (New York: Oxford University Press, 1982).

Colin McGinn, *The Problem of Consciousness* (Oxford: Blackwell, 1991).

John R. Searle, *Mind: A Brief Introduction* (New York: Oxford University Press, 2004).

John R. Searle, *The Rediscovery of the Mind* (Cambridge, MA: MIT Press, 1992).

Michael Tye, *Ten Problems of Consciousness* (Cambridge, MA: MIT Press, 1995).

Part III Know Thyself

On the Mind–Body Problem

David Chalmers, *Philosophy of Mind: Classical and Contemporary Readings* (New York: Oxford University Press, 2002).

David Rosenthal, *The Nature of Mind* (New York: Oxford University Press, 1997).

Stephen Stich, *Blackwell Guide to Philosophy of Mind* (Oxford: Blackwell, 2003).

On Identity Theory

C.V. Borst, ed., *The Mind-Brain Identity Theory* (New York: St Martin's Press, 1970).

David Rosenthal, ed., *Materialism and the Mind–Body Problem* (Englewood Cliffs, NJ: Prentice-Hall, 1971).

On Functionalism

David Chalmers, *The Conscious Mind* (New York: Oxford University Press, 1996).

Dan Dennett, *Brainstorms* (Newton Center, MA: Bradford Books, 1979).

Dan Dennett, *Consciousness Explained* (Boston: Little Brown, 1991).

Jay L. Garfield, *Foundations of Cognitive Science* (New York: Paragon House, 1990).

Joseph Margolis, *The Philosophy of Psychology* (Englewood Cliffs, NJ: Prentice-Hall, 1983).

On Panpsychism

D.S. Clarke, *Panpsychism: Past and Recent Selected Readings* (Albany: State University of New York Press, 2004).

David Skrbina, *Panpsychism in the West* (Cambridge, MA: MIT Press, 2005).

CHAPTER 5

SELF AND FREEDOM

'I'm not myself today, you see,' Alice said to the caterpillar. 'I don't see,' said the caterpillar.

Lewis Carroll

'Just be yourself!' How often have you heard that? What is it to be a 'self'? And what does it mean to be a particular self? In the abstract, these questions seem obscure. But in everything that you do, you adopt some conception of your identity, both as a person and as an individual, whether you are called upon to articulate it or not. As a student, you walk into a classroom with certain conceptions of your own abilities and intelligence, your status among other students, your role vis-à-vis the professor, some haunting memories, perhaps some embarrassment or a certain vanity about your looks, your clothes, your grades, or just your new pair of shoes.

If you had to identify yourself as an individual, describe what makes you *you*, how would you do it? What features are essential to being a person? What features are essential to being the person you are, and what features distinguish you from other persons? Think for a moment of yourself in an office, applying for a job or a scholarship for professional school or just filling out one of those dozens of forms that bombard you during the year. You dutifully fill in your birthdate, where you were born, your grades in school, awards you have received, past work experience or academic qualifications, arrests and other troubles, your sex, and perhaps your marital status. This list of facts about yourself would be one way of identifying 'you'. But at some point, you have likely felt that sense of absurdity and rebellion—'this isn't me!' or 'this is all irrelevant!' What may seem more relevant to your self-identity are your political views, your religious beliefs, your cultural background, your tastes in art and music, your favourite books and movies, your loves and hates, habits and beliefs, or just the fact, perhaps, that you think your own thoughts. These more personal, or 'internal', features as well as the 'cold facts', or 'external' features, are important for identifying you as an individual different from other individuals.

In one sense, your **self-identity** is the way you characterize yourself as an individual. The philosophical problem of self-identity is thus concerned in part with what these characterizing qualities are. Are they just concerned with status and roles among other people? Or is there something that can truly be called 'your self', your '**essence**', or maybe even your soul? How, in other words, should you identify yourself?

There is another sense in which we might talk about a person's self-identity. You may know someone who has experienced a religious conversion or who has just undergone treatment for alcoholism; or perhaps you've encountered an old friend who told you, 'I'm not the same person.' What does this mean, and how is it possible to say you are not the

ESSENCE

The necessary or defining characteristics or properties of a thing.

same person? When someone says, 'I'm not the same person I was', he or she is pointing to the fact that some significant aspects of himself or herself have changed; this person has a new self-identity. Yet, in another sense, this is still the same person; the old identity and the new identity are both identities of the same person.

So we have a second sense of 'self-identity'. Here your self-identity is what makes you the same person over time. The philosophical problem of how to identify an individual as the *same* individual over time has often concerned philosophers. What is it about you without which you wouldn't be you? Presumably you would still be you if you changed your religious beliefs or tastes in music. But what if you had a sex-change operation? Or what if you completely lost your memory, all recollection of your family and friends? Or what if you physically disappeared altogether, remaining only as a wispy consciousness, a spirit, or a ghost without a body? Would it then make sense to say that you are still you?

There is yet a third sense in which we talk about self-identity. What is it that *allows* us to be individual people at all? Interestingly, the fact of consciousness—of having thoughts and feelings—seems the most private and individual thing a person possesses, and yet it is the very thing that we tend to believe *all* people possess. Whatever our attempts to answer the problems of self-identity, they begin with a single 'fact'—our own consciousness. This was the logical beginning for Descartes, who used the fact of his own consciousness as the starting point for his whole philosophy. It was true for Locke, as well, who argued that our identity is to be found in the continuity of our consciousness rather than in the continuity of our bodies. It was even used by Hume, who used his own consciousness as the basis of his denial that there is any such thing as the self!

Of course, these questions assume some metaphysical claims that can and have been questioned. Later in this chapter, we will look at some of these assumptions and some criticisms of them. Must a person have only one 'self', or might he or she in fact have several or many selves? Is there such a thing as a 'self' at all? Or is the self, as many Eastern philosophers have argued, an illusion? Should self-lessness be our ideal self-identity?

And we mustn't ignore questions about the relation between the concept of *self* and the concept of *freedom*? Right now, as you are reading this, you may be firmly convinced that you are a free agent and that what you do is ultimately up to you; but think about it for another minute or two, and you may not feel so sure. Ask yourself: To what extent is your self-identity your own free creation? Can you *choose* your identity? Or is it something that is imposed on you—by God or nature, history or society—and hence something for which you bear no real **responsibility**? In other words, are you responsible for who you are and what you do? How can you ever act freely if there exists a God who already knows exactly how the future will unfold? Again, how can you ever act freely if the past fixes or determines the future in conformity with the laws of nature?

Before we attempt to tackle such questions, we must boldly face another, more fundamental one—namely, What is meant by 'free will'? In what does the difference between free and unfree actions consist? Free actions, like unfree ones, must have causes; but are their causes different in kind? Some philosophers have maintained that a free action is caused by something *within* the self, such as internal desires, as opposed to being caused by something external to the self, such as brute force or violence. Are they right? Is that all there is to it? Or are free actions caused not by anything within the self (such as desires) but simply by the self alone? In that case, however, what kind of thing would the self have to be?

By now, one thing should be crystal clear to you: questions about the self lead us to questions about freedom, and questions about freedom lead us back to questions about the self. In this chapter, therefore, we shall explore a number of different questions about self-identity and freedom. We begin with an important and still influential tradition in philosophy, from Descartes and Locke to Hume and Kant, which focuses on self-consciousness as the sole key to personal identity.

FREEDOM

The idea that a decision or action is a person's own responsibility and that praise and blame may be appropriately ascribed.

A. Consciousness and the Self: From René Descartes to Immanuel Kant

Sometimes we act out our identities without being aware of it at all. At other times, particularly when we talk about ourselves or are placed in a situation where we are forced to 'look at ourselves as others see us', we are very much aware—even painfully aware—of our identities. At such times we say we are **self-conscious**. In general, most modern philosophers and psychologists would argue that you can't have a concept of who you are unless you are also sometimes (not necessarily always) self-conscious. Conversely, you can't be self-conscious unless you have some sense of identity, no matter how crude. The two concepts, in other words, go hand in hand and cannot be separated from each other.

Many philosophers have argued that not only is self-consciousness crucial to having a concept of one's own individuality, but it is also crucial for establishing that one is an enduring self, that is, the same person over time. Descartes is such a philosopher. Remember how he characterized himself:

> I am, however, a real thing and really exist; but what thing? . . . A thing which thinks. . . . What is a thing which thinks? It is a thing which doubts, understands, affirms, denies, wills, refuses, which also imagines and feels.[1]

He goes on to say that he is a thing with desires, who perceives light and noise and feels heat. Clearly, Descartes' concept of 'self' is of thought, or consciousness—a human essence—which each person has and with which each person identifies himself or herself. He also claims to show by his method of doubt that all of this might be so even if he were not to have a body at all. Perhaps, he argues, he is fooled about his 'having' a body just as he might be fooled about all sorts of other things. Therefore, he concludes, it is not his body that provides him with an identity or with the self from which he begins his philosophy. It follows from this that the particular aspects of his self—whether he is male or female, black or white, tall or short, handsome or ugly, strong or weak—are associated with his body only and cannot be essential to his identity. His self-identity is in his mind, in his thinking, doubting, feeling, perceiving, imagining, and desiring. He is, essentially, 'a thing which thinks'.

From 'Meditation VI'
By René Descartes

Therefore, just because I know certainly that I exist, and that meanwhile I do not remark that any other thing necessarily pertains to my nature or essence, excepting that I am a thinking thing, I rightly conclude that my essence consists solely in the fact that I am a thinking thing [or a substance whose whole essence or nature is to think]. And although possibly (or rather certainly, as I shall say in a moment) I possess a body with which I am very intimately conjoined, yet because, on the one side, I have a clear and distinct idea of myself inasmuch as I am only a thinking and unextended thing, and as, on the other, I possess a distinct idea of body, inasmuch as it is only an extended and unthinking thing, it is certain that this I [that is to say, my soul by which I am what I am], is entirely and absolutely distinct from my body, and can exist without it.

It is important to appreciate the kind of step Descartes has taken here. What he is saying is that self-identity depends on consciousness. Our identity does not depend in any way on our body remaining the same, and so human identity is different from the identity of anything else in the world.

> • What is the connection between self-consciousness and self-identity? Do you think (some) animals are self-conscious? If so, do you think that they might have a self-identity?
> • What does Descartes identify as the 'self'? Is this anything unique to individuals? In what sense (if any) does it individuate you from someone else?

John Locke, like Descartes, sees self-consciousness as the key to self-identity. But unlike Descartes, he argues that this identity does not depend on our remaining the same thinking substance, that is, on our having the same soul. Indeed, in the course of our life our soul might be replaced with new souls just as in the course of a tree's growth its cells are replaced with new cells. What makes the tree the same tree is the fact that the same life is present in spite of changes in its physical structure; and what makes a person the same person is that the same consciousness and memories are present. Thus Locke differs from Descartes in distinguishing between the soul (a substance) and consciousness. It is our consciousness that we call our 'self'. In *An Essay Concerning Human Understanding*, Locke argues:

On Personal Identity
By John Locke

Self is that conscious thinking thing . . . which is sensible or conscious of pleasure and pain, capable of happiness or misery, and so is concerned for itself, as far as that consciousness extends.

To find wherein personal identity consists, we must consider what *person* stands for;—which, I think, is a thinking intelligent being, that has reason and reflection, and can consider itself as itself, the same thinking thing, in different times and places; which it does only by that consciousness which is inseparable from thinking, and as it seems to me, essential to it: it being impossible for anyone to perceive without *perceiving* that he does perceive. When we see, hear, smell, taste, feel, meditate, or will anything, we know that we do so. Thus it is always as to our present sensations and perceptions: and by this everyone is to himself that which he calls *self*:—it not being considered, in this case, whether the same self be continued in the same or divers substances. For, since consciousness always accompanies thinking, and it is that which makes everyone to be what he calls self, and thereby distinguishes himself from all other thinking things, in this alone consists personal identity, i.e., the sameness of a rational being: and as far as this consciousness can be extended backwards to any past action or thought, so far reaches the identity of that person; it is the same self now it was then; and it is by the same self with this present one that now reflects on it, that that action was done.

Consciousness makes personal Identity.—But it is further inquired, whether it be the same identical substance. This few[2] would think they had reason to doubt of, if these perceptions, with their consciousness, always remained present in the mind, whereby the same thinking thing would be always consciously present, and, as would be thought, evidently the same to itself. But that which seems to make the difficulty is this, that this consciousness being interrupted always by forgetfulness, there being no moment of our lives wherein we have the whole train of all our past actions before our eyes in one view, but even the best memories losing the sight of one part whilst they are viewing another; and we sometimes, and that the greatest part of our lives, not reflecting on our past selves, being intent on our present thoughts, and in sound sleep having no thoughts at all, or at least none with that consciousness which remarks our waking thoughts,—I say, in all these cases, our consciousness being interrupted, and we losing the sight of our past selves, doubts are raised whether we are the same thinking thing, i.e. the same *substance* or no. Which, however reasonable or unreasonable, concerns not *personal* identity at all. The question being what makes the same person; and not whether it be the same identical substance, which always thinks in the same person, which, in this case, matters not at all: different substances, by the same consciousness (where they do partake in it) being united into one person, as well as different bodies by the same life are united into one animal, whose identity is preserved in that change of substances by the unity of one continued life. For, it being the same consciousness that makes a man be himself to himself, personal identity depends on that only, whether it be annexed solely to one individual substance, or can be continued in a succession of several substances. For as far as any intelligent being *can* repeat the idea of any past action with the same consciousness it had of it at first, and with the same consciousness it has of any present action; so far it is the same personal self. For it is by the consciousness it has of its present thoughts and actions, that it is *self to itself* now, and so will be the same self, as far as the same consciousness can extend to actions past or to come; and would be by distance of time, or change of substance, no more two persons, than a man be two men by wearing other clothes today than he did yesterday, with a long or a short sleep between: the same consciousness uniting those distant actions into the same person, whatever substances contributed to their production.

Personal Identity in Change of Substance.—That this is so, we have some kind of evidence in our very bodies, all whose particles, whilst vitally united to this same thinking conscious self, so that *we feel* when they are touched, and are affected by, and conscious of good or harm that happens to them, are a part of ourselves; i.e. of our thinking conscious self. Thus, the limbs of his body are to everyone a part of himself; he sympathizes and is concerned for them. Cut off a hand, and thereby separate it from that consciousness he had of its heat, cold, and other affections, and it is then no longer a part of that which is himself, any more than the remotest part of matter. Thus, we see the *substance* whereof personal self consisted at one time may be varied at another, without the change of personal identity; there being no question about the same person, though the limbs which but now were a part of it, be cut off.

* * *

If the same consciousness (which, as has been shown, is quite a different thing from the same numerical figure or motion in body) can be transferred from one thinking substance to another, it will be possible that two thinking substances may make but one person. For the same consciousness being preserved, whether in the same or different substances,

the personal identity is preserved. Whether the same immaterial being, being conscious of the action of its past duration, may be wholly stripped of all the consciousness of its past existence, and lose it beyond the power of ever retrieving it again: and so as it were beginning a new account from a new period, have a consciousness that *cannot* reach beyond this new state. All those who hold pre-existence are evidently of this mind; since they allow the soul to have no remaining consciousness of what it did in the pre-existing state, either wholly separate from body, or informing any other body; and if they should not, it is plain experience would be against them. So that personal identity, reaching no further than consciousness reaches, a pre-existent spirit not having continued so many ages in a state of silence, must needs make different persons. Suppose a Christian Platonist or a Pythagorean should, upon God's having ended all his works of creation the seventh day, think his soul hath existed ever since; and should imagine it has revolved in several human bodies; as I once met with one, who was persuaded his had been the *soul* of Socrates (how reasonably I will not dispute; this I know, that in the post he filled, which was no inconsiderable one, he passed for a very rational man, and the press has shown that he wanted not parts of learning) —would anyone say, that he, being not conscious of any of Socrates' actions or thoughts, could be the same *person* with Socrates? Let any one reflect upon himself, and conclude that he has in himself an immaterial spirit, which is that which thinks in him, and, in the constant change of his body keeps him the same: and is that which he calls *himself*.

The body, as well as the soul, goes to the making of a Man.—And thus may we be able, without any difficulty, to conceive the same person at the resurrection, though in a body not exactly in make or parts the same which he had here,—the same consciousness going along with the soul that inhabits it. But yet the soul alone, in the change of bodies, would scarce to anyone but to him that makes the soul the man, be enough to make the same man. For should the soul of a prince, carrying with it the consciousness of the prince's past life, enter and inform the body of a cobbler, as soon as deserted by his own soul, everyone sees he would be the same *person* with the prince, accountable only for the prince's actions: but who would say it was the same *man*? The body

(Continued)

too goes to the making the man, and would, I guess, to everybody determine the man in this case, wherein the soul, with all its princely thoughts about it, would not make another man: but he would be the same cobbler to everyone besides himself. I know that, in the ordinary way of speaking, the same person, and the same man, stand for one and the same thing.

Consciousness alone unites actions into the same Person.—But though the same immaterial substance or soul does not alone, wherever it be, and in whatsoever state, make the same *man*; yet it is plain, consciousness, as far as ever it can be extended—should it be to ages past—unites existences and actions very remote in time into the same *person*, as well as it does the existences and actions of the immediately preceding moment: so that whatever has the consciousness of present and past actions, is the same person to whom they both belong. Had I the same consciousness that I saw the ark and Noah's flood, as that I saw an overflowing of the Thames last winter, or as that I write now, I could no more doubt that I who write this now, that saw the Thames overflowed last winter, and that viewed the flood at the general deluge, was the same *self*,—place that self in what *substance* you please—than that I who write this am the same *myself* now whilst I write (whether I consist of all the same substance, material or immaterial, or no) that I was yesterday. For as to this point of being the same self, it matters not whether this present self be made up of the same or other substances—I being as much concerned, and as justly accountable for any action that was done a thousand years since, appropriated to me now by this self-consciousness, as I am for what I did the last moment.

Self depends on Consciousness, not on Substance.—Self is that conscious thinking thing,—whatever substance made up of, (whether spiritual or material, simple or compounded, it matters not)—which is sensible or conscious of pleasure and pain, capable of happiness or misery, and so is concerned for itself, as far as that consciousness extends. Thus everyone finds that, whilst comprehended under that consciousness, the little finger is as much a part of himself as what is most so. Upon separation of this little finger, should this consciousness go along with the little finger, and leave the rest of the body, it is evident the little finger would be the person, the same person; and self then would have nothing to do with the rest of the body. As in this case it is the consciousness that goes along with the substance, when one part is separate from another, which makes the same person, and constitutes this inseparable self: so it is in reference to the substances remote in time. That with which the consciousness of this present thinking thing *can* join itself, makes the same person, and is one self with it, and with nothing else; and so attributes to itself, and owns all the actions of that thing, as its own, as far as that consciousness reaches, and no further.

The main thesis of Locke's argument is this: Personal self-identity is based upon self-consciousness, in particular, upon memories about one's former experiences. In this, he argues, man is different from animals, whose identity (that is, 'the same dog' or 'the same horse') is based on the continuity of the body, just as you would say that you have had 'the same car' for ten years even if almost every part except the chassis has been replaced during that time. The identity of a 'person', that is, 'personal' identity, depends on self-consciousness.

Locke's idea that memory is what constitutes a self-identity is inspired by the distinctly Cartesian notion that a person's relationship to his or her own thoughts is unique. You cannot think your friend's thoughts and she cannot think yours. Since memory is a species of thought, it follows that you cannot remember your friend's experiences, nor she yours. For example, you may remember your first day of school. Because *you* are remembering that experience as one that happened to *you*, you are self-identical to the person who had the earlier experience. According to Locke, then, memory provides an infallible link between what we might call different 'stages' of a person. Memory seems to guarantee the identity of the person who is now remembering with the person who was then having the experience.

While Locke's theory has the advantage over Descartes' of allowing us to understand self-identity in terms of consciousness without requiring that we posit the existence of a persisting immaterial soul, it is not without its own difficulties. First, much of what we experience, we later forget. Do you remember everything that has ever happened to you?

Undoubtedly, the answer is no. Even if you have a very good memory, you likely do not remember being born, learning to walk, or what you had for breakfast on 28 June 2010. Probably you have completely forgotten some fairly long stretches of your past. What are we to make of these forgotten periods, with regard to our personal identity?

Second, our memories are not always accurate. Sometimes we remember things that never happened. For example, you might clearly remember lending your dictionary to a friend, only to find later that you had, in fact, been using it as a doorstop. Even more disturbing, though fortunately less frequent, cases of inaccurate memory occur when a person sincerely remembers experiences that, in fact, happened, but didn't happen to him. There are people who now remember fighting in the War of 1812, discovering insulin with Frederick Banting, or playing lead guitar with George, John, Paul, and Ringo at Carnegie Hall. What are we to say of such memories? They are not *genuine* memories, but are only *apparent* memories. Clearly, Locke did not intend merely apparent memories to count among those that guarantee identity. We must, then, find a way to distinguish between those cases in which a memory is genuine and those in which it is not. But to do this, it seems that we would have to say that the memories are in fact the correct memories *of that person*. If this is so, it would appear that our memory theory is circular.

A genuine memory, as opposed to a merely apparent one, is, of course, a memory of an experience the rememberer actually had. Now you can see that in distinguishing genuine from apparent memory, we have presupposed the existence of a persisting, self-identical person. That would be all very well were it not for the fact that the concept of self-identity is precisely what we are trying to explain. We cannot use the concept of memory to explain self-identity and then use the concept of self-identity to explain memory. Moreover, once we reflect on the nature of genuine memory, we can see that Locke was, indeed, putting the cart before the horse. When a person says, 'I remember when I learned to ride my bike', the truth of his statement presupposes, rather than establishes, that he is self-identical to the little boy with the scabby knees.

There are other problems with Locke's theory of personal identity; and critics have not been slow to call our attention to them. According to Thomas Reid, for instance, it is a consequence of Locke's account of identity that 'a man may be, and at the same time not be, the person that did a particular action'. But that consequence is logically impossible: X cannot both be identical with Y and not identical with Y. So Locke's theory, Reid concludes, must be false.

Now why does Reid think that Locke's view implies that 'a man may be, and at the same time not be, the person that did a particular action'? Reid makes his case for this claim with the aid of a memorable example.

From *Essays on the Intellectual Powers of Man*
By Thomas Reid

There is another consequence of this doctrine, which follows no less necessarily, though Mr Locke probably did not see it.

There is another consequence of this doctrine, which follows no less necessarily, though Mr Locke probably did not see it. It is, that a man may be, and at the same time not be, the person that did a particular action.

Suppose a brave officer to have been flogged when a boy at school, for robbing an orchard, to have taken a standard from the enemy in his first campaign, and to have been made a general in advanced life. Suppose also, which must he admitted to be possible, that, when he took the standard, he was conscious of his having been flogged at school, and that when made a general he was conscious of his taking the standard, but had absolutely lost the consciousness of his flogging.

Imagine an elderly general, says Reid. When this general was a brave young army officer, he captured the enemy's standard in battle; and when he was even younger than that—a mere schoolboy—he was soundly thrashed for stealing fruit from an orchard. While the general remembers doing what the officer did (that is, capturing the enemy's standard), the general no longer remembers doing what the boy did (that is, being beaten for robbing the orchard). However, the officer remembered doing what the boy did.

You may be wondering what this charming little fable has to do with Locke. Here is Reid's answer:

These things being supposed, it follows, from Mr Locke's doctrine, that he who was flogged at school is the same person who took the standard, and that he who took the standard is the same person who was made a general. Whence it follows, if there be any truth in logic, that the general is the same person with him who was flogged at school. But the general's consciousness does not reach so far back as his flogging—therefore, according to Mr Locke's doctrine, he is not the person who was flogged. Therefore, the general is, and at the same time is not the same person with him who was flogged at school.

If Locke is right about the nature of personal identity, Reid argues, we can immediately draw two conclusions. First, since the general remembers doing what the officer did, the general is the same person as the officer. Second, since the officer remembers doing what the boy did, the officer is the same person as the boy. Now, it is a law of logic that if $X = Y$, and if $Y = Z$, then $X = Z$. (This is known as the *transitivity of identity*.) So if the general is the same person as the officer, and the officer is the same person as the boy, it follows that *the general and the boy are one and the same person*. But—and this is crucial—we can also conclude that *the general and the boy cannot be the same person*. Why? Because the general does not remember doing what the boy did. So if Locke's theory of personal identity is correct, then the general both is, and is not, the same person as the boy. Since that is logically impossible—indeed, it is a manifest contradiction—we must conclude that Locke's simple, sensible-sounding account of personal identity is flawed.

- Can you think of any reply Locke might make to Reid's objection?
- How does the role of consciousness differ in the accounts of self-identity of Locke and Descartes?
- Can you think of a time when you were 'unaware' of your self; that is, contrary to Locke, you were not aware of your awareness and you did not perceive that you were perceiving?
- What is the difference between individual substance and personal identity for Locke? What constitutes individual substance? What constitutes personal identity?
- Does Locke think that the pre-existence of the soul entails the pre-existence of one's self?
- What is the difference between 'person' and 'man' for Locke? What is required for each?

Even before Reid released his *Essays on the Intellectual Powers of Man*, Hume critiqued Locke's philosophy of the self in *A Treatise of Human Nature*. In this work, Hume completely undercuts Descartes' and Locke's view of self-identity. Relying on his belief that any idea must be derived from an impression, Hume argues that when we are self-conscious we are only aware of fleeting thoughts, feelings, and perceptions; we do not have an impression of the self or a thinking substance. He concludes that the idea of the self is simply a fiction. Moreover, since we are never aware of any enduring self, we are never justified in claiming we are the same person we were a year or a minute ago.

On 'There Is No Self'
By David Hume

I may venture to affirm of the rest of mankind, that they are nothing but a bundle or collection of different perceptions, which succeed each other with an inconceivable rapidity, and are in a perpetual flux and movement.

There are some philosophers, who imagine we are every moment intimately conscious of what we call our Self, that we feel its existence and its continuance in existence and are certain, beyond the evidence of a demonstration, both of its perfect identity and simplicity. The strongest sensation, the most violent passion, say they, instead of distracting us from this view, only fix it the more intensely, and make us consider their influence on *self* either by their pain or pleasure. To attempt a further proof of this were to weaken its evidence; since no proof can be derived from any fact, of which we are so intimately conscious; nor is there anything of which we can be certain, if we doubt of this.

Unluckily all these positive assertions are contrary to that very experience, which is pleaded for them, nor have we any idea of *self*, after the manner it is here explained. For from what impression could this idea be derived? This question 'tis impossible to answer without a manifest contradiction, and absurdity; and yet 'tis a question which must necessarily be answered, if we would have the idea of self pass for clear and intelligible. It must be some one impression, that gives rise to every real idea. But self or person is not any one impression, but that to which our several impressions and ideas are supposed to have a reference. If any impression gives rise to the idea of self, that impression must continue invariably the same, thro' the whole course of our lives; since self is supposed to exist after that manner. But there is no impression constant and invariable. Pain and pleasure, grief and joy, passions and sensations succeed each other, and never all exist at the same time. It cannot, therefore, be from any of these impressions, or from any other, that the idea of self is derived; and consequently there is no such idea.

But further, what must become of all our particular perceptions upon this hypothesis? All these are different, and distinguishable, and separable from each other and may be separately considered, and may exist separately, and have no need of anything to support their existence. After what manner, therefore, do they belong to self and how are they connected with it? For my part, when I enter most intimately into what I call *myself*, I always stumble on some particular perception or other, of heat or cold, light or shade, love or hatred, pain or pleasure. I never can catch *myself* at any time without a perception, and never can observe anything but the perception. When my perceptions are removed for any time, as by sound sleep; so long am I insensible of myself, and may truly be said not to exist. And were all my perceptions removed by death, and could I neither think, nor feel, nor see, nor love, nor hate after the dissolution of my body, I should be entirely annihilated, nor do I conceive what is further requisite to make me a perfect nonentity. If anyone upon serious and unprejudiced reflection, thinks he has a different notion of *himself*, I must confess I can reason no longer with him. All I can allow him is, that he may be in the right as well as I, and that we are essentially different in this particular. He may, perhaps, perceive something simple and continued, which he calls *himself*; tho' I am certain there is no such principle in me.

But setting aside some metaphysicians of this kind, I may venture to affirm of the rest of mankind, that they are nothing but a bundle or collection of different perceptions, which succeed each other with an inconceivable rapidity, and are in a perpetual flux and movement. Our eyes cannot turn in their sockets without varying our perceptions. Our thought is still more variable than our sight; and all our other senses and faculties contribute to this change; nor is there any single power of the soul, which remains unalterably the same, perhaps for one moment. The mind is a kind of theatre, where several perceptions successively make their appearance; pass, repass, glide away, and mingle in an infinite variety of postures and situations. There is properly no *simplicity* in it at one time, nor *identity* in different; whatever natural propension we may have to imagine that simplicity and identity. The comparison of the theatre must not mislead us. They are the successive perceptions only, that constitute the mind: nor have we the most distant notion of the place, where these scenes are represented, or of the materials, of which it is composed.

What then gives us so great a propension to ascribe an identity to these successive perceptions, and to suppose ourselves possessed of any invariable and uninterrupted existence thro' the whole course of our lives?

To answer this question, Hume draws an analogy between the fictitious identity we ascribe to persons and the equally fictitious identity we ascribe to things. Just as we can never find an impression of the self that will explain human identity, so we can never find an impression of an object or substance to explain the identity of plants, animals, and things. According to Hume, then, we are never justified in claiming that, for example, a tree we see now is the same tree we saw five years ago or even five minutes ago. The cells and parts of the tree are continuously being replaced so that at no time is it ever literally the same tree. But Hume's argument goes further than this; even if that were not so, we would still have no way of justifying our belief that this tree is the same one we saw some time ago, rather than another, reasonably similar to it, but yet different. How do we know, for example, that someone has not come along and replaced it with another?

The temptation to ascribe identity to things and persons, Hume thinks, arises in part from the spatiotemporal continuity of the thing; the tree is in the same place at different times. People, however, have the troublesome habit of moving around, going to Europe for the summer or college for the semester; we still see the continuity of an individual's movement, receive postcards from the appropriate places at the appropriate times, and so we conclude that it is the same person. In addition to spatiotemporal continuity, we ordinarily rely on **resemblance** as a **criterion** of identity. We tolerate small changes, a haircut or a new scar, even a lost leg or a bit of plastic surgery. As long as there is a strong resemblance between two individuals, for example before and after a haircut, we think of them as the same. Only when there is a great change, as from Dr Jekyll to Mr Hyde, do we question the identity of the two individuals.

Hume, however, argues that spatiotemporal continuity and resemblance do not in fact guarantee identity:

The identity, which we ascribe to the mind of man, is only a fictitious one, and of a like kind with that which we ascribe to vegetables and animal bodies. It cannot, therefore, have a different origin, but must proceed from a like operation of the imagination upon his objects.

We have a distinct idea of an object, that remains invariable and uninterrupted thro' a supposed variation of time; and this idea we call that of *identity* or *sameness*. We have also a distinct idea of several different objects existing in succession, and connected together by a close relation; and this to an accurate view affords as perfect a notion of *diversity*, as if there was no manner of relation among the objects. But tho' these two ideas of identity, and a succession of related objects be in themselves perfectly distinct, and even contrary, yet 'tis certain, that in our common way of thinking they are generally confounded with each other. That action of the imagination, by which we consider the uninterrupted and invariable object, and that by which we reflect on the succession of related objects, are almost the same to the feeling, nor is there much more effort to thought required in the latter case than in the former. The relation facilitates the transition of the mind from one object to another, and renders its passage as smooth as if it contemplated one continued object. This resemblance is the cause of the confusion and mistake, and makes us substitute the notion of identity, instead of that of related objects.

Our last resource is to . . . boldly assert that these different related objects are in effect the same, however interrupted and variable. In order to justify to ourselves this absurdity, we often feign some new and unintelligible principle, that connects the objects together, and prevents their interruption or variation. Thus we feign the continued existence of the perceptions of our senses, to remove the interruption; and run into the notion of a *soul*, and *self*, and *substance*, to disguise the variation. But we may further observe, that where we do not give rise to such a fiction, our propension to confound identity with relation is so great, that we are apt to imagine something unknown and mysterious connecting the parts, beside their relation; and this I take to be the case with regard to the identity we ascribe to plants and vegetables. And even when this does not take place, we still feel a propensity to confound these ideas, tho' we are not able fully to satisfy ourselves in that particular, nor find anything invariable and uninterrupted to justify our notion of identity.

* * *

Suppose any mass of matter, of which the parts are contiguous and connected, to be placed before us; 'tis plain we must attribute a perfect identity to this mass, provided all the parts continue uninterruptedly and invariably the same, whatever motion or change of place we may observe either in the whole or in any of the parts. But supposing some very *small* or *inconsiderable* part to be added to the mass, or subtracted from it; tho' this absolutely destroys the identity of the whole, strictly speaking; yet as we seldom think so accurately, we scruple not to pronounce a mass of matter the same, where we find so trivial an alteration. The passage of the thought from the object before the change to the object after it, is so smooth and easy, that we scarce perceive the transition, and are apt to imagine, that 'tis nothing but a continued survey, of the same object.

- How do you understand Hume's claim that the self is nothing but a bundle of perceptions? Where, then, do we get our idea of identity, according to Hume?

Hume's argument is familiar to us from our discussion of empiricism in Chapter 3. All we perceive, he says, is a sequence of impressions, and nowhere do we encounter an impression either of a substance (an enduring object) or of the self. What right do we have, therefore, to identify the object of this impression with the object of another? What right do we have to identify the person we are now with someone in the past?

But Hume's argument that 'I never can catch *myself*' suffers from a peculiar but obvious form of self-contradiction. He can't even deny that there is a self without in some sense pointing to himself in order to do it. This point was not missed by Kant. Kant agrees with Hume that the enduring self is not to be found in self-consciousness. The enduring self is not an object of experience—Hume was right on this point and both Descartes and Locke were mistaken. In Kant's words, the enduring self is not empirical. It is transcendental.

By 'transcendental' Kant means what is a necessary condition for the possibility of *any* experience. Kant saw that if there were a different self at each moment of consciousness, we would not be able to perceive anything. In order to experience an object, we must be able to combine our various impressions of it in a unified consciousness. Thus, if we do in fact experience objects, we must assume that we have a unified consciousness that combines these impressions into the perception of an object. Or, to take a different example, Hume talks of different sorts of relations of impressions, for example, succession. In order for an individual to perceive two impressions as successive, these impressions must have been perceived by the *same* consciousness.

The self of 'I' for Kant, then, is the necessary logical subject of any thought, perception, feeling, and so on. It is not an object of experience but transcends and is presupposed by all experience.

Hume's error, as in other matters, was in confusing the supposed experience of self-consciousness with the transcendental rules with which we tie these various experiences together. Accordingly, Kant argues, Descartes and Locke are both correct in equating self-identity and self-consciousness, but it must not be thought that the self is therefore a 'thing' (as Descartes said) that we find in experience.

According to Kant, the self is the activity of consciousness, in particular the activity of organizing our various experiences. Kant borrows Hume's argument, but he turns it toward the opposite conclusion: True, I never find a self 'in' my experiences, but I can always find myself in that 'I' that has the experience. Kant's 'self', in other words, is the act of having experiences rather than anything that we experience itself. But for Kant this self is not merely the passive recipient of experiences, and here is where the notion of self as activity becomes all-important. The self is the activity of applying the rules by which we organize our experience. Moreover, Kant argues that one of the most basic rules of this activity is that the self organize its experience as its own experience. The rule is that we must always 'synthesize' our various experiences into a unity, for we could not come to have any knowledge whatever of a scattering of various impressions and sensations without this synthesis. This basic rule of synthesis allows Kant to say that not only is the self the activity that applies the various rules to experience but its existence as a unified self with a unified synthesis of experiences is itself a rule.

Kant gives this curious idea of the self as a rule a formidable name, 'the transcendental unity of apperception'. What is important in this concept is that the self for Kant is indeed essential to self-consciousness, but it is not 'in' self-consciousness. Metaphorically, it is often said that it is 'behind' self-consciousness, that is, it is the activity of bringing our various experiences together in accordance with the basic rules of our experience. Accordingly, Kant refers to this self as the **transcendental ego**, 'transcendental' because it is basic and necessary for all possible human experience. The difference between Hume and Kant is sometimes illustrated in this way: Hume looks for the self among our experiences and doesn't find it; Kant agrees with Hume but argues that he looked in the wrong place. The self, Kant says, is the thread that ties together our various experiences. Accordingly, the self is not in the bundle of our experiences; it is rather the 'transcendental' thread that holds them all together and is as real as any experience.

Kant returns to Descartes and challenges his main theses, even while agreeing with parts of them. First, while Descartes thought that we had to be self-conscious all the time, Kant insists that it is only necessary for 'the "I think" to be able to accompany all experiences'. It is not necessary to be always conscious of our selves but only to be, at any point in our experience, capable of becoming self-conscious; we can turn our attention when we want to from whatever we are doing and watch ourselves doing what we are doing. This is an important point: Our concern with self-consciousness is given impetus just because we are often not self-conscious. In fact, several philosophers (and many mystics) have argued that self-consciousness is bad, a useless thing, and should be avoided as much as possible. According to Descartes, this is not possible, for to exist at all as a human being is to exist self-consciously. According to Kant, on the other hand, to exist as a human being is 'to be able' to be self-conscious.

Second, Kant objects to Descartes' belief that the thinking self is a thinking thing. He objects to this, first of all, because of his insistence (as a result of Hume's argument) that the self (or 'transcendental ego') is not in our experience but rather 'behind' it and responsible for it. More literally, he says that the self must be thought of as an activity. You can see what a radical move this is when you recall the traditional doctrine of the soul in Plato, in Christianity, and in much of modern thought. The soul, quite simply, is the self conceived of as a thing, an enduring thing that can survive the death of the body. By saying that the self is an activity, Kant undermines (as Hume had intended to undermine) the traditional concept of soul.[3]

TRANSCENDENTAL EGO

The bare, logical fact of one's own self-consciousness.

Against the Soul
By Immanuel Kant

Life is the subjective condition of all our possible experience; consequently we can only infer the permanence of the soul in life, for the death of a man is the end of all experience.

Pure reason requires us to seek for every predicate of a thing its own subject, and for this subject, which is itself necessarily nothing but a predicate, its subject, and so on indefinitely (or as far as we can reach). But hence it follows that we must not hold anything at which we can arrive to be an ultimate subject.

Now we appear to have this substance in the consciousness of ourselves (in the thinking subject), and indeed in an immediate intuition; for all the predicates of an internal sense refer to the *ego*, as a subject, and I cannot conceive myself as the predicate of any other subject. Hence completeness in the reference of the given concepts as predicates to a subject—not merely an Idea, but an object—that is, the absolute subject itself, seems to be given in experience. But this expectation is disappointed. For the ego is not a concept, but only the indication of the object of the inner sense, so far as we know it by no further predicate. Consequently it cannot indeed be itself a predicate of any other thing; but just as little can it be a definite concept of an absolute subject, but is, as in all other cases, only the reference of the inner phenomena to their unknown subject. Yet this idea (which serves very well as a regulative principle totally to destroy all materialistic explanations of the internal phenomena of the soul) occasions by a very natural misunderstanding a very specious argument, which infers its nature from this supposed knowledge of the substance of our thinking being. This is specious so far as the knowledge of it falls quite without the complex of experience.

But though we may call this thinking self (the soul) 'substance', as being the ultimate subject of thinking which cannot be further represented as the predicate of another thing, it remains quite empty and without significance if permanence—the quality which renders the concept of substances in experience fruitful—cannot be proved of it.

But permanence can never be proved of the concept of a substance as a thing in itself, but for the purposes of experience only.

If, therefore, from the concept of the soul as a substance we would infer its permanence, this can hold good as regards possible experience only, not of the soul as a thing in itself and beyond all possible experience. Life is the subjective condition of all our possible experience; consequently we can only infer the permanence of the soul in life, for the death of a man is the end of all experience which concerns the soul as an object of experience, except the contrary be proved—which is the very question in hand. The permanence of the soul can therefore only be proved (and no one cares to do that) during the life of man, but not, as we desire to do, after death. The reason for this is that the concept of substance, so far as it is to be considered necessarily with the concept of permanence, can be so combined only according to the principles of possible experience, and therefore for the purposes of experience only.

Third, Kant argued that we need two very different conceptions of self. He saw that this conception of self as self-consciousness was not sufficient to do the whole job that philosophers had wanted it to do. One part of Descartes' enterprise was to find out what was essential to his existence, what could not be doubted and so could serve as a first premise for his *Meditations*. So too Locke and Hume had tried to find (though Locke did and Hume didn't) that self that defined us through our various changes, which identified Jekyll and Hyde and identifies us from year to year, day to day, and mood to mood. But the function of the self was also to serve as a way of identifying ourselves in distinction from other people and other things. Thus Descartes' concept of the self as a thinking thing was not sufficient to tell us what makes one person different from another, and he found it necessary to supplement his concept of self with an account of how a person is composed of a self and a body in some special way.

> - How does Kant answer Hume's challenge that there is no enduring self of which we are aware?
> - Why is the transcendental self lacking as an explanation for self-identity? What does Kant introduce into his theory that would account for the differences we observe among persons?

Similarly, Locke distinguishes between personal identity and identity as a man (that is, as a biological example of the species *Homo sapiens*) and tells us that both are necessary for us to understand how one particular person is different from another particular person. We can now clearly see that the question of self-identity divides into two questions: (1) What is essential to being a self? and (2) What is essential to being a particular self? Kant's conception of self as that which has experiences, the transcendental self, only answers the first question. Nothing in the notion of transcendental self allows us to distinguish between different people and tell them apart. Accordingly, he identifies another 'self' that he calls the **empirical ego**, which includes all of those particular things about us that make us different people. Differences in our bodies, our looks, our size, our strength would be such differences. So too would our different personalities, our different thoughts and memories. It is the empirical self that identifies us as individual persons. The transcendental self makes possible human consciousness.

These have been the traditional answers to the philosophical problem of self-identity. What is it that makes one 'the same person' from moment to moment and year to year? The spatiotemporal **continuity** of the body would seem to be a part of the answer. But philosophers since (and before) Descartes have seen quite clearly that this is never enough, that it is also self-consciousness that provides the key to self-identity.

B. Existentialism: Self-identity, Responsibility, and Radical Freedom

The traditional conception of self-identity has held that there is some essential property of identity in which we all share. In the Western Judeo-Christian view, we are all the same 'before God', and our identities are to be judged accordingly. From a non-religious perspective, most of us would insist on a common ideal—being 'a good person'—that transcends individual considerations. Even where cultural differences would suggest the possibility of different conceptions of self-identity, we might still reduce any variance between individuals to mere 'accidental differences', insisting that we are 'essentially the same'. Of course, people are different and think differently of themselves; but it does not follow that those differences are essential, nor does it follow that relativism must be true. Ultimately, when we say that all people are 'essentially the same', we believe that there are, indeed, universal criteria for self-identity and that the differences between people, though we need not deny them, are merely superficial.

Yet, must there be a single answer to the problem of self-identity that is 'correct' for everyone? According to some philosophers, there is nothing necessary about this, or even desirable. For them, the problem of self-identity is the problem of deciding which of the many possible characteristics an individual should choose as his or her own standards for self-identity. And that choice is not just one that philosophers make, but one that each person makes at some point or points during his or her life.

In this view, self-identity is, by nature, a highly individualistic concept. It is a mask that *you* wear in every social encounter (though you might wear slightly different masks for different encounters). It is the way *you* think of yourself and the standards by which *you* judge yourself in every moment of reflection. It is the self-image *you* follow when you decide how to act in any given circumstance. And there *is* a certain relativity to self-identity. Consider that a very handsome but stupendously dumb bully will surely have a very different conception of self-identity than an extremely intelligent and talented mathematics major. Likewise, an elderly farmer in rural China will likely think of and judge himself in a way very different from that in which a university student in Canada will think of and judge herself.

One of the most powerful schools of contemporary thought has been dedicated to the idea that self-identity, in every case, is a matter of individual choice. This school is **existentialism**. Its most powerful advocate is the twentieth-century French philosopher Jean-Paul Sartre, whose philosophy is the culmination of a full century of existentialist thought, beginning with Søren Kierkegaard in the 1840s. According to Sartre, there are no set standards for self-identity, either for individuals or for people in general. There is, he argues, no such thing as 'human nature', and what we are—and what it means to be a human being—are always matters of decision. There is no correct choice; there are only choices.

EMPIRICAL EGO

Characteristics that distinguish each of us from other persons.

EXISTENTIALISM

The philosophy that puts great emphasis on individual choice and the voluntary acceptance of all values.

On Existentialism

By Jean-Paul Sartre

When we say that man is responsible for himself, we do not mean that he is responsible only for his own individuality, but that he is responsible for all men.

What existentialists have in common is simply the fact that they believe that *existence* comes before *essence*—or, if you will, that we must begin from the subjective. What exactly do we mean by that?

If one considers an article of manufacture—as, for example, a book or paper-knife—one sees that it has been made by an artisan who had a conception of it; and he has paid attention, equally, to the conception of a paper-knife and to the pre-existent technique of production which is a part of that conception and is, at bottom, a formula. Thus the paper-knife is at the same time an article producible in a certain manner and one which, on the other hand, serves a definite purpose, for one cannot suppose that a man would produce a paper-knife without knowing what it was for. Let us say, then, of the paper-knife that its essence—that is to say the sum of the formulae and the qualities which made its production and its definition possible—precedes its existence. The presence of such-and-such a paper-knife or book is thus determined before my eyes. Here, then, we are viewing the world from a technical standpoint, and we say that production precedes existence.

When we think of God as the creator, we are thinking of him, most of the time, as a supernal artisan. Whatever doctrine we may be considering, whether it be a doctrine like that of Descartes, or of Leibniz himself, we always imply that the will follows, more or less, from the understanding or at least accompanies it, so that when God creates he knows precisely what he is creating. Thus, the conception of man in the mind of God is comparable to that of the paper-knife in the mind of the artisan: God makes man according to a procedure and a conception, exactly as the artisan manufactures a paper-knife, following a definition and a formula. Thus each individual man is the realization of a certain conception which dwells in the divine understanding. In the philosophic atheism of the eighteenth century, the notion of God is suppressed, but not, for all that, the idea that essence is prior to existence; something of that idea we still find everywhere, in Diderot, in Voltaire, and even in Kant. Man possesses a human nature; that 'human nature', which is the conception of human being, is found in every man; which means that each man is a particular example of an universal conception, the conception of Man. In Kant, this universality goes so far that the wild man of the woods, man in the state of nature and the bourgeois are all contained in the same definition and have the same fundamental qualities. Here again, the essence of man precedes that historic existence which we confront in experience.

* * *

What do we mean by saying that existence precedes essence? We mean that man first of all exists, encounters himself, surges up in the world—and defines himself afterwards. If man as the existentialist sees him is not definable, it is because to begin with he is nothing. He will not be anything until later, and then he will be what he makes of himself. Thus, there is no human nature, because there is no God to have a conception of it. Man simply is. Not that he is simply what he conceives himself to be, but he is what he wills, and as he conceives himself after already existing—as he wills to be after that leap towards existence. Man is nothing else but that which he makes of himself. That is the first principle of existentialism. And this is what people call its 'subjectivity', using the word as a reproach against us. But what do we mean to say by this, but that man is of a greater dignity than a stone or a table? For we mean to say that man primarily exists—that man is, before all else, something which propels itself towards a future and is aware that it is doing so. Man is, indeed, a project which possesses a subjective life, instead of being a kind of moss, or a fungus, or a cauliflower. Before that projection of the self nothing exists; not even in the heaven of intelligence: man will only attain existence when he is what he purposes to be. Not, however, what he may wish to be. For what we usually understand by wishing or willing is a conscious decision taken—much more often than not—after we have made ourselves what we are. I may wish to join a party, to write a book, or to marry—but in such a case what is usually called my will is probably a manifestation of a prior and more spontaneous decision. If, however, it is true that existence is prior to essence,

(Continued)

man is responsible for what he is. Thus, the first effect of existentialism is that it puts every man in possession of himself as he is, and places the entire responsibility for his existence squarely upon his own shoulders. And, when we say that man is responsible for himself, we do not mean that he is responsible only for his own individuality, but that he is responsible for all men.

When we say that man chooses himself, we do mean that every one of us must choose himself; but by that we also mean that in choosing for himself he chooses for all men. For in effect, of all the actions a man may take in order to create himself as he wills to be, there is not one which is not creative, at the same time, of an image of man such as he believes he ought to be.

- To what extent is self-identity a matter of choice?

But this existentialist doctrine of choice doesn't make the problem of self-identity any easier. In fact, it complicates it enormously. Earlier in this chapter, we considered whether the facts about a person are sufficient to determine his or her identity. We said surely not all of them are necessary; some are more essential than others. But this isn't yet an answer to the question, for it may be that all the essential facts are still not sufficient to determine a person's identity.

According to the existentialist, this is made even more complex by the fact that a person chooses which facts are to be considered as essential. Are the facts alone ever sufficient to determine our identity? Sartre's answer, which he adapted from German existentialist Martin Heidegger, is 'never!' The facts that are true of a person are always, at least so long as that person is alive, only indicative of what that person has been and done so far. In judging a person's identity, we must always consider more than the facts that are true of him or her (which Sartre and Heidegger collectively name, somewhat technically, a person's **facticity**); we must also consider that individual's projections into the future, his or her ambitions, plans, intentions, hopes, and fantasies. (Sartre calls these considerations a person's **transcendence**. Notice that this is the third way in which *transcendence* has been used in our discussion, so be careful.) This way of viewing the person makes the question of self-identity impossibly complex, in fact, irresolvable. For example, consider Sartre's example of what he calls 'bad faith' in one of his most important works, *Being and Nothingness* (1943).

Bad faith, quite simply, is refusing to accept yourself.[4] This can happen in two different ways. Either you can refuse to accept the facts and actions as relevant to your self-identity (for example, denying that your repeated cowardly behaviour establishes your identity as a coward). Or you can go too far in the opposite direction, believing that your actions conclusively and unalterably establish your self-identity (for example, denying that you could ever alter your cowardly self-identity through an act of heroism).

On Bad Faith
By Jean-Paul Sartre

Let us take an example: Suppose a certain homosexual frequently has an intolerable feeling of guilt, and his whole existence is determined in relation to this feeling.[5] One will readily foresee that he is in bad faith. In fact it frequently happens that this man, while recognizing his homosexual inclination, while avowing each and every particular misdeed which he has committed, refuses with all his strength to consider himself '*a homosexual*'. His case is always 'different', peculiar; there enters into it something of a game, of chance, of bad luck; the mistakes are all in the past; they are explained by a certain conception of the beautiful which women cannot satisfy; we should see in them the results of a restless search, rather than the manifestations of a deeply rooted tendency, etc., etc. Here is assuredly a man in bad faith who borders on the comic since, acknowledging all the facts which are imputed to him, he refuses to draw from them the conclusion which they impose. His friend, who is his most severe critic, becomes irritated with this duplicity. The critic asks only one thing—and perhaps then he will show himself indulgent: that the guilty one recognize himself as guilty, that the homosexual declare frankly—whether humbly or boastfully matters little—'I am a homosexual.' We ask here: Who is in bad faith? The homosexual or the champion of sincerity?

The homosexual recognizes his faults, but he struggles with all his strength against the crushing view that his mistakes constitute for him a *destiny*. He does not wish to let himself be considered as a thing. He has an obscure but strong feeling that a homosexual is not a homosexual as this table is a table or as this red-haired man is red-haired. It seems to him that he has escaped from each mistake as soon as he has posited it and recognized it; he even feels that the psychic duration by itself cleanses him from each misdeed, constitutes for him an undetermined future, causes him to be born anew. Is he wrong? Does he not recognize in himself the peculiar, irreducible character of human reality? His attitude includes then an undeniable comprehension of truth. But at the same time he needs this perpetual rebirth, this constant escape in order to live; he must constantly put himself beyond reach in order to avoid the terrible judgment of collectivity. Thus he plays on the word *being*. He would be right actually if he understood the phrase, 'I am not a homosexual' in the sense of 'I am not what I am'. That is, if he declared to himself, 'To the extent that a pattern of conduct is defined as the conduct of a [homosexual] and to the extent that I have adopted this conduct, I am a homosexual. But to the extent that human reality cannot be finally defined by patterns of conduct, I am not one.' But instead he slides surreptitiously toward a different connotation of the word 'being'. He understands 'not being' in the sense of 'not-being-in-itself'. He lays claim to 'not being a homosexual' in the sense in which this table *is not* an inkwell. He is in bad faith.

- What is the difference between 'facticity' and 'transcendence'? How does Sartre employ these concepts to claim that there is no self-identity?
- What is 'bad faith'? Can you think of a time when you acted in 'bad faith'?

Sartre then lays bare the heart of his theory. Bad faith points to the most important single fact about personal self-identity—there isn't any. In somewhat paradoxical terminology, Sartre tells us, 'one is what one is not, and one is not what one is'. In other words, whatever the facts about you, you are always something more than those facts. The homosexual in Sartre's example is a homosexual to the extent that all his past actions and desires are those of a homosexual. He falls into bad faith by refusing to see that his past actions point to his having a self-identity as a homosexual. Yet at the same time, there is a genuine sense in which he is not a homosexual: In the future, he may radically alter his lifestyle. It would, then, also be bad faith were he to totally accept his self-identity as a homosexual, denying that he could be anything else. As long as a person is alive, he or she is identified by intentions, plans, dreams, and hopes as much as by what is already true by virtue of the facts. Given this complexity, the problem of deciding 'who I am' takes on dramatic and extravagant complications. Consider the following scene from Sartre's famous play *No Exit*, in which one of the characters (now dead and 'living' in hell) tries to justify his image of himself as a hero, despite the facts of his life, which would indicate that he was a coward.

From *No Exit*
By Jean-Paul Sartre

It's what one does, and nothing else, that shows the stuff one's made of.

GARCIN: They shot me.

ESTELLE: I know. Because you refused to fight. Well, why shouldn't you?

GARCIN: I—I didn't exactly refuse. [*In a far-away voice*] I must say he talks well, he makes out a good case against me, but he never says what I should have done instead. Should I have gone to the general and said: 'General I decline to fight'? A mug's game; they'd have promptly locked me up. But I wanted to show my colours, my true colours, do you understand? I wasn't going to be silenced. [*To ESTELLE*] So I—I took the train. . . . They caught me at the frontier.

ESTELLE: Where were you trying to go?

GARCIN: To Mexico. I meant to launch a pacifist newspaper down there. [*A short silence.*] Well, why don't you speak?

ESTELLE: What could I say? You acted quite rightly, as you didn't want to fight. [*GARCIN makes a fretful gesture.*] But, darling, how on earth can I guess what you want me to answer?

INEZ: Can't you guess? Well, *I* can. He wants you to tell him that he bolted like a lion. For 'bolt' he did, and that's what's biting him.

GARCIN: 'Bolted', 'went away'—we won't quarrel over words.

ESTELLE: But you *had* to run away. If you'd stayed they'd have sent you to jail, wouldn't they?

GARCIN: Of course. [*A pause.*] Well, Estelle, am I a coward?

ESTELLE: How can I say? Don't be so unreasonable, darling. I can't put myself in your skin. You must decide that for yourself.

GARCIN: [*wearily*] I can't decide.

ESTELLE: Anyhow, you must remember. You must have had reasons for acting as you did.

GARCIN: I had.

ESTELLE: Well?

GARCIN: But were they the real reasons?

ESTELLE: You've a twisted mind, that's your trouble. Plaguing yourself over such trifles!

GARCIN: I'd thought it all out, and I wanted to make a stand. But was that my real motive?

INEZ: Exactly. That's the question. Was that your real motive? No doubt you argued it out with yourself, you weighed the pros and cons, you found good reasons for what you did. But fear and hatred and all the dirty little instincts one keeps dark—they're motives too. So carry on, Mr Garcin, and try to be honest with yourself—for once.

GARCIN: Do I need you to tell me that? Day and night I paced my cell, from the window to the door, from the door to the window. I pried into my heart, I sleuthed myself like a detective. By the end of it I felt as if I'd given my whole life to introspection. But always I harked back to the one thing certain—that I had acted as I did, I'd taken that train to the frontier. But why? Why? Finally I thought: My death will settle it. If I face death courageously, I'll prove I am no coward.

INEZ: And how did you face death?

GARCIN: Miserably. Rottenly. [*INEZ laughs.*] Oh, it was only a physical lapse—that might happen to anyone; I'm not ashamed of it. Only everything's been left in suspense, forever. [*To ESTELLE*] Come here, Estelle. Look at me. I want to feel someone looking at me while they're talking about me on earth. . . . I like green eyes.

INEZ: Green eyes! Just hark to him! And you, Estelle, do you like cowards?

ESTELLE: If you knew how little I care! Coward or hero, it's all one—provided he kisses well.

GARCIN: There they are, slumped in their chairs, sucking at their cigars. Bored they look. Half-asleep. They're thinking: 'Garcin's a coward.' But only vaguely, dreamily. One's got to think of something. 'That chap Garcin was a coward.' That's what they've decided, those dear friends of mine. In six months' time they'll be saying: 'Cowardly as that skunk Garcin.' You're lucky, you two; no one on earth is giving you another thought. But I—I'm long in dying.

GARCIN: [*putting his hands on (INEZ's) shoulders*] Listen! Each man has an aim in life, a leading motive; that's so, isn't it? Well, I didn't give a damn for wealth, or for love. I aimed at being a real man. A tough, as they say. I staked everything on the same horse. . . . Can one possibly be a coward when one's deliberately courted danger at every turn? And can one judge a life by a single action?

INEZ: Why not? For thirty years you dreamt you were a hero, and condoned a thousand petty lapses—because a hero, of course, can do no wrong. An easy method obviously. Then a day came when you were up against it, the red light of real danger—and you took the train to Mexico.

GARCIN: I 'dreamt', you say. It was no dream. When I chose that hardest path, I made my choice deliberately. A man is what he wills himself to be.

INEZ: Prove it. Prove it was no dream. It's what one does, and nothing else, that shows the stuff one's made of.

GARCIN: I died too soon. I wasn't allowed time to—to do my deeds.

INEZ: One always dies too soon—or too late. And yet one's whole life is complete at that moment, with a line drawn neatly under it, ready for the summing up. You are—your life, and nothing else.

To speak of 'bad faith' in Sartre's sense is, inevitably, to speak of freedom. In *Being and Nothingness*, Sartre argued that we are, always, absolutely free. This means that insofar as we act (and Sartre says that we are always acting) our decisions and our actions cannot be viewed as having any causes whatsoever. We must make decisions, and no amount of information and no number of causal circumstances can ever replace our need to make them. We can, of course, refuse to make decisions, acting as if they were made for us, as if circumstances already determined them, as if the fates had already established the outcome. But even in these cases, we are making decisions, and, to use a classic Sartrean phrase, in 'choosing not to choose, we are condemned to be free'. Again, desires may enter into consideration, but only as 'consideration'. We can always act against a desire, any desire, no matter how strong, if only we are sufficiently decided that we shall do so. A starving man may yet refuse food if, for example, he is taking part in a hunger strike for a political cause to which he is dedicated. A mother may refuse to save her own life if it would be at the expense of her children. A student may miss his favourite television show if he has resolved to study for tomorrow's test. Whether trivial or grandiose, our every act is a decision, and our every decision is free. Even if we fail to live up to our decisions or find that we 'cannot' make them, we are responsible nevertheless. There is no escape from freedom or responsibility.

On Absolute Freedom
By Jean-Paul Sartre

From the instant of my upsurge into being, I carry the weight of the world by myself alone without anything or any person being able to lighten it.

Although the considerations which are about to follow are of interest primarily to the ethicist, it may nevertheless be worthwhile after these descriptions and arguments to return to the freedom of the for-itself and try to understand what the fact of this freedom represents for human destiny.

The essential consequence of our earlier remarks is that man being condemned to be free carries the weight of the whole world on his shoulders; he is responsible for the world and for himself as a way of being. We are taking the word 'responsibility' in its ordinary sense as 'consciousness (of) being the incontestable author of an event or of an object'. In this sense the responsibility of the for-itself is overwhelming since he is the one by whom it happens that *there is* a world; since he is also the one who makes himself be, then whatever may be the situation in which he finds himself, the for-itself must wholly assume this situation with its peculiar coefficient of adversity, even though it be insupportable. He must assume the situation with the proud consciousness of being the author of it, for the very worst disadvantages or the worst threats which can endanger my person have meaning only in and through my project; and it is on the ground of the engagement which I am that they appear. It is

(Continued)

therefore senseless to think of complaining since nothing foreign has decided what we feel, what we live, or what we are.

Furthermore this absolute responsibility is not resignation; it is simply the logical requirement of the consequences of our freedom. What happens to me happens through me, and I can neither affect myself with it nor revolt against it nor resign myself to it. Moreover everything which happens to me is *mine*. By this we must understand first of all that I am always equal to what happens to me *qua* man, for what happens to a man through other men and through himself can be only human. The most terrible situations of war, the worst tortures do not create a non-human state of things; there is no non-human situation. It is only through fear, flight, and recourse to magical types of conduct that I shall decide on the non-human, but this decision is human, and I shall carry the entire responsibility for it. But in addition the situation is *mine* because it is the image of my free choice of myself, and everything which it presents to me is *mine* in that this represents me and symbolizes me. Is it not I who decide the coefficient of adversity in things and even their unpredictability by deciding myself?

Thus there are no *accidents* in life; a community event which suddenly burst forth and involves me in it does not come from the outside. If I am mobilized in a war, this war is *my* war; it is in my image and I deserve it. I deserve it first because I could always get out of it by suicide or by desertion; these ultimate possibles are those which must always be present for us when there is a question of envisaging a situation. For lack of getting out of it, I have *chosen* it. This can be due to inertia, to cowardice in the face of public opinion, or because I prefer certain other values to the value of the refusal to join in the war (the good opinion of my relatives, the honour of my family, etc.). Any way you look at it, it is a matter of choice. This choice will be repeated later on again and again without a break until the end of the war. Therefore we must agree with the statement by J. Romains, 'In war there are no innocent victims.' If therefore I have preferred war to death or to dishonour, everything takes place as if I bore the entire responsibility for this war. Of course others have declared it, and one might be tempted perhaps to consider me as a simple accomplice. But this notion of complicity has only a juridical sense, and it does not hold here. For it depended on me that for me

and by me this war should not exist, and I have decided that it does exist. There was no compulsion here, for the compulsion could have got no hold on a freedom. I did not have any excuse; . . . the peculiar character of human-reality is that it is without excuse. Therefore it remains for me only to lay claim to this war.

But in addition the war is *mine* because by the sole fact that it arises in a situation which I cause to be and that I can discover it there only by engaging myself for or against it, I can no longer distinguish at present the choice which I make of myself from the choice which I make of the war. To live this war is to choose myself through it and to choose it through my choice of myself. There can be no question of considering it as 'four years of vacation' or as 'reprieve', as a 'recess', the essential part of my responsibilities being elsewhere in my married, family, or professional life. In this war which I have chosen I choose myself from day to day, and I make it mine by making myself. If it is going to be four empty years, then it is I who bear the responsibility for this.

Finally, . . . each person is an absolute choice of self from the standpoint of a world of knowledges and of techniques which this choice both assumes and illumines; each person is an absolute upsurge at an absolute date and is perfectly unthinkable at another date. It is therefore a waste of time to ask what I should have been if this war had not broken out, for I have chosen myself as one of the possible meanings of the epoch which imperceptibly led to war. I am not distinct from this same epoch; I could not be transported to another epoch without contradiction. Thus *I am* this war which restricts and limits and makes comprehensible the period which preceded it. In this sense we may define more precisely, the responsibility of the for-itself if to the earlier quoted statement, 'There are no innocent victims', we added the words, 'We have the war we deserve'. Thus, totally free, undistinguishable from the period for which I have chosen to be the meaning, as profoundly responsible for the war as if I had myself declared it, unable to live without integrating it in *my* situation, engaging myself in it wholly and stamping it with my seal, I must be without remorse or regrets as I am without excuse; for from the instant of my upsurge into being, I carry the weight of the world by myself alone without anything or any person being able to lighten it.

Yet this responsibility is of a very particular type. Someone will say, 'I did not ask to be born.' This is a naive way of throwing greater emphasis on our facticity. I am responsible for everything, in fact, except for my very responsibility, for I am not the foundation of my being. Therefore everything takes place as if I were compelled to be responsible. I am *abandoned* in the world, not in the sense that I might remain abandoned and passive in a hostile universe like a board floating on the water, but rather in the sense that I find myself suddenly alone and without help, engaged in a world for which I bear the whole responsibility without being able, whatever I do, to tear myself away from this responsibility for an instant. For I am responsible for my very desire of fleeing responsibilities. To make myself passive in the world, to refuse to act upon things and upon Others is still to choose myself, and suicide is one mode among others of being-in-the-world. Yet I find an absolute responsibility for the fact that my facticity (here the fact of my birth) is directly inapprehensible and even inconceivable, for this fact of my birth never appears as a brute fact but always across a projective reconstruction of my for-itself. I am ashamed of being born or I am astonished at it or I rejoice over it, or in attempting to get rid of my life I affirm that I live and I assume this life as bad. Thus in a certain sense I *choose* being born. This choice itself is integrally affected with facticity since I am not able not to choose, but this facticity in turn will appear only in so far as I surpass it toward my ends. Thus facticity is everywhere but inapprehensible; I never encounter anything except my responsibility. That is why I cannot ask, '*Why* was I born?' or curse the day of my birth or declare that I did not ask to be born, for these various attitudes toward my birth—i.e., toward the *fact* that I realize a presence in the world—are absolutely nothing else but ways of assuming this birth in full responsibility and of making it *mine*. Here again I encounter only myself and my projects so that finally my abandonment—i.e., my facticity—consists simply in the fact that I am condemned to be wholly responsible for myself. I am the being which *is* in such a way that in its being its being is in question. And this 'is' of my being *is* as present and inapprehensible.

Under these conditions since every event in the world can be revealed to me only as an *opportunity* (an opportunity made use of, lacked, neglected, etc.) or better yet since everything which happens to us can be considered as a *chance* (i.e., can appear to us only as a way of realizing this being which is in question in our being) and since others as transcendences-transcended are themselves only *opportunities* and *chances*, the responsibility of the for-itself extends to the entire world as a peopled-world. It is precisely thus that the for-itself apprehends itself in anguish; that is, as a being which is neither the foundation of its own being nor of the Other's being nor of the in-itselfs which form the world, but a being which is compelled to decide the meaning of being—within it and everywhere outside of it. The one who realizes in anguish his condition as *being* thrown into a responsibility which extends to his very abandonment has no longer either remorse or regret or excuse; he is no longer anything but a freedom which perfectly reveals itself and whose being resides in this very revelation. But as we pointed out . . . , most of the time we flee anguish in bad faith.

- How is Sartre's view of freedom similar to Kant's? How is thinking that you are free proof that in some important sense you are free?
- What does Sartre mean by in 'choosing not to choose, we are condemned to be free'?
- Do you agree with Sartre that we are always responsible insofar as everything in our life is, in effect, a free choice (including war: in war, 'there are no innocent victims')?

Though expressed with pith and vigour, Sartre's views about freedom and bad faith are frequently misunderstood, even caricatured. To help us grasp what Sartre is really saying, we need some help and guidance from an expert. In our next reading, written for this text, Canadian philosopher Alia Al-Saji provides us with just that.

'Sartrean Freedom and Bad Faith: Social Identities and Situations'
By Alia Al-Saji

In *Being and Nothingness*, Sartre's concept of 'freedom' can be understood to ground 'bad faith' in three ways: Freedom is the condition of possibility, the motivation, and the means for bad faith. To understand these connections, we must first understand Sartre's conception of consciousness. As 'for-itself', consciousness is activity and freedom; more precisely, it is intentionality (in the phenomenological sense).[6] Sartre understands this activity oppositionally in terms of what he calls 'nihilation'.[7] Consciousness, as 'nihilating activity', both constitutes the sense of its objects and makes them objects— that is, objects are constituted as 'other to' consciousness. More so, consciousness has this nihilating relation not only to objects in the world, but also to its own past, its body and its situation. Since this relation is one of non-identity, consciousness is emptied of any substantive content. Nihilation is the foundation of freedom for Sartre;[8] we are free to the extent that we are 'nihilating activity', or 'nothingness'.[9]

It is from this basis that Sartre approaches the question of the being of consciousness in relation to bad faith—'[w]hat must be the being of man [sic] if he is to be capable of bad faith?'[10] This question points to the structure of consciousness as for-itself or freedom, an active becoming or 'nothingness' that Sartre's paradoxical formula for consciousness renders as 'a being which is what it is not and which is not what it is'.[11] It is this perpetual activity, at once becoming and disintegrating, that consciousness attempts to escape in bad faith. Moreover, this attempt at escape is only possible if consciousness is not a thing but a freedom. Thus freedom proves to be both *the condition of possibility* and *the motivation for bad faith*. This does not imply that bad faith is necessary, but that it is a project that takes its point of departure from freedom as ground in order to negate that very ground.[12] This also shows freedom to be *the means for bad faith*: Bad faith adopts the very nihilating operation that defines the freedom of consciousness and directs that negation towards the activity of consciousness itself. Such self-nihilation attempts to freeze the activity of consciousness, to reify or deny it, in a project of escape.

Yet we may find a deeper connection between freedom and bad faith in Sartre's philosophy: Sartre's diagnosis of bad faith as a phenomenon of escape follows from the absolute nature of freedom in his account.[13] For Sartre, one of the principal modalities of bad faith occurs when consciousness attempts to be *something* 'in-itself' and unqualifiedly, thus attempting to escape its own freedom (along with the responsibility that is the other side of this freedom) in a project of avoidance.[14] But what makes the contamination of the for-itself with an in-itself—the appearance of consciousness to itself *as something*—a phenomenon of 'bad' faith? The conception of consciousness as pure emptiness (or absolute freedom) seems to imply that the attribution of definite qualities to consciousness goes against its very nature. Were consciousness to be understood as already incorporating a dimension of passivity, this diagnosis of bad faith may not apply.

Sartre does, of course, acknowledge the 'facticity', or givenness, of freedom.[15] Freedom cannot even be described as an essence, since that would make freedom the foundation of its own being and imply that we might be free not to be free.[16] Freedom is rather coextensive with the nihilating structure of consciousness; to exist as consciousness is to be free. But it is precisely in this sense that there can be no external limits to freedom.[17] Although it does not form its own foundation, *freedom is the ground by which all the rest receives meaning*. Hence one's body, past, place, surroundings, situation, and world take on meaning through one's free project—through the choice of a particular way of being in the world. Consciousness does not create the situation in which it finds itself, but it does constitute the meaning of that situation (including the sense of the situation as obstacle or aid), by choosing itself as a particular manner of living that situation.[18] It is then 'our freedom which constitutes the limits which it will subsequently encounter'.[19]

Is there passivity to this absolute and free subjectivity? This question is not meant to appeal to determinism but to ask after the real limitations on consciousness that arise in social and historical situations. Specifically, Sartre's theory of freedom seems to evacuate the ambiguity between acting and undergoing that characterizes our lived experiences.[20] It is this lived mixture of activity and passivity that the dualism of the Sartrean ontology of for-itself and in-itself artificially disentangles. There is no doubt that Sartre's philosophy can accommodate the phenomenon of undergoing, or suffering, but, to paraphrase Sartre, *at what cost*? On Sartre's account, to undergo an emotion, for example, is to actively constitute oneself as suffering that emotion; consciousness makes itself emotional while hiding that constitutive activity from itself.[21] Even though Sartre is clear that this act is neither voluntary nor reflective, being rather pre-reflective, the meaning-making activity of consciousness remains absolute. Though consciousness has motivations for Sartre, it must be understood to have constituted the meaning and value of those motives through its actions, rather than to have endured their effects.[22] On this model, subjectivity appears as the absolute source of meaning. While Sartre insists that subjectivity must exist 'in situation', the meaning of the situation reflects the attitude and comportment that the subject adopts toward it. The situation is made meaningful through our choice; it does not weigh on the form that this choice takes. The movement of meaning-bestowal is, it seems, an asymmetrical one, a movement that issues solely from the subject.

This account of freedom becomes troubling in considerations of social identity and the social-historical situatedness of subjects—a situatedness that would seem to mitigate the freedom of those subjects. In particular, when dimensions of race, gender, class, and sexuality are taken into account, subjectivity appears to be constituted along lines of meaning that it does not always choose but that belong to social structures that undergird individual expression. Sartre gives several examples of social identities, including the woman on a date who denies her status as object of desire for the male gaze,[23] the homosexual man who attempts to escape classification by his friend,[24] and the Jewish man who recovers his 'being-a-Jew' as an identity by assuming what he is in the eyes of anti-Semites.[25] Is social identity the free assumption and responsibility of a consciousness? Can such identities be assimilated to instances where consciousness reifies itself, attempting to escape its freedom by adopting the mantel of the 'in-itself'? The naturalization of absolute freedom to subjectivity makes experiences of limitation, passivity, and oppression appear as phenomena of hidden or forgotten freedom, of avoidance and 'bad faith'. This constructs subjects as equally free in all situations,[26] so that

oppressed subjects come to bear, at least in part, the responsibility of their oppressive situations.[27] Sartre's radical anti-essentialism may lead us to assume that all identities are essentializing and objectifying, cases of bad faith. Though this is certainly the case when consciousness takes itself to be *something unqualifiedly*, a more nuanced reading of the question of social identity is possible.[28]

An alternative, and more generous, reading is made possible by focussing on (1) the different modalities of bad faith and (2) the complex structure of freedom in situation. In this regard, the concepts of freedom and bad faith become central to understanding the nuanced ways in which Sartre attempts to broach the question of identity—in particular, how subjects take up, while differing from, their social positions and situations, their socially and historically defined identities.

We can be in bad faith in two ways according to Sartre.[29] The first way, the one that we have discussed so far, is to identify with the in-itself unqualifiedly—to attempt to make oneself *something* so as to escape the perpetual becoming and freedom that is consciousness. Sartre illustrates this type of bad faith with an example of a waiter in a café who plays at being a waiter, and nothing but a waiter, reducing his movements to stereotyped mechanisms in order to coincide with the social image that corresponds to his function.[30] This form of bad faith can be directed towards others as well, as Sartre demonstrates with his example of the 'champion of sincerity' who asks of his friend to declare himself a homosexual, as if that identity were an essence and being-homosexual a thing.[31] The second way that we can be in bad faith is exemplified by the homosexual man's reaction in Sartre's example. This man refuses the label 'homosexual', not merely in the sense in which he recognizes that he is not a thing, but in the categorical sense of rejecting any relation to the social identity, situated though it may be, of homosexuality.[32] In so doing, he cuts himself off from his facticity and his situation—refusing to assume it or give it meaning—positing himself as pure transcendence or freedom. But this transcendence is without concrete form; it is an abstract freedom without insertion in the world. It is a freedom that refuses to take responsibility for the meaning it produces in the world (meaning that even an attitude of denial will inevitably produce). This form of bad faith forgets that freedom is grounded in

(Continued)

a nihilating and meaning-making relation to the in-itself, and is hence always situated freedom.

Heterosexist as his example may seem, Sartre is attempting to portray the difficulty for homosexuals in negotiating the bigoted social regard of a homophobic society. The homosexual man, Sartre notes, 'must constantly put himself beyond reach in order to avoid the terrible judgment of collectivity'.[33] Given this recognition of oppressive social conditions, we could ask whether Sartre's philosophy allows for a relation to social identity that negotiates these conditions without bad faith. The duality in bad faith already hints at a response. The Sartrean concept of bad faith designates two disproportionate attitudes with respect to social identity—two ways in which the relation of consciousness to its situation can be distorted. On the one hand, the unqualified identification with the in-itself—with one's body, past, place, social position, or situation—is an attempt to reify consciousness, to make it a thing. On the other hand, the refusal of any relation to the in-itself tries to deny the situated character of consciousness and the need to deal with the situation one finds oneself in. So, to designate these two attitudes as bad faith is not to reject social identities altogether but to call for a more nuanced, fluid, and lived understanding of identity-formation.

Sartre is certainly critical of the objectified and static forms of identity that stem from social histories of oppression—racialized,[34] stereotyped, or reified identities that are naturalized to particular groups as part of the justification for their oppression.[35] However, the response to such social constructions cannot be mere avoidance: We cannot pretend to live in a colour-blind, gender-neutral, non-heterosexist, individualist world. As subjects, we exist in an inter-subjective world in which certain social identities define for each of us a situation. Sartre's insight is that we are free to take up, and give meaning to, these identities in different ways, but we are not free not to reckon with them. All that I can do is to recognize that I *must assume* my social situation, and in this sense am responsible for it, but that I *remain free in the manner* in which I relate to it—affirmatively, indifferently, oppositionally, resistantly, hesitatingly, and so on.[36] There can be no coincidence with social identity on this model of subjectivity, but neither can social constructs, the ways in which others see and label us, be shed like clothes. To assume oneself as a pattern of conduct, a past, a member of a social group, part of a history of oppression or revolt, is not to be locked into that past or that identity as in a prison, but to already nihilate and give meaning to that conduct, that past, and that identity in one's manner of assuming it—that is, through its place in one's present activity or project.[37]

Thus Sartrean freedom, though absolute, is not abstract. Freedom is not an escape from situation. Rather, as Sartre notes, 'there is freedom only in a *situation*, and there is a situation only through freedom'.[38] Since consciousness must be a nihilating relation to the in-itself (whether that be its body, past, surroundings, social position, or situation), freedom cannot arise in isolation or abstraction; rather, 'freedom is originally *a relation to the given*'.[39] But as freedom is not the foundation of its own existence, since it does not choose itself as free, neither can it choose the conditions wherein it exists. The contingency of our situation mirrors the facticity of our freedom for Sartre; the fact that we are 'condemned to be free' also means that consciousness has to arise as a being in the midst of the world, in a contingent situation not of its own making.[40] The remarkable consequence of this contingent freedom is that consciousness is confronted with the need to make sense of a situation that it did not create. Situation, then, does not imply an external limitation on freedom but an open exigency to meaning. Since freedom is fundamentally relational, since it is 'being-in-situation', consciousness *must* assume the situation in which it finds itself, at once giving it meaning and making that situation its own (whether in an appropriative or critical attitude).[41] Sartrean freedom is therefore a peculiar kind of choice: You do not *create* the situation in which you must be free, but you *constitute* its meaning by 'choosing' yourself—not in your 'being' but in your 'manner of being', by choosing how you act and live any given situation.[42] It is in this sense of authorship of meaning that we can understand Sartrean responsibility as responsibility not only for oneself but also for one's world.[43]

To illustrate this point, Sartre employs an example of a cliff. Only if your project is to scale this cliff, will the cliff appear to be 'unscalable'; yet the cliff would appear in a different light if you were, for example, set on a project of aesthetic appreciation.[44] Thus the meaning of the situation reflects back to consciousness its freedom, the particular manner it has of 'being-in-the-world'.[45] It is in terms of that freedom, in light of the project that consciousness chooses to be, that the situation appears with a particular 'coefficient of adversity'.[46] This means that although your freedom cannot determine whether the cliff will lend itself to scaling, the resistance of the cliff to scaling and the role it plays as an obstacle or aid to climbing cannot be separated from your project of scaling. This points, for Sartre, to the *ambiguity of situation*—a 'phenomenon in which it is impossible for the for-itself to distinguish the contribution of freedom from that of the brute existent'.[47]

We may now ask whether this reference to ambiguity and to a 'coefficient of adversity' constitutes a recognition of the passivity and limitations of consciousness. That Sartre attributes ambiguity to the structure of situation, rather than to freedom, is telling, for it allows consciousness to remain the clear source of meaning. What the ambiguity of situation means is that the part of situation which owes to the given, to the in-itself, is finally inapprehensible. We have access to the in-itself only as meaning, as constituted by consciousness. Moreover, the in-itself does not contribute to this meaning; it does not motivate or call for a particular sense (since this would require that the in-itself determine or demand a particular conduct from consciousness, a dependency that Sartre's picture of consciousness cannot admit). Even when consciousness is confronted with limits, it is only in view of a particular end posited as a free project of consciousness that these limits are constituted as limits. Limitation, resistance, and passivity are hence experiential structures that are constituted as a function of the free activity of consciousness, not of the brute existent as such. Indeed, in his example of the cliff, Sartre notes that '[t]he rock will not be an obstacle if [the climber] wish[es] at any cost to arrive at the top of the mountain'.[48] For Sartre, it remains freedom that constitutes its own limits.[49] The autonomy of consciousness in meaning-making is paramount.

But there would seem to be situations where consciousness confronts real limitations that are not of its own making—specifically, situations where the meaning of the limit is already constituted by others. Such are the social identities discussed above. These identities seem to provide consciousness with limitations that arise not in virtue of the project that consciousness chooses but of its situatedness in a social world. How does Sartre account for such phenomena? He addresses these experiences as part of the 'being-for-others' dimension of consciousness. When I am confronted with another freedom in the world, another consciousness that confers meaning upon me, I experience a certain alienation of my being; I suffer the identity that the other constitutes for me as something that I have not chosen to be.[50] Sartre calls such an identity 'unrealizable'.[51] It is unrealizable in three senses. First, this identity is constituted not by my consciousness but through another freedom, a consciousness that I cannot capture and with which I cannot coincide; in this sense, the identity remains external to me. But, second, this identity can only be given through others, for it involves the constitution of my freedom and my situation as *objects*; it is this objectification that makes me appear as an existent in the world with external or 'objective' features and limits.[52] Third, since this identity is an *object*, an in-itself, which consciousness cannot *be*, it can only be given as *unrealizable for my consciousness*.[53]

Through the freedom of others, we therefore find 'a *real* limit to our freedom'.[54] This limit, however, cannot be encountered unless it is assumed by consciousness—and even then it remains un-*real*-izable, that is, it is not given as a *real* limit.[55] To be experienced as 'unrealizable' requires that identities 'must be revealed in the light of some project aiming at realizing them'.[56] Sartre's theory remains consistent here: Meaning cannot be passively received, but must be freely assumed by consciousness that, in choosing itself as a manner of being, constitutes that meaning relative to its choice. In the case of social identities, it is by freely recognizing the freedom of others that you assume your being-for-others and hence choose yourself in an intersubjective world where another's freedom is limiting for you; in so doing, you choose your own passivity.[57] The exteriority and limitation that social identities present are finally experienced only if one recovers them—indeed, interiorizes them—as part of one's project.[58] The difficulty of Sartre's account is reflected in his example of the Jewish man who recovers the identity of 'being-a-Jew' by taking up what he is in the eyes of anti-Semites. Sartre notes that 'it is his pride of being a Jew, his shame, or his indifference which will reveal to him his being-a-Jew; *and this being-a-Jew is nothing outside the free manner of adopting it*'.[59] On the one hand, Sartre is clearly right that Jewish identity is more than the definition anti-Semitism gives it; he is also right that this identity is altered in the multitude

(Continued)

ways in which it is lived and taken up. On the other hand, can this identity be so *freely* assumed and interpreted given the social-historical situation?[60] More precisely, is it the case that, if one is a Jew, one is *equally free* (in a project of denial, or Sartrean bad faith) to ignore this identity by 'consider[ing] the anti-Semites as pure *objects*'?[61]

This brings us to the crux of the difficulty with Sartrean freedom in *Being and Nothingness*: Although freedom must arise in situation, it remains free consciousness with respect to that situation. It is freedom that constitutes the meaning of its situation by choosing itself as a particular manner of being in that situation. But this manner of being cannot be understood to have been really motivated by the situation. Situation, in other words, does not weigh on, or limit, the choices that freedom makes. Situation is presented as material to which consciousness must give form; there is an exigency to make sense of the situation, but no limitation on what form that meaning can take. This means that consciousness is not internally affected or formed by its situation.[62] And it is in this sense that situations are understood to be equal for Sartre (so that the slave is as free as the master). What is elided is the way in which oppression not only structures a situation with a pregiven social meaning but also affects the meaning-making activity of subjectivity itself. Other existentialist thinkers have noted in response to Sartre that oppression can mutilate and fragment the freedom of consciousness, its ability to produce meaning in the world.[63] This recognition of the formative power of situations goes beyond the Sartrean theory of freedom to acknowledge a social dimension constitutive of, not only constituted by, consciousness, a passivity that intermingles with its activity.

> • What is 'bad faith'? What are some ways in which you can be in bad faith?

Sartre's very strong sense of responsibility goes even so far as to ascribe an act of choice to those situations in which we seem clearly to be only victims, for example, in war. 'There are no accidents in life,' he argues. It is always the individual's choice as to how he or she will deal with a situation. One can always complain, 'I didn't ask to be born,' Sartre says, but this is only an attempt to avoid responsibility. Given the fact that we have been born, raised in certain conditions, and so forth, it is now entirely up to us as to what we shall make of all this. Instead of looking at the events of the world as problems and intrusions, Sartre ultimately says, we should learn to look at everything as an opportunity. Here is the optimistic note to his very strong defence of human freedom.

What all of these arguments demand is the following: In making a decision, you can never appeal to determinism, even if determinism is true. Whatever might be theoretically determined, in practice, you must choose. Since freedom is the key to our self-esteem and our pride in ourselves, some people will demand it at any cost.

The most brilliant, if bizarre, example of this existentialist demand is formulated by a strange character in Dostoyevsky's short novel *Notes from the Underground*. The argument is simple. Any prediction can be thwarted as long as you know about it. If they say, 'you'll do *x*'; do *y*. Now, suppose that determinism is true. In particular, suppose that psychological determinism is true and that its basic law is this: 'People always act to their own advantage.' Now, what does this have to do with the predictability of a person's actions? Absolutely nothing, if you are sufficiently determined not to be predictable. Accordingly, the character in this novel is, more than anything else, spiteful. His main concern is to avoid being predictable, to prove his freedom even if it means making himself miserable. Now you might say that his spite itself is the determinant of his behaviour, and of course it is. But the very point of the argument is that causes and explanations of any kind are simply beside the point. Let the underground man know what you expect him to do, and he'll do precisely the opposite. If you predict he'll act spiteful, he'll be as agreeable as can be—just out of spite!

From 'The Most Advantageous Advantage'
By Fyodor Dostoyevsky

I am a sick man . . . I am a spiteful man. I am an unpleasant man. I think my liver is diseased. However, I don't know beans about my disease, and I am not sure what is bothering me. I don't treat it and never have, though I respect medicine and doctors. Besides, I am extremely superstitious, let's say sufficiently so to respect medicine. (I am educated enough not to be superstitious, but I am.) No, I refuse to treat it out of spite. You probably will not understand that. Well, but *I* understand it.

* * *

Why, in the first place, when in all these thousands of years has there ever been a time when man has acted only for his own advantage? What is to be done with the millions of facts that bear witness that men, *knowingly*, that is, fully understanding their real advantages, have left them in the background and have rushed headlong on another path, to risk, to chance, compelled to this course by nobody and by nothing, but, as it were, precisely because they did not want the beaten track, and stubbornly, wilfully, went off on another difficult, absurd way seeking it almost in the darkness. After all, it means that this stubbornness and wilfulness were more pleasant to them than any advantage. Advantage! What is advantage? And will you take it upon yourself to define with perfect accuracy in exactly what the advantage of man consists of? And what if it so happens that a man's advantage *sometimes* not only may, but even must, consist exactly in his desiring under certain conditions what is harmful to himself and not what is advantageous. And if so, if there can be such a condition then the whole principle becomes worthless.

* * *

The fact is, gentlemen, it seems that something that is dearer to almost every man than his greatest advantages must really exist, or (not to be illogical) there is one most advantageous advantage (the very one omitted of which we spoke just now) which is more important and more advantageous than all other advantages, for which, if necessary, a man is ready to act in opposition to all laws, that is, in opposition to reason, honour, peace, prosperity—in short, in opposition to all those wonderful and useful things if only he can attain that fundamental, most advantageous advantage which is dearer to him than all.

What is that 'advantageous advantage'? Nothing other than

One's own free unfettered choice, one's own fancy, however wild it may be, one's own fancy worked up at times to frenzy. That is the 'most advantageous advantage', which is always overlooked.

> • To what extent is it possible to choose otherwise or 'to negate' certain facts about yourself? Could you choose to be taller, better looking, or more intelligent? How would Sartre or Dostoyevsky reply?

Freedom in other words, is itself what we most demand, whatever the cost, whatever the difficulties, and whatever the arguments against it. Whatever else may be true, we will refuse to see ourselves as anything but free. For it is freedom that makes us human.

C. One Self? Any Self? Questioning the Concept of Personal 'Essence'

So far, we have talked as if your self is something singular, a unified set of ideals and characteristics according to which you identify yourself. But should we think of the 'self' in this way?

According to Robert Louis Stevenson in his classic tale *The Strange Case of Dr Jekyll and Mr Hyde*, the answer is no. At the end of the novel, Stevenson's guilt-ridden narrator writes of a shocking discovery he has made—a discovery about the very nature of human identity and selfhood:

From *The Strange Case of Dr Jekyll and Mr Hyde*
By Robert Louis Stevenson

Man is not truly one, but truly two. I say two, because the state of my own knowledge does not pass beyond that point.

With every day, and from both sides of my intelligence, the moral and the intellectual, I thus drew steadily nearer to that truth by whose partial discovery I have been doomed to such a dreadful shipwreck: that man is not truly one, but truly two. I say two, because the state of my own knowledge does not pass beyond that point. Others will follow, others will outstrip me on the same lines; and I hazard the guess that man will be ultimately known for a mere polity of multifarious, incongruous, and independent denizens. I, for my part, from the nature of my life, advanced infallibly in one direction, and in one direction only. It was on the moral side, and in my own person, that I learned to recognize the thorough and primitive duality of man; I saw that, of the two natures that contended in the field of my consciousness, even if I could rightly be said to be either, it was only because I was radically both; and from an early date, even before the course of my scientific discoveries had begun to suggest the most naked possibility of such a miracle, I had learned to dwell with pleasure, as a beloved daydream, on the thought of the separation of these elements.

Why does Stevenson's tormented narrator deny that the self is a unity, or a thing existing in its own right? Not (as in Hume) because he thinks that there is no self, but because he is persuaded that the self is *plural* or *multiple*. The self is not one, we are now told, because it is many; not one, because it is more—not less—than one. Each of us, according to this view, has *at least* two identities; so what we call 'a person' is not an integrated and harmonious whole, but an unruly school of contrary selves—'a mere polity of multifarious, incongruous, and independent denizens'.

> • How is what Stevenson describes—the lack of unity within a person—reminiscent of Freud's model of the mind? (See Chapter 4, pp. 313–14, for a discussion of Freud's theories.) Do you see any differences?

Suppose each of us is 'not truly one, but truly two', as Stevenson says. What can we do about this? How are we to cope with the experience of being fragmented and divided, with our refined consciences pulling us in one direction while our wild desires pull us in another? If each of us is not one self, but many; if integrity is an impossibility; if the metaphysical and moral unity of a person is the stuff of myth—if all of this is true, you may ask, then, *how am I to live*? Confronted with this painful and pregnant problem, Stevenson's narrator proposes a radical solution:

If each, I told myself, could but be housed in separate identities, life would be relieved of all that was unbearable; the unjust might go his way, delivered from the aspirations and remorse of his more upright twin; and the just could walk steadfastly and securely on his upward path, doing the good things in which he found his pleasure, and no longer exposed to disgrace and penitence by the hands of this extraneous evil. It was the curse of mankind that these incongruous faggots were thus bound together—that in the agonized womb of consciousness these polar twins should be continuously struggling.

> • Do you think the narrator's solution is a good one? Why or why not?

In his novel *Steppenwolf*, Hermann Hesse presents a character—Harry Haller—who, like Stevenson's narrator, is a *multiple* or *pluralistic* self, a collection of 'selves', with no one of them 'real' or 'essential'. Like many of us, Harry Haller lives with the myth of 'two selves', one human, rational, and well behaved, the other beastly, wild, and wolf-like. He is torn between the two. But, Hesse tells us, Harry's unhappiness is not, as he thinks, a result of his 'war between the selves' at all but rather the result of an oversimplified notion of self. 'The Steppenwolf is a fiction,' writes Hesse, a 'mythological simplification.' The idea of two selves is as old as the mind–body distinction, as old as the Christian division between the body and the soul—even older, in fact, dating back to Pythagoras and Plato. Hesse's argument is that this simple self is a strictly 'bourgeois convention', a middle-class argument for the simplicity and unity of the self; indeed, Harry is unhappy because of the tension and complexity of only two selves: the 'human' who has culture and cultivated thoughts and feelings and the 'wolf' who is savage and cruel, the dark world of Freud's **unconscious** instincts and raw, untamed nature.

From *Steppenwolf*
By Hermann Hesse

Suppose that Harry tried to ascertain in any single moment of his life, any single act, what part the man had in it and what part the wolf, he would find himself at once in a dilemma, and his whole beautiful wolf theory would go to pieces. For there is not a single human being . . . not even the idiot, who is so conveniently simple that his being can be explained as the sum of two or three principal elements; and to explain so complex a man as Harry by the artless division into wolf and man is a hopelessly childish attempt. Harry consists of a hundred or a thousand selves, not of two. His life oscillates, as everyone's does, not merely between two poles, such as the body and the spirit, the saint and the sinner, but between thousand and thousands.

Why is it, Hesse asks, that we all seem to have this need to think of ourselves in such deceptive terms and regard the self as a single unit? Because, he suggests, we are deluded by an analogy; since each of us has but one body, we assume that we each have a single soul. From this analogy we assume that there must be one self within each body. But it is here that Hesse contrasts our view with the views of ancient India and notes with admiration that there is no trace of such a notion in the poems of the ancient Asiatics. He then offers us his own analogy:

Man is an onion made up of a hundred integuments, a texture made up of many threads. The ancient Asiatics knew this well enough, and in the Buddhist Yoga an exact technique was devised for unmasking the illusion of the personality. The human merry-go-round sees many changes: The illusion that cost India the efforts of thousands of years to unmask is the same illusion that the West has laboured just as hard to maintain and strengthen.

> • What would it mean to have a pluralistic self or selves? Do you find this view plausible? Have you ever felt as though you were somehow a multiplicity of selves or identities?

Hesse refers to Buddhist concepts of the self with approval and enthusiasm. Although he remains entrenched in Western ideas, Hesse is already more than half way to one of the ancient Eastern conceptions of self, which is essentially a denial of the self as we are accustomed to think of it. As we've seen in Chapter 2, the Buddhist says, 'give up your self-identity', 'give up your self-consciousness', and finally, 'give up your self'. Now, just what does the Buddhist think we are giving up when we give up 'the self'? And why are we to give it up? Are there metaphysical, as well as moral, reasons for doing so?

If you are interested in learning more about these questions, you should read *The Questions of King Milinda* (or *Milinda Panha*), a classic Buddhist dialogue composed almost two thousand years ago. In its pages we meet two sharp-witted debaters: King Milinda (also known as Menander), an Indo-Greek ruler, and Nagasena, a Buddhist monk with a great reputation for wisdom.

On being introduced to Nagasena, King Milinda politely asks the monk who he is and what his name is. Nagasena, evidently not one for small talk, answers the king's conventional questions with a mind-blowing paradox.

From *The Questions of King Milinda*

And King Milinda asked him: 'How is your Reverence known, and what is your name, Sir?' 'As Nagasena I am known, O great king, and as Nagasena do my fellow religious habitually address me. But although parents give such names as Nagasena, or Surasena, or Virasena, or Sihasena, nevertheless this word 'Nagasena' is just a denomination, a designation, a conceptual term, a current appellation, a mere name. For no real person can here be apprehended.'

Yes, you read that right: Nagasena has just told King Milinda that there is no such person as Nagasena. This bizarre speech leaves King Milinda stunned and puzzled—and no wonder. After all, how would you react if tonight at dinner your roommate, let's call her Emily, solemnly informed you that there is no such person as Emily? Would you agree with her, pass her the salt, and then excuse her from paying next month's rent on metaphysical grounds? Probably not. But what would you do? Perhaps you would object to the statement as King Milinda does:

But King Milinda explained: 'Now listen, you 500 Greeks and 80,000 monks, this Nagasena tells me that he is not a real person! How can I be expected to agree with that!'

So is the poor monk out of his mind, or is he just pulling Milinda's regal leg? Neither. Nagasena is not mad or mischievous, but he is a philosopher, and as such, he is prepared to defend his thesis with a thought-provoking argument. That argument begins with what initially seems an irrelevant question posed by Nagasena: How did you travel here today, King Milinda?

Thereupon the Venerable Nagasena said to King Milinda: 'As a king you have been brought up in great refinement and you avoid roughness of any kind. If you would walk at midday on this hot, burning, and sandy ground, then your feet would have to tread on the rough and gritty gravel and pebbles, and they would hurt you, your body would get tired, your mind impaired, and your awareness of your body would be associated with pain. How then did you come—on foot, or on a mount?' 'I did not come, Sir, on foot, but on a chariot.'

It is at this point that Nagasena gets down to business. King Milinda, he says, do you grant that there are chariots? Yes? Very well. But what, exactly, *is* a chariot? Answering this childish-sounding question is much harder than it seems, as the king soon learns:

'If you have come on a chariot, then please explain to me what a chariot is. Is the pole the chariot?'—'No, reverend Sir!'—'Is then the axle the chariot?'—'No, reverend Sir!'—'Is it then the wheels, or the framework, or the flag-staff, or the yoke, or the reins, or the goad-stick?'—'No, reverend Sir!'—'Then is it the combination of pole, axle, wheels, framework, flagstaff, yoke, reins, and goad which is the "chariot"?'—'No, reverend Sir!'—'Then is this "chariot" outside the combination of pole, axle, wheels, framework, flagstaff, yoke, reins, and goad?'—'No, reverend Sir!'—'Then, ask as I may, I can discover no chariot at all. Just a mere sound is this "chariot". But what is the real chariot? Your Majesty has told a lie, has spoken a falsehood! There really is no chariot! Your Majesty is the greatest king in the whole of India. Of whom then are you afraid, that you do not speak the truth?' And he exclaimed: 'Now listen, you 500 Greeks and 80,000 monks, this king Milinda tells me that he has come on a chariot. But when asked to explain to me what a chariot is, he cannot establish its existence. How can one possibly approve of that?'

The 500 Greeks thereupon applauded the Venerable Nagasena and said to king Milinda: 'Now let your Majesty get out of that if you can!'

Faced with Nagasena's polite but persistent request—'[P]lease explain to me what a chariot is'—many of us, falling back on common sense, might be tempted to reply that a chariot is a thing with various attributes or parts: wheels, axle, pole, yoke, framework, flag-post, reins, and so forth. Is this a good answer? No, because it sidesteps a basic metaphysical question: How is the chariot *related* to all the parts we have just mentioned? Are we to think of 'the chariot' as something over and above those parts—as a thing in its own right, distinct from the pole, the axle, the wheels, and all the rest? Surely not. If we took away each and every one of these parts—gradually subtracting wheels, axle, pole, yoke, framework, flag-post, reins, and so on—in the end there would be absolutely nothing left over (and hence no 'chariot'). So if by 'chariot' we mean a *substance*—that is, a thing existing in its own right, independently of its various attributes—then there is no such thing as a chariot. And this is what Nagasena tells Milinda: 'I can discover no chariot at all.'

Yet King Milinda has sworn that there are such things as chariots, including the chariot that has brought him to see Nagasena. So was the king mistaken? Has he spoken a falsehood? Listen carefully to how Milinda defends himself:

'I have not, Nagasena, spoken a falsehood. For it is in dependence on the pole, the axle, the wheels, the framework, the flagstaff, etc., that there takes place this denomination 'chariot', this designation, this conceptual term, a current appellation and a mere name'.

And here is Nagasena's triumphant conclusion, in which things finally come full circle:

'Your Majesty has spoken well about the chariot. It is just so with me. In dependence on the thirty-two parts of the body and the five skandhas there takes place this denomination 'Nagasena', this designation, this conceptual term, a current appellation and a mere name. In ultimate reality, however, this person cannot be apprehended. And this has been said by our Sister Vajira when she was face to face with the Lord:

Where all constituent parts are present,
The word 'a chariot' is applied.
So likewise where the skandhas are,
The term a 'being' commonly is used.

Nagasena's point? As it is with 'chariot', so it is with 'person'. Like 'chariot', 'person' refers not to a substance—there are no substances in the Buddhist scheme—but simply to a set of attributes that we can directly apprehend or know. In the case of a chariot, those attributes are the axle, the wheels, the poles, the yoke, the reins, the flag-post, and so forth. In the case of a person, those attributes are transient phenomena known to Buddhist as 'the five skandhas': 'forms, feelings, perceptions, impulses, and consciousness'. So if a person is nothing more than a bundle of ever-changing attributes, then there is nothing to him over and above those attributes; and if there is nothing to him over and above those ever-changing attributes, then there is nothing to which a name such as 'Nagasena' can correspond or refer. There is no fixed 'I', no substantial soul, no rock-solid self, no enduring ego, no static core of being hidden beneath the flimsy wrapping of phenomenal fact.

Understood as the conclusion of this argument, Nagasena's original claim—'[T]his word "Nagasena" is . . . a mere name. For no real person can be here apprehended'—no longer seems so absurd. Indeed, even King Milinda is now beginning to see the light:

'It is wonderful, Nagasena, it is astonishing, Nagasena! Most brilliantly have these questions been answered! Were the Buddha himself here, he would approve what you have said. Well spoken, Nagasena, well spoken!'

Eastern religions have long criticized the notion of the unified 'self'. Of course, they admit that people have 'personalities' and 'egos' in some sense; most people most of the time think of 'themselves'. Some Eastern religions claim, however, that this vision of 'ourselves' is a false image. It is just an illusion that one accepts out of moral weakness or backwardness. Thus, in these religions, the multiple self or the non-self is an ideal understanding that can be achieved only with enlightenment.

An early Buddhist work, *The Dhammapada* (*c.* 250 BCE), contains several passages about this ideal.

From *The Dhammapada*

Chapter XII Self

Let each man first direct himself to what is proper, then let him teach others; thus a wise man will not suffer.

If a man make himself as he teaches others to be, then, being himself well-subdued, he may subdue others; for one's own self is difficult to subdue.

Self is the lord of self, who else could be the lord? With self well-subdued, a man finds a lord such as few can find.

The evil done by one's self, born of one's self, begotten by one's self, crushes the foolish, as a diamond breaks even a precious stone.

* * *

The foolish man who scorns the instruction of the saintly, of the elect [*ariya*], of the virtuous, and follows a false doctrine—he bears fruit to his own destruction, like the fruits of the *Katthaka* reed.

By one's self the evil is done, by one's self one suffers; by one's self evil is left undone; by one's self one is purified. The pure and the impure stand and fall by themselves; no one can purify another.

Let no one forget his own duty for the sake of another's, however great; let a man after he has discerned his own duty, be faithful to his duty.

All forms are unreal—he who knows and sees this is at peace though in a world of pain; this is the way that leads to purity.

* * *

Through zeal knowledge is gained, through lack of zeal knowledge is lost; let a man who knows this two-fold path of gain and loss thus place himself that knowledge may grow.

Cut down the whole forest of desires, not a tree only! Danger comes out of the forest of desires. When you have cut down both the forest of desires and its undergrowth, then, *bhikshus*, you will be rid of the forest and of desires!

* * *

Cut out the love of self, like an autumn lotus with your hand! Cherish the road to peace. *Nirvāna* has been shown by the Blessed One.

Sections of the *Dao De Jing* touch on the same theme:

From *Dao De Jing*
By Lao-zi

> *The reason I have an enemy is because I have 'self'. If I no longer had a 'self', I would no longer have an enemy.*

13

Success is as dangerous as failure,
and we are often our own worst enemy.
What does it mean that success is as dangerous as failure?
He who is superior is also someone's subordinate.
Receiving favour and loosing it both cause alarm.
That is what is meant by success is as dangerous as failure.
What does it mean that we are often our own worst enemy?
The reason I have an enemy is because I have 'self'.
If I no longer had a 'self', I would no longer have an enemy.
Love the whole world as if it were your self;
then you will truly care for all things.

22

If you want to become whole,
first let yourself become broken.
If you want to become straight,
first let yourself become twisted.
If you want to become full,
first let yourself become empty.
If you want to become new,
first let yourself become old.
For this reason the Master embraces the Dao,
as an example for the world to follow.
Because she isn't self-centred,
people can see the light in her.
Because she does not boast of herself,
she becomes a shining example.
Because she does not glorify herself,
she becomes a person of merit.

(Continued)

Because she wants nothing from the world,
the world cannot overcome her.
When the ancient Masters said,
'If you want to become whole,
then first let yourself be broken,'
they weren't using empty words.
All who do this will be made complete.

These Eastern examples are certainly not the only alternatives to the early modern European notion of the self accepted by Descartes and his philosophical descendants. Islamic, Christian, and Jewish mystics in the West as well as other Eastern traditions also offered alternatives to this conception. While we do not have space in this text to discuss all of these alternatives, you should know that the Western view of the unified self is not the only view available.[64]

- What is the Buddhist argument against belief in the self? Do you find it convincing? Why or why not?
- What do you think Buddhists would agree with in Hume's views about the self? Where might they disagree?
- What do you think we gain if we 'give up the self'? What do you think we lose?

We have now said all that we are going to say about the unity, substantiality, and identity of the self. We shall now turn to a closer examination of the concept of freedom. Simply put, the question before us is this: Are we, as selves or as persons, truly free agents? To begin our examination, we must think hard about a host of related topics—fatalism, karma, predestination, and determinism, as well as chance, causation, moral responsibility, and the very nature of agency. We will begin with fatalism and karma.

D. Fatalism and Karma

Are we cogs in the universe? Are we pawns of the fates? People have often thought so. Our tendency to believe in fate goes back to the ancient Greeks. Most of the ancient Greeks believed that our destinies were already decided for us; no matter what our actions, the outcome was settled. Today, many people believe our actions and character are the causal result of our genes and our upbringing, and perhaps also the result of unconscious fears and desires that we may never even recognize. Then too, astrology and other theories of external determination have always been popular. And we can see why they would be—the more our actions are the results of other forces and not our own doing, the less we need feel responsible for them, and the less we need worry about deciding what to do. It is already decided, and not by us.

FATALISM

The thesis that some (perhaps all) events will happen even if we try to prevent them.

The ancient Greek tragedies depend upon **fatalism**, the view that whatever a person's actions and circumstances, however free they may seem, his or her predetermined end is inevitable. The story of Oedipus, most famously recounted in Sophocles' tragedy *Oedipus the King*, is perhaps the most stirring picture of Greek determinism. Oedipus and his wife, Iocasta, both scoffed at the prophets and made efforts to avoid their prophesied destinies:

From *Oedipus the King*
By Sophocles

OEDIPUS: I went to Delphi. Phoebus . . . declared
A thing most horrible: he foretold that I
Should mate with my own mother, and beget
A brood that men would shudder to behold,
And that I was to be the murderer
Of my own father.
Therefore, back to Corinth
I never went—the stars alone have told me
Where Corinth lies—that I might never see
Cruel fulfillment of that oracle.

IOCASTA: Listen to me
And you will hear the prophetic art
Touches our human fortunes not at all.
I soon can give you proof.—An oracle
Once came to [my husband] . . .
His fate it was, that he should have a son
By me, that son would take his father's life.
But he was killed—or so they said—by
Strangers.
By brigands, at a place where three ways meet.
As for the child, it was not three days old
When [my husband] fastened both its feet together
And had it cast off a precipice.
Therefore Apollo failed . . .
So much for what prophetic voices have uttered.

Unbeknown to either of them, of course, the 'brigand' who killed Iocasta's husband was Oedipus himself, Iocasta's son, saved as a baby from the precipice and adopted by the man he had thought was his father, from whom he had fled. Thus, both their destinies had been fulfilled. Neither had any control over—nor even knowledge of—what happened to them, and so neither acted freely at all. Thus, the Chorus of observers declares:

I pray that I might pass my life in reverent holiness of word and deed
For there are laws enthroned above,
Heaven created them,
Olympus was their father,
And mortal men had no part in their birth.

How should we deal with our fate? Should we try to know it? Iocasta advocates that 'ignorance is bliss', and tries hard throughout the play not to acknowledge her growing suspicions. If we can't do anything about our fate, she reasons, then we shouldn't even think about it. But Oedipus insists on finding out the truth, and as a whole the play seems to advocate facing the fact of our destinies.

IOCASTA: Why should we fear, seeing that man is ruled
By chance, and there is room for no clear forethought?
No: live at random, live as best one can. . . .
Whoever thinks
The least of this, he lives most comfortably.
OEDIPUS: Alas! you generations of men!
Even while you live you are next to nothing!
Has any man won for himself
More than the shadow of happiness? . . .
Time sees all, and Time, in your despite
Disclosed and punished your unnatural marriage
CREON:[65] Seek not to have your way in all things.
Where you had your way before,
Your mastery broke before the end.

The anthropomorphic Greek gods were integral to the ancient Greek notion of 'fate'. Human choices were considered impotent to change one's fate, because human beings were thought to be at the mercy of the gods' whims. But another conception of fate, the Buddhist conception, sees human choices as tremendously important—not because they are free, but precisely the opposite. In Buddhism, all human choices are gestures of *attachment* to the physical world, each one binding its maker more and more to a difficult fate. The effects of a person's choices, as we have seen in Chapter 2, are called his or her *karma*, which the individual can only escape by paying the long-term debt that he or she has built up. Thus, there is a concept of freedom here, called *Nirvāna*, but it is not a freedom of the self or the individual. In fact, it is a freedom *from* the self and the individual, achieved only when there is no longer a self at all. It is our foolish attachment to this world, the Buddhist claims, that fosters the illusion that we are individuals at all. In a sense then, our fate is entirely determined; yet ironically, if we submit ourselves to fate and accept its authority, if we can stop making choices that further delude us into believing we are free, then and only then, can we ultimately become free.

Consider the following excerpt from a contemporary Japanese philosopher, Keiji Nishitani, who has written extensively on the Buddhist concept of 'nothingness' and the Western concept of 'nihilism', which he says has now infected Japan.

On Fate
By Keiji Nishitani

Karma is freedom determined by causal necessity within the whole infinite nexus, a freedom of spontaneity in 'attachment' and, therefore, a freedom totally bound by fate.

From that viewpoint [the standpoint of nothingness] the world of karma is a world where each individual is determined by its ties and causal kinship within an endless world nexus, and yet each instance of individual existence and behaviour, as well as each moment of their time, arises as something totally new, possessed of freedom and creativity.

Although the ebb and flow of the total nexus 'since time past without beginning' is conceived as an infinite chain of causal necessity, its having no beginning implies, conversely, a *before* previous to any and all conceivable pasts. For such time to have no end means that it has an *after* that is future even to the most remote of possible futures. Any such before and after (beyond any definite before and after) lies in the present of every man and makes the present into free and creative activity.

* * *

The karmic deeds that make manifest this restless, incessant becoming always return thereby at the same time to the home-ground of karma, to the home-ground of the present. In other words, doing opens itself up on each occasion to the openness of nihility and thus preserves the dimension of ecstatic transcendence.

This means that the self is at all times itself. Even as in my karma I constantly constitute my existence as a becoming *qua* being, in the home-ground of that karma I am ever in my own home-ground: I am always myself. This is why restless, incessant becoming within time is at all times *my* existence. Karma is at all times *my* karma. And this means that it is free karma, that it implies an ecstatic transcendence to nihility.

Of course, although we call it freedom or creativity, it is not at this point true freedom or creativity. Freedom here is one with an inner necessity compelling us constantly to be doing something. It is in unison with that infinite drive and that infinite drive in turn is in unison with freedom. To be within the limitless world-nexus ceaselessly relating to something or other, and to be conditioned and determined in these relations by the world-nexus, is, seen from the other side, a self-determination. While the present karma is here the free work of the self, it appears at the same time to be possessed of the character of fate. Fate arises to awareness in unison with that freedom. Here the present karma reaches awareness under its form of infinity as infinite drive, in its 'willful' essence.

The self's relation with something, seen as a self-determination, is the self's exercise of free will. Of its own accord, the self accepts a thing as good or rejects it as bad. But insofar as it is determined through causal kinship within the total nexus, this free will is a fate, a causal necessity, without thereby ceasing to be free will. To accept or reject something implies a simultaneous 'attachment' to it. The karma that relates to something by lusting after it is at once voluntary and compulsory. The being of the self that comes about in that karma is at once a freedom and a burden. Here spontaneity becomes a burden and a debt.

* * *

All of this indicates how deeply rooted self-centredness is. So deeply underground do the roots of the self extend that no karmic activity can ever reach them. The karma of the self at all times returns to its own home-ground, namely, to the self itself, but it cannot get back to the home-ground of the self as such. Karma can do no more than go back to its own home-ground in the self and there reinstate its debt-laden existence. In karma, the self is constantly oriented inward to the home-ground of the self; and yet the only thing it achieves by this is the constant reconstitution of being *qua* becoming in a time without beginning or end. To transit endlessly through time in search of the home-ground of the self is the true form of our karma, that is, of our being in time, our life.

The karma of 'time past without beginning' is the true form of our life. It implies a sense of essential 'despair'. Karma is what Kierkegaard calls the 'sickness unto death'. Its despair rises to awareness from directly underfoot of the work of our present deed, word, and thought, from the fountainhead of time without beginning or end, and of being within that time, in short from our self-centredness. We can see an awareness of that despair also underlying the confession of the Buddhist *Verse of Repentance*, which suggests that every sort of karma stemming from the body, mouth, and mind of the self is grounded in a greed, anger, and folly without beginning.

* * *

Karma here comes to bear the marks of guilt and sin. In a certain sense, it takes on the character of original sin, namely, sin that is as equally elemental as the free work and existence of man. Karma is freedom determined by causal necessity within the whole infinite nexus, a freedom of spontaneity in 'attachment' and, therefore, a freedom totally *bound* by fate. At the same time, having reduced the whole causal nexus to its own centre, it is a freedom altogether *unbound*. In karma these two aspects of freedom and causal necessity become one. Consequently, as a freedom that derives entirely from the determining force of causal necessity, as a freedom chased out and driven away from necessity, karma binds itself in attachment to the other, while at the same time it remains an altogether unbound freedom, gathering every other into the centre of the self. This freedom is in the mode of an original sin.

> • What are the similarities and differences between the notion of fate and the notion of karma? How is the notion of luck different from both of them?

E. Predestination

Fatalism, in its Greek or Buddhist sense, is the claim that our future is determined by a play of forces beyond our understanding. But what if these forces are understood and in fact *created* by one superhuman being? **Predestination** has been the view of many theologians, according to whom our every action (and every event in the universe) is known, if not also caused in advance, by God. Predestination, like fatalism, does not depend upon any particular antecedent conditions (unless we want to say that God is an antecedent condition).

All the Western theologians have had to ponder the problem of predestination and freedom, since all the Western religions' scriptures claim that God created, or caused, everything. As we saw in Chapter 2, this is of particular concern when considering evil. There, the 'problem of evil' was described as the question of how evil could be caused by a good God. We now can see that the crux of the 'problem of evil' is the question of freedom. It would be easy to explain much evil if human beings were free—in that case, we, not an all-good God, would be the **cause** of evil. But if, as is stated in scripture, God created and caused everything, then surely, God creates our human actions, too. Humans sin—and so it seems we are back to the drawing board. How can an all-good God cause us or let us be free to sin?

The following dialogue from St Augustine summarize the problem of freedom and one Christian solution to it. God made human beings free, because He is all good, and free actions are better than unfree ones. However, since freedom allows us to sin, we are responsible for bringing evil into the world.

From *On Free Choice of the Will*
By St Augustine

1. Why Did God Give Freedom of the Will to Men, since It Is by This that Men Sin?

EVODIUS: Now, if possible, explain to me why God gave man free choice of the will since if he had not received it he would not be able to sin.

AUGUSTINE: Are you perfectly sure that God gave to man what you think ought not to have been given?

EVODIUS: As far as I seem to understand the discussion in the first book, we have freedom of will, and could not sin if we were without it.

AUGUSTINE: I, too, remember that this was made clear to us. But I just asked you whether you know that it was God who gave us that which we possess, through which it is clear that we commit sin.

EVODIUS: No one else. For we are from Him, and whether we sin or whether we do right, we earn reward or punishment from Him.

AUGUSTINE: I want to ask, as well: Do you know this clearly, or do you believe it willingly without really knowing it, because you are prompted by authority?

EVODIUS: I admit that at first I trusted authority on this point. But what can be more true than that all good proceeds from God, that everything just is good, and that it is just to punish sinners and to reward those who do right? From this it follows that through God sinners are afflicted with unhappiness, and those who do right endowed with happiness.

AUGUSTINE: I do not object, but let me ask another question: how do you know that we are from God? You did not answer that; instead, you explained that we merit punishment and reward from God.

EVODIUS: The answer to *that* question, too, is clear, if for no other reason than the fact that, as we have already agreed, God punished sins. All justice is from God, and it is not the role of justice to punish foreigners, although it is the role of goodness to bestow benefits on them. Thus it is clear that we belong to God, since He is not only most generous in bestowing benefits upon us, but also most just in punishing us. Also, we can understand that man is from God through the fact, which I proposed and you conceded, that every good is from God. For man himself, insofar as he is a man, is a good, because he can live rightly when he so wills.

AUGUSTINE: If this is so, the question that you proposed is clearly answered. If man is a good, and cannot act rightly unless he wills to do so, then he must have free will, without which he cannot act rightly. We must not believe that God gave us free will so that we might sin, just because sin is committed through free will. It is sufficient for our question, why free will should have been given to man, to know that without it man cannot live rightly. That it was given for this reason can be understood from the following: if anyone uses free will for sinning, he incurs divine punishment. This would be unjust if free will had been given not only that man might live rightly, but also that he might sin. For how could a man justly incur punishment who used free will to do the thing for which it was given? When God punishes a sinner, does He not seem to say, 'Why have you not used free will for the purpose for which I gave it to you, to act rightly?' Then too, if man did not have free choice of will, how could there exist the good according to which it is just to condemn evildoers and reward those who act rightly? What was not done by will would be neither evildoing nor right action. But punishment and reward would be unjust if man did not have free will. Moreover, there must needs be justice both in punishment and in reward, since justice is one of the goods that are from God. Therefore, God must needs have given free will to man.

One's opinion on the question of freedom was a crucial determinant of one's sectarian alliance in early Islam. Islam is sometimes understood in the West as a 'fatalist' religion; in other words, it is thought that all Muslims believe that human beings are not free. However, the Mu'tazilites, one of the first Islamic sects, claimed that the human will is free, despite passages in the Koran that would lead one to believe the contrary, such as the following:

'No misfortune befalls except by Allah's [God's] will. He guides the hearts of those who believe in him. Allah has knowledge of all things.' (64:11)

'Every misfortune that befalls the earth or your own persons, is ordained before we bring it into being.' (57:22–3)

Thus, Islam provides an interesting breadth of argument on the question of freedom. The Mu'tazilites claimed that human freedom is consistent with God's power, by distinguishing between two types of action, or causality. God's actions are 'necessary', or law-like—they must happen. Human actions, however, are 'intentional'—they are contingent upon God's actions. Thus, a person is free, for instance, to hit a billiard ball with his or her pool cue. But he or she is not free to hit the ball and have it stay still, or to hit it in one direction and have it go in another. Only God is 'free' to make necessary, physical, laws. For the Mu'tazilites, human freedom amounts to directing God's actions along various possible paths. We are responsible for how we direct God's creations, and so we are rightly rewarded or punished by God for our choices.

Another very important Islamic school, the Ash'arites, reacted against the Mu'tazilites in favour of a more liberal interpretation of scriptural passages like the ones above. The Ash'arites, however, wound up making a distinction with regard to the question of freedom that was similar to that of the Mu'tazilites. The Ash'arites claimed that only God is free, and that all human actions are determined by God. God's 'predestination' here, however, is more like an offer of a gift. God offers to human beings various actions, which they can accept, acquire, or pass. Only God, therefore, can create an action, according to the

Ash'arites. Human beings merely acquire actions 'secondhand'. When we acquire good actions, we deserve our reward. When we acquire bad ones, we deserve our punishment.

Although one may take it overall, then, that Islamic tradition does seem to believe more in God's predestination than does Christianity, the Islamic stance on the question of freedom is really a very complex one. The debate within Islam about freedom continues to this day. Here is an example from an important twentieth-century Islamic thinker and theologian, Mohammad Iqbal.

From *The Reconstruction of Religious Thought in Islam*
By Mohammad Iqbal

[Fatalism] is life and boundless power which recognizes no obstruction, and can make a man calmly offer his prayers when bullets are showering around him.

Does the ego then determine its own activity? If so, how is the self-determination of the ego related to the determination of the spatio-temporal order? Is personal causality a special kind of causality, or only a disguised form of the mechanism of Nature? It is claimed that the two kinds of determinism are not mutually exclusive and that the scientific method is equally applicable to human action. The human act of deliberation is understood to be a conflict of motives which are conceived, not as the ego's own present or inherited tendencies of action or inaction, but as so many external forces fighting one another, gladiator-like, on the arena of the mind. Yet the final choice is regarded as a fact determined by the *strongest* force, and not by the resultant of contending motives, like a purely physical effect. I am, however, firmly of the opinion that the controversy between the advocates of Mechanism and Freedom arises from a wrong view of intelligent action which modern psychology, unmindful of its own independence as a science, possessing a special set of facts to observe, was bound to take on account of its slavish imitation of physical sciences.

* * *

Thus the element of guidance and directive control in the ego's activity clearly shows that the ego is a free personal causality. He shares in the life and freedom of the Ultimate Ego who, by permitting the emergence of a finite ego, capable of private initiative, has limited this freedom of His own free will. This freedom of conscious behaviour follows from the view of ego-activity which the Quran takes. There are verses which are unmistakably clear on this point:

'And say: The truth is from your Lord: Let him, then, who will, believe: and let him who will, be an unbeliever.' (18: 28)

'If ye do well to your own behoof will ye do well: and if ye do evil against yourselves will ye do it.' (17: 7)

Indeed Islam recognizes a very important fact of human psychology, i.e., the rise and fall of the power to act freely, and is anxious to retain the power to act freely as a constant and undiminished factor in the life of the ego. The timing of the daily prayer, which according to the Quran restores 'self-possession' to the ego by bringing it into closer touch with the ultimate source of life and freedom, is intended to save the ego from the mechanizing effects of sleep and business. Prayer in Islam is the ego's escape from mechanism to freedom.

The fatalism implied in this attitude is not negation of the ego . . . it is life and boundless power which recognizes no obstruction, and can make a man calmly offer his prayers when bullets are showering around him.

- How do predestination and fatalism differ? In what respects are they similar? Is predestination a version of fatalism?
- How does predestination relate to the problem of evil? What account does St Augustine offer to tie them together? How is there room for free will?
- What are the differences between the two Islamic schools' (Mu'tazilites and Ash'arites) conceptions of human freedom and predestination?

F. Determinism

As we have seen, the problem of freedom occurs in different contexts, from pagan fatalism to Christian predestination. The problem occurs in terms of the most abstract thesis that the universe as a whole is a single great machine or 'substance' (as in Newton or Spinoza) and in very localized theories about the psychology of the human personality. At all levels, however, the problem relates to **determinism**. We were briefly introduced to determinism in Chapter 1: Spinoza defended it in his metaphysical system; Newton gave it a convincing scientific interpretation with his physical theories. Determinism can be characterized by a principle already familiar to us from Chapter 3—the 'principle of universal causation'. Determinism is the thesis that everything that happens in the universe is determined according to the *laws of nature*. The problem is that human actions, whatever else they might be, are also events in the physical universe. But if human action is just another law-determined natural occurrence, can it be free? Would it make sense to start praising people (or blaming them) for obeying the law of gravity? What else could they possibly do?

Determinism is related to, but different from, fatalism and predestination. According to fatalism, despite what happens, the end is inevitable. In predestination, God's will has power over *both* human choices and natural law. According to determinism, however, an event will necessarily happen if its antecedent conditions are fulfilled. Determinism, on the other hand, does not say that a specific event is inevitable, it insists only that *if* certain conditions exist, *then* a certain kind of event will take place (for example, if a pot of water is heated sufficiently, then it will boil; if a person is forced to choose between losing his life and killing an insect, then he will take the life of the insect). This 'if . . . then' structure is essential to determinism. (There need be no such 'ifs' or 'thens' to fatalism or predestination.)

Determinism is the theory that every event in the universe, including every human action, has its natural causes; given certain antecedent conditions, an event will take place necessarily, according to the laws of nature. But we must fill out the determinist's premise by at least one more step. It is not enough to say that 'every event has its natural cause(s)', since this would leave open the possibility that although every event requires certain **antecedent conditions** in order to take place, the event might still be a matter of chance, at least to some extent, or a matter of human choice. We must say that 'every event has its *sufficient* natural cause(s)'. A **sufficient cause** is capable of bringing the event about by itself. In this definition, there is no room for chance and no room for choice. This view, which we shall call 'hard' determinism ('hard' as in 'hardhearted' as well as a 'hard' conclusion to accept), clearly leaves no room for human freedom. Without choice, there can be no freedom, and without freedom, there is no reason to hold a person responsible for his action, no matter how virtuous or how vicious it might be. According to the hard determinist thesis, we can barely be said to be 'acting' at all, for our 'actions' are nothing but the result of antecedent conditions and laws of nature that leave no room for our 'doing something' at all.

1. Hard Determinism

The hard determinist premise received its greatest impetus from Newton's physics and his picture of the universe as 'matter in motion', determined according to the laws of motion and gravitation that he so elegantly formulated. But his followers applied these laws not only to the movements of the planets and the stars or to the ball rolling down an inclined plane. According to them, we too are 'matter in motion', physical bodies that are subject to all of the laws of nature. What we 'do' is just as determined by these laws as any other event in nature.

This 'hardheaded' determinism has maintained a powerful hold on philosophers ever since Isaac Newton published his theories in the seventeenth century. The philosopher Pierre-Simon Laplace had such confidence in the Newtonian system that he claimed that if he knew the location and motion of every object in the universe, he could predict the location and motion of every object in the universe at any time in the future. (He could also

DETERMINISM

The view that every event in the universe is dependent upon other events, which are its causes.

retrodict, or look back to, every past state of the universe.) This means that if he had a proper map of the universe, including the material parts of our own bodies, he could predict everything that would ever happen and everything that we would ever do. If this is so, what possible sense could we make of our vain claims to have choices of actions, to decide what to do, or to hold ourselves and others responsible for what we have done?

Laplace's confidence in the hard determinist thesis was common among the immediate successors and enthusiasts of Newton. For example, one of the philosophers of the French Enlightenment, Paul Henri d'Holbach, defended the hard determinist viewpoint so uncompromisingly that he shocked even his colleagues as well as the many traditionalists.

From *System of Nature*

By Paul Henri d'Holbach

The actions of man are never free; they are always the necessary consequence of his temperament, of the received ideas, and of the notions, either true or false, which he has formed to himself of happiness; of his opinions, strengthened by example, by education, and by daily experience.

In whatever manner man is considered, he is connected to universal nature, and submitted to the necessary and immutable laws that she interposes on all beings she contains, according to their peculiar essences or to the respective properties with which, without consulting them, she endows each particular species. Man's life is a line that nature commands him to describe upon the surface of the earth, without his ever being able to swerve from it, even for an instant. He is born without his own consent; his organization does in nowise depend upon himself; his ideas come to him involuntarily; his habits are in the power of those who cause him to contract them; he is unceasingly modified by causes, whether visible or concealed, over which he has no control, which necessarily regulate his mode or existence, give the hue to his way of thinking, and determine his manner of acting. He is good or bad, happy or miserable, wise or foolish, reasonable or irrational, without his will being for anything in these various states. Nevertheless, in spite of the shackles by which he is bound, it is pretended he is a free agent, or that independent of the causes by which he is moved, he determines his own will, and regulates his own condition.

However slender the foundation of his opinion, of which everything ought to point out to him the error, it is current at this day and passes for an incontestable truth with a great number of people, otherwise extremely enlightened; it is the basis of religion, which supposing relations between man and the unknown being she has placed above nature, has been incapable of imagining how man could merit reward or deserve punishment from this being, if he was not a free agent. Society has been believed interested in his system; because an idea has gone abroad, that if all the actions of man were to be contemplated as necessary, the right of punishing those who injure their associates would no longer exist. At length human vanity accommodated itself to a hypothesis which, unquestionably, appears to distinguish man from all other physical beings, by assigning to him the special privilege of a total independence of all other causes, but of which a very little reflection would have shown him the impossibility.

The will, as we have elsewhere said, is a modification of the brain, by which it is disposed to action, or prepared to give play to the organs. This will be necessarily determined by the qualities, good or bad, agreeable or painful, of the object or the motive that acts upon his sense, or of which the idea remains with him, and is resuscitated by his memory. In consequence, he acts necessarily, his action is the result of the impulse he receives either from the motive, from the object, or from the idea which has modified his brain, or disposed his will. When he does not act according to his impulse, it is because there comes some new cause, some new motive, some new idea, which modified his brain in a different manner, gives him a new impulse, determines his will in another way, by which the action of the former impulse is suspended: thus, the sight of an agreeable object, or its idea, determines his will to set him in action to procure it; but if a new object or a new idea more powerfully attracts him, it gives a new direction to his will, annihilates the effect of the former, and prevents the action by which it was to be procured. This is the mode in which reflection, experience, reason, necessarily arrests or suspends the action of man's will: without this he would of necessity have followed the anterior impulse which carried him toward a then desirable object. In all this he always acts according to necessary laws from which he has no means of emancipating himself.

* * *

In short, the actions of man are never free; they are always the necessary consequence of his temperament, of the received ideas, and of the notions, either true or false, which he has formed to himself of happiness; of his opinions, strengthened by example, by education, and by daily experience. So many crimes are witnessed on the earth only because everything conspires to render man vicious and criminal; the religion he has adopted, his government, his education, the examples set before him, irresistibly drive him on to evil: under these circumstances, morality preaches virtue to him in vain. In those societies where vice is esteemed, where crime is crowned, where venality is constantly recompensed, where the most dreadful disorders are punished only in those who are too weak to enjoy the privilege of committing them with impunity, the practice of virtue is considered nothing more than a painful sacrifice of happiness. Such societies chastise, in the lower orders, those excesses which they respect in the higher ranks; and frequently have the injustice to condemn those in the penalty of death, whom public prejudices, maintained by constant example, have rendered criminal.

Man, then, is not a free agent in any one instant of life; he is necessarily guided in each step by those advantages, whether real or fictitious, that he attaches to the objects by which his passions are roused: these passions themselves are necessary in a being who unceasingly tends towards his own happiness; their energy is necessary, since that depends on his temperament; his temperament is necessary, because it depends on the physical elements which enter into his composition; the modification of his temperament is necessary, as it is the infallible and inevitable consequence of the impulse he receives from the incessant action of moral and physical beings.

- Define determinism and explain how 'hard' determinism modifies this definition. How does hard determinism eliminate human freedom?
- What are the implications to giving up the determinists' premise that every event has a sufficient natural cause? Does this seem to solve the problem of freedom?
- How might we say that our acts are still free, yet determined?

Given the scientific paradigm that is still widespread in philosophy, determinism is still an influential thesis, despite the shifts in science that make d'Holbach's conception of nature quite outdated. But is that thesis true? That is the question before us.

2. Determinism versus Indeterminism

So should we accept the determinist's premise? Without it, determinism cannot get to first base. In earlier chapters, we saw the traditional arguments in support of this premise. The most general argument is that only by assuming from the outset that every event has its (sufficient natural) cause(s) can we ever understand anything. Otherwise, we should have auto mechanics always giving us back our cars (and our bills) with the unhelpful statement that 'there's no cause for our troubles'. We could expect the same from doctors whenever a diagnosis gave them the least bit of trouble, and we would use it ourselves every time a problem began to get difficult.

A much stronger argument is made by Kant, who says that the basic rule of determinism, the principle of universal causation, is one of the rules by which we must interpret every experience. But even Hume, who denies that this principle can be justified either through reason or through experience, insists that it is a 'natural habit' or custom that is indispensable to us and that we could not give up even if we wanted to. The consensus, then, has been that the principle itself is inescapable. Even Leibniz, who rejected the idea of causation altogether, insisted on his 'Principle of Sufficient Reason', which came to the same end, that is, 'every event has its sufficient reason'.

The agreement of so many philosophers indicates the strength of the hard determinist position. Without the assumption that 'every event has its sufficient natural cause(s)', human knowledge would seem to be without one of its most vital presuppositions. Not only scientific research but even our most ordinary, everyday beliefs would be forced to an intolerable skeptical standstill. Our every experience would be unintelligible, and our universe would appear to be nothing but a disconnected stream of incoherent happenings from which nothing could be **predicted** and nothing understood. So the answer to the question, 'Why should we accept the determinist's premise?' seems to be, 'We cannot give it up; how could we possibly do without it?' For no matter how it is rephrased or philosophically altered (for example, by Leibniz, who eliminates the concept of 'cause' from it), the assumption that every event in the universe, including our own actions, can be explained and understood, if only one knows enough about it and its antecedent conditions, is a presupposition of all human thinking.

Even if the hard determinist's premise seems undeniable, it is not yet clear how we are to understand that premise. The older determinists of the Newtonian period (Laplace, d'Holbach) understood the idea of a cause as a literal push or **compulsion**, as if one were given a shove down the stairs. On this model, our actions are no different, except in complexity, from the 'actions' of billiard balls on a felt-covered table, the motion of each wholly determining the motion of the next. The exact movements of every ball, of course, are not always predictable. In the opening break, for example, even the most expert player cannot predict with accuracy where each ball will go. But we can be sure that each one is absolutely determined by the movements of the other balls that make contact with it, just as with the simple predictable case of a single ball hitting another straight on.

If we view human beings as nothing more than physical bodies—bones, muscles, nerve cells, and the like—then this mechanical billiard ball model might make some sense. But a much weaker interpretation of the hard determinist premise does not require us to so radically reduce people to mere bodies. Instead of talking about actual physical pushes and compulsions, we can interpret the determinist premise in the following way: To say that every event has its cause(s) is to say that if certain antecedent conditions are satisfied, then we can predict that such and such will occur. On the stronger mechanistic determinist interpretation, causes are actual pushes and, on such an interpretation, the notion of freedom is clearly impossible. But the weaker interpretation, of determinism as predictability, may yet offer room for us to talk about freedom of action. For example, we may be able to predict our friend's decision, but that does not seem to mean that he was forced to make it. We may be able to predict his action, but only because, knowing him, we know what he will probably do. On the second interpretation, perhaps we can have determinism and freedom.

Many philosophers defend determinism only as predictability on the basis of probability. We might easily be wrong. To say that every event is determined, on this view, means only that it is predictable if we know enough about antecedent conditions. But it has been objected, against the determinist, that the fact of such predictability is not sufficient to defend determinism in anything like the 'hard' sense. It is one thing to say that all events, including human actions, are actually caused or compelled by physical forces. It is something quite different to say that all events including human actions, are predictable. They might be predictable, for example, only on the basis of certain statistical probabilities. 'Most people in this circumstance would do that.' 'The odds are for it,' in other words. Or, in the case of human actions, the predictability might still be due to human choices; we can predict each other's actions because we know how we would probably choose in the same circumstances. But there is no need here to talk about 'causes' or compulsions. Nor, it has been argued, should we even talk any longer about 'determinism', if this is all that we mean by it.

In contrast, the antideterminist thesis, called **indeterminism**, rejects both versions of determinism. Indeterminism claims that not every event has its sufficient natural cause(s). This theory at least appears to leave room for **free will**, for as soon as we allow that there are some events that are uncaused, human actions might be among them. Thus it would seem that we can be held properly responsible for our actions. But is the indeterminist thesis plausible?

The indeterminist argument has recently received a boost from physics, the very science that gave rise to the determinist threat in the first place. But it has been shown in recent physics that such knowledge is impossible. One of the most important discoveries of modern physics is the **Heisenberg uncertainty principle** (named after its discoverer, Werner Heisenberg), which says that we cannot know both the location and the momentum of a subatomic particle. In coming to know the one, we make it impossible for us to know the other at the same time.

From this principle, the British physicist-philosopher Sir Arthur Eddington advanced the indeterminist argument that determinism is false on physical grounds. Not every event in the universe is predictable. Furthermore, many scientists now agree, on the basis of such considerations, that the concept of 'cause' does not apply to certain subatomic particles either. The determinist premise that 'every event in the universe has its sufficient natural cause' is false. Some events—namely, those involving some subatomic particles—are not caused, not predictable, and therefore not determined, on any interpretation. But if not all events are determined, then perhaps human actions are not determined; if they are predictable, it is not because they are caused.

The object of indeterminism is to deny the determinist position in order to make room for human freedom. But there are, unfortunately, two serious objections to the indeterminist argument. First, even if we suppose that the conclusions of modern physical ('quantum') theory are correct (a matter still in dispute among physicists), it is clear that determinism is of importance to us primarily as a theory of macroscopic bodies (that is, bodies of visible size—people, trees, cars), not subatomic particles. No one has ever concluded that quantum theory and modern physics actually refute Newton's theories. Rather, it supplements them, puts them in their place, and qualifies them in ways that would have been unthinkable in the eighteenth century. But as for the determinism of the gravitation of the planets or the rolling of a ball down an inclined plane, the spectacular discoveries of modern particle physics don't affect them in the least. With regard to the physical determinism of our own bodies, the case remains as before. It might be true that it is impossible to predict what a subatomic particle in our bodies might do, but it does not follow that it is impossible to predict what our bodies will do. Falling out of a plane, we still fall at exactly the same speed as a sack of potatoes, which is all the determinist needs to continue his attack on our concept of freedom. Second, even if there should be such indeterminism, indeterminism is not the same as freedom. Suppose there should be a 'gap' in the causal determinism of our decisions by the various neurological processes of our brains; that would mean, at most, that what we do is not determined at all—or is determined only randomly. Suppose that all of a sudden your legs started moving and you found yourself kicking a fire hydrant; surely this is not what we mean by a 'free action'. Freedom means, at least, that we are free to choose what we shall do and that our decisions are effective. Indeterminism robs us of our freedom, therefore, just as much as determinism. And the argument against determinism, in any case, is not yet sufficiently persuasive to allow the indeterminist his conclusions.

INDETERMINISM

The thesis that at least some events in the universe are not caused by antecedent conditions and may not be predictable.

Below, philosopher Robert Kane expands on this second objection to the indeterminist argument:

On Indeterminism
By Robert Kane

[There is] a further problem that has haunted free will debates for centuries: If this deeper freedom is not compatible with determinism, it does not seem to be compatible with *indeterminism* either. An event which is undetermined might occur or might not occur, given the entire past. (A determined event *must* occur, given the entire past.) Thus, whether or not an undetermined event actually occurs, given its past, is a matter of chance. But chance events occur spontaneously and are not under the control of anything, hence not under the control of agents. How then could they be free actions? If, for example, a choice occurred by virtue of a quantum jump or other undetermined event in one's brain, it would seem a fluke or accident rather than a responsible choice. Undetermined events in the brain or body it seems would inhibit or interfere with our freedom, occurring spontaneously and not under our control. They would turn out to be a nuisance—or perhaps a curse, like epilepsy—rather than an enhancement of our freedom.

Or look at the problem in another way that goes a little deeper. If my choice is really undetermined, that means I could have made a different choice *given exactly the same past* right up to the moment when I did choose. That is what indeterminism and the denial of determinism mean: exactly the same past, different outcomes. Imagine, for example, that I had been deliberating about where to spend my vacation, in Hawaii or Colorado, and after much thought and deliberation had decided I preferred Hawaii and chose it. If the choice was undetermined, then exactly the same deliberation, the same thought processes, the same beliefs, desires, and other motives—not a sliver of difference—that led up to my favouring and choosing Hawaii over Colorado, might by chance have issued in my choosing Colorado instead. That is very strange. If such a thing happened it would seem a fluke or accident, like that quantum jump in the brain just mentioned, not a rational choice. Since I had come to favour Hawaii and was about to choose it, when by chance I chose Colorado, I would wonder what went wrong and perhaps consult a neurologist. For reasons such as these, people have argued that undetermined free choices would be 'arbitrary', 'capricious', 'random', 'irrational', 'uncontrolled', and 'inexplicable', not really free and responsible choices at all. If free will is not compatible with determinism, it does not seem to be compatible with indeterminism either.

- How have modern developments in physics (the Heisenberg uncertainty principle, quantum physics) undermined the determinist thesis?
- What are the objections to indeterminism? Does indeterminism entail freedom?

---

3. Soft Determinism

The philosophers of the Newtonian tradition, those 'hard' determinists who believe that determinism precludes the possibility of freedom of choice and action, have always had a powerful and simple argument on their side. But because of the urgency of our demand that we hold ourselves and each other responsible for our actions, most philosophers have not accepted 'hard' determinism, even though they have accepted the determinist argument. Accordingly, many philosophers have espoused what has been called **soft determinism**. (The name was coined by William James.) Soft determinists, unlike the uncompromising hard determinists, believe that human freedom and determinism are compatible positions. On the one hand, they accept the determinist's argument, but, on the other, they refuse to give up the all-important demand for human freedom and responsibility. (Accordingly, they are often called compatibilists, and their position, **compatibilism**.)

COMPATIBILISM

The thesis that both determinism and free action can be true.

The key to the 'soft determinist' position is that an action or a decision, though fully determined, is free if it 'flows from the agent's character'. John Stuart Mill, for example, defends such a position in the following way:

On Causation and Necessity
By John Stuart Mill

Given the motives which are present to an individual's mind, and given likewise the character and disposition of the individual, the manner in which he will act might be unerringly inferred.

The question, whether the law of causality appears in the same strict sense to human actions as to other phenomena, is the celebrated controversy concerning the freedom of the will; which, from at least as far back as the time of Pelagius, has divided both the philosophical and the religious world. The affirmative opinion is commonly called the doctrine of Necessity, as asserting human volitions and actions to be necessary and inevitable. The negative maintains that the will is not determined, like other phenomena, by antecedents, but determines itself; that our volitions are not, properly speaking, the effects of causes, or at least no causes which they uniformly and implicitly obey.

I have already made it sufficiently apparent that the former of these opinions is that which I consider the true one; but the misleading terms in which it is often expressed, and in the indistinct manner in which it is usually apprehended, have both obstructed its reception, and perverted its influence when received. The metaphysical theory of free-will, as held by philosophers (for the practical feeling of it, common in a great or less degree to all mankind, is in no way inconsistent with the contrary theory), was invented because the supposed alternative of admitting human actions to be *necessary* was deemed inconsistent with everyone's instinctive consciousness, as well as humiliating to the pride and even degrading to the moral nature of man. Nor do I deny that the doctrine, as sometimes held, is open to these imputations; for the misapprehension in which I shall be able to show that they originate, unfortunately is not confined to the opponents of the doctrine, but is participated in by many, perhaps we might say by most, of its supporters.

Correctly conceived, the doctrine called Philosophical Necessity is simply this: that, given the motives which are present to an individual's mind, and given likewise the character and disposition of the individual, the manner in which he will act might be unerringly inferred; that if we knew the person thoroughly, and knew all the inducements which are acting upon him, we could foretell his conduct with as much certainty as we can predict any physical event. This proposition I take to be a mere interpretation of universal experience, a statement in words of what everyone is internally convinced of. No one who believed that he knew thoroughly the circumstances of any case, and the characters of the different persons concerned, would hesitate to foretell how all of them would act. Whatever degree of doubt he may in fact feel, arises from the uncertainty whether he really knows the circumstances, or the character of some one or other of the persons, with the degree of accuracy required; but by no means from thinking that if he did know these things, there could be any uncertainty what the conduct would be. Nor does this full assurance conflict in the smallest degree with what is called our feeling of freedom. We do not feel ourselves the less free, because those to whom we are intimately known are well assured how we shall will to act in a particular case. We often, on the contrary, regard the doubt what our conduct will be, as a mark of ignorance of our character, and sometimes even resent it as an imputation. The religious metaphysicians who have asserted the freedom of the will, have always maintained it to be consistent with divine foreknowledge of our actions: and if with divine, then with any other foreknowledge. We may be free, and yet another may have reason to be perfectly certain what use we shall make of our freedom. It is not, therefore, the doctrine that our volitions and actions are invariable consequents of our antecedent states of mind, that is either contradicted by our consciousness, or felt to be degrading.

(Continued)

But the doctrine of causation, when considered as obtaining between our volitions and their antecedents, is almost universally conceived as involving more than this. Many do not believe, and very few practically feel, that there is nothing in causation but invariable, certain, and unconditional sequence. There are few to whom mere constancy of succession appears a sufficient stringent bond of union for so peculiar a relation as that of cause and effect. Even if the reason repudiates, the imagination retains, the feeling of some more intimate connection, of some peculiar tie, or mysterious constraint exercised by the antecedent over the consequent. Now this it is which, considered as applying to the human will, conflicts with our consciousness, and revolts our feelings. We are certain that, in the case of our volitions, there is not this mysterious constraint. We know that we are not compelled, as by a magical spell, to obey any particular motive. We feel, that if we wished to prove that we have the power of resisting the motive, we could do so (that wish being, it needs scarcely be observed, a *new antecedent*); and it would be humiliating to our pride, and (what is of more importance) paralyzing to our desire of excellence, if we thought otherwise. But neither is any such mysterious compulsion now supposed, by the best philosophical authorities, to be exercised by any other cause over its effect. Those who think that causes draw their effects after them by a mystical tie, are right in believing that the relation between volitions and their antecedents is of another nature. But they should go farther, and admit that this is also true of all other effects and their antecedents. If such a tie is considered to be involved in the word Necessity, the doctrine is not true of human actions; but neither is it then true of inanimate objects. It would be more correct to say that matter is not bound by necessity, than that mind is so.

* * *

A fatalist believes, or half believes (for nobody is a consistent fatalist), not only that whatever is about to happen will be the infallible result of the causes which produce it (which is the true necessitarian doctrine), but moreover that there is no use in struggling against it; that it will happen however we may strive to prevent it. Now, a necessitarian, believing that our actions follow from our characters, and that our characters follow from our organization, our education, and our circumstances, is apt to be, with

more or less of consciousness on his part, a fatalist as to his own actions, and to believe that his nature is such, or that his education and circumstances have so moulded his character, that nothing can now prevent him from feeling and acting in a particular way, or at least that no effort of his own can hinder it. In the words of the sect which in our own day has most perseveringly inculcated and most perversely misunderstood this great doctrine, his character is formed *for* him, and not *by* him; therefore his wishing that it had been formed differently is of no use; he has no power to alter it. But this is a grand error. He has, to a certain extent, a power to alter his character. Its being, in the ultimate resort, formed for him, is not inconsistent with its being, in part formed *by* him as one of the intermediate agents. His character is formed by his circumstances (including among these his particular organization); but his own desire to mould it in a particular way, is one of those circumstances, and by no means one of the least influential. We cannot, indeed, directly will to be different from what we are. But neither did those who are supposed to have formed our characters directly will that we should be what we are. Their will had no direct power except over their own actions. They made us what they did make us, by willing, not the end, but the requisite means; and we, when our habits are not too inveterate, can, by similarly willing the requisite means, make ourselves different. If they could place us under the influence of certain circumstances, we, in like manner, can place ourselves under the influence of other circumstances. We are exactly as capable of making our own character, *if we will*, as others are of making it for us.

Yes (answers the Owenite),[66] but these words, 'if we will', surrender the whole point: since the will to alter our own character is given us, not by any efforts of ours, but by circumstances which we cannot help, it comes to us either from external causes, or not at all. Most true: if the Owenite stops here, he is in a position from which nothing can expel him. Our character is formed by us as well as for us; but the wish which induces us to attempt to form it is formed for us; and how? Not, in general, by our organization, nor wholly by our education, but by our experience; experience of the painful consequences of the character we previously had; or by some strong feeling of admiration or aspiration, accidentally aroused. But to think that we have no power of altering our character, and to think that we shall not use our power unless we desire to use it, are very different things, and have a very different effect on the mind. A person who does not wish to alter his character, cannot be the person who is supposed to feel discouraged or paralyzed by thinking himself unable to do it. The depressing effect of the fatalist doctrine can only be felt where there *is* a wish to do what that doctrine represents as impossible. It is of no consequence what we think forms our character, when we have no desire of our own about forming it; but it is of great consequence that we should not be prevented from forming such a desire by thinking the attainment impracticable, and that if we have the desire, we should know that the work is not so irrevocably done as to be incapable of being altered.

And indeed, if we examine closely, we shall find that this feeling, of our being able to modify our own character *if we wish*, is itself the feeling of moral freedom which we are conscious of. A person feels morally free who feels that his habits or his temptations are not his masters, but he theirs; who, even in yielding to them, knows that he could resist; that were he desirous of altogether throwing them off, there would not be required for the purpose a stronger desire than he knows himself to be capable of feeling. It is of course necessary, to render our consciousness of freedom complete, that we should have succeeded in making our character all we have hitherto attempted to make it; for if we have wished and not attained, we have, to that extent, not power over our own character; we are not free. Or at least, we must feel that our wish, if not strong enough to alter our character, is strong enough to conquer our character when the two are brought into conflict in any particular case of conduct. And hence it is said with truth, that none but a person of confirmed virtue is completely free.

In this section, Mill glides between the harsh alternatives of 'hard determinism' and indeterminism. He begins by accepting determinism and the idea that all human actions are 'necessary and inevitable', given their causes. But he then goes on to say that these causes are themselves within human control, that we can alter the causes of events and even, by taking certain steps, alter our own characters. But this is not in the least to deny determinism; nor does it deny that we are in control and have 'free will' in an important sense. Human actions, following from their various causes (including 'character', or personality), are as predictable as any other events. But predictability is not incompatible with freedom, for freedom means, according to Mill, nothing other than acting in accordance with one's own character, desires, and wishes. Since these are the causes of our actions, Mill's definition of freedom allows him to defend both determinism and freedom at the same time.

David Hume is also a 'soft determinist', and he too argues that the reconciliation of 'liberty and necessity' is to be found in the fact that one's actions 'flow from one's character or disposition'. In defending soft determinism, Hume argues that we cannot mean by a free action one that is uncaused, a matter of chance, for this flies in the face of our common assumption that every event must have a cause. Such a view of freedom is also incoherent: The free-will advocate wants to ensure that we can hold people responsible for their actions; but if people's actions were merely a matter of chance, over which they have no control, we surely would not hold them responsible. On the contrary, actions that we praise or blame are precisely those determined by the person's character.

Although Hume defends a soft determinist position, there is a sense in which Hume is not a determinist at all. Recall from Chapter 3 that Hume thinks that causality is a fiction and our penchant for seeking out causes merely a habit. Thus he can argue that just as we are never rationally justified in claiming that a particular event has a cause, so we are never fully justified in claiming that human actions have causes.

On Causation and Character
By David Hume

By liberty, . . . we can only mean a power of acting or not acting according to the determinations of the will.

But to proceed in this reconciling project with regard to the question of liberty and necessity; the most contentious question of metaphysics, the most contentious science; it will not require many words to prove, that all mankind have ever agreed in the doctrine of liberty as well as in that of necessity, and that the whole dispute, in this respect also, has been hitherto merely verbal. For what is meant by liberty, when applied to voluntary actions? We cannot surely mean that actions have so little connection with motives, inclinations, and circumstances, that one does not follow with a certain degree of uniformity from the other, and that one affords no inference by which we can conclude the existence of the other. For these are plain and acknowledged matters of fact. By liberty, then, we can only mean *a power of acting or not acting according to the determinations of the will*; that is, if we choose to remain at rest, we may; if we choose to move, we also may. Now this hypothetical liberty is universally allowed to belong to everyone who is not a prisoner and in chains. Here then is no subject of dispute.

Whatever definition we may give of liberty, we should be careful to observe two requisite circumstances: *first*, that it be consistent with plain matter of fact; *secondly*, that it be consistent with itself. If we observe these circumstances and render our definition intelligible, I am persuaded that all mankind will be found of one opinion with regard to it.

It is universally allowed that nothing exists without a cause of its existence, and that chance, when strictly examined, is a mere negative word and means not any real power which has anywhere a being in nature. But it is pretended that some causes are necessary, some not necessary. Here then is the advantage of definitions. Let anyone *define* a cause without comprehending it, as part of the definition, a *necessary connection* with its effect, and let him show distinctly the origin of the idea expressed by the definition, and I shall readily give up the whole controversy. But if the foregoing explication of the matter be received, this must be absolutely impracticable. Had not objects a regular conjunction with each other, we should never have entertained any notion of cause and effect; and this regular conjunction produces that inference of the understanding which is the only connection that we can have any comprehension of. Whoever attempts a definition of cause exclusive of these circumstances will be obliged either to employ unintelligible terms or such as are synonymous to the term which he endeavours to define. And if the definition above mentioned be admitted, liberty, when opposed to necessity, not to constraint, is the same thing with chance, which is universally allowed to have no existence. . . .

All laws being founded on rewards and punishments, it is supposed as a fundamental principle, that these motives have a regular and uniform influence on the mind, and both produce the good and prevent the evil actions. We may give to this influence what name we please; but, as it is usually conjoined with the action, it must be esteemed a *cause*, and be looked upon as an instance of that necessity, which we would here establish.

The only proper object of hatred or vengeance is a person or creature, endowed with thought and consciousness; and when any criminal or injurious actions excite that passion, it is only by their relation to the person, or connection with him. Actions are, by their very nature, temporary and perishing; and where they proceed not from some *cause* in the character and disposition of the person who performed them, they can neither redound to his honour, if good; nor infamy, if evil. The actions themselves may be blameable; they may be contrary to all the rules of morality and religion: But the person is not answerable for them; and as they proceeded from nothing in him that is durable and constant, and leave nothing of that nature behind them, it is impossible he can, upon their account, become the object of punishment or vengeance. According to the principle, therefore, which denies necessity, and consequently causes, a man is as pure and untainted, after having committed the most horrid crime, as at the first moment of his birth, nor is his character anywise concerned in his actions, since they are not derived from it, and the wickedness of the one can never be used as a proof of the depravity of the other.

Men are not blamed for such actions as they perform ignorantly and casually, whatever may be the consequences. Why? but because the principles of these actions are only momentary, and terminate in them alone. Men are less blamed for such actions as they perform hastily and unpremeditatedly than for such as proceed from deliberation. For what reason? but because a hasty temper, though a constant cause or principle in the mind, operates only by intervals, and infects not the whole character. Again, repentance wipes off every crime, if attended with a reformation of life and manners. How is this to be accounted for? but by asserting that actions render a person criminal merely as they are proofs of criminal principles in the mind; and when, by an alteration of these principles, they cease to be just proofs, they likewise cease to be criminal. But, except upon the doctrine of necessity, they never were just proofs, and consequently never were criminal.

It will be equally easy to prove, and from the same arguments, that *liberty*, according to that definition above mentioned, in which all men agree, is also essential to morality, and that no human actions, where it is wanting, are susceptible of any moral qualities, or can be the objects either of approbation or dislike. For as actions are objects of our moral sentiment, so far only as they are indications of the internal character, passions, and affections; it is impossible that they can give rise either to praise or blame, where they proceed not from these principles, but are derived altogether from external violence.

In other words, Hume too suggests that not only is freedom of choice and action possible within the framework of determinism, but determinism is even necessary if we are to make sense out of the notion of freedom of choice and responsibility. His language is convoluted, but his point is plain: We can make sense of the notion of voluntary action only because there is a uniform ('necessary') connection between our motives, inclinations, circumstances, and characters and what we do. But 'soft determinism' raises the same old questions yet again. Can we be said to be responsible even for those acts that are caused by our character? Can we choose our character, as Mill suggests? Could we have done other than what we did, even if we had wanted to?

- Do you agree with compatibilists that freedom and determinism are compatible? (Just because you are unwilling to give up either one of them doesn't mean that they are compatible.)
- How does Mill address the 'common-sense' objection to determinism that it conflicts with our experience of freedom? How does he distinguish between different ideas of causation?
- Hume suggests that determinism is necessary for us to make sense of action and responsibility. Is acting from character sufficient for freedom?

---

4. Incompatibilism Revisited: Libertarianism

At this point, it may seem as if compatibilism has a lot going for it. For one thing, compatibilism promises you that you can have your cake and eat it too. All you need to do is agree that 'free' and 'determined' are not mutually exclusive descriptions, and you can embrace the modern scientific picture of Nature as law-governed without needing to give up our age-old image of ourselves as morally responsible beings. The enticing philosophical sales pitch here is plain: *Compatibilism's synthesis will give you the best of both worlds with a clean logical conscience.* Next, compatibilism generously estimates the extent of your freedom. If freedom is a matter of doing what you choose to do rather than doing what someone else forces you to do, then many of your everyday deeds, from getting out of bed in the morning to eating a midnight snack, will qualify as free actions. (No wonder Hume says, in *An Enquiry Concerning Human Understanding*, that compatibilist freedom 'is universally allowed to belong to everyone who is not a prisoner and in chains'.) Finally, compatibilism takes the philosophical mystery out of freedom. If freedom is nothing more than 'a power of acting or not acting, according to the determinations of the will',[67] then there is much less to the problem of free will versus determinism than meets the eye of the metaphysician. Indeed, strictly speaking, there *is* no such problem for the compatibilist, because she flatly denies that free will and determinism are at odds. The sooner you agree with her about this, she declares, the sooner you shall have one less dusty philosophical problem to worry about.

Compatibilism, in short, can seem both radical and reassuring, daring yet sensible, imaginative but sane. What more could anyone ask for in a philosophical theory? And yet compatibilism has always had its share of fierce and distinguished opponents. Immanuel Kant, for example, famously called compatibilism 'a wretched subterfuge'; and William James denounced soft determinism—a compromise he thought misguided—as 'a quagmire of evasion'. A more recent but no less formidable critic is the **libertarian** Roderick Chisholm, whose classic essay 'Human Freedom and the Self' sheds a great deal of light on the problem of free will.

One way of seeing what separates Chisholm from the soft determinist is to compare the ways in which the two reply to a simple argument for hard determinism. Here, in a nutshell, is that argument:

> (1) *Our actions are caused.*
> (2) *If our actions are caused, then determinism is true.*
> (3) *If determinism is true, then none of our actions are free.*

Therefore,

> (4) *None of our actions are free.*

Both Chisholm and the soft determinist reject (4), the hard determinist's conclusion. Note, however, that the hard determinist's argument is formally valid. Because (4) follows logically from (1), (2), and (3), Chisholm and the soft determinist must find fault with one or more of the argument's three premises. But which one(s) should they discard? That is the question we need to think about.

Neither side wishes to contest premise (1); and it is to their credit that they don't. For one thing, denying (1) would be tantamount to denying the time-honoured principle that every event has a cause; for if actions aren't events, what on earth are they? Also, it would be perversely inconsistent for a believer in free actions to deny (1); for how could anyone think uncaused actions free, or free actions uncaused?

With premise (1) off-limits, a would-be critic can only attack premise (2) or (3). And so we face a choice: if one of these two premises has got to go, which should it be? According to the soft determinist, premise (3) must be abandoned: freedom, properly understood, is perfectly consistent with the truth of determinism. Not so, retorts Chisholm: the offending premise is not (3), but (2). The hard determinist is quite right in thinking that freedom and determinism are incompatible, but quite wrong in thinking that causation and freedom are incompatible.

So we have three ways in which we can respond to the argument for hard determinism. The following table summarizes these positions:

	HARD DETERMINISM	**SOFT DETERMINISM**	**CHISHOLM'S LIBERTARIANISM**
Accepts	Premises 1, 2, and 3	Premises 1 and 2	Premises 1 and 3
Rejects	None	Premise 3	Premise 2

- Where do Chisholm and the hard determinist agree? Where do they disagree?
- Where do Chisholm and the soft determinist agree? Where do they disagree?
- Where do the hard determinist and the soft determinist agree? Where do they disagree?

LIBERTARIAN

An incompatibilist who affirms the reality of free will.

Now, here's how things look from Chisholm's point of view. Since your actions are events, your actions must have causes. So far, so good. However, if there are any free actions in the libertarian's sense of 'free', it seems that those actions cannot be caused by other *events*; for that way lies determinism. What follows? Two things, according to Chisholm: 'We must not say that every event involved in the act is caused by some other event; and we must not say that the act is something that is not caused at all.' So what on earth causes your free actions (if there are any)? Simple, says Chisholm: *you and you alone are ultimately the cause of your free actions*. In other words, free actions are caused by the *agent* (or *person*, or *self*) whose actions they are. As Chisholm points out, this view of free agency implies that 'we have a prerogative which some would attribute only to God: each of us, when we act is a prime mover unmoved. In doing what we do, we cause certain events to happen, and nothing—or no one—causes us to cause those events to happen.' In short: if free will isn't a fiction, **agent causation** must be a fact.

AGENT CAUSATION

The metaphysical thesis that agents or selves, not events, are the ultimate causes of free actions.

From 'Human Freedom and the Self'
By Roderick Chisholm

In doing what we do, we cause certain events to happen, and nothing—or no one—causes us to cause those events to happen.

1. The metaphysical problem of human freedom might be summarized in the following way: Human beings are responsible agents; but this fact appears to conflict with a deterministic view of human action (the view that every event that is involved in an act is caused by some other event); and it *also* appears to conflict with an indeterministic view of human action (the view that the act, or some event that is essential to the act, is not caused at all.) To solve the problem, I believe, we must make somewhat far-reaching assumptions about the self or the agent—about the man who performs the act.

   Perhaps it is needless to remark that, in all likelihood, it is impossible to say anything significant about this ancient problem that has not been said before.

2. Let us consider some deed, or misdeed, that may be attributed to a responsible agent: one man, say, shot another. If the man *was* responsible for what he did, then, I would urge, what was to happen at the time of the shooting was something that was entirely up to the man himself. There was a moment at which it was true, both that he could have fired the shot and also that he could have refrained from firing it. And if this is so, then, even though he did fire it, he could have done something else instead. (He didn't find himself firing the shot 'against his will', as we say.) I think we can say, more generally, then, that if a man is responsible

for a certain event or a certain state of affairs (in our example, the shooting of another man), then that event or state of affairs was brought about by some act of his, and the act was something that was in his power either to perform or not to perform.

But now if the act which he *did* perform was an act that was also in his power *not* to perform, then it could not have been caused or determined by any event that was not itself within his power either to bring about or not to bring about. For example, if what we say he did was really something that was brought about by a second man, one who forced his hand upon the trigger, say, or who, by means of hypnosis, compelled him to perform the act, then since the act was caused by the *second* man it was nothing that was within the power of the *first* man to prevent. And precisely the same thing is true, I think, if instead of referring to a second man who compelled the first one, we speak instead of the *desires* and *beliefs* which the first man happens to have had. For if what we say he did was really something that was brought about by his own beliefs and desires, if these beliefs and desires in the particular situation in which he happened to have found himself caused him to do just what it was that we say he did do, then since *they* caused it, *he* was unable to do anything other than just what it was that he did do. It makes no difference whether the cause of the deed was internal or external; if the cause was some state or event for

(Continued)

which the man himself was not responsible, then he was not responsible for what we have been mistakenly calling his act. If a flood caused the poorly constructed dam to break, then, given the flood and the constitution of the dam, the break, we may say, *had* to occur and nothing could have happened in its place. And if the flood of desire caused the weak-willed man to give in, then he, too, had to do just what it was that he did do and he was no more responsible than was the dam for the results that followed. (It is true, of course, that if the man is responsible for the beliefs and desires that he happens to have, then he may also be responsible for the things they lead him to do. But the question now becomes: *is* he responsible for the beliefs and desires he happens to have? If he is, then there was a time when they were within his power either to acquire or not to acquire, and we are left, therefore, with our general point.)

One may object: But surely if there were such a thing as a man who is really *good*, then he would be responsible for things that he would do; yet, he would be unable to do anything other than just what it is that he does do, since, being good, he will always choose to do what is best. The answer, I think, is suggested by a comment that Thomas Reid makes on an ancient author. The author had said of Cato, 'He was good because he could not be otherwise', and Reid observes: 'This saying, if understood literally and strictly, is not the praise of Cato, but of his constitution, which was no more the work of Cato than his existence.' If Cato was himself responsible for the good things that he did, then Cato, as Reid suggests, was such that, although he had the power to do what was not good, he exercised his power only for that which was good.

All of this, if it is true, may give a certain amount of comfort to those who are tender-minded. But we should remind them that it also conflicts with a familiar view about the nature of God—with the view that St Thomas Aquinas expresses by saying that 'every movement both of the will and of nature proceeds from God as the Prime Mover'. If the act of the sinner *did* proceed from God as the Prime Mover, then God was in the position of the second agent we just discussed—the man who forced the trigger finger, or the hypnotist—and the sinner, so-called, was *not* responsible for what he did. (This may be a bold assertion, in view of the history of Western theology, but I must say that I have never encountered a single good reason for denying it.)

There is one standard objection to all of this and we should consider it briefly.

3. The objection takes the form of a stratagem—one designed to show that determinism (and divine providence) is consistent with human responsibility. The stratagem is one that was used by Jonathan Edwards and by many philosophers in the present century, most notably G.E. Moore.

One proceeds as follows: The expression

(a) He could have done otherwise,

it is argued, means no more nor less than

(b) If he had chosen to do otherwise, then he would have done otherwise.

(In place of 'chosen', one might say 'tried', 'set out', 'decided', 'undertaken', or 'willed'.) The truth of statement (b), it is then pointed out, is consistent with determinism (and with divine providence); for even if all of the man's actions were causally determined, the man could still be such that, if he had chosen otherwise, then he would have done otherwise. What the murderer saw, let us suppose, along with his beliefs and desires, *caused* him to fire the shot; yet he was such that *if*, just then, he had chosen or decided *not* to fire the shot, then he would not have fired it. All of this is certainly possible: Similarly, we could say, of the dam, that the flood caused it to break and also that the dam was such that, *if* there had been no flood or any similar pressure, then the dam would have remained intact. And therefore, the argument proceeds, if (b) is consistent with determinism, and if (a) and (b) say the same thing, then (a) is also consistent with determinism; hence we can say that the agent *could* have done otherwise even though he was caused to do what he did do; and therefore determinism and moral responsibility are compatible.

Is the argument sound? The conclusion follows from the premises, but the catch, I think, lies in the first premise—the one saying that statement (a) tells us no more nor less than what statement (b) tells us. For (b), it would seem, could be true while (a) is false. That is to say, our man might be such that, if he had chosen to do otherwise, then he would have done otherwise, and yet *also* such that he could not have done otherwise. Suppose, after all, that our murderer could not have *chosen*, or could not have *decided*, to do otherwise. Then the fact that he happens also to be a man such that, if he had chosen not to shoot he would not have shot, would make no difference. For if he could *not* have chosen *not* to shoot, then he could not have done anything other than just what it was that he did do. In a word: from our statement (b) above ('If he had chosen to do otherwise, then he would have done otherwise'), we cannot make an inference to (a) above ('He could have done otherwise') unless we can *also* assert:

(c) He could have chosen to do otherwise.

And therefore, if we must reject this third statement (c), then, even though we may be justified in asserting (b), we are not justified in asserting (a). If the man could not have chosen to do otherwise, then he would not have done otherwise— *even* if he was such that, if he *had* chosen to do otherwise, then he would have done otherwise.

The stratagem in question, then, seems to me not to work, and I would say, therefore, that the ascription of responsibility conflicts with a deterministic view of action.

4. Perhaps there is less need to argue that the ascription of responsibility also conflicts with an indeterministic view of action—with the view that the act, or some event that is essential to the act, is not caused at all. If the act—the firing of the shot—was not caused at all, if it was fortuitous or capricious, happening so to speak out of the blue, then, presumably, no one—and nothing—was responsible for the act. Our conception of action, therefore, should be neither deterministic nor indeterministic. Is there any other possibility?

5. We must not say that every event involved in the act is caused by some other event; and we must not say that the act is something that is not caused at all. The possibility that remains, therefore, is this: We should say that at least one of the events that are involved in the act is caused, not by any other events, but by something else instead. And this something else can only be the agent—the man. If there is an event that is caused, not by other events, but by the man, then there are some events involved in the act that are not caused by other events. But if the event in question is caused by the man then it *is* caused and we are not committed to saying that there is something involved in the act that is not caused at all. But this, of course, is a large consequence, implying something of considerable importance about the nature of the agent or the man.

6. If we consider only inanimate natural objects, we may say that causation, if it occurs, is a relation between *events* or *states of affairs*. The dam's

breaking was an event that was caused by a set of other events—the dam being weak, the flood being strong, and so on. But if a man is responsible for a particular deed, then, if what I have said is true, there is some event, or set of events, that is caused, *not* by other events or states of affairs, but by agent, whatever he may be.

I shall borrow a pair of medieval terms, using them, perhaps, in a way that is slightly different from that for which they were originally intended. I shall say that when one event or state of affairs (or set of events or states of affairs) causes some other event or state of affairs, then we have an instance of *transeunt* causation. And I shall say that when an *agent*, as distinguished from an event, causes an event or state of affairs, then we have an instance of *immanent* causation.

The nature of what is intended by the expression 'immanent causation' may be illustrated by this sentence from Aristotle's *Physics*: 'Thus, a staff moves a stone, and is moved by a hand, which is moved by a man.'[68] If the man was responsible, then we have in this illustration a number of instances of causation—most of them transeunt but at least one of them immanent. What the staff did to the stone was an instance of transeunt causation, and thus we may describe it as a relation between events: 'The motion of the staff caused the motion of the stone.' And similarly for what the hand did to the staff: 'The motion of the hand caused the motion of the staff.' And, as we know from physiology, there are still other events which caused the motion of the hand. Hence we need not introduce the agent at this particular point, as Aristotle does—we *need* not, though we *may*. We *may* say that the hand was moved by the man, but we may *also* say that the motion of the hand was caused by the motion of certain muscles; and we may say that the motion of the muscles was caused by certain events that took place within the brain. But some event, and presumably one of those that took place within the brain, was caused by the agent and not by any other events.

* * *

11. If we are responsible, and if what I have been trying to say is true, then we have a prerogative which some would attribute only to God: each of us, when we act, is a prime mover unmoved. In doing what we do, we cause certain events to happen, and nothing—or no one—causes us to cause those events to happen.

- How does Chisholm formulate 'the metaphysical problem of human freedom'?
- What is Chisholm's solution to that problem? What questions do you have about it?
- What is the difference between 'transeunt causation' and 'immanent causation'?
- Some philosophers have thought that 'he could have done otherwise' means the same as 'if he had chosen to do otherwise, then he would have done otherwise'. Why does Chisholm think that philosophers who think this are mistaken? If Chisholm is right about this, where does that leave the case for compatibilism?

SUMMARY AND CONCLUSION

Self-identity is a question of essential properties: What is it about you that makes you a particular person and the same person over time? In this chapter we have reviewed a series of different answers to this question. The tradition from Descartes and Locke to Kant stresses the importance of consciousness in our conception of ourselves, that is, the importance of our minds over our bodies. (Even Hume, who denies that there is a self, is part of this tradition.) And despite many objections to these early doctrines of the self, modern theories of personal identity have, by and large, appealed to some notion of memory, self-consciousness, or psychological continuity. (Ancient philosophers did not believe this. For Aristotle, for example, self-identity was essentially bodily identity, without any particular reference to self-consciousness.) Today, the questions persist. How much is the self something that we can choose, and how much is it something that is determined for us? Does each person have just one self, one set of essential properties, or might a single 'person' be several people, with several selves? Or might there really be no self at all? None of these questions has any firmly agreed-upon answers, but all of us adopt one view or another, even if just

for a short time, every time we attempt to define ourselves or just 'be ourselves'.

And this brings us to freedom. To say that a person's act is free is to be able to ascribe responsibility. The defence of freedom therefore becomes extremely important to us. Our confidence in the universality of scientific explanations, however, may seem to imply the thesis of determinism, which holds that every event has its sufficient natural cause. Human actions, as events, thus seem to be determined and thus not free. Philosophers have attempted to reconcile these two vital beliefs—that at least some human acts are free and that science can ultimately (at least in principle) explain everything—in various ways. Some philosophers have defended determinism ('hard determinism') to the exclusion of freedom. Others have defended freedom to the exclusion of determinism ('indeterminists'). Most philosophers, however, have tried to defend both theses ('compatibilists'). They have argued that determinism does not preclude freedom if an act flows from a person's decision or character ('soft determinists'), that we can be more and less susceptible to determinists, or that even if determinism is true, we cannot help but think of ourselves as free.

REVIEW QUESTIONS

1. What is Locke's analysis of personal identity? Why does Reid think Locke's analysis is flawed?

2. In Kant's view of the self, what is the difference between the transcendental ego and the empirical ego? Why does Kant need both notions?

3. Can an empiricist believe in a substantial self? If you answer 'Yes', what do you think is wrong with the Humean (and Buddhist) case against the self? If you answer 'No', does your assertion prove that there really is no self, or just that empiricism is flawed?

4. What role, if any, does the body play in self-identity or identity of personhood? Do you think that consciousness, memory, or some mental aspect is sufficient to establish personal identity? Could you conceive of your consciousness and memory states inhabiting some other body? What would make that person you?

5. How does Sartre's conception of the self complicate the idea of an individual self? How does he explain the paradox that he creates between the self as 'a being which is what it is not and which is not what it is'? Why does he believe this?

6. Compare and contrast the ideas of a universe ruled by chance, divine predestination, fatalism, and karma. Which view do you find most appealing? Which view do you find most plausible?

7. Suppose your friend advances the following argument: '(1) Determinism is either true or false. (2) If determinism is true, then we don't have free will (because whatever we do, we couldn't have done otherwise). And (3) if determinism is false, then we don't have free will (because our actions, lying outside the order of nature, are just the products of blind chance). Therefore, (4) we do not have free will.' Do you agree with your friend's argument? What seems right to you about it? What seems wrong with it?

8. Discuss the relationship between moral responsibility and freedom.

KEY TERMS

agent causation
antecedent conditions
bad faith
cause
compatibilism
compulsion
continuity (spatiotemporal continuity)
criterion
determinism
dualism
empirical ego

essence
existentialism
facticity
fatalism
free will
freedom
Heisenberg uncertainty principle
indeterminism
libertarian
predestination
prediction

resemblance
responsibility
retrodiction
self-consciousness
self-identity
soft determinism
sufficient cause
transcendence
transcendental ego
unconscious

FURTHER READING

On Self-identity

Owen J. Flanagan and Amélie O. Rorty, eds, *Identity, Character, and Morality: Essays in Moral Psychology* (Cambridge, MA: MIT Press, 1993).

John Perry, ed., *Personal Identity* (New York: Lieber-Atherton, 1975).

Sydney Shoemaker, *Self-Knowledge and Self-Identity* (Ithaca, NY: Cornell University Press, 1963).

On Eastern Conceptions of the Self

C. Moore, ed., *The Individual in East and West* (Honolulu: East-West Center Press, 1967).

D.T. Suzuki, *Zen Buddhism*, ed. W. Barrett (New York: Doubleday, 1956).

On the History of the Self

Richard Ashmore and Lee Jussim, *Self and Identity* (New York: Oxford University Press, 1997).

Quassim Cassam, *Self-Knowledge* (New York: Oxford University Press, 1994).

Charles Taylor, *Sources of the Self* (Cambridge, MA: Harvard University Press, 1994).

On the Problem of Free Will

Bernard Berofsky, ed., *Free Will and Determinism* (New York: Harper and Row, 1966).

Daniel C. Dennett, *Elbow Room* (Cambridge, MA: MIT Press, 1984).

James A. Harris, *Of Liberty and Necessity: The Free Will Debate in Eighteenth-Century British Philosophy* (New York: Oxford University Press, 2005).

Ted Honderich, *Are You Free? The Determinism Problem* (New York : Oxford University Press, 1993).

Robert Kane, ed., *The Oxford Handbook of Free Will* (New York: Oxford University Press, 2002).

John Martin Fischer, Robert Kane, Derk Pereboom, and Manuel Vargas, *Four Views on Free Will* (Oxford: Blackwell, 2007).

Peter Van Inwagen, *An Essay on Free Will* (New York: Oxford University Press, 1983).

Gary Watson, ed., *Free Will* (New York: Oxford University Press, 2003).

PART IV
THE GOOD AND THE RIGHT

CHAPTER 6

ETHICS

All things excellent are as difficult as they are rare.
Benedictus de Spinoza

What should we do, and what should we not do? What acts should we praise? What acts should we condemn and blame? These are questions of **ethics**, the concern for which Socrates was willing to give up his life. The core of ethics is **morality**. Morality is a set of fundamental rules that guide our actions; for example, they may forbid us to kill each other, encourage us to help each other, tell us not to lie, and command us to keep our promises.

Most of the moral rules we accept and follow are ones that we have learned and adopted from parents, friends, teachers, and our own society. At times, though, others may challenge our moral rules, demanding that we defend them. Why should we help each other? Why shouldn't we ever cheat? What reasons can we give to defend one sexual ethic rather than another? New social and technological developments may also force us to re-evaluate our morality. Since minorities and women have participated more and more in public debates on moral issues, we now find ourselves constantly confronted with the injustices of discrimination on the basis of race or sex. The development of sophisticated life-sustaining devices has forced both physicians and philosophers to question whether it is always a moral duty to preserve life whenever possible.

Whenever we try to defend or criticize a moral belief, we enter the realm of ethics. Ethics, or 'moral philosophy'—we shall use these two terms interchangeably—is not concerned with specific moral rules but with the foundation of morality and with providing general principles that will both help us evaluate the validity of a moral rule and choose between different moralities (different sets of moral rules). For example, some ethical theorists, those called **utilitarians**, hold that any good moral rule should promote the greatest **happiness** for the greatest number. Other theorists, for example, Aristotle and Kant, have argued that a good moral rule helps us act in the most rational way possible.

Ethics is also concerned with whether or not to take into account others' or our own interests and desires when deciding what we ought to do. For some ethicists, morality is tied to self-interest at least in an abstract way, and they argue that morality is the best way of satisfying everyone's interests. Other philosophers retain the rigid distinction between morality and self-interest, and they insist that obedience to morality is good for its own sake, or equivalent to being rational, or simply required in order to make us human. And yet other authors have argued that morality is only one among many sets of principles, which we may but need not choose to obey.

In this chapter, we will begin by raising some of the perennial problems of ethics, including the nature of morality and the problem of moral relativism. Then, we will address the familiar claim that the basis of all human behaviour—moral behaviour included—is selfishness, or **egoism**. Next, we will examine several different ethical theories, different ways of conceiving of morals and (or) justifying moral beliefs:

- The ethics of Aristotle, who based his view of morality on the concept of 'virtue' and his idea that man is by nature a social and rational animal. Aristotle argues that being virtuous—controlling our feelings and acting rationally—enables us to become fully human.
- Modern adaptations of Aristotle's ethics, which suggest that we can still learn a great deal from Aristotle about how to live our lives.
- The view that morality is essentially a matter of feeling; David Hume and Jean-Jacques Rousseau are its representatives.
- The monumental ethical theory of Immanuel Kant, who insisted that morality is strictly a matter of practical reason, divorced from our personal interests and desires and based solely on universal principles or **laws**. Thus, according to Kant, we cannot justify the morality of our actions simply by appealing to the good consequences of our actions for others or ourselves.
- The ethical theories of the utilitarians, who argued (in contrast to Kant) that moral rules are merely rules of thumb for achieving the greatest good for the greatest number of people, and who thereby tried to reconcile the interests of each individual with the interests of everyone else.
- The radical theories of Nietzsche and the **existentialists**, who insist that, in an important sense, we choose our moralities and that this choice cannot be justified in any of the ways argued by other modern philosophers.
- Feminist theories and the implications for practical and personal ethics.

Finally, we shall ponder the nature of *ethics in the modern age*. Here, two issues shall engage our attention:

- Is our modern way of thinking about morality significantly different from what preceded it? If it is different, how—and why—is it different? Here we will look at Charles Taylor's influential discussion of what he calls 'the ethics of authenticity'.
- When you find people whose values differ significantly from your own—and that is only to be expected in today's diverse and pluralistic world—how can you reason with them about right and wrong? In other words, how is dialogue possible where there is so much disagreement on fundamentals? Here we will look at Margaret Somerville's response to this problem: the search for 'a shared ethics'.

Before we can explore any of these topics, however, we need to say a bit more about what moral philosophy is—as well as what it isn't.

A. Moral Philosophy

What, then, is moral philosophy all about? What are moral philosophers trying to do? What, exactly, do they hope to accomplish? Attending to these questions will help us to understand what moral philosophers are up to so that we will be in a good position to judge whether or not they have succeeded. We must establish the right set of expectations—we must know what moral philosophers are trying to do—in order to see the point of what they have to say to us. If we misinterpret their intentions, we might end up feeling let down, disappointed, even cheated, but only because we expected them to do things that they never dreamt of attempting.

So just what should we expect from moral philosophers? Some people believe that moral philosophers are supposed to say lofty, inspiring, encouraging things—things that will

EGOISM

The thesis that people act for their own interests.

LAW

An objective rule that is binding on individuals whether they personally accept it or not.

awaken in us a burning desire to live well, to reform our conduct, or to perfect our character. Others believe that the moral philosopher should have wise, profound, and penetrating things to say about life and society in general, or about human nature, or about the cosmos and our place in it. Some great philosophers have done all of these things. Certainly, we find moral philosophers who have produced uplifting, sermon-like writings in which they praise virtue and goodness with great eloquence and beauty (think of Plato); and we find moral philosophers who have been uncommonly shrewd and insightful observers of the human condition (think of Nietzsche). The real question, however, isn't whether individual moral philosophers have done these things; it is whether these things are actually *part* of moral philosophy. In other words, are moral philosophers *supposed* to be edifying preachers, perceptive moralists, cultural critics, prophets, teachers of a new morality, or something similar? Are any of these things part of their official 'job description', so to speak?

According to Canadian philosopher A.R.C. Duncan, the answer to this question is an uncompromising 'No'. In the opening chapter of his book *Moral Philosophy*, Duncan argues that the moral philosopher must not be confused with the moralist, the moral teacher, the moral preacher, or even the maker of moral rules. Instead, the moral philosopher's job, or special function, is 'to understand and reflect on moral experience'.

From *Moral Philosophy*
By A.R.C. Duncan

The moral philosopher is sometimes mistaken for the moralist, he is often confused with the moral teacher, and on occasion he is accused of being a moral preacher.

Since the fifth century BC, moral philosophy has attracted the energies of nearly all the outstanding philosophers in the Western tradition. None of them has underestimated the difficulty or the importance of this branch of philosophy. Plato put the problem very succinctly when he observed that 'it is no light matter to discuss the course we must follow if we are to live our lives to the best advantage'. No light matter indeed, but in the twentieth century the task of the moral philosopher has been greatly complicated by a number of factors that produce considerable confusion concerning the nature of that task and his hopes of achieving it. If we do not begin by attempting to remove some of the causes of this confusion, there is a serious danger that our whole discussion will be shipwrecked on the jagged rocks of misunderstanding.

* * *

Not only does the philosopher in general have to explain the nature of his subject and its methods, but the moral philosopher in particular must make it clear that he is not doing a number of things that he is frequently alleged to be doing. The moral philosopher is sometimes mistaken for the moralist, he is often confused with the moral teacher, and on occasion he is accused of being a moral preacher. A moralist is someone who seeks to draw a moral lesson either from an edifying story, from some event that has taken place, or from his observations on human behaviour. It is quite possible that someone listening to a moral philosopher may draw for himself a moral lesson from something that the philosopher has said or from an example he has used. But when this happens—and there is no reason why it should not happen—it is entirely accidental and forms no part of the philosopher's primary intention. The works of the great moralists like Bacon, La Rochefoucauld, or La Bruyère, are among the finest in our Western literature, but they are not specimens of moral philosophy. A moral teacher is a person whose express function is to inculcate a proper set of moral beliefs in the young. These teachers have an important role to play in any society. Without persons who were prepared to assume this role there would be no continuity in the moral tradition of society, indeed there would be no continuity in social life at all. However, the work of the moral philosopher, which consists largely in critical reflection on the grounds of moral beliefs, cannot even begin until long after the work of the moral teacher has been completed. In recent years philosophers appear to have been particularly afraid of being mistaken for preachers (i.e. people who exhort us to follow a way of life or live up to certain standards). This fear has its roots in the mistaken belief that philosophy should imitate the example of science and adopt a position of strict moral neutrality. If a philosopher decides for one solution to a problem rather than another, then he has abandoned the position of moral neutrality. However, if his position is supported by solid arguments, I see no reason why he should not do so. To present an argument is neither to exhort nor is it to give advice. It is to make an appeal to common human reason, the only authority recognized by a philosopher.

In this connection there is a possible source of misunderstanding that I would like to remove at once. Although the moral philosopher is engaged in discussing various moral rules and principles, he is most emphatically not concerned to lay down or establish a set of moral principles that must be recognized by everyone, nor does he attempt to formulate policy about the ends to be pursued by mankind at large. The moral philosopher is in no sense a moral legislator or a moral policy maker. Moral philosophers have indeed talked about establishing some principle of morality. Kant in the eighteenth century and John Stuart Mill in the nineteenth century were both concerned to establish moral principles. This is true, but we must be careful to understand the sense in which they were using the word 'establish'. Neither Kant nor Mill thought of themselves as establishing a new principle of morality in the way in which a body of legislators might enact or establish new laws, which the citizens would then have to obey. In arguing for the principle of the greatest happiness for the greatest number, Mill claimed that he was simply clarifying something that was implicit in the ordinary moral consciousness, but which had not yet been accurately formulated. In so doing he was engaged in critical analysis and reasoned argument designed to establish a conclusion. Kant not only stated that this was what he was doing, but he also poured scorn on a critic who had complained that his book contained no new principle of morality. 'Who would think,' Kant wrote, 'of introducing a new principle of all morality, and making himself as it were the first discoverer of it, just as if all the world before him were ignorant of what duty was or had been in

thoroughgoing error.' Both Kant and Mill—and to them we can add the names of their great Greek predecessors Plato and Aristotle—interpreted their task as moral philosophers to be that of careful analytic reflection on the morality of ordinary men and women, including themselves, with a view to separating the wheat from the chaff among moral beliefs by means of rational criticism. They did not legislate, they presented arguments for our consideration.

* * *

If the moral philosopher neither moralizes nor preaches nor legislates nor functions as an adviser on practical moral problems, you may well begin to wonder just what he does do. Perhaps the simplest and the least misleading positive description I can give is to say that the moral philosopher seeks to understand and to interpret moral experience. In so far as understanding and interpreting are theoretical activities, his task is theoretical—like that of the physicist seeking to understand the behaviour of matter. But what distinguishes the moral philosopher from any kind of scientist, including the social scientist, is that he has to try to understand moral experience from the inside. He cannot make moral experience an object to which he can adopt a wholly detached attitude in the manner regarded as appropriate to a scientist. While examining moral experience, the philosopher remains a moral being, subject to all the usual duties and obligations characteristic of moral living and experience. Indeed it is only because this is so that he is in a position to try to understand moral experience. Moral experience itself is not something that can be caught and put under a microscope. It is something dynamic and constantly changing, something found only in the lives of actual persons. There is an important sense in which the practice of moral philosophy is a means to self-knowledge, and indeed the founder of the subject, Socrates, explicitly did regard it in that way.

An important consequence of this conception of the philosopher's task—and this is true for all branches of philosophy—is that every man must do his own philosophizing for himself. In this respect philosophy differs from either science or history. In order to read or learn about physics or history, I don't need to become a physicist or a historian. The results of the work of physicists and historians are to

(Continued)

be found, partly at least, in the books they write. Those of us who are not professional physicists or historians more or less have to accept what they say on authority. But you may say, 'Isn't this true of philosophers who also have been known to write books?' The answer to that is quite emphatically 'No'. And the reason is that the philosopher is not concerned to state a number of facts about anything, facts that could be learnt or accepted on authority.

He is concerned to understand, and understanding is an intensely personal activity. When a philosopher writes a book or makes any type of public utterance, what he is doing is inviting his readers or hearers to join him in the task of thinking about some aspect of human experience in the hope that through that activity of thinking some measure of understanding can be achieved. To join in that type of thinking is to philosophize.

- Why does Duncan think that 'every man must do his own philosophizing for himself'? How is this claim related to his conception of the moral philosopher's task?

B. Morality

Morality gives us the rules by which we live with other people. It sets limits to our desires and our actions. It tells us what is permitted and what is not. It gives us guiding principles for making decisions. It tells us what we ought and what we ought not to do. But what is this 'morality' that sounds so impersonal and 'above' us? Let us begin to answer this question by considering a metaphor that Nietzsche uses in *Thus Spoke Zarathustra*: 'A tablet of virtues hangs over every people.'

The 'tablet of virtues' is morality. The prototype of morality, in this view, is those ancient codes, carved in stone, with commands that are eternal and absolute, such as the two tablets on which were inscribed what we call the Ten Commandments. And they are indeed *commandments*. 'Thou shalt' and 'Thou shalt not' is all they say. This is the essence of morality. It consists of commands. These commands do not appeal to individual pleasures or desires. They do not make different demands on different individuals or societies. Quite to the contrary, they are absolute rules that tell us what we must or must not do, no matter who we are, no matter what we want, and regardless of whether or not our interests will be served by the command. 'Thou shalt not kill' means that even if you want to, even if you have the power to, and even if you can escape all punishment, you are absolutely forbidden to kill.

The image of morality as coming 'from above' is appropriate. First, moral laws are often said, and not only in our society, to come from God. Second, we learn these laws from our parents, who literally 'stand over us' and indoctrinate us with these laws through shouts, commands, examples, threats, and gestures. Finally and most importantly, morality itself is 'above' any given individual or individuals, whether it is canonized in the laws of society or not. Morality is not just another aid in getting us what we want; it is entirely concerned with right and wrong. And these considerations are 'above' tampering by any individual, no matter how powerful, as if they have a life of their own.

This characteristic of morality as independent of individual desires and ambitions has led many people to characterize morality simply in terms of some absolute and independent agency. Most often, this absolute and independent agency is God. St Augustine, for example, talks about morality in this way:

From *On Freedom*
By St Augustine

Unless you turn to Him and repay the existence that He gave you, you won't be 'nothing'; you will be wretched. All things owe to God, first of all, what they are insofar as they are natures. Then, those who have received a will owe to Him whatever better thing they can will to be, and whatever they ought to be. No man is ever blamed for what he has not been given, but he is justly blamed if he has not done what he should have done; and if he has received free will and sufficient power, he stands under obligation. When a man does not do what he ought, God the Creator is not at fault. It is to His glory that a man suffers justly; and by blaming a man for not doing what he should have done, you are praising what he ought to do. You are praised for seeing what you ought to do, even though you see this only through God, who is immutable Truth.

St Thomas Aquinas noted, 'It is apparent that things prescribed by divine law are right, not only because they are put forth by law, but also because they are in accord with nature.' He also noted that 'by divine law precepts had to be given, so that each man would give his neighbour his due and would abstain from doing injuries to him.'[1] And in the Bible we read, 'When thou shalt harken—to the voice of the Lord thy God, to keep all his commandments, which I command thee this day, to do that which is right in the eyes of the Lord thy God.'[2]

But whether or not we believe in God, it is clear that something further is needed to help us define morality. Even assuming that there is a God, we need a way of determining what His moral commands must be. One might say that He has given these commands to various individuals, but the fact is that different people seem to have very different ideas about the morality that God has given them. Some, for example, would say that it explicitly rules out abortion and infanticide. Others would argue that God does not rule these out but makes it clear that they are, like other forms of killing (a 'holy war', for example), justifiable only in certain circumstances. In view of such disagreements, we cannot simply appeal to God but must, for reasons that we can formulate and defend, define our morality for ourselves. There is a further question, which has often been debated, but was raised originally by Plato, in his dialogue, *Euthyphro*: Should we follow God's laws just because they are His or, rather, because His laws are good? If the latter, then we have to decide what is good in order to know that God is good. If the former, then we have to decide whether or not to believe in God precisely on the basis of whether we can accept those laws. Either way, we have to decide for ourselves what laws of morality we are willing to accept.

Similar considerations hold true for that familiar appeal to conscience in determining what we ought or ought not to do. Even if one believes that conscience is God-given, the same problems emerge again. Should we follow our consciences just because 'conscience tells us to'? Or do we follow our conscience just because we know that what our conscience commands is good? How do we decide whether a nagging thought is or is not the prompting of God? Probably on the basis of whether what it demands is good or not. (Thus you might readily attribute to conscience the nagging reminder that you shouldn't have cheated an unsuspecting child, but you would not attribute to conscience the nagging thought that you could have gotten away with shoplifting if only you had had the daring to do it.) If we believe that conscience is simply the internalization of the moral teachings of our parents and society, then the question takes an extra dimension: Should we accept or reject what we have been taught? Since our consciences often disagree, we must still decide whose conscience and which rules of conscience we ought to obey. Identifying morality with the promptings of conscience is both plausible and valuable, but philosophically it only moves the question one step back: How do you know what is, and what is not, the prompting of conscience? And is it always right to follow your conscience? But these two questions are in fact just another way of asking what is moral: 'What should I do?'

Morality is not just obedience—whether obedience to a king, a pope, the law, or a personal conscience. Morality is doing what is *right*, whether or not it is commanded by any person or law and whether or not you 'feel' it in your conscience. One way of putting this—which was defended by Immanuel Kant—is to say that morality involves **autonomy**, that is, the ability to think for oneself and decide, for oneself, what is right and what is wrong, whom to obey and whom to ignore, what to do and what not to do. The danger is that this conception of morality as autonomy seems to leave us without a place to learn morality in the first place. How do we learn to judge right and wrong but from our parents, our friends, our teachers, and our society and its models? But if we try to tie morality too closely to our upbringing and our society, then it looks as if there is no room for autonomy, no way in which we could disagree with our family or society, no way to criticize the way in which we have been raised. Furthermore, tying morality to particular societies raises an additional question, and that is whether morality (or moralities) might not be relative to particular societies and cultures.

- In your opinion, are the 'tablets of virtue' justified because they have been commanded by authority or because they are good? In other words, is what is right right because God (or gods) command(s) it? Or does God (or do gods) command it because it is right? What are the advantages and disadvantages with each view?
- Why does it make you uncomfortable when you ignore your conscience? Does it help if others tell you that your action is right (even if you know that it's not)?

C. Is Morality Relative?

Moralities, like lifestyles, vary from culture to culture and even from person to person. But while there is nothing surprising about the fact that lifestyles vary, there is a problem in the variation of moralities. Morality, by its very nature, is supposed to be a set of universal principles, principles that do not distinguish between cultures or peoples or lifestyles. If it is morally reprehensible to kill for fun, then it is morally reprehensible in every society, in every culture, for every lifestyle, and for every person, no matter who he or she is. This will be true even if the society or person in question does not agree with that moral principle.

Aristotle, for example, discusses at length what he calls 'the wicked man' who does evil because he believes in immoral principles and therefore acts without regret, unlike the person who acts badly from momentary weakness, force of circumstances, desperation, or misinformation. But on what grounds can one society or person claim that another society's or person's principles are immoral? How could European Christians in the early nineteenth century, for example, be justified in criticizing the sexual morality of Polynesians in the South Pacific? The Polynesians were a separate society, with their own mores and principles that worked quite well for them, possibly even better in certain ways than the European customs worked in Europe. Yet European missionaries felt no hesitation whatever in condemning their sexual practices as 'immoral'. Similarly, but with more serious implications, what gives us the right to criticize a culture across the world that still believes in genocide as a legitimate consequence of war or in torture as a way of keeping civil order? We surely feel that we have the right to speak up in such cases, but then we too are asserting the universality of our morality, extending it even to people who might explicitly reject our principles. How can we do this? What justifies such an extension?

The problem of **relativism** has become extremely controversial since the nineteenth century, when anthropologists began telling us of exotic societies with moralities so different from ours. In a sense, relativism has always been a threat to established morality, for even the Greeks came into contact with societies that were much different from theirs. (Thus they tended to immediately label anything non-Greek 'barbarian', so that they didn't have to consider the possibility of relativism.) Kant was the most vigorous opponent of relativism, for his conception of morality was such that if a human being was to count as rational at all, he or she had to agree to at least the basic principles of a universal morality. There were people and societies that did not, but that, according to Kant, only proved that they were less than rational (and therefore less than human as well). Today we tend to be more liberal in our acceptance of different styles of life, but few people would deny that at least some moral principles hold for every society. The principle that unnecessary cruelty is wrong, for example, would be such a principle, although people might well disagree about what is 'cruel' and what is 'unnecessary'.

Philosophers generally distinguish two theses when considering relative moralities. The first—**cultural relativism**—is the factual claim that different societies have different moralities. The difficult question is whether these different moralities are only different superficially or whether they are fundamentally different. For example, it's been said that some Inuit tribes kill their elders by leaving them to freeze on the ice; we consider that grossly immoral (we send most of our elders to frigid 'old-age homes' instead). But the question of cultural relativity is whether this difference is merely the reflection of different interpretations of some basic moral principle (such as, don't kill anyone unless it is absolutely necessary for the survival of the rest) or whether it really is a wholly different morality. This is among the most controversial anthropological questions of our time. But philosophers are interested in a second, somewhat different question: Assuming that two moralities really are fundamentally different, is it possible that each is as correct as the other? The philosopher who says 'yes' is an **ethical relativist**, and ethical relativism is what occupies us here.

In the following selection, Gilbert Harman presents a contemporary defence of the relativist position.

ETHICAL RELATIVISM

The thesis that different moralities can be equally correct even if they contradict each other.

From 'Moral Relativism Defended'
By Gilbert Harman

My thesis is that morality arises when a group of people reach an implicit agreement or come to a tacit understanding about their relations with one another. Part of what I mean by this is that moral judgments—or, rather, an important class of them—make sense only in relation to and with reference to one or another such agreement or understanding. This is vague, and I shall try to make it more precise in what follows. But it should be clear that I intend to argue for a version of what has been called moral relativism.

In doing so, I am taking sides in an ancient controversy. Many people have supposed that the sort of view which I am going to defend is obviously correct—indeed, that it is the only sort of account that could make sense of the phenomenon of morality. At the same time there have also been many who have supposed that moral relativism is confused, incoherent, and even immoral, at the very least obviously wrong.

Most arguments against relativism make use of a strategy of dissuasive definition; they define moral relativism as an inconsistent thesis. For example, they define it as the assertion that (a) there are no universal moral principles and (b) one ought to act in accordance with the principles of one's own group, where this latter principle, (b), is supposed to be a universal moral principle. It is easy enough to show that this version of moral relativism will not do, but that is no reason to think that a defender of moral relativism cannot find a better definition.

My moral relativism is a soberly logical thesis—a thesis about logical form, if you like. Just as the judgment that something is large makes sense only in relation to one or another comparison class, so too, I will argue, the judgment that it is wrong of someone to do something makes sense only in relation to an agreement or understanding. A dog may be large in relation to chihuahuas but not large in relation to

(Continued)

dogs in general. Similarly, I will argue, an action may be wrong in relation to one agreement but not in relation to another. Just as it makes no sense to ask whether a dog is large, period, apart from any relation to a comparison class, so too, I will argue, it makes no sense to ask whether an action is wrong, period, apart from any relation to an agreement.

There is an agreement, in the relevant sense, if each of a number of people intends to adhere to some schedule, plan, or set of principles, intending to do this on the understanding that the others similarly intend. The agreement or understanding need not be conscious or explicit; and I will not here try to say what distinguishes moral agreements from, for example, conventions of the road or conventions of etiquette, since these distinctions will not be important as regards the purely logical thesis that I will be defending.

Although I want to say that certain moral judgments are made in relation to an agreement, I do not want to say this about all moral judgments. Perhaps it is true that all moral judgments are made in relation to an agreement; nevertheless, that is not what I will be arguing. For I want to say that there is a way in which certain moral judgments are relative to an agreement but other moral judgments are not. My relativism is a thesis only about what I will call 'inner judgments', such as the judgment that someone ought or ought not to have acted in a certain way or the judgment that it was right or wrong of him to have done so. My relativism is not meant to apply, for example, to the judgment that someone is evil or the judgment that a given institution is unjust.

In particular, I am not denying (nor am I asserting) that some moralities are 'objectively' better than others or that there are objective standards for assessing moralities. My thesis is a soberly logical thesis about logical form.

I. Inner Judgments

We make inner judgments about a person only if we suppose that he is capable of being motivated by the relevant moral considerations. We make other sorts of judgment about those who we suppose are not susceptible of such motivation. Inner judgments include judgments in which we say that someone should or ought to have done something or that someone was right or wrong to have done something. Inner judgments do not include judgments in which we call someone (literally) a savage or say that

someone is (literally) inhuman, evil, a betrayer, a traitor, or an enemy.

Consider this example. Intelligent beings from outer space land on earth, beings without the slightest concern for human life and happiness. That a certain course of action on their part might injure one of us means nothing to them; that fact by itself gives them no reason to avoid the action. In such a case it would be odd to say that nevertheless the beings ought to avoid injuring us or that it would be wrong for them to attack us. Of course we will want to resist them if they do such things and we will make negative judgments about them; but we will judge that they are dreadful enemies to be repelled and even destroyed, not that they should not act as they do.

Similarly, if we learn that a band of cannibals has captured and eaten the sole survivor of a shipwreck, we will speak of the primitive morality of the cannibals and may call them savages, but we will not say that they ought not to have eaten their captive.

Again, suppose that a contented employee of Murder, Incorporated was raised as a child to honour and respect members of the 'family' but to have nothing but contempt for the rest of society. His current assignment, let us suppose, is to kill a certain bank manager, Bernard J. Ortcutt. Since Ortcutt is not a member of the 'family', the employee in question has no compunction about carrying out his assignment. In particular, if we were to try to convince him that he should not kill Ortcutt, our argument would merely amuse him. We would not provide him with the slightest reason to desist unless we were to point to practical difficulties, such as the likelihood of his getting caught. Now, in this case it would be a misuse of language to say of him that he ought not to kill Ortcutt or that it would be wrong of him to do so, since that would imply that our own moral considerations carry some weight with him, which they do not. Instead we can only judge that he is a criminal, someone to be hunted down by the police, an enemy of peace-loving citizens, and so forth.

* * *

Of course, I do not want to deny that for various reasons a speaker might pretend that an agent is or is not susceptible to certain moral considerations. For example, a speaker may for rhetorical or political reasons wish to suggest that someone is beyond the pale, that he should not be listened to, that he can be treated as an enemy. On the other hand, a speaker may pretend that someone is susceptible to certain moral considerations in an effort to make that person or others susceptible to those considerations. Inner judgments about one's children sometimes have this function. So do inner judgments made in political speeches that aim at restoring a lapsed sense of morality in government.

II. The Logical Form of Inner Judgments

Inner judgments have two important characteristics. First, they imply that the agent has reasons to do something. Second, the speaker in some sense endorses these reasons and supposes that the audience also endorses them. Other moral judgments about an agent, on the other hand, do not have such implications; they do not imply that the agent has reasons for acting that are endorsed by the speaker.

* * *

Now we need not suppose that the agreement or understanding in question is explicit. It is enough if various members of society knowingly reach an agreement in intentions—each intending to act in certain ways on the understanding that the others have similar intentions. Such an implicit agreement is reached through a process of mutual adjustment and implicit bargaining.

Indeed, it is essential to the proposed explanation of this aspect of our moral views to suppose that the relevant moral understanding is thus the result of *bargaining*. It is necessary to suppose that, in order to further our interests, we form certain conditional intentions, hoping that others will do the same. The others, who have different interests, will form somewhat different conditional intentions. After implicit bargaining, some sort of compromise is reached.

Seeing morality in this way as a compromise based on implicit bargaining helps to explain why our morality takes it to be worse to harm someone than to refuse to help someone. The explanation requires that we view our morality as an implicit agreement about what to do. This sort of explanation could not be given if we were to suppose, say, that our morality represented an agreement only about the facts (naturalism). Nor is it enough simply to suppose that our morality represents an agreement in attitude, if we forget that such agreement can be reached, not only by way of such principles as are mentioned, . . . but also through bargaining.

- Why does Harman insist that he is giving only the 'logical' form of relativism? What does this mean? What is he not claiming?
- What is ethical relativism? How does it undermine morality's claim to authority? Can you think of a way in which one might account for the variety of moral principles (cultural relativism) without adopting ethical relativism?
- What is ethical absolutism? Does this capture how you think of morality? What problems do you see with it?

D. Egoism and Altruism

Most moral rules, whether about sexuality or otherwise, enjoin us to take into account the interests, feelings, or welfare of other people. The commands not to lie, not to kill, and not to steal, as well as the commands to keep our promises, treat others fairly, and be generous, are all commands that concern our relations to other persons. (There can, of course, be moral rules that require us to take into account our own interests; for example, the prohibition of suicide or, as Kant thought, the **obligation** to develop our talents.)

One of the important assumptions of any morality, then, is that it is possible for us to act in the interests of other people. In addition, morality assumes that it is possible for us to do so *because* we are concerned about others' welfare or because we recognize that we ought to be. Someone who refrains from cheating, for example, simply because he or she is afraid of being caught acts purely self-interestedly; we would not think this person is morally praiseworthy. Again, a person who visits a dying relative in the hospital because he or she wants to ensure a substantial inheritance is not acting morally. Only if actions are motivated by a concern for others' interests do we call them truly moral actions.

One important theory, though, denies that we can be motivated simply by a concern for others. This is **psychological egoism**. Psychological egoism is the thesis that everyone, in fact, acts for his or her own advantage, and the only reason why people act respectfully or kindly toward each other is that that too, for one reason or another, is to their advantage. It might be fear of punishment that makes them act 'correctly'. Some have 'ulterior motives'; that is, they expect other things later on, perhaps a favour in return or a reward in heaven after they die, or they are trying to avoid guilt or want a feeling of self-satisfaction. In popular language, the egoist position is often called **selfishness**.

One should be careful, though, to distinguish psychological egoism from ethical egoism. Psychological egoism asserts that our psychology is such that we cannot help but act in our own interests. In contrast, **ethical egoism** claims that even though we *can* act in others' interests because we are concerned for others, we *ought* always to act in our own interest.

It is psychological, not ethical, egoism that challenges the very possibility of any morality. One of Socrates' opponents in *The Republic* states the psychological egoist's view with brutal clarity:

ETHICAL EGOISM

The thesis that people ought to act in their own interests.

From *The Republic*
By Plato

They say that to do wrong is naturally good, to be wronged is bad, but the suffering of injury so far exceeds in badness the good of inflicting it that when men have done wrong to each other and suffered it, and have had a taste of both, those who are unable to avoid the latter and practise the former decide that it is profitable to come to an agreement with each other neither to inflict injury nor to suffer it. As a result they begin to make laws and covenants, and the law's command they call lawful and just. This, they say, is the origin and essence of justice; it stands between the best and the worst, the best being to do wrong without paying the penalty and the worst to be wronged without the power of revenge. The just then is a mean between two extremes; it is welcomed and honoured because of men's lack of the power to do wrong. The man who has that power, the real man, would not make a compact with anyone not to inflict injury or suffer it. For him that would be madness. This then, Socrates, is, according to their argument, the nature and origin of justice.

Even those who practise justice do so against their will because they lack the power to do wrong. This we could realize very clearly if we imagined ourselves granting to both the just and the unjust the freedom to do whatever they liked. We could then follow both of them and observe where their desires led them, and we would catch the just man redhanded travelling the same road as the unjust. The reason is the desire for undue gain which every organism by nature pursues as a good, but the law forcibly sidetracks him to honour equality. The freedom I just mentioned would most easily occur if these men had the power which they say the ancestor of the Lydian Gyges possessed. The story is that he was a shepherd in the service of the ruler of Lydia. There was a violent rainstorm and an earthquake which broke open the ground and created a chasm at the place where he was tending sheep. Seeing this and marvelling, he went down into it. He saw, besides many other wonders of which we are told, a hollow bronze horse. There were window-like openings in it; he climbed through them and caught sight of a corpse which seemed of more than human stature, wearing nothing but a ring of gold on its finger. This ring the shepherd put on and came out. He arrived at the usual monthly meeting which reported to the king on the state of the flocks, wearing the ring. As he was sitting among the others he happened to twist the hoop of the ring toward himself, to the inside of his hand, and as he did this he became invisible to those sitting near him and they went on talking as if he had gone. He marvelled at this and, fingering the ring, he turned the hoop outward again and became visible. Perceiving this he tested whether the ring had this power and so it happened: if he turned the hoop inwards he became invisible, but was visible when he turned it outwards. When he realized this, he at once arranged to become one of the messengers to the king. He went, committed adultery with the king's wife, attacked the king with her help, killed him, and took over the kingdom.

Now if there were two such rings, one worn by the just man, the other by the unjust, no one, as these people think, would be so incorruptible that he would stay on the path of justice or bring himself to keep away from other people's property and not touch it, when he could with impunity take whatever he wanted from the market, go into houses and have sexual relations with anyone he wanted, kill anyone,

free all those he wished from prison, and do the other things which would make him like a god among men. His actions would be in no way different from those of the other and they would both follow the same path. This, some would say, is a great proof that no one is just willingly but under compulsion, so that justice is not one's private good, since wherever either thought he could do wrong with impunity he would do so. Every man believes that injustice is much more profitable to himself than justice, and any exponent of this argument will say that he is right. The man who did not wish to do wrong with that opportunity, and did not touch other people's property, would be thought by those who knew it to be very foolish and miserable. They would praise him in public, thus deceiving one another, for fear of being wronged.

Both egoist positions are contrasted with what is usually called altruism, that is, acting for the sake of other people's interests. There are degrees of altruism. One may be altruistic because one acts morally, because one recognizes an obligation to other people. Or one may be altruistic in actually taking another person's interests as important or even more important than one's own interests, an act one often finds between lovers or brothers and sisters. Altruism can also be divided into two distinct theses, although these are not so often distinguished. *Psychological altruism* says that people 'naturally' act for each other's sakes. (We shall see this thesis defended by several important philosophers in later sections.) It has rarely been argued, however, that people are compelled to act altruistically. Thus psychological egoism is usually defended for all cases; psychological altruism, in contrast, is only defended for some cases. **Ethical altruism**, on the other hand, says that people ought to act with each other's interests in mind. This is, of course, a basic statement of morality, best summarized in the so-called **Golden Rule**: 'Do unto others as you would have them do unto you.' (We shall see a modern version of this ancient teaching in the philosophy of Kant.)

The most familiar and most difficult question is about psychological egoism: Is it true that people only act for their own self-interest? A famous story about Abraham Lincoln, past president of the United States, is an apt illustration of the thesis. As he was arguing the psychological egoist position with a friend, his coach was passing a mud slide where a mother pig was squealing as her piglets were drowning. Lincoln stopped the coach, saved the piglets, then moved on. His friend asked him whether that wasn't a clear case of altruism. Lincoln replied: 'Why that was the very essence of selfishness. I should have had no peace of mind all day had I gone on and left that suffering old sow worrying over those piglets. I did it to get peace of mind, don't you see?'[3]

Many actions are based upon self-interest and are 'selfish' without any question. The question is, are there any actions that are not based on self-interest? Lincoln's response is an excellent example because it would seem as if his action is not for selfish reasons at all. Yet, according to him, there was a selfish reason behind his actions—his own sense of satisfaction and 'peace of mind'. Could this be true of all our actions?

> **ETHICAL ALTRUISM**
>
> The thesis that one ought to act for the sake of the interests of others.

- What is the point of Plato's story about the Ring of Gyges?

E. Are We Naturally Selfish? A Debate

At the bottom of the ongoing debates about justice, government, and the role of society in constituting and enforcing justice, a deeper debate about human nature is always just under the surface. In the Western tradition, we know this debate by way of two thousand years of arguments about so-called original sin, that is, the idea that people are essentially flawed just by virtue of the fact that they are human. If this is so, if people are, for instance, naturally selfish, then that fact would seem to dictate corrective governmental or cultural sanctions. (Hobbes' view of man in the state of nature makes this quite clear.) On the other hand, if we were to take a more benign view of human nature, as, for example, that found in the philosophy of Jean-Jacques Rousseau, then the sanctions of the state should be more modest, perhaps even minimal.

But here we will look at a different version of that debate, one carried out for an even longer period of time, in the philosophies of ancient China. On the one hand, there is the philosophy of Mencius, a disciple of the great Chinese philosopher Confucius, who argues that humanity is basically benevolent, that every person has a sense of compassion for others. Against this view, there is the later philosopher Xun-zi, who argues to the contrary that people are naturally selfish and cultivation is necessary to correct their evil dispositions.

On Human Nature: Man Is Good
By Mencius

6. Mencius said, 'No man is devoid of a heart sensitive to the suffering of others. Such a sensitive heart was possessed by the Former Kings and this manifested itself in compassionate government. With such a sensitive heart behind compassionate government, it was as easy to rule the Empire as rolling it on your palm.

'My reason for saying that no man is devoid of a heart sensitive to the suffering of others is this. Suppose a man were, all of a sudden, to see a young child on the verge of falling into a well. He would certainly be moved to compassion, not because he wanted to get in the good graces of the parents, nor because he wished to win the praise of his fellow villagers or friends, nor yet because he disliked the cry of the child. From this it can be seen that whoever is devoid of the heart of compassion is not human, whoever is devoid of the heart of shame is not human, whoever is devoid of the heart of courtesy and modesty is not human, and whoever is devoid of the heart of right and wrong is not human. The heart of compassion is the germ of benevolence; the heart of shame, of dutifulness; the heart of courtesy and modesty, of observance of the rites; the heart of right and wrong, of wisdom. Man has these four germs just as he has four limbs. For a man possessing these four germs to deny his own potentialities is for him

to cripple himself; for him to deny the potentialities of his prince is for him to cripple his prince. If a man is able to develop all these four germs that he possesses, it will be like a fire starting up or a spring coming through. When these are fully developed, he can take under his protection the whole realm within the Four Seas, but if he fails to develop them, he will not be able to serve his parents.'

7. Mencius said, 'Is the maker of arrows really more unfeeling than the maker of armour? He is afraid lest he should fail to harm people, whereas the maker of armour is afraid lest he should fail to protect them. The case is similar with the sorcerer-doctor and the coffin-maker. For this reason one cannot be too careful in the choice of one's calling.

'Confucius said, "The best neighbourhood is where benevolence is to be found. Not to live in such a neighbourhood when one has the choice cannot by any means be considered wise." Benevolence is the high honour bestowed by Heaven and the peaceful abode of man. Not to be benevolent when nothing stands in the way is to show a lack of wisdom. A man neither benevolent nor wise, devoid of courtesy and dutifulness, is a slave. A slave ashamed of serving is like a maker of bows ashamed of making bows, or a maker of arrows ashamed of making arrows. If one is ashamed, there is no better remedy than to practise benevolence. Benevolence is like archery: an archer makes sure his stance is correct before letting fly the arrow, and if he fails to hit the mark, he does not hold it against his victor. He simply seeks the cause within himself.'

- Mencius argues that human beings 'by nature' have sympathy for one another. Why do you think, then, that some people display utter callousness toward others? Why do we all find it difficult to sympathize with some people?
- What do you think Mencius means when he says that 'a man neither benevolent nor wise, devoid of courtesy and dutifulness, is a slave'?

From 'Human Nature Is Evil'
By Xun-zi

Crooked wood needs to undergo steaming and bending by the carpenter's tools; then only is it straight. Blunt metal needs to undergo grinding and whetting; then only is it sharp. Now the original nature of man is evil, so he must submit himself to teachers and laws before he can be just.

The nature of man is evil; his goodness is acquired.

His nature being what it is, man is born, first, with a desire for gain. If this desire is followed, strife will result and courtesy will disappear. Second, man is born with envy and hate. If these tendencies are followed, injury and cruelty will abound and loyalty and faithfulness will disappear. Third, man is born with passions of the ear and eye as well as the love of sound and beauty. If these passions are followed, excesses and disorderliness will spring up and decorum and righteousness will disappear. Hence to give rein to man's original nature and to yield to man's emotions will assuredly lead to strife and disorderliness, and he will revert to a state of barbarism. Therefore it is only under the influence of teachers and laws and the guidance of the rules of decorum and righteousness that courtesy will be observed, etiquette respected, and order restored. From all this it is evident that the nature of man is evil and that his goodness is acquired.

Crooked wood needs to undergo steaming and bending by the carpenter's tools; then only is it straight. Blunt metal needs to undergo grinding and whetting; then only is it sharp. Now the original nature of man is evil, so he must submit himself to teachers and laws before he can be just; he must submit himself to the rules of decorum and righteousness before he can be orderly. On the other hand, without teachers and laws, men are biased and unjust; without decorum and righteousness, men are rebellious and disorderly. In ancient times the sage-kings knew that man's nature was evil and therefore biased and unjust, rebellious and disorderly. Thereupon they created the codes of decorum and righteousness and established laws and ordinances in order to bend the nature of man and set it right, and in order to transform his nature and guide it. All men are thus made to conduct themselves in a manner that is orderly and in accordance with the Way. At present, those men who are influenced by teachers and laws, who have accumulated culture and learning, and who are following the paths of decorum and righteousness, are the gentlemen. On the other hand those who give rein to their nature, who indulge in their willfulness, and who disregard decorum and righteousness, are the inferior men. From all this it is evident that the nature of man is evil and that his goodness is acquired.

Mencius says: 'The reason man is ready to learn is that his nature is originally good.' I reply: This is not so. This is due to a lack of knowledge about the original nature of man and of understanding of the distinction between what is natural and what is acquired. Original nature is a heavenly endowment; it cannot be learned, and it cannot be striven after. As to rules of decorum and righteousness, they have been brought forth by the

(Continued)

sages, they can be attained by learning, and they can be achieved by striving. That which cannot be learned and cannot be striven after and rests with Heaven is what I call original nature. That which can be attained by learning and achieved by striving and rests with man is what I call acquired character. This is the distinction between original nature and acquired character. Now by the nature of man, the eye has the faculty of seeing and the ear has the faculty of hearing. But the keenness of the faculty of sight is inseparable from the eye, and the keenness of the faculty of hearing is inseparable from the ear. It is evident that keenness of sight and keenness of hearing cannot be learned.

Mencius says: 'The original nature of man is good; but because men all ruin it and lose it, it becomes evil.' I reply: In this he is gravely mistaken. Regarding the nature of man, as soon as he is born, he tends to depart from its original state and depart from its natural disposition, and he is bent on ruining it and losing it. From all this, it is evident that the nature of man is evil and that his goodness is acquired.

To say that man's original nature is good means that it can become beautiful without leaving its original state and it can become beneficial without leaving its natural disposition. This is to maintain that beauty pertains to the original state and disposition and goodness pertains to the heart and mind in the same way as the keenness of the faculty of sight is inseparable from the eye and the keenness of the faculty of hearing is inseparable from the ear, just as we say that the eye is keen in seeing or the ear is keen in hearing. Now as to the nature of man, when he is hungry he desires to be filled, when he is cold he desires warmth, when he is tired he desires rest. This is man's natural disposition. But now a man may be hungry and yet in the presence of elders he dare not be the first to eat. This is because he has to yield precedence to someone. He may be tired and yet he dare not take a rest. This is because he has to labour in the place of someone. For a son to yield to his father and a younger brother to yield to his older brother, for a son to labour in the place of his father and a younger brother to labour in the place of his older brother—both of these kinds of actions are opposed to man's original nature and contrary to man's feeling. Yet they are the way of the filial son and in accordance with the rules of decorum and righteousness. It appears if a person follows his natural disposition he will show no courtesy, and if he shows courtesy he is acting contrary to his natural disposition. From all this it is evident that the nature of man is evil and that his goodness is acquired.

It may be asked: 'If man's original nature is evil, whence do the rules of decorum and righteousness arise?' I reply: All rules of decorum and righteousness are the products of the acquired virtue of the sage and not the products of the nature of man. Thus, the potter presses the clay and makes the vessel—but the vessel is the product of the potter's acquired skill and not the product of his original nature. Or again, the craftsman hews pieces of wood and makes utensils—but utensils are the product of the carpenter's acquired skills and not the product of his original nature. The sage gathers many ideas and thoughts and becomes well versed in human affairs, in order to bring forth the rules of decorum and righteousness and establish laws and institutions. So then the rules of decorum and righteousness and laws and institutions are similarly the products of the acquired virtue of the sage and not the products of his original nature.

* * *

Man wishes to be good because his nature is evil. If a person is unimportant he wishes to be important, if he is ugly he wishes to be beautiful, if he is confined he wishes to be at large, if he is poor he wishes to be rich, if he is lowly he wishes to be honoured—whatever a person does not have within himself, he seeks from without. But the rich do not wish for wealth and the honourable do not wish for position, for whatever a person has within himself he does not seek from without. From this it may be seen that man wishes to be good because his nature is evil. Now the original nature of man is really without decorum and righteousness, hence he strives to learn and seeks to obtain them.

- If men are by nature evil and unjust and require teachers and laws to become good and just, then how can we be sure that our teachings and laws are just and good since they are made and taught by evil men? Doesn't this require some kernel of natural goodness? Does Xun-zi offer a solution to this problem?

The arguments that are still considered to be the most powerful and definitive against psychological egoism were formulated as sermons by an English bishop, Joseph Butler. Butler argued that the psychological egoist's reasonings based on the thesis that people only ever act out of self-interest turn on a number of fallacies. Butler begins by accepting the distinction between 'private good and a person's own preservation and happiness' and 'respect to society and the promotion of public good and the happiness of society'. But then he insists that these are not, as the egoists argue, always in conflict and fighting against each other. To the contrary, they are almost always in perfect harmony.

Against Egoism
By Joseph Butler

If it be said that there are persons in the world who are in great measure without the natural affections toward their fellow creatures, there are likewise instances of persons without the common natural affections to themselves; but the nature of man is not to be judged of by either of these, but by what appears in the common world, in the bulk of mankind.

From this review and comparison of the nature of man as respecting self and as respecting society, it will plainly appear that there are as real and the same kind of indications in human nature that we were made for society and to do good to our fellow creatures, as that we were intended to take care of our own life and health and private good; and that the same objections lie against one of these assertions as against the other.

First, there is a natural principle of *benevolence* in man, which is in some degree to *society* what *self-love* is to the *individual*. And if there be in mankind any disposition to friendship; if there be any such thing as compassion, for compassion is momentary love; if there be any such thing as the paternal or filial affections; if there be any affection in human nature the object and end of which is the good of another—this is itself benevolence or the love of another. Be it ever so short, be it in ever so low a degree, or ever so unhappily confined, it proves the assertion and points out what we were designed for, as really as though it were in a higher degree and more extensive. I must however remind you that though benevolence and self-love are different, though the former tends most directly to public good, and the latter to private, yet they are so perfectly coincident that the greatest satisfactions to ourselves depend upon our having benevolence in a due degree, and that self-love is one chief security of our right behaviour toward society. It may be added that their mutual coinciding, so that we can scarce promote one without the other, is equally a proof that we were made for both.

* * *

Secondly, this will further appear, from observing that the *several passions and affections*, which are distinct both from benevolence and self-love, do in general contribute and lead us to *public* good as really as to *private*. It might be thought too minute and particular, and would carry us too great a length, to distinguish between and compare together the several passions or appetites distinct from benevolence, whose primary use and intention is the security and good of society; and the passions distinct from self-love, whose primary intention and design is the security and good of the individual. It is enough to the present argument that desire of esteem from others, contempt and esteem of them, love of society as distinct from affection to the good of it, indignation against successful vice—that these are public affections or passions, have an immediate respect to others, naturally lead us to regulate our behaviour in such a manner as will be of service to our fellow creatures. If any or all of these may be considered likewise as private affections, as tending to private good, this does not hinder them from being public affections, too, or destroy the good influence of them upon society, and their tendency to public good. It may be added that as persons without any conviction from reason of the desirableness of life would yet of course preserve it merely from the appetite of hunger, so by acting merely from regard (suppose) to reputation, without any consideration of the good of others, men often contribute to public good. In both these instances they
(Continued)

are plainly instruments in the hands of another, in the hands of Providence, to carry on ends, the preservation of the individual and good of society, which they themselves have not in their view or intention. The sum is, men have various appetites, passions, and particular affections, quite distinct both from self-love and from benevolence—all of these have a tendency to promote both public and private good, and may be considered as respecting others and ourselves equally and in common; but some of them seem most immediately to respect others, or tend to public good, others of them most immediately to respect self, or tend to private good; as the former are not benevolence, so the latter are not self-love; neither sort are instances of our love either to ourselves or others, but only instances of our Maker's care and love both of the individual and the species, and proofs that He intended we should be instruments of good to each other, as well as that we should be so to ourselves.

Thirdly, there is a principle of reflection in men by which they distinguish between, approve and disapprove, their own actions. We are plainly constituted such sort of creatures as to reflect upon our own nature. The mind can take a view of what passes within itself, its propensions, aversions, passions, affections, as respecting such objects and in such degrees, and of the several actions consequent thereupon. In this survey it approves of one, disapproves of another, and toward a third is affected in neither of these ways, but is quite indifferent. This principle in man by which he approves or disapproves his heart, temper, and actions, is conscience. . . . That this faculty tends to restrain men from doing mischief to each other, and leads them to do good, is too manifest to need being insisted upon. Thus a parent has the affection of love to his children; this leads him to take care of, to educate, to make due provision for them; the natural affection leads to this, but the reflection that it is his proper business, what belongs to him, that it is right and commendable so to do—this added to the affection becomes a much more settled principle and carries him on through more labour and difficulties for the sake of his children than he would undergo from that affection alone, if he thought it, and the course of action it led to, either indifferent or criminal. This indeed is impossible, to do that which is good and not to approve of it; for which reason they are frequently not considered as distinct, though they really are, for men often approve of the actions of others which they will not imitate, and likewise do that which they approve not. It cannot possibly be denied that there is this principle of reflection or conscience in human nature. Suppose a man to relieve an innocent person in great distress, suppose the same man afterwards, in the fury of anger, to do the greatest mischief to a person who had given no just cause of offence; to aggravate the injury, add the circumstances of former friendship and obligation from the injured person, let the man who is supposed to have done these two different actions coolly reflect upon them afterwards, without regard to their consequences to himself; to assert that any common man would be affected in the same way toward these different actions, that he would make no distinction between them, but approve or disapprove them equally, is too glaring a falsity to need being confuted. There is therefore this principle of reflection or conscience in mankind.

* * *

If it be said that there are persons in the world who are in great measure without the natural affections toward their fellow creatures, there are likewise instances of persons without the common natural affections to themselves; but the nature of man is not to be judged of by either of these, but by what appears in the common world, in the bulk of mankind.

In short, Butler argues that merely acting on one's own desires does not make an action selfish, for all actions are, in some sense, based on our desires, but at least some of those desires are desires to serve someone else's interests. Thus the 'object' of desire is what makes an act selfish or unselfish, not merely the fact that one's own desire is acted upon. Nor can simply acting with some benefit to oneself make an action selfish, for even if we agreed that an act gives us some benefit (for example, peace of mind), it may still be the case that most of the benefit is for someone else. Even if peace of mind typically follows virtuous actions, that does not show that our motivation is selfish. The satisfaction that accompanies good acts is itself not the motivation of the act. So how would Butler respond to Lincoln's reasoning? He would undoubtedly say that Lincoln's act was an altruistic one; his satisfaction was not the motive of the act but only its consequence.

- Distinguish between psychological egoism and ethical egoism. Do you agree with either?
- Are ethical altruism and psychological egoism compatible? How does Butler reconcile the two?

F. Morality as Virtue: Aristotle

Aristotle's *Ethics* (properly called *The Nicomachean Ethics*) is the best systematic guide to ancient Greek moral and ethical thinking. The significant feature of Greek ethics is its stress on being virtuous as opposed to merely following moral rules. Aristotle's concept of virtue is based on a very special conception of man as a rational being. **Virtue**, accordingly, is rational activity, activity in accordance with a rational principle. Having defined virtue in this way, Aristotle can then defend, for example, courage as a virtue by showing that the courageous man is more rational than the coward.

Aristotle arrives at his conception of man as an essentially rational being by asking what 'the natural good for man' is. This, he argues, will be discovered by finding what all men desire 'for its own sake' and not 'for the sake of anything else'.

From *The Nicomachean Ethics*
By Aristotle

Since . . . it is the reason that in the truest sense is the man, the life that consists in the exercise of the reason is the best and pleasantest for man—and therefore the happiest.

Every art and every kind of inquiry, and likewise every act and purpose, seems to aim at some good; and so it has been well said that the good is that at which everything aims. But a difference is observable among these aims or ends. What is aimed at is sometimes the exercise of a faculty, sometimes a certain result beyond that exercise. And where there is an end beyond that act, there the result is better than the exercise of the faculty. Now since there are many kinds of actions and many arts and sciences, it follows that there are many ends also; e.g. health is the end of medicine, ships of shipbuilding, victory of the art of war, and wealth of economy. But when several of these are subordinated to some one art or science,—as the making of bridles and other trappings to the art of horsemanship, and this in turn, along with all else that the soldier does, to the art of war, and so on,—then the end of the master art is always more desired than the end of the subordinate arts, since these are pursued for its sake. And this is equally true whether the end in view be the mere exercise of a faculty or something beyond that, as in the above instances.

If then in what we do there be some end which we wish for on its own account, choosing all the others as means to this, but not every end without exception as a means to something else (for so we should go on *ad infinitum*, and desire would be left void and objectless),—this evidently will be the good or the best of all things.

We see here the same logical strategy that we saw Aristotle use in our discussion of his metaphysics in Chapter 1—the idea that every act is for the sake of something else (we want to earn a dollar to buy ourselves some food, and we want that to satisfy our hunger).

But since there can be no 'infinite regress', there must be some ultimate end. Aristotle examines two popular conceptions of this ultimate end that is the natural good for man: pleasure and success. He rejects both because neither pleasure nor success is desired for its own sake. Rather, happiness is what all men desire for its own sake; therefore, happiness is the natural good for man.

It seems that men not unreasonably take their notions of the good or happiness from the lives actually led, and that the masses who are the least refined suppose it to be pleasure, which is the reason why they aim at nothing higher than the life of enjoyment. For the most conspicuous kinds of life are three: this life of enjoyment, the life of the statesman, and, thirdly, the contemplative life. The mass of men show themselves utterly slavish in their preference for the life of brute beasts, but their views receive consideration because many of those in high places have the tastes of Sardanapalus. Men of refinement with a practical turn prefer honour; for I suppose we may say that honour is the aim of the statesman's life. But this seems too superficial to be the good we are seeking: for it appears to depend upon those who give rather than upon those who receive it; while we have a presentiment that the good is something that is peculiarly a man's own and can scarce be taken away from him. Moreover, these men seem to pursue honour in order that they may be assured of their own excellence,—at least, they wish to be honoured by men of sense, and by those who know them, and on the ground of their virtue or excellence. It is plain, then, that in their view, at any rate, virtue or excellence is better than honour; and perhaps we should take this to be the end of the statesman's life, rather than honour. But virtue or excellence also appears too incomplete to be what we want; for it seems that a man might have virtue and yet be asleep or be inactive all his life, and, moreover, might meet with the greatest disasters and misfortunes; and no one would maintain that such a man is happy, except for argument's sake. But we will not dwell on these matters now, for they are sufficiently discussed in the popular treatises. The third kind of life is the life of contemplation: we will treat of it further on. As for the money-making life, it is something quite contrary to nature; and wealth evidently is not the good of which we are in search, for it is merely useful as a means to something else. So we might rather take pleasure and virtue or excellence to be ends than wealth; for they are chosen on their own account. But it seems that not even they are the end, though much breath has been wasted in attempts to show that they are.

* * *

Let us return once more to the question, what this good can be of which we are in search. It seems to be different in different kinds of action and in different arts,—one thing in medicine and another in war, and so on. What then is the good in each of these cases? Surely that for the sake of which all else is done. And that in medicine is health, in war is victory, in building is a house,—a different thing in each different case, but always, in whatever we do and in whatever we choose, the end. For it is always for the sake of the end that all else is done. If then there be one end of all that man does, this end will be the realizable good,—or these ends, if there be more than one.

By this generalization our argument is brought to the same point as before. This point we must try to explain more clearly. We see that there are many ends. But some of these are chosen only as means, as wealth, flutes, and the whole class of instruments. And so it is plain that not all ends are final. But the best of all things must, we conceive, be something final. If then there be only one final end, this will be what we are seeking—or if there be more than one, then the most final of them. Now that which is pursued as an end in itself is more final than that which is pursued as means to something else, and that which is never chosen as means than that which is chosen both as an end in itself and as means, and that is strictly final which is always chosen as an end in itself and never as means.

Happiness seems more than anything else to answer to this description: for we always choose it for itself, and never for the sake of something else; while honour and pleasure and reason, and all virtue or excellence, we choose partly indeed for themselves (for, apart from any result, we should choose each of them), but partly also for the sake of happiness, supposing that they will help to make us happy. But no one chooses happiness for the sake of these things, or as a means to anything else at all. We seem to be led to the same conclusion when we start from the notion of self-sufficiency. The final good is thought to be self-suffing [or all-suffing]. In applying this term we do not regard a man as an individual leading a solitary life, but we also take account of parents, children, wife, and, in short, friends and fellow-citizens generally, since man is naturally a social being. Some limit must indeed be set to this; for if you go on to parents and descendants and friends of friends, you will never come to a stop. But this we will consider further on: for the present we will take self-suffing to mean what by itself makes life desirable and in want of nothing. And happiness is believed to answer to this description. And further, happiness is believed to be the most desirable thing in the world, and that not merely as one among other good things: if it were merely one among other good things [so that other things could be added to it], it is plain that the addition of the least of other goods must make it more desirable; for the addition becomes a surplus of good, and of two goods the greater is always more desirable. Thus it seems that happiness is something final and self-suffing, and is the end of all that man does.

We need some idea of what happiness is, and Aristotle here gives us his idea: Happiness is living according to **rationality**, the exercise of our most vital faculties.

RATIONALITY

Acting in the best possible way; according to reason.

But perhaps the reader thinks that though no one will dispute the statement that happiness is the best thing in the world, yet a still more precise definition of it is needed. This will best be gained, I think, by asking, What is the function of man? For as the goodness and the excellence of a piper or a sculptor, or the practiser of any art, and generally of those who have any function or business to do, lies in that function, so man's good would seem to lie in his function, if he has one. But can we suppose that, while a carpenter and a cobbler has a function and a business of his own, man has no business and no function assigned him by nature? Nay, surely as his several members, eye and hand and foot, plainly have each his own function, so we must suppose that man also has some function over and above all these.

What then is it? Life evidently he has in common even with the plants, but we want that which is peculiar to him. We must exclude, therefore, the life of mere nutrition and growth. Next to this comes the life of sense; but this too he plainly shares with horses and cattle and all kinds of animals. There remains then the life whereby he acts—the life of his rational nature, with its two sides or divisions, one rational as obeying reason, the other rational as having and exercising reason. But as this expression is ambiguous, we must be understood to mean thereby the life that consists in the exercise [not the mere possession] of the faculties; for this seems to be more properly entitled to the name.

The function of man, then, is exercise of his vital faculties [or soul] on one side in obedience to reason, and on the other side with reason. But what is called the function of a man of any profession and the function of a man who is good in that profession are, generically the same, e.g. of a harper and of a good harper; and this holds in all cases without exception, only that in the case of the latter his superior excellence at his work is added; for we say a harper's function is to harp, and a good harper's to harp well. Man's function then being, as we say, a kind of life—that is to say, exercise of his faculties and action of various kinds with reason—the good man's function is to do this well and beautifully [or nobly]. But the function of anything is done well when it is done in accordance with the proper excellence of that thing. If this be so the result is that the good of man is exercise of his faculties in accordance with excellence or virtue, or, if there be more than one, in accordance with the best and most complete virtue. But there must also be a full term of years for this exercise; for one swallow or one fine day does not make a spring, nor does one day or any small space of time make a blessed or happy man.

It is important to notice the structure of Aristotle's argument here, for we shall see it emerge often in philosophy as well as in our own thought. The argument rests on a definition of what is 'natural' to man. The good for man is that which is 'natural' to him, and that means, according to Aristotle, what is special or unique to him as well. Thus mere 'nutrition and growth', that is, eating and keeping physically healthy, cannot in themselves be happiness (although they are necessary for happiness) because even plants, Aristotle says, have these 'goals'. Nor can happiness lie in simple experience, even exciting experiences, since even a cow has this as the 'end' of its life. What is unique to man, Aristotle concludes, is his rationality, his ability to act on rational principles. But action according to rational principles, is, as we shall see, precisely what Aristotle thinks virtue is. Thus happiness turns out to be an 'activity of the soul in accordance with perfect virtue'. (This is the key phrase of his work.) This 'perfect virtue' is also called 'excellence', and thus Aristotle's ethics is often called an ethics of self-realization, the goal of which is to make each individual as perfect as possible in all ways:

Indeed, in addition to what we have said, a man is not good at all unless he takes pleasure in noble deeds. No one would call a man just who did not take pleasure in doing justice, nor generous who took no pleasure in acts of generosity, and so on. If this be so, the manifestations of excellence will be pleasant in themselves. But they are also both good and noble, and that in the highest degree—at least, if the good man's judgment about them is right, for this is his judgment. Happiness, then, is at once the best and noblest and pleasantest thing in the world.

So far, however, it sounds as if virtue and happiness are strictly individual matters. But this is not the case. Aristotle's well-known belief that man is a social animal is as important as these other principles. Thus, the principles of reason and rationality that enter into his *Ethics* will have the interests of society as well as those of the individual built into them. (Aristotle even says that there is no real distinction between ethics and politics and that the proper end of ethics is politics.) Virtue, accordingly, is also a social conception, and most of the virtues Aristotle discusses, for example, justice and courage, have much to do with one's role in society. Happiness in general, therefore, has its social dimensions. For example, Aristotle argues that both respect and honour are ingredients in the good life. For Aristotle, the happy person, the virtuous person, is a good citizen. It is necessary to add, however, that the only people who could qualify for Aristotle's good life were Greek citizens, which meant that women, children, slaves, and anyone who did not have the good fortune to be born Greek did not even have a chance at being happy, in Aristotle's sense.[4]

Not only does happiness have a social dimension and not only are the virtues socially defined, but the good life, according to Aristotle, must be taught us by society. Accordingly, Aristotle talks a great deal about the need for 'good education', and he goes so far as to say that if a person has not been brought up 'properly', then no amount of philosophy will be able to make him either virtuous or happy. He also says that young people, because they are 'inexperienced in the actions of life' and are 'so ruled by their passions', should not try to learn moral philosophy, which depends upon maturity and rationality. On this point, however, we will ignore Aristotle's warnings—growing older and more 'mature' is certainly no guarantee of wisdom, and the passions of youth are sometimes more virtuous than the 'rationality' of established maturity.

We have already seen Aristotle's beginning: Every act has its goal (or 'good'), and ultimately there is a goal (or 'chief good') toward which all human acts aim, and that goal is generally called happiness (**eudaimonia**). But, Aristotle adds, this is not much help, for people give very different accounts of what they take to be the ingredients in happiness. Some say that it is pleasure, others say it is wealth or honour. We have seen Aristotle's arguments against these views and his conclusion that happiness must be 'activity in accordance with rational principle', and that means virtuous activity. The key to Aristotle's ethics, then, lies in his concept of virtue.

> • What does Aristotle mean by happiness? How does this conception differ from the way in which we normally think of happiness?

Aristotle distinguishes two kinds of virtues, the practical or moral virtues (courage, generosity, and so on) and the intellectual virtues (skill at mathematics and philosophy). Although Aristotle thinks the highest virtue is the intellectual virtue of philosophic **contemplation**, most of his discussion of virtue centres on the moral virtues. We will now take a closer look at how moral virtues are acquired, what Aristotle means by a moral virtue, and what the moral virtues are.

Excellence, then, being of these two kinds, intellectual and moral, intellectual excellence owes its birth and growth mainly to instruction, and so requires time and experience, while moral excellence is the result of habit or custom and has accordingly in our language received a name formed by a slight change from the word for custom. From this it is plain that none of the moral excellences or virtues is implanted in us by nature; for that which is by nature cannot be altered by training. For instance, a stone naturally tends to fall downwards, and you could not train it to rise upwards, though you tried to do so by throwing it up ten thousand times, nor could you train fire to move downwards, nor accustom anything which naturally behaves in one way to behave in any other way. The virtues, then, come neither by nature nor against nature, but nature gives the capacity for acquiring them, and this is developed by training.

Again, where we do things by nature we get the power first, and put this power forth in act afterwards: as we plainly see in the case of the senses; for it is not by constantly seeing and hearing that we acquire those faculties, but, on the contrary, we had the power first and then used it, instead of acquiring the power by the use. But the virtues we acquire by doing the acts, as is the case with the arts too. We learn an art by doing that which we wish to do when we have learned it; we become builders by building, and harpers by harping. And so by doing just acts we

become just, and by doing acts of temperance and courage we become temperate and courageous.

* * *

Again, both the moral virtues and the corresponding vices result from and are formed by the same acts; and this is the case with the arts also. It is by harping that good harpers and bad harpers alike are produced: and so with builders and the rest; by building well they will become good builders, and bad builders by building badly. Indeed, if it were not so, they would not want anybody to teach them, but would all be born either good or bad at their trades. And it is just the same with the virtues also. It is by our conduct in our intercourse with other men that we become just or unjust, and by acting in circumstances of danger, and training ourselves to feel fear or confidence, that we become courageous or cowardly. So too, with our animal appetites and the passion of anger; for by behaving in this way or in that on the occasions with which these passions are concerned, some become temperate and gentle, and others profligate and ill-tempered. In a word, acts of any kind produce habits or characters of the same kind. Hence we ought to make sure that our acts be of a certain kind; for the resulting character varies as they vary. It makes no small difference, therefore, whether a man be trained from his youth up in this way or in that, but a great difference, or rather all the difference.

Aristotle's point here is not just that the virtues are acquired by practice; he is also arguing that virtue is a state of character. The virtuous person wants to do virtuous acts and he does them 'naturally'. We sometimes think that we are moral just because we believe in moral principles. But believing isn't enough; virtuous action is required. Yet not even virtuous action by itself is enough to make us virtuous. While we sometimes think that a person is virtuous because he 'forces himself' to do what he is supposed to, Aristotle identifies a virtuous person as one who does what he is supposed to do because he wants to, because it is built into his very character. It is even essential, according to Aristotle, that the virtuous man enjoys being virtuous:

And, further, the life of these men is in itself pleasant. For pleasure is an affection of the soul, and each man takes pleasure in that which he is said to love,—he who loves horses in horses, he who loves sight-seeing in sight-seeing, and in the same way he who loves justice in acts of justice, and generally the lover of excellence or virtue in virtuous acts or the manifestation of excellence. And while with most men there is a perpetual conflict between the several things in which they find pleasure, since these are not naturally pleasant, those who love what is noble take pleasure in that which is naturally pleasant. For the manifestations of excellence are naturally pleasant, so that they are both pleasant to them and pleasant in themselves. Their life, then, does not need pleasure to be added to it as an appendage, but contains pleasure in itself.

Here Aristotle gives us perhaps his most famous doctrine, the idea that virtues are **'means between the extremes'**. This is often misinterpreted, however, to read, 'everything in moderation'. In a way, what Aristotle teaches is very different from this; he tells us that we can't do too much of a good thing, that is, if it is a virtue. One can't be too courageous (as opposed to being rash or cowardly), or too just. What he intends by 'the means between the extremes' is this:

By the absolute mean, or mean relatively to the thing itself, I understand that which is equidistant from both extremes, and this is one and the same for all. By the mean relatively to us I understand that which is neither too much nor too little for us; and this is not one and the same for all. For instance, if ten be too large and two too small, six is the mean relatively to the thing itself: for it exceeds one extreme by the same amount by which it is exceeded by the other extreme: and this is the mean in arithmetical proportion. But the mean relatively to us cannot be found in this way. If ten pounds of food is too much for a given man to eat, and two pounds too little, it does not follow that the trainer will order him six pounds: for that also may perhaps be too much for the man in question, or too little; too little for Milo, too much for the beginner. The same holds true in running and wrestling. And so we may say generally that a master in any art avoids what is too much and what is too little, and seeks for the mean and chooses it—not the absolute but the relative mean.

If, then, every art or science perfects its work in this way, looking to the mean and bringing its work up to this standard (so that people are wont to say of a good work that nothing could be taken from it or added to it, implying that excellence is destroyed by excess or deficiency, but secured by observing the mean; and good artists, as we say, do in fact keep their eyes fixed on this in all that they do), and if virtue, like nature, is more exact and better than any art, it follows that virtue also must aim at the mean—virtue of course meaning moral virtue or excellence; for it has to do with passions and actions, and it is these that admit of excess and deficiency and the mean. For instance, it is possible to feel fear, confidence, desire, anger, pity, and generally to be affected pleasantly and painfully, either too much or too little, in either case wrongly; but to be thus affected at the right times, and on the right occasions, and toward the right persons, and with the right object, and in the right fashion, is the mean course and the best course, and these are characteristics of virtue. And in the same way our outward acts also admit of excess and deficiency, and the mean or due amount. Virtue, then, has to deal with feelings or passions and with outward acts, in which excess is wrong and deficiency also is blamed, but the mean amount is praised, and is right—both of which are characteristics of virtue. Virtue, then, is a kind of moderation inasmuch as it aims at the mean.

Again, there are many ways of going wrong (for evil is infinite in nature, to use a Pythagorean figure, while good is finite), but only one way of going right; so that the one is easy and the other hard—easy to miss the mark and hard to hit. On this account also, then, excess and deficiency are characteristic of vice, hitting the mean is characteristic of virtue.

* * *

Virtue, then, is a habit or trained faculty of choice, the characteristic of which lies in moderation or observance of the mean relatively to the persons concerned, as determined by reason, i.e., by the reason by which the prudent man would determine it. And it is a moderation, firstly, inasmuch as it comes in the middle or mean between two vices, one on the side of excess, the other on the side of defect; and, secondly, inasmuch as, while these vices fall short of or exceed the due measure in feeling and in action, it finds and chooses the mean, middling, or moderate amount. Regarded in its essence, therefore, or according to the definition of its nature, virtue is a moderation or middle state, but

viewed in its relation to what is best and right it is the extreme of perfection.

But it is not all actions nor all passions that admit of moderation; there are some whose very names imply badness, or malevolence, shamelessness, envy, and, among acts, adultery, theft, murder. These and all other like things are blamed as being bad in themselves, and not merely in their excess or deficiency. It is impossible therefore to go right in them; they are always wrong: rightness and wrongness in such things (e.g. in adultery) does not depend upon whether it is the right person and occasion and manner, but the mere doing of any one of them is wrong. It would be equally absurd to look for moderation or excess or deficiency in unjust cowardly or profligate conduct; for then there would be moderation in excess or deficiency, and excess in excess, and deficiency in deficiency. The fact is that just as there can be no excess or deficiency in temperance or courage because the mean or moderate amount is, in a sense, an extreme, so in these kinds of conduct also there can be no moderation or excess or deficiency, but the acts are wrong however they be done. For, to put it generally, there cannot be moderation in excess or deficiency, nor excess or deficiency in moderation.

We see that Aristotle defines 'moral virtue' as a mean both in feeling and action. Thus courage is a virtue because the courageous man feels neither too little nor too much fear. His fear is appropriate to the dangerousness of his situation. Because the courageous person feels the right amount of fear, he acts in the right way, neither plunging rashly into danger nor fleeing from it in terror. Now, finally, Aristotle gives us his examples of virtue:

Moderation in the feelings of fear and confidence is courage: of those that exceed, he that exceeds in fearlessness has no name (as often happens), but he that exceeds in confidence is foolhardy, while he that exceeds in fear, but is deficient in confidence, is cowardly. Moderation in respect of certain pleasures and also (though to a less extent) certain pains is temperance, while excess is profligacy. But defectiveness in the matter of these pleasures is hardly ever found, and so this sort of people also have as yet received no name: let us put them down as 'void of sensibility'. In the matter of giving and taking money, moderation is liberality, excess and deficiency are prodigality and illiberality. But

both vices exceed and fall short in giving and taking in contrary ways: the prodigal exceeds in spending, but falls short in taking; while the illiberal man exceeds in taking, but falls short in spending. . . . But, besides these, there are other dispositions in the matter of money: there is a moderation which is called magnificence (for the magnificent is not the same as the liberal man: the former deals with large sums, the latter with small), and an excess which is called bad taste or vulgarity, and a deficiency which is called meanness . . . . With respect to honour and disgrace, there is a moderation which is pride, an excess which may be called vanity, and a deficiency which is humility.

(Continued)

But just as we said that liberality is related to magnificence, differing only in that it deals with small sums, so here there is a virtue related to high-mindedness, and differing only in that it is concerned with small instead of great honours. A man may have a due desire for honour, and also more or less than a due desire: he that carries this desire to excess is called ambitious, he that has not enough of it is called unambitious, but he that has the due amount has no name. . . . In the matter of anger also we find excess and deficiency and moderation. The characters themselves hardly have recognized names, but as the moderate man is here called gentle, we will call his character gentleness; of those who go into extremes, we may take the term wrathful for him who exceeds, with wrathfulness for the vice, and wrathless for him who is deficient, with wrathlessness for his character.

* * *

In the matter of truth, then, let us call him who observes the mean a true [or truthful] person, and observance of the mean truth [or truthfulness]: pretence, when it exaggerates, may be called boasting, and the person a boaster; when it understates, let the names be irony and ironical. With regard to pleasantness in amusement, he who observes the mean may be called witty, and his character wittiness; excess may be called buffoonery, and the man a buffoon; while boorish may stand for the person who is deficient, and boorishness for his character. With regard to pleasantness in the other affairs of life, he who makes himself properly pleasant may be called friendly, and his moderation friendliness; he that exceeds may be called obsequious if he have no ulterior motive, but a flatterer if he has an eye to his own advantage; he that is deficient in this respect, and always makes himself disagreeable, may be called a quarrelsome or peevish fellow.

Moreover, in mere emotions and in our conduct with regard to them, there are ways of observing the mean; for instance, shame is not a virtue, but yet the modest man is praised. For in these matters also we speak of this man as observing the mean, of that man as going beyond it (as the shamefaced man whom the least thing makes shy), while he who is deficient in the feeling, or lacks it altogether, is called shameless; but the term modest is applied to him who observes the mean. Righteous indignation, again, hits the mean between envy and malevolence. These have to do with feelings of pleasure and pain at what happens to our neighbours. A man is called righteously indignant when he feels pain at the sight of undeserved prosperity, but your envious man goes beyond him and is pained by the sight of anyone in prosperity, while the malevolent man is so far from being pained that he actually exults in the misfortunes of his neighbours.

It is worth making a short list of Aristotle's moral virtues. Many of them are our own virtues also, but some of them are far more appropriate to an aristocratic, warrior society than they are to our own. To illustrate Aristotle's idea that virtues are the means between the extremes, we have included 'the extremes' in parentheses for contrast:

- *Courage*, particularly courage in battle (extremes: cowardice, rashness). What motivates courage, Aristotle tells us, is a sense of honour, not fear of punishment nor desire for reward, nor merely a sense of duty. The courageous man is afraid, he adds, because without fear there would be no courage. The man who feels no fear in the face of danger is rather rash.
- *Temperance*, particularly concerning bodily pleasures, such as sex, food, and drinking (extremes: self-indulgence or piggishness, insensitivity). Notice that Aristotle does not say, along with many modern moralists, that pleasures are either 'bad' or unimportant; in fact, he attacks the man who does not enjoy sex, food, and drinking as much as he attacks the man who overindulges himself. He says that such people 'are not even human'.
- *Liberality*, or, as we would say, 'charity' (extremes: prodigality or waste, meanness or stinginess). Aristotle ridicules the man who gives more than he can afford to charity as much as he chastises the man who will not give at all.
- *Magnificence*, in other words, how extravagantly you live (extremes: vulgarity, miserliness). Aristotle says that one ought to live 'like an artist' and spend lavishly. (There is little of the ascetic in Aristotle.)

- *Pride* (extremes: humility, vanity). It is worth noting that pride is one of the seven deadly sins in Christian morality while humility is a virtue. In Aristotle's ethics, this is reversed.
- *Good temper* (extremes: irascibility or bad temper, being too easygoing). It is important to get angry, according to Aristotle, about the right things, but not too angry (which 'makes a person impossible to live with').
- *Friendliness* (extremes: obsequiousness, churlishness). Friendship, for Aristotle, is one of the most important ingredients in the good life, and being friendly, therefore, is an extremely important virtue. But Aristotle does not say that we should be friendly to everyone; the person who is indiscriminately friendly toward everyone is not worth being a friend with at all.
- *Truthfulness* (extremes: lying, boasting). Aristotle notes that this virtue is most important in relation to telling the truth about oneself.
- *Wittiness* (extremes: buffoonery, boorishness). We think of wittiness as a personal asset, but rarely as a virtue. Aristotle thinks that people who are incapable of telling a joke or who tell bad jokes are actually inferior. Fun is an important ingredient in Greek virtuousness.
- *Shame* (extreme: shamelessness). Aristotle calls this a 'quasi-virtue'. We all make mistakes and it is a sign of virtue, according to Aristotle, that the good man feels shame when he does them. Shamelessness is a sign of wickedness. Aristotle does not even talk of the other extreme, which he did not consider a problem. (We certainly would. We call it excessive guilt.)
- *Justice,* the cardinal virtue of the Greeks. The need for lawful and fair (which does not mean equal) treatment of other men. (The sense in which justice is a mean between extremes is too complex to discuss here. Aristotle spends a full chapter explaining it.)

Finally, Aristotle gives us his view of the good life for humankind; it is the life of activity in accordance with virtue, but it is also, ideally, a life of intellectual activity, or what he calls 'the life of contemplation'. In other words, the happiest person is the philosopher:

We said that happiness is not a habit or trained faculty. If it were, it would be within the reach of a man who slept all his days and lived the life of a vegetable, or of a man who met with the greatest misfortunes. As we cannot accept this conclusion, we must place happiness in some exercise of faculty, as we said before. But as the exercises of faculty are sometimes necessary (i.e. desirable for the sake of something else), sometimes desirable in themselves, it is evident that happiness must be placed among those that are desirable in themselves, and not among those that are desirable for the sake of something else: for happiness lacks nothing; it is sufficient in itself.

Now, the exercise of faculty is desirable in itself when nothing is expected from it beyond itself. Of this nature are held to be (1) the manifestations of excellence; for to do what is noble and excellent must be counted desirable for itself: and (2) those amusements which please are more apt to be injured than to be benefitted by them, through neglect of their health and fortunes. Now, most of those whom men call happy have recourse to pastimes of this sort. And on this account those who show a ready wit in such pastimes find favour with tyrants; for they make themselves pleasant in that which the tyrant wants, and what he wants is pastime. These amusements, then, are generally thought to be elements of happiness, because princes employ their leisure in them. But such persons, we may venture to say, are no criterion. For princely rank does not imply the possession of virtue or of reason, which are the sources of all excellent exercise of faculty. And if these men, never having tasted pure and refined pleasure, have recourse to the pleasures of the body, we should not on that account think these more desirable; for children also fancy that the things which they value are better than anything else. It is only natural, then, that as children differ from men in their estimate of what is valuable, so bad men should differ from good.

(Continued)

As we have often said, therefore, that is truly valuable and pleasant which is so to the perfect man. Now, the exercise of those trained faculties which are proper to him is what each man finds most desirable; what the perfect man finds most desirable, therefore, is the exercise of virtue. Happiness, therefore, does not consist in amusement; and indeed it is absurd to suppose that the end is amusement, and that we toil and moil all our life long for the sake of amusing ourselves. We may say that we choose everything for the sake of something else, excepting only happiness; for it is the end. But to be serious and to labour for the sake of amusement seems silly and utterly childish; while to amuse ourselves in order that we may be serious, as Anacharsis says, seems to be right; for amusement is a sort of recreation, and we need recreation because we are unable to work continuously. Recreation then, cannot be the end; for it is taken as a means to the exercise of our faculties.

Again, the happy life is thought to be that which exhibits virtue; and such a life must be serious and cannot consist in amusement. Again, it is held that things of serious importance are better than laughable and amusing things, and that the better the organ or the man, the most important is the function; but we have already said that the function or exercise of that which is better is higher and more conducive to happiness. Again, the enjoyment of bodily pleasures is within the reach of anybody, of a slave no less than the best of men; but no one supposes that a slave can participate in happiness, seeing that he cannot participate in the proper life of man. For indeed happiness does not consist in pastimes of this sort, but in the exercise of virtue, as we have already said.

But if happiness be the exercise of virtue, it is reasonable to suppose that it will be the exercise of the highest virtue; and that will be the virtue or excellence of the best part of us. Now, that part or faculty—call it reason or what you will—which seems naturally to rule and take the lead, and to apprehend things noble and divine—whether it be itself divine, or only the divinest part of us—is the faculty the exercise of which, in its proper excellence, will be perfect happiness. . . . this consists in speculation or theorizing.

This conclusion would seem to agree both with what we have said above, and with known truths. This exercise of faculty must be the highest possible; for the reason is the highest of our faculties and of all knowable things those that reason deals with are the highest. Again, it is the most continuous; for speculation can be carried on more continuously than any kind of action whatsoever. We think too that pleasure ought to be one of the ingredients of happiness; but of all virtuous exercises it is allowed that the pleasantest is the exercise of wisdom. At least philosophy is thought to have pleasures that are admirable in purity and steadfastness; and it is reasonable to suppose that the time passes more pleasantly with those who possess, than with those who are seeking knowledge. Again, what is called self-sufficiency will be most of all found in the speculative life. The necessaries of life, indeed, are needed by the wise man as well as by the just man and the rest; but, when these have been provided in due quantity, the just man further needs persons toward whom, and along with whom, he may act justly; and so does the temperate and the courageous man and the rest; while the wise man is able to speculate even by himself, and the wiser he is the more is he able to do this. He could speculate better, we may confess, if he had others to help him, but nevertheless he is more self-sufficient than anybody else. Again, it would seem that this life alone is desired solely for its own sake; for it yields no result beyond the contemplation, but from the practical activities we get something more or less besides action.

* * *

[It] follows that the exercise of reason will be the complete happiness of man, i.e. when a complete term of days is added; for nothing incomplete can be admitted into our idea of happiness. But a life which realized this idea would be something more than human; for it would not be the expression of man's nature, but of some divine element in that nature—the exercise of which is as far superior to the exercise of the other kind of virtue, as this divine element is superior to our compound human nature. If then reason be divine as compared with man, the life which consists in the exercise of reason will also be divine in comparison with human life. Nevertheless, instead of listening to those who advise us as men and mortals not to lift our thoughts above what is human and mortal, we ought rather, as far as possible, to put off our mortality and make every effort to live in the exercise of the highest of our faculties; for though it be but a small part of us, yet in power and value it far surpasses all the rest. And indeed this part would even seem to constitute our true self, since it is the sovereign and the better part. It would be strange, then, if a man were to prefer the life of something else to the life of his true self. Again, we may apply here what we said above—for every being that is best and pleasantest which is naturally proper to it. Since, then, it is the reason that in the truest sense is the man, the life that consists in the exercise of the reason is the best and pleasantest for man—and therefore the happiest.

But you must not think that Aristotle's ideal philosopher does nothing but contemplate. He may also enjoy pleasure, wealth, honour, success, and power. As a man among men, he is also virtuous and chooses to act virtuously like all good men. But in addition, he has an understanding and an appreciation of reason that makes him 'dearest to the Gods and presumably the happiest among men'. This is surely a flattering portrait of the place of the philosopher! But if we ignore this final self-congratulation, we can see in Aristotle a powerful conception of morality, with its emphasis on virtue, excellence, and a kind of heroism (whether intellectual or moral) that is in some ways very different from our own conception of morality and the good life.

- What role does society, or the community, play in Aristotle's ethics?
- How does Aristotle define virtue? What does he mean by 'the mean between extremes'? What are some examples of the virtues? In what sense are they the mean between the extreme? Can you identify any virtues that do not seem to have a corresponding extreme (whether excess or deficiency)?
- How does Aristotle characterize human excellence? How does this differ from your own conception of the good life?

G. Beyond Aristotle: Happiness, Human Nature, and Perfectionism

When we step back and survey Aristotle's ethics from our present perspective, we can't help but ask certain basic questions about what we see. Of course, we will have plenty of questions about specific parts of the *Ethics*, including questions on how some of those parts fit with others; but we may also wonder about the 'big picture', the fundamental orientation and presuppositions of Aristotle's ethical thought as a whole.

Can we, as twenty-first-century Canadians, accept that 'big picture'—Aristotle's ethical vision—in its entirety? It is very tempting to say no. After all, you may think, we are not members of that ancient Athenian world that shaped his thought so profoundly. If this is your immediate reaction, here are four questions you need to ask yourself. First, what do you think it is about us—about our culture, our history, our way of looking at ourselves and at others— that prevents us from living our lives according to the ideals that Aristotle sets forth? Second, what elements of Aristotle's ethical vision do you think we *can* accept? Third, how wise, inspiring, or valuable do you find these elements? Fourth, how might we adapt what is best in Aristotle—his deepest insights, his most compelling thoughts—to the needs of our own time?

These questions are not easy, and different philosophers have given very different answers to them. One writer whose answers are instructive is the Canadian humanitarian Jean Vanier.[5] In his book-length study of *The Nicomachean Ethics*, entitled *Made for Happiness: Discovering the Meaning of Life with Aristotle*, Vanier argues that Aristotle was right about a great many things that matter. In the first place, Vanier thinks that Aristotle was absolutely right to connect ethics with our pursuit of happiness:

From *Made for Happiness*
By Jean Vanier

Happiness, whatever else people may say, is the great concern of our life . . . Aristotle is one of the great witnesses to this quest for happiness.

Happiness, whatever else people may say, is the great concern of our life. A brief inquiry will easily bear this out. We would only have to ask people rushing to work, strolling about the streets, or chatting over a drink, 'What are you looking for in life?' Some might say, 'success at work, promotion'; others, 'marriage, starting a family', or 'a peaceful life without conflict', or 'a salary increase, a holiday in the sun, a good time with friends'. But if we were to press them further, 'Why do you want to be successful, earn a salary increase, start a family, or have an enjoyable holiday?' their answer would no doubt be, 'because it would make me happy'.

To be happy, to know happiness, is the great desire of every man and woman. We may differ perhaps in the means by which we attain happiness, but we all want to be happy. That is our great aspiration.

* * *

Aristotle is one of the great witnesses to this quest for happiness. His thinking was not that of an ideologue, but based on human facts and personal experience. That was what led him to propound his ethics of happiness in order to help people to look more clearly into themselves and to find their own fulfillment. He did so 2,400 years ago, but his thinking spans the centuries and is still relevant to us today.

In the second place, Vanier applauds the way in which Aristotle does justice to the respective roles of intelligence and desire, of reason and aspiration, in human life:

Aristotle believes in human intelligence. He is convinced that what distinguishes human beings from animals is the capacity to think, to know and analyze reality, to make choices, to orient our lives in one direction or another. He does not accept that we are merely a collection of predestined desires or impulses. He thinks that each of us is, to a greater or lesser extent, master of our own life and destiny.

Aristotle does not, however, seek merely to reiterate moral axioms. Nor does he wish to prompt people

by external means to be just, to seek the truth, and to obey laws. What he wants to do is lay the foundations of a moral science with thinking that stems from humanity's deep desires. His fundamental question is not 'What ought we to do?' but 'What do we really want?' His ethics are not those of law. Rather, they look closely at humanity's deepest inclinations in order to bring them to their ultimate fulfillment. Aristotle's ethics are not therefore based on an idea but on the desire for fullness of life inscribed in every human being.

In the third place, he praises the way in which Aristotle's ethics invites us to reflect on what we are and on what we can make of ourselves:

Aristotle's ethics require that we work on ourselves. We might be disappointed that they do not provide us with the clear moral guidelines for action that we are seeking, or with the principles that we might expect ethics to propound. Instead Aristotle invites us

to look for and discern those guidelines within ourselves. 'What is your deepest desire, hidden perhaps beneath other, more superficial desires?' It is for us to work that out.

* * *

Even though Aristotelian ethics have their limitations, they nevertheless set down some essential principles. They call upon each one of us to use our intelligence to reflect upon what we are and what we could become, and not to allow ourselves to be guided by illusions, dreams, or sophisms—by what everyone else does and says—but to seek the truth about humanity. Ethical reflection is essential. Human beings are not simply assemblies of predetermined or completely chaotic desires. With help, we are capable of taking hold of our lives, of being responsible for our own lives and making choices. Ethics call upon us to become more aware of ourselves and our fundamental motivation. They invite us to ask ourselves what we want out of life and what we are looking for, in order then to orient ourselves with greater truth toward the good that we are capable of choosing, and the happiness we are capable of attaining.

In the fourth place, Vanier finds Aristotle's understanding of happiness appropriately broad and inclusive; for although Aristotle is 'a believer in human intelligence' who prizes contemplation and the search for truth, he also recognizes that pleasure, affection, and friendship all matter deeply to us:

If there are deficiencies in Aristotle's thinking, there are also things of significant value. He wants to take into account the whole of human reality, not to create a system of ethics that is purely ideological. His ethics integrate the dimension of the body and affectivity, as well as that of pleasure. They afford friendship a generous place, for Aristotle is convinced that it is impossible to be happy all on one's own: 'For without friends no one would choose to live.'[6] In a broader sense, happiness has a social or *civic* dimension. The man who wishes to be fully human cannot remain a stranger to city life.

It is this profound sense of reality and human reality that has always interested me about Aristotle. . . .

In the fifth place, Vanier approves of Aristotle's realistic but edifying assessment of human beings. According to Aristotle, human beings are neither gods nor brutes, neither invulnerable nor helpless, neither infallible nor irredeemably flawed:

The Value of Aristotelian Ethics

Aristotelian ethics are realistic. They stem from what is human and come back to what is human. On the one hand, Aristotle knows that most men allow themselves to be led by their passions; on the other, he recognizes the grandeur of man, who is specifically different from the animals.

Man is a being who endlessly seeks the keys to happiness. Frequently he stops at mirages, believing he has found the ultimate sources of happiness and healing, only to discover that they are just illusions. So he sets out again on his interminable quest. From generation to generation, human beings have sought to quench their thirst for the limitless: the search for God, the search for the infinite in nature and the heavens, the search for the infinite in love, the search for omnipotence. Human beings cannot stop the quest that so torments them because, if they are conscious of their being, they are also conscious of not being masters of their own destiny. Accidents, illness, the death of those near to us and the prospect of our own death, wars, man's hatred, storms, earthquakes—all go to show that we are not masters of our own future. The universe and its forces are beyond our control. We are but small, mortal fragments in the vast whole. We exist, but we do not have within us all the resources to be fully alive and live forever. That is our tragedy.

Aristotelian ethics do not then rely on a fully developed theory, but on the *desire* in every human being to be happy. Just as a seed planted in the earth will grow to fullness of life, provided it is watered, so a human being aspires to his own fullness of life.

(Continued)

The difference between plants and human beings is that the seed, provided it is nourished, will unfailingly spring up and bear fruit, that is to say, it will reach its fullness of life. The human being, for his part, can attain his only through knowledge, choices, and even struggle. This involves, for Aristotle, education and good laws. Man is capable of correctly orienting his life toward happiness, but he is also capable of going astray under the impetus of his passions, which orient him toward false happiness.

We can see then the necessity for a moral science as a science of man—different from psychology—that seeks to clarify the nature of happiness. Knowledge alone cannot make for happiness, insists Aristotle, telling us that there is no point in studying ethics if we are not resolved to seek happiness actively.

Not only does Aristotle base his ethics on the desire for happiness, but the ethics themselves are developed by constantly resorting to the sayings of the many, or at least of the wisest of them, and this is acknowledged. In order to know what is man and a fully lived life, let us ask men. Therein lies Aristotle's wisdom and his realism. In order to understand man, let us listen to man.

Nevertheless, Vanier is not uncritical of Aristotle. Though sympathetic to Aristotle's 'big picture', he does not hesitate to point out what he regards as the most serious shortcomings and limitations of Aristotle's ethical vision. For the most part, what he calls attention to are Aristotle's blind spots: that is, things that Aristotle overlooks, ignores, neglects, or dismisses. And just what are these blind spots, according to Vanier?

Aristotle . . . affirms that it is the *logos* that defines a human being. On the strength of this, he establishes a whole hierarchy. Only men, and of them, only those who are free and well born, are capable of perfect happiness. Women and slaves can experience a certain happiness because they are capable of a virtuous life within their particular parameters, but they are there to serve the family in some way. Aristotle underlines the importance of the family and therefore of respect for women. . . . [H]e refers to women's virtue and the friendship that is possible with their husbands.[7] He also appeals for justice in relation to slaves, because they too are human beings. But for him, women and slaves remain inferior to men. They cannot attain the most complete happiness.

* * *

Aristotle also succumbs to actual racism and elitism when he cites Euripides: '"It is meet that Hellenes should rule over barbarians"; as if they thought that the barbarian and the slave were by nature one.'[8] It is not inconceivable that Aristotle's words may have been used to justify slavery or the idea of superiority of one race over another.

The Absence of Heart

This rigid vision of things and of the hierarchy of people derives, it seems to me, from the fact that Aristotle bases the value of human beings on their rational and intellectual capacity alone. That is why he gives no human value to children with severe mental handicaps who seem deprived of reason.

For him, what is essential is the exercise of reason and intelligence that make a greater or lesser degree of autonomy possible, and autonomy draws a man closer to God, or the gods. Friendship, for him, is a pinnacle of human life, a marvellous fruit of virtue. But he is ignorant of the importance of the life of relationship, which exists even before the burgeoning of reason.

He cannot therefore conceive of the supreme value of an encounter between two people of the kind Martin Buber describes in his book *I and Thou*. Friendship between unequals, for example, between a rich person and a poor person, is considered by Aristotle only from a perspective that is almost mercantile. For him, the rich or magnanimous person is happy because he can *give*. *Receiving* implies a lack of autonomy, inferiority. Similarly, a man's virtue is to command, a woman's to obey. Aristotle does not see what they can bring one another, not merely in terms of their capacities, but also in terms of their love. On this basis, a *communion* can develop between them that is the sharing not merely of great and fine activities, beautiful thoughts, and generosity, but also of their shortcomings, their weaknesses, and their affective needs. Happiness then consists not of achieving the greatest possible autonomy, in which we appear strong and capable, but of a sharing of hearts and humility in relation to one another. Thus the child can humanize the man in the same way that a person who is weak and bereft can release the goodness, tenderness, and compassion in him, and thereby help him to discover a new inner unity and communion.

The human sciences teach us that the capacity to love develops in the very first months of a child's life through his relationship with his mother. He needs the experience of a first love that is unconditional. That is the mystery of human beings. This first relationship, of the child with his mother and father, is crucial and forms the basis of subsequent deliberate choices. If the small child is wounded by rejection or the absence of this first love, he is likely to lack self-confidence and have great difficulty in acquiring human virtues in later life. Aristotle could not grasp the role of the parent/child relationship in the development of human beings and human intelligence.

Yet Aristotle is not the father of intellectualism that he has at times been accused of being. He has been reproached for the dryness of his philosophy and people have applauded in contrast the affective dimensions of Eastern and Jewish thought. It is true that Aristotle is seeking to understand the universe, whereas the Jewish people receive their knowledge and laws from the God who loves, watches over, and guides them. So it is that in Judaism, the affective is afforded a certain primacy. To stop short at the discursive intelligence seeking to understand, however, is to misunderstand Aristotle. For him, knowledge begins with astonishment and wonder at the universe and culminates in the wonder, peace, and rest of contemplation, or in works of justice in the city-state. He bases his whole approach on a relationship of trust with the world, a relationship that is almost affective with reality as perceived through the senses. He insists on knowledge and the search for truth, provided they are oriented toward others or toward the divinity. In this way Aristotle differs from those for whom the starting (and the finishing) point is in the consciousness of the subject who is thinking.

For Aristotle it is friendship that opens a definitive door to the heart. Between two friends true love exists. The friend is *another self*. He wants what is good for the other person. Both seek the same values. Together they devote themselves to the pursuit of truth and justice in the city-state. The heart element is present, but friendship implies also that the friend is strong and capable and devotes himself to great things. In this way friendship becomes, as we have seen, a pinnacle of human life.

A Lack of Compassion

Aristotle does not reject affectivity, but he does not consider the heart to be the mainspring of human life and relationship. The fact that he does not afford the heart primacy prevents Aristotle from seeing human evolution as a growth toward greater and more universal justice, justice for every human being. Evolution is neither an ancient Greek concept nor an Aristotelian one. For the Greeks, time was cyclical and could not contain the notion of progress. Kindness and a desire for justice for the weak, the sick, the orphaned, and the poor in general appear to be lacking. With him there is no real compassion. Can we say that, in this respect, he comes close to Nietzsche, who despised the weak and those who treated them kindly? No, even if Aristotle does not call for compassion for the weak, he does affirm that the master should deal justly with his slave.

His model is always the magnanimous, the most perfect man. The magnanimous man does great things in the city-state: He brings about reform, he works for justice. While he does not despise weak people or slaves, he does not waste his time on them. Aristotle could not conceive of the fact that weak people might be able to help a man to become more human, to grow in his humanity. In order to do good, the magnanimous man draws upon his personal virtue.

Aristotle does not work out a morality of compassion. In this respect, his ethics differ fundamentally from the Egyptian religion of 2,800 years ago, which stresses the importance of taking care of the weak, and the Jewish religion, which stresses the importance of looking after widows, orphans, and immigrants.[9] In the time of Isaiah, God revealed what behaviour pleased him: It was not first and foremost the sacrificing of animals in the temple or fasting, but working for the hungry, the poor, and the weak.[10] And, in the jubilee year, slaves were to be set free.[11]

(Continued)

Religions that afford compassion a place allow for an important human experience. Through relationship with the poor or weak person or with the child, the heart, compassion, and goodness are awakened, and a new inner unity is established between body and soul. It is as if the tension between the intelligence and the body finds a mysterious resolution in the experience of being present to the poor. Compassion engages the body and it is through the body that we draw nearer to others. We discover that the fragile person can help us to accept ourselves with our own frailties and we undergo an inner transformation. We become more human, more welcoming, and more open to others. Aristotle was enclosed behind city walls, the walls of the small world of Greek freemen. How was he to imagine what it was like to be open to others, and to non-Greeks in particular?

Why does Aristotle glorify the intelligence and the capacity for command in freemen and refuse to recognize the same potential in the intelligence of women, slaves, and barbarians? Is this just a problem of culture, or is there something more profound that Aristotle did not or could not grasp?

- What are Vanier's main criticisms of Aristotle? What things does he think Aristotle overlooks? Do you think Aristotle's ethical framework could be enlarged to make room for any of these things? Why or why not?

Jean Vanier, it is plain, admires Aristotle; but he isn't afraid to criticize him. This attitude is not uncommon: in recent decades, many moral philosophers have tried to save what they have thought best in Aristotle—that is, to preserve his most vital and enduring insights—while abandoning ideas that strike them as outmoded, antiquated, or moribund. Two excellent examples of such 'friendly critics' are Canadians Christine McKinnon and Thomas Hurka. While neither McKinnon nor Hurka agrees with everything in *The Nicomachean Ethics*—who does?—both authors write approvingly of Aristotle's 'big picture'. Like Vanier, McKinnon and Hurka are convinced that Aristotle was right about something that matters. And what was he right about? According to McKinnon, Aristotle was right to insist that we cannot talk sensibly about morality without talking about *human nature*. According to Hurka, Aristotle was right to call attention to a distinctive and promising moral view—a view Hurka calls Aristotelian **perfectionism**.

PERFECTIONISM

The view that the best life is one devoted to the full exercise and development of our highest faculties.

From *Character, Virtue Theories, and the Vices*
By Christine McKinnon

Morality is for human beings. It is possible because of certain facts of human nature, and it is necessary because of other facts of human nature.

Human Nature and Ethics

Morality is for human beings. It is possible because of certain facts of human nature, and it is necessary because of other facts of human nature. Because humans are the sorts of beings who can be self-consciously aware of their desires and can self-reflexively shape their motivational profiles in response to judgments that they make about the worthiness or otherwise of some of their desires, morality is a possibility for us. And because humans are the sorts of beings who experience a wide range of desires, the satisfaction of some of which do not conduce to the well-being of the person having them or to the well-being of other persons, morality is needed to evaluate desires and to adjudicate between desires. Morality is thus deeply rooted in facts of human nature and the human needs, desires, and capacities to which these give rise.

* * *

The ancient Greeks argued that the central question in moral philosophy was the ethical one, 'what kind of life should one live?' This was not simply a practical question about how to attain standards of success current at the time. It was a question informed by the thought that humans had a certain kind of nature which circumscribed quite closely what kinds of life choices would, enough other things being equal, conduce to a flourishing, harmonious, fulfilled, good human life. A happy life was never guaranteed (luck or fortune could always intervene), but certain kinds of choices and certain kinds of circumstances served as necessary conditions for a good human life. One criticism of this ancient account is that its characterization of the good life was unduly narrow and restrictive, and in particular, that it overemphasized the intellectual side of humans. This criticism would seem to be justified by one of Aristotle's accounts of the proper end for humans,[12] where he does seem to value the contemplative life and all those features which make its exercise possible at the expense of other features of a human life. But philosophers have offered another, more general, criticism. It is not that Aristotle valued the wrong aspect of human nature, but that he was wrong to suppose that there is such a thing as human nature, the harmonious exercise of certain aspects of which serves as a necessary condition for leading a good life.

In this century, natural scientists of all stripes as well as social scientists and philosophers have debated the question of whether humans have a nature, and, if so, what it is. Many factors appear to motivate the denial that humans have a nature. One is an attempt to protect an inchoate kind of freedom for human beings. Another arises from fear of invidious assimilation to the 'lesser' creatures of the animal kingdom. Another may be due to fears of manipulation by those in political power. These fears may be genuine or misplaced, but they themselves cannot provide support for the claim that humans lack a nature. Closer inspection of these fears might, however, expose the ways in which they have been used to make this claim more plausible.

Beings that have a nature are thought to function according to that nature. This might seem to compromise their freedom, and so a threat is posed to a treasured conception of human beings as free agents. This exposes a double misunderstanding. First, the behaviour of beings that have natures, especially beings that have complicated natures and that can interact with their environments in complex ways, is at best constrained—and not determined—by their natures. And, second, the idea of absolute freedom is confused: all freedom is relative to a specific set of constraints.

No one who argues that human beings have a nature would want to argue that everything that a human does is explicable solely in terms of that nature. Nor would they want to claim this for any animal whose nature is at all complex. They couldn't. Any being with a complex nature will have several kinds of wants, some of them in direct conflict with others, and many of them not simultaneously satisfiable. So a being's nature could never determine which want gets satisfied in every instance. It is one factor in explaining behaviour. Particular internal chemistry, environmental context, and social relationships provide other factors. When the relatively modest role claimed for human nature in explanations of particular instances of behaviour is recognized, the supposed threat of biological determinism diminishes.

Perhaps even this claim that human nature provides a modest constraint on choices and available behaviours compromises human freedom unduly? Some, including existentialists, have thought so. They have argued that human beings are radically undetermined and that humans must be totally free to make radical choices, to create a self from nothing. But no self can be created from nothing, and no choices can be without antecedent choices or preferences. Choices must be made in the context of wants and needs, and these latter are not completely arbitrary. Wants and needs arise from somewhere: human freedom consists in choosing which ones to satisfy when and why; it does not consist in fabricating from nothing the needs and wants.[13]

The fears based on claims that human nature compromises human freedom and makes humans into 'mere' animals can be allayed if the claims made on behalf of the causal powers of human nature are not exaggerated and if a reasonable sense of human freedom is being defended. The fear that persons can be more easily manipulated if their nature is known seems to be a more legitimate fear, but conceding this fear does not establish that humans lack a nature. And the knowledge can cut both ways: while humans may be more open to manipulation once more is known about their wants and their motivational structures,

(Continued)

they may also become more transparent to themselves and others in ways that further self and mutual comprehension, as well as empathetic concern.

Humans are animals, and if it is to be admitted that other animals possess natures but humans do not, then there will have to be some explanation of how humans evolved 'out of' having a nature. This kind of explanation is very different from the kind that is sometimes offered for the presence of consciousness or self-consciousness in higher animals, including humans. Sometimes these explanations are in terms of mental properties 'emerging' out of exceedingly complex material properties, but no story about emergence could account for humans 'outgrowing' their nature. At best, a story about these special features of humans permitting them to 'override' their nature could be had. The commitment to the constraining role of human nature I was advocating above permits many particular instances of 'overriding', even if it insists on quite a robust picture of human nature.

- What is the meaning of McKinnon's remark that '[m]orality is for human beings'? Would Aristotle agree with her?
- What reasons are there for doubting that there is such a thing as 'human nature'? What reasons are there for thinking there is such a thing? Which set of reasons impresses you the most?

From 'The Well-Rounded Life'
By Thomas Hurka

Perfectionism holds that there are certain intrinsically valuable states of human beings, and that each of us should maximize the achievement of these states both in herself and in others. Like utilitarianism, then, it is a species of consequentialism. It thinks the morally right act is the one which produces the most good. But perfectionism differs from utilitarianism about what this good is. Whereas utilitarians identify the good with happiness, perfectionists find it in such states as knowledge, artistic creation (or contemplation), the carrying out of complex and difficult projects, and friendship. They want us to lead the best life, and to make its conditions available to others. But what determines the best life is not pleasure or satisfaction, it is the achievement of certain objective goods. Perfectionism is the morality of Plato, Aristotle, Thomas Aquinas, G.W. Leibniz, G.W.F. Hegel, Karl Marx, Friedrich Nietzsche, F.H. Bradley, and (in part) G.E. Moore and Hastings Rashdall. So it has been prominent in our tradition. But, for several bad reasons, it has been ignored by philosophers since about 1920. It is time for a reconsideration.

Perfectionism might seem less important, if the activities best by its lights were always most satisfying or brought the most happiness. In various forms, this has been held by Aristotle, J.S. Mill, and John Rawls. But the view is surely naive. It is a commonplace that knowledge can be painful, and serious achievement a strain. An artist's life, balancing joy in successful creation with the frequent anguish of failure, can be less contented overall than the life of an idle clubman. And it is clearly less contented than life in *Brave New World*. So it matters that perfectionism finds it better. And, even when good activities are most satisfying, a question of theory remains. Are the activities good because they are perfect, or because they are pleasant? Here perfectionism says, as Bradley did, that, even if life without pleasure is inconceivable, 'what we hold to against every possible modification of Hedonism, is that the standard and test is in higher and lower function, not in more or less pleasure'.[14]

The problem I want to discuss can arise in any perfectionism, but it is most usefully discussed with a specific version in view. So let me briefly describe what I consider the most plausible perfectionism, a theory called *Aristotelian perfectionism*.

Like Aristotle's, this theory starts from the idea that, at the deepest level, the intrinsic goods develop properties fundamental to human nature. A little vaguely, they develop properties essential to us qua human organisms. This idea generates three major goods, of which the first is *physical perfection*. This perfection develops the bodily properties we share with other animals, and is present to a low degree in ordinary good health, and more completely in vigorous athletic activity, especially at the highest, perhaps Olympic levels. So the first Aristotelian claim is that a life is better and more completely human, if it is free of disease or injury and marked by some demanding physical feats. The remaining goods—the more important ones, it will emerge—are exercises of rationality, both theoretical and practical. On the theoretical side, the side of our beliefs, we achieve more theoretical perfection the more knowledge we have. The more we understand the world, and ourselves, and our place in the world, the better and more choiceworthy our lives. Of course, not all knowledge has equal value. Knowing the co-stars in some 1930s movie is not as important as knowing a fundamental law of the universe, or understanding the workings of a friend's personality. We need a test for the best knowledge, and I suggest it is the most organized or systematic knowledge, with general principles unifying and explaining derived particulars. This is most clearly present when we grasp a whole scientific theory from first principles down to particular explanations. But it is also present in interpersonal understanding and even

the craft knowledge of skilled artisans. In any case, the second Aristotelian claim is that a life is better the more it is informed and aware, and the more it has unified its knowledge in one structure. The last good is *practical perfection*, or the exercise of rationality in action. Parallel to knowledge is the successful achievement of one's goals, given a justified belief that this would happen, or, more briefly, non-lucky achievement. This is the basic practical value, but, again, some achievements are more valuable and exhibit more rationality than others. Just as it is better to know a scientific law than to know about 1930s movies, so it is better to achieve a fundamental reform of one's society than to light a cigarette successfully. The question how goals are ranked is difficult, but I would say the best achievements involve the same organizing structure in a person's intentions as is present in the best knowledge. On this view, there is practical perfection in any life which is organized around a single end, or in which large parts have one end, so many activities serve a long-term goal; in activities that are complex, challenging, and difficult, especially if they require precise, and precisely ordered decisions; in political leadership and co-operation with others, which spread one's concerns beyond the self; and in friendship, especially when it is expressed in a nuanced emotional responsiveness. These are all practical excellences or exercises of rationality in action, and they make a life better by their presence.

- What is 'Aristotelian perfectionism'? What is ***Aristotelian*** about it?
- What different ***kinds*** of perfections does Aristotelian perfectionism recognize? Are there any perfections that Aristotelian perfectionism ignores or overlooks?

H. Morality and Sentiment: David Hume and Jean-Jacques Rousseau

Morality for Aristotle depended upon rules embedded and learned in a particular society, an elite society of the privileged males of the Greek aristocracy. Modern conceptions of morality, on the other hand, are usually thought to be universal, that is, not restricted to a particular society or a particular elite. They apply to women, men, poor people, rich people, adults, and children, even if they are only a few years old. At the same time, however, most modern conceptions of morality minimize Aristotle's emphasis on society and upbringing, preferring to place morals on some individual basis. For example, the key to morality in Kant's moral philosophy is *individual autonomy*, the idea that every person can find for himself or herself, just through the use of reason, what acts are moral and what acts are not. Before Kant, the ruling conception of morality was based upon a conception of personal feelings of a special moral kind, a 'natural desire' to help one's fellow man. (As in Aristotle, this philosophy insisted that morality had to be viewed as a part of nature.)

It should be clear how this conception of morality has a distinct advantage in reconciling personal interests and moral principles. Since strong moral feelings are a kind of personal interest, one can satisfy his personal feelings and the demands of morality at the same time. (Again, this lies in the heart of Butler's arguments.) Of course, other personal feelings—jealousy, greed, and envy—can act against these moral feelings. But at least some of our feelings are satisfied by moral action. According to these philosophers, such moral feelings can be found in virtually all of us.

The two most famous philosophers to argue this position are David Hume and Jean-Jacques Rousseau. The key to both of their philosophies is the notion of **sentiment** ('feeling') and the notion of **sympathy** ('fellow feeling' or feeling pity for other people and taking their interests into account as well as our own). Hume says:

> The hypothesis which we embrace is plain. It maintains that morality is determined by sentiment. It defines virtue to be whatever mental action or quality gives to a spectator the pleasing sentiment of approbation; and vice the contrary.[15]

The central concern in Hume's moral philosophy distinguishes those who defend morality as a function of reason from those who say that it is rather a matter of sentiment and passion. Elsewhere Hume gives us his very strong opinion that 'reason is, and ought to be, the slave of the passions'. Here is his argument:

On 'Reason as Slave of the Passions'
By David Hume

The distinct boundaries and offices of reason and of taste are easily ascertained. The former conveys the knowledge of truth and falsehood; the latter gives the sentiment of beauty and deformity, vice and virtue.

There has been a controversy started of late, much better worth examination, concerning the general foundation of *morals*; whether they be derived from *reason* or from *sentiment*; whether we attain the knowledge of them by a chain of argument and induction or by an immediate feeling and finer internal sense; whether, like all sound judgment of truth and falsehood, they should be the same to every rational, intelligent being, or whether, like the perception of beauty and deformity, they be founded entirely on the particular fabric and constitution of the human species.

The ancient philosophers, though they often affirm that virtue is nothing but conformity to reason, yet, in general, seem to consider morals as deriving their existence from taste and sentiment. On the other hand, our modern inquirers, though they also talk much of the beauty of virtue and deformity of vice, yet have commonly endeavoured to account for these distinctions by metaphysical reasonings and by deductions from the most abstract principles of the understanding. Such confusion reigned in these subjects that an opposition of the greatest consequence could prevail between one system and another, and even in the parts of almost each individual system, and yet nobody, till very lately, was ever sensible of it.

* * *

It must be acknowledged that both sides of the question are susceptible of specious arguments. Moral distinctions, it may be said, are discernible by pure *reason*; else, whence the many disputes that reign in common life, as well as in philosophy with regard to this subject, the long chain of proofs often produced on both sides, the examples cited, the authorities appealed to, the analogies employed, the fallacies detected, the inferences drawn, and the several conclusions adjusted to their proper principles? Truth is disputable, not taste: what exists in the nature of things is the standard of our judgment: what each man feels within himself is the standard of sentiment. Propositions in geometry may be proved, systems in physics may be controverted, but the harmony of verse, the tenderness of passion, the brilliancy of wit must give immediate pleasure. No man reasons concerning another's beauty, but frequently concerning the justice or injustice of his actions. In every criminal trial, the first object of the prisoner is to disprove the facts alleged and deny the actions imputed to him; the second, to prove that, even if these actions were real, they might be justified as innocent and lawful. It is confessedly by deductions of the understanding that the first point is ascertained; how can we suppose a different faculty of the mind is employed in fixing the other?

On the other hand, those who would resolve all moral determinations into *sentiments* may endeavour to show that it is impossible for reason ever to draw conclusions of this nature. To virtue, say they, it belongs to be *amiable* and vice *odious*. This forms their very nature or essence. But can reason or argumentation distribute these different epithets to any subjects and pronounce beforehand that this must produce love and that hatred? Or what other reason can we ever assign for these affections but the original fabric and formation of the human mind, which is naturally adapted to receive them?

The end of all moral speculations is to teach us our duty, and, by proper representations of the deformity of vice and beauty of virtue, beget correspondent habits and engage us to avoid the one and embrace the other. But is this ever to be expected from inferences and conclusions of the understanding, which of themselves have no hold of the affections or set in motion the active powers of men? They discover truths. But where the truths which they discover are indifferent and beget no desire or aversion, they can have no influence on conduct and behaviour. What is honourable, what is fair, what is becoming, what is noble, what is generous takes possession of the heart and animates us to embrace and maintain it. What is intelligible, what is evident, what is probable, what is true procures only the cool assent of the understanding and, gratifying a speculative curiosity, puts an end to our researches.

* * *

Extinguish all the warm feelings and prepossessions in favour of virtue, and all disgust or aversion to vice; render men totally indifferent toward these distinctions, and morality is no longer a practical study nor has any tendency to regulate our lives and actions.

These arguments on each side (and many more might be produced) are so plausible that I am apt to suspect they may, the one as well as the other, be solid and satisfactory and that *reason* and *sentiment* concur in almost all moral determinations and conclusions. The final sentence, it is probable, which pronounces characters and actions amiable or odious, praiseworthy or blamable; that which stamps on them the mark of honour or infamy, approbation or censure; that which renders morality an active principle and constitutes virtue our happiness, and vice our misery—it is probable, I say, that this final sentence depends on some internal sense of feeling which nature has made universal in the whole species.

It is worth noting here that Hume's moral philosophy, like his philosophy of knowledge, is strictly empiricist:

Men are now cured of their passion for hypotheses and systems in natural philosophy and will hearken to no arguments but those which are derived from experience. It is full time they should attempt a like reformation in all moral disquisitions and reject every system of ethics, however subtle or ingenious, which is not founded on fact and observation.

Reason, Hume argues, may be of use in deciding how we can get what we want, but it is incapable of ever telling us what we ultimately want. Notice the familiar argument against an infinite regress; notice also Hume's sharp distinction between reason (which is concerned with knowledge, truth, and falsehood) and taste or sentiment (that judges values, which ultimately depend upon pleasure and pain):

It appears evident that the ultimate ends of human actions can never, in any case, be accounted for by *reason*, but recommend themselves entirely to the sentiments and affections of mankind without any dependence on the intellectual faculties. Ask a man *why he uses exercise*; he will answer, *because he desires to keep his health*. If you then inquire *why he desires health*, he will readily reply, *because sickness is painful*. If you push your inquiries further and desire a reason *why he hates pain*, it is impossible he can ever give any. This is an ultimate end and is never referred to any other object.

Perhaps to your second question, *why he desires health*, he may also reply that *it is necessary for the exercise of his calling*. If you ask *why he is anxious on that head*, he will answer, *because he desires to get money*. If you demand, *why? It is the instrument of pleasure*, says he. And beyond this, it is an absurdity to ask for a reason. It is impossible there can be a progress *in infinitum* and that one thing can always be a reason why another is desired. Something must be desirable on its own account and because of its immediate accord or agreement with human sentiment and affection.

Now, as virtue is an end and is desirable on its own account, without fee or reward, merely for the immediate satisfaction which it conveys, it is requisite that there should be some sentiment which it touches—some internal taste or feeling, or whatever you please to call it, which distinguishes moral good and evil and which embraces the one and rejects the other.

Thus, the distinct boundaries and offices of *reason* and of *taste* are easily ascertained. The former conveys the knowledge of truth and falsehood; the latter gives the sentiment of beauty and deformity, vice and virtue. The one discovers objects as they really stand in nature, without addition or diminution; the other has a productive faculty; and gliding or straining all natural objects with the colours borrowed from internal sentiment, raises, in a manner, a new creation. Reason, being cool and disengaged, is no motive to action and directs only the impulse received from appetite or inclination by showing us the means of attaining happiness or avoiding misery. Taste, as it gives pleasure or pain, and thereby constitutes happiness or misery, becomes a motive to action and is the first spring or impulse to desire and volition. From circumstances and relations, known or supposed, the former leads us to the discovery of the concealed and unknown. After all circumstances and relations are laid before us, the latter makes us feel from the whole a new sentiment of blame or approbation.

Elsewhere Hume argues a razor-sharp distinction between facts and values. He argues with characteristic conciseness that 'it is impossible to derive an "ought" from an "is", that is, any notions of value or what we *ought to do* cannot be derived from any statements of fact. For example, you may know, as a matter of fact, that pushing a certain button will kill a thousand innocent children, but from that fact alone, it does not follow that you ought not push the button. What you ought to do—or ought not to do—depends on something that is not a matter of fact or reason at all: your moral feelings or sentiments. Without these sentiments, no action is either moral or immoral, praiseworthy or blameworthy, or of any value whatever. Accordingly, in one of his most shocking statements Hume says that it would not be irrational for him to prefer the death of half the world to the pricking of his little finger. This is not to say that he would prefer this, but there is *nothing in reason* to forbid it. Values are a matter of sentiment, not of reason.

A similar theory of sentiment is defended by the French philosopher Jean-Jacques Rousseau. Although he is often characterized as the first great 'Romantic', Rousseau is not nearly so antagonistic to reason as his reputation suggests. Sentiment, by his theory, is tied to a kind of 'natural reason'. The key to his theory, therefore, is the concept of **conscience**, a powerful kind of moral feeling that has its own kind of divine reason. As in Hume, detached reason offers us no guidance. Notice that Rousseau too reconciles 'self-love' and 'moral goodness' as ultimately having the same goals:

CONSCIENCE

A sense or feeling about what is right and wrong, usually without argument.

From *Émile*
By Jean-Jacques Rousseau

To know good is not to love it; this knowledge is not innate in man; but as soon as his reason leads him to perceive it, his conscience impels him to love it; it is this feeling which is innate.

Let us lay it down as an incontrovertible rule that the first impulses of nature are always right; there is no original sin in the human heart, the how and why of the entrance of every vice can be traced. The only natural passion is self-love or selfishness taken in a wider sense. This selfishness is good in itself and in relation to ourselves; and as the child has no necessary relations to other people he is naturally indifferent to them; his self-love only becomes good or bad by the use made of it and the relations established by its means. Until the time is ripe for the appearance of reason, that guide of selfishness, the main thing is that the child shall do nothing because you are watching him or listening to him; in a word, nothing because of other people, but only what nature asks of him; then he will never do wrong.

I do not mean to say that he will never do any mischief, never hurt himself, never break a costly ornament if you leave it within his reach. He might do much damage without doing wrong, since wrong-doing depends on the harmful intention which will never be his. If once he meant to do harm, his whole education would be ruined; he would be almost hopelessly bad.

* * *

The morality of our actions consists entirely in the judgments we ourselves form with regard to them. If good is good, it must be good in the depth of our heart as well as in our actions; and the first reward of justice is the consciousness that we are acting justly. If moral goodness is in accordance with our nature, man can only be healthy in mind and body when he is good. If it is not so, and if man is by nature evil, he cannot cease to be evil without corrupting his nature, and goodness in him is a crime against nature. If he is made to do harm to his fellow creatures, as the wolf is made to devour his prey, a humane man would be as depraved a creature as a pitiful wolf; and virtue alone would cause remorse.

My young friend, let us look within, let us set aside all personal prejudices and see whither our inclinations lead us. Do we take more pleasure in the sight of the sufferings of others or their joys? Is it pleasanter to do a kind action or an unkind action, and which leaves the more delightful memory behind it? Why do you enjoy the theatre? Do you delight in the crimes you behold? Do you weep over the punishment which overtakes the criminal? They say we are indifferent to everything but self-interest; yet we find our consolation in our sufferings in the charms of friendship and humanity, and even in our pleasures we should be too lonely and miserable if we had no one to share them with us. If there is no such thing as morality in man's heart, what is the source of his rapturous admiration of noble deeds, his passionate devotion to great men? What connection is there between self-interest and this enthusiasm for virtue?

* * *

Take from our hearts this love of what is noble and you rob us of the joy of life. The mean-spirited man in whom these delicious feelings have been stifled among vile passions, who by thinking of no one but himself comes at last to love no one but himself, this man feels no raptures, his cold heart no longer throbs with joy, and his eyes no longer fill with the sweet tears of sympathy, he delights in nothing; the wretch has neither life nor feeling, he is already dead.

There are many bad men in this world, but there are few of these dead souls, alive only to self-interest, and insensible to all that is right and good. We only delight in injustice so long as it is to our own advantage; in every other case we wish the innocent to be protected. If we see some act of violence or injustice in town or country, our hearts are at once stirred to their depths by an instinctive anger and wrath, which bids us go to the help of the oppressed; but we are restrained by a stronger duty, and the law deprives us of our right to protect the innocent. On the other hand, if some deed of mercy or generosity meets our eye, what reverence and love does it inspire! Do we not say to ourselves, 'I should like to have done that myself'? What does it matter to us that two thousand years ago a man was just or unjust? and yet we take the same interest in ancient history as if it happened yesterday. What are the crimes of Cataline to me? I shall not be his victim. Why then have I the same horror of his

(*Continued*)

crimes as if he were living now? We do not hate the wicked merely because of the harm they do to ourselves, but because they are wicked. Not only do we wish to be happy ourselves, we wish others to be happy too, and if this happiness does not interfere with our own happiness, it increases it. In conclusion, whether we will or not, we pity the unfortunate; when we see their suffering we suffer too. Even the most depraved are not wholly without this instinct, and it often leads them to self-contradiction. The highwayman who robs the traveller, clothes the nakedness of the poor; the fiercest murderer supports a fainting man.

Men speak of the voice of remorse, the secret punishment of hidden crimes, by which such are often brought to light. Alas! who does not know its unwelcome voice? We speak from experience and we would gladly stifle this imperious feeling which causes us such agony. Let us obey the call of nature; we shall see that her yoke is easy and that when we give heed to her voice we find a joy in the answer of a good conscience. The wicked fears and flees from her; he delights to escape from himself; his anxious eyes look around him for some object of diversion; without bitter satire and rude mockery he would always be sorrowful; the scornful laugh is his one pleasure. Not so the just man, who finds his peace within himself; there is joy not malice in his laughter, a joy which springs from his own heart; he is as cheerful alone as in company, his satisfaction does not depend on those who approach him; it includes them.

* * *

It is no part of my scheme to enter at present into metaphysical discussions which neither you nor I can understand, discussions which really lead nowhere. I have told you already that I do not wish to philosophize with you, but to help you to consult your own heart. If all the philosophers in the world should prove that I am wrong, and you feel that I am right, that is all I ask.

For this purpose it is enough to lead you to distinguish between our acquired ideas and our natural feelings; for feeling precedes knowledge; and since we do not learn to seek what is good for us and avoid what is bad for us, but get this desire from nature, in the same way the love of good and the hatred of evil are as natural to us as our self-love. The decrees of conscience are not judgments but feelings. Although all our ideas come from without, the feelings by which they are weighed are within us, and it is by these feelings alone that we perceive fitness or unfitness of things in relation to ourselves, which leads us to seek or shun these things.

To exist is to feel; our feeling is undoubtedly earlier than our intelligence, and we had feelings before we had ideas. Whatever may be the cause of our being, it has provided for our preservation by giving us feelings suited to our nature; and no one can deny that these at least are innate. These feelings, so far as the individual is concerned, are self-love, fear, pain, the dread of death, the desire for comfort. Again, if, as it is impossible to doubt, man is by nature sociable, or at least fitted to become sociable, he can only be so by means of other innate feelings, relative to his kind; for if only physical well-being were considered, men would certainly be scattered rather than brought together. But the motive power of conscience is derived from the moral system formed through this twofold relation to himself and to his fellow men. To know good is not to love it; this knowledge is not innate in man; but as soon as his reason leads him to perceive it, his conscience impels him to love it; it is this feeling which is innate.

So I do not think, my young friend, that it is impossible to explain the immediate force of conscience as a result of our own nature, independent of reason itself. And even should it be impossible, it is necessary; for those who deny this principle, admitted and received by everybody else in the world, do not prove that there is no such thing; they are content to affirm, and when we affirm its existence we have quite as good grounds as they, while we have moreover the witness within us, the voice of conscience, which speaks on its own behalf. If the first beams of judgment dazzle us and confuse the objects we behold, let us wait till our feeble sight grows clear and strong, and in the light of reason we shall soon behold these very objects as nature has already showed them to us. Or rather let us be simpler and less pretentious; let us be content with the first feelings we experience in ourselves, since science always brings us back to these, unless it has led us astray.

Conscience! Conscience! Divine instinct, immortal voice from heaven; sure guide for a creature ignorant and finite indeed; yet intelligent and free; infallible judge of good and evil, making man like to God! In these consists the excellence of man's nature and the morality of his actions; apart from thee, I find nothing in myself to raise me above the beasts—nothing but the sad privilege of wandering from one error to another, by the help of an unbridled understanding and a reason which knows no principle.

But, as we pointed out before, there is a problem with this notion of conscience and with all appeals of morality to personal feeling. What if different people disagree? Whose conscience or whose feelings should we accept? And even if we find ourselves in agreement, how do we know that our consciences or feelings are right? It is with these questions in mind that we turn to the moral philosophy of Kant.

- How can morality be based on natural, human sentiment? Does this view seem too 'subjective'? How might it be made less so?
- Why is morality usually thought to be based on reason, according to Hume? What argument does he give to support the claim that morality is based on sentiment? How does Hume envision the relationship between reason and the passions or sentiments? Do you agree?
- What does Rousseau mean when he claims that a child will never do wrong if left to act according to his nature? How could you defend this bold claim?
- How is it that for Rousseau, our capacity for morality is a natural response?

I. Morality and Practical Reason: Immanuel Kant

Aristotle, Hume, and Rousseau all give feeling an important place in their conceptions of morality. For Aristotle, the virtuous man wants to act virtuously and enjoys doing so. For Hume and Rousseau, sentiment defines morality. On all such accounts, our concept of *duty*—what we ought to do—is derivative, at least in part, from such feelings and from our upbringing. But what if feelings disagree? What if people are brought up to value different things? What are we to say of a person who is brought up by criminals to value what is wicked and to enjoy cruelty? And what are we to say, most importantly of all, in those familiar cases in which a person's feelings draw him or her toward personal interests but duty calls in the opposite direction? This is the problem that Kant considered, and because of it, he rejected all attempts to base morality on feelings of any kind. Morality, he argued, must be based solely on reason and reason alone. Its central concept is the concept of duty, and so morality is a matter of **deontology** (from the Greek word *dein*, or 'duty').

Hume had restricted the notion of reason to concern with knowledge, truth, and falsity; Kant replies that reason also has a practical side, one that is capable of telling us what to do as well as how to do it. Rousseau had said that morality must be universal, common to all men, even in a presocietal 'state of nature'; Kant (who very much admired Rousseau) agrees but says that the nature of this universality cannot lie in people's feelings, which may vary from person to person and society to society, but only in reason, which by its very nature must be universal. And Aristotle had insisted that morality must be taught within society and that morals were a matter of public opinion and practices; but, unlike most modern philosophers, Kant insists on the independence of morality from society. What is most important, he argues, is that morality be autonomous, a function of individual reason, such that every rational person is capable of finding out what is right and what is wrong for himself or herself. Where Hume and Rousseau had looked for morality in individual feeling, Kant again insists that it must be found through an examination of reason, nothing else. This is the key to Kant's moral philosophy: Morality consists solely of *rational* principles.

Since morality is based on reason, according to Kant, it does not depend on particular societies or particular circumstances; it does not depend on individual feelings or desires (Kant summarizes all such personal feelings, desires, ambitions, impulses, and emotions as **inclinations**). The purpose of moral philosophy, therefore, is to examine our ability to

DEONTOLOGY

Ethics based on duty.

WILL

The power of mind that allows us to choose our own actions, or, at least, what we try to do.

reason practically and to determine from this examination the fundamental principles that lie at the basis of every morality, for every person, and in every society. In direct contrast to Aristotle, Kant begins by saying that what is ultimately good is none of those benefits and virtues that make up Greek happiness, but rather what he calls a good **will**. And a good will, in turn, is the will that exercises pure practical reason.

From *Fundamental Principles of the Metaphysics of Morals*
By Immanuel Kant

An action done from duty must wholly exclude the influence of inclination, and with it every object of the will.

Nothing can possibly be conceived in the world, or even out of it, which can be called good without qualification, except a *good will*. Intelligence, wit, judgment, and other *talents* of the mind, however they may be named, or courage, resolution, perseverance, as qualities of temperament, are undoubtedly good and desirable in many respects; but these gifts of nature may also become extremely bad and mischievous if the will which is to make use of them, and which, therefore, constitutes what is called *character*, is not good. It is the same with the *gifts of fortune*. Power, riches, honour, even health, and the general well-being and contentment with one's condition which is called *happiness*, inspire pride and often presumption, if there is not a good will to correct the influence of these on the mind, and with this also to rectify the whole principle of acting, and adapt it to its end. The sight of a being who is not adorned with a single feature of a pure and good will, enjoying unbroken prosperity, can never give pleasure to an impartial rational spectator. Thus a good will appears to constitute the indispensable condition even of being worthy of happiness.

The argument behind this opening move is this: It makes no sense to blame or praise a person for his or her character or abilities or the consequences of his or her actions. Many factors contribute to a person's circumstances. Whether or not a person is wealthy, intelligent, courageous, witty, and so on (Aristotle's virtues) is often due to his or her upbringing and heredity rather than any personal choice. But what we *will*, that is, what we try to do, is wholly within our control. Therefore it is the only thing that is ultimately worth moral consideration. Notice that Kant is concerned with questions of morality and not questions of the good life in general. What makes us happy is not particularly his concern. He is only concerned with what makes a person morally *worthy* of being happy.

A good will is good not because of what it performs or effects, not by its aptness for the attainment of some proposed end, but simply by virtue of the volition— that is, it is good in itself, and considered by itself is to be esteemed much higher than all that can be brought about by it in favour of any inclination, nay, even of the sum-total of all inclinations. Even if it should happen that, owing to special disfavour of fortune, or the niggardly provision of a stepmotherly nature, this will should wholly lack power to accomplish its purpose, if with its greatest efforts it should yet achieve nothing, and there should remain only the good will (not, to be sure, a mere wish, but the summoning of all means in our power), then, like a jewel, it would still shine by its own light, as a thing which has its whole value in itself. Its usefulness or fruitlessness can neither add to nor take away anything from this value. It would be, as it were, only the setting to enable us to handle it the more conveniently in common commerce, or to attract it to the attention of those who are not yet connoisseurs, but not to recommend it to true connoisseurs, or to determine its value.

There is, however, something so strange in this idea of the absolute value of the mere will, in which no account is taken of its utility, that notwithstanding the thorough assent of even common reason to the idea, yet a suspicion must arise that it may perhaps really be the product of mere high-flown fancy, and that we may have misunderstood the purpose of nature in assigning reason as the governor of our will. Therefore we will examine this idea from this point of view.

Kant's argument here is surprisingly similar to Aristotle's argument in his *Ethics*. You remember that Aristotle argues that the good for man must be found in man's nature, in that which is unique to him. The assumption is that since man is singularly endowed with reason, then reason must have a special significance in human life. Kant's argument also begins with the observation that man, unlike other creatures, is capable of reasoning. But why should he have such a capacity? Not in order to make him happy, Kant argues, because any number of instincts would have served that end more effectively. (Remember that Kant is presupposing God as Creator here, so he believes, like Leibniz, that everything exists for some sufficient reason.)

[Our] existence has a different and far nobler end, for which and not for happiness, reason is properly intended, and which must, therefore, be regarded as the supreme condition to which the private ends of man must, for the most part, be postponed.

This 'far nobler end' and 'supreme condition' is what Kant calls *duty*. 'The notion of duty,' he tells us, 'includes that of a good will'—but a good will that subjects itself to rational principles. Those rational principles are moral laws, and it is action in accordance with such laws that alone makes a man good.

It is important, however, to make a distinction, which Aristotle makes too: It is one thing to do what duty requires for some personal interest, and it is something else to do one's duty just because it is one's duty. For example, a grocer might refuse to cheat his customers (which is his duty) because it would be bad for business; then he is not acting for the sake of duty, but for personal interests. But he may refuse to cheat his customers just because he knows that he ought not to. This does count as doing his duty and thereby makes him morally worthy.

I omit here all actions which are already recognized as inconsistent with duty, although they may be useful for this or that purpose, for with these the question whether they are done *from duty* cannot arise at all, since they even conflict with it. I also set aside those actions which really conform to duty, but to which men have *no* direct *inclination*, performing them because they are impelled thereto by some other inclination. For in this case we can readily distinguish whether the action which agrees with duty is done *from duty* or from a selfish view. It is much harder to make this distinction when the action accords with duty, and the subject has besides a *direct* inclination to it. For example, it is always a matter of duty that a dealer should not overcharge an inexperienced purchaser; and wherever there is much commerce the prudent tradesman does not overcharge, but keeps a fixed price for everyone, so that a child buys of him as well as any other. Men are thus *honestly* served; but this is not enough to make us believe that the tradesman has so acted from duty and from principles of honesty; his own advantage required it;

(Continued)

it is out of the question in this case to suppose that he might besides have a direct inclination in favour of the buyers, so that, as it were, from love he should give no advantage to one over another. Accordingly the action was done neither from duty nor from direct inclination, but merely with a selfish view.

On the other hand, it is a duty to maintain one's life; and, in addition, everyone has also a direct inclination to do so. But on this account the often anxious care which most men take for it has no intrinsic worth, and their maximum has no moral import. They preserve their life *as duty requires*, no doubt, but not *because duty requires*. On the other hand, if adversity and hopeless sorrow have completely taken away the relish for life, if the unfortunate one, strong in mind, indignant at his fate rather than desponding or dejected, wishes for death, and yet preserves his life without loving it—not from inclination or fear, but from duty—then his maxim has a moral worth.

To be beneficent when we can is a duty; and besides this, there are many minds so sympathetically constituted that, without any other motive of vanity or self-interest, they find a pleasure in spreading joy around them, and can take delight in the satisfaction of others so far as it is their own work. But I maintain that in such a case an action of this kind, however proper, however amiable it may be, has nevertheless no true moral worth, but is on a level with other inclinations, for example, the inclination to honour, which, if it is happily directed to that which is in fact of public utility and accordant with duty, and consequently honourable, deserves praise and encouragement, but not esteem. For the maxim lacks the moral import, namely, that such actions be done *from duty*, not from inclination. Put the case that the mind of that philanthropist was clouded by sorrow of his own extinguishing all sympathy with the lot of others, and that while he still has the power to benefit others in distress he is not touched by their trouble because he is absorbed with his own; and now suppose that he tears himself out of this dread insensibility and performs the action without any inclination to it, but simply from duty, then first has his action its genuine moral worth. Further still, if nature has put little sympathy in the heart of this or that man, if he, supposed to be an upright man, is by temperament cold and indifferent to the sufferings of others, perhaps because in respect of his own he is provided with the special gift of patience and fortitude and supposes, or even requires, that others should have the same—and such a man would certainly not be the meanest product of nature—but if nature had not specially framed him for a philanthropist, would he not still find in himself a source from whence to give himself a far higher worth than that of a good-natured temperament could be? Unquestionably. It is just in this that the moral worth of the character is brought out which is incomparably the highest of all, namely, that he is beneficent, not from inclination, but from duty.

In two short paragraphs, Kant tells us that we have a duty to make ourselves happy, not because we want to be happy (wants are never duties) but because happiness is necessary for us to do our other duties. Then, with reference to the Bible, Kant makes a famous (or infamous) distinction between two kinds of love: practical love, which is commanded as a duty, and pathological love, in other words, what we would call the *emotion* of love.

To secure one's own happiness is a duty, at least indirectly; for discontent with one's condition, under a pressure of many anxieties and amidst unsatisfied wants, might easily become a great *temptation to transgression of duty*. But here again, without looking to duty, all men have already the strongest and most intimate inclination to happiness, because it is just in this idea that all inclinations are combined in one total. But the precept of happiness is often of such a sort that it greatly interferes with some inclinations, and yet a man cannot form any definite and certain conception of the sum of satisfaction of all of them which is called happiness. It is not then to be wondered at that a single inclination, definite both as to what it promises and as to the time within which it can be gratified, is often able to overcome such a fluctuating idea, and that a gouty patient, for instance, can choose to enjoy what he likes, and to suffer what he may, since, according to his calculation, on this occasion at least, he has

[only] not sacrificed the enjoyment of the present moment to a possibly mistaken expectation of a happiness which is supposed to be found in health. But even in this case, if the general desire for happiness did not influence his will, and supposing that in his particular case health was not a necessary element in this calculation, there yet remains in this, as in all other cases, this law—namely, that he should promote his happiness not from inclination but from duty, and by this would his conduct first acquire true moral worth.

It is in this manner, undoubtedly, that we are to understand those passages of Scripture also in which we are commanded to love our neighbour, even our enemy. For love, as an affection, cannot be commanded, but beneficence for duty's sake may, even though we are not impelled to it by any inclination—nay, are even repelled by a natural and unconquerable aversion. This is *practical* love, and not *pathological*—a love which is seated in the will, and not in the propensions of sense—in principles of action and not of tender sympathy; and it is this love alone which can be commanded.

Having thus defended his primary proposition that what is ultimately good is a good will acting in accordance with practical reason, in other words, from duty, Kant moves on to two corollary propositions:

The second proposition is: That an action done from duty derives its moral worth, *not from the purpose* which is to be attained by it, but from the maxim by which it is determined, and therefore does not depend on the realization of the object of the action, but merely on the *principle of volition* by which the action has taken place, without regard to any object of desire. It is clear from what precedes that the purposes which we may have in view in our actions, or their effects regarded as ends and springs of the will cannot give to actions any unconditional or moral worth. In what, then, can their worth lie if it is not to consist in the will and in reference to its expected effect? It cannot lie anywhere but in the *principle of the will* without regard to the ends which can be attained by the action. For the will stands between its *a priori* principle, which is formal, and its *a posteriori* spring which is material, as between two roads, and as it must be determined by something, it follows that it must be determined by the formal principle of volition when an action is done from duty, in which case every material principle has been withdrawn from it.

The third proposition, which is a consequence of the two preceding, I would express thus: *Duty is the necessity of acting from respect for the law.* I may have *inclination* for an object as the effect of my proposed action, but I cannot have *respect* for it just for this reason that it is an effect and not an energy of will. Similarly, I cannot have respect for inclination, whether my own or another's; I can at most, if my own, approve it; if another's, sometimes even love it, that is, look on it as favourable to my own interest. It is only what is connected with my will as a principle, by no means as an effect—what does not subserve my inclination, but overpowers it, or at least in case of choice excludes it from its calculation—in other words, simply the law of itself, which can be an object of respect, and hence a command. Now an action done from duty must wholly exclude the influence of inclination, and with it every object of the will, so that nothing remains which can determine the will except objectively the *law*, and subjectively *pure respect* for this practical law, and consequently the maxim that I should follow this law even to the thwarting of all my inclinations.

Thus the moral worth of an action does not lie in the effect expected from it, nor in any principle of action which requires to borrow its motive from this expected effect. For all these effects—agreeableness of one's condition, and even the promotion of the happiness of others—could have been also brought about by other causes, so that for this there would have been no need of the will of a rational being; whereas it is in this alone that the supreme and unconditional good can be found. The pre-eminent good which we call moral can therefore consist in nothing else than *the conception of law* in itself, *which certainly is only possible in a rational being*, in so far as this conception, and not the expected effect, determines the will. This is a good which is already preset

(Continued)

in the person who acts accordingly, and we have not to wait for it to appear first in the result.

By what sort of law can that be the conception of which must determine the will, even without paying any regard to the effect expected from it, in order that this will may be called good absolutely and without qualification? As I have deprived the will of every impulse which could arise to it from obedience to any law, there remains nothing but the universal conformity of its actions to law in general, which alone is to serve the will as a principle.

- What role does reason play in Kant's morality? Kant claims to be following Rousseau, but how is he like Rousseau? How does he differ from Rousseau?
- What does Kant mean by a 'good will'? What makes the will good, according to Kant?
- What makes an act 'morally worthy', according to Kant?

The conception of 'universal conformity to law' is Kant's central notion of duty. He defines it, as we shall see, as a generalized version of the Golden Rule: 'Do unto others as you would have them do unto you.' The point is, decide what you ought to do by asking yourself the question, 'What if everyone were to do that?' The rule, as he states it, is

I am never to act otherwise than so, *that I could also will that my maxim should become a universal law*. Here, now, it is the simple conformity to law in general, without assuming any particular law applicable to certain actions, that serves the will as its principle, and must so serve it if duty is not to be a vain delusion and a chimerical notion. The common reason of men in its practical judgments perfectly coincides with this, and always has in view the principle here suggested. Let the question be, for example: May I when in distress make a promise with the intention not to keep it? I readily distinguish here between the two significations which the question may have: whether it is prudent or whether it is right to make a false promise? The former may undoubtedly often be the case. I see clearly indeed that it is not enough to extricate myself from a present difficulty by means of this subterfuge, but it must be well considered whether there may not hereafter spring from this lie much greater inconvenience than that from which I now free myself, and as, with all my supposed *cunning*, the consequences cannot be so easily foreseen but that credit once lost may be much more injurious to me than any mischief which I seek to avoid at present, it should be considered whether it would not be more *prudent* to act herein according to a universal maxim, and to make it a habit to promise nothing except with the intention of keeping it. But it is soon clear to me that such a maxim will still only be based on the fear of consequences. Now it is a wholly different thing to be truthful from duty, and to be so from apprehension of injurious consequences. In the first case, the very notion of the action implies a law for me; in the second case, I must first look about elsewhere to see what results may be combined with it which would affect myself. For to deviate from the principle of duty is beyond all doubt wicked; but to be unfaithful to my maxim of prudence may often be very advantageous to me, although to abide by it is certainly safer. The shortest way, however, and an unerring one, to discover the answer to this question whether a lying promise is consistent with duty, is to ask myself, Should I be content that my maxim (to extricate myself from difficulty by a false promise) should hold good as a universal law, for myself as well as for others; and should I be able to say to myself, 'Every one may make a deceitful promise when he finds himself in a difficulty from which he cannot otherwise extricate himself'? Then I presently become aware that, while I can will the lie, I can by no means will that lying should be a universal law. For with such a law there would be no promises at all, since it would be in vain to allege my intention in regard to my future actions to those who would not believe this allegation, or if they over-hastily did so, would pay me back in my own coin. Hence my maxim, as soon as it should be made a universal law, would necessarily destroy itself.

The impressive name Kant gives to this general formulation of his notion of duty is the *categorical imperative*. An **imperative**, however, is just what we called a command in our preliminary discussion of morality. It is of the form 'do this!' or 'don't do this!' The word that distinguishes moral commands in general is the word **ought**, and this tells us something about the term *categorical*. Some imperatives tell us to 'do this!' but only in order to get or do something else. Kant calls these '**hypothetical imperatives**'. For example, 'go to law school' (if you want to be a lawyer) or 'don't eat very hot curry' (unless you don't mind risking an ulcer). But imperatives with a moral *ought* in them are not tied to any such 'if' or 'in order to' conditions. They are simply 'do this' or 'don't do this', whatever the circumstances, whatever you would like or enjoy personally; for example, 'don't lie' (no matter what). This is what Kant means by '*categorical*'.

CATEGORICAL IMPERATIVE

For Kant, a command that is unqualified and not dependent on any conditions or qualifications

HYPOTHETICAL IMPERATIVE

For Kant, a command that is conditional, depending upon particular aims or inclinations.

Now all *imperatives* command either *hypothetically* or *categorically*. The former represent the practical necessity of a possible action as means to something else that is willed (or at least which one might possibly will). The categorical imperative would be that which represented an action as necessary of itself without reference to another end, that is, as objectively necessary.

Since every practical law represents a possible action as good, and on this account, for a subject who is practically determinable by reason as necessary, all imperatives are formulae determining an action which is necessary according to the principle of a will good in some respects. If now the action is good only as a means *to something else*, then the imperative is *hypothetical*; if it is conceived as good *in itself* and consequently as being necessarily the principle of a will which of itself conforms to reason, then it is *categorical*.

With hypothetical imperatives, what is commanded depends upon particular circumstances. With moral or categorical imperatives, there are universal laws that tell us what to do in every circumstance. (A **maxim**, according to Kant, is a 'subjective principle of action', or what we would call an *intention*. It is distinguished from an 'objective principle', that is, a universal law of reason.)

There is therefore but one categorical imperative, namely, this: *Act only on that maxim whereby thou canst at the same time will that it should become a universal law.*

Now if all imperatives of duty can be deduced from this one imperative as from their principle, then, although it should remain undecided whether what is called duty is not merely a vain notion, yet at least we shall be able to show what we understand by it and what this notion means.

Since the universality of the law according to which effects are produced constitutes what is properly called *nature* in the most general sense (as to form)—that is, the existence of things so far as it is determined by general laws—the imperative of duty may be expressed thus: *Act as if the maxim of thy action were to become by thy will a universal law of nature.*

We will now enumerate a few duties, adopting the usual division of them into duties to ourselves and to others, and into perfect and imperfect duties.

1. A man reduced to despair by a series of misfortunes feels wearied of life, but is still so far in possession of his reason that he can ask himself whether it would not be contrary to his duty to himself to take his own life. Now he inquires whether the maxim of his action could become a universal law of nature. His maxim is: From self-love I adopt it as a principle to shorten my life when its longer duration is likely to bring more evil than satisfaction. It is asked then simply whether this principle founded on self-love can become a universal law of nature. Now we see at once that a system of nature of which it should be law to destroy life by means of the very feeling whose special nature it is to impel to the improvement of life would

(Continued)

contradict itself, and therefore could not exist as a system of nature; hence that maxim cannot possibly exist as a universal law of nature, and consequently would be wholly inconsistent with the supreme principle of all duty.

2. Another finds himself forced by necessity to borrow money. He knows that he will not be able to repay it, but sees also that nothing will be lent to him unless he promises stoutly to repay it in a definite time. He desires to make this promise, but he has still so much conscience as to ask himself: Is it not unlawful and inconsistent with duty to get out of a difficulty in this way? Suppose, however, that he resolves to do so, then the maxim of his action would be expressed thus: When I think myself in want of money, I will borrow money and promise to repay it, although I know that I never can do so. Now this principle of self-love or of one's own advantage may perhaps be consistent with my whole future welfare; but the question now is, Is it right? I change then the suggestion of self-love into a universal law, and state the question thus: How would it be if my maxim were a universal law? Then I see at once that it could never hold as a universal law of nature, but would necessarily contradict itself. For supposing it to be a universal law that everyone when he thinks himself in a difficulty should be able to promise whatever he pleases, with the purpose of not keeping his promise, the promise itself would become impossible, as well as the end that one might have in view in it, since no one would consider that anything was promised to him, but would ridicule all such statements as vain pretenses.

3. A third finds in himself a talent which with the help of some culture might make him a useful man in many respects. But he finds himself in comfortable circumstances and prefers to indulge in pleasure rather than to take pains in enlarging and improving his happy natural capacities. He asks, however, whether his maxim of neglect of his natural gifts, besides agreeing with his inclination to indulgence, agrees also with what is called duty. He sees then that a system of nature could indeed subsist with such a universal law, although men (like the South Sea islanders) should let their talents rest and resolve to devote their lives merely to idleness, amusement, and propagation of their species—in a word, to enjoyment; but he cannot possibly *will* that this should be a universal law of nature, or be implanted in us as such by a natural instinct. For, as a rational being, he necessarily wills that his faculties be developed, since they serve him, and have been given him, for all sorts of possible purposes.

4. A fourth, who is in prosperity, while he sees that others have to contend with great wretchedness and that he could help them, thinks: What concern is it of mine? Let everyone be as happy as Heaven pleases, or as he can make himself; I will take nothing from him nor even envy him, only I do not wish to contribute anything to his welfare or to his assistance in distress! Now no doubt, if such a mode of thinking were a universal law, the human race might very well subsist, and doubtless even better than in a state in which everyone talks of sympathy and goodwill, or even takes care occasionally to put it into practice, but, on the other side, also cheats when he can, betrays the rights of men, or otherwise violates them. But although it is possible that a universal law of nature might exist in accordance with that maxim, it is impossible to *will* that such a principle should have the universal validity of a law of nature. For a will which resolved this would contradict itself, inasmuch as many cases might occur in which one would have need of the love and sympathy of others, and in which, by such a law of nature, sprung from his own will, he would deprive himself of all hope of the aid he desires.

These are a few of the many actual duties, or at least what we regard as such, which obviously fall into two classes on the one principle that we have laid down. We must be *able to will* that a maxim of our action should be a universal law. This is the canon of the moral appreciation of the action generally. Some actions are of such a character that their maxim cannot without contradiction be even *conceived* as a universal law of nature, far from it being possible that we should *will* that it *should* be so. In others, this intrinsic impossibility is not found, but still it is impossible to *will* that their maxim should be raised to the universality of a law of nature, since such a will would contradict itself. It is easily seen that the former violate strict or rigorous (inflexible) duty; the latter only laxer (meritorious) duty. Thus it has been completely shown by these examples how all duties depend as regards the nature of the obligation (not the object of the action) on the same principle.

- What is a categorical imperative? How does it differ from a hypothetical imperative? What is a maxim? How does Kant first formulate the categorical imperative in terms of maxims? How does he use this to show that lying is wrong?

Another way of describing the categorical imperative, using a term from Kant that we've already encountered, is to say that it is an **a priori** principle, in this case, independent of any particular circumstances. Moral principles are necessary for the same reason that certain principles of knowledge are necessary, according to Kant, that is, because they are essential to human nature. It is important, therefore, for Kant to insist that moral principles, as a priori principles of reason, hold for every human being, in fact, even more generally, for every rational creature. (There is an extremely important point hidden in this phrase; traditionally, morality has always been defended on the basis of God's will, that is, we ought to be moral because God gave us the moral laws. According to Kant, however, God does not give the laws, but as a rational creature He is bound to them just as we are. Thus, in answer to the question, 'Are the laws of morality good because God is good or is God good because he obeys the laws of morality?' Kant would accept the latter.)

Kant's discussion of the categorical imperative is made confusing because after he has told us that 'there is but one categorical imperative', he then goes on to give us others. He calls these 'alternative formulations of the categorical imperative', but their effect on most readers is to confuse them unnecessarily. In actuality, for Kant there are a great many categorical imperatives. The first one Kant gave us is merely the most general. More specific examples are 'don't lie!' and 'keep your promises!' Another general categorical imperative is 'never use people!' There is, however, a sense in which 'using people' may be perfectly innocent. For example, you 'use' a friend in order to play tennis, since you could not play alone. In such a case, your friend derives as much benefit from your 'using' her as you do, and we could say that she is 'using' you as well. But there are cases in which we are tempted to 'use' people for our own benefit without any regard to their interests. This is what Kant forbids.

Now I say: man and generally any rational being *exists* as an end in himself, *not merely as a means* to be arbitrarily used by this or that will, but in all his actions, whether they concern himself or other rational beings, must be always regarded at the same time as an end. All objects of the inclinations have only a conditional worth; for if the inclinations and the wants founded on them did not exist, then their object would be without value. But the inclinations themselves, being sources of want, are so far from having an absolute worth for which they should be desired that, on the contrary, it must be the universal wish of every rational being to be wholly free from them. Thus the worth of any object which is *to be acquired* by our action is always conditional. Beings whose existence depends not on our will but on nature's, have nevertheless, if they are not rational beings, only a relative value as means, and are therefore called *things*; rational beings, on the contrary, are called *persons*, because their very nature points them out as ends in themselves, that is, as something which must not be used merely as means, and so far therefore restricts freedom of action (and is an object of respect). These, therefore, are not merely subjective ends whose existence has a worth *for us* as an effect of our action, but *objective ends*, that is, things whose existence is an end in itself—an end, moreover, for which no other can be substituted, which they should subserve *merely* as means, for otherwise nothing whatever would possess *absolute worth*; but if all worth were conditioned and therefore contingent, then there would be no supreme practical principle of reason whatever.

If then there is a supreme practical principle or, in respect of the human will, a categorical imperative, it must be one which, being drawn from the conception of that which is necessarily an end for everyone because it is *an end in itself*, constitutes an *objective* principle of will, and can therefore serve as a universal practical law. The foundation of this principle is:

(Continued)

rational nature exists as an end in itself. Man necessarily conceives his own existence as being so; so far then this is a *subjective* principle of human actions. But every other rational being regards its existence similarly, just on the same rational principle that holds for me; so that it is at the same time an objective principle from which as a supreme practical law all laws of the will must be capable of being deduced. Accordingly the practical imperative will be as follows: *So act as to treat humanity, whether in thine own person or in that of any other in every case as an end withal, never as means only*. We will now inquire whether this can be practically carried out.

To abide by the previous examples:

First, under the head of necessary duty to oneself: He who contemplates suicide should ask himself whether his action can be consistent with the idea of humanity *as an end in itself*. If he destroys himself in order to escape from painful circumstances, he uses a person merely as *a mean* to maintain a tolerable condition up to the end of life. But a man is not a thing, that is to say, something which can be used merely as means, but must in all his actions be always considered as an end in himself. I cannot, therefore, dispose in any way of a man in my own person so as to mutilate him, to damage or kill him. (It belongs to ethics proper to define this principle more precisely, so as to avoid all misunderstanding, for example, as to the amputation of the limbs in order to preserve myself; as to exposing my life to danger with a view to preserve it, etc. This question is therefore omitted here.)

Secondly, as regards necessary duties, or those of strict obligation, toward others: He who is thinking of making a lying promise to others will see at once that he would be using another man *merely as a mean*, without the latter containing at the same time the end in himself. For he whom I propose by such a promise to use for my own purpose cannot possibly assent to my mode of acting toward him, and therefore cannot himself contain the end of this action. This violation of the principle of humanity in other men is more obvious if we take in examples of attacks on the freedom and property of others. For then it is clear that he who transgresses the rights of men intends to use the person of others merely as means, without considering that as rational beings they ought always to be esteemed also as ends, that is, as beings who must be capable of containing in themselves the end of the very same action.

Thirdly, as regards contingent (meritorious) duties to oneself: It is not enough that the action does not violate humanity in our own person as an end in itself, it must also *harmonize with it*. Now there are in humanity capacities of greater perfection which belong to the end that nature has in view in regard to humanity in ourselves as the subject; to neglect these might perhaps be consistent with the *maintenance of* humanity as an end in itself, but not with the *advancement* of this end.

Fourthly, as regards meritorious duties toward others: The natural end which all men have is their own happiness. Now humanity might indeed subsist although no one should contribute anything to the happiness of others, provided he did not intentionally withdraw anything from it; but after all, this would only harmonize negatively, not positively, with *humanity as an end in itself*, if everyone does not also endeavour, as far as in him lies, to forward the ends of others. For the ends of any subject which is an end in himself ought as far as possible to be *my* ends also, if that conception is to have its *full* effect with me.

This principle that humanity and generally every rational nature is *an end in itself* (which is the supreme limiting condition of every man's freedom of action), is not borrowed from experience, *first*, because it is universal, applying as it does to all rational beings whatever, and experience is not capable of determining anything about them; *secondly*, because it does not present humanity as an end to men (subjectively), that is, as an object which men do of themselves actually adopt as an end; but as an objective end which must as a law constitute the supreme limiting condition of all our subjective ends, let them be what we will; it must therefore spring from pure reason.

- What does it mean to say that we are 'ends'? How do you treat someone as an end? What does Kant mean when he tells us not to treat others as a means only? What would be an example of treating another person as a means only? Under what circumstances might it be permissible to do so?

In Kant's own terms, every human will is capable of acting according to universal laws of morality, not based upon any personal inclinations or interests but obeying rational principles that are categorical. Using this as a definition of morality, Kant then looks back at his predecessors:

Looking back now on all previous attempts to discover the principle of morality, we need not wonder why they all failed. It was seen that man was bound to laws by duty, but it was not observed that the laws to which he is subject are *only those of his own giving*, though at the same time they are *universal*, and that he is only bound to act in conformity with his own will—a will, however, which is designed by nature to give universal laws. For when one has conceived man only as subject to a law (no matter what), then this law required some interest, either by way of attraction or constraint, since it did not originate as a law from *his own will*, but this will was according to a law obliged by *something else* to act in a certain manner. Now by this necessary consequence all the labour spent in finding a supreme principle of *duty* was irrevocably lost. For men never elicited duty, but only a necessity of acting from a certain interest.

Any morality worthy of the name, in other words, must be a product of a person's own autonomous reason yet universal at the same time, as a product of rational will and independent of personal feeling or interest. All previous philosophy, however, had insisted upon appealing to such personal feelings and interests and thus ended up with principles that were in every case hypothetical and not, according to Kant, categorical or moral. Thus morality for Aristotle depended upon a person's being a male Greek citizen. For Kant, morality and duty are completely set apart from such personal circumstances and concerns. Morality and duty have no qualifications, and, ultimately, they need have nothing to do with the good life or with happiness. In a perfect world, perhaps, doing our duty might also bring us happiness. But this is not such a world, Kant observes, and so happiness and morality are two separate concerns, with the second always to be considered the most important. (It is at this point, however, that Kant introduces his 'Postulates of Practical Reason', and God in particular, in order to give us some assurance that, at least in the [very] long run, doing our duty will bring us some reward.)

Kant's conception of morality is so strict that it is hard for most people to accept. What is most difficult to accept is the idea that morality and duty have nothing to do with our personal desires, ambitions, and feelings, which Kant called our inclinations. We can agree that at least sometimes our duties and our inclinations are in conflict. But many philosophers have felt that Kant went much too far the other way in separating them entirely. Furthermore, Kant's emphasis on the categorical imperative systematically rules out all reference to particular situations and circumstances. In response to Kant, one may ask: Isn't the right thing to do often determined only within the particular context or situation? Don't we have to know the particular problems and persons involved? What is right in one situation might very well be wrong in another, just because of different personalities, for example. Some people may be extremely hurt if we tell them the 'truth' about themselves. On the other hand, a 'little white lie' may make them feel much better. Other people are offended at any lie, however, and prefer even hurtful truths to the ignorant bliss of not knowing. Must not all moral rules be tempered to the particular situation?[16]

The Kantian response to this objection would be that there are many ways to avoid hurting people other than telling lies. One can say, 'no comment'. One can cough conveniently, or drop the platter in one's hand. The fact that certain deceptions are institutionalized in our society (such as 'regrets' for a dinner party) does not mean that a Kantian should defend them. The question, then, becomes how one formulates an accurate description of the options in such cases. Is it ever simply the case that one has a choice—hurt someone or tell a lie?

In a more general way, it has been objected that Kant's unqualified concept of morality is much too general to help us decide what to do in any particular situation. As an example, take the categorical imperative 'don't steal!' Although the imperative itself, as a categorical one, must be unqualified, in order to apply it at all, we have to understand the kinds of circumstances to which it applies. Can't we have a right to steal in certain circumstances? Or, to put the same point differently, aren't there some circumstances in which 'stealing' isn't really stealing at all? But what then of the situation in which a starving man steals a loaf of bread from an extremely wealthy baker. He *is* stealing, but wouldn't we say that, under the circumstances, he is justified in doing so? The Kantian reply here is to distinguish between the question of whether that man is *wrong* in stealing and the question of whether (or how) he should be punished. In this case, we can presume, Kant would insist that the man did wrong, but he would nevertheless agree that the man should not be punished.

How do we decide 'under which circumstances' a moral law is to be applied? Kant's formulation of the categorical imperative only tells us that we must act in such a way that anyone in similar circumstances would act the same way. What defines these 'similar' circumstances? Suppose a woman were to say, 'Anyone in my own circumstances, namely, anyone who is five-foot-seven, has blond hair and blue eyes, was born in Toronto in 1942, and graduated from C. High School, may steal.' According to her formulation, anyone in the same circumstances can steal, but, she has defined the circumstances in such a way that it is extremely unlikely that anyone but herself will ever qualify. How can we avoid such trickery? Not by any considerations within the categorical imperative itself, for by its very nature it is incapable of telling us under what circumstances a moral law applies. Another way of making the same objection is to complain that there is no way of deciding how detailed the imperative must be. For example, should we simply say, 'don't steal!' or rather, 'don't steal unless you're starving and the other person is not!' or else, 'don't steal unless you're blond and blue-eyed!' and so on? Kant's reply, to prevent such abuses, is to quite clearly leave out all mention of particular circumstances in the formulation of principles. Nevertheless we have to decide in what circumstances to apply what principles, and here the question comes up once again: How narrowly must we define the circumstances? Which circumstances are relevant to the formulation of a categorical imperative? Surely the answer won't be to say that *none* of the circumstances are relevant; at least we must know enough to know whether or not this act is an instance of stealing.

There have been other objections to Kant's severe philosophy. For example, if moral principles are categorical, then what do we do when two different moral principles conflict? The rule that tells us 'don't lie!' is categorical; so is the rule that tells us 'keep your promises!' Suppose that your brother promises not to tell anyone where you will be this weekend. Then some people wishing to kill you force him to tell. He has to say something. Either he breaks the promise or he lies. Kant gives us no adequate way of choosing between the promise and the lie. He has ruled out any appeal to the consequences of our actions. In Kant's argument, even if your enemies are trying to kill you, it is not morally relevant. Most importantly, Kant has ruled out any appeal to what will make people happy, not only the person who must either lie or break a promise but everyone else who is involved as well. Kant would reply, presumably, that such cases of apparent conflict are due to a misrepresentation of the case. To continue with our example, your brother could respond to the intruders by playing dumb, or refusing to say anything, or trying to make them go away with force. The question of moral conflict thus becomes critical for Kant's moral philosophy. If moral principles conflict, we need a way of choosing between them. If they do not conflict, then we need a way of accounting for apparent conflicts and resolving them. But it is not clear that the Kantian theory gives us either a satisfactory criterion for getting out of moral quandaries or for explaining away some of the very painful moral conflicts in which we occasionally find ourselves.

- Do you find Kant's view that moral worth has nothing to do with our own personal inclinations, passions, and feelings convincing? Do you find it problematic? Why is he so concerned with separating morality from inclinations?

J. Utilitarianism

In response to the harsh Kantian view of morality, with its neglect of happiness and the good life, a number of British philosophers, chiefly Jeremy Bentham, James Mill, and Mill's son John Stuart Mill, developed a conception of morality that is called utilitarianism. This philosophy was an attempt to bring back personal inclinations and interests into moral considerations. Utilitarians wished to reconsider the consequences as well as the 'will' of an action and to consider the particular circumstances of an action in an attempt to determine what is morally right. Most importantly, they wanted to return morality to the search for the personally satisfying life that Kant had neglected.

The basis of utilitarianism is a form of **hedonism**, the conception of the good life that says that the ultimate good is pleasure and that we want and ought to want this pleasure. But where traditional hedonism is concerned only with one's personal pleasure, utilitarianism is concerned with pleasure in general; that is, with one's own pleasure and the pleasure of other people. In many utilitarian writings, the notions of pleasure and happiness are used interchangeably. From our earlier discussions (and especially our discussion of Aristotle), we know that we must be cautious of such an exchange. Many short-lived pleasures do not make us happy, and happiness is much more than mere pleasure. But this is a major concern for the utilitarians; their whole theory revolves around a single aim: to make the most people as happy as possible, sometimes sacrificing short-term pleasures for enduring ones. Their central principle is often summarized as 'the greatest good for the greatest number'.

Jeremy Bentham was motivated to formulate his utilitarian theories not so much by the strict moralism of Kant's philosophy as by the absurd complexity of the British legal system. Just as Kant sought a single principle that would simplify all morality, Bentham looked for a single principle that would simplify the law. Bentham began with the fact that people seek pleasure and avoid pain and developed the '**principle of utility**' on just this basis:

> **PRINCIPLE OF UTILITY**
>
> The principle that one ought to do what gives the greatest pleasure to the greatest number of people.

From *An Introduction to the Principles of Morals and Legislation*
By Jeremy Bentham

An action . . . may be said to be conformable . . . to utility . . . when the tendency it has to augment the happiness of the community is greater than any it has to diminish it.

I. Nature has placed mankind under the governance of two sovereign masters, pain and pleasure. It is for them alone to point out what we ought to do, as well as to determine what we shall do. On the one hand the standard of right and wrong, on the other the chain of causes and effects, are fastened to their throne. They govern us in all we do, in all we say, in all we think; every effort we can make to throw off our subjection, will serve but to demonstrate and confirm it. In words a man may pretend to abjure their empire; but in reality he will remain subject to it all the while. The principle of utility recognizes the subjection, and assumes it for the foundation of that system, the object of which is to tear the fabric

(*Continued*)

of felicity by the hands of reason and of law. Systems which attempt to question it, deal in sounds instead of sense, in caprice instead of reason, the darkness instead of light.

But enough of metaphor and declamation: it is not by such means that moral science is to be improved.

II.   The principle of utility is the foundation of the present work; it will be proper therefore at the outset to give an explicit and determinate account of what is meant by it. By the principle of utility is meant that principle which approves or disapproves of every action whatsoever, according to the tendency which it appears to have to augment or diminish the happiness of the party whose interest is in question; or, what is the same thing in other words, to promote or to oppose that happiness. I say of every action whatsoever; and therefore not only of every action of a private individual, but of every measure of government.

III.   By utility is meant that property in any object, whereby it tends to produce benefit, advantage, pleasure, good, or happiness, (all this in the present case comes to the same thing) or (what comes again to the same thing) to prevent the happening of mischief, pain, evil, or unhappiness to the party whose interest is considered: if that party be the community in general, then the happiness of the community: if a particular individual, then the happiness of that individual.

IV.   The interest of the community is one of the most general expressions that can occur in the phraseology of morals: no wonder that the meaning of it is often lost. When it has a meaning, it is this. The community is a fictitious body, composed of the individual persons who are considered as constituting as it were its members. The interest of the community then is, what?—the sum of the interests of the several members who compose it.

V.   It is in vain to talk of the interest of the community, without understanding what is the interest of the individual. A thing is said to promote the interest, or to be for the interest, of an individual, when it tends to add to the sum total of his pleasures: or, what comes to the same thing, to diminish the sum total of his pains.

VI.   An action then may be said to be conformable to the principle of utility, or, for shortness' sake, to utility, (meaning with respect to the community at large) when the tendency it has to augment the happiness of the community is greater than any it has to diminish it.

VII.   A measure of government (which is but a particular kind of action, performed by a particular person or persons) may be said to be conformable to or dictated by the principle of utility, when in like manner the tendency which it has to augment the happiness of the community is greater than any which it has to diminish it.

Morality, according to Bentham's principle of utility, means nothing other than action that tends to increase, rather than diminish, the amount of pleasure for any group of people.

X.   Of an action that is conformable to the principle of utility, one may always say either that it is one that ought to be done, or at least that it is not one that ought not to be done. One may say also, that it is right it should be done; at least that it is not wrong it should be done: that it is a right action; at least that it is not a wrong action. When thus interpreted, the words ought, and right and wrong, and others of that stamp, have a meaning: when otherwise, they have none.

How does one defend this principle of utility? One cannot. To try to prove the principle is 'as impossible as it is needless'. People quite 'naturally', whether they admit to it or not, act on the basis of it. This is not to say that they always act on it, but that is only because, according to Bentham, people do not always know what is best for them. That is the reason for formulating the principle in philosophy.

The heart of Bentham's theory is the formulation of a procedure for deciding, in every possible case, the value of alternative courses of action. The procedure simply involves the determination of alternative amounts of pleasures and pain, according to what has appropriately been called the **happiness calculus**.

I. Pleasures then, and the avoidance of pains, are the *ends* which the legislator has in view; it behoves him therefore to understand their *value*. Pleasures and pains are the *instruments* he has to work with: it behoves him therefore to understand their force, which is gain, in other words, their value.

II. To a person considered *by himself*, the value of a pleasure or pain considered *by itself*, will be greater or less, according to the four following circumstances.
   1. Its *intensity*.
   2. Its *duration*.
   3. Its *certainty* or *uncertainty*.
   4. Its *propinquity* or *remoteness*.

III. These are the circumstances which are to be considered in estimating a pleasure or a pain considered each of them by itself. But when the value of any pleasure or pain is considered for the purpose of estimating the tendency of any *act* by which it is produced, there are two other circumstances to be taken into the account; these are,
   5. Its *fecundity*, or the chance it has of being followed by sensations of the *same* kind: that is, pleasures, if it be a pleasure: pains, if it be a pain.
   6. Its *purity*, or the chance it has of *not* being followed by sensations of the *opposite* kind: that is, pains, if it be a pleasure: pleasures, if it be a pain.

Then he reveals the test itself:

V. To take an exact account then of the general tendency of any act by which the interests of a community are affected, proceed as follows. Begin with any one person of those whose interests seem most immediately to be affected by it; and take an account,
   1. Of the value of each distinguishable *pleasure* which appears to be produced by it in the *first* instance.
   2. Of the value of each *pain* which appears to be produced by it in the *first* instance.
   3. Of the value of each pleasure which appears to be produced by it *after* the first. This constitutes the *fecundity* of the first *pleasure* and the *impurity* of the first *pain*.
   4. Of the value of each *pain* which appears to be produced by it after the first. This constitutes the *fecundity* of the first *pain*, and the *impurity* of the first pleasure.
   5. Sum up all the values of all the *pleasures* on the one side, and those of all the pains on the other. The balance, if it be on the side of pleasure, will give the *good* tendency of the act upon the whole, with respect to the interests of that *individual* person; if on the side of pain, the *bad* tendency of it upon the whole.
   6. Take an account of the *number* of persons whose interests appear to be concerned; and repeat the above process with respect to each. *Sum up* the numbers expressive of the degrees of *good* tendency, which the act has, with respect to each individual, in regard to whom the tendency of it is *good* upon the whole: do this again with respect to each individual, in regard to whom the tendency of it is *bad* upon the whole. Take the balance; which, if on the side of *pleasure*, will give the general *good* tendency of the act, with respect to the total number of community of individuals concerned; if on the side of pain the general *evil tendency*, with respect to the same community.

Let us take an example. Bentham himself discusses the problem of lust, which he says is always bad. Why? 'Because if the effects of the motive are not bad, then we do not call it lust.' Lust, in other words, is sexual desire that is so excessive that it brings about more pain than pleasure. Suppose you are sexually attracted to another person. How do you decide (assuming that there is already mutual agreement) whether to follow through or not? First, you must estimate the amount of pleasure that you and your potential partner will gain. Then, you must estimate how the act will impact the pleasure of others. If it is a question of adultery, you must consider the interests of at least a third person. But assuming that no such direct complications are involved, you must consider even the indirect interests of the rest of society. (If you and your potential lover are sufficiently young, should the happiness of your parents enter into your decision?) After you have considered its initial pleasure, you must estimate the initial pain. (In this case, we may presume it will be slight.) Then you must ask about the longer-term pleasures and pains for each person involved. If a sexual relationship will leave you feeling happy about yourself and the other person, then the subsequent pleasure will be considerable. If either person will have regrets or feel de-graded, or if sex will spoil a good friendship, or if a sexual relationship will set up expecta-tions that one or both of you is unwilling to fulfill, the amount of subsequent pain may be overwhelming. Finally, you must add up the pleasures and pains for each person and match the total amount of pleasure against the total amount of pain. If the balance is posi-tive, you may go ahead. If the balance is negative, you shouldn't do it.

Suppose, for example, you each expect a great deal of initial pleasure, and one of you expects nothing but good feelings afterward while the other expects only mild regrets. No one else need even know, and so the balance, clearly, is very positive. But suppose neither of you expects to enjoy it all that much, and the subsequent hassles will be a prolonged and troublesome bother; then, very likely, the balance will be negative. We don't often make this kind of decision in this way; we simply do what we want to do at the time. And this is precisely what Bentham says we shouldn't do. He argues that it is because we so often act on the basis of impulses without rational calculations that we end up unhappy. In other words, the fact that we are usually irrational is not an argument against Bentham's princi-ples. Their purpose is precisely to make us rational, to help us get what we really want.

> • What is the principle of utility? Is pleasure quantifiable? How does Bentham suggest that we calculate utility? Consider two courses of action and compare them according to the Benthamite calculus.

There are problems with Bentham's theory. The greatest problem is that his 'happiness calculus' only considers the amount of pleasure and pain that will result from any act. But some of you, in response to our preceding example, might well say, 'It doesn't matter how much pleasure and how little pain two people will gain if they get into a sexual relationship. Under certain circumstances (if it is adultery, or simply if they are not married) such behaviour is wrong! Mere happiness is not enough!' Here we see the beginning of a swing back toward Kant. To see why such a move is necessary, let us examine the following objection to Bentham.

Suppose a great many people would get a great deal of pleasure out of seeing some in-nocent person tortured and slaughtered like a beast. Of course the victim would suffer a great deal of pain, but by increasing the size of the crowd we could eventually obtain an amount of pleasure on the part of everyone else that more than balanced the suffering of the victim. Bentham's calculus has no way of rejecting such a gruesome outcome. A less horrible example is this: If a person gets great pleasure from some activity and no pain, there are no other considerations that apply to him or her (assuming that his or her actions do not affect others). Are we then to say that a life of sloth and self-indulgence, if it satisfies everyone and gives them a lot of pleasure and no pain, is to be preferred to any other life of any kind? Does Bentham give us any reason to try for anything 'better' than being happy pigs? This was the problem that bothered Bentham's godson, John Stuart Mill.

Mill's version of utilitarianism added an important qualification to Bentham's purely quantitative calculus. Mill said that it is not only the quantity of pleasure that counts, but the quality as well. Needless to say, this makes the calculations much more complicated. In fact, it makes them impossible, for there cannot be precise calculations of quality, even though there can be precise calculations of quantity. Mill's now-famous example is the following: If a pig can live a completely satisfied life, while a morally concerned and thoughtful individual like Socrates cannot ever be so satisfied, is the life of the pig therefore preferable? Mill's answer is this:

> It is better to be a human being dissatisfied than a pig satisfied; better to be Socrates dissatisfied than a fool satisfied.

On what grounds can he say this? Aren't the pig and the fool happier?

> If the fool, or the pig, are of a different opinion, it is because they only know their own side of the question. The other party [Socrates] knows both sides.[17]

Some problems emerge from this theory. How are we to evaluate different 'qualities' of pleasure, even if we have tried them all? But first let us look to Mill's revision of utilitarianism, as summarized in his popular pamphlet, appropriately called *Utilitarianism*. (It was Mill, not Bentham, who invented this term.) It begins with a general consideration of morality and of Kant's moral philosophy in particular.

From *Utilitarianism*
By John Stuart Mill

Of two pleasures, if there be one to which all or almost all who have experience of both give a decided preference, irrespective of a feeling of moral obligation to prefer it, that is the more desirable pleasure.

Our moral faculty, according to all those of its interpreters who are entitled to the name of thinkers, supplies us only with the general principles of moral judgments; it is a branch of our reason, not of our sensitive faculty; and must be looked to for the abstract doctrines of morality, not for perception of it in the concrete. The intuitive, no less than what may be termed the inductive, school of ethics, insists on the necessity of general laws. They both agree that the morality of an individual action is not a question of direct perception, but of the application of a law to an individual case. They recognize also, to a great extent, the same moral laws; but differ as to their evidence, and the source from which they derive their authority. According to the one opinion, the principles of morals are evident a priori, requiring nothing to command assent, except that the meaning of the terms be understood. According to the other doctrine, right and wrong, as well as truth and falsehood, are questions of observation and experience. But both hold equally that morality must be deduced from principles; and the intuitive school affirm as strongly as the inductive, that there is a science of morals. Yet they seldom attempt to make out a list of the a priori principles which are to serve as the premises of the science; still more rarely do they make any effort to reduce those various principles to one first principle, or common ground of obligation. They either assume the ordinary precepts of morals as of a priori authority, or they lay down as the common groundwork of those maxims, some generality much less obviously authoritative than the maxims themselves, and which has never succeeded in gaining popular acceptance. Yet to support their pretensions there ought either to be some one fundamental principle or law, at the root of all morality, or if there be several, there should be a

(Continued)

determinate order of precedence among them; and the one principle, or the rule for deciding between the various principles when they conflict, ought to be self-evident.

To inquire how far the bad effects of this deficiency have been mitigated in practice, or to what extent the moral beliefs of mankind have been vitiated or made uncertain by the absence of any distinct recognition of an ultimate standard, would imply a complete survey and criticism of past and present ethical doctrine. It would, however, be easy to show that whatever steadiness or consistency these moral beliefs have attained, has been mainly due to the tacit influence of a standard not recognized. Although the non-existence of an acknowledged first principle has made ethics not so much a guide as a consecration of men's actual sentiments, still, as men's sentiments, both of favour and of aversion, are greatly influenced by what they suppose to be the effects of things upon their happiness, the principle of utility, or as Bentham latterly called it, the Greatest Happiness Principle, has had a large share in forming the moral doctrines even of those who most scornfully reject its authority. Nor is there any school of thought which refuses to admit that the influence of actions on happiness is a most

material and even predominant consideration in many of the details of morals, however unwilling to acknowledge it as the fundamental principle of morality, and the source of moral obligation. I might go much further, and say that to all those a priori moralists who deem it necessary to argue at all, utilitarian arguments are indispensable. It is not my present purpose to criticize these thinkers; but I cannot help referring, for illustration, to a systematic treatise by one of the most illustrious of them, the *Metaphysics of Ethics*, by Kant. This remarkable man, whose system of thought will long remain one of the landmarks in the history of philosophical speculation, does, in the treatise in question, lay down a universal first principle as the origin and ground of moral obligation; it is this:—'So act, that the rule on which thou actest would admit of being adopted as a law by all rational beings.' But when he begins to deduce from this precept any of the actual duties of morality, he fails, almost grotesquely, to show that there would be any contradiction, any logical (not to say physical) impossibility, in the adoption by all rational beings of the most outrageously immoral rules of conduct. All he shows is that the *consequences* of their universal adoption would be such as no one would choose to incur.

Then Mill gets down to the business of redefining utilitarianism. Like Bentham, he insists that the principle of utility cannot be proven as such, for it is the ultimate end in terms of which everything else is justified. But there is, Mill tells us, a 'larger sense of the word *proof*':

On the present occasion, I shall, without further discussion of the other theories, attempt to contribute something toward the understanding and appreciation of the Utilitarian or Happiness theory, and toward such proof as it is susceptible of. It is evident that this cannot be proof in the ordinary and popular meaning of the term. Questions of ultimate ends are not amenable to direct proof. Whatever can be proved to be good must be so by being shown to be a means to something admitted to be good without proof. The medical art is proved to be good by its conducing to health; but how is it possible to prove that health is good? The art of music is good, for the reason, among others, that it produces pleasure; but what proof is it possible to give that pleasure is good? If, then, it is asserted that

there is a comprehensive formula, including all things which are in themselves good, and that whatever else is good, is not so as an end, but as a mean, the formula may be accepted or rejected, but is not a subject of what is commonly understood by proof. We are not, however, to infer that its acceptance or rejection must depend on blind impulse, or arbitrary choice. There is a larger meaning of the word proof, in which this question is as amenable to it as any other of the disputed questions of philosophy. The subject is within the cognizance of the rational faculty; and neither does that faculty deal with it solely in the way of intuition. Considerations may be presented capable of determining the intellect either to give or withhold its assent to the doctrine; and this is equivalent to proof.

Mill concerns himself with dispelling a popular misconception that views the principle of utility as advocating 'usefulness' in opposition to pleasure. Here he points out that, by utility, proponents of the theory have always meant 'not something to be contradistinguished from pleasure, but pleasure itself, together with exemption from pain'. The 'Greatest Happiness Principle', in turn, holds that actions are right to the extent that they promote happiness and are wrong to the extent that they diminish happiness. By happiness, of course, Mill means pleasure and the absence of pain. Pleasure or happiness, according to Mill, is the only thing desirable as an end (it is therefore an *intrinsic good*) and all other desirable things are so desired for the pleasure that they produce. These other goods are simply means toward pleasure (and are therefore *instrumental goods*).

A passing remark is all that needs be given to the ignorant blunder of supposing that those who stand up for utility as the test of right and wrong, use the term in that restricted and merely colloquial sense in which utility is opposed to pleasure. An apology is due to the philosophical opponents of utilitarianism, for even the momentary appearance of confounding them with anyone capable of so absurd a misconception; which is the more extraordinary, inasmuch as the contrary accusation, of referring everything to pleasure, and that too in its grossest form, is another of the common charges against utilitarianism: and, as has been pointedly remarked by an able writer, the same sort of persons, and often the very same persons, denounce the theory 'as impracticably dry when the word *utility* precedes the word pleasure, and as too practically voluptuous when the word pleasure precedes the word utility'. Those who know anything about the matter are aware that every writer, from Epicurus to Bentham, who maintained the theory of utility, meant by it, not something to be contradistinguished from pleasure, but pleasure itself, together with exemption from pain; and instead of opposing the useful to the agreeable or the ornamental, have always declared that the useful means these, among other things. Yet the common herd, including the herd of writers, not only in newspapers and periodicals, but in books of weight and pretension, are perpetually falling, into this shallow mistake. Having caught up the word utilitarian, while knowing nothing whatever about it but its sound, they habitually express by it the rejection, or the neglect, of pleasure in some of its forms; of beauty, of ornament, or of amusement. Nor is the term thus ignorantly misapplied solely in disparagement, but occasionally in compliment; as though it implied superiority to frivolity and the mere pleasures of the moment. And this perverted use is the only one in which the word is popularly known, and the one from which the new generation are acquiring their sole notion of its meaning. Those who introduced the word, but who had for many years discontinued it as a distinctive appellation, may well feel themselves called upon to resume it, if by doing so they can hope to contribute anything toward rescuing it from this utter degradation.

The creed which accepts as the foundation of morals, Utility or the Greatest Happiness Principle, holds that actions are right in proportion as they tend to promote happiness, wrong as they tend to produce the reverse of happiness. By happiness is intended pleasure, and the absence of pain; by unhappiness, pain, and the privation of pleasure. To give a clear view of the moral standard set up by the theory, much more requires to be said; in particular, what things it includes in the ideas of pain and pleasure; and to what extent this is left an open question. But these supplementary explanations do not affect the theory of life on which this theory of morality is grounded—namely, that pleasure, and freedom from pain, are the only things desirable as ends; and that all desirable things (which are as numerous in the utilitarian as in any other scheme) are desirable either for the pleasure inherent in themselves, or as means to the promotion of pleasure and the prevention of pain.

After defining the principle of utility, Mill turns his attention to the objection (one often levied against the Epicureans) that to claim that pleasure is the highest good for human beings is to degrade human life to the level of pigs. Mill responds that it is not the advocates of pleasure who degrade human life; rather, it is their critics who degrade this life by assuming that humans are only capable of the same types of pleasures as swine. Mill distinguishes between higher and lower pleasures and says that humans, unlike pigs, are capable of both since we possess higher cognitive faculties. Hence, when Mill says that the highest good is pleasure, he is referring to the higher types of pleasures.

How do we know which pleasures are higher or what makes one pleasure higher than another? Mill's answer is quite simple: If we are considering two pleasures, then the higher pleasure will be the one that is preferred by those who have experienced both. Human beings will prefer to satisfy their higher faculties than their lower, even though the higher faculties are much more difficult to satisfy. Few among us would consent to exchange his or her life with the life of a satisfied pig, even if he or she seems to be less satisfied than a pig. We hardly think that the life of a satisfied pig is a dignified one. Thus, Mill claims that 'it is better to be a human being dissatisfied than a pig satisfied; better to be Socrates dissatisfied than a fool satisfied'.

Now, such a theory of life excites in many minds, and among them in some of the most estimable in feeling and purpose, inveterate dislike. To suppose that life has (as they express it) no higher end than pleasure— no better and nobler object of desire and pursuit—they designate as utterly mean and grovelling; as a doctrine worthy only of swine, to whom the followers of Epicurus were, at a very early period, contemptuously likened; and modern holders of the doctrine are occasionally made the subject of equally polite comparisons by its German, French, and English assailants.

When thus attacked, the Epicureans have always answered, that it is not they, but their accusers, who represent human nature in a degrading light; since the accusation supposes human beings to be capable of no pleasures except those of which swine are capable. If this supposition were true, the charge could not be gainsaid, but would then be no longer an imputation; for if the sources of pleasure were precisely the same to human beings and to swine, the rule of life which is good enough for the one would be good enough for the other. The comparison of the Epicurean life to that of beasts is felt as degrading, precisely because a beast's pleasures do not satisfy a human being's conceptions of happiness. Human beings have faculties more elevated than the animal appetites, and when once made conscious of them, do not regard anything as happiness which does not include their gratification. I do not, indeed, consider the Epicureans to have been by any means faultless in drawing out their scheme of consequences from the utilitarian principle. To do this in any sufficient manner, many Stoic, as well as Christian elements require to be included. But there is no known Epicurean theory of life which does not assign to the pleasures of the intellect, of the feelings and imagination, and of the moral sentiments, a much higher value as pleasures than to those of mere sensation. It must be admitted, however, that utilitarian writers in general have placed the superiority of mental over bodily pleasures chiefly in the greater permanency, safety, uncostliness, etc., of the former—that is, in their circumstantial advantages rather than in their intrinsic nature. And on all these points utilitarians have fully proved their case; but they might have taken the other, and, as it may be called, higher ground, with entire consistency. It is quite compatible with the principle of utility to recognize the fact, that some *kinds* of pleasure are more desirable and more valuable than others. It would be absurd that while, in estimating all other things, quality is considered as well as quantity, the estimation of pleasures should be supposed to depend on quantity alone.

If I am asked, what I mean by difference of quality in pleasures, or what makes one pleasure more valuable than another, merely as a pleasure, except its being greater in amount, there is but one possible answer. Of two pleasures, if there be one to which all or almost all who have experience of both give a decided preference, irrespective of a feeling of moral obligation to prefer it, that is the more desirable pleasure. If one of the two is, by those who are competently acquainted with both, placed so far above the other that they prefer it, even though knowing it to be attended with a greater amount of discontent, and would not resign it for any quantity of the other pleasure which their nature is capable of, we are justified in ascribing to the preferred enjoyment a superiority in quality, so far outweighing quantity as to render it, in comparison, of small account.

Now it is an unquestionable fact that those who are equally acquainted with, and equally capable of appreciating and enjoying, both, do give a most marked preference to the manner of existence which employs their higher faculties. Few human creatures would consent to be changed into any of the lower animals, for a promise of the fullest allowance of a beast's pleasures; no intelligent human being would consent to be a fool, no instructed person would be an ignoramus, no person of feeling and conscience would be selfish and base, even though they should be persuaded that the fool, the dunce, or the rascal is better satisfied with his lot than they are with theirs. They would not resign what they possess more than he for the most complete satisfaction of all the desires which they have in common with him. If they ever fancy they would, it is only in cases of unhappiness so extreme, that to escape from it they would exchange their lot for almost any other, however undesirable in their own eyes. A being of higher faculties requires more to make him happy, is capable probably of more acute suffering, and certainly accessible to it at more points, than one of an inferior type; but in spite of these liabilities, he can never really wish to sink into what he feels to be a lower grade of existence. We may give what explanation we please of this unwillingness; we may attribute it to pride, a name which is given indiscriminately to some of the most and to some of the least estimable feelings of which mankind are capable: we may refer it to the love of liberty and personal independence, an appeal to which was with the Stoics one of the most effective means for the inculcation of it; to the love of power,

or to the love of excitement, both of which do really enter into and contribute to it: but its most appropriate appellation is a sense of dignity, which all human beings possess in one form or other, and in some, though by no means in exact, proportion to their higher faculties, and which is so essential a part of the happiness of those in whom it is strong, that nothing which conflicts with it could be, otherwise than momentarily, an object of desire to them. Whoever supposes that this preference takes place at a sacrifice of happiness—that the superior being, in anything like equal circumstances, is not happier than the inferior—confounds the two very different ideas, of happiness, and content. It is indisputable that the being whose capacities of enjoyment are low, has the greatest chance of having them fully satisfied; and a highly endowed being will always feel that any happiness which he can look for, as the world is constituted, is imperfect. But he can learn to bear its imperfections, if they are at all bearable; and they will not make him envy the being who is indeed unconscious of the imperfections, but only because he feels not at all the good which those imperfections qualify. It is better to be a human being dissatisfied than a pig satisfied; better to be Socrates dissatisfied than a fool satisfied. And if the fool, or the pig, are of a different opinion, it is because they only know their own side of the question. The other party to the comparison knows both sides.

Mill does recognize that cultivating the higher faculties is a very difficult thing to do. We know many among us who do not pursue the higher pleasures but seem to constantly seek bodily satisfaction. Mill explains the behaviour of these types of people in a number of ways: they may be lazy, they may have had little opportunity for cultivating their higher faculties in the past and are now incapable of doing so, they might be ignorant, or they may have what is referred to as 'weakness of will'. Weakness of will refers to that familiar experience of knowing what the right or good thing to do is yet, at the time of choosing it, somehow giving in to temptation and failing to do what is right or good.

Mill thinks that the cultivation of noble character is a necessity for the utilitarian. Not only will noble types be more receptive to cultivating their higher faculties and therefore more apt to pursue higher pleasures, but noble or virtuous people tend to make others happy. Since the goal of utilitarianism is to increase not just the agent's happiness but the greatest total amount of happiness of everyone, then the utilitarian is obligated to cultivate the virtues in himself and in others. Hence, we see an important modification of Bentham's view.

It may be objected, that many who are capable of the higher pleasures, occasionally, under the influence of temptation, postpone them to the lower. But this is

quite compatible with a full appreciation of the intrinsic superiority of the higher. Men often, from infirmity of character, make their election for the nearer
(*Continued*)

good, though they know it to be the less valuable; and this no less when the choice is between two bodily pleasures, than when it is between bodily and mental. They pursue sensual indulgences to the injury of health, though perfectly aware that health is the greater good. It may be further objected, that many who begin with youthful enthusiasm for everything noble, as they advance in years sink into indolence and selfishness. But I do not believe that those who undergo this very common change, voluntarily choose the lower description of pleasures in preference to the higher. I believe that before they devote themselves exclusively to the one, they have already become incapable of the other. Capacity for the nobler feelings is in most natures a very tender plant, easily killed, not only by hostile influences, but by mere want of sustenance; and in the majority of young persons it speedily dies away if the occupations to which their position in life has devoted them, and the society into which it has thrown them, are not favourable to keeping that higher capacity in exercise. Men lose their high aspirations as they lose their intellectual tastes, because they have not time or opportunity for indulging them; and they addict themselves to inferior pleasures, not because they deliberately prefer them, but because they are either the only ones to which they have access, or the only ones which they are any longer capable of enjoying. It may be questioned whether anyone who has remained equally susceptible to both classes of pleasures, ever knowingly and calmly preferred the lower; though many, in all ages, have broken down in an ineffectual attempt to combine both.

From this verdict of the only competent judges, I apprehend there can be no appeal. On a question which is the best worth having of two pleasures, or which of two modes of existence is the most grateful to the feelings, apart from its moral attributes and from its consequences, the judgment of those who are qualified by knowledge of both, or, if they differ, that of the majority among them, must be admitted as final. And there needs be the less hesitation to accept this judgment respecting the quality of pleasures, since there is no other tribunal to be referred to even on the question of quantity. What means are there of determining which is the acutest of two pains, or the intensest of two pleasurable sensations, except the general suffrage of those who are familiar with both? Neither pains nor pleasures are homogeneous, and pain is always heterogeneous with pleasure. What is there to decide whether a particular pleasure is worth purchasing at the cost of a particular pain, except the feelings and judgment of the experienced? When, therefore, those feelings and judgment declare the pleasures derived from the higher faculties to be preferable *in kind*, apart from the question of intensity, to those of which the animal nature, disjoined from the higher faculties, is susceptible, they are entitled on this subject to the same regard.

I have dwelt on this point, as being a necessary part of a perfectly just conception of Utility or Happiness, considered as the directive rule of human conduct. But it is by no means an indispensable condition to the acceptance of the utilitarian standard; for that standard is not the agent's own greatest happiness, but the greatest amount of happiness altogether; and if it may possibly be doubted whether a noble character is always the happier for its nobleness, there can be no doubt that it makes other people happier, and that the world in general is immensely a gainer by it. Utilitarianism, therefore, could only attain its end by the general cultivation of nobleness of character, even if each individual were only benefitted by the nobleness of others, and his own, so far as happiness is concerned, were a sheer deduction from the benefit. But the bare enunciation of such an absurdity as this last, renders refutation superfluous.

According to the Greatest Happiness Principle, as above explained, the ultimate end, with reference to and for the sake of which all other things are desirable (whether we are considering our own good or that of other people), is an existence exempt as far as possible from pain, and as rich as possible in enjoyments, both in point of quantity and quality; the test of quality, and the rule for measuring it against quantity, being the preference felt by those who in their opportunities of experience, to which must be added their habits of self-consciousness and self-observation, are best furnished with the means of comparison. This, being, according to the utilitarian opinion, the end of human action, is necessarily also the standard of morality; which may accordingly be defined, the rules and precepts for human conduct, by the observance of which an existence such as has been described might be, to the greatest extent possible, secured to all mankind; and not to them only, but, so far as the nature of things admits, to the whole sentient creation.

- Why is Mill's modification of Bentham's view so significant? Can you provide examples of higher pleasures? (Lower pleasures are pretty obvious.) Why, according to Mill, do humans not always seek higher pleasures?
- Is Mill a hedonist? What is hedonism? How does hedonism differ from Aristotle's view of the good life? In what ways does Mill's notion of higher pleasure seem closer to Aristotle's conception of *eudaimonia*?
- What problems do you find in trying to base a morality on considerations of pain and pleasure?

K. The Creation of Morality: Friedrich Nietzsche and Existentialism

The single term *morality* must not mislead us. We have been discussing not simply different theories of morality (ethics) but different conceptions of morality, and that means different moralities, even if they should have many principles in common. So we can see that the problem of relativism is not confined to the comparison of exotically different cultures. It faces us in a far more urgent form in our own conceptions of morality. We might agree that killing without extreme provocation is wrong. But why do we believe that it is wrong? One person claims that it is wrong because the Ten Commandments (and therefore God) forbid it. Another says it is wrong because it is a mark of insensitivity and therefore a flaw in character. Another says it is wrong because it violates people's rights, while still another says it increases the amount of pain in the world without equally adding to happiness. They all agree that killing is wrong, but the different reasons point to different circumstances in which each would kill: the first, if God commanded him or her to kill; the second, if the killing could be seen as a sign of strength and heroism; the third, if he or she found a way to take away people's right to live or found another right that was overriding; the fourth, as a utilitarian, if the death of one person was more than balanced by the increased welfare of the others (as in a criminal execution).

As we have seen in this chapter, different moral philosophies may promote different principles. Even when they agree on a certain principle, they often hold widely different reasons for supporting that principle. Of the moral philosophies we have studied thus far, we find the most dramatic differences between Aristotle's ancient Greek morality and Kant's modern morality of duty. Kant's morality may be taken as a fair representation of the modern Judeo-Christian morality in its strictest form: the emphasis on moral principle and laws, the emphasis on reason and individual autonomy, the emphasis on good intentions ('a good will') and doing one's duty. There are small differences that we have already pointed out: the Greek emphasis on pride as a virtue in contrast to the Christian condemnation of pride as a 'deadly sin' (or at least a personality flaw) and its emphasis on humility. One of Aristotle's first virtues was courage in battle, while most modern moralities consider that as a special case, not as a matter of being an everyday 'good person'. This difference might well be attributed to the different political climates of the two societies. But that is not enough. As we shall see, the differences are much deeper.

There are crucial differences between ancient and modern moral perspectives; the most striking is the difference in the scope of their applicability. In Aristotle's moral philosophy, only a small elite is thought to be capable of true happiness (*eudaimonia*) through virtuous action and contemplation. Other people (women, slaves, non-citizens) may live comfortably enough and do their duties and chores efficiently, but they cannot be called 'happy'. In Kant's conception of morality, by contrast, there are no elites; all people who are rational are to be judged by the same moral standards.

These two moral philosophies also hold different conceptions of 'what it is to be moral'. For Aristotle, the emphasis is on *individual achievement*. The elite are to be characterized by their excellence—their wealth, power, honour, intelligence, wit, and all of those rewards that come with an aristocratic upbringing, the best of education, and a life that is guaranteed in basic comforts from birth. For Kant, the emphasis is on *duty*, and a person's moral worth is to be judged solely on the basis of his or her *intentions*. Here, 'external' advantages are not relevant to a person's goodness or badness. In fact, in Kant's view it is possible that a perfectly 'good' person would, with only the best intentions, cause chaos and unhappiness around him wherever he goes.[18] (Aristotle would find this laughable. How could we call a man virtuous just because of his intentions? How can a perfect failure be an example of ideal goodness?)

Now notice that both moralities have many of the same results. Aristotle's morality will praise many and condemn most of the same acts as are praised and condemned by Kant's morality: killing needlessly and stealing are wrong; telling the truth and keeping promises are right. Yet, as we have seen, their conceptions of morality and their conceptions of people are distinctively different. As we appreciate the nature of this difference, we will be in a position to understand one of the most dramatic moral revolutions of modern times, that was initiated by Friedrich Nietzsche.

Nietzsche called himself an **immoralist**, and he attacked morality as viciously as he attacked Christianity. But though he has often been interpreted as saying that we should give up morality and feel free to kill, steal, and commit crimes of all kinds, his moral philosophy does not in fact say that at all. What he did was to attack modern morality, as summarized by Kant and Christianity, and urge us to return to ancient Greek morality as summarized by Aristotle. He also attacked utilitarianism, which he considered 'vulgar'.

Like a great many philosophers of the nineteenth century (particularly German philosophers: Fichte, Hegel, Marx), Nietzsche saw in the ancient Greeks a sense of personal harmony and a sense of excellence that had been lost in the modern world. Nietzsche, like Aristotle, saw the concept of duty as fit for servants and slaves, but such a morality was wholly inadequate to motivate us to personal excellence and achievement. And Nietzsche, like Aristotle, was an unabashed elitist. Only a few people were capable of this 'higher' morality. For the rest, the '**slave morality**' of duty would have to suffice. But for those few, nothing was more important than to give up the 'thou shalt not . . .' of Judeo-Christian morality and seek out one's own virtues and abilities. This does not mean that such a person need ever violate the laws of morality, although it must be said that Nietzsche's belligerent style and often warlike terminology certainly suggest that his **master morality** will include a good amount of cruelty and immorality.[19] But it is clear that Nietzsche does not consider obedience to laws as the most important thing in life. Nor does this mean that Nietzsche is (as he is often thought to be) an ethical egoist. To say that a person should develop his or her own virtues and become excellent in as many ways as possible is not at all to say that one must act only in one's own interests. As in Aristotle, the excellence of the individual is part of and contributes to the excellence of mankind as a whole.

Nietzsche takes his central project as a philosopher to be what he calls 'the creation of values'. In this he is rightly listed as one of the existentialist philosophers, or at least as one of their most important predecessors. The phrase is perhaps misleading, however. What Nietzsche is doing is not inventing new values so much as reasserting very old ones. Furthermore, Nietzsche, like Aristotle, takes ethics to be based solely upon human nature, and so it is not a question of 'creating values' so much as finding them in oneself. But since Nietzsche, unlike Aristotle, did not believe that every human 'nature' was the same, he taught that different individuals would most assuredly find and follow different values, different conceptions of excellence and thus have different moralities. For this reason, students who read Nietzsche looking for concrete moral advice, a set of principles to act on, are always disappointed. His central teaching is rather 'follow yourself, don't follow me'.

IMMORALIST

A person who rejects the ultimate claims of morality.

Consequently, he can't—and won't—try to tell you how to live. But he does tell you to live and to give up the servile views that we have held of ourselves for many centuries.

Nietzsche's moral philosophy is largely critical, and most of his efforts have gone into the rejection of Kant's conception of morality in order to make room for individual self-achieving as found in Aristotle. His argument, however, is not a refutation in the usual sense. Instead, he undermines morality by showing that the motivation behind it is decrepit and weak. Categories of Nietzsche's philosophy are strength and weakness, and he considers the Greek tradition of personal excellence a source of strength, the modern conception of morality a facade for weakness. Accordingly, he calls the first a 'master morality' and the second a 'slave morality' or, with reference to modern mass movements, a 'herd-instinct'.

The excerpts that follow illustrate Nietzsche's general attack on morality. But never forget that his purpose is not merely destructive but, in his eyes, creative, and the point is to get us to look to ourselves for values and to excel, each in our own ways (the phrase '**will to power**' refers to just this effort to excel as individuals).

> **WILL TO POWER**
>
> The thesis that every act is ultimately aimed at superiority, according to one's own standards.

On 'Morality as Herd-Instinct'
By Friedrich Nietzsche

By morality the individual is taught to become a function of the herd, and to ascribe to himself value only as a function.

Wherever we meet with a morality we find a valuation and order of rank of the human impulses and activities. These valuations and orders of rank are always the expression of the needs of a community or herd: that which is in the first place to *its* advantage—and in the second place and third place—is also the authoritative standard for the worth of every individual. By morality the individual is taught to become a function of the herd, and to ascribe to himself value only as a function. As the conditions for the maintenance of one community have been very different from those of another community, there have been very different moralities; and in respect to the future essential transformations of herd and communities, states and societies, one can prophesy that there will still be very divergent moralities. Morality is the herd-instinct in the individual.

On 'Master and Slave Morality'
By Friedrich Nietzsche

Apart from the value of claims like 'there is a categorical imperative in us', the question remains: what does this sort of claim tell us about the ones who make it? There are moralities that are meant to justify their creator in the eyes of others, and other moralities that are meant to calm him and help him to be content with himself; still others allow him to crucify and humiliate himself. With others he wants to take revenge, with others to hide, with others to transfigure himself and remove himself to the heights. There are moralities that help their creators to forget, and others that allow him—or something about him—to be forgotten. Many moralists want to exercise their power and creative whims on humanity, some others, perhaps even Kant himself, suggest with their morality: 'What deserves respect in me is that I can obey—and you *ought* not to be different than me! —in short, morality is merely a *sign language of the passions!*

* * *

On a journey through the many finer and coarser moralities that have so far ruled or still rule on earth I found that certain properties recurred regularly

(*Continued*)

together and were closely related: until at last I found two fundamental types and one fundamental difference. There are *master morality* and *slave morality*—I add immediately that in all the higher and mixed cultures there also appear attempts at a blending of both moralities, and still more often the interpenetration and mutual misunderstanding of both, indeed at times they are hard against one another—even in the same human being, within a *single* soul. The moral discrimination of values has originated either in a ruling group whose understanding of its difference from the ruled was felt with well-being—or among the ruled, the slaves and dependents of every grade. In the first case, when it is the rulers who determine what is 'good', the lofty proud states of soul are experienced as conferring distinction and determining the order of rank. The noble human distances from himself those in whom the contrary of such lofty proud states finds expression: he despises them. One should immediately note that in this first kind of morality the opposition of 'good' and 'bad' means about the same as 'noble' and 'contemptible'—the opposition of 'good' and 'evil' has a different origin. Despised are the cowardly, the anxious, the petty, those who think about narrow utility; even so the suspicious with their constrained glances, those who humble themselves, the dog-kind of humans who allow themselves to be maltreated, the fawning flatterers, above all the liars. It is a fundamental belief of all aristocrats that the common people lie. 'We truthful ones' thus the nobility of ancient Greece named itself. It is obvious that moral designations that were everywhere first applied to humans and only derivatively and late to actions: which is why it is a serious error when historians of morality begin with questions like 'why was the pitying act praised?' The noble kind of human feels itself as establishing values, it has no need for approval, it judges 'what is harmful to me is harmful in itself', it knows itself to be that which

first grants things their honour, it is value-creating. It honours everything that it knows as part of itself: such a morality is self-glorification.

It is different with the second type of morality, slave morality. Suppose the raped, oppressed, suffering, bound, timorous, and exhausted moralize: what will their moral valuations have in common? Probably a pessimistic suspicion about the whole human condition will make itself known, perhaps a condemnation of humankind along with its condition. The glance of the slave is adverse to the virtues of the powerful: he has skepticism and mistrust, he has subtle mistrust of all the 'good' that is honoured there, he would like to persuade himself that even their happiness is not real. Conversely, those qualities are brought forth and brightly illuminated that serve to lighten existence for the suffering: here pity, the obliging helpful hand, the warm heart, patience, industry, humility, and friendliness come to be honoured, for here these are the most useful qualities and nearly the sole means for enduring the stress of existence. Slave morality is essentially a morality of utility. Here is the place for the source of that famous opposition between good and 'evil': into evil were projected power and dangerousness, a certain fearfulness, subtlety, and strength, that does not permit contempt to arise. For slave morality the 'evil' therefore inspire fear; for master morality it is precisely the 'good' that inspire and want to inspire fear, while the 'bad' are felt to be contemptible. The opposition comes to a peak when, as a direct consequence of slave morality, a touch of scorn comes along with the 'good' of this morality. This may be slight and benevolent because the good must be harmless in the slave's way of thinking: he is good-natured, easy to deceive, a bit stupid perhaps, *un bonhomme* ['a nice person']. In general, where slave morality becomes predominant language tends to bring the words 'good' and 'stupid' closer together.

Nietzsche's ethics is not all criticism, however. He also vigorously argues for an alternative morality, a heroic morality, not unlike that of the ancient Greeks. In his long quasi-Biblical epic called *Thus Spoke Zarathustra*, he introduces his famous idea of the *Übermensch*, the superman who is more than human and superior in his virtues. Our virtues, in turn, should be aimed at making such a supervirtuous person possible (for example, by defending our own idealism and by educating future generations to be better than we are).

From *Thus Spoke Zarathustra*
By Friedrich Nietzsche

Man is a rope stretched between the animal and the *Übermensch*, a rope over an abyss.

A dangerous crossing, a dangerous on-the-way, a dangerous looking-back, a dangerous trembling and halting.

What is great in man is that he is a bridge and not a goal: what is lovable in man is that he is an over-going and a going under.

I love those that do not know how to live except by going under, for they are those who go over.

I love the great despisers, because they are the great adorers and arrows of longing for the other shore.

I love those who do not first seek a reason beyond the stars for going under and being sacrifices, but sacrifice themselves to the earth, that the earth may some day belong to the *Übermensch*.

I love him who lives in order to know, and seeks to know in order that the *Übermensch* may live some day. And thus he wants to go under.

I love him who loves his virtue: for virtue is the will to going under, and an arrow of longing.

I love him who reserves not one drop of spirit for himself, but wants to be wholly the spirit of his virtue: thus he strides as spirit over the bridge.

I love him who makes his virtue his addiction and his catastrophe: thus, for the sake of his virtue, he wants to live on and to live no more.

I love him whose soul is so overfull that he forgets himself, and all things are in him: thus all things become his going under.

I love him who has a free spirit and a free heart: thus his head is only the guts of his heart; his heart, however, causes his going under.

Behold, I am a herald of the lightning, and a heavy drop out of the cloud: the lightning, however, is the *Übermensch*.

And, in his next book, *Beyond Good and Evil*, Nietzsche examines the role of the philosopher:

From *Beyond Good and Evil*
By Friedrich Nietzsche

True philosophers . . . are commanders and legislators: they say, 'thus it shall be!' First they determine the 'where to' and the 'what for' of humankind, and thus they have at hand the preliminary work of all philosophical labourers, of everyone who has overcome the past. With a creative hand they reach for the future, and all that is and has been becomes a means for them, a tool, a hammer. Their 'knowing' is creating, their creating is a legislating, their will to truth is—will to power.—Are there such philosophers today? Have there been such philosophers yet? Must there not be such philosophers?

- Do you see affinities between Nietzsche and Aristotle on ethics?
- What are 'master morality' and 'slave morality'? What do these two ethical perspectives suggest about the nature of morality?

Nietzsche is often viewed as the most extreme of the antimoralists, those who attack the traditional duty-bound Kantian-Christian conception of morality. In fact, he is but one among many philosophers who have rejected that morality in exchange for a more personal and individual set of principles. Given his emphasis on human 'nature', we can say that even Nietzsche is much more traditional than is usually supposed (though he is traditional within the Aristotelian, not the Kantian, tradition). In the past few decades, however, morality has become far more personalized than even Nietzsche suggested. In Anglo-American philosophy, largely in the wake of **logical positivism**, ethics has been reduced to a matter of emotions, prescriptions, and attitudes rather than principles and rational laws. (Ironically, Nietzsche has always been in extreme disfavour among such philosophers while Kant has been considered with extreme favour.)

The attack on the absolute moral principles of reason, which are the same for everyone, has been one of the most vigorous philosophical movements of the past century, so much so that many philosophers, religious leaders, and moralists have become alarmed at the destruction of uniform moral codes and have attempted to reassert the old moral laws in new ways. The problem is one of relativism. Is there a single moral code? Or are there possibly as many moralities as there are people? There are intermediary suggestions, such as relativizing morals to particular groups or societies, but the question is still the same: 'Is there ultimately any way of defending one moral code against any other?

The most extreme relativist position of all has emerged from Nietzsche's existentialist successors, particularly Jean-Paul Sartre. Sartre's rejects not only the idea of a uniform morality but the idea of a human nature upon which this morality might be based—not because different people might have different 'natures', as in Nietzsche, but because our values are quite literally a question of creation, of personal **commitment**. In answer to any question about morality, the only ultimate answer is 'because I choose to accept these values'. But what is most fascinating about Sartre's conception of morality as choice is that he does not therefore abandon general principles as Nietzsche does. Quite the contrary, he adopts an almost Kantian stance about the need to choose principles for all mankind, not just oneself. The difference is that Sartre, unlike Kant, makes no claims about the singular correctness of these principles. All he can say is 'this is what I choose mankind to be'. Thus Sartre's moral philosophy is a curious mixture of the most radical relativism and the most traditional moralizing.

From *Existentialism as a Humanism*
By Jean-Paul Sartre

When we say that man is responsible for himself, we do not mean that he is responsible only for his own individuality, but that he is responsible for all men.

Man is nothing else but that which he makes of himself. That is the first principle of existentialism. And this is what people call its 'subjectivity', using the word as a reproach against us. But what do we mean to say by this, but that man is of a greater dignity than a stone or a table? For we mean to say that man primarily exists—that man is, before all else, something which propels itself toward a future and is aware that it is doing so. Man is, indeed, a project which possesses a subjective life, instead of being a kind of moss, or a fungus or a cauliflower. Before that projection of the self nothing exists; not even in the heaven of intelligence; man will only attain existence when he is what he purposes to be. Not, however, what he may wish to be. For what we usually understand by wishing or willing is a conscious decision taken—much more often than not—after we have made ourselves what we are. I may wish to join a party, to write a book or to marry—but in such a case what is usually called my will is probably a manifestation of a prior and more spontaneous decision. If, however, it is true that existence is prior to essence, man is responsible for what he is. Thus, the first effect of existentialism is that it puts every man in possession of himself as he is, and places the entire responsibility for his existence squarely upon his own shoulders. And, when we say that man is responsible for himself, we do not mean that he is responsible only for his own individuality, but that he is responsible for all men. The word 'subjectivism' is to be understood in two senses, and our adversaries play upon only one of them. Subjectivism means, on the one hand, the freedom of the individual subject and, on the other, that man cannot pass beyond human subjectivity. It is the latter which is the deeper meaning of existentialism. When we say that man chooses himself, we do mean that every one of us must choose himself; but by that we also mean that in choosing for himself he chooses for all men. For in effect, of all the actions a man may take in order to create himself as he wills to be, there is not one which is not creative, at the same time, of an image of man such as he believes he ought to be. To choose between this or that is at the same time to affirm the value of that which is chosen; for we are unable ever to choose the worse. What we choose is always the better and nothing can be better for us unless it is better for all. If, moreover, existence precedes essence and we will to exist at the same time as we fashion our image, that image is valid for all and for the entire epoch in which we find ourselves. Our responsibility is thus much greater than we had supposed, for it concerns mankind as a whole. If I am a worker, for instance, I may choose to join a Christian rather than a Communist trade union. And if, by that membership, I choose to signify that resignation is, after all, the attitude that best becomes a man, that man's kingdom is not upon this earth, I do not commit myself alone to that view. Resignation is my will for everyone, and my action is, in consequence, a commitment on behalf of all mankind. Or if, to take a more personal case, I decide to marry and to have children, even though this decision proceeds simply from my situation, from my passion or my desire, I am thereby committing not only myself, but humanity as a whole, to the practice of monogamy. I am thus responsible for myself and for all men, and I am creating a certain image of man as I would have him to be. In fashioning myself I fashion man.

* * *

Who can prove that I am the proper person to impose, by my own choice, my conception of man upon mankind? I shall never find any proof whatever; there will be no sign to convince me of it.

* * *

If I regard a certain course of action as good, it is only I who choose to say that it is good and not bad. . . . nevertheless I also am obliged at every instant to perform actions which are examples. Everything happens to every man as though the whole human race had its eyes fixed upon what he is doing and regulated its conduct accordingly.

* * *

As an example by which you may the better understand this state of abandonment, I will refer to the case of a pupil of mine, who sought me out in the following circumstances. His father was quarrelling with his mother and was also inclined to be a 'collaborator'; his elder brother had been killed in the German offensive of 1940 and this young man, with a sentiment somewhat primitive but generous, burned to avenge him. His mother was living alone with him, deeply afflicted by the semi-treason of his father and by the death of her eldest son, and her only consolation was in this young man. But he, at this moment, had the choice between going to England to join the Free French Forces or of staying near his mother, and helping her to live. He fully realized that this woman lived only for him and that his disappearance—or perhaps his death—would plunge her into despair. He also realized that, concretely and in fact, every action he performed on his mother's behalf would be sure of effect in the sense of aiding her to live, whereas anything he did in order to go and fight would be an ambiguous action which might vanish like water into sand and serve no purpose. For instance, to set out for England he would have to wait indefinitely in a Spanish camp on the way through Spain; or, on arriving in England or in Algiers he might be put into an office to fill up forms. Consequently, he found himself confronted by two very different modes of action; the one concrete, immediate, but directed toward only one individual; and the other an action addressed to an end infinitely greater, a national collectivity, but for that very reason ambiguous—and it might be frustrated on the way. At the same time, he was hesitating between two kinds of morality; on the one side the morality of sympathy, of personal devotion and, on the other

(Continued)

side, a morality of wider scope but of more debatable validity. He had to choose between those two. What could help him to choose? Could the Christian doctrine? No. Christian doctrine says: Act with charity, love your neighbour, deny yourself for others, choose the way which is hardest, and so forth. But which is the harder road? To whom does one owe the more brotherly love, the patriot or the mother? Which is the more useful aim, the general one of fighting in and for the whole community, or the precise aim of helping one particular person to live? Who can give an answer to that a priori? No one. Nor is it given in any ethical scripture. The Kantian ethic says, Never regard another as a means, but always as an end. Very well; if I remain with my mother, I shall be regarding her as the end and not as a means: but by the same token I am in danger of treating as means those who are fighting on my behalf; and the converse is also true, that if I go to the aid of the combatants I shall be treating them as the end at the risk of treating my mother as a means.

If values are uncertain, if they are still too abstract to determine the particular, concrete case under consideration, nothing remains but to trust in our instincts. That is what this young man tried to do; and when I saw him he said, 'In the end, it is feeling that counts; the direction in which it is really pushing me is the one I ought to choose. If I feel that I love my mother enough to sacrifice everything else for her—my will to be avenged, all my longings for action and adventure—then I stay with her. If, on the contrary, I feel that my love for her is not enough, I go.' But how does one estimate the strength of a feeling? The value of his feeling for his mother was determined precisely by the fact that he was standing by her. I may say that I love a certain friend enough to sacrifice such or such a sum of money for him, but I cannot prove that unless I have done it. I may say, 'I love my mother enough to remain with her', if actually I have remained with her. I can only estimate the strength of this affection if I have performed an action by which it is defined and ratified. But if I then appeal to this affection to justify my action, I find myself drawn into a vicious circle.

* * *

In other words, feeling is formed by the deeds that one does; therefore I cannot consult it as a guide to action. And that is to say that I can neither seek within myself for an authentic impulse to action, nor can I expect, from some ethic, formulae that will enable me to act. You may say that the youth did, at least, go to a professor to ask for advice. But if you seek counsel—from a priest, for example—you have selected that priest; and at bottom you already knew, more or less, what he would advise. In other words, to choose an adviser is nevertheless to commit oneself by that choice. If you are a Christian, you will say, Consult a priest; but there are collaborationists, priests who are resisters and priests who wait for the tide to turn: which will you choose? Had this young man chosen a priest of the resistance, or one of the collaboration, he would have decided beforehand the kind of advice he was to receive. Similarly, in coming to me, he knew what advice I should give him, and I had but one reply to make. You are free, therefore choose—that is to say, invent. No rule of general morality can show you what you ought to do.

To say that it does not matter what you choose is not correct. In one sense choice is possible, but what is not possible is not to choose. I can always choose but I must know that if I do not choose, that is still a choice. This although it may appear merely formal, is of great importance as a limit to fantasy and caprice. For, when I confront a real situation—for example, that I am a sexual being, able to have relations with a being of the other sex and able to have children—I am obliged to choose my attitude to it, and in every respect I bear the responsibility of the choice which, in committing myself, also commits the whole of humanity. . . . Man finds himself in an organized situation in which he is himself involved: his choice involves mankind in its entirety, and he cannot avoid choosing. Either he must remain single, or he must marry without having children, or he must marry and have children. In any case, and whichever he may choose, it is impossible for him, in respect of this situation, not to take complete responsibility. Doubtless he chooses without reference to any pre-established values, but it is unjust to tax him with caprice. Rather let us say that the moral choice is comparable to the construction of a work of art.

* * *

No one can tell what the painting of tomorrow will be like; one cannot judge a painting until it is done. What has that to do with morality: We are in the same creative situation. We never speak of a work of art as irresponsible; when we are discussing a canvas by Picasso, we understand very well that the composition became what it is at the time when he was painting it, and that his works are part and parcel of his entire life.

It is the same upon the plane of morality. There is this in common between art and morality, that in both we have to do with creation and invention. We cannot decide a priori what it is that should be done. I think it was made sufficiently clear to you in the case of that student who came to see me, that to whatever ethical system he might appeal, the Kantian or any other, he could find no sort of guidance whatever; he was obliged to invent the law for himself. Certainly we cannot say that this man, in choosing to remain with his mother—that is, in taking sentiment, personal devotion, and concrete charity as his moral foundations—would be making an irresponsible choice, nor could we do so if he preferred the sacrifice of going away to England. Man makes himself; he is not found ready-made; he makes himself by the choice of his morality, and he cannot but choose a morality, such is the pressure of circumstances upon him.

Sartre says that 'man makes himself'. He believes this to be true both individually and collectively. It is through your actions that you commit yourself to values, not through principles you accept a priori or rules that are imposed upon you by God or society. If you accept the voice of some authority, you have chosen to accept that authority rather than some other. If you appeal for advice or help, you have chosen to seek that kind of advice rather than some other kind. If you refuse to choose between alternatives, then you are responsible for neglecting both or all the alternatives, for 'copping-out'. In any case, you must do something, even if what you do is 'doing nothing' (that is, not taking one of the important alternatives before you).

Here is Sartre's reply to his predecessors: We are no longer in the position of Aristotle, in which morality appears to us as a given, as 'natural' and without alternatives of the most irresolvable kind. We can no longer trust our 'sentiments', as Hume did, for we now find ourselves torn with conflicting sentiments of every kind. We can no longer accept the a priori moralizing of Kant, for we now see that the circumstances in which we must act are never so uncomplicated that they will allow for a simple 'categorical' imperative. And even 'the greatest good for the greatest number' no longer provides a guide for our actions, for we no longer pretend that we can calculate the consequences of our actions with any accuracy. Besides, who is to say what 'the greatest good' or, for that matter, 'the greatest number' is today? Against all of this, Sartre argues that there is simply our choice of actions and values, together with their consequences, whatever they are. There is no justification for these and no 'right' or 'wrong'. But this does not mean that we need not choose or that it is all arbitrary. To the contrary, the upshot of Sartre's thesis is precisely that we are always choosing and that morality is nothing other than our commitments, at least for the present, to those values we choose to follow through our actions.

> • Does anything make an act good for Sartre? How is Sartre's view still in the Kantian tradition? (Hint: 'In choosing for himself he chooses for all men.') How is it very different?

As we have seen, both Nietzsche and Sartre are critics of 'morality' as it has traditionally been understood in modern European philosophy. But how, exactly, are their positions related? Where do they agree, and where do their views diverge? To help us make progress on these questions, we now turn to an essay, written specifically for this text, by Canadian philosopher Christine Daigle, author of *Le nihilisme est-il un humanisme? Étude sur Nietzsche et Sartre*:

'Nietzsche and Sartre on the Creation of Morality'

By Christine Daigle

Friedrich Nietzsche and Jean-Paul Sartre are both fierce critics of traditional moralities. The ones they target in particular are those that present the human being as a rational agent that has to use reason to follow rules and principles erected as absolutes. Each philosopher has different reasons for rejecting such moralities, but they do share one strong objection: they both consider traditional rationalistic moralities to be detrimental to the flourishing of the human being. However, their critiques are not dismissive of any and all morality. They criticize in order to clear the ground and generate the right conditions for the moral development of the human being. For both philosophers, a key condition is the creation of a new type of morality.

One major problem with traditional moralities, as Nietzsche and Sartre see it, is that they impose moral principles on the human being rather than grounding these principles in human nature. In traditional moralities, moral principles are erected as absolutes and oftentimes are founded in an otherworldly reality. For example, in Plato's view, worldly morality is grounded in the form of the Good that is at the foundation of the world of the forms. For its part, Christian morality rests on a notion of the good as enacted by the divine commander. Kant's morality is an interesting case: he tries to erect a moral principle upon human nature. Nietzsche and Sartre would agree with his attempt if only Kant did not conceive of the human being solely as a rational animal. Kant's categorical imperative is a principle that only a purely rational being could follow. According to Kant, the human being, as a rational being, ought to disregard any other urge and follow it. But Nietzsche and Sartre conceive of the human differently.

Both philosophers reject a rationalist view of the human being. According to the rationalist view, when faced with a moral decision the individual will, using his reason, determine the right course of action. In this view, morality seems to be reduced to a rational process whereby one may gear one's will to any end one determines; morality becomes a matter of analyzing a situation, recognizing or knowing the principles one must obey, and setting out on a course of action that will follow those principles. Nietzsche and Sartre both think that such a

process fails to acknowledge the human being for what it is. They do not argue that the human being is a non-rational being; rather, they see the human being as much more than a rational being. Nietzsche insists that the human is a body that thinks. The body that is in the world uses its reason to understand the world, but being conscious involves more than just thinking rationally. Sartre proposes something similar by defining the human being as an embodied consciousness. This consciousness can be rational (he calls it reflective), but most of its activity is to be conscious of the world and of itself in the world, and that is not a rational process: it is more like a being-aware, a being-there as conscious. For both philosophers then, the body, the emotions, and non-rational conscious processes are just as important as reason in defining a human being. Traditional moralities that focus solely on the agent as a rational being thus misconceive of the human and try to put him in a box in which he cannot fit. Such misconceptions led Nietzsche to assert that under traditional moralities such as the Christian one, one will inevitably be a sinner. Traditional moralities simply make it impossible for the individual to be moral.

According to Nietzsche and Sartre, it is imperative that we dismiss any traditional morality that impairs the human's capacity to be moral. For Nietzsche, it is necessary to destroy in order to erect a new order; for Sartre, fierce criticism of the old ways is necessary in order to better construct new ways. Neither are nihilists who wish to abolish all moral systems and see the human live in a state of immorality or amorality. When Nietzsche declares himself to be a great immoralist, he means that he is against the flawed traditional moralities in which followers must blindly obey transcendent moral principles. He is an immoralist insofar as he wants to see a better morality emerge, and he believes that this will happen once we properly understand the beings that we are and once we thrive to flourish as those beings.

For Nietzsche, this better morality takes the form of a morality based on the notion of *will to power*. The human being is, in either a declining or ascending form, will to power. Therefore, the morality that will best suit the human being is one that fosters its development as will to power. Will to power is the force that drives humans and all things on earth to grow. For the human being, this means that the individual who lives as will to power will feel a constant urge to overcome him- or herself. It is crucial to understand that will to power is not simply the exercise of brute force, as it has sometimes been conceived. For Nietzsche, there is no doubt that acts of cruelty on the part of strong people toward weaker people are reprehensible. Such acts are, in fact, the expression of descending will to power, which does not strive toward human flourishing and overcoming. In contrast, Nietzsche approves of moral acts—those acts that are conducive to growth and the augmentation of life under his own system of morality—as expressions of ascending will to power. Nietzsche thinks that once they have discarded old moralities, humans need to erect new tables of values. Indeed, humans need values to live. The human being is a creator of values—he is the animal that values, as Nietzsche puts it in his *Genealogy of Morals*. This valuing is driven by will to power. Creating values for oneself as a being that is will to power is Nietzsche's moral ideal. When one achieves this ideal, one finds oneself on the path of the Overhuman (*Übermensch*); one becomes one's self-master (which is the sense of the master morality Nietzsche champions: to be the master of oneself).

A similar moral ideal emerges in Sartre's thinking as he attempts to build a new morality around the central notion of *freedom*. The human being is freedom, and each individual is a project that must unfold. Any morality that prevents the flourishing of the human as a free being must be discarded. Therefore, moralities that impose values on the human being must be discarded, and the individual must create values for him- or herself. Furthermore, the individual should create his or her values based on the moral principle according to which any act that fosters freedom is good and any act that impairs freedom is bad. Sartre thinks that one ought always to respect freedom in oneself and in others. That principle may be followed in a variety of ways, and this is why the individual needs to invent while confronted with a particular decision in a concrete situation. No individual is the same, and no situation is the same, so rules cannot apply universally. Therefore, the individual must create his or her own values via decision-making. This, according to Sartre, is the only way to become authentic and to enact one's own existential project. To give in to the temptation of following pre-established rules is to be in bad faith and to refuse to acknowledge oneself as the free being one is. Authenticity is Sartre's moral ideal, and everyone should strive to be authentic—that is, we must strive to be the free creators of values that we are by nature.

Both Nietzsche and Sartre share the same critical stance toward traditional moralities that they deem detrimental for the human being. These moralities are attractive for humans because they represent easy paths: it requires much less moral strength to follow transcendent rules than to actually create values for oneself and engage on the path of self-overcoming. As Sartre put it, freedom is a condemnation. One is entirely free but also entirely responsible for oneself and one's actions. Individuals are often afraid of bearing the weight of such responsibility. But, as Sartre says, morality is tough! Nietzsche and Sartre both propose a similar solution to the situation generated by the traditional moralities that they qualify as alienating for human beings. They both propose a moral ideal that corresponds to what the human being is: will to power in one case, freedom in the other. This ideal entails for both a morality in which every human being must create values for him- or herself. There are no pre-determined rules, only an operating principle whereby the individual must respect his or her own nature. The creation of values that will operate under such a principle will foster the flourishing of the individual. It will lead to the individual's self-actualization. Thus one will be authentic, thus one will be an Overhuman.

- What do Nietzsche and Sartre think is wrong with traditional morality? What does each philosopher seek to put in its place?

L. Ethics and Gender

One of the most obvious features of so much of the moral philosophy we have been examining is its focus on (or occasionally its denial of) the centrality of abstract principles of reason. Kant, most obviously, celebrates the a priori dictates of practical reason as the core of morality, and Mill, though the nature of his utilitarian principles may be quite different, nevertheless emphasizes the importance of a calculative impersonal principle in the determination of right and wrong. In recent decades, however, an enormous volume of literature has appeared challenging this view of morality as something essentially rational, principled, and impersonal. Thirty years ago, Harvard University psychologist Carol Gilligan argued at some length that women tended to think about moral issues differently than men did, and ever since, there has been a booming business in trying to define and sort out the differences between the two. Of course, many of the features emphasized in feminist ethics, for instance, a healthy attention to personal feelings as well as (or rather than) impersonal reason, were anticipated by earlier male philosophers, such as Hume and Rousseau. Yet some of the features of feminist ethics, such as considerations of the ability to give birth to a child and the experience of motherhood, are indeed distinctively female. In the following essay, Canadian philosopher and feminist Susan Sherwin ponders the significance of these differences for ethics.

From 'Ethics, Feminism, and Caring'
By Susan Sherwin

Caring, on its own, may be a dangerous basis for a feminist ethics.

I found myself greatly disillusioned with traditional ethical theory because of its failure to provide a clear critique of sexism; I then turned to an examination of the nature of moral theory to try to understand what makes it oblivious to this serious form of culturally pervasive injustice. In addition to its tolerance of patriarchy, I found a number of other features of traditional moral theory disturbing. One difficulty I had was that both of the most prominent of the philosophical moral theories evaluated moral behaviour in terms of abstract properties of isolated acts. Utilitarianism, for instance, says that actions are right if the consequences of those acts produce more overall happiness (or less suffering) than any alternative action available at the time. It does not say whose happiness is significant; it is happiness, itself, and not the individuals who experience it which determines moral judgments.

Consider what this means for the sorts of problems feminists concern themselves with, for example, pornography. Many men presumably enjoy pornography; it is a huge industry, and many people profit from it. Many women participate in the production of pornography, and, although for some, participation is

a consequence of their sexual enslavement, others say they choose this work and would suffer if it were not available to them. To be sure, many women and children are severely harmed by the effects of producing and consuming pornography, and many of us are distressed by knowledge of its pervasive occurrence. From the perspective of utilitarianism, we would need to find some way of measuring the relative enjoyment and despair produced by pornography and anticipate the consequences of restrictive legislation; only if the harms of current practice outweigh the pleasures it produces, and only if the benefits of its regulation could outweigh the loss of freedom associated with such control, would we be able to justify legislative restrictions on pornography. Yet from a feminist perspective, we must consider a very deep set of consequences for pornography in addition to the direct harm it causes. We must also try to recognize the harm produced by the ways in which pornography reinforces and extends sexism in our culture. The image it presents is one of women and children portrayed as sexual objects to be used, rather than as autonomous persons to be respected, of the sexualization of dominance and violence, and of sexual experience as anonymous sensation rather than a product of mutually caring relationships. These attitudes affect all aspects of social life and influence the way women are perceived in the streets and in the workplace as well as in the bedroom. Such measures are not easily determined by empirical tests. Further, if it should (though I do not believe that it would) turn out to be the case that the happiness men derive from pornography and sexism should somehow quantitatively outweigh the misery it produces for women, then, on utilitarian grounds we would not only have to tolerate, but perhaps even support pornography as a 'beneficial social institution'. Clearly, then, there is something wrong with the utilitarian way of deciding moral norms.

A further problem with this means of calculating moral value is that we are to measure happiness and unhappiness wherever it is found, but, from a feminist perspective, we are particularly aware of the ways that some people's interests seem to take precedence over the interests of others. In particular, the interests of women and children are often overlooked . . .; moreover, since women are socialized to define their interest in terms of others, if their interests are taken into account, they are skewed in such a way as to double count the interests of others without really meeting the needs of women. For example, women tend to define their happiness in terms of the success of their partners and children; I doubt that women's focus on second-order happiness does, in fact, constitute the best way of making women happy, but it is difficult to prove this empirically. Nonetheless, it seems clear that social change is necessary to allow women more autonomy and to protect them from punishment when men do not succeed (and sometimes even when they do), whatever the utility calculations turn out to be.

The other leading mainstream moral theory is the Kantian variety which directs us to act according to rules we can will to be universal. It argues that moral truths are matters of purely rational calculations and that our duties ought to apply to rational persons equally without regard to individual particulars. Kantian theory underlies a conception that is widespread in our culture; it suggests that individuals are rational, isolated, and independent from one another and that interaction between such beings is an anomaly that requires moral duties to govern such unusual experiences. Women have a difficult time thinking of morality as an arrangement governing relationships between independent rational beings. Women commonly have the responsibility of looking after those who are not fully rational and independent, namely the young, the very old, the infirm, and the ill; they also feel the responsibility of looking after the needs of those who are quite strong and 'independent', including their husbands, fathers, bosses, and co-workers. Women's views of society are not of isolated, rational, autonomous beings who develop rights to protect themselves from one another, but of a social network of complex relationships of varying degrees of dependency and interaction. Kantian conceptions do not easily fit women's model of social and moral arrangements.

Hence, when I tried to apply a Kantian framework to feminist issues, I found it worked quite well for protection against others, e.g., in the area of battery, rape, and sexual harassment, but when I tried to consider questions of justice, e.g., affirmative action programmes, or when I tried to deal with broad social policy issues, e.g., access to developing reproductive technologies, I found that a conceptual scheme which focussed on individual rights was simply inadequate. Hence, I began to consider what a moral theory might look like if it was to be compatible with my feminist objectives.

Like many feminists, I was excited and stimulated by Carol Gilligan's important empirical work on the effect of gender on moral reasoning, spelled out in her book *In a Different Voice*. Her research has helped women to name what they find dissatisfying about mainstream ethical theories. Gilligan found that females (girls and women) often differ from males (boys and men) in the considerations they bring to bear on moral dilemmas. Males tend to speak in Kantian voices whereby they seek general rules to resolve all conflicts, applying what Gilligan calls an ethic of justice; in contrast, females tend to focus on relationships and seek out alternative solutions to conflicts in which no one need lose. Where males seem to feel uneasy about intimate relationships and prefer a precise set of rules and rights, females, generally, focus on the primacy of relationships with others and evaluate moral dilemmas in terms of responsibilities to others. This she names an ethic of responsibility. It seems that women tend to resist general solutions to ethical questions that are indifferent to the character and relationship of those involved in favour of an approach that attends to the details of a

(Continued)

specific, ethical problem and that is fair to the actual individuals concerned. Though the empirical claims cannot be generalized as true of all individual women and men, she found that women generally seek to find a place for love in ethics, where male theorists argue that ethics must remain impersonal. Gilligan describes the feminine voice as articulating an ethic of caring.

The different voice of women with respect to ethics has been noted by philosophers as well. In her provocative article called 'What Do Women Want in a Moral Theory?', Annette Baier notes that most women who write on questions in the area of philosophical ethics tend to avoid system-building and focus on specific, contextually defined issues. She notes that men have built ethical theories on a conceptual foundation based on obligation; obligation, in fact, has been accepted as the key moral concept. But women tend to seek an ethics that can be connected with feeling. Both Gilligan and Baier assume that an adequate approach to ethics must include both masculine and feminine voices and have room for both an ethics of justice or obligation and also one of caring. Baier recommends we pursue such a theory by making the concept of trust the key moral concept since it can serve to mediate between these different approaches. She has been developing a theory to help determine when trust in another is appropriate and when distrust (or anti-trust) might be a more suitable response. Such a theory, she hopes, will be attractive to both men and women.

* * *

Nonetheless, many feminists have been cautious in their enthusiasm for these paradigm shifts and have issued strong warnings against accepting any conclusion that women share a common approach to moral matters which must be preserved. A number of concerns have been cited. One level addresses the cultural specificity of the particular female and mothering virtues cited. . . . We must be wary of generalizing from a culturally specific perspective, for mothering may be quite different at different times and places, varying even between different ethnic groups and classes among us. . . .

Personally, I think it is of some reassurance that these 'feminine' moral traits are not universalizable, for, if they were, that would imply that there is some biological essentialism governing the differences between human males and females. Such a conclusion

would be discouraging for feminism because it would suggest that the structures of gender relations are far deeper than we usually assume, and that we must find ways of modifying biological properties or their effect if we are to transform the power relations that constitute patriarchy. If it is not the case that all and only women tend to approach morality in this so-called 'feminine' way, then it is easier to consider ways of extending the parts of this morality we value to men, and to change the aspects of women's role that are connected with their subordinate social position. We must move from an essentialist feminism to one that has been labelled 'cultural feminism'. Cultural feminists believe that there are universal female experiences and attitudes, but attribute these common features to social conditioning rather than biological necessity. Further, cultural feminists generally value qualities associated with women.

But if it is the case that women have acquired their particular moral character through social conditioning and not through biological causes, then we must address the fact that caring is the sort of response women have learned under patriarchy. In the dominance relationships of patriarchy, those who are relegated to the subordinate position learn to be very sensitive to the emotional pulse of others, to see things in relational terms, to be pleasing and compliant. The nurturing and caring which women do so well are, to a large degree, the skills of survival for an oppressed group living in close contact with their oppressors. As Joan Ringleheim challenges, 'Is women's culture liberating? How can it be if it was nourished in oppression?'[20]

Still, the fact that caring is the product of oppression does not necessarily mean that it is not valuable or significant from a moral point of view, but it does caution us against unbridled enthusiasm for these capacities. We must investigate the ways in which women's tendency to adopt caring perspectives may in fact contribute to their continued subordinate position. We can see, for instance, that a caring orientation makes it difficult for women to make significant changes in their lives, because it keeps them sensitive to the unease and disappointment which their own independence may produce. So long as no one else is caring for the dependent members of their families and society, women pursuing a caring orientation will find it difficult to pursue their own interests when they are in conflict with the needs of others. As Gilligan noted, women tend to make moral decisions by considering their responsibilities to others, often at the expense of denying any responsibility to themselves. If men do not accept the moral injunction to care, or if they do accept the injunction but learn that their conditioning prevents them from being effective carers, women may find it difficult to abandon their role of caring for the helpless out of fear that no one else will assume responsibility. Or, it may turn out that women's caring skills are simply a necessary condition of their subordination which might wither away in a truly equal society. In other words, women's tendency to care may be primarily a product of subordination and not a particularly female aspect of character. We should consider Barbara Houston's observation

> that women's distinctive morality is self-defeating, or highly dubious, when exercised in our relations with men, with those more powerful than ourselves, or when exercised in conditions in which the social structures are likely to deform our caring or disguise it as a form of consent to the status quo.[21]

Hence, caring, on its own, may be a dangerous basis for a feminist ethics. Values and virtues must be evaluated in context; even such an attractive trait as caring may not be intrinsically good, independent of social context.

Moreover, as [Nel] Noddings works it out,[22] caring is a specifically apolitical ethics. Since she resists universals and principles, claiming that all moral decisions must be addressed in their particular concrete details, Noddings insists that political analysis, including the general view that women are oppressed, is incompatible with ethical responses. By directing us to focus on individual relationships, she denies the significance of social patterns which constitute the heart of feminist theory. As most feminists agree, there are no individual solutions to the problems of patriarchy, and collective action must be taken based on bonds among strangers—sometimes, even, in the face of conflict with loved ones.

Like Houston, I believe that 'for feminists, the moral and the political are necessarily bound to each other'. Whatever morality we endorse must make the subordination of women a primary moral concern and should help ensure the elimination of such subordination. Hence, it is important that a feminist ethic challenge the status quo and not serve, in the existing social context, to further women's oppression.

A feminist must, then, seek an ethics that helps her sort through her personal relationships, but also helps define the injustice of sexism and explicitly works to correct its abuses. I imagine that caring will be a part of any such moral theory, but I do not expect that it will be the whole of it. Women have long followed a personal ethic of caring which may, in fact, have worked to strengthen the bonds of our oppression. Women need a moral theory that addresses the gender basis of our oppression and offers direction for the elimination of hierarchical relationships. While it is important to credit women's moral achievements, it is not enough for women to accept the *status quo*. We must struggle to find a way to transform our society so that caring will not be a means to facilitate oppression, but rather an element of trusting relationships in the context of a keen sense of justice. And we must be very clear about to whom and in what forms we extend our caring.

- What are some major differences between traditional morality and feminist morality?
- What does Sherwin think is wrong with utilitarianism? What does she think is wrong with Kantian ethical theories?
- Why does Sherwin think that 'caring, on its own, may be a dangerous basis for feminist ethics'? What conclusions does she draw from this statement?

M. Ethics in the Modern Age

In this chapter, we have surveyed a wide range of 'classic' ethical theories—theories that have their origins in different historical periods as well as in different places. We have sampled the moral thought of the ancients (Plato, Aristotle, Mencius, Xun-zi), the middle ages (St Augustine), the eighteenth century (Butler, Hume, Rousseau, Kant, Bentham), the nineteenth century (Mill, Nietzsche), and the twentieth century (Sartre, Vanier, Harman, Hurka, Sherwin, McKinnon).

The fact that the writings we have been studying span almost 2,500 years is worth pondering. Think, for just a moment, about how different everyday life was for most people when Kant or Mill wrote, let alone when Aristotle or Mencius taught. Think, too, about how many things have changed in the last 250 years of human history, let alone in the last 2,500. Ask yourself: How many things did our ancestors take for granted that we do not? How many moral assumptions seemed perfectly natural to them but now strike us as implausible, even unintelligible? How many moral assumptions seem perfectly natural to us, but would have struck them as outlandish or perverse? Sexuality, gender roles, marriage, family life, friendship, law, power, political authority, government, social class, justice, race, equality, freedom, compassion, suffering, pleasure, beauty, violence, war, death, work, leisure, the meaning of life—how have ages and cultures other than our own understood these things and their interconnections? And just how do we understand them today?

One thing is clear: not everyone has thought about morality in the way we do now. This may sound terribly complacent and self-congratulatory, as if we were saying that we are somehow more 'enlightened', 'humane', or 'high-minded' than people in earlier ages. But to draw that self-serving conclusion is to miss the point entirely. Rather, we must ask another question: if our way of thinking about morality is different, *how* is it different? And—here is yet another, pregnant question—*why* is it different? What happened, historically, to bring about this change in sensibility and values? If the moral space that we currently inhabit is new, how did we get here? What roads or paths did human beings have to travel in order to arrive here?

For anyone interested in seeking answers to these difficult questions, Canadian philosopher Charles Taylor is an excellent guide. In his CBC Massey Lectures, *The Malaise of Modernity*—and in his magisterial study *Sources of the Self: The Making of the Modern Identity*—Taylor describes the emergence of a distinctively modern moral ideal: the ideal of **authenticity**. According to Taylor, this ideal is implicit in popular forms of individualism that affirm the value of self-fulfillment:

From *The Malaise of Modernity*
By Charles Taylor

The ethic of authenticity is something relatively new and peculiar to modern culture.

The Inarticulate Debate

We can pick it up through a very influential recent book in the United States, Allan Bloom's *The Closing of the American Mind*. The book itself was a rather remarkable phenomenon: a work by an academic political theorist about the climate of opinion among today's students, it held a place on the *New York Times* bestseller list for several months, greatly to the surprise of the author. It touched a chord.

The stance it took was severely critical of today's educated youth. The main feature it noted in their outlook on life was their acceptance of a rather facile relativism. Everybody has his or her own 'values', and about these it is impossible to argue. But as

Bloom noted, this was not just an epistemological position, a view about the limits of what reason can establish; it was also held as a moral position: one ought not to challenge another's values. That is their concern, their life choice, and it ought to be respected. The relativism was partly grounded in a principle of mutual respect.

In other words, the relativism was itself an offshoot of a form of individualism, whose principle is something like this: everyone has a right to develop their own form of life, grounded on their own sense of what is really important or of value. People are called upon to be true to themselves and to seek their own self-fulfillment. What this consists of, each must, in the last instance, determine for him- or herself. No one else can or should try to dictate its content.

This is a familiar enough position today. It reflects what we could call the individualism of self-fulfillment, which is widespread in our times and has grown particularly strong in Western societies since the 1960s.

* * *

The moral ideal behind self-fulfillment is that of being true to oneself, in a specifically modern understanding of that term. A couple of decades ago, this was brilliantly defined by Lionel Trilling in an influential book, in which he encapsulated that modern form and distinguished it from earlier ones. The distinction is expressed in the title of the book, *Sincerity and Authenticity*, and following him I am going to use the term 'authenticity' for the contemporary ideal.

Expressions of the ideal of authenticity now pervade our culture, observes Taylor; and it is hard to disagree with him about this. We talk about 'being in touch with ourselves' and 'finding ourselves'; we prize 'self-discovery' and 'self-expression'; we stress the need to find and follow a path in life that is truly ours and no one else's; we agree that each person should 'do her own thing', 'go her own way', and 'be true to herself'; we acknowledge the value of 'self-development' and 'self-fulfillment'—and whenever we talk this way, we are speaking the language of authenticity, whether we realize it or not.

Central to this new language of authenticity is the modern understanding of the self as an inner space with rich and potentially inexhaustible depths. Once we think of the self in this way—that is, as a subjective sphere whose unique contents may never be fully fathomed or articulated—we find it natural to say that each person should express what is deepest in herself and aspire to live in her own way. Each of us, in other words, should strive to be authentic: you should express yourself; she should express herself; and he should express himself. But since individuals are fundamentally different from one another—since what is deepest in your nature isn't the same as what is deepest in your roommate's nature—the expression of the self will be different for every person. And this means that each of us, as individuals, may be called to lead very different kinds of lives.

Taylor is plainly interested in understanding authenticity not simply as a sociological trend, but as a *moral ideal*. But what does he mean by 'moral ideal'? He tells us:

What do I mean by a moral ideal? I mean a picture of what a better or higher mode of life would be, where 'better' and 'higher' are defined not in terms of what we happen to desire or need, but offer a standard of what we ought to desire.

If this is what a moral ideal amounts to—'a picture of what a better or higher mode of life would be, where "better" and "higher" . . . offer a standard of what we ought to desire'— then is it clear that authenticity qualifies as a moral ideal? Some writers and thinkers have vehemently denied that it does, because they are firmly convinced that authenticity does not offer 'a standard of what we should desire'. From their perspective, talk of 'authenticity' is just a cover for various disreputable commitments and ignoble practices: egoism, hedonism, narcissism, self-indulgence, moral laxity, and antinomianism, not to mention a facile 'anything goes' brand of relativism (as in 'Each person has his own values, about which there can be no argument; and no one should impose his values on anyone else').

According to Taylor, authenticity's staunchest critics are not entirely wrong. Some contemporary expressions of authenticity *really are* self-centred, self-indulgent, shallow, and debased; and some enthusiastic defenders of authenticity *really have* embraced fatuous forms of relativism without giving the matter a second thought. Nevertheless, Taylor insists that this is not the whole story:

What we need to understand here is the moral force behind notions like self-fulfillment. Once we try to explain this simply as a kind of egoism, or a species of moral laxism, a self-indulgence with regard to a tougher, more exigent earlier age, we are already off the track. Talk of 'permissiveness' misses this point. Moral laxity there is, and our age is not alone in this. What we need to explain is what is peculiar to our time. It's not just that people sacrifice their love relationships, and the care of their children, to pursue their careers. Something like this has perhaps always existed. The point is that today many people feel called to do this, feel they ought to do this, feel their lives would be somehow wasted or unfulfilled if they didn't do it.

Thus what gets lost in this critique is the moral force of the ideal of authenticity. It is somehow being implicitly discredited, along with its contemporary forms. That would not be so bad if we could turn to the opposition for a defence. But here we will be disappointed. That the espousal of authenticity takes the form of a kind of soft relativism means that the vigorous defence of any moral ideal is somehow off limits. For the implications, as I have just described them above, are that some forms of life are indeed *higher* than others, and the culture of tolerance for individual self-fulfillment shies away from these

claims. This means, as has often been pointed out, that there is something contradictory and self-defeating in their position, since the relativism itself is powered (at least partly) by a moral ideal. But consistently or not, this is the position usually adopted. The ideal sinks to the level of an axiom, something one doesn't challenge but also never expounds.

In adopting the ideal, people in the culture of authenticity, as I want to call it, give support to a certain kind of liberalism, which has been espoused by many others as well. This is the liberalism of neutrality. One of its basic tenets is that a liberal society must be neutral on questions of what constitutes a good life. The good life is what each individual seeks, in his or her own way, and government would be lacking in impartiality, and thus in equal respect for all citizens, if it took sides on this question. Although many of the writers in this school are passionate opponents of soft relativism (Dworkin and Kymlicka among them), the result of their theory is to banish discussions about the good life to the margins of political debate.

The result is an extraordinary inarticulacy about one of the constitutive ideals of modern culture. Its opponents slight it, and its friends can't speak of it. The whole debate conspires to put it in the shade, to render it invisible. This has detrimental consequences.

So what is Taylor's own take on authenticity? What does he make of it? Simple: while he affirms the validity of authenticity as a moral ideal, he denies that *all* contemporary expressions of that ideal are worthy of respect. Hence he avoids two extremes: on the one hand, that of the hypercritical and censorious 'knockers', according to whom authenticity is not even a moral ideal, and, on the other hand, that of the uncritical and wildly enthusiastic 'boosters', according to whom all manifestations of that ideal are (equally) good or deserving of respect:

What I am suggesting is a position distinct from both boosters and knockers of contemporary culture. Unlike the boosters, I do not believe that everything is as it should be in this culture. Here I tend to agree with the knockers. But unlike them, I think that authenticity should be taken seriously as a moral ideal. I differ also from the various middle positions, which hold that there are some good things in this culture (like greater freedom for the individual), but that these come at the expense of certain dangers (like a weakening of the sense of

citizenship), so that one's best policy is to find the ideal point of trade-off between advantages and costs.

The picture I am offering is rather that of an ideal that has degraded but that is very worthwhile in itself, and indeed, I would like to say, unrepudiable by moderns. So what we need is neither root-and-branch condemnation nor uncritical praise; and not a carefully balanced trade-off. What we need is a work of retrieval, through which this ideal can help us restore our practice.

If, as Taylor thinks, authenticity is a distinctively *modern* moral ideal, where did it come from? What is its history? What developments—philosophical, religious, cultural, political, social—made its articulation possible? And what conditions have conspired to make the ideal of authenticity so appealing to so many of us?

The Sources of Authenticity

The ethic of authenticity is something relatively new and peculiar to modern culture. Born at the end of the eighteenth century, it builds on earlier forms of individualism, such as the individualism of disengaged rationality, pioneered by Descartes, where the demand is that each person think self-responsibly for him- or herself, or the political individualism of Locke, which sought to make the person and his or her will prior to social obligation. But authenticity also has been in some respects in conflict with these earlier forms. It is a child of the Romantic period, which was critical of disengaged rationality and of an atomism that didn't recognize the ties of community.

One way of describing its development is to see its starting point in the eighteenth-century notion that human beings are endowed with a moral sense, an intuitive feeling for what is right and wrong. The original point of this doctrine was to combat a rival view, that knowing right and wrong was a matter of calculating consequences, in particular those concerned with divine reward and punishment. The notion was that understanding right and wrong was not a matter of dry calculation, but was anchored in our feelings. Morality has, in a sense, a voice within.

The notion of authenticity develops out of a displacement of the moral accent in this idea. On the original view, the inner voice is important because it tells us what is the right thing to do. Being in touch with our moral feelings would matter here, as a means to the end of acting rightly. What I'm calling the displacement of the moral accent comes about when being in touch takes on independent and crucial moral significance. It comes to be something we have to attain to be true and full human beings.

To see what is new in this, we have to see the analogy to earlier moral views, where being in touch with some source—God, say, or the Idea of the Good—was considered essential to full being. Only now the source we have to connect with is deep in us. This is part of the massive subjective turn of modern culture, a new form of inwardness, in which we come to think of ourselves as beings with inner depths. At first, this idea that the source is within doesn't exclude our being related to God or the Ideas; it can be considered our proper way to them. In a sense, it can be seen just as a continuation and intensification of the development inaugurated by Saint Augustine, who saw the road to God as passing through our own reflexive awareness of ourselves.

The first variants of this new view were theistic, or at least pantheist. This is illustrated by the most important philosophical writer who helped to bring about this change, Jean-Jacques Rousseau. I think Rousseau is important not because he inaugurated the change; rather I would argue that his great popularity comes in part from his articulating something that was already happening in the culture. Rousseau frequently presents the issue of morality as that of our following a voice of nature within us. This voice is most often drowned out by the passions induced by our dependence on others, of which the key one is 'amour propre', or pride. Our moral salvation comes from recovering authentic moral contact with ourselves. Rousseau even gives a name to the intimate contact with oneself, more fundamental than any moral view, that is a source of joy and contentment: 'le sentiment de l'existence'.

Rousseau also articulated a closely related idea in a most influential way. This is the notion of what I want to call self-determining freedom. It is the idea that I am free when I decide for myself what concerns me, rather than being shaped by external influences. It is a standard of freedom that obviously goes beyond what has been called negative liberty, where I am free to do what I want without interference by others because that is compatible with my being shaped and influenced by society and its laws of conformity. Self-determining freedom demands that I break the hold of all such external impositions, and decide for myself alone.

I mention this here not because it is essential to authenticity. Obviously the two ideals are distinct. But they have developed together, sometimes in the works of the same authors, and their relations have been complex, sometimes at odds, sometimes closely bound together. As a result, they have often been confused, and this has been one of the sources of the

(Continued)

deviant forms of authenticity, as I shall argue. I will return to this later.

Self-determining freedom has been an idea of immense power in our political life. In Rousseau's work it takes political form, in the notion of a social contract state founded on a general will, which precisely because it is the form of our common freedom can brook no opposition in the name of freedom. This idea has been one of the intellectual sources of modern totalitarianism, starting, one might argue, with the Jacobins. And although Kant reinterpreted this notion of freedom in purely moral terms, as autonomy, it returns to the political sphere with a vengeance with Hegel and Marx.

But to return to the ideal of authenticity: it becomes crucially important because of a development that occurs after Rousseau and that I associate with Herder—once again its major early articulator rather than its originator. Herder put forward the idea that each of us has an original way of being human. Each person has his or her own 'measure' is his way of putting it. This idea has entered very deep into modern consciousness. It is also new. Before the late eighteenth century no one thought that the differences between human beings had this kind of moral significance. There is a certain way of being human that is my way. I am called upon to live my life in this way, and not in imitation of anyone else's. But this gives a new

importance to being true to myself. If I am not, I miss the point of my life, I miss what being human is for *me*.

This is the powerful moral ideal that has come down to us. It accords crucial moral importance to a kind of contact with myself, with my own inner nature, which it sees as in danger of being lost, partly through the pressures toward outward conformity, but also because in taking an instrumental stance to myself, I may have lost the capacity to listen to this inner voice. And then it greatly increases the importance of this self-contact by introducing the principle of originality: each of our voices has something of its own to say. Not only should I not fit my life to the demands of external conformity; I can't even find the model to live by outside myself. I can find it only within.

Being true to myself means being true to my own originality, and that is something only I can articulate and discover. In articulating it, I am also defining myself. I am realizing a potentiality that is properly my own. This is the background understanding to the modern ideal of authenticity and to the goals of self-fulfillment or self-realization in which it is usually couched. This is the background that gives moral force to the culture of authenticity including its most degraded, absurd, or trivialized forms. It is what gives sense to the idea of 'doing your own thing' or 'finding your own fulfillment'.

- What, according to Taylor, are some of the philosophical sources of the ideal of authenticity?
- Can you think of specific examples of things you do that reflect a commitment to the ideal of authenticity?
- Do you agree with Taylor that authenticity is a valid moral ideal? Why or why not?

If Taylor is right, then any thinker seeking to make sense of ethics in the modern age must come to terms with authenticity. But that isn't the only thing such thinkers must come to terms with. They must also think—and think hard—about how to cope with disagreement between individuals or cultures whose basic ethical commitments differ dramatically. When this happens—and we know that it does, living as we do in an increasingly interconnected world—what can you do? Absolutely nothing, declares the pessimist. After all, how can you reason about right and wrong with people who do not share your fundamental values? And how can there be any fruitful dialogue where there is deep-rooted discord? It seems patently impossible.

Are we forced to accept the pessimist's conclusion? Margaret Somerville, a prominent Canadian ethicist, does not think so. She rejects the all-or-nothing assumption on which the pessimist's argument depends: the assumption, namely, that *either* we start with *complete* agreement on fundamentals *or* we cannot reason with each other at all. According to

Somerville, we need to draw a distinction between 'a universal ethics' (where every group agrees with every other group about *all* values) and 'a shared ethics' (where every group agrees with every other group about *some* value or values). Understanding this idea of a shared ethics—explaining what it requires, what it permits, and why it matters—is a central project of Somerville's recent book, *The Ethical Imagination: Journeys of the Human Spirit.*

From *The Ethical Imagination*
By Margaret Somerville

Can we truly find a shared ethics for a globalized world?

Journeys of the Human Spirit

Before looking at how and where we might find a shared ethics, I want to explain in more detail what I mean by this idea. I do not mean that we will have one monolithic, universal ethics. Nor do I mean that we will all just accept one another's ethics—what is called an 'ethical pluralism'. Nor do I accept moral relativism—that everyone's views on ethics are as good as anyone else's. Nor do I accept ethical cosmopolitanism, if that means that we must be equally concerned for and equally bonded to everyone.

* * *

I see a difference between a shared ethics (with each group we can find some values we share) and a universal ethics (we all agree on the same values). In a shared ethics, we would find consensus on some matters with some people or groups, and on other matters with other people or groups. I'm assuming that our consensus represents a genuine commitment to those matters and is not just indifference or simply disengaged tolerance with respect to them. The fact that there are some values, concepts, or ideas that we share would create a different tone for discussion of those on which we disagree—perhaps in some instances we would see these disagreements as less divisive. At present, we focus only on our disagreements, especially in media reporting. This is not neutral in its impact. Imagine a family that focussed only on its disagreements. It would be astonishing if such a family survived intact. We need to create a general climate of agreement about what ethics requires in given circumstances, but our climate must also accommodate disagreements as the exception. At present, we have a general climate of disagreement, with agreement as the exception. I am proposing we start our 'ethics talk' from where we agree and move to our disagreements

rather than vice versa. This change may seem inconsequential, but it can have major impact. We have seen that in the relation between law and ethics. Starting from law means law informs ethics; starting from ethics that ethics informs law. The outcome can be radically different.

In order to start from consensus, not disagreement, we might need to agree on three things: that we should seek to identify the values on which we agree that fall in a shared middle range between the poles at each extreme, a process that must be understood as excluding unethical compromises; that the search is a continuous process; and that it involves ways of knowing that include, but are not limited, to, reason—for instance, that we require imagination as well. We can then identify how broad the middle is—that is, we would accept that there are matters at either end of the spectrum of values that are not acceptable to all and that we will never agree upon, but we hope we would also discover there is much that all of us can accept. I am proposing a thick overlap of borders concept—that we might start from different poles, but there is a big (one hopes) overlap of common territory in the middle, in which we all are, in fact, 'at home'.

My concept of a shared ethics can be most easily explained, perhaps, by another metaphor: Imagine building a hotel. The ground floor must be open to everyone and large enough to accommodate all who want to enter. The second floor might have some special facilities where only certain groups of people want to go. Upper floors might have private rooms that are each decorated differently according to the occupants' personal preferences. The ground floor is the shared ethics; the second floor might be different cultural, national, or religious practices or beliefs; the upper floors are smaller groups such as families or

(Continued)

individuals. For the structure to be viable, it must have a ground floor strong enough to support the entire building; that ground floor must be open to everyone; people must reach their communal or private rooms by way of the ground floor; and what they do on those upper floors must not threaten the structural integrity of the hotel as a whole.

Now the crucial question is, Can we truly find a shared ethics for a globalized world? As I explained earlier, we cannot any longer rely on a shared religion to provide our shared ethical base. But might we be able to find some universals that are common to all people whether or not they are religious and, if so, no matter what religion they espouse? Might we be able to say that these universals are so widely shared over such a long period of time across so many different cultures that they can be taken as characteristics of being human—that is, they are innate to being human?

The danger in that approach is that some of our worst characteristics, as well as our best, are innate to being human. Can we deal with that danger by using a concept of maintaining and promoting human good as a touchstone for a shared base? That concept might include: Respect for individuals and their relationships to others—intimates and strangers—and for all life. Respect for community and its maintenance. Recognition of a shared desire to fully live fully human lives. Acknowledgement of obligations to fulfill certain physical and non-physical needs of others. Respect for freedom. And not harming the deep human need to experience creativity, imagination, and play. Might the search for meaning be the most fundamental characteristic of humanness? Could that be a manifestation of an innate moral element in humans as individuals and collectives that we can use to found a base against which we can test the rightness or wrongness of what we do? We can't prove there is such an element—but, when we can't be certain either way, we are better off assuming that there is than that there is not.

- Why does Somerville think we should focus more on our agreements and less on our disagreements?
- Explain Somerville's hotel metaphor. What truth(s) is it meant to convey?

SUMMARY AND CONCLUSION

In this chapter, we have reviewed a half dozen or so theories of morality. (1) Aristotle takes the key to morality to be the concept of 'virtue', which he argues to be activity in accordance with rational principles. He bases this argument on a concept of what is 'natural' for man, but his discussion is clearly limited to a small class of Greek male citizens, whom he views as the ideal specimens of humanity. As we saw, however, some contemporary philosophers think that this doesn't mean that there isn't an enormous amount that we can still learn from Aristotle. (2) Hume and Rousseau both argue that morality must be based on certain kinds of feelings or 'sentiments'. 'Reason is and ought to be the slave of the passions,' Hume argues, and Rousseau similarly argues that man is 'naturally' good. (3) Kant insists that morality is strictly a matter of rational principle divorced from all personal interests and desires ('inclinations'). This includes a rejection of Hume and Rousseau, who base morality on feelings (which are inclinations in Kant's sense). This also includes a rejection of Aristotle. Although both philosophers use the notion of a 'rational principle', Kant intends his notion to apply to every human being, and therefore every person has the same duties and obligations. (4) The utilitarians, Bentham and Mill, reject Kant's divorce between morality and personal interest and argue that morality is our guide to the satisfaction of the greatest number of interests of the greatest number of people. (5) Nietzsche rejects both Kant and the utilitarians, preferring a return to the elitism and 'virtue' orientation of Aristotle's ethics. He argues that we create our values and live with them according to our personal needs. Following him, the existentialists, particularly Jean-Paul Sartre, argue that all values are chosen by us; there is no 'true' morality, only those values to which we have voluntarily committed ourselves. (6) Recent feminists have challenged the 'male bias' of these traditional theories, raising questions about what a truly feminist ethics should look like. (7) Finally, we explored two issues central to understanding ethics in the modern age: 'the ethics of authenticity' (Charles Taylor) and the idea of 'a shared ethics' (Margaret Somerville).

REVIEW QUESTIONS

1. Compare Rousseau's notion of conscience to Hume's notion of sentiment. Does one theory seem to be stronger than the other, based on the differences and similarities between the notions of sentiment and conscience?

2. Does Aristotle's model of virtue ethics depend only upon social expectations, or does it also leave room for individual autonomy?

3. Aristotle claims that 'actions are called just or temperate when they are the sort that a just or temperate person would do'. Does this account seem circular to you? How would Aristotle deny this?

4. What insights do Vanier, McKinnon, and Hurka give Aristotle credit for? What good ideas do they find in *The Nicomachean Ethics*?

5. Consider how one might reconcile the rule-based system of Kant with the consequence-based system of utilitarianism. Do the two ethical systems complement one another, or are they at odds?

6. Here is one objection to utilitarianism: '(1) Some actions are morally wrong, no matter what (that is—regardless of the consequences). But (2) if some actions are morally wrong regardless of the consequences, utilitarianism must be false (since it makes right and wrong a matter of consequences). Therefore (3) utilitarianism must be false.' What seems right to you about this argument? What seems wrong? Explain.

7. What are the moral dangers of suggesting, as Nietzsche and Sartre do, that individuals create their own value systems? Could a prison guard in a Nazi concentration camp describe himself as a 'good person' on existentialist grounds?

8. How plausible is the idea that men and women make their moral choices using different rules and criteria? Given the choice between saving your own child's life and the lives of someone else's two children, what would you do and why? What do you think Aristotle would say? Kant? Mill?

9. What is 'authenticity'? In what sense is it a moral ideal, according to Taylor? Can we say that some forms of authenticity are superior to others? How? By what standard?

10. What does Somerville mean by 'a shared ethics'? Why does she think it matters? How does a shared ethics differ from universal ethics, on the one hand, and relativism, on the other?

KEY TERMS

a priori	ethical egoism	inclination
authenticity	ethical relativism	law
autonomy	ethics	logical positivism
categorical imperative	*eudaimonia*	master morality
commitment	existentialism	maxim
conscience	Golden Rule	mean (between the extremes)
contemplation (the life of)	happiness	morality
cultural relativism	happiness calculus (also	obligation
deontology	felicity calculus)	ought
duty	hedonism	perfectionism
egoism	hypothetical imperative	principle of utility
ethical absolutism	immoralist	psychological egoism
ethical altruism	imperative	rationality

relativism	slave morality	virtue
selfishness	sympathy	will
sentiment	utilitarians	will to power

FURTHER READING

On Ethics in General
Simon Blackburn, *Being Good: A Short Introduction to Ethics* (Oxford and New York: Oxford University Press, 2001).

Gordon Graham, *Living the Good Life: An Introduction to Moral Philosophy* (New York: Paragon House, 1990).

George Grant, *Philosophy in the Mass Age* (Toronto: Copp Clark, 1959).

J.L. Mackie, *Ethics: Inventing Right and Wrong* (London: Penguin, 1977).

G.E. Moore, *Principia Ethica* (Cambridge: Cambridge University Press, 1903).

John Rist, *Real Ethics: Reconsidering the Foundations of Morality* (New York: Cambridge University Press, 2002).

Peter Singer, *A Companion to Ethics* (Oxford: Blackwell, 2000).

Bernard Williams, *Morality: An Introduction to Ethics* (New York: Harper and Row, 1972).

On the History of Ethics and Its Problems
Richard R. Brandt, *Ethical Theory* (Englewood Cliffs, NJ: Prentice-Hall, 1959).

W. Frankena, *Ethics*, 2nd edn (Englewood Cliffs, NJ: Prentice-Hall, 1973).

A. MacIntyre, *A Short History of Ethics* (New York: Macmillan, 1966).

J.B. Schneewind, *The Invention of Autonomy: A History of Modern Moral Philosophy* (Cambridge: Cambridge University Press, 1998).

On Modern Moral Sensibility
Charles Taylor, *Sources of the Self: The Making of the Modern Identity* (Cambridge, MA: Harvard University Press, 1989).

On Virtue Ethics
Philippa Foot, *Virtues and Vices* (Berkeley and Los Angeles: University of California Press, 1978).

Alasdair MacIntyre, *After Virtue*, 3rd edn (Notre Dame, IN: University of Notre Dame, 2007).

Christine McKinnon, *Character, Virtue Theories, and the Vices* (Peterborough, ON: Broadview Press, 1999).

On Perfectionism
Thomas Hurka, *Perfectionism* (New York: Oxford University Press, 1993).

On Ethical Thought in Ancient China
E.R. Hughes, ed., *Chinese Philosophy in Classical Times* (London: Dent, 1942).

Benjamin Schwartz, *The World of Thought in Ancient China* (Cambridge, MA: Harvard University Press, 1985).

On Classic Arguments against Egoism
J. Butler, *Fifteen Sermons upon Human Nature* (London: Macmillan, 1900).

T. Nagel, *The Possibility of Altruism* (New York: Oxford University Press, 1970).

On Aristotle's Ethics
W.D. Ross, *Aristotle* (New York: Meridian, 1959).

Francis Sparshott, *Taking Life Seriously: A Study of the Argument of The Nicomachean Ethics* (Toronto: University of Toronto Press, 1994).

Jean Vanier, *Made for Happiness: Discovering the Meaning of Life with Aristotle*. Trans. Kathryn Spink (Toronto: Anansi, 2001).

J. Walsh and H. Shapiro, eds, *Aristotle's Ethics* (Belmont, CA: Wadsworth, 1967).

On Kant's Ethics
Christine Korsgaard, *The Sources of Normativity* (Cambridge: Cambridge University Press, 1996).

Onora O'Neill, *Acting on Principle: An Essay on Kantian Ethics* (New York: Columbia University Press, 1975).

On Utilitarianism
J.J.C. Smart and Bernard Williams, *Utilitarianism: For and Against* (Cambridge: Cambridge University Press, 1973).

On Existential Ethics
M. Warnock, *Existentialist Ethics* (New York: St Martin's Press, 1967).

On Feminist Ethics
Alison M. Jaggar and Paula S. Rothenberg, eds, *Feminist Frameworks*, 3rd edn (New York: McGraw-Hill, 1993).

Janet McCracken, *Thinking about Gender: A Historical Anthology* (Fort Worth, TX: Harcourt Brace, 1997).

CHAPTER 7

JUSTICE

Man, when perfected, is the best of animals, but, when separated from law and justice, he is the worst of all.

Aristotle

'Man is a social animal,' wrote Aristotle. And because we are social, we are political animals as well. We live with other people, not just our friends and families but thousands and millions of others, most of whom we will never meet and many of whom we come across in only the most casual way—while crossing the street or buying a ticket at the movie theatre. Yet we have to be concerned about them, and they about us, for there is a sense in which we are all clearly dependent upon each other. For example, we depend on them not to attack us without reason or steal our possessions. Of course, our confidence varies from person to person and from city to city. But it is clear that, in general, we have duties toward people we never know, for example, the duty not to contaminate their water supply or place their lives in danger. And they have similar duties to us. We also claim certain **rights** for ourselves: for example, the right not to be attacked as we walk down the street, the right to speak our mind about politically controversial issues without being thrown in jail, the right to believe in this religion or that religion or no religion without having our jobs, our homes, or our **freedom** taken from us.

Political and social philosophy is the study of people in societies with particular attention to the abstract claims they have on each other in the form of 'rights', 'duties', and 'privileges', and their demands for 'justice', 'equality', and 'freedom'. (It is important to distinguish this sense of *political* freedom from the causal or metaphysical freedom that we discussed earlier.) At least ideally, politics is continuous with morality. Our political duties and obligations are often the same as our moral duties and obligations. Our claims to certain 'moral rights' are often claims to political rights as well, and political rights—particularly those very general and absolute rights that we call human rights (for example, the right not to be tortured or degraded, the right not to be exploited by powerful institutions or persons)—are typically defended on the basis of moral principles. The virtues of **government** are ideally the virtues of individuals: Government should be just, temperate, courageous, honest, humane, considerate, and reasonable.

Plato and Aristotle, for example, portrayed their visions of the ideal **state** in precisely these terms. (Both Plato and Aristotle, unlike most modern philosophers, actually had the opportunity to set up such governments; both failed, but for reasons that were hardly their fault.) This is not to say that all politics or all politicians are moral; we know much better than that. But it is to say that our politics are constrained and determined by our sense of morality. Morality is concerned more with relations between particular people while politics

RIGHTS

Demands that a member of society is entitled to make upon his or her society.

is concerned more with large and impersonal groups. But the difference is one of degree. In ancient Greece, Plato and Aristotle lived in relatively small 'city-states' (each called a *polis*), with fewer citizens than even most Canadian towns. It was much easier for them to treat morality and politics together. But even today, we still speak hopefully of 'the human family' and 'international brotherhood', which is to reassert our enduring belief that politics—even at the international level—ought to be based on interpersonal moral principles.

The key to a successful **society** is cooperation. If people do not cooperate, the success of society requires that some authority has the power to bring individual interests into line with the public interest. This authority is generally called the state. The state passes laws and enforces them; its purpose is to protect the public interest. But is this its only purpose? We would probably say *no*. Its purpose is also to protect individual rights, for example, against powerful corporations and against strongly mobilized pressure groups that try to interfere with individual lives. In general, we might say that the function of the state is to protect justice. But there has been disagreement ever since ancient times about what that means and how much the primary emphasis should be placed on the public interest and how much on individual rights and interests.

Our concept of the state and the extent of its power and **authority** depends very much on our conception of human nature and of people's willingness to cooperate without being forced to do so. At one extreme are those who place such strong emphasis on the smooth workings of society that they are willing to sacrifice most individual rights and interests; they are generally called 'authoritarians', and their confidence in willing individual cooperation is very slight compared to their confidence in a strong authoritarian state. ('He makes the trains run on time' was often said of the **fascist** Italian dictator Benito Mussolini.) At the other extreme are people with so much confidence in individual cooperation and so little confidence in the state that they argue that the state should be eliminated altogether; they are called **anarchists**. Between these extremes are more moderate positions, for example, people who have some confidence both in individual cooperation and in the possibility of a reasonably just state, but don't have complete confidence in either. The vast majority of mainstream politicians, for example, believe in a government that is at least partially run by the people themselves but with sufficient power to enforce its laws over individual interests whenever necessary. All these people believe in varying solutions to the same central problem: the problem of a balance between the public interest and the need for cooperation on the one hand and individual rights and interests on the other—in other words, the problem of **justice**.

JUSTICE

The virtues of an ideal society; the balance of public interest and individual rights, the fair sharing of goods, the proper punishment of criminals, and the fair restitution to victims.

A. The Problem of Justice

When we think of justice, we first tend to think of criminal cases and of punishment. Justice, in this sense, is catching the criminal and 'making him pay for his crime'. The oldest sense of the word *justice*, therefore, is what philosophers call **retributive justice**, or simply, 'getting even'. Retribution for a crime is making the criminal suffer or pay an amount appropriate to the severity of the crime. In ancient traditions, the key phrase was 'an eye for an eye, a tooth for a tooth'. If a criminal caused a person to be blind, he was in turn blinded. We now view this as brutal and less than civilized. But is it so clear that we have in fact given up this retributive sense of justice? Do we punish our criminals (that is, demand retribution), or do we sincerely attempt to reform them? Or is the purpose of prison simply to keep them off the street? Should we ever punish people for crimes, or should we simply protect ourselves against their doing the same thing again? If a man commits an atrocious murder, is it enough that we guarantee that he won't commit another one? Or does he deserve punishment even if we know that he won't do it again?

But retributive justice and the problems of punishment are really only a small piece of a much larger concern. Justice is not just 'getting even' for crimes and offences. It concerns the running of society as a whole in day-to-day civil matters as well as the more dramatic criminal concerns. Given the relative scarcity of wealth and goods, how should they be distributed? Should everyone receive exactly the same amount? Should the person who works hard at an unpleasant job receive no more than the person who refuses to work at all and prefers to watch TV all day and just amuse himself or herself? Should the person who uses his wealth to the benefit of others receive no more than the person who 'throws away' his or her money on gambling, drinking, and debauchery? If a class of people has historically been deprived of its adequate share because of the colour of their skin, their religious beliefs, or their sex or age, should that class now be given more than its share in compensation, or is this too an injustice against other people?

Not only wealth and goods are at issue here, however. Distribution of privileges and power are equally important. Who will vote? Will everyone's vote count exactly the same? Should an illiterate person who does not even know the name of his political leaders have as much say in the government as a political scientist or economist who has studied these matters for years? Should everyone be allowed to drive? Or to drink? Should everyone receive exactly the same treatment before the law? Or are there concerns that would indicate that some people (for example, foreign diplomats) should receive special privileges?

Enjoyment of society's cultural gifts is also at issue. Should everyone receive the same education? What if that turns out to be 'impractical' (since job training is much more efficient than 'liberal arts' learning)? But doesn't that mean that some—the workers and career persons who are trained to do a job—are deprived of the education necessary to enjoy great books, music, poetry, philosophy, intellectual debate, or proficiency in foreign languages?

There are also questions of status. Should there be social classes? What if it could be proved that such divisions make a society run more smoothly? How minimal should distinctions in status be? This in turn leads to the more general question: Shouldn't all members of society be able to expect equal treatment and respect not only by the law but in every conceivable social situation?

All of these are the concerns of justice. But what is just? Who decides? And how?

These are among the hardest questions in political philosophy. They are also among the most practical questions you and I face as 'social animals', as engaged citizens, and as voters. Indeed, what we think about these questions—how thoughtfully each of us answers them—will shape the kind of country we create together. Whom we vote for (or against!), what party governs us from Ottawa, how federal and provincial governments divide up power and responsibility, what our health care system looks like, what social welfare and unemployment programs are available, how much we pay in taxes, what laws we pass, what immigration policies we adopt, what foreign policy we support, how much aid we give to countries in need, even whether Canada remains a country—all of these things (and many others) depend on what we think about justice and its demands. Far from being mere abstractions remote from the so-called 'real world', then, our thoughts about justice have concrete practical implications.

The centrality of justice to our conception of ourselves was affirmed by Prime Minister Pierre Trudeau, who presented us with a vision of Canada as a 'just society'. In the following excerpt, taken from a 1968 speech, Trudeau defines the just society of his vision:

From 'The Just Society'
By Pierre Trudeau

The Just Society will be one in which all of our people will have the means and the motivation to participate. The Just Society will be one in which personal and political freedom will be more securely ensured than it has ever been in the past. The Just Society will be one in which the rights of minorities will be safe from the whims of intolerant majorities. The Just Society will be one in which those regions

(Continued)

and groups which have not fully shared in the country's affluence will be given a better opportunity. The Just Society will be one where such urban problems as housing and pollution will be attacked through the application of new knowledge and new techniques. The Just Society will be one in which our Indian and Inuit population will be encouraged to assume the full rights of citizenship through policies which will give them both greater responsibility for their own future and more meaningful equality of opportunity. The Just Society will be a united Canada, united because all of its citizens will be actively involved in the development of a country where equality of opportunity is ensured and individuals are permitted to fulfill themselves in the fashion they judge best.

In a later reflection on his time as prime minister, Trudeau tells us that his sense of justice had its roots in his own experiences as a young student growing up in Montreal:

My notion of justice is the old Aristotelian one: that every individual should receive what is due to him or her. It's simply a question of fairness. At college I realized that some of my classmates had to do their homework on the kitchen table, surrounded by the rest of the family, while I had a room of my own at home. I was always ambitious, I always wanted to be head of the class, but I didn't want to compete with special advantages while my opponents had one hand tied behind their backs. So a just society means equal opportunities.

Saint-Exupéry told a story of travelling by train from France to Poland and seeing on board a little boy, the son of poor immigrants. Maybe this is a Mozart, he thought, but he'd never have the chance to learn an instrument because his parents have nothing to eat. And I used to think of all the wasted potential in the organization of societies that don't give equal opportunities to all. That doesn't mean that everyone should have a piano and be able to play it. It means that everyone should have a chance, to fulfill him- or herself according to his or her potential.

Rather than trying to build a society that is founded on concepts of quantity, the governments that I had the honour of leading tried to make more and more of their decisions based on quality. We didn't reject the material values, the civilization of the 'more' that brought Canada to a very advanced degree of progress and gave Canadians one of the very highest standards of living in the world. But we were saying that now, having reached the point where there are enough goods and enough technological skills, we should be able to help the less fortunate and trade off some of our material aims and goals for more spiritual, more qualitative values.

It won't have escaped your attention that Trudeau mentions Aristotle, but just what is 'Aristotelian' about Trudeau's definition of justice? What do our modern conceptions of justice have in common with those of societies that existed 2,500 years ago? To see these parallels, let's examine some philosophical conceptions of justice from ancient Greece.

B. Two Ancient Theories of Justice: Plato and Aristotle

Theories of justice, in one sense, are as old as human society. The ancient codes of the Hebrews, the Persians, and the Babylonians were theories of justice in the sense that they tried, in their various ways, to develop rules to cover fair dealing and distribution of goods, the punishment of criminals, and the settling of disputes. A fully developed theory of justice, however, should go beyond establishing specific rules; it should try to analyze the nature of justice itself. The first great theories of justice to try to do this were those of Plato and Aristotle. In *The Republic*, Plato argues that justice in the state is precisely the same as justice in the individual, that is, a harmony between the various parts for the good of the whole. In other words, cooperation among all for the sake of a successful society is the key to justice. But this means that the interests of the individual take a secondary role to the interests of society. In ancient Greece, this may have been only rarely true for the wealthy and powerful, but for the majority of people—especially the slaves—this secondary role was the norm. Because their docile submission was seen as necessary to the overall success of society, their individual interests and rights were extremely minimal. They expected to be rewarded and satisfied only insofar as their efforts benefitted their betters, and then they expected their betters to reap far more reward from their labour than they themselves. In Plato's universe, everyone has his or her 'place', and justice means that they act and are treated accordingly:

From *The Republic*
By Plato

The doing of one's own job by the moneymaking, auxiliary, and guardian groups, when each group is performing its own task in the city . . . is justice and makes the city just.

I think that justice is the very thing, or some form of the thing which, when we were beginning to found our city, we said had to be established throughout. We stated, and often repeated, if you remember, that everyone must pursue one occupation of those in the city, that for which his nature best fitted him.

Yes, we kept saying that.

Further, we have heard many people say, and have often said ourselves, that justice is to perform one's own task, and not to meddle with that of others.

We have said that.

This then, my friend, I said, when it happens, is in some way justice, to do one's own job. And do you know what I take to be a proof of this?

No, tell me.

I think what is left over of those things we have been investigating, after moderation and courage and wisdom have been found, was that which made it possible for those three qualities to appear in the city and to continue as long as it was present. We also said that what remained after we found the other three was justice.

It had to be.

And surely, I said, if we had to decide which of the four will make the city good by its presence, it would be hard to judge whether it is a common belief among the rulers and the ruled, or the preservation among the soldiers of a law-inspired belief as to the nature of what is, and what is not, to be feared, or the knowledge and guardianship of the rulers, or whether it is, above all, the presence of this fourth in child and woman, slave and free, artisan, ruler and subject, namely that each man, a unity in himself, performed his own task and was not meddling with that of others.

How could this not be hard to judge?

It seems then that the capacity for each in the city to perform his own task rivals wisdom, moderation, and courage as a source of excellence for the city.

It certainly does.

You would then describe justice as a rival to them for excellence in the city?

Most certainly.

Look at it this way and see whether you agree: you will order your rulers to act as judges in the courts of the city?

Surely.

And will their exclusive aim in delivering judgment not be that no citizen should have what belongs to another or be deprived of what is his own?

That would be their aim.

That being just?

Yes.

In some way then possession of one's own and the performance of one's own task could be agreed to be justice.

That is so.

Consider then whether you agree with me in this: if a carpenter attempts to do the work of a cobbler, or a cobbler that of a carpenter, and they exchange their tools and the esteem that goes with the job, or the same man tries to do both, and all the other exchanges are made, do you think that this does any great harm to the city?

No.

But I think that when one who is by nature a worker or some other kind of moneymaker is puffed up by wealth, or by the mob, or by his own strength, or some other such thing, and attempts to enter the warrior

(Continued)

class, or one of the soldiers tries to enter the group of counsellors or guardians, though he is unworthy of it, and these exchange their tools and the public esteem, or when the same man tries to perform all these jobs together, then I think you will agree that these exchanges and this meddling bring the city to ruin.

They certainly do.

The meddling and exchange between the three established orders does very great harm to the city and would most correctly be called wickedness.

Very definitely.

And you would call the greatest wickedness worked against one's own city injustice?

Of course.

That then is injustice. And let us repeat that the doing of one's own job by the moneymaking, auxiliary, and guardian groups, when each group is performing its own task in the city, is the opposite, it is justice and makes the city just.

I agree with you that this is so.

EGALITARIANISM

The view that all people are equal in rights and respect just by virtue of their being human.

Plato's rigid hierarchy of social classes and insistence on the inequality of people offends our sense of universal **equality**, but it is important to see that equality (or, more properly, **egalitarianism**) is a position that must be argued and is not a 'natural' state of affairs or a belief that has always been accepted by everyone.

The same is true of Aristotle's theory of justice. In his *Politics*, he gives an unabashed defence of slavery, not only on the grounds that slaves are efficient and good for society as a whole, but because those who are slaves are 'naturally' meant to be slaves and would be unhappy and unable to cope if they were granted freedom and made citizens. For Aristotle as for Plato, treating unequals equally is as unjust as treating equals unequally. Both philosophers would consider the view that children, foreigners, and people with intellectual impairments deserve the same respect and treatment as citizens ridiculous. So too would they find the contemporary argument that we should treat men and women as equals.[1]

But despite these opinions, Plato and Aristotle laid the foundations of much of our own conceptions of justice. We share their idea that equals must be treated as equals, although we differ from them in that we consider every person to be an equal. Similarly, the theory of what is called **distributive justice**, the fair distribution of wealth and goods among the members of society, is a current international as well as national concern that owes much to Aristotle's original formulations. The idea that individuals are due certain rewards for their labour is also Aristotle's idea. But despite his aristocratic opinions and his harsh elitism, Aristotle saw quite clearly that the members of society who depended most upon an adequate theory of justice were the poorer and less powerful members. It was for them that the just society was most vital (since the powerful and wealthy had a much better chance of taking care of themselves). It was also Aristotle who made the vital distinction, with which we began this section, between a restricted concern for justice that rights certain wrongs (in crimes, in bad business deals, and in public misfortunes) and the general concern of justice for a well-balanced and reasonable society.

From *The Nicomachean Ethics*
By Aristotle

To go to the judge is to go to justice; for the nature of the judge is to be a sort of animate justice.

Let us take as a starting-point, then, the various meanings of 'an unjust man'. Both the lawless man and the greedy and unfair man are thought to be unjust, so that evidently both the law-abiding and the fair man will be just. The just, then, is the lawful and the fair, the unjust the unlawful and the unfair.

Since the lawless man was seen to be unjust and the law-abiding man just, evidently all lawful acts are in a sense just acts; for the acts laid down by the legislative art are lawful, and each of these, we say, is just. Now the laws in their enactments on all subjects aim at the common advantage either of all or of the best of those who hold power, or something of the sort; so that in one sense we call those acts just that tend to produce and preserve happiness and its components for the political society. And the law bids us do both the acts of a brave man (e.g. not to desert our post nor take to flight nor throw away our arms), and those of a temperate man (e.g. not to commit adultery nor to gratify one's lust), and those of a good-tempered man (e.g., not to strike another nor to speak evil), and similarly with regard to the other virtues and forms of wickedness, commanding some acts and forbidding others; and the rightly framed law does this rightly, and the hastily conceived one less well.

This form of justice, then, is complete virtue, but not absolutely, but in relation to our neighbour. And therefore justice is often thought to be the greatest of virtues, and 'neither evening nor morning star' is so wonderful; and proverbially 'in justice is every virtue comprehended'. And it is complete virtue in its fullest sense, because it is the actual exercise of complete virtue. It is complete because he who possesses it can exercise his virtue not only in himself but toward his neighbour also; for many men can exercise virtue in their own affairs, but not in their relations to their neighbour.

* * *

But at all events what we are investigating is the justice which is a *part* of virtue; for there is a justice of this kind, as we maintain. Similarly it is with injustice in the particular sense that we are concerned.

That there is such a thing is indicated by the fact that while the man who exhibits in action the other forms of wickedness acts wrongly indeed, but not graspingly (e.g. the man who throws away his shield through cowardice or speaks harshly through bad temper or fails to help a friend with money through meanness), when a man acts graspingly he often exhibits none of these vices—no, nor all together, but certainly wickedness of some kind (for we blame him) and injustice. There is, then, another kind of injustice which is a part of injustice in the wide sense, and a use of the word 'unjust' which answers to a part

of what is unjust in the wide sense of 'contrary to the law'. Again, if one man commits adultery for the sake of gain and makes money by it, while another does so at the bidding of appetite though he loses money and is penalized for it, the latter would be held to be self-indulgent rather than grasping, but the former is unjust, but not self-indulgent; evidently, therefore, he is unjust by reason of his making gain by his act. Again, all other unjust acts are ascribed invariably to some particular kind of wickedness, for example adultery to self-indulgence, the desertion of a comrade in battle to cowardice, physical violence to anger; but if a man makes gain, his action is ascribed to no form of wickedness but injustice. Evidently, therefore, there is apart from injustice in the wide sense another, 'particular', injustice which shares the name and nature of the first, because its definition falls within the same genus; for the significance of both consists in a relation to one's neighbour, but the one is concerned with honour or money or safety—or that which includes all these, if we had a single name for it—and its motive is the pleasure that arises from gain; while the other is concerned with all the objects with which the good man is concerned.

It is clear, then, that there is more than one kind of justice, and that there is one which is distinct from virtue entire; we must try to grasp its genus and differentia.

* * *

Of particular justice and that which is just in the corresponding sense, (A) one kind is that which is manifested in distributions of honour or money or the other things that fall to be divided among those who have a share in the constitution (for in these it is possible for one man to have a share either unequal or equal to that of another), and (B) one is that which plays a rectifying part in transactions between man and man. Of this there are two divisions; of transactions (1) some are voluntary, and (2) others involuntary—voluntary such transactions as sale, purchase, loan for consumption, pledging, loan for use, depositing, letting (they are called voluntary because the origin of these transactions is voluntary), while of the involuntary (a) some are clandestine, such as theft, adultery, poisoning, procuring, enticement of slaves, assassination, false witness, and (b) others are violent, such as assault, imprisonment, murder, robbery with violence, mutilation, abuse, insult.

(Continued)

* * *

(A) We have shown that both the unjust man and the unjust act are unfair or unequal; now it is clear that there is also an intermediate between the two unequals involved in either case. And this is the equal; for in any kind of action in which there is a more and a less there is also what is equal. If, then, the unjust is unequal, the just is equal, as all men suppose it to be, even apart from argument. And since the equal is intermediate, the just will be an intermediate. Now equality implies at least two things. The just, then, must be both intermediate and equal and relative (*i.e.* for certain persons). And *qua* intermediate it must be between certain things (which are respectively greater and less); *qua* equal, it involves *two* things; *qua* just, it is for certain people. The just, therefore, involves at least four terms; for the persons for whom it is in fact just are two, and the things in which it is manifested, the objects distributed, are two. And the same equality will exist between the persons and between the things concerned; for as the latter—the things concerned—are related, so are the former; if they are not equal, they will not have what is equal, but this is the origin of quarrels and complaints—when either equals have and are awarded unequal shares, or unequals equal shares. Further, this is plain from the fact that awards should be 'according to merit'; for all men agree that what is just in distribution must be according to merit in some sense, though they do not all specify the same sort of merit, but democrats identify it with the status of freeman, supporters of oligarchy with wealth (or with noble birth), and supporters of aristocracy with excellence.

This, then, is what the just is—the proportional; the unjust is what violates the proportion. Hence one term becomes too great, the other too small, as indeed happens in practice, for the man who acts unjustly has too much, and the man who is unjustly treated too little, of what is good. In the case of evil the reverse is true; for the lesser evil is reckoned a good in comparison with the greater, and what is worthy of choice is good, and what is worthier of choice a greater good.

This, then, is one species of the just.

* * *

(B) The remaining one is the rectificatory, which arises in connection with transactions both voluntary and involuntary. This form of the just has a different specific character from the former. For the justice which distributes common possessions is always in accordance with the kind of proportion mentioned above (for in the case also in which the distribution is made from the common funds of a partnership it will be according to the same ratio which the funds put into the business by the partners bear to one another); and the injustice opposed to this kind of justice is that which violates the proportion. But the justice in transactions between man and man is a sort of equality indeed, and the injustice a sort of inequality; not according to that kind of proportion, however, but according to arithmetical proportion. For it makes no difference whether a good man has defrauded a bad man or a bad man a good one, nor whether it is a good or a bad man that has committed adultery; the law looks only to the distinctive character of the injury, and treats the parties as equal, if one is in the wrong and the other is being wronged, and if one inflicted injury and the other has received it. Therefore, this kind of injustice being an inequality, the judge tries to equalize it; for in the case also in which one has received and the other has inflicted a wound, or one has slain and the other has been slain, the suffering and the action have been unequally distributed; but the judge tries to equalize things by means of the penalty, taking away from the gain of the assailant. For the term 'gain' is applied generally to such cases, even if it be not a term appropriate to certain cases, for example to the person who inflicts a wound—and 'loss' to the sufferer; at all events when the suffering has been estimated, the one is called loss and the other gain. Therefore the equal is intermediate between the greater and less in contrary ways; more of the good and less of the evil are gain, and the contrary is loss; intermediate between them is, as we saw, the equal, which we say is just; therefore corrective justice will be the intermediate between loss and gain. This is why, when people dispute, they take refuge in the judge; and to go to the judge is to go to justice; for the nature of the judge is to be a sort of animate justice; and they seek the judge as an intermediate; and in some states they call judges mediators, on the assumption that if they get what is intermediate they will get what is just. The just, then, is an intermediate, since the judge is so. The judge restores equality.

- What is retributive justice? What is distributive justice? Provide an example for each. Do you think that one concept (theory) fits them both, or are they very different?
- Why must individuals submit themselves to the authority of the state for the sake of justice?
- Plato's conception of justice is anti-egalitarian. In what respects are we still anti-egalitarian (or inegalitarian) today?
- Aristotle gives one definition of justice that requires that each individual be given his due according to merit. Is Aristotle's notion of justice compatible with equality?
- Can you think of circumstances in which it is unjust to treat people equally? Why should we treat others equally?
- What does Aristotle mean when he claims that the just is 'the proportional'?

C. Two Modern Theories of Justice: David Hume and John Stuart Mill on Utility and Rights

In contrast to the Greeks, the premise of most modern theories of justice has been the equality of everyone with everyone else. No one is 'better' than anyone else, whatever his or her talents, achievements, wealth, family, or intelligence. This view rules out slavery on principle, whatever the benefits to society as a whole and whatever the alleged benefits to the slaves. Slavery is inequality and is thus to be condemned. But this egalitarian principle has its problems too. It is obvious that, as a matter of fact, all people are not equally endowed with intelligence or talent, good looks or abilities. Is it therefore to the good of all that everyone should be treated equally? One person is a doctor, capable of saving many lives; another is a chronic profligate and drunkard. If they were to commit exactly the same crime, would it be to the public interest to give them equal jail terms? Obviously not. But would it be just to give them different terms? It doesn't appear so. One problem that recent theorists have tried to answer is connected with cases in which the public interest seems at odds with the demands for equal treatment. A similar problem gives rise to one of the 'paradoxes of democracy' that we mentioned before. Does it make sense to treat the opinions of an ignorant person whose only knowledge of current events comes from fifteen minutes (at best) of television news a day in the way that we treat the opinions of a skilled political veteran? You might say no, but the ballots we vote on make no such distinction. And it is obvious that our society, despite its egalitarian principles, treats people who are cleverer at business or power-brokering much better than everyone else. Is this an example of systematic injustice? Or are there cases, even for us, in which inequality can still be justified as justice?

The theory of justice has been one of the central concerns of British philosophy for several centuries. Thomas Hobbes developed a theory that began with equality as a 'natural fact' and took justice to be that which 'assured peace and security to all' enforced by the government. There is no justice in 'the state of nature', Hobbes argued; justice, like law, comes into existence only with society, through a 'social compact' in which everyone agrees to abide by certain rules and to cooperate rather than compete—all for their mutual benefit. Several years later, John Locke and then David Hume argued a similar theory of justice; again, equality was the premise, and mutual agreement the basis of government authority. For both philosophers, the ultimate criterion of justice was utility—acting for the public interest and therefore the satisfaction of the interests of at least most citizens. This would have been rejected by Plato and Aristotle.

Hume exemplifies this modern view—that justice is to be characterized not just in terms of the structure of the overall society and everyone's 'place' in it, but by the interests and well-being of each and every individual. But what about an instance, Hume asks, in which a particular act of justice clearly is contrary to the public interests, such as the case in which an obviously guilty criminal is released for technical reasons or a disgusting pornographer is allowed to publish and sell his or her wares under the protection of 'free speech'? Hume replies that there is a need to distinguish between the utility of a single act and the utility of an overall system; he says that although a specific act of justice might go against the public interest, the system of justice necessarily will be in the public interest. This means that a single unjust act is to be challenged not as an isolated occurrence but as an example of a general set of rules and practices.

On 'Justice and Utility'
By David Hume

To make this more evident, consider, that though the rules of justice are established merely by interest, their connection with interest is somewhat singular, and is different from what may be observed on other occasions. A single act of justice is frequently contrary to *public interest*; and were it to stand alone, without being followed by other acts, may, in itself, be very prejudicial to society. When a man of merit, of a beneficent disposition, restores a great fortune to a miser, or a seditious bigot, he has acted justly and laudably, but the public is a real sufferer. Nor is every single act of justice, considered apart, more conducive to private interest, than to public; and it is easily conceived how a man may impoverish himself by a single instance of integrity, and have reason to wish that with regard to that single act, the laws of justice were for a moment suspended in the universe. But however single acts of justice may be contrary, either to public or private interest, it is certain, that the whole plan or scheme is highly conducive, or indeed absolutely requisite, both to the support of society, and the well-being of every individual.

The most explicitly utilitarian statement of justice as utility is found, however, in John Stuart Mill's influential pamphlet, *Utilitarianism*.

From *Utilitarianism*
By John Stuart Mill

When we call any thing a person's right, we mean that he has a valid claim on society to protect him in the possession of it, either by the force of law, or by that of education and opinion.

In the case of this, as of our other moral sentiments, there is no necessary connection between the question of its origin and that of its binding force. That a feeling is bestowed on us by nature does not necessarily legitimate all its promptings. The feeling of justice might be a peculiar instinct, and might yet require, like our other instincts, to be controlled and enlightened by a higher reason. If we have intellectual instincts leading us to judge in a particular way, as well as animal instincts that prompt us to act in a particular way, there is no necessity that the former should be more infallible in their sphere than the latter in theirs: it may as well happen that wrong judgments are occasionally suggested by those, as wrong actions by these.

* * *

In the first place, it is mostly considered unjust to deprive anyone of his personal liberty, his property, or any other thing which belongs to him by law. Here, therefore, is one instance of the application of the terms *Just* and *Unjust* in a perfectly definite sense; namely, that it is just to respect, unjust to violate, the *legal rights* of anyone. But this judgment admits of several exceptions, arising from the other forms in which the notions of justice and injustice present themselves. For example: the person who suffers the deprivation may (as the phrase is) have *forfeited* the rights which he is so deprived of; a case to which we shall return presently.

* * *

Secondly, the legal rights of which he is deprived may be rights which *ought* not to have belonged to him: in other words, the law which confers on him these rights may be a bad law. When it is so, or when (which is the same thing for our purpose) it is supposed to be so, opinions will differ as to the justice or injustice of infringing it. Some maintain that no law, however bad, ought to be disobeyed by an individual citizen; that his opposition to it, if shown at all, should only be shown in endeavouring to get it altered by competent authority. This opinion (which condemns many of the most illustrious benefactors of mankind, and would often protect pernicious institutions against the only weapons, which, in the state of things existing at the time, have any chance of succeeding against them) is defended, by those who hold it, on grounds of expediency; principally on that of the importance, to the common interest of mankind, of maintaining inviolate the sentiment of submission to law. Other persons, again, hold the directly contrary opinion, that any law, judged to be bad, may blamelessly be disobeyed, even though it be not judged to be unjust, but only inexpedient; while others would confine the license of disobedience to the case of unjust laws. But, again, some say that all laws which are inexpedient are unjust, since every law imposes some restriction on the natural liberty of mankind; which restriction is an injustice, unless legitimated by tending to their good. Among these diversities of opinion, it seems to be universally admitted that there may be unjust laws, and that law, consequently, is not the ultimate criterion of justice, but may give to one person a benefit, or impose on another an evil, which justice condemns. When, however, a law is thought to be unjust, it seems always to be regarded as being so in the same way in which a breach of law is unjust—namely, by infringing somebody's right; which, as it cannot in this case be a legal right, receives a different appellation, and is called a moral right. We may say, therefore, that a second case of injustice consists in taking or withholding from any person that to which he has a *moral right*.

Thirdly, it is universally considered just, that each person should obtain that (whether good or evil) which he *deserves*; and unjust, that he should obtain a good, or

be made to undergo an evil, which he does not deserve. This is, perhaps, the clearest and most emphatic form in which the idea of justice is conceived by the general mind. As it involves the notion of desert, the question arises, What constitutes desert? Speaking in a general way, a person is understood to deserve good if he does right; evil, if he does wrong: and, in a more particular sense, to deserve good from those to whom he does or has done good, and evil from those to whom he does or has done evil. The precept of returning good for evil has never been regarded as a case of the fulfillment of justice, but as one in which the claims of justice are waived, in obedience to other considerations.

Fourthly, it is confessedly unjust to *break faith* with anyone; to violate an engagement, either express or implied; or disappoint expectations raised by our own conduct, at least if we have raised those expectations knowingly and voluntarily. Like the other obligations of justice already spoken of, this one is not regarded as absolute, but as capable of being overruled by a stronger obligation of justice on the other side, or by such conduct on the part of the person concerned as is deemed to absolve us from our obligation to him, and to constitute a *forfeiture* of the benefit which he has been led to expect.

Fifthly, it is, by universal admission, inconsistent with justice to be *partial*; to show favour or preference to one person over another in matters to which favour and preference do not properly apply. Impartiality, however, does not seem to be regarded as a duty in itself, but rather as instrumental to some other duty; for it is admitted that favour and preference are not always censurable, and indeed the cases in which they are condemned are rather the exception than the rule. A person would be more likely to be blamed than applauded for giving his family or friends no superiority in good offices over strangers, when he could do so without violating any other duty; and no one thinks it unjust to seek one person in preference to another as a friend, connection, or companion. Impartiality, where rights are concerned, is of course obligatory; but this is involved in the more general obligation of giving to everyone his right. A tribunal, for example, must be impartial, because it is bound to award, without regard to any other consideration, a disputed object to the one of two parties who has the right to it. There are other cases in which impartiality means, being solely influenced by desert; as with those who, in the capacity of judges, preceptors, or parents, administer reward and

(Continued)

punishment as such. There are cases, again, in which it means being solely influenced by consideration for the public interest; as in making a selection among candidates for a government employment. Impartiality, in short, as an obligation of justice, may be said to mean being exclusively influenced by the considerations which it is supposed ought to influence the particular case in hand, and resisting the solicitation of any motives which prompt to conduct different from what those considerations would dictate.

Nearly allied to the idea of impartiality is that of *equality*; which often enters as a component part both into the conception of justice and into the practice of it, and, in the eyes of many persons, constitutes its essence. But, in this still more than in any other case, the notion of justice varies in different persons, and always conforms in its variations to their notion of utility. Each person maintains that equality is the dictate of justice, except where he thinks that expediency requires inequality. The justice of giving equal protection to the rights of all is maintained by those who support the most outrageous inequality in the rights themselves. Even in slave countries, it is theoretically admitted that the rights of the slave, such as they are, ought to be as sacred as those of the master,

and that a tribunal which fails to enforce them with equal strictness is wanting in justice; while, at the same time, institutions which leave to the slave scarcely any rights to enforce are not deemed unjust, because they are not deemed inexpedient. Those who think that utility requires distinctions of rank do not consider it unjust that riches and social privileges should be unequally dispensed; but those who think this inequality inexpedient think it unjust also. Whoever thinks that government is necessary sees no injustice in as much inequality as is constituted by giving to the magistrate powers not granted to other people. Even among those who hold levelling doctrines, there are as many questions of justice as there are differences of opinion about expediency. Some Communists consider it unjust that the produce of the labour of the community should be shared on any other principle than that of exact equality; others think it just that those should receive most whose wants are greatest; while others hold that those who work harder, or who produce more, or whose services are more valuable to the community, may justly claim a larger quota in the division of the produce. And the sense of natural justice may be plausibly appealed to in behalf of every one of these opinions.

Mill then goes on to define a right:

When we call any thing a person's right, we mean that he has a valid claim on society to protect him in the possession of it, either by the force of law, or by that of education and opinion. If he has what we consider a sufficient claim, on whatever account, to have something guaranteed to him by society, we say that he has a right to it. If we desire to prove that any thing does not belong to him by right, we think this done as soon as it is admitted that society ought not to take measures for securing it to him, but should leave him to chance, or to his own exertions. Thus a person is said to have a right to what he can earn in fair professional competition, because society ought not to allow any other person to hinder him from endeavouring to earn in that manner as much as he can. But he has not a right to three hundred a year, though he may happen to be earning it, because society is not called on to provide that he shall earn that sum. On the contrary, if he owns ten thousand pounds three-per-cent stock, he *has* a right to three

hundred a year, because society has come under an obligation to provide him with an income of that amount.

To have a right, then, is, I conceive, to have something which society ought to defend me in the possession of. If the objector goes on to ask why it ought, I can give him no other reason than general utility. If that expression does not seem to convey a sufficient feeling of the strength of the obligation, nor to account for the peculiar energy of the feeling, it is because there goes to the composition of the sentiment, not a rational only, but also an animal element—the thirst for retaliation; and this thirst derives its intensity, as well as its moral justification, from the extraordinarily important and impressive kind of utility which is concerned. The interest involved is that of security; to everyone's feelings, the most vital of all interests. All other earthly benefits are needed by one person, not needed by another; and many of them can, if necessary, be cheerfully foregone, or replaced by something else. But security no human being can possibly do without: on it we depend for all our immunity from evil, and for the whole value of all and every good, beyond the passing moment; since nothing but the gratification of the instant could be of any worth to us if we could be deprived of everything the next instant by whoever was momentarily stronger than ourselves. Now, this most indispensable of all necessaries, after physical nutriment, cannot be had, unless the machinery for providing it is kept unintermittedly in active play. Our notion, therefore, of the claim we have on our fellow creatures to join in making safe for us the very groundwork of our existence, gathers feelings around it so much more intense than those concerned in any of the more common cases of utility, that the difference in degree (as is often the case in psychology) becomes a real difference in kind. The claim assumes that character of absoluteness, that apparent infinity, and incommensurability with all other considerations, which constitute the distinction between the feeling of right and wrong and that of ordinary expediency and inexpediency. The feelings concerned are so powerful, and we count so positively on finding a responsive feeling in others (all being alike interested), that *ought* and *should* grow into *must*, and recognized indispensability becomes a moral necessity, analogous to physical, and often not inferior to it in binding force.

Mill's utilitarian theory of justice is a logical extension of his ethical theories: What is good and desirable is what is best for the greatest number of people. But although it might at first seem as if the greatest happiness of the greatest number leaves no room for such abstract concerns as justice, Mill argues that, to the contrary, only utility can give that abstract sense of justice some concrete basis in human life.

The problem with the utilitarian theory of justice is identical to the problem we saw with the utilitarian theory of morals. Could there not be a case in which the public interest and general utility would be served only at the clearly unjust expense of a single unfortunate individual? Suppose we lived in a society that ran extremely well, such that we had few if any complaints about our government and the way it was run, when a single muckraking journalist started turning the peace upside down with his insistence that something was very wrong in the government. We might easily suppose that, at least in the short run, the public confusion and trauma would be much more harmful to the public interest than the slight correction that would result from public exposure. Should the government forcefully silence the journalist? We would say no. He has a right to his inquiries and a right to speak his mind. Or suppose that the most efficient way to solve a series of ongoing crimes was to torture a recently captured suspect and hold him without evidence? Here again public interest and justice are at odds. Or more generally, should the government have the authority to throw people in jail just because it has reason (even good reason) to believe that they will create a public disturbance or commit certain crimes? Public interest says yes; justice says no.

This is the problem with utilitarian theories of justice in general: although we may well agree that justice *ought* to serve the public interest and every individual's interests as well, the utilitarian view is always in an awkward position when it must choose to serve the public interest at the intolerable expense and injustice of a small number of individuals or even a single individual. Consider the extreme example of an entire city that would prosper if it would sacrifice the life of one innocent child. Arguably, utilitarianism would seem to defend the sacrifice; justice, however, says that such a sacrifice is inexcusable.

- In what important respect do modern conceptions of justice differ from conceptions of justice in ancient Greece? How are interests and rights important considerations for justice?
- Can justice demand that we break a law? How does Mill argue this point? Can you think of an example where breaking the law would be the just thing to do? How so?
- How does Mill define a right? Does his definition agree with our general use of rights? Is utilitarianism compatible with rights? (Jeremy Bentham, whose 'principle of utility' we encountered in Chapter 6, didn't think so.) Why might they be incompatible?

D. The Social Contract

The single most influential conception of justice in modern times has been called the 'social contract theory'. The **social contract** is an agreement among people to share certain interests and make certain compromises for the good of them all. It is a contract based on the 'consent of the governed'. In one form or another, it existed even in ancient times. For example, recall from the Introduction Socrates' argument that by staying in Athens he had implicitly agreed to abide by its laws, even when those laws condemned him to death. What is most important in understanding the nature of this social contract is that, as in Socrates' argument, there need not have been any actual, physical contract or even oral agreement in order for the agreement to exist. We are bound by social contract, in other words, even if we never signed or saw such a contract. Moreover, such a contract might never have existed, even in past history. Simply to live in a society, according to this argument, is to have agreed, at least implicitly, to such an agreement. (Thus, living in a society you are expected to obey its laws; 'ignorance is no excuse', and you cannot get out of an arrest by saying 'I don't really live here', much less 'I don't recognize your right to arrest me'.)

Two very different pictures of the original social contract are presented to us by the English philosopher Thomas Hobbes and the French philosopher Jean-Jacques Rousseau. Both begin by considering man in 'the state of nature', without laws and without society, before men and women came together to accept the social contract. Hobbes bases his conception of the social contract, however, on an extremely unfavourable conception of human nature. He attacks the idealistic political philosophies of Plato and Aristotle for being unrealistic and assuming wrongly that people are naturally capable of virtue and wisdom. Like Machiavelli, whom he follows with praise, he considers himself a 'realist'. And for him, as for many others, being a realist means seeing the nasty side of things. So, according to his theory of human nature, natural man is a selfish beast, fighting for his own interests against everyone else. Human life is a 'war of all against all' and a person's life, consequently, is 'nasty, brutish, and short'. He dismisses reason and appeals to human passions, particularly the passion for self-preservation. The social contract, therefore, is mainly an agreement of equally selfish and self-seeking persons not to commit mutual murder.

From *Leviathan*
By Thomas Hobbes

If a covenant be made, wherein neither of the parties perform presently, but trust one another; in the condition of mere nature, which is a condition of war of every man against every man, upon any reasonable suspicion, it is void: but if there be a common power set over them both, with right and force sufficient to compel performance, it is not void.

Of the Natural Condition of Mankind as Concerning Their Felicity, and Misery

Men by nature equal. Nature hath made men so equal, in the faculties of the body, and mind; as that though there be found one man sometimes manifestly stronger in body, or of quicker mind than another; yet when all is reckoned together, the difference between man, and man, is not so considerable, as that one man can thereupon claim to himself any benefit, to which another may not pretend, as well as he. For as to the strength of the body, the weakest has strength enough to kill the strongest, either by secret machination or by confederacy with others, that are in the same danger with himself.

* * *

For such is the nature of men, that howsoever they may acknowledge many others to be more witty,

Chapter 7 Justice   **491**

or more eloquent, or more learned; yet they will hardly believe there be many so wise as themselves; for they see their own wit at hand, and other men's at a distance. But this proveth rather that men are in that point equal, than unequal. For there is not ordinarily a greater sign of the equal distribution of any thing, than that every man is contented with his share.

From equality proceeds diffidence. From this equality of ability, ariseth equality of hope in the attaining of our ends. And therefore if any two men desire the same thing, which nevertheless they cannot both enjoy, they become enemies; and in the way to their end, which is principally their own conservation, and sometimes their delectation only, endeavour to destroy, or subdue one another. And from hence it comes to pass, that where an invader hath no more to fear, than another man's single power; if one plant, sow, build, or possess a convenient seat, others may probably be expected to come prepared with forces united, to dispossess, and deprive him, not only of the fruit of his labour, but also of his life, or liberty. And the invader again is in the like danger of another.

From diffidence war. And from this diffidence of one another, there is no way for any man to secure himself, so reasonable, as anticipation; that is, by force, or wiles, to master the persons of all men he can, so long, till he see no other power great enough to endanger him: and this is no more than his own conservation requireth, and is generally allowed. Also because there be some, that taking pleasure in contemplating their own power in the acts of conquest, which they pursue farther than their security requires; if others, that otherwise would be glad to be at ease within modest bounds, should not by invasion increase their power, they would not be able, long time, by standing only on their defence, to subsist. And by consequence, such augmentation of dominion over men being necessary to a man's conservation, it ought to be allowed him.

Again, men have no pleasure, but on the contrary a great deal of grief, in keeping company, where there is no power able to over-awe them all. For every man looketh that his companion should value him, at the same rate he sets upon himself: and upon all signs of contempt, or undervaluing, naturally endeavours, as far as he dares (which amongst them that have no common power to keep them in quiet, is far enough to make them destroy each other), to extort a greater value from his contemners, by damage; and from others, by the example.

So that in the nature of man, we find three principal causes of quarrel. First, competition; secondly, diffidence; thirdly, glory.

The first, maketh men invade for gain; the second, for safety; and the third, for reputation. The first use violence, to make themselves masters of other men's persons, wives, children, and cattle; the second, to defend them; the third, for trifles, as a word, a smile, a different opinion, and any other sign of undervalue, either direct in their persons, or by reflection in their kindred, their friends, their nation, their profession, or their name.

Out of civil states, there is always war of every one against every one. Hereby it is manifest, that during the time men live without a common power to keep them all in awe, they are in that condition which is called war; and such a war, as is of every man, against every man. For war, consisteth not in battle only, or the act of fighting, but in a tract of time, wherein the will to contend by battle is sufficiently known.

* * *

The incommodities of such a war. Whatsoever therefore is consequent to a time of war, where every man is enemy to every man; the same is consequent to the time, wherein men live without other security, than what their own strength, and their own invention shall furnish them withal. In such condition, there is no place for industry; because the fruit thereof is uncertain: and consequently no culture of the earth; no navigation, nor use of the commodities that may be imported by sea; no commodious building; no instruments of moving, and removing, such things as require much force; no knowledge of the face of the earth; no account of time; no arts; no letters; no society; and which is worst of all, continual fear, and danger of violent death; and the life of man, solitary, poor, nasty, brutish, and short.

It may seem strange to some man, that has not well weighed these things; that nature should thus dissociate, and render men apt to invade, and destroy one another: and he may therefore, not trusting to this inference, made from the passions, desire perhaps to have the same confirmed by experience. Let him therefore consider with himself, when taking a journey, he arms himself, and seeks to go well accompanied; when going to sleep, he locks his doors; when even in his house he locks his chests; and this when he knows there be laws, and public officers,

(Continued)

armed to revenge all injuries shall be done him; what opinion he has of his fellow-subjects, when he rides armed; of his fellow citizens, when he locks his doors; and of his children, and servants, when he locks his chests. Does he not there as much accuse mankind by his actions, as I do by my words? But neither of us accuse men's nature in it. The desires, and other passions of man, are in themselves no sin. No more are the actions, that proceed from those passions, till they know a law that forbids them: which till laws be made they cannot know: nor can any law be made, till they have agreed upon the person that shall make it.

It may peradventure be thought, there was never such a time, nor condition of war as this; and I believe it was never generally so, over all the world: but there are many places, where they live so now. For the savage people in many places of America, except the government of small families, the concord whereof dependeth on natural lust, have no government at all; and live at this day in that brutish manner, as I said before. Howsoever, it may be perceived what manner of life there would be, where there were no common power to fear, by the manner of life, which men that have formerly lived under a peaceful government, use to degenerate into, in a civil war.

Of the First and Second Natural Laws, and of Contracts

Right of nature. The right of nature, which writers commonly call *jus naturale*, is the liberty each man hath, to use his own power, as he will himself, for the preservation of his own nature; that is to say, of his own life; and consequently, of doing any thing, which in his own judgment, and reason, he shall conceive to be the aptest means thereunto.

Liberty. By liberty, is understood, according to the proper signification of the word, the absence of external impediments: which impediments, may oft take away part of a man's power to do what he would; but cannot hinder him from using the power left him, according as his judgment, and reason shall dictate to him.

A law of nature. A law of nature, *lex naturalis*, is a precept or general rule, found out by reason, by which a man is forbidden to do that, which is destructive of his life, or taketh away the means of preserving the same; and to omit that, by which he thinketh it may be best preserved.

Difference of right and law. For though they that speak of this subject, use to confound *jus*, and *lex*, *right* and *law*: yet they ought to be distinguished; because right, consisteth in liberty to do, or to forbear: whereas law, determineth, and bindeth to one of them: so that law, and right, differ as much, as obligation, and liberty; which in one and the same matter are inconsistent.

Naturally every man has right to every thing. And because the condition of man, as hath been declared in the precedent chapter, is a condition of war of every one against every one; in which case every one is governed by his own reason; and there is nothing he can make use of, that may not be of help unto him, in preserving his life against his enemies; it followeth, that in such a condition, every man has a right to every thing; even to one another's body. And therefore, as long as this natural right of every man to every thing endureth, there can be no security to any man, how strong or wise soever he be, of living out the time, which nature ordinarily alloweth men to live.

The fundamental law of nature. And consequently it is a precept, or general rule of reason, *that every man, ought to endeavour peace, as far as he has hope of obtaining it; and when he cannot obtain it, that he may seek, and use, all helps, and advantages of war.*

* * *

The second law of nature. From this fundamental law of nature, by which men are commanded to endeavour peace, is derived this second law; *that a man be willing, when others are so too, as far-forth, as for peace, and defence of himself he shall think it necessary, to lay down this right to all things; and be contented with so much liberty against other men, as he would allow other men against himself.* For as long as every man holdeth this right, of doing any thing he liketh; so long are all men in the condition of war. But if other men will not lay down their right, as well as he; then there is no reason for any one, to divest himself of his: for that were to expose himself to prey, which no man is bound to, rather than to dispose himself to peace. This is that law of the Gospel; *whatsoever you require that others should do to you, that do ye to them.*

* * *

What it is to lay down a right. To *lay down* man's *right to* any thing, is to *divest* himself of the *liberty*, of hindering another of the benefit of his own right to the same. For he that renounceth, or passeth away his right, giveth not to any other man a right which he had not before; because there is nothing to which every man had not right by nature: but only standeth out of his way, that he may enjoy his own original right, without hindrance from him; not without hindrance from another. So that the effect which redoundeth to one man, by another man's defect of right, is but so much diminution of impediments to the use of his own right original.

* * *

Not all rights are alienable. Whensoever a man transferreth his right, or renounceth it; it is either in consideration of some right reciprocally transferred to himself; or for some other good he hopeth for thereby. For it is a voluntary act: and of the voluntary acts of every man, the object is some *good to himself*. And therefore there be some rights, which no man can be understood by any words, or other signs, to have abandoned, or transferred. As first a man cannot lay down the right of resisting them, that assault him by force, to take away his life; because he cannot be understood to aim thereby, at any good to himself. The same may be said of wounds, and chains, and imprisonment; both because there is no benefit consequent to such patience; as there is to the patience of suffering another to be wounded, or imprisoned: as also because a man cannot tell, when he seeth men proceed against him by violence, whether they intend his death or not. And lastly the motive, and end for which this renouncing, and transferring of right is introduced, is nothing else but the security of man's person, in his life, and in the means of so preserving life, as not to be weary of it. And therefore if a man by words, or other signs, seem to despoil himself of the end, for which those signs were intended; he is not to be understood as if he meant it, or that it was his will; but that he was ignorant of how such words and actions were to be interpreted.

Contract. The mutual transferring of right, as that which men call CONTRACT.

* * *

Covenants of mutual trust, when invalid. If a covenant be made, wherein neither of the parties perform presently, but trust one another; in the condition of mere nature, which is a condition of war of every man against every man, upon any reasonable suspicion, it is void: but if there be a common power set over them both, with right and force sufficient to compel performance, it is not void. For he that performeth first, has no assurance the other will perform after; because the bonds of words are too weak to bridle men's ambition, avarice, anger, and other passions, without the fear of some coercive power; which in the condition of mere nature, where all men are equal, and judges of the justness of their own fears, cannot possibly be supposed. And therefore he which performeth first, does but betray himself to his enemy; contrary to the right, he can never abandon, of defending his life, and means of living.

But in a civil estate, where there is a power set up to constrain those that would otherwise violate their faith, that fear is no more reasonable; and for that cause, he which by the covenant is to perform first, is obliged so to do.

The cause of fear, which maketh such a covenant invalid, must be always something arising after the covenant made; as some new fact, or other sign of the will not to perform: else it cannot make the covenant void. For that which could not hinder a man from promising, ought not to be admitted as a hindrance of performing.

Right to the end, containeth right to the means. He that transferreth any right, transferreth the means of enjoying it, as far as lieth in his power. As he that selleth land, is understood to transfer the herbage, and whatsoever grows upon it: nor can he that sells a mill turn away the stream that drives it. And they that give to a man the right of government in sovereignty, are understood to give him the right of levying money to maintain soldiers; and of appointing magistrates for the administration of justice.

- What is a social contract? Does it matter whether there is an actual meeting or agreement? To what extent is our own society or government based on a social contract?
- What is meant by the 'state of nature'? Given that the state of nature does not describe an actual historical state of affairs, what purpose does referring to the state of nature serve?

Hobbes begins his argument with the perhaps surprising observation that people are basically equal in nature. He is not talking here about legal equality or equal rights (for there are no laws and no legal rights) but rather equality in abilities, talents, and power. This seems strange, because the problem of equality usually pays attention to the great differences between people. Instead Hobbes points out our similarities. In particular, he points out that almost everyone is strong enough and smart enough to kill or inflict grievous injury on others. Even a puny moron can, with a knife or a handgun, kill the strongest and smartest person on earth. Accordingly, the basis of the social contract (or 'covenant') according to Hobbes is our mutual protection. Everyone agrees not to kill other people and in return is guaranteed that he or she won't be killed. Although it is a cynical view of human nature, it also continues to be one of the most powerful arguments for strong governments. (Hobbes himself was a conservative monarchist.)

Rousseau, quite to the contrary, had an extremely optimistic view of human nature, as we saw in the preceding chapter. He believed that people are 'naturally good', and it is only the corruptions of society that makes them selfish and destructive. Rousseau does not take the social contract, therefore, to be simply a doctrine of protection between mutually brutish individuals. For him, the function of the state is rather to allow people to develop the 'natural goodness' that they had in the absence of any state at all. This is not to say (although Rousseau is often interpreted this way) that he was nostalgic and wanted to 'go back to the state of nature'. That is impossible. (It is not even clear that Rousseau believed that there ever was a 'state of nature' as such; his example, like Hobbes' example, is a way of giving a picture of 'human nature', whether or not it is historically accurate.) We are already in society; that is a given fact. So Rousseau's aim is to develop a conception of the state that will allow us to live as morally as possible. This is important, for Rousseau, unlike most social contract theorists, is not at all a utilitarian; he sees goodness, rather than happiness, as the most important end. (Hobbes, by way of contrast, took utility, pleasure, and well-being, in addition to self-preservation, to be the purpose of the social contract.)

Rousseau's ambition, therefore, is not to 'get us back to nature' but rather to revise our conception of the state. His 'revision', however, is one of the most radical documents in modern history and has rightly been said to be one of the causes of both the American and the French revolutions. The main thesis is one that Rousseau inherits from Locke: the state has legitimate power only so long as it serves the people it governs. The revolutionary corollary is that when a state ceases to serve its citizens, the citizens have a right to overthrow that government. This was a radical claim, again reminiscent of Locke. Even Rousseau was not comfortable with it. (Locke had made his statement *after* the English Revolution.) He called revolution 'the most horrible alternative', to be avoided wherever possible. But subsequent French history took his theories quite literally and demonstrated too the 'horror' that may follow too radical and abrupt a change in the authority that citizens accept as legitimate.

In earlier works, Rousseau argued his famous thesis that 'natural man' is 'naturally good' and that contemporary society has corrupted him (and her). He went on to say that competition and the artificiality of our lust for private property are responsible for this corruption, and he even included marriage and romantic love as forms of this 'lust for private property'. In the state of nature, he suggests, people mated when they felt like it, with whomever they felt like, and duels fought between rivals were unheard of. Rousseau does not suggest that we return to that prehistoric custom, but he does use it as a wedge to pry open even the most sacred of our modern civil institutions. All of these, he argues, must be re-examined, and the tool for that re-examination is the social contract.

The key to his most famous book, appropriately called *The Social Contract,* is that man must regain his freedom within society. This does not mean, however, that a person can do whatever he or she would like to do. Quite the contrary—to be a citizen, according to Rousseau, is to want and do what is good for the society as well. To be free is precisely to want to do what is good for the society. In fact, in one of the most problematic statements of the social contract, Rousseau says that a person who does not so act for the good of the society may have to 'be forced to be free'. Here is the basis for a strange paradox. On the one hand, Rousseau has properly been regarded as the father of the most liberal and revolutionary political theories of our time. (Marx, for example, claims a great debt to Rousseau). His political philosophy stresses individual freedom and rights above all, even above the state itself. But another side to Rousseau emerges in his paradoxical phrase; his stress on the state as an entity in itself ('the **sovereign**', presumably the king, but essentially any government) and the subservience of the individual to the state has also caused him to be labelled an authoritarian and the forerunner of totalitarian and fascist governments.

This paradox is not easily resolved, but we can at least explain how it comes about. Rousseau believes that the state is subject to and receives its **legitimacy** from the people it governs. But that does not mean that individual people need have any real power in determining the form or functions of government. Rousseau is not a democrat. What he says instead is that the state is subject to what he calls 'the general will', which is not simply a collection of individuals but something more. For example, we talk about 'the spirit of the revolution' or 'the discontent of the working class', but this spirit or discontent is not simply the product of each individual person. A poll of workers or revolutionaries would not show it either way. The revolution may have spirit even though some participants do not; indeed, they may even dislike the whole idea. Here is the source of the paradox: Legitimacy is given to the state by the general will, not by every individual person. The person who does not agree with the general will, therefore, may very well find himself or herself forced into compliance with the state ('forced to be free'). How much force, however, is a matter about which Rousseau is not very clear; and his many followers have not agreed on that crucial point either. On one extreme, Rousseau's authoritarian followers have insisted that all dissent from the general will must be stifled; on the other extreme, Rousseau's most libertarian and anarchist followers have insisted that the rights of the individual to be free from government intervention and to live according to his or her own 'natural goodness' outweigh any claims that the state may have. What follows are a few selections from *The Social Contract*, beginning with one of Rousseau's best-known slogans.

LEGITIMACY

The right to have authority; sanctioned power.

From *The Social Contract*
By Jean-Jacques Rousseau

Each individual, in making a contract, as we may say, with himself, is bound in a double capacity; as a member of the Sovereign he is bound to the individuals, and as a member of the State to the Sovereign.

Man is born free; and everywhere he is in chains. One thinks himself the master of others, and still remains a greater slave than they. How did this change come about? I do not know. What can make it legitimate? That question I think I can answer.

If I took into account only force, and the effects derived from it, I should say: 'As long as a people is compelled to obey, and obeys, it does well; as soon as it can shake off the yoke, and shakes it off, it does still better; for, regaining its liberty by the same right as took it away, either it is justified in resuming it, or there was no justification for those who took it away.' But the social order is a sacred right which is the basis of all other rights. Nevertheless, this right does not come from nature, and must therefore be founded on conventions. Before coming to that, I have to prove what I have just asserted.

The First Societies

The most ancient of all societies, and the only one that is natural, is the family: and even so the children remain attached to the father only so long as they need him for their preservation. As soon as this need ceases, the natural bond is dissolved. The children, released from the obedience they owed to the father, and the father, released from the care he owed his children, return equally to independence. If they remain united, they continue so no longer naturally, but voluntarily; and the family itself is then maintained only by convention.

(Continued)

This common liberty results from the nature of man. His first law is to provide for his own preservation, his first cares are those which he owes to himself; and, as soon as he reaches years of discretion, he is the sole judge of the proper means of preserving himself, and consequently becomes his own master.

The family then may be called the first model of political societies; the ruler corresponds to the father, and the people to the children; and all, being born free and equal, alienate their liberty only for their own advantage. The whole difference is that, in the family, the love of the father for his children repays him for the care he takes of them, while, in the State, the pleasure of commanding takes the place of the love which the chief cannot have for the peoples under him.

* * *

The Social Contract

I suppose men to have reached the point at which the obstacles in the way of their preservation in the state of nature show their power of resistance to be greater than the resources at the disposal of each individual for his maintenance in that state. That primitive condition can then subsist no longer; and the human race would perish unless it changed its manner of existence.

But, as men cannot engender new forces, but only unite and direct existing ones, they have no other means of preserving themselves than the formation, by aggregation, of a sum of forces great enough to overcome the resistance. These they have to bring into play by means of a single motive power, and cause to act in concert.

This sum of forces can arise only where several persons come together: but, as the force and liberty of each man are the chief instruments of his self-preservation, how can he pledge them without harming his own interests, and neglecting the care he owes to himself? This difficulty, in its bearing on my present subject, may be stated in the following terms:

'The problem is to find a form of association which will defend and protect with the whole common force the person and goods of each associate, and in which each, while uniting himself with all, may still obey himself alone, and remain as free as before.' This is the fundamental problem of which the *Social Contract* provides the solution.

The clauses of this contract are so determined by the nature of the act that the slightest modification would make them vain and ineffective; so that, although they have perhaps never been formally set forth, they are everywhere the same and everywhere tacitly admitted and recognized, until, on the violation of the social compact, each regains his original rights and resumes his natural liberty, while losing the conventional liberty in favour of which he renounced it.

These clauses, properly understood, may be reduced to one—the total alienation of each associate, together with all his rights, to the whole community; for, in the first place, as each gives himself absolutely, the conditions are the same for all; and, this being so, no one has any interest in making them burdensome to others.

Moreover, the alienation being without reserve, the union is as perfect as it can be, and no associate has anything more to demand: for, if the individuals retained certain rights, as there would be no common superior to decide between them and the public, each, being on one point his own judge, would ask to be so on all; the state of nature would thus continue, and the association would necessarily become inoperative or tyrannical.

Finally, each man, in giving himself to all, gives himself to nobody; and as there is no associate over which he does not acquire the same right as he yields others over himself, he gains an equivalent for everything he loses, and an increase of force for the preservation of what he has.

If then we discard from the social contract what is not of its essence, we shall find that it reduces itself to the following terms:

'Each of us puts his person and all his power in common under the supreme direction of the general will, and, in our corporate capacity, we receive each member as an indivisible part of the whole.'

At once, in place of the individual personality of each contracting party, this act of association creates a moral and collective body, composed of as many members as the assembly contains voters, and receiving from this act its unity, its common identity, its life, and its will. This public person, so formed by the union of all other persons, formerly took the name of *city*, and now takes that of *Republic* or *body politic*; it is called by its members *State* when passive, *Sovereign* when active, and *Power* when compared with others like itself. Those who are associated in it take collectively the name of *people*, and severally are called *citizens*, as sharing in the sovereign power, and *subjects*, as being under the laws of the State. But these terms are often confused and take one for another: it is enough to know how to distinguish them when they are being used with precision.

The Sovereign

This formula shows us that the act of association comprises a mutual understanding between the public and the individuals, and that each individual, in making a contract, as we may say, with himself, is bound in a double capacity; as a member of the Sovereign he is bound to the individuals, and as a member of the State to the Sovereign. But the maxim of civil right, that no one is bound by undertakings made to himself, does not apply in this case; for there is a great difference between incurring an obligation to yourself and incurring one to a whole of which you form a part.

Attention must further be called to the fact that public deliberation, while competent to bind all the subjects to the Sovereign, because of the two different capacities in which each of them may be regarded, cannot, for the opposite reason, bind that Sovereign to itself; and that it is consequently against the nature of the body politic for the Sovereign to impose on itself a law which it cannot infringe. Being able to regard itself in only one capacity, it is in the position of an individual who makes a contract with himself; and this makes it clear that there neither is nor can be any kind of fundamental law binding on the body of the people—not even the social contract itself. This does not mean that the body politic cannot enter into undertakings with others, provided the contract is not infringed by them; for in relation to what is external to it, it becomes a simple being, an individual.

But the body politic or the Sovereign, drawing its being wholly from the sanctity of the contract, can never bind itself, even to an outsider, to do anything derogatory to the original act, for instance, to alienate any part of itself, or to submit to another Sovereign. Violation of the act by which it exists would be self-annihilation; and that which is itself nothing can create nothing.

As soon as this multitude is so united in one body, it is impossible to offend against one of the members without attacking the body, and still more to offend against the body without the members resenting it. Duty and interest therefore equally oblige the two contracting parties to give each other help; and the same men should seek to combine, in their double capacity, all the advantages dependent upon that capacity.

Again, the Sovereign, being formed wholly of the individuals who compose it, neither has nor can have any interest contrary to theirs; and consequently the sovereign power need give no guarantee to its subjects, because it is impossible for the body to wish to hurt all its members.

* * *

In fact, each individual, as a man, may have a particular will contrary or dissimilar to the general will which he has as a citizen. His particular interest may speak to him quite differently from the common interest: his absolute and naturally independent existence may make him look upon what he owes to the common cause as a gratuitous contribution, the loss of which will do less harm to others than the payment of it is burdensome to himself; and, regarding the moral person which constitutes the State as a *persona ficta*, because not a man, he may wish to enjoy the rights of citizenship without being ready to fulfill the duties of a subject. The continuance of such an injustice could not but prove the undoing of the body politic.

In order then that the social compact may not be an empty formula, it tacitly includes the undertaking, which alone can give force to the rest, that whoever refuses to obey the general will shall be compelled to do so by the whole body. This means nothing less than that he will be forced to be free; for this is the condition which, by giving each citizen to his country, secures him against all personal dependence. In this lies the key to the working of the political machine; this alone legitimizes civil undertakings, which, without it, would be absurd, tyrannical, and liable to the most frightful abuses.

The Civil State

The passage from the state of nature to the civil state produces a very remarkable change in man, by substituting justice for instinct in his conduct, and giving his actions the morality they had formerly lacked. Then only, when the voice of duty takes the place of physical impulses and right of appetite, does man, who so far had considered only himself, find that he is forced to act on different principles, and to consult his reason before listening to his inclinations. Although, in this state, he deprives himself of some advantages which he got from nature, he gains in return others so great, his faculties are so stimulated and developed, his ideas so extended, his feelings so ennobled, and his whole soul so uplifted, that, did not the abuses of this new condition often degrade him below that which he left,

(Continued)

he would be bound to bless continually the happy moment which took him from it for ever, and, instead of a stupid and unimaginative animal, made him an intelligent being and a man.

Let us draw up the whole account in terms easily commensurable. What man loses by the social contract is his natural liberty and an unlimited right to everything he tries to get and succeeds in getting; what he gains is civil liberty and the proprietorship of all he possesses. If we are to avoid mistake in weighing one against the other, we must clearly distinguish natural liberty, which is bounded only by the strength of the individual, from civil liberty, which is limited by the general will; and possession, which is merely the effect of force or the right of the first occupier, from property, which can be founded only on a positive title.

We might, over and above all this, add, to what man acquires in the civil state, moral liberty, which alone makes him truly master of himself; for the mere impulse of appetite is slavery, while obedience to a law which we prescribe to ourselves is liberty.

Although Rousseau shares with Hobbes a belief in the social contract theory, the differences between them could not be more striking. Where Hobbes begins with a brutal view of human nature forced into agreement by fear of mutual violence, Rousseau begins by saying that 'man is born free'. For Rousseau, the social contract is not an instrument of mutual protection but a means of improving people and bringing out what is best in them. His central theme is not antagonism but humanity's 'natural goodness'. With unmistakable clarity, Rousseau rejects all might-makes-right theories and insists that legitimacy must always be a matter of the consent of the governed. 'The general will' is not a general compromise but the creation of a new power, the power of the people, which for Rousseau is the ultimate voice of authority.

- What does Hobbes mean when he claims that we are all 'by nature equal'?
- How does Hobbes describe human nature? How does this differ from Plato's, Aristotle's, and Rousseau's views of human nature?
- Does the social contract function differently in Hobbes's view than it does in Rousseau's view?
- What does it mean to be free for Rousseau? What is the difference between natural liberty and civil liberty? How are we free with the latter?

E. Classical Conservatism: Tradition and Attachment

The modern idea of a social contract was given an intriguing twist by Irish-born political thinker Edmund Burke in the late eighteenth century. In his famous *Reflections on the Revolution in France*—a work that has been remarkably influential, especially (though not exclusively) among conservatives—Burke invites us to re-examine the nature of this 'contract':

From *Reflections on the Revolution in France*
By Edmund Burke

Society is . . . a partnership not only between those who are living, but between those who are living, those who are dead, and those who are to be born.

Society is indeed a contract. Subordinate contracts for objects of mere occasional interest may be dissolved at pleasure—but the state ought not to be considered as nothing better than a partnership agreement in a trade of pepper and coffee, calico or tobacco, or some other such low concern, to be taken up for a little temporary interest, and to be dissolved by the fancy of the parties. It is to be looked on with other reverence; because it is not a partnership in things subservient only to the gross animal existence of a temporary perishable nature. It is a partnership in all science; a partnership in all art; a partnership in every virtue and in all perfection. As the ends of such a partnership cannot be obtained in many generations, it becomes a partnership not only between those who are living, but between those who are living, those who are dead, and those who are to be born.

Whether or not we agree with Burke, it isn't too hard to see what he is driving at. Society *is* a contract, but it is a very special kind of contract. For, unlike ordinary trade agreements that have 'temporary' material goods as their ultimate ends, society aims at the realization of ideals that are constitutive of civilized life: 'art', 'science', 'virtue', and 'perfection'. And these goods take a great deal of time to obtain. Consequently, society must be thought of as a partnership across the generations—past, present, and future.

Once we feel this in our bones—once we acknowledge that we are a link in a chain spanning centuries—we shall see ourselves in a new light: as descendants bound to ancestors by gratitude, and as ancestors joined to descendants by duty; as creatures of the past, and as creators of the future; as humble debtors, and as wise stewards. Above all, we shall recognize our obligation to preserve the very best things we possess, for good and precious things, being fragile, are easily ruined, and future generations are depending on us for their inheritance. So we must do unto the future as the past did unto us:

[O]ne of the first and most leading principles on which the commonwealth and the laws are consecrated, is lest the temporary possessors and life-renters in it, unmindful of what they have received from their ancestors, or of what is due to their posterity, should act as if they were the entire masters; that they should not think it amongst their rights to cut off the entail, or to commit waste on the inheritance by destroying at their pleasure the whole original fabric of their society; hazarding to leave to those who come after them, a ruin instead of an habitation—and teaching these successors as little to respect their contrivances, as they had themselves respected the institutions of their forefathers. By this unprincipled facility of changing the state as often, and as much, and in as many ways as there are floating fancies or fashions, the whole chain and continuity of the commonwealth would be broken. No one generation could link with the other. Men would become little better than the flies of a summer.

* * *

You will observe, that from Magna Charta to the Declaration of Right, it has been the uniform policy of our constitution to claim and assert our liberties, as an *entailed inheritance* derived to us from our forefathers, and to be transmitted to our posterity; as an estate specially belonging to the people of this kingdom without any reference whatever to any other more general or prior right. By this means our constitution preserves an unity in so great a diversity of its parts. We have an inheritable crown; an inheritable peerage; and an house of commons and a people inheriting privileges, franchises, and liberties, from a long line of ancestors.

This policy appears to me to be the result of profound reflection; or rather the happy effect of following nature, which is wisdom without reflection, and above it. A spirit of innovation is generally the result of a selfish temper and confined views. People will not look forward to posterity, who will never look backward to their ancestors.

* * *

I cannot conceive how any man can have brought himself to that pitch of presumption, to consider his country as nothing but *carte blanche*, upon which he may scribble whatever he pleases. A man full of warm speculative benevolence may wish his society otherwise constituted than he finds it; but a good patriot, and a true politician, always considers how he shall make the most of the existing materials of his country. A disposition to preserve and an ability to improve, taken together, would be my standard of a statesman.

(Continued)

We can see why tradition is very important to Burke and his followers. Without a shared or common tradition, Burke declares, 'no one generation could link with the other', and we would be in no better position than that of 'the flies of a summer'. Tradition, in short, ensures a measure of continuity and stability; and without such things, society—along with the rights and freedoms established within society—would simply break down.

Yet tradition does much more than simply make society work. According to classical conservatives, tradition is the crucible in which our very identity is formed. History and community, languages and institutions, customs and conventions, manners and mores—all these things have conspired to make us who and what we are. It follows that self-respect is ultimately inseparable from respect for tradition and that the beliefs we have inherited from our ancestors inform our current understanding of what is just. As distinguished Canadian historian W.L. Morton suggests in his 1959 essay on conservatism, it is the inherited belief in 'human fallibility' that informs the conservative's respect for authority as the rightful provider of law and order:

From 'Canadian Conservatism Now'
By W.L. Morton

It is because he knows that the individual man is weak . . . that the conservative believes that men need to be sustained by authority and guided by tradition.

[O]ne of the first principles of a conservative is respect for authority; not for authority merely as the right to command, but for authority as the expression of that law and order, and that civil decency without which society dissolves in anarchy.

And the next first principle is a similar respect for tradition, for that which is handed down from the experience of the race, or the wisdom of our ancestors. This is not ancestor worship, but merely the realization that, important as the individual is, he is what he is largely in virtue of what he is by blood and breeding, and of what he has absorbed, consciously or unconsciously, formally or informally, from home, church, school, and neighbourhood. He subscribes, in short, to Burke's definition of the social contract as a partnership in all virtue, a partnership between the generations, a contract not made once for all time, but one perennially renewed in the organic processes of society, the birth, growth, and death of successive generations.

Authority and tradition, then, are cornerstones of conservative belief. And the quarry from which they are dug is a particular belief about the nature of man. To the theologian this is the belief in original sin, the belief, that is, that man by his nature is imperfect, and is to be made perfect only by redemption and grace. In philosophic terms, it is a denial of the fundamental liberal and Marxist belief that human nature is inherently perfectible, that man may realize the perfection that is in him if only the right environment is created. And, I need not tell you, this belief in human fallibility, or the other belief in human perfectibility, are what unmistakably and for all time separate the conservative from the liberal.

The belief in human imperfection need not, of course, be derived only from Christian theology. It is present by implication both in Stoicism and in Aristotle's *Politics*.

It is because he knows that the individual man is weak, imperfect, and limited that the conservative believes that men need to be sustained by authority and guided by tradition, the formulated experience of society.

This human need of fellowship, of the support of the church, or of the Aristotelian *polis*, gives rise, of course, to the next fundamental conservative principle. That is Loyalty. Loyalty is the instinct to do for others what is expected of one, it may be by one's superiors, it may be by one's inferiors. So important in the conservative creed is this great principle that Lord Hugh Cecil once defined conservatism as simply 'loyalty to persons'. He meant, of course, that the conservative not only regards loyalty as a cardinal virtue, but that he gives loyalty not to institutions or abstractions, but to persons, not to the Crown but to Queen Elizabeth, not to the Conservative party but to John Diefenbaker. But if loyalty is a personal matter, it is also a peculiarly conservative thing, for the conservative prefers the concrete to the abstract, and persons to ideas.

Finally, the conservative holds firmly to the need for continuity in human affairs. He does so because he believes in what Coleridge calls the Principle of Permanence in society. But today's conservative believes in permanence while recognizing the fact of change in human affairs. But change should come, he firmly believes, by way of organic growth, not by deliberate revolution or skilful manipulation. The good society of the conservative ideal, the society which would be just and admit of the good life, would not be static. It would change, but it would change as insensibly as a child grows, or as a river runs. Such change leads to the continuity that makes permanence possible.

The conservative, that is, is devoted to actual life, with all its imperfections. That is why, when the Whig is extinct and the Liberal as rare as the whooping crane, the Conservative continues perennial. He lives for the simple, organic things, children, dogs, the elm on the skyline, the water lapping at the rock. He is interested in family; he instinctively wants to know who your people were and where you come from. He sees society as persons knit by kinship and neighbourhood. And, he endows society and nation with the same sense of organic life, and believes that men in their particular communities are members one of another.

That is how I define the conservative.

According to Morton, 'the conservative . . . is devoted to actual life, with all its imperfections'. His meaning is plain enough: conservatives don't dream wildly about a perfect world, but instead appreciate and cherish what the real world has to offer. This idea also informs the writings of Michael Oakeshott, whom many regard as the most outstanding English conservative thinker of the twentieth century. Oakeshott says that conservatism is not so much a philosophical theory as it is a concrete disposition grounded in a powerful sense of attachment to familiar things. This attachment is deep and intense, not because its objects are perfect, but because they are *known*—and known as *good*.

From 'On Being Conservative'
By Michael Oakeshott

The general characteristics of this disposition are not difficult to discern, although they have often been mistaken. They centre upon a propensity to use and to enjoy what is available rather than to wish for or to look for something else; to delight in what is present rather than what was or what may be. Reflection may bring to light an appropriate gratefulness for what is available, and consequently the acknowledgement of a gift or an inheritance from the past; but there is no mere idolizing of what is past and gone. What is esteemed is the present; and it is esteemed not on account of its connections with a remote antiquity, nor because it is recognized to be more admirable than any possible alternative, but on account of its familiarity. . . .

To be conservative, then, is to prefer the familiar to the unknown, to prefer the tried to the untried, fact to mystery, the actual to the possible, the limited to the unbounded, the near to the distant, the sufficient to the superabundant, the convenient to the perfect, present laughter to utopian bliss. Familiar relationships and loyalties will be preferred to the allure of more profitable attachments; to acquire and to enlarge will be less important than to keep, to cultivate, and to enjoy; the grief of loss will be more acute than the excitement of novelty or promise. It is to be equal to one's own fortune, to live at the level of one's own means, to be content with the want of greater perfection which belongs alike to oneself and one's circumstances. With some people this is itself a choice; in others it is a disposition which appears, frequently or less frequently, in their preferences and aversions, and is not itself chosen or specifically cultivated.

- What does Burke's interpretation of the social contract add to our understanding of society as a contract?
- What does being conservative mean to Morton and to Oakeshott? How are their conceptions of conservatism similar? How do they differ?
- What does justice mean for conservatives? To whom do they give the power to decide what is just?

F. Two Contemporary Theories of Justice: John Rawls and Robert Nozick

In the last few decades, a very different conception of justice has once again begun to dominate—a set of views that recognizes the desirability of serving every individual's interests while having a primary concern for justice, not in terms of utility but in terms of *rights*. Thus, public interest is important, but respect for every individual's rights is even more important. This view dates back (at least) to Kant, who defended the notions of 'duty' and 'obligation' as morally basic to any concern for utility. In its modern conception, this view is most ably defended by Harvard philosopher John Rawls in his seminal work entitled *Theory of Justice*.

For nearly six hundred pages, Rawls essentially defends two principles in order of priority. The first (and more fundamental) principle asserts that we all have basic rights and equal rights, in particular with reference to our personal freedom. The second principle (which assumes the first) asserts that although we cannot expect everyone in society to enjoy equal wealth, equal health, and equal opportunities, we can and should insist that all inequalities are to every individual's advantage. For example, it should not be such that society allows that 'the rich get richer and the poor get poorer'. Rawls' actual statement from *Theory of Justice* is as follows:

*First: each person is to have an equal right to the most extensive basic **liberty** compatible with a similar liberty for others.*

Second: social and economic inequalities are to be arranged so that they are both (a) reasonably expected to be to everyone's advantage, and (b) attached to positions and offices open to all.

Rawls' justification for establishing the rationality and necessity of these 'liberal' principles derives from his view that all of us (or our ancestors) might be in 'the original position'—like Hobbes' 'state of nature'—and 'unencumbered' by any of our particular traits or interests. In such a situation, what would be rational for us to choose by way of the principles according to which society should be run? Because we do not know, in the essential sense, who we will be in that society, it does us no good to adopt principles that benefit the persons we are now. For example, in a society composed entirely of purple people and green people (remembering that in the original position we do not know which we will be), it would only be rational, Rawls argues, to enact a law that would treat all people equally, whether purple or green. It is much like (but much more complicated and uncertain than) the childhood example involving one of us being asked to cut a pie into sections, giving everyone else first choice. The only rational decision—even if you suspect that the other children are dullards—is to divide the pie equally. So too, the aim of Rawls' dual principles is to cut for all of us—if not equal pieces of the social pie, at least pieces that are as equal as possible.

The following selection is from one of Rawls' early essays.

LIBERTY

In the sense of *political freedom*, the ability to act without restraint or threat of punishment.

From 'Justice as Fairness'
By John Rawls

Inequalities are arbitrary unless it is reasonable to expect that they will work out for everyone's advantage.

Throughout I consider justice only as a virtue of social institutions, or what I shall call practices.[2] The principles of justice are regarded as formulating restrictions as to how practices may define positions and offices, and assign thereto powers and liabilities, rights and duties. Justice as a virtue of particular actions or of persons I do not take up at all. It is important to distinguish these various subjects of justice, since the meaning of the concept varies according to whether it is applied to practices, particular actions, or persons. These meanings are, indeed, connected, but they are not identical. I shall confine my discussion to the sense of justice as applied to practices, since this sense is the basic one. Once it is understood, the other senses should go quite easily.

The conception of justice which I want to develop may be stated in the form of two principles as follows: first, each person participating in a practice, or affected by it, has an equal right to the most extensive liberty compatible with a like liberty for all; and second, inequalities are arbitrary unless it is reasonable to expect that they will work out for everyone's advantage, and provided the positions and offices to which they attach, or from which they may be gained, are open to all. These principles express justice as a complex of three ideas: liberty, equality, and reward for services contributing to the common good.

The term 'person' is to be construed variously depending on the circumstances. On some occasions it will mean human individuals, but in others it may refer to nations, provinces, business firms, churches, teams, and so on. The principles of justice apply in all these instances, although there is a certain logical priority to the case of human individuals. As I shall use the term 'person', it will be ambiguous in the manner indicated.

The first principle holds, of course, only if other things are equal: that is, while there must always be a justification for departing from the initial position of equal liberty (which is defined by the pattern of rights and duties, powers and liabilities, established by a practice), and the burden or proof is placed on him who would depart from it, nevertheless, there can be,

and often there is, a justification for doing so. Now, that similar particular cases, as defined by a practice, should be treated similarly as they arise, is part of the very concept of a practice; it is involved in the notion of an activity in accordance with rules. The first principle expresses an analogous conception, but as applied to the structure of practices themselves. It holds, for example, that there is a presumption against the distinctions and classifications made by legal systems and other practices to the extent that they infringe on the original and equal liberty of the persons participating in them. The second principle defines how this presumption may be rebutted.

It might be argued at this point that justice requires only an equal liberty. If, however, a greater liberty were possible for all without loss or conflict, then it would be irrational to settle on a lesser liberty. There is no reason for circumscribing rights unless their exercise would be incompatible, or would render the practice defining them less effective. Therefore no serious distortion of the concept of justice is likely to follow from including within it the concept of the greatest equal liberty.

The second principle defines what sorts of inequalities are permissible; it specifies how the presumption laid down by the first principle may be put aside. Now by inequalities it is best to understand not *any* differences between offices and positions, but differences in the benefits and burdens attached to them either directly or indirectly, such as prestige and wealth, or liability to taxation and compulsory services. Players in a game do not protest against there being different positions, such as batter, pitcher, catcher, and the like, nor to there being various privileges and powers as specified by the rules; nor do the citizens of a country object to there being the different offices of government such as president, senator, governor, judge, and so on, each with their special rights and duties. It is not differences in the resulting distribution established by a practice, or made possible by it, of the things men strive to attain or avoid. Thus they may complain about the pattern of honours and rewards set up by

(Continued)

a practice (e.g. the privileges and salaries of government officials) or they may object to the distribution of power and wealth which results from the various ways in which men avail themselves of the opportunities allowed by it (e.g. the concentration of wealth which may develop in a free price system allowing large entrepreneurial or speculative gains).

It should be noted that the second principle holds that an inequality is allowed only if there is reason to believe that the practice with the inequality, or resulting from it, will work for the advantage of *every* party engaging in it. Here it is important to stress that *every* party must gain from the inequality.

Since the principle applies to practices, it implies that the representative man in every office or position defined by a practice, when he views it as a going concern, must find it reasonable to prefer his condition and prospects with the inequality to what they would be under the practice without it. The principle excludes, therefore, the justification of inequalities on the grounds that the disadvantages of those in one position are outweighed by the greater advantages of those in another position. This rather simple restriction is the main modification I wish to make in the utilitarian principle as usually understood.

> • What does Rawls mean by 'justice as fairness'? When are inequalities tolerable?

Rawls, like Hume in particular, ties the concept of 'justice' to the concept of 'equality'. The main theme of his work is an attempt to develop this connection and to state precisely the kind of 'equality' that is most important for justice. Against the laissez-faire idea that people are equal in legal rights and 'opportunities' alone, without any right to material goods and social services, he argues that a just society will consider the welfare of the worst-off members of society as an obligation. Here he differs with Mill and the utilitarians, who would say that such help is a matter of utility; for Rawls, it is more like a Kantian duty. Moreover, Rawls clearly distinguishes himself from socialists, who would argue that all property should be shared; he says only that it is obligatory to help out the worst-off members of society. Justice, in his definition, does not equate *fair distribution* with *equal distribution*. In Rawls' liberalism, therefore, equality becomes a far more complex notion than simple egalitarianism often takes it to be.

Is equality the primary concern of justice? Even Rawls admits that a society in which everyone has exactly equal shares of social goods is impossible. But why is it impossible? We can all imagine a situation—and some radical thinkers even propose it—in which all material goods (at least) would be collected and cataloged by the state, then redistributed to every citizen in precisely equal shares. Most of us, including Rawls, find this suggestion intolerable. Yet why, if it realizes the equality that justice demands? Something stops us, and it is not simply the idea that we might lose our own goods, for many of us would in fact benefit from such a redistribution scheme. What bothers us initially is the very idea of anyone, including (perhaps especially) the government, intruding into our lives and exerting such power. However, we also sense that such a scheme for redistributing wealth violates something very basic to justice—namely, the rights we have to our possessions. Rawls, of course, gives rights top priority in his theory; but they are rights having to do with liberty in general, not rights having to do with possession as such. We all feel, with whatever reservations, that we have a right to what we earn and that we have a right to keep what we already possess. We resent that the government takes from us a substantial percentage of our earnings to use in ways not directly (or perhaps even indirectly) under our control. And we believe we have the right, for instance, to the modest sum that grandfather left us in his will (presumably the residue of earlier taxation), even though we did not earn it in any sense. Thus many philosophers have become increasingly aware of another kind of right that is not treated adequately by such liberal theories of Rawls'—in fact, a right that goes against the modest scheme of redistribution (for example, through taxation) encouraged by his principles. This other kind of right, known as **entitlement**, gives rise to a very different kind of theory of justice.

The popular name for this alternative theory is **libertarianism**. The basic idea, an 'entitlement theory', puts the right to private property first and foremost and couples with it a deep skepticism as to the wisdom or fairness of government. The original entitlement theory was developed by John Locke, who argued that the right to private property was so basic that it preceded any social conventions or laws and existed quite independent of any government or state. What gave a person the right to a piece of property (particularly land), Locke argued, was that he had 'mixed his labour with it', in other words, worked with it and improved it and so had the right to it. In today's terms—where what is at stake consists mainly of salaries and what we can buy with them—we would say that a person has the basic right to keep what he or she earns. Recently, Locke's theory has been updated considerably and argued forcefully by Rawls' younger Harvard colleague Robert Nozick. In *Anarchy, State, and Utopia*, Nozick argues for the entitlement theory and against any attempt to set 'patterns' of fair distribution, for the enforcement of any such pattern must result in the violation of people's rights.

> **LIBERTARIANISM**
>
> The view that government interference with individual freedom should be kept to a minimum.

From *Anarchy, State, and Utopia*
By Robert Nozick

A minimal state, limited to the narrow functions of protection against force, theft, fraud, enforcement of contracts, and so on, is justified.

Individuals have rights, and there are things no person or group may do to them (without violating their rights). So strong and far-reaching are these rights that they raise the question of what, if anything, the state and its officials may do. How much room do individual rights leave for the state? . . . Our main conclusions about the state are that a minimal state, limited to the narrow functions of protection against force, theft, fraud, enforcement of contracts, and so on, is justified; that any more extensive state will violate persons' rights to not be forced to do certain things, and is unjustified; and that the minimal state is inspiring as well as right. Two noteworthy implications are that the state may not use its coercive apparatus for the purpose of getting some citizens to aid others, or in order to prohibit activities to people for their *own* good or protection.

* * *

The Entitlement Theory

The subject of justice in holdings consists of three major topics. The first is the *original acquisition of holdings*, the appropriation of unheld things. This includes the issues of how unheld things may come to be held, the process, or processes, by which unheld things may come to be held, the things that may come to be held by these processes, the extent of what comes to be held by a particular process, and so on. We shall refer to the complicated truth about this topic, which we shall not formulate here, as the principle of justice in acquisition. The second topic concerns the *transfer of holdings* from one person to another. By what processes may a person transfer holdings to another? How may a person acquire a holding from another who holds it? Under this topic come general descriptions of voluntary exchange, and gift and (on the other hand) fraud, as well as reference to particular conventional details fixed upon in a given society. The complicated truth about this subject (with placeholders for conventional details) we shall call the principle of justice in transfer. (And we shall suppose it also includes principles governing how a person may divest himself of a holding, passing it into an unheld state.)

(Continued)

If the world were wholly just, the following inductive definition would exhaustively cover the subject of justice in holdings.

1. A person who acquires a holding in accordance with the principle of justice in acquisition is entitled to that holding.
2. A person who acquires a holding in accordance with the principle of justice in transfer, from someone else entitled to the holding, is entitled to the holding.
3. No one is entitled to a holding except by (repeated) applications of 1 and 2.

The complete principle of distributive justice would say simply that a distribution is just if everyone is entitled to the holdings they possess under the distribution.

A distribution is just if it arises from another just distribution by legitimate means. The legitimate means of moving from one distribution to another are specified by the principle of justice in transfer. The legitimate first 'moves' are specified by the principle of justice in acquisition. Whatever arises from a just situation by just steps is itself just.

* * *

Not all actual situations are generated in accordance with the two principles of justice in holdings: the principle of justice in acquisition and the principle of justice in transfer. Some people steal from others, or defraud them, or enslave them, seizing their product and preventing them from living as they choose, or forcibly exclude others from competing in exchanges. None of these are permissible modes of transition from one situation to another. And some persons acquire holdings by means not sanctioned by the principle of justice in acquisition. The existence of past injustice (previous violations of the first two principles of justice in holdings) raises the third major topic under justice in holdings: the rectification of injustice in holdings. If past injustice has shaped present holdings in various ways, some identifiable and some not, what now, if anything, ought to be done to rectify these injustices? What obligations do the performers of injustice have toward those whose position is worse than it would have been had the injustice not been done? Or, than it would have had compensation been paid promptly? How, if at all, do things change if the beneficiaries and those made worse off are not the direct parties in the act of injustice, but, for example, their descendants? Is an injustice done to someone whose holding was itself based upon an unrectified injustice? How far back must one go in wiping clean the historical slate of injustices? What may victims of injustice permissibly do in order to rectify the injustices being done to them, including the many injustices done by persons acting through their government? I do not know of a thorough or theoretically sophisticated treatment of such issues. Idealizing greatly, let us suppose theoretical investigations will produce a principle of rectification. This principle uses historical information about previous situations and injustices done in them (as defined by the first two principles of justice and rights against interference), and information about the actual course of events that flowed from these injustices, until the present, and it yields a description (or descriptions) of holdings in the society.

* * *

Historical Principles and End-Result Principles

The general outlines of the entitlement theory illuminate the nature and defects of other conceptions of distributive justice. The entitlement theory of justice in distribution is *historical*; whether a distribution is just depends upon how it came about. In contrast, *current time-slice principles* of justice hold that the justice of a distribution is determined by how things are distributed (who has what) as judged by some *structural* principle(s) of just distribution. A utilitarian who judges between any two distributions by seeing which has the greater sum of utility and, if the sums tie, applies some fixed equality criterion to choose the more equal distribution, would hold a current time-slice principle of justice. As would someone who had a fixed schedule of trade-offs between the sum of happiness and equality. According to a current time-slice principle, all that needs to be looked at, in judging the justice of a distribution, is who ends up with what; in comparing any two distributions one need look only at the matrix presenting the distributions. No further information need be fed into a principle of justice. It is a consequence of such principles of justice that any two structurally identical distributions are equally just. (Two distributions are structurally identical if they present the same profile, but perhaps have different persons occupying the particular slots. My having ten and your having five, and my having five and your having ten are structurally identical distributions.) Welfare economics is the theory of current time-slice principles of justice. The subject is conceived as operating on matrices representing only current information about distribution. This, as well as some of the usual conditions (for example, the choice of distribution is invariant under relabelling of columns), guarantees that welfare economics will be a current time-slice theory, with all of its inadequacies.

Most persons do not accept current time-slice principles as constituting the whole story about distributive shares. They think it relevant in assessing the justice of a situation to consider not only the distribution it embodies, but also how that distribution came about. If some persons are in prison for murder or war crimes, we do not say that to assess the justice of the distribution in the society we must look only at what this person has, and that person has, and that person has, . . . at the current time. We think it relevant to ask whether someone did something so that he *deserved* to be punished, deserved to have a lower share. Most will agree to the relevance of further information with regard to punishments and penalties. Consider also desired things. One traditional socialist view is that workers are entitled to the product and full fruits of their labour; they have earned it; a distribution is unjust if it does not give the workers what they are entitled to. Such entitlements are based upon some past history. No socialist holding this view would find it comforting to be told that because the actual distribution *A* happens to coincide structurally with the one he desires *D*, therefore is no less just than *D*; . . . This socialist rightly, in my view, holds onto the notions of earning, producing, entitlement, desert, and so forth, and he rejects current time-slice principles that look only to the structure of the resulting set of holdings. . . . His mistake lies in his view of what entitlements arise out of what sorts of productive processes.

- How does the entitlement theory differ from Rawls' conception of justice as fairness? Which view is more similar to Aristotle's conception of justice?

G. Socialism: Equality and Community

While Rawls' notion of 'justice as fairness' has been attacked by some political philosophers— such as the state-wary libertarians for whom Nozick is a hero—for being too egalitarian, others have said that it is not egalitarian enough. While socialists would agree with many of Rawls' assertions—especially his insistence on the equal division of the 'social pie'—they would have a more restricted definition of the types of inequalities that are acceptable within a just society. In particular, for socialists absolute justice can be found only in a social system in which everyone is *absolutely equal* in terms of *opportunity*.

To get a sense of how socialist theory defines justice and equality, we will turn to ingenious but accessible defence of a radically egalitarian socialist framework offered by G.A. Cohen, a distinguished Canadian philosopher very sympathetic to Marxism. What Cohen calls his 'preliminary case for socialism' begins with a thought experiment. Imagine, he says, that we are going on a camping trip together. If our trip is going to be a success, we shall need to cooperate in certain ways. For example, we will have to share the work, divide up the chores, and make use of the possessions each of us brings on the trip. (I have a tent, you have a cooler, he has a canoe, she has a fishing rod, they have life jackets, and so on). Ask yourself: How should we run things? That is, what principles should we follow for the duration of the trip if we want it to be enjoyable for all concerned? According to Cohen, the principles we find it natural and reasonable to follow when we organize our camping trip turn out to be socialist principles. To see why he is persuaded that this is so, consider what he says about how camping trips typically work:

From 'Why Not Socialism?'
By G.A. Cohen

Socialist equality of opportunity seeks to correct for all unchosen disadvantages, disadvantages, that is, for which the agent cannot herself reasonably be held responsible . . . .

You and I and a number of other people go on a camping trip. There is no hierarchy among us; our common aim is that each of us should have a good time, doing, so far as possible, the things that he or she likes best (some of those things we do together; others we do individually). We have facilities with which to carry out our enterprise: we have, for example, pots and pans, oil, coffee, fishing rods, canoes, a soccer ball, decks of cards, and so forth. And, as is usual on camping trips, we avail ourselves of those facilities collectively: even if they are privately owned things, they are under collective control for the duration of the trip, and we have shared understandings about who is going to use them when, under what circumstances, and why. Somebody fishes, somebody else prepares the food, and another person cooks it. People who hate cooking but enjoy washing up may do all the washing up, and so on. There are plenty of differences, but our mutual understandings, and the spirit of the enterprise, ensure that there are no inequalities to which anyone could mount a principled objection.

It is commonly true on camping trips, and on certain small-scale projects of other kinds, that we co-operate within a concern that, so far as is possible, everybody has a roughly similar opportunity to flourish. In these contexts most people, even most *anti*-egalitarians, accept, indeed, take for granted, a norm of equality. So deeply do most people take it for granted that there is no occasion to question it: to question it would contradict the spirit of the trip.

You could imagine a camping trip where everyone asserts her rights over the pieces of equipment and the talents that she brings, and where bargaining proceeds with respect to who is going to pay what to whom to be allowed, for example, to use a knife to peel the potatoes, and how much he is then going to charge others for those now peeled potatoes which he bought in an unpeeled condition from another camper, and so on. You could base a camping trip on the principles of market exchange and strictly private ownership of the required facilities.

Most people would hate that. Most people would be more drawn to the first kind of camping trip than to the second, primarily on grounds of fellowship. And this means that most people are drawn to the socialist ideal, at least in certain restricted settings.

To reinforce this point, here are some conjectures about how most people would react in various imaginable camping scenarios.

a. Harry loves fishing, and Harry is very good at fishing. Consequently, he brings back more fish than others do. Harry says: 'It's unfair, how we're running things. I should have better fish when we dine. I should have only perch, not the mix of perch and catfish that we've all been having.' But his fellow campers say: 'Oh, for heaven's sake, Harry, don't be such a shmuck. You sweat and strain no more than the rest of us do. So, you're very good at fishing. We don't begrudge you that special endowment, which is, quite properly, a source of satisfaction to you, but why should we *reward* that pre-eminence?'

b. Following a three-hour, time-off-for-personal-exploration period, an excited Sylvia returns to the campsite and announces: 'I've found a huge apple tree, full of perfect apples.' 'Great,' others exclaim, 'now we can all have apple sauce, and apple pie, and apple strudel!' 'Provided, of course,' so Sylvia rejoins, 'that you reduce my labour burden, and/or furnish me with more room in the tent, and/or with more bacon at breakfast.' Her claim to (a kind of) ownership of the tree revolts the others, but exactly such a claim, expressed or implicit, is, of course, at the heart of the constitution of private property: private property renews itself, every day, because such a claim is enforced, and/or accepted.

c. Morgan recognizes the campsite. 'Hey, this is where my father camped thirty years ago. This is where he dug a special little pond on the other side of that hill, and stocked it with specially good fish. Dad knew I might come camping here one day, and he did all that so that I could eat better when I'm here. Great. Now I can have better food than you guys have.'

The rest frown, or smile, at Morgan's greed.

Note that Cohen isn't assuming that camping is something we all do or should enjoy. His point is about how such trips should be organized, not about whether anyone should want to go on one. Cohen's key contention is simple: *if* you were going on a camping trip, and *if* you wanted everybody to have a good time on that trip, then the way of doing things that he describes has a great deal to recommend it.

Of course, not everybody likes camping trips. I do not myself enjoy them much, because I am not outdoorsy, or, at any rate, I am not outdoorsy overnight-wise. There is a limit to the outdoorsiness to which an urban Jew can be expected to submit: I would rather have my communism in the warmth of All Souls College than in the wet of the Laurentians, and I love modern plumbing. But the question I am asking is not: wouldn't you like to go on a camping trip? but: isn't this the socialist way, with collective property and planned mutual giving, rather obviously the right way to run a camping trip, whether or not you actually like camping.

Now, Cohen thinks that his ideal camping trip realizes two socialist principles. The first is a principle of equality; the second, a principle of community. Here is what Cohen says about his first principle—that of 'socialist equality of opportunity':

Socialist equality of opportunity seeks to correct for *all* unchosen disadvantages, disadvantages, that is, for which the agent cannot herself reasonably be held responsible, whether they be disadvantages that reflect social misfortune or disadvantages that reflect natural misfortune. When socialist equality of opportunity prevails, differences of outcome reflect nothing but differences of taste and choice, not differences in natural and social capacities and powers.

So, for example, under socialist equality of opportunity income differences are acceptable when they reflect nothing but different income/leisure preferences. People differ in their tastes, not only across consumer items, but also between working only a few hours and consuming rather little on the one hand, and working long hours and consuming rather more on the other. Preferences across income and leisure are not in principle different from preferences across apples and oranges, and there can be no objection to differences in people's benefits and burdens that reflect nothing but different preferences, and do not, therefore, constitute inequalities of benefits and burdens.

Let me spell out the analogy at which I have just gestured. A table is laden with a dozen apples and a dozen oranges. Each of us is entitled to take six pieces of fruit, with apples and oranges appearing in any combination to make up that six. Suppose, now, I complain that Sheila has five apples whereas I have only three.

Then it should extinguish my (totally idiotic) sense of grievance if you point out that Sheila has only one orange whereas I have three, and that I could have had a bundle just like Sheila's had I forgone a couple of oranges. So, similarly, under a system in which each gets the same income per hour but can choose how many hours she works, it is not an intelligible complaint that people who work longer hours have more take-home pay than others. The income/leisure trade-off is relevantly like the apples/oranges trade-off: that I have more income than you do no more shows, just as such, that we are unequally placed than my having four apples from the table when you have two represents, just as such, an objectionable inequality.

Now, you might think that I have misused the term 'socialist' in the phrase 'socialist equality of opportunity', for the simple reason that it is a familiar socialist policy to insist on equality both of income and of hours of work: have not kibbutzim, those paradigms of socialism, worked that way?

In reply, I would distinguish between socialist principles and socialist modes of organization, the first, of course, being the putative justifications of the second. What I call 'socialist equality of opportunity' is, as expounded here, a principle, which, so I say, is satisfied on the camping trip, but I have not said what modes of organization would, and would not, satisfy it in general. And, although the suggested

(Continued)

strictly equal work/wage regime would indeed contradict it, I acknowledge that socialists have advocated such regimes, and I have no wish, or need, to deny that those regimes can be called socialist work/wage regimes. What I do need to insist is that such systems contradict the fundamental principles animating socialists, when those principles are fully thought through. No defensible fundamental principle of equality, or, indeed, of community, taken by itself, warrants such a system, which may nevertheless be justifiably advocated by socialists as an appropriate 'second-best' in light of the constraints of a particular place and time.

What I have called socialist equality of opportunity is consistent with three forms of inequality, the second and third forms being sub-types of one type. The first form of inequality is unproblematic, the second form is a bit problematic, and the third is very problematic.

(i) The first type, or form, of inequality is unproblematic because it does not constitute an inequality, all things considered. Variety of preference across lifestyle options means that some people will have more goods of a certain sort than others do, but that is no inequality to which anyone can object when those who have fewer such goods have simply chosen differently, and therefore have more goods of another sort. That was the lesson of the apples/oranges example, and of its application to income/leisure choices.

(ii) The second type of inequality *is* an inequality, all things considered. For socialist equality of opportunity tolerates inequalities of outcome, inequalities, that is, of benefit in outcome, where those inequalities reflect the genuine choices of parties who are initially equally placed and who may therefore reasonably be held responsible for the consequences of those choices. And this type of inequality takes two forms: inequality due to differences in amounts of *chosen effort*, and inequality due to differences in amounts of *chosen option luck*.

(ii-a) To illustrate the first of these forms, imagine that one apple/orange chooser (but not the other) carelessly waits so long that, by the time he picks up the number of them to which he is entitled, they have lost their full savour: the resulting inequality of benefit represents no grievance. And the same holds true for someone in a work/pay regime whose ultimate fortune is inferior because she did not bother to examine her job opportunities properly.

These inequalities of outcome are justified by differential exercises of effort and/or care by people, who are, initially, absolutely equally placed, and who are equal even in their capacities to expend effort and care. If you believe (against the grain, I wager, of your reactions to people in ordinary life) that there is no such thing, ultimately, as being 'truly responsible', you believe that greater negligence, for example, can reflect nothing but a smaller capacity for attentiveness, in the given circumstances, than others have, which should not be penalized, then you will not countenance this second form of inequality. But even if, like me, you are not firmly disposed to disallow it, then the question remains, how large is this inequality likely to be? That is a very difficult question, and my own view, or hope, is that it would not be very large, on its own. It can, however, contribute to very high degrees of inequality when it is in synergy with the third and truly problematic form of inequality that is consistent with socialist equality of opportunity.

(ii-b) That truly problematic inequality, the substantial inequality that is consistent with socialist equality of opportunity, is the inequality that reflects differences in what Ronald Dworkin calls option luck. The paradigm case of option luck is a deliberate gamble. We start out equally placed, each with $100, and we are relevantly identical in all respects, in character, in talents, and in circumstances. One of the features that we share is a penchant for gambling, so we flip a coin on the understanding that I give you $50 if it comes up heads, and you give me $50 if it comes up tails. I end up with $150 and you end up with $50, and with no extra any things to offset that monetary shortfall.

This inequality is consistent with socialist equality of opportunity, and it does not occur only as a result of gambling narrowly so called. Some market inequalities have that sort of option luck genesis, or are sufficiently marked by option luck, within a complex causal story, that justice, understood as socialist equality of opportunity, cannot condemn them, or, better, cannot condemn them entirely. Such inequalities are broadly compatible with, and, indeed, justified by, socialist equality of opportunity.

Although inequalities of type (ii) are not condemned by justice, they are nevertheless repugnant to socialists, when they obtain on a sufficiently large scale, because they then contradict community: community is put under strain when large inequalities come to obtain.

And this brings us to Cohen's second socialist principle: the 'principle of community'.

The sway of socialist equality of opportunity must therefore be tempered by a principle of community, if society is to display the socialist character that makes the camping trip attractive.

'Community' can mean many things, but the requirement of community that is central here is that people care about, and, where necessary and possible, care for, one another, and, too, care that they care about one another. There are two modes of communal caring that I want to discuss here. The first is the mode that curbs socialist equality of opportunity. The second mode of communal caring is not strictly required for equality, but it is nevertheless of supreme importance in the socialist conception.

We cannot enjoy full community, you and I, if you make, and keep, say, ten times as much money as I do, because my life will then labour under challenges that you will never face, challenges that you could help me to cope with, but do not, because you keep your money. Compare the case where you and I have radically different physical vulnerabilities. You have serious ones, and I could assist you, but I turn my back on you: community cannot, therefore, obtain between us. Analogously, widely divergent incomes produce widely divergent social vulnerabilities, and they, too, destroy community, when those who could attenuate them let them persist.

To be sure, the sick and the healthy can enjoy community with each other. But, so I am suggesting, they can do so only when the healthy are fully prepared, as they may be, to do what they can for the sick, within reasonable limits of self-sacrifice. And if the rich do what they can for the poor, even within reasonable limits of self-sacrifice, then they will give away rather a lot of their money, and community will indeed obtain, but inequality will be reduced. Community is consistent with widely different earnings, but not, in relevantly realistic ranges, with, so to speak, widely different keepings, and, therefore, widely different powers to care for oneself, to protect and care for offspring, to avoid danger, and so forth.

So, to return to the camping trip, if we eat meagrely, but you have your special high-grade fish pond, which you got neither by inheritance nor by chicanery nor as a result of the brute luck of your superior exploratory talent, but as a result of an absolutely innocent option luck that no one can impugn from the point of view of justice: you got it through a lottery that we all entered; then, even so, even though there is no injustice here, you are cut off from our common life, and the ideal of community condemns that.

The other expression of communal caring instantiated on the camping trip is a communal form of reciprocity, which contrasts with the market form of reciprocity, as I shall presently explain. Where starting points are equal, and there are independent (of equality of opportunity) limits put on inequality of outcome, communal reciprocity is not required for equality, but it is nevertheless required for human relationships to take a desirable form.

Communal reciprocity is the non-market principle according to which I serve you not because of what I can get in return but because you need my service, and you, for the same reason, serve me. Communal reciprocity is not the same thing as market reciprocity, since the market motivates productive contribution not on the basis of commitment to one's fellow human beings and a desire to serve them while being served by them, but on the basis of cash reward. The immediate motive to productive activity in a market society is typically some mixture of greed and fear, in proportions that vary with the details of a person's market position and personal character. In greed, other people are seen as possible sources of enrichment, and in fear they are seen as threats. These are horrible ways of seeing other people, however much we have become habituated and inured to them, as a result of centuries of capitalist civilization.

I said that, within communal reciprocity, I produce in a spirit of commitment to my fellow human beings: I desire to serve them while being served by them. To be sure, there is, in such motivation, an expectation of reciprocation, but it differs critically from the expectation of reciprocation in market motivation. If I am a marketeer, then I am willing to serve, but only in order to be served: I would not serve if doing so were not a means to get service. Accordingly, I give as little service as I can in exchange for as much service as I can get: I want to buy cheap and sell dear. I serve others either in

(Continued)

order to get something that I desire—that is the greed motivation—or in order to ensure that something I seek to avoid is avoided—that is the fear motivation. A marketeer, considered just as such, does not value cooperation with others for its own sake: she does not value the conjunction, serve-and-be-served, as such.

A non-marketeer relishes cooperation itself: what I want, as a non-marketeer, is that we serve each other. To be sure, I serve you in the expectation that (if you are able to) you will also serve me. I do not want to be a sucker who serves you regardless of whether you are going to serve me (unless you are unable to), but I nevertheless find value in each part of the conjunction—I serve you and you serve me—and in that conjunction itself I do not regard the first part—I serve you—as simply a means to my real end, which is that you serve me. The relationship between us under communal reciprocity is not the market-instrumental one in which I give because I get, but the wholly non-instrumental relationship in which I give because you need, or want, and in which I enjoy a comparable generosity from you.

Because motivation in market exchange consists of greed and fear, nobody cares fundamentally, within the economic game, about how well or badly anyone other than herself fares. You cooperate with other people not because you believe that cooperating with other people is a good thing in itself, not because you want yourself and the other person to flourish, but because you seek to gain and you know that you can do so only if you cooperate with others. In every type of society people perforce provision one another: a society is a network of mutual provision. But in market society, that mutuality is only a by-product of a wholly unmutual and non-reciprocating attitude.

And this brings us, at long last, to Cohen's challenge. It might be put this way: If we are inclined to endorse these two principles of equality and community—and Cohen's camping trip example is presented as evidence that we *are* so inclined—then why shouldn't we apply them to our society as a whole? In other words, why not accept socialism?

- What is Cohen's principle of equality? What is the principle of community? Do you think that these principles are essential to a just society?
- Do you agree with Cohen that his example of the camping trip shows that we are inclined to favour his principles of equality and community? If so, why? If not, what conclusion do you draw from his example?
- How do you think Nozick would respond to Cohen's argument? How do you think Rawls would respond?

Socialism, as propounded by philosophers like Cohen, is an abstract theory, wrought with nuanced logic and subtle distinctions. For Canadian politician Tommy Douglas, however, socialism was a concrete, all-consuming passion that grew out of an unshakeable faith in fairness. Inspired in part by his religious convictions (he was an ordained Baptist minister), Douglas spent decades trying to make Canada a fairer place for the poor and the vulnerable, particularly where access to medical services was concerned. As premier of Saskatchewan, the first province to have its own public health insurance program (in 1961), Douglas insisted that no one should be turned away by a doctor or hospital because of an inability to pay. As federal leader of the CCF (Cooperative Commonwealth Federation), a forerunner of today's NDP, he was convinced that so-called 'ordinary Canadians' needed a socialist party to look after their interests. But why did he think this? The answer can be found in Douglas' charming fable 'Mouseland'.

From 'Mouseland'
By Tommy Douglas

Watch out for the little fellow with an idea.

It's the story of a place called Mouseland. Mouseland was a place where all the little mice lived and played, were born and died. And they lived much the same as you and I do.

They even had a Parliament. And every four years they had an election. Used to walk to the polls and cast their ballots. Some of them even got a ride to the polls. And got a ride for the next four years afterward too. Just like you and me. And every time on election day all the little mice used to go to the ballot box and they used to elect a government. A government made up of big, fat, black cats.

Now if you think it strange that mice should elect a government made up of cats, you just look at the history of Canada for last ninety years and maybe you'll see that they weren't any stupider than we are.

Now I'm not saying anything against the cats. They were nice fellows. They conducted their government with dignity. They passed good laws— that is, laws that were good for cats. But the laws that were good for cats weren't very good for mice. One of the laws said that mouseholes had to be big enough so a cat could get his paw in. Another law said that mice could only travel at certain speeds— so that a cat could get his breakfast without too much effort.

All the laws were good laws. For cats. But, oh, they were hard on the mice. And life was getting harder and harder. And when the mice couldn't put up with it any more, they decided something had to be done about it. So they went en masse to the polls. They voted the black cats out. They put in the white cats.

Now the white cats had put up a terrific campaign. They said: 'All that Mouseland needs is more vision.' They said: 'The trouble with Mouseland is those round mouseholes we got. If you put us in we'll establish square mouseholes.' And they did. And the square mouseholes were twice as big as the round mouseholes, and now the cat could get both his paws in. And life was tougher than ever.

And when they couldn't take that anymore, they voted the white cats out and put the black ones in again. Then they went back to the white cats. Then to the black cats. They even tried half black cats and half white cats. And they called that coalition. They even got one government made up of cats with spots on them: they were cats that tried to make a noise like a mouse but ate like a cat.

You see, my friends, the trouble wasn't with the colour of the cat. The trouble was that they were cats. And because they were cats, they naturally looked after cats instead of mice.

Presently there came along one little mouse who had an idea. My friends, watch out for the little fellow with an idea. And he said to the other mice, 'Look fellows, why do we keep on electing a government made up of cats? Why don't we elect a government made up of mice?' 'Oh,' they said, 'he's a Bolshevik. Lock him up!' So they put him in jail.

But I want to remind you: that you can lock up a mouse or a man but you can't lock up an idea.

- Who do you think the mice are supposed to represent? What about the cats? What do you think the difference is between the white cats and the black cats?
- Do you agree with Douglas that it is impossible for the political equivalent of cats to look after the political equivalent of mice? Why or why not? What would justice mean in such a society?
- Why do the mice react against 'the one little mouse who had an idea'? What does their reaction suggest about the possibility of individual freedom in such a society?

H. Justice or Care: A Feminist Perspective

The debate about justice has gone on for almost 2,500 years. But it might be noted that most of the voices in the debate have been male voices, and this raises the question whether there is some male bias to the perspective in which justice has been debated, or, indeed, some male bias in the very notion of justice itself. Cheshire Calhoun has argued that this is the case. Here is an excerpt of her argument.

From 'Justice, Care, Gender Bias'
By Cheshire Calhoun

The exclusion of the care perspective from the ethics of justice simultaneously undermines the adequacy of the ethics of justice . . . and renders it gender biased.

Carol Gilligan poses two separable, though in her work not separate, challenges to moral theory. The first is a challenge to the adequacy of current moral theory that is dominated by the ethics of justice. The ethics of justice, on her view, excludes some dimensions of moral experience, such as contextual decision making, special obligations, the moral motives of compassion and sympathy, and the relevance of considering one's own integrity in making moral decisions. The second is a challenge to moral theory's presumed gender neutrality. The ethics of justice is not gender neutral, she argues, because it advocates ideals of agency, moral motivation, and correct moral reasoning which women are less likely than men to achieve; and because the moral dimensions excluded from the ethics of justice are just the ones figuring more prominently in women's than men's moral experience.

The adequacy and gender-bias charges are, for Gilligan, linked. She claims that the ethics of justice and the ethics of care are two different moral orientations. Whereas individuals may use both orientations, the shift from one to the other requires a Gestalt shift, since 'the terms of one perspective do not contain the terms of the other'. The exclusion of the care perspective from the ethics of justice simultaneously undermines the adequacy of the ethics of justice (it cannot give a complete account of moral life) and renders it gender biased.

Some critics have responded by arguing that there is no logical incompatibility between the two moral orientations. Because the ethics of justice does not in principle exclude the ethics of care (even if theorists within the justice tradition have had little to say about care issues), it is neither inadequate nor gender biased. Correctly applying moral rules and principles, for instance, requires, rather than excludes, knowledge of contextual details. Both orientations are crucial to correct moral reasoning and an adequate understanding of moral life. Thus, the ethics of justice and the ethics of care are not in fact rivalling, alternative moral theories. The so-called ethics of care merely makes focal issues that are already implicitly contained in the ethics of justice.

Suppose the two are logically compatible. Would the charge of gender bias evaporate? Yes, so long as gender neutrality only requires that the ethics of justice could, consistently, make room for the central moral concerns of the ethics of care. But perhaps gender neutrality requires more than this. Since the spectre of gender bias in theoretical knowledge is itself a moral issue, we would be well advised to consider the question of gender bias more carefully before concluding that our moral theory speaks in an androgynous voice. Although we can and should test the ethics of justice by asking whether it could consistently include the central moral issues in the ethics of care, we might also ask what ideologies of the moral life are likely to result from the repeated inclusion or exclusion of particular topics in moral theorizing.

Theorizing that crystallizes into a tradition has non-logical as well as logical implications. In order to explain why a tradition has the contours it does, one may need to suppose general acceptance of particular beliefs that are not logically entailed by any particular theory and might be denied by individual theorists were those beliefs articulated. When behavioural researchers, for example, focus almost exclusively on aggression and its role in human life, neglecting other behavioural motives, their doing so has the non-logical implication that aggression is, indeed, the most important behavioural motive. This is because only a belief like this would explain the rationality of this pattern of research. Such non-logical implications become ideologies when politically loaded (as the importance of aggression is when coupled with observations about women's lower level of aggression).

When understood as directed at moral theory's non-logical implications, the gender-bias charge takes a different form. Even if the ethics of justice could consistently accommodate the ethics of care, the critical point is that theorists in the justice tradition have not said much, except in passing, about the ethics of care, and are unlikely to say much in the future without a radical shift in theoretical priorities; and concentrating almost exclusively on rights of non-interference, impartiality, rationality, autonomy, and principles creates an ideology of the moral domain which has undesirable political implications for women. This formulation shifts the justice-care debate from one about logical compatibility to a debate about which theoretical priorities would improve the lot of women.

• In what sense are notions of justice 'masculine'? What contribution or revisions can a feminist perspective offer?

I. Individual Rights and Freedom

If our concern were only the smooth workings of society, almost any government would do—the stronger the better, the more authoritarian, the more efficient. But efficiency is only one of several concerns and probably not the most important. You might argue that the public interest could be served by such a government, but it is clear that justice and individual rights could not. The importance of the social contract theory (and 'consent of the governed' theories in general) is the clear emphasis on justice and rights. However, the social contract theory by itself is not entirely clear about the status of individual rights, as Nozick makes clear in his criticism of Rawls. Those rights concerning personal freedom are of particular concern here. Thus any discussion of justice and the state must include some special concern for the status of basic freedoms and **unalienable rights**, such as freedom to speak one's political opinions without harassment, freedom to worship (or not worship) without being penalized or punished, freedom to defend oneself against attack ('the right to bear arms' in the United States is a controversial case), and the freedom to pursue one's own interests (where these do not interfere with the rights of others). In addition, we can add the right not to be imprisoned without reason, or accused without a fair trial, or punished unduly for a crime committed.

In Canada, the Canadian Charter of Rights and Freedoms lists the rights and freedoms guaranteed to each of us, 'subject only to such reasonable limits prescribed by law as can be demonstrably justified in a free and democratic society'. Here are just a few of those rights and freedoms:

> **UNALIENABLE RIGHTS**
>
> Those rights that no one and no government can take away.

From the Canadian Charter of Rights and Freedoms

Guarantee of Rights and Freedoms

Rights and Freedoms in Canada

1. The Canadian Charter of Rights and Freedoms guarantees the rights and freedoms set out in it subject only to such reasonable limits prescribed by law as can be demonstrably justified in a free and democratic society.

Fundamental Freedoms

Fundamental Freedoms

2. Everyone has the following fundamental freedoms:
   (*a*) freedom of conscience and religion;
   (*b*) freedom of thought, belief, opinion, and expression, including freedom of the press and other media of communication;
   (*c*) freedom of peaceful assembly; and
   (*d*) freedom of association.

(Continued)

Democratic Rights

Democratic Rights of Citizens

3. Every citizen of Canada has the right to vote in an election of members of the House of Commons or of a legislative assembly and to be qualified for membership therein.

* * *

Legal Rights

Life, Liberty, and Security of Person

7. Everyone has the right to life, liberty, and security of the person and the right not to be deprived thereof except in accordance with the principles of fundamental justice.

Search or Seizure

8. Everyone has the right to be secure against unreasonable search or seizure.

Detention or Imprisonment

9. Everyone has the right not to be arbitrarily detained or imprisoned.

* * *

Equality Rights

Equality before and under Law and Equal Protection and Benefit of Law

15. (1) Every individual is equal before and under the law and has the right to the equal protection and equal benefit of the law without discrimination and, in particular, without discrimination based on race, national or ethnic origin, colour, religion, sex, age, or mental or physical disability.

Affirmative Action Programs

15. (2) Subsection (1) does not preclude any law, program, or activity that has as its object the amelioration of conditions of disadvantaged individuals or groups including those that are disadvantaged because of race, national or ethnic origin, colour, religion, sex, age, or mental or physical disability.

* * *

General

Multicultural Heritage

27. This Charter shall be interpreted in a manner consistent with the preservation and enhancement of the multicultural heritage of Canadians.

Rights Guaranteed Equally to Both Sexes

28. Notwithstanding anything in this Charter, the rights and freedoms referred to in it are guaranteed equally to male and female persons.

But even if the importance of such rights is indisputable, the precise formulation and extent of those rights are highly debatable. Some speak of 'unalienable rights', but should such rights be left unrestricted, for example, even in wartime? It is clear, to mention the most common example, that freedom of speech does not extend so far as the right to falsely yell 'fire' in a crowded theatre. Freedom of speech, therefore, like other rights, is limited by considerations of public welfare and utility. But how limited? Is mere annoyance to the government or general boredom among the populace sufficient cause to limit a right? Similarly, we can go back to the difficult examples we raised in earlier sections. Are the rights against imprisonment and harsh punishment always valid against overwhelming public interest? For example, are they valid in the case of a criminal who has repeatedly committed crimes? Or, to take a difficult example, is 'free enterprise' an 'unalienable' right in our society? Or is free enterprise rather a theory (and a debatable one) that suggests that public interest and justice will best be served by open competition and a free market? But that theory evolved before modern monopolies developed and before it was obvious that 'free' markets could be manipulated so as not to be either free or in the public interest at all. Is that 'freedom' still a right? Or should it also be tempered by other concerns?

One of the most important basic rights is the presumed right to own private property. John Locke, writing just after the English ('Glorious') Revolution of 1688, listed three basic rights that would become the main ingredients of the still-prominent political philosophy called liberalism. Foremost among them were 'life, liberty, and the right to own private property'. For Locke, private property is the bulwark of freedom and the basis of other human rights. One's own body is private property in the most basic sense; no one else has the authority to violate or use it without permission. Most contemporary societies recognize this right to one's own body as fundamental. But then Locke adds that the right to own property that one has helped cultivate with his or her body ('hath mixed his labour with it') is also basic to freedom and human dignity:

From *The Second Treatise on Government*
By John Locke

For his labour being the unquestionable property of the labourer, no man but he can have a right to what that is once joined to, at least where there is enough, and as good left in common for others.

Though the earth and all inferior creatures be common to all men, yet every man has a *property* in his own *person*. This nobody has any right to but himself. The *labour* of his body and the *work* of his hands, we may say, are properly his. Whatsoever, then, he removes out of the state that nature hath provided and left it in, he hath mixed his labour with it, and joined to it something that is his own, and thereby makes it his property. It being by him removed from the common state nature placed it in, it hath by this labour something annexed to it that excludes the common right of other men. For his labour being the unquestionable property of the labourer, no man but he can have a right to what that is once joined to, at least where there is enough, and as good left in common for others.

He that is nourished by the acorns he picked up under an oak, or the apples he gathered from the trees in the wood, has certainly appropriated them to himself. Nobody can deny but the nourishment is his. I ask, then, when did they begin to be his? when he digested? or when he ate? or when he boiled? or when he brought them home? or when he picked them up? And 'tis plain, if the first gathering made them not his, nothing else could. That labour put a distinction between them and common. That added something to them more than Nature, the common mother of all, had done, and so they became his private right. And will anyone say he had not right to those acorns or apples he thus appropriated because he had not the consent of all mankind to make them his? Was it a robbery thus to assume to himself what belonged to all in common? If such a consent as that was necessary, man had starved, notwithstanding the plenty God had given him. We see in commons, which remain so by compact, that 'tis the taking any part of what is common, and removing it out of the state Nature leaves it in, which begins the property, without which the common is of no use. And the taking of this or that part does not depend on the express consent of all the commoners. Thus, the grass my horse has bit, the turfs my servant has cut, and the ore I have digged in any place, where I have a right to them in common with others, become my property without the assignation or consent of anybody. The labour that was mine, removing them out of that common state they were in, hath fixed my property in them.

* * *

And thus, I think, it is very easy to conceive, without any difficulty, how labour could at first begin a title of property in the common things of nature, and how the spending it upon our uses bounded it; so that there could then be no reason of quarrelling about title, nor any doubt about the largeness of possession it gave. Right and conveniency went together. For as a man had a right to all he could employ his labour upon, so he had no temptation to labour for more than he could make use of. This left no room for controversy about the title, nor for encroachment on the right of others. What portion a man carved to himself was easily seen; and it was useless as well as dishonest to carve himself too much, or take more than he needed.

It is important to point out that discussions of rights should never be set apart from discussions of political duties and obligations. As the several versions of the social contract make clear, these are always part of one and the same agreement—certain rights in return for certain obligations. To discuss freedom of speech, for example, without also discussing the obligation to be well informed and logically coherent, is to provide a dangerously one-sided view of the problem. One way of developing this idea of an exchange of rights and obligations has been to distinguish two different senses of 'freedom': a *negative* freedom from interference and a *positive* freedom to realize one's own potential and find one's place in society. Freedom from interference may be necessary for a person to enjoy life and contribute to the welfare of those around him or her, but a person also needs positive goods—health and education, for example. Thus freedom takes on a double meaning, freedom *from* interference but freedom *to* participate in society too. Since positive freedom also includes a person's being able to take on responsibilities, some philosophers have pointed out a paradox in the idea of being 'free to perform obligations'.

The idea that one is 'free to perform obligations' may sound odd to us because we are so used to talking exclusively about freedom from constraints and the demands made by authority. But one theme that has recurred since the ancient Greeks is that all rights and 'freedoms from' must be coupled with duties and obligations and the freedom to perform them. In Rousseau, for example, the citizen's obligations to the state are just as important as the state's obligations to its citizens. Many philosophers are concerned that simple freedom from constraint leaves people without direction or morality and can easily degenerate into chaos and anarchy. Thus these philosophers stress the necessity of laws and guidelines as an essential part of freedom. This is why they call it 'positive' freedom, since it necessarily includes 'positive' goods (health and education) as well as a set of roles, duties, obligations, and constraints. This notion can be abused easily, however, for 'positive freedom' can be made compatible with the most authoritarian state. But despite possible abuses, it is important to see that there is more to freedom than simple freedom from interference. Whenever someone demands freedom, it is important to ask not only 'from what?' but also 'for what?'

It is also worth distinguishing several different kinds of rights. We can distinguish between 'negative' and 'positive' rights as well as freedoms; one has a right not to be interfered with, and one has rights *to* certain goods that society can provide. We have mostly been discussing negative rights (the right to be left alone, the right not to be arrested without good reason). But there are positive rights that are equally important, although they are often more controversial in this society, for example, the right to a minimal income regardless of the work one performs, the right to adequate health care regardless of one's ability to pay for it. Many rights are clearly localized to a particular state or a particular community, as, for example, the right of university regents to free hockey game tickets and lunches at taxpayers' expense. These rights exist by convention only and cannot be generalized from one community to another.

Then, more generally, there are **civil rights**, rights that are guaranteed in a particular state. One example can be the right to equal treatment despite differences in skin colour or sex or religion, as are described in the Canadian Charter of Rights and Freedoms. These are clearly much more important than the conventional rights, and they have a clearly moral basis. For that reason, even though they are defined by reference to a particular society, they are often generalized to other societies as well. Insofar as they are generalized in this way, they become *moral* rights or **human rights**, extendable to all people, in any society, regardless of the laws and customs of the society in which they live. Some apparent human rights have been hotly debated: for example, whether our government has the moral authority to interfere with the harsh abuses of human right in, say, China. If the right in question is harsh punishment for a seemingly minor crime

CIVIL RIGHTS

Those rights that are determined by a particular state and its laws.

HUMAN RIGHTS

Those rights that are considered to be universal, 'unalienable', and common to every person.

it might be argued that their system of punishment is simply more severe than ours, and we should not apply our values. If the right in question is the ability of citizens to speak out against the government without threat of imprisonment or worse, a strong argument has been made that our government does indeed have that moral authority. But if the right in question is one of those basic human rights against torture or debasement or pointless murder, then it can be argued that everyone has a moral obligation to defend such rights. Human rights are those that transcend all social and national boundaries; they demand that people deserve certain treatment just because they are human, regardless of all else.

The vocabulary of rights, it is fair to say, has come to dominate the political discourse of our age. No matter who is speaking—politicians, citizens, activists, protesters, journalists, lawyers, civil servants, talk-show hosts, bloggers—it seems as if the medium of expression is always the same: the new *lingua franca* of rights. Torture, abortion, same-sex marriage, gender equality, affirmative action, multiculturalism, free speech, religious expression, education, animal welfare, health care, the treatment of disabled persons—debates around all of these issues (and many more besides) are commonly framed in terms of individual or collective rights. Now, what is so striking about this? It isn't just that we tend to think and talk in terms of rights; it is that we find it *perfectly natural and normal* to do so—so natural, in fact, that many of us would have a very hard time articulating our views about socio-political issues without using the vocabulary of rights. For many of us, indeed, 'rights talk' seems as indispensable as oxygen, as irresistible as gravity.

How did this happen, and what does it mean? Understanding the near-ubiquity of 'rights talk' in our culture is no easy task; but it is one of the principal aims of Michael Ignatieff's recent Massey Lectures, *The Rights Revolution*. Another of Ignatieff's aims, however, is to illuminate Canada's role in bringing about the 'rights revolution'.

From *The Rights Revolution*
By Michael Ignatieff

Canada has become one of the most distinctive rights cultures in the world.

In these lectures, I am going to talk about a fundamental change that has come over us in our lifetime. I'm calling this change the rights revolution, to describe the amazing way in which rights talk has transformed how we think about ourselves as citizens, as men and women, and as parents. The rights revolution took off in the 1960s in all industrialized countries, and it is still running its course. Just think for a minute about how much rights talk there is out there: women's rights, rights of gays and lesbians, Aboriginal rights, children's rights, language rights, and constitutional rights. In one sense, the rights revolution is a story of inclusion, of how previously excluded groups obtained rights of equality. In this regard, the extension of rights has widened and deepened our democracy. In a second sense, however, the rights revolution has been about protecting certain groups from the effects of democracy. Group rights to language and Aboriginal rights to land and resources are designed to enable minorities to protect that which is essential to their survival from the power of elective majorities.

In other words, rights have a double-sided relationship to democracy. Rights enacted into law by democratically elected representatives express the will of the people. But there are also rights whose purpose is to protect people from that will, to set limits on what majorities can do. Human rights and constitutionally guaranteed rights are supposed to have a special immunity from restriction by the majority. This allows them to act as a bulwark for the freedom of the vulnerable. So the rights revolution has a double aspect: it has been about both enhancing our right to be equal and protecting our right to be different. Trying to do both—that is, enhancing

(*Continued*)

equality while safeguarding difference—is the essential challenge of the rights revolution, and this is what I want to explore with you in these lectures.

* * *

Canada has become one of the most distinctive rights cultures in the world. First, on moral questions such as abortion, capital punishment, and gay rights, our legal codes are notably liberal, secular, and pro-choice. In this, they approximate European standards more closely than American ones. Despite the fact that we share our way of life and our public media with our neighbours to the south, our habits of mind on rights questions are very much our own. Second, our culture is social democratic in its approach to rights to welfare and public assistance. Canadians take it for granted that citizens do have the right to free health care, as well as to unemployment insurance and publicly funded pensions. Again, the comparison with the republic to the south is noteworthy. The third distinguishing feature of our rights culture, of course, is our particular emphasis on group rights. This is expressed, first, in Quebec's Charte de la langue française (Bill 101) and, second, in the treaty agreements that have given land and resources to Aboriginal groups. Apart from New Zealand, no other country has given such recognition to the idea of group rights.

The fourth distinguishing feature of Canadian rights culture is that we are one of the few states that has actually put in writing, in recent Supreme Court decisions and in federal legislation, the terms and conditions for breaking our federation apart. Having survived two referenda on the future of the country, Canadians rightly feared we might not survive a third. So both communities, English- and French-speaking, have sought to define the conditions under which national groups have a right to secede, how referenda on secession should be framed so that the mandate is clear, and how negotiations should take place between those departing and those remaining in the federation. Viewed from the outside, this search for 'clarity' on the question of secession probably seems both crazy and dangerous. Doesn't talking about it make it more likely to happen? The Canadian gamble—or is it a strange kind of genius?—is that clarity will make breakup less likely. The idea is counterintuitive, but it is not stupid: if everybody knows the rules, nobody will be caught by surprise. Unilateral secessions are ruled out. Both sides must negotiate the terms of a divorce. If both sides understand the consequences of their actions, the chances of violence and conflict can be reduced.

- What, exactly, is the 'rights revolution'?
- In what way do rights have a 'double-sided relation' to democracy?
- According to Ignatieff, Canada has become 'one of the most distinctive rights cultures in the world'. In what ways is it distinctive?

A right is a kind of demand, the demand that one is owed something by society and the state, usually a certain sort of consideration or treatment. But most of the rights we have been discussing are in fact rights to freedom or to liberty, that is, the right to be left alone and not interfered with. A belief in individual freedom forms the basis of the liberal political philosophy, which is defined most of all by a commitment to the right of each individual to be free to do whatever he or she wishes as long as it doesn't interfere with similar rights of others. The classic statement of this position appears in another pamphlet by John Stuart Mill, *On Liberty* (1859). In it, he defends the rights of individuals and minorities against the tyranny of democratic majorities, for Mill sees that liberty can be as endangered in a **democracy** as it can in an authoritarian state. Mill goes on to offer a 'very simple principle', that individual liberty is to be considered inviolable except when other people are threatened with harm.

DEMOCRACY

That form of government in which policies or at least the makers of policy are chosen by popular mandate.

From *On Liberty*
By John Stuart Mill

The only freedom which deserves the name, is that of pursuing our own good in our own way, so long as we do not attempt to deprive others of theirs, or impede their efforts to obtain it.

The object of this essay is to assert one very simple principle, as entitled to govern absolutely the dealings of society with the individual in the way of compulsion and control, whether the means used be physical force in the form of legal penalties, or the moral coercion of public opinion. That principle is, that the sole end for which mankind are warranted, individually or collectively, in interfering with the liberty of action of any of their number, is self-protection. That the only purpose for which power can be rightfully exercised over any member of a civilized community, against his will, is to prevent harm to others. His own good, either physical or moral, is not a sufficient warrant. He cannot rightfully be compelled to do or forbear because it will be better for him to do so, because it will make him happier, because, in the opinions of others, to do so would be wise, or even right. These are good reasons for remonstrating with him, or reasoning with him, or persuading him, or entreating him, but not for compelling him, or visiting with any evil in case he do otherwise. To justify that, the conduct from which it is desired to deter him must be calculated to produce evil to someone else. The only part of the conduct of anyone, for which he is amenable to society, is that which concerns others. In the part which merely concerns himself, his independence is, of right, absolute. Over himself, over his own body and mind, the individual is sovereign.

It is, perhaps, hardly necessary to say that this doctrine is meant to apply only to human beings in the maturity of their faculties. We are not speaking of children, or of young persons below the age which the law may fix as that of manhood or womanhood. Those who are still in a state to require being taken care of by others, must be protected against their own actions as well as against external injury. For the same reason, we may leave out of consideration those backward states of society in which the race itself may be considered as in its nonage. The early difficulties in the way of spontaneous progress are so great, that there is seldom any choice of means for overcoming them; and a ruler full of the spirit of improvement is warranted in the use of any expedients that will attain an end, perhaps otherwise unattainable. Despotism is a legitimate mode of government in dealing with barbarians, provided the end be their improvement,[3] and the means justified by actually affecting that end. Liberty, as a principle, has no application to any state of things anterior to the time when mankind have become capable of being improved by free and equal discussion.

It is proper to state that I forego any advantage which could be derived to my argument from the idea of abstract right, as a thing independent of utility. I regard utility as the ultimate appeal on all ethical questions; but it must be utility in the largest sense, grounded on the permanent interests of a man as a progressive being. Those interests, I contend, authorize the subjection of individual spontaneity to external control, only in respect to those actions of each, which concern the interest of other people. If anyone does an act hurtful to others, there is a *prima facie* case for punishing him, by law, or, where legal penalties are not safely applicable, by general disapprobation. There are also many positive acts for the benefit of others, which he may rightfully be compelled to perform; such as to give evidence in a court of justice; to bear his fair share in the common defence, or in any other joint work necessary to the interest of the society of which he enjoys the protection; and to perform certain acts of individual beneficence, such as saving a fellow creature's life, or interposing to protect the defenceless against ill-usage, things which whenever it is obviously a man's duty to do, he may rightfully be made responsible to society for not doing. A person may cause evil to others not only by his actions but by his inaction, and in either case is justly accountable to them for the injury. The latter case, it is true, requires a much more cautious exercise of compulsion than the former. To make anyone answerable for doing evil to others is the rule; to make him answerable for not preventing evil is, comparatively speaking, the exception. Yet there are many cases clear enough and grave enough to justify that exception. In all things which regard the external relations of the individual, he is *de jure* amenable to those whose interests are concerned, and, if need be, to society as their protector. There are often

(Continued)

good reasons for not holding him to the responsibility; but these reasons must arise from the special expediencies of the case: either because it is a kind of case in which he is on the whole likely to act better, when left to his own discretion, than when controlled in any way in which society have it in their power to control him; or because the attempt to exercise control would produce other evils, greater than those which it would prevent. When such reasons as these preclude the enforcement of responsibility, the conscience of the agent himself should step into the vacant judgment seat, and protect those interests of others which have no external protection; judging himself all the more rigidly, because the case does not admit of his being made accountable to the judgment of his fellow creatures.

But there is a sphere of action in which society, as distinguished from the individual, has, if any, only an indirect interest; comprehending all that portion of a person's life and conduct which affects only himself, or if it also affects others, only with their free, voluntary, and undeceived consent and participation. When I say only himself, I mean directly, and in the first instance; for whatever affects himself, may affect others through himself; and the objection which may be grounded on this contingency, will receive consideration in the sequel. This, then, is the appropriate region of human liberty. It comprises, first, the inward domain of consciousness; demanding liberty of conscience in the most comprehensive sense; liberty of thought and feeling; absolute freedom of opinion and sentiment on all subjects, practical or speculative, scientific, moral, or theological. The liberty of expressing and publishing opinions may seem to fall under a different principle, since it belongs to that part of the conduct of an individual which concerns other people; but, being almost of as much importance as the liberty of thought itself, and resting in great part on the same reasons, is practically inseparable from it. Secondly, the principle requires liberty of tastes and pursuits; of framing the plan of our life to suit our own character; of doing as we like, subject to such consequences as may follow: without impediment from our fellow creatures, so long as what we do does not harm them, even though they should think our conduct foolish, perverse, or wrong. Thirdly, from this liberty of each individual, follows the liberty, within the same limits, of combination among individuals; freedom to unite, for any purpose not involving harm to others: the persons combining being supposed to be of full age, and not forced or deceived.

No society in which these liberties are not, on the whole, respected, is free, whatever may be its form of government and unqualified. The only freedom which deserves the name, is that of pursuing our own good in our own way, so long as we do not attempt to deprive others of theirs, or impede their efforts to obtain it. Each is the proper guardian of his own health, whether bodily, *or* mental and spiritual. Mankind are greater gainers by suffering each other to live as seems good to themselves, than by compelling each to live as seems good to the rest.

Mill's main concern in his essay is the extent to which government and public interest have authority over individuals and individual actions. If an action harms other people or presents a public menace, then government does have the authority to prevent it or punish a person for doing it. But if an action is not harmful to others, the government has no such authority. In the question of freedom of speech, for example, this means that governments have no authority to censor some comment or publication unless it clearly harms other people, not merely annoys or personally offends them. Mill is particularly concerned with protecting individuals against 'the tyranny of the majority'. The public interest is authoritative to 'a limit', but that limit does not include interfering with personal affairs or opinions.

- What is a right? What does it mean to say that rights are inalienable? Are rights ever absolute or inalienable in practice?
- What is the difference between a civil right and a human right?
- What is the only justification for the exercise of power, according to Mill? When is despotism a legitimate form of government?
- How is liberty related to a notion of rights? Which of the rights guaranteed under the Canadian Charter of Rights and Freedoms can you identify in Mill's pamphlet? What would Mill think of our Charter?

J. Obeying the Law: Civil Disobedience and Anarchism

If one accepts Mill's argument for limited government, one might also be tempted to take one more radical step—no government at all. The idea that people can get along and work together without government requires a robust confidence in the capacity of both the common man and the most powerful members of society to cooperate without the need of force from above, the very opposite of Thomas Hobbes' view of men as selfish and requiring a sovereign in order to get along. Or else, one might question the need for living in society at all. The American author and philosopher Henry David Thoreau is well known for his grand experiment of living out in the Massachusetts woods at Walden Pond, minimizing his needs and for the most part living virtually alone. Of course one might object that he was able to do so only with the support of society (not least because the land itself was owned by his friend, Ralph Waldo Emerson); but the point, of course, repeated by many defenders of 'the simple life' over the centuries, is that we can all get along with much less than we typically think we can, living in 'civilized' society. It is a point that is being widely promoted in Canada, America, and other 'advanced' societies today, in the name of the environment and the ultimate viability of life on earth. But Thoreau's experiment spoke to something quite different: the independence and self-reliance of the individual.

Thoreau, however, lived in society like the rest of us and could thus be argued to be beholden to its laws. But should one obey the laws of the land? As we have seen, Socrates certainly thought so, even in the case where those laws were unfairly turned against him. But not everyone agrees, and many have argued that the right to rebel against unjust laws and an oppressive government is directly entailed by the very idea of a social contract. Thoreau makes just such an argument in his essay 'Civil Disobedience', in which he defends his decision not to pay his taxes. Indeed, he claims that for a person to obey the laws of a government that behaves unjustly would be the same as his behaving unjustly himself. While 'lesser men'— degraded, immoral, and unthinking pawns of government—might go along year after year, obeying the laws, casting their important and thoughtless vote, no man of moral character would do so, claimed Thoreau. But being a man of moral character himself, he absolved himself of any obligations to his country other than to 'do what he believed right'.

On 'Civil Disobedience'
By Henry David Thoreau

Must the citizen ever for a moment, or in the least degree, resign his conscience to the legislator? Why has every man a conscience, then?

I heartily accept the motto,—'That government is best which governs least'; and I should like to see it acted up to more rapidly and systematically. Carried out, it finally amounts to this, which also I believe,— 'That government is best which governs not at all'; and when men are prepared for it, that will be the kind of government which they will have. Government is at best but an expedient; but most governments are usually, and all governments are sometimes, inexpedient. The objections which have been brought against a standing army, and they are many and weighty, and deserve to prevail, may also at least be brought against a standing government. The standing army is only an arm of the standing government. The government itself, which is only the mode which the people have chosen to execute their will, is equally liable to be abused and perverted before the people can act through it. Witness the present Mexican war, the work of comparatively a few individuals using the standing government as their tool; for, in the outset, the people would not have consented to this measure.

This American government,—what is it but a tradition, though a recent one, endeavouring to transmit

(*Continued*)

itself unimpaired to posterity, but each instant losing some of its integrity? It has not the vitality and force of a single living man; for a single man can bend it to his will. It is a sort of wooden gun to the people themselves; and, if ever they should use it in earnest as a real one against each other, it will surely split. But it is not the less necessary for this; for the people must have some complicated machinery or other, and hear its din, to satisfy that idea of government which they have. Governments show thus how successfully men can be imposed on, even impose on themselves, for their own advantage. It is excellent, we must allow; yet this government never of itself furthered any enterprise, but by the alacrity with which it got out of its way. *It* does not keep the country free. *It* does not settle the West. *It* does not educate. The character inherent in the American people has done all that has been accomplished; and it would have done somewhat more, if the government had not sometimes got in its way. For government is an expedient by which men would fain succeed in letting one another alone; and, as has been said, when it is most expedient, the governed are most let alone by it. Trade and commerce, if they were not made of India rubber, would never manage to bound over the obstacles which legislators are continually putting in their way; and, if one were to judge these men wholly by the effects of their actions, and not partly by their intentions, they would deserve to be classed and punished with those mischievous persons who put obstructions on the railroads.

But, to speak practically and as a citizen, unlike those who call themselves no-government men, I ask for, not at once no government, but *at once* a better government. Let every man make known what kind of government would command his respect, and that will be one step toward obtaining it.

After all, the practical reason why, when the power is once in the hands of the people, a majority are permitted, and for a long period continue, to rule, is not because they are most likely to be in the right, nor because this seems fairest to the minority, but because they are physically the strongest. But a government in which the majority rule in all cases cannot be based on justice, even as far as men understand it. Can there not be a government in which majorities do not virtually decide right and wrong, but conscience?—in which majorities decide only those questions to which the rule of expediency is applicable? Must the citizen ever for a moment, or in the least degree, resign his conscience to the

legislator? Why has every man a conscience, then? I think that we should be men first, and subjects afterward. It is not desirable to cultivate a respect for the law, so much as for the right. The only obligation which I have a right to assume, is to do at any time what I think right. It is truly enough said, that a corporation has no conscience; but a corporation of conscientious men is a corporation *with* a conscience. Law never made men a whit more just; and, by means of their respect for it, even the well-disposed are daily made the agents of injustice. A common and natural result of an undue respect for law is, that you may see a file of soldiers, colonel, captain, corporal, privates, powder-monkeys and all, marching in admirable order over hill and dale to the wars, against their wills, aye, against their common sense and consciences, which makes it very steep marching indeed, and produces a palpitation of the heart. They have no doubt that it is a damnable business in which they are concerned; they are all peaceably inclined. Now, what are they? Men at all? or small moveable forts and magazines, at the service of some unscrupulous man in power?

* * *

Under a government which imprisons any unjustly, the true place for a just man is also a prison. The proper place today, the only place which Massachusetts has provided for her freer and less desponding spirits, is in her prisons, to be put out and locked out of the State by her own act, as they have already put themselves out by their principles. It is there that the fugitive slave, and the Mexican prisoner on parole, and the Indian come to plead the wrongs of his race, should find them; on that separate, but more free and honourable ground, where the State places those who are not *with* her but *against* her,—the only house in a slave-state in which a free man can abide with honour. If any think that their influence would be lost there, and their voices no longer afflict the ear of the State, that they would not be as an enemy within its walls, they do not know by how much truth is stronger than error, nor how much more eloquently and effectively he can combat injustice who has experienced a little in his own person. Cast your whole vote, not a strip of paper merely, but your whole influence. A minority is powerless while it conforms to the majority; it is not even a minority then; but it is irresistible when it clogs by its whole weight. If the alternative is to keep all just men in prison, or give up war and slavery, the State will not hesitate which to choose. If a thousand men were not to pay their tax-bills this year, that would not be a violent and bloody measure, as it would be to pay them, and enable the State to commit violence and shed innocent blood. This is, in fact, the definition of a peaceable revolution, if any such is possible. If the tax-gatherer, or any other public officer, asks me, as one has done, 'But what shall I do?' my answer is, 'If you really wish to do any thing, resign your office.' When the subject has refused allegiance, and the officer has resigned his office, then the revolution is accomplished. But even suppose blood should flow. Is there not a sort of blood shed when the conscience is wounded? Through this wound a man's real manhood and immortality flow out, and he bleeds to an everlasting death. I see this blood flowing now.

* * *

Thus the State never intentionally confronts a man's sense, intellectual or moral, but only his body, his senses. It is not armed with superior wit or honesty, but with superior physical strength. I was not born to be forced. I will breathe after my own fashion. Let us see who is the strongest. What force has a multitude? They only can force me who obey a higher law than I. They force me to become like themselves. I do not hear of *men* being *forced* to live this way or that by masses of men. What sort of life were that to live? When I meet a government which says to me, 'Your money or your life', why should I be in haste to give it my money? It may be in a great strait, and not know what to do: I cannot help that. It must help itself; do as I do. It is not worth the while to snivel about it. I am not responsible for the successful working of the machinery of society. I am not the son of the engineer. I perceive that, when an acorn and a chestnut fall side by side, the one does not remain inert to make way for the other, but both obey their own laws, and spring and grow and flourish as best they can, till one, perchance, overshadows and destroys the other. If a plant cannot live according to its nature, it dies; and so a man.

- On what basis is civil disobedience justified, according to Thoreau? In what respects is Thoreau's view similar to Rousseau's or Locke's?

Thoreau did not reject the idea of living in society, despite his insistence on independence and self-reliance, nor did he reject the idea of government as such. He rather insisted on a just government and just laws as the precondition of his cooperation. But there is a much more radical argument for the rejection of government, not only unjust governments and laws, but the rejection of any government. This is the position called anarchism, and it presupposes, as Hobbes does not, that people are naturally capable and willing to live together in harmony. Government only interferes. Anarchism, however, is often confused with anarchy, which in most people's minds means chaos and utter confusion. It is not this, however. It is much more like natural order, a vision that is articulated by the Canadian writer and literary critic George Woodcock in *Anarchism: A History of Libertarian Ideas and Movements*:

From *Anarchism*
By George Woodcock

Mere unthinking revolt does not make an anarchist.

What is anarchism? And what is it not? These are the questions we must first consider.

* * *

All anarchists deny authority; many of them fight against it. But by no means all who deny authority and fight against it can reasonably be called anarchists.

(Continued)

Historically, anarchism is a doctrine which poses a criticism of existing society; a view of a desirable future society; and a means of passing from one to other. Mere unthinking revolt does not make an anarchist, nor does a philosophical or religious rejection of earthly power. Mystics and stoics seek not anarchy, but another kingdom. Anarchism, historically speaking, is concerned mainly with man in his relation to society. Its ultimate aim is always social change; its present attitude is always one of social condemnation, even though it may proceed from an individualist view of man's nature; its method is always that of social rebellion, violent or otherwise.

* * *

To describe the essential theory of anarchism is rather like trying to grapple with Proteus, for the very nature of the libertarian attitude—its rejection of dogma, its deliberate avoidance of rigidly systematic theory, and, above all, its stress on extreme freedom of choice and on the primacy of the individual judgment—creates immediately the possibility of a variety of viewpoints inconceivable in a closely dogmatic system. Anarchism, indeed, is both various and mutable, and in the historical perspective it presents the appearance, not of a swelling stream flowing on to its sea of destiny (an image that might well be appropriate to Marxism), but rather of water percolating through porous ground—here forming for a time a strong underground current, there gathering into a swirling pool, trickling through crevices, disappearing from sight, and then re-emerging where the cracks in the social structure may offer it a course to run. As a doctrine it changes constantly; as a movement it grows and disintegrates, in constant fluctuation, but it never vanishes. It has existed continuously in Europe since the 1840s, and its very Protean quality has allowed it to survive where many more powerful but less adaptable movements of the intervening century have disappeared completely.

* * *

All anarchists, I think, would accept the proposition that man naturally contains within him all the attributes which make him capable of living in freedom and social concord. They may not believe that man is naturally good, but they believe very fervently that man is naturally social. His sociality is expressed, according to Proudhon, in an immanent sense of justice, which is wholly human and natural to him:

An integral part of a collective existence, man feels his dignity at the same time in himself and in others, and thus carries in his heart the principle of a morality superior to himself. This principle does not come to him from outside; it is secreted within him, it is immanent. It constitutes his essence, the essence of society itself. It is the true form of the human spirit, a form which takes shape and grows toward perfection only by the relationship that every day gives birth to social life. Justice, in other words, exists in us like love, like notions of beauty, of utility, of truth, like all our powers and faculties.

Not merely is man naturally social, the anarchists contend, but the tendency to live in society emerged with him as he evolved out of the animal world. Society existed before man, and a society living and growing freely would in fact be a natural society, as Kropotkin emphasizes in *Modern Science and Anarchism*:

The anarchists conceive a society in which all the mutual relations of its members are regulated, not by laws, not by authorities, whether self-imposed or elected, but by mutual agreements between the members of that society, and by a sum of social customs and habits not petrified by law, routine, or superstition, but continually developing and continually readjusted, in accordance with the ever-growing requirements of a free life, stimulated by the progress of science, invention, and the steady growth of higher ideals. No ruling authorities, then. No government of man by man; no crystallization and immobility, but a continual evolution—such as we see in Nature.

If man is naturally capable of living in such a free society, if society is in fact a natural growth, then clearly those who attempt to impose man-made laws, or to create what Godwin called 'positive institutions' are the real enemies of society, and the anarchist who rebels against them, even to the extent of violence and destruction, is not antisocial after all; according to anarchist reasoning he is the regenerator, a responsible individual striving to adjust the social balance in its natural direction.

The emphasis on the natural and prehuman origin of societies has made almost every anarchist theoretician, from Godwin to the present, reject Rousseau's idea of a Social Contract.

* * *

[T]he anarchist sees progress not in terms of a steady increase in material wealth and complexity of living, but rather in terms of the moralizing of society by the abolition of authority, inequality, and economic exploitation. Once this has been achieved, we may return to a condition in which natural processes resume their influence over the lives of societies and individuals, and then man can develop inwardly in accordance with the spirit that raises him above the beast.

- If you deny or defy authority, does that automatically make you an anarchist? Why doesn't Woodcock think so?
- Is anarchism a purely negative doctrine, according to Woodcock? Why do anarchists oppose authority? What, if anything, do they ultimately hope to achieve by doing so?

K. Multiculturalism and Race

Everyone knows that Canada is a 'multicultural society'. Indeed, we've all heard this so often that we probably are inclined to agree without giving the matter too much thought. But perhaps we *should* give it some thought. Let's start with a simple question: What, exactly, does it mean to say that Canada is a 'multicultural society'?

If the idea behind this familiar phrase is just that Canada's citizenry is remarkable for its cultural, ethnic, and linguistic diversity—that many people have come to Canada from all over the world, bringing with them the traditions, customs, religions, and languages (not to mention cuisine!) of their places of origin—then this claim simply states an indisputable truth that anyone can verify by looking at the relevant census data. But is this really all that 'multiculturalism' means to us? No; it is evident that many people have much more than this in mind when they press that word into service, as pundits frequently do. When we watch Canadian news programs, read Canadian newspapers, listen to the speeches of Canadian politicians, or hearken to the slogans of Canadian protesters and activists, we find that 'multiculturalism' is frequently presented as proof of our deep commitment to certain basic democratic values: equality, justice for all, respect for the rights and freedoms of others, tolerance, goodwill, openness, a courteous pluralism, and the like. Multiculturalism, in this richer sense, is not so much a sociological fact as it is a political ideal; not so much a datum as an achievement; not so much a destiny as a collective aspiration.

Multiculturalism, then, is not the stuff of dry-as-dust census data, but high-octane fuel for the engine of national pride—this, for a good many of us, is the real meaning of Canadian multiculturalism. Canada, as we may have been told, is not meant to be a giant melting pot, but a great mosaic. *Not a melting pot*, because immigrants are not expected to 'melt away' the distinctive cultural heritages they bring with them, as if their cultural identities were nothing but a burden or a liability. *A mosaic*, because we understand that Canada as a whole is enriched when its diverse parts preserve their distinctive qualities and excellences. Just as a mosaic composed of only one cut and colour of tile would be a dull monotonous space, a society made up of people whose ethnocultural backgrounds are all alike would inevitably be the poorer for it.

Anyone seeking an eloquent exposition of the virtues of Canadian multiculturalism need look no further than the writings of former prime minister Pierre Trudeau. As leader of the first federal government to champion multiculturalism in Canada—almost forty years ago—Trudeau was convinced that embracing multiculturalism would lead to a more inclusive—and ultimately more just—society. But why did he believe that multiculturalism would be so good for Canada? To answer this question, here is a selection of his remarks on multiculturalism:

From 'Multiculturalism'
By Pierre Trudeau

Uniformity is neither desirable nor possible in a country the size of Canada.

National unity, if it is to mean anything in the deeply personal sense, must be founded on confidence in one's own *individual* identity; out of this can grow respect for that of others and a willingness to share ideas, attitudes, and assumptions. A vigorous policy of multiculturalism will help create this initial confidence. It can form the basis of a society which is founded on fair play for all.

* * *

We have concluded in Canada almost without debate that true greatness is not measured in terms of military might or economic aggrandizement. On a planet of finite size, the most desirable of all characteristics is the ability and desire to cohabit with persons of differing backgrounds, and to benefit from the opportunities which this offers.

* * *

The decision by the Canadian government that a second language be given increased official recognition is, in indirect fashion, support for the cultivation and use of many languages, because it is a breach of the monopoly position of one language and an elevation of the stature of languages that are 'different'.

* * *

Every single person in Canada is now a member of a minority group. Linguistically our origins are one-third English, one-third French, and one-third neither. We have no alternative but to be tolerant of one another's differences. Beyond the threshold of tolerance, however, we have countless opportunities to benefit from the richness and variety of a Canadian life which is the result of this broad mix. The fabric of Canadian society is as resilient as it is colourful. It is a multicultural society; it offers to every Canadian the opportunity to fulfill his or her own cultural instincts and to share those from other sources. This mosaic pattern, and the moderation which it includes and encourages, makes Canada a very special place.

* * *

Uniformity is neither desirable nor possible in a country the size of Canada. We should not even be able to agree upon the kind of Canadian to choose as a model, let alone persuade most people to emulate it. There are surely few policies potentially more disastrous for Canada than to tell all Canadians that they must be alike. There is no such thing as a model or ideal Canadian. What could be more absurd than the concept of an 'all-Canadian' boy or girl? A society which emphasizes uniformity is one which creates intolerance and hate. A society which eulogizes the average citizen is one which breeds mediocrity. What the world should be seeking, and what we in Canada must continue to cherish, are not concepts of uniformity but human values: compassion, love, and understanding.

No doubt many people still agree with Trudeau's optimistic view of multiculturalism. Not everyone does, however. Indeed, Canadian multiculturalism now has no shortage of vocal home-grown critics. Their main argument is easily stated: by encouraging groups to think of themselves in terms of their inherited cultural identity (as opposed to encouraging them to understand themselves first and foremost as Canadian citizens), multiculturalist policies have effectively promoted forms of ethnocultural separatism that threaten the cause of national unity. According to these critics, the truth is there for all to see: Trudeau's dream of a creating a truly open, vital, and diverse society has been defeated by the fact of ever-increasing fragmentation along ethnocultural lines. In other words, they think the old 'mosaic' metaphor breaks down badly: instead of a country whose diverse parts form an integrated whole, we now have a land where each part is on its way to becoming a whole of its own.

These are serious criticisms. Is there anything to them? In our next reading, Canadian political philosopher Will Kymlicka examines some popular objections to multiculturalism. Kymlicka's conclusion? When one takes a good look at the evidence available to us, there is every reason to believe that the experiment of Canadian multiculturalism has proven a resounding success.

From *Finding Our Way*
By Will Kymlicka

How has the adoption of multiculturalism in 1971 affected the integration of ethnic groups in Canada?

In 1971 Canada embarked on a unique experiment by declaring a policy of official 'multiculturalism'. According to Pierre Trudeau, the prime minister who introduced it in the House of Commons, the policy had four aims: to support the cultural development of ethnocultural groups; to help members of ethnocultural groups overcome barriers to full participation in Canadian society; to promote creative encounters and interchange among all ethnocultural groups; and to assist new Canadians in acquiring at least one of Canada's official languages.[4] This policy was officially enshrined in law in the 1988 Multiculturalism Act.

* * *

The debate over multiculturalism has heated up recently, largely because of two best-selling critiques: Neil Bissoondath's *Selling Illusions: The Cult of Multiculturalism in Canada* (1994) and Richard Gwyn's *Nationalism without Walls: The Unbearable Lightness of Being Canadian* (1995).[5] Bissoondath and Gwyn make very similar claims about the results of the policy. In particular, both argue that multiculturalism has promoted a form of ethnic separatism among immigrants. According to Bissoondath, multiculturalism has led to 'undeniable ghettoization'.[6] Instead of promoting integration, it encourages immigrants to form 'self-contained' ghettos 'alienated from the mainstream', and this ghettoization is 'not an extreme of multiculturalism but its ideal: a way of life transported whole, a little outpost of exoticism preserved and protected'. He approvingly quotes Arthur Schlesinger's claim that multiculturalism reflects a 'cult of ethnicity' that 'exaggerates differences, intensifies resentments and antagonisms, drives even deeper the awful wedges between races and nationalities', producing patterns of 'self-pity and self-ghettoization' that lead to 'cultural and linguistic apartheid'.[7] According to Bissoondath, multiculturalism policy does not encourage immigrants to think of themselves as Canadians; even the children of immigrants 'continue to see Canada with the eyes of foreigners. Multiculturalism, with its emphasis on the importance of holding on to the former or ancestral homeland, with its insistence that *There* is more important than *Here*, encourages such attitudes.'

Gwyn makes the same claim, in very similar language. He argues that 'official multiculturalism encourages apartheid, or to be a bit less harsh, ghettoism'.[8] The longer multiculturalism policy has been in place, 'the higher the cultural walls have gone up inside Canada'. Multiculturalism encourages ethnic leaders to keep their members 'apart from the mainstream', practising 'what can best be described as mono-culturalism'. In this way the Canadian state 'encourages these gatekeepers to maintain what amounts, at worst, to an apartheid form of citizenship'.

Bissoondath and Gwyn are hardly alone in these claims; they are repeated endlessly in the media. To take just one example, Robert Fulford recently argued in *The Globe and Mail* that the policy encourages people to maintain a 'freeze-dried' identity, reducing intercultural exchange and relationships, and that time will judge it to be one of Canada's greatest 'policy failures'.[9]

It is important—indeed urgent—to determine whether such claims are true. Surprisingly, however, neither Bissoondath nor Gwyn provides any empirical evidence for his views. In order to assess their claims, therefore, I have collected some statistics that may bear on the question of whether multiculturalism has promoted ethnic separatism, and discouraged or impeded integration. I will start with evidence from within Canada, paring ethnic groups before and after the adoption of the multiculturalism policy in 1971.

* * *

How has the adoption ... lism in 1971 affected the integrati... Canada? To answer this ques... count of what 'integration' invo... puzzling features of the Gwyn and ... tiques that neither defines exactly what he means by integration. However, we can piece together some of the elements they see as crucial: adopting a Canadian identity rather than clinging exclusively to one's ancestral identity; participating in broader Canadian

(Continued)

institutions rather than participating solely in ethnic-specific institutions; learning an official language rather than relying solely on one's mother tongue; having inter-ethnic friendships or even mixed marriages, rather than socializing entirely within one's ethnic group. Such criteria do not form a comprehensive theory of 'integration', but they seem to be at the heart of Gwyn's and Bissoondath's concerns about multiculturalism, so they are a good starting point.

Let us begin with the most basic form of integration: the decision of an immigrant to become a Canadian citizen. If the Gwyn/Bissoondath thesis were true, one would expect naturalization rates to have declined since the adoption of multiculturalism. In fact, naturalization rates have increased since 1971.[10] This is particularly relevant because the economic incentives to naturalize have lessened over the last 25 years. Canadian citizenship is not needed in order to enter the labour market in Canada, or to gain access to social benefits. There are virtually no differences between citizens and permanent residents in their civil rights or social benefits; the right to vote is the only major legal benefit gained by naturalization.[11] The primary reason for immigrants to take out citizenship, therefore, is that they identify with Canada; they want to formalize their membership in Canadian society and to participate in the political life of the country.

Moreover, if we examine which groups are most likely to naturalize, we find that it is the 'multicultural groups'—immigrants from non-traditional source countries, for whom the multiculturalism policy is most relevant—that have the highest rates of naturalization. By contrast, immigrants from the United States and United Kingdom, who are not seen in popular discourse as 'ethnic' or 'multicultural' groups, have the lowest rates of naturalization.[12] In other words, those groups that are most directly affected by the multiculturalism policy have shown the greatest desire to become Canadian, while those that fall outside the multiculturalism rubric have shown the least desire to become Canadian.

Let's move now to political participation. If the Gwyn/Bissoondath thesis were true, one would expect the political participation of ethnocultural minorities to have declined since the adoption of multiculturalism in 1971. After all, political participation is a symbolic affirmation of citizenship, and reflects an interest in the political life of the larger society. Yet there is no evidence of decline in such participation.[13] To take one relevant indicator, between Confederation and the 1960s, in the period prior to the adoption of multiculturalism, ethnic groups became increasingly underrepresented in Parliament, but since 1971 the trend has been reversed, so that today they have nearly as many MPs as one would expect, given their percentage of the population.[14]

It is also important to note the way ethnocultural groups participate in Canadian politics. They do not form separate ethnic-based parties, either as individual groups or as coalitions, but participate overwhelmingly within pan-Canadian parties. Indeed, the two parties in Canada that are closest to being ethnic parties were created by and for those of French or English ancestry: the Parti/Bloc Quebecois, whose support comes almost entirely from Quebecers of French ancestry, and the Confederation of Regions Party, whose support came almost entirely from New Brunswickers of English Loyalist ancestry.[15] Immigrants themselves have shown no inclination to support ethnic-based political parties, and instead vote for the traditional national parties.

This is just one indicator of a more general point: namely, that immigrants are overwhelmingly supportive of, and committed to protecting, the country's basic political structure. We know that, were it not for the 'ethnic vote', the 1995 referendum on secession in Quebec would have succeeded. In that referendum, ethnic voters overwhelmingly expressed their commitment to Canada. More generally, all the indicators suggest that immigrants quickly absorb and accept Canada's basic liberal-democratic values and constitutional principles, even if their home countries are illiberal or non-democratic.[16] As Freda Hawkins puts it, 'the truth is that there have been no riots, no breakaway political parties, no charismatic immigrant leaders, no real militancy in international causes, no internal political terrorism . . . . immigrants recognize a good, stable political system when they see one.'[17] If we look at indicators of legal and political integration, then, we see that since the adoption of multiculturalism in 1971 immigrants have been more likely to become Canadians, and more likely to participate politically. And when they participate, they do so through pan-ethnic political parties that uphold Canada's basic liberal-democratic principles.

This sort of political integration is the main aim of a democratic state. Yet from the point of view of individual Canadians, the most important forms of immigrant integration are probably not political, but societal. Immigrants who participate in politics may be good democratic citizens, but if they can't speak English or French, or are socially isolated in self-contained ethnic groups, then Canadians will perceive a failure of integration. So let us shift now to two indicators of societal integration: official language acquisition and intermarriage rates.

If the Gwyn/Bissoondath thesis were true, one would expect to find that the desire of ethnocultural minorities to acquire official language competence has declined since the adoption of multiculturalism. If immigrant groups are being 'ghettoized', are 'alienated from the mainstream', and are attempting to preserve their original way of life intact from their homeland, then presumably they have less reason than they did before 1971 to learn an official language.

In fact, demand for classes in English and French as second languages (ESL; FSL) has never been higher, and actually exceeds supply in many cities. According to the 1991 Census, 98.6 per cent of Canadians report that they can speak one of the official languages.[18] This figure is staggering when one considers how many immigrants are elderly and/or illiterate in their mother tongue, and who therefore find it extremely difficult to learn a new language. It is especially impressive given that the number of immigrants who arrive with knowledge of an official language has declined since 1971.[19] If we set aside the elderly—who make up the majority of the Canadians who cannot speak an official language—the idea that there is a general decrease in immigrants' desire to learn an official language is absurd. The overwhelming majority do learn an official language, and insofar as such skills are lacking, the explanation is the lack of accessible and appropriate ESL/FSL classes, not lack of desire.[20]

Another indicator worth looking at is intermarriage rates. If the Gwyn/Bissoondath thesis were true, one would expect intermarriage to have declined since the adoption of a policy said to have driven 'even deeper the awful wedges between races and nationalities' and to have encouraged groups to retreat into 'monocultural' ghettos and hide behind 'cultural walls'. In fact, intermarriage rates have consistently increased since 1971. There has been an overall decline in endogamy, both for immigrants and for their native-born children. Moreover, and equally important, we see a dramatic increase in social acceptance of mixed marriages.[21] Whereas in 1968 a majority of Canadians (52 per cent) disapproved of Black-White marriages, the situation is now completely reversed, so that by 1995 an overwhelming majority (81 per cent) approved of such marriages.[22]

Unlike the previous three indicators of integration, intermarriage is not a deliberate goal of government policy; it is not the business of governments either to encourage or to discourage intermarriage. But changes in intermarriage rates are useful as indicators of a broader trend that is a legitimate government concern: namely, the extent to which Canadians feel comfortable living and interacting with members of other ethnic groups. If Canadians feel comfortable living and working with members of other groups, inevitably some people will become friends with, and even lovers of, members of other ethnic groups. The fact that intermarriage rates have gone up is important, therefore, not necessarily in itself, but rather as evidence that Canadians are more accepting of diversity. And we have direct evidence for this more general trend. Canadians today are much more willing to accept members of other ethnic groups as co-workers, neighbours, or friends than they were before 1971.[23]

Other indicators point to the same trends. For example, despite Gwyn's and Bissoondath's rhetoric about the proliferation of ethnic 'ghettos' and 'enclaves', studies of residential concentration have shown that permanent ethnic enclaves do not exist in Canada. Indeed, 'it is scarcely sensible to talk of "ghettos" in Canadian cities.'[24] What little concentration does exist is more likely to be found among older immigrant groups, like the Jews and Italians, whose arrival preceded the multiculturalism policy. Groups that have arrived primarily after 1971, such as Asians and Afro-Caribbeans, exhibit the least residential concentration.[25]

In short, whether we look at naturalization, political participation, official language competence, or intermarriage rates, we see the same story. There is no evidence to support the claim that multiculturalism has decreased the rate of integration of immigrants, or increased the separatism or mutual hostility of ethnic groups. As Orest Kruhlak puts it, 'irrespective of which variables one examines, including [citizenship acquisition, ESL, mother-tongue retention, ethnic association participation, intermarriage] or political participation, the scope of economic involvement, or participation in mainstream social or service organizations, none suggest a sense of promoting ethnic separateness.'[26]

- What arguments do Bissoondath and Gywn present against multiculturalism? How does Kymlicka respond?
- Do you find Kymlicka's arguments convincing? Why or why not?
- How has Canada benefitted from being a multicultural society? Do you think that our focus on multiculturalism since 1971 has brought us closer to Trudeau's ideal of the 'just society'?

As we have noted, some authors have criticized multiculturalism on primarily *political* grounds. (According to Neil Bissoondath and Richard Gwyn, for instance, multiculturalist policies are tearing the country apart, weakening the ties that bind Canadians together, and destroying an already fragile national identity.) However, it is worth noting that multiculturalism has been attacked on *philosophical* grounds as well. For example, some have worried that multiculturalism rests on a noxious form of relativism—a relativism that says that there are no objective truths or standards independent of one's culture by which that culture can be judged or criticized. Here, you will observe, the worry isn't just that widespread adherence to such radical relativism would be a disaster in practice (though that might well be true); it is that this relativistic view of truth is as grotesquely mistaken as it is naive.

The argument we want to think about now runs as follows: 'Multiculturalism is a form of radical relativism; but such relativism is absurd; therefore, multiculturalism must be wrong.' Now, is this a good argument? How we answer this question depends crucially on whether or not we accept the premise that multiculturalism *is* a form of radical relativism. According to Charles Taylor, this premise is faulty. In his essay 'The Other and Ourselves: Is Multiculturalism Inherently Relativist?', Taylor contends that we can accept and respect cultural differences without giving up on the idea of objective truth.

From 'The Other and Ourselves'
By Charles Taylor

Understanding 'the other' will pose the twenty-first century's greatest social challenge. The days are over when 'Westerners' could consider their experience and culture as the norm and other cultures merely as earlier stages in the West's development. Nowadays, most of the West senses the arrogant presumption at the heart of that old belief.

Sadly, this newfound modesty, so necessary for understanding other cultures and traditions, threatens to veer into relativism and a questioning of the very idea of truth in human affairs. For it may seem impossible to combine objectivity with the recognition of fundamental conceptual differences between cultures. So cultural openness poses the risk that we debase the currency of our values.

To grapple with this dilemma, we must understand culture's place in human life. Culture, self-understanding, and language mediate whatever we identify as fundamental to a common human nature. Across human history, always and everywhere, these basic faculties have demonstrated endless extraordinary innovation.

In accounting for such variety, some people anchor our understanding of human nature at a level below that of culture. Sociobiology, for example, seeks to discover human motivation in the ways that human beings evolved. Advocates of this view claim that cultural variation is but the surface play of appearances.

But we can never discover species-wide laws, because we can never operate outside of our historically and culturally specific understanding of what it is to be a human being. Our account of the decline of the Roman Empire is not and *cannot* be the same as that put forward in eighteenth-century England, and it will differ from accounts offered in twenty-second-century Brazil or twenty-fifth-century China.

Here the charge of relativism arises. But it is wrong to believe that accepting cultural differences requires abandoning allegiance to truth. The seventeenth-century scientific revolution's great achievement was to develop a language for nature that purged the purpose- and value-terms bequeathed by Plato and Aristotle to earlier scientific languages, which were nourished by earlier civilizations.

But the universality of the language of natural science cannot be applied to the study of human beings, where a host of theories and approaches compete. One reason for this is that the language of human science draws on our ordinary understanding of what it is to be human, to live in society, to have moral convictions, aspire to happiness, and so on. No matter how much our everyday views may be questioned by a theory, we nonetheless draw on our understanding of basic features of human life that seem so obvious as to need no formulation. It is these tacit understandings that make it difficult to understand people of another time or place.

Ethnocentrism results from the unchallenged understandings that we unwittingly carry with us, and which we cannot dispel by adopting another attitude. If our tacit sense of the human condition can block our understanding of others, and if it is so fundamental to who we are that we cannot merely wish it away, are we utterly imprisoned in our own outlooks, unable to know others?

True understanding in human affairs requires a patient identification and undoing of those facets of our implicit assumptions that distort the reality of 'the other'. This can happen when we begin to see our own peculiarities clearly, as facts *about us*, and not simply as taken-for-granted features of the general human condition. At the same time, we must begin to perceive, without distorting, corresponding features in the lives of others.

Our understanding of the 'other' will be improved through these corrections, but it will remain imperfect. If the historiography of the Roman Empire in twenty-fifth-century China turns out to be different from our own, this will not be because the facts will be found to be different than we (or twenty-second-century Brazilians) thought. The difference will be that different questions will be asked, different issues raised, and different features will stand out as remarkable. Of course, as in our time, some accounts will be more ethnocentric and distortive, others more superficial. In short, some will be more 'right' and come closer to truth than others.

Avoiding distortion requires acknowledging that our way of being is not uniquely 'natural', that it merely represents one among many possible forms. We can no longer relate to our way of doing or construing things as if it were too obvious to mention. There can be no understanding of 'the other' without a changed understanding of the self—an identity shift that alters our understanding of ourselves, our goals, and our values. This is why multiculturalism is so often resisted. We have a deep investment in our distorted images of others.

Most of us recognize that we are enriched by understanding other human possibilities. It cannot be denied, however, that the path to acknowledging their existence and value can be painful. The crucial moment occurs when the 'other's' differences can be perceived not as error, or as a fault, or as the product of a lesser, undeveloped version of what we are, but as the challenge posed by a viable human alternative.

Other societies present us with different and often disconcerting ways of being human. Our task is to acknowledge the humanity of these 'other' ways while still living our own. That this may be difficult to achieve, that it will demand a change in our self-understanding and hence in our way of life, is the challenge our societies must reckon with in the years ahead.

- What does Taylor mean by 'the other'? Why is understanding 'the other' so important in the twenty-first century?
- According to Taylor, understanding 'the other' requires that we change our self-understanding. What does he mean by this?
- Why does Taylor think multiculturalism 'is so often resisted'? Do you agree?

One pressing problem facing multicultural and multiethnic societies such as Canada is racism. What can we do to address this grave problem? In 'Modern Racism in Canada', Phil Fontaine, speaking as National Chief of the Assembly of First Nations, outlines one possible response:

From 'Modern Racism in Canada'
By Phil Fontaine

The heinous violations of human rights which have been perpetuated upon our people for generations, merely because of our race, cannot go unmarked.

As far as Aboriginal people are concerned, racism in Canadian society continues to invade our lives institutionally, systematically, and individually. The Aboriginal Justice Inquiry in Manitoba, the Donald Marshall Inquiry in Nova Scotia, the Cawsey Report in Alberta, and the Royal Commission on Aboriginal Peoples all agree. The question now is, What is to be done?

Anti-racism strategies, to the extent that they exist, are all about the relative value of human lives. A negative response to racism is a statement that victims of racism are valued members of our society. Recognizing the harms of racism and the need to strengthen our dangerously fickle collective commitment to equality requires us to *listen* to those who suffer from discrimination, and to hear their stories. Sustainable solutions toward equality between Aboriginal and non-Aboriginal Canadians can be developed, but the truth of the present and past must be told.

Patricia Monture, a Mohawk woman and legal scholar, stated that if the white society cannot bring itself to understand the pain that Aboriginal men, women, and children go through, then they are never going to understand anything. All the equality promises in the world will not get us anywhere because without that understanding, the theories do not reflect social reality, and do not reflect peoples' experiences. To combat racism, we must give up on monolithic, ethnocentric reality and believe that there is something to be learned and a better society to be achieved by listening to formerly silenced people. Listening to the powerless may, in turn, lead to the understanding that some groups and group members have enjoyed disproportionate privilege, including the power to define, to appropriate, and to control the realities of others.

It must be understood that racists have no interest or desire to investigate the reality of others different from themselves nor the injustices that result when others' realities are imposed upon them. Their objectives are to roll back progress through the mobilization of fear, resentment, ignorance, and intolerance. For them, difference is dealt with by making it disappear, by treating everyone the same. Non-Aboriginal Canadians must understand that this never has been and never will be good enough, because it will only perpetuate racism, indefinitely. Equality requires a commitment to the proposition that there are alternative claims to the 'truth'.

Another prerequisite to future equality is an accounting of the past. The heinous violations of human rights which have been perpetuated upon our people for generations, merely because of our race, cannot go unmarked. Their extent should be catalogued, their detail exposed, and their causes explored. Once all this has been done, the results must be published so that society will have a lasting record and guide to avoid future repetition of the violations we have suffered. If the truth of residential schools, religious persecution, cultural destruction, and mass abductions of our children remains unexplored and obscure, I fear that equality, peace, and justice will elude our grasp. Only when misconduct is exposed and addressed can we begin to build a fence around it and move confidently and purposefully toward the full achievement of equality, dignity, and respect. Some progress has been made. A first step was taken with the establishment of the Healing Fund and the apology for residential school abuse. Many other steps remain which will require the partnership of goodwill of both Aboriginal and non-Aboriginal Canadians.

I look forward to travelling this path with all Canadians.

- What can we do to end racial injustice in Canada, according to Fontaine?
- Compare Fontaine's position with what Taylor says about the need to understand 'the other'. Where do you think they agree? Where do they disagree?

GLOSSARY

Abrahamic religions The Western monotheisms: Judaism, Christianity, and Islam (they all trace their roots from the prophet Abraham).

absolute space and **absolute time** The view that space and time exist independently of objects and events 'in' them, a view defended by Newton. In general, *absolute*, as used in philosophy, means 'independent and non-relative, unqualified and all-inclusive'.

absolutism The thesis that there is but one correct view of reality. Opposed to relativism (See *relations of ideas*).

abstract Overly general, not concrete, independent of particular concerns or objects. For example, a philosopher may attempt to ascertain the nature of justice without particular reference to any concrete practical case.

action-at-a-distance The idea that one object can have a causal effect on another from a distance, as in Newton's laws of gravitational attraction. Leibniz's rejection of this idea as 'absurd' led him to develop a non-causal interpretation of the same phenomena.

ad hominem **argument** An argument against the person instead of the position; for example, attacking a philosopher's living habits instead of his or her theories.

agent causation The metaphysical thesis that agents or selves, not events, are the ultimate causes of free actions. Theories of agent causation have been defended by libertarians such as Thomas Reid (in the eighteenth century) and Roderick Chisholm (in the twentieth).

agnosticism The refusal to believe either that God exists or that He does not exist, usually on the grounds that there can be no sufficient evidence for either belief.

Ahura Mazda The God of Zoroastrianism.

alienation In Marx, the unnatural separation of a person from the products he or she makes, from other people, or from oneself.

analytic (of a sentence or truth) Demonstrably true (and necessarily true) by virtue of the logical form or the meanings of the component words. The concept was introduced by Kant, who defined it in terms of a sentence (he called it a 'judgment') in which the 'predicate was contained in the subject' and 'added nothing to it'. For example, in 'a horse is an animal', he would say that the concept of 'horse' already includes the concept of being an animal; we would say that 'horse' means 'an animal that . . .' and thus 'is an animal' adds nothing to what we already know just from 'horse'. Kant also says that the *criterion* or test for analytic sentences (or analyticity) is the principle of contradiction; an analytic sentence is one for which denial yields a self-contradiction.

analytic philosophy See *linguistic philosophy*.

anarchism The view that no government has the legitimate authority to coerce people and that the public interest and individual rights can only be served without a state of any kind.

Angra Mainyush The evil spirit of Zoroastrianism.

animism The view that things (or, at the extreme, all things) are alive. It may also be the view that the universe as a whole is one gigantic organism.

antecedent conditions Those circumstances, states of affairs, or events that regularly precede and can be said to cause an event. The antecedent conditions of boiling water, for example, are the application of heat to water under normal atmospheric pressure, and so on. A determinist would say that the antecedent conditions of a human action would be the state of his or her nervous system, a developed character (with personality traits), certain desires and beliefs, and the circumstances (or 'stimulus') in which the action takes place.

anthropomorphic Humanlike. An anthropomorphic conception of God ascribes human attributes to Him.

apeiron In Anaximander, 'the unlimited', the basic stuff of the universe.

aphorism A short, striking general observation, usually just a sentence or two.

a posteriori (knowledge) 'After experience', or empirical. (See *empirical*.)

appearance The way something seems to us, through our senses. Usually philosophers worry about something's being a mere appearance, such that it bears no faithful resemblance to the reality of which it is the appearance.

a priori (knowledge) 'Before experience', or more accurately, independent of all experience. A priori knowledge is always necessary, for there can be no imaginable instances that would refute it and no intelligible doubting of it. One might come to know something a priori through experience (for example, you might find out that no parallel lines ever touch each other by drawing tens of thousands of parallel lines), but what is essential to a priori knowledge is that no such experience is needed. Knowledge is a priori if it can be proven independently of experience. The most obvious examples of a priori knowledge are analytic sentences, such as 'a horse is an animal' and 'if all men are mammals and Socrates is a man, then Socrates is a mammal'.

argument The process of reasoning from one claim to another. An argument may, but need not, be directed against an explicit alternative. A philosophical argument does not require an opponent or a disagreement.

argument from design See *teleological argument*.

asceticism A life of self-denial and material simplicity, often to further philosophical or religious goals.

Asha Immortal spirit or 'righteousness' in Zoroastrianism.

assertion A statement or declaration, taking a position. Mere assertion, when presented as an argument, is a fallacy; arguments consist not only of assertions but of reasons for them as well.

association of ideas A central idea of empiricist philosophy, according to which all knowledge is composed of separate ideas that are connected by their resemblance to one another (for example, 'this one looks exactly like that one'), by their contiguity in space and time (for example, 'every time I see this, I see that as well'), and by their causality (for example, 'every time a thing of that sort happens, it is followed by something of this sort'). (The three different 'associations' here are Hume's.)

assumption A principle taken for granted, without argument or proof.

atheism The belief that there is no God. A person who believes that there is no God is an *atheist*.

attribute In Spinoza, an essential property of God; for example, having a physical nature, having thoughts. In general, an attribute is a property (as in Aristotle).

authenticity Modern moral ideal that stresses individual self-fulfillment and self-fidelity. When we speak about being true to one's own nature, being in touch with oneself, expressing oneself, doing one's own thing, or following one's own path in life, we are speaking the language of authenticity.

authority That which controls; usually, that which has the right to control. (For example, the government has the authority to tax your income.)

autonomy Intellectual independence and freedom from authority. Moral autonomy is the ability of every rational person to reach his or her own moral conclusions about what is right and what is wrong. (This does not mean that they will therefore come to different conclusions.)

axiom A principle that is generally accepted from the beginning and so may be used without further debate as a starting point of argument.

bad faith Sartre's characterization of a person's refusal to accept himself or herself. This sometimes means not accepting the facts that are true about you. More often it means accepting the facts about you as conclusive about your identity, as in the statement 'Oh, I couldn't do that, I'm too shy'.

Becoming (in Plato) The 'world of Becoming' is the changing world of our daily experience, in which things and people come into being and pass away.

begging the question Merely restating as the conclusion of an argument one of its premises. For example, 'Why do oysters give me indigestion? Because they upset my stomach.'

behaviourism In psychology, the radical methodological thesis that insists that only what is publicly observable can be used as subject matter or as evidence in scientific research regarding human beings. In particular, all talk of 'minds' and 'mental events', 'desires', 'purposes', 'ideas', 'perceptions', and 'experiences' is to be given up in favour of terms that refer only to the experimental situation or the behaviour of the creature (or person) in question (for example, 'stimulus', 'response', 'reinforcements'). In philosophy and metaphysics, behaviourism is the logical thesis that there are no 'covert' or 'private' mental events, only patterns of behaviour and psychological ways of talking about behaviour as 'intelligent', 'deceitful', 'calculating', or 'inattentive'. All of these must

be understood not in terms of some process ('intelligence', 'deceitful thinking', 'calculating', or 'lack of attending') going on 'in the mind' but rather as ways of interpreting, predicting, and otherwise describing and evaluating behaviour.

Being (in Plato) The 'world of Being' is the realm of eternal Forms, in which nothing ever changes. It is, for him, reality. In general, Being is used by philosophers to refer to whatever they consider ultimately real (substance, God, etc.).

best of all possible worlds Leibniz's view that God demands a perfect universe and makes it 'the best possible', all things considered.

Bhagavadgītā (Gītā) The 'Song of God' of ancient Hinduism; the epic poem of Krishna, who is God incarnate.

Brahma (Brahman) Precursor of God in Hindu theism; the idea of the One, the unity underlying all things.

Buddha 'The awakened one'; the historical founder of Buddhism.

Cartesianism Concerning Descartes. In particular, concerning his philosophical method. (Descartes' followers are generally called 'Cartesians' and their method 'Cartesianism'.) The Cartesian method is essentially a deductive method, as in geometry, starting with self-evident axioms and deducing the rest.

categorical imperative In Kant's philosophy, a moral law, a command that is unqualified and not dependent on any conditions or qualifications. In particular, that rule that tells us to act in such a way that we would want everyone else to act the same way.

categories Kant's word (borrowed from Aristotle) for those most basic and a priori concepts of human knowledge, for example, 'causality' and 'substance'.

causal interactionism The theory that mind and body causally interact, that mental events (for example, an 'act of will') can cause a bodily consequence (for example, raising one's arm) and that a bodily change (for example, a puncture of the skin) can cause a mental consequence (for example, a pain).

causal theory of perception The view that our experience (our sensations and ideas) are the effects of physical objects acting upon our sense organs (which are thereby the causes).

causation (or causality) The relation of cause and effect, one event's bringing about another according to natural law. In Hume, (1) one event's following another necessarily (or so it seems to us); (2) one type of event regularly following another (see *association of ideas*).

cause That which brings something about. On the hard determinist interpretation, a cause is an antecedent condition that, together with other antecedent conditions, is sufficient to make the occurrence of some event necessary, according to the laws of nature. On a weaker interpretation, a cause may simply be an event (or condition) that regularly precedes another event and thus can be used to predict when the latter will occur. (For example, if we say 'a cause of forest fires is lightning', we mean 'whenever lightning strikes a sufficiently dry forest, fire will occur'.) In Aristotle, 'cause' means something like 'reason', and he distinguishes four different kinds of 'causes' of a change: (1) the *formal* cause, the principle or essential idea according to which a change comes about (think of a blueprint for a building); (2) the *material* cause, the matter that undergoes the change (think of the raw materials for building a house); (3) the *efficient* cause, that which initiates the change (for example, the construction workers and their tools); (4) the *final* cause, or the purpose of the change (to build a place where a family can live, for example).

cause-of-itself (*causa sui*) That which explains its own existence, often said of God. It also follows from the usual definitions of substance.

certainty Beyond doubt. The term is used in a more specific sense in philosophy than it is in psychology, for example, where *certain* means '*feeling*, beyond a doubt, that you know something' (this feeling could be wrong). One can be certain, in the philosophical sense, only if one can prove that the matter is beyond doubt, that no reasons for doubt could be raised.

civil rights Those rights that are determined by a particular state and its laws; constitutional rights, for example, are civil rights in this sense, guaranteed by the law of the land.

cogito, ergo sum ('I think, therefore I am') Descartes' only principle that he finds 'beyond doubt' and 'perfectly certain'. ('Think' here refers to any kind of idea or experience in the mind, not just what we would call 'thinking'.) It is the premise of his entire philosophy.

coherence Logical connection. A statement by a witness in a courtroom coheres with other testimony and evidence when it fits in and follows from that other testimony and evidence. A philosophy is coherent if its various principles fit together in an orderly and logically agreeable fashion.

coherence theory of truth A statement or a belief is true if and only if it 'coheres' with a system of statements or beliefs. A truth of mathematics is 'true' because it forms part of the nexus in the complex of mathematical truths. A geometrical theorem is 'true' because it can be proven from other theorems (axioms, definitions) of the geometrical system. A 'factual' statement is 'true' insofar as other 'factual' statements, including general statements about experience that are logically relevant to the original statement, support it. Since we can never get 'outside' our experience, the only sense in saying that a belief is true (according to this theory) is that it 'coheres' with the rest of our experience.

commitment To form a binding obligation voluntarily. In Sartre's moral philosophy, a commitment is a freely chosen adoption of a moral principle or project that one thereby vows to defend and practise, even in the absence of any other reasons for doing so. Since, according to Sartre, there are never conclusive reasons for adopting any particular moral position, one must always defend his or her position through commitment and nothing else.

compatibilism The thesis that both determinism (on some interpretations) and free action can be true. Determinism does not rule out free action and the possibility of free action does not require that determinism be false. They are compatible positions.

compulsion Being forced to do something. One acts from compulsion (or is compelled to act) when he or she could not have done otherwise. Some philosophers distinguish between *external* compulsions (for example, a push) and *internal* compulsions (for example, a neurotic obsession).

conceptual truth A statement that is true and that we can see to be true by virtue of the meanings of the words (or we should say, the 'concepts') that compose it. For example, 'a horse is an animal' is a conceptual truth because anyone who speaks English and knows the meaning of the words 'horse' and 'animal' knows that such a statement must be true; part of the definition of the word *horse* is 'an animal'. In Plato, a conceptual truth is a truth about Forms. In Aristotle, a conceptual truth is a matter of describing the essence of a thing. (See *essence, Form*.)

conscience A sense or feeling about what is right and wrong, usually without argument. (It is like intuition in matters of knowledge.) In Christian moral theory, it is a moral sense instilled in us by God. In Freudian psychology, it is the internalization of the moral lessons given us as children by our parents and teachers.

consistent Fitting together in an orderly logical way. Two principles are consistent if they do not contradict each other. A philosophy is consistent if none of its principles contradict each other.

constitute To put together, 'set up', or synthesize experience through categories or concepts. First used by Kant, later by Husserl.

contemplation, the life of According to Aristotle (and other philosophers), the happiest life, the life of thought and philosophy.

contingent (truth) Dependent on the facts; neither logically necessary nor logically impossible. A contingent state of affairs could have been otherwise. One test to see if a state of affairs is contingent is to see if it is conceivable that it could be other than it is. It is contingent, for example, that heavy objects fall toward the earth, since it is easily imaginable what it would be like if they did not. This is so even though, in another sense, we say that it is (physically) necessary that heavy objects fall. The philosophical terms *contingent* and *necessary* refer to logical possibility, not to the factual question of whether a statement is true or not.

continuity (spatiotemporal continuity) The uninterrupted identifiability of an object over time in the same location or in a sequence of tangent locations.

contradiction The logical relation of two principles in which the truth of one requires the falsity of the other. A witness's statement in court contradicts other testimony if both statements cannot be true.

correspondence theory of truth A statement or belief is true if and only if it 'corresponds' with 'the facts'. (Even when restricting our attention to statements of fact, however, this commonsensical 'theory' gets into trouble as soon as it tries to pick out what corresponds to what. How can we identify a 'fact', for example, apart from the language we use to identify it? And what does it mean to say that a statement 'corresponds' to a fact?)

cosmogony The study of the origins of the universe in its entirety.

cosmological argument An argument (or set of arguments) that undertakes to 'prove' that God exists on the basis of the idea that there must have been a first cause or an ultimate reason for the existence of the universe (the cosmos).

cosmology The study of the universe in its entirety (from the Greek word for 'universe'—*cosmos*).

counter-example An example that contradicts a generalization, such as 'all elephants have tusks'. A counter-example would be an elephant without tusks.

criterion The test or standard according to which a judgment or an evaluation can be made. For example, a test for a substance's being an acid is whether or not it turns litmus paper red. In ancient skepticism, a sufficient guarantee of truth.

critical Thinking so as to be mindful of mistakes in reasoning; to be critical is not necessarily to be unpleasant.

cultural relativism The descriptive anthropological thesis that different societies have different moralities. These moralities must be fundamentally different, not only different in details. For example, different societies might have slightly different definitions of 'theft' yet be very similar to one another in other respects, but a society that does not have a conception of private property would likely be fundamentally different from one that does.

Cynics Group of post-Socratic philosophers who taught that the good life was a life of complete autonomy. They minimized the social values of success, wealth, and honour and focussed their attention on what makes a person wholly self-sufficient. For Diogenes, this consisted of the simplest life possible, based upon simple pleasures and simple virtues. For Aristippus, this consisted of a life of immediate pleasure.

Dao The 'Way'. In Confucianism, the 'way' to be a gentleman, for example, following the rituals; in Daoism, the underlying and ineffable 'way' of nature or reality.

datum Latin, literally, 'what is given'. (plural, *data*)

deduction (deductive argument) A process of reasoning from one principle to another by means of accepted rules of inference. In a deductive argument, a conclusion follows necessarily from the premises, and so if you are certain of the premises, you can be certain of the conclusion, too.

deism Popular in the science-minded eighteenth century, deism holds that God must have existed to create the universe with all of its laws (and thereby usually accepts some form of the cosmological argument) but also holds that there is no justification for our belief that

God has any special concern for man, any concern for justice, or any of those anthropomorphic attributes for which we worship Him, pray to Him, and believe in biblical stories about Him.

democracy That form of government in which policies or at least the makers of policy are chosen by popular mandate.

deontology Ethics based on duty (from the Greek *dein*). Kant's ethic is deontological in that it stresses obedience to principle rather than attention to consequences (including happiness).

dependent being In metaphysics, a being that depends on some other being(s) for its existence. In other words, a thing that derives its existence from something outside itself.

determinism The view that every event in the universe is dependent upon other events, which are its causes. On this view, all human actions and decisions, even those that we would normally describe as 'free' and 'undetermined', are totally dependent on prior events that cause them.

Deus absconditus Latin phrase meaning 'hidden God'.

dharma In Hinduism, righteousness, the way of the good.

dialectic Argument through dialogue, disagreement, and successive revisions, out of which comes agreement. Alternatively, a 'logic' developed by Hegel in which different forms or philosophies are arranged according to increasing sophistication and scope; the 'logic' is a development from one form, whose inadequacies are demonstrated, to another, which corrects these inadequacies, and so on. Marx borrows this 'dialectic' and gives it a social interpretation. (The 'logic' need not be anything like the form 'thesis-antithesis-synthesis'.)

distributive justice The ideal of everyone receiving his or her fair share. For example, concerns over ownership of land, just wages, and fair prices are all matters of distributive justice.

divine pre-ordination God's knowledge of and power over all that will happen, including our own future actions.

doubt Lack of certainty; lack of reasons to believe, and perhaps having reasons not to believe. It is important to distinguish doubt in this philosophical sense from doubt in the ordinary psychological sense. Mere personal uncertainty or distrust is not sufficient; there must be a demonstrable reason for doubt, that is, reasons for not accepting the beliefs in question.

dual aspect theory The theory (for example, in Spinoza) that mind and body are simply different aspects (or 'attributes') of one and the same substance, thus avoiding the problem of interaction between substances.

dualism In general, the distinction between mind and body as separate substances, or very different kinds of states and events with radically different properties.

duty What one is morally bound to do.

egalitarianism The view that all people are equal in rights and respect.

egoism The thesis that people act for their own interests. *Psychological egoism* is merely the thesis that they in fact

act in their own interests; *ethical egoism* is the thesis that people ought to act in their own interests.

eliminative materialism The thesis that increasing knowledge of neurology eventually will allow us to give up our 'folk-psychological' terminology of mental states.

empirical (knowledge) Derived from and to be defended by appeal to experience. Empirical knowledge can only be so derived and so defended (as opposed to a priori knowledge, which need not be).

empirical ego All those characteristics of a person that can be discovered through experience and that distinguish each of us from other persons qualitatively; that which makes each of us a particular man or woman and gives us a particular 'character'. Compare *transcendental ego*.

empiricism The philosophy that demands that all knowledge, except for certain logical truths and principles of mathematics, comes from experience. British empiricism is often used to refer specifically to Locke, Berkeley, and Hume. It is still very much alive, however, and includes Bertrand Russell in the twentieth century and a great many philosophers of the past fifty or so years who have called themselves 'logical empiricists' (better known as logical positivists).

Enlightenment A cultural and philosophical movement in the eighteenth century in Europe defined by a new confidence in human reason and individual autonomy. In France, some of the major figures of this movement were René Descartes, Paul Henri d'Holbach, Jean-Jacques Rousseau, and Voltaire. In Great Britain, Enlightenment philosophers were John Locke and David Hume; in Germany, Immanuel Kant.

entitlement A right; for instance, a right to own property.

epiphenomenalism The thesis that mental events are epiphenomena, that is, side effects of various physical processes in the brain and nervous system but of little importance themselves. The model is a one-way causal model: Body states cause changes in the mind, but mental states have no effect in themselves on the body.

epistemology The study of human knowledge, its nature, its sources, its justification. The term was coined by James Frederick Ferrier.

equality In political philosophy, the non-discriminatory treatment of every person, regardless of sex, race, religion, physical or mental abilities, wealth, social status, and so forth.

essence (or an essential property) The necessary or defining characteristics or properties of a thing. The essence of a person is that without which we would not say one is *that* particular person (Fred rather than Mary, for example). Husserl borrowed the term from Aristotle (and the medieval philosophers) and used it in much the same way, except that Husserl's notion of essence is always tied to 'intuition' and consciousness. In Husserl's writings, 'essence' or 'essential intuition' refers to those ideal objects and laws that constitute necessary truths.

ethical absolutism The thesis that there is one and only one correct morality.

ethical altruism The thesis that one ought to act for the sake of the interests of others.

ethical egoism The thesis that people ought to act in their own interests.

ethical relativism The thesis that different moralities should be considered equally correct even if they directly contradict each other. A morality is 'correct', by this thesis, merely if it is correct according to the particular society that accepts it.

ethics A system of general moral principles and a conception of morality and its foundation. Or, the study of moral principles.

eudaimonia Aristotle's word for 'happiness,' or, more literally, 'living well'.

existentialism The modern movement in philosophy that puts great emphasis on individual choice and the voluntary acceptance of all values. In Sartre's terms, existentialism is the philosophy that teaches that 'man's existence precedes his essence'. That is, people have no given self-identity, they have to choose their identities and work for them through their actions. (Neglect and omission, however, are also actions. One can be a certain type of person just by not bothering to do the appropriate activities.)

explanation An account—usually a causal account—of something; it is opposed to *justification*, which also defends. One can, for example, explain one's action (say, by claiming that he or she was drunk) without thereby justifying it, that is, showing it to be right. Hume ultimately explains our knowledge but does not justify it.

extended Having spatial dimensions. Philosophers (for example, Descartes, Leibniz, and Spinoza) often define bodies as 'extended', while minds and ideas are 'unextended'.

extended (substance) Physical matter in space and time, material objects.

facticity Sartre's term (borrowed from Heidegger) for the totality of facts that are true of a person at any given time.

faith In theology, faith usually refers to the trust that a believer should have in God's ultimate grace and fairness. Sometimes, faith is defended as a rational belief in God (for example, in Kant). More often, faith is defended against rationality (as in Kierkegaard).

fallacy An apparently persuasive argument that is really an error in reasoning; an unsound or invalid argument.

fascism The view that the best government is the strongest, and that the government has the right—and perhaps the duty—to control the lives of every citizen for the sake of the most efficient society.

fatalism The thesis that certain events (or perhaps all events) are going to happen inevitably, regardless of what we take to prevent them.

first principles Those axioms and assumptions with which a philosophy begins. These must be indisputable principles; they need not be the principles that one happens to first believe.

Form (in Plato) An independently existing entity in the world of Being, which determines the nature of the particular things of this world. In Aristotle, forms have no independent existence.

Four Noble Truths Among the most important teachings of the Buddha: 'All is suffering (and transitory)', the need to eliminate desire, the way to eliminate desire, and the right path to the good.

freedom The idea that a human decision or action is a person's own responsibility and that praise and blame may be appropriately ascribed. The most extreme interpretation of 'freedom' is the absence of any causes or determinations. Thus an indeterminist would say that an event is free if it has no causes; a libertarian would say that a human act is free only if it is self-caused (not determined by anything else, including a person's character). Certain determinists, however ('soft determinists'), would say that an act is free only if it is 'in character' and based upon a person's desire and personality. Most generally, we say that a person's act is free—whether or not it is the result of a conscious decision and whether or not certain causes may be involved—if he or she could do otherwise. (See also *liberty*.)

freedom of the will Actions undetermined by external causes, including the power of God (though how God can leave us this 'indeterminacy' in spite of God's power and knowledge over us is and must be incomprehensible to us).

free will Among philosophers, a somewhat antiquated expression (as in 'he did it of his own free will') that means that a person is capable of making decisions that are not determined by antecedent conditions. Of course, there may be antecedent considerations, such as what a person wants or believes, but free will means that such considerations never determine a person's decision. At most they 'enter into the decision'.

functionalism The view that the mind is the product of a pattern in the brain, as in a computer, rather than a product of the matter of the brain as such.

generalization Usually, a proposition about all of a group or set of things on the basis of a limited acquaintance with some of its members. In logic, however, a generalization may be universal ('all *x*'s are *y*'s') or existential ('there are some *x*'s that are *y*'s').

generalization from experience (or inductive generalization) Inference from observation, experience, and experiment to a generalization about all members of a certain class. For example, in a laboratory, a researcher finds that certain experiments on tobacco plants always have the same result. He or she generalizes, through induction, from experimental observations to a claim (or *hypothesis*) about all tobacco plants. But notice that this generalization is never certain. It might always turn out there was a fluke in the experiment or that the researcher chose a peculiar sample of plants.

God In traditional Judeo-Christian theology, that being who created the universe and exists independently of it, who is all-powerful, all-knowing, everywhere at once, and concerned with justice and the ultimate welfare of humankind. When spelled with a small 'g' the word refers to any supernatural being worthy of worship or at least extraordinary respect.

Golden Rule 'Do unto others as you would have them do unto you.'

government The instrument of authority; that body that rules, passes and enforces laws, and so forth.

happiness The achievement of the good life. In Aristotle, the name we all agree to give to the good life, whatever it is. Happiness, in this sense, must not be confused with pleasure, which is but one (among many) concerns and conceptions of the good life.

happiness calculus (also *felicity calculus*) Bentham's technique for quantifying and adding up pleasures and pains as a way of deciding what to do.

hedonism The conception of the good life that takes pleasure to be the ultimate good. Hedonism is the premise of most forms of utilitarianism. It is often the premise—though sometimes a consequence—of ethical egoism. (These two are not the same: hedonism refers to *the end*; egoism refers to *whose ends*.)

Heisenberg uncertainty principle An important principle of physics, first proposed in the early twentieth century, that demonstrates that we cannot know both the position and the momentum of certain subatomic particles, for in our attempts to know one, we make it impossible to know the other. This principle has been used to attack the very idea of 'determinism' in its classical formulations, for determinism requires just the 'certainty' of possible prediction that the Heisenberg uncertainty principle rejects.

hermeneutics The discipline of interpretation of texts. Broadly conceived (as by Heidegger, Gadamer), it is the 'uncovering' of meanings in everyday life, the attempt to understand the signs and symbols of one's culture and tradition in juxtaposition with other cultures and traditions.

historicism A philosophy that localizes truth and different views of reality to particular times, places, and peoples in history. It is generally linked to a very strong relativist thesis as well, that there is no truth apart from these various historical commitments.

human rights Those rights that are considered to be universal, 'unalienable', and common to every person regardless of where or when he or she lives. For example, freedom from torture and degradation would be a human right.

Hume's fork Hume's insistence that every belief be justified either as a 'relation between ideas' or as a 'matter of fact'.

hypothesis A provisional conclusion, accepted as most probable in the light of the known facts or tentatively adopted as a basis for analysis.

hypothetical imperative In Kant, a command that is conditional, depending upon particular aims or inclinations. For example, 'if you want to be a doctor, then go to medical school'. According to Kant, all other philosophers act in their own interests; *ethical egoism* is the thesis that people ought to act in their own interests.

eliminative materialism The thesis that increasing knowledge of neurology eventually will allow us to give up our 'folk-psychological' terminology of mental states.

empirical (knowledge) Derived from and to be defended by appeal to experience. Empirical knowledge can only be so derived and so defended (as opposed to a priori knowledge, which need not be).

empirical ego All those characteristics of a person that can be discovered through experience and that distinguish each of us from other persons qualitatively; that which makes each of us a particular man or woman and gives us a particular 'character'. Compare *transcendental ego*.

empiricism The philosophy that demands that all knowledge, except for certain logical truths and principles of mathematics, comes from experience. British empiricism is often used to refer specifically to Locke, Berkeley, and Hume. It is still very much alive, however, and includes Bertrand Russell in the twentieth century and a great many philosophers of the past fifty or so years who have called themselves 'logical empiricists' (better known as logical positivists).

Enlightenment A cultural and philosophical movement in the eighteenth century in Europe defined by a new confidence in human reason and individual autonomy. In France, some of the major figures of this movement were René Descartes, Paul Henri d'Holbach, Jean-Jacques Rousseau, and Voltaire. In Great Britain, Enlightenment philosophers were John Locke and David Hume; in Germany, Immanuel Kant.

entitlement A right; for instance, a right to own property.

epiphenomenalism The thesis that mental events are epiphenomena, that is, side effects of various physical processes in the brain and nervous system but of little importance themselves. The model is a one-way causal model: Body states cause changes in the mind, but mental states have no effect in themselves on the body.

epistemology The study of human knowledge, its nature, its sources, its justification. The term was coined by James Frederick Ferrier.

equality In political philosophy, the non-discriminatory treatment of every person, regardless of sex, race, religion, physical or mental abilities, wealth, social status, and so forth.

essence (or an essential property) The necessary or defining characteristics or properties of a thing. The essence of a person is that without which we would not say one is *that* particular person (Fred rather than Mary, for example). Husserl borrowed the term from Aristotle (and the medieval philosophers) and used it in much the same way, except that Husserl's notion of essence is always tied to 'intuition' and consciousness. In Husserl's writings, 'essence' or 'essential intuition' refers to those ideal objects and laws that constitute necessary truths.

ethical absolutism The thesis that there is one and only one correct morality.

ethical altruism The thesis that one ought to act for the sake of the interests of others.

ethical egoism The thesis that people ought to act in their own interests.

ethical relativism The thesis that different moralities should be considered equally correct even if they directly contradict each other. A morality is 'correct', by this thesis, merely if it is correct according to the particular society that accepts it.

ethics A system of general moral principles and a conception of morality and its foundation. Or, the study of moral principles.

eudaimonia Aristotle's word for 'happiness,' or, more literally, 'living well'.

existentialism The modern movement in philosophy that puts great emphasis on individual choice and the voluntary acceptance of all values. In Sartre's terms, existentialism is the philosophy that teaches that 'man's existence precedes his essence'. That is, people have no given self-identity, they have to choose their identities and work for them through their actions. (Neglect and omission, however, are also actions. One can be a certain type of person just by not bothering to do the appropriate activities.)

explanation An account—usually a causal account—of something; it is opposed to *justification*, which also defends. One can, for example, explain one's action (say, by claiming that he or she was drunk) without thereby justifying it, that is, showing it to be right. Hume ultimately explains our knowledge but does not justify it.

extended Having spatial dimensions. Philosophers (for example, Descartes, Leibniz, and Spinoza) often define bodies as 'extended', while minds and ideas are 'unextended'.

extended (substance) Physical matter in space and time, material objects.

facticity Sartre's term (borrowed from Heidegger) for the totality of facts that are true of a person at any given time.

faith In theology, faith usually refers to the trust that a believer should have in God's ultimate grace and fairness. Sometimes, faith is defended as a rational belief in God (for example, in Kant). More often, faith is defended against rationality (as in Kierkegaard).

fallacy An apparently persuasive argument that is really an error in reasoning; an unsound or invalid argument.

fascism The view that the best government is the strongest, and that the government has the right—and perhaps the duty—to control the lives of every citizen for the sake of the most efficient society.

fatalism The thesis that certain events (or perhaps all events) are going to happen inevitably, regardless of what efforts we take to prevent them.

first principles Those axioms and assumptions from which a philosophy begins. These must be solid and indisputable principles; they need not be those principles that one happens to first believe.

Form (in Plato) An independently existing entity in the world of Being, which determines the nature of the particular things of this world. In Aristotle, forms have no independent existence.

Four Noble Truths Among the most important teachings of the Buddha: 'All is suffering (and transitory)', the need to eliminate desire, the way to eliminate desire, and the right path to the good.

freedom The idea that a human decision or action is a person's own responsibility and that praise and blame may be appropriately ascribed. The most extreme interpretation of 'freedom' is the absence of any causes or determinations. Thus an indeterminist would say that an event is free if it has no causes; a libertarian would say that a human act is free only if it is self-caused (not determined by anything else, including a person's character). Certain determinists, however ('soft determinists'), would say that an act is free only if it is 'in character' and based upon a person's desire and personality. Most generally, we say that a person's act is free—whether or not it is the result of a conscious decision and whether or not certain causes may be involved—if he or she could do otherwise. (See also *liberty*.)

freedom of the will Actions undetermined by external causes, including the power of God (though how God can leave us this 'indeterminacy' in spite of God's power and knowledge over us is and must be incomprehensible to us).

free will Among philosophers, a somewhat antiquated expression (as in 'he did it of his own free will') that means that a person is capable of making decisions that are not determined by antecedent conditions. Of course, there may be antecedent considerations, such as what a person wants or believes, but free will means that such considerations never determine a person's decision. At most they 'enter into the decision'.

functionalism The view that the mind is the product of a pattern in the brain, as in a computer, rather than a product of the matter of the brain as such.

generalization Usually, a proposition about all of a group or set of things on the basis of a limited acquaintance with some of its members. In logic, however, a generalization may be universal ('all *x*'s are *y*'s') or existential ('there are some *x*'s that are *y*'s').

generalization from experience (or inductive generalization) Inference from observation, experience, and experiment to a generalization about all members of a certain class. For example, in a laboratory, a researcher finds that certain experiments on tobacco plants always have the same result. He or she generalizes, through induction, from experimental observations to a claim (or *hypothesis*) about all tobacco plants. But notice that this generalization is never certain. It might always turn out that there was a fluke in the experiment or that the researcher chose a peculiar sample of plants.

God In traditional Judeo-Christian theology, that being who created the universe and exists independently of it, who is all-powerful, all-knowing, everywhere at once, and concerned with justice and the ultimate welfare of humankind. When spelled with a small 'g' the word refers to any supernatural being worthy of worship or at least extraordinary respect.

Golden Rule 'Do unto others as you would have them do unto you.'

government The instrument of authority; that body that rules, passes and enforces laws, and so forth.

happiness The achievement of the good life. In Aristotle, the name we all agree to give to the good life, whatever it is. Happiness, in this sense, must not be confused with pleasure, which is but one (among many) concerns and conceptions of the good life.

happiness calculus (also *felicity calculus*) Bentham's technique for quantifying and adding up pleasures and pains as a way of deciding what to do.

hedonism The conception of the good life that takes pleasure to be the ultimate good. Hedonism is the premise of most forms of utilitarianism. It is often the premise—though sometimes a consequence—of ethical egoism. (These two are not the same: hedonism refers to *the end*; egoism refers to *whose ends*.)

Heisenberg uncertainty principle An important principle of physics, first proposed in the early twentieth century, that demonstrates that we cannot know both the position and the momentum of certain subatomic particles, for in our attempts to know one, we make it impossible to know the other. This principle has been used to attack the very idea of 'determinism' in its classical formulations, for determinism requires just the 'certainty' of possible prediction that the Heisenberg uncertainty principle rejects.

hermeneutics The discipline of interpretation of texts. Broadly conceived (as by Heidegger, Gadamer), it is the 'uncovering' of meanings in everyday life, the attempt to understand the signs and symbols of one's culture and tradition in juxtaposition with other cultures and traditions.

historicism A philosophy that localizes truth and different views of reality to particular times, places, and peoples in history. It is generally linked to a very strong relativist thesis as well, that there is no truth apart from these various historical commitments.

human rights Those rights that are considered to be universal, 'unalienable', and common to every person regardless of where or when he or she lives. For example, freedom from torture and degradation would be a human right.

Hume's fork Hume's insistence that every belief be justified either as a 'relation between ideas' or as a 'matter of fact'.

hypothesis A provisional conclusion, accepted as most probable in the light of the known facts or tentatively adopted as a basis for analysis.

hypothetical imperative In Kant, a command that is conditional, depending upon particular aims or inclinations. For example, 'if you want to be a doctor, then go to medical school'. According to Kant, all other philosophers

(Aristotle, Hume, Rousseau) took morality to be a hypothetical imperative; he does not.

idea In epistemology, almost any mental phenomenon (not, as in Plato, with existence independent of individual minds). The terminology varies slightly; Locke uses 'idea' to refer to virtually any 'mental content'; Hume reserves 'idea' for those mental atoms that are derived by the mind from impressions. In Plato, a Form.

idealism The metaphysical view that only minds and their ideas exist.

Identity of Indiscernibles A principle of Leibniz's philosophy according to which no two things can possibly have all of the same properties or be absolutely identical in all respects.

identity theory The thesis that the mind and brain are ontologically one and the same, or, more accurately, that mental states and events are in fact certain brain and nervous system processes. The theory is usually presented as a form of materialism, but, unlike many materialistic theories, it does not deny the existence of mental events; it denies only that they have independent existence. Mental events are nothing other than certain bodily events.

illusion A false belief motivated by intense wishes. According to Marx, religion is an illusion that is intended to compensate for an intolerable social situation. According to Freud, religion is an illusion that attempts to hold onto our childhood desires for fatherly protection and security.

immaterialism The metaphysical view that accepts the existence of non-spatial, non-sensory entities such as numbers, minds, and ideas. The weak version asserts merely that there are such entities. The strong version asserts that there are *only* such entities (that is, there are no physical objects).

immediate For certain and without need for argument.

immoralist A person who rejects the ultimate claims of morality. An immoralist need not actually break the rules of morality; he or she does not consider them absolute rules and claims that other considerations (even personal considerations) may override them.

immortality The idea that the soul survives death (and, in some belief systems, precedes birth).

imperative A command.

implication One statement logically follows from another. Statements imply one another: we infer one from the other.

impression Hume's word for sensations or sense-data, that which is given to the mind through the senses.

inclination Kant's term for all personal considerations: desires, feelings, emotions, attitudes, moods, and so on.

inconsistent Not compatible; contradictory. One might also say that a person's actions are inconsistent with his or her principles. People as well as other principles can be inconsistent with a principle.

incorrigibility Impossible to correct; cannot be mistaken. It has long been argued that our claims about our own mental states are incorrigible—we cannot be mistaken about them.

independent being In metaphysics, a being that does not depend on any other being for its existence. In other words, a thing that derives its existence from its own nature, not from something outside itself.

indeterminism The thesis that at least some events in the universe are not determined, are not caused by antecedent conditions, and may not be predictable.

induction; inductive reasoning; inductive generalization Induction is the process of inferring general conclusions (for example, 'all swans are white') from a sufficiently large sample of particular observations ('this swan is white, that swan is white, and that one, and that one . . .'). It is usually contrasted with *deduction*, in that, while deductive reasoning guarantees that the conclusion shall be as certain as the premises, induction never gives us a conclusion as certain as the premises. Its conclusions are, at most, merely probable. ('There might always be some swans that are not white'; indeed, there are black swans in Australia.) (See 'A Brief Introduction to Logic', pp. 35–9.)

inductive argument A process of reasoning in which the characteristics of an entire class or set of things is inferred on the basis of an acquaintance with some of its members. In an inductive argument, although the conclusion is supported by the premises, it does not follow necessarily from the premises and its truth is not guaranteed by them.

ineffable Indescribable.

inference Reasoning from one set of principles to another, as in an argument. Deductive inference is but a single kind of inference.

infinite regress A sequence going back endlessly. For example, 'A is caused by B, and B by C, and C by D . . . and so on to infinity'. Aristotle believed such a regress to be an intellectual absurdity.

innate ideas Ideas that are 'born into the mind'; knowledge that is 'programmed' into us from birth and need not be learned. Experience may be necessary to 'trigger off' such ideas, but they are already 'in' all of us. In Plato, the theory of innate ideas is part of a general theory of the immortality of the soul. Locke's famous attack on such ideas took them to be literally ideas that all men share from birth. The rationalist philosophers he was attacking, however, held a much more sophisticated notion; they did not believe that ideas were literally 'born into us', but they did believe that we are born with certain 'innate' capacities and dispositions, which develop with proper education (and mental health). And these ideas, most importantly, can be defended or justified without appeal to any particular experiences or experiments. This is the claim that Locke ultimately rejected.

intentionality The 'aboutness' of mental states. A belief is always *about* something. A desire is always *for* something. An emotion is *directed* at someone or some situation. The concept was used by Husserl's teacher, Franz Brentano, who borrowed it from some medieval philosophers, before Husserl used it and made it famous.

intuition Immediate knowledge of the truth, without the aid of any reasoning and without appeal to experience. Intuition, as rational intuition (there are other kinds), is a central concern of the rationalist philosophers, who consider intuition one of the main functions of reason. But because of its very nature, intuition cannot be argued for, nor can it be defended by experience. Accordingly, many philosophers, especially empiricists, reject the notion of intuition and accept it only when absolutely unavoidable. In the twentieth century, Edmund Husserl defended the appeal to intuition in his phenomenology.

invalid An argument that does not correctly follow agreed-upon rules of inference. Always applies to arguments, not to statements. (Opposite of *valid*.)

justice In the general sense, the virtues of an ideal society. In the more particular sense, the balance of public interest and individual rights, the fair sharing of the available goods of society, the proper punishment of criminals, and the fair restitution to victims of crime and misfortune within society.

justification An attempt to defend a position or an act, to show that it is correct (or at least reasonable). (Compare with *explanation*.)

karma In Hinduism, the tendency of any course of action to be repeated; the limitation of one's free will by one's own habits and dispositions (even into the next life).

Krishna In Hinduism, God incarnate.

law An objective rule that is binding on individuals whether they personally accept it or not. Contrasted with *maxim*.

law of contradiction That basic rule of logic that demands that a sentence and its denial cannot both be true: 'not (*P* and not *P*)'. This law is used by many philosophers (Kant, Leibniz, and Hume, for example) as criterion for analyticity or analytic truth.

law of the excluded middle That rule of logic that says either a sentence or its denial must be true: 'either *P* or not *P*'. In formal logic, this law, together with the law of contradiction, forms the basis of a great many arguments (for example, that form of *reductio ad absurdum* argument in which the consequences of one premise are shown to be absurd, and therefore its denial is accepted). Many logicians are now reconsidering this law, for it is becoming evident that not all sentences are either true or false. For example, consider Russell's famous example, 'the King of France is bald' (when there is no king of France); is that true or false? It surely isn't true, but neither can it be false, for there is no king of France who is not bald. Or what of 'green ideas sleep furiously'? Many philosophers would say that such statements are neither true nor false, thus rejecting the law of the excluded middle.

legitimacy The right to have authority; sanctioned power (for example, through the grace of God, by means of legal succession, by appeal to justice, or to the general consent of the people governed).

libertarian In metaphysics, an incompatibilist who affirms the reality of free will. Like hard determinists, libertarians think that free will and determinism are mutually exclusive; but unlike hard determinists, libertarians maintain that some of our actions are free. In political philosophy, the view that government interference with individual freedom should be kept to a minimum.

liberty (political freedom) The ability to act without restraint or threat of punishment. For example, the ability to travel between states without a passport, the ability to speak one's opinions without prosecution, or the ability to work for or choose one's own profession or career. This ability, however, is not mere physical or mental ability; one might have the liberty to travel or to try to become a doctor without having the means to do so. This political sense of *liberty* differs from the metaphysical or causal sense of the term. The latter refers to freedom in relation to the causes of human behaviour; the former refers only to freedom in relation to legislation and political forces that constrain or liberate our behaviour.

linguistic philosophy The movement in twentieth-century philosophy, particularly in North America and Britain, that focuses its primary attention on language and linguistic analysis. Also called 'analytic philosophy'.

logic The study of the rules of valid inference and 'rational argument'. In general, a sense of order.

logical positivism A powerful school of philosophy that originated in Vienna around 1929 with a group of scientists and philosophers of anti-Nazi, liberal, and anti-metaphysical persuasion. Against the horrendous superstitions propagandized by the Nazis, these philosophers used the clarity of science to dispel nonsense and to defend common sense. The main thrust of logical positivism is its total rejection of metaphysics in favour of science and verifiability through experience. The method of the logical positivists is strongly empiricist and has much in common with the method of Hume, according to which all knowledge is to be defended either as a matter of empirical fact to be verified (that is, confirmed) through experience or as a matter of logic and language to be demonstrated through analysis. Arithmetic and geometry, for the logical positivists, consist of analytic truths. The group was broken up by the Nazis in 1938, and most of its members left for the United States, England, and Holland.

logical truth A sentence that can be shown to be true by virtue of its logical form alone (by virtue of the connectives, 'and', 'or', etc.).

master morality In Nietzsche, a morality that takes personal self-realization as primary, so-called because it was the morality of the 'masters' in the slave states of the ancient world (including Greece).

materialism The metaphysical view that only physical matter and its properties exist. Such intangible entities as numbers, minds, and ideas are really properties of physical bodies. To talk about energy, for example, is, in a way, to talk about physical potential; to talk about minds is, as a kind of shorthand, to talk about behaviour; to talk about ideas is, in a misleading way, to talk about the various structures and interrelationships between objects. Numbers have no existence of their own but only represent sets of sets of objects (the set of all sets of eight things is the number eight, for example). Materialism has always been a powerful worldview in modern scientific culture. It is also the most common view among the pre-Socratic philosophers.

matter of fact (in Hume) An empirical claim, to be confirmed or falsified through experience.

maxim In Kant, a personal rule or intention. Contrasted with *law*.

mean (between the extremes) In Aristotle, the middle course, not too much, not too little. Courage, for example, is a mean because a person with courage is neither too timid to fight nor so lacking in fear that he or she is rash or reckless in the face of danger.

metaphysics Most simply, the study of the most basic (or 'first') principles. Traditionally, the study of ultimate reality, or 'Being as such'. Popularly, any kind of very abstract or obscure thinking. Most philosophers today would define metaphysics as the study of the most general concepts of science and human life, for example, 'reality', 'existence', 'freedom', 'God', 'soul', 'action', and 'mind'. In general, we can divide metaphysics into ontology, cosmology, and an ill-defined set of problems concerning God and the immortality of the human soul. (See *ontology*, *cosmology*.)

method (sometimes, methodology) An approach and strategy for resolving philosophical problems. For example, the appeal to experience, the appeal to divine revelation, the insistence upon mathematical logic, confidence in reason, or trust in authority—all of these are aspects of philosophical methodology.

method of doubt (or methodological doubt) Descartes' technique for discovering those principles of which we can be 'perfectly certain'; namely, doubt everything until you discover those principles that cannot be doubted.

modes (in Spinoza) Inessential properties or modifications of attributes.

monad (in Leibniz) The simple immaterial substances that are the ultimate constituents of all reality. God, the one uncreated monad, created all of the others as self-enclosed ('windowless'), predetermined entities.

monism The metaphysical view that there is ultimately only one substance, that all reality is one. Less strictly, it may be applied to philosophers who believe in only one kind of substance.

monotheism Belief in one God.

morality In general, the rules for right action and prohibitions against wrong acts. Sometimes morality is that single set of absolute rules and prohibitions that are valid for all men at all times and all societies. More loosely, a morality can be any set of ultimate principles, and there might be any number of moralities in different societies.

mysticism The belief that one can come to grasp certain fundamental religious truths (the existence of God, the oneness of the universe) through direct experience, but of a very special kind, different from ordinary understanding.

naturalism The belief that ultimate reality is a natural property.

necessary (truth) Cannot be otherwise and cannot be imagined to be otherwise. In philosophy, it is not enough that something be 'necessary' according to physical laws (for example, the law of gravity) or 'necessary' according to custom or habit (for example, the 'necessity' of laws against rape or the felt necessity of having a cigarette after dinner). *Necessary* allows for not even imaginary counter-examples; thus it is a necessary truth that two plus two equals four. Not only do we believe this with certainty and find ourselves incapable of intelligibly doubting it, but we cannot even suggest what it might be for it to be false, no matter how wild our imaginations.

necessary and sufficient conditions A is necessary and sufficient for B when A is both logically required and enough to guarantee B ('A if and only if B').

necessity In accordance with a necessary truth.

nihility 'The Nothing', 'nothingness'.

obligation Bound by duty. For example, 'you have an obligation to keep your promises'.

omnipotent All-powerful, usually said of God.

omnipresent Everywhere at once, usually said of God.

omniscient All-knowing, usually said of God.

ontological argument An argument (or set of arguments) that tries to 'prove' the existence of God from the very concept of 'God'. For example, 'God', by definition, is that being with all possible perfection; existence is a perfection; therefore, God exists.

ontology The study of being. That is, that part of metaphysics that asks such questions as 'What is there?', 'What is it for something to exist?', 'What is an individual thing?', and 'How do things interact?' Traditionally, these questions were formulated as questions about substance. Today, much of ontology is part of logic and linguistics and is the study of the concepts we use to discuss such matters. Sometimes ontology is used as a synonym for metaphysics, but usually the latter is the broader discipline.

ought The term most often used to express moral duty or obligation. Sometimes 'should' is used, but this is ambiguously between 'ought' and merely 'preferable'. Sometimes 'must' or 'have to' is used, but this is ambiguously between 'ought to' and 'forced to'. In Hume's ethics (and in many others as well), 'ought' is contrasted with 'is' as the hallmark of value (especially moral) judgment.

panpsychism In metaphysics and the philosophy of mind, the view that everything is invested with some degree of mentality or consciousness.

pantheism The belief that God is identical to the universe as a whole, everything is divine, or that God is in everything. Spinoza, for example, was a pantheist. Hinduism is a form of pantheism in that it includes a conception of the divine in all things, rather than as a separate Creator.

paradox A self-contradictory conclusion drawn from seemingly acceptable premises. For example, suppose you decide to help *all* and *only* those people who do not help themselves. That sounds reasonable enough. But then, do you help yourself? If you do not help yourself, you place yourself among those people who do not help themselves; therefore, you will be obliged to help yourself. But if you help yourself, you can no longer include yourself among those people who do not help themselves; therefore, you will have gone against your decision to help *only* those who do not help themselves. This is a paradox.

parallelism The thesis that mental events and bodily events parallel each other and occur in perfect coordination but do not interact.

participation Plato's obscure and unexplained relationship between the things of this world and the Forms of which they are manifestations. He tells us that individual things 'participate' in their Forms.

perceptions A source of information; sense experience.

perfectionism In ethics, the view that the best life for human beings is one devoted to the full exercise and development of our highest faculties. For perfectionists, a well-lived human life aims at excellence, not pleasure; the cultivation of our talents, not happiness; achievement, not passive enjoyment.

phenomenology A contemporary European philosophy, founded by the German-Czech philosopher Edmund Husserl, that begins with a 'pure description of consciousness'. Originally developed as an answer to certain questions of necessary truth in the foundations of arithmetic, it was later expanded to answer more general philosophical questions and, in the hands of its later practitioners, it became a 'philosophy of man' as well as a theory of knowledge.

pluralism The metaphysical view that there are many distinct substances in the universe and, perhaps, many different kinds of substances as well.

polytheism Belief in many gods.

pragmatic theory of truth A statement or a belief is true if and only if it 'works', that is, if it allows us to predict certain results and function effectively in everyday life, and if it encourages further inquiry and helps us lead better lives.

pragmatism A distinctly American philosophical movement founded by Charles Sanders Peirce in the late nineteenth century and popularized by William James and John Dewey. Its central thesis is obvious in its name, that truth (etc.) is always to be determined by reference to practical (pragmatic) considerations. Only those metaphysical distinctions that make some difference in practice are worth considering, and the only ultimate defence of any belief is that 'it works'.

predestination The thesis (usually in a theological context) that every event is destined to happen (as in fatalism) whatever efforts we make to prevent it. The usual version is that God knows and perhaps causes all things to happen, and therefore everything must happen precisely as He knows (and possibly causes) it to happen.

predicate That which is asserted or denied of a thing, which refers to a property of things. Some familiar predicates are 'is red' and 'is an animal'.

prediction To say that some event will happen before it happens. Determinism normally includes the thesis that if we know enough about the antecedent conditions of an event, we can always predict that it will occur. But prediction does not require determinism. One might predict the outcome of some state of affairs on the basis of statistical probabilities without knowing any antecedent conditions and perhaps even without assuming that there are any such conditions (in quantum physics, for example). It is also possible that a person might predict the future on the basis of lucky guesses or ESP, again without necessarily accepting determinism.

pre-established harmony The belief that the order of the universe is prearranged by God. In Leibniz, this view allows him an alternative to Newton's theory of causal relationships, namely that the coordination between our ideas and the physical events of the world and our bodies was set up by God in perfect order.

premise The principle, or one of the principles, upon which an argument is based. The starting point of an argument.

presupposition A principle that is assumed as a precondition for whatever else one believes, which itself may remain unexamined and uncriticized throughout the argument. For example, a lawyer presupposes that the court aims at justice and has some idea what is just. It is the philosopher, not the lawyer, who challenges those claims.

primary qualities In Locke, those properties ('qualities') that inhere in the object.

prime mover (in Aristotle) The 'cause-of-itself', the first cause, which (Who) initiates all changes but is not itself (Himself) affected by anything prior. Aristotle believes there must be a prime mover if we are to avoid an infinite regress, which he considers an absurdity. Aristotle also refers to the prime mover as 'God', and medieval philosophers (for example, St Thomas Aquinas) have developed these views into Christian theology.

principle of induction The belief that the laws of nature will continue to hold in the future as they have in the past. (Crudely, 'the future will be like the past'.)

Principle of Sufficient Reason (in Leibniz) The insistence that all events must have a justification and that ultimately all events must be justified by God's reasons. The principle is sometimes invoked to assert that everything must have some explanation, whether or not God is involved. (For example, scientists use such a principle in their work.)

principle of universal causation The belief that every event has its cause (or causes). In scientific circles, it is usually added, 'its sufficient *natural* cause', in order to eliminate the possibility of miracles and divine intervention (which are allowed in Leibniz's similar but broader Principle of Sufficient Reason).

principle of utility In Bentham, the principle that one ought to do what gives the greatest pleasure to the greatest number of people.

principles of common sense Fundamental assumptions or beliefs that virtually all human beings find irresistible and take for granted in their everyday lives. According to Reid, such principles include belief in perception, belief in reason, belief in the self, belief in personal identity, belief in other minds, belief in substance, belief in Nature's uniformity, belief in the reality of moral distinctions, and belief in (libertarian) free will. We cannot prove any of these things, says Reid; but skeptics like Hume cannot coherently call them into question.

privacy The seeming inaccessibility of mental states and events to anyone other than the person who 'has' them.

privileged access The technical term used by philosophers to refer to the curious fact that a person usually (if not always) can immediately know, simply by paying attention, what is going on in his or her own mind, while other people can find out what is going on—if they can at all—only by watching the person's behaviour, listening to what he or she says, or asking (and hoping they get a truthful answer). It is important to distinguish *privileged access* from *incorrigibility*. The first means that a person knows directly what is 'in his or her mind' without having to observe his or her behaviour; the second means that he or she knows for certain and beyond the possibility of error.

probable Likely; or supported by the evidence (but not conclusively). The empiricist's middle step between the extremities of certainty and doubt. (Probability is the measure of how probable something is.)

problem of evil The dilemma that emerges from trying to reconcile the belief that God is omnipotent, omniscient, and just with the suffering and evil in the world.

problem of divine hiddenness An objection to theism that can be represented as a variation on the classic problem of evil. If God is perfect, knowledge of Him must be a great good; but many of us are deprived of that good. Why is this? Is it that God does not exist? Or is some other explanation available?

proof In a deductive argument, a proof is a sequence of steps, each according to an acceptable rule of inference, to the conclusion to be proved.

property Properties are generally distinguished from the substances in which they 'inhere' by pointing to the fact that a property cannot exist without being a property of something; for example, there can be any number of red things but no redness that exists independently. (Many philosophers have challenged this idea, but this problem, which is called the 'problem of universals', is discussed in this introductory textbook.)

proposition An assertion that is either true or false.

psychological egoism The thesis that people always act for their own self-interest, even when it seems as if they are acting for other people's benefit (for example, in giving to charity, the egoist would say, the person is simply making himself or herself feel self-righteous).

quality In Locke (and other authors), a property.

rational In accordance with the rules of effective thought: coherence, consistency, practicability, simplicity, comprehensiveness, looking at the evidence and weighing it carefully, not jumping to conclusions, and so forth. Rationality

may not guarantee truth; all of the evidence and everything we believe may point to one conclusion, while later generations, who know things that we do not, may see that our conclusion was incorrect. Yet it would still be, for us, the rational conclusion. Rationality points to the manner of thinking rather than its ultimate conclusions. Philosophically, the stress on rationality takes the emphasis off reality and places it on our manner of philosophizing.

rationalism The philosophy that is characterized by its confidence in reason, and intuition in particular, to know reality independently of experience. *Continental rationalism* is usually reserved for three European philosophers: Descartes, Spinoza, and Leibniz. (See *reason, intuition*.)

rationality Acting in the best possible way; according to reason. Sometimes, rationality means simply doing what is best under the circumstances, without insisting that there is only one rational way of acting. In other words, rationality is considered relative to particular interests and circumstances. In Kant's philosophy, however, rationality refers to that faculty that allows us to act in the correct way, without reference to particular interests and circumstances.

realism The thesis that reality exists in itself and it is independent of our consciousness of it.

reason The ability to think abstractly, to form arguments and make inferences. It is sometimes referred to as a 'faculty' of the human mind (a leftover from eighteenth-century philosophy). In rationalism, the term describes the faculty that allows us to know reality, through intuition. In empiricism, reason is simply the ability to recognize certain principles that are 'relations of ideas', for example, trivial truths ('a cat is an animal') and, more complicated, principles of arithmetic and geometry. Empiricists deny that reason allows us special insight into reality, however; it tells us only relations between ideas. In metaphysics, however, reason often has a more controversial meaning, namely, that human ability to go beyond experience to determine, through thought alone, what reality is really like.

reasons Explanations, justifications, evidence, or some other basis for accepting a proposition.

reductio ad absurdum A form of argument in which one refutes a statement by showing that it leads to self-contradiction or an otherwise intolerable conclusion.

reflection To think about something, to 'put it in perspective'. We often do this with our beliefs and our emotions. For example, 'this morning I was furious at you, but after reflecting on it at lunch, I decided that it was nothing to be angry about'. One might say that philosophy is reflection about life and knowledge in general.

relations of ideas In empiricism, knowledge that is restricted to the logical and conceptual connections between ideas, not to the correspondence of those ideas to experience or to reality. Such knowledge can therefore be demonstrated without appeal to experience. Arithmetic and geometry were taken to be paradigm examples of 'relations of ideas'.

relativism The thesis that there is no single correct view of reality, no single truth. Relativists often talk about the possibility of 'different conceptual frameworks', 'alternative lifestyles', and various 'forms of consciousness'. They are opposed, often violently, to realists and absolutists. Also, the thesis that morals are relative to particular societies, particular interests, particular circumstances, or particular individuals. (See *cultural relativism*, *ethical relativism*.)

resemblance Having the same features. All people resemble each other (or at least most do) in having one and only one head; you resemble yourself five years ago in (perhaps) having the same texture hair, the same colour eyes, the same fear of spiders, and the same skill at chess.

responsibility Answerability or accountability for some act or event presumed to be within a person's control.

retributive justice 'Getting even' or 'an eye for an eye'.

retrodiction To say, on the basis of certain present evidence, what must have happened in the past. For example, the astronomer who looks at the present course of a comet can retrodict certain facts about its history. For the determinist, retrodiction is as important to his thesis as prediction.

rhetoric The persuasive use of language to convince other people to accept your beliefs.

rights Demands that a member of society is entitled to make upon his or her society. Everyone, for example, has a right to police protection.

rule of inference A generally accepted principle according to which one may infer one statement from another; those rules of logic according to which validity is defined. All such rules are analytic, but there is considerable disagreement whether all are so by virtue of their own logical form or whether some are so because they are derived from other, more basic rules. There is also the following question: Given that these rules define correct logical form, how is it possible to say that they have correct logical form?

secondary qualities In Locke, those properties ('qualities') that are caused in us by objects, but do not inhere in the objects themselves (for example, colour).

self-consciousness Being aware of oneself, whether 'as others see you' (looking in a mirror or 'watching yourself play a role' at a party) or just 'looking into yourself' (as when you reflect on your goals in life or wonder whether you really exist or not). Self-consciousness requires having some concept of your 'self'. Accordingly, it is logically tied to questions of self-identity.

self-evident Obvious without proof or argument; for Descartes, a 'clear and distinct idea', one about which there could be no doubt and it is obvious that there could be no doubt.

self-identity The way you characterize yourself, either in general (as a human being, as a man or as a woman, as a creature before God, or as one among many animals) or in particular (as the person who can run the fastest mile, as an all-'C' student, or as the worst-dressed slob in your class). Self-identity, on this characterization, requires self-consciousness. The self-identity of a person, in other words, is not merely the same as the identity of a 'thing', for example, the identity of a human body.

selfishness Acting in one's own interest to the exclusion of others' interests. The word has a negative connotation—it often implies that an action is condemnable and blameworthy—and so should be separated from the more neutral claims of the psychological egoist. (It is possible to act for one's own interests and not be selfish; an act may be both in one's own interest and in the interests of others.)

semantics The meanings of a sentence and its various components. Also, the study of those meanings. (So, we can talk about the semantics of a sentence, and we can talk about doing semantics.) 'Merely semantic' is a nasty way of referring to conceptual truths, analytic sentences that are true just by virtue of meanings.

semantic theory of truth A formal theory, best known from the work of Alfred Tarski, that defines 'true' in terms of a technical notion of *satisfaction*. According to the theory, every sentence in the language is either satisfied or not by a distinct class of individuals. This is adequate, however, only for artificially constructed languages. Generalizing the theory to natural language (for example, American English), we can say that the theory suggests that we (but not each of us personally) set up the rules according to which our sentences do or do not 'correspond with the facts' of the world.

sensation The experimental result of the stimulation of a sense organ, for example, *seeing* red, *hearing* a ringing noise, *smelling* something burning. Sensations are the simplest of mental phenomena.

sense-data That which is given to the senses, prior to any reasoning or organization on our part.

sentiment Feeling, emotion; particularly moral feelings (as in Hume, Rousseau).

skepticism A philosophical belief that knowledge is not possible, that doubt will not be overcome by any valid arguments. A philosopher who holds this belief is called a skeptic. Skepticism is not mere personal doubt; it requires systematic doubt with reasons for that doubt.

slave morality In Nietzsche's moral philosophy, a morality that takes duties and obligations as primary, so called because it was the morality of the slaves who were not allowed to aspire any higher than mere efficiency and personal comfort.

social contract An agreement, tacit or explicit, that all members of society shall abide by the laws of the state in order to maximize the public interest and ensure cooperation among themselves. No actual contract need ever have been signed; every member of a society, by choosing to remain in that society, implicitly agrees to such an agreement.

society A group of people with common historical and cultural ties; usually but not always, members of the same state and ruled by the same government.

soft determinism A thesis that accepts determinism but claims that certain kinds of causes, namely, a person's character, still allow us to call his or her actions 'free'. The soft determinist is therefore a compatibilist, for he believes in both freedom and determinism.

sophists Ancient Greek philosophers and teachers who believed that no reality exists except for what we take to be reality.

sound An argument whose premises are true and that is valid.

sovereign Independent. A sovereign state is one that is subject to the laws of no other state. A sovereign is a person (for example, a king) who is not subject or answerable to the commands of anyone else. A people are sovereign when their wishes are ultimate in the same way and not subject to commands by anyone else or any government. (To say that a people is sovereign is not to say that the will of any individual or group is sovereign within it.)

Spenta Mainyush The good spirit of Zoroastrianism.

state The centre of authority in a society, for example, the largest political unit in a society. Most often, a state is a nation (for example, Canada). A state is usually, but not always, coextensive with a society, and it is usually, but not always, distinguished by a single form of government and a single government (for example, the Canadian federal government).

Stoics An ancient movement in philosophy that taught self-control and minimized passion, with a willingness to endure whatever fate has in store. Some believers were Zeno of Citium in Greece (not the same as Zeno of the paradoxes), Seneca, and Marcus Aurelius in Rome.

subjective idealism The view that only ideas and mind exist, and that there are no substances, matter, or material objects. In particular, the philosophy of Berkeley.

subjective truth In Kierkegaard, the 'truth' of strong feelings and commitment.

substance A 'unit' of existence, a being; something that 'stands by itself'; the essential reality of a thing or things that underlies the various properties and changes of properties. Its most common definitions: 'that which is independent and can exist by itself' and 'the essence of a thing, which does not and cannot change'. In traditional metaphysics, substance is the same as 'ultimate reality', and the study of substance is that branch of metaphysics that studies reality, namely, ontology. In Descartes, a thing that so exists that it needs no other thing in order to exist (God). Created substances need only the occurrence of God to exist. (See *essence*, *ontology*.)

sufficient cause Capable of bringing something about by itself (for example, four healthy people are sufficient to push a Volkswagen up a hill).

Sufism Islamic mysticism.

syllogism A three-line deductive argument; the best-known examples are those arguments of the following form:

All *P*'s are *Q*'s. (Major premise)
S is a *P*. (Minor premise)
Therefore *S* is a *Q*. (Conclusion)

The major premise asserts something about the predicate of the conclusion (in this case, *Q*). The minor premise asserts something about the subject of the conclusion (in this case, *S*).

sympathy Fellow feeling; felt concern for other people's welfare. In the ethics of Hume and Rousseau, the necessary and universal sentiment without which morals—and society—would be impossible.

synonym 'Meaning the same.' Two words are synonymous if they are interchangeable in a sentence without losing the meaning of the sentence. For example, 'criminal' and 'felon' are synonyms in most contexts. The test of a supposedly conceptual truth is to replace certain words with synonyms and then see if its denial yields a self-contradiction. In other words, substituting synonyms turns a conceptual truth into an analytic truth. For example, 'ferns are plants'; substituting for 'fern' its synonym (or, in this case, its definition) 'a primitive plant that bears spores, etc.' we have 'a primitive plant is a plant', whose denial ('a plant is not a plant') is a contradiction; the statement is thus an analytic truth.

synthetic (statement) A non-contradictory proposition in which the predicate is not entailed by the subject, for example, 'horses are generally obstinate'. ('Synthetic' is opposed, in this sense, to 'analytic'.) A synthetic sentence cannot be shown to be true by appeal to the logical form or the meanings of the component words. Kant defined a 'synthetic' sentence as one that 'adds an idea to the subject that is not already contained in it'. For example, 'a horse is the source of a large income for some people' is a strictly synthetic sentence. No appeal to the meaning of 'horse' will help you find out whether the sentence is true or not, and its denial surely does not result in self-contradiction. But, according to Kant, it must not be concluded that all synthetic sentences can be shown to be true solely by appeal to experience. Some, he claimed, are known a priori.

synthetic a priori knowledge Knowledge that is necessary and known independently of experience (and thus a priori), but that does not derive its truth from the logic or meaning of sentences (thus synthetic). This is the focal concept of Kant's philosophy.

system An orderly formulation of principles (together with reasons, implications, evidence, methods, and presuppositions) that is comprehensive, consistent, and coherent and in which the various principles are interconnected as tightly as possible by logical implications.

tabula rasa In Locke's philosophy, the 'blank tablet' metaphor of the mind, in which the mind is a 'blank' at birth and everything we know must be 'stamped in' through experience. This conception of the mind stands in opposition to the doctrine of innate ideas.

tautology A trivial truth that is true by virtue of logical form alone and tells us nothing about the world. (Popularly, a bit of repetitive nonsense, for example, 'a rose is a rose is a rose'. Technically, [in logic] a sentence that can be shown to be true no matter what the truth or falsity of its component parts.)

teleological argument An argument that attempts to 'prove' that God exists because of the intricacy and 'design' of nature. It is sometimes called the 'argument from design', as the basis of the argument is that since the universe is evidently designed, it must have a designer. The analogy most often used is our inference from finding a complex mechanism on a beach (for example, a watch) that some intelligent being must have created it.

teleology (teleological) The belief that all phenomena have a purpose, end, or goal (from the Greek *telos*, meaning 'purpose'). Aristotle's metaphysics is a teleology, which means that he believes that the universe itself—and consequently everything in it—operates for purposes and can be explained according to goals.

theism Belief in God.

transcendence (in Sartre) Sartre's term for a person's plan, ambitions, intentions, and hopes for the future. (Note that Sartre's definition differs from common use, where *transcendence* usually refers to something that is beyond, or independent of, human experience.)

transcendent Independent of. In the philosophy of religion, a *transcendent God* is one who is distinct and separate from the universe he created. This is contrasted with the concept of an immanent God, for example, in pantheism, where God is identical with his creation, or, to take a different example, in certain forms of humanism, in which God is identical with humankind. (Hegel argued such a thesis.)

transcendental Referring to the basic rules of human knowledge, usually with an absolutist suggestion that there can be but a single set of such basic rules. Thus Kant's 'transcendental deduction' attempted to deduce the one possible set of basic rules for human understanding, and Husserl's transcendental phenomenology attempted to lay bare the one set of basic ('essential') laws of human consciousness. Contemporary philosophers sometimes talk about 'the transcendental turn' in philosophy, in other words, the attempt to move beyond claims that might apply only to ourselves and our way of viewing things to the way that things must be viewed.

transcendental deduction Kant's elaborate attempt to prove that there is but one set of categories (basic rules or a priori concepts) that all rational creatures must use in constituting their experience.

transcendental ego The bare, logical fact of one's own self-consciousness: Descartes' 'I think'; the self 'behind' all of our experiences; the mental activity that unifies our various thoughts and sensations. (The term comes from Kant's *Critique of Pure Reason*.)

trivial Obvious and not worth saying.

truth of reason In traditional rationalism, a belief that can be justified solely by appeal to intuition or deduction from premises based upon intuition. Arithmetic and geometry were, for the rationalists as for the empiricists, a paradigm case of such truths. The rationalists disagreed with the empiricists mainly on the scope of such truths and the restrictions to be placed on the problematic appeal to intuition.

unalienable rights Those rights that no one and no government can take away, for example, the right of a person to protect his or her own life. In other words, *human rights*.

unconscious Freud's famous way of referring to the fact that there are ideas, desires, memories, and experiences in our minds to which we do not have privileged access, which we may be wrong about (and, therefore, about which our claims are not incorrigible), and which may be more evident to other people than to oneself. He also distinguishes a *preconscious* ('the antechamber of consciousness'). Preconscious ideas can be made conscious simply by being attended to. (For example, you do know what the capital of Canada is, but you weren't conscious of it before I mentioned it; it was preconscious.) Truly unconscious ideas, however, cannot be made conscious, even when one tries to do so.

unextended Not having spatial dimensions. Philosophers (for example, Descartes, Leibniz, and Spinoza) often define mind and ideas as unextended.

unsound An argument whose premises are false or that is invalid.

Upanishads The 'secret doctrines' that form the basis of Hinduism.

utilitarianism The moral philosophy that says that we should act in such ways as to make the greatest number of people as happy as possible.

valid An argument that correctly follows agreed-upon rules of inference. Always applies to arguments, not to statements.

vicious circle Use of two propositions or arguments to support one another with no other support. For example, 'He must be guilty because he's got such a guilty look on his face. . . . Well, I can tell it's a guilty look because he's the one who is guilty.'

virtue Moral excellence. In Aristotle's philosophy, a state of character according to which we enjoy doing what is right. In Kant, willing what is right (whether or not we enjoy it, in fact, especially if we don't enjoy it).

void Empty space.

will The power of mind that allows us to choose our own actions, or, at least, what we shall try to do. In Kant, a good will is the only thing that is good 'without qualification', in other words, acting for the right reasons and good intentions.

will to power In Nietzsche's philosophy, the thesis that every act is ultimately aimed at superiority, sometimes over other people, but, more importantly, superiority according to one's own standards. In other words, it is what Aristotle meant by excellence. (Nietzsche has often been interpreted, however, to mean political power.)

Zend-Avesta The scripture of Zoroastrianism.

Zoroastrianism The religion of ancient Persia.

NOTES

Introduction

1. The word was invented by Pythagoras. When he was asked if he was already a wise man, he answered, 'No, I am not wise, but I am a lover of wisdom.'
2. Lao-zi is sometimes referred to by variants such as Laosi, Lao Tse, or Lao-Tzu; the *Dao De Jing* is sometimes referred to as the *Tao Te Ching*.
3. Not, at that point in history, *hers* as well. The concept of a woman's autonomy and right to choose is a late-nineteenth-century idea.
4. See Plato's dialogue *Theaetetus*, 155d.
5. Ralph Waldo Emerson, 'Self Reliance', in *Essays: First Series* (1841).

Chapter 1

1. Heraclitus, Fragment 23, trans. John Burnet.
2. Heraclitus, Fragment 21, trans. John Burnet.
3. Heraclitus, Fragment B30, trans. John Burnet.
4. Heraclitus, Fragment 17, trans. John Burnet.
5. The Sanskrit text is ambiguous between these two meanings; the first suggests Buddhist doctrines, and the alternative suggests Hindu theism.
6. Some of these doctrines clearly have forerunners in the Upanishads; it is noteworthy that the Buddha upholds certain lines of continuity between his and previous spiritual figures' teachings. Others are distinctively Buddhist, in particular the 'insubstantiality' doctrines.
7. *The Odyssey* 11, 489–90, where Achilles says to Odysseus, on the latter's visit to the underworld, that he would rather be a servant to a poor man on earth than king among the dead. [Translator's note.]
8. Notice that 'form' is written with a lowercase *f* here, although Aristotle uses the same word as Plato, *eidos*. His word for the matter is *hyle*.
9. Aristotle rejected a theory of natural selection argued by Empedocles twenty-three hundred years before Darwin because it was not a teleological theory.
10. We are all determined by the nature of God or the universe. But then, here is a problem: Are we not then compelled to struggle? If so, what is the point of Spinoza's urging us not to?

Chapter 2

1. An efficient cause is an event (or an agent) that brings something about. The term comes from Aristotle. See *cause* in the glossary.
2. While Clarke admits that the cosmological argument *alone* is not sufficient to prove the existence of God, he does think that it is a rock-solid foundation on which to build a case for the existence of God, as he does in the remainder of *A Demonstration of the Being and Attributes of God*. In this text, after establishing to his own satisfaction that '[t]here has existed from eternity some one unchangeable and independent being' (Proposition II), Clarke goes on to argue the existence of God along with certain attributes which that being must possess: self-existence (Proposition III), eternity (Proposition V), omnipresence (Proposition VI), uniqueness (Proposition VII), intelligence (Proposition VIII), freedom (Proposition IX), omnipotence (Proposition X), infinite wisdom (Proposition XI), and infinite goodness (Proposition XII).
3. William Shakespeare, *Macbeth* 2.1.33–9.
4. I have considered this in *God and Other Spirits* (New York: Oxford University Press, 2004), 195–202. [Wiebe's note.]

5. See *Collected Papers of Charles Saunders Peirce, Volumes V and VI, Pragmatism and Pragmaticism and Scientific Metaphysics*, ed. Charles Hartshorne and Paul Weiss (Cambridge, MA: Harvard University Press, 1935), vol. 5, bk 1, lec. 6 and 7. This kind of 'inference' is sometimes called 'inference to the best explanation', but the word '*best*' creates many difficulties. [Wiebe's note.]

6. *Visions of Jesus* (New York: Oxford University Press, 1997).

7. *Vancouver Sun*, 12 December 2000; cf. Emma Heathcote-James, *Seeing Angels* (London: Blake, 2002), 46–7.

8. Blaise Pascal, *Pensées*, #233 (New York: Modern Library, 1941).

9. The following texts are from the Bhagavadgītā 1.31b–35, 3.9–12, 3.15, 4.6–8, 4.11, 4.14–19, 4.22–24, 4.31–33, 4.36–37, and 4.42b. Trans. Steve Phillips.

10. Literally, 'wish-fulfilling cow'.

11. A *hypothetical syllogism* is a type of deductive argument with the following logical form: Premise (1): If A is true, then B is true. Premise (2): If B is true, then C is true. Conclusion: If A is true, then C is true. Example: If God does not exist, then life has no meaning; if life has no meaning, then it doesn't matter what we do with our lives; therefore, if God does not exist, then it doesn't matter what we do with our lives.

12. *Modus tollens* is a type of deductive argument with the following logical form: Premise (1): If P is true, then Q is true. Premise (2): But Q is false. Conclusion: P is false. Example: If your brother is eligible to vote this year, he must be at least 18 years of age. But your brother is under 18. Therefore, your brother is not eligible to vote this year.

13. *Modus ponens* is a type of deductive argument with the following logical form: Premise (1): If P is true, then Q is true. Premise (2): P is true. Conclusion: Q is true. Example: If you paid your health club membership fee early this year, then you may use the new pool at the club whenever you want. Now, I paid my health club membership fee early this year. Therefore, I may use the new pool at the club whenever I want.

14. The first and third readings are from Søren Kierkegaard, *Concluding Unscientific Postscript*, and the second reading is from Søren Kierkegaard, *Philosophical Fragments*. All three have been translated from the Danish by Clancy Martin and reprinted with his permission.

15. Trans. Clancy Martin.

Chapter 3

1. Herbert A. Giles, trans., *Chuang-Tzu: Taoist Philosopher and Chinese Mystic* (London: George Allen and Unwin, 1961 [1889]), 47.

2. Berkeley travelled to the United States. Berkeley, California, is named after him.

3. E.S. Haldane and G.R.T. Ross, eds, *The Philosophical Works of Descartes*, vol. 1 (New York: Dover, 1955), 148.

4. British empiricism has traditionally considered itself the defender of 'common sense' against the excesses of metaphysics. This was even true of Berkeley and Hume, who reached conclusions more outrageous than any metaphysician. It was also true of Bertrand Russell and G.E. Moore in the twentieth century.

5. Bertrand Russell, *A History of Western Philosophy* (New York: Simon and Schuster, 1945).

6. David Hume, *An Enquiry Concerning Human Understanding*, 2nd edn, ed. L.A. Selby-Bigge (Oxford: Oxford University Press, 1902).

7. Modern philosophers have given a great deal of attention to inductive inferences that are not based upon any obvious causes, for example, statistical probabilities (as in genetics or in gambling).

8. It is important to remember that Hume, like Locke, models his philosophy-psychology after Newton's physics. So even if he rejects Locke's 'causal theory of perception', the Newtonian model, in which causality is central, remains at the heart of his theories.

9. David Hume, *A Treatise of Human Nature*, ed. L.A. Selby-Bigge (Oxford: Oxford University Press, 1888).

10. Thomas Reid, 'An Inquiry into the Human Mind on the Principles of Common Sense', in *Philosophical Works* (Hildesheim: Georg Olms Verlagsbuchhandlung, 1967), 108.

11. Reid lists such principles in both his *Essays on the Intellectual Powers* and in his *Essays on the Active Powers*.

12. Today, many philosophers would rather say that these concepts through which we constitute the world are part of a language, which raises the intriguing but controversial possibility that the world might be quite different for people who speak different languages. (Kant himself did not believe this.)

13. The familiar doctrine of Hegel's dialectic is often known only in terms of 'thesis-antithesis-synthesis'. In fact these categories are rarely used by either Hegel or Marx.

14. Translations are by Clancy Martin.

15. Friedrich Nietzsche, 'On Truth and Lie in Extra-Moral Sense', in Walter Kaufmann, ed. and trans., *The Viking Portable Nietzsche* (New York: The Viking Press, 1954), 46–7.

16. Richard Rorty, 'Pragmatism, Relativism, and Irrationalism', in *Proceedings and Addresses of the American Philosophical Association,* vol. 53 (1980), 12.

17. Richard Rorty, *Consequences of Pragmatism (Essays: 1972–1980)* (Minneapolis: University of Minnesota Press, 1982), xiii.

18. Richard Rorty, *Objectivity, Relativism and Truth: Philosophical Papers*, vol. 1 (Cambridge: Cambridge University Press, 1991), 13.

19. Richard Rorty, *Consequences of Pragmatism*, 73.

20. Rorty, *Objectivity, Relativism and Truth: Philosophical Papers*, vol. 1, 193–4.

21. Rorty, *Consequences of Pragmatism*, xli–xliii.

22. Richard Rorty, 'Human Rights, Rationality, and Sentimentality', in S. Shute and S. Hurley, eds, *On Human Rights* (New York: Basic Books, 1993), 127.

23. Rorty, *Objectivity, Relativism and Truth: Philosophical Papers*, vol. 1, 36.

24. Rorty, *Objectivity, Relativism and Truth: Philosophical Papers*, vol. 1, 38.

25. Rorty, *Objectivity, Relativism and Truth: Philosophical Papers*, vol. 1, 214.

26. Rorty, *Consequences of Pragmatism*, 44.

27. Rorty, *Objectivity, Relativism and Truth: Philosophical Papers*, vol. 1, 199.

28. Richard Rorty, *Achieving Our Country* (Cambridge, MA: Harvard University Press, 1998), 28.

29. From Plato's *Cratylus*, 385b.

30. Charles Sanders Peirce, *Collected Papers*, vols 1–6, ed. Charles Hartshorne and Paul Weiss (Cambridge, MA: Belknap Press of Harvard University, 1931–5), 1.14.

31. Ibid., 5.402.

32. Ibid., 5.407.

33. Ibid., 5.525.

34. Kant speaks in the Preface to the *Critique of Pure Reason* of the desirability of setting metaphysics 'on the secure path of a science'. [Migotti's note.]

35. Ibid., 7.605.

36. William James, *The Meaning of Truth*, in *William James: Writings 1902–1910* (New York: The Library of America, 1987), 823.

37. William James, *Pragmatism: A New Name for Some Old Ways of Thinking*, in *William James: Writings 1902–1910* (New York: The Library of America, 1987), 515.

38. Richard Rorty, *Consequences of Pragmatism (Essays: 1972–1980)* (Minneapolis: University of Minnesota Press, 1982), xiii.

39. Thomas S. Kuhn, *The Structure of Scientific Revolutions*, 2nd edn (Chicago: The University of Chicago Press, 1970), 4.

40. This is an application of Piaget's principle of equilibration at a phylogenetic level. [Code's note.]

41. Christine Pierce, 'Philosophy', in *Signs: Journal of Women in Culture and Society*, vol. I, no. 2 (1975), 493.

42. See Sally McConnell-Ginet, 'Intonation in a Man's World', in *Signs: Journal of Women in Culture and Society*, vol. 3, no.3 (1978), 541–59.

43. Robin Lakoff, *Language and Woman's Place* (New York: Harper and Row, 1973).

44. Casey Miller and Kate Swift, *Words and Women* (Garden City, NY: Doubleday Anchor Books, 1977).

45. C. Kramer, B. Thorne, and N. Henley, 'Perspectives on Language and Communication', in *Signs: Journal of Women in Culture and Society*, vol. 3, no. 3 (1978), 644.

46. The same authors suggest that 'language renders females invisible' (loc. cir.), citing the generic 'he' as evidence, for example 'everyone take his seat'. This may be a valid condemnation of the English language but it cannot apply to languages where the gender of the noun determines the gender of the possessive pronoun. Consider the French equivalent: 'Tout le monde à sa place'. [Code's note.]

47. Kramer, Thorne, and Henley, op. cit., 646.

48. Susanne Langer, *Philosophical Sketches* (Baltimore, MD: The Johns Hopkins Press, 1962), 11.

49. Here I am adopting the spirit of Bertrand Russell's terminology as he spells it out, for example, in *The Problems of Philosophy* (Oxford, OUP Paperback edition, 1970, 26–8). I am using the acquaintance/description distinction in a very broad derivative sense. In this broad sense the distinction is useful for my purposes here, at least where its epistemological, as opposed to its ontological, implications are concerned. [Code's note.]

Chapter 4

1. As a matter of fact, Descartes believed that there were three kinds of substances, the third being God. But we need not worry about that third substance in this chapter. Here, we will consider Descartes to be a dualist.

2. It is logically possible, although extremely unlikely, that scientific research could show that the brain and our mind have very little to do with each other, that the presumed coordination between the two does not exist. It once was thought (by Aristotle and by Descartes, for example) that the heart had to do with emotions. Science has proven this belief wrong. But science cannot do more than lay the groundwork for the problem.

3. The gland Descartes is referring to is what is now called the pineal gland, a small endocrine gland at the base of the brain. It had only recently been discovered in Descartes' time, and its functions are still not fully understood. It is currently understood to regulate sleep patterns and control mating cycles in higher animals; it may also play a role in any number of other activity cycles.

4. John Watson, *Behaviourism* (New York: Norton, 1930).

5. Both refer to the planet Venus, but it took many years for this identity to be discovered.

6. This is the so-called Turing Test, named after logician/computer scientist Alan Turing (1912–1954).

7. Maurice Merleau-Ponty, *The Structure of Behaviour*, trans. Alden L. Fisher (Boston: Beacon Press, 1963).

8. One psychological study showed short movies of little triangles moving around on a screen, sometimes bumping into each other and engaging in a variety of motions. Observers, including both adults and young children, uniformly reported what they saw in terms of simple stories that treated the dots as intelligent agents engaged in purposeful activity (for example, 'the big triangle is trying to catch the little one, who is hiding'). [Seager's note.]

9. The classic novel *Frankenstein* is partly inspired by the question of whether life can come from mere matter plus, in Dr Frankenstein's case, a little jolt of electricity—a phenomenon under intense scientific investigation and popular wonder at the time Mary Shelley was writing. [Seager's note.]

10. In an interesting 2002 experiment, scientists synthesized the poliovirus from its constituent DNA (mail ordered from standard chemical suppliers). The artificial virus could fully replicate and infect animal hosts. While the chemical formula of human DNA is somewhat more complex than that of the poliovirus, it is no less purely chemical. [Seager's note.]

11. Gottfried Wilhelm Leibniz, *Monadology*, in Robert Latta, trans., *The Monadology and Other Philosophical Writings* (Oxford: Clarendon Press, 1898).

12. William James, *The Principles of Psychology*, vol. 1 (New York: Henry Holt and Company, 1890).

13. Thomas Nagel, *The View from Nowhere* (Oxford: Oxford University Press, 1986), 49.

Chapter 5

1. From 'Meditation II'.

2. Locke refers here to Descartes.

3. It is worth mentioning that Kant held onto the Christian concept of soul; to do so, he defended it as a 'postulate of practical reason', in other words, as a strictly moral claim, much as he had defended his belief in God. Later philosophers borrowed Kant's arguments to get rid of the concept of the soul altogether.

4. This is, however, the main concept of *Being and Nothingness* and takes well over seven hundred pages to analyze correctly.

5. Sartre's example here reveals the extreme prejudice of his time. Writing in France in the early 1940s, where homosexuality was widely viewed as a serious social transgression, Sartre openly aligns 'homosexuality' with 'criminal behaviour' of which one can be 'guilty'.

6. For more on Sartrean freedom as intentionality, see Dagfinn Føllesdal, 'Sartre on Freedom', in *The Philosophy of Jean-Paul Sartre* (*The Library of Living Philosophers, vol. XVI*), ed. Paul Arthur Schilpp (La Salle, IL: Open Court, 1981), 392–407. [All notes in this piece are from Al-Saji.]

7. Jean-Paul Sartre, *Being and Nothingness: An Essay on Phenomenological Ontology*, trans. Hazel E. Barnes (London: Philosophical Library, 1956), 439.

8. Ibid., 440.

9. Ibid., 453.

10. Ibid., 55.

11. Ibid., 58.

12. Ibid., 49.

13. Despite Sartre's disavowal of a moral or normative reading, 'bad faith' is negatively inflected with the sense of 'lying to oneself', 'reification', and 'evasion' (Ibid., 49).

14. Ibid., 70.

15. Ibid., 486–7. Note that this is the meaning of his famous remark that we are 'condemned to be free' (Ibid., 439, 485, and 553).

16. Ibid., 438–9, 484–6.

17. Sartre distinguishes between the empirical concept of freedom as success in obtaining ends and the philosophical concept of freedom as autonomy of choice (*Ibid.*, 483). This is not a choice that precedes action but a choice that is already acting; existing is choosing, 'a choice in the making' (Ibid., 479). In this second sense, freedom is an absolute that we cannot not be, although we may try to hide from or escape this fact in bad faith.

18. Ibid., 548–9.
19. Ibid., 482.
20. To recall the critique that Maurice Merleau-Ponty levelled against Sartre in *Phenomenology of Perception*, trans. Colin Smith (London: Routledge & Kegan Paul, 1962), 434–42.
21. This makes emotion generally an instance of bad faith (Sartre, *Being and Nothingness*, 61). See also Jean-Paul Sartre, *Sketch for a Theory of the Emotions*, trans. Philip Mairet (London and New York: Routledge, 2002), 52–3.
22. Sartre, *Being and Nothingness*, 34.
23. Ibid., 55–6.
24. Ibid., 63–4.
25. Ibid., 526–7, 529.
26. Hence Sartre's claim that the slave is as free as the master (Ibid., 550).
27. Ibid., 550.
28. So far I have presented a critical reading of the Sartrean account of freedom in *Being and Nothingness*—a reading that, while it has its basis in the text, does not take into account Sartre's own concern for the social dimensions of experience. The previous examples, paraphrased from Sartre's work, are evidence of this concern.
29. Sartre calls these 'good faith' and 'bad faith' at the end of the chapter on bad faith, though both prove to be versions of bad faith on his analysis (Ibid., 70).
30. Ibid., 59.
31. Ibid., 63–5.
32. Ibid., 64.
33. Ibid., 64.
34. For a Sartrean consideration of racism as bad faith, see Lewis R. Gordon, *Bad Faith and Anti-Black Racism* (Amherst, NY: Humanity Books, 1999).
35. We can think here of the construction of homosexuality as deviance, of femininity as sexual and reproductive service, or of blackness as inferiority.
36. 'Although I have at my disposal an infinity of ways of assuming my being-for-others, *I am not able not to assume it*' (Sartre, *Being and Nothingness*, 529).
37. Ibid., 64, 487.
38. Ibid., 489. Sartre calls this 'the paradox of freedom'.
39. Ibid., 486. Moreover, Sartre notes that '*to do* supposes the nihilation of a given. One does something *with* or *to* something' (Ibid., 485).
40. Ibid., 485–6.
41. Ibid., 548, 554.
42. Ibid., 548.
43. Ibid., 553.
44. Ibid., 488. The cliff would then no longer be seen as 'scalable' or 'unscalable', but rather as 'beautiful', 'ugly', and so on.
45. Ibid., 549.
46. Ibid., 482.
47. Ibid., 488.
48. Ibid., 488.
49. Ibid., 482. Cited above.
50. Ibid., 524.
51. Ibid., 527. For more on identity as 'unrealizable' for Sartre, see Robert Bernasconi, 'Can Race Be Thought in Terms of Facticity? A Reconsideration of Sartre's and Fanon's Existential Theories of Race', in François Raffoul and Eric Sean Nelson, eds, *Rethinking Facticity* (Albany, NY: State University of New York Press, 2008), 195–213.
52. Sartre, *Being and Nothingness*, 525.
53. 'For-myself I am not a professor or a waiter in a café, nor am I handsome or ugly,

Jew or Aryan, spiritual, vulgar, or distinguished. We shall call these characteristics *unrealizables*.' (Ibid., 527)

54. Ibid., 524.
55. Ibid., 531.
56. Ibid., 528.
57. Ibid., 526.
58. Ibid., 527.
59. Ibid., 529, my emphasis.
60. Recall that Sartre is writing in occupied France.
61. Ibid., 527. Sartre seems to have a more nuanced consideration of the oppressive weight of situation in *Anti-Semite and Jew*, trans. George J. Becker (New York: Schocken Books, 1948), 89.
62. Sartre's note: 'The given in no way enters into the constitution of freedom since freedom is interiorized as the internal negation of the given.' (Ibid., 487)
63. Namely, Frantz Fanon and Simone de Beauvoir. See Frantz Fanon, *Black Skin, White Masks*, trans. Charles Lam Markmann (New York: Grove Press, 1967), in particular the chapter entitled 'The Fact of Blackness [*L'expérience vécue du Noir*]'. Also see Simone de Beauvoir, *The Second Sex*, trans. H.M. Parshley (New York: Vintage Books, 1989).
64. If you are interested in exploring this subject further, you will find a great deal of material to read, much of it uncommonly rich.
65. Oedipus' uncle/brother-in-law.
66. From Robert Owen (1771–1858), a political reformer.
67. David Hume, *An Enquiry Concerning Human Understanding*.
68. VII, 5, 256a, 6–8.

Chapter 6

1. St Thomas Aquinas, *Summa Contra Gentiles*, bk III (New York: Doubleday, 1955).
2. Deuteronomy 13:18.
3. Quoted in F. Sharp, *Ethics* (New York: Appleton-Century-Crofts, 1928).
4. It is necessary to say something about Aristotle's special notion of happiness; it is not at all like our conception of 'feeling happy'. Aristotle's term (*eudaimonia*) means something like 'living well', and it includes such matters as one's status in society and virtuous acts as well as good feelings. No matter how good you feel about yourself—even if you are in a state of ecstasy all of the time—you would not be happy in Aristotle's sense unless you had these other advantages and acted virtuously as well.
5. You may recognize Vanier as the founder of L'Arche, an international network of communities in which intellectually disabled persons and committed assistants live together.
6. Aristotle, *The Nicomachean Ethics*, 1155a3.
7. Aristotle, *The Nicomachean Ethics*, 1162a24.
8. Aristotle, *Politics*, 1127b23–32.
9. See Deuteronomy 10, 17–19.
10. Isaiah 58.
11. Leviticus 25.
12. Aristotle, *The Nicomachean Ethics*, bk X, trans. W.D. Ross (Oxford: Oxford University Press, 1980), Ch. 7.
13. Mary Midgley, *The Ethical Primate* (London: Routledge, 1994), Ch. 10.
14. F.H. Bradley, 'Mr Sidgwick's Hedonism', in *Collected Essays*, vol. I (New York: Oxford, 1935), 97.
15. David Hume, *Enquiry Concerning the Principles of Morals* (La Salle, IL: Open Court, 1912).

16. In the twentieth century, the moral philosophy called 'situation ethics' renewed this ancient demand that 'what is moral' can be defined only in relation to a specific context.

17. John Stuart Mill, *Utilitarianism* (London: J.M. Dent, 1910).

18. Dostoyevsky wrote one of his greatest novels, *The Idiot*, about just this—a perfectly good man, with all the right intentions, causes suffering and even death every time he tries to do good.

19. While Aristotle's philosophy was in agreement with most of the thinking of his times, Nietzsche's thought was a radical disruption of the usual Kantian style of thinking of the modern period and so takes on the tone of violent destructiveness rather than—as in Aristotle—the self-satisfied tones of a gentleman.

20. Joan Ringelheim, 'Women and the Holocaust: A Reconsideration of Research', *Signs: Journal of Women in Culture and Society*, vol. 10, no. 4 (1985), 759.

21. Barbara Houston, 'Rescuing Womanly Virtues: Some Dangers of Moral Reclamation', in M. Hanen and K. Nielsen, eds, *Science, Morality and Feminist Theory* (Calgary: University of Calgary, 1987), 252.

22. Nel Noddings, *Caring: A Feminine Approach to Ethics and Moral Education* (Berkeley: University of California Press, 1984).

Chapter 7

1. Plato did venture that women as well as men ought to be rulers.

2. I use the word *practice* throughout as a sort of technical term meaning any form of activity specified by a system of rules which defines offices, roles, moves, penalties, defences, and so on, and which gives the activity its structure. As examples one may think of games and rituals, trials and parliaments, markets and systems or property. I have attempted a partial analysis of the notion of a practice in a paper, 'Two Concepts of Rules', *Philosophical Review, vol.* 64 (1955), 3–32. [Rawls' note.]

3. Notice the political implications for this qualification, however, in 'underdeveloped' countries and colonies. The principle of paternalism—that one ought to take care of those who cannot take care of themselves—is easily abused and therefore dangerous.

4. Trudeau in *House of Commons Debates*, 8 Oct. 1971: 8545–6. [All notes in this piece are from Kymlicka.]

5. Neil Bissoondath, *Selling Illusions: The Cult of Multiculturalism in Canada* (Toronto: Penguin, 1994); Richard Gwyn, *Nationalism without Walls: The Unbearable Lightness of Being Canadian* (Toronto: McClelland and Stewart, 1995).

6. The passages quoted in this paragraph can be found on pages 111, 110, 98, and 113 of *Selling Illusions*.

7. A.M. Schlesinger, *The Disuniting of America* (New York: Norton, 1992), 138. According to his analysis, the United States is witnessing the 'fragmentation of the national community into a quarrelsome spatter of enclaves, ghettoes, tribes . . . encouraging and exalting cultural and linguistic apartheid' (137–8). Bissoondath argues that the same process is occurring in Canada.

8. The passages quoted in this paragraph are from pages 274, 8, and 234 of *Nationalism without Walls*.

9. Robert Fulford, 'Do Canadians Want Ethnic Heritage Freeze-dried?', in the *Globe and Mail*, 17 Feb. 1997.

10. Citizenship and Immigration Canada, *Citizenship and Immigration Statistics* (Ottawa: Public Works, 1997), Table G2 and Table 1.

11. The remaining differences between citizens and permanent residents relate to (a) minority language rights; (b) protection against deportation; and (c) access to a few sensitive bureaucratic positions, none of which are relevant to most immigrants.

12. The average length of residence before naturalization is 7.61 years, with immigrants from the UK taking the longest (13.95 years); immigrants from China, Vietnam, and the Philippines all take under five years on average (Citizenship Registrar, Multiculturalism and Citizenship Canada, 1992). In 1971, only 5 per cent of the Americans eligible to take out citizenship in Canada chose to do so. See Karol Krotki and Colin Reid, 'Demography of Canadian Population by Ethnic Group', in J.W. Berry and Jean Laponce, eds, *Ethnicity and Culture in Canada: The Research Landscape* (Toronto: University of Toronto Press, 1994), 26.

13. For surveys of the political participation of ethnocultural groups in Canadian politics, see the three research studies in Kathy Megyery, ed., *Ethnocultural Groups and Visible Minorities in Canadian Politics: The Question of Access*, vol. 7 of the Research Studies of the Royal Commission on Electoral Reform and Party Financing (Ottawa: Dundurn Press, 1991); Jean Laponce, 'Ethnicity and Voting Studies in Canada: Primary and Secondary Sources 1970–1991', in Berry and Laponce, eds, *Ethnicity and Culture*, 179–202; and Jerome Black and Aleem Lakhani, 'Ethnoracial Diversity in the House of Commons: An Analysis of Numerical Representation in the 35th Parliament', in *Canadian Ethnic Studies*, vol. 29 no. 1 (November 1997), 13–33.

14. Daiva Stasiulus and Yasmeen Abu-Laban, 'The House the Parties Built: (Re)constructing Ethnic Representation in Canadian Politics', in Megyery, ed., *Ethnocultural Groups*, 14; cf. Alain Pelletier, 'Politics and Ethnicity: Representation of Ethnic and Visible-Minority Groups in the House of Commons', in ibid., 129–30.

15. Geoffrey Martin, 'The COR Party of New Brunswick as an "Ethnic Party"', in *Canadian Review of Studies in Nationalism*, vol. 23 no. 1 (1996), 1–8.

16. For evidence of the quick absorption of liberal-democratic values by immigrants, see James Frideres, 'Edging into the Mainstream: Immigrant Adults and Their Children', in S. Isajiw, ed., *Multiculturalism in North America and Europe: Comparative Perspectives on Interethnic Relations and Social Incorporation in Europe and North America* (Toronto: Canadian Scholars' Press, 1997); Jerome Black, 'The Practice of Politics in Two Settings: Political Transferability among Recent Immigrants to Canada', in *Canadian Journal of Political Science*, vol. 20, no. 4 (1987), 731–53. Studies show that students born outside Canada, as well as students for whom English was not a first or home language, knew and valued their rights as much as their Canadian-born, English-speaking counterparts. See, for example, Charles Ungerleider, 'Schooling, Identity and Democracy: Issues in the Social-Psychology of Canadian Classrooms', in R. Short et al., eds, *Educational Psychology: Canadian Perspectives* (Toronto: Copp Clark, 1991), 204–5.

17. Freda Hawkins, *Critical Years in Immigration: Canada and Australia Compared* (Montreal: McGill-Queen's University Press, 1989), 279.

18. Some 63 per cent of immigrants have neither English nor French as their mother tongue, yet only 309,000 residents in the 1991 Census couldn't speak an official language. Most of these were elderly (166,000 were over 55). See Brian Harrison, 'Non parlo né inglese, né francese' (Statistic Canada: Census of Canada Short Article Series, #5, September 1993).

19. Derrick Thomas, 'The Social Integration of Immigrants', in Steven Globerman, ed., *The Immigration Dilemma* (Vancouver: Fraser Institute, 1992), 224.

20. Susan Donaldson, 'Un-LINC-ing Language and Integration: Future Directions for Federal Settlement Policy' (MA thesis, Department of Linguistics and Applied Language Studies, Carleton University, 1995).

21. Morton Weinfeld, 'Ethnic Assimilation and the Retention of Ethnic Cultures', in Berry and Labonce, eds, *Ethnicity and Culture*, 244–5.

22. Jeffrey Reitz and Raymond Breton, *The Illusion of Difference: Realities of Ethnicity in Canada and the United States* (Toronto: C.D. Howe Institute, 1994), 80; Leo Driedger, *Multi-ethnic Canada: Identities and Inequalities* (Toronto: Oxford University Press, 1996), 277.

23. Driedger, *Multi-ethnic Canada*, 263.

24. John Mercer, 'Asian Migrants and Residential Location in Canada', in *New Community*, vol. 15, no. 2 (1989), 198.

25. Thomas, 'Social Integration', 240, 247.

26. Orest Kruhlak, 'Multiculturalism: Myth versus Reality', unpublished paper prepared for the Institute for Research on Public Policy project 'Making Canada Work: Towards a New Concept of Citizenship' (1991), 10.

BRIEF BIOGRAPHIES

Note: An asterisk (*) denotes Canadian figures.

al-Ghazali, Mohammad (1058–1111) Islamic philosopher and theologian, known especially for his criticisms of Aristotelianism and Avicenna. His most famous work is called *The Incoherence of the Philosophers*.

*****Al-Saji, Alia** Canadian philosopher who teaches at McGill University, specializing in continental philosophy, feminist thought, and critical race theory.

Anaximander (*c.* 611–547 BCE) Pre-Socratic philosopher who taught that reality is ultimately composed of an indeterminate something that we can never know directly through experience.

Anaximenes (6th century BCE) Pre-Socratic philosopher who taught that the basic element of reality was air and that all things in the universe are different forms of air.

Anselm, St (*c.* 1033–1109) Archbishop of Canterbury and author of the ontological argument for God's existence. He was one of the main defenders of the intellect and understanding against the then current anti-intellectualism of the Church. He is best known for his *Monologion* and *Proslogion*, in which he develops the ontological argument.

Aquinas, St Thomas (1225–1274) Architect of the most comprehensive theological structure of the Roman Catholic Church, the *Summa Theologica*, which has long been recognized as the official statement of orthodox Christian beliefs by many theologians. Aquinas drew many of his arguments from Aristotle, as can be seen in his five ways of demonstrating the existence of God.

Aristophanes (*c.* 450–385 BCE) Ancient Greek writer of comedies. A contemporary of Socrates, he poked fun at his fellow Athenians in his play *The Clouds*.

Aristippus (*c.* 435–356 BCE) One of the Cynics and a student of Socrates, who taught that the good life consists solely of immediate pleasures.

Aristotle (384–322 BCE) One of the greatest Western philosophers, Aristotle was born in northern Greece (Stagira). His father was the physician to Philip, king of Macedonia, and he himself was to become the tutor to Philip's son, Alexander the Great. For eighteen years Aristotle was a student in Plato's academy in Athens, where he learned and parted from Plato's views. After Plato's death, he turned to the study of biology, and many of his theories ruled Western science until the Renaissance. He was with Alexander until 335 BCE, when he returned to Athens to set up his own school, the Lyceum. After Alexander's death, the anti-Macedonian sentiment in Athens forced Aristotle to flee (commenting that the Athenians would not sin twice against philosophy). In addition to his biological studies, Aristotle virtually created the sciences of logic and linguistics, developed extravagant theories in physics and astronomy, and made significant contributions to metaphysics, ethics, politics, and aesthetics. His *Metaphysics* is still a basic text on the subject, and *The Nicomachean Ethics* codified ancient Greek morality. This latter work stresses individual virtue and excellence for a small elite of Greek citizens. The best life of all, according to Aristotle, is the life of contemplation, that is, the life of a philosopher, for it is the most self-contained and the closest to the gods. But such contemplation must be together with the pleasures of life, honour, wealth, and virtuous action.

Augustine, St (354–430) The main figure in the development of medieval Christian thought from its roots in classical Greece and Rome. Augustine was born in North Africa and lived during the decline of the Roman Empire. After exploring various pagan beliefs, he was converted to Christianity and became bishop of Hippo in North Africa. He is best known for his theological treatise *The City of God* and for his very personal *Confessions*.

Bentham, Jeremy (1748–1832) A leader in the legal reform movement in England and the founding father of that ethical position called utilitarianism. His *principle of utility*, which says that one should act to produce the greatest good for the greatest number of people, was the central theme of utilitarianism and slowly worked its way into the confusion of rules and statutes that constituted the English legal system of his day. His best-known work is *An Introduction to the Principles of Morals and Legislation* (1789).

Berkeley, Bishop George (1685–1753) Irish philosopher; as a student he immersed himself in the writings of the important philosophers of the time, particularly Locke, Newton, and some of the French metaphysicians. He wrote virtually all the works that made him famous before he turned twenty-eight. In later life, Berkeley became an educational missionary, visiting America and Bermuda, and then a bishop, eventually moving to Oxford. Unlike Locke and Hume, whose interests spread across the whole of philosophy, science, and human affairs, Berkeley restricted himself to a single problem—perception—and his entire philosophy is aptly summarized in his famous phrase 'to be is to be perceived' (*esse est percipi*). His arguments for this position are most thoroughly outlined in his *Treatise Concerning the Principles of Human Knowledge* (1710).

Borges, Jorge Luis (1899–1986) Influential Argentinian writer whose intricate fictions and poems are rich in philosophical motifs. Borges was a great admirer of Berkeley, Hume, and Schopenhauer.

Braddon-Mitchell, David Professor of philosophy at the University of Sydney in Australia and co-author, with Frank Jackson, of *The Philosophy of Mind and Cognition* (1996).

Buddha (*c.* 563–483 BCE) The Awakened One; a name for the founder of the Buddhist religion, the ancient Indian prince Siddhãrtha Gautama, after his enlightenment.

Burke, Edmund (1729–1797) Irish writer, statesman, and orator famous for his eloquence and for his skeptical brand of conservatism. Author of *Reflections on the Revolution in France* (1790) and *A Philosophical Enquiry into the Origin of Our Ideas of the Sublime and Beautiful* (1757).

Butler, Joseph (1692–1752) Powerful English clergyman who formulated what are still recognized as the standard arguments against psychological egoism in his *Fifteen Sermons* (1726).

Calhoun, Cheshire (1954–) Teaches philosophy at Colby College in Maine and is the author of *Feminism, the Family, and the Politics of the Closet: Lesbian and Gay Displacement* (2002).

Chisholm, Roderick (1916–1999) A leading American analytic philosopher who taught at Brown University, Chisholm made major contributions to the fields of epistemology and metaphysics. Author of *Theory of Knowledge* (three editions: 1966, 1977, 1989), *The Foundations of Knowing* (1982), and *On Metaphysics* (1989).

*****Churchland, Paul M.** (1942–) Canadian-born philosopher who teaches at the University of California, San Diego; specialist in cognitive science and the interplay between philosophy, computer science, and neurology. Author of *Matter and Consciousness* (1984) and *Neurophilosophy at Work* (2007).

Clarke, Samuel (1675–1729) One of the leading British philosophers of his time, as well as a prominent Anglican clergyman and theologian. He defended the views of Isaac Newton against the criticisms of Leibniz, with whom he corresponded. Clarke is the author of two impressive works in the philosophy of religion: *A Demonstration of the Being and Attributes of God* (1704) and *A Discourse Concerning the Unchangeable Obligations of Natural Religion and the Truth and Certainty of the Christian Revelation* (1705).

*****Code, Lorraine** (1937–) Canadian feminist philosopher who teaches at York University. Author of *What Can She Know? Feminist Theory and the Construction of Knowledge* (1991) and *Rhetorical Spaces: Essays on (Gendered) Locations* (1995).

*****Cohen, G.A.** (1941–2009) Canadian political philosopher who taught at University College in London and at Oxford University. Author of *Karl Marx's Theory of History: A Defence* (1978), *If You're an Egalitarian, How Come You're So Rich?* (2000), and *Why Not Socialism?* (2009).

Confucius (*c.* 551–479 BCE) Ancient Chinese sage whose philosophies of moral virtue developed into the school of philosophy known as *Confucianism*. His doctrine sought gentlemanly conduct, which was to be achieved through adherence to ritual.

*****Daigle, Christine** Canadian philosopher who teaches at Brock University. Author of *Le nihilisme est-il un humanisme? Étude sur Nietzsche et Sartre* (2005) and *Jean-Paul Sartre* (2009).

Damascene, St John (*c.* 676–749) Eastern Orthodox Christian monk known for his piety and for his seminal contributions to theology. Author of *An Exact Exposition of the Orthodox Faith*.

Dao De Jing **Poets** (*c.* 6th century BCE) Ancient Chinese mystics whose doctrine was that the Dao or Way was the ineffable underpinning of existence.

Davies, Paul (1946–) English author, physicist, and cosmologist who currently teaches at Arizona State University. He has written over twenty books, including *God and the New Physics* (1983), *The Mind of God* (1992), and, most recently, *The Eerie Silence* (2010).

Dawkins, Richard (1941–) Kenyan-born biologist who was, between 1995 and 2008, the occupant of the prestigious Simonyi Professorship for the Public Understanding of Science at Oxford University. He is the author of many best-selling books, including *The Selfish Gene* (1976), *The Blind Watchmaker* (1986), and *The God Delusion* (2006).

Democritus (5th century BCE) Pre-Socratic philosopher who taught that reality is divisible into small atoms, which combine to make up all things but which themselves are eternal and indivisible.

Descartes, René (1596–1650) French philosopher who is usually considered the father of modern philosophy. He was raised in the French aristocracy and educated at the excellent Jesuit College of La Flèche. He became skilled in the classics, law, and medicine; however, he decided that they fell far short of proper knowledge, and so he turned to modern science and mathematics. His first book was a defence of Copernicus, which he prudently did not publish. He discovered, while still a young man, the connections between algebra and geometry (which we now call analytic geometry) and used this discovery as a model for the rest of his career. Basing the principles of philosophy and theology on a similar mathematical basis, he was able to develop a method in philosophy that could be carried through according to individual reason and no longer depended upon appeal to authorities whose insights and methods were questionable. In *Discourse on Method* (1637), he set out these basic principles, which he had already used in *Meditations on First Philosophy* (not published until 1641), to re-examine the foundations of philosophy. He sought a basic premise from which, as in a geometrical proof, he could deduce all those principles that could be known with certainty.

Dewey, John (1859–1952) American pragmatist, social critic, educational theorist, and reformer. Author of *Reconstruction in Philosophy* (1920) and *The Quest for Certainty* (1929).

d'Holbach, Baron Paul Henri (1723–1789) French philosopher and one of the leaders of the Enlightenment. An ardent materialist and atheist, he represented the most radical fringe of the brilliant free-thinkers of prerevolutionary France.

Diogenes (*c.* 412–323 BCE) Cynic philosopher who lived an extremely simple life. Offered anything he wanted by Alexander the Great, he replied, 'Get out of my light.'

Dostoyevsky, Fyodor (1821–1881) Russian writer whose best-known novels—*Notes from Underground* (1864), *Crime and Punishment* (1866), *The Idiot* (1868–69),

The Possessed (1871–72), and *The Brothers Karamazov* (1879–80)—are a repository of psychological truth and philosophical insight.

*Douglas, Tommy (1904–1986) Scottish-born Canadian politician voted 'The Greatest Canadian' in a CBC television program of the same name in 2004. An ordained Baptist minister, a gifted public speaker, and a passionate democratic socialist, Douglas was for many years a prominent member of the CCF (Cooperative Commonwealth Federation), a forerunner of today's NDP (New Democratic Party). He served as premier of Saskatchewan (1944–1961) and as the first leader of the NDP at the federal level (1961–71). Because of his commitment to the idea that access to health care services should not depend on one's ability to pay for them, Douglas is often called 'the father of medicare'. In 1961, Douglas' CCF government introduced medicare in Saskatchewan, making Saskatchewan the first province to have its own public health insurance program. The federal Liberal government, led by Prime Minster Lester B. Pearson, introduced a similar nationwide program in 1966.

*Duncan, A.R.C. (1915–) Scottish-born Canadian philosopher and emeritus professor of philosophy at Queen's University. Author of *Practical Reason and Morality* (1957) and *Moral Philosophy* (1965).

Einstein, Albert (1879–1955) Swiss physicist responsible for the special and general theories of relativity. In addition to pursuing his strictly scientific investigations, the mature Einstein spent a good deal of time pondering questions of a broadly philosophical character: questions about science, religion, politics, world affairs, human nature, morality, and the meaning of life. His thoughts on these subjects are collected in two books: *The World as I See It* (1934) and *Out of My Later Years* (1950).

Emerson, Ralph Waldo (1803–1882) American essayist, poet, philosopher, and sage whose writings stress the value of self-reliance and principled non-conformity. Friend and mentor to Henry David Thoreau.

Epicurus (*c.* 342–270 BCE) Greek philosopher who argued that the good life was pleasure, but not just the immediate pleasure talked about by Aristippus. Some pleasures last longer than others; some have a lower price than others. Accordingly, he taught self-control and avoidance of violent pleasures, which often caused more pain than ultimate pleasure. Ultimately what was most pleasurable, according to Epicurus, was a life of peace and quiet. Today we use the word *Epicurean* to describe someone who often indulges in pleasures, particularly sophisticated pleasures (gourmet food, for example).

Fackenheim, Emil (1916–2003) Distinguished philosopher and rabbi whose influential works explore Judaism, the Holocaust, German idealism, and the philosophy of religion. Born in Germany, Fackenheim was ordained a rabbi there in 1938. In 1940, after spending time in a Nazi concentration camp, he emigrated to Canada, where he taught at the University of Toronto.

His works include *Metaphysics and Historicity* (1961), *The Religious Dimension in Hegel's Thought* (1968), *Encounters between Judaism and Modern Philosophy* (1973), *To Mend the World: Foundations of Future Jewish Thought* (1982), and *The God Within: Kant, Schelling, and Historicity* (1996).

Ferrier, James Frederick (1808–1864) Scottish philosopher who taught at the University of St Andrews. His masterpiece, *The Institutes of Metaphysic* (1854), presents a rigorous and original defence of idealism.

Fichte, Johann Gottlieb (1762–1814) German philosopher who turned Kant's transcendental philosophy into a practically oriented and relativistic ethical idealism. He taught that the kind of philosophy a man chooses depends upon the kind of man he is. He was one of the first German nationalists.

*Fontaine, Phil (1944–) A member of the Sagkeeng First Nation, Manitoba-born Fontaine was national chief of the Assembly of First Nations for three terms: from 1997 until 2000, from 2003 until 2006, and from 2006 until 2009.

Foucault, Michel (1926–1984) French post-structuralist, follower of Nietzsche. He wrote influential books on knowledge, power, sexuality, and selfhood.

Frege, Gottlob (1848–1925) Brilliant logician whose work on the foundations of arithmetic inspired Bertrand Russell and Alfred North Whitehead and turned the current of logical thinking from the Mill-like empiricism that was then reigning (in Germany as well as in England) to a hard-headed mathematical discipline. He is often said to have been the pioneer and innovator of modern mathematical logic. Most important, perhaps, is his *Foundations of Arithmetic* (1884).

Freud, Sigmund (1856–1939) Austrian psychiatrist and neurologist; founder of the psychoanalytic school of psychology.

Gadamer, Hans-Georg (1900–2002) Leading German promoter of hermeneutics. Author of *Truth and Method* (1960).

*Gooch, Paul Canadian philosopher who teaches at the University of Toronto. Author of *Partial Knowledge: Philosophical Studies in Paul* (1987) and *Reflections on Jesus and Socrates: Word and Silence* (1996).

*Grant, George (1918–1988) A Canadian political and social philosopher who taught at Dalhousie University and McMaster University. Grant's writings offer a critique of modernity from a standpoint shaped by Platonism and Christianity. Author of *Philosophy in the Mass Age* (1959), *Lament for a Nation: The Defeat of Canadian Nationalism* (1965), and *English-Speaking Justice* (1974).

Grosz, Elizabeth Australian philosopher and professor of women's and gender studies at Rutgers University. She has published several texts in feminist philosophy.

Harman, Gilbert (1938–) American philosopher who specializes in ethics, epistemology, and cognition science. He teaches at Princeton University. Author of *The Nature of Morality* (1977).

Hartshorne, Charles (1897–2000) Was emeritus professor of philosophy at the University of Texas at Austin and the author of a great many books over his long and distinguished career. He is, perhaps, best known for his work in the philosophy of religion.

Hegel, Georg Wilhelm Friedrich (1770–1831) German philosopher who, during the age of Napoleon, wrote his *Phenomenology of Spirit* (1807), which was the single most powerful influence in European philosophy—after Kant's works—for the next hundred years. He argued that there were many different views of the world, that none of them should be thought to be wholly correct or incorrect in exclusion of the others, but that these various views could still be compared and evaluated according to a dialectic, in which some views are shown to be more developed, more inclusive, and more adequate than others.

Heidegger, Martin (1889–1976) German phenomenologist and student of Edmund Husserl, whose rebellion against his teacher began the existential movement in phenomenology. His best-known work is *Being and Time* (1927). Although focussing on metaphysics and phenomenology, this work is also one of the first existentialist studies of human nature. The significance of Heidegger's membership in the Nazi party is still being debated by scholars.

Heraclitus (*c.* 535–470 BCE) Pre-Socratic philosopher who taught that the basic element of reality was fire and that all things are in constant flux but yet are unified by an underlying logic or *logos*.

Hesse, Hermann (1877–1962) German writer and winner of the Nobel Prize for Literature (1946). Author of *Demian* (1919), *Siddhartha* (1922), *Steppenwolf* (1927), *Narcissus and Goldmund* (1930), and *The Glass Bead Game* (1943).

Hobbes, Thomas (1588–1679) The author of *Leviathan* (1651) and one of England's first great modern philosophers. He is generally credited with the formulation of the theory of the social contract for the establishment of governments and society, and he was one of the first philosophers to base his theory of government on a conception of man prior to his civilization, in what he called the 'state of nature'. This was, according to Hobbes, solitary, poor, nasty, brutish, and short. Therefore, people were motivated to become part of society for their mutual protection. Hobbes also defended a materialist conception of the universe. Even the human mind, he argued, was nothing more than matter in motion.

Hume, David (1711–1776) Often admired as the outstanding genius of British philosophy. Born in Scotland (Edinburgh), where he spent much of his life, he often travelled to London and Paris. After a vacation in France, he wrote the *Treatise of Human Nature* (1739). He achieved notoriety as well as literary fame in his lifetime, was involved in scandals, and was proscribed by the Church. He was refused professorships at the leading universities for his heresies. Yet he was, by all accounts, an utterly delightful man who never lost his sense of humour, and he has long set the standard of the ideal thinker for British philosophers. Hume's *Enquiry*

Concerning the Principles of Morals (1751) created as much of a stir in the intellectual world as his *Enquiry Concerning Human Understanding* (1748). Both texts were heavily based on his youthful *Treatise*, which never received the attention it deserved. Hume's thesis in moral philosophy was as skeptical and shocking as his thesis in epistemology. According to Hume, there is no knowledge of right and wrong and no rational defence of moral principles; these are based upon sentiment or feeling and, as such, cannot be defended by argument.

*****Hurka, Thomas** Canadian moral philosopher who teaches at the University of Toronto. Author of *Perfectionism* (1993) and *Vice, Virtue, and Value* (2001).

Husserl, Edmund (1859–1938) German-Czech philosopher and mathematician who was the founder of phenomenology, a modern form of rational intuitionism. With Gottlob Frege, he fought against the empiricist view of necessary truth defended by John Stuart Mill and developed an alternative view in which matters of necessity were not matters of ordinary experience but rather of a special kind of intuition. His best-known works are *Ideas* (Vol. 1) (1913) and *Cartesian Meditations* (1931).

*****Ignatieff, Michael** (1947–) Canadian author, journalist, academic, and politician who is the current leader of the Liberal Party of Canada and of the official opposition in Parliament. A scholar of human rights, Ignatieff was the director of the Carr Center for Human Rights Policy at Harvard University's John F. Kennedy School of Government from 2000 to 2005. Author of *The Needs of Strangers* (1984), *The Rights Revolution* (2000), *Human Rights as Politics and Idolatry* (2001), and *The Lesser Evil: Political Ethics in an Age of Terror* (2004).

Iqbal, Mohammad (1877–1938) Muslim philosopher, poet, and politically engaged man of letters whose writings played a role in the creation of Pakistan as an independent state. Author of *The Development of Metaphysics in Persia* (1908) and *The Reconstruction of Religious Thought in Islam* (1930).

Jackson, Frank (1943–) Australian philosopher and professor at Australian National University and co-author, with David Braddon-Mitchell, of *The Philosophy of Mind and Cognition* (1996).

James, William (1842–1910) Perhaps the greatest American philosopher (and psychologist) to this day. James was born in New York City and graduated from Harvard with a medical degree, but he decided to teach (at Harvard) rather than to practice medicine. He developed the particularly American philosophy of pragmatism from the brilliant but obscure formulations of his colleague at Harvard, Charles Sanders Peirce, into a popular and still very powerful intellectual force. His best-known works in philosophy are *The Varieties of Religious Experience* (1902) and *Pragmatism: A New Name for Some Old Ways of Thinking* (1907). He also established himself as one of the fathers of modern psychology with his *Principles of Psychology* (1890).

Jaspers, Karl (1883–1969) German existentialist philosopher. Author of *Way to Wisdom: An Introduction to Philosophy* (1951), *The Origin and the Goal of History* (1953), and a wonderfully eclectic two-volume survey entitled *The Great Philosophers* (1962, 1966).

Juhl, Cory Teaches philosophy at the University of Texas at Austin. His areas of specialty include logic, philosophy of science, and philosophy of mind.

Kane, Robert (1938–) Teaches philosophy at the University of Texas at Austin. Author of *Through the Moral Maze* (1994) and *The Significance of Free Will* (1996).

Kant, Immanuel (1724–1804) German philosopher, probably the greatest philosopher since Plato and Aristotle, who lived his entire life in a small town in East Prussia (Königsburg). He was a professor at the university there for more than thirty years; he led a quiet life, he never married, and his neighbours said that his habits were so regular that they could set their watches by him. Yet, from a safe distance, he was one of the most persistent defenders of the French Revolution and, in philosophy, created no less a revolution himself. His philosophical system, embodied in three huge volumes called *Critique of Pure Reason* (1781), *Critique of Practical Reason* (1788), and *Critique of Judgment* (1790), changed the thinking of philosophers as much as the revolution changed France. His central thesis was the defence of what he called synthetic a priori judgments (and their moral and religious equivalents) by showing their necessity for all human experience. In this way, he escaped from Hume's skepticism and avoided the dead-end intuitionism of his rational predecessors.

Kierkegaard, Søren (1813–1855) Danish philosopher and theologian who is generally recognized as the father of existentialism and the founder of many varieties of contemporary religious irrationalism. He dedicated himself to religious writing after a short and not altogether successful attempt at the wild life and a brief engagement, which he broke off in order to devote himself to his work. The basic tenet of Kierkegaard's philosophy is the need for each individual to choose his own way of life. In his view, Christianity, as one of the possible choices, cannot be considered anything other than just such a choice, a passionate choice, which has nothing to do with doctrines, churches, social groups, and ceremonies. Author of *Either/Or* (1843), *Fear and Trembling* (1843), *Philosophical Fragments* (1844), *Concluding Unscientific Postscript* (1846), *The Sickness unto Death* (1849), and *Training in Christianity* (1850).

***Kymlicka, Will** Canadian philosopher who teaches at Queen's University, where he holds the title of Canada Research Chair in Political Philosophy. Author of *Multicultural Citizenship: A Liberal Theory of Minority Rights* (1995), *Finding Our Way: Rethinking Ethnocultural Relations in Canada* (1998), *Politics in the Vernacular: Nationalism, Multiculturalism and Citizenship* (2001), and *Multicultural Odysseys: Navigating the New International Politics of Diversity* (2007).

Lao-zi (See *Dao De Jing* **Poets**)

Leibniz, Gottfried Wilhelm von (1646–1716) Leibniz has been called the last of the universal geniuses. He was one of the inventors of the calculus, the father of modern formal linguistics, the inventor of a primitive computer, a military strategist (who may have influenced Napoleon), a physicist who in his own time was thought to be the rival of Newton, and most of all a great philosopher. He grew up in Leipzig but travelled considerably (to Paris and Amsterdam and all over Germany). He spoke personally with most of the great philosophers of his time and often debated with them. His metaphysics is a curious combination of traditional theology and a radical alternative to the physical doctrines of Newton, to whose philosophy he had once been attracted but which he had given up as absurd. His short *Monadology* (1714) is a summary of his mature metaphysical theories.

Locke, John (1632–1704) Generally credited as not only the founder of British empiricism but also the father of modern political liberalism. He spent his early life in the English countryside, and he taught philosophy and the classics at Oxford until he earned a medical degree and turned to medicine. Much of Locke's mature life, however, was spent in politics, and he joined a more or less revolutionary group that was fighting for the overthrow of the government. He was forced to flee England in 1683, and he lived in Holland until the Glorious Revolution of 1688. For his part in the struggle, he received a government position, although he spent most of his time writing his two *Treatises on Government* (1689) to justify the revolution and its political principles and defending his *Essay Concerning Human Understanding* (1690), which he had written while in exile.

***Lonergan, Bernard** (1904–1984) Canadian theologian, philosopher, and Jesuit priest who, after extensive studies in Montreal, Guelph, London, and Rome, taught in Europe (at Rome's Gregorian University) and North America (at Regis College in Toronto, at Harvard University, and at Boston College). Author of *Insight* (1957) and *Method in Theology* (1972).

Maimonides, Moses (1135–1204) Spanish-born Jewish philosopher, scholar, and medical doctor who spent most of his adult life in exile, dying in Egypt. One of the greatest philosophers of the Middle Ages, Maimonides was the author of *The Guide for the Perplexed*.

Marx, Karl (1818–1883) German philosopher and social theorist who formulated the philosophical basis for one of the most cataclysmic political ideologies of the twentieth century. He received a doctorate in philosophy but could not teach in Germany because of his radical views. He spent most of his life abroad, in Paris, Brussels, and London, developing his theories and writing for various journals and newspapers (including the *New York Herald Tribune*). His savage attacks on established beliefs and his advocacy of revolution were constant throughout his life and forced him into exile. As a young man he wrote a devastating critique of G.W.F. Hegel, whom he had studied and followed as a young student, and whose concept of dialectic he used in developing a powerful social-political philosophy of class conflict and economic determination.

McGinn, Colin (1950–) British philosopher specializing in philosophy of mind. Currently teaches at the University of Miami.

*McKinnon, Christine Canadian philosopher who teaches at Trent University. Author of *Character, Virtue Theories, and the Vices* (1999).

Mencius (372–289 BCE) A Confucian philosopher who emphasized man's natural compassion and virtue.

Merleau-Ponty, Maurice (1908–1961) French existentialist, the most serious of the existential phenomenologists who followed Husserl in France. His most important work is his *Phenomenology of Perception* (1945). He is also well known for his political writings and his art criticism. In his early *Structure of Behavior* (1942), he argued that the human body cannot be considered merely another fragment of matter—in other words, merely a body—but must be viewed as the centre of our experience.

Midgley, Mary (1919–) English moral philosopher who taught at Newcastle University. Author of *Beast and Man* (1978), *Wickedness* (1984), and *Utopias, Dolphins and Computers: Problems of Philosophical Plumbing* (1996).

*Migotti, Mark Canadian philosopher who teaches at the University of Calgary, specializing in nineteenth-century thought, ancient Greek philosophy, and ethics.

Mill, John Stuart (1806–1873) Son of James Mill, also a philosopher, and one of the documented geniuses of modern history. His intellectual feats by the age of ten would have been to the credit of most scholars at the age of sixty. He pushed himself so hard, however, that he suffered a nervous breakdown at the age of twenty, at which time he and turned his attention from the hard sciences to poetry and political reform. He is best known for his moral and political writings, particularly *On Liberty* (1859) and *Utilitarianism* (1861). His logic and epistemology are the best to be found in the British empiricist tradition of the nineteenth century. His views on mathematics, for example, became one of those positions that every writer on the subject had either to accept or to fight forcefully.

*Misak, Cheryl Canadian pragmatist philosopher who teaches at the University of Toronto. Author of *Truth and the End of Inquiry* (two editions: 1990, 2004), *Verificationism: Its History and Prospects* (1995), and *Truth, Politics, Morality: Pragmatism and Deliberation* (2000).

Moore, G.E. (1873–1958) English philosopher who taught at Cambridge University. Moore's work in a variety of areas—ethics, epistemology, and metaphysics—profoundly influenced many Anglo-American philosophers. His mature writings are remarkable for their painstaking exploration of philosophical questions, their allegiance to common sense, and their plain yet cautious style. Author of *Principia Ethics* (1903), *Ethics* (1912), *Philosophical Studies* (1922), *Some Main Problems of Philosophy* (1953), and *Philosophical Papers* (1959).

*Morton, W.L. (1908–1980) Manitoba-born historian of Canada who taught at the University of Manitoba and at Trent University. Author of *Manitoba: A History* (1957), *The Canadian Identity* (1961), *The Kingdom of Canada* (1963), and *Contexts of Canada's Past: Selected Essays of W.L. Morton* (1980).

Nagel, Thomas (1937–) American philosopher at New York University and a broad-ranging thinker who has written on a spectrum of topics from sex and death to political philosophy and racism in South Africa. He is the author of *Mortal Questions* (1979), *The View from Nowhere* (1986), and *The Last Word* (1997).

Nietzsche, Friedrich (1844–1900) German philosopher who declared himself the archenemy of traditional morality and Christianity and spent much of his life writing polemics against them. His most sustained and vicious attack is in one of his last books, *Antichrist* (1888). Although generally known as an immoralist (a name he chose for himself), Nietzsche's moral philosophy is actually an attack on one conception of morality in order to replace it with another. The morality he attacked was the morality of traditional Christianity, as defined by Kant. The morality he sought to defend was the ancient morality of personal excellence, as defined by Aristotle. He referred to the first as slave morality, suggesting that it was suitable only for the weak and servile, and to the latter as master morality, suggesting that it was the morality of the strong and independent few.

Nishitani, Keiji (1900–1990) Japanese philosopher, a representative of the Kyoto School, founded by Kitaro Nishida (1870–1945). Their work was devoted to incorporating Western thought, especially existentialism, into Buddhism.

Nozick, Robert (1938–2002) American philosopher at Harvard University and author of several influential books on political philosophy, including *Anarchy, State and Utopia* (1974) and *Philosophical Explanations* (1981).

Oakeshott, Michael (1901–1990) English political philosopher who taught at the London School of Economics (LSE). Author of *Rationalism in Politics and Other Essays* (1962).

Paley, William (1743–1805) English philosopher and Anglican priest who taught at Cambridge University. Paley's *Natural Theology* (1802) presents a classic version of the teleological proof for the existence of God.

Parmenides (5th century BCE) Pre-Socratic philosopher who taught that reality was eternal and unchanging and that therefore we could not know it as such.

Pascal, Blaise (1623–1662) French scientist and philosopher with mildly mystical tendencies. He stressed confidence in the heart rather than in reason, and many of his best-known writings are concerned with the problems of religious faith. However, he was also a famous mathematician and inventor. His best-known work is *Pensées* (*Thoughts*), published posthumously.

Peirce, Charles Sanders (1839–1914) American philosopher, logician, and scientist credited with founding the philosophical movement known as pragmatism.

Plato (427–347 BCE) One of the greatest philosophers in ancient Greece. Plato was born into a family of wealth and political power, but in Athens he fell under the influence of Socrates and turned his talents to philosophy. He conceived of a philosopher-king, the ideal wise ruler, who certainly did not exist in Athens. He was disillusioned by Socrates' execution and devoted his life to continuing his mentor's work. Plato set up the Academy for this purpose and spent the rest of his life teaching there. He first set down his reminiscences of Socrates' life and death, and, using the dialogue form, with Socrates as his mouthpiece, he extended Socrates' thought into entirely new areas, notably, metaphysics and the theory of knowledge. Plato incorporated a theory of morality into his metaphysics and politics, particularly in *The Republic*. Like all Greeks, he saw ethics as part of politics and the good life for the individual in terms of the strength and harmony of the society. In *The Republic*, accordingly, Socrates argues against the various views of selfishness and hedonism that would interfere with such a conception. Virtue, he argues, is the harmony of the individual soul as well as the harmony of the individual within the society. It is still difficult, since we have nothing from Socrates himself, to know how much is original Plato and how much is transcribed Socrates.

Plotinus (*c*. 204–270) Egyptian-born philosopher who moved to Rome at the age of forty, where he achieved fame as an exponent of the mystical system expounded in *The Enneads*, a set of six treatises dealing with the nature of the soul, beauty, goodness, evil, and reality. The philosophy of Plotinus is usually described as a form of Neoplatonism: *Platonism*, because Plotinus draws heavily on Plato's philosophy; *Neo*, because Plotinus, being an original thinker and not a mere commentator, added something genuinely new to that philosophy. Though not himself an adherent of any religion, Plotinus was a significant influence on early Christian philosophers and theologians such as St Augustine.

Popper, Karl (1902–1994) Austrian-born philosopher of science who taught for many years at the London School of Economics (LSE). Author of *The Open Society and Its Enemies* (1945), *The Logic of Scientific Discovery* (1959), and *Conjectures and Refutations* (1963).

Pythagoras (*c*. 580–500 BCE) A pre-Socratic philosopher and religious mystic. He believed that numbers were the essence of all things.

Radhakrishnan, Sarvepalli (1888–1975) Indian philosopher, scholar, politician, and president of India from 1962 until 1967. Author of *The Hindu View of Life* (1927), *An Idealist View of Life* (1929), and *Indian Philosophy* (1929), a remarkably rich and lucid historical survey.

Rawls, John (1921–2002) Professor of philosophy at Harvard University. Author of *A Theory of Justice* (1971) and *Political Liberalism* (1993).

Reid, Thomas (1710–1796) Scottish philosopher widely regarded as the founder of the so-called Scottish Common Sense school of philosophy. According to Reid, skepticism is fundamentally misguided: we have no choice but to trust our basic cognitive faculties (in other words—perception, consciousness, memory, and reason) and our most fundamental assumptions about reality (for example—that nature is uniform, that there are other minds, that we have free will, that there is a real difference between right and wrong). Though an astute critic of David Hume, Reid was an original philosopher in his own right; and his views on a wide range of topics have attracted considerable attention from philosophers during the last few decades. Written with exemplary clarity, Reid's principal works are *An Inquiry into the Human Mind on the Principles of Common Sense* (1764), *Essays on the Intellectual Powers of Man* (1785), and *Essays on the Active Powers of Man* (1788).

Rorty, Richard (1931–2007) American philosopher who taught at Stanford University. Rorty defended a controversial version of pragmatism that called into question traditional conceptions of truth, objectivity, and knowledge. Author of *Philosophy and the Mirror of Nature* (1979), *Consequences of Pragmatism* (1982), *Contingency, Irony, and Solidarity* (1989), and *Philosophy and Social Hope* (2000).

Rousseau, Jean-Jacques (1712–1778) Stormy Enlightenment philosopher who fought with most of his peers (including David Hume) and developed a dramatic conception of natural morality, which he contrasted to what he saw as the fraud and hypocrisy of contemporary civilized man. He formulated a picture of man in the state of nature, before civilization, in which his natural goodness was not yet corrupted by society. The key to this idea was his conception of moral sentiment, which was innate in all people and not learned from society. His writings were condemned, and he spent much of his life running from the police. He died in total poverty, but only a few years after his death his political ideas became the central ideology of the French Revolution.

Russell, Bertrand (1872–1970) One of the greatest philosophers of the twentieth century. As a young man, he wrote, with Alfred North Whitehead, a book called *Principia Mathematica* (1903), which set the stage for modern logic and foundations of mathematics and gave logic a central role as a philosophical tool. He wrote an enormous number of philosophical books on virtually every topic, including several notorious polemics in favour of what was branded free love and atheism. He was a persistent and harsh critic of religion in general, and Christianity in particular, as a source of what he called superstition and legitimized murder. Russell was a committed pacifist during World War I and wrote at least one of his most famous books while sitting in prison for his antiwar activities. Like his famous predecessor, David Hume (with whom he had much in common), Russell was too controversial for most universities, and a famous court case prevented him from teaching at the City College of New York. He won the Nobel Prize for Literature in 1950.

***Russon, John** Canadian philosopher who teaches at the University of Guelph. Author of *Human Experience: Philosophy, Neurosis and the Elements of Everyday Life* (2003) and *Reading Hegel's Phenomenology* (2004).

Ryle, Gilbert (1900–1978) Oxford ordinary-language philosopher whose book *The Concept of Mind* (1949) set the stage for several decades of debate over his quasi-behaviouristic resolution of the mind–body problem. His main thesis is that the distinction between mind and body rests on what he calls a category mistake, that is, wrongly believing something to be one kind of thing when it is really another. In particular, it has been thought that mental events were events on a par with, but wholly different from, bodily events. Instead, Ryle argues, to talk about mind is to talk about behavioural dispositions and abilities. (To say that a person *wants* to do something is to say that he *would* do that if given the opportunity.)

Sartre, Jean-Paul (1905–1980) French philosopher who began as a literary writer and a phenomenologist, in the style of Edmund Husserl, but who converted that austere philosophy to his own radical ends. He is generally regarded as the main proponent of the philosophy of existentialism. Sartre's existentialism is a moral philosophy as well as a philosophy of freedom. It denies that there is any such thing as human nature and therefore insists that man makes himself. That is, through our various choices and moral commitments we define what we want humanity to be. According to Sartre, we do not simply find moral principles upon which we should act, but rather we *choose* those moral principles *through our acting*. Thus Sartre's moral philosophy places most of its emphasis on action and minimizes the importance of moral deliberation and all that sort of moralizing in which we simply talk about what is good, rather than simply a good will as in Kant. In his novels and plays, Sartre's characters are always torn by alternative identities, suffering just because they cannot make up their minds. In his greatest work, *Being and Nothingness* (1943), Sartre argues that a man is who he is not, and is not who he is, by which Sartre means (in a paradoxical phrase) that our identity is never simply the totality of facts (facticity) that are true of us; we always identify ourselves with our plans and intentions for the future (our transcendence) as well, which means that so long as we are alive, we have no fixed identity at all.

***Schellenberg, J.L.** Canadian philosopher of religion who teaches at Mount Saint Vincent University. Author of *Divine Hiddenness and Human Reason* (1993), *Prolegomena to a Philosophy of Religion* (2005), *The Wisdom to Doubt: A Justification of Religious Skepticism* (2007), and *The Will to Imagine: A Justification of Skeptical Religion* (2009).

Schopenhauer, Arthur (1788–1860) German philosopher; famous pessimist and man of letters. His main work, *The World as Will and Idea*, was an elaboration on Kant's philosophy. Yet instead of Kant's rationality, irrationality of the will became the centrepiece of Schopenhauer's philosophy. The book was first published in 1819, but did not become popular and earn its author the fame he much desired until the second half of the nineteenth century.

***Seager, William** Canadian philosopher of mind who teaches at the University of Toronto. Author of *Metaphysics of Consciousness* (1991) and *Theories of Consciousness* (1999).

Searle, John R. (1932–) American philosopher at the University of California at Berkeley. Author of *Minds, Brains, and Science* (1984), *The Rediscovery of the Mind* (1992), and *Mind, Language, and Society* (1998).

Shaffer, Jerome (1929–) American philosopher and emeritus professor of philosophy at University of Connecticut. One of the best-known critics of the now influential identity theory of mind and body.

***Sherwin, Susan** Canadian philosopher, emeritus professor of philosophy at Dalhousie University, and prominent philosophical feminist. Author of *No Longer Patient: Feminism, Ethics, and Health Care* (1992).

Singer, Isaac Bashevis (1902–1991) Polish-born Yiddish writer and winner of the Nobel Prize for Literature (1978). Author of *Gimpel the Fool and Other Stories* (1957), *The Magician of Lublin* (1960), *The Spinoza of Market Street and Other Stories* (1961), and *Enemies, A Love Story* (1972).

Skinner, B.F. (1904–1990) American psychologist and author who taught at Harvard University. He is best known in philosophy for developing the school of thought known as *radical behaviourism*.

Smart, J.J.C. (1920–) Australian philosopher and emeritus professor of philosophy at Monash University. He is a classic defender of the mind–body identity theory.

Socrates (*c.* 469–399 BCE) Athenian philosopher with a gift for rhetoric and debating. He had a notoriously poor marriage, had several children, and lived in poverty most of his life. Socrates began his studies in the physical sciences but soon turned to the study of human nature, morality, and politics. He became famous debating with the many sophists who wandered about giving practical training in argument and persuasion (the ancient equivalent of law school). Socrates found their general skepticism intolerable and urged a return to the absolute ideals of wisdom, virtue, justice, and the good life. In his philosophy, he approached these questions as matters of finding the exact definitions of these concepts in order to clarify our pursuit of them. In doing so, he developed a brilliant technique of dialogue or dialectic in which he would discover these definitions by constant debating, forcing his opponents or students to advance varying theories, which he in turn would knock down. In the process, the correct definition would slowly emerge. This is not always a tactful way to search for truth, however, and Socrates made many enemies, who eventually had him condemned to death, a cruel and unfair verdict he accepted with dignity.

*Somerville, Margaret (1942–) Australian-born Canadian ethicist who teaches at McGill University, where she founded the Centre for Medicine, Ethics, and the Law. Author of *The Ethical Canary: Science, Society, and the Human Spirit* (2000) and *The Ethical Imagination: Journeys of the Human Spirit* (2006).

Sophocles (c. 496–406 BCE) Ancient Greek writer of tragedies. Best known for his three plays about the royal house of Thebes: *Antigone*, *Oedipus the King*, and *Oedipus at Colonus*.

*Sparshott, Francis (1926–) English-born Canadian poet and philosopher who is emeritus professor at the University of Toronto. Author of *Taking Life Seriously: A Study of the Nicomachean Ethics* (1994) and *The Future of Aesthetics* (1996).

Spinoza, Benedictus de (1632–1677) Spinoza was born Baruch ben Michael, the son of Jewish refugees from the Spanish Inquisition. He was born and grew up in Amsterdam, a relative haven of toleration in a world still dangerous because of religious hatreds. He studied to be a rabbi, making himself familiar with Christian theology as well. He was always a recluse who wandered about the country making a living by grinding lenses, and he was later ostracized by his fellow Jews for his heretical beliefs. His best-known book is *Ethics* (1677); it is a radical reinterpretation of God as identical to the universe (pantheism) and a protracted argument concerning the uselessness of human struggle in the face of a thoroughly determined universe.

Stevenson, Robert Louis (1850–1894) Scottish essayist, critic, poet, novelist, travel writer, and teller of stylish tales of suspense and adventure. Author of *New Arabian Nights* (1882), *Treasure Island* (1883), *Kidnapped* (1886), *The Strange Case of Dr Jekyll and Mr Hyde* (1886), *The Master of Ballantrae* (1889), and *Island Nights' Entertainments* (1893).

Strawson, Galen (1952–) English philosopher of mind based at the University of Reading. Author of *Mental Reality* (1994) and *Selves* (2009).

*Stroud, Barry (1935–) Canadian-born professor of philosophy at the University of California at Berkeley. Author of *Hume* (1977) and *The Significance of Philosophical Scepticism* (1984).

*Taylor, Charles (1931–) Canadian philosopher who has spent much of his career at McGill University, though he has also occupied the prestigious Chichele Chair of Social and Political Theory at Oxford University. Author of *Hegel* (1975), *Philosophical Papers* (1985; in 2 volumes), *Sources of the Self* (1989), *The Malaise of Modernity* (1992), and *A Secular Age* (2007).

Thales (c. 624–545 BCE) The first known Greek philosopher, who taught that all things were ultimately composed of water.

Thoreau, Henry David (1817–1862) American essayist, naturalist, and philosopher; a champion of individualism. His most famous work was *Walden* (1854).

Tillich, Paul (1886–1965) German-born philosopher who spent many of his later years teaching in the United States. He is among the best known of those modern theologians who, like the Romantics of the nineteenth century, place emphasis on emotion and concern rather than on reason in religion. In Tillich's theology, God is no longer the transcendent judge of the scriptures but simply the symbol of our ultimate concern. He is the author of *Systematic Theology* (1953–63), *The Dynamics of Faith* (1957), and *The Courage to Be* (1952).

*Trudeau, Pierre (1919–2000) Canada's fifteenth prime minister (1968–1979, 1980–1984). A cosmopolitan intellectual with a strong background in political philosophy and law, Trudeau defended his distinctive (and not uncontroversial) vision of Canada with verve and argument. Trudeau-led Liberal governments were responsible for the development of our federal multiculturalism policy (in 1971) and the Canadian Charter of Rights and Freedoms (in 1982).

*Vanier, Jean (1928–) Canadian founder of L'Arche, an international network of communities in which intellectually disabled persons and committed assistants live together as a family. Trained as a philosopher, Vanier taught at the University of Toronto before founding the first L'Arche community outside Paris in 1964. Author of *An Ark for The Poor: The Story of L'Arche* (1995), *Made For Happiness: Discovering the Meaning of Life with Aristotle* (2001), *Finding Peace* (2003), and *Becoming Human* (2008).

Vivekananda, Swami (1863–1902) Indian religious teacher and writer who explained the rudiments of Hinduism to Western audiences, beginning with his famous addresses to the Parliament of Religions in 1893 in Chicago. A fervent believer in the idea of a universal religion, Vivekananda stressed what various faiths had in common, advocating tolerance and pluralism in the face of religious disagreement. His *Collected Works*, containing lectures, poems, and travel sketches, run to nine volumes.

Watson, John (1878–1958) American psychologist generally recognized as the founder of behaviourism. He attacked the notion of consciousness as a remnant of the age-old religious belief in the soul and urged that we give up what he called such magical nonsense in favour of a purely scientific view, which allows us to talk sensibly only about observables, in other words, human behaviour rather than the human mind. He is the author of *Behaviorism* (1924).

Weil, Simone (1909–1943) French philosopher, writer, and mystic whose works explore themes from Platonism and Christianity in a mutually illuminating way. Author of *Gravity and Grace* (1952), *Waiting on God* (1959), and *The Need for Roots* (1960).

*Wiebe, Phillip Canadian philosopher of religion who teaches at Trinity Western University. Author of *Visions* *of Jesus: Direct Encounters from the New Testament to Today* (1997) and *God and Other Spirits: Intimations of Transcendence in Christian Faith* (2004).

Wisdom, John (1904–1993) English philosopher who taught at Cambridge University. Though influenced significantly by Ludwig Wittgenstein, Wisdom's writings have a charm that is all their own. Author of *Other Minds* (1952) and *Philosophy and Psychoanalysis* (1953).

Wittgenstein, Ludwig (1889–1951) Austrian-born philosopher who became the single most powerful influence on twentieth-century analytic philosophy. He entered philosophy as an engineer, studied with Bertrand Russell, and wrote the book *Tractatus Logico-Philosophicus* (1922), which inspired logical positivism. Giving up philosophy for a number of years and changing his mind about his arguments in the *Tractatus*, he returned to philosophy at Cambridge and developed that therapeutic brand of philosophy that became known as ordinary-language philosophy. In his later works, culminating in his *Philosophical Investigations* (1953, published posthumously), Wittgenstein initiated a devastating attack on Cartesian dualism and the problems it carried with it. His so-called private-language argument, in fact culled from a series of aphorisms, argues that even if there were such private occurrences as mental events, we should have no way of talking about them and no way of knowing about them, even in our own case. But although he is often described as a behaviourist, Wittgenstein is better described as one of those philosophers who was groping for an entirely new conception of a person or at least attempting to reject all the old ones.

*****Woodcock, George** (1912–1995) Canadian writer, poet, and literary critic who taught at the University of British Columbia. His *Anarchism: A History of Libertarian Ideas and Movements* (1962) has been hailed as a classic.

Xenophanes (*c.* 570–475 BCE) Founder of the Eleatic school and a severe critic of Greek popular religion.

Xun-zi (*c.* 300–230 BCE) A Confucian philosopher who emphasized the importance of culture in replacing man's natural selfishness with virtue.

*****Young, James O.** Canadian philosopher who teaches at Victoria University. Author of *Global Anti-realism* (1995), *Art and Knowledge* (2001), and *Cultural Appropriation and the Arts* (2008).

Zeno of Elea (5th century BCE) Pre-Socratic philosopher and student of Parmenides who taught that motion was unreal and developed a series of brilliant paradoxes in order to prove it.

Zoroaster (Zarathustra) (*c.* 628–551 BCE) Ancient Persian reformer and prophet of the first monotheistic religion, Zoroastrianism.

CREDITS

Mohammad al-Ghazali. *The Deliverance from Error*, from *The Faith and Practice of al-Ghazali*, trans. William Montgomery Watt, London: Allen & Unwin, 1953.

St Anselm. 'On the Ontological Argument', from *Proslogion*, in *A Scholastic Miscellany*, Vol. 10, The Library of Christian Classics, ed. and trans. Eugene R. Fairweather, 1956. Used by permission of Westminster John Knox Press.

St Thomas Aquinas. 'On the Cosmological Argument' and 'On the "Fifth Way"', from *Summa Theologica*, trans. Fathers of the English Dominican Province, New York: Benziger, Bruce & Glencoe, 1948.

Aristophanes. *The Clouds*, in *The Complete Plays of Aristophanes*, ed. Moses Hadas. Copyright © 1962 by Bantam Books, a division of Random House, Inc.

Aristotle. *De Anima*, in the *Loeb Classical Library from Aristotle: Minor Works*, Volume XIV, trans. W.S. Hett, Cambridge, MA: Harvard University Press, 1936. Reprinted by permission of the publishers. *Metaphysics* (excerpt on p. 318), T.1.1003a21, Z.1.1028a10, trans. W.D. Ross, Oxford: Oxford University Press, 1924. *Metaphysics* (excerpts on pp. 53, 85), reprinted by permission of the publishers and the Loeb Classical Library from *Aristotle: Metaphysics*, Vol. XVII, trans. H. Tredennick, Cambridge, MA: Harvard University Press, 1933. *Metaphysics* (excerpt on p. 80), from *Metaphysics*, T.1.1003a21, Z.1.1028a10, trans. W. D. Ross, Oxford: Oxford University Press, 1924. *The Nicomachean Ethics* (excerpt on p. 407), 8th edn, trans. by F.H. Peters, London: K. Paul, Trench, Tubner & Co., Ltd, 1888. *The Nicomachean Ethics* (excerpt on p. 482), trans. W.D. Ross, Oxford: Oxford University Press, 1925. *Physics*, II.1.193a9; II.1.193, I.8.191a24, trans. W.D. Ross, Oxford: Oxford University Press, 1936.

St Augustine. *Confessions*, Bk. VII, trans. R.S. Pine-Coffin. Copyright © 1961 by R. S. Pine-Coffin. Penguin Classics, 1961, pp. 136–149. Reprinted by permission of Penguin Books, Ltd. *On Free Choice of the Will*, trans. Anna S. Benjamin and L.H. Hackstaff. Copyright © 1964. Reprinted by permission of Pearson Education, Inc., Upper Saddle River, NJ. *On Freedom*, New York: Bobbs-Merrill, 1956.

Bhagavadgita. The following texts are from Bhagavadgita 1.31b-35, 3.9–12, 3.15, 4.6–8, 4.11, 4.14–19, 4.22–24, 4.31–33, 4.36–37, and 4.42b. Trans. Steve Phillips.

Jeremy Bentham. *An Introduction to the Principles of Morals and Legislation*, Oxford: Clarendon, 1879.

Bishop George Berkeley. *Treatise Concerning the Principles of Human Knowledge*, London: Brown & Sons, 1907.

Jorge Luis Borges. 'Things', in *Selected Poems*, Alexander Coleman, ed., Alastair Reid, trans. (New York: Penguin Group, 2000), 277.

David Braddon-Mitchell and Frank Jackson. *Philosophy of Mind and Cognition*, London: Blackwell, 1996.

Edmund Burke. *Reflections on the Revolution in France and on the Proceedings in Certain Societies in London Relative to That Event*, ed. Conor Cruise O'Brien, London: Penguin Books, 1968, 119, 192–5, 266–7.

Joseph Butler. 'Against Egoism', from *Sermons*, Boston: Hillard, Gray, Little, and Wilkins, 1827.

Cheshire Calhoun. 'Justice, Care, Gender Bias', in *Journal of Philosophy* 85, 1988. Reprinted by permission of *The Journal of Philosophy*.

Canadian Charter of Rights and Freedoms, Part I of the *Constitution Act, 1982*.

Roderick M. Chisholm. 'Human Freedom and the Self', in *On Metaphysics*, Minneapolis: University of Minnesota, 1989, 5–9, 12. Reprinted by permission of the publisher.

Paul M. Churchland. 'On Eliminative Materialism', from *Matter and Consciousness: A Contemporary Introduction to the Philosophy of Mind*, Cambridge, MA: mit Press, 1988, 43–9. Copyright © 1988 Massachusetts Institute of Technology, by permission of The MIT Press.

Samuel Clarke. *A Demonstration of Being and Attributes of God*, ed. Ezio Vailati, Cambridge: Cambridge University Press, 1998, 8, 10–11.

Lorraine B. Code. 'Is the Sex of the Knower Epistemologically Significant?', *Metaphilosophy* 12, no. 3 and 4 (July/October 1981), 267–76.

G.A. Cohen. 'Why Not Socialism?', *Democratic Equality: What Went Wrong?*, ed. Edward Broadbent, Toronto: University of Toronto Press, 2001, 58–60, 62–7. Reprinted by permission of the publisher.

Confucius. *The Analects of Confucius*, trans. and annotated by Arthur Waley, New York: Vintage, 1938.

St John Damascene. *An Exact Exposition of the Orthodox Faith*, in *Saint John of Damascus Writings*, trans. Frederic H. Chase, Jr, Washington: The Catholic University of America Press, 1958, 169–70.

Paul Davies. *The Mind of God*. Reprinted by permission of Simon & Schuster Adult Publishing Group. Copyright © 1992 by Orion Productions.

Richard Dawkins. *The Blind Watchmaker*, New York: W.W. Norton & Company Inc., 1986, 5–6, 21. Reprinted by permission of SLL/Sterling Lord Literistic, Inc. Copyright by Richard Dawkins.

René Descartes. *Discourse on Method*, trans. Elizabeth S. Haldane and G.R.T. Ross, 1911. Reprinted with the permission of Cambridge University Press. 'Letter of Dedication to the Dean and Doctors of the Faculty of Sacred Theology of Paris', from *Meditations on First Philosophy*; *Meditations on First Philosophy*; 'On Substance', from *Principles of Philosophy*; 'On the Ontological Argument' and 'Meditation VI', from *Meditations on First Philosophy*; and 'The Passions of the Soul', in *The Philosophical Works of Descartes*, ed. E. Haldane and G.R.T. Ross, 1911. Reprinted with the permission of Cambridge University Press.

The Dhammapada. Parts reprinted in *The Teachings of the Compassionate Buddha: Early Discourses, the Dhammapada, and Later Basic Writings*, ed. E.A. Burtt, New York:

New American Library, 1955. Reprinted by permission of W.B. Brinster.

Baron Paul Henri d'Holbach. *System of Nature*, London: Kearsley, 1797.

Fyodor Dostoyevsky. *The Brothers Karamazov*, trans. Constance Barnett, New York: Modern Library, 1929. 'The Most Advantageous Advantage', from *Notes from the Underground*, in *Notes from the Underground and The Grand Inquisitor*, trans. Ralph Matlaw, New York: E.P. Dutton, 1960.

Tommy Douglas. Quoted in L.D. Lovick, *Tommy Douglas Speaks*, Vancouver: Douglas & McIntyre, 1980, 80–1.

A.R.C. Duncan. *Moral Philosophy*, Toronto: cbc Enterprises, 1965, 1, 5–7, 9–10.

Albert Einstein. 'On the Design of the Universe', from 'Religion and Science', in *Ideas and Opinions*, trans. Sonia Bargmann, New York: Crown, 1954.

Emil L. Fackenheim. 'On the Eclipse of God', *Quest for Past and Future: Essays in Jewish Theology*, Boston: Beacon Press, 1968, 229–31. Reprinted by permission of Georges Borchardt, Inc., on behalf of the Estate of Emil L. Fackenheim.

James Frederick Ferrier. *Institute of Metaphysic*, in *Philosophical Works of James Frederick Ferrier*, Bristol: Thoemmes Press, 2001, 1–5.

'Fire-Sermon' from *Mah -Vagga*. Reprinted by permission of the publishers from *Buddhism in Translation: Passages Selected from the Buddhist Sacred Texts and Translated from the Original Pali into English* by Henry Clark Warren, Student's Edition, Harvard Oriental Series 3. Cambridge, MA: Harvard University Press, 1896/1922, 351–3. Copyright © 1953 by the President and Fellows of Harvard College.

Phil Fontaine. 'Modern Racism in Canada', 1998 Donald Gow Lecture, School of Policy Studies, Queen's University, 1998.

Sigmund Freud. *The Future of an Illusion*, from *The Standard Edition of the Complete Psychological works of Sigmund Freud*, translated and edited by James Strachey, published by The Hogarth Press. Reprinted with permission. 'On the "Unconscious"', from *New Introductory Lectures on Psychoanalysis*, ed. and trans. James Strachey, New York: Norton, 1964.

Paul W. Gooch. *Reflections on Jesus and Socrates: Word and Silence*, New Haven: Yale University Press, 1996, 13–15. Reprinted by permission of the publisher.

George Grant. 'What Is Philosophy', in *The George Grant Reader*, ed. William Christian and Sheila Grant, Toronto: University of Toronto Press, 1998, 33–7, 38–9. Reprinted by permission of the publisher.

Elizabeth Grosz. 'On Feminist Knowledge, from 'Philosophy', in *Feminist Knowledge: Critique and Construct*, ed. Sneja Gunew, London: Routledge, 1990. Reprinted by permission of Elizabeth Grosz.

Gilbert Harman. 'Moral Relativism Defended', in *Philosophical Review* 75 (1975), 3–22. The *Philosophical Review* is published by Duke University Press.

Charles Hartshorne. 'On the Ontological Argument', from *Man's Vision of God and the Logic of Theism*. Copyright © 1941 by Charles Hartshorne, renewed 1969. Reprinted by permission of HarperCollins Publishers.

G.W.F. Hegel. *The Phenomenology of Spirit*, trans. A.V. Miller, New York: Oxford University Press, 1977. *Reason in History*, trans. Robert S. Hartman, Upper Saddle River, NJ: Pearson Education, Inc., 1995, 25–9. Copyright © 1995. Reprinted by permission of Pearson Education, Inc., Upper Saddle River, NJ.

Hermann Hesse. *Steppenwolf*, trans. Basil Creighton and Rev. Joseph Mileck, New York: Holt, Rinehart and Winston, 1929.

Thomas Hobbes. *Leviathan*, New York: Hafner, 1926.

David Hume. *An Enquiry Concerning Human Understanding*, 2nd edn, ed. L.A. Selby-Bigge, Oxford: Oxford University Press, 1902. 'On an Imperfect Universe', from *Dialogues Concerning Natural Religion*, ed. Norman Kemp Smith, Oxford: Oxford University Press, 1935. 'On Causation and Character', from *An Enquiry Concerning Human Understanding*, 2nd edn, ed. L.A. Selby-Bigge, Oxford: Oxford University Press, 1902. 'On "Justice and Utility"' and 'On "Reason as Slave of the Passions"', from *Enquiry Concerning the Principles of Morals*, La Salle, IL: Open Court, 1912. 'On "There Is No Self"', from *A Treatise of Human Nature*, ed. L.A. Selby-Bigge, Oxford: Oxford University Press, 1888. *A Treatise of Human Nature*, ed. L.A. Selby-Bigge, Oxford: Oxford University Press, 1888.

Thomas Hurka. 'The Well-Rounded Life', *The Journal of Philosophy, Inc.* 2 (1987), 727–46. Reprinted by permission of *The Journal of Philosophy* and Thomas Hurka.

Edmund Husserl. *The 1929 Paris Lectures*, trans. Peter Koestenbaum, Hague: Nijhoff, 1975. Reprinted with permission by Springer Science and Business Media. 'Philosophy as Rigorous Science', in *Phenomenology and the Crisis of Philosophy*, trans. Quentin Lauer, New York: Harper & Row, 1965.

Michael Ignatieff. *The Rights Revolution*, Toronto: House of Anansi Press Inc./cbc, 2000, 1–2, 7–9. Reprinted by permission of House of Anansi Press. www.anansi.ca.

Mohammad Iqbal. *The Reconstruction of Religious Thought in Islam*, London: Oxford University Press, 1934.

William James. 'Does Consciousness Exist?', in *Journal of Philosophy, Psychology and Scientific Methods*, 1 September 1904. *The Varieties of Religious Experience*. New York: Random House, 1929, 370–2, 414–5, 427–9. 'The Will to Believe', in *The Will to Believe and Other Essays in Popular Philosophy*, New York: Longmans, Green, 1896.

Karl Jaspers. 'The "Axial Period"', in *Basic Philosophical Writings—Selections*, ed., trans., and with introductions by Edith Ehrlich, Leonard H. Ehrlich, and George B. Pepper, Athens, OH: Ohio University Press, 1986, 382–7.

Cory Juhl. 'On the "Fine-Tuning" Argument'. Reprinted by permission of the author.

Robert Kane. 'On Indeterminism', courtesy of Robert Kane, University Distinguished

Teaching Professor of Philosophy Emeritus and Professor of Law.

Immanuel Kant. 'Against the Ontological Argument', from *The Critique of Pure Reason*, rev. 2nd edn, trans. Max Müller, London: Macmillan, 1927. 'Against the Soul', from *Prolegomena to Any Future Metaphysics*, trans. Lewis White Beck. Copyright © 1959. Reprinted by permission of Pearson Education, Inc., Upper Saddle River, NJ. *The Critique of Pure Reason*, rev. 2nd edn, trans. Max Müller, London: Macmillan, 1927. *Fundamental Principles of the Metaphysics of Morals*, trans. T.K. Abbott, New York: Longmans, Green, 1898. 'On God and Morality', from *The Critique of Practical Reason*, 3rd ed., trans. Lewis White Beck, Upper Saddle River, NJ: Prentice-Hall, Inc., 1993, 130–2. Copyright © 1993 reprinted by permission of Pearson Education, Inc. *Prolegomena to Any Future Metaphysics*, trans. Lewis White Beck. Copyright © 1959. Reprinted by permission of Pearson Education, Inc., Upper Saddle River, NJ.

Søren Kierkegaard. *The Sickness unto Death*, ed. and trans. Howard V. Hong and Edna H. Hong, Princeton: Princeton University Press, 1980, 92. 'On the Subjective Truth' (excerpt on p. 174): The first and third readings are from Søren Kierkegaard, *Concluding Unscientific Postscript*, and the second reading is from Søren Kierkegaard, *Philosophical Fragments*. All three have been translated from the Danish by Clancy Martin and reprinted with his permission.

Will Kymlicka. *Finding Our Way: Rethinking Ethnocultural Relations in Canada*, Toronto: Oxford University Press Canada, 1998, 15–21. © Will Kymlicka. Reprinted by permission of Beverley Slopen Literary Agency.

Lao-zi (Lao-Tzu). *Tao Te Ching*, trans J.H. McDonald, 1996 (for the public domain).

Gottfried Wilhelm von Leibniz. 'Leibniz's Rebuttal', from *New Essays on Human Understanding*, trans. A.G. Langley. Reprinted by permission of Open Court Publishing Company, a division of Carus Publishing Company, Peru, IL. Copyright © 1949 by Open Court Publishing. *Monadology* (excerpt on p. 98), in *The Rationalists*, trans. George Montgomery, New York: Doubleday, 1968. *Monadology* (excerpt on p. 132), in *The Rationalists*, trans. George Montgomery, New York: Anchor Press, 1974, 460.

John Locke. *An Essay Concerning Human Understanding*, ed. A.C. Fraser, Oxford: Clarendon Press, 1894. 'On Personal Identity', from *An Essay Concerning Human Understanding*, ed. A.C. Fraser, Oxford: Clarendon Press, 1894. *The Second Treatise on Government*, Oxford: Clarendon, 1690, 26–7, 51.

Bernard Lonergan. 'Method in Theology', in *The Lonergan Reader*, ed. Mark D. Morelli and Elizabeth A. Morelli, Toronto: University of Toronto Press, 1997, 476–7. Reprinted with permission of the publisher.

Colin McGinn. 'On the "Mystery of Consciousness"', from 'Consciousness and Content', *Proceedings of the British Academy 74* (1988), 219–39.

Christine McKinnon. *Character, Virtue Theories, and the Vices*, Peterborough: Broadview Press, 1999, 5, 7–8. Copyright © 1999 by Christine McKinnon. Reprinted by permission of Broadview Press.

Moses Maimonides. *The Guide for the Perplexed*, 2nd edn, trans. M. Friedländer, New York: Dover Publications, Inc., 1956, 384–5.

Karl Marx. *Critique of Hegel's Philosophy of Right in Early Writings*, trans. T. Bottomore. Copyright © 1964. Reprinted by permission of The McGraw-Hill Companies.

Mencius. 'On Human Nature: Man Is Good', from *Human Nature*, trans. D.C. Lau, Penguin Classics, 1970, 82–3. Copyright © 1970 by D.C. Lau. Reprinted by permission of Penguin Books, UK.

Mary Midgley. 'Water and Thought', in *Utopias, Dolphins, and Computers: Problems of Philosophical Plumbing*, London: Routledge, 2006, 1–2. Reproduced by permission of Taylor & Francis Books UK.

John Stuart Mill. 'On Causation and Necessity', from *A System of Logic*, 8th edn, New York: Harper & Row, 1874. *On Liberty*, London: Longmans, 1859. *Utilitarianism*, London: J.M. Dent, 1910.

Cheryl Misak. *Truth, Politics, Morality*, London: Routledge, 2000, 12–13, 17–18. Reproduced by permission of Taylor & Francis Books UK.

George Edward Moore. *Some Main Problems of Philosophy*, London: George Allen & Unwin Ltd, 1966, 119–20, 125–6.

W.L. Morton. 'Canadian Conservatism Now', *Contexts of Canada's Past: Select Essays of W.L. Morton*, ed. A.B. McKillop, Toronto: Macmillan of Canada, 1980, 243–5.

Thomas Nagel. *Mortal Questions*. Copyright © 1979. Reprinted with the permission of Cambridge University Press.

Friedrich Nietzsche. Excerpts from *The Antichrist, Beyond Good and Evil, The Gay Science, On Truth,* and *Thus Spoke Zarathustra*, trans. Clancy Martin. 'On "Master and Slave Morality"', from *Beyond Good and Evil*, trans. Clancy Martin. 'On "Morality as Herd-Instinct"', from *The Gay Science*, trans. Walter Kaufmann, New York: Random House, 1974. 'On the "Genius of the Species"', from *The Gay Science*, trans. Clancy Martin.

Keiji Nishitani. 'On Fate' and 'What Is Religion?', from *Religion and Nothingness*, ed. and trans. Jan Van Bragt. Copyright © 1982 by Keiji Nishitani. Published by University of California Press. Reprinted with permission.

Robert Nozick. *Anarchy, State, and Utopia*. Copyright © 1974 by Basic Books, Inc. Reprinted by permission of Basic Books, a member of Perseus Books, L.L.C.

Michael Oakeshott. 'On Being Conservative', *Rationalism in Politics and Other Essays*, Indianapolis, Liberty Fund, Inc., 1991, 408–9.

William Paley. *Natural Theology*, ed. Matthew D. Eddy and David Knight, Oxford: Oxford University Press, 2008, 7.

Parmenides. *Fragments* (B2; B3; B6, 11 1–2; B8, 11 3–9), trans. Paul Woodruff.

Blaise Pascal. *Pensées and Other Writings*, #13, #18, #233, #260, #266–7, #271, #274–5, #644, #681, #708–9, trans Honor Levi, Oxford: Oxford University Press, 1995.

Plato. *The Apology* (excerpts on pp. 3, 9), in *Five Dialogues,* 2nd edition, trans G.M.A. Grube, rev. John M. Cooper, 35, 40, 41–2. Copyright © 2002 by Hackett Publishing Company, Inc. Reprinted by permission of Hackett Publishing Company, Inc. All rights reserved. *The Apology* (excerpt on p. 19), in The *Last Days of Socrates*, trans. Hugh Tredennick, Harmondsworth, Middlesex: Penguin, 1954. *The Crito* (excerpt on p. 4), in *Five Dialogues,* 2nd edition, trans G.M.A. Grube, rev. John M. Cooper. Copyright © 2002 by Hackett Publishing Company, Inc. Reprinted by permission of Hackett Publishing Company, Inc. All rights reserved. *The Meno* (excerpts on pp. 10, 75), Five Dialogues, 2nd edition, trans G.M.A. Grube, rev. John M. Cooper, 68–9. Copyright © 2002 by Hackett Publishing Company, Inc. Reprinted by permission of Hackett Publishing Company, Inc. All rights reserved. *The Phaedo* (excerpt on p. 7), *Five Dialogues,* 2nd edition, trans G.M.A. Grube, rev. John M. Cooper. Copyright © 2002 by Hackett Publishing Company, Inc. Reprinted by permission of Hackett Publishing Company, Inc. All rights reserved. *The Republic* (excerpts on pp. 8, 71, 400, 481), trans. G.M.A. Grube. Copyright © 1974 by Hackett Publishing Company, Inc. Reprinted by permission. All rights reserved. *The Symposium* (excerpt on p. 13), *Five Dialogues,* 2nd edition, trans G.M.A. Grube, rev. John M. Cooper, 65–8. Copyright © 2002 by Hackett Publishing Company, Inc. Reprinted by permission of Hackett Publishing Company, Inc. All rights reserved. *The Symposium* (excerpt on p. 71), trans. Alexander Nehamas and Paul Woodruff. Copyright © 1989 by A. Nehamas and P. Woodruff. Reprinted by permission of Hackett Publishing Company, Inc. All rights reserved. *Theaetetus* (excerpt on p. 191), reprinted in The Collected Dialogues of Plato, trans. F. M. Cornford, ed. Edith Hamilton and Huntington Cairns, Bollingen Series, Princeton: Princeton University Press, 1980, 61.

Plotinus. *The Enneads*, 3rd edn, trans. Stephen MacKenna, London: Faber & Faber Limited, 1962, 353–5, 357.

Karl R. Popper. 'The Spell of Plato', in *The Open Society and Its Enemies,* Vol. 1, Princeton: Princeton University Press, 1971, 193–4.

The Questions of King Milinda. Edward Conze, trans., *Buddhist Scriptures*, London: Penguin Group, 1959, 147–9. Reprinted by permission of Penguin Group, UK.

Sarvepalli Radhakrishnan. *An Idealist View of Life*, London: George Allen & Unwin Ltd, 1932, 84, 89, 90–1.

John Rawls. 'Justice as Fairness', in *The Philosophical Review* 67 (April 1958). Copyright © 1958 by Cornell University. Reprinted by permission of the publisher. The *Philosophical Review* is published by Duke University Press.

Thomas Reid. 'Essays on the Intellectual Powers of Man' and 'An Inquiry into the Human Mind on the Principles of Common Sense', in *Philosophical Works*, Hildesheim: Georg Olms Verlagsbuchhandlung, 1967, 101, 108, 183–5, 351, 442–53. Reprinted with permission from Georg Olms Verlag AG.

Richard Rorty. 'Solidarity or Objectivity?' from *Philosophical Papers, Vol. 1: Objectivity, Relativism, and Truth*. Reprinted with the permission of Cambridge University Press.

Jean-Jacques Rousseau. *Émile*, trans. Barbara Foxley, New York: E.P. Dutton, 1968. Reprinted by permission of Everyman's Library, an imprint of Alfred A. Knopf. *The Social Contract and Discourses*, trans. G.D.H. Cole, J.M. Dent, Ltd, 1947. Reprinted by permission of Everyman's Library, an imprint of Alfred A. Knopf.

Bertrand Russell. *The Problems of Philosophy* (excerpts on pp. 26, 189), Oxford: Oxford University Press, 1912. Excerpt from *A History of Western Philosophy*, New York: Simon and Schuster, 1945.

John Russon. Reprinted by permission from *Human Experience: Philosophy, Neurosis, and the Elements of Everyday Life*, by John Russon, the State University of New York Press © 2003, 9–11, 20. State University of New York. All rights reserved.

Gilbert Ryle. *The Concept of Mind*, London: Hutchinson, 1949. Reprinted with permission of Taylor and Francis Books UK, with the permission of the Principal, Fellows, and Scholars of Hertford College in the University of Oxford.

Jean-Paul Sartre. *Existentialism as a Humanism*, trans. Philip Mairet, New York: Philosophical Library of New York, 1949. Reprinted by permission. *No Exit*, in *No Exit and The Flies*, trans. Stuart Gilbert. Copyright © 1946 by Stuart Gilbert, renewed 1974, 1975 by Maris Agnes Mathilde Gilbert. Reprinted by permission of Alfred A. Knopf, a division of Random House, Inc., and Editions Gallimard, Paris. 'On Absolute Freedom' and 'On Bad Faith', from *Being and Nothingness*, trans. Hazel E. Barnes, New York: Philosophical Library of New York, 1956. Copyright © 1956. Courtesy of the Philosophical Library of New York. 'On Existentialism', from *Existentialism as a Humanism*, trans. Phillip Mairet, New York: Philosophical Library of New York, 1949. Courtesy of the Philosophical Library of New York

Arthur Schopenhauer. *The World as Will and Representation*, trans. E.F. Payne, 275 et supra. Copyright © 1966 by Dover Publications, Inc.

John R. Searle. *Minds, Brains, and Science*, Cambridge: Harvard University Press, 1984, 32–3. Reprinted by permission of the publisher. 'The Myth of the Computer', in the *New York Review of Books*. Reprinted with permission from *The New York Review of Books*. Copyright © 1982 by NYREV, Inc.

Jerome Shaffer. 'Against the Identity Theory', from *Philosophy of Mind*. Copyright © 1994. Reprinted by permission of the author.

William Shakespeare. Macbeth, from *The Complete Works of William Shakespeare*, general editors Stanley Wells and Gary Taylor, Oxford: Clarendon Press, 1986, p. 1107.

Susan Sherwin. 'Ethics, Feminism, and Caring', *Queen's Quarterly* 96, No. 1 (Spring 1989), 5–8, 10–13. Reprinted by permission of Susan Sherwin.

Isaac Bashevis Singer. 'Joy', in *Gimpel the Fool and Other Sto-*

ries, New York: The Noonday Press, Farrar, Straus and Giroux, 1985, 131–2.

J.J.C. Smart. 'Sensations and Brain Processes', in *Philosophical Review* 68 (1959). Copyright © 1959 by Cornell University. Reprinted by permission of the publisher. The *Philosophical Review* is published by Duke University Press.

Margaret Somerville. *The Ethical Imagination: Journeys of the Human Spirit*, Toronto: House of Anansi Press, 2006, 34–5, 39–42. Copyright © 2006 by Margaret Sommerville and the Canadian Broadcasting Corporation. Reprinted by permission of House of Anansi Press. www.anansi.ca.

Sophocles. *Oedipus the King*, in *Three Tragedies: Antigone, Oedipus the King, Electra*, trans. H.D.F. Kitto, Oxford University Press, 1962. Reprinted with permission.

Francis Sparshott. 'Philosopher', *A Cardboard Garage*, Toronto: Clarke, Irwin, 1969.n Reprinted by permission of Francis Sparshott.

Benedictus de Spinoza. *Ethics*, in *The Rationalists*, trans. R.H.M. Elwes, New York: Doubleday, 1960.

Robert Louis Stevenson. *Dr Jekyll & Mr Hyde, The Merry Men, and Other Tales*, London: J.M. Dent & Sons Ltd. 1961, 48–9.

Galen Strawson. 'On "Cognitive Experience"', from 'Intentionality and Experience: Terminological Preliminaries', in *Phenomenology and the Philosophy of Mind*, eds David Woodruff Smith and Amie L. Thomasson, New York: Oxford University Press, 2005.

Barry Stroud. *The Significance of Philosophical Scepticism*, Oxford: Clarendon Press, 1987, 12–14.

Charles Taylor. 'The Other and Ourselves: Is Multiculturalism Inherently Relativist?', *Project Syndicate* (July 2002). www.project-syndicate.org. *The Malaise of Modernity*, Toronto: cbc/House of Anansi, 1991, 13–18, 22–3, 25–9. Copyright © 1991 by Charles Taylor and the Canadian Broadcasting Corporation. Reprinted by permission of House of Anansi Press. www.anansi.ca.

Henry David Thoreau. 'On "Civil Disobedience", from 'Resistance to Civil Government', 1849.

Paul Tillich. 'On the Ultimate Concern', from 'Religious Symbols', 'Symbols of Faith', in *The Dynamics of Faith* by Paul Tillich. Copyright © 1957 by Paul Tillich, renewed 1985 by Hannah Tillich. Reprinted by permission of HarperCollins Publishers.

Pierre Elliott Trudeau. 'The Just Society' and 'Multiculturalism', *The Essential Trudeau*, ed. Ron Graham, Toronto: McClelland & Stewart Inc., 1998, 15–16, 18–19, 144–6. Courtesy of The Pierre Elliott Trudeau Foundation; Excerpts from The Essential Trudeau by Pierre Elliott Trudeau, edited by Ron Graham © 1998. Published by McClelland & Stewart Ltd. Used with permission of the Estate and the Publisher.

Upanishads. Unless noted otherwise, all passages from the Upanishads were translated by Stephen Phillips.

Jean Vanier. *Made for Happiness: Discovering the Meaning of Life with Aristotle*, trans. Kathryn Spink, Toronto: House of Anansi Press Ltd, 2001, ix–xii, 183, 184–9, 194–6. Copyright © 1991 by Jean Vanier. Reprinted with permission of House of Anansi Press Inc. www.anansi.ca.

Swami Vivekananda. 'Maya and Illusion', in *The Complete Works of Swami Vivekananda*, 10th edn, Kolkata: Advaita Ashrama, 2003, 103.

Simone Weil. *First and Last Notebooks*, trans. Richard Rees, London and New York: Oxford University Press, 1970.

John Wisdom. 'Gods', in *Proceedings of the Aristotelian Society*, XLV, London: Harrison & Sons, 1944–5.

George Woodcock. *Anarchism: A History of Libertarian Ideas and Movements*, Cleveland: Meridian Books/The World Publishing Company, 1962, 9, 17–18, 22–3, 29–30.

Xun-zi. 'Human Nature Is Evil', in Wing-Tsit Chan, *Sourcebook in Chinese Philosophy*. Copyright © 1963, renewed 1991 by Princeton University Press. Reprinted by permission.

Zend-Avesta. All passages from the Yasna are taken from the Zend-Avesta, Part III, trans. L.H. Mills; part of the series, *The Sacred Books of the East*, ed. F. Max Muller, Westport, CT: Greenwood Press, 1972 (Oxford, 1887). All passages from the Yashts are taken from the Zend-Avesta, Part II, trans. James Darmesteter; part of the series, *The Sacred Books of the East*, ed. F. Max Muller, Motilal Banarsidass: Delhi, 1965 (Oxford, 1883).

INDEX